Ref 920 Enc v.8
Encyclopedia of world biography /

CYF $64.41

P9-EGJ-753

ENCYCLOPEDIA OF WORLD BIOGRAPHY

8

ENCYCLOPEDIA OF WORLD BIOGRAPHY

SECOND EDITION

Hoxha
Kierkegaard

8

GALE

DETROIT • NEW YORK • TORONTO • LONDON

Staff

Senior Editor: Paula K. Byers
Project Editor: Suzanne M. Bourgoin
Managing Editor: Neil E. Walker

Editorial Staff: Luann Brennan, Frank V. Castronova, Laura S. Hightower, Karen E. Lemerand, Stacy A. McConnell, Jennifer Mossman, Maria L. Munoz, Katherine H. Nemeh, Terrie M. Rooney, Geri Speace

Permissions Manager: Susan M. Tosky
Permissions Specialist: Maria L. Franklin
Permissions Associate: Michele M. Lonoconus
Image Cataloger: Mary K. Grimes

Production Director: Mary Beth Trimper
Production Manager: Evi Seoud
Production Associate: Shanna Heilveil
Product Design Manager: Cynthia Baldwin
Senior Art Director: Mary Claire Krzewinski

Research Manager: Victoria B. Cariappa
Research Specialists: Michele P. LaMeau, Andrew Guy Malonis, Barbara McNeil, Gary J. Oudersluys
Research Associates: Julia C. Daniel, Tamara C. Nott, Norma Sawaya, Cheryl L. Warnock
Research Assistant: Talitha A. Jean

Graphic Services Supervisor: Barbara Yarrow
Image Database Supervisor: Randy Bassett
Imaging Specialist: Mike Lugosz

Manager of Data Entry Services: Eleanor M. Allison
Data Entry Coordinator: Kenneth D. Benson

Manager of Technology Support Services: Theresa A. Rocklin
Programmers/Analysts: Mira Bossowska, Jeffrey Muhr, Christopher Ward

While every effort has been made to ensure the reliability of the information presented in this publication, Gale Research Inc. does not guarantee the accuracy of the data contained herein. Gale accepts no payment for listing; and inclusion in the publication of any organization, agency, institution, publication, service, or individual does not imply endorsement of the editors or publisher. Errors brought to the attention of the publisher and verified to the satisfaction of the publisher will be corrected in future editions.

∞™ This book is printed on acid-free paper that meets the minimum requirements of American National Standard for Information Sciences— Permanence Paper for Printed Library Materials, ANSI Z39.48-1984.

This publication is a creative work fully protected by all applicable copyright laws, as well as by misappropriation, trade secret, unfair competition, and other applicable laws. The authors and editors of this work have added value to the underlying factual material herein through one or more of the following: unique and original selection, coordination, expression, arrangement, and classification of the information. All rights to this publication will be vigorously defended.

Copyright © 1998
Gale Research
835 Penobscot Bldg.
Detroit, MI 48226-4094

ISBN 0-7876-2221-4 (Set)
ISBN 0-7876-2548-5 (Volume 8)

Library of Congress Cataloging-in-Publication Data

Encyclopedia of world biography / [edited by Suzanne Michele Bourgoin and Paula Kay Byers].
     p. cm.
    Includes bibliographical references and index.
    Summary: Presents brief biographical sketches which provide vital statistics as well as information on the importance of the person listed.
    ISBN 0-7876-2221-4 (set : alk. paper)
    1. Biography—Dictionaries—Juvenile literature. [1. Biography.]
I. Bourgoin, Suzanne Michele, 1968- . II. Byers, Paula K. (Paula Kay), 1954- .
CT 103.E56 1997
920′ .003—dc21
                             97-42327
                             CIP
                             AC

Printed in the United States of America
10 9 8 7 6 5 4 3

ENCYCLOPEDIA OF WORLD BIOGRAPHY

8

Enver Hoxha

Enver Hoxha (1908-1985) was the preeminent Albanian political leader of the 20th century. He was the leader of the Communist Party of Albania from its formation in 1941 and led the effort to force German withdrawal in 1944. He headed the Albanian government for the next four decades, longer than any other postwar European leader.

During the years from its proclamation of independence (1912) to its final liberation from German occupation (1944), Albania's history was characterized by dismal economic and political conditions at home and almost continuous intrigue and interference in the affairs of the country from abroad. Independence was declared during a period of chaotic internal conditions and occupation of much of the Albanians' lands by the armies of Serbia, Greece, and Montenegro, allies in a war against the Ottoman Empire, of which Albania was a part. World War I followed, and Albania was occupied by several regional and great power belligerents.

A tenuous independence was finally established after the war, but it was marked by increasing domestic political instability, culminating in the rise to power of Ahmet Zogu (later, King Zog I). Zog's regime was one of ever greater authoritarianism at home and political and economic subservience to fascist Italy abroad. Rome invaded Albania outright in 1939 and proclaimed the country's union with the Italian crown. In the fall of 1943, following the collapse of Mussolini's regime, German troops occupied Albania.

These conditions formed the environment in which Hoxha was born and matured.

Rise of Albanian Communism

Hoxha was born on October 16, 1908, the son of a Muslim landowner from the southern Albanian town of Gjirokastër. Graduating from the French lycée of Korçë—an institution of decidedly liberal inclinations—Hoxha in 1930 received an Albanian state scholarship to study engineering in France. He apparently soon became involved in socialist and communist activities there, however, and the grant was suspended. After a period in which he wrote articles critical of the Zog regime for the French Communist newspaper *L'Humanité,* he briefly served as private secretary to the Albanian consul in Brussels. He studied law but did not earn a degree. In 1936 Hoxha returned to Korçë, where he obtained a teaching post at the lycée and became active with one of the few groups of Communists operating in Albania.

When Hoxha returned to Albania there was no single, Comintern-recognized, Communist Party there; rather, there were several independent and mutually antagonistic groups. The Italian occupation found these groups at odds with one another, and the possibilities for united resistance were limited. The German invasion of the Soviet Union in 1941, however, forced the Albanian Communists to submerge their differences, and, with the assistance of emissaries sent by the Communist Party of Yugoslavia (CPY), the Communist Party of Albania (CPA) was formed on November 8, 1941. Hoxha was elected general secretary—that is, leader—of the party.

Hoxha and his colleagues immediately set about organizing the numerous, disparate resistance groups operating in Albania. The outgrowth of this activity was a meeting organized by the party in Pezë in September 1942 at which

1

the National Liberation Movement (NLM)—of which Hoxha became chief commissar—was formed. Later, in July 1943, the first brigades of the NLM's Army of National Liberation were activated and began large scale operations against the occupiers. While some prominent non-communists joined the NLM's ranks, many others who felt the NLM was merely a communist front remained aloof. Their organizations gradually were discredited by the fact that NLM was better organized and fought the occupation forces, whereas they lapsed into inactivity and even cooperation with the Axis. By November 1944 the NLM's brigades succeeded in forcing the Germans to withdraw completely from the country. This achievement was accomplished entirely in the absence of Allied troops. The leadership of the NLM assumed control of the country, with Hoxha—the dominant personality in the organization—filling the posts of prime minister, minister of defense, minister of foreign affairs, and commander-in-chief of the army.

The years between 1944 and 1948 were marked by the Hoxha government's attempts to solidify its position and put the country on the road to socialism. A number of trials of the government's opponents were held, including some of individuals who had cooperated with the occupation regimes. In 1945 and 1946 Hoxha ordered expropriation of nearly all significant private industry and large landed estates, eliminating the influence of foreign companies and the pre-war Albanian elite. These years also saw increasingly blatant attempts by the Yugoslav government of Josip Broz Tito to control Albania politically and economically through pro-Belgrade Albanian communist leaders such as

Koçi Xoxe, the minister of interior. The expulsion of the CPY from the Cominform in June 1948 enabled Hoxha and his supporters to denounce the Yugoslavs and execute Xoxe in May 1949.

Thereafter, Hoxha enthusiastically embraced the Soviet Union and its model of socialism as propounded by Stalin. The early 1950s saw a continuation of Hoxha's campaign against "Titoism" both at home and abroad, as well as the crushing of several attempts by the United States and Britain to foment an anti-communist insurgency using Albanian exiles trained abroad and covertly returned to Albania. During this period Hoxha's government received large amounts of Soviet aid for the initial phases of socialist construction; at the same time it became a fully integrated member of the socialist bloc, participating in both the Council for Mutual Economic Assistance and the Warsaw Pact.

Although Hoxha formally relinquished his governmental titles in 1953 and 1954, he retained his position as leader of the renamed CPA, the Party of Labor of Albania (PLA). In the years after Stalin's death, Hoxha grew increasingly distressed by the policies of the Soviet leadership and of Khrushchev in particular. Hoxha especially was not prepared to accept either the Soviet leader's attempts at de-stalinization in the USSR and elsewhere or his overtures to Tito's Yugoslavia. China, too, was for its own reasons disillusioned with Soviet behavior at this time, and Hoxha found common ground with Mao Zedong's criticisms of Moscow. By 1961 Hoxha's attacks on the "revisionist" Soviet leadership had so infuriated Khrushchev that he elected first to terminate Moscow's economic aid to Albania and ultimately to sever diplomatic relations entirely.

China's Ally in Europe

The end of relations with Moscow forced Hoxha to align himself still more closely with the Chinese. During the 1960s Chinese aid and technicians largely replaced assistance formerly given by the Soviet Union and its East European allies. Hoxha frequently denounced Soviet "social imperialism" in tones not unlike those reserved for American "imperialism." In 1968, following Hoxha's blistering condemnation of the Soviet invasion of Czechoslovakia, Albania formally withdrew from the Warsaw Pact (in which it had not participated since 1961).

The 1960s saw an Albanian version of China's Cultural Revolution. Unlike that in China, the Albanian variant was closely controlled by Hoxha from the outset as he sought to rekindle revolutionary fervor in Albanian life and eliminate the last vestiges of the old order. Perhaps best known of this campaign were Hoxha's speeches of 1967 on the subjects of liberation of Albanian women and the elimination of bureaucratism. At the same time Hoxha spearheaded a parallel drive against religion which resulted in a September 1967 decree banning all religious activity and proclaiming Albania the "first atheist state in the world."

By the mid-1970s Hoxha grew critical of China's policies, particularly in the wake of Beijing's opening to the United States and its rapprochement with Yugoslavia. Branding the Chinese theory of the "three worlds" as "revisionism," he charged that Mao's successors aimed to make China a great power by aligning themselves with Washington and betraying revolutionary movements in developing countries. In mid-1978 the Chinese suspended their aid program and recalled their technicians. The loss of this assistance forced a re-evaluation of Albanian foreign policy which some analysts regard as the explanation for the mysterious suicide in December 1981 of Mehmet Shehu, the longtime prime minister of Albania and formerly Hoxha's most trusted associate. These observers theorize that Shehu favored a greater opening to Western countries in the wake of the Chinese rift. Hoxha later charged that Shehu was simultaneously an agent of the U.S. Central Intelligence Agency, the Soviet KGB, and the Yugoslav intelligence service.

In his last years, as Albania strove to maintain his policy of "self-reliance," Hoxha withdrew more and more from public view, apparently for reasons of health and to finish his voluminous reminiscences. He died on April 11, 1985, having shaped Albania into a land vastly different from that into which he was born. Hoxha was survived by his wife, Nexhmije, herself a leading figure in the PLA. They had two sons and a daughter.

To succeed Hoxha the Albanian Communist Party selected Ramiz Alia (born 1925), a strict Marxist who had been propaganda chief of the Albanian Workers' Party.

Further Reading

There is at present no full-length biography of Hoxha available in English. There are, however, several surveys of contemporary Albania which include information on Hoxha's life. The official Albanian chronology may be found in Stefanaq Pollo and Arben Puto, *The History of Albania from its Origins to the Present Day* (1981). Anton Logoreci's *The Albanians, Europe's Forgotten Survivors* (1977) is an account by an Albanian exile. Nicholas Pano's *The People's Republic of Albania* (1968) and Peter R. Prifti's *Socialist Albania Since 1944: Domestic and Foreign Developments* (1978) are very useful studies by Albanian-American scholars. *Albania and the Albanians* (1975) by Ramadan Marmullaku is a somewhat sympathetic work by an Albanian in Yugoslavia.

Finally, and most importantly, are Hoxha's own writings. Many are available in English, such as his five volume *Selected Works* (1974-1985) and certain of his memoirs including *Reflections on China* (1979, 2 volumes), *With Stalin* (1979), *The Anglo-American Threat to Albania* (1982), and others. Read carefully, Hoxha's words present the most illuminating insights available into his theories and activities. □

Aleš Hrdlička

American physical anthropologist Aleš Hrdlička (1869-1943) made important contributions to the study of human origins and variation, as well as playing a major role in shaping the professional contours of the discipline in the United States.

Aleš Hrdlička was born in Humpolec, Bohemia (now the Czech Republic), on March 29, 1869, the first of seven children born to Maximilian and Koralina (Wagner) Hrdlička. In 1881 the family moved to the United States, settling in New York City, where young Hrdlička completed his secondary education and in 1889 began his medical studies at the New York Eclectic Medical College. On graduating with honors from this school in 1892 he entered general practice on the Lower East Side, while at the same time continuing his medical education at the New York Homeopathic College (1892-1894).

In 1895 he secured a position as a junior physician at the State Homeopathic Hospital for the Insane at Middletown, New York. It was while in this position that he became interested in the application of anthropometry to medicine, and as a direct result of his researches at the Middletown asylum he was invited in 1896 to join a multidisciplinary team being assembled to staff the newly created Pathological Institute in New York City. Under the direction of the neurologist and histochemist Ira Van Gieson this institute had been charged with the task of investigating the "modus operandi" of insanity. To prepare for this work, Hrdlička spent the winter of 1896 at the Ecole de Medécine in Paris studying anthropology under Léonce Manouvrier, who exerted an important and enduring influence on his intellectual development.

Hrdlička remained at the Pathological Institute until 1899, when he was invited by Frederic Ward Putnam to join the Hyde Expeditions of the American Museum of Natural History as a "field anthropologist." In this capacity Hrdlička conducted four intensive surveys among the Native Americans of the southwestern U.S. and northern Mexico between 1899 and 1902. A summary of these and later surveys (1903-1906) can be found in his monograph *Physiological and Medical Observations among the Indians of Southwestern United States and Northern Mexico* (1908). In 1903 he was selected to head the newly created Division of Physical Anthropology (DPA) at the National Museum of Natural History (Smithsonian Institution) in Washington, D.C., a position he held for the next 40 years.

During his tenure at the National Museum, Hrdlička built the DPA into a major research center housing one of the finest human osteological collections in the world. He also did much to promote physical anthropology as a legitimate academic discipline in the United States. In this regard, he endeavored to organize the then-nascent profession along the lines Paul Broca had taken French anthropology. Although his ambition of founding an American Institute of Physical Anthropology was never realized, he did succeed in launching the *American Journal of Physical Anthropology* in 1918 and the American Association of Physical Anthropologists in 1930, both of which were fundamental elements of his particular vision of the future of American physical anthropology. He also did much to promote physical anthropology in his native country. Besides making substantial donations that launched and sustained Jindrich Matiegka's journal *Anthropologie* (published at Charles University in Prague until 1941), he donated money to the Czech Academy of Arts and Sciences for the exploration of prehistoric sites in Moravia and also to Charles University for the foundation of the Museum of Man that is now named in his honor.

Throughout his long career Hrdlička received many awards and honors which indicated appreciation for his prodigious labors in the discipline. He was elected to membership in the American Philosophical Society in 1918 and in the National Academy of Sciences in 1921 and served as president of the American Anthropological Association (1925-1926), the Washington Academy of Science (1928-1929), and the American Association of Physical Anthropologists (1930-1932). He was also a recipient of the prestigious Huxley Medal (1927).

Although Hrdlička's research interests ranged over almost every aspect of modern physical anthropology, the primary focus of his scientific endeavors was on the question of the origin and antiquity of the American aborigines. He commenced this work with an exhaustive study of all the available evidence attributed to early humans in North and South America, the results of which are summarized in two major publications: *The Skeletal Remains Suggesting or Attributed to Early Man in North America* (1907) and *Early Man in South America* (1912). These studies indicated the presence of only anatomically modern humans in the Western hemisphere, which led him to reject the view that the Native Americans had either evolved in the New World or had entered the continent in early glacial or preglacial times. Following this he began orchestrating evidence to support a case for hominid origins in the western sector of the Old World and the subsequent peopling of the New World from Asia during the late Pleistocene-early Holocene period.

It was Hrdlička's growing conviction that anatomically modern *Homo sapiens* had been derived from a basically Neanderthaloid population that had initially been restricted to Europe and Africa. As these early transitional hominids spread slowly eastward across the Old World, Hrdlička contended, they became separated into a number of discrete geographical breeding units that led to their subsequent differentiation into the various racial groups that characterize the modern human family. He first presented an outline of this hypothesis in a paper presented to the American Philosophical Society in Philadelphia in 1921, under the title "The Peopling of Asia" (*Proceedings, American Philosophical Society*, 60 [1922]). This period of Hrdlička work culminated with the delivery of the 1927 Huxley Memorial Lecture in London in which he summarized his arguments for a "Neanderthal Phase of Man" (*Journal of the Royal Anthropological Institute*, 57 [1927]), and the subsequent publication of his now classic work, *The Skeletal Remains of Early Man* (1930).

After 1926 Hrdlička pursued evidence to document the thesis that the first Americans had entered the New World from Asia. His work in the Yukon and Alaskan coast (1926-1930), Kodiak Island (1931-1935), and the Aleutian and Commander Islands (1936-1938) is summarized in two posthumously published volumes: *The Anthropology of Kodiak Island* (1944) and *The Aleutian and Commander Islands and their Inhabitants* (1945). One of the main objec-

tives of his work in the Commander and Aleutian islands had been to investigate the possibility that they had served as stepping stones from Kamchatka to the American mainland. Excavations proved, however, that the Commanders had been uninhabited in pre-Russian times. Thus, on the basis of this negative evidence, he concluded that the earlier and later inhabitants of the Aleutians must have entered these islands from Alaska. After 1938 he had intended to initiate a program of research on the Siberian mainland in an effort to prove the Asiatic origins of the American aborigines. These plans, however, were scotched by the outbreak of World War II. Hrdlička died of a heart attack at his home in Washington, D.C., on September 5, 1943.

Further Reading

For further biographical details see Frank Spencer, *Aleš Hrdlička M.D., 1869-1943: A Chronicle of the Life and Work of an American Physical Anthropologist* (2 volumes, 1979); and Frank Spencer and Fred H. Smith, "The Significance of Aleš Hrdlička's "Neanderthal Phase of Man: A Historical and Current Assessment" in *American Journal of Physical Anthropology* (1981). □

Hsia Kuei

Hsia Kuei (active 1190-1225) was a Chinese painter who, with Ma Yüan, was the creator of the "Ma-Hsia school" of landscape painting.

H sia Kuei, also named Yüyü, was a native of Ch'ien-t'ang, the modern Hangchou in Chekiang Province. Of his life it is known only that he served in the painting academy of Emperor Ning-tsung (reigned 1195-1224), who awarded him the Golden Belt, symbolizing the highest artistic achievement. Hsia's name is commonly linked with that of Ma Yüan to characterize the most distinctive and influential landscape style of the late Sung period.

Chinese landscape painting of the 10th and 11th centuries had been a monumental vision of the great universe, the macrocosm, of towering granite cliffs, deep valleys, and broad, shadowed marshlands. By the mid-11th century a more amiable, personal style had become dominant; and in the art of Li T'ang landscape was conceived in dramatically expressive intimacy, a reflection of the emotions of man rather than his mind. Hsia Kuei and Ma Yüan developed from Li T'ang and realized the final subtleties of poetic suggestion.

No painter displays greater mastery of the subtleties of brush and ink than Hsia Kuei. In his masterpiece, *Twelve Views from a Thatched Cottage,* a hand scroll 7 inches high and (originally) 16 feet long, this technical virtuosity is allied with perhaps the most profoundly affecting response to the moods of nature in Chinese art. In this scroll, beginning with *Wandering the Hills by the River* and ending with *Evening Mooring by a Misty Bank*, the painter passes through the hours of the day in a succession of vignettes describing the life along a river. Each scene is subtly related to the next in a continuous sequence remarkably like modern cinematic techniques, but also with a complexity of mood, pace, tonal variation, and theme similar to musical composition. As the scroll opens, one is swept into the busy activities of the early hours, and one scene follows another in quick succession. But as the day lengthens, the pace slows gradually, mist sweeps into the picture, light begins to fade; the *Clear and Lonely Sound of the Fisherman's Flute* is rendered. As the scroll ends, the banks and trees are cloaked in shadow, the fishing boats are silent, and night obliterates sight.

From the breathtaking sweep of the conception as a whole to the infinite subtleties of pulsating life in the smallest detail, Hsia Kuei reveals the mind and the hand of the supreme master. With the crackling poetry of Ma Yüan and the evocative Zen mystery of the monk Much'i, Hsia Kuei stands at the end of a long era in Chinese art history. For centuries the artist had sought to capture in ink the profound powers of nature. When the infinity of space itself was brought under the control of his brush, the quest was finished. Henceforward, Chinese painters turned toward the expression of inner realities.

Further Reading

Hsia Kuei is extensively discussed in Oswald Siren, *Chinese Painting: Leading Masters and Principles,* vol. 1 (1956). The art of the Southern Sung period as a whole is treated by James Cahill, *The Art of Southern Sung China* (1962). □

Wei Hsiao-Wen-ti

Wei Hsiao-wen-ti (467-499) was the sixth emperor of the Northern Wei dynasty. His reign represents the apogee of the dynasty's power and probably sowed the seeds for its subsequent decline.

Wei Hsiao-wen-ti was born T'o-pa Hung on Oct. 13, 467, in P'ing-ch'eng (east of the present Ta-t'ung, Shansi, south of the Great Wall), eldest son of Emperor Hsien-wen. He was perfectly white, and there were the usual "supernatural" signs of an imperial birth. His father, a fervent Buddhist, abdicated in 471, and four-year-old Hsiao-wen ascended the throne. The first 19 years of his reign, under the regency of his grandmother, the formidable empress dowager Feng (442-490), were devoted to studies which enabled him to become versed in all aspects of Chinese literary culture, as well as in Buddhism.

Until his grandmother's death Hsiao-wen was only titular head of state, all real decisions being taken by her with the counsel of her Chinese officials. He gave up hunting at the age of 14 to devote himself entirely to preparing himself for his future imperial tasks. He is traditionally thought of as a paragon of rulers, exceptionally attentive to the needs of his people, considerate of others, and profoundly filial.

The two most outstanding events of Emperor Hsiao-wen's reign were the promulgation of the "equal-field"

(*chün-t'ien*) system and his removal of his capital from Ta-t'ung to Loyang, with the accompanying Sinicization that removal symbolized. The equal-field agrarian reform was promulgated in 485, during a period of severe famine, and was an attempt to redistribute the land so that it would be more extensively cultivated. This reform greatly influenced later, similar attempts at land reform and has been passionately debated in China and Japan in recent years.

Hsiao-wen's most important influence in Chinese history was the steps he took to achieve the total Sinicization of his Hsien-pi (proto-Mongol or Turkish) compatriots, to whose T'o-pa clan the Emperor belonged. His own deep interest in Chinese culture had led him to feel he was the true son of heaven and should rule over the entire Chinese Empire from the ancient capital of Loyang, which was in the southern part of his domains. Against the bitter opposition of the entire court, he had the capital moved in 494. Barbarian dress and hair style were prohibited in the same year, and a year later the Hsien-pi language was prohibited in court by all except those who were too old (over 30) to learn Chinese. Finally, in 496, he changed his tribal name from T'o-pa to the Chinese name of Yüan, had other tribes also take Chinese names, and encouraged the intermarriage of the Hsien-pi noblemen with Chinese girls of aristocratic families.

This nostalgia for China and things Chinese weakened the Northern Wei empire, taking its people away from their homeland, putting them into an inferior position vis-à-vis the culturally superior Chinese officialdom, and generally sowing the seeds of Hsien-pi discontent that was to split the dynasty in two in a little over 3 decades. Hsiao-wen's Sinophilia was also the direct cause of his early end, for he died, exhausted by his campaigning in his attempt to unite all of China, in what is now northern Hupei on April 26, 499, at the age of 32. In 500 his son, Hsüan-wu, had a memorial carved for Hsiao-wen and his wife in the famous caves at Lung-men near Loyang. He remains in history as a man of culture, intelligence, and humanity in an era when this last virtue, in particular, was exceptionally rare.

Further Reading

A good study of Wei Hsiao-wen-ti is in Dun J. Li, *The Ageless Chinese: A History* (1965). An interesting, somewhat personal view of his equal-field reform is in Etienne Balazs, *Chinese Civilization and Bureaucracy* (trans. 1964). For general historical background see Wolfram Eberhard, *A History of China* (1950). □

Hsieh Ling-yün

Hsieh Ling-yün (385-433), Duke of K'ang-lo, was a Chinese poet. An aristocrat of philosophic temper, he was China's first systematic nature poet to explore the mountains and gorges of South China and write poems about them.

Hsieh Ling-yün, whose ancestral home was Yang-hsia (in presentday Honan Province), belonged to one of the most illustrious families who moved to South China with the Chin court when North China was invaded by barbarian tribes from across the Chinese border. Besides Hsieh Ling-yün, there were several poets of the Hsieh clan who achieved fame during the 4th and 5th centuries.

Upon his father's death, Ling-yün acquired his hereditary title as the Duke of K'ang-lo and would have seemed assured of a brilliant career at court; yet this persistently eluded him. Partly to blame were his aristocratic arrogance and his lavish style of maintaining himself. When the Eastern Chin collapsed in 419, he served the Liu Sung dynasty. He was, however, demoted to Marquis of K'ang-lo.

In 422 his enemies, jealous of his friendship with the heir to the throne, the prince of Lu-ling, exiled him to Yung-chia (in present-day Chekiang) and murdered the prince. It is from this period that Ling-yün matured as a poet. As prefect of Yung-chia, he recorded the scenic attractions around it with a fresh, observant eye; at the same time, suffering had deepened his outlook so that a philosophic vein now ran through his descriptive verse. For the next 10 years he alternated between intervals of seclusion on his estate and spells of discontented service as an official. Finally, he contracted the enmity of a powerful clique at court, was exiled to Canton, and was executed there on a trumped-up charge.

Brought up as a Taoist, Hsieh Ling-yün became in his youth a fervent convert to Buddhism. He once joined the intellectual community on Mt. Lu, under the famous monk Hui-yüan, and distinguished himself by his essays on Buddhist philosophy and his translation of several sutras. But his real contribution to Chinese literature lies in his nature poetry, which grew out of his love for the mountains and waters of Chekiang and Kiangsi. He wrote mainly in the five-word style, using a bookish and allusive vocabulary fashionable at his time. For this reason modern Chinese critics tend to belittle him by placing his achievement alongside that of his contemporary T'ao Ch'ien, a much greater poet. Nevertheless, with all his stylistic faults, Hsieh Ling-yün's passionate love for nature shines through his verse, and he remains the most important landscape poet of the pre-T'ang period.

Further Reading

For a sampling of Hsieh Ling-yün's poetry see J. D. Frodsham with the collaboration of Ch'eng Hsi, compilers, *An Anthology of Chinese Verse: Han, Wei, Chin, and the Northern and Southern Dynasties* (1967). The standard work is J. D. Frodsham, *The Murmuring Stream: The Life and Works of the Chinese Nature Poet Hsieh Ling-yün (385-433), Duke of K'ang-lo* (2 vols., 1967), which contains a full biography of the poet as well as copious translations of his verse. □

Hsüan Tsang

Hsüan Tsang (ca. 602-664) was the most famous Chinese Buddhist pilgrim and traveler in India and a translator of Buddhist texts. His "Hsi-yü Chi," or "Record of Western Countries," remains an indispensable source book to students of 7th-century India and central Asia.

Hsüan Tsang, also spelled Hsüan Chuang, whose name is romanized in a wide variety of ways, is the Buddhist designation of the Chinese holy monk whose family name was Ch'en and personal name, Chen. He was born in Honan midway in the brief Sui dynasty (589-617), which represented the first successful attempt at reunifying the Chinese Empire since the end of the Han dynasty (220). The intervening centuries saw much chaos and suffering together with a phenomenal expansion of Buddhism. Hsüan Tsang followed the example of an elder brother and joined the Buddhist monastic order in Loyang at the age of 12. The boy monk traveled extensively in China in pursuit of Buddhist learning, particularly the Vijnanavadin school.

Travel to India

A burning desire for firsthand clarification prompted Hsüan Tsang to leave for India in 627, stealthily, as it was against the law to travel abroad. Surviving the rigors of forbidding deserts and mountains and narrowly escaping the jaws of death, he passed through the central Asiatic regions of Turfan, Karashahr, Tashkent, Samarkand, and Bactria. He kept a journal of his unique experiences and observations during his 19-year sojourn, which later became known as the *Hsi-yü Chi*. This *Record of Western Countries* stands today as the single written record of conditions at that time in India and central Asia. After visiting some 34 "kingdoms" along the way, he finally entered India in 631 by crossing the Hindu Kush into Kapisa. His first impressions of the Hindus inhabiting northwest India were recorded as follows: "The people are accustomed to a life of ease and prosperity and they like to sing. However, they are weak-minded and cowardly, and they are given to deceit and treachery. In their relations with each other there is much trickery and little courtesy. These people are small in size and unpredictable in their movements."

Study and Travel in India

After a 2-year study period in northwest India, Hsüan Tsang sailed down the Ganges to visit the holy land of Buddhism. His itinerary included Kapilavastu, the birthplace of Buddha; Benares; Sarnath, where Buddha delivered his first sermon; and Bodhgaya, where Buddha attained his nirvana under the bodhi tree. The trip terminated at Nalanda, the leading center of Buddhist learning in India, where Hsüan Tsang took up the study of Vijnanavada in earnest under the tutelage of the grand, old Silabhadra, the authoritative representative of the Asanga-Vasubandhu tradition.

After a study period of 15 months at Nalanda, Hsüan Tsang resumed his travel, going south along the east coast. Being unable to visit Ceylon because of local civil strife, he made his way north along the west coast, returning finally to Nalanda. In his *Records,* Hsüan Tsang made entries of more than 100 "kingdoms" scattered over all of the "Five (Regions of) Indias." Hsüan Tsang devoted his second stay at Nalanda to the study of Indian philosophy. His scholarly achievements began to attract the attention of kings and princes as well as men of learning.

Through the introduction of the king of Kamarupa (Assam), Hsüan Tsang was received with full honors by Harsha, the emperor of India. The Emperor convened a grand assembly to honor the visitor from afar and to give the Brahmins and Hinayana followers a lesson. The disputations lasted 18 days among the contestants, and Hsüan Tsang emerged triumphant against all challengers. He was accorded the exalted titles of Moksadeva and Mahayanadeva.

Return to China

In spite of the respect and affection shown him by many people in India, Hsüan Tsang was determined to return to China. Emperor Harsha provided him with escorts and gifts. Hsüan Tsang took the southern route across central Asia and arrived back in Ch'ang-an in 645. He was received with royal honors and elaborate ceremonials. To Emperor T'ai Tsung, Hsüan Tsang presented the 657 Buddhist texts which were packed in 520 cases and carried by a caravan of 20 horses.

Rejecting all other offers, Hsüan Tsang settled down to the monastic routine and devoted himself to the translation of the texts which he had brought back. Working almost to his dying day, he was able to complete the translation of 75 items, totaling 1,335 fascicles. The superior quality of Hsüan Tsang's translations was to be expected, as he was completely at home in both Chinese and Sanskrit. At the Emperor's suggestion he also wrote the *Hsi-yü Chi* in Chinese and translated the *Tao Te Ching* into Sanskrit. When Hsüan Tsang died at the age of 62, the Emperor canceled his audiences for 3 days, and just about every resident of Ch'ang-an marched in the funeral procession.

The Ta-yen-t'a, a pagoda of seven stories 194 feet high, built in the southern suburb of Ch'ang-an at Hsüan Tsang's request to house the Buddhist sutras and mementos brought back from India, is still standing. Popularly referred to as the Big Geese Pagoda, this rare T'ang-dynasty structure stands as a vivid reminder of the great Buddhist monk, traveler, and translator.

Further Reading

Works that have information on Hsüan Tsang are Shaman Hwui-li, *The Life of Hiuen-Tsiang* (1911); René Grousset, *In the Footsteps of the Buddha* (1929; trans. 1932); and Arthur Waley, *The Real Tripitaka and Other Pieces* (1952). □

T'ang Hsüan-tsung

T'ang Hsüan-tsung (685-762) was the seventh emperor of the T'ang dynasty. Although he was an able man, his long reign ended with his abdication after the massive rebellion of An Lu-shan broke out in 755.

Hsüan-tsung was the third son of Emperor Jui-tsung (reigned 685, 710-713). In the year he was born, his great-aunt, Empress Wu, deposed Jui-tsung and replaced him with her young son Chung-tsung (reigned 685-690, 705-710).

Hsüan-tsung spent his youth in Ch'ang-an and Loyang, the T'ang capitals. During the years after the successful coup d'etat against Empress Wu in 705, there was almost constant maneuvering behind the scenes in the palace. Cliques formed around empresses, deposed emperors, and princes. Hsüan-tsung was deeply involved in these intrigues and, after helping to restore his father to the throne in 710, became emperor in 713.

Administration of the Empire

At the beginning of his reign Hsüan-tsung was an active and vigorous ruler. He continued the efforts of earlier rulers to centralize the empire and put it on a sound financial basis. During his reign a variety of institutional innovations were introduced in an effort to meet the political and economic changes that had developed since the founding of the dynasty in 618. To carry out his reforms, he used individuals and groups that could help implement his policies. In doing this, however, he introduced new political elements, including the notorious eunuchs, that eventually usurped power and authority.

Hsüan-tsung's reign was also a period of expansion abroad. Although there were genuine defensive considerations, much of the incentive for an aggressive foreign policy was simply the desire for conquest and glory. There was also a major effort to strengthen the borders of China against foreign enemies, but the policy produced unexpected and disastrous results as the border commanders became strong and independent. The tragic consequences were obvious when the most powerful of the regional commanders, An Lu-shan, led his soldiers against the dynasty in 755. Hsüan-tsung was forced to flee the capital and, soon thereafter, to abdicate. The rebellion was put down only after 8 years of bitter fighting.

Although it is usually quite difficult to penetrate the aura of sanctity which surrounded the person of the Chinese emperor, something is known of Hsüan-tsung's capacities and personality. His success in achieving power in a time of political intrigue and instability certainly testifies to his political ability and tenacity. It was clear when he first ascended the throne that he would not, at the beginning at least, be dominated by any person or faction. But although he was capable of ruling vigorously, he was also artistically inclined and fond of a luxurious life. In addition to having a large harem, he patronized musicians, artists, and poets, and his reign is traditionally characterized as a period of great cultural brilliance.

Further Reading

There is much information on Hsüan-tsung's reign in Edwin G. Pulleyblank, *The Background of the Rebellion of An Lu-shan* (1955). Concerning the lives of the two great poets of the period see Arthur Waley, *The Poetry and Career of Li Po* (1950), and William Hung, *Tu Fu: China's Greatest Poet* (1952). □

Hsün-tzu

The Chinese philosopher Hsün-tzu (ca. 312-ca. 235 B.C.) is one of the important early Confucian philosophers. He is famous for his theory that human nature is basically evil.

Hsün-tzu, or Hsün K'uang, is frequently referred to as Hsün Ch'ing. Almost the only information about his life comes from a short biography written by the historian Ssu-ma Ch'ien in the *Records of the Historian*. It mentions that Hsün-tzu was a native of Chao, a state in modern western Hopei and northern Shansi provinces in north-central China.

The first mention of Hsün-tzu is when, at the age of 50, he arrived in Ch'i, a state in modern Shantung Province. Ch'i by this time had become one of the major centers of learning in China. The ruling family of Ch'i, which had usurped the throne in 386 B.C., was interested in promoting scholarship in order to enhance the state's prestige. They established at the Ch'i capital an academy known as the Chi-hsia and invited the most illustrious scholars of the realm to come and study there. Hsün-tzu arrived in Ch'i around 264, when the Chi-hsia was in decline.

Apparently he left Ch'i several times and visited the western state of Ch'in. After one of these visits, upon his return to Ch'i Hsün-tzu found himself slandered at court, perhaps because of his association with the state of Ch'in, which was one of Ch'i's enemies. Hsün-tzu then traveled south to the state of Ch'u, where the prime minister, the lord of Ch'un-shen, gave him a position as prefect of Lan-ling, a small city-state in southern Shantung. The lord of Ch'un-shen was assassinated in 238, and Hsün-tzu resigned his post. Hsün-tzu remained in Lanling, where he established a school. His students included the philosopher Han Fei Tzu and the future prime minister of Ch'in, Li Ssu. Hsün-tzu died at Lan-ling approximately in the year 235.

Hsün-tzu is attributed with a work originally titled *New Writings of Minister Hsün*, which in the 9th century was given the current designation, *Hsün-tzu*. Parts of the book are undoubtedly spurious, but much of the material appears to be an accurate representation of Hsün-tzu's teachings, even if it does not come directly from his hand. Hsün-tzu is important in the history of Chinese thought for his theory that human nature is basically evil and that only through

study and moral training can one attain goodness. He placed strong emphasis on rites and music as edifying influences. Hsün-tzu anticipated the later authoritarian Legalists, such as Han Fei Tzu, by stressing the importance of harsh punishment of wrongdoers. He was particularly intolerant of superstitions and attacked a number of the religious observances of his time.

Further Reading

For further information in English on Hsün-tzu's life and ideas see Homer H. Dubs, *Hsüntze: The Moulder of Ancient Confucianism* (1927). Highly recommended is Burton Watson, *Hsün Tzu: Basic Writings* (1963). □

Huang Ch'ao

Huang Ch'ao (died 884) was a Chinese rebel leader. From 875 to 884 he conducted a major rebellion against the T'ang dynasty.

Huang Ch'ao was born to a family of merchants living in northeast China on the Shantung peninsula. His family was wealthy enough to provide him with some education, and he tried to pass the civil service examination. His failure to do so embittered him against the ruling T'ang dynasty.

Although the T'ang had nearly been overthrown by the An Lu-shan rebellion in the middle of the 8th century, there had been a period of imperial recovery lasting until about 820. The following half century was one of steady decline for the ruling house.

In 874 the 11-year-old emperor Hsi-tsung succeeded to the throne. This boy was, of course, unable to give any positive direction to imperial policy. The result was tragic, because the beginning of his reign coincided with a period of severe drought in China. The central government was incapable of helping the desperate people, and by 875 full-scale rebellion had broken out.

The leader of the rebellion was Wang Hsien-chih; Huang Ch'ao was one of his lieutenants. In 878, after 3 years of hard fighting, Wang was killed in battle and Huang Ch'ao became commander of the rebel troops. In 879 they occupied Canton and its outlying areas. Success began to follow success for the rebels. Huang Ch'ao led a major campaign toward the north and by the winter of 880 occupied the eastern capital, Loyang, which had put up no resistance. Early in 881, just weeks after taking Loyang, Huang Ch'ao took Ch'ang-an, the western capital.

Huang's first act was to proclaim himself emperor. In an effort to create a government, he preserved the bureaucratic structure, putting his own followers in the top posts. This effort was short-lived, however, as imperial troops recovered the capital in the spring of 881.

The military situation fluctuated for the next 2 years, although the rebels were able to regain and hold Ch'angan. They could not obtain provisions, however, and their situation became desperate. The real turning point came when the T'ang enlisted the aid of non-Chinese armies, which drove Huang Ch'ao and his troops out of the capital. The rebels struggled to the east, but within a year their army was dispersed and their leader dead. The T'ang dynasty survived, in name at least, for 2 more decades, but in 907 the same armies which had driven Huang Ch'ao out of the capital in 883 overthrew the dynasty.

Further Reading

Howard S. Levy's edition of Hsiu Ou-Yang, *Biography of Huang Ch'ao* (1955), is recommended. For background information see the excellent, detailed work by Wang Gungwu, *The Structure of Power in North China during the Five Dynasties* (1963).

Additional Sources

Huang, Chao-chin, *Grandpa Huang Chao-chin's memoirs: for his grandchildren,* Taipei, Taiwan, R.O.C.: Huang Chen In-lien, 1986. □

Huang Tsung-hsi

Huang Tsung-hsi (1610-1695) was a Chinese scholar and political philosopher who, with other Chinese intellectuals, sought to provide a philosophical framework that would open up new vistas of scholarship and restore morality and equity to Chinese politics.

Huang Tsung-hsi was the son of Huang Tsun-su, a prominent official in Peking and a member of the Eastern Grove Society (Tung-lin), which opposed the rapacious activities of Wei Chung-hsien, a powerful and unscrupulous eunuch, who managed to dominate the young emperor and thus rose to almost absolute control in the court. The Tung-lin group advocated a return to political morality, and they often held secret meetings in Huang's home to discuss political problems and strategy.

In 1625 Huang Tsun-su was dismissed from office and killed in prison during the following year for criticizing Wei Chung-hsien. Huang Tsung-hsi set forth for the capital, determined to avenge his father's death by killing the officials involved. But before he could carry out his planned revenge, a new emperor was enthroned who purged the eunuch faction, and Wei Chung-hsien committed suicide.

While still in his youth Huang developed a keen interest in history and literature which was further stimulated by his marriage to the daughter of a well-known writer and playwright. But until 1649 Huang's primary role was that of political critic and activist. In the 1630s he had joined the Fu-she, a society similar to that in which his father had participated, and once he was almost arrested for signing a petition deploring corruption in the court of the late Ming dynasty.

Fight against the Manchu

In spite of his forthright criticisms, however, Huang remained loyal to the Ming dynasty and was outraged by the Manchu conquest of China in 1644. Like many other talented scholars of his day, Huang spent much of the 1640s engaged in anti-Manchu resistance movements which centered on various descendants of the Ming imperial house in South China. Huang attained very high political office in the administration of one of these claimants to the throne of the fallen Ming dynasty. But the cause was hopeless, and Huang Tsung-hsi retired from his political and military activities in 1649.

From 1649 to his death in 1695, Huang refused to accept service under the Manchus, the Ch'ing dynasty, and instead followed the path of several of his associates in choosing to dedicate his life to scholarship. Even in 1679, when the emperor, K'ang-hsi, offered him a chance to compete in a special examination and to help compile the official history of Huang's beloved Ming dynasty, Huang refused to accept. Except for visits to a number of important scholars, he spent most of his later life near his birthplace in the coastal province of Chekiang.

Scholarship and Political Philosophy

Huang's writings are characterized by their breadth of interest and their systematic and factual content. Huang had a deep interest in the Chinese classics and wrote many critical analyses dealing with earlier periods in Chinese philosophy. Among his several works of criticism was his *Ming-ju hsüeh-an* (Records of Confucian Thought in the Ming Period), a monumental multi-volume accomplishment, which was one of the first comprehensive attempts at a systematic analysis of a period in intellectual history. As a historian, Huang is known as the founder of the Eastern Chekiang school, which advocated general interpretation as well as objective research and which had a great influence on later historians. He wrote several works of history and spent considerable effort on histories of the Southern Ming loyalist regimes which sprouted up after the Manchu conquest. Huang was also interested in literature and compiled several anthologies, as well as writing his own prose and poetry.

Huang Tsung-hsi's most famous work was his *Ming-i tai-fang lu* (1662; A Plan for a Prince). In this volume he developed his political philosophy by making not only a number of general premises but also suggesting practical reforms. He was deeply disturbed by the nature of Chinese government and society during the late Ming and early Ch'ing periods, and he wrote this treatise in the hope that some later regime would implement his recommendations. Like the ancient Chinese philosopher Mencius, Huang argued that government must promote the happiness of the people.

Feeling that the imperial government had become too autocratic, Huang urged emperors to place more responsibility in the hands of their ministers and to revise the law codes in the interests of the common people. His proposed reforms were in some instances strikingly similar to those of the great 11th-century statesman Wang An-shih. Huang held that the influence of eunuchs should be greatly diminished and considerably more attention should be paid to the often corrupt clerks and assistants in local government. A universal system of public education should be established in order to broaden the pool of talent in the empire. The civil service examinations should concentrate more on contemporary affairs, and all land should be publicly owned and distributed by the government on the basis of need.

In *Ming-i tai-fang lu* Huang reflected the late Ming revival of interest in current problems and in political morality. Although Huang was certainly not suggesting a democratic government, he was attempting to provide more equitable guidelines for imperial China. As a man of exceptional talent and dedication, Huang deserves to be remembered as a remarkable figure in the late years of Chinese traditional philosophy.

Further Reading

A biography of Huang Tsung-hsi is in Arthur Hummel, ed., *Eminent Chinese of the Ch'ing Period* (2 vols., 1943; 1 vol., 1964). A study of his *Ming-i tai-fang lu* is W. T. De Bary, "Chinese Despotism and the Confucian Ideal: A Seventeenth-century View," in John K. Fairbank, ed., *Chinese Thought and Institutions* (1957). A fine survey of 17th-century Chinese thought with special attention to Huang and with some translations of his writings is in W. T. De Bary, ed., *Sources of Chinese Tradition* (1960). □

Edwin Powell Hubble

The American astronomer Edwin Powell Hubble (1889-1953) established the scale of the universe and laid the observational basis for the cosmological theory of the expanding universe.

Edwin Hubble was born on Nov. 20, 1889, in Marshfield, Mo., where his father, a lawyer, was in the insurance business. Hubble received scholarship aid to go to the University of Chicago. He chose law for a career, and after receiving his bachelor's degree in 1910, he went as a Rhodes scholar to Oxford University, England. In 1913 he returned to the United States, was admitted to the bar in Kentucky, and practiced law for about a year in Louisville.

Quite suddenly, Hubble decided that he would devote his life to astronomy, and in 1914 he left for the University of Chicago's Yerkes Observatory in Williams Bay, Wis. In 1917 he completed his doctorate and enlisted in the infantry. He served in France as a line officer in the American Expeditionary Force.

Early Work at Mount Wilson

As a student at Chicago, Hubble had attracted the attention of the well-known astronomer G. E. Hale, and after the war Hale offered him a staff position at Mount Wilson Observatory near Pasadena, Calif. Except for the period 1942-1946, when Hubble was with the Ordnance

Department in Aberdeen, Md., he was connected with the Mount Wilson Observatory for the rest of his life.

Hubble's early observations at Mount Wilson were made with its 60-inch reflecting telescope and concentrated on objects within our own galaxy, for example, novae, nebulous stars, and variable stars. Gradually he began to observe more distant objects. To determine the distances of the spiral nebulae (galaxies), he used Cepheid variable stars. This method derived from Henrietta S. Leavitt's 1912 discovery that the period of variation in the intensity of these stars is directly related to their absolute magnitude, so that by measuring the former, one may easily determine the latter. By knowing the star's absolute magnitude and measuring its apparent magnitude, its (relative) distance may be readily calculated from the inverse-square law.

In 1923 Hubble definitely recognized a Cepheid variable in the Andromeda Nebula, known to astronomers as M31. Others were soon found in M31 and its companion nebula M33. To obtain his photographs, Hubble used Mount Wilson's 100-inch telescope. Once he had located the variables and determined their periods and apparent magnitudes, he used Leavitt's period-luminosity relationship to determine their distances. He concluded that the great spiral Andromeda Nebula is roughly 900,000 light-years away, a fantastically large distance, placing it clearly outside our own galaxy and proving that, in general, galaxies are islands in the universe. To allow for interstellar absorption, Hubble's distance estimate had to be later reduced to roughly 750,000 light-years, a figure that stood until shortly before Hubble's death.

Hubble continued to determine galactic distances and to study galactic characteristics. By 1925 he had enough observations to propose a scheme for their classification: he imagined concentrated, very luminous, spheroidal galaxies to merge into ellipsoidal ones, which in turn branched into "normal spirals" on the one hand, and "barred spirals" on the other. Hubble tended to avoid drawing evolutionary conclusions from his scheme, but it was clearly very suggestive in that direction. Furthermore, it proved invaluable in statistical studies of the universe. At the time of his death, Hubble was attempting to revise his scheme in order to make it more complete.

Expanding Universe

In the late 1920s Hubble laid the observational groundwork for the most spectacular astronomical discovery of this century: the expanding universe. V. M. Silpher had, over a period of years, made spectroscopic observations on tens of nebulae (galaxies) which indicated, on the basis of the Doppler shifts recorded, that these nebulae were receding from the earth at velocities between roughly 300 and 1,800 kilometers per second. Hubble realized the great importance of Silpher's observations for cosmological theories and organized a plan for measuring both the distances and (radial) velocities of as many galaxies as possible, down to the faintest ones detectable with Mount Wilson's 100-inch telescope.

While an assistant, M. L. Humason photographed galactic spectra and analyzed the observed Doppler shifts. Hubble photographed the galaxies themselves, searched for Cepheid variable stars, and computed the distances to the galaxies. By 1929 Hubble had distance data on Silpher's nebulae and announced what became known as Hubble's law: the velocity of recession of a galaxy is directly proportional to its distance from the earth. By the early 1940s this law had been confirmed for galactic velocities up to roughly 45,000 kilometers per second, corresponding to galactic distances up to roughly 220 million light-years.

During the 1930s Hubble became more and more cautious over the interpretation to be placed on the observed Doppler displacements, preferring to refer to them by the neutral (theory-free) term "red shifts." Thus, if at some future time these red shifts were found to be due, not to recessional velocity, but to some presently unknown physical law, the term "red shift" could still be retained as a description.

Postwar Work

After World War II Hubble devoted a great deal of time to planning the research program of the 200-inch Hale telescope at Mount Palomar; he was almost entirely responsible for conceiving and executing the National Geographic Society-Palomar Observatory Sky Survey carried out with the 48-inch Schmidt telescope. He received many honors, including a number of honorary degrees and medals, as well as membership in the National Academy of Sciences and other honorary societies. For his war research he received the Medal of Merit for 1946. In 1948 he was elected an honorary fellow of Queen's College, Oxford. He died of a coronary thrombosis in San Marino, Calif., on Sept. 28, 1953. In 1990, NASA launched the Hubble Space Telescope, which was named in his honor.

Further Reading

Hubble discusses his own work in *The Realm of the Nebulae* (1937) and *Observational Approach to Cosmology* (1937). For brief treatments of his life and work see Bernard Jaffe, *Men of Science in America* (1944; rev. ed. 1958); Otto Struve and Velta Zebergs, *Astronomy of the 20th Century* (1962); and Harlow Shapley, *Through Rugged Ways to the Stars* (1969). □

Ricarda Huch

Ricarda Huch (1864-1947), German novelist, poet, and cultural historian, won renown as a talented writer in several genres.

Ricarda Huch was born in Brunswick (Braunschweig) on Aug. 18, 1864, the daughter of a merchant. She became the first female student admitted to the University of Zurich at a time when women could not study at any German university; she obtained her doctorate in history in 1892. The next years she spent working first as a librarian in Zurich and later as a schoolteacher in Bremen. Her Swiss experiences she later described in a charming book of memoirs, *Frühling in der Schweiz* (1938).

Huch's first creative phase (1890-1900) is marked by several volumes of lyrical poetry written in neoromantic style: *Gedichte* (1891) and *Neue Gedichte* (1907), both later issued under the title *Liebeslyrik* (1913). Their central theme is that of her love for her cousin Richard Huch, whom she married in 1907 after divorcing her first husband, an Italian dentist, Ermanno Ceconi. Her second marriage lasted only 3 years.

Huch's first novel was a highly romantic book on which her early fame rested: *Erinnerungen von Ludolf Ursleu dem Jüngeren* (1892). *Aus der Triumphgasse* (1902) mixes realistic and romantic elements in describing the slum districts of Trieste. But her basic theme, the will to live, finds expression here and in her next novel, *Vita somnium breve* (1903).

Huch won prominence during the years 1902 to 1910 as a master of the historical novel. Best known are two brilliant works dealing with the romantic period in German history: *Blütezeit der Romantik* (1899) and *Ausbreitung und Verfall der Romantik* (1902). Several of her books from this period center on the theme of the unification of Italy in the 19th century: *Die Geschichten von Garibaldi* (1906-1907), *Die Verteidigung Roms* (1906), and *Der Kampf um Rom* (1907). Later she turned to the historical works that assure her a lasting place in the history of German letters: Her trilogy, *Deutsche Geschichte* (1912-1949), deals respectively with Germany during the Thirty Years War, the Reformation, and the collapse of the Holy Roman Empire. Lighter works include a successful series of *novellen* (short tales)

enry Hudson's life is undocumented prior to his famous voyages. He is first recorded in 1607 as commander of an English Muscovy Company ship that attempted to reach the Orient by sailing northward and southward across the polar sea. This hopeless quest led Hudson to explore the eastern coast of Greenland, gain more accurate information about Spitsbergen, and discover Hudson's "Tutches" (Jan Mayen Island).

The next year Hudson sailed to the Arctic again, hoping to find the passage to Asia via Novaya Zemlya. Failing, as the Dutch navigator Willem Barents had earlier failed, Hudson returned to England. There he was approached by agents of the Dutch East India Company, which had not abandoned hopes of a Northeast Passage. In 1609 the Dutch company gave the explorer command of the *Half Moon* and perhaps another ship called *Good Hope,* with crews largely recruited from Dutch seamen.

The search for a Northeast Passage took Hudson again to Novaya Zemlya, where his passage was blocked by ice and his crews grew increasingly mutinous. He then changed plans, disregarding orders, and decided to seek a passage through North America. In doing this Hudson was clearly influenced by Capt. John Smith, who had corresponded with him and lent him maps. Hudson's expeditionary fleet, now reduced to the *Half Moon,* crossed the Atlantic and explored a stretch of North American coast extending southward to New York Bay.

Although nearly a century earlier the Italian navigator Giovanni da Verrazano, sailing in the service of France, had

and a psychological detective novel, *Der Fall Daruga* (1917).

At the time of Hitler's rise to power in Germany the writer was one of her country's most respected members of the Preussische Dichterakademie (Academy of Prussian Writers). However, in protest to Hitler's dictatorship, she refused to join the newly founded Nazi Academy of Writers.

The numerous honors awarded to Huch included appointment as honorary senator of the University of Munich (1924), the Goethe Prize of Frankfurt (1931), and an honorary doctorate at the University of Jena (1946). She died while visiting in Frankfurt am Main on Nov. 17, 1947.

Further Reading

Material on Ricarda Huch in English is scarce. For her place in German Literature see J. G. Robertson, *A History of German Literature* (rev. ed. 1947); H. Boeschenstein, *The German Novel, 1934-44* (1949); and Ronald Gray, *The German Tradition in Literature, 1871-1945* (1965). □

Henry Hudson

Henry Hudson (active 1607-1611) was an English navigator who explored areas of America for England and the Netherlands.

entered New York Bay, Hudson in the *Half Moon* ascended the river nearly to present-day Albany. The ascent of the river, later named in Hudson's honor, gave the Dutch claim to the area, but it failed to satisfy Hudson, for it still offered no water route to Asia. He returned to England in November 1609, and the English authorities ordered him not to return to the Netherlands but to resume exploration for his own country.

English explorers had already carried the search for a Northwest Passage to the strait (ultimately named for Hudson) between Baffin Island and Labrador. A number of English merchants now sent Hudson, in command of the *Discovery,* to find a way through to the "South Sea" (Pacific Ocean). Crew discontent plagued him from the start. (The ringleader, Robert Juet, had sailed on the previous voyage with Hudson and had written a first hand account of it.) Hudson and his crew entered Hudson Strait on June 24-25, 1610, then followed the narrower passage into Hudson's Bay, whose eastern coast they explored to the southern extremity of James Bay. After a vain search for a western way out of this bay, their ship became icebound on November 10, and they passed a miserable winter, nearly starving. When warmer weather came, mutineers, led by Juet, placed Hudson and a few loyal crew members in an open boat and set it adrift; the mutineers sailed for England. Many died on the way, including Juet; and the survivors, when the truth leaked out, received prison sentences. Nothing more is known of Hudson, but as the weather was still very cold, he and his friends must have died of exposure.

Further Reading

Robert Juet's and other accounts of Hudson's career may be consulted in G. M. Asher, ed., *Henry Hudson the Navigator: The Original Documents* (1860). Thomas A. Janvier, *Henry Hudson* (1909), was written to commemorate the third centennial of Hudson's voyage up the Hudson River. See also Llewelyn Powys, *Henry Hudson* (1928). Edward Heawood, *A History of Geographical Discovery in the Seventeenth and Eighteenth Centuries* (1912), devotes substantial space to Hudson. □

Victoriano Huerta

Victoriano Huerta (1854-1916) was a Mexican general and political leader who, in 1913, overthrew the first government to emerge from the Mexican Revolution and became the executive of a counterrevolutionary regime.

Victoriano Huerta was born of Huichol Indian parents in Colotlán, Jalisco, on Dec. 23, 1854. He received military training at the Chapultepec Military College. During the rule of Porfirio Díaz, Huerta's abilities brought him recognition and advancement to the rank of general. In 1901 he was in command of the military campaign which crushed the resistance of the Maya Indians. When Díaz's regime collapsed in 1911 and the aging dictator was forced into exile, Gen. Huerta commanded the escort which accompanied Díaz safely to Veracruz.

At the very time that Francisco Madero was endeavoring to arrange for the peaceful discharge of the revolutionary forces in Morelos, interim president Francisco de la Barra ordered Gen. Huerta to crush the peasant followers of Emiliano Zapata. When Madero, who wanted a peaceful solution, assumed the presidency, Huerta was sent into temporary retirement. Nonetheless, the impatient agrarians of Morelos rebelled against the new administration less than 3 weeks after it took office. When Pascual Orozco pronounced against Madero in February 1912 in northern Mexico with conservative backing, Huerta was recalled to active duty and, after careful preparations, crushed the rebellion. Returning to the capital, he was rankled by Madero's treatment of him.

The revolt led by Bernardo Reyes and Félix Díaz in February 1913 made it necessary for Madero once more to place his fate in the hands of Huerta. After the carnage in Mexico City known as the "Ten Tragic Days," Huerta made a deal with Félix Díaz to betray the Madero government. Madero and his vice president, Pino Suárez, were seized and, influenced by promises that they and their associates would be protected, resigned their posts. Huerta assumed the provisional presidency and, on the night of Feb. 22, 1913, while being transferred from the National Palace to prison, Madero and Pino Suárez were assassinated by their escort.

Although there is no evidence of Huerta's direct responsibility in the tragic events, he and his administration could not escape blame for the bloody trail which led to his secretary of war. Madero's martyrdom unified the divided revolutionaries, and United States president Woodrow Wilson refused to recognize a regime which had come to power through murder. Having outmaneuvered Félix Díaz, Huerta became president in a farcical October election and tended to conduct national business behind a bottle of cognac in the Café Colón.

The regime of the heavy-drinking Huerta became more oppressive the more desperate the leader became. Opposition was suppressed, and critics like Senator Belisario Domínguez met violent death. With the dissolution of Congress, all pretense of representative government ended. Venustiano Carranza became the first chief of the Constitutionalist movement to avenge Madero and reestablish constitutional government. These forces, led by Carranza, Pancho Villa, and Álvaro Obregón in the north and Zapata's guerrilla army in the south, were aided by the lifting of the United States arms embargo.

The brief arrest of some American sailors at Tampico (April 1914) became an "affair of honor" for President Wilson, who, to prevent a German arms shipment from reaching Huerta, ordered the occupation of Veracruz. This almost permitted Huerta to rally the nation behind him. Military victories by revolutionary forces—Villa at Torreón and at Zacatecas and Obregón on the west coast—splintered Huerta's army, and on July 15, 1914, Huerta escaped to Veracruz.

After living for a time in Forest Hills, N.Y., Huerta traveled to the southwest border to join other antiregime plotters. Arrested for conspiracy, he died at El Paso, Tex., on Jan. 13, 1916, shortly after being released for health reasons from Fort Bliss.

Further Reading

While there have been no full biographical studies of Huerta, there recently has developed a revisionist effort emphasizing the need for serious restudying of the man and his regime. This need was pointed out by William L. Sherman and Richard E. Greenleaf in *Victoriano Huerta: A Reappraisal* (1960). Details of Huerta's role in the De la Barra and Madero periods are to be found in Stanley R. Ross, *Francisco I. Madero: Apostle of Mexican Democracy* (1955). Two scholarly studies of diplomatic relations during Huerta's government are available: Peter Calvert, *The Mexican Revolution, 1910-1914: The Diplomacy of Anglo-American Conflict* (1968), and Kenneth J. Grieb, *The United States and Huerta* (1969). See also John Womack, *Zapata and the Mexican Revolution* (1969). □

Sir William Huggins

The English astronomer Sir William Huggins (1824-1910) pioneered in applying the techniques of spectrum analysis, or spectroscopy, to the study of the stars.

William Huggins was born in London on Feb. 7, 1824, to a family of considerable means. Educated by tutors and under no obligation to earn a living, he occupied his early years with the study of physics, chemistry, and physiology. Only in 1856 did his interests settle on astronomy, and upon building a private observatory during that same year at Tulse Hill, South London, he began making routine types of observations. Then, in 1859, Gustav Kirchhoff and Robert Bunsen published their epochal interpretation of spectral lines, according to which each of the chemical elements emits and absorbs light of various characteristic frequencies. Huggins became one of the small band of astronomers who utilized this discovery to forge a new branch of science—astrophysics.

Much of the early spectroscopy work concerned the sun, whose spectrum displayed numerous dark lines, the significance of which could scarcely be guessed. The analogous spectra of stars were so faint that little more could be done than group them into various types, in the hope (eventually fulfilled) that each type would correspond to a particular type of star, or even a particular phase in an evolutionary cycle of star development. Huggins, however, determined to perfect his instruments to the point of permitting some genuine analysis of stellar spectra. By 1863 he had succeeded to the extent of being able to name some of the chemical constituents of several stars on the basis of numerous stellar emission lines. Similar attempts on comets and planets were less successful, but those on the nebulae were nothing short of spectacular. For about a century these hazy spots of light had been cataloged by the thousands. As

telescopes were improved, many nebulae had been resolved into millions of individual stars grouped into what are now termed other galaxies. Whether all nebulae could be so resolved, or whether some of them were something other than a collection of stars, was decided by Huggins in 1864, when he discovered, in the constellation Draco, a bright nebula whose spectrum clearly stamped it a mass of glowing gas.

Interesting as these early findings were, their very novelty militated against appreciation of the real significance of the new tool—spectroscopy. In 1868, however, Huggins established the truly revolutionary character of spectroscopy beyond all doubt. Celestial movements were what astronomers understood, and movements were what he gave them—movements of a kind unobtainable in any other way. By drawing an analogy to the shift of pitch that accompanies a moving source of sound waves (the Doppler effect), he inferred, by measuring a shift in its spectral lines, that the bright star Sirius was moving away from the sun at a rate of 29 miles per second.

Huggins worked until the day of his death, on May 12, 1910, following the lines of research opened in his first decade of spectroscopic inquiry and pioneering in the use of photography. In recognition of his contributions he was knighted (1897), awarded the Order of Merit (1902), and showered with honors from all parts of the scientific world.

Further Reading

The only biography of Huggins is John Montefiore and others, *A Sketch of the Life of Sir William Huggins, K. C. B., O. M.* (1936), from material collected by Lady Huggins. ☐

Charles Evans Hughes

The American jurist and statesman Charles Evans Hughes (1862-1948) served as secretary of state in two administrations and was a chief justice of the Supreme Court.

Charles Evans Hughes was born at Glens Falls, N.Y., on April 14, 1862, the son of a minister. Precocious and gifted with a phenomenal memory, Hughes entered Madison University at the age of 14, transferring later to Brown University. He graduated from Cornell Law School in 1884. For the next 20 years he practiced law, briefly interrupting his work to teach law at Cornell.

At the age of 43 Hughes was chosen by a legislative committee to investigate the gas and electric industry in New York. His brilliant success in exposing extortionate rates led to his appointment as investigator of the insurance scandals in New York. In 1906 he was nominated as the Republican gubernatorial candidate. He won in a bitter campaign against William Randolph Hearst.

Hughes was a vigorous governor. He won a battle for the regulation of public utilities, strove to stamp out racetrack gambling, and was interested in conservation and in an employment compensation law. He was an exacting administrator, demanding high standards.

After a second term as governor, Hughes was appointed an associate justice of the Supreme Court by President William Howard Taft. He distinguished himself by supporting national railroad rate regulation and wrote one of the most important decisions in this field. In 1916 Hughes resigned from the Court to accept the Republican presidential nomination. He was beaten by a narrow margin in the ensuing campaign against Woodrow Wilson. In 1920 Hughes advocated ratification of the League of Nations treaty with reservations and urged the election of Warren Harding to implement acceptance. However, once appointed Harding's secretary of state, he made no effort to secure American adherence to the League Covenant.

Hughes was a brilliant secretary of state. He began by calling the Washington Conference on the Limitation of Armaments, at which he electrified the delegates by proposing a specific schedule for reducing the battleship force of the great naval powers. After some jockeying, a treaty was signed. In a significant concession to Japan, the United States agreed not to increase its fortifications in the Far Pacific. Hughes also brought about a partial settlement of the vexing question of German World War I reparations, gave a more precise definition to the Monroe Doctrine, and improved the quality of the U.S. Foreign service.

After 1925 Hughes for the most part practiced law until, in 1930, he was nominated by President Herbert Hoover as chief justice of the United States. Hughes presided over a Court badly divided and hostile to the New Deal of incoming president Franklin D. Roosevelt. He joined in the Court's decision to set aside the National Recovery Act of 1934 and in the ruling against the Agricultural Recovery Act of 1935. When President Roosevelt advanced his famous Court-packing plan in 1937, Hughes carefully pulverized the President's argument that the Court was behind in its work. This sparring ended when Hughes joined four other justices in sustaining the Wagner Labor Relations Act, an important piece of New Deal legislation. Hughes always maintained that he acted on the basis of the law, not political considerations.

Hughes took an advanced stand on civil rights, especially in cases involving African American rights, and he was a firm advocate of freedom of the press. He resigned from the Court in 1941 and died on Aug. 27, 1948.

Further Reading

The authorized biography of Hughes is Merlo J. Pusey, *Charles Evans Hughes* (2 vols., 1951). A briefer study is Dexter Perkins, *Charles Evans Hughes and American Democratic Statesmanship* (1956). A study of the Progressive movement in New York State, with the focus upon Hughes's years as governor, is Robert F. Wesser, *Charles Evans Hughes: Politics and Reform in New York, 1905-1910* (1967).

Additional Sources

Perkins, Dexter, *Charles Evans Hughes and American democratic statesmanship,* Westport, Conn.: Greenwood Press, 1978.
Pusey, Merlo John, *Charles Evans Hughes,* New York: Garland Pub., 1979. □

Howard Robard Hughes

Howard Robard Hughes (1905-1976) was a flamboyant entreprenuer who used an inherited fortune to achieve a national reputation in the motion picture and aviation industries, remaining in the news in later years because of his paranoid concern for privacy.

oward Robard Hughes was born in Houston, Texas, on December 24, 1905, the only child of Howard Robard Hughes and Alene Gano Hughes. He attended private schools in California and Massachusetts, Rice Institute in Houston, and the California Institute of Technology. His mother died when Hughes was 16 and his father when he was 18, leaving him an orphan but with an estate worth $871,000 and a patent for a drill bit used in most oil and gas drilling that brought large revenues to the family's Hughes Tool Company that manufactured the bit. Hughes left school to take control of the company, using its profits to finance a variety of projects which he hoped would make him a legend in his own time. In 1925, when he was 20, Hughes married Ella Rice and moved to Los Angeles (they separated in 1928). In 1927 Hughes entered the motion picture business and produced such films as "Hell's Angels" (1930), "Scarface" (1932), and "The Outlaw" (1941). He discovered actors Jean Harlow and Paul Muni and made Jane Russell a well-known star.

In 1928 Hughes obtained a pilot's license. His interest in aviation led him to found the Hughes Aircraft Company in Glendale in 1932 and to design, build, and fly record-breaking airplanes. He set a world speed record in 1935, transcontinental speed records in 1936 and 1937, and a world flight record in 1938. Hughes was honored with the Harmon Trophy and a New York City ticker-tape parade after his world flight. He was awarded the Collier Trophy in 1939, the Octave Chanute Award in 1940, and a Congressional Medal in 1941.

In 1939 he began work on an experimental military aircraft, and in 1942 he received a contract to design and build the world's largest plane, a wooden seaplane, later nicknamed the "Spruce Goose," which was supposed to serve as a troop carrier in World War II. Hughes suffered a nervous breakdown in 1944 and was critically injured in the crash of his experimental military plane in 1946, but he recovered and flew the huge seaplane the next year, blunting the congressional investigation of his war contracts. As a result of these aviation activities, Hughes became a popular public figure because he seemed to embody the traditional American qualities of individuality, daring, and ingenuity. He was named to the Aviation Hall of Fame in 1973.

The Hughes Aircraft Company became a major defense contractor after World War II. As the profits of the company increased, Hughes became obsessed with avoiding taxes and in 1953 created the Howard Hughes Medical Institute as a sophisticated tax shelter to which he transferred the assets of the aircraft company. In 1956 Hughes loaned $205,000 to Richard Nixon's brother Donald in a successful effort to influence an Internal Revenue Service ruling on the medical institute. Hughes made secret contributions of $100,000 to the Nixon campaign in 1970 and was able to prevent enforcement of the Tax Reform Act against the medical institute. Hughes continued to use profits from the tool company for other ventures, including the creation of Trans World Airlines (TWA), in which he had begun investing in 1939.

In 1950 he went into seclusion, beginning a lifestyle which would ultimately turn him into a recluse, although he did marry actress Jean Peters in 1957, divorcing her in 1971. Hughes refused to appear in court or even give a deposition, and in a 1963 antitrust case over his ownership of 78 percent of TWA, his failure to appear resulted in a default ruling that led him to sell his holdings in 1966. The $566 million received from this sale was invested by Hughes in Las Vegas hotels, gambling casinos, golf courses, a television station, an airport, and land. In 1972 the Hughes Tool Division, the basis of the Hughes fortune, was sold. The holding company was renamed Summa Corporation and its headquarters relocated to Las Vegas, where Hughes had moved his residence.

From this point in his career, Hughes' accomplishments were minimal. His obsession to control every aspect of his environment turned him into a recluse seen by a few associates and isolated from the operations of his company. In 1970 he left the United States, abruptly moving from place to place—the Bahamas, Nicaragua, Canada, England, and Mexico. He always arrived unannounced in luxury hotels and took extreme precautions to ensure privacy. Hughes saw only a few male aides, worked for days without sleep in a black-curtained room, and became emaciated from the effects of a meager diet and the excessive use of drugs. His concern for privacy ultimately caused controversy, resulting in a scandal over his supposed memoirs by author Clifford Irving that sold for $1 million before being proven fraudulent. The Hughes conglomerate became involved with the Central Intelligence Agency (CIA), and in 1975 it built an undersea exploratory drilling ship which was actually for use by the CIA to attempt to recover a sunken Soviet submarine. The company retained a Washington, D.C., public relations firm that was also involved with the CIA, which led the Hughes corporation to become involved in the Watergate affair.

Hughes died, a hopeless psychotic, on April 5, 1976, on an airplane that was taking him from Acapulco, Mexico, to a hospital in Houston for medical attention. Hughes was controversial even after his death. Several wills appeared, one of which was found in the Mormon church in Salt Lake City, Utah, but all were declared to be forgeries after protracted litigation.

Further Reading

There are numerous books devoted to the controversial Hughes. The best biography is Donald L. Barlett and James B. Steele, *Empire: The Life, Legend, and Madness of Howard Hughes* (1979). John Keats, *Howard Hughes* (1972) is excellent on the qualities which made Hughes popular with Americans in the 1930s and 1940s. Noah Dietrich and Bob Thomas, *Howard: The Amazing Mr. Hughes* (1972) provide an insider's view of Hughes' business affairs. James Phelan, *Howard Hughes: The Hidden Years* (1976) is the best book on Hughes' final years as a recluse. Michael Drosnin, *Citizen Hughes: In His Own Words—How Howard Hughes Tried To Buy America* (1985) is an example of studies which are extremely critical of Hughes' methods. □

John Joseph Hughes

Irish-born John Joseph Hughes (1797-1864) was the first Catholic archbishop of New York and an outspoken defender of American Catholicism against Protestant attacks.

John Hughes emigrated from Ireland to the United States in 1817. Denied admission to Mount Saint Mary's Seminary, he served as that institution's gardener. After diligent study he finally matriculated as a regular student and in 1826 received ordination. As a young priest in Philadelphia, he soon was embroiled in a dispute over lay trusteeism. Throughout the history of Catholicism the administration of Church property had been the bishop's responsibility; in America, however, laymen claimed the right to manage the Philadelphia Cathedral, as well as the authority to name their own pastor. The clergy's efforts to establish their traditional prerogatives angered Protestants, who regarded the Catholic hierarchy as somehow subversive and the principle of lay control as more consonant with American democracy. Hughes's newspaper debates with Protestant critics soon made him famous.

In 1838 Hughes became coadjutor bishop of New York and the following year was made administrator in his own right. Once again he was involved in an episode of anti-Catholic sentiment—the struggle over the New York City public schools. Hughes objected to the Protestant religious practices required of Catholic students in the supposedly nonsectarian educational system. The ensuing turmoil resulted in complete reorganization of the school system, although Hughes's demand for tax money for parochial schools went unheeded. Soon the Native American party began attacking Hughes for allegedly having driven the Bible out of the classroom.

In 1850 Rome elevated New York to a province and made Hughes its first archbishop. He opposed a bill pend-

ing in the state legislature that would prevent bishops from holding Church property in their own name; although the bill passed, the state never enforced it. He also carried the burden of defending his Church against the attacks of the Know-Nothing party, while reflecting the conservatism of New York City in his stand on slavery. He rejected abolition, fearing that African Americans would not be prepared for freedom. But when the South seceded, he remained a staunch unionist. During the Civil War he undertook a diplomatic mission to France for President Abraham Lincoln and, in July 1863, helped New York's governor put down the draft riots. Hughes died on Jan. 3, 1864.

Further Reading

There is no recent biography of Hughes. Henry A. Brann, *Most Reverend John Hughes* (1892), is uncritically laudatory but presents a complete account. Contemporary scholars have given attention to selected aspects of his career. Ray Allen Billington, *The Protestant Crusade, 1800-1860* (1964), is a comprehensive study of 19th-century nativism, which focused so much of its attention on Hughes. Vincent P. Lannie, *Public Money and Parochial Education: Bishop Hughes, Governor Seward, and the New York School Controversy* (1968), gives intensive coverage to Hughes's role in the debate over public schools.

Additional Sources

Shaw, Richard, *Dagger John: the unquiet life and times of Archbishop John Hughes of New York,* New York: Paulist Press, 1977. □

River," which marked this development, appeared in the *Crisis* in 1921.

Hughes returned to America and enrolled at Columbia University; meanwhile, the *Crisis* printed several more of his poems. Finding the atmosphere at Columbia uncongenial, Hughes left after a year. He did odd jobs in New York. In 1923 he signed on as steward on a freighter. His first voyage took him down the west coast of Africa; his second took him to Spain. In 1924 he spent 6 months in Paris. He was relatively happy, produced some prose, and experimented with what he called "racial rhythms" in poetry. Most of this verse appeared in African American publications, but *Vanity Fair,* a magazine popular among middle-and upper-class women, published three poems.

Later in 1924 Hughes went to live with his mother in Washington, D.C. He hoped to earn enough money to return to college, but work as a hotel busboy paid very little, and life in the nation's capital, where class distinctions among African Americans were quite rigid, made him unhappy. He wrote many poems. "The Weary Blues" won first prize in 1925 in a literary competition sponsored by *Opportunity,* a magazine published by the National Urban League. That summer one of his essays and another poem won prizes in the *Crisis* literary contest. Meanwhile, Hughes had come to the attention of Carl Van Vechten, a white novelist and critic, who arranged publication of Hughes's first volume of verse, *The Weary Blues* (1926).

This book projected Hughes's enduring themes, established his style, and suggested the wide range of his poetic

Langston Hughes

American author Langston Hughes (1902-1967), a moving spirit in the artistic ferment of the 1920s often called the Harlem Renaissance, expressed the mind and spirit of most African Americans for nearly half a century.

Langston Hughes was born in Joplin, Mo., on Feb. 1, 1902. His parents soon separated, and Hughes was reared mainly by his mother, his maternal grandmother, and a childless couple named Reed. He attended public schools in Kansas and Illinois, graduating from high school in Cleveland, Ohio, in 1920. His high school companions, most of whom were white, remembered him as a handsome "Indian-looking" youth whom everyone liked and respected for his quiet, natural ways and his abilities. He won an athletic letter in track and held offices in the student council and the American Civic Association. In his senior year he was chosen class poet and yearbook editor.

Hughes spent the next year in Mexico with his father, who tried to discourage him from writing. But Hughes's poetry and prose were beginning to appear in the *Brownie's Book,* a publication for children edited by W. E. B. Du Bois, and he was starting work on more ambitious material dealing with adult realities. The poem "A Negro Speaks of

talent. It showed him committed to racial themes—pride in blackness and in his African heritage, the tragic mulatto, the everyday life of African Americans—and democracy and patriotism. Hughes transformed the bitterness which such themes generated in many of his African American contemporaries into sharp irony, gentle satire, and humor. His casual-seeming, folklike style, reflecting the simplicity and the earthy sincerity of his people, was strengthened in his second book, *Fine Clothes to the Jew* (1927).

Hughes had resumed his education in 1925 and graduated from Lincoln University in 1929. *Not without Laughter* (1930) was his first novel. The story deals with an African American boy, Sandy, caught between two worlds and two attitudes. The boy's hardworking, respectability-seeking mother provides a counterpoint to his high-spirited, easy-laughing, footloose father. The mother is oriented to the middle-class values of the white world; the father believes that fun and laughter are the only virtues worth pursuing. Though the boy's character is blurred, Hughes's attention to details that reveal African American culture in America gives the novel strength.

The relative commercial success of his novel inspired Hughes to try making his living as an author. In 1931 he made the first of what became annual lecture tours. He took a trip to Soviet Union the next year. Meanwhile, he turned out poems, essays, book reviews, song lyrics, plays, and short stories. He edited five anthologies of African American writing and collaborated with Arna Bontemps on another and on a book for children. He wrote some 20 plays, including *Mulatto, Simply Heavenly,* and *Tambourines to Glory.* He translated Federico Garcia Lorca, the Spanish poet, and Gabriela Mistral, the Latin American Nobel laureate poet, and wrote two long autobiographical works.

As a newspaper columnist, Hughes created "Simple," probably his most enduring character, brought his style to perfection, and solidified his reputation as the "most eloquent spokesman" for African Americans. The Simple sketches, collected in five volumes, are presented as conversations between an uneducated, African American city dweller, Jesse B. Semple (Simple), and an educated but less sensitive African American acquaintance. The sketches, which ran in the *Chicago Defender* for 25 years, are too varied in subject, too relevant to the universal human condition, and too remarkable in their display of Hughes's best writing for any quick summary. That Simple is a universal man, even though his language, habits, and personality are the result of his particular experiences as an African American man, is a measure of Hughes's genius.

Hughes received numerous fellowships, awards, and honorary degrees, including the Anisfield-Wolf Award (1953) for a book on improving race relations. He taught creative writing at two universities; had his plays produced on four continents; and made recordings of African American history, music commentary, and his own poetry. He was elected to the American Academy of Arts and Sciences and to the National Institute of Arts and Letters. His work, some of which was translated into a dozen languages, earned him an international reputation unlike any other African American writer except Richard Wright and Ralph Ellison. Forty-seven volumes bear Hughes's name. He died in New York City on May 22, 1967.

Further Reading

The chief sources of biographical data are Hughes's autobiographical *The Big Sea* (1940) and *I Wonder as I Wander: An Autobiographical Journey* (1956); Donald C. Dickinson, *A Bio-Bibliography of Langston Hughes, 1902-1967* (1967); James A. Emanuel, *Langston Hughes* (1967); Milton Meltzer, *Langston Hughes: A Biography* (1968); and Charlemae H. Rollins, *Black Troubadour: Langston Hughes* (1970). Hughes gets extensive critical treatment in Saunders Redding, *To Make a Poet Black* (1939); Hugh M. Gloster, *Negro Voices in American Fiction* (1948); John Milton Charles Hughes, *The Negro Novelist, 1940-1950* (1953); and Robert A. Boone, *The Negro Novel in America* (1958). Historical background is provided by Benjamin O. Brawley, *The Negro in Literature and Art in the United States* (1918); John Hope Franklin, *From Slavery to Freedom: A History of Negro Americans* (1947; 3d ed. 1967); and Vernon Loggins, *The Negro Author: His Development in America to 1900* (1959). □

Ted Hughes

Ted Hughes (born 1930) was an eminent English poet who led a resurgence of English poetic innovation starting in the late 1950s. He was named poet laureate in 1985.

Ted Hughes was born in 1930 in the Yorkshire town of Mytholmroyd in England. His home backed onto a canal, while close by was the main road from the Yorkshire woolen towns to the cotton centers of Lancashire over the Pennine hills. This landscape was indelibly to shape his future poetry as he struggled to create a usable language that could accommodate poetry and literature to the demands of an increasingly post-literate society.

In the 1950s Hughes went to Pembroke College, Cambridge, where he started to "read" English but changed to anthropology as he felt that the academic study of English literature conflicted with his search for poetic creativity. It was at Cambridge in 1956 that he met the American poet Sylvia Plath whom he later married. The marriage produced a son and a daughter before Plath's suicide in 1963. During the time they were together an important process of mutual aesthetic stimulation took place, and it is a relationship that has fascinated some critics almost as much as that between Scott and Zelda Fitzgerald.

In 1957 Hughes' first book of poetry, *Hawk in the Rain,* was published to immediate acclaim and placed him as a leading exponent of what the critic A. Alvarez called the "new depth poetry." Hughes' poetry revolted against the depiction of landscape in romantic and genteel terms—this had been a dominant tradition in English poetry from the time of the Lake poets of the early 19th century and had received a new impetus from the Georgians before World War I. However, Hughes was also reacting to the modernism of such poets as W. B. Yeats and T. S. Eliot and the

Pike too immense to stir, so immense and old/That past nightfall I dared not cast.'' The discovery of this England was clearly an immense task as the weight and burden of tradition was lifted away from English culture. For Hughes, though, this was an opportunity for the affirmation of a relationship with the surrounding landscape which, in his early period at least, was not burdened by Christian myth and ritual. His employment of pagan imagery thus, to some extent, distinguished him from the more religious concerns of Plath.

In the case of the poem "Hawk Roosting" in *Lupercal,* however, he was accused by some critics of writing a paean to fascist power as he depicted an animal in anthropomorphic terms: "I kill where I please because it is all mine. /There is no sophistry in my body: /My manners are tearing off heads.'' Similarly in the later collection *Crow* (1970) where he had chosen a considerably less aggressive natural symbol, "A Childish Prank" was seen as demeaning the relation between men and women as "Crow laughed. / He bit the Worm, God's only son, /Into two writhing halves.'' On the other hand, in Hughes' later poetry the beginnings of a healing process can be seen to have occurred as Hughes celebrated a more varied view of nature beyond that of struggle and survival. In *Moortown* (1978) the "Birth of Rainbow" offers a more optimistic view of procreation as the birth of a calf is described, while Hughes moved towards a fuller acceptance of the Christian tradition:'' . . . then the world blurred/And disappearing in forty-five degree hail/And a gate-jerking blast. We got to cover. / Left to God the calf and his mother.''

Hughes' poetry established his pre-eminence in English poetry at an early stage and indicated a resurgence of English poetic innovation after a long period of Welsh, Scottish, and Irish dominance. *Hawk in the Rain* won the First Publications Award in New York in 1957 and *Lupercal* won the Hawthornden Prize in 1961. Hughes won the Guinness Poetry Award in 1958 and the Somerset Maughan Award in 1960 and was a John Simon Guggenheim Fellow in 1959-1960. He also became a children's poet, publishing *Meet My Folks* in 1961, *The Earth-Owl and Other Moon People* in 1963, and *Nessie, The Mannerless Monster* in 1964, together with collections of children's stories. Hughes saw children's verse as a vital accompaniment to his poetry for he saw children as an important potential audience for poets, especially through the use of tapes and videos in schools.

Hughes' varied contributions to poetry led to his finally succeeding the late Sir John Betjeman as poet laureate in 1985. The appointment marked a radical departure from the genteel view of poetry of his popular predecessor. While clearly a major English poet, Hughes cannot be described as simply celebrating *Englishness* from a standpoint of inward-looking nationalism. Many of his early poems especially share a more general post-modernist concern with struggle and the violent affirmation of identity, and some more traditionally-minded critics have seen them as rather alien to the English spirit of harmony and compromise.

Since becoming poet laureate in 1985, Hughes' publications include verse: *Flowers and Insects* (1989),

concern for ritual and ceremony and was instead preoccupied with developing a more vital and direct link with animals and nature. In many ways this was a brutal and violent depiction of struggle and a Darwinian interest in the survival of the fittest. Hughes later stated that as a boy he had been fascinated by animals, seeing them as representatives of another world which was "the true world.'' The only relationship, though, as a boy from the town was one of catching or killing animals, and this reinforced the idea that animals were by nature victims of man's aggressive impulses.

Hughes' attitude to animals was a direct and self-conscious one, and he did not see them as strange and alien creatures and as representatives of mysterious hidden forces like D. H. Lawrence. The poem "The Horses," for instance, in *The Hawk in the Rain* speaks of horses as "Grey silent fragments of a grey silent world" and ends with the poet's later memory of meeting the horses in "hour-before-dawn dark'': "In din of crowded streets, going among the years, the faces, /May I still meet my memory in so lonely a place.''

Hughes became especially known for his graphic depiction of struggle and conflict such as the poem "Pike" in his second volume *Lupercal* in 1960: "Three we kept behind glass, /Jungled in weed: three inches, four, /And four and a half: fed fry to them-/Suddenly there were two. Finally one.'' The poem was also important for linking this natural struggle to the search for another England with which a number of poets of Hughes' generation were concerned. The pond in which Hughes used to fish in "Pike" had: "Stilled, legendary depth:/It was as deep as England. It held/

Moortown Diary (1989), *Rain-charm for the Duchy* (1992), *New Selected Poems 1957-1994* (1995); libretti: *Wedekind, Spring Awakening* (1995); stories: *Tales of the Early World* (1988), *The Iron Woman* (1993), *The Dreamfighter* (1995), *Collected Animal Poems* (1995); and prose: *Shakespeare and the Goddess of Complete Being* (1992), *Winter Pollen* (1994), and *Difficulties of a Bridegroom* (1995). In 1996, Hughes translated and published two dozen passages from Latin poet Publius Ouidius Naso's *Metamorphoses*.

Further Reading

Additional information on Ted Hughes can be found in Keith Sagar, *The Art of Ted Hughes* (Cambridge, 1975); Margaret D. Uroff, *Sylvia Plath and Ted Hughes* (1979); Terry Gifford and Neil Roberts, *Ted Hughes: A Critical Study* (London, 1981); Keith Sagar (editor), *The Achievement of Ted Hughes* (Manchester University Press, 1983); David Porter, ''Ted Hughes'' in *The American Poetry Review* (1971); Anthony Libby, ''God's Lioness and the Priest of Sycorax: Plath and Hughes'' in *Contemporary Literature* (1974); and Michael Wood, ''We All Hate Home: English Poetry since World War II'' in *Contemporary Literature* (1977). ☐

William Morris Hughes

William Morris Hughes (1864-1952) was an English-born Australian statesman. Displaying political acumen and unbridled ambition, he rose through the rough and tumble of the labor movement and became prime minister at the age of 51.

The son of Welsh parents, William Morris Hughes was born in London on Sept. 25, 1864. He attended grammar schools and was teaching school before he emigrated to Sydney in 1884. Several years spent as an itinerant worker in country areas gave him a sound knowledge of the life of the underdog in the hinterland. Rural workers were being unionized, and Hughes returned to Sydney to organize maritime workers into a union, becoming its secretary.

Emergence as Labour Leader

Elected as a member of the New South Wales Legislative Assembly in 1894, Hughes supported federation and was a candidate for the House of Representatives in 1901, when the Commonwealth Constitution came into force. Having studied law, he took up legal practice in addition to his parliamentary duties.

Hughes was appointed minister for external affairs in the short-lived Labour ministry of John Watson (1904) and was attorney general under Andrew Fisher in 1908-1909, 1910-1913, and 1914. Hughes's stature had been enhanced by his forceful tract *The Case for Labour* (1910), but he was too prickly to gain the approval of most rank-and-file members, who feared his mercurial independence. Nevertheless, on Fisher's appointment as high commissioner in London, Hughes was chosen Labour party leader, and he became

prime minister in October 1915. His ascendancy soon widened the growing rift between the parliamentary leadership and the party in general.

Wartime Prime Minister

War disillusionment was already apparent. In spite of heavy Australian losses, the ill-starred Gallipoli campaign, begun with high hopes in April 1915, had achieved little, and a withdrawal was seen as inevitable. Long casualty lists had soured many to the war, and the labor movement was highly critical of the parliamentary leadership's abandonment of legislation for social betterment. Labour was in an uproar as Hughes left for England, at the invitation of the United Kingdom War Cabinet, in January 1916. In his absence Labour's anticonscription attitude hardened; party and trade union conferences declared uncompromising opposition, while extremist groups campaigned actively against the entire war effort.

Heavy British casualties in the Battle of the Somme convinced Hughes of the need to follow the United Kingdom's lead and introduce conscription, but his Cabinet generally did not favor this course. In a compromise move Hughes gained approval for a poll on the issue. After the enabling act was passed, overt opposition to the war flared among extremist groups, particularly in Sydney. The referendum held in October rejected Hughes's proposal, but the rift within the Labour party widened, and the party voted to expel him and others who supported him.

Hughes formed a new Cabinet and continued in office with Liberal party support. Early in 1917 his ''National Labour'' group and the Liberals merged as the Nationalist party; a general election returned the new party. Hughes intensified recruiting but did not push for conscription legislation, preferring instead to put the issue to a second referendum (December 1917). The campaign was even more vituperative than in 1916, but again the proposal was rejected.

Hughes was determined to claim a major voice in Pacific affairs for Australia. In London and in Washington he pressed for the postwar cession of former German island territories and enunciated an Australian ''Monroe Doctrine.'' After gaining British Cabinet approval for his plan, he found that U.S. president Woodrow Wilson favored placing the former German colonies under League of Nations control. At the Versailles Peace Conference, Hughes agreed to accept a League mandate for German New Guinea (including the northern Solomons), with the safeguard of control over immigration into the territory. Hughes returned to Australia in August 1919 to a hero's welcome as the ''Little Digger,'' a reference to his frail and gnomish physique.

However, the plethora of wartime controls affecting the lives of citizens had built up resentment, and when Hughes intervened directly in wage determination (by passing the Arbitration Court), popular support began to fade. His parliamentary majority was trimmed in 1920, and after the 1922 election the Nationalists could govern only with Country party support. In 1923 Hughes was replaced by Stanley Bruce.

Hughes remained in Parliament, a thorn in the side of both Labour and Nationalists. From the mid-1920s he became a brooding and cantankerous critic of Bruce's measures, and in 1929 he sided with Labour to defeat a bill designed to pass to the states responsibility for virtually all wage arbitration matters. Bruce and the Nationalists were defeated in the ensuing election; for his part in the debacle Hughes was expelled from the party.

Final Years

When the United Australia party was formed from a merger of Labour breakaways and the Nationalists, Hughes joined it. He became minister for repatriation and health (1934), and subsequently he became minister for external affairs (1934-1939). On the death of Joseph Lyons in April 1939, Hughes was a candidate for the prime ministership, but he was narrowly defeated for the party leadership by Robert Gordon Menzies, under whom he became minister for the navy and attorney general (1939-1941).

With the changeover to the Labour administration of John Curtin, Hughes continued his diligent support of the war effort and refused to withdraw from the Advisory War Council when his party instructed him to do so; again he was expelled. In 1944 he supported Labour in its appeal for wider federal powers. In 1945 Hughes was invited to join the new Liberal party, successor to the United Australia party. He remained a member of the House of Representatives until his death, Oct. 28, 1952, having held a seat in the House since federation.

Further Reading

Hughes's early life is dealt with in L. F. Fitzhardinge, *A Political Biography of William Morris Hughes,* part 1: *That Fiery Particle, 1862-1914* (1964). See also Douglas Sladen, *From Boundary-rider to Prime Minister* (1916); F. C. Browne, *They Called Him Billy* (1946); and W. F. Whyte, *William Morris Hughes: His Life and Times* (1957). The period of Hughes's rise as a Labour leader is covered in R. A. Gollan, *Radical and Working Class Politics: A Study of Eastern Australia, 1850-1910* (1960); R. N. Ebbels, *The Australian Labor Movement, 1850-1907* (1965); and W. G. Spence, *Australia's Awakening: Thirty Years in the Life of an Australian Agitator* (1919).
The split within Labour is explored in V. G. Childe, *How Labour Governs* (1923; repr. 1966); Louise Overacker, *The Australian Party System* (1952); H. V. Evatt, *Australian Labour Leader: The Story of W. A. Holman and the Labour Movement* (1954); and D. W. Rawson, *Labor in Vain?* (1966). The rise of conservative opposition to Hughes is explained in U. R. Ellis, *A History of the Australian Country Party* (1963), and Earle Page, *Truant Surgeon: The Inside Story of Forty Years of Australian Political Life* (1963). Background on the parliamentary maneuvers involved in Hughes's replacement is in Frank C. Green, *Servant of the House* (1969).

Additional Sources

Booker, Malcolm, *The great professional: a study of W.M. Hughes,* Sydney; New York: McGraw-Hill, 1980.
Horne, Donald, *In search of Billy Hughes,* South Melbourne: Macmillan Co. of Australia, 1979. □

Vicomte Victor Marie Hugo

The French author Victor Marie, Vicomte Hugo (1802-1885), was the supreme poet of French romanticism. He is noted for the breadth of his creation, the versatility that made him as much at ease in the novel as in the short lyric, and the mystical grandeur of his vision.

Victor Hugo had a nomadic and anxious childhood. He was erratically schooled, a fact which accounts in part for the eclectic and unsystematic aspect of his poetic thought. At age 14 he wrote, "I want to be Chateaubriand or nothing." He had begun to write in every poetic genre—odes, satires, elegies, riddles, epics, madrigals—and to receive recognition while still in his adolescence, never having to fact the long years of obscurity and struggle that are the lot of most poets.

In 1822 Hugo married his childhood sweetheart, Adèle Foucher, one and a half years after the death of his mother, who opposed the match. They later had four children, and their apartment, on the rue Cherche-midi in Paris, became the meeting place for the avant-garde of the romantic movement. In 1822 Hugo also published his first signed book, *Odes et poésies diverses.* In the preface to this book, which contains many poems celebrating his love for Adèle, the poet wrote, "Poetry is the most intimate of all things."

Hugo's work may be roughly divided into three periods. First in time is the intimate lyrical vein typical of the odes. Second is an involved or committed poetry speaking directly to political and social conditions. The epic novel *Les Misérables,* for example, fits into this group. (But this vein is also present in the very first volume, where a number of poems praise the throne and the altar; Hugo, who was to end as a staunch republican, began as a royalist.) In the last phase of his career Hugo rose to the heights of mysticism and poetic vision, as in *La Fin de Satan.*

Development of Romanticism

In 1824 some of Hugo's friends founded a review called *Muse française* which claimed as its contributors Alfred de Musset, Charles Nodier, and Hugo himself. All were young writers who were beginning to break with neoclassicism. After his visit to Alphonse de Lamartine and his discovery of German balladry, in 1826 Hugo published *Odes et ballades,* in which his rejection of neoclassicism became increasingly clear.

The years 1826 and 1827 were triumphant ones for the *Cénacle,* the name given to the young romantics who recognized Hugo as their chief and called him the "prince of poets." What Lamartine and the Vicomte de Chateaubriand had begun, Hugo was dedicated to complete. He ceased writing complimentary odes to King Charles X and began praising Napoleon I instead. With critics like Nodier and Charles Sainte-Beuve to advise him and with the support of geniuses such as the painter Eugène Delacroix and the poets Musset and Gerard de Nerval, Hugo formulated the doc-

trine of romanticism. This doctrine was expressed in the preface to his unproduced play, *Cromwell,* published in October 1827. Where classics and neoclassics had repudiated the Middle Ages as "barbaric," Hugo saw richness and beauty in this period, and he called for a new poetry inspired by medieval Christianity. He vindicated the ugly and grotesque as elements of the "new beauty." Poetry, he said, should do as nature does, "mixing in its creations yet without confusion shadow with light, the grotesque with the sublime, in other words, the body with the soul, the bestial with the spiritual." The vivifying sources of this new literature were to be the Bible, Homer, and Shakespeare.

Convinced that the new vision must prove itself in the theater, Hugo followed *Cromwell* with a number of other plays. On Feb. 25, 1830, the famous "battle of *Hernani*" took place, with Hugo's supporters outshouting the neoclassicists and antiromantics who had come to hiss the play. *Hernani* was performed 45 times (an unusual success for those days) and brought Hugo the friendship of such notable figures as Dumas *père* and George Sand.

But Hugo did not confine himself to the drama. In 1831 he published his magnificent novel *Notre Dame de Paris,* the work for which he is best known in the United States. He was originally inspired by Sir Walter Scott, on whom he hoped to improve by adding "sentiment" and "poetry" to the historical novel. In addition, he wished to convey the true spirit of the late Middle Ages through his evocation of the Cathedral of Notre Dame and his characters: Frollo the archdeacon, Quasimodo the hunchback, and Esmeralda the gypsy girl. Hugo wrote the novel nonstop during the fall and early winter of 1830 in order to meet his publisher's deadline. Although some readers were shocked that Frollo (who had taken holy orders) should fall in love with Esmeralda, the tale was an immense success. Théophile Gautier compared it to Homer's *Iliad.*

Also in 1831 Hugo published one of his most beautiful collections of poetry, *Les Feuilles d'automne.* Once again, Hugo wrote in the intimate vein: "Poetry speaks to man, to man as a whole. . . . Revolution changes all things, except the human heart." This volume expressed the sadness of things past as the poet approached his significant thirtieth birthday. The tone was personal and elegiac, sometimes sentimental.

It was not merely the passage of time that accounted for Hugo's melancholy. His wife, tired of bearing children and frustrated by the poet's immense egoism (*Ego Hugo* was his motto), turned for consolation to the poet's intimate friend, the waspish critic Sainte-Beuve. The sadness of this double betrayal is felt in *Feuilles d'automne* .

Tormented by his wife's coldness and his own inordinate sexual cravings, Hugo fell in love with the young actress and courtesan Juliette Drouet and took it upon himself to "redeem" her. He paid her debts and forced her to live in poverty, with her whole being focused entirely upon him. For the next 50 years Juliette followed the poet wherever he went. She lived in his shadow, unable to take a step without his permission, confined to a room here, a mere hovel there, but always near the magnificent houses where Hugo settled with his family. She lived henceforth solely for the poet and spent her time writing him letters, of which many thousands are extant.

With the advent of the July Monarchy, which ended the Bourbon succession and brought Louis Philippe of the house of Orléans to power, Hugo achieved wealth and recognition, and for 15 years he was the official poet of France. During this period a host of new works appeared in rapid sequence, including three plays: *Le Roi s'amuse* (1832), *Lucrézia Borgia* (1833), and the triumph *Ruy Blas* (1838).

In 1835 came *Chants du crépuscule,* which included many love lyrics to Juliette, and in 1837 *Les Voix intérieures,* an offering to the memory of his father, who had been a Napoleonic general. *Les Rayons et les ombres* (1840) showed the same variety of inspiration, the same sonorous harmony, the same brilliance of contrasting images. His devotion to Juliette here found its deepest poetic expression in the beautiful poem entitled *Tristesse d'Olympio,* which directly rivals Lamartine's *Le Lac* and Alfred de *Vigny's Maison du berger* . Like these famous poets, Hugo evoked the past, searching for permanence of love; but unlike the pantheistic Lamartine or the skeptical Vigny, Hugo found permanence in memory.

Political Involvement

Hugo published no more lyric poetry until 1853. He was now seized with a new ambition: he wished to become a statesman. At first a royalist, then a moderate, Hugo moved steadily toward liberalism. After the July Revolution he wrote in a more stirring vein than he ever had before: "I hate oppression with a profound hatred. . . . I curse those kings who ride in blood up to the bridle!'' Hugo claimed that he had a ''crystal soul'' that reflected the same evolution as that the French people had gone through: from royalism to opposition to royalism, from the cult of Bonaparte to republicanism.

When Louis Philippe was deposed in the Revolution of 1848, Hugo at first found it hard to identify himself with the provisional government of Lamartine, for he still believed that a constitutional monarchy was the best form of government for France. Nevertheless, he allowed himself to be elected a deputy to the Assembly.

When Louis Napoleon, the nephew of the great man Hugo had always idolized, began to achieve notoriety, Hugo supported him. But his enthusiasm for the new president was short-lived. He wrote: ''Upon the barricades I defended order. Before dictatorship I defended liberty.'' He made a stirring plea for freedom of the press and clemency to the rebel elements; at last, in 1849, he broke with Napoleon III with the words, ''Because we have had a Great Napoleon must we now have a Little one?''

Louis Napoleon seized power by a coup d'etat on the night of Dec. 2, 1850, and proclaimed himself emperor. Hugo called for armed resistance and, witnessing the ensuing slaughter, Hugo believed the ''Little Napoleon'' to be a murderer. At great peril to her own life, Juliette saved the poet, found him shelter, and organized his escape to Brussels. From there he went to the British Channel islands of Jersey and Guernsey.

In November 1853 Hugo's fiercely anti-Napoleonic verse volume, *Les Châtiments,* was published in Belgium. Two different editions—one published under a false name with rows of dots in place of the individuals attacked, and the other, which was complete, with only ''Geneva and New York'' in place of the author's name—were culled from the 6,000 verses of the original manuscript. Though banned in France, the books were smuggled in (a favorite trick being to stuff them into hollow busts of the Emperor) and widely circulated.

In *Les Châtiments* Hugo wrote in the same polemical but exalted vein as did Pierre Ronsard in some of his *Discours,* Agrippa d'Aubigne in his *Les Tragiques,* André Chénier in his *lambs.* Comparisons between the Great and the Little Napoleons recur frequently in the poem, and the poet repeatedly calls on Nature to punish the hideous crime against her. Only the vision of an avenging future can placate the poet's hatred of Little Napoleon. The definitive edition of *Les Châtiments,* with numerous additions, was published in 1870, when Hugo returned to Paris after the fall of Napoleon III.

His Mysticism

During his exile Hugo gave vent to the mystical side of his personality. There were many séances in his home, first on Jersey, then in his splendid Hauteville House overlooking the coast of Guernsey. For Hugo, the supernatural was merely the natural. He had always felt premonitions, always heard premonitory sounds and messages during the night. Now, under the influence of a female voyante, he

believed that he was communicating with spirits, among them Dante, Shakespeare, Racine, and even Jesus. But the ''visit'' that touched him most was that of his favorite daughter, Léopoldine, tragically drowned in the Seine with her young husband in 1843.

Indeed, Hugo's family was stricken with multiple tragedies. While exile refreshed and nourished his poetry, his wife and children languished. They longed for their friends and the familiar surroundings of Paris. His daughter, Adèle, retreated into a fantasy world, till at last she ran away in pursuit of an English officer who was already married. Hugo's wife left him to live in Brussels, where she died in 1868. Only Juliette remained loyal during the 17 years the poet spent in Hauteville House.

Hugo continued his experiments with the supernatural until stopped by the threatened insanity of his son, Charles. He never abandoned, however, the syncretic and magical religious views that he reached at this time. He believed that all matter was in progress toward a higher state of being, and that this progress was achieved through suffering, knowledge, and the love that emanates from God. Evil was not absolute but rather a necessary stage toward the Good. Through suffering and the experience of evil, man made progress toward higher states of being.

In 1856 Hugo published *Les Contemplations,* a work which he described as follows: ''*Les Contemplations* are the memoirs of a soul; they are life itself beginning with the dawn of the cradle and finishing with the dawn of the tomb, they are a spirit which marches from gleam to gleam through youth, love, work, struggle, sorrow, dreams, hope, and which stops distraught on the brink of the infinite. It begins with a smile, continues with a sob, and ends with a trumpet blast from the abyss.''

Many of these poems anticipate Hugo's next major work, the epic cycle *La Légende des siècles* (1859), conceived as part of an enormous uncompleted work whose mission was to ''express humanity.'' Like his heroes Homer, Shakespeare, Dante, and his own contemporary Honoré de Balzac, Hugo dreamed of an all-inclusive cosmic poem. It would show the ascent of the universal soul toward the Good, and the emergence of Spirit from Matter.

In 1862 Hugo published *Les Misérables,* an immense novel, the work of many years. His guiding interest was similar to that of Charles Dickens, a social and humanitarian concern for the downtrodden. The book was meant to show the ''threefold problem of the century'': the degradation of proletarian man, the fall of woman through hunger, and the destruction of children. The sympathetic portrayal of the waif, Gavroche, and the escaped convict, Jean Valjean, won a vast readership for Hugo. The book was not merely an adventure story but a love story and a mystery as well. It crystallized Hugo's concern for social injustice and once again astounded the reading public with the scope of his literary powers.

When Victor Hugo died on May 22, 1885, it was as a venerable man, crowned with worldwide glory, still robust and emotionally ardent to the last.

Further Reading

The best life of Hugo in English is Matthew Josephson, *Victor Hugo: A Realistic Biography of the Great Romantic* (1942). Elliott M. Grant, *The Career of Victor Hugo* (1945), amplifies and complements Josephson with additional details on Hugo's publications and literary career. A partial account of the poet is Adèle Hugo, *Victor Hugo, by a Witness of His Life,* translated by Charles E. Wilbour (1964). Other studies are André Maurois, *Olympio: The Life of Victor Hugo* (1954; trans. 1956), and Richard B. Grant, *The Perilous Quest: Image, Myth, and Prophecy in the Narratives of Victor Hugo* (1968). A bibliography of works by and about Hugo is Elliott M. Grant, *Victor Hugo: A Select and Critical Bibliography* (1967). See also Horatio Smith, *Masters of French Literature* (1937).

Additional Sources

Decaux, Alain, *Victor Hugo,* Paris: Perrin, 1984.

Ionesco, Eugene, *Hugoliad, or, The grotesque and tragic life of Victor Hugo,* New York: Grove Press, 1987.

Juin, Hubert, *Victor Hugo,* Paris: Flammarion, 1980-c1986.

Peyre, Henri, *Victor Hugo: philosophy and poetry,* University: University of Alabama Press, 1980.

Richardson, Joanna, *Victor Hugo,* New York: St. Martin's Press, 1976.

Stevens, Philip, *Victor Hugo in Jersey,* Shopwyke Hall, Chichester, Sussex: Phillimore, 1985. □

Hui-Tsung

The Chinese emperor Hui-Tsung (1082-1135) was the eighth Sung emperor, an outstanding painter and calligrapher and a great patron of the arts, whose reign ended in disaster.

Son of Emperor Shen-tsung and a gifted concubine, Lady Ch'en, Hui-tsung came to the throne unexpectedly on the death of the young emperor Che-tsung, largely because he was supported by the empress dowager Hsiang. Initially Hui-tsung tried to reconcile reformers who looked back to Wang An-shih and their conservative opponents, but after the death of the empress dowager in 1101, Huitsung turned to the reform party led by Chief Minister Ts'ai Ching.

Together Hui-tsung and Ts'ai revived many of the reform programs while adding such innovations as the establishment of new charity hospitals and the extension of the educational system, but the Emperor also condoned the proscription of all opponents of the reforms and shared responsibility for the decline in political standards, the depletion of the treasury, and the heavy burden of taxes and exactions which formed part of the essential background of the Fang-la Rebellion (1120-1122). Especially notorious was the collection of rare plants, stones, and novelties which were taken from the people without compensation to grace a large garden Hui-tsung had constructed.

Hui-tsung was devoted to the arts. His delicate paintings of flowers and birds rendered in fine detail and the "slender gold" style of his calligraphy reveal a refined esthetic sensibility. He was responsible for the flourishing painting academy at court and extended his patronage to archeology, music, and poetry. His enthusiasm for art is further indicated by the catalog of the paintings in his collection, which lists 6,396 works by 231 artists. Also in harmony with these interests was his patronage of Taoism, including the building of temples. He has the further distinction of being the most prolific Sung emperor, for he was the father of no less than 63 children.

The worst failure of Hui-tsung's reign was in foreign policy. The eunuch T'ung Kuang, who rose to the command of the Sung armies, was instrumental in the formation of an alliance with the Chin (Jürchen) against the Liao (Khitan) which led to war between the Chin and the Sung, the defeat of the latter, and what proved to be the irreversible loss of the North. On Jan. 18, 1126, with enemy forces threatening the capital, Hui-tsung abdicated in favor of his son Ch'in-tsung, but in 1127, after the fall of the capital, father and son were captured by the Chin. Hui-tsung ended his life in captivity in northeastern Manchuria, where he died on June 4, 1135.

Further Reading

For Hui-tsung as a painter see Laurence Sickman and Alexander Soper, *The Art and Architecture of China* (1956), or any other standard history of Chinese art. Charles P. Fitzgerald, *China: A Short Cultural History* (1935; 3d ed. 1961), contains a short section on Huitsung. □

Hui-yüan

Hui-yüan (334-416) was the most famous monk of the early period of Chinese Buddhism, combining in his person and in his thought profound understanding of Chinese culture and philosophy with real faith in Buddhist doctrine and religion.

In the 4th century China was torn in two by continual warfare. The North was occupied by barbarian dynasties who were generally very fond of Buddhism and who had close ties with Buddhists of central Asia. The South remained Chinese, and the Buddhism practiced there was really an amalgam of native, Taoist philosophy and Indian Buddhism. Hui-yüan was at once the most perfect practician of southern "gentry" Buddhism and the adumbration of what Chinese Buddhism was to become when it was completely assimilated and digested.

Throughout his life Hui-yüan, whose family name was Chia, gives witness of having been a man of great refinement and culture. His family came from northern Shansi, and he went with his maternal uncle to Loyang and Hsüch'ang to study the Confucian and Taoist classics, showing that the family were literati. Hui-yüan and his younger brother joined the Buddhist monk Tao-an in 355 and became Buddhist monks. Tao-an's lectures on the

Prajnaparamita showed Hui-yüan that Buddhism was indeed the true religion, and in 375 Hui-yüan began to preach, using analogies from the *Chuang-tzu* and other secular literature to help explain points difficult for his Chinese audience to grasp. He followed Tao-an to Hsiang-yang and remained with him there until 378, when the community was disbanded. Hui-yüan left with some disciples and about 380 set up his own monastery on one of the most beautiful mountains in China, Lushan (Mt. Lu, near Chiu-chiang in northern Kiangsi).

Mt. Lu Monastery

Until the end of his life, Hui-yüan did not leave Mt. Lu and, although he never seems to have had many more than 100 disciples at a time, his reputation spread throughout North and South China. This reputation seems to have been based on the profound seriousness, sincerity, and intelligence with which he invested his monastery.

Hui-yüan was able to converse elegantly with his famous and often powerful lay visitors, indulging in the fashionable "pure conversations" (*ch'ing-t'an*) with the correct number of bons mots, but that only made his Buddhist faith all the more impressive. He developed a new style of preaching, adding a sermon to the formal ritual of early religious meetings, and he earnestly sought new texts and new translations of Buddhist works, asking the Sarvastivadin monk Sanghadeva to help translate two philosophical texts in 391 and sending disciples to the West in search of new materials in 393.

Worship of Amitabha

On Sept. 11, 402, Hui-yüan, with 123 of his disciples, took a vow before an image of the Buddha Amitabha that they all would earnestly strive for rebirth in the Western Paradise and help one another to reach it. The fact that both laymen and monks took part in this ceremony, that they made their vow in front of an image, and that Hui-yüan and his disciples practiced "invoking" the name of the Buddha makes this ceremony seem like the beginning of Pure Land Buddhism, one of the most popular Buddhist sects in China.

Much later sources say Hui-yüan's group was called the White Lotus Society and that it was indeed the direct ancestor of the sect, but there is actually no real assurance that there is any direct filiation between Hui-yüan's group and later Pure Land Buddhists. What is more important is to see that this ceremony shows that Hui-yüan was "popularizing" Buddhism, taking it out of the realm of pure philosophical speculation and making it a true, personal religion.

His Philosophy

This religious fervor that is characteristic of Hui-yüan's community probably helped him defend Buddhist autonomy against secular authority. His theoretical arguments are given in one of his most famous works, "That a Monk Should Not Pay Homage to the King," a letter written in 404 to Huan Hsüan, who had just usurped the imperial throne and who had been in correspondence with Hui-yüan for many years on this topic. His eloquent and firm arguments

in this series of essays helped keep the Buddhist communities independent of imperial control—no mean achievement in a country in which the state was, theoretically at least, omnipotent.

These essays, and his correspondence with Kumarajiva, begun in 405 or 406, are Hui-yüan's lengthiest works. In them he develops his theories on the "immortality of the soul" and on the *dharmakāya,* the "body of Buddha." These essays are not easy to understand and are highly technical, but they do show that Hui-yüan had an extremely good grasp of Buddhist doctrine. They also show that he had not completely understood the Madhyamika philosophy that Kumarajiva expounded and that he was still, in part at least, a Chinese thinker, inclined to seek a concrete, down-to-earth explanation for what were in fact highly abstract Indian speculations.

This tendency of mind is also apparent in what seems to be the last event in Hui-yüan's life that can be dated: the painting he had made of the "shadow of the Buddha" and that he had placed in a chapel on May 27, 412. He had probably heard about this image from a Sarvastivadin Kashmirian monk named Buddhabhadra, who came to Mt. Lu in 410 or 411. This painting, like the image of Amitabha before which he and his disciples took their vow, shows that Hui-yüan was seeking some more concrete form of worship than the prevalent metaphysical schools could furnish. He died on Sept. 13, 416 (some sources give 417), on Mt. Lu, where he is still buried.

Further Reading

In English, the most complete studies of Hui-yüan are in Erik Zürcher, *The Buddhist Conquest of China* (1959), and, for the philosophy, in Richard H. Robinson, *Early Madhyamika in India and China* (1967). There is also a short résumé in Kenneth K. S. Ch'ên, *Buddhism in China: A Historical Survey* (1964). □

Johan Huizinga

The Dutch historian Johan Huizinga (1872-1945) is known for his books on cultural history and essays on the philosophy of history.

Johan Huizinga was born on Dec. 7, 1872, in Groningen. Trained as a linguist and a specialist in Sanskrit at the universities of Groningen and Leipzig, he received his doctorate in 1897 and went on to become a high school teacher in Haarlem and a teacher of Indic studies in Amsterdam. His interests soon turned to the history of his own country, however, and in 1905 he published *The Origins of Haarlem.* The same year he was appointed professor at Groningen University; in 1915 he was named professor at Leiden University.

Like Swiss historian Jacob Christoph Burckhardt, Huizinga was a cultural conservative, strongly elitist, and in later years deeply despondent over the future of European civilization. Like Burckhardt, he took as his professional task the description of periods of cultural history. Whereas the Swiss historian had conceived of culture as the spontaneous creation of free individuals, Huizinga defined culture as the state of a community "when the domination of nature in the material, moral, and spiritual realms permits a state of existence which is *higher* and *better* than the given natural conditions," a state of "harmonious balance of material and social values."

Huizinga's first major work, and his greatest, was *The Waning of the Middle Ages* (1919), in which he portrayed "the forms of life, thought, and art" in the Burgundian state of the 14th and 15th centuries. He saw it as a period of violence, terrified by the image of death, from which men escaped by creating a "dream of life," coloring life with fancy. By their idealized style of knighthood, their conventions of love, their images of religious sensibility, they transformed or hid the real world in which they lived. Huizinga recaptured these colors of late medieval life with great vividness of style.

To Huizinga several aspects of this late medieval culture were essentially forms of play. In *Homo Ludens* (1938) he addressed the problem directly: to what extent does human culture result from play and to what extent does it express itself in the forms of play? His concern was not with games but with the play element of law, war, poetry, philosophy, science, and art, the sportive qualities of serious concerns. Along with the earnest, he argued, play is necessary to true culture.

Huizinga also wrote *Men and Mass in America* (1918), a biography *Erasmus of Rotterdam* (1924), *Holland's Culture in the Seventeenth Century* (1932), and numerous essays on historiography and the contemporary scene. When Leiden University was closed by the Germans in 1940, Huizinga was interned as a hostage. Released for reasons of ill health, he died in the village of De Steeg on Feb. 1, 1945.

Further Reading

A brief analysis of Huizinga's conception of culture is presented by Karl J. Weintraub, *Visions of Culture* (1966). Pieter Geyl gives a critical view of Huizinga's work in *Encounters in History* (1961). □

Hulagu Khan

Hulagu Khan (ca. 1216-1265) was a Mongol conqueror and the founder of the dynasty of the Il-Khans of Iran. He also suppressed the Ismaili sect and defeated the last Abbasid caliph.

Hulagu—the native form of his name is Hüle'ü, whence the Alau of Marco Polo—was a grandson of Genghis Khan and the younger brother of the Great Khans Mangu (Möngkë) and Kublai. At a *kuriltai,* or assembly of the Mongol princes, held in 1251 at the time of Mangu's accession, it was decided that Hulagu should consolidate the conquests in western Asia by suppressing the sect of the Ismailis, or Assassins of Alamut, in northwestern Persia and then, if necessary, attacking the caliphate.

Hulagu left Mongolia in the autumn of 1253 at the head of a large army. Traveling slowly along a carefully prepared route, from which all natural obstacles had been removed, he did not cross the Oxus, then the frontier between the Chaghatai Khanate and Persia, until the beginning of 1256. By the end of that year the greater part of the Ismaili castles had been captured, and the Grand Master himself was a prisoner in Mongol hands. He was sent to Mongolia, where he was executed by the order of the Great Khan, and with the wholesale massacre of the Ismailis that followed, the sect was all but wiped out.

The summer of 1257 was spent in diplomatic exchanges with the caliph al-Mustasim from Hulagu's headquarters in the Hamadan area. The Caliph refused to accede to Mongol demands for submission, and in the autumn Hulagu's forces began to converge on Baghdad. On Jan. 17, 1258, the Caliph's army was defeated in battle; on the 22nd Hulagu appeared in person before the walls of Baghdad; the city surrendered on February 10, and 10 days later al-Mustasim was put to death. The story, familiar from the pages of Marco Polo and Longfellow's *Kambalu,* of the Caliph's being left to starve in a tower full of gold and silver is apocryphal; he was probably rolled in a carpet and beaten or trampled to death in order not to shed royal blood, such being the Mongols' custom in the execution of their own princes. With his death the Islamic institution of the caliphate came to an end, although it was artificially preserved by the Mamluk rulers of Egypt and the title was afterward assumed by the Ottoman sultans.

From Baghdad, Hulagu withdrew into Azerbaijan, henceforward destined to be the seat of the Il-Khanid dynasty, and from here in the autumn of 1259 he set out to conquer Syria. Aleppo was taken after a short siege, Damascus surrendered without a blow, and by the early summer of 1260 the Mongols had reached Gaza on the frontier with Egypt. However, news of the death of his brother the Great Khan Mangu in China caused Hulagu to return to Persia, and the depleted army that he had left behind was decisively defeated by the Egyptians at Ain Jalut in Palestine on Sept. 3, 1260.

In 1262-1263 Hulagu was involved in hostilities in the Caucasus area with his cousin Berke, the ruler of the Golden Horde and the ally of his enemies, the Mamluk rulers of Egypt. Hulagu's troops were at first victorious, crossing the Terek into Berke's territory, but were then driven back with heavy losses; many were drowned in the river when the ice gave way under their horses' hooves. Apart from the quelling of risings in Mosul and Fars, this was the last of Hulagu's campaigns. He died on Feb. 8, 1265, and was buried on a great rock rising 1,000 feet above the shore of the island of Shahi in Lake Urmia. He was the last of the Mongol princes to be accorded the traditional heathen burial, several young women being interred with him to serve their master in the hereafter.

The kingdom which Hulagu had founded comprised, in addition to Persia and the states of the southern Caucasus, the present-day Iraq and eastern Turkey. He and his successors bore the title of Il-Khan (subordinate khan) as vassals of the Great Khan in Mongolia and afterward in China. He himself either still adhered to the shamanist beliefs of his forefathers or was a convert to Buddhism, but his chief wife, Dokuz, was a Nestorian Christian, as Hulagu's mother had been, and special favor was shown to the Christians during his reign. Like several of his successors, he was a great builder, the most celebrated of his edifices being a great observatory on a hill north of Maragha, where Moslem, Christian, and Far Eastern scientists carried out their researches.

Further Reading

René Grousset, *The Empire of the Steppes: A History of Central Asia* (1939; trans. 1970), is a useful study. For a treatment incorporating more recent research see J. A. Boyle, ed., *The Cambridge History of Iran,* vol. 5 (1968). □

Clark Leonard Hull

The American psychologist Clark Leonard Hull (1884-1952) was a primary representative of the neobehaviorist school. He was also the first known psychologist to apply quantitative experimental methods to the phenomena of hypnosis.

Clark L. Hull was born in a country farmhouse near Akron, N.Y., on May 24, 1884. He attended high school for a year in West Saginaw, Mich., and the academy of Alma College. His education was interrupted by bouts of typhoid fever and poliomyelitis, giving him pause to consider possible vocational choices; he decided upon psychology. He then matriculated at the University of Michigan, took his bachelor's degree, and went on to the University of Wisconsin, receiving his doctorate in 1918. Staying on at Wisconsin to teach, Hull was at first torn between two schools of psychological thought which prevailed at the time: early behaviorism and Gestalt psychology. He was not long in deciding in favor of the former.

After an experimental project on the influence of tobacco smoking on mental and motor efficiency, Hull was offered the opportunity to teach a course in psychological tests and measurements. Gladly accepting it, he changed the name to "aptitude testing" and worked hard at developing it as a sound basis for vocational guidance. The material which he collected in this course was gathered into a book, *Aptitude Testing* (1928). Next, with the help of a grant from the National Research Council, he built a machine that automatically prepared the correlations he needed in his test-construction work.

In 1929 Hull became a research professor of psychology at the Institute of Psychology at Yale University, later incorporated into the Institute of Human Relations. He came to certain definite conclusions about psychology, and in 1930 he stated that psychology is a true natural science, that its primary laws are expressible quantitatively by means

of ordinary equations, and that quantitative laws even for the behavior of groups as a whole could be derived from the same primary equations.

The next 10 years were filled with projects dealing not only with aptitude testing but with learning experiments, behavior theory, and hypnosis. As a representative of behaviorism, Hull fell into that school's neobehaviorist period of the 1930s and early 1940s. His basic motivational concept was the "drive." His quantitative system, based on stimulus-response reinforcement theory and using the concepts "drive reduction" and "intervening variables," was highly esteemed by psychologists during the 1940s for its objectivity.

Hull was probably the first psychologist to approach hypnosis with the quantitative methodology customarily used in experimental psychology. This combination of experimental methods and the phenomena provided by hypnosis yielded many appropriate topics for experimental problems by his students. *Hypnosis and Suggestibility,* the first extensive systematic investigation of hypnosis with experimental methods, was published in 1933, incorporating the earlier, and better, part of the hypnosis program that Hull had carried out at the University of Wisconsin.

In 1940 Hull published, jointly with C. I. Hovland, R. T. Ross, M. Hall, D. T. Perkins, and F. B. Fitch, *Mathematico-Deductive Theory of Rote Learning.* Three years later his *Principles of Behavior* was published, followed by a revision of his theories in *Essentials of Behavior* (1951). Hull expressed learning theory in terms of quantification, by means of equations which he had derived from a method of scaling originally devised by L. L. Thurstone. In his last book, *A Behavior System* (1952), Hull applied his principles to the behavior of single organisms. His system stands as an important landmark in the history of theoretical psychology. He died in New Haven, Conn., on May 10, 1952.

Further Reading

There is a short biography of Hull by Frank A. Beach in *Biographical Memoirs* of the National Academy of Sciences, vol. 33 (1959), and an autobiographical narrative in Edwin G. Boring and others, eds., *A History of Psychology in Autobiography,* vol. 4 (1952). An interesting exposition of Hull and of the various movements in psychology contemporary with and preceding neobehaviorism is in Melvin H. Marx and William A. Hillix, *Systems and Theories in Psychology* (1963). □

Cordell Hull

Cordell Hull (1871-1955) was an American congressman, secretary of state, and winner of the Nobel Peace Prize in 1945.

Cordell Hull was born on Oct. 2, 1871, in Pickett County, Tenn. He attended normal school at Bowling Green, Ky., and had a year at the National

Normal University at Lebanon, Ohio. He then enrolled in the Cumberland Law School at Lebanon, Tenn., completing a 10-month course in 5 months.

Hull was elected to the Tennessee Legislature at the age of 21, and in 1903 he was appointed to fill an unexpired term as judge of the Fifth Judicial Circuit of the States. In 1906 he was elected to the House of Representatives, where he served, with one interruption, until 1931. In 1930, elected to the U.S. Senate, he took special interest in the tariff, consistently advocating freer trade relations for the United States. He authored the income tax law of 1913 and several subsequent tax laws. He was a devoted supporter of Woodrow Wilson and of the League of Nations.

In 1933 President Franklin Roosevelt appointed Hull secretary of state, and Hull served in this office longer than any other incumbent—until 1944. During Roosevelt's first two administrations, Hull's great contribution was his development of the good-neighbor policy, involving the establishment of more cordial relations with Latin America. In 1933, at the conference of Montevideo (Uruguay), he signed a protocol declaring intervention in the affairs of the independent states of the New World illegal; this was strengthened by a new declaration at the Conference of Buenos Aires in 1937. Hull fought vigorously and successfully for freer trade relationships, lower tariff duties, and reciprocal trade arrangements. The cooperation of the Latin American republics during World War II was largely due to his influence.

Hull conducted the negotiations in the developing crisis with Japan in the late 1930s and early 1940s. He took a firm stand against Japanese imperialism, while seeking to avoid actual armed conflict. During World War II Hull's role was less significant, however, for Roosevelt leaned on other advisers. Hull did, however, visit Moscow in 1943, where he won Premier Stalin's assent to the projected United Nations. Hull worked vigorously for the realization of the United Nations, though he resigned from the State Department in late 1944, partly because of failing health. In 1945 he was awarded the Nobel Peace Prize. Hull died at Bethesda Naval Hospital on July 23, 1955.

Further Reading

Hull left *The Memoirs of Cordell Hull* (2 vols., 1948). For his career as secretary of state see Julius W. Pratt, *Cordell Hull, 1933-44* (2 vols., 1964). He is discussed in Norman A. Graebner, ed., *An Uncertain Tradition: American Secretaries of State in the Twentieth Century* (1961). □

William Hull

William Hull (1753-1825), American military commander, surrendered United States troops at Detroit to the British during the War of 1812, dealing a severe blow to the American war effort.

William Hull was born June 24, 1753, in Derby, Conn. After graduating from Yale College, he studied law in Litchfield and was admitted to the bar in 1775. That July he joined the American army besieging Boston and served actively throughout the Revolutionary War, rising to the rank of lieutenant colonel. After the war Hull set up law practice in Newton, Mass., the home of his wife, Sarah Fuller. He participated in the suppression of Shays' Rebellion and served as a state senator and as a judge of the court of common pleas.

In March 1805 President Thomas Jefferson appointed Hull governor of the newly organized Michigan Territory. Hull was instrumental in obtaining land cessions from the Indians, which added to their growing unrest. In the spring of 1812, after the declaration of war on Great Britain, he accepted a commission as brigadier general and command of the army which was to defend Michigan and to invade Upper Canada. Hull stressed the necessity of controlling Lake Erie, but he incorrectly argued that a large American army at Detroit might compel the British to abandon their naval forces on the lake.

Hull brought a 2,200-man army into Detroit, crossed the Detroit River into Canada on July 12, and occupied Sandwich. There he hesitated. When British commander Gen. Isaac Brock concentrated his forces on him, Hull retreated to Detroit and tried to reopen his lines of communication. This failed, and on August 12 Hull surrendered to Brock. This left Lake Erie and the Michigan country in British control. In defense of his actions Hull claimed that the army

had had only a month's provisions and that continued resistance would have provoked the Michigan Indians, who were with the British, to massacre the civilian population.

A court-martial found Hull guilty of cowardice and neglect of duty, but he was pardoned because of past services. He lost his army position and retired to Newton, where he died on Nov. 29, 1825.

Further Reading

There is no good biography of Hull. His daughter, Maria Campbell, wrote *Revolutionary Services and Civil Life of General William Hull* (1848), which was published together with a work by Hull's grandson James Freeman Clarke, *The History of the Campaign of 1812, and Surrender of the Post of Detroit.* Since Clarke's essay was written to defend Hull, it should be read critically. An account condemning Hull is found in volume 6 of Henry Adams, *History of the United States of America* (9 vols., 1889-1891). A good brief account of Hull's western campaign is in Harry L. Coles, *The War of 1812* (1965).

Additional Sources

Hull, William H. (William Henry), *The good ol' boys,* Edina, Minn.: W.H. Hull, 1994. □

Baron Friedrich Heinrich Alexander von Humboldt

Baron Friedrich Heinrich Alexander von Humboldt (1769-1859) was a German scientist who made substantial contributions to geography, geology, geophysics, and meteorology. For much of his life he was associated with the Prussian court, ultimately as a scientific adviser of its rulers.

Of German and French Huguenot parentage, Alexander von Humboldt was born in Berlin on Sept. 14, 1769. His father, an officer in the Prussian army, died early, and Alexander was educated by a private tutor with his brother, Wilhelm. The household was marred by the mother's "cold and aloof" temperament. Alexander never married but derived great happiness from friendships with colleagues and others and also from his brother's friendly household.

Humboldt studied at the universities of Frankfurt an der Oder and Göttingen from 1787 and later went to the School of Mines at Freiburg in Saxony. In 1792 he joined the mining department of the Prussian government, and promotion came swiftly. One observation he made which proved crucial in his later researches was on the magnetic qualities of rocks; he also invented a safety lamp.

Explorations and Scientific Observations

In 1796 Humboldt's mother died, and he became sufficiently wealthy to plan a 5-year period of exploration. He started out in June 1799, after studying various techniques of botanical research, meteorological observation, and height estimation from barometric readings.

With Aimé Boupland, a botanist, Humboldt spent 5 years traveling in South America and Mexico, with visits to Cuba and finally to the United States, returning home in August 1804. The achievement was magnificent, for it included new material on volcanoes and on the structure of the Andes, with a vast array of data on climate and on plant geography. The *Personal Narrative* of this expedition was published in French in 1814-1819, and an English translation appeared in 1825; among its admiring readers was Charles Darwin. Humboldt was a splendid scientific observer. He saw that excessive tree felling could be followed by soil erosion, eagerly noted the relics of the Inca and Aztec civilizations, and in France carefully worked out the climatic conditions under which vines could be grown.

From 1804 to 1827 Humboldt lived mainly in Paris as a writer and scientist, still following researches into geomagnetism which eventually, in 1838, led to the discovery of the magnetic pole. From 1827 he lived in Berlin and in 1829 spent 9 months in Siberia on a mining survey with some botanical and geological work. In 1830 he became an adviser to the King of Prussia and acquired increasing influence at court.

Humboldt's *Asie Centrale* appeared in three volumes in Paris in 1843, and the great *Kosmos* in five volumes in Stuttgart from 1845 to 1862. These works cover a vast range of physical and human phenomena. Caustic in comment, Humboldt was benevolent in disposition, but he was quite unable to manage money. He died on May 6, 1859, in Berlin.

Further Reading

Charlotte Kellner, *Alexander von Humboldt* (1963), is a sympathetic study. Gerald R. Crone, *Modern Geographers* (1951), includes a short treatment. Humboldt's influence on modern geography is discussed in Thomas W. Freeman, *A Hundred Years of Geography* (1961). □

Baron Wilhelm von Humboldt

The German educator, statesman, political theorist, and philologist Baron Wilhelm von Humboldt (1767-1835) reformed the Prussian school system and founded the University of Berlin. He was influential in developing the science of comparative philology.

Wilhelm von Humboldt was born in Potsdam on June 22, 1767. He studied law in Berlin and Göttingen. In his essay *Über das Studium des Klassischen Altertums* (1793) he summarized his program for educational reform, which was basically the program of German neohumanism. In Jena (1794-1797) he was a member of Friedrich von Schiller's circle. After traveling through Spain and France, during which Humboldt became interested in philology, he was appointed Prussian resident minister in Rome (1802-1808).

Humboldt was influenced by the educational principles of Johann Pestalozzi. As Prussian minister of education (1809-1810), he sent teachers to Switzerland to study Pestalozzi's methods, and he founded the University of Berlin (1809). Humboldt's ideas profoundly influenced European and American elementary education.

From 1810 to 1819 Humboldt served the government as minister in Vienna, London, and Berlin. He resigned from the ministry in protest against the reactionary policies of the government. His philological works on the Basque language (1821) and on Kavi, the ancient language of Java, published posthumously (1836-1840), were landmarks in their field. He died at Tegel on April 8, 1835.

Political Theory

In *The Sphere and Duties of Government* (published in part in 1792 and completely in 1851) Humboldt held that although the nation-state is a growing body, government is only one of the means aiding its welfare, a means whose sole aim should be to provide security for social development. As in biological evolution, all growth is good, as it brings forth an organism more complex, more diverse, and richer, and government—while a major agent in fostering this development—is not the only one. If it tries to do too much, it interferes with and retards the beneficial effects of other agencies.

Under the influence of romanticism Humboldt became almost mystical as he placed more stress on supra-individual and historically conditioned nationality and viewed individual nationality in turn as part of the universal spiritual and divine life which was the characteristic expression of humanity. In essays on the German (1813) and Prussian (1819) constitutions he advocated a liberalism which would preserve the unique character and traditions of individual states, provinces, and regions, with the constitution of any state adapted to the particular genius of its national character. He rejected both the artificial and atomistic liberalism of the French Revolution, which derived the state from the isolated and arbitrary wills of individuals, and the ultraconservative program to revive the old feudal estates. He advocated a liberalism grounded in tradition with regional self-governing bodies participating in governing a monarchical civil service state.

Further Reading

There is no definitive biography in English on Humboldt. One work is Hermann Klencke, *Lives of the Brothers Humboldt, Alexander and William* (trans. 1952). Humboldt is discussed or mentioned in the following works: Henry Barnard, *Pestalozzi and His Educational System* (1881); Eugene Newton Anderson, *Nationalism and the Cultural Crisis in Prussia, 1806-15* (1939); Leonard Kreiger, *The German Idea of Freedom* (1957); and Walter Horace Bruford, *Culture and Society in Classical Weimar, 1775-1806* (1962).

Additional Sources

Sweet, Paul Robinson, *Wilhelm von Humboldt: a biography,* Columbus: Ohio State University Press, 1978-c1980. □

David Hume

The Scottish philosopher David Hume (1711-1776) developed a philosophy of "mitigated skepticism," which remains a viable alternative to the systems of rationalism, empiricism, and idealism.

If one was to judge a philosopher by a gauge of relevance—the quantity of issues and arguments raised by him that remain central to contemporary thought—David Hume would be rated among the most important figures in philosophy. Ironically, his philosophical writings went unnoticed during his lifetime, and the considerable fame he achieved derived from his work as an essayist and historian. Immanuel Kant's acknowledgment that Hume roused him from his "dogmatic slumbers" stimulated interest in Hume's thought.

With respect to Hume's life there is no better source than the succinct autobiography, *My Own Life,* written 4 months before his death. He was born on April 26, 1711, on the family estate, Ninewells, near Edinburgh. According to Hume, the ''ruling passion'' of his life was literature, and thus his story contains ''little more than the History of my writings.'' As a second son, he was not entitled to a large inheritance, and he failed in two family-sponsored careers in law and business because of his ''unsurmountable aversion to everything but the pursuits of Philosophy and general learning.'' Until he was past 40, Hume was employed only twice. He spent a year in England as a tutor to a mentally ill nobleman, and from 1745 to 1747 Hume was an officer and aide-de-camp to Gen. James Sinclair and attended him on an expedition to the coast of France and military embassies in Vienna and Turin.

Major Works

During an earlier stay in France (1734-1737) Hume had written his major philosophic work, *A Treatise of Human Nature.* The first two volumes were published in 1739 and the third appeared in the following year. The critical reception of the work was singularly unfortunate. In Hume's own words, the *Treatise* ''fell dead born from the press.'' Book I of the *Treatise* was recast as *An Enquiry concerning Human Understanding* and published in 1748. The third volume with minor revisions appeared in 1751 as *An Enquiry concerning the Principles of Morals.* The second volume of the *Treatise* was republished as Part 2 of *Four Dissertations* in 1757. Two sections of this work dealing with liberty and necessity had been incorporated in the first *Enquiry.* Hume's other important work, *Dialogues concern-*

ing Natural Religion, was substantially complete by the mid-1750s, but because of its controversial nature it was published posthumously.

During his lifetime Hume's reputation derived from the publication of his *Political Discourses* (1751) and six-volume *History of England* (1754-1762). When he went to France in 1763 as secretary to the English ambassador, Hume discovered that he was a literary celebrity and a revered figure among the *philosophes.* He led a very happy and active social life even after his retirement to Edinburgh in 1769. He died there on Aug. 25, 1776. He specified in his will that the gravestone be marked only with his name and dates, ''leaving it to Posterity to add the rest.''

''Mitigated Skepticism''

Skepticism is concerned with the truthfulness of human perceptions and ideas. On the level of perception, Hume was the first thinker to consistently point out the disastrous implications of the ''representative theory of perception,'' which he had inherited from both his rationalist and empiricist predecessors. According to this view, when I say that I perceive something such as an elephant, what I actually mean is that I have in my mind a mental idea or image or impression. Such a datum is an internal, mental, subjective *representation* of something that I assume to be an external, physical, objective fact. But there are, at least, two difficulties inherent in ascribing any truth to such perceptions. If truth is understood as the conformity or adequacy between the image and the object, then it is impossible to establish that there is a true world of objects since the only evidence I have of an external world consists of internal images. Further, it is impossible to judge how faithfully mental impressions or ideas represent physical objects.

Hume is aware, however, that this sort of skepticism with regard to the senses does violence to common sense. He suggests that a position of complete skepticism is neither serious nor useful. Academic skepticism (the name derives from a late branch of Plato's school) states that one can never know the truth or falsity of any statement (except, of course, this one). It is, however, a self-refuting theory and is confounded by life itself because ''we make inferences on the basis of our impressions whether they be true or false, real or imaginary.'' Total skepticism is unlivable since ''nature is always too strong for principle.'' Hume therefore advances what he calls ''mitigated skepticism.'' In addition to the exercise of caution in reasoning, this approach attempts to limit philosophical inquiries to topics that are adapted to the capacities of human intelligence. It thus excludes all metaphysical questions concerning the origin of either mind or object as being incapable of demonstration.

Theory of Knowledge

Even though an ultimate explanation of both the subject or object of knowledge is impossible, Hume provides a description of how man senses and understands. He emphasizes the utility of knowledge as opposed to its correctness and suggests that experience begins with feeling rather than thought. He uses the term ''perception'' in its traditional sense—that is, whatever can be present to the mind from the senses, passions, thought, or reflection. Nonetheless he distinguishes between impressions which are felt and ideas which are thought. In this he stresses the difference between feeling a toothache and thinking about such a pain, which had been obscured by both rationalists and empiricists. Both impressions and ideas are subdivided further into simple and complex; for example, the idea of heat is simple, while the idea of combustion is complex.

These simple divisions are the basis for Hume's "phenomenalism" (that is, knowledge consists of "appearances" in the mind). Hume distinguishes the various operations of the mind in a descriptive psychology, or "mental geography." Impressions are described as vivacious and lively, whereas ideas are less vivid and, in fact, derived from original impressions. This thesis leads to the conclusion that "we can never think of any thing which we have not seen without us or felt in our own minds." Hume often overestimates the importance of this discovery with the suggestion that the sole criterion for judging ideas is to remove every philosophical ambiguity by asking "from what impression is that supposed idea derived." If there is no corresponding impression, the idea may be dismissed as meaningless. This assumption that all ideas are reducible, in principle, to some impression is a primary commitment of Hume's empiricism. Hume did admit that there are complex ideas, such as the idea of a city, that are not traceable to any single impression. These complex ideas are produced by the freedom of the imagination to transform and relate ideas independently of impressions; such ideas are not susceptible to empirical verification. This represents the major paradox of Hume's philosophy—the imagination which produces every idea beyond sensible immediacy also denies the truth of ideas.

Theory of Ideas

Hume accepts the Cartesian doctrine of the distinct idea—conceivability subject only to the principle of contradiction—as both the unit of reasoning and the criterion of truth. But the doctrine of the distinct idea means that every noncontradictory idea expresses an a priori logical possibility. And the speculative freedom of the imagination to conceive opposites without contradiction makes it impossible to demonstrate any matter of fact or existence. This argument leads to a distinction between relations of ideas (demonstrations which are true a priori) and matters of fact (the opposite of which is distinctly conceivable). And this distinction excludes from the domain of rational determination every factual event, future contingent proposition, and causal relation. For Hume, since truth is posterior to fact, the ideas of reason only express what the mind thinks about reality.

Distinct ideas, or imaginative concepts, are pure antinomies apart from experience as every factual proposition is equally valid a priori. But Hume does acknowledge that such propositions are not equally meaningful either to thought or action. On the level of ideas, Hume offers a conceptual correlative to the exemption of sensation as a form of cognition by his recognition that the meaning of

ideas is more important than their truth. What separates meaningful propositions from mere concepts is the subjective impression of belief.

Belief, or the vivacity with which the mind conceives certain ideas and associations, results from the reciprocal relationship between experience and imagination. The cumulative experience of the past and present—for example, the relational factors of constancy, conjunction, and resemblance—gives a bias to the imagination. But it is man's imaginative anticipations of the future that give meaning to his experience. Neither the relational elements of experience nor the propensive function of the imagination, from the viewpoint of the criterion of truth, possesses the slightest rational justification. Hence the interplay between the criterion of truth and the logic of the imagination explains both Hume's skepticism and his conception of sensation and intellection.

The most celebrated example of this argument is Hume's analysis of the causal relation. Every statement which points beyond what is immediately available to the senses and memory rests on an assumption and/or extension of the cause and effect relation. Let us examine two cases: I see lightning and hear thunder; I see a rabbit and then a fox. The question is why I am right in concluding that lightning causes thunder but wrong in believing that rabbits cause foxes. Experience, in both instances, reveals an A that is followed by B, and repeated experiences show that A is always followed by B. While the constant conjunction of A and B might eliminate the rabbit-fox hypothesis, it is of no help in explaining causality because there are all sorts of objects, such as tables and chairs, which are similarly conjoined but not supposed to be causally related. Thus experience reveals only that constant conjunction and priority are sufficient but not necessary conditions for establishing a causal connection. And it is necessity, understood as that which cannot be otherwise than it is, which makes a relation causal in the propositional form of "If A then B *must* appear and if no A then no B."

But if necessary connection explains causality, what explains necessity? Experience yields only a particular instance and tells us nothing about the past or the future. Nor is there any necessity discoverable in repeated experiences. That the sun will rise tomorrow because it has in the past is an assumption that the past necessarily causes the future which is, of course, the connection that is to be demonstrated. If experience cannot account for necessity, then reason fares no better. I can always imagine the opposite of any matter of fact without contradiction. If someone tells me that Caesar died of old age or that thunder is uncaused or that the sun will not rise tomorrow, I will not believe him, but there is nothing logically incorrect about such statements since for every probability "there exists an equal and opposite possibility." Thus there is no justifiable knowledge of causal connections in nature, although this is not a denial that there are real causes. Man's supposed knowledge results from repeated associations of A and B to the point where the imagination makes its customary transition from one object to its usual attendant, that is, "an object followed by another, and whose appearance always conveys the thought to that other."

Because of his skeptical attitude toward the truths of reason Hume attempted to ground his moral theory on the bedrock of feeling—"Reason is, and ought only to be, the slave of the passions." In this, Hume followed the "moral sense" school and, especially, the thought of Francis Hutcheson. The notion that virtue and vice are to be derived ultimately from impressions of approbation and blame or pleasure and pain shows that Hume anticipated Jeremy Bentham's utilitarianism, a debt which the latter acknowledged. Although Hume considered himself to be primarily a moralist, this doctrine is the least original part of his philosophical writings.

Further Reading

Ernest C. Mossner, who edited several volumes of Hume's correspondence, also wrote the best biography, *The Life of David Hume* (1954). John H. Burton, *Life and Correspondence of David Hume* (1846; repr. 1967), is still useful. Good studies of Hume include John A. Passmore, *Hume's Intentions* (1952); Farhang Zabeeh, *Hume, Precursor of Modern Empiricism* (1960); and Charles W. Hendel, *Studies in the Philosophy of David Hume* (1963). Also useful are Alfred B. Glathe, *Hume's Theory of the Passions and of Morals* (1950); and Antony Flew, *Hume's Philosophy of Belief* (1961), a study of the first *Enquiry*. Various aspects of Hume's work are considered in several anthologies of critical opinion: D. F. Pears, ed., *David Hume: A Symposium* (1963); Alexander Sesonske and Noel Fleming, eds., *Human Understanding: Studies in the Philosophy of David Hume* (1965); and V. C. Chappell, ed., *Hume* (1966). ☐

Hubert Horatio Humphrey Jr.

Hubert Horatio Humphrey, Jr. (1911-1978), the pharmacist turned politician, served different constituencies as mayor of Minneapolis, United States senator from Minnesota, and vice-president of the United States. He was an unsuccessful candidate for the presidency of the United States in 1968.

For 35 years, 1943-1978, Hubert Horatio Humphrey, Jr., held various public offices. At all times he was the liberal candidate for these public positions. Rather early Humphrey knew the meaning of the term "empirical collectivism," which, applied to government, meant providing answers to various *bona-fide* public problems that confronted the American people. When the people were faced with problems to which they could not find solutions individually or by group actions, they could call upon government to resolve those problems. On various occasions Humphrey proposed that government take over responsibility from the individuals or the groups.

Probably the experiences of his family and of neighbors and farmers in the state of South Dakota were responsible for Humphrey's proposals. The people of the state ran into problems of various kinds, including dust bowls, bank failures, farm failures, and depressed economic situations.

Hubert's father was a small businessman, a pharmacist and owner of several different drug stores in South Dakota, first in Wallace, then in Dorland, and finally in Huron. Actually, he was not successful before the 1930s. The Huron drug store succeeded, becoming the first Walgreen Agency in the United States. Before this there were ups and downs in the business which reflected economic conditions in South Dakota. They also affected the family and Hubert. For example, in 1927 Humphrey's father was forced to sell their home to pay off debts of his business. The same thing had happened in 1932, when Humphrey was forced to withdraw from the University of Minnesota.

Education for Public Service

Humphrey was educated in the Dorland public schools and graduated from high school in 1929. He enrolled at the University of Minnesota in that year, remaining as a student for the next three years. Failure of his father's business forced Humphrey out of the university in 1932. In December of 1932 he was enrolled as a student at Capitol College of Pharmacy in Denver, Colorado. He graduated from this intensive program in six months. He then returned to the new drug store in Huron and was employed by his father. In Humphrey's words, "The drug store was my life and it seemed then it might always be." He remained as a druggist

during the years 1933-1937. He was married to Muriel Buck in 1936, and they became a small town family. But Humphrey proved that he could do other things. Again he enrolled at the University of Minnesota in 1937 and received his Bachelor of Arts degree in 1939. He entered the master's program in political science at Louisiana State University and was awarded his graduate degree in 1940. He and his family returned to Minneapolis, and Humphrey did further graduate work at the University of Minnesota. He did not receive his Doctor of Philosophy degree because he did not complete his dissertation.

Other things were more important than becoming a professor of political science. From 1941 to 1945 Humphrey had various public service jobs, including state director of war production training and reemployment, assistant director of the War Manpower Commission, and mayor of Minneapolis. These positions served as stepping stones in his later political career.

Political Career

Humphrey's first attempt at elected public office occurred in 1943 when he attempted to win election as a mayoral candidate. He was narrowly defeated, but he benefitted from his loss. In 1945 he was elected mayor and won reelection in 1947.

Humphrey had his first chance to put at least one of his proposals into practice. He believed in the civil rights of all Americans, including African Americans. He successfully proposed to the city council that it adopt a fair employment practices ordinance. In 1948 Humphrey had an opportunity to do something about civil rights at the Democratic national convention. He and other liberal Democrats who were members of the platform committee were opposed to the proposed weak plank on civil rights. These liberals challenged the leadership of the party, and Humphrey gave a minority report before the convention. Among other things, he said, "There are those who say: This issue of civil rights is an infringement on State's rights. The time has arrived for the Democratic Party to get out of the shadow of State's rights and walk forth-rightfully into the bright sunshine of human rights."

The delegates were so excited at Humphrey's statements that they paraded around the convention floor and voted in favor of the stronger civil rights position set forth in the minority report. One of the consequences was that conservative Southern Democrats walked out of that convention and established a splinter party, the Dixiecrats. President Truman had to face the Republican candidate (Tom Dewey) and two splinter party candidates from the right (J. Strom Thurman) and the left (Henry A. Wallace) of the Democratic Party. He won reelection in part because of the victories of various strong senatorial candidates, including Guy Gillette of Iowa, Paul Douglas of Illinois, Estes Kefauver of Tennessee, Bob Kerr of Oklahoma, Matt Neely of West Virginia, and Hubert Humphrey of Minnesota.

Although the Democrats were in complete control of the Congress, no law guaranteeing the civil rights of African Americans could be passed. The first modern civil rights law was adopted in 1957 under a Republican president, Dwight

Eisenhower. This law of 1957 was followed by other civil rights and voting rights laws in 1960, 1964, 1965, 1968, and 1972.

Civil rights was only one of the political goals of Hubert Humphrey. On other occasions he proposed the establishment of the Peace Corps, the creation of a Food for Peace program, and legislation favoring labor unions, farmers, and the unemployed. Humphrey was concerned about the bigotry confronting Jews, discrimination against African Americans, better working conditions for labor, economic protection for American farmers, and laws in the public interest.

Humphrey was in the Senate from 1949 to 1965 and from 1971 to January 1978. He was vice president from 1965 to 1969. During those years Humphrey had a number of opportunities to talk about his proposals. His reelections went hand in hand with his concerns about these various groups. The question was whether these groups would follow a two way street, maintaining their support for Humphrey and his political success.

Communists, Conservatives, and Liberal Democrats

Humphrey was challenged by, and in turn challenged, three major groups of foes at some time in his political life. During World War II, and especially in 1943 and 1944, Humphrey had trouble with the Communists and the extreme left wingers. He was chiefly responsible for the establishment of a non-communist liberal organization, Americans for a Democratic Society. During the same period of time Humphrey expressed concern over the two progressive parties in the State of Minnesota, the Democrats and the Farmer-Laborites. He had recognized that the left wing of the Farmer-Labor Party was controlled by the left, and he and others wanted to unify these two parties without any support from the radicals. Humphrey and others had gone to a state party convention in 1944, but they were forced to withdraw and establish a "rump convention" elsewhere. This was just one occasion when Humphrey was called a fascist and a war monger.

While Humphrey believed that he was an anti-communist, conservatives within the Democratic and Republican parties would not accept his claim. This was especially true within that period known as McCarthyism (1950-1954), when Humphrey and the liberal Democrats were accused of being "soft on Communism." It was at this time that the liberals under the leadership of Senator Humphrey proposed that Congress adopt the toughest anti-communist bill, the Communist Control Bill. What the liberals had done was to accuse the conservatives of being "soft on Communism," and they forced Congress to adopt this legislation. So many constitutional questions were present in this law, it was never enforced.

The conservatives and Humphrey challenged each other on other occasions. For example, as a freshman senator Humphrey had spoken about a conservative, Senator Harry Flood Byrd of Virginia, who was not present in the Senate. Humphrey was not concerned about the rules of the Senate nor the fact that he did not have the support of the inner circle in the Senate. Humphrey had made mistakes in this attack, and he decided thereafter to follow the Senate rules. He later became a member of the inner circle, as was demonstrated in 1961 when he was chosen the majority whip of the Senate.

Whenever Humphrey wanted to run for the presidency of the United States he was challenged by liberal Democrats, including Jack and Bobby Kennedy, Gene McCarthy, and George McGovern. In 1960 Humphrey entered several state presidential primaries. He did not have much money and had to campaign on a bus. Jack Kennedy flew from place to place and campaigned with the support of celebrities from Hollywood. In Humphrey's words: "I heard a plane overhead. On my cot, bundled in layers of uncomfortable clothes, both chilled and sweaty, I yelled, 'Come down here, Jack, and play fair.'"

Humphrey almost lost the 1960 presidential primary in Wisconsin and did lose the presidential primary in West Virginia. Immediately thereafter he withdrew from that presidential race and ran again for the United States Senate. He believed that he would spend the rest of his political life in the Senate. In 1964 this changed once again. President Lyndon Johnson selected Humphrey to be his running mate. While Johnson was overwhelmingly reelected, he still lost the confidence of the American people in the next four years as a consequence of increasing involvement in the war in Vietnam. Johnson almost lost the 1968 presidential primary in New Hampshire, and then he told the American people that he would not run for reelection.

Humphrey and other liberals—Gene McCarthy, George McGovern, and Bobby Kennedy—entered the 1968 primaries. Because Humphrey was part of the establishment and therefore responsible for the Vietnamese venture, he was opposed by many liberals, including McCarthy, McGovern, and Bobby Kennedy. Bobby Kennedy's effort ended in June when he was assassinated, but Kennedy's supporters would not join with Humphrey. Humphrey became the Democratic candidate for the presidency in 1968, but during the national convention the streets of Chicago were filled with anti-war rioters. At most Humphrey could only count on lukewarm support from McCarthy and McGovern. When Humphrey campaigned on college campuses and in major American cities he was heckled by anti-war activists. So many of these people refused to vote in that year that Humphrey lost the election to Richard Nixon.

Defeated and no doubt disappointed Humphrey returned to Minnesota and for the next two years served as a professor of public affairs at the university. This career did not last long, because in 1970 and again in 1976 Humphrey was reelected to the U.S. Senate.

In 1968 and again in 1977 doctors operated on Humphrey for cancer. In October 1977 Humphrey knew that his death was imminent and made his last trip to the Senate. On October 25 Humphrey was applauded by the senators and their guests, and several praised him in their speeches. On January 14, 1978, there was to be a tribute to Hubert Humphrey. Humphrey died the evening before. His Senate term was completed by his wife.

Further Reading

There are various books by Humphrey and about Humphrey and his ideas. There is an autobiography, *The Education of a Public Man* (1976), and a biography, *Hubert Humphrey: The Man and His Dream* (1978) by S. D. Engelmayer and R. J. Wagman. Humphrey was the author of *Beyond Civil Rights: A New Day of Equality* (1968), *Intergration vs. Segregation* (1964), *War on Poverty* (1964), and *Young American in the "Now" World* (1971). Humphrey was an able orator, and his notable statements were compiled by Perry D. Hall, *The Quotable Hubert H. Humphrey.* □

Friedensreich Hundertwasser

Austrian born visionary painter and spiritual ecologist Friedensreich Hundertwasser (Friedrich Stowasser; born 1928) consistently worked with spiral motifs, primitive forms, spectral colors, and repetitive patterns. Although influenced by other Viennese artists, Hundertwasser was never formally affiliated with any "ism."

Friedensreich Hundertwasser was born Friedrich Stowasser in Vienna on December 15, 1928, of a Jewish mother and a Christian father. His father died in 1929. Hundertwasser was baptized in 1937 and supposedly joined the Hitler Youth Corps in 1941. In 1943 69 of his maternal relatives were deported and killed in Nazi concentration camps. During the war and the Russian occupation Hundertwasser lived in a Viennese cellar with his mother. Decades after the Hitler period he could be seen carrying a satchel containing a passport, foreign currencies, and a portable painting set, among other essentials. Hundertwasser married in 1958, while in Gibraltar, and was subsequently divorced in 1960. In 1962, after spending a year in Japan, he married Juuko Ikewada in Venice. They were divorced four years later.

Hundertwasser is viewed as an international, independent artist. He traveled, lived, and worked in various locations throughout Europe, the East, North Africa, New Zealand, and Australia and was never formally affiliated with any school of painting or "ism." In 1949 he selected and assumed the name Hundertwasser (Hundred Water), and in 1969 Friedensreich (Kingdom of Peace), often adding Regenstag (Rainy Day), a name that he originally invented for the converted sailing ship upon which he sometimes lived.

From 1936 to 1937 Hundertwasser attended Montessori School in Vienna, a learning experience to which he would later credit the choice of color in his paintings. His formal art training included three months at the Academy of Fine Arts in Vienna in 1948 and a day at the Ecole des Beaux-Arts in Paris in 1950. As a mature artist he professed an intense dislike for all art theory, including color theory.

Hundertwasser believed that painting is a religious experience. Opting always for spiritualism over rationalism, he preferred to be viewed as a "magician of vegetation." In 1954 the artist developed a quasi-mystical philosophy of artistic creation and perception called "Transautomatism" which he later developed into a "Grammar of Vision."

Hundertwasser's early paintings were heavily influenced by the Vienna Secession tradition of Egon Schiele and Gustav Klimt. His works from 1949 through 1953 also display close affinity with well-known paintings by Paul Klee. In 1953 the spiral motif first appeared in his work and became the most consistent formal element of his mature style. The artist, who first recognized the spiral while viewing a film called "Imagery of the Insane," defined the motif as a "biological spiral" and "a symbol of life." Throughout his career Hundertwasser used the six spectral colors almost exclusively. His later work combined these with metallic colors such as gold, silver, bronze, or aluminum. His forms are archaic and primitive and his picture surfaces are often covered by repetitive patterns.

It was the artist's intention to offer his viewers a glimpse of Paradise, constructed while the creator is in a dream state. The work is rarely disturbing and almost always highly decorative. Hundertwasser made no attempt to identify universals with his primitivized forms, and as a result his language remains relatively private. The audience is given only limited access to the painter's fantasy experiences. Hundertwasser's dreams were more than a little repetitive, but usually pleasant.

Numerous exhibitions of Hundertwasser's paintings have been mounted, including one-man shows at the Art Club, Vienna (1952); Studio Paul Facchetti, Paris (1954, 1960, 1965, and 1974); Tokyo Gallery (1961); Austrian Pavilion, Binnale, Venice (1962); Kestner-Gesellschaft, Hannover (1966); University of California, Berkeley (1968); Auckland City Art Gallery, New Zealand (1973); and a retrospective at the Haus der Kunst, Munich (1975). In 1957 Hundertwasser was awarded the Prix du Syndicat d'Initiative, Première Bordeaux (France) Biennale, and in 1959 the Sanbra Prize at the Fifth São Paulo (Brazil) Biennale. That same year he assumed a guest lectureship in Hamburg at the Kunsthochschule der Freien und Hansestadt, only to be asked to leave his post because he performed the "endless line," a ten mile, two days and nights spiral. He was also awarded the Mainichi Prize at the Sixth International Art Exhibition, Tokyo, in 1961.

The artist's public lectures and manifestations include: "Art Is Always Changing" (Salzburg, 1949); "My Aspiration: To Free Myself from the Universal Bluff of our Civilization" (Vienna, 1952); "Mouldiness Manifesto: Against Rationalism in Architecture" (Austria and Germany, 1958); "Les Ortilles" (Paris, 1959); "Naked Speech" (Munich, 1968); "Intensive Naked Demonstration" (Vienna, 1968); and "Your right to windows—your duty to the trees" (1972).

A diverse artist, Hundertwasser also designed a church in 1987 and a day-care center in Frankfurt, Germany (1987). He created postage stamp designs for Austria, Senegal, and the Cape Verde Islands. He also designed relief medallions for the Austrian Mint, environmental posters donated to various environmental groups, and various architectural models.

Hundertwasser received the Austrian State Award for Arts in 1980 and the Austrian Protection of Nature Award in 1981. He resided in Vienna.

Further Reading

Friedrich Hundertwasser, by Herschel B. Chipp and Brenda Richardson, published in conjunction with the University of California, Berkeley's 1968 Hundertwasser exhibition, is of particular value to the English speaking audience. The catalogue includes an informed introductory essay, the artist's "Mouldiness Manifesto," commentaries by graduate students who participated in a Hundertwasser seminar, and a personal reminiscence by collector Joachim Hean Aberbach. *Hundertwasser,* a small scale but well-executed catalogue published by Aberbach Fine Art, New York (1973), is another good source, as is *Hundertwasser Rainy Day,* by Manfred Bockelmann (1972). □

Hung Hsiu-ch'üan

Hung Hsiu-ch'üan (1814-1864) was a Chinese religious leader and founder of the Taiping sect. His beliefs led to the Taiping Rebellion.

Hung Hsiu-ch'üan was born on Jan. 1, 1814, not far from Canton to a poor peasant family of the Hakka minority group. Because the young boy displayed some intelligence, his family pooled its resources in order to give him an education. In 1827 Hung participated in the official civil service examinations for the first time, and, although he passed the preliminary examination, he failed the district examination in Canton. Despite repeated attempts he was never successful and became one of those frustrated scholars who eked out a living as a low-paid teacher and who in times of crisis often provided the leaders and supporters of rebellious movements.

Birth of a Religion

In 1836, when in Canton for another unsuccessful attempt at the examinations, Hung heard a Christian missionary preach and was given some religious tracts. In the following year, after failing again, he suffered a nervous collapse. While in a coma he had visions of a fatherly old man who complained that men had forsaken him and were worshiping demons. A middle-aged man also appeared who instructed Hung in the slaying of demons. The true significance of his visions did not become apparent to Hung until 1843, when he took the trouble to read the Christian tracts he had been given 7 years earlier. Hung suddenly realized that the old man was God the Father and the middle-aged man, Jesus Christ, the Elder Brother and that Hung, as the Younger Brother, was commissioned to stamp out the worship of demons.

In 1844 Hung converted the members of his family to his new religion and then, because of local Chinese animosity, went to Kwangsi to preach among the Hakka. The religious group that Hung founded was known as the God Worshipers Society and was initially a purely religious organization, but government persecution and local opposition eventually forced it to assume a political role.

Taiping Rebellion

In July 1850 Hung and his followers decided to resist the government forces that had been sent to wipe them out, and the Taiping Rebellion began. As avowed rebels with dynastic aspirations, the God Worshipers changed their name to the T'ai-p'ing T'ien-kuo, "Celestial Kingdom of Peace," and Hung was declared T'ien-wang, or "Celestial King." The Taiping forces swept northward in the spring of 1852 and by March of 1853 had taken Nanking, which became the "Celestial Capital."

Thousands of desperate peasants joined Hung's theocratic state. Although his understanding of Christianity was rather limited, it did not prevent Hung from developing his own ideas, which were accepted by his followers as the word of God. Prostitution, foot-binding, and slaves were prohibited, as were opium smoking, adultery, gambling, and the use of wine and tobacco. All property belonged to the state, which in turn provided for the needs of the people. Women were allowed to hold land and serve in the army and administration, but the sexes were rigidly separated. Monogamy was the rule, and, contrary to the Chinese custom of religious tolerance, all followers had to believe in the one true God. The Manchus, whom Hung regarded as alien conquerors and the personification of evil, were slated to be eliminated, as were Confucian culture and the gentry-literati-official class.

The competent leadership, tight military organization, and fanatical devotion to the cause which had made the Taiping forces almost invincible was, however, dissipated by jealousy and intrigue. In 1856, after an attempted usurpation, Hung ordered a bloodbath of his closest advisers, withdrew to his harem, and left the governing of the Taiping kingdom, which encompassed most of central China, to his incompetent relatives.

Under the leadership of Tseng Kuo-fan, the imperial forces began to reverse the tide in 1860. With two new imperial armies in the field, one under Li Hung-chang in Kiangsu and the other under Tso Tsung-t'ang in Chekiang, Nanking was finally taken on July 19, 1864. Hung Hsiu-ch'üan, who had placed his trust in divine guidance, had committed suicide on June 1. The victors found his body wrapped in yellow satin embroidered with dragons in a sewer under his palace.

Further Reading

A full biography of Hung appears in Arthur W. Hummel, ed., *Eminent Chinese of the Ch'ing Period, 1644-1912* (2 vols., 1943-1944). The most extensive study of the Taiping Rebellion in English is Franz H. Michael, *The Taiping Rebellion*, vol. 1 (1966). Vincent Yu-chung Shih, *The Taiping Ideology* (1967), discusses in depth the sources, interpretations, and influences of Taiping thought. □

Hung-wu

Hung-wu (1328-1398) was the founder of the Ming dynasty of China. He provided the basis for much of China's subsequent development and expansion.

Born into a poor peasant family in modern Anhwei Province, Chu Yüan-chang, as Hung-wu was originally named, had no schooling and was orphaned at the age of 16. He entered a monastery for subsistence, became a mendicant monk in the Huai River valley, and participated in the popular uprisings organized by the White Lotus—Maitreya secret societies against the Mongol rule.

Rise to Power

In April 1352 Chu joined the local leader Kuo Tzuhsing and soon gained his confidence. By marrying Kuo's foster daughter, Chu succeeded to the command after Kuo's death in 1355 and set out to contest power with his rivals. Chu differed from other rebels in restraining his men from killing and plunder and in his effort to recruit educated people to his service.

After some initial success Chu led his forces across the Yangtze, capturing Nanking (1356) and defeating his leading opponent, Ch'en Yu-liang (1363); he proclaimed himself the prince of Wu in 1364. He continued campaigning to eliminate his adversaries, first Chang Shihch'eng, then Fang Kuo-chen in 1364-1367, while his general captured Peking in 1368. On Jan. 23, 1368, Chu, not yet 40, ascended the throne of Ming (Brilliance), adopted the reign title Hung-wu (Grand Military Achievement), and made his capital in Nanking.

Emperor of China

Hung-wu directed his lieutenants to complete the unification of China. In 1368-1369 his general Hsü Ta campaigned against the Mongols in Shansi and Shensi. Szechwan was captured in 1371, and Ming forces moved into Manchuria. Yünnan became a Chinese province in 1381. Ming forces went as far as Karakorum and Hami (in Dzungaria). In the east, Korea and Japan both acknowledged Chinese suzerainty, while traditional vassals in Southeast Asia such as Annam and Champa also submitted.

On the other hand, Hung-wu devoted himself to restructuring the political and military institutions by synthesizing the traditional system with Mongol precedent. The Emperor took personal supervision over the six ministries: personnel, revenue, rites, war, justice, and works. The branch central secretariat, which once exercised overall power in a province, was changed to a system of administrative commissioners. The central military commission created in 1361 was fragmented into five military commissions in 1380. National defense fell on "military families," who alternated between military duties and cultivating their fields for subsistence. The system of civil service was revived, and traditional institutions such as the Censorate, Hanlin Academy, and the National University were restored. In 1382 the Emperor organized a secret service known as the "Embroidered-uniform Guard" with unlimited police and judicial authority over every individual in the state.

In social and economic spheres the Emperor devised various measures for control over the population and the inflow of revenue. Foremost of these was a scheme of population registration known as the *li-chia* system. Every 10 households formed a *chia* with one man as chief; 10 *chia* made a *li,* which, together with 10 *chia* chiefs, made a total of 110 households headed by a *li* leader. This served as a basis for labor services as well as a security check.

In addition the Emperor revived the Yüan system of population classification, under which people were grouped under three heads, military, civil, and crafts, and were forbidden to shift from one class to another. The Emperor was known for his benevolent treatment of the peasants. He established a special agricultural bureau to assist farmers and reduced or suspended their tax payment in times of distress. However, he treated the rich differently. The head of a wealthy family was usually chosen as "tax captain" for the collection and delivery of the allotted quota of revenue to the government. For effective collection of taxes, population and land registers were compiled and kept up to date.

Assessment of His Reign

Hung-wu's reign, despite its achievement, was marred by excessive violence against officials and scholars whom the Emperor regarded as dangerous to his throne. The terror was a product of the Emperor's uneasiness over the arrogance of the intellectuals who secretly despised his humble origin. While it was common for officials to suffer harsh treatment, the Emperor inaugurated three successive purges against his former comrades which took a heavy toll of lives.

The most notorious was the case of Hu Wei-yung, the prime minister who was executed on the charge of sedition in 1380. The second and third purges, in 1385 and 1393, were designed to eliminate military officials whom the Emperor considered too powerful to be acquiesced to. Altogether, several tens of thousands of innocent people were put to death on trumped-up charges.

Hung-wu died in June 1398 and received the posthumous temple name T'ai-tzu (Grand Progenitor). Hungwu was a controversial figure in history. Condemned as a ruthless dictator and cruel tyrant for the notorious means to achieve his ends, he was also praised as a vigorous ruler for founding a new dynasty out of ruins and for laying the foundation of the Chinese systems and achievements of the subsequent centuries. Hung-wu was quick to learn from his tutors and became quite conversant with the literary tradition. About 20 titles of works attributed to his authorship are still extant today.

Further Reading

There is no book-length biography of Hung-wu in English, although several substantial contributions have lately appeared in Sinological journals. A brief but out-of-date biographical notice is included in H. A. Giles, *A Chinese Biographical Dictionary* (1898). A succinct résumé of Hung-wu's rise to power is in F. W. Mote, *The Poet Kao Ch'i, 1336-1374* (1962). For details on the government institutions founded by Hungwu see Charles O. Hucker, *The Traditional Chinese State in Ming Times, 1368-1644* (1961) and *Chinese Government in Ming Times* (1969). Recommended for background are C. P. Fitzgerald, *China: A Short Cultural History* (1935); L. Carrington Goodrich, *A Short History of the Chinese People* (1943); and Edwin O. Reischauer and John K. Fairbank, *East Asia: The Great Tradition* (1958). □

Hun Sen

A Cambodian political leader, Hun Sen (born 1951) early in 1985, at the age of 33, became the then youngest premier of any country in the world.

Hun Sen was born the second son of a family of poor peasants on April 8, 1951, in a hamlet in Cambodia's southeastern Kompong Cham province, which borders Vietnam. The location of the area of his birth was to prove significant for his career in the 1970s, as it early on was to bring him in contact with nearby Vietnamese political and military leaders and their Cambodian allies.

Hun Sen's formal schooling was haphazard. Reportedly he received primary education in Phnom Penh while living with relatives. But he did not go beyond this, and instead was soon swept up as an adolescent participant in various revolutionary youth movements. These movements themselves reflected the turbulent power struggle among Cambodian communists, including Hanoi-oriented leaders, during the middle 1960s. This struggle culminated in the founding of the Communist Party of Kampuchea (CPK) in 1966. Hun Sen appears to have drifted between farming work with his family in Kompong Cham and underground organizational activity, including for a supposed "youth wing" of the party. The continued communist factional squabbling left Hun Sen relatively untainted. And, in any case, the establishment of the government of Marshal Lon Nol after the overthrow on March 18, 1970, of the longtime regime of Prince Norodom Sihanouk solidified the communist struggle. This solidification for the moment strengthened the common cause of communist Cambodian dissidents in or on the fringes of the CPK with the general leadership of Hanoi and its Cambodian followers.

Member of the Khmer Rouge

Already in late 1968 Hun Sen formally had joined the CPK, conventionally called the "Khmer Rouge." Cadre course training followed, and in subsequent years he was to distinguish himself in guerrilla combat against the U.S.-backed Lon Nol forces. Hun Sen is said to have lost his left eye and to have been severely wounded four more times in the fighting, which included the Khmer Rouge's Eastern Zone area of operations. This area included his home province of Kompong Cham.

On April 17, 1975, the victorious Khmer Rouge forces, having driven Lon Nol into exile and consolidated their hold on Phnom Penh and on most major Cambodian towns, proclaimed the birth of the state of "Democratic Kampuchea" (DK). By this time Hun Sen, though barely 24 years old, had risen to the rank of Khmer Rouge division commander. He was asked to participate in at least one of the major Khmer Rouge victory celebrations in Phnom Penh during April 1975, an indication that he was trusted by Pol Pot, Khieu Sampan, Ieng Sary, and other senior CPK and DK leaders.

This spirit of trust and amity was not to last long, however. Hun Sen returned to Kompong Cham as Khmer Rouge commander and senior CPK cadre while the Pol Pot holocaust designed to "cleanse" Cambodian society was being unleashed. The extent of Hun Sen's own involvement in the deliberate campaign of killing and maltreatment that was to cost a million Cambodian lives remains to be determined.

Break With Pol Pot

A number of factors influenced Hun Sen's position in the 1975-1977 period prior to his break with Pol Pot and the DK. Because of his limited formal education and youth, he had escaped the maniacal suspicion among the Pol Pot entourage of all those Cambodians who, because of their education or maturity, automatically were perceived as poisoned by the ideologies of the hated regimes of the past. Hun Sen's combat service also helped. But it was precisely in the Eastern Zone, particularly Kompong Cham, that underground Khmer Rouge opposition to the bloody "year zero" tactics of the Pol Pot regime first manifested itself.

This opposition centered around the older, Vietnamese influenced Cambodian communists and their younger followers, about 2,000 of whom had gone to Hanoi after the 1954 Geneva peace conference which had partitioned Vietnam and given separate status to Cambodia and Laos. They had seen little chance of developing the communist resistance in Cambodia at the time, and they largely returned to Cambodia only after Prince Norodom Sihanouk's fall in 1970 in order to ally themselves with Pol Pot's Khmer Rouge in the struggle against Lon Nol's regime. Though identified early with Pol Pot's CPK and its guerrillas, Hun Sen's posting in Kompong Cham through most of the 1970s and the proximity of Vietnamese communist cadres across the border in neighboring South Vietnam had their effect. Being too young and not senior enough in party affairs to be suspected by his Khmer Rouge mentors, Hun Sen escaped the purges of the older Vietnamese-oriented communists ordered by Pol Pot in the Eastern Zone after he had established his DK regime in Phnom Penh in 1975.

Mutual suspicion between the Cambodian communist factions continued to mount in the years after 1975, catching Hun Sen in the middle. This suspicion was fed by ancient Cambodian-Vietnamese ethnic hostility and by resentment felt by Cambodian communists who had not gone to Hanoi believing that the Socialist Republic of Vietnam unifying North and South Vietnam since 1975 meant to dominate Cambodia and Laos, in keeping with Ho Chi Minh's old dream of a single communist Indochina state. Perhaps well before September 24, 1977, Hun Sen had made a major irrevocable life decision. On that date, Khmer Rouge forces, on orders of Pol Pot, crossed into South Vietnam's Tay Ninh province hunting for suspected Vietnam sympathizers among CPK cadres. There is some, but not conclusive, evidence that Khmer Rouge forces already had gone on similar "hunting" missions in Tay Ninh during the months before this incursion.

If Hun Sen, even before that date, already quietly had decided to defect, the September incursion wholly committed him to cast his lot with his pro-Vietnamese party companions. In one press interview a decade later he was to declare that already early in 1977 he had refused Khmer Rouge command orders to arrest and search for suspected CPK comrades in his territory.

Along with other Eastern Zone Cambodian communist dissidents, Hun Sen now went to Hanoi, receiving further training (as he was to put it later) in "people's leadership." He also almost certainly supplied his Vietnamese mentors with information on Khmer Rouge tactical military intentions of "rectifying" the DK's long disputed southeastern border with Vietnam. He also joined a fellow former Eastern Zone Khmer Rouge division commander, Heng Samrin, in organizing a Vietnam-sponsored Kampuchean National

Front for National Salvation (KNUFNS)—a shadow government and movement to replace Pol Pot's CPK and DK regime.

After a 110,000-man Vietnamese army invaded Cambodia on December 30, 1978, drove out the Pol Pot-controlled DK regime from Phnom Penh, and occupied virtually all of the country, most of the KNUFNS leadership reconstituted itself as the cabinet of a new People's Republic of Kampuchea (PRK), formally proclaimed in Phnom Penh on January 10, 1979. On that same date, Hun Sen became minister of foreign affairs of the PRK and a Politburo member of the new government's guiding political party, the Kampuchean People's Revolutionary Party (KPRP).

Hun Sen Becomes Premier

On December 24, 1984, the PRK's chairman of the council of ministers, Prime Minister Chan Sy, died while undergoing medical treatment in the Soviet Union. On January 14, 1985, the Eighth Session of the PRK National Assembly elected Hun Sen to the premiership. Toward the end of 1986 Hun Sen, in a gradual transfer, initially passed his foreign affairs minister's post over to KPRP Politburo member Kong Korm. However, by the first week of December 1987, in a general cabinet shake-up that reflected a leadership need for stronger and independent initiatives in economic development and foreign policy discussions, Hun Sen resumed the foreign minister's office along with his premiership. Hun Sen also was elected chairman of the PRK National Assembly at its January 1985 session.

Along with his membership in the Politburo, the Central Committee, and the secretariat of the KPRP, the joint cabinet seats of premier and foreign minister unquestionably have made Hun Sen the second most powerful figure in his government after head of state Heng Samrin. On April 30, 1989, there came a technical change in Hun Sen's position as the PRK formally changed its name to State of Cambodia. This name change was in accordance with a new peace strategy of inclusion, so as to broaden the appeal of the Heng Samrin-Hun Sen government to various opposition groups, among them the remnants of Pol Pot's DK and Khmer Rouge organization.

As premier, and for more than a decade also as foreign minister, Hun Sen showed remarkable political skills in retaining support—or at least not incurring strong hostility—among different factions in his party and government, including the older, Vietnam-oriented dissidents of the original Khmer Rouge who left Pol Pot; the hard-line, avowedly more "nationalistic," younger KPRP cadres suspicious of both Hanoi and foreign support from the USSR; a pro-Soviet faction around former premier Pen Sovan; and other lesser factions.

In the years from 1979 to 1983, Hun Sen's efforts primarily were designed to win as broad acceptance as possible for the PRK, not only among other communist regimes of the world, but also in the Third World generally. This strategy was designed, among other goals, to minimize the influence of China, which, alone among the major powers, continued to support Pol Pot's DK diplomatically and with military supplies. Hun Sen initially also emphasized

the importance of close PRK political and military relations with Vietnam, but later joined Hanoi in approving the Vietnamese military withdrawal and in stressing Cambodia's need to be self-reliant. At the beginning of 1981, in part as a result of frequent visits to various world capitals by Hun Sen, the PRK regime had already secured official diplomatic recognition from some 30 countries and had neutralized much hostility in the Third World, although the PRK continued to be refused a seat in the United Nations as Cambodia's legitimate government.

The Long Search for Peace

After 1983 Hun Sen increasingly entered into dialogue with Indonesian and Thai officials and with other nations to find a Cambodian peace settlement. He helped defuse the potentially explosive Cambodian border conflict with Thailand between 1985 and 1987. But he continued to voice strong reservations at various international conferences over a possible interim United Nations regime in Cambodia, perhaps headed by Prince Norodom Sihanouk, pending general elections.

After June 1982 Hun Sen and his government faced the unification of major Cambodian opposition groups that stepped-up guerrilla attacks, including attacks by the 40,000-man Khmer Rouge. The vehicle of this combined opposition was the UN-and U.S.-recognized Coalition Government of Democratic Kampuchea (CGDK). At the same time, economic stagnation and international pressure also were compelling Vietnam to accelerate withdrawing forces from Cambodia. In an almost endless series of direct discussions between Hun Sen and Southeast Asian leaders on the implications of these developments, recognition grew that the PRK (State of Cambodia) represented the only real alternative to a probable return of the Khmer Rouge, whose guerrillas along the Thai border still were being supplied by China with the concurrence of some senior Thai military.

Hun Sen's policy became to widen this Southeast Asian, and indeed international, recognition of his regime as the only option other than the Khmer Rouge. By March 1986, in an agreement at Beijing, leaders of the Association of Southeast Asian Nations (ASEAN) accepted the need to include the PRK in a future Cambodian interim government. By August 1987 Hun Sen, in turn, had offered a "national reconciliation" proposal designed to include all opposition factions except the Khmer Rouge in the existing PRK government. During 1988-1990, however, frequent international conferences at Fère-en-Tardenois, near Paris in France, between Hun Sen and Sihanouk and two informal meetings in Jakarta attended by all the Cambodian factions, ASEAN, and some of the UN Security Council's permanent members failed to provide a desired consensus on a Cambodian peace settlement.

Finally, on October 23, 1991, all the warring factions agreed on a peace plan to share power under a Supreme National Council pending elections in 1993. Under UN supervision, the nation's administration was to be in the hands of Prince Sihanouk. The 1993 landmark elections yielded an impressive 90 percent voter turn-out, despite Khmer Rouge threats. The majority of the ballots were cast for King Sihanouk's royalist party, FUNCINPEC. Hun Sen and his Cambodian People's Party (CPP) used violence to intimidate competitors, duly recorded by the UN, but not prevented. The four provinces most dominated by the CPP threatened to secede, which would have initiated another civil war. Because the non-Communist parties lacked the military muscle to prevent this, a compromise was reached and a coalition government was the result. Hun Sen, representing the electoral losers, and Silhanouk's son Prince Ranariddh, representing the winners, became co-prime ministers.

The first two years of their collaborative form of government were relatively peaceful, marked by only the occasional spat. In 1995, they publicly announced their intention to stay together until 2010. At one point in 1996, Hun Sen said of his co-prime minister in an interview, "It is not a friendship but rather like brothers, although I am not a royal family member. He's older than me, I respect him, and our two families have good relations. So I consider him my elder brother. We enjoy an understanding with each other in our work." The specter of the 1998 elections seemed to fuel the infighting between Hun Sen and Ranariddh that escalated steadily in the months prior to a Hun Sen staged coup d'etat in early July 1997, a move he vehemently defended as legal and denied as ebing a coup. Hun Sen publicly announced that anyone who negotiates with the remaining hard-line Khmer Rouge rebels should be arrested. Ranariddh was negotiating with the Khmer Rouge, as Hun Sen had done the year before. Although Hun Sen was a one-time Khmer Rouge commander, he is reviled by his former comrades. Ranariddh, however, was living in exile and reportedly "desperately seeking" Khmer Rouge support to supplement his own army that is said to be smaller than Hun Sen's forces. Foreign Minister Ung Huot was elected to Ranariddh's post on July 30, 1997, in an election by what many consider an incomplete parliament due to the fact that many of Ranariddh's supporters had fled the country.

In keeping with present Cambodian practices, little is known officially of Hun Sen's private life. He was said to have married a fellow worker in the original CPK in 1972, and they had four children. In July 1997, Hun Sen revisited the site of the grave of his firstborn son, who died at birth 21 years prior. In late June 1997, Hun Sen dedicated a reconstructed school to his wife. Hun Sen's younger brother, Nun Nong, was head of the KPRP's provincial executive committee of Kompong Cham and also was a member of the national KPRP's Central Committee.

Further Reading

There is no book, or even any published biographical article of any length, on Hun Sen in any language. Brief biographical sketches of Hun Sen based on a few official government handouts have appeared in the international press. See, for example, *Washington Post,* National Weekly Edition, June 26 and July 2, 1989. Other snippets of information on Hun Sen or his political affiliations from open sources are provided by the *Asia Year-Book* annuals (published by the *Far Eastern Economic Review,* Hong Kong) from 1980 onward; Ben Kiernan, "Origins of Khmer Communism," in *Southeast Asian Affairs 1981* (Institute of Southeast Asian Studies, Singapore: 1981); Peter Schier, "Kampuchea in 1985," in *Southeast Asian Af-*

fairs 1986; Nayan Chanda, *Brother Enemy. The War After the War* (1986); Michael Vickery, *Kampuchea, Politics, Economics and Society* (1986); and Elizabeth Becker, *When the War Was Over: Cambodia's Revolution and the Voices of Its People* (1986). □

H. L. Hunt

H. L. Hunt (1889-1974) was an entrepreneur who built a financial empire from a small early investment in oil in Arkansas. In his later years he was perhaps the world's richest man.

Born on his father's farm near Vandalia, Illinois, on February 17, 1889, Haroldson Lafayette Hunt worked nearly full-time on the farm as a boy, reaching only the fifth grade in the public schools. At age 16 he left home, travelling across the United States working as a farmhand, cowboy, lumberjack, and mule skinner. When his father died in 1911 he left the young man an inheritance of about $6,000. With that money Hunt bought himself a cotton plantation near Lake Valley, Arkansas, in the Mississippi Delta.

Not content with simply farming, Hunt began speculating in cotton and timber land near Lake Providence, Louisiana. By 1920 he owned some 15,000 acres of land in Arkansas and Louisiana on which he planted cotton to take advantage of the high prices during World War I. With the end of the war, however, the cotton market collapsed, and the value of Hunt's cotton lands plummeted accordingly. He then began looking for more lucrative sources of income. Upon hearing rumors of an oil strike in El Dorado, Arkansas, he decided to strike out for the area. A more conventional man would undoubtedly have sold his land, but not Hunt. Recognizing that the land would someday rise in value, he borrowed $50 and headed for El Dorado.

Once there he began trading in oil leases. His mode of operation was to ask a farmer how much he wanted for his land, go back into town and offer to sell the land to an oil prospector for a higher price, and then buy and sell the land practically simultaneously, making a profit without investing a penny of his own money. After six months of this trading, Hunt had enough money to lease a half-acre of land on his own. Paying freight and demurrage, he brought in an old rotary rig, drilled, and struck oil. Within a short time he owned some 44 producing wells in the El Dorado area. In 1924 he sold a half interest in 40 of these wells for $600,000.

Throughout the rest of the 1920s Hunt continued to drill wells in Arkansas and also in Oklahoma and Louisiana. By the end of the decade he had 100 producing wells throughout the South and Southwest. Hunt's greatest coup came in September 1930 when he joined forces with a wildcatter named C. M. "Tex" Joiner. Joiner had discovered a vein of oil on his 4,000 acre spread in Rusk County, Texas, but lacked the capital to drill and was too far in debt to borrow any. At that point he decided to sell his land, but the

large oil companies were not interested because they were afraid that his titles were not in good order. Since most independent oilmen had been hard hit by the crash in October of 1929 they were not able to invest either.

Hunt went to Joiner and offered him a deal. In return for $30,000 in cash and an agreement to pay him $1.2 million in oil (if and when it was produced), Hunt acquired rights to the site of the greatest oil discovery in the world up until that time and the first major strike in what later would become the lucrative oil terrain of East Texas. A leading historian of the industry has commented that "More independent oil fortunes came out of the East Texas field than from any other place in the world." It was primarily because of the great size of the field. This, in turn, became a great turning point in Texas history. Prior to this time local oil men always had to go hat in hand to the major oil companies to solicit funds for expansion and development. But Hunt, like some others, was able to build his own pipelines and to supply Sinclair Oil Company tank cars with his own oil.

To exploit this new field, the Hunt Oil Company was founded in 1936. First headquartered in Tyler, Texas, it later moved to Dallas where it grew to become the largest independent oil producer in the United States. During World War II the amount of oil Hunt sold to the Allies exceeded the total German output. He also supplied 85 percent of the natural gas piped into the eastern United States in 1946 to help relieve the critical fuel shortage of that year. It was during these years that Hunt began to develop large holdings in real estate, and at one time he was also the largest pecan grower in the country. In later years he began getting

involved in the production of canned goods, health products, and cosmetics, all of which were placed under the umbrellas of HLH Products of Dallas. By the time of his death in 1974 Hunt's fortune was estimated at between $2 and $3 billion, and he was earning about $1 million a week.

During the early 1950s Hunt increasingly turned his interest to politics. Deeply concerned with what he felt was a serious communist menace to the United States, he founded the Facts Forum in 1951 as an educational foundation. This organization produced and distributed radio and television programs and subsidized the mass distribution of anticommunist and patriotic books and pamphlets. After having spent some $3.5 million on the organization, Hunt suspended its operation in 1956. Two years later it was revived under the name of Life Line, producing 15 minute radio programs. In 1964 Hunt began writing a conservative newspaper column and also wrote several books dealing with aspects of conservative ideology.

Hunt also got increasingly involved in electoral politics. In 1952 he headed the MacArthur for President movement, and it was rumored that he put up $150,000 for the effort. He agreed to support Eisenhower only reluctantly in that year and in 1956. In 1960 Hunt pushed hard for the nomination of Lyndon B. Johnson, since Johnson had supported oil depletion allowances (for tax purposes) throughout his career in the House and the Senate. After Johnson failed to gain the presidential nomination, but agreed to become John F. Kennedy's running mate, Hunt supported the latter with a contribution of some $100,000. Kennedy, however, did not reciprocate. Smarting under that rebuff and disgusted with Johnson's liberal policies after assuming the presidency in 1963, Hunt supported Barry Goldwater in 1964.

Hunt had four sons, and three of the four achieved some notoriety. Lamar Hunt owned the Kansas City Chiefs of the National Football League; Herbert Hunt supervised the operation of Hunt Oil Company, the $735 million family held oil corporation; and in 1979-1980 Nelson Bunker Hunt led a family attempt to corner the world silver market, which ended in near disaster for the world monetary system, the American economy, and the Hunt family fortune, with losses estimated at some $300 million.

An unpretentious man and a bit of an eccentric, Hunt lived in a relatively modest home in Dallas. There he cut the grass himself each week and took his lunch to work daily in a brown paper bag. Despite this unassuming demeanor, Hunt was often overheard introducing himself to strangers by proclaiming: "Hello, I am H. L. Hunt, the world's richest man. . . ." He died in Dallas on November 29, 1974.

Further Reading

There is no biography of Hunt, but there is valuable information in James Presley, *A Saga of Wealth: The Rise of the Texas Oilmen* (1978). Additional information on the industry and its political thrust can be found in Carl Solberg, *Oil Power* (1976).

Additional Sources

Brown, Stanley H., *H. L. Hunt,* Chicago: Playboy Press, 1976.

Burst, Ardis, *The three families of H.L. Hunt,* New York: Weidenfeld & Nicolson, 1988.
Hurt, Harry, *Texas rich: the Hunt dynasty, from the early oil days through the Silver Crash,* New York: W. W. Norton, 1981. □

Richard Morris Hunt

The American architect Richard Morris Hunt (1827-1895) was a major contributor to the eclectic style of the 19th century.

R ichard Morris Hunt was born in Brattleboro, Vt. His father was a lawyer and member of Congress, his mother a painter. He graduated from the Boston Latin School in 1843. He was sent to a military school in Geneva but soon tired of it and entered the studio of the architect Samuel Darier. In 1845 Hunt went to Paris to work with the architect Hector Martin Lefuel. The following year he was admitted to the École des Beaux-Arts. To round out his artistic training, he also studied painting and sculpture. For long periods he traveled in Europe, Asia Minor, and Egypt, evidently determined to see everything before beginning his career.

By 1854 Lefuel had appointed Hunt an inspector of construction at the Louvre in Paris. Though urged to remain in Paris, Hunt returned to America. He worked as a draftsman in Washington, and in 1858 he opened his own office in New York. He married Catharine Clinton Howland in 1861.

Hunt's early work was of little consequence; perhaps aware of this, he went to Europe again in the early 1860s. In 1868 he returned to New York and reopened his office. Bolstered by strong determination, Hunt finally profited from his long period of study and architectural gestation as he secured a number of commissions from wealthy New Yorkers. Hunt designed the Studio Building (1857) in New York City, the first building in America strictly for artists. More important, he built one of New York's first skyscrapers, the Tribune Building (1873-1875).

However, Hunt's genius lay in other directions. His home (1870-1871) at Newport, R.I., was a modest precursor of the great residences he was to build. This house combined the style of the Swiss chalet with a French mansard roof, colonial clapboards, and Gothic and Greek revival motifs. In spite of this heterogeneous heritage, the design had unity. Hunt was not an inventor but a clever reinterpreter of styles. As rich patrons began commissioning him to do houses, his designs became larger and more resplendent, remarkable for their richness of materials, color, and ingenuity of design. Some were overgrown and bulky; others were burdened with porches, hanging decorations, and bay windows in a variety of shapes; all were covered by highly irregular roofs.

In the late 1880s and the 1890s Hunt tended to simplify his homes by adhering more closely to adaptations of a single style, usually late French Gothic or Renaissance and Italian Renaissance. "Ochre Court" (1888-1891) in Newport and the William K. Vanderbilt House (1881) in New York City are in the French château style; "The Breakers" (1892-1895), built for Cornelius Vanderbilt, and "Marble House" (1892), both in Newport, are in the Italian Renaissance style. These houses were more homogeneous than Hunt's earlier designs. For George Washington Vanderbilt he designed an enormous country estate, probably the largest in America, called "Biltmore" (1890-1895), near Asheville, N.C. This French château, with ornate Gothic decorations, cost over $4 million and covers 5 acres of the 130,000-acre estate.

More important for the future of architecture than Hunt's buildings were his insistence on high professional standards, his help in founding the American Institute of Architects, and his willingness to train the architects of the next generation in his office.

Further Reading

No attempt has yet been made to write Hunt's biography or to publish a critical catalog of his architectural works. John V. Van Pelt wrote *A Monograph of the William K. Vanderbilt House* (1925). Biographical information is in Wayne Andrews, *Architecture, Ambition and Americans* (1955), and James Philip Noffsinger, *The Influence of the École des Beaux-Arts on the Architects of the United States* (1955).

Additional Sources

Baker, Paul R., *Richard Morris Hunt,* Cambridge, Mass.: MIT Press, 1980. □

William Holman Hunt

The English painter William Holman Hunt (1827-1910) was one of the founding members of the Pre-Raphaelite Brotherhood and the only one to remain faithful to its precepts throughout his life.

W illiam Holman Hunt was born in London. His father, a warehouse manager, reluctantly allowed him to enter the Royal Academy schools in 1844, where he met John Everett Millais. Profoundly influenced by his discovery of John Keats and his reading of John Ruskin's *Modern Painters* in 1847, Hunt developed a new approach to painting which involved the expression of significant moral ideas in a completely natural manner. To this end he evolved an intensely realistic technique, using brilliant, clear colors on a white ground instead of the traditional dark underpainting. These new ideas are embodied in his illustration inspired by Keats's *The Eve of St. Agnes*.

Dante Gabriel Rossetti, Hunt, and Millais founded the Pre-Raphaelite Brotherhood. Despite Ruskin's defense of the brotherhood in the *Times,* the hostile reception of Hunt's paintings in the academy, for example, *Christians Sheltering a Priest from the Druids* (1850), almost caused him to abandon painting. However, with Ruskin's praise for the *Light of the World* and the *Awakening Conscience*

(1853), Hunt began to gain recognition, and he turned almost exclusively to the portrayal of religious themes.

Hunt was passionately determined to ensure absolute truth to nature in the rendering of his subjects. He painted most of the *Light of the World* outside by moonlight, and the *Scapegoat* (1854) was painted beside the Dead Sea on the first of Hunt's many journeys to the Holy Land in search of authentic settings for his biblical scenes.

In 1865 Hunt married Fanny Waugh; within a year, after the birth of their son, she died. In 1873 he married Edith Waugh. After about 1860 Hunt was acknowledged as a leading English painter, but he became increasingly isolated from contemporary trends by his long absences abroad and his continuing adherence to the ideals and realistic technique of the Pre-Raphaelite style. Following Rossetti's death (1882), Hunt began a vigorous defense of these ideals and of his role in their formation with a series of articles which culminated in his remarkable autobiography (1905-1906).

Although Hunt was obsessed throughout his life with light and its effect on color, his popularity was to a large extent founded on his vivid religious imagery, which received wide circulation in the form of engravings. The *Miracle of the Sacred Fire* (1899), painted in Jerusalem, shows the same scrupulous attention to minute detail which may have caused his eyesight to fail in the last years.

Hunt was awarded the Order of Merit in 1905, and his importance was recognized in a series of major exhibitions. He died on Sept. 7, 1910.

Further Reading

The most important book on Hunt is his autobiography, *Pre-Raphaelitism and the Pre-Raphaelite Brotherhood* (2 vols., 1905-1906; 2d ed. rev. 1914). Fascinating sidelights on his character are in Diana Holman-Hunt, *My Grandmothers and I* (1960). Background on the period is provided in Robin Ironside, *Pre-Raphaelite Painters* (1948), and Graham Reynolds, *Victorian Painting* (1966).

Additional Sources

Amor, Anne Clark, *William Holman Hunt: the true Pre-Raphaelite,* London: Constable, 1989. □

Floyd Hunter

American social worker and administrator, community worker, professor, and author, Floyd Hunter (born 1912) was an originator of the "power structure" or elite concept in contemporary sociology.

Floyd Hunter was born on February 26, 1912, in Richmond, Kentucky, son of Jesse Hunter, a farmer, and Dovie Benton. He attended Richmond public schools and received both his B.A. (1939) in social science and his M.A. (1941) in social service administration from the University of Chicago. He married Ester Araya Rojas on December 23, 1937, and the couple had four children.

Hunter's mother and father were divorced when he was four and he lived at different times with each parent; with his mother in Bloomington, Illinois, and with his father on a Richmond tobacco farm. Both parents had been descended from British Isle ancestors who had placed great value upon political liberty and independence. This political heritage, along with Hunter's life experiences and intellectual development, formed the bone and sinew out of which he would fashion his controversial theory of "elite" social power.

Hunter's early life experiences were molded by two main influences: both familial and social "marginality" and the effects of the Great Depression on the American economy and polity. His marginality stemmed first from the transitory, shifting role he played in two families. Because both families suffered economic losses, Hunter's social status was unstable, allowing him an "observer's" eye on community status and family systems.

Meanwhile, his experiences in the Depression strengthened an already wary eye toward business interests and the government. He was shocked at the "petty and shoddy" practices of businessmen (the "ownership establishment") as they exploited the "dispossessed" customers. Unemployed and often famished during school breaks, Hunter hitchhiked to Washington, D.C., where he broke bread with the the Bonus Marchers two days before they were routed by General MacArthur's armed troops. Disenchanted by the use of military force in this and in other potentially disruptive occurrences, such as bank closings, he began to question the "relationship between our representative government and the people it was supposed to 'represent.'" Local political leaders who exploited New Deal policies for their own benefit, and thereby took a "root hog or die" attitude toward the poor, only alienated the young Hunter even further. "No milk of human kindness seemed to course through the political sieve," he felt. Economic and political injustice, then, formed a theme in Hunter's thought even before he had developed the intellectual tools necessary to craft an academic argument.

Hunter began his career as a social worker in Texas in the 1930s, moved to Chicago, and then to Indianapolis around 1940 as a social work administrator. From there he went to Atlanta in 1943 to head the southeastern regional office of the U.S.O. From 1946 to 1948 he headed the Atlanta Community Council, an experience which only provided real-life fodder for the growth of his power scheme. Following a political dispute with business leaders over the use of public property for a Henry Wallace campaign rally in the 1948 election (which had been allowed in the case of the Republican campaign), Hunter was fired from his position. With his wife and four children, he then moved to the University of North Carolina (U.N.C.), where he received his Ph.D. (1951) in sociology and anthropology. His doctoral dissertation, *Community Power Structure* (1953), became his most famous published work. A penetrating look at the power of business elites in Atlanta, it was followed up by his 1979 *Community Power Succession.*

These two works, more than any others, established Hunter as a leading progenitor of the power elite model of political sociology, a theme later picked up by C. Wright Mills and G. William Domhoff. In broad terms, Hunter and his intellectual descendants represented a crystallization of a 20th-century American paradigm which followed the earlier "conflict" model of economic domination established by Marx in 19th-century Europe. The main assumption of this model—that society was dominated by a relatively small group of social, economic, and political elites who make self-interested decisions in the absence of significant countervailing power—represented a challenge to the more consensually-oriented theory of structural functionalism that had held sway on American sociology for decades. Both of Hunter's studies on Atlanta held firmly to his basic theme.

Hunter was a professor at U.N.C. until 1960. Through the 1960s he headed two research firms, Social Science Research and Development Corporation and Decision Data, both based in the San Francisco area, where Hunter continued to reside in 1990. He was a Fulbright research professor at the University of Chile in 1964, and from the early through the late 1970s he was a visiting professor at several universities, including the University of California, the University of Kentucky, Eastern Kentucky University, and Harvard.

Meanwhile, Hunter wrote many books and articles, both fiction and nonfiction. Aside from the 1953 and 1979 works already mentioned, he published *The Big Rich and the Little Rich* (1965), *Top Leadership, U.S.A.* (1959), and *Community Organization: Action and Inaction* (1956). His

unpublished efforts as of the 1990s included several works of fiction and a 1989 attempt to combine the natural and social sciences into a "social physics" or "social relativity." Even his unpublished fiction works, however, such as *Chilean Rooms* (1964), were often attempts to weave himself "autobiographically into materials of social observation."

His detached, critical viewpoint was finely honed in his other nonfiction work as well. *The Big Rich and the Little Rich,* which asked, "What is the community function of great personal wealth?" essentially argued the "dysfunctions" of both large and small wealth. Both groups, Hunter believed, "do nothing that others could not do as well and much less expensively." *Top Leadership, U.S.A.* continued his methodological use of the "reputational" model of power he had developed in *Community Power Structures,* whereby leading organizations and individuals were asked to weigh the relative influence of others on them. In *Radical Democracy: One Man, One Vote; One Man, One Share,* a 1972 unpublished manuscript, Hunter broadened his critical view of elitism in society to include communist as well as capitalist states and unabashedly called for "complete trust in the people." Another unpublished work, *The Unrepresented* (1965), applied the elite model to the particular American context of communities and government.

Hunter's influence on theoretical developments in sociology and other disciplines that utilize the concept of "power" was substantial. Likewise, his methodology, which consisted of the "reputational" approach, also had a profound influence on the debate over how scholars should conduct "power" studies.

Further Reading

Hunter was cited in connection with the power elite theory and/ or the reputational method in almost any standard sociology text. His *Community Power Structure* is favorably reviewed by C. Wright Mills (whose 1956 *The Power Elite* had a profound influence on American sociology) in *Social Forces* (October 1953). *Community Power Succession* was reviewed, among many other places, in the *American Journal of Sociology* (July 1982). For versions of the power elite theory, see such works by G. William Domhoff as *The Higher Circles: The Governing Class in America* (1970), *Who Rules America* (1967), and *Power Structure Research* (1980). A work that utilized Hunter's work was Domhoff and Thomas, editors, *Power Elites and Organizations* (1987). The leading competitive model with elite theory was represented by the "pluralist" school. See Robert Dahl's *Who Governs?* (1962) and David Riesman, *The Lonely Crowd* (1953). For a critique of the reputational approach see Martin's *The Sociology of Power* (1977). Both critiques and extensions of the elite model may be found in Domhoff's and Ballard Hoyt's 1968 *C. Wright Mills and the Power Elite.*

The Special Collections Department of Emory University's Woodruff Library was the repository for Hunter's papers. These papers (47 boxes, 19.50 linear feet) consisted primarily of Hunter's notes, drafts, writings, and related materials from 1933 to 1989. Also included was a correspondence file and sets of autobiographical materials. The Hunter Papers were used extensively for this biographical sketch. □

Madeline Cheek Hunter

Influential American educator Madeline Cheek Hunter (1916-1994) developed a model for teaching and learning that was widely adopted by schools during the last quarter of the 20th century.

Madeline Hunter was one of two daughters born to Alexander Cheek, grandson of a Cherokee Indian. He had been orphaned at eight years old and had to drop out of school to work. Eventually he became a barber and, as a result of hard effort and intelligence, owned shops all over the United States and Canada. Her mother, Anna Keis, was the daughter of a Bohemian nobleman and a peasant woman.

Madeline's family originally lived in Canada where she was born. Her father was an avid hunter who liked Canada because "the duck hunting was better there." As Madeline was a "sickly" child, the family ultimately moved to California to avoid the terrible Canadian winters in Saskatchewan. Although they returned to Canada from May to October for many years, most of her schooling was in California. She and her father became naturalized United States citizens when she was about 14 years old. There was never a question that she and her sister would receive an education, a privilege denied her parents.

In junior high school she was placed in an experimental school to test some of Stanford University professor Louis Terman's psychological theories on intelligence. The school used her to score intelligence tests. Hunter later reported that, "As a result of that 'chore' and the stimulation from an outstanding school psychologist and teacher, Christine Cook, I became interested in human intelligence. That and classical ballet were my passions in life." As a 16-year-old (1932) she entered the University of California at Los Angeles as a combination pre-medicine and psychology major while continuing her ballet dancing. Eventually she had to choose between going to South America on tour with the Ballet Russe or finishing her degree. After choosing the latter, she discovered that limited eye-hand coordination would deny her the chance of a career as a neurological surgeon.

Two additional events influenced her choice of a career in school psychology. The first occurred many years before when waiting to be assigned to her seventh grade classroom in junior high school. Unknowingly, she would be assigned to an experimental class. While sitting in an auditorium, she watched as nearly every other student's name was called first and left for an assigned classroom. The feelings of hurt associated with a child being labeled last or dumb was not forgotten in her later works. As a consequence, a theme that runs consistently throughout her career is the need to give positive reinforcement to students in schools—"Never put a kid down, always build the kid up." A second defining moment that shaped her thinking occurred after graduation during her first work experiences at Children's Hospital in Los Angeles and at Juvenile Hall. From these situations she soon concluded that interventions in helping children in such situations were "too little, too late." She knew she needed to turn to children in schools and work there on the preventative side rather than the remedial side.

During World War II she married an engineer, Robert Hunter, who continued to work at Lockheed Aviation until his retirement. In 1944 they had a daughter, Cheryl, whose later career was that of a film editor, and in 1946 they had a son, Robin, who later became a school principal. When the children no longer needed a mother at home, Madeline went back to work full time in education, holding a series of positions in Los Angeles, namely, school psychologist, then principal, followed by director of research, and finally as an assistant superintendent who was used for "trouble shooting" difficult situations in the inner city, often involving multicultural groups. After 1963 she was associated with the University of California at Los Angeles (UCLA), first at the University Elementary School and later as a professor in the College of Education. During those years she worked closely with her colleague John Goodlad and was given the opportunity to implement her educational model in that laboratory school setting. She was named one of the hundred most influential women of the 20th century and one of the ten most influential in education by the Sierra Research Institute and the National Women's Hall of Fame.

Dissatisfaction with the quality of instruction in American schools during the 1970s and 1980s led many educators to call for fundamental changes. Madeline Hunter's model was turned to by many as a solution, and eventually it was implemented in 16 states formally in the 1980s and was widely used in others. Her education model is a "teacher decision-making model that is applicable to any mode or style of teaching, to any learner, and for any objective." Her method enables teachers to understand how particular behaviors can be attained by a student and how those desirable behaviors can be transferred and repeated in new situations.

A brief list of instructional and curricular decisions an English teacher might make in preparing for class are: (1) What can the students do as a result of this class? (2) What skills or information will the students need for attaining what they need to learn? (3) What learning behaviors can the teacher facilitate in the students which will result in the highest probability of being satisfying and successful? and (4) How will the teacher artistically use research and intuition to make students' satisfying achievement more probable?

By using her pre-medical background and her work in psychology, Hunter skillfully translated research from academic disciplines into teacher language and educational practice. She argued that teaching is like ballet or surgery; that is, teachers have to automate many behaviors so they can perform them artistically at high speed when a situation requiring them arises. As a consequence of applying her model, students learn behaviors that they can creatively transfer into new situations.

In response to a question asking her to assess the current educational situation in the 1990s, she said, "I believe the future of education is bright! We are beginning to unlock the mystery of the human brain and how it processes and learns. We, now, can enable teachers to use that knowledge to accelerate that learning process. No longer is teaching a 'laying on of hands.' It has become a profession that combines science with art to create a better and a more productive world for humankind." She died in 1994.

Further Reading

A brief biography and discussion of ideas can be found in two journals: *Newsmakers* 91, "Madeline Hunter," by David Collins; and *Educational Leadership,* "Portrait of Madeline Hunter," by Mark F. Goldberg (February 1990). Two journal articles that discuss and apply her education model are: *Educational Leadership,* "On Teaching and Supervising: A Conversation with Madeline Hunter," by Ron Brandt (February 1985); and *English Journal,* "Madeline Hunter in the English Classroom," by Madeline Hunter (September 1989). Selected books by her that introduce and apply her education model are published by TIP Publications, P.O. Box 514, El Segundo, California. They are: *Motivation* (1967); *Reinforcement* (1967); *Retention* (1967); *Teach More—Faster* (1969); *Improve Instruction* (1976); *Mastery Teaching* (1982); and, with Doug Russell, *Mastering Coaching & Supervision* (1989).

☐

William Hunter

The Scottish anatomist and obstetrician William Hunter (1718-1783) was instrumental in improving the practice of obstetrics and establishing it as a medical discipline.

Villiam Hunter was born on May 23, 1718, near East Kilbride, Lanarkshire. At the age of 13 he entered the University of Glasgow to study theology, but after 5 years there he decided instead to study medicine and became an assistant to William Cullen, a well-known physician. Hunter spent 3 years with Cullen, attended the University of Edinburgh for a year, and in 1740 went to London, where he studied with James Douglas, who encouraged him in anatomy, and William Smellie, from whom he developed his interest in obstetrics. Hunter decided to teach anatomy and opened a series of private lectures on anatomy and surgery in 1746 in London. He was a popular and respected teacher.

While teaching, Hunter was also engaged in obstetrical practice. In 1747 he was appointed assistant to the accoucheur at Middlesex Hospital, and in 1748 he became surgeon-accoucheur at the British Lying-in Hospital. Before Hunter, obstetrics had been the domain of the midwife, but his skill and methods helped elevate the discipline to a respected practice in medicine. In recognition of his achievements he was awarded a medical degree by the University of Glasgow in 1750. His fame led to his appointment as physician extraordinary to Queen Charlotte in 1764 and as professor of anatomy at the newly opened Royal Academy of London 5 years later.

In the mid-1760s Hunter outlined a project for a museum to improve the teaching of medicine, surgery, and anatomy through illustration. This museum was opened in London in 1768 and contained natural-history specimens, medals, and a fine library of rare books as well as anatomical and pathological specimens. Hunter published on many subjects, including fossil elephants, but his most famous work is the handsomely illustrated *The Anatomy of the Human Gravid Uterus* (1774), which includes accurate descriptions of the parts of the uterus and of the placenta. Together with his brother John Hunter, he also charted the system of the lymphatics. John was a surgeon who achieved greater fame than William, and although the brothers had studied and worked together, they became rivals and were embroiled in many disputes over priority of discovery.

William Hunter died on March 30, 1783. He gave his museum into trusteeship to be given to the University of Glasgow.

Further Reading

The standard biography is by Hunter's contemporary S. F. Simmons, *An Account of the Life and Writings of the Late William Hunter, M. D.* (1783). An entertaining, recent biography, written in the first person, is Sir Charles Illingworth, *The Story of William Hunter* (1967). The student should also consult R. Hingston Fox, *William Hunter* (1901); George C. Peachey, *A Memoir of William and John Hunter* (1924); and Jane M. Oppenheimer, *New Aspects of John and William Hunter* (1946).

Additional Sources

Royal Academy of Arts (Great Britain) and Hunterian Museum (University of Glasgow), *Dr. William Hunter at the Royal Academy of Arts,* Glasgow: University of Glasgow Press, 1975.

William Hunter and the eighteenth-century medical world, Cambridge; New York: Cambridge University Press, 1985. □

Collis Potter Huntington

Collis Potter Huntington (1821-1900), American railroad builder, was a promoter and manager of the Central Pacific Railway and was prominent later in the Southern Pacific Company.

Collis P. Huntington was born on Oct. 22, 1821, at Harwinton, Conn. His early life was hard. At the age of 14 he left school and went to work. A year later he migrated to New York City, where he arranged to sell watches in the South. He gradually acquired enough capital to open a general store in Oneonta, N.Y., which was very successful. In 1849, after the California gold strike, Huntington decided to go west and try his luck. After a one-day fling at mining, he opened a store in Sacramento, specializing in mining supplies.

Good fortune smiled on Huntington in 1860, when Theodore Judah, an engineer, convinced Huntington, Leland Stanford, Mark Hopkins (Huntington's store partner), and Charles Crocker of the practically of a railroad from Sacramento across the Sierra Nevada. This line would be part of a transcontinental route linking East and West. The U.S. Congress chartered the railroad in 1862 and authorized construction in both directions. Huntington's group, the Central Pacific, built eastward from California, while the Union Pacific pushed westward from Omaha, Nebr. The two met at Promontory Point, Utah, on May 10, 1869. Most of the construction had been financed by government loans, and Huntington made huge profits by controlling the Central Pacific's construction company.

After completing the transcontinental railroad, Huntington's group constructed tracks to southern California and eventually to El Paso, Tex., and to New Orleans, which virtually constituted a second transcontinental route. In 1884 the various companies were merged into the Southern Pacific Company.

Huntington served in several capacities with the Southern Pacific. As its financial agent, he sold the company's stocks and bonds and arranged bank borrowing. During the depression of the 1870s the system remained viable because of Huntington's abilities. He also acted as the railroad's lobbyist in Washington, where he successfully blocked efforts to secure aid for a potential competitor, the Texas and Pacific.

Huntington also controlled the Chesapeake and Ohio Railroad from 1869 until the 1890s. He was involved with the Pacific Mail Steamship Company and several other steamship firms. In 1890 he replaced Stanford as president of the Southern Pacific. Huntington died on Aug. 13, 1900, near Raquette Lake, N.Y.

Further Reading

The only full-scale treatments of Huntington are Cerinda W. Evans, *Collis Potter Huntington* (2 vols., 1954), and David Lavender, *The Great Persuader* (1970). He is discussed at length in Oscar Lewis, *The Big Four* (1938). For unfriendly views see Gustavus Myers, *History of the Great American Fortunes* (3 vols., 1910; 1 vol., 1937), and Matthew Josephson, *The Robber Barons: The Great American Capitalists, 1861-1901* (1934).

Additional Sources

Lewis, Oscar, *The big four: the story of Huntington, Stanford, Hopkins, and Crocker, and of the building of the Central Pacific,* New York: Arno Press, 1981, 1938. □

Huntley and Brinkley

Chet Huntley (1911-1974) and David Brinkley (born 1920), American journalists and radio and television news broadcasters, were the most popular dual anchormen in broadcasting history.

In October 1956 NBC News replaced the "Camel News Caravan" with the "Huntley-Brinkley Report," which was apparently a third choice as a replacement after author John Hershey and Ambassador Henry Cabot Lodge. The success of the Huntley and Brinkley combination, which soon became the ratings leader, was unprecedented. Previously the great names in American broadcasting were solo performers: H. V. Kaltenborn, Lowell Thomas, Gabriel Heatter, and Edward R. Murrow. It is inconceivable that those giants of broadcast news would have shared a podium. Huntley and Brinkley did. Their format has often been imitated, but their success has never been equaled.

The two partners were similar in their backgrounds, yet also quite different. Chester Robert Huntley, a Westerner, was born in Montana, the only son of P. A. and Blanche Wadine (Tathan) Huntley, the former a descendant of John Adams and the latter of Western pioneer stock. At an early age, Chet Huntley excelled in speech and debate. Those skills earned him a scholarship in 1929 to Montana State College, where he was a premedical student for three years. Another scholarship took him to the Cornish School of Arts in Seattle, Washington. From there he transferred to the University of Washington, earning his BA degree in 1934.

That same year Huntley was hired by a Seattle radio station, where he worked about two years. From 1935 to 1939 he worked for radio stations in Spokane, Washington; Portland, Oregon; and Los Angeles, California. Then he began a 12-year employment with the Columbia Broadcasting System (CBS) at Los Angeles. In 1951 he moved to the American Broadcasting Company (ABC), where he broadcast daily news at that network's Los Angeles radio and television stations. When Huntley joined the National Broadcasting Company (NBC) in 1955, he had been recognized with the prestigious George Peabody Award twice (1942 and 1954), as well as several other professional citations.

While Huntley was a Westerner and retained ties to that region and its style of life, Brinkley's roots were in the border South. He was born in Wilmington, North Carolina, one of five children of William Graham and Mary MacDonald (West) Brinkley. He began his journalistic career as a high school student when asked to write a weekly column by a relative who owned a newspaper. From 1938 to 1940 he was a reporter for the Wilmington *Star-News* and attended classes at the University of North Carolina (Chapel Hill).

Following service in the United States Army (1940-1941) Brinkley worked for the United Press (UP) in Atlanta, Georgia; Montgomery, Alabama; Nashville, Tennessee; and Charlotte, North Carolina. In 1943 he moved to Washington, D.C., where he joined NBC as a news writer. By the end of that year he was also broadcasting news on television, one of the first persons in the field of television newscasting. Initially his broadcast duties also involved radio, but by 1950 he was a television news commentator and soon thereafter he became the Washington correspondent for his network's "Camel News Caravan."

The Huntley-Brinkley Report

The first collaborative efforts of Huntley and Brinkley occurred at the 1956 presidential nominating conventions. The merger was largely coincidental. NBC had been grooming Huntley for major responsibilities since he joined the network. His skills had been utilized on both radio and television before he was transferred to New York in early 1956. He began his half-hour Sunday news and features program, "Outlook," in April. Media observers saw him as the likely candidate to challenge the preeminence of CBS in television news. That contention was reinforced by his designation to be the on-camera chief of NBC's coverage at the national conventions.

The joint efforts of the Westerner and the Southerner at the political conventions were rewarded by favorable ratings, which led to the launching of the "Huntley-Brinkley Report" on October 29, 1956. The events of those days were unusually newsworthy. The Suez War had begun and ended a few weeks before; the Hungarian Revolution was raging, and Dwight D. Eisenhower was concluding a successful re-election campaign. Huntley and Brinkley did not immediately overwhelm the opposition, but their viewer ratings were respectable and continued to improve. With the 1960 conventions, the duo demonstrated their viewer approval was not restricted to the evening news; they could outshine their opposition in coverage of special events as well. Throughout the 1960s, the NBC team was the front-runner among the evening news broadcasts. On July 31, 1970, the last "Report" was broadcast as Huntley retired.

Sources of Success

Why was the Huntley-Brinkley combination so popular? The answer is neither obvious nor certain. Reference is often made to Brinkley's sardonic sense of humor or his dry wit. He did frequently offer brief comment on the paradoxical or illogical implications of a news item, but that trait in itself would not explain the pair's popularity. Huntley was often characterized as serious. That is not to say that he was a straight man for Brinkley's punch line or that Brinkley was frivolous. Rather, it denotes that in his presentation of the news, in his writings, and in his interaction with his colleagues Huntley repeatedly indicated his awareness of the immense responsibility he felt to report the news fairly, accurately, and professionally. Neither Huntley nor Brinkley presumed that the facts would speak for themselves. Both sought to present the facts, put them in context, and suggest likely consequences. To a greater extent than any broadcasters before them, except possibly Edward R. Murrow, the NBC co-anchors offered commentary, not merely news reports.

Both broadcasters were handsome; Huntley received a legendary amount of mail from females. Both were well spoken. Those attributes no doubt contributed to Huntley and Brinkley having a greater public recognition than movie stars and heads of states.

Upon the final "Goodnight David ... Goodnight Chet," Brinkley became sole anchor for the "NBC Nightly News" until John Chancellor assumed that role the next year. Then Brinkley was intermittently either co-anchor or commentator on that program until October 1979, after which he devoted himself to specials and eventually to "NBC Magazine," which featured four correspondents, each of whom reported on a topical subject that varied from week to week. In September 1981 Brinkley unexpectedly announced his retirement from NBC. Two months later he broadcast his first "This Week with David Brinkley" on ABC television—a position he would hold for over 15 years.

In addition to his weekly series, Brinkley provided political commentary for *World News Tonight* and national election coverage. It was just such coverage that led to his retirement from ABC in 1996. At the end of ABC's election coverage, Brinkley declared that President Clinton was "boring" and would subject the American public to more "goddamned nonsense" during the next four years. Brinkley began his final appearance on *This Week with David Brinkley* on Nov. 10, 1996 with a personal apology to President Bill Clinton. "I'm reminded of something I wrote years ago," Brinkley said. "It may be impossible to be objective, I said, but we must always be fair. Well, after a long election day and seven hours on the set, what I said on the election night coverage was both impolite and unfair. I'm sorry. I regret it." Clinton appeared on the show and accepted the apology with a smile, saying he had often said things he regretted late at night when he was tired. The show marked the end of Brinkley's 53-year network news career and he spoke his last commentary on the program on September 28, 1997.

Huntley's off-camera activities were touched with controversy. Unlike Brinkley, he crossed picket lines during a 1967 strike against the networks. The Federal Communications Commission admonished him in 1968 for his failure to inform his audience of his financial interests in the cattle feeding industry when he criticized on the air governmental meat inspection requirements. Subsequently he sold his New Jersey cattle farm following incidents of vandalism there. After retirement, Huntley devoted himself to the development of the Big Sky recreational complex in Montana, a project opposed by conservationists. As the facility was about to be dedicated, he died on March 20, 1974, following abdominal surgery for cancer.

Further Reading

A brief but interpretive account of the Huntley-Brinkley collaboration is William Whitworth's "Profiles: An Accident of Casting," *The New Yorker* (August 3, 1968). Huntley provided a delightful autobiographic account of his youth in Montana in *The Generous Years: Remembrances of a Frontier Boyhood* (1968). He described his professional chores in *Chet Huntley's New Analysis* (1961). He stated his professional principles in *The Reporter* (January 27, 1955). The final days of Brinkley's career are taken from several newspaper articles. They include: *Los Angeles Times*, November 11, 1996, "Brinkley Apologizes to Clinton, Exits as TV Host"; October 17, 1996, "Brinkley's Weeks Ahead Will Include Documentaries"; articles were also used from *MediaWeek,* 1/15/96. □

John Hunyadi

John Hunyadi (1385?-1456) was regent of Hungary, 1446-1452, and commander of the Hungarian army, 1452-1456. A national hero, he led the struggle against the Ottoman Turks.

John Hunyadi spent his youth at the court of the emperor Sigismund, and he distinguished himself in arms from an early age. The last years of Sigismund and the short reign of his son-in-law Albert (1437-1439) witnessed increasing Turkish pressure in southern Hungary. Under both kings John Hunyadi held military commands: he was made ban of Szörény in 1439 and voivode of Transylvania and captain of Belgrade in 1440. From 1441 on Hunyadi was constantly in the field. He inflicted severe defeats upon the Turks in 1442-1443. By 1444 Hunyadi, with the aid of Cardinal Caesarini and the Serbian George Branković, forced the sultan Murad II to a truce. For the first time since their invasions in the late 14th century, the Turks had been fought to a standstill by a Hungarian army. King Úlászló, however, was persuaded by Caesarini to violate the truce and in 1444 led a Hungarian army to the slaughter at the battle of Varna, where he died; Hunyadi barely escaped with his life.

The death of Úlászló again plunged Hungary into a domestic crisis. The new king, Ladislas Posthumus, was a minor, and Hunyadi was appointed regent of Hungary in 1446. Hunyadi's skill as a general was equaled by his skill as a statesman. In the face of disruptive activities of bands of Czech soldiers in the north and jealous rivals from the higher aristocracy, Hunyadi maintained political order by balancing the interests of the lesser nobility against those of the great magnates and by shaping the Hungarian army into an effective fighting force.

After the Turkish capture of Constantinople in 1453, Hungary once again became the target of the Turkish armies. In a final heroic effort Hunyadi shattered the army of Sultan Mohammed II at Belgrade in 1456. Three weeks after his victory, however, John Hunyadi died of the plague, which had broken out in the army. After King Ladislas died in 1457, the Hungarians elected John Hunyadi's second son, Matthias Corvinus, king of Hungary; under his rule Hungary flourished.

John Hunyadi is known to history as *törökverö*, conqueror of the Turks. His role in the history of Hungary is that of a protector at a time when Hungary's nominal protectors—its kings—were ineffective and when Hungary's enemies—the Turks and internal factionalism—were strong.

Further Reading

There is no biography of Hunyadi in English. *The Cambridge Medieval History,* vol. 8 (1936), contains a good account of Hunyadi's career by the greatest modern Hungarian historian, Bálint Hóman. Other accounts may he found in Denis Sinor, *A History of Hungary* (1959), and C. A. Macartney, *Hungary: A Short History* (1962).

Additional Sources

Held, Joseph, *Hunyadi: legend and reality,* Boulder: East European Monographs; New York: Distributed by Columbia University, 1985. □

Douglas Hurd

After a classic education and diplomatic career, Douglas Hurd (born 1930) turned to English Conservative Party politics. He became home secretary in 1985 and, under Margaret Thatcher (and later John Major), foreign secretary of Great Britain in 1989.

No prominent Briton since Benjamin Disraeli has so successfully combined careers in Conservative Party politics and novel-writing as Douglas Hurd. Hurd also shares with Disraeli a romantic fascination for the workings of politics and the conduct of foreign affairs, and, like Disraeli, has written cleverly about both. Unlike Disraeli, however, Hurd was never an outsider to the British political elite; indeed, his background, education, and career molded him into an almost archetypal English parliamentary gentleman.

Born on March 8, 1930, in Marlborough, England, Hurd was the eldest son of Sir Anthony (later Baron) Hurd and his wife Stephanie. Anthony Hurd pursued a farming career during Douglas' boyhood and wrote on agricultural developments for the London *Times*. The elder Hurd later became both the director of several major companies and a Conservative MP (Member of Parliament). The Hurd family had a strong connection with Conservative politics: Anthony Hurd's father was himself a Tory MP.

Douglas Hurd attended public school at Eton, where he excelled both in sports and in academics. After leaving Eton in 1948, Hurd performed his military service in the British Army, becoming a second lieutenant. In 1949 he entered Trinity College, Cambridge, where he once again excelled in his studies, in particular history. He also participated in extracurricular activities, becoming president of the Cambridge Union (the university debating society) in 1952 and chairman of the University Conservative Association.

Although he had long since decided on a political career, Hurd followed his father's advice against doing so immediately after Cambridge, and instead entered the Diplomatic Service. As a diplomat Hurd was posted to Peking (1954-1956) and to the United Kingdom mission to the United Nations (1956-1960), served as private secretary to the permanent under-secretary of state at the Foreign Office in London (1960-1963), and then was posted again, this time to Rome, where he served as first secretary from 1963 to 1966. Hurd found Rome a dull place for diplomacy in the mid-1960s, and in his spare time wrote his first novel, the political thriller *Send Him Victorious,* with one of his colleagues, Andrew Osmond. He and Osmond also wrote three other novels between 1969 and 1982. At about the same time he decided to leave the Diplomatic Service, in which he felt his career had stagnated.

A Rising Star in the Conservative Party

Accordingly, in 1966 Hurd resigned and joined the Conservative Party's Research Department. He did very well in this new job, rising to head of the Foreign Affairs Section in 1968 and greatly impressing party leaders, in particular Edward Heath. In 1968 Hurd resigned from the Research Department to become private secretary to Heath, then leader of the Conservative Party, which was out of power. In 1970, when Heath became prime minister, Hurd was made Health's political secretary, a position which he found both fascinating and frustrating.

By 1974 Hurd was tired of politics behind the scenes and determined that he would try to enter Parliament himself. His close connection with Heath proved to be a disadvantage, and he was rejected by five constituencies before being adopted as the candidate for the Conservative Party for Mid-Oxfordshire. Hurd won this seat in the February 1974 general election, but Heath and his government lost the election, and within the next year Health also lost the leadership of the party to Margaret Thatcher. As a Heath protegé, Hurd was not in favor with the new order and could not hope for rapid political advancement. Nonetheless, to enhance party unity Thatcher appointed him opposition spokesman on European affairs in 1976. In 1979, when the Tories returned to power, he was appointed to the sub-Cabinet post of minister of state at the Foreign Office, where he enjoyed working with Foreign Secretary Lord Carrington and where he became the effective deputy foreign secretary after Carrington's resignation over the Falklands War. From 1983 to 1984 Hurd served as minister of state at the Home Office, another sub-Cabinet post.

Perhaps because of Hurd's solid performance in his sub-Cabinet posts, and perhaps in part because of Lord Carrington's enthusiastic support, Hurd at last reached the Cabinet when Thatcher appointed him secretary of state for Northern Ireland on September 10, 1984. At the time of his appointment, Northern Ireland was experiencing renewed violence. Hurd's most important achievement in the job was his promotion of the peace process: in May 1985 he was appointed to oversee British talks with Ireland on the Northern Ireland issue. The talks culminated successfully in November with an agreement which allowed Ireland to serve as a consultant on Northern Irish affairs.

Meanwhile, however, on September 2, 1985, Hurd had been appointed to one of the three most important positions in the British Government, the secretary of state for home affairs, or home secretary. This appointment was something of a surprise, not only because he had been in the midst of the Irish negotiations as Northern Ireland secretary, but also because it was a sign of Thatcher's ultimate approval. As the Cabinet officer in charge of domestic affairs, Hurd was responsible for a wide range of issues, and his tenure at the Home Office was characterized by a firm adherence to the principles of law and order. The week after his appointment he was faced with the problem of serious race riots in Birmingham. Hurd refused to rationalize the destruction because of the rioters' poverty: at a news conference he said, "There is no justification why those conditions should lead people to loot, burn, and put people's lives at risk." Hurd responded to the problem with the Public Order Bill of 1985, which provided additional authority to the police to deal with race riots and other sorts of violence, such as labor unrest, street demonstrations, and "football hooliganism."

In 1986 Hurd served as chairman of an emergency meeting of European Community interior ministers to deal with international terrorism. The meeting resulted in an agreement to coordinate efforts to "harry and disrupt" terrorists. Hurd also combated terrorists at home by banning radio and television appearances by members of the IRA (Irish Republican Army), the Sinn Fein, and the Ulster Defence Association. During the Salman Rushdie affair in 1989, Hurd attempted to defuse high tension in the British Muslim community with a speech at the Central Mosque in Birmingham. He was sensitive, he indicated, to the pain Muslims felt because of the perceived sacrilege in Rushdie's novel, *The Satanic Verses,* and they had every right to express this pain through protests. "But to turn such protests towards violence or the threat of violence," he stressed, "is wholly unacceptable."

An Exemplary Foreign Secretary

In October 1989 a reshuffle in the Thatcher Cabinet allowed Hurd to achieve what he described as his life-long dream when he became foreign secretary. His appointment was nearly universally applauded because of his vast expe-

rience in foreign affairs. One of his first duties as foreign secretary was a November 1989 visit to the Berlin Wall after East Germany had opened its borders. Hurd used this visit to emphasize the need for Britain and its Western allies to develop new policies to cope with the fast-breaking changes in Eastern Europe. In January 1990 he visited Hong Kong, where he assuaged the concerns of residents about the 1997 Chinese takeover. During the Persian Gulf crisis commencing in August 1990, Hurd proved to be a coolly authoritative foreign secretary and a staunch supporter of U.S. policy, working for a UN resolution about the Kuwait invasion, keeping the British embassy in Kuwait open despite Iraqi demands, and leaving the military option open.

A continuing and pressing challenge to Foreign Secretary Hurd was Britain's role in the impending European Community economic union. Such a union clearly had strong political overtones, and many Britons, including Thatcher, remained highly suspicious about the possibility of infringement on Britain's national sovereignty. Although cautious on this matter, Hurd was much more pro-European than Thatcher, and it was through the tactful influence of Hurd and then Chancellor of the Exchequer John Major that Thatcher agreed to allow Britain's entry in the Exchange Rate Mechanism of the European Monetary System—the first step toward economic union—in October 1990.

The Tory leadership struggle in November 1990 solidified Hurd's reputation as a perfect English gentleman. He deplored former Cabinet minister Michael Heseltine's November 14 challenge to Thatcher as a "mistake—from the point of view of the government, the party, and the country," and he loyally supported his leader during the first vote on November 20, 1990. When Thatcher resigned on November 22, he entered the race for the party leadership (and the prime ministership), issuing a joint statement with fellow candidate John Major which emphasized their desire to have a "friendly contest so that our party colleagues . . . can choose which of us is better placed to unite the party." Hurd was viewed by many as the candidate with the best credentials because of his knowledge of foreign affairs, experience in the Home Office, broad base of support, and freedom from ideological narrowness. His opponents, however, decried his lack of charisma, lack of knowledge of economics, and the fact that he, the son and grandson of Tory MPs and an Eton and Cambridge graduate, would represent a return to the sort of Tory politics that Thatcher's revolutions had overthrown. When he lost to Major on November 27, he good-naturedly conceded to the victor, who immediately re-appointed him as foreign secretary.

Hurd's Waterloo

In a surprise move, Hurd offered his resignation as foreign secretary after six years in the post and just a day after then Prime Minister John Majors announced that he would move the party leadership election from November to July. Hurd said he wanted to "disentangle" himself as a possible target in the leadership fight. Hurd said he will not resign his parliamentary seat and will remain an active "backbencher." In the past, Hurd had emerged virtually unscathed from scandals—the British government's indirect support for the Khmer Rouge in Cambodia, a massive aid and arms deal for the Suharto regime in Indonesia—that would have left a less canny politician bruised or beaten. Bosnia, it appears, was Hurd's Waterloo.

More than any other European politician, Hurd shaped the disastrous European policy toward the former Yugoslavia, and perhaps the best postmortem on that policy is a close look at Hurd's career since 1991. That was when Hurd took a leading role in staving off recognition of Slovenia and Croatia, well after Yugoslavia had irretrievably collapsed. Hurd agreed to their independence only after Serbian President Slobodan Milosevic had acquiesced on the condition that a UN presence in the Serb-held areas help to safeguard the interests of the Serb population there. That UN presence was later secured through the Vance Plan, an arrangement in which the British Foreign Office took full part.

Hurd personally crafted the British, and ultimately the European, policy of eschewing military intervention. As early as September 1991 he announced that Europe would offer no military deterrent in the former Yugoslavia. That same month, he led the way to imposing, through the Security Council, a blanket arms embargo that handicapped the victims and helped the aggressors. The next year he masterminded the dispatch of UN troops, inadequately equipped and on a fudged mandate, into a war zone.

What was Hurd's strategy, and what lay behind it? Hurd and his colleagues in the Foreign Office said that a solution could not "be imposed by force," rhetoric that led, in turn, to the tortuous reasoning that force should not be used at all and that a negotiated political settlement, backed by humanitarian aid, was the only way to end the Balkan conflict. This position was partly based on the perceived strategic interest of allying Britain with the Serbs as the natural successor to Yugoslavia and as a counterweight to any possible extension of German influence in the Balkans. Through this policy, Hurd hoped to bring Russia on board and to help open economic opportunities within Russian markets. An off-the-cuff remark made by someone close to the Foreign Office is illuminating: "It would be better to have the Russians in the Adriatic than the Germans." It may also have been in the nature of the former foreign secretary, the old Etonian and the son and grandson of Tory MPs, to prefer dealing with Milosevic, "the strong man of Europe," or with the "irrepressible" Radovan Karadzic than with Bosnian "Muslims."

For all these reasons, Hurd opposed the major European powers, including France, Germany, Italy, and Holland, when they supported a European Community initiative to send a peacekeeping force to Yugoslavia in the summer of 1991. In light of what followed, the significance of this stand cannot be underestimated. At a time when the casualty toll was still in the hundreds (as opposed to the hundreds of thousands) and the battlefield confined to Croatia, the British foreign secretary "led the consensus" at the European Community Foreign Ministers' meeting on September 19, 1991. It resulted in the terse communiqué: "No military intervention contemplated."

Within days, Serbian forces, fortified by word that Europe would stay neutral, unleashed a massive onslaught by land, sea and air. They blockaded Croatia's main ports, sent dozens of tanks to the Croatian border and began a large-scale attack on Vukovar and Dubrovnik. The same week, the UN Security Council passed Resolution 713, which banned arms imports to Yugoslavia. The ban left Croatia, whose territorial army had been dismantled earlier in the year, unable to defend itself against the onslaught of the Serb-led Yugoslav national army and Serbian paramilitaries. Most Bosnia watchers know that Britain's government has been the most consistently opposed to lifting the arms embargo. What they are less likely to know is that Britain, again in September 1991, went to the Serb-dominated Yugoslav government and quietly suggested it request a blanket arms embargo on all Yugoslav republics—a move that ratified the imbalance of arms between the Serbs and all other ethnic groups. Hurd then resisted lifting the embargo; he was reluctant, as he put it, to create "a level killing field," a phrase whose ironies seemed lost on him.

The foreign secretary has often stated, in parliament and elsewhere, that the other major powers back Britain's policy in former Yugoslavia. But this is not quite the case. True, in the summer of 1991, as Hurd stood out in opposition to his European colleagues, the U.S. took a back seat and let the Europeans get on with it. But at other times the British Foreign Office actively slowed momentum to intervene against the Serbs. In the summer of 1992, for example, with the exposure of Serb-run concentration-type camps and the expulsion of hundreds of thousands from Bosnia, the U.S. and many European states called for a tougher stand against the Serbs. Just in the nick of time, Hurd came up with another concept: "protective support." That meant providing armed escort, including 1,800 lightly armed UN troops from Britain, for UN aid convoys in Bosnia. In the short term, this policy had advantages. It staved off world pressure for firmer action, and it endorsed British policies established the previous year. With UN peacekeepers on the ground, it was unthinkable to bomb from the sky or to lift the arms embargo and escalate hostilities between the "warring factions."

The British decision to dispatch UN troops as aid escorts to a war zone might have been viewed as a mere misreading of the ground situation were it not for a decision of British UN Commander Lt. General Michael Rose. In April 1994 Rose dispatched to Gorazde 168 British soldiers whom the Bosnian Serbs had stripped of their ammunition and personal cameras. To send a battalion of British troops, minus much of their equipment, into an enclave totally surrounded by Serbian General Ratko Mladic's forces could only be interpreted as an unequivocal signal to the Serbs of British support. For, without the acquiescence of the Serbs, these troops would be unable to exit safely from the "safe" area. (French President Francois Mitterrand, on the other hand, opted at the last minute to pull back the French troops about to be dispatched to Gorazde and let the British soldiers continue without them.)

Throughout the Balkan conflict, the support of the French has been vital to Hurd, who feared that Britain would be isolated in Europe by its Bosnia policy. One of the foreign secretary's frequent gambits in the House of Commons was to insist that the French and British were at one on Bosnia. But this has never been entirely true—and has been still less so since the election of Jacques Chirac as president. Indeed, the tension between the two countries over Bosnia can be linked with Hurd's policy. The first hint of rupture in Anglo-French Bosnian policy came during the hostage debacle, when the British and French announced the joint decision to send in a Rapid Reaction Force to Bosnia. It soon emerged that, while Britain's intention was merely that the force protect the UN soldiers on the ground, Chirac had hoped it would also establish a protected route for aid to Sarajevo and the enclaves. This would have involved combat action, of course, a prospect the British government resisted from the outset. While the French partly retracted from their more ambitious plans and appeared reconciled to the British proposals on the role of the Rapid Reaction Force, the two countries' views on the way forward in Bosnia seemed, at the time of Hurd's resignation, to be seriously at odds. Chirac's explicit charge that Britain was engaging in Chamberlain-like appeasement cut too deep to be deftly parried, though Hurd's chosen successor, Malcolm Rifkind, tried to do so at the July 17 European Union meeting. In the British press, Hurd's resignation had been accompanied by none of the usual accolades for a departing figure of his stature. That may be an indication of the long-term judgment to come on his Bosnia policy.

Hurd married twice. With his first wife, Tatiana, whom he married in 1960, he had three sons. They separated in 1976, Tatiana Hurd saying, "Really, politics don't mix with marriage," and divorced in 1982. In that year he married Judy Smart, his former parliamentary secretary. They had two children, a boy and a girl.

Hurd was a polite, charming, witty man of great intelligence. Loyalty, however, was the hallmark of Hurd's political career. He was loyal to Edward Heath, Margaret Thatcher, and John Major. For Hurd's loyalty transcends mere personalities and is indicative of anunshakable adherence to more profound matters: the Conservative Party and what it stands for—courage, steadfastness, individual freedom, and responsibility—all, in short, that is in his view best and worth preserving in the British way of life.

Further Reading

There are no biographies of Douglas Hurd. For an important profile of Hurd's career, achievements, and characteristics to 1985, see Patrick Cosgrave, "The Diplomat with a Touch of Acid," in the London *Times* (September 12, 1985). For a revealing view of Hurd as seen from the Left, Andrew Roth's "Thatcher's Second XI" in the *New Statesman* (September 14, 1984) is excellent. Another *New Statesman* portrait, "A Flawed Vision" (April 29, 1988), is critical of his "Hobbesian" views while being sympathetic to Hurd as "one of the few humane and flexible intelligences remaining on the Tory front bench."

Hurd's own writings—his seven novels and, to some extent, his two historical works—provide a great deal of information about Hurd's ideals and values. Although Hurd's first book, *The Arrow War* (1967), is a simple history of a brief Anglo-Chinese confrontation in the 1850s, his next three books, thrillers written with Andrew Osmond, are much more revealing. *Send Him Victorious* (1968), *The Smile on the Face of* the Tiger (1969), and *Scotch on the Rocks* (1971), a series of novels with continuing characters, are all clever, witty novels with a piquant dollop of cynicism regarding the civil service, the military, politicians, and the media, as is his novel *Truth Game* (1972). They nonetheless show Hurd's idealism and his belief in the basic correctness of the Conservative Party. The best of Hurd's novels, *Vote to Kill* (1975), clearly based on his experiences as Edward Heath's political secretary, like his others is clever, cynical, well-written, and well-plotted. In *An End to Promises* (1979), Hurd describes his activities as Heath's political secretary and indicates his great admiration for Heath and what Heath attempted to achieve. *The Palace of Enchantment* (1985), written with Stephen Lamport, reiterates his feelings about the addictive nature of politics and takes a strongly Disraelian and romantic view of Parliament and the role of the MP. □

Zora Neale Hurston

Zora Neale Hurston (1903-1960), folklorist and novelist, was best known for her collection of African American folklore *Mules and Men* (1935) and her novel *Their Eyes Were Watching God* (1937), in which she charted a young African American woman's journey for personal fulfillment.

Zora Neale Hurston was born on January 7, 1903, in Eatonville, Florida, to Reverend John and Lucy Hurston. Zora's mother died when she was nine years old, and her father soon remarried. Her relationship with her stepmother rapidly deteriorated, and her father sent her to school in Jacksonville. In her early teens she became a wardrobe girl in a Gilbert and Sullivan repertory company touring the South. Eighteen months later she enrolled in Morgan Academy in Baltimore in 1917. She graduated a year later and went to Howard University, where she completed a year and a half of course work between 1919 and 1924. She secured a scholarship which allowed her to transfer to Barnard College, where she earned her B.A. in 1928. From 1928 to 1932 she studied anthropology and folklore at Columbia University under Franz Boas, the renown anthropologist. In 1936 she was awarded a Guggenheim Fellowship for travelling and collecting folklore in Haiti and the British West Indies.

Hurston worked at a variety of jobs, from manicurist, to Fannie Hurst's secretary, to writer for Paramount and Warner Brothers Studios, to librarian at the Library of Congress, to drama coach at North Carolina College for Negroes. Hurston began her writing career while at Howard when she wrote her first short story for *Stylus*, a college literary magazine. She continued to write stories, and in 1925 won first prize in the *Opportunity* literary contest for "Spunk." In 1939 Morgan College awarded her an honorary doctorate. In 1943 she received the Annisfield Award for the autobiographical *Dust Tracks on the Road;* also in 1943 Howard University bestowed its alumni award upon her.

Although Hurston worked all of her life at many jobs and was a prolific writer, money was always a serious

problem. In the late 1940s she returned to Florida and worked as a maid in Riva Alto. After several efforts to re-kindle her writing career, she died in poverty in the town of her birth.

Hurston's most famous work is her novel *Their Eyes Were Watching God* (1937), in which she created the por-trait of an African American female, Janie, growing into adulthood searching for her identity and fulfillment. Through a series of marriages Janie comes to know and define herself in terms of her relationship with whites. For several years after the novel's publication critics saw this work as a sentimental love story. However, if the novel is read with the understanding that love was the traditional way in which a woman was supposed to find fulfillment, then love can be seen as the vehicle for emotional, spiritual, and intellectual development. The novel also portrays the awakening of a woman's sexuality. With the advent of the women's movement of the 1970s and the subsequent growth of female awareness, many critics cited this novel as the central text in the canon of literature by African Ameri-can women writers, specifically, and by women writers in general.

Hurston was also a famous folklorist who applied her academic training to collecting African American folklore around her hometown in Florida. This work produced two collections of folklore, *Mules and Men* (1935) and *Tell My Horse* (1939). All of her work is characterized by her use of African American folk idioms, which are intrinsic to her character portrayals.

Hurston wrote three other novels: *Jonah's Gourd Vine* (1934), an autobiographical novel about her father's rise from an illiterate laborer to become a respected Baptist minister; *Moses, Man of the Mountain* (1939), which recre-ated Mosaic biblical myth in an African context; and *Seraph on the Suwanee* (1948), which is about a woman's search for selfhood within the confines of marriage to a man who sees all women as inferior.

Hurston also wrote several plays: *Fast and Furious* (1931), *The First One* (1927), *Mule Bone: A Comedy of Negro Life in Three Acts* (1931), and *Polk County* (1944), as well as many articles and short stories.

Further Reading

Hurston tells her life story in the autobiography *Dust Tracks on the Road* (1942, 1985). For the best critical biographical source see Robert Hemenway, *Zora Neale Hurston: A Literary Biography* (1977). Barbara Christian summarized Hurston's career and placed her in the context of her female contempo-raries in *Black Women Novelists* (1980). Also see Daryl C. Dance, "Zora Neale Hurston," in *American Women Writers: Bibliographical Essays,* edited by Maurice Duke, et al.; Quandra P. Stadler, "Visibility and Difference: Black Women in History and Literature: Pieces of a Paper and Some Rumina-tions," in *The Future of Difference* (1980), edited by Alice Jardine. See also citations for Hurston in *Black American Writers Past and Present,* edited by Theressa G. Rush, et al., and Alice Walker's Hurston reader *I Love Myself When I'm Laughing . . .* for Hurston's posthumously published essay. *Spunk: The Selected Short Stories of Zora Neale Hurston* was published in 1985. □

Jan Hus

Jan Hus (1369-1415), a fifteenth-century religious reformer, was (along with John Wycliffe) one of the most important forerunners of the 16th-century Reformation.

Among the many, no doubt apocryphal, stories of Jan Hus's life is one that relates an incident in his youth, which foreshadowed his fate as a Christian martyr. According to the account, the youthful Hus was sitting be-side a fire one winter evening reading about the martyrdom of St. Lawrence. Suddenly, he thrust his hand into the flames. When a fellow pupil pulled him away from the fire and questioned his intentions, Hus replied: "I was only trying what part of the tortures of this holy man I might be capable of enduring."

What truth, if any, there is in the story cannot be determined. But what is historical fact is that on July 6, 1415, condemned as an arch-heretic by the Council of Constance and turned over to the state for execution, Jan Hus sang a hymn as the flames engulfed his body in a meadow just outside the city walls of Constance. Hus was charged with propagating the heretical teachings of the late 14th-century English reformer John Wycliffe, "the Morning Star of the Reformation," whose bones the Council of Constance ordered disinterred and burned. One hundred years later, Martin Luther was charged with heresy by the church hierarchy for espousing views associated with Hus and condemned as heresy by the Council of Constance. Therein lies the historical significance of Jan Hus. He was a vital link in the chain of reformers who sought to reform the late-medieval church, and whose efforts, often punctuated by martyrdom, culminated in the 16th-century Reformation.

The period of the Renaissance church (roughly the mid-14th through 16th centuries) was, spiritually speaking, the bleakest chapter in Church history. In 1303, Pope Boniface VIII was taken captive by the French king Philip IV, and the papal court moved to Avignon in southern France. An attempt in 1378 to end the "Babylonian Captivity" and return the papal court to Rome led only to the election of two rival popes, one in Avignon and the other in Rome. Both were dominated by men who often made no pretense to spiritual interests. But as destructive as it was, the worldliness of the Renaissance popes did not damage the spiritual authority of the church nearly so much as the Great Schism, the scandal of two popes.

According to the teachings of the medieval church, the pope, or bishop of Rome, was "the vicar of Christ, the successor to St. Peter, the keeper of the keys, the *servus servorum Dei,* the servant of the servants of God." How then could the authority of Christ be divided? Only one of the two popes could be the true successor of St. Peter according to apostolic succession. The other had to be an antipope. But which was the pope and which was the antipope? And were the sacraments, held to be necessary for the salvation of the individual, valid if performed under the authority of the antipope?

It is within the context of this crisis of faith within the late-medieval church that the life of Jan Hus must be considered. But it also must be viewed against the backdrop of imperial politics within the Holy Roman Empire and the emergence of Bohemian (or Czech) nationalism. The two are so closely intertwined that they cannot be separated. The cause of religious reform in Bohemia at the turn of the 15th century was also the cry of Bohemian nationalism within the Holy Roman Empire.

The exact date of Jan Hus's birth cannot be determined. It has been variously given as the year 1369, 1372, 1373 or 1375. Popular legend placed the exact date as July 6, 1369, but *July 6* is believed to be nothing more than an imaginative analogy with the date of his martyrdom. In any event, he was born in Husinec (meaning "Goosetown") in southern Bohemia on the border of Bavaria.

In his youth, Jan Hus was known simply as "Jan, son of Michael," since it was customary in Bohemia to identify a man by giving his Christian name and the name of his father. In the register of the University of Prague, he is inscribed as "Jan of Husinec," or "Jan from the village of Husinec." Between 1398 and 1400, he signed his name as "Jan Hus," or "Jan Hus of Husinec." After 1400, he always signed his name as simply "Jan Hus." Thus he derived his last name "Hus" from the name of his birthplace, and his actual family name is lost to history.

Of Jan Hus's family even less is known. It is assumed that his parents were humble people of peasant background. Nothing is known of his father, who apparently died when Jan was very young. His mother was a very pious woman. A casual mention in one of his surviving letters leads scholars to assume that Jan Hus had brothers, but nothing is known of them or any possible sisters.

Jan Hus received his "elementary" schooling in the Latin school of the nearby town of Prachatice. When 18 years old, he enrolled at the University of Prague. From then until his death in 1415, his life and fate were shaped by the political and religious struggles that characterized this divided university. In 1393 or 1394, he received his bachelor's degree, and by 1396, his master of arts. That same year, he became a member of the faculty of arts at the university. At first, he lectured on the philosophy of the ancient Greek philosopher Aristotle and the realist philosophy of John Wycliffe. While teaching, Hus also pursued theological studies and in 1404, he earned a bachelor of divinity degree. Three years later, he was in the process of earning his doctorate but never received it. Instead, he earned the martyr's crown.

At what point in his life Jan Hus made the transition to a religious reformer is also unknown. He once commented that the reason he wanted to become a priest was "to secure a good livelihood and dress and be held in esteem by men." During his early years at the university, he lived what he characterized as a lighthearted lifestyle. Hus nowhere records a "conversion" experience as do Martin Luther and other religious reformers. Rather, he simply states that "when the Lord gave me knowledge of the Scriptures, I

discarded from my foolish mind that kind of stupid fun making.''

Following his ordination in 1402, he was appointed rector and preacher of the Bethlehem Chapel in Prague. Founded in 1391, the Bethlehem Chapel was the point at which the Czech national movement coalesced with the cause of religious reform. Under the patronage of Charles IV, king of Bohemia, and his son Wenceslas IV, both of whom were also Holy Roman Emperors, Bethlehem Chapel was a refuge for a group of reform-minded Bohemian clergy, including John Milič of Kroměříž and Matthew of Janov. They preached in the Czech language, rather than Latin, and hence were very popular with the common people.

Jan Hus soon became the leader of the reform party centered in the Bethlehem Chapel and shared their condemnation of the corrupt clergy. Matthew of Janov characterized the priests as:

> worldly, proud, mercenary, pleasure-loving, and hypocritical. . . . They do not regard their sins as such, do not allow themselves to be reproved, and persecute the saintly preachers. There is no doubt that if Jesus lived among such people, they would be the first to put him to death.

Such outspoken opinions ran the risk of incurring the wrath of the church hierarchy. But so long as Hus and his associates enjoyed the protection of Wenceslas and Zybněk Zajic, the young reform-minded Archbishop of Prague, they were safe.

What drew upon the reformers the charge of heresy was their acceptance of many of the theological teachings of John Wycliffe, a leading exponent of the philosophical position known as ''realism.'' Prior to 1401, Hus knew only Wycliffe's philosophical works, but this was enough to incur the enmity of the German-dominated faculty of the university, for they were committed to the opposite philosophical position, ''nominalism.'' The realists believed that universals have objective reality, whereas the nominalists held that universals or abstract concepts are mere names. For Wycliffe and his followers, this meant that in theology they emphasized the priority of faith over reason and the authority of the Scriptures (Bible) over church tradition.

After the marriage of Wenceslas's half-sister Anne of Bohemia to Wycliffe's patron and defender, Richard II of England, a number of Bohemian students went to study under Wycliffe at Oxford University. As these students returned to the University of Prague, they brought with them the theological works of Wycliffe. Many of Wycliffe's views were congenial to the Bohemian reformers of the Bethlehem Chapel and accepted by them. Among them was Wycliffe's doctrine of the true Church. According to Wycliffe's understanding of Scripture, which he held to be authoritative, the true Church consisted of all those—past, present, and future—predestined by God to salvation. Since the Roman Catholic Church included both those predestined to salvation and those ''foreknown'' to damnation, it was not, as it believed itself to be, the true body of Christ. Hence, Wycliffe

rejected the divine origin of the Roman Catholic Church and the alleged authority of the pope.

Wycliffe also advocated ''territorial churches, each protected, regulated, and supported by the territorial lords and princes.'' There was, of course, much more to Wycliffe's theological teaching, but the attraction it held for the Bohemians trying to liberate themselves from German cultural domination should be clear. Likewise, the connection with the 16th-century Reformation is clear. The fundamental doctrines of the Protestant Reformation are present in Wycliffe's teaching, and hence that of Hus, also.

Jan Hus did not accept carte blanche all that Wycliffe taught. He did not, for example, accept Wycliffe's doctrine of remanence with respect to the Eucharist, or Mass. The doctrine of remanence held that in the celebration of the Eucharist, the bread and wine retain their material substance. Thus it denied the alleged miracle of transubstantiation by which, according to the Roman Catholic Church, the bread and wine became the flesh and blood of Christ. Transubstantiation was the key to the whole edifice of medieval theology. Remove it, and one removed the need for the priesthood and the medieval institutional church as it then existed.

Although Hus did not agree with all that Wycliffe taught, and which his associates at Bethlehem Chapel and the university were teaching, he refused to denounce those views which he did not hold. The Bohemian party at the university was locked in a struggle with the German party for control of that institution. The Germans soon realized that their most effective way of countering the Bohemian party was to focus on its Wycliffism. Many of Wycliffe's teachings had been condemned by Pope Gregory XI and the English prelates, although Wycliffe died officially orthodox (''conforming to established doctrine'').

In 1403, Johann Hübner, one of the German masters at the university, drew up a list of 45 articles from Wycliffe's writings. Among them were the doctrine of remanence and the teaching that the Bible is the sole source of Christian doctrine. Hübner was able to have the 45 articles condemned as heresy. As they became a test of orthodoxy at the university, Hus was in danger of being branded a heretic and soon lost the support of both Archbishop Zbyněk and King Wenceslas, although for different reasons. The change of events grew out of efforts to end the Great Schism.

Wenceslas and the king of France (Charles VI) sought to end the Great Schism by convening a church council in Pisa in 1409. The Council deposed both Gregory XII (Rome) and Benedict XIII (Avignon), and elected Alexander VI, who was succeeded in 1410 by John XXIII. Since neither of the former two resigned, the number of popes was merely increased by one.

The Council of Pisa and its aftermath sealed Hus's fate. Hus supported Wenceslas and recognized Alexander VI as pope. Zbyněk and the German masters at the University of Prague refused to do so. When many of the German masters chose to leave Prague to found a new university at Leipzig in Germany, Zybněk began to take a closer look at Hus's teachings.

In 1410, Archbishop Zybněk confiscated Wycliffe's books and ordered them burned. When Hus defended the books, Zybněk excommunicated him, and the following year Hus was ordered to appear in Rome. Refusing to go, Hus was excommunicated for disobedience. Having lost the support of his onetime ally, the Archbishop, Hus would next lose the support of his King.

John XXIII proclaimed a crusade against King Ladislas of Naples, a supporter of John XXIII's rival, Gregory XII. The cost of the crusade was to be paid for by the sale of indulgences in, among other areas, Bohemia. Since Wenceslas was to receive a portion of the income from the sale of indulgences, he supported the crusade. Hus, however, openly condemned both and accused John XXIII of "trafficking in sacred things." Such action cost him and his associates the support of Wenceslas. Shortly thereafter, three members of the reform party who spoke out against indulgences were arrested and beheaded.

In September 1412, a papal bull of excommunication of Hus was published in Prague. The city was placed under an interdict, and Bethlehem Chapel closed. An interdict was still a powerful weapon against heretics or other enemies of the church hierarchy. An area under interdict was denied the sacraments: "All masses and sermons, all religious functions, even burial with the Christian rites were prohibited." It was intended to turn the people of an area against the one—in this case Hus—who was defying the church authorities. To spare the city the rigors of being under an interdict, Hus withdrew from Prague and took refuge with various Bohemian nobles.

The final act of Hus's life was played out at the Council of Constance (1414-18), called to bring an end to the Great Schism and to deal with the problem of heresy, especially Hus. Zygmunt, the king of Hungary and brother of Wenceslas, was elected Holy Roman Emperor in 1410. To strengthen his position in Germany, he pressured John XXIII to call the Council. Then, in the spring of 1415, offering a guarantee of safe conduct, Zygmunt invited Hus to attend. At first Hus hesitated, but with the urging of Wenceslas, he accepted.

Once in Constance, Hus was lured into the papal residence, then imprisoned in a Dominican dungeon. What followed were months of interrogation and suffering. Zygmunt withdrew his safe conduct in January 1415. It was only due to great pressure exerted by Bohemian noblemen that Hus was given any semblance of a public hearing on June 5, 7, and 8, but he was not allowed to respond to the charges made against him. Presented with a list of 30 articles allegedly drawn from his writings but in fact drawn from the writings of John Wycliffe, Hus was ordered to renounce them upon oath. He refused, unless instructed from Scripture as to where his teachings were in error. The Council rejected his appeal to the Bible as a superior authority.

On July 6, Hus was given a final opportunity to recant. Again he refused, saying that since he did not hold all of the views as stated, to recant would be to commit perjury. He was then declared an arch-heretic and a disciple of Wycliffe. He was ceremoniously degraded from the priesthood, his soul was consigned to the devil, and he was turned over to the secular authorities for execution. That same day, he was led to a meadow outside the city wall and burned alive.

Although the Council had consigned his soul to the devil, Hus—singing loudly as the flames consumed him—consigned his soul to God: "Jesus Christ! The Son of the living God! Have mercy upon me." His ashes were then gathered up and cast into the Rhine River.

Further Reading

de Bonnechose, Emile. *The Reformers Before the Reformation.* Harper and Brothers, 1844.

Estep, William R. *Renaissance & Reformation.* Eerdmans, 1986.

Foxe, John. *Foxe's Book of Martyrs.* Whitaker House, 1981.

Kaminsky, Howard. "John (Jan) Hus," in *Dictionary of the Middle Ages.* Vol. VI. Scribners, 1985.

Lutzow, Count. *The Life & Times of Master John Hus.* J. M. Dent, 1909.

Palmer, R. R., and Joel Colton. *A History of the Modern World.* 6th ed. Knopf, 1984.

Spinka, Matthew. "Jan Hus," in *The New Encyclopedia Britannica.* Vol. IX. 15th ed. 1973.

Bartok, Josef Paul. *John Hus at Constance.* Cokesbury Press, 1935.

Loserth, Johann. *Wiclif and Hus.* Hodder & Stoughton, 1884.

Previte-Orton, C. W. and Z. N. Brooke, eds. *The Cambridge Medieval History, Vol. VIII: The Close of the Middle Ages.* Cambridge University Press, 1964.

Roubiczek, Paul, and Joseph Kalmer. *Warrior of God.* Nicholson and Watson, 1947.

Schwarze, William Nathaniel. *John Hus: The Martyr of Bohemia.* Revell, 1915.

Spinka, Matthew. *John Hus: A Biography.* 1968. □

Gustáv Husák

Gustáv Husák (1913-1991) became general secretary of the Central Committee of the Communist Party of Czechoslovakia in 1971 and president of the Czechoslovak Socialist Republic in 1975. He held both of these political positions through the latter 1980s. During this period he brought Czechoslovakia back to orthodox Marxism and unswerving loyalty to the Soviet Union. (Czechoslovakia is now comprised of two separate countries, the Czech Republic and Slovakia.)

L ittle is known of Husák's personal life, especially the early years. He was born on January 10, 1913, in Dúbravka, near Bratislava, the capital city of Slovakia, then part of the Austro-Hungarian Empire. He first came into focus in the 1930s as a brilliant and hard working law student at Comenius University in Bratislava, now part of Slovakia. At this young age he already displayed two chief interests—a devotion to the cause of Slovak nationalism and political autonomy, and a penchant for Marxist theory and socialist causes. In 1934 he joined the Slovak Communist Party. He also became part of a group of intellectuals affiliated with the periodical *Dav,* Slovakia's leading Communist journal before World War II.

Husák received his law degree in 1937 and joined a law firm in Bratislava. Between 1940 and 1943 he was arrested and imprisoned several times for illegal Communist activities in the clerico-fascist Slovak Republic created by Nazi Germany in 1939. In late 1943, as a deputy chairman of the Slovak Communist Party, he helped create a coalition of underground resistance groups called the Slovak National Council. In the fall of 1944 this coalition organized an armed revolt against the government. Although short-lived, the Slovak National Uprising occupies a proud place in Slovak history. Husák wrote his personal account of it in 1964: *Svedectvo o Slovenskom národnom povstaní* ("Testimony on the Slovak National Uprising"). He fled to the Soviet Union in December 1944, returning to his home country with the liberating Soviet armies in February 1945.

In liberated and reunified Czechoslovakia after the war, and especially after the Communists took control of the country in February 1948, Husák quickly moved into a long series of important party and governmental positions. For example, from 1946 to 1950 he chaired the Slovak Board of Commissioners, Slovakia's regional governing body. From 1949 to 1951 he was a member of the Central Committee of the Czechoslovak Communist Party. He also held a seat in the Czechoslovak National Assembly (parliament). All this ended in 1951 when he fell victim to the wave of purges launched throughout the East European satellites by Joseph Stalin. All of the new Soviet-style regimes were ordered to

seek out their "national Communists," potential imitators of Marshall Tito, who had taken Yugoslavia out of the Soviet camp in 1948. Husák became a likely target because of his long-term personal affiliation with Vladimír Clementis, the prominent Slovak Communist who had become Czech foreign minister after the Communist coup d'état only to be convicted and executed as a "bourgeois nationalist" and foreign agent. In addition, Husák's own well-known Slovak nationalistic sentiments helped lead to his arrest in February 1951 on charges of treason and sabotage. He was taken to Prague's infamous Ruzyně Prison, where he was tortured and forced to confess to these spurious crimes. In April 1954 he was sentenced to life imprisonment.

Slovak nationalism revived as part of the national Czechoslovak movement in the 1960s to "humanize" and "de-Sovietize" the domestic Communist regime (its slogan was "Socialism with a Human Face"). Many previously convicted political prisoners were freed, including Husák, who was released in the "Prague Spring" beginning in 1960. Three years later he was formally "rehabilitated"— his conviction reversed and his party membership, which he had lost in 1951, restored to him. For several years he led the quiet life of a scholarly writer. But in late 1967 he again became prominent with a series of published attacks on Antonín Novotný, the Stalinist first secretary of the Czechoslovak Communist Party, and demands for the federalization of Czechoslovakia, with autonomy for the Slovaks and equal status with the Czechs.

At the height of the liberalization movement, in the spring and summer of 1968, Husák emerged as a close associate of Alexander Dubček, the fellow Slovak who replaced Novotný as head of the Czechoslovak Communist Party, and as one of the chief architects of Dubček's "action program" of reform. However, when the armed forces of the Warsaw Pact invaded Czechoslovakia on August 20, 1968, he quickly turned his coat. He thanked the invaders for their "act of international assistance" against the "right-wing anti-socialist and counter-revolutionary forces" he claimed had penetrated Dubček's movement. He counseled "realism" and "compromise" to his countrymen and unquestioning alliance with the Soviet Union as the only proper Czechoslovak policy. His advertisement of himself to the Soviets as a suitable new leader for the country was successful. By April 1969, with Soviet blessing, he had succeeded Dubček as first secretary of the Czechoslovak Communist party (in 1971 his title was changed to general secretary) and set about "normalizing" Czechoslovakia for them in systematic, uncompromising, often brutal fashion.

In short order, "liberal" Communists were removed from the party and government and replaced by trusted hard-liners. Of the 1968 reform program, only the federalization of Czechoslovakia, Husák's own pet project, was put into effect, in 1969. The country's lively press and innovative culture were stifled by a renewed emphasis on dogmatic Marxism. Those dissidents who dared to challenge Husák's regime, such as the courageous group called Charter 77, suffered persecution and violence, with little concern for world opinion. Soviet troops were stationed in Czechoslovakia, and the country became notorious, even among its East European neighbors, as a slavish follower of the Soviet Union in international affairs.

A new government was formed in 1989 with dissent over the maintenance of a union between the Czechs and the Slovaks. A decision to form two countries was made in 1992 and the land was divided into the Czech Republic and Slovakia in 1993.

Further Reading

There is no biography of Gustáv Husák in English, but there are some useful books on the major historical events and periods with which his life was connected. Tad Szulc's *Czechoslovakia since World War II* (1971) is a readable account of the period 1945 to 1968 by an experienced journalist. H. Gordon Skilling's *Czechoslovakia's Interrupted Revolution* (1976) is unquestionably the most comprehensive treatment of the "Prague Spring" reform movement of 1968 and its antecedents. Vladimir V. Kusin, *From Dubček to Charter 77: A Study of "Normalization" in Czechoslovakia, 1968-1978* (1978) analyzes the techniques the Husák regime employed to return Czechoslovakia to its pre-1968 orthodoxy and docility. □

Taha Husayn

Taha Husayn (sometimes spelled Hussein)(1889-1973) is considered one of Egypt's leading men of letters. Blind from early childhood, he devoted his life to intellectual freedom for the writer, critic, and scholar and to the introduction of Western learning into his country.

Taha Husayn was born on Nov. 4, 1889, in Maghagha, a mill town in Minya Province, Egypt. One of 11 children, he became blind at the age of three from a combination of eye disease and folk medicine. After completing studies at the village mosque school, Taha was sent to Cairo (1902) to attend al-Azhar, the mosque university that served as a theological seminary to much of the Moslem world. Because of his outspoken opposition to the school's teaching system at al-Azhar, Husayn was failed in his final examinations. He enrolled in the new, secular Egyptian University, where he studied with some of the leading scholars of the time, Egyptian and European, in the field of Arabic and Islamic studies. In this heady new atmosphere, Husayn received the first doctorate awarded by the university (1914) for his thesis on Abu-l-Ala al-Maarri, the blind Syrian philosopher of the 11th century.

Study in France

In 1915 Husayn won a scholarship for study in France, first to Montpellier and then to Paris. In Montpellier he employed a young Frenchwoman and student, Suzanne Bresseau, as his reader, and she later became his wife. His fields of study were literature and philosophy, including classical, and he became deeply interested in contemporary French literature.

Upon his return to Egypt after earning his doctorate in 1919, Husayn became a lecturer in ancient history at Egyptian University, and in 1925 he was given the chair in Arabic language and literature. Soon after he was elected dean of the faculty, the first Egyptian to hold the post.

A Provocative Career

In 1926 the young professor caused a public uproar with his work on pre-Islamic poetry that scandalized conservative Moslem opinion by criticizing traditional assumptions. The outcry almost caused the fall of the government, and the book was eventually withdrawn and reissued in a less provocative version.

Husayn's boldness and fervent support of academic freedom were not forgotten, however, and in 1932 he was dismissed. He wrote prodigiously for literary magazines and newspapers, as well as more substantial works. He became a prime mover in the founding of Alexandria University, and was minister of education and chairman of the cultural committee of the League of Arab States. In later years he was awarded many domestic and foreign honors.

Publications

Hasayn retired from academic life in 1952 to continue his writings, which he did until his death in 1973. The vast body of his works places him at the forefront of the Egyptian literary renaissance of the 20th century. He worked on the edition of classical Arabic texts and translated ancient Greek and modern French classics into Arabic.

Husayn's more purely literary studies were, on classical Arabic poetry, *Ma al-Mutanabbi* (1937; With al-Mutanabbi); and on modern Arabic poets, *Hafiz wa-Shawqi* (1933; Hafiz and Shawqi). His studies of the political and social history of early Islam include *Al-Fitnah al-Kubra* (The Great Time of Troubles), an interpretation of major political and ideological clashes.

Husayn's fiction includes numerous short stories as well as novels such as *Ala Hamish al-Sirah* (3 vols., 1933-1943; On the Margin of the Prophet's Life) and novellas with modern, often Upper Egyptian settings such as *Dua al-Karawan* (1934; The Appeal of the Caravan) and *Shajarat al-Bus* (1944; The Tree of Despair).

Husayn's fiction often became a vehicle to attack the Egyptian "system" that he knew. One of his most important works on educational and cultural policy is the major study *Mustaqbal al-Thaqafah fi Misr* (2 vols., 1938; The Future of Culture in Egypt), in which he developed his thesis that Egyptian culture was part of Mediterranean culture and hence any attempt to "orientalize" it was a dangerous error.

In his moving autobiography, *Al-Ayyam* (3 vols., 1929-1955; The Days), Husayn retells in simple language his own story, from village life and childhood blindness through educational trials and maturity. The value and appeal of this work are suggested by the fact that it has been translated into at least nine languages, including Chinese, English, Hebrew, and Russian.

Further Reading

The major critical study of Husayn is Pierre Cachia, *Taha Husayn: His Place in the Egyptian Literary Renaissance* (1956). Recommended for general background is Albert Hourani, *Arabic Thought in the Liberal Age, 1798-1939* (1962). □

Al-Hajj Amin al-Husayni

The preeminent Palestinian leader during most of the British mandate over Palestine, 1922 to 1948, was Al-Hajj Amin al-Husayni (1895-1974), the mufti of Jerusalem. As a Moslem scholar/leader he sought to establish an Arab state in Palestine. Unable to end Jewish immigration, he led a violent Arab revolt (1936-1939) against the Zionists and the British but failed, as did his attempt to stop the creation of Israel in 1948.

Al-Hajj Amin al-Husayni was born in 1895 in Jerusalem to a prominent Palestinian Muslim family. He studied in Cairo at al-Azhar and at the military academy in Istanbul. He served in the Ottoman army in 1916 but, because of Turkish attempts to impose their language and culture on their Arab subjects, he left for Palestine. There he assisted in the 1916 Arab revolt against the Ottomans and in the effort to form an Arab nation. Because he feared Zionism would cause the eventual domination or expulsion of the Palestinians from their homeland, he participated in an anti-Zionist demonstration in 1920. He fled to Damascus, but a year later he was pardoned and appointed to succeed his brother as mufti of Jerusalem.

In 1922 the new mufti was appointed president of the Supreme Muslim Council, with authority over religious institutions and with a budget of 50,000 pounds annually. These resources allowed him to extend his influence throughout Palestine. During the 1929 riots he was perceived as having stood up to the Zionists. The disturbance made him famous among Palestinians and infamous among Zionists.

In reality, he neither organized nor led the riots. Indeed, he cooperated with the British Palestine government in the 1920s and early 1930s, attempting to change British policy by appealing to the British and by holding a General Islamic Congress in 1931 to galvanize the Arab and Islamic world against Zionism and to goad them to pressure Britain. Instead, the British allowed Jewish immigration to increase to 61,854 in 1935, which radicalized the Palestinians. That year a revolutionary, Izz al-Din al-Qassam, was killed by British troops, which further embittered the Palestinians, who challenged the mufti's methods of cooperation. Until 1936 the mufti served two masters: his British employers, and his people. However, when the Arab revolt began in 1936, activists called on him to lead them against Zionism and British rule. As soon as he agreed to lead the

revolt, as president of the Arab Higher Committee, he put himself on a collision course with the British government.

The British stripped him of his offices and tried to arrest him in 1937. He fled to Lebanon, from where he continued the revolt until it was suppressed in 1939. He then fled to Iraq, where he encouraged a pan-Arab revolt against the British in 1941. Prime Minister Winston Churchill authorized his assassination in Baghdad but the British and Zionist mission to assassinate him failed. Once again he fled, this time to Rome, then Berlin, where he negotiated with Hitler. The Nazis promised to help the Arab countries liberate themselves from British rule, for which the mufti helped with anti-British and anti-Jewish propaganda and recruited Muslim volunteers for the war effort. He sought but failed to limit the number of Jews leaving for Palestine. His association with the Nazis tainted his name and cause.

After the war he escaped to the Middle East to resume his struggle against Zionism and to establish a Palestine state. Subsequent to a British announcement of their intent to leave Palestine, the United Nations passed a partition resolution in 1947. The Zionists accepted but the Arabs, including the mufti, opposed it because it gave the Zionists 55 percent of Palestine although they owned only 7 percent. In the war that followed the establishment of Israel in 1948, the Arab armies were defeated and some 725,000 Palestinians left or were expelled. Within a few years the mufti lost his political following and became a Muslim leader, settling first in Cairo, then in Beirut, where he died in 1974.

An assessment of Husayni's political role indicates that both his policy of cooperation and, after 1935, of resistance failed to achieve any nationalist goals. Yet the overriding factors that frustrated the Palestinians had less to do with the mufti than with historical processes and the balance of forces. Vigorous Zionist efforts to establish a Jewish commonwealth in Palestine and the sometimes pro-Zionist British policy enabled the Zionists to grow from 50,000 to 600,000 and to establish quasi-governmental and military institutions. The Palestinians were a weak and traditional society and never a match for the occupying British and later the Zionists.

Further Reading

Until the 1970s biographies of the mufti were written by Zionists, such as Moshe Pearlman, Joseph Schechtman, and Eliahu Elath, who attempted to vilify him, or by Arab nationalists, such as Zuhayr al-Mardini, who praised him. An early scholarly account of the mufti's rise to power in the 1920s was a chapter in Y. Porath's *Emergence of the Palestinian Arab-National Movement, 1918-1929* (1974). Majid Khadduri wrote a critical biographical sketch in his *Arab Contemporaries* (1973). A revisionist account is found in the author's succinct biography of Husayni's life, *The Mufti of Jerusalem* (1988, revised in 1992).

Additional Sources

Elpeleg, Z. (Zvi), *The grand mufti: Haj Amin al-Hussaini, founder of the Palestinian national movement,* London, England; Portland, Or.: Frank Cass, 1992.

Jabarah, Taysir, *Palestinian leader, Hajj Amin al-Husayni, Mufti of Jerusalem,* Princeton, N.J.: Kingston Press, 1985.

Mattar, Philip, *The Mufti of Jerusalem: Al-Hajj Amin al-Husayni and the Palestinian National Movement,* New York: Columbia University Press, 1992.

Taggar, Yehuda, *The Mufti of Jerusalem and Palestine: Arab politics, 1930-1937,* New York: Garland, 1986, 1987. □

Husein ibn Ali

Husein ibn Ali (ca. 1854-1931) was an Arab nationalist and political leader who proclaimed the Arab Revolt against the Ottoman Empire and became king of the Hejaz.

Born in Istanbul, the capital of the Ottoman Empire, Husein ibn Ali was a member of an important Arab family which claimed descent from the prophet Mohammed and the hereditary position of Meccan leadership. Following the Young Turk Revolution in 1908, the new Ottoman government named Husein to the traditional family position of sharif of Mecca, the governor and protector of the Islamic holy places. When, on the eve of World War I, Arabs and Turks were unable to reach a proper political balance for the multinational Ottoman Empire, Husein developed ambitions of his own for more extensive authority in Arab affairs and for Arab home rule.

His son Abdullah had discretely contacted British officials in Egypt as to Great Britain's attitude toward his father's aspirations in the event of Turkish involvement in war. When the war actually began, Husein found excuses for not sending Arab troops in support of his political and religious overlord, the Ottoman sultan.

During 1915 and 1916 Husein exchanged a famous series of letters with Sir Henry McMahon, the British high commissioner in Egypt, a follow-up to Abdullah's earlier inquiries. In the Husein-McMahon correspondence, the sharif of Mecca thought that the British had promised to support the establishment of an independent Arab state in southwest Asia with himself as the ruler in return for his proclamation of an Arab Revolt against the Ottoman Empire. In the meantime his third son, Faisal, had made an unsuccessful attempt to find a compromise with the Ottoman Turks.

Arab Revolt

In the spring of 1916 Turkish repression and execution of Arab leaders in Damascus and Beirut and the movement of Ottoman troops down the Hejaz railway into Arabia forced Husein's hand. Husein proclaimed the Arab Revolt in June 1916 and his own new title of king of the Arabs, which others recognized merely as king of the Hejaz. Husein, now in his mid-60s, remained behind in Mecca during the war, while his sons Abdullah and Faisal led Arab troops against the Ottoman troops in northwest Arabia and in what is present-day Syria. Husein thus lost control of the nationalist movement he had played such an important and symbolic role in starting.

Following World War I, Great Britain found itself enmeshed in several conflicting promises and agreements. Power politics led it to acquiesce in the French occupation of what became Syria and Lebanon, and in the Zionist aspirations for Palestine which had been ambiguously proclaimed in the Balfour Declaration of 1917. Britain and France partitioned southwest Asia, including unmistakenly Arab lands, between themselves, formalizing the decision at the San Remo Conference in 1920. It was legitimatized through the awarding of mandates by the League of Nations soon thereafter.

Husein bitterly rejected the peace settlements for greater Syria and scorned the British offer of recognition as king of the Hejaz and of a financial subsidy. He was scarcely assuaged when, in 1921, the British named his sons Abdullah and Faisal as emir of Transjordan and king of Iraq, respectively. Husein quarreled with Egypt over the pilgrimage trade to Mecca and with his increasingly powerful neighbor and rival, Ibn Saud of the Nejd in central Arabia, over religious issues. In 1924 after republican Turkey had abolished the Ottoman caliphate, Husein arrogantly proclaimed himself the new religious leader of Islam, a claim as caliph accepted by almost no one. The enraged Saudis, who considered Husein a sinful Moslem and a Europeanized Arab and who coveted the profits of the pilgrimage trade for themselves, took his self-proclamation as caliph as the last straw, besieged Mecca in 1924, and forced him to abdicate and flee. Husein lived in Cyprus as an embittered and frustrated exile until he had a serious stroke in 1930 and went to live his final year with his son Abdullah in Amman, Transjordan, where he died on June 4, 1931.

Further Reading

There is no biography of Husein, but there is a popular account of his dynasty in James Morris, *The Hashemite Kings* (1959). The classic Arab account of the rise of Arab nationalism and the Arab Revolt of 1916 is George Antonius, *The Arab Awakening: The Story of the Arab National Movement* (1939), which may be read in conjunction with a recent study by an Arab historian, Zeine N. Zeine, *The Emergence of Arab Nationalism* (1958; rev. ed. 1966). For Britain's role see Elie Kedourie, *England and the Middle East* (1956), and Elizabeth Monroe, *Britain's Moment in the Middle East, 1914-1956* (1963). □

Hu Shih

The Chinese philosopher Hu Shih (1891-1962) was in the literary and intellectual avant-garde during the New Thought movement of 1915-1919. As the premier Chinese disciple of John Dewey, he applied the principles of instrumentalism to scholarship and politics.

Hu Shih was born in Shanghai, where his father, a literatus from Anhwei, was serving as a government official. When Hu Shih was 4 years old, his father died. By this time the child prodigy already knew 1,000 Chinese characters. While in primary school, Hu received an education in the Chinese classics and was an avid reader of vernacular fiction.

Determined to obtain a modern education, Hu spent 4 years studying English, mathematics, and science, as well as traditional subjects, at several schools in Shanghai. From 1906 to 1908 he was enrolled at the China National Institute, where he edited a student newspaper. In 1908 he found himself financially unable to continue his schooling but remained in Shanghai teaching English and doing editorial work. During his years in Shanghai, Hu read, in translation, T. H. Huxley's *Evolution and Ethics,* J. S. Mill's *On Liberty,* and Montesquieu's *Spirit of the Laws,* as well as Liang Ch'i-ch'ao's essays on Western history and thought. In 1910 Hu went to Peking and passed the examination for a Boxer Indemnity scholarship to the United States.

Study Abroad

Believing technical skills to be essential for China's salvation, Hu enrolled in the College of Agriculture at Cornell University. In 1912, however, he transferred to the College of Arts and Sciences, where he majored in philosophy. He was elected to Phi Beta Kappa in 1913 and graduated in 1914. During his first year of graduate study in philosophy at Cornell, Hu discovered John Dewey's writings on experimentalism. He entered Columbia University

in 1915 to study under Dewey and received a doctorate in 1917. In his dissertation, "The Development of the Logical Method in Ancient China," Hu explored "pragmatic" tendencies in early Chinese thought.

While in the United States, Hu's basic political attitudes developed apace with his philosophical ideas. He was a member of the Cornell Cosmopolitan Club and the International Federation of Students and of several pacifist groups. When fellow Chinese students responded to Japan's "Twenty-one Demands" by urging a massive return to China, Hu urged them to seek national salvation through study rather than by precipitous political action. This remained his basic attitude toward student activism.

Professor at Peita

Through his writings while in the United States, Hu became well known in China for his intellectual individualism and especially for his advocacy of the replacement of the traditional *wen-yen* style in Chinese literature with the vernacular *pai-hua.* Upon his return in 1917, he was appointed professor of philosophy at National Peking University (Peita).

Except for brief absences, Hu remained in Peking until 1926. During this decade he gained fame as a champion of instrumentalism in both scholarship and politics. Between January 1917 and April 1918 three of his essays on literary reform appeared in Ch'en Tu-hsiu's prestigious periodical *Hsin ch'ing-nien* (New Youth). As a member of the *Hsin ch'ing-nien* circle, he also participated in the discussion of overall cultural change. An essay on Ibsenism in June 1918 raised the issue of the relationship between the individual and society. This was followed by essays on feminism, immortality, and experimentalism. The last, published in February 1919 in anticipation of Dewey's arrival, introduced Chinese to the principles of pragmatism. Hu served as an interpreter during Dewey's lecture tour (1919-1921). He also took advantage of his master's presence to promote a rational, scientific, gradualistic approach to social problems.

In his essay "Problems and Isms" (summer 1919) Hu advocated this approach over the totalistic ideological solutions of Marxism. He continued to expound a non-revolutionary attitude toward politics in the magazine *Nu-li choupao* (Endeavor), which he and others founded in May 1922. His manifesto, "Our Political Proposals," published in its second issue, attracted a wide range of signators, including Li Ta-chao, a founder of the Chinese Communist party. As an advocate of continuity in the midst of change, Hu found himself at one with neoconservatives such as Liang Ch'i-ch'ao. However, in the great debate of the mid-1920s over science and Western civilization, Hu argued that Western "materialism" was basically more humane than Eastern "spiritualism."

The years at Peita were creative ones for Hu as a scholar. He applied his experimentalist methodology to the study of the great vernacular novels, the *Shui-hu chuan* (The Water Margin, translated by Pearl Buck as *All Men Are Brothers*) and the *Hung-lou meng* (Dream of the Red Chamber). He also published widely on the history of Chinese philosophy, seeking in traditional thought precedents for modern scientific ideas.

Hu and the Kuomintang

In 1926 Hu traveled abroad on behalf of the British Boxer Indemnity Fund Committee. En route to London he visited the Soviet Union, where he was impressed with the accomplishments of the Communist revolution, still in its experimental stage. He was still abroad during the first phase of Chiang Kai-shek's Northern Expedition, and he returned in the spring of 1927 to find China south of the Yangtze in Nationalist hands. For the next 3 years Hu taught philosophy at Kuanghua University and from April 1928 to May 1930 served as president of the China National Institute. During these years he was critical of the Nanking government, and he secured official registration for the institute only by resigning his presidency. In 1930 Hu returned to Peking and in 1931 became dean of the College of Arts at Peita under the university's new president, his old friend, Chiang Monlin. Except for a brief trip to deliver the Haskell Lectures at the University of Chicago in 1933, Hu remained at Peita until the beginning of the Second Sino-Japanese War in 1937.

From 1932 to 1937 Hu edited *Tu-li tsa-chih* (The Independent Critic), the title of which reflected his own political posture. While other intellectuals and students clamored for war against the Japanese aggressor, Hu continued to hope for a peaceful solution that would permit the undisturbed development of China's educational and cultural institutions.

Further Years Abroad

During the last 25 years of Hu's life he spent only 2 years on the Chinese mainland. From September 1938 until September 1942 he served as ambassador to the United States. After his abrupt replacement by Wei Taoming, Hu remained in the United States until 1946 as a lecturer and writer. In 1945 he served, consecutively, as a member of the Chinese delegation to the United Nations Conference on International Organization and as acting head of the Chinese delegation to the first United Nations Educational, Scientific, and Cultural Organization conference.

Hu was appointed president of Peita after Chiang Monlin's resignation in June 1945. Hu returned to China to assume the post in mid-1946 and remained at Peita until the eve of Communist take-over 2 1/2 years later. In November 1946 he was a delegate to the National Assembly that drafted China's constitution. In 1948 he declined a personal invitation from Chiang Kai-shek to run for the Chinese presidency and spurned an opportunity to serve as premier.

From Nanking, Hu moved to Shanghai and then to New York, where he lived in semiretirement until the autumn of 1958, when he went to Taiwan to become president of the Academia Sinica. While heading this official research institute, Hu continued to lend his weight to governmental critics through sponsorship of *Tzu-yu chung-kuo* (Free China Fortnightly). However, he was unable to prevent the arrest of the editor, Lei Chen, and the termination of publication in 1960.

During these final years in Taiwan, Hu's intellectual following was confined in large measure to the older generation of mainland refugee intellectuals who had survived from the period of the New Thought movement. His vigorous criticism of the Peking regime, moreover, did not protect him from Kuomintang conservatives, who accused him of undermining China's traditions and opening the gateway to communism. Meanwhile, on the mainland, Hu was vilified as the archetype of the American-trained liberal intellectual and was denounced by his own son. On Feb. 24, 1962, Hu died of a heart attack.

Hu's approach to modern China's problems was gradualistic, experimental, cosmopolitan, and liberal. To the extent that these attitudes have been submerged by revolutionary tides of voluntarism, radicalism, extreme nationalism, and apocalyptic change, Hu may be deemed a failure. However, his contributions to modern China's language and scholarship have had an undeniable impact on his country's 20th-century transformation.

Further Reading

A major scholarly biography is Jerome B. Grieder, *Hu Shih and the Chinese Renaissance: Liberalism in the Chinese Revolution, 1917-1937* (1970). For more information on Hu Shih and China see C. P. FitzGerald, *The Birth of Communist China* (1952; rev. ed. 1966); Orville Schell and Franz Schurmann, eds., *The China Reader* (3 vols., 1967); Henry McAleavy, *The Modern History of China* (1967); and Immanuel Chung-yueh Hsü, *The Rise of Modern China* (1970).

Additional Sources

Chou, Min-chih, *Hu Shih and intellectual choice in modern China,* Ann Arbor: University of Michigan Press, 1984. □

Hussein ibn Talal

Hussein ibn Talal (born 1935) became at the age of 18 the king of the Hashemite Kingdom of Jordan, a strategic central state in the Middle East. He was regarded in the West as a moderate Arab leader.

King Hussein, born in Amman, was the scion of the illustrious Hashemite family from which the Prophet Mohammed sprang in the sixth century. His great-grandfather Hussein ibn Ali and his grandfather Abdullah were leaders of the Arab revolt against the Ottoman Empire during World War I. The latter was also founder of the modern state of Jordan, originally called Transjordan. Hussein's early life is described as happy but the family's lifestyle was not elaborate. They lived in a modest villa in what was still an unspoiled desert kingdom.

The young Prince Hussein attended primary and secondary schools in Amman, Egypt, and England, after which he was a student at Britain's Sandhurst. At Sandhurst he learned military principles and attitudes that helped in future years with his own Jordan Arab Army, which in turn became a key to his longevity on Jordan's throne. The most important formative influence on the prince, though, was his grandfather King Abdullah, who was his tutor and guide. From him Hussein learned both respect for tradition and openness to change. Crown Prince Talal, Hussein's father, suffered from schizophrenia and the King took a special interest in his grandson Hussein, the only member of the family King Abdullah believed could rule Jordan.

When Abdullah was assassinated in the Haram al-Sharif mosque in Jerusalem in 1951 Hussein was at his side, and the memory of that event would affect his personal attitude toward danger as well as his view of the significance of Jerusalem. Following the assassination Talal, Hussein's father, was crowned king, but he was removed by the Jordanian parliament within a year due to his mental illness. After a brief regency in 1953 Hussein took the constitutional oath as king. In the 1980s he became the longest ruling head of state in the world.

"The King and country were alike—young, inexperienced, poor and uncompromising" wrote John Newhouse in the *New Yorker*. The young Hussein inherited a country which was extremely poor, filled with refugees, and subject to the political turmoil that was characteristic of the Middle East. Considered a pawn of the West, the young king spent the early portion of his reign just trying to survive in a time when Arab nationalism was thriving. For Jordan, the results of the 1948 Arab-Israeli war were threefold. The West Bank of the Jordan River and its Palestinian population were included in the Hashemite Kingdom of Jordan; hundreds of thousands of refugees from other parts of Palestine found their way to Jordan; and the state of Israel was created on

Jordan's western border. Within this context King Hussein faced challenges to his throne emanating from disgruntled citizens, from radical Arab nationalism and interference from neighboring Arab states, and from occasional conflicts with Israeli military forces in Jordan's West Bank. With the key support of the army, which was recruited from Jordan's tribes, and other loyal political leaders, King Hussein and his regime were able to consolidate control by the late 1950s, although they still faced periodic challenges. Despite political tumult and tensions, King Hussein's regime made strides in building up the country's social and economic infrastructure—most significantly in education, which paid off in the following decades.

The 1967-1970 period was undoubtedly the most threatening to King Hussein's rule. In 1967 King Hussein along with Egypt and Syria fought the Six Day War against Israel and was defeated. For King Hussein the defeat was a severe setback, because Jordan lost the West Bank which, despite its small size, contained half the country's people, a little less than half of the economic activity, and the important religious shrines of East Jerusalem and Bethlehem.

Equally important, this defeat gave rise to the Palestinian guerrilla movements. Initially they attacked the state of Israel, which would retaliate by hitting their camps in Jordan. In 1970 the guerrillas turned their attacks on the government of Jordan. At the same time a Syrian tank force threatened the country's northern border, creating a second front which Jordan's military had to defend. With diplomatic support from the United States King Hussein won on both fronts, but not without considerable death and destruction, particularly in Amman in the struggle with the Palestinian guerrillas.

From 1967 through 1973 Jordan's economy suffered greatly as a result of the fighting and punitive actions on the part of some radical Arab regimes. In the post-1974 oil boom, however, Jordan's fortunes improved significantly. Jordan's trained population and loyal military performed valuable services for the Arab petroleum producing countries for which they were well paid. The king and his brother, Crown Prince Hassan, also sought and received grants and concessional loans from the same countries. The infrastructure built in the 1950s and 1960s allowed these funds to fuel economic expansion. Not only were there rapid advances in socio-economic development in the 1970s and 1980s, but also King Hussein allowed his people personal and economic freedom in an environment of civil order. Neither of the Hashemite monarchs, however, has allowed extensive political freedom or participation. Apparently to fill this void, King Hussein recalled parliament in 1984 after a ten-year hiatus.

Another major theme during King Hussein's reign was his difficult search for peace with Israel in the context of a realization of the just rights of the Palestinians. In the aftermath of the 1967 war with Israel he was the chief Arab negotiator in the formulation of the United Nations Security Council Resolution 242 which stipulated the principle of exchange of territory for peaceful relations with Israel as well as the inadmissibility of acquisition of territory by war. In 1972 the king followed up on this resolution with a proposal for a United Arab Kingdom which would be composed of East Jordan and the West Bank, the latter of which would enjoy local autonomy under the Jordanian crown.

In 1974 Hussein surrendered leadership in negotiations over the West Bank and Jerusalem to the Palestinian Liberation Organization (PLO), which was recognized by the Rabat summit as the sole legitimate representative of the Palestinian people. Consistent with this position, he refused to participate in the autonomy talks envisaged by the Camp David agreements of 1978, which had in fact been rejected by the PLO. But when Egypt and Israel signed a subsequent peace treaty in 1979 Jordan became the first Arab nation to cut diplomatic ties with Egypt.

President Ronald Reagan's Middle East peace initiative of 1982 was similar to a combination of Resolution 242 and the Hussein 1972 proposal. In the following years, King Hussein worked at realizing the 1982 initiative through talks and negotiations with American, Arab, and Palestinian leaders. But peace remained elusive.

In the 1991 Persian Gulf War, which was prompted by Iraq's invasion of Kuwait, King Hussein remained neutral initially, but eventually supported Saddam Hussein. After Iraq's defeat, King Hussein's relations with surrounding nations and the West were strained.

In the mid 1990s Hussein relinquished his strangle hold over the government and permitted political parties to field candidates in the first multi-party elections since 1956. Another crucial change in Jordan's relations with its neighbors occurred in 1994, when Israel and Jordan ended their 46-year state of war with the signing of a peace treaty. After the signing of the historic treaty, Hussein admitted that the Six Day War of 1967 was a mistake. However, the road to peace was not smooth, especially after the assassination of Yitzhak Rabin, Israel's prime minister. Rabin's successors chose not to honor all of the peace accords and this caused Hussein much anger and loss of face within his own country.

King Hussein is married to his fourth wife, Queen Noor, the former Lisa Halaby, an American citizen. They had two sons and two daughters. Previously the king had seven children (plus one adoption) from three earlier marriages.

Further Reading

There are one biography and one autobiography of Hussein, respectively, Peter Snow, *Hussein: A Biography* (1972), and Hussein, King of Jordan, *Uneasy Lies the Head* (1962). A more recent, comprehensive book on Hussein's kingdom is Peter Gubser, *Jordan: Crossroads of Middle Eastern Events* (1983). Hassan bin Talal, Crown Prince of Jordan and brother of Hussein, wrote a perceptive book explaining the Hashemites' thinking and accomplishments which is titled *Search for Peace* (1984). Other noteworthy books which deal with Jordan and King Hussein are P. J. Vatikiotis, *Politics and the Military in Jordan* (1967); John B. Glubb, *A Soldier with the Arabs* (1957); and Benjamin Shwadran, *Jordan: A State of Tension* (1959). □

Edmund Husserl

The German philosopher Edmund Husserl (1859-1938) is considered the father of phenomenology, one of the most important trends in 20th-century philosophy.

Edmund Husserl was born on April 8, 1859, in Prossnitz, Moravia. After finishing his elementary education in Prossnitz, he attended schools in Vienna and Olmütz. In 1876 he entered the University of Leipzig, pursuing physics, astronomy, and mathematics. He proved to be especially gifted in mathematics, and in 1878 he moved to the University of Berlin to study with a number of the leading mathematicians of that era. He became profoundly interested in the question of the foundations of mathematical reasoning, and he took his doctoral degree in mathematics at Vienna in 1883. Thereafter, however, his interest turned increasingly to philosophy, and he followed the lectures of Franz Brentano with great interest.

Husserl began his teaching career at Halle, initially as an assistant to the distinguished psychologist Carl Stumpf. Here Husserl published his first research into the foundations of mathematics, volume 1 of his *Philosophy of Arithmetic* (1891). Following British empiricism, he tried to show how the foundations were to be found in acquired habits of thought. But, yielding to sharp criticisms by Gottlob Frege, he soon revised his opinions. He then pushed the question further back into the ultimate foundations of all rational thought. Gradually he became convinced that the ultimate justification of thought patterns rested in the synthetic powers of consciousness—not in mere habits of thought but rather in indispensable concepts and relations, which, as underlying all thought, were seen to be necessary. These ultimate *phenomena* became now the constant objects of his tireless research.

Husserl's first preparatory studies in phenomenology were published as *The Logical Investigations* (2 vols., 1900-1901). Called to a professorship at Göttingen (1901-1916), he continued to write extensively. Works from this period include *The Idea of Phenomenology, Philosophy as a Rigorous Science,* and the first part of his *Ideas toward a Pure Phenomenology* (1913).

In 1916 Husserl was called to Freiburg as a full professor. Here he published the second and third parts of his *Ideas,* together with three other long works. He retired in 1929 and, remaining in Freiburg, continued to write. From this period date the *Cartesian Meditations* and the *Crisis of the European Sciences.* In all of these works Husserl doggedly pursued his vision of a radical foundation for rational thought. His passionate dedication to clarity and fundamental insight were what most impressed his students. Never satisfied with his results, however, he referred to himself at the end of his life as "a true beginner." Husserl died at Freiburg on April 27, 1938.

Further Reading

A definitive study of Husserl's work must await the complete publication of his papers. Meanwhile, a generally reliable and elementary guide is Joseph J. Kockelmans, *A First Introduction to Husserl's Phenomenology* (1967). For general background and for assessing Husserl's influence on other authors, Herbert Spiegelberg, *The Phenomenological Movement: A Historical Introduction* (2 vols., 1960-1965), is indispensable. □

Robert Maynard Hutchins

Reform-minded educator Robert Maynard Hutchins (1899-1977) aroused controversy over his views on liberal education in America. Critical of overspecialization, he fought for a balance between college curriculum and Western intellectual tradition at the University of Chicago in the 1930s and 1940s. Until his retirement in 1974, three years before his death in 1977, Hutchins was chairman of the Board of Editors of *Encyclopaedia Britannica*.

Robert M. Hutchins was born in Brooklyn, New York, Jan. 17, 1899, but grew up in Oberlin, Ohio, where his father was professor of theology at Oberlin College. Hutchins himself entered Oberlin at the age of 16, only to have his academic career interrupted by World War I. He enlisted in the army and served as an ambulance driver in Italy, earning the Italian medal, Croce di Guerra, in 1918. Home once more, he completed his education at Yale University, where he graduated with honors in 1921.

Hutchins was on a fast career track for the next seven years. He taught at Lake Placid School in New York from 1921 to 1923, while attending Yale Law School, where he graduated with honors in 1925. He was secretary of Yale from 1923 to 1927, named a full professor of the law school in 1927 and dean the following year.

The University of Chicago Years

Hutchins was just 29 years old when he took over Yale Law School, but he was already making his views known concerning American education. His plan to raise entrance requirements and set higher scholastic standards was regarded as "refreshing" in one so young. However, when he became president of the University of Chicago in 1929, at the age of 30, he began to be regarded as controversial.

In Chicago, Hutchins became the era's most exciting and discussed figure in education. He asserted that universities should be centers of independent thought and criticism, operating to change things from the way they are to the way they ought to be. "We have confused science with information, ideas with facts, and knowledge with miscellaneous data," he said. He decried the tendency toward specialization and vocationalism.

In the late 1930s, Hutchins introduced his Chicago Plan for liberal education, based on his belief that the last two years of high school in America duplicated the first two years of college. Its main element was a drastic reorganization that began collegiate education in the third year of high school and ended after the second year of college. The curriculum consisted of 14 year-long comprehensive courses, each integrating a basic field—the physical, biological, and social sciences and the humanities. Students demonstrated mastery of a subject by passing a comprehensive examination that could be administered at any time, whether they attended classes or not. Instruction was primarily by discussion. Hutchins believed that "dialogue" rather than lecturing was the best means of learning.

The controversial Hutchins also introduced a Great Books course at the university to encourage a wider breath of knowledge. Also, his belief that colleges placed undue emphasis on extracurricular activities brought an end to intercollegiate football at Chicago in 1939.

By 1942, the University of Chicago was awarding the bachelor's degree for those who completed the new program. Students were admitted to the college on the basis of placement tests rather than high school records.

Continuing Controversy

Most educators reacted to the Chicago Plan with outrage. Many universities refused to recognize the "two-year degree." Nevertheless, Hutchins had stirred up a hornet's nest in liberal education. Even those who opposed his ideas introduced some of his general courses into their own institutions.

In 1935, the state legislature investigated the University of Chicago on charges of "communistic influences" in the school. Hutchins eloquently defended the freedom to teach, which set the tone in the wave of similar investigations that swept educational institutions during this era.

Hutchins was against U.S. participation in World War II for which he said the country was "morally unprepared." Ironically, his university had a large part in the development of the atomic bomb. A government grant of $2 billion led to the first "controlled" chain reaction experiment just five days before the Japanese attacked Pearl Harbor, on December 7, 1941, and brought the United States into the war.

The Later Years

Leaving the university in 1951, after serving the last six years as chancellor, Hutchins became the associate director of the Ford Foundation, whose purpose is to further the cause of peace. In 1954, he was named president of the Fund for the Republic, which advocated no restrictions on freedom of thought and expression in the United States. In 1959, he founded the Center for the Study of Democratic Institutions, which approached his ideal of a community of scholars, in Santa Barbara, CA. Besides his own published works on education, Hutchins was chairman of the Board of Editors of *Encyclopaedia Britannica* from 1943 until his retirement in 1974.

Hutchins's first marriage, to sculptress Maude Phelps McVeigh in 1921, ended in divorce in 1948. The couple had three daughters, Mary Frances, Joanna, and Clarissa. In 1949, he married Vesta Sutton Orlick. The controversial educator died in Santa Barbara, CA, on May 17, 1977.

Further Reading

Hutchins wrote of his Chicago experience in *The Higher Learning in America* (1936), *No Friendly Voice* (1937), and *The Great Conversation: The Substance of a Liberal Education* (1952). There is no full-scale biography; Thomas C. Reeves, *Freedom and the Foundation: The Fund for the Republic in the Era of McCarthyism* (1969), is the fullest interpretation. Good secondary accounts of the Hutchins years at Chicago are Chauncey S. Boucher, *The Chicago College Plan* (1935), and Reuben Frodin and others, *The Idea and Practice of General Education: An Account of the College of the University of Chicago by Present and Former Members of the Faculty* (1950). Arthur A. Cohen, ed., *Humanistic Education and Western Civilization: Essays for Robert M. Hutchins* (1964), has a chapter on Hutchins. □

Anne Marbury Hutchinson

English-born Anne Marbury Hutchinson (1591-1643) was banished from the Massachusetts colony and excommunicated from its church for dissenting from the Puritan orthodoxy. Her "case" was one of several prefiguring the eventual separation of church and state in America.

Anne Marbury was born in Alford, Lincolnshire, the eldest daughter of a strong-willed Anglican priest who had been imprisoned and removed from office because of his demand for a better-educated clergy. In 1605 the family moved to London, where her father was reinstated to the clergy. He died in 1611, leaving his daughter a legacy of biblical scholarship and religious independence. The following year Anne returned to her birthplace as the bride of William Hutchinson, a prosperous cloth merchant. For the next 20 years she operated the household, acquired a knowledge of medicinal herbs, and cared for over a dozen children.

Her Early Puritanism

Hutchinson also continued her father's religious individualism. Adopting Puritanism, she often journeyed to St. Botolph's Church in Boston, England, to hear John Cotton, one of England's outstanding Puritan ministers. When the Anglican Church silenced him and he left for the colony of Massachusetts in America, Hutchinson became extremely distraught. She finally persuaded her husband to leave for America, so that she could follow her religious mentor.

The Hutchinson family was well received in Massachusetts. William Hutchinson was granted a desirable house lot in Boston, and both husband and wife quickly became church members. William Hutchinson resumed his career as a merchant, became a landowner, and was elected a town selectman and deputy to the General Court. Hutchinson's experience with medicinal herbs made her much in demand as a nurse, and she made many friends. When she

was criticized for failing to attend weekly prayer meetings in the homes of parishioners, she responded by holding meetings in her own home. She began by reiterating and explaining the sermons of John Cotton but later added some of her own interpretations, a practice that was to be her undoing.

Puritan Orthodoxy

John Cotton was an intelligent and subtle theologian who had articulated an extremely fine balance between the value of God's grace and the value of good works in achieving salvation. While the Puritans believed that salvation was the result of God's grace, freely given to man, they also maintained that good works, or living the moral life, were important signs of that salvation and necessary preparation for the realization that one had received God's grace. But grace and works had to be kept in proper balance. To overemphasize works was to argue that man could be responsible for his own salvation and thus would deny God's power over man. On the other hand, to overemphasize grace was to assert a religious individualism that denied the necessity of moral living and by implication rejected clerical leadership, church discipline, and civil authority. While Cotton had maintained his balance in this most difficult of issues, Hutchinson did not, and she finally came to stress grace to the exclusion of works in determining salvation. The origin of her views is difficult to discover. Certainly Cotton had influenced her. She probably held her beliefs prior to her arrival in Boston, but she evidently did not advance them until the meetings in her home.

As her meetings became more popular, Hutchinson drew some of Boston's most influential citizens to her home. Many of these were town merchants and artisans who had been severely criticized for profiteering in prices and wages; they saw in Hutchinson's stress on grace a greater freedom regarding morality and therefore more certainty of their own salvation. But others came in search of a more meaningful and personal relationship with their God. As she attracted followers and defenders, the orthodox Puritans organized to oppose her doctrines and her advocates.

Antinomian Controversy

The issue of grace as opposed to works assumed political significance and ultimately divided Massachusetts into hostile camps. The orthodox Puritans called the Hutchinson group "Antinomians," or those who denied the applicability of moral law to the saved, and the Hutchinsonians referred to orthodox Puritans as "Legalists," or those who trusted only the observance of church laws as a sign of salvation. The orthodox Puritans, always a majority in the colony, came to demand repudiation of what seemed not only religious error but also potential social chaos. If Hutchinson's views predominated, they reasoned, individual conscience would replace clerical and civil authority as the standard for public conduct.

The Puritan orthodoxy began its assault on the dissenters in the May 1637 election. Henry Vane, a Hutchinson defender, was defeated for reelection to the governorship by John Winthrop, an opponent of her views. In the summer a synod was called in order that the "errors" of the Hutchinsonians could be identified and dealt with by the government. Following a special election in October, in which the orthodoxy increased its political strength, the government moved against individuals. Boston's pro-Hutchinson deputies were not permitted to take their seats in the General Court, and Hutchinson's brother-in-law John Wheelwright (previously convicted for sedition and contempt because of a sermon preached in defense of grace) was banished.

Anne Hutchinson Banished

The court then moved against Hutchinson. It was a difficult situation. As a woman, her words had not been public and she had not participated in the political maneuvers surrounding the controversy. Called before the court, she was accused of sedition and questioned extensively. She defended herself well, however, demonstrating both biblical knowledge and debating skill. She returned the next morning to be aided by John Cotton's testimony about her beliefs, which differed from the report of the clergymen who had spoken for the court. This conflicting evidence would have cleared her, but she brashly intervened and, before it was over, had declared herself the recipient of direct revelations from God, without aid of either Scripture or clergy. This assertion of direct communion with God was regarded as the vilest heresy by all, and it sealed her doom. She was banished as a woman "not fit for [Massachusetts] society."

While Hutchinson's trial was, by modern standards, a gross miscarriage of justice, it was not unjust according to the standards of 17th-century England, where, generally, in sedition cases a formal defense was not permitted and a jury was not used. Yet even by 17th-century standards, a mistrial occurred when the same men sat both as prosecution and judge, for her guilt had been thus "known" by the General Court long before she even presented herself to it.

After her sentencing, Hutchinson's importance waned. Her strongest supporters had either left Massachusetts or been banished, and her idol, John Cotton, had finally allied himself with the orthodoxy. The result of her investigation by the Boston congregation was a foregone conclusion. Her attempt to renounce her former errors was taken as incomplete by the clergy, and she was excommunicated for the sin of lying. Within a week she and her family departed for Rhode Island, where she was free to practice her religious views. In 1642 her husband died, and Hutchinson moved with her six youngest children to Long Island and then to the New Netherland (New York) mainland. In the late summer of 1643, Hutchinson and all but one of her children were killed in an Indian attack.

It was a sad end for an important religious figure. Hutchinson's emphasis on grace as the only requirement for salvation was an important step toward the achievement of religious freedom—that is, the ability to follow the dictates of one's own conscience in matters of belief—in America.

Further Reading

The best biography of Anne Hutchinson is Emery John Battis, *Saints and Sectaries: Anne Hutchinson and the Antinomian Controversy in the Massachusetts Bay Colony* (1962). Other useful biographies are Helen Auguer, *An American Jezebel: The Life of Anne Hutchinson* (1930); Edith R. Curtis, *Anne Hutchinson* (1930); and Winnifred King Rugg, *Unafraid: A Life of Anne Hutchinson* (1930). Relevant documents dealing with the Antinomian controversy were published in David D. Hall, ed., *The Antinomian Controversy, 1636-1638: A Documentary History* (1968). Background material is in Charles F. Adams, *Three Episodes of Massachusetts History: The Settlement of Boston Bay; the Antinomian Controversy; A Study of Church and Town Government* (2 vols., 1892; 5th ed. 1896); James T. Adams, *The Founding of New England* (1921); Thomas J. Wertenbaker, *The Puritan Oligarchy* (1947); Edmund S. Morgan, *The Puritan Dilemma: The Story of John Winthrop* (1958); and Larzer Ziff, *The Career of John Cotton: Puritanism and the American Experience* (1962). □

Thomas Hutchinson

Thomas Hutchinson (1711-1780), American governor of colonial Massachusetts and a staunch defender of English colonial policy, was also a jurist and historian.

Thomas Hutchinson was born in Boston on Sept. 9, 1711. He entered Harvard at the age of 12, graduating 3 years later. Entering his father's commercial house, Hutchinson continued to further his education through extensive reading. By the time he was 25 he was worth £5,000 and was part owner of a ship. On May 16, 1734, he married Margaret Sanford of Newport, R.I., who bore him three sons and two daughters before her death in 1753.

Politics in Massachusetts

In 1737 Hutchinson was elected selectman for Boston. That same year he gained a seat in the Massachusetts House of Representatives, where he served every year, except 1739, and was speaker for 3 years (1746-1748) until his defeat in the election of 1749. In 1750 he was chosen a member of the governor's council (and served continuously until 1766). In 1740 he was sent to England to represent Massachusetts in the boundary dispute with New Hampshire. He gained favor with the Massachusetts merchants when, in the fight against the Land Bank, he advocated sound money. In 1752 he was appointed judge of probate and justice of common pleas for Suffolk County.

As a representative of Massachusetts at the Albany Congress in 1754, he gave his support to Benjamin Franklin's plan of union for the Colonies. He was appointed lieutenant governor of Massachusetts in 1758 and became chief justice for the colony 2 years later. Because of his continuing interest in commerce, he opposed general search warrants by the governor, insisting that they be issued by the courts. By 1763 Hutchinson was one of the most influential men in Massachusetts politics, but he had earned the enmity of fiery prerevolutionary patriots Samuel Adams and James Otis by his opposition to the Land Bank and his support of the issuance of general writs by proper authority.

In February 1764 the General Court sent Hutchinson to England to protest the proposed sugar duties. Although he opposed the Sugar Act and the Stamp Act on the grounds that they would injure trade, he never denied the right of Parliament to tax the Colonies. It was this attitude and the fact that his brother-in-law Andrew Oliver was stamp master that led a Boston mob to sack his home in 1765. He lost an estimated £3,000 in personal property and the manuscript of his *History of Massachusetts Bay,* the first volume of which had been published in 1764. This violence led Hutchinson to believe that more stringent policies should be adopted by Parliament.

Uneasy Governorship

Although expressing opposition to the Townshend duties, Hutchinson felt that they should be enforced as the law. He was acting governor of Massachusetts from 1769 to 1771. Appointed royal governor of Massachusetts in 1771, he faithfully followed instructions from the Crown. His popularity waned when he twice called out troops to quell disturbances and constantly disputed with the House over such trivialities as its place of meeting. On Jan. 6, 1773, he addressed the General Court, urging the case of parliamentary supremacy.

Hutchinson's position became untenable when Benjamin Franklin sent from England the "Hutchinson Letters," which had been written to friends in 1768 and 1769. These documents, published in Massachusetts in 1773, were interpreted so as to make it seem that Hutchinson had secretly urged the British government to exert more stringent authority over the Colonies. The Tea Act precipitated a crisis, not only because the governor's two sons had been designated tea consignees, but because Hutchinson refused to issue clearance papers for the tea ships until the tea had been landed. The Boston Tea Party was the result.

In 1774 Gen. Thomas Gage replaced Hutchinson as governor. Hutchinson sailed for England, hoping to return as soon as the general's presence was no longer necessary. Unaware of the gravity of the colonial crisis, he urged a policy of conciliation toward the Colonies. Although he had many friends in England and Oxford University conferred upon him an honorary degree, he remained homesick for New England. His writings include a reply to the Declaration of Independence and the three-volume *History of Massachusetts Bay*. On June 3, 1780, he died and was buried at Croydon, England.

Further Reading

Portions of Hutchinson's own account, badly edited by Peter O. Hutchinson, are in *The Diary and Letters of His Excellency Thomas Hutchinson* (2 vols., 1884-1886). The Lawrence S. Mayo edition of Hutchinson's *History* (3 vols., 1936) is the most useful. James K. Hosmer, *The Life of Thomas Hutchinson, Royal Governor of the Province of Massachusetts Bay* (1896), the only biography, is superseded by the sketch of Hutchinson in Clifford K. Shipton, *Sibley's Harvard Graduates: Biographical Sketches of Those Who Attended Harvard College in the Classes 1726-1730,* vol. 8 (1951).

Additional Sources

Bailyn, Bernard, *The ordeal of Thomas Hutchinson,* Cambridge, Mass., Belknap Press of Harvard University Press, 1974.
Freiberg, Malcolm, *Prelude to purgatory: Thomas Hutchinson in provincial Massachusetts politics, 1760-1770,* New York: Garland, 1990. □

Ulrich von Hutten

The German imperial knight and humanist Ulrich von Hutten (1488-1523) advocated the dissolution of Germany's ties with the papacy. He advanced an unrealistic program, however, for solving German national problems by reversion to medieval knighthood and feudalism.

U lrich von Hutten, born in a castle near Fulda in Hesse, was sent at age 11 to a monastery to become a Benedictine monk. After 6 years he escaped and led a vagabond life, attending four German universities. In Erfurt he befriended Crotus Rubianus and other humanists. He went to Italy, took service as a soldier, and attended universities, spending some time in Pavia and Bologna. In Germany he served in the imperial army (1512). Because of the death of a cousin, Hans, at the hands of Duke Ulrich of Württemberg, he published sharp Latin diatribes

against the duke, which have been compared with the *Philippics* of Demosthenes and which brought him fame. In 1519 he played a part in the expulsion of the duke.

A second visit to Italy took Hutten to Bologna and Rome (1515-1517). In 1517 he was crowned poet laureate by Emperor Maximilian I in Augsburg for his Latin poems. His protector was Archbishop-Elector Albrecht of Mayence, at whose court he often appeared. In 1517 too he played a part in the defense of Johann Reuchlin against the Cologne Dominicans; he probably wrote the second part of the famous *Epistolae obscurorum virorum*. His *Colloquia* followed in 1518 (in German, 1520-1521). The bitter dialogues *Vadiscus* (1520), directed against the papacy, cost him the protection of Albrecht. His German work *Aufwecker der teutschen Nation* (1520; *Arouser of the German Nation*), which opens with his motto ''Ich hab's gewagt'' (I have dared to do it), was bold and forward-looking and announced his support of Martin Luther. The hostility aroused by this work forced him to flee to Basel.

In Basel, Hutten hoped to find help from Erasmus, but the two humanists soon feuded. His dream of enlisting Luther and the unsuccessful freedom fighter Franz von Sickingen in his struggle for a stronger, independent empire also failed, as did attempts to interest Maximilian and his successor, Charles V. Efforts to war against the Catholic clergy had degenerated into a robber-baron adventure. In Switzerland, Huldreich Zwingli took an interest in him and sheltered him on the island of Ufenau in Lake Zurich, where Hutten died in 1523.

Further Reading

Two biographical studies of Hutten are David Friedrich Strauss, *Ulrich von Hutten,* translated by Mrs. George Sturge (1874; new ed. 1927), and Hajo Holborn, *Ulrich von Hutten and the German Reformation,* translated by Roland H. Bainton (1937). Recommended for general background is Harold J. Grimm, *The Reformation Era, 1500-1650* (1954; rev. ed. 1965).

Additional Sources

Holborn, Hajo, *Ulrich von Hutten and the German Reformation,* Westport, Conn.: Greenwood Press, 1978, 1937. □

James Hutton

The Scottish naturalist James Hutton (1726-1797), the founder of modern geology, is best known for his *Theory of the Earth.*

James Hutton was born in Edinburgh on June 3, 1726. He entered Edinburgh University in 1740 to study the humanities, but he developed an intense and long-lasting interest in chemistry. At 17 Hutton was placed as an apprentice in a lawyer's office; however, performing chemistry experiments during office hours led to his dismissal, and he then chose medicine as a profession. For 3 years he pursued medical studies at Edinburgh University in spite of the fact that no degree of medicine could be obtained from that institution. Therefore, in 1747 he went to Paris to study chemistry and anatomy. He received a medical degree at Leiden in 1749.

Back in London, Hutton realized that even medicine would not give him sufficient spare time for his scientific interests. He therefore abandoned medicine for agriculture. In 1752 he went to a farm in Norfolk, where the scenery apparently turned his mind to mineralogy and geology.

Theory of the Earth

In 1754 Hutton visited Flanders allegedly to compare husbandry methods with those practiced in Norfolk. Actually he spent most of his time making geological observations later to be included in his *Theory of the Earth.* At the end of the year he settled down at his family property in Berwickshire, where he managed a farm according to the most scientific methods. In 1768 he abandoned his country life and settled in Edinburgh, spending all his time on scientific studies. His interests, however, were by no means confined to geology, for he published treatises on physics and metaphysics and investigated all branches of science except mathematics.

The spectacular geological features around Edinburgh provided Hutton with numerous fundamental observations to combine with his broad knowledge of many parts of Great Britain. Eventually he was led to formulate a definite theory, or system, of the earth, and although he had discussed it at length with his friends, he did not write it down until he was persuaded to address in 1785 one of the first meetings of the newly founded Royal Society of Edinburgh. The full text was published in the *Transactions* in 1788 under the title "Theory of the Earth; or, An Investigation of the Laws Observable in the Composition, Dissolution and Restoration of Land upon the Globe." The paper attracted little attention, perhaps because of its misleading title of "Theory" and its publication in the transactions of a learned society which had just been founded. However, when the paper was criticized in 1793, Hutton revised and developed his theory in greater detail. The result was the *Theory of the Earth, with Proofs and Illustrations* (2 vols., 1795). A projected third volume remained incomplete and was published by the Geological Society of London in 1899.

Hutton's Doctrine

In Hutton's opinion, the purpose of geology is first to collect objective data by observing the earth's crust and second to interpret the evidence with a minimum amount of imagination, rather than to begin with an artificial hypothesis and then attempt to fit the observations into a rigid theoretical framework. Hutton's theory evolved in such a natural fashion from his observations that it achieved the prerequisite of involving very little speculation. His basic assumption is that the past history of the globe should be interpreted in the light of what is happening today or has happened in recent times. This dominant idea that the present is the key to the past is so commonplace in modern geological thinking that one often fails to fully appreciate the genius of the man who first formulated it in modern times.

Hutton first turned his attention to sedimentary rocks, observing that they consist of debris of older rocks. He drew a parallel between such rocks and present-day marine deposits, comparing conglomerates with gravels, sandstones with sands, limestones with accumulations of organic debris, and shales with silts and muds. From the wide distribution of these beds—which form the continents—he understood that they could only have been deposited in the sea. Hutton's first conclusion was that the continents consisted of indurated sediments which, eroded from some preexisting emerged land, had been spread in strata over the sea floor. Since all these sedimentary rocks were originally deposited as soft sediments but appear today as indurated rocks, he attributed this change to the combined action of pressure and subterranean heat.

Hutton's next problem was to explain how beds originally deposited in a horizontal fashion on the sea floor could occur in mountains such as the Alps, tilted, ruptured, and contorted in a spectacular fashion. Hutton understood that such occurrences resulted from powerful revolutions which at different times in the past seem to have affected the entire earth's crust. After having demonstrated the existence of episodes of large-scale deformation which had uplifted the sea bottom with its indurated sediments and folded them in a complex manner to build the existing continents, he investigated the possible cause of these processes. He assumed the existence of forces acting vertically and upward which were probably related to deep-seated reservoirs of heat. The action of these vertical forces interfering with gravity and the resistance of the rocks would create a lateral and oblique component responsible for the contortions of the beds.

Hutton considered volcanoes as safety valves through which some of the earth's internal heat could escape, but he understood that the heat was not due to the combustion of coal seams or the oxidation of pyritic shales, as believed for a long time, but to a deep-seated and molten mass. By means of this concept, Hutton attempted to explain the origin of the various types of nonstratified rocks, either massive or in veins, which he had observed in different places. He called them whinstones (basic rocks, including basalts), porphyries, and granites, and interpreted them as material that once had been in a molten condition and subsequently had been injected upward during the great disturbances of the earth's crust.

Most of the modern ideas on geomorphology are to be found in the Huttonian theory, including the importance of the erosion and transportation power of mountain glaciers. However, these concepts were ignored or even rejected for many years.

Hutton died on March 26, 1797. His *Theory of the Earth* is marred by a rather obscure style and defective organization. One of his friends, John Playfair, the mathematician and natural philosopher, was able to give the work a well-organized and elegant presentation, combined with a series of personal comments, under the title *Illustrations of the Huttonian Theory of the Earth* (1802).

Further Reading

A modern biography of Hutton, including excerpts of his major works, is Edward Battersby Bailey, *James Hutton: The Founder of Modern Geology* (1967). Other accounts of Hutton's life and contribution to geology are in Sir Archibald Geikie, *The Founders of Geology* (1897; 2d ed. 1905); Karl Alfred von Zittel, *History of Geology and Palaeontology to the End of the Nineteenth Century* (1899; trans. 1901); and F. D. Adams, *The Birth and Development of the Geological Sciences* (1938). □

Aldous Leonard Huxley

The novels, short stories, and essays of the English author Aldous Leonard Huxley (1894-1963) explore crucial questions of science, religion, and philosophy.

Aldous Huxley was born into a family of intellectual prominence. His father, Leonard, was the son of T. H. Huxley, the famous proponent of Darwinism when it was first finding acceptance; his mother, Julia, was the niece of the poet and critic Matthew Arnold. Aldous attended Eton on a scholarship and specialized in biology, intending to become a doctor, but he contracted keratitis and soon was almost blind. However, he learned to read Braille and continued his studies under tutors. When one eye recovered enough so that he could read with a magnifying glass, he turned to English literature and philosophy at Oxford, taking a degree in 1915.

After World War I Huxley engaged in literary journalism and was on the staff of the *Athenaeum,* edited by John Middleton Murry. For the greater part of 1923-1930 he lived in Italy; after 1926 he spent much time there with D. H. and Frieda Lawrence. Lawrence was a strong influence on Huxley, particularly in his mistrust of intellect and trust in vital promptings.

Huxley's early period was characterized by skeptical, brilliant portraits of a decadent society. This was the period of the novels *Crome Yellow* (1921), *Antic Hay* (1923), and *Point Counter Point* (1928), in which the characterizations of D. H. and Frieda Lawrence as the Mark Rampions are practically the only favorable ones. Huxley's disgust with much of the modern world became explicit in *Brave New World* (1932) and *Eyeless in Gaza* (1936).

In 1938 Huxley encountered the Bates method of eye training and moved to southern California, where facilities for it were unusually good. He said of the method that it demonstrated in that particular sphere "the possibility of becoming the master of one's circumstances. . . . Similar techniques for controlling other unfavorable circumstances have been independently developed. . . . All these techniques, however, are secondary . . . to a great central technique. This central technique, which teaches the art of obtaining freedom from the fundamental human disability of egotism, has been repeatedly described by the mystics of

all ages and countries. It is with the problem of personal, psychological freedom that I now find myself predominantly concerned."

Huxley's *The Perennial Philosophy* (1945) was in a sense a documentation of this statement. Through its initial statement of somatic psychology, it illustrated well the modern interest in psychological necessity. But Huxley's most famous dramatization of the possibility of dehumanizing kinds of control through the use of conditioning, drugs, and economic necessity was *Brave New World*. In a sequel, *Brave New World Revisited,* he considered ways of solving the threat of the so-called population explosion.

Huxley's "mystical" phase is linked to his long association with Gerald Heard. Huxley's most successful later work was *The Devils of Loudon* (1952), which dealt with the hysteria that swept a French Ursuline convent in the 17th century and the martyrdom of a priest. All along, of course, Huxley had shown interest in any means of liberation from the bondage of the ego, and his *The Doors of Perception* (1954), dealing with the drug mescaline, can be seen as an interesting anticipation of the interest more than a decade later in the psychedelic experience. He said that he had helped his wife, Maria, die by using the medieval *Ars moriendi,* and it is said that while he was dying, his mind was "liberated" by drugs.

Of Huxley's general direction, Charles J. Rolo (1947) said: "When Huxley came of age, human behavior, it seemed to the modernist, was entirely explicable in terms of Libido, Instinct, glandular function or conditioned re-

flex. . . . While repudiating the Gods and Goods, Huxley implicitly continued to search for them, applying to the task an integrity that bit like acid through illusion, sentimentality and convention. All his work is a quest for values in the face of scepticism." Jocelyn Brooke (1954) found Huxley, "despite the homogeneity of his writings . . . , a strangely paradoxical figure: an intellectual who profoundly distrusts the intellect, a sensualist with an innate loathing for the body, a naturally religious man who remains an impenitent rationalist."

Further Reading

A good introduction and survey is *The World of Aldous Huxley: An Omnibus of His Fiction and Non-fiction over Three Decades,* edited with an introduction by Charles J. Rolo (1947). A brief survey of Huxley's career is in Jocelyn Brooke, *Aldous Huxley* (1954). See also David S. Savage, *Mysticism and Aldous Huxley: An Examination of Heard-Huxley Theories* (1947), and the essay by M. Lebowitz in John Crowe Ransom, ed., *The Kenyon Critics: Studies in Modern Literature from the Kenyon Review* (1951). Other studies of Huxley include John A. Atkins, *Aldous Huxley: A Literary Study* (1956; rev. ed. 1967); Julian S. Huxley, ed., *Aldous Huxley, 1894-1963: A Memorial Volume* (1965); and Laura Archera Huxley, *The Timeless Moment: A Personal View of Aldous Huxley* (1968). ☐

Julian Huxley

The English biologist and author Julian Huxley (1887-1975) helped establish the modern synthetic theory of evolution by natural selection and served as first director of the United Nations Educational and Scientific Organization (UNESCO).

Sir Julian Sorell Huxley was born June 22, 1887, in London, England. His father, Leonard Huxley, master of Charterhouse School and later an editor, encouraged his children Julian, Trevenen, Aldous, and Margaret to live up to the achievements of their grandfather, the famous evolutionist Thomas Henry Huxley. Julian traced his thinking in many fields to this influence of T. H. Huxley maintained by his father. It was the origin of his creed of rationalism, atheism, and general, as opposed to specialized, thinking. Leonard encouraged his son's early interest in natural history, which found opportunity in the rural setting of their home in Surrey. Julian's mother, who founded a school in the area, was also a great influence and encouraged his intellectual interests, including a passion for poetry.

After taking a degree in zoology at Oxford in 1909, Huxley went to the Naples Zoological Station in Italy for a year of research on sponges. This led to his first book, *The Individual in the Animal Kingdom* (1912), upon his return to an Oxford lectureship in zoology. In 1912 the newly opened Rice Institute in Houston, Texas, hired him. He effectively developed and headed the biology department, but during World War I he felt called to duty for his country.

He returned to England in 1916 and served in the Army Intelligence Corps until the end of the war. He remained in England, returning once again to Oxford. He married Juliette Baillot in 1919. They had two sons.

Teaching, Research, Writing

The young Huxley became a driving force in the zoology department, promoting new teaching and research priorities and organizing an ecological research expedition to Spitsbergen Island in the Arctic. Huxley himself had already produced studies not only of morphology and development but also of bird ecology and bird behavior during courtship. He wanted to move zoology away from its classical morphological and descriptive base, toward the new excitement of dynamic ecology and of genetics and physiology.

To that end, he began his own laboratory researches in developmental morphology, choosing to examine growth rates. He developed the idea that an organism's form depends on differential growth rates in the separate parts of the body. Begun at Oxford, this work was continued after 1925 at King's College, London, where he had been appointed professor of zoology. Although he kept the laboratory until 1935, he served only as an honorary lecturer after 1927, having resigned in order to gain more time for research and for the large amount of writing he had begun. By the time of the publication of *Problems of Relative Growth* in 1932, Huxley had become widely known as a talented popularizer of biology.

Huxley combined his writing talent with his broad interests in biology in the collaboration with H. G. Wells and his son G. P. Wells to produce *The Science of Life* (1931), an encyclopedic textbook. Other Huxley books during this time included *Essays of a Biologist, Religion without Revelation, Essays in Popular Science, The Stream of Life, What Darwin Really Said, Ants,* and *Bird-Watching and Bird-Behaviour.* Notable were his breadth of interests and his willingness to entertain the controversy created by his adherence to rationalist views, held with the Huxley commitment to intellectual integrity and public responsibility. He tackled evolution and its meaning for human life, religion, and ethics; he also explored the impact for society of the latest biological knowledge. Huxley believed in the self-directed evolution and progress of humanity. He called his view an evolutionary "religious humanism," but Huxley's views nonetheless eschewed the need for belief in a personal God. He looked toward scientific method and knowledge as the new guide and promoted concentration on science teaching and research as an aid to social problems. This theme continued through the 1930s in such books as *If I Were Dictator* and *Scientific Research and Social Needs.*

Other controversial applications of science to human life included Huxley's early commitments to eugenics and birth control. His thinking about population regulation in nature and the ecological problems of over-population fostered a concern for family planning, and he campaigned for the birth control movement. Because of his reputation as a eugenicist, he was invited to join in the writing of a book refuting Hitler's pure race theories; *We Europeans* appeared in 1935. The authors argued that ethnic characteristics are determined mainly by environment and cultural history, not genetics.

Explaining "Natural Selection"

In his scientific researches, Huxley in 1932 began a second phase of his career, devoted to synthetic works. With Gavin de Beer he wrote *Principles of Experimental Embryology* (1934), in which they attempted to survey the various approaches to the subject. They concluded that organized regions, with chemical influences spreading outward, led development. Stimulated by much new work on the theory of natural selection, Huxley also wrote *Evolution: The Modern Synthesis* (1942). His earlier bird researches had led him to revive biologists' interest in sexual selection, and now in the 1930s he gathered supporting arguments for the theory of natural selection from the new mathematical genetics of J. B. S. Haldane, R. A. Fisher, and Sewall Wright. Darwinism had declined in popularity since the late 1800s, with many biologists—especially in the new field of genetics—rejecting the operation of natural selection in nature. Huxley's book played a major role in establishing the "modern synthesis," an updated version of Darwinism incorporating Mendelian genetics and the latest findings in all biological fields. The theory holds that a major cause of evolution is the action of natural selection on small genetic differences within populations, creating adaptation; separation of different populations in a species can lead to new species through various "isolating mechanisms." Exemplifying the value of Huxley's generalist approach to science, the book was his proudest achievement and his most influential.

The final phase of Huxley's career found him involved in even more public activities for science. As secretary of the Zoological Society from 1935 to 1942 he worked to improve the London Zoo. During World War II he lectured frequently on war aims and postwar problems. In 1946 he became the first director-general of the United Nations Educational and Scientific Organization (UNESCO), and his ideas about applying scientific findings to world problems were influential in determining the future of the organization. After retirement he continued until his death in 1975 to write popular works about science, covering such topics as Soviet genetics and politics, current evolutionary theory, cancer, and humanism.

Further Reading

Julian Huxley wrote about his personal and professional life in two books, *Memories* (1970) and *Memories II* (1973). In addition, the famous Huxley family members are depicted in Ronald W. Clark, *The Huxleys* (1968). □

Thomas Henry Huxley

The English biologist Thomas Henry Huxley (1825-1895) is most famous as "Darwin's bulldog," that is, as the man who led the fight for the acceptance of Darwin's theory of evolution.

On May 4, 1825, T. H. Huxley was born at Ealing, the seventh child of George and Rachel Withers Huxley. Perhaps because two brothers-in-law were doctors, Thomas decided to enter the medical profession and in the fashion of the time became an apprentice to a brother-in-law at the age of 15. In 1842 he won a free scholarship to the medical school attached to Chairing Cross Hospital in London and completed the course in 1846.

Huxley then sought a position in the medical service of the Royal Navy and was assigned to the *Rattlesnake,* a surveying ship bound for New Guinea and Australia. The *Rattlesnake* sailed on Dec. 3, 1846, and returned to England on Nov. 9, 1850. During two stopovers in Sydney, Australia, Huxley met Henrietta Heathorn, whom he married in 1855.

A Naturalist in Spite of Himself

Although another man held the post of naturalist on the expedition, Huxley found time amidst his duties as ship's surgeon to study those delicate marine animals that float near the surface of the sea. He worked up reports of his discoveries and sent them to England for publication. Those on the medusae, or jellyfish, were especially important and original. Soon after his return to England, and primarily on the basis of this work on the medusae, Huxley was elected a fellow of the Royal Society in 1851 and was awarded one of its royal medals in 1852.

Though still in his 20s, Huxley was now recognized as an accomplished investigator. But opportunities for a scientific career were rare in England, and from 1851 through 1853 Huxley sought in vain for a teaching position and for funds to cover the costs of publishing his complete researches. Finally, in 1854, he was appointed lecturer on natural history at the Government School of Mines in London. To supplement the meager income from this post, he was a year later named naturalist to the Geological Survey. This position carried with it certain duties with regard to fossils. Huxley accepted both positions with reservations. He "did not care for fossils" and "species work was a burden" to him. "There was," he wrote, "little of the genuine naturalist in me." What he hoped eventually to find was a position in physiology, but this was not to be. He spent all of his active career at the School of Mines and became a genuine naturalist in spite of himself.

In 1859 Huxley's monograph *On the Oceanic Hydrozoa* was published, but his research interests had expanded greatly by then. He ranged all over the field of zoology, but vertebrate morphology and paleontology had become his leading concerns. His most important single paper during this period was his Croonian lecture of 1858, "On the Theory of the Vertebrate Skull." In this work, as in that on the medusae and other marine animals, Huxley demonstrated the value of embryological development as a criterion for determining the significance of the anatomical features of adult animals.

Huxley and Evolution

Until Darwin published his theory of evolution, Huxley doubted that a transmutation of species had taken place. He considered the prior evidence for this idea insufficient, and he was unimpressed by previous attempts to provide a causal mechanism for evolution. Although Huxley was among the privileged few to hear the outlines of Darwin's theory in advance of publication, his active support for the theory seems to begin with the publication in November 1859 of the *Origin of Species*. Here at last was presented a mass of scientific evidence in favor of transmutation and, more importantly, a plausible mechanism as to how it had occurred—namely, by the "natural selection" of favored variations in the struggle for existence. "My reflection," Huxley wrote, "when I first made myself master of the central idea of *Origin* was 'How extremely stupid not to have thought of that!'" Even now he retained certain reservations about Darwin's theory, pointing out that no new species had been known to result from artificial selection and that Darwin had not given an adequate explanation of how variations are produced in the first place. Huxley suggested to Darwin that he had committed himself too exclusively to the notion of insensible gradations in variation; Huxley believed that variation might sometimes take place in larger and more clearly defined steps (what might today be called mutations).

But even with these reservations Huxley thought that Darwin's theory was a "well-founded working hypothesis" and a "powerful instrument of research." By comparison, the old doctrine that each species was an immutable special creation of God seemed "a barren virgin." Foreseeing that Darwin would be subjected to "considerable abuse" for his heresy, Huxley promised his less combative friend that he was "sharpening up my claws and beak in readiness." He was determined that Darwin's theory should receive a fair hearing, and he opened the campaign with a review appearing in the *London Times* the day after Christmas, 1859.

For his part in the open clash which resulted between science and the church, Huxley became a famous public figure. Neither among the public nor among scientists did Huxley ever really settle the question of the origin of species, but his fair and fearless advocacy of Darwin's theory did much to advance the cause.

Scientific Work

From 1860 to 1870 Huxley devoted himself largely to the question of man's origin and place in nature and to the study of paleontology. Along with W. H. Flower he produced apparently irrefutable evidence against Richard Owen's view that the brain of man possessed unique anatomical features. In *Evidences as to Man's Place in Nature* (1863) Huxley emphasized that the differences in the foot, hand, and brain between man and the higher apes were no greater than those between the higher and lower apes.

By 1871 Huxley had published 38 paleontological papers, including several on dinosaur fossils. Largely as a result of these papers and of more purely morphological work suggested by them, the evolutionary relationships between reptiles and the birds (the Sauropsida) and between amphibia and fishes (the Ichthyopsida) became more clearly understood. Huxley's work was also important in establishing the view that the Sauropsida and Mammalia had diverged from some common ancestor. Also during these years Huxley erected a new and largely successful classificatory scheme for the birds.

Administrator, Reformer, and Lecturer

Huxley was Fullerian professor of physiology at the Royal Institution (1856-1858), examiner in physiology and comparative anatomy for the University of London (1856-1863, 1865-1870); and Hunterian professor at the Royal College of Surgeons (1863-1870). Thereafter he devoted an increasing portion of his time to administrative and public duties.

Throughout his career Huxley published review articles and delivered a vast number of public lectures, both on scientific and more general topics. Gradually he acquired the lucid, forceful, and witty style for which he is so justly celebrated. Many consider him the greatest master of English prose of his time. His fervent belief that science should be diffused among the masses found expression in his famous lectures to working men, delivered from 1855 on.

Huxley's views on science, education, and philosophy gained an especially wide audience after he published *Lay Sermons, Addresses and Reviews* (1870). With regard to education in general, he insisted on the evils of one-sided education, whether classical or scientific, and on the need to cultivate the physical and moral as well as the intellectual capacities of children. But his main point was to chastise the English schools and universities for failing to recognize that science formed an essential part of Western culture.

In his philosophical essays Huxley placed himself in the tradition of "active skepticism" represented by René Descartes and David Hume. In essays like his famous "On the Physical Basis of Life" (1869) he insisted that life and even thought were at bottom molecular phenomena. For such ideas he was accused of being a materialist, but Huxley argued that "materialism and spiritualism are opposite poles of the same absurdity." To express his philosophical and theological position, Huxley in 1870 invented the word "agnostic." Because he thus denied that the existence of God could be proven, rejected the biblical account of creation and supported instead Darwin's theory of evolution, and tended toward liberalism or even radicalism in his political views, Huxley's name was anathema in respectable Anglican homes. But by his fair and courageous support of the truth as he saw it, he contributed greatly to an increased toleration toward free thought in Victorian England. In many ways Huxley is a mirror and a measure of his age.

In 1885 Huxley retired from all active duties and gave himself almost entirely to his philosophical and theological essays. He died at Eastbourne on June 29, 1895.

Further Reading

The basic source on Huxley is Leonard Huxley, *Life and Letters of Thomas Henry Huxley* (1900). Although no adequate account of Huxley's scientific work exists, an attempt is made in P.

Chalmers Mitchell, *Thomas Henry Huxley: A Sketch of His Life and Work* (1900). A work focusing on Huxley's role in education is Harold Cyril Bibby, *T. H. Huxley: Scientist, Humanist and Educator* (1959). Ronald W. Clark, *The Huxleys* (1968), is a popular, literate biography of Huxley and his famous grandsons Andrew, Julian, and Aldous Huxley.

Additional Sources

Autobiographies, Oxford Oxfordshire; New York: Oxford University Press, 1983.

Clodd, Edward, *Thomas Henry Huxley,* New York: AMS Press, 1977.

Di Gregorio, Mario A., *T.H. Huxley's place in natural science,* New Haven: Yale University Press, 1984.

Huxley, Thomas Henry, *Life and letters of Thomas Henry Huxley,* New York: AMS Press, 1979, 1900.

Huxley, Thomas Henry, *The major prose of Thomas Henry Huxley,* Athens: University of Georgia Press, 1997.

Irvine, William, *Apes, angels & Victorians: the story of Darwin, Huxley, and evolution,* Lanham, MD: University Press of America, 1983, 1955.

Jensen, J. Vernon (John Vernon), *Thomas Henry Huxley: communicating for science,* Newark: University of Delaware Press; London: Associated University Presses, 1991.

Paradis, James G., *T. H. Huxley: man's place in nature,* Lincoln: University of Nebraska Press, 1978.

Peterson, Houston, *Huxley, prophet of science,* New York: AMS Press, 1977. □

Christiaan Huygens

The Dutch mathematician, astronomer, and physicist Christiaan Huygens (1629-1695) was the first to recognize the rings of Saturn, made pioneering studies of the dynamics of moving bodies, and was the leading advocate of the wave, or pulse, theory of light.

Born in The Hague on April 14, 1629, Christiaan Huygens was the second son of Constantin Huygens, a brilliant diplomat and Renaissance scholar. Privately tutored at home until he was 16, Christiaan early showed signs of intellectual brilliance, devoting much time to drawing and making mechanical models and devices as well as demonstrating exceptional skill in geometry. He studied law and mathematics at the University of Leiden and after 2 years moved on to Breda, where he completed his studies.

Telescopes and Observations of Saturn

Huygens's first published work, on the quadrature of various mathematical curves, appeared in 1651. In addition, as a result of his study of collision phenomena between hard, elastic bodies, by 1656 he had demonstrated the incorrectness of René Descartes's laws of motion and impact, although he did not announce his conclusions until some 12 years later, and his complete study of such phenomena was published posthumously. The best-known of his early researches, however, were his efforts to improve telescope lenses and his observations of the planet Saturn.

In 1655 Huygens spent several months in Paris. He attended the informal gatherings of the so-called Montmort Academy, an important precursor of the French Academy of Sciences and, to at least some of its members, reported on his discovery of Titan, the first of Saturn's moons to be observed. He had initially been attracted to Saturn by its apparently anomalous shape, described by Galileo as "three spheres which almost touch each other, which never change their relative positions, and are arranged in a row along the zodiac so that the middle sphere is three times as large as the others." Intrigued by this peculiar shape, Huygens realized that its resolution would depend on constructing improved telescopes, less subject to various aberrations and more capable of producing detailed images.

Upon returning from Paris, Huygens devoted full time to his efforts to construct such improved eyepieces and lens systems, and although he was unsuccessful in his attempts to produce lenses with hyperbolic or elliptical surfaces, he and his elder brother did succeed in figuring and polishing lenses with an accuracy never before attained. With telescopes utilizing these improved components, great progress was made toward solving the problem of Saturn's appearance. What had originally appeared as a "trispherical" form now appeared as simply some sort of band passing across the middle of the planet, and, early in 1656, utilizing a still better telescope, Huygens was able to clearly distinguish a thin ring surrounding the planet at a slight angle to the ecliptic. In 1659 he published his complete study of Saturn in a work entitled *Systema Saturnium.*

Huygens's interest in improving telescopes continued throughout his life. For measuring the angular diameter of planets, he invented a type of micrometer consisting of a series of small brass plates of varying widths which could be slipped across the focal plane of the telescope. Recognizing that the eyepiece could be made to partially correct for certain defects in the objective lens of a telescope, he designed a special eyepiece which still bears his name, and his improved methods of grinding lenses allowed him to construct longer telescopes with greater powers of magnification. These "aerial telescopes" exceeded 30 feet in length and dispensed entirely with the usual tubular enclosure, utilizing instead two shorter tubes, one for the eyepiece and one for the objective lens. Huygens never was, however, a regular astronomical observer; with the exception of his observations of Saturn, his contributions to astronomy exhibited a strong practical bias.

Pendulum Clock

This practical aspect of Huygens's work is also manifested in the great time and energy he devoted to the perfection of the pendulum clock. Although he had been working on it for some years, Huygens first described his successful application of the pendulum to the escapement mechanism of the standard mechanical clock in 1658.

Sometime after he had produced the first pendulum clock, Huygens became interested in its obvious application to the problem of determining longitude at sea. One of the simplest solutions to this important navigation problem involved the construction of an extremely accurate time keeping device with which local time could be compared with a standard time at, say, Paris or London. Although the pendulum clock was the most accurate such device then available, its motion was easily disturbed by the movement of the ship at sea. In an effort to overcome this difficulty, Huygens invented a pendulum whose period of oscillation was independent of the amplitude of its swing (for regular pendulums this isochronous property exists only for very small amplitudes). Although the discovery of a pendulum whose path was a cycloidal arc provided such an isochronous device, it did not solve the problem of constructing a marine clock or chronometer whose accuracy would not be affected by the pitching of a ship.

Paris and the Study of Dynamics

In 1660 Huygens returned to Paris, where he again attended meetings of the Montmort Academy. By 1661 he had discovered a basic principle of mechanics which allowed him to solve with ease certain types of problems which English mathematicians at the time found especially difficult. Now fundamental, this principle stated that the center of gravity of a body or system of bodies, acting solely under the influence of gravity, cannot rise above the level from which it initially falls. In recognition of the significance of this and other aspects of his work, he was in 1663 elected a fellow of the Royal Society.

The French Academy of Sciences was officially formed in 1666, and at the invitation of Louis XIV's chief minister, Huygens returned to Paris and a position as a leader and foundation member of the new academy. He was one of the chief influences in guiding the early affairs of the academy and, profiting from his contacts with English men of science, he emphasized the need for careful observation and experiment. With the exception of two trips to The Hague because of illness, he remained in Paris until 1681.

In the years after his return to Paris, Huygens's interests turned increasingly from astronomy to terrestrial mechanics, and as the result of his work in this field, he has rightfully been regarded as one of the founders of the science of dynamics. His earliest studies in this area dealt with impact phenomena, and although he had completed this work as early as 1656, his results were reported only in 1669, when he presented to the Royal Society a clear and concise statement of the laws governing the collision of elastic bodies. Although of great significance because of their statement of the conservation of mechanical energy in the collision of perfectly elastic bodies and because of their refutation of the incorrect laws of impact earlier presented by Descartes, Huygens's results were presented without proof, and their complete demonstration was published posthumously in 1703.

One of the great scientific treatises of the 17th century, Huygens's masterpiece, *Horologium oscillatorium,* appeared in 1673. More than just a summary of his researches on the pendulum clock, it in fact was a general work on dynamics containing numerous original discoveries. In it he demonstrated the isochronous nature of a body moving freely under the influence of gravity along a cycloidal path. He showed how to calculate the period of oscillation of a simple pendulum. He provided a definitive solution to the problem of compound and physical pendulums, demonstrating how to calculate the "center of oscillation" and the length of an equivalent simple pendulum. And, in an appendix, he presented the basic laws of centrifugal force governing bodies moving with uniform circular motion. The significance of this monumental work was immediately recognized.

Wave, or Pulse, Theory of Light

Perhaps the best-known of Huygens's varied pursuits is his work on physical optics and his development of the wave, or, more accurately, pulse, theory of light. First presented before the Academy of Sciences in 1678, his *Traité de la lumière* (*Treatise on Light*) was, characteristically, not published until 1690. The theory of light put forth in it, however, was the direct result of his study of impact phenomena and represented the union of the physical and mathematical aspects of the study of optics.

Light, Huygens suggested, consisted of the longitudinal vibrations of an all-pervasive ether composed of small, hard, elastic particles, each of which transmitted the impulses it received to all contiguous particles without itself suffering any permanent displacement. The propagation of light was thus reduced to the transmission of motion. Each particle of a luminous body, such as a candle flame, sent out its own set of concentric, spherical wavelets. Formulating what is today known as Huygens's principle, he conceived of each ether particle itself as also being the source of a new wavelet, which was likewise propagated to the adjacent particles. Within the boundaries where these individual wavelets reinforced each other and formed a coherent wave envelope, light was propagated. Outside the boundaries, there being no reinforcement of the wavelets, was shadow and no propagation of light.

Return to Holland and Later Life

In 1681 Huygens returned to The Hague. Although ill health was the immediate cause, additional personal and religious pressures combined to make permanent his return to his native country. He had never married, and his later years were characterized by considerable solitariness; in his correspondence he often lamented the absence of anyone with whom to discuss scientific topics. He did, however, maintain his extensive correspondence, and although his mathematical and abstract studies suffered a marked diminution after 1680, the general pattern of his life remained little changed until his death on July 8, 1695.

Unlike many men of science in the 17th century, Huygens never occupied himself to any significant extent with either philosophy or theology. He devoted his efforts entirely to the pursuit of science, and his contributions to astronomy, dynamics, and optics were of fundamental importance.

Further Reading

Huygens's correspondence and collected works were published in Dutch in a 22-volume edition under the auspices of the Dutch Academy of Sciences (1888-1950). His *Treatise on Light* was translated into English by Silvanus P. Thompson (1912). Huygens's life and the historical significance of his work are covered in Arthur Ernest Bell, *Christian Huygens and the Development of Science in the Seventeenth Century* (1947). □

Joris Karl Huysmans

The novelist Joris Karl Huysmans (1848-1907) was a leading French exponent of the decadent movement. His works, though intensely personal, present artistic and intellectual life in late-19th-century France.

Charles Marie Georges Huysmans, who wrote under the pseudonym of Joris Karl Huysmans was born in Paris on Feb. 5, 1848, the only son of a French mother and a Dutch father. In 1866 he entered the civil service and was employed by the Ministry of the Interior until his retirement in 1898.

Huysmans' earliest works reflect the influence of contemporary French masters. His first publication, *Le Drageoir à épices* (1874), was a collection of Baudelairian prose poems. He next wrote a series of naturalistic novels that focused on the sordidness and futility of everyday life:

Marthe (1876), *Les Soeurs Vatard* (1879), and *En ménage* (1881). These works were early indexes of the distinctive style and the talent for precise, detailed description which were to characterize all of Huysmans' writing. While he was a member of Émile Zola's Médan group of naturalist writers, his wartime anecdote *Sac au dos* was published in the collective volume *Les Soirées de Médan* (1880).

Huysmans remained a disciple of Zola for only a short time and soon asserted his independence from codified naturalism. His subsequent novels formed a loosely linked series in which the author, under various guises, traced his quest for happiness.

The first of this group was *A vau-l'eau* (1882; *Down Stream*), a pessimistic account of the empty existence of an obscure functionary. It was followed in 1884 by *À rebours* (*Against the Grain*), the most characteristic and best known of Huysmans' novels. The jaded protagonist, Des Esseintes, quickly became the prototype for the finde-siècle decadent hero. Distancing himself still further from Zola's doctrine, Huysmans wrote *En rade* (1887), a curious blend of naturalistic descriptions and surrealistic dream sequences, and *Là-bas* (1891; *Down There*), a study of medieval and modern satanism.

Huysmans' last novels are primarily an intellectual and spiritual self-portrait: *En route* (1895) recounts his return to Catholicism; *La Cathédrale* (1898) is an erudite study of the Chartres Cathedral; and *L'Oblat* (1903) depicts the author's life as a lay monk in a Benedictine monastery from 1899 to 1901.

Huysmans also ranks as one of the foremost art critics of his generation and was one of the first to appreciate the impressionists in *L'Art moderne* (1883) and in *Certains* (1889). Huysmans died of cancer on May 12, 1907, in Paris.

Further Reading

Robert Baldick, *The Life of J. -K. Huysmans* (1955), is the most comprehensive work on Huysmans in English and the first fully documented biography of the novelist. It is a detailed and authoritative account of Huysmans' life and works and of the milieus in which he lived. For background see A. E. Carter, *The Idea of Decadence in French Literature, 1830-1900* (1958), and George R. Ridge, *The Hero in French Decadent Literature* (1961).

Additional Sources

Audoin, Philippe., *J.K. Huysmans,* Paris: Editions H. Veyrier, 1985.

Banks, Brian R., *The image of Huysmans,* New York, N.Y.: AMS Press, 1990.

Vircondelet, Alain, *Joris-Karl Huysmans,* Paris: Plon, 1990. □

Douglas Hyde

The scholar and writer Douglas Hyde (1860-1949) led the Irish language revival and was president of Ireland from 1938 to 1945.

D ouglas Hyde was born at Frenchpark, County Roscommon, on Jan. 17, 1860, the son of the local Protestant rector. As a child, he learned the Irish language from surviving native speakers in the area and developed a love and enthusiasm for Irish which were to characterize his later life. He graduated from Trinity College in 1884 and soon concentrated his attention on Irish literary studies. During his career he published a number of scholarly works, notably *The Love Songs of Connacht* (1893) and *A Literary History of Ireland* (1899).

In 1893 Hyde played the leading role in the foundation of the Gaelic League and then served as its president until 1915. The purpose of the league was to revive the disappearing culture and traditions, and its work stimulated considerable popular enthusiasm for the study of the Irish language. At the turn of the century Hyde led a successful fight to prevent the exclusion of Irish from the curriculum of secondary schools. In 1908 he was appointed professor of modern Irish in the newly established National University of Ireland and helped to make Irish a compulsory subject for matriculation at the university.

Hyde insisted that the Gaelic League must remain nonpolitical so that it might have the widest possible appeal. This condition was formally observed, but the league's efforts to revive Irish inevitably encouraged political separatism, and its strongest supporters were nationalists, who saw restoration of the native language as a means of helping to establish and maintain a distinct national identity.

Hyde successfully resisted attempts to turn the league to political ends until 1915, when the annual convention passed a resolution which added the objective of national freedom to the league's statement of aims. Hyde at once resigned the presidency and remained aloof from the struggle for Irish independence which began in 1916. He served briefly as a senator in the Irish state which was established in 1922, and in 1938 he was elected unopposed as the first president of Ireland under the new Constitution of 1937. He died 4 years after, completing his term of office, on July 12, 1949.

Hyde's work, more than that of any other individual, preserved the Irish language from extinction and began its revival, a revival which became a matter of state policy after 1922. P. H. Pearse, one of the leaders of the Easter Rising of 1916, called the Gaelic League "the most revolutionary force that has ever come into Ireland" and observed that the Irish Revolution really began with its foundation.

Further Reading

The most detailed study of Hyde is Diarmuid Coffey, *Douglas Hyde* (1938). Good brief studies of Hyde are in Conor Cruise O'Brien, ed., *The Shaping of Modern Ireland* (1960), and Kevin B. Nowlan, ed., *Making of 1916* (1969).

Additional Sources

Daly, Dominic, *The young Douglas Hyde; the dawn of the Irish revolution and renaissance, 1874-189,* Totowa, N.J., Rowman and Littlefield 1974.

Dunleavy, Gareth W., *Douglas Hyde,* Lewisburg Pa., Bucknell University Press 1974.

Dunleavy, Janet Egleson, *Douglas Hyde: a maker of modern Ireland,* Berkeley: University of California Press, 1991. □

Libbie Henrietta Hyman

Libbie Henrietta Hyman (1888-1969) was a specialist in invertebrate and vertebrate zoology. She produced a six-volume set of reference books titled *The Invertebrates.*

Libbie Henrietta Hyman earned an international reputation for her monumental six-volume work on the classification of invertebrates . Although she considered her invertebrate treatise essentially a "compilation" of the literature, others have called it a remarkable synthetic work. Compiled by one independent woman with enormous knowledge of the field and a great facility for translating European languages, it represents a textbook of the invertebrate animal kingdom that whole academies might have attempted. Hyman's treatise consists of judicious analysis and integration of previously scattered information; it has had a lasting influence on scientific thinking about a number of invertebrate animal groups, and the only works that can be compared with hers are of composite authorship. Hyman also influenced the teaching of zoology classes nationwide with the publication of her laboratory manuals.

Hyman was born on December 6, 1888 in Des Moines, Iowa, the third of four children and the only daughter. Her parents were Jewish immigrants; her father, Joseph Hyman, came to the United States from Konin, Poland, at age fourteen, and her mother, Sabina Neumann, was born in Stettin, Germany. Hyman's childhood and youth were spent in Fort Dodge, Iowa, where her father kept an unsuccessful clothing store. Her home life was strict and without affection. Her father, twenty years older than her mother, worried about his declining fortunes and ignored his children, although he did have scholarly inclinations, keeping volumes of Dickens and Shakespeare, which Hyman read. In her brief autobiography, Hyman remembered her mother as being "thoroughly infiltrated with the European worship of the male sex." Her mother required her to do "endless housework" caring for her brothers, whom Hyman believed were "brought up in idleness and irresponsibility."

From an early age, Hyman demonstrated an interest in nature. She learned the scientific names of flowers from a high-school botany book that belonged to her brothers, and she made collections of butterflies and moths. She remembered being initially puzzled by classification, until she suddenly realized that the flowers of a common cheeseweed were the same as the flowers of a hollyhock. In 1905, she graduated from Fort Dodge High School. She was class valedictorian but had failed to attract the attention of her science teachers. Although she passed the state examination for teaching in the country schools, she was too young to be appointed to a teaching position and so re-

turned to high school during 1906 for advanced studies in science and German. When these classes ended, she took a factory job, pasting labels on oatmeal cereal boxes.

On her way home from the factory one fall afternoon, she met Mary Crawford, a Radcliffe graduate and high school language teacher who was "shocked" to learn what she was doing. Crawford arranged for Hyman to attend the University of Chicago with scholarship money that was available to top students. "To the best of my recollection," Hyman said, "it had never occurred to me to go to college. I scarcely understood the purpose of college." At the university, she began a course in botany, but was discouraged by anti-semitic harassment from a laboratory assistant. Instead, she majored in zoology and graduated in 1910 with a B.S. degree. Professor Charles Manning Child, from whom she had taken a course during her senior year, encouraged her to enter the graduate program. As Child's graduate assistant, she directed laboratory work for courses in elementary zoology and comparative vertebrate anatomy.

Hyman was not free from family responsibilities, however. Her father had died in 1907; her possessive mother moved to Chicago with her brothers, and Hyman was again required to keep house for them and endure their continuing disapproval of her career.

Hyman received her Ph.D. in 1915, when she was twenty-six years old, for a dissertation entitled, "An Analysis of the Process of Regeneration in Certain Microdrilous Oligochaetes." She then accepted an appointment as Child's research assistant, a position she held until he neared retirement. Her work in Child's laboratory consisted of conducting physiological experiments on lower invertebrates, including hydras and flatworms. It was during this time that Hyman realized that many of these common animals were misidentified because they had not been carefully studied taxonomically. She became a taxonomic specialist in these invertebrate groups. Hyman's interest in invertebrates had a strong aesthetic component; she confessed a deep fondness for "the soft delicate ones, the jellyfishes and corals and the beautiful microscopic organisms."

During her time as a laboratory assistant, helping Child direct his classes, Hyman had felt that a better student guide book was needed, and now she wrote one. *A Laboratory Manual for Elementary Zoology* was published in 1919 by the University of Chicago Press. The first printing quickly sold out, and in 1929 she wrote an expanded edition. She also published, in 1922, *A Laboratory Manual for Comparative Vertebrate Anatomy,* which also enjoyed brisk sales. The second edition of this manual was published in 1942 as *Comparative Vertebrate Anatomy.* She was never excited about vertebrates, however, and she refused to consider a third edition. (The third edition was published in 1979, the work of eleven contributors.)

By 1930, Hyman had realized she could live on the royalties from the sale of her laboratory manuals, and she resigned her position in the zoology department, leaving Chicago in 1931 to tour western Europe for fifteen months. She never again worked for wages. When she returned from her travels, she settled near the American Museum of Natural History in New York City, where she lived modestly, close to the museum's "magnificent" library, determined to devote all of her time to writing a treatise on the invertebrates. In 1937, she was made an honorary research associate of the museum. Although unsalaried, she was given an office, where she placed food and water at the window for pigeons. The first volume of *The Invertebrates* appeared in 1940.

Hyman had always wanted to live in the country and indulge her interest in gardening. In 1941, she bought a house in Millwood, Westchester County, about thirty-five miles north of Times Square. She commuted to her work at the museum until 1952, when she sold the house and returned to New York City. Although she said that gardening and commuting had taken time away from her treatise, during those years of residence in the country she completed the second and third volumes, which were both published in 1951. At the museum, Hyman spent most of her time in the library. She read, made notes, digested information, composed in her head, and typed the first and only draft of her books on her manual typewriter. She also taught herself drawing, and her books contain her own illustrations. She apparently never had a secretary or an assistant. The fourth volume of the treatise was published in 1955, and the fifth in 1959.

Hyman loved music and regularly attended performances of the Metropolitan Opera and the New York Philharmonic. Her physical appearance had been altered by a bungled sinus operation in 1916, and to many she presented a brusque and formidable exterior, but she was not a recluse. She carried on a lively correspondence with scientists who sent her specimens or consulted her. She encouraged young scientists and contributed to charitable causes. She acquired a small, but valuable art collection, and made summer collecting trips to marine laboratories.

Hyman's recognition began with publication of her first invertebrate volume. The University of Chicago awarded her an honorary doctor of science degree in 1941, and honorary degrees followed from other colleges. She received the Daniel Giraud Elliot Medal of the National Academy of Sciences in 1951, the Gold Medal of the Linnaean Society of London in 1960, and the American Museum presented her with its Gold Medal for Distinguished Achievement in Science in April 1969, a few months before she died.

Hyman served as president of the Society of Systematic Zoology in 1959, and she edited the society's journal, *Systematic Zoology,* from 1959–1963. She was vice president of the American Society of Zoologists in 1953 and a member of the National Academy of Sciences, as well as Phi Beta Kappa, Sigma Xi, the American Microscopical Society, the American Society of Naturalists, the Marine Biological Laboratory of Woods Hole, the American Society of Limnology and Oceanography, and the Society of Protozoologists. In addition to her books, she published 135 scientific papers between 1916 and 1966. Her early papers represent contributions to Child's physiological projects; her taxonomic and anatomical papers began to appear in 1925.

In the last decade o Hyman's life, her health was poor and her work on invertebrates had become more difficult. In 1967, at the age of seventy-eight and suffering from Parkinson's disease, she published the sixth volume of her treatise. She announced in its preface that this would be the last volume of *The Invertebrates* from her hands, although McGraw-Hill intended to continue the series with different authors. "I now retire from the field," Hyman wrote, "satisfied that I have accomplished my original purpose—to stimulate the study of invertebrates." She died on August 3, 1969.

Further Reading

Hyman, Libbie H., and G. Evelyn Hutchinson, "Libbie Henrietta Hyman: December 6, 1888-August 3, 1969," in *Biographical Memoirs,* National Academy of Sciences, Volume 60, 1991, pp. 103–14.

Rossiter, Margaret W., *Women Scientists in America: Struggles and Strategies to 1940,* Johns Hopkins University Press, 1982, pp. 210–11, 294, 373, 374.

Sicherman, Barbara, and Carol Hurd Green, editors, *Notable American Women: The Modern Period,* Belknap Press of Harvard University Press, 1980, pp. 365–67.

Stunkard, Horace W., "In Memoriam: Libbie Henrietta Hyman, 1888–1969," in *Biology of the Turbellaria,* Riser, Nathan W., and M. Patricia Morse, editors, McGraw-Hill, 1974, pp. 9–13.

Winston, Judith E., "Great Invertebrate Zoologists: Libbie Henrietta Hyman (1888–1969)," in *American Society of Zoologists, Division of Invertebrate Zoologists Newsletter,* fall, 1991. ☐

Hypatia of Alexandria

Hypatia of Alexandira (370–415) was the only famous woman scholar in ancient Egypt. She became a teacher and wrote many books on mathematics along with criticisms of philosophical and mathematical concepts.

Although all of her work has been lost or destroyed, history regards Hypatia of Alexandria as the only famous female scholar of ancient times. She was the first woman ever known to teach and analyze highly advanced mathematics.

Hypatia probably studied mathematics and astronomy under the tutelage of her father, Theon of Alexandria (fl. c. 4th century A.D.), the last recorded member of the city's great Museum. The Museum of Alexandria in Egypt was a prominent cultural and intellectual center which resembled a large modern university. It consisted of several schools, public auditoriums, and the famous library, once one of the most comprehensive repositories of books in antiquity. Although the Museum was in Egypt, its dominant culture and a considerable portion of its population were Greek. At one time, scholars came from across the Roman Empire and even from as far away as Ethiopia and India to hear lectures on the latest scientific and philosophical ideas and to study in the city's library.

Hypatia became a teacher at Alexandria's Neoplatonic School and was appointed its director in 400 A.D. Her lively lectures won her popular esteem, and she wrote a number of books on mathematics and other subjects, as well as criticisms of philosophical and mathematical concepts which her contemporaries regarded as perceptive. She corresponded with many distinguished scholars, some of whose letters to her survive and testify to their estimation of her abilities.

Although written records are sketchy, it appears that Hypatia invented or helped to invent mechanical devices such as the plane astrolabe, an instrument used by Greek astronomers to determine the position of the sun and stars. This device was probably developed with Synesius of Cyrene (c. 370-413 A.D.), a scholar who had attended Hypatia's classes. A letter to Hypatia from Synesius, who later became a Christian and the bishop of Ptolomais, exists

in which he asks her advice on the construction of the device. Synesius also worked with Hypatia on a graduated brass hydrometer, which measured the specific gravity of liquids, and a hydroscope, which was used to observe objects submerged in water.

At the age of 45 Hypatia was brutally murdered by a mob. The reasons behind her violent death are in dispute, though her personal independence and pagan beliefs seem to have created hostility among Alexandria's Christian community. Another contributing factor appears to have been her alliance with Orestes, the pagan governor of the city, and a political adversary of Cyril (c. 375-444 A.D.), the Alexandrian bishop. After Hypatia was killed, her works

perished, along with many other records of ancient learning, when mobs burned the library, destroying the entire collection. □

Lido (Lee) Anthony Iacocca

After a 32-year career with Ford Motor Company, including eight years as president, Lido (Lee) Anthony Iacocca (born 1924) engineered one of business history's greatest comebacks at Chrysler Corporation. His success, coupled with appearances in television commercials and his best-selling book, made him one of the nation's best-known and most admired businessmen.

Lido (Lee) Anthony Iacocca was born October 15, 1924 in Allentown, Pennsylvania, the son of Italian immigrants Nicola and Antionette. Iacocca grew up in comfortable surroundings learning the nuts and bolts of business from his father. Nicola was an entrepreneur who taught his son about the responsibilities of borrowing money and the need for a hard-driving vision in order to build a thriving business. Nicola Iacocca worked as a cobbler, hot-dog restaurant and theater owner. He also ran one of the first car rental agencies in the country and passed on his love of the automobile to his son. Iacocca was deferred during World War II because of having had rheumatic fever as a child. He earned his BS and MS degrees in engineering from Lehigh University and Princeton University, respectively. Even as a teenager, Iacocca decided that he was going to be an auto company executive and focused his studies in that direction. His degrees are in industrial engineering. He secured a coveted engineering trainee job at Ford in 1946, but deferred his start until he completed his masters degree at Princeton.

Joining Ford Motor Company as an engineering trainee in 1946, Iacocca soon entered the fast lane of sales. With the force of a muscle car and the maneuverability of a racing vehicle, in 1960, at age 36, he sped into the vice-presidency and general managership of the company's most important unit, Ford Division. In 1964, with others on his staff, he launched the Mustang, which, thanks to brilliant styling and marketing, introduced a new wave of sports cars, set a first-year sales record for any model, gave its name to a generation, and landed its creator's picture on the covers of *TIME* and *Newsweek* simultaneously.

In 1960 Iacocca was named Ford's vice-president, car and truck group; in 1967, executive vice-president; and in 1970, president. Pocketing an annual salary and bonus of $977,000, the flamboyant executive also earned a reputation as one of the greatest salesmen in U.S. history. Of Iacocca, it has been said that he was always selling, whether products, ideas—or himself.

From Ford to Chrysler

Iacocca was discharged from Ford Motor Company in June 1978 by Chairman Henry Ford II for reasons Ford never disclosed, but obviously relating to the chairman's distaste for having Iacocca succeed him. Though bitter at being dismissed from Ford, Iacocca was not out of the car business for long. Five months after his firing, Iacocca was named president of Chrysler (becoming chairman in 1979) and began transforming the number three automaker from corporate history's number one deficits manufacturer into a highly-profitable enterprise.

How was Chrysler turned around? By downsizing expenses to a much lower break-even point, by winning approval of $1.5 billion in federal loan guarantees, by selling off profitable units such as the tank division, and by intro-

Folk Hero

By the mid-1980s Iacocca had achieved folk-hero status. Typically, the *Saturday Evening Post* described him as "the sex symbol of America"; the *Reader's Digest* as "the living embodiment of the American dream"; and *TIME* as "a corporate capitalist with populist appeal, an 'eminence terrible' admired by working class and ruling class alike." Talk of Iacocca-for-President became increasingly widespread, and a 1985 poll of 1988 presidential preferences showed that the cocky industrialist trailed Vice-President George Bush by only three percentage points (41 to 38 points).

The late 1980s and early nineties were not as kind to Iacocca. His public image, like Chrysler's earnings, began to fall off. At a time when the American people, in the grip of a recession, renounced the huge paychecks of executives whose companies were ailing, Iacocca who had once achieved a publicity coup when, for a time, he only accepted one dollar a year from Chrysler, was paid a 1987 salary of $18 million. In addition, Iacocca, lambasted Japanese trading practices, blaming them for the ills that American car manufacturers had suffered. Critics cited that the American public believed that Japanese cars were superior and instead of criticizing the Japanese, Iacocca's car company should have been emulating them. At the end of 1992, Iacocca was forced to retire after he had bettered the position of the company for a merger or takeover. He remained a consultant to Chrysler (with a $500,000 a year salary and use of the company jet) until the end of 1994.

In 1995, Iacocca announced that he was suing Chrysler, claiming that it unlawfully blocked him from exercising $42 million in share options that he had earned while he was the chairman. Chrysler claimed that Iacocca's role as an adviser to Kirk Kerkorian, the investor who wanted to purchase the company, violated the share option plan agreement. Although Kerkorian's bid failed to materialize because he was unable to raise the financing, Chrysler agreed to pay Iacocca $21 million to settle the lawsuit. Iacocca continued to work as Kerkorian's consultant.

Iacocca and Mary McCleary were married in 1956 and had two daughters, Kathi and Lia. Mary died of diabetes in 1983, and in her memory, Iacocca donated his book earnings to diabetes research. In 1986 Iacocca married Peggy Johnson (born 1950), an advertising executive from whom he was divorced in 1996.

Further Reading

The primary source of information about Iacocca is the executive's best-selling *Iacocca: An Autobiography* (1984), although critics say it was written mostly to stroke Iacocca's ego and to vilify Henry Ford II. David Abodaher's *Iacocca* (1982), written by an employee of Chrysler's advertising agency, ceaselessly praises the automaker while providing interesting anecdotal material. Perhaps the best of the numerous magazine and newspaper stories on the magnate are *New Republic*'s "What's So Great About Lee Iacocca?," July 16 and 23, 1984; *Newsweek*'s "Behind the Wheels," October 8, 1984; the *New York Times*'s "The Importance of Being Iacocca," December 23, 1984; and *Time*'s "A Spunky Tycoon Turned Superstar," April 1, 1985. *Detroit News,*

ducing timely products. In addition, Chrysler welcomed, for the first time in U.S. corporate history, a union president to a board of directors. In 1984 the company posted profits of $2.4 billion (higher than in the previous 60 years combined), and in 1985 it bought Gulfstream Aerospace Corporation for $637 million and E. F. Hutton Credit Corporation for $125 million.

In the early 1980's Chrysler issued the K-car and what would later become its meal ticket—the minivan. Just as the Mustang re-established the sports car for Ford, the minivan would be loved by the young family in need of room and efficiency and revitalize Chrysler. In 1983, Chrysler paid the government back its loans and Iacocca became a star, a symbol of success and the achievement of the American Dream.

Along with spearheading Chrysler's resurgence, Iacocca assumed various civic responsibilities, most notably the chairmanship of the President's Statue of Liberty-Ellis Island Centennial Commission, set up to raise funds for and to oversee restoration of the two monuments. If Iacocca attained prominence through business stewardship, television commercials, and identification with the Statue of Liberty, he gained much additional exposure through his 1984 autobiography. *Iacocca: An Autobiography,* the best-selling nonfiction hard cover book in history, had two million copies in print by July 1985. Most readers seemed to accept the volume as near-gospel, while others ventured that Iacocca's achievements had lost nothing in the telling and that the author was overly vindictive toward Henry Ford II.

''Retirement has been a rough ride for Iacocca,'' June 1996; *Automotive News,* June 1996. □

Carlos Ibáñez del Campo

Carlos Ibáñez del Campo (1877-1960) was a Chilean general and twice president of the republic. A self-styled populist leader, he attempted to secure for the middle and lower classes a greater voice in the nation's economic and political life.

Carlos Ibáñez was born in Linares on Nov. 3, 1877. Entering the military school in Santiago, he graduated and received his commission. In 1903 he was appointed military adviser to the army of El Salvador, and after his return to Chile he held the directorship of the cavalry school and police academy. He rose to political prominence as a result of the military coup in September 1924 and was one of the leaders of the second coup of January 1925, which restored Arturo Alessandri, the legal president, to power. Ibáñez was rewarded by being named minister of war. He emerged as a spokesman for reformist-minded and politically ambitious officers and steadily increased his influence in the government.

Popular Dictatorship

Alessandri resigned after a clash with Ibáñez in October 1925, and the new president, Emiliano Figueroa Larrain, was forced to keep him in the Cabinet. Figueroa, a weak leader, was eventually eased out in April 1927, and Ibáñez was now the most powerful leader of the nation. Elections were called, and he was almost unanimously elected president. Ibáñez governed dictatorially, exiling his opponents and restricting citizens' rights. His dictatorship was popular, however, as Chile was enjoying prosperity, foreign loans were available, and the government instituted public works projects to keep employment at a high level.

Ibáñez's popularity declined when the effects of the world depression were felt in Chile, and in July 1931, after popular demonstrations broke out, he was forced to flee. His subsequent career centered on rehabilitating his image and attempting to regain power. He ran for the presidency in 1938 as the standard-bearer of the Nazis and in 1942 as the candidate of the conservatives and liberals. In 1949 he was elected to the Senate.

An ''Aging Lion''

In 1952 Ibáñez organized his party, the Agrarian-Labor, and appealed to the electorate as an independent, not tied to the vested interests, one who could resolve the social and economic problems of the country. The traditional parties, split and discredited, accused Ibáñez of wishing to install a *peronista* -style dictatorship in Chile. But the voters expressed their desire for strong government and gave a plurality of votes to Ibáñez. Once in office, he found it difficult to govern. Congress was in the hands of his ene-

mies, and he was old and unable to offer effective leadership. He served out his term increasingly powerless and in 1958 turned over the presidency to Jorge Allessandri, his elected successor. Ibáñez died on April 28, 1960.

Further Reading

There is no detailed study of Ibáñez's career in English. Federico G. Gil deals with Chile during the Ibáñez era in *The Political System of Chile* (1966). John Reese Stevenson covers the Ibáñez dictatorship in *The Chilean Popular Front* (1942), and Fredrick B. Pike ably discusses both administrations in *Chile and the United States, 1880-1962* (1963). □

Dolores Ibárruri Gómez

Dolores Ibárruri Gómez (1895-1989) became famous during the Spanish Civil War (1936-1939) as an eloquent propagandist for the Republican (Loyalist) cause. Ibárruri was known to most of the world as ''La Pasionaria'' (the Passion Flower), a nom de plume which became identified with her indomitable will and gift as a fiery orator.

Born in the Basque mining village of Gallarta, Ibárruri was the eighth of eleven children. From an early age she seems to have been affected by the abominable working conditions that her father and other miners were forced to endure in order to earn a meager income. Perhaps equally influential in her formative years was her strict religious upbringing. As a youth she impressed others by her devoutness, a trait that later molded her attitude towards politics. Up to the time she left home, however, there was no indication that Ibárruri would one day become a flaming revolutionary. Yet this is precisely what happened. At the age of 20 she married an Asturian miner, Julián Ruiz, who introduced her to the world of left-wing ideas. Not long afterwards she renounced Catholicism, deciding to join the Spanish Communist Party (Partido Comunista de España, PCE) shortly before it was formally established in 1921.

After becoming involved in politics, Ibárruri was at first obliged to divide her time between raising a family and campaigning for a Marxist revolution. But her home life eventually proved to be so miserable—four of her six children died in infancy and she was unhappily married—that she decided to devote herself completely to a political career. During the Primo de Rivera dictatorship (1923-1930) she distinguished herself as a journalist and dedicated party activist. Then, following the proclamation of the Spanish Second Republic (1931), she moved to Madrid where her writing talents were put to use on the editorial board of *Mundo Obrero,* the principal mouthpiece of the PCE. As her reputation as a communist agitator grew, Ibárruri increasingly fell under government suspicion. As a result, she was arrested several times between 1931 and 1934.

Within the communist movement, though, Ibárruri's self-sacrificing and tireless agitation propelled her rise

through the party's ranks. In 1930 she was appointed to the PCE's Central Committee, and two years later she was elected to the politburo as Secretary of Women's Affairs. The next year she was sent to Moscow as the PCE's fraternal delegate to the Thirteenth Plenary of the Executive Committee of the Communist International (Comintern).

During the period when the right ruled the republic (1933-1935), Ibárruri belonged to the current within the PCE that sought better cooperation between the communists and other left-wing groups. To this end, she helped to organize the Spanish branch of the nonsectarian World Committee of Women Against War and Fascism in 1933, and she campaigned in behalf of the thousands of workers and their families who had fallen victim to the fierce government repression that followed the Asturian rising of October 1934.

Ibárruri's efforts to enlarge the PCE's political base not only represented a departure from the party's past factionalism, but also anticipated the communists' highly successful Popular Front strategy. This policy was adopted at the Seventh World Congress of the Communist International in August 1935. Above all, the new program called for the formation of alliances among a broad spectrum of parties, including the working classes and the bourgeoisie, as a means of checking the rise of fascism. Not surprisingly, it was a policy that Ibárruri herself enthusiastically promoted in the following months. In Spain's national elections of February 1936, the Popular Front electoral bloc formed by several major left-wing parties emerged victorious. Ibárruri was one of 17 communists elected to the Cortes

(Parliament). By the time the Civil War broke out in July 1936, she had already achieved national attention for her fervent and vitriolic speeches against her enemies.

Civil War and Exile, 1936-1977

The Spanish Civil War thrust Ibárruri into many new roles, but most notably as the leading propagandist for the Republican side. Soon after the July military rebellion began, she took to the radio and became instantly famous for uttering "!No pasarán!" (They shall not pass!) This, along with other slogans she coined—such as, "It is better to die on your feet than to live on your knees"—were so frequently repeated that they became rallying cries of Republican resistance against the Nationalists, led by General Francisco Franco. Whether she was addressing a mass public meeting or speaking on the radio, Ibárruri's deep, resonant voice and lyrical phrases exerted a spellbinding effect on her audiences. One of her most memorable speeches was a tribute to the International Brigades on November 15, 1938. Ibárruri deeply moved the vast crowd in Barcelona who had come to bid farewell to the Americans and other departing foreign volunteers when she proclaimed them national heroes and examples "of democracy's solidarity and universality."

While Ibárruri's meteoric rise to fame during the war was based in part on her own abilities, it is also true that her reputation owed a great deal to the communists' successful efforts to present her as a symbol of the Republican cause. By the end of the war, the iconography that had grown up around Ibárruri had transformed her into a legendary figure. Her own custom of appearing in public dressed in black, unadorned by jewelry and with her hair modestly fastened in a bun, helped to reinforce the image of her as the archetypical self-abnegating revolutionary. It was a powerful image, one that would be associated with her for the rest of her life.

Though Ibárruri's politics rarely deviated from the official party line, during the civil war she went farther than most official communists in championing women's rights. She was almost alone in the party hierarchy in demanding that women must be treated as men's equals and that their economic and political emancipation should be a primary goal of the communist movement. Yet her main preoccupation was the war effort. Apart from her role as a propagandist, she worked in a variety of capacities in the rearguard, including as a coordinator of the evacuation of children from the war zone to safer havens elsewhere in Spain and abroad.

On the other hand, Ibárruri's religious-like devotion to Marxism and strong emotional attachment to the Soviet Union led her to support some causes that later became politically embarrassing for many communists. For example, during the civil war the communists ruthlessly persecuted their political rivals. Ibárruri herself vigorously supported the communists' campaign to liquidate the anti-Stalinist POUM (Partido Obrero de Unificación Marxista). Years after the war there were still vestiges of her malice.

In the aftermath of the civil war, Ibárruri was among the tens of thousands of Republicans who fled Franco's Spain.

Like many other communists, Ibárruri found refuge in the Soviet Union, where, apart from brief spells abroad, she lived for the next 36 years.

The year 1942 was a decisive one for Ibárruri. In the spring the PCE's secretary-general, José Díaz, died, and Ibárruri was asked to lead the party. Later that year her son Ruben, who along with his sister Amaya had been living in Russia since 1935, was killed in the battle of Stalingard. However, the combined weight of taking on new political responsibilities and coping with a personal tragedy did not break her spirit. She successfully managed to hold together a party that was frequently at the point of disintegration.

During the 1940s and early 1950s Ibárruri's strategy for the party was guided by the erroneous assumption that the demise of Franco's regime was imminent. Ibárruri thus lost standing within the party, particularly among the younger generation of reformist-minded communists who were now in the ascendant. She was asked to step down as secretary-general at the VI PCE Congress held in Prague in 1960. From then on, Ibárruri served as the president of the PCE, a post specially created to honor her many contributions to the party.

No longer active in daily party affairs, Ibárruri turned to other projects. She presided over a historical commission that wrote a multi-volume history of the Spanish Civil War from the communist perspective, and she also completed the first part of her autobiography. From time to time she also continued her propaganda work, making several public appearances at communist rallies (Montreuil, France, 1971, and Geneva, 1974) and broadcasting messages to Franco's Spain over Radio Pirenaica (Pyrenean Radio).

Return to Spain, 1977-1989

Following Franco's death in 1975, Ibárruri grew more and more eager to return home. Finally, in May 1977, one month after the PCE had been legalized, she arrived in Madrid. Ibárruri's triumphant homecoming was generally viewed as a sign that Spain's war wounds were finally healing. Largely for this reason, she was asked to stand for a parliamentary seat in the June 1977 national elections, the first free elections since 1936. Once again Ibárruri was elected as a deputy from Asturias, thus completing a political circle that had begun a half century earlier.

When she died in November 1989, many Spaniards believed that her death marked an end to an era, not least because it coincided with a time when much of the communist world which she had known and had fought for was in an advanced state of collapse.

Further Reading

Ibárruri's two autobiographical works, *El único camino* (translated into English in 1966 as *They Shall Not Pass*) and *Memorias de Pasionaria* (1984), are ultimately disappointing because they provide few insights into her adult personal life and offer an uncritical analysis of her political career. An anthology of her civil war speeches was published in 1968, *En la lucha,* and the publications of the historical project she directed, *Guerra y Revolución en España,* appeared between 1966 and 1977. For the most part, Ibárruri has been treated reverentially in biographical studies. See, for example, the article on her in Marie Marmo Mullaney's *Revolutionary Women* (1983). One exception is Teresa Pàmies' revealing *Una española llamada Dolores Ibárruri* (Mexico: 1965). □

Sieur d'Iberville

Pierre Le Moyne, Sieur d'Iberville (1661-1706), was a French soldier, naval captain, and adventurer. He harried the British forces in North America and laid the foundations for Louisiana.

Pierre Le Moyne, Sieur d'iberville, was born in July 1661 at Montreal, Quebec. Son of a wealthy fur trader ennobled for valiant service, Pierre grew up on the frontier and spent much of his youth voyaging across the Atlantic on his father's supply ship.

In 1686 Iberville accompanied the overland expedition, led by Pierre de Troyes, which captured three Hudson's Bay Company posts in James Bay. Given command of the area in 1688, Iberville defeated an English attempt to recapture the posts. With 16 Canadians he captured 85 Hudson's Bay Company men and returned to Quebec with a rich haul of furs. He suffered defeat on another front, however. In 1688 the Sovereign Council at Quebec found him guilty in a paternity suit.

In February 1690 Iberville was second in command of the Canadian war party that destroyed Schenectady. By 1694 the English had driven the French out of Hudson Bay. Iberville returned to capture York Fort in October 1694, but after his departure the English once again seized control.

During these years Iberville also harried the English unmercifully in Newfoundland and along the Atlantic coast. Then, in 1697, he was sent back to Hudson Bay. In his one ship of 44 guns he engaged three English men-of-war, sank one, and captured another. At that the English governor of Hudson Bay was constrained to surrender. Leaving his brother Serigny in command, Iberville went to France, never to return to these ice-clogged waters.

Founding of Louisiana

When Louis XIV decided to establish a colony at the mouth of the Mississippi, Iberville was given command. In 1699 he established Ft. Maurepas in Biloxi Bay, and on his return to France he was awarded the Cross of the Order of St. Louis. The following year he established a fort at Mobile, then he began welding the Indian nations of the region into a commercial and military alliance to contain the English colonies.

In 1705 Iberville was given command of a naval expedition to harass the English in the West Indies. His forces captured Nevis in April 1706 and laid waste to the island. Before he could assault other of the enemy-held islands, he was struck down by fever and died aboard his flagship at Havana on July 9, 1706.

Throughout his career Iberville had unscrupulously availed himself of every opportunity to put money in his purse. He bequeathed a sizable estate to his widow and five children, but the Crown demanded restitution of 112,000 livres acquired during his last campaign. He was, however, one of the outstanding men of his age.

Further Reading

A biography in English of Iberville is Nellis M. Crouse, *Lemoyne d'Iberville: Soldier of New France* (1954). For historical background see W. J. Eccles, *Canada under Louis XIV, 1663-1701* (1964). □

Muhyi al-Din Ibn al-Arabi

Muhyi al-Din Ibn al-Arabi (1165-1240) was an outstanding Spanish-born Moslem thinker and mystic. One of the most prolific writers of the Islamic Middle Ages on the subject of mysticism, he also wrote love poetry.

Ibn al-Arabi was from Murcia, of a family which prided itself on ancient Arabian lineage. He received his education in Seville, where his father was a friend of the philosopher Averroës. A vision experienced during a youthful illness deepened Ibn al-Arabi's religious tendencies, and he began the serious study of *tasawwuf,* or Islamic mysticism. Until the age of 30 he studied with several Sufi (guides to the mystic life), both in Spain and in North Africa.

Ibn al-Arabi began to write in Morocco. His first pilgrimage to Mecca, in 1202, was (as for countless other Moslems) a deeply moving experience. He stayed 2 years in the holy city, writing there his encyclopedic exposé of mystic philosophy, *Meccan Revelations,* which he claimed was dictated to him by supernatural beings. At the same time and place he also composed a collection of love poetry inspired by a beautiful Persian woman named Nizam, although one of the introductory passages of the volume disclaims any worldly intention.

Pilgrims from Konya to Mecca induced Ibn al-Arabi to return with them and visit the Seljuk domains in Anatolia, which he did in 1205. He appears to have spent a good deal of time traveling, with passing references in his works to sojourns in Baghdad, Aleppo, Damascus, Jerusalem, Cairo, and again Mecca. He finally settled in Damascus, under the patronage of a wealthy family, and in his last years composed there one of his most important works, *Bezels of Wisdom.* The book is Ibn al-Arabi's summary of the teachings of the 28 persons recognized by the Moslems as prophets, from Adam to Mohammed, the author claiming that it was dictated to him in a dream by the prophet Mohammed himself. Ibn al-Arabi's tomb still exists in Damascus, where he died.

Ibn al-Arabi's importance for Islamic mysticism lies in the fact that he was a speculative thinker of the highest order, albeit diffuse and difficult to understand. His central doctrine is the unity of all existence: all things preexist in God's knowledge, and the world and everything in it is an outward aspect, the inward aspect of which is God. Man, more exactly the idea of man, is a microcosm uniting all the divine attributes. There is a "Perfect Man," and there have been several incarnations of the "Perfect Man," beginning with Adam and ending with Mohammed. With Ibn al-Arabi, Sufism moves away from anguished and ascetic searchings of the heart and conscience and becomes a matter of speculative philosophy and theosophy.

In terms of his influence Ibn al-Arabi, the mystic speculator, prepared the ground from which was to spring the rich harvest of Islamic—especially Persian—mystical poetry. There seems some evidence also that Ibn al-Arabi may have influenced Christian thinkers such as the Catalan Raymond Lull and possibly also Dante Alighieri.

Further Reading

Reynold A. Nicholson translated and edited Ibn al-Arabi's book of poems, *The Tarjuman al-Ashwaq: A Collection of Mystical Odes* (1911). A. E. Affifi analyzes his thought in *The Mystical Philosophy of Muhyid Din-Ibnul Arabi* (1939). Majid Fakhry, *A History of Islamic Philosophy* (1970), is recommended for general background. For Ibn al-Arabi's possible influence on Dante see Miguel Asín Palácios, *Islam and the Divine Comedy,* translated and abridged by Harold Sunderland (1926). □

Muhammad ibn Battuta

Muhammad ibn Battuta (1304-c. 1368) was a Moorish traveler whose extensive voyages as far as Sumatra and China, southern Russia, the Maldives, the East African coast, and Timbuktu made him one of the greatest medieval travelers.

Muhammad ibn Battuta was born in Tangier. His family was of Berber origin and had a tradition of service as judges. After receiving an education in Islamic law, Ibn Battuta set out in 1325, at the age of 21, to perform the obligatory pilgrimage to Mecca and to continue his studies in the East. He reached Mecca in 1326 by way of Egypt and Syria. This journey aroused in him the passion to see the world. From Mecca he made a trip to Iraq and western Persia as far as Tabriz and in 1327 returned via Baghdad to Mecca, where he spent the next 3 years.

Ibn Battuta then traveled by ship along the Red Sea shores to Yemen and from Aden to Mogadishu and the East African trading ports. He returned by way of Oman and the Persian Gulf to Mecca in 1332. Next he passed through Egypt and Syria and by ship reached Anatolia, where he visited local Turkish rulers and religious brotherhoods. He crossed the Black Sea to the Crimea in the territories of the Golden Horde and visited its khan in the Caucasus. He then journeyed to Sarai, the capital of the Golden Horde east of the lower Volga, and then through Khwarizm, Transoxiana, and Afghanistan to the Indus valley.

From 1333 to 1342 Ibn Battuta stayed at Delhi, where Sultan Muhammad ibn Tughluq gave him a position as judge, and then he traveled through central India and along the Malabar coast to the Maldives. His next trip took him to Ceylon, back to the Maldives, Bengal, Assam, and Sumatra. He landed in China at the port of Zayton and probably reached Peking. Returning via Sumatra to Malabar in 1347, he took a ship to the Persian Gulf. He revisited Baghdad, Syria, Egypt, Mecca, and Alexandria, traveled by ship to Tunis, Sardinia, and Algeria, and reached Fez by an over-land route in 1349. After a visit to the Moslem kingdom of Granada, he made a final trip through the Sahara to the black Moslem empire on the Niger, returning to Fez in 1354.

During his travels Ibn Battuta sometimes lost his diaries and had to rewrite them from memory. His travel book was written from his reports by Ibn Juzayy, a man of letters commissioned by the ruler of Fez. These circumstances may account for some inaccuracies in chronology and itineraries and other shortcomings of the work which affect some parts in particular. However, the book contains invaluable and sometimes unique information on the countries Ibn Battuta visited.

Further Reading

An annotated translation of selections from Ibn Battuta's *Travels,* with an introduction to his life, work, and the historical back-ground of his travels, is by H. A. R. Gibb (1929). A complete translation with detailed notes by Gibb is *The Travels of Ibn Battuta* (2 vols., 1958-1962). An annotated translation of the sections on India, the Maldives, and Ceylon was published by Agha Mahdi Husain, *The Rehla of Ibn Battuta* (1953). Ibn Battuta is also discussed in Charles Raymond Beazley, *The Dawn of Modern Geographical Science* (3 vols., 1897-1906); Arthur Percival Newton, ed., *Travel and Travellers of the Middle Ages* (1926); and Merriam Sherwood and Elmer Mantz, *The Road to Cathay* (1928).

Additional Sources

Dunn, Ross E., *The adventures of Ibn Battuta, a Muslim traveler of the fourteenth century,* Berkeley: University of California Press, 1986; London: Croom Helm, 1986.

Ibn Batuta, *The travels of Ibn Battuta, A.D. 1325-1354,* Mil-lwood, N.Y.: Kraus Reprint, 1986, 1971.

Timofeev, Igor, *Ibn Battuta,* Moskva: "Molodaia gvardiia," 1983. □

Solomon ben Judah ibn Gabirol

Solomon ben Judah ibn Gabirol (ca. 1021-ca. 1058) was an outstanding Spanish Hebrew poet and philos-opher of the Middle Ages.

Solomon ibn Gabirol was born in Málaga and was orphaned at an early age. He spent his formative years in Saragossa, where he found a generous patron in Yekutiel ibn Hassan. The latter died when Ibn Gabirol was 17, and the youthful poet was forced to resume his wandering. The poetry he wrote during this period reflects his melancholy mood.

In Granada, Ibn Gabirol found a new patron in Samuel he-Nagid, the famous Spanish Jewish statesman, poet, and Talmudist, but when Samuel died, Ibn Gabirol again suf-fered want and need. It seems that he never married. He died at a young age, some believe before his fortieth birth-day (1058), but more probably at the age of 48 (1069).

Ibn Gabirol distinguished himself both in his secular and religious poems. The former were written generally in a light vein, but some of them depict loneliness and despair. About half of his 300 verses that have survived are religious in character. His greatest and longest masterpiece of reli-gious poetry is his *Keter Malkhut* (Royal Crown), a partly philosophical meditation on struggling man's insignificance before the sublime mystery of the universe and God.

Ibn Gabirol ranks as the first great Spanish Jewish thinker. His chief work, the *Mekor Hayyim (Fons vitae,* or Fountain of Life), written originally in Arabic, accepts the Neoplatonic ideas of Emanation, expounded primarily by Plotinus. But Ibn Gabirol's view of Emanation differs from that of the Neoplatonists in that his Emanations are the result of the Will of God and not a mere mechanical necessity or flow from the Divine Source. Matter is spiritual and as such streams directly from the Godhead; it becomes corporeal only at a distance from its origin. Perhaps because Ibn Gabirol omitted all biblical allusion in *Mekor Hayyim,* Jews did not read it; in fact, it was regarded by many as the product either of a Christian scholastic writer or of a Mos-lem, and "Ibn Gabirol" was frequently corrupted to Avicebron or Avicembril.

Tikkun Middot Ha-nephesh (Improvement of the Moral Qualities), Ibn Gabirol's ethical treatise, despite its many biblical quotations, represented a system of ethics indepen-dent of the Jewish tradition. It was based largely on a psychological and physiological approach and urged man to attain harmony in body and soul by disciplining his senses along the lines of Aristotle's golden mean. Although Ibn Gabirol exercised a relatively minor influence on later Jewish thinkers, his Neoplatonic ideas penetrated the medi-eval Cabala, or Jewish mystic lore.

Further Reading

Israel Davidson, ed. *The Selected Religious Poems of Solomon ibn Gabirol* (1923), contains an informative introduction by the editor and a splendid collection of Ibn Gabirol's poetic works, including his *Keter Malkhut,* translated by Israel Zangwill. Abraham E. Millgram, ed., *The Anthology of Medi-eval Hebrew Literature* (1935), presents a brief sketch of Ibn Gabirol's life and includes a small selection of his secular and religious poems. A good review of Ibn Gabirol's philosophy may be found in Julius Guttman, *The Philosophy of Judaism* (trans. 1964). □

Abu Muhammad Ali ibn Hazm

Abu Muhammad Ali ibn Hazm (994-1064) was a Spanish-born Arab theologian, philosopher, and jurist whose most important work was a book on comparative religious history.

Ibn Hazm was born in Cordova. His father, who was chief minister at the Umayyad court, died when Ibn Hazm was 18 years old, during the violent political upheavals of the time. After a careful education in the usual legal and literary style of the time, Ibn Hazm entered active politics himself, being at various times vizier to reigning members of the Umayyad house, a fugitive in neighboring Andalusian statelets, and a political prisoner.

At the age of 32 Ibn Hazm finally renounced political life and devoted himself wholeheartedly to scholarship, but his outspokenness in legal writings which attacked the jurists of the dominant Maliki rite led to efforts to silence him. The latter half of his life seems to have been spent on his family estates, writing and teaching informally those who sought him out.

As a jurist, Ibn Hazm was one of the strongest spokesmen for the Zahiri, or literalist, school of legal interpretation, in local opposition in Spain to the predominant Maliki school. This insistence upon a meticulous basis in the Koran and the Traditions for legal decisions naturally led Ibn Hazm to philology and a heightened consciousness of the importance of the Arabic language for Moslems. He was aware of Aristotelian logic but saw it as definitely a handmaiden to religion, to be used to reconcile the Koran and the Traditions of the Prophet on the rare occasions when these did not seem to agree on the surface.

His Writings

Perhaps Ibn Hazm's most important work is the *Book of Religions and Sects,* a work on comparative religious history, one of the earliest of this genre, which examines, in a polemical way, Judaism, Christianity, Zoroastrianism, and Islam. There is evidence of careful, firsthand investigation by Ibn Hazm and awareness of the historical evolution of each of these religions. The section on Islam is chiefly devoted to the sectarian movements and philosophically dissident schools of thought. Second only in importance to his work on comparative religion is the *Ring of the Dove,* a treatise on love in its psychological and ethical complexities.

Further Reading

The translation by A. J. Arberry of *The Ring of the Dove: A Treatise on the Art and Practice of Arab Love* (1953) and that by Israel Friedlaender of *The Heterodoxies of the Shiites in the Presentation of Ibn Hazm* (1909) are almost the only works by Ibn Hazm in English. They both have material about the author. Ibn Hazm is discussed at length in De Lacy O'Leary, *Arabic Thought and Its Place in History* (1922; rev. ed. 1939).

See also Philip K. Hitti, *History of the Arabs: From the Earliest Times to the Present* (1937; 10th ed. 1970). □

Abd al-Rahman ibn Muhammad ibn Khaldun

Abd al-Rahman ibn Muhammad ibn Khaldun (1332-1406) was an Arab historian, philosopher, and statesman whose treatise, the *Muqaddima,* in which he pioneered a general sociological theory of history, shows him as one of the most original thinkers of the Middle Ages.

Ibn Khaldun was born on May 27, 1332, in Tunis. His family, of southern Arabian origin, settled in Seville after the Moslem conquest of Spain and distinguished themselves in the political and intellectual life of the city. Shortly before the Christian reconquest they left and eventually settled in Tunis. Ibn Khaldun always felt attached to the cultural tradition of Moslem Spain.

Growing up in Tunis, Ibn Khaldun studied the traditional religious sciences including law according to the Maliki school as well as the rational sciences. He also was trained in the arts necessary for a career in government. Among his teachers, he was most impressed by al-Abili, who came to Tunis in 1347 and introduced him to philosophy.

Early Wanderings

In 1352 the Hafsid ruler of Tunis gave Ibn Khaldun a minor position in the chancery, but he left soon to join al-Abili, who had returned to Fez. During his stay in Fez (1354-1362) Ibn Khaldun pursued his scholarly interests and was actively involved in the political life at the Merinid court. Suspected of plotting against the ruler, he was imprisoned in 1357 for 22 months. Under a later ruler he again held high positions but became discouraged by court intrigues.

Prevented by the Merinid court from joining the rival court at Tlemcen, Ibn Khaldun turned to Granada, where he was accorded a royal welcome by the young ruler, Muhammad V, and his vizier, Ibn al-Khatib, an outstanding man of letters, whose friendship he had gained during Ibn al-Khatib's exile in Fez. In 1364 Muhammad V sent Ibn Khaldun to Seville on a mission to Pedro I, King of Castile. Ibn Khaldun declined an offer of Pedro to have his ancestors' possessions reinstated if he would enter royal service. Ibn Khaldun's intimacy with Muhammad V, whom he tried to direct toward his ideal of philosopher king, aroused the suspicion of Ibn al-Khatib, and Ibn Khaldun was forced to leave Granada, though with official honors, in 1365.

Ibn Khaldun accepted an invitation from the Hafsid ruler of Bougie and became his minister. When the ruler was defeated and killed by his cousin a year later, Ibn Khaldun entered the service of the cousin but soon left as a result of court intrigue. The next 9 years were the most turbulent of his life. Thoroughly disappointed with his court experiences, he tried to keep away from politics and spent most of the time in research and teaching in Biskra, at the sanctuary of the saint Abu Madyan near Tlemcen, and in Fez. He felt, however, repeatedly obliged to assume political missions for various rulers among the Arab tribes in the area. In 1375 he briefly returned to Granada but was expelled.

Writing the *Muqaddima*

Soon afterward Ibn Khaldun retreated to the castle of Ibn Salama in central Algeria, where he spent over 3 years in complete seclusion under tribal protection. He intended writing a history of the contemporary Maghreb and began the introduction (*muqaddima*) setting forth his ideas about critical historiography. The *Muqaddima* rapidly grew into a general theory of history, or science of civilization, as he termed it. He now widened his plans to include a universal history based on his new science. In 1379 he returned to Tunis with the permission of the new Hafsid ruler to avail himself of books and archives for his work. Under the ruler's patronage he wrote the history of the Maghreb and sections of the history of the East. His influence with the ruler and popularity among students again provoked court intrigues, and he left in 1382 for Egypt under pretext of a pilgrimage to Mecca.

The last 2 decades of his life Ibn Khaldun lived in Cairo, the splendid capital of the Mamluk empire, enjoying the patronage of the sultans Barquq and Faraj. He was granted professorships in several colleges. Six times he was appointed Maliki chief judge, though only for brief terms. Most of his time was devoted to teaching and research. He completed his history and continued improving it. He made a pilgrimage to Mecca and two trips to Damascus, the second one occasioned by the campaign of Faraj against Tamerlane in 1400. Tamerlane invited Ibn Khaldun to visit his camp; his conversations with the world conqueror, reported in his autobiography, turned mostly around the political conditions in Egypt and the Maghreb. Ibn Khaldun died on March 17, 1406.

Theory of Civilization

Ibn Khaldun's fame rests on his *Muqaddima,* in which he set forth the earliest general theory of the nature of civilization and the conditions for its development, intending it as a tool for understanding and writing history. He considered the permanent conflict between primitive Bedouin and highly developed urban society as a crucial factor in history. Civilization is for him an urban phenomenon to be realized only by local concentration and cooperation of men united under a strong dynastic rule. He saw group solidarity (*asabiyya*) as the driving force for this cooperation and the establishment of dynastic rule. The group with the strongest feeling of solidarity establishes its predominance and the rule of its leading family. The division of labor resulting from cooperation makes possible the production of conveniences and luxuries beyond the elementary necessities of life and the development of sciences. Indulgence in luxuries, however, causes degeneration and

loss of group solidarity and thus results in the disintegration of the state and the group supporting the civilization. Another, less civilized group with an unspoiled sense of solidarity takes over and becomes heir to the earlier civilization.

Ibn Khaldun's history of the Maghreb, written with the insight of an active participant, presents a penetrating description of the rise and fall of dynasties and the role of Berber and Arab tribes. It is an invaluable source for the medieval history of North Africa. The other parts of his universal history generally lack such insight and source value. His autobiography, the most detailed one in medieval Moslem literature, offers a perspicacious description of his life until 1405. Of his early works, which were scholastic exercises in various fields of learning, only two are known to be extant.

Further Reading

Ibn Khaldun's *The Muqaddimah: An Introduction to History,* edited and translated by Franz Rosenthal (3 vols., 1958; 2d ed. 1967), contains a complete translation of the *Muqaddima* with a detailed introduction to Ibn Khaldun's life and work. Muhsin Mahdi, *Ibn Khaldun's Philosophy of History* (1957), is a penetrating study. The reports concerning Ibn Khaldun's meeting with Tamerlane were translated and edited by Walter J. Fischel in *Ibn Khaldun and Tamerlane* (1952). Other useful sources are Nathaniel Schmidt, *Ibn Khaldun: Historian, Sociologist and Philosopher* (1930), and Muhammad Abdullah Enan, *Ibn Khaldun: His Life and Work* (trans. 1941).

Additional Sources

Ali, Shaukat, Dr., *Intellectual foundations of Muslim civilization,* Lahore: Publishers United, 1977.

Schmidt, Nathaniel, *Ibn Khaldun, historian, sociologist, and philosopher,* Lahore: Universal Books, 1978. □

Abd al-Aziz ibn Saud

Abd al-Aziz ibn Saud (1880-1953) was an Arab political leader who founded the kingdom of Saudi Arabia. During his rule, from 1932 to 1953, much of the Arabian peninsula developed from a group of desert sheikhdoms to a politically unified kingdom with new wealth from oil fields.

Ibn Saud was born in Riyadh in the central Arabian principality of Nejd. He escaped with his father, Abd al-Rahman, to exile in Kuwait in 1891, when the rival Rashidi family seized Saudi lands. In 1902 the young Ibn Saud with a small number of warriors recaptured Riyadh in a daring raid.

Although the modern history of Arabia dates from the Saudi reoccupation of Riyadh, there was much history and tradition in the young sheikh's policy. Ibn Saud revived the family alliance with the Wahhabis, an 18th-century puritanical reform movement within Islam which had spread over central Arabia. Skillfully combining the Wahhabi religious zeal with his own personal charisma and political capability as a desert sheikh, Ibn Saud expanded his authority over most of the peninsula. Especially important were the Ikhwan, settled military and agricultural colonies which protected and extended the Saudi domain while beginning the settling-down process for the once nomadic Bedouin.

In 1913 Ibn Saud occupied the Ottoman province of al-Hasa on the Persian Gulf, a territory in which oil would soon be found. Two years later he accepted British protection and a financial subsidy in return for agreeing not to attack British interests in the gulf area or the sharif Husein ibn Ali of Mecca. The political ambitions of Ibn Saud and Husein inevitably clashed following World War I. While Husein had dissipated his resources in inefficient administration, in the Arab Revolt of 1916, and in a vain attempt to establish himself as king of all the Arabs, Ibn Saud consolidated his status and power in Arabia. In addition, the puritanical Wahhabis felt shame and contempt for the more worldly practices of the Islamic holy cities ruled by Husein since 1908. Ibn Saud also realized his need for the profits of the pilgrimage trade for his expansionist policies. In 1924, with Husein's self-proclamation as caliph as the last straw, Ibn Saud's forces besieged Mecca and forced his rival's abdication and exile. In 1926 Ibn Saud assumed the title of king of the Hejaz, a year later that of the Nejd; in 1932 he joined them in the kingdom of Saudi Arabia.

In 1933 Ibn Saud granted the first oil concession to an American company later known as ARAMCO, but the worldwide depression and World War II prevented much further development. Following the war, oil production and government revenues from oil royalties grew very quickly. Government income, synonymous with the King's personal funds, jumped from less than $1 million in 1920 to $7 million in 1939 to over $200 million in 1953, when Ibn Saud died.

Further Reading

There are several good studies of Ibn Saud: H. St. J. B. Philby, *Arabian Jubilee* (1953); Jacques Benoist-Méchin, *Arabian Destiny* (trans. 1957); and two studies by David Howarth, *The Desert King: Ibn Saud and His Arabia* (1964) and *The Desert King: The Life of Ibn Saud* (1968). K. S. Twitchell, *Saudi Arabia* (1947; 3d ed. 1958), and H. St. J. B. Philby, *Sa'udi Arabia* (1955), are good general histories. □

Yusuf ibn Tashufin

Yusuf ibn Tashufin (died 1106) was a North African Almoravid ruler and conqueror who created the first Berber Empire uniting North Africa and Spain.

Before 1061, when he was appointed commander of the Almoravid armies in Morocco by his cousin Abu Bakr, virtually nothing is known of Ibn Tashufin except that he belonged to the Berber family which, together with Abdullah ibn Yasin, had founded the Almoravid movement some 10 years earlier. Apparently Ibn Tashufin's appointment was to have been temporary, to enable Abu Bakr to put down tribal uprisings in the Sahara, but since Ibn Tashufin chose not to relinquish command and Abu Bakr agreed to confine his activities to the desert and black Africa, from 1061 on Ibn Tashufin was virtual leader of the Almoravids.

Ibn Tashufin's career is divided in two phases: the conquest of western North Africa to Algiers and the conquest of Spain. The first step Ibn Tashufin took in consolidating the victories previously won in southern Morocco and in pushing toward the north was the foundation of Marrakesh, henceforth to be the Almoravid capital. Beginning in 1063, Ibn Tashufin undertook the subjugation of the cities held by the Zenata Berbers of central Morocco, a campaign which was culminated in 1069 with the final conquest of Fez. Firmly entrenched in south and central Morocco, Ibn Tashufin then led the Almoravid armies over the next 12 years in expeditions to the north and east; by 1082 he had conquered virtually all of Morocco and western Algeria, stopping only when he reached territory governed by a related Sanhaja tribe.

The spectacular victories of the Almoravid armies had not gone unnoticed across the straits in Moslem Spain, which just at this time was under attack from the Christian powers of northern Spain led by Alfonso VI of León and Castile. Weakened and divided among themselves, the party kings of Spain were unable to defend themselves from the Christian advance and after the fall of Toledo in 1085 invited Ibn Tashufin to bring the Almoravid armies to their aid.

In all, Ibn Tashufin crossed into Spain four times. The first expedition, in 1086, resulted in the famous victory of al-Zallaqa, in which Alfonso's armies were decisively defeated. Two years later, in 1088, Ibn Tashufin was defeated by the revived Christian forces and decided that the only way to strengthen the Moslems in Spain was to unite them by force. Accordingly, in 1090 he returned again to Spain, this time campaigning against the Moslem kings on the grounds that they had failed in their duty as Moslem sovereigns. Still a fourth expedition was required, in 1097, which ended in Almoravid control over the southern half of the Iberian Peninsula.

Thus at the end of the 11th century Ibn Tashufin had succeeded in uniting Morocco and Moslem Spain under Berber rule. Since Ibn Tashufin, like the founder of the Almoravids, was an austere man, intent on implementing a strict Maliki version of Islamic law, the territories which he had conquered had also a degree of religious unity at his death in 1106.

Further Reading

There is no biography of Ibn Tashufin. Gailbraith Welch, *North African Prelude* (1949), gives historical background and biographical details. For Ibn Tashufin's exploits in Spain see Edwyn Hole, *Andalus: Spain under the Muslims* (1958), and S. M. Imamuddin, *A Political History of Muslim Spain* (1961). □

Abu Bakr Muhammad ibn Tufayl

Abu Bakr Muhammad ibn Tufayl (ca. 1110-1185) was a Spanish Moslem philosopher and physician, author of the celebrated allegorical tale "Hayy Ibn Yaqzan."

Known to medieval Christian scholastics as Abubacer (from Abu Bakr), Ibn Tufayl was born in the town known in modern times as Guadix near Granada. He was trained as a physician but also followed the career of a government functionary, serving as secretary to the governors of Granada, and later of Ceuta and Tangier in North Africa (1154). Ultimately, he became court physician to the Almohad sultan Abu Yaqub Yusuf, who ruled in Marrakesh from 1163 to 1184.

Ibn Tufayl used his considerable influence at court to forward the career of the young Averroës; the Sultan seems to have taken a lively interest in philosophy, and Averroës wrote his commentary on Aristotle at the Almohad court, encouraged by Ibn Tufayl. After the latter's retirement as court physician, Averroës took his place. Ibn Tufayl died in Marrakesh.

"Alive, Son of Awake"

Little of Ibn Tufayl's work has survived except for *Hayy Ibn Yaqzan*, whose title means "Alive, Son of Awake," although medieval Arabic bibliographies credit him with an additional two books on medicine and some writings on astronomy. The title is borrowed from Avicenna, but the ideas put forward in Ibn Tufayl's work are quite contrary to Avicenna's.

The setting of the narrative is an island in the Indian Ocean, inhabited solely by a youth named Hayy, who grew up there quite alone, suckled as a child only by a gazelle, and completely cut off from humanity. Despite this cultural deprivation, Hayy stays alive and even thinks through and evolves a system of philosophy and metaphysics of the most refined order. Through fasting and meditation, moreover, he seeks and attains mystical experiences.

Ibn Tufayl then introduces into the narrative a devout man named Asal, from a neighboring island, who is seeking an uninhabited retreat from the world. He meets Hayy, teaches him to speak, and is astonished to find that the natural youth has evolved—all untaught—a system comparable but superior to Asal's own philosophy.

Hayy and Asal return to civilization, determined that Hayy's *aperçus* will be shared with mankind. The attempt fails, however, and the two philosophers return to the desert island and leave the common people to the undisturbing practice of their ancestral religion.

Translated into Latin in 1671, Ibn Tufayl's work has evoked interesting speculations. Translations into English and European languages soon followed, and it has been suggested that Defoe's *Robinson Crusoe,* which was published in 1719, may have been inspired by the English translation of 1708. The interpretations of scholars of the meaning of the allegory have varied greatly, although all agree, at least, that it is a tour de force intended to show the almost limitless capabilities of the human intellect.

Further Reading

The 1708 English translation, revised by A. S. Fulton, *The History of Hayy Ibn Yaqzan, by Abu Bakr Ibn Tufayl* (1929), presents Ibn Tufayl's philosophical romance on the "awakening of the soul." Z. A. Siddiqi, *Philosophy of Ibn Tufayl* (1965), is a study of Ibn Tufayl's work. □

Muhammad ibn Tumart

Muhammad ibn Tumart (ca. 1080-1130) was a North African religious revolutionary leader who founded the Almohad movement in North Africa. His organization of Berber tribesmen led to the end of Almoravid rule in North Africa.

A Masmuda Berber born in a mountain village in southern Morocco, Ibn Tumart showed remarkable piety as a youth; in pursuit of religious learning he left home in 1105 to visit the principal cities of Islamic civilization, studying Islamic theology and jurisprudence in Marrakesh, Cordova, Baghdad, Damascus, and Alexandria. About 1118 he returned to North Africa, where he preached in towns and villages against the immoral behavior of the inhabitants, calling upon them to act in accordance with the strictures of Islamic law. More specifically, he denounced such impious actions as drinking wine, the playing of musical instruments, and the appearance of women in public places without the veil. Public criticism of the Almoravid sultan Ali ibn Yusuf and of prominent theologians led to Ibn Tumart's banishment from Marrakesh, the Almoravid capital, and his withdrawal to his birthplace in the Atlas Mountains, where he set about recruiting disciples among his fellow Masmuda tribesmen.

Religious Rebellion

In 1121 Ibn Tumart began the more militant phase of his career when he proclaimed himself to be the long-awaited Mahdi—the infallible, divinely inspired guide who would lead erring mankind to righteousness and restore justice on earth. Righteousness was to be attained by belief in Ibn Tumart's doctrine of the absolute unity (Arabic, *tawhid;* from this doctrine the groups called the Muwahhidun, or Unifiers, and the Spanish Almohads developed) of God and adoption of the Koran and prophetic tradition (*hadith*) as the sole sources of Islamic law; justice was to be restored by fighting in Ibn Tumart's armies to overthrow the heretical Almoravid government.

An attempt by the Almoravid rulers to smash the nascent movement led Ibn Tumart to emigrate in 1125 from his birthplace to an even more inaccessible mountain village, Tinmel. For the next 5 years he recruited the bulk of his warrior disciples. But because the Masmuda Berbers were unacquainted with anything but the most rudimentary Islam, Ibn Tumart's mission was partly education and included even the rote teaching of the Koran in Arabic. Furthermore, in order to give some basis of solidarity to his followers, he transformed the loose tribal ties of the Berbers into a highly stratified, almost hierarchical form of political and social organization which was undoubtedly designed to reinforce the religious loyalty due to him as Mahdi.

Once Ibn Tumart had won a sufficient number of disciples and had organized them into an obedient and disciplined fighting force, he launched a military campaign against Marrakesh in 1130. Unaccustomed both to siege warfare and to fighting in the plains, Ibn Tumart's Berbers were defeated and retreated into their mountain fortress. Shortly thereafter, Ibn Tumart fell ill and died in the same year.

The fact that Ibn Tumart's lieutenants kept his death a secret for a period estimated by some historians as 3 years before venturing to install Abd al-Mumin as his successor is an indication of the strong force of his personal leadership on his followers. Although Ibn Tumart died before the spectacular victories in North Africa and Spain were achieved by his followers, there is no doubt that these conquests would have been impossible without the religious inspiration and sociopolitical organization which he gave the movement.

Further Reading

Ibn Tumart is discussed at length in De Lacy O'Leary, *Arabic Thought and Its Place in History* (1922; rev. ed. 1939). See also Reynold A. Nicholson, *A Literary History of the Arabs* (1907), and Philip K. Hitti, *History of the Arabs: From the Earliest Times to the Present* (1937; 10th ed. 1970).

Additional Sources

Bourouiba, Rachid, *Ibn Tumart,* Alger: SNED, 1974. □

Ibrahim Pasha

Ibrahim Pasha (1789-1848) was an outstanding Turkish military and administrative leader in the eastern Mediterranean area of the Ottoman Empire.

I brahim Pasha was born in Kavalla in what is now Greek Macedonia but was then an important Ottoman provincial center. He joined his father, Mohammed Ali, in Egypt in 1805, the same year that the Ottoman sultan had reluctantly accepted Mohammed Ali as his governor and representative. Ibrahim became his father's right-hand man in military affairs, and Mohammed Ali's success in beginning the modernization of Egypt and in establishing an autonomous Egypt ruled by his own dynasty was due to the prowess and skill of both father and son.

In 1811 Mohammed Ali sent Ibrahim to Upper Egypt to defeat the remaining Mamluks, to control the Bedouin, and to assert the power of the new government. Ibrahim remained as local governor until 1816, when the Sultan rewarded him for his services to the Ottoman Empire with the title of pasha. In the same year Mohammed Ali transferred him to western Arabia, where the puritanical Wahhabi Moslems, in alliance with the Saudi family of central Arabia, were menacing the Islamic holy cities of Mecca and Medina and challenging the political hegemony of the Ottoman sultan. Ibrahim succeeded in defeating the Saudi-Wahhabi alliance and in restoring Ottoman authority over western Arabia by 1819. In 1821 he returned for additional campaigns in the northern Sudan, particularly to meet his father's requirements for more troops and laborers for developing Egyptian armies and factories.

Campaign in Greece

In 1824 at the request of Sultan Mahmud II, Mohammed Ali sent Ibrahim and the new Egyptian army to the Peloponnesus to subdue Greek nationalist rebels. Ibrahim's well-trained troops routed the Greeks but lost the war and had to evacuate Egypt because of the naval intervention of the major European powers, whose combined fleets destroyed the joint Ottoman-Egyptian naval force at the battle of Navarino off the southern Greek coast in 1827. This cut the supply and communications route between Mohammed Ali in Egypt and Ibrahim in the Peloponnesus. Mohammed Ali had no alternative but to recall his otherwise triumphant son.

Disagreement with the Ottoman sultan over the Greek conflict covered Mohammed Ali's increasingly ambitious plans for a powerful Near Eastern state based on Egypt and led to his sending Ibrahim into Syria in 1831. This again demonstrated the superiority of the Egyptian army and the skillful military leadership of Ibrahim in defeating the Ottoman troops in a series of battles to within a hundred miles of Istanbul, the imperial capital. Bolstered by Russian intervention in 1833, Sultan Mahmud II secured a treaty with Mohammed Ali in which Egypt agreed to withdraw its troops from Anatolia in return for the administrative cession of the districts of Adana and Syria.

Governor of Syria

Mohammed Ali appointed Ibrahim as governor of the new areas. To win the support of the suspicious European powers, who with the exception of France feared the destruction of the status quo by Mohammed Ali's threat to Ottoman integrity and stability, Ibrahim opened greater Syria to the penetration of Western merchants and missionaries.

Ibrahim's 10 years in Syria permanently disrupted traditional society in the area and started the transition process already begun in Egypt by Napoleon's 1798 invasion. As a political ruler, Ibrahim proved less capable than in his military exploits. His utilization of tight and centralized control, his seizure of arms and conscription of troops, and his catering to Christian minorities for support caused dissatisfaction and, ultimately, rejection of Egyptian overrule by many Syrians.

The struggle between Sultan Mahmud II and his supposed subordinate, Mohammed Ali, the pasha of Egypt, continued. In 1839 the Sultan felt strong enough to challenge Ibrahim in Syria, but again Ibrahim overwhelmed the Ottoman forces on the Anatolian border. Mahmud II died before the news of his further defeat reached Istanbul. With the Sultan dead, Ibrahim victorious on the Anatolian border, the army scattered, and the navy already deserted to Egypt, the major European powers, except France, feared the final disintegration of the Ottoman Empire.

Intervention of the powers in 1840 by blockading the Syrian coast, by landing troops near Mt. Lebanon, and by encouraging already dissident groups to revolt forced Ibrahim to withdraw to Egypt and Mohammed Ali to yield his claims to Syria and Adana. In return, the Ottoman Empire and the European powers recognized Mohammed Ali's hereditary rights to the position of pasha of Egypt.

Ibrahim participated in no further military campaigns and remained largely in Cairo assisting his father in administrative duties. Because of Mohammed Ali's apparent senility, Ibrahim became viceroy in September 1848 but died 2 months later. His widespread and capable military campaigns in support of Mohammed Ali's plans and ambitions made Ibrahim one of the leading figures in the 19th-century Near East.

Further Reading

The only biography of Ibrahim is Pierre Crabitès, *Ibrahim of Egypt* (1935). See also the classic study of his father, Mohammed Ali, by Henry Dodwell, *Founder of Modern Egypt* (1931). For Near Eastern diplomacy, the latest and best book is Matthew Smith Anderson, *The Eastern Question, 1774-1923* (1966). William R. Polk, *The Opening of South Lebanon, 1788-1840: A Study of the Impact of the West on the Middle East* (1963), is an excellent study that deals with Ibrahim's activities in part of greater Syria. For general background on 19th-century Egypt see John A. Marlowe, *A History of Modern Egypt and Anglo-Egyptian Relations, 1800-1956* (1954; 2d ed. 1965), and Tom Little, *Modern Egypt* (1967). □

Henrik Ibsen

The Norwegian playwright Henrik Ibsen (1828-1906) developed realistic techniques that changed the entire course of Western drama. There is very little in modern drama that does not owe a debt to him.

Henrik Ibsen was born on March 20, 1828, in the town of Skien. His father, a businessman, went bankrupt when Ibsen was 8, a shattering blow to the family. Ibsen left home at 15, spending the next six, difficult years as a pharmacist's assistant in Grimstad, where he wrote his first play. In 1850 he moved to Christiania (Oslo) to study. In 1851 he became resident dramatist, later director, of a new theater in Bergen. Although he never became a good director and his plays were mostly unsuccessful, the years in Bergen gave him invaluable experience in practical stagecraft.

Ibsen returned to Christiania in 1857, where he spent the worst period of his life. His plays were either rejected or failures, he went into debt, and his talent was publicly questioned. He left Norway in 1864, spending the next 27 years in Italy and Germany. While bitter and humiliating personal memories explain, in part, his long exile, it seems also that only by distancing himself from everything he held dear could he devote himself completely to his art. When he left Norway, he looked like a rather dissolute bohemian. In the following years he changed his appearance, habits, and even his handwriting. He became the "Sphinx" he still is to many people—unapproachable, secretive, an avid collector of medals and honors which he wore to protect himself from the real and imagined hostility of others. Long before he returned home in 1891, he had become the world's most famous dramatist.

Early Plays

For all its youthful excesses, *Catiline* (1850), his first play, is remarkably Ibsenian. The theme, as Ibsen wrote later, is the discrepancy between ability and aspiration, which he called "mankind's and the individual's tragedy and comedy at the same time." Like the characters in many of Ibsen's later plays, Catiline is torn between two women

who represent conflicting forces in himself: one of them embodies domestic virtues, the other his calling and, significantly, his death. Also, the play begins with words which could be uttered by many later Ibsen heroes and heroines: "I must, I must, a voice deep in my soul urges me on—and I will heed its call."

The six following plays (*The Warrior's Barrow,* 1850; *St. John's Eve,* 1853; *Lady Inger of Østraat,* 1855; *The Feast at Solhaug,* 1856; *Olaf Liljekrans,* 1857; and *The Vikings in Helgeland,* 1858) are all in the spirit of romanticism and show Ibsen struggling to find a form and techniques which would embody his personal vision. The two plays he wrote during his second stay in Christiania deserve to be better known, both for their merits and for the light they shed on Ibsen's authorship: *Love's Comedy* (1862), a satire on bourgeois versus romantic love, and *The Pretenders* (1864), a magnificent historical and psychological tragedy.

In the first 10 years of his "exile" Ibsen wrote four plays. The immensely successful *Brand* (1866) is a towering drama of a man who strives to realize himself in terms of Søren Kierkegaard's "either/or" and of the consequences of such an effort. His next play, *Peer Gynt* (1867), made Ibsen Scandinavia's most discussed dramatist. Peer Gynt is Brand's opposite, a man who evades his problems until he loses everything, including himself. Peer is Ibsen's most universally human character.

The League of Youth (1869), a political satire, shows Ibsen moving toward the later "realistic" plays. Ibsen called *Emperor and Galilean* (1873), a 10-act play about Julian the

Apostate, "a world-historical drama." In Julian's rejection of Christianity, his futile attempt to restore the pagan cult of man, and his doomed quest to found "the third kingdom," a Hegelian synthesis of the two ways of life, Ibsen dramatized what he saw as Western man's, and his own, dilemma. The play is a failure, but one can glimpse Julian's quest beneath the polished, modern surfaces of many of Ibsen's later plays.

Plays of Contemporary Life

Inspired by the demand of the critic Georg Brandes that literature begin to take up contemporary problems for discussion, and influenced by changing public taste, Ibsen now set out to develop a dramatic form in which serious matters could be dealt with in the "trivial" guise of everyday life. Since there were models for such a drama, Ibsen cannot be said to have invented the realistic, or social reform, play. However, he brought it to perfection and, in doing so, made himself the most famous, reviled and praised dramatist of the 19th century. It should be stressed, however, that Ibsen had no intention of becoming merely a dramatist whose plays reflected contemporary manners and attacked social evils. He remained what he had always been, essentially antisociety, concerned with the individual and his problems.

Ibsen solved the technical difficulties involved in translating his tragic vision from the romantic forms to a realistic form in two central ways. First, he developed a retrospective technique whereby, as the play progresses, the past events leading to the climax are gradually brought to light through the words and acts of the characters. In Ibsen's hands (but not always in those of his followers), the past is not just dead matter: it grips the present and changes its significance. Ibsen's characters live in a continual, exciting "now," moving toward the truth about themselves and their condition.

Second, and equally important, was Ibsen's exploitation of visual imagery, whereby he gave his plays, through set, costume, and stage direction, much of the poetry denied the dramatist who deals with modern people speaking in everyday prose.

The term "Ibsenite," as used by G. B. Shaw, Ibsen's disciple and champion in England, describes a play which exposes individual and social hypocrisy. It can be used, in the narrowest sense, only about *Pillars of Society* (1877) and *A Doll's House* (1879), which do seem to stress the aspects of society and personal dishonesty that hinder personal development. But even Nora, in the latter play, is a sufficiently complex character to suggest other interpretations. Already in *Ghosts* (1881), however, the heroine, Mrs. Alving, discovers that the forces working against human development are not just dead social conventions: there are forces in the individual that are more elusive and destructive than the "doll house" of marriage and society. The last of the "Ibsenite" plays, *An Enemy of the People* (1882), takes the consequences of Mrs. Alving's discovery and laughs at the social reformer. The laughter, however, is compassionate—the hero has a certain resemblance to Ibsen himself—and the play is one of Ibsen's finest comedies.

Plays after 1882

After 1882 Ibsen concentrated more and more on the individual and his dilemma, as he had done prior to 1877, and on those timeless forces, reflected in individual psychology and working through social institutions, that hinder individual growth. *The Wild Duck* (1884) might be said to introduce Ibsen's last period by showing how the average man needs illusions to survive and what happens to a family when something that may be truth is introduced into it. Here Ibsen also moved toward a new symbolism, rising from and intimately bound up with his realistic surfaces.

In *Rosmersholm* (1886), a man raised in a tradition of Christian duty and sacrifice tries, under the influence of a free, "pagan" woman, to break with his past. *The Lady from the Sea* (1888) is considered a remarkable anticipation of psychotherapy, but the heroine's "cure" makes unconvincing theater. *Hedda Gabler* (1890) is a savage portrait of a frustrated woman, spiritually, sexually, and socially. There is, however, much of Ibsen, as he saw himself at the time, in Hedda Gabler.

With the exception of *Little Eyolf* (1894), the weakest of the later plays, the last plays are, to a great extent, confessional. *The Master Builder* (1892) is one of Ibsen's most beautiful dramas, essentially a dialogue between a guilt-burdened artist and the youth he betrayed, played against the wife and children he has "murdered" for his ambition. *John Gabriel Borkman* (1896), Ibsen's bleakest play, is a study of a man (he could be today's industrialist) who has sacrificed everything to his vision, until he is killed by the forces in nature he has sought to control. Glimpsed in the background, in scenes alternately comic and pathetic, is the alternative to Borkman's way of life, the life of sensual pleasure. But no synthesis seems possible of the spirit and the flesh: the "third kingdom" of which Ibsen had dreamed so long is farther away than ever.

Ibsen's last play, *When We Dead Awaken* (1899), more symbolic than even those which immediately precede it, is an artist's confession of his failure as a man and of his doubts about his achievement. The play is not, however, just about the cost of great achievement: it is also about that achievement and about the man who, as Ibsen expressed it in his first words as a dramatist, hears a voice urging him on and heeds that voice. Soon after this play, Ibsen suffered a stroke that ended his career. He died on May 23, 1906.

Further Reading

Ibsen's collected works, together with all draft material, lists of English translations and criticism, and introductions by the editor, were translated in *Ibsen*, edited by James W. McFarlane (7 vols., 1960-70). The standard biography is by Halvdan Koht, *The Life of Ibsen* (2 vols., trans. 1931). Ibsen's daughter-in-law, Bergljot Ibsen, in *The Three Ibsens* (trans. 1951), gives valuable information on his life. More specialized is Brian W. Downs, *The Intellectual Background* (1946).

On Ibsen's plays generally, George Bernard Shaw's classic *The Quintessence of Ibsenism* (1913) stresses the social reform aspects, and Herman J. Weigand, *The Modern Ibsen: A Reconsideration* (1925), emphasizes Ibsen the psychologist. John Northam, *Ibsen's Dramatic Method* (1953), is invaluable for the light it sheds on Ibsen's visual imagery. See also Eric

Bentley, *The Life of the Drama* (1964), and Maurice Valency, *The Flower and the Castle* (1964), on Ibsen and August Strindberg and their contribution to modern drama. The prefaces to Rolf Fjelde's excellent translations of some of Ibsen's plays (Signet paperbacks) are well worth reading.

Additional Sources

Bull, Francis, *Ibsen, the man and the dramatist,* Philadelphia: R. West, 1977.

Duve, Arne, *The real drama of Henrik Ibsen?,* Oslo: Lanser forl., 1977.

Gosse, Edmund, *Henrik Ibsen,* Norwood, Pa.: Norwood Editions, 1978 c1907.

Jorgenson, Theodore, *Henrik Ibsen: a study in art and personality,* Westport, Conn.: Greenwood Press, 1978, 1945.

Macfall, Haldane, *Ibsen: the man, his art & his significance,* Norwood, Pa.: Norwood Editions, 1978; Folcroft, Pa.: Folcroft Library Editions, 1976.

Shafer, Yvonne, *Henrik Ibsen: life, work, and criticism,* Fredericton, N.B., Canada: York Press, 1985. □

Harold LeClaire Ickes

As U.S. secretary of the interior for 13 years, Harold LeClaire Ickes (1874-1952) played a key role in developing New Deal policies.

Harold L. Ickes was born March 15, 1874, on a farm near Holidaysburg, Pa. He grew up in nearby Altoona, where his father ran a store and dabbled in local politics. At the age of 16, after his mother's death, he went to Chicago to live with his aunt and uncle. Following his graduation from high school, Ickes attended the University of Chicago part time, graduating in 1897. Ten years later he also received his law degree from the university, although he never maintained a regular practice. In 1907 he married Anna Wilmarth Thompson, a wealthy widow, with whom he had a son.

Ickes was a prominent local and regional political adviser and campaign organizer for reform-minded Republican office seekers in Illinois. However, his political irregularity was notorious in party circles. In 1912 he fervently backed Theodore Roosevelt's presidential candidacy on the Progressive party ticket. In 1920, after he failed in his attempt to get the Republican presidential nomination for California Progressive Hiram Johnson, Ickes voted for the Democratic candidate. In 1924 and 1928 he again voted for Democratic presidential candidates.

Ickes worked hard in Franklin Roosevelt's presidential campaign in 1932. After Roosevelt's overwhelming victory Ickes actively sought appointment as Indian commissioner in the Interior Department. He first met Roosevelt in February 1933, after which the president-elect named him secretary of the interior.

Besides his duties as Interior secretary in a greatly stepped-up Federal conservation program, Ickes served as administrator of the National Recovery Administration's code for the petroleum industry and as head of the Public

Works Administration. He economically administered the letting of billions of dollars in Federal contracts for a great variety of undertakings, including much new naval construction. Despite Ickes's disputes with fellow New Dealers and his generally cantankerous disposition, Roosevelt appreciated his abilities. During World War II as petroleum administrator for war, Ickes coordinated the conservation, acquisition, and allocation of the nation's oil resources.

Roosevelt's death in April 1945 was a deep personal loss to Ickes. He never really got along with Roosevelt's successor, Harry Truman. In 1946, when President Truman tried to appoint an oil company executive as undersecretary of the Navy, Ickes attacked the administration for lack of interest in oil conservation and angrily announced his resignation. His tenure as secretary of the interior had been the longest in the department's history.

Ickes's wife had died in 1935. Three years later Ickes had married Jane Dahlman, a recent college graduate; they had two children. Now, leaving government service, Ickes lived in semiretirement with his family on his farm near Olney, Md. He wrote a syndicated newspaper column and contributed regularly to the liberal weekly *New Republic*. On Feb. 3, 1952, he died in a Washington hospital.

Further Reading

Ickes's rambling, sardonic personal recollections appeared in 1943 under the title *The Autobiography of a Curmudgeon*. Of much greater value for understanding his life is *The Secret Diary of Harold L. Ickes* (3 vols., 1953-1954), which covers the period 1933-1941 week by week. Ickes's role in the early years of the New Deal is treated in Arthur M. Schlesinger, Jr., *The Age of Roosevelt* (3 vols., 1957-1960).

Additional Sources

Clarke, Jeanne Nienaber, *Roosevelt's warrior: Harold L. Ickes and the New Deal*, Baltimore: Johns Hopkins University Press, 1996.

Ickes, Harold L. (Harold LeClair), *The autobiography of a curmudgeon*, Westport, Conn.: Greenwood Press, 1985, 1943.

Lear, Linda J., *Harold L. Ickes: the aggressive progressive, 1874-1933*, New York: Garland Pub., 1981.

Watkins, T. H. (Tom H.), *Righteous pilgrim: the life and times of Harold L. Ickes, 1874-1952*, New York: H. Holt, 1990.

White, Graham J., *Harold Ickes of the New Deal: his private life and public career*, Cambridge, Mass.: Harvard University Press, 1985. □

Ictinus

Ictinus (active second half of 5th century B.C.) was a Greek architect and the chief designer of the Parthenon. In addition, he is known to have prepared a design for the Telesterion, the great hall of the Mysteries at Eleusis.

Of what city Ictinus was a citizen is not known, but the importance of the building projects assigned to him in Athens makes it not unlikely that he was an Athenian. Like Phidias, he may have been part of a coterie of artists and intellectuals who were particularly favored by Pericles and who were assigned the task of formulating and giving external expression to the ideals of Periclean Athens.

The intellectual side of Ictinus's activity is confirmed by Vitruvius, who records the existence of a treatise about the Parthenon written by the architect and an associate named Carpion. This treatise presumably dealt with the well-known "refinements" of Greek temple architecture— proportional relationships, curvature of horizontal lines, and inclination of vertical members—which Ictinus brought to their highest point of development in the Parthenon.

Ictinus seems to have been particularly interested in the development of interior space in Greek architecture. In the Parthenon he integrated the colossal cult image of Athena with the cella in which it stood by using the superimposed rows of Doric columns which supported the ceiling of the cella as a three-sided frame for the image. He also incorporated elements of the Ionic order into the Doric cella— notably the famed Ionic frieze around its exterior and Ionic columns to support the ceiling of its west room. Both Vitruvius and the archeological evidence suggest that the distinctive feature of Ictinus's design for the Telesterion at Eleusis, a project never completed, was to reduce greatly the number of interior supports so that there would have been more unobstructed space than ever before for witnessing the most secret rites of the Mysteries.

The traveler Pausanias states that the temple at Bassae was a votive offering to Apollo for aid in averting the plague of 430/429 B.C. Some architectural historians find it difficult to believe that the old-fashioned exterior of this temple could have been built by Ictinus after his work on the Parthenon. The design of its interior, on the other hand, incorporating the first use of the Corinthian order, engaged Ionic columns, and an Ionic frieze, seems to represent an imaginative extension of the innovations in the Parthenon.

It may therefore be that the temple was begun by another architect around the middle of the fifth century B.C. but left unfinished for a time and that Ictinus was invited to complete it by designing its interior somewhat after 430 B.C.

Further Reading

The literary sources regarding Ictinus are collected in Jerome J. Pollitt, *The Art of Greece, 1400-31 B.C.: Sources and Documents* (1965). A detailed discussion of Ictinus's buildings is in William Bell Dinsmoor, *The Architecture of Ancient Greece* (1950). For illustrations see Helmut Berve and Gottfried Gruben, *Greek Temples, Theatres, and Shrines* (1963). The archeological evidence for the Telesterion at Eleusis is summarized in George E. Mylonas, *Eleusis and the Eleusinian Mysteries* (1961). □

Idris I

His full name was Sidi Muhammad Idris Al-Mahdi As-sanusi (1889-1983). The first and only king of Libya, he reigned as Idris I from 1950 to 1969. Although he led his country to independence, his conservatism finally brought about his overthrow in a military coup under the direction of the controversial leader, Muammar al-Qaddafi.

Libya's future king was born on March 13, 1890, in Jaghbub, an oasis in the eastern province of Cyrenaica. At the time, Libya was part of the Ottoman Empire. Idris I died in exile in Cairo, Egypt, in 1983.

Leader in Exile

When his father died in 1902, Idris became head of the Sanusiyah, an Islamic mystical brotherhood. Still a minor, he did not assume active leadership until 1916. His main problem over the next few years was how to deal with the Italians, who had invaded Libya in 1922 in an effort to build a North African empire. Italy never established its rule much beyond the coast, and in 1917, Idris was able to secure a ceasefire and confirm his own authority in Cyrenaica while acknowledging Italian supremacy in the area.

Given the title of emir, Idris established a parliament and secured financial grants from Italy. But when he proved unable or unwilling to disarm his tribal supporters, Italy invaded in the spring of 1922. Idris saw little point in resisting and went into exile in Egypt.

The War Years

Idris continued to direct his followers while in exile. Through the years, the Sanusiyah brotherhood had been changing into a much more political organization. Idris's support came from conservative tribesmen who were mainly concerned with restoring his rule to the province of Cyrenaica. But a younger faction in this area wanted a union of the Libyan provinces of Cyrenaica, Tripolitania, and Fezzan.

Libya was the scene of heavy fighting in World War II, and Idris recruited guerrillas and scouts to aid the British, who eventually occupied Cyrenaica and Tripolitania. Fezzan came under control of the French.

Idris returned to his homeland in 1947, but the issue of a Libyan union was not solved until two years later. In November 1949, the United Nations resolved that representatives of the three provinces in question should meet in a national assembly to decide their future. The assembly decided on a constitutional monarchy and offered the throne to Idris.

Independence and Exile

Libya declared its independence in December 1951, with Idris I as king. Two capitals were established, one in Tripoli (Tripolitania), home of the parliament, and one in Bangasi, meeting place of the king and his cabinet.

As the reigning monarch, Idris had complete control of the army and a good deal of influence over the parliament, which was mainly composed of powerful tribal leaders. In addition Libya, an arid, impoverished country with crop production limited to the narrow coastline, could not flourish without heavy aid from Western powers. In time, younger citizens, especially the military, grew tied of the king's conservative policies and extreme dependence on the West.

Idris I had the misfortune to require medical treatment at a Turkish spa in September 1969. While he was out of the country, he was toppled from power in a military coup led by controversial Libyan leader, Muammar al-Qaddafi, then an army colonel. As of 1997, al-Qaddafi remained in power.

Immediately following the 1969 coup, Idris I and his family fled to Greece. They then asked for and received political asylum in Cairo, Egypt. Idris had married his cousin in 1933 and, according to Islamic law, was allowed to take another wife. In 1955, Idris married the daughter of an Egyptian landowner. He remained in exile in Cairo until his death on May 25, 1983.

Further Reading

Idris is discussed in studies of Libya such as Ismail R. Khalidi, *Constitutional Development in Libya* (1956); H. S. Willard, *Libya: The New Arab Kingdom of North Africa* (1956); and Majid Khadduri, *Modern Libya: A Study in Political Development* (1963). See also Nicola A. Ziadeh, *Sanusiyah: A Study of a Revivalist Movement in Islam* (1958). □

Muhammad ibn Muhammad al-Idrisi

The Arab geographer Muhammad ibn Muhammad al-Idrisi (1100-1165) wrote the *Book of Roger*, a world geography, for King Roger II of Sicily. His work, marking the end of the classical age of Arab geography, sums up much of its achievement.

Al-Idrisi was born in Ceuta in Morocco, a descendant of the sharifian Hammudid dynasty, which had ruled over Málaga until 1057 and over Ceuta and Tangier until 1084. He studied at Cordova, the center of scholarship in Moslem Spain. In his youth he traveled widely, visiting Asia Minor, North Africa, Spain, France, and probably the English coast. At the invitation of Roger II, Norman king of Sicily, he went, not later than 1144, to live at the latter's court in Palermo. Roger's motives in inviting him may have been partly political. Al-Idrisi, as a descendant of a dynasty ruling in Moslem Spain and North Africa, and having an intimate knowledge of these regions, must have seemed a useful tool in Roger's designs on establishing his hegemony over the western Mediterranean.

Roger also had, however, a keen theoretical interest in geography. Since 1139 he had sponsored an ambitious project for a world geography to be based on the Greek, Latin, and Arabic geographical literature as well as on contemporary reports and research. He appointed a commission to gather and sift the material. Al-Idrisi soon became its leading member and in this function developed into one of the great Arab geographers.

Book of Roger

At the order of the King, al-Idrisi produced a silver celestial sphere and an enormous map of the world in disk form cast on a silver base. As a commentary to it, he wrote his large geography of the world. It was completed in January 1154 and became known as the *Book of Roger* in recognition of the King's important role in sponsoring it.

In this work al-Idrisi divided the known world, in accordance with the Greek tradition, into seven climes and described each clime in detail moving from west to east. A world map and 70 sectional maps accompany the description. His conception of the world as reflected in the maps is more influenced by the Ptolemaic than the Arab tradition. Al-Idrisi used the geography of Ptolemy and many works of the Arab geographers as sources, though some important ones escaped him.

Al-Idrisi also relied on reports of contemporary travelers and, for the regions he had visited, on his own observations. Quite original and generally precise is his description of the countries of Europe, for which he had to rely almost exclusively on contemporary reports. Although an abridged version of the *Book of Roger* was published in Rome in 1592 and a Latin translation of it in 1619, the full text has never been edited. A complete edition was under preparation in Italy in the early 1970s.

After the death of Roger in 1154, al-Idrisi produced an enlarged version of his geography for Roger's son and successor, William I. This work is lost. Al-Idrisi left Sicily, perhaps as a result of the anti-Moslem riots in Palermo in 1161. Later he composed a shorter compendium of world geography which is extant in manuscript. Al-Idrisi also wrote a pharmacological treatise and some poetry. According to a conjecture on the basis of a poor source, he died in Ceuta in 1165.

Further Reading

The section of al-Idrisi's geography on India and the neighboring countries was translated into English by S. Maqbul Ahmad as *Al-Sharif al-Idrisi: India and the Neighbouring Territories* (1960). It contains biographical notes and a discussion of al-Idrisi's method. □

Tokugawa Ieyasu

Tokugawa Ieyasu (1542-1616) was the founder and first shogun of the Tokugawa shogunate, or military government, which maintained effective rule over Japan from 1600 until 1867.

The period from 1477 until 1568 was a time of disorder and disunity in Japan. The traditional government of the country, the imperial court at Kyoto, had 1 1/2 centuries earlier delegated ruling authority to the shogunate of the warrior family of Ashikaga, which also had its offices in Kyoto. But, although the Ashikaga shoguns had managed to maintain a loose control over much of the land until about 1477, thereafter their central power virtually disappeared. For the remainder of the 15th century and during the first half of the 16th, warrior families everywhere were constantly at war.

By about the 1550s, however, a group of daimyos (regional barons) had succeeded in establishing stable territorial domains throughout much of the country. In 1568 one of these daimyos, Oda Nobunaga, entered Kyoto, where, with the approval of the imperial court, he established himself as the new de facto hegemon of the central provinces of the main island of Honshu.

One of the chief reasons for Nobunaga's early success was the alliance he made with Tokugawa Ieyasu, the young daimyo of a neighboring domain. When Nobunaga under-

took his campaign westward to Kyoto, Ieyasu provided invaluable service by protecting him from attack by potential enemies to the east.

From 1568 until his death in 1582, Nobunaga destroyed or secured the allegiance of his enemies near Kyoto and gradually began to spread his control to other parts of the country. He was treacherously killed by one of his leading generals, Akechi Mitsuhide, who in turn was almost immediately attacked and killed by another of Nobunaga's generals, Toyotomi Hideyoshi.

Having avenged his lord's death, Hideyoshi undertook to complete the task of unification of Japan that Nobunaga had begun. By 1590 he had made himself the undisputed master of the country.

Rise of Ieyasu

After unifying the country, Hideyoshi arranged to have Ieyasu move his domain from the region of the Nagoya Plain to the eastern provinces of the Kanto. His intent was presumably to remove Ieyasu as far as possible from his own base in the central provinces. Yet in so doing he allowed Ieyasu to establish himself in the most agriculturally wealthy part of the country, from which the Tokugawa leader was able to assert his power on the national level after Hideyoshi's death.

Hideyoshi's final years were darkened by two unsuccessful attempts to invade Korea—in 1592 and 1597. Moreover, when he died in 1598, his successor, Hideyori, was a mere child of 5. Hideyoshi extracted vows of allegiance to Hideyori from the various leading daimyos, including Ieyasu. Yet no sooner had Hideyoshi died than the daimyos began to contend for power among themselves. Before long they had divided into two major factions, one headed by Ieyasu and the other in opposition to him. In 1600 they clashed in a great battle at Sekigahara which brought victory to Ieyasu and determined the course of Japanese history for the next 2 1/2 centuries.

Establishment of the Tokugawa
Shogunate

After the battle of Sekigahara all those daimyos who had not yet accepted Ieyasu's overlordship were obliged to do so. Although Ieyasu did not actually receive the title of shogun from the imperial court until 1603, for all practical purposes the rule of the Tokugawa shogunate, whose headquarters he established in Edo (present-day Tokyo) in the eastern provinces, began in 1600.

The establishment of the Tokugawa shogunate was in great measure a logical outcome of the institutional developments of the preceding century. Rather than seeking to pursue and completely humble his chief opponents after Sekigahara, Ieyasu settled for an overall national hegemony under which the daimyos retained virtually complete autonomy over their domains but in return paid allegiance to Edo and were under certain circumstances personally subject to its jurisdiction.

Three types of daimyos ruled the feudal domains that constituted Japan during the Tokugawa period: *fudai,* or

hereditary daimyos, who had become the vassals of Ieyasu before the battle of Sekigahara; *tozama,* or outside daimyos, including both Ieyasu's allies and opponents at Sekigahara; and a small number of *shimpan,* or collateral daimyos, who were directly related to the Tokugawa family.

Of the two major types of daimyos, hereditary and outside, the former, as long-standing vassals, were allowed to hold posts in the Tokugawa shogunate, whereas the outside daimyos were theoretically barred from any participation whatever in the administrative affairs of the Edo government. However, all daimyos, with only a few exceptions based on special circumstances, were obliged to spend part of their time each year in attendance at the Shogun's court at Edo. This system of "alternate attendance," which was evolved during the first few decades of Tokugawa rule, was the chief means by which the Tokugawa exercised surveillance over the daimyos. When the daimyos were not in Edo, moreover, they were obliged to leave their wives and children there as hostages.

Ieyasu was immensely rich. By the time of the establishment of the shogunate he had acquired roughly one-quarter of the rice-producing land of the country as the private domain of the Tokugawa family. In addition, as shogun, he "nationalized" most of the important cities—including Kyoto (the seat of the imperial court), Osaka, and Nagasaki—as well as certain mining and other important sites. The additional revenues he was able to draw from these sources handsomely augmented his already preponderant income from agriculture.

Ieyasu and the Europeans

In 1600, the year of the battle of Sekigahara, the first English and Dutch arrived in Japan. These newcomers were Protestants and were quite willing to trade without engaging also in missionary activities. Ieyasu even elevated one of them, an Englishman named Will Adams, to the rank of retainer and made him the shogunate's official adviser on foreign affairs.

Yet, even though Ieyasu (like Hideyoshi before him) was personally most anxious to develop trade with the Europeans, and the arrival of the Protestants seemed to present an opportunity to dispense with the Christianizing which the Catholics insisted upon, there remained the problem of how to deal with the Portuguese and Spanish who were still in Japan.

Ieyasu became increasingly convinced that Christianity must be banned, and in his final years he took steps to enforce and to expand the original injunctions of Hideyoshi against the foreign religion and its missionaries. He even executed some native Christians who did not comply with his will, but it was not until the time of the second shogun, Hidetada, that the persecution of both European and Japanese Christians was undertaken with ferocity.

The leaders of the Tokugawa shogunate had become inordinately fearful that Christianity was subversive to Japanese society and that Tokugawa rule might be threatened by a league of foreign Christians (especially Portuguese and Spanish) and daimyos of the western provinces. This fearfulness contributed importantly to the final decision made in the 1630s to institute a national seclusion policy. According to the seclusion policy, all Japanese were forbidden henceforth to leave the country, and only the Dutch and Chinese were allowed to engage in trade on a strictly limited basis at the single port of Nagasaki in Kyushu.

It would be difficult to overstress the importance of the national seclusion policy on the history of the Tokugawa period. Without question it was the chief reason for the longevity of Tokugawa rule: more than 2 1/2 centuries of almost unbroken peace. Yet the Japanese had to pay a price for this age of peace, which was based on withdrawal from the outside world. It was during this period that the West surged ahead into the scientific and industrial revolutions; and when Japan finally reentered the international community in the mid-19th century, it was forced to deal with the Westerners on radically different terms.

Consolidation of Tokugawa Rule

Ieyasu was by nature an exceedingly cautious man. Mindful that many prominent chieftains earlier in Japanese history (as well as his two immediate predecessors, Nobunaga and Hideyoshi) had failed to perpetuate the rule of their families, he sought by careful stages to consolidate the governing position of the Tokugawa after the battle of Sekigahara.

Despite Ieyasu's great military victory in 1600, there remained the widespread feeling that Hideyoshi's young son Hideyori should by right ultimately succeed his father as national hegemon. Accordingly, although he took the title of shogun in 1603, Ieyasu allowed the Toyotomi and their supporters to harbor at least the hope that power would be transferred to Hideyori after he reached adulthood. This hope was greatly reduced in 1605, however, when Ieyasu resigned the office of shogun in favor of his own son Hidetada. Clearly this move could be interpreted only as an effort to minimize disruption within the shogunate after Ieyasu's death and thus to perpetuate Tokugawa rule.

But it was not until 1614 that Ieyasu finally decided to settle the Toyotomi issue once and for all. By means of highly contrived charges of rebellious intent on the part of Hideyori, he forced the Toyotomi and their supporters to take up a position of armed opposition to the Tokugawa in the great castle at Osaka, which had originally been constructed by Hideyoshi. In 1614 Ieyasu personally laid siege to the castle with a great force. But, much to his chagrin, he was unable to force its defenders (numbering perhaps 90,000) to capitulate.

To avoid further embarrassment, Ieyasu offered peace if Hideyori would agree to having the castle's outer defenses leveled. Yet no sooner had this been done than Ieyasu renewed his attack on the castle and slaughtered nearly all of its occupants, including Hideyori. Ieyasu had acted treacherously, but very efficiently, in eliminating the last major threat to the superiority of the Tokugawa.

Although Ieyasu had resigned the office of shogun in 1605 and had even "retired" to the town of Sumpu to the west of Edo, he had in no sense relinquished his rulership of the shogunate. Until his death in 1616, one year after victory at the battle of Osaka Castle, he remained the guiding influence in shogunate affairs.

The Tokugawa shogunate, even though it was based on a hegemony which allowed extensive autonomy to the various daimyo domains, was the first government in Japanese history (apart from Hideyoshi's, which had lasted only a few years) that was in a position to rule on a truly national scale. It had been founded by professional warriors, and many of its offices were organized along military lines. Nevertheless, it became the government of a country securely at peace, and the attitude of its officials was inevitably transformed more and more into that of civilian administrators.

The philosophy of rule and maintenance of social order that came to appeal most to the leaders of Tokugawa Japan was Confucianism or, more precisely, Neo-Confucianism, which had long been established as the orthodox sociopolitical creed of China. Neo-Confucian ideas had been introduced to Japan several centuries earlier from China, but they were of little practical value to the warring chieftains of the medieval age. The Tokugawa, however, found in this philosophy an eminently appropriate set of precepts for their exercise of national rule.

Neo-Confucianism "legitimized" the division of Japanese society into four major classes—samurai, peasants, artisans, and merchants—and the enforcement of strictly hierarchical personal relations as embodied particularly in the virtues of filial piety and loyalty. Neo-Confucian doctrine also endorsed the essentially anticommercial bias of a state whose chief form of economic wealth was agriculture. Commerce did, in fact, advance greatly during the Tokugawa period, but the shogunate always maintained the official attitude that artisans and merchants were less socially respectable than either samurai or peasants.

Ieyasu in History

When Ieyasu died in 1616, his son Hidetada had already been shogun for 11 years. Hidetada and his son, the third shogun, Iemitsu, continued the general policies of the shogunate's founder. By the time of Iemitsu's death in 1651, the Tokugawa regime was firmly set in the form that it was to retain for 2 more centuries.

Whereas Nobunaga undertook unification and Hideyoshi completed it, Ieyasu made it enduring. The magnitude of Ieyasu's achievement as a dynastic founder is unchallengeable; yet his capacity as a military commander has perhaps been underrated because of unfortunate comparison with the superb generalship of Hideyoshi. Nevertheless, Ieyasu was without doubt one of the greatest field commanders and one of the greatest governmental administrators in Japanese history.

Following Japan's defeat in World War II there was a distinct emotional reaction against the historical memory of the Tokugawa period. It was felt that this age, with its stern "feudal" polity and, in particular, its unnatural policy of national seclusion, had somehow "perverted" Japan and had caused it to pursue the course that led ultimately to disaster in war. Since Japan's remarkable economic recovery in the 1950s and 1960s, however, there has been a mellowing of feeling and a greater willingness to note the praiseworthy features of the Tokugawa period and its rulers. One result of this has been a particular revival of interest in Ieyasu. He now enjoys a historical popularity commensurate with his distinguished role in the evolution of Japan.

Further Reading

A biography of Tokugawa Ieyasu in English, although dated, is Arthur L. Sadler, *The Maker of Modern Japan: The Life of Tokugawa Ieyasu* (1937). George Sansom, *A History of Japan, 1334-1615* (1961), and John W. Hall, *Government and Local Power in Japan, 500 to 1700* (1966), contain excellent accounts of the process of unification in the late 16th century. Another good source for information about the founding of the Tokugawa shogunate by Ieyasu is Conrad Totman, *Politics in the Tokugawa Bakufu, 1600-1843* (1967). Two important books that deal with the Western presence in Japan during the late 16th and early 17th centuries are Charles R. Boxer, *The Christian Century in Japan* (1951), and Michael Cooper, *They Came to Japan* (1965). □

Enrique V. Iglesias

The Uruguayan economist, banker, and public official Enrique V. Iglesias (born 1930) was active in economic development in Uruguay and Latin America for many years before becoming president of the Inter-American Development Bank in 1988. He also served in the United Nations and other international organizations involved in economic development, energy, and environmental issues.

A man of humble origins—the son of an immigrant Spanish grocer—Enrique V. Iglesias was born in the northwest province of Asturias, Spain, in 1930. He later became a naturalized citizen of Uruguay. Enrique Iglesias attended the University of the Republic of Uruguay and majored in economics and business administration, graduating in 1953. He went on to pursue specialized programs of study in the United States and France. After finishing his studies, Iglesias worked in the private banking sector before he initiated his long career of public service.

At the University of the Republic of Uruguay, Enrique V. Iglesias held the Chair on Economic Development and served as director of the Institute of Economics from 1952 to 1967. He also served on the board of the Latin American Social Sciences Council (CLACSO) and took part in various training courses organized by the Economic Commission for Latin America and the Caribbean (ECLAC), the Institute for Latin American Integration (INTAL), and the Latin American Institute for Economic and Social Planning (ILPES). He joined the board of directors of ILPES in 1965, was its chairman from 1967 to 1972, and served as interim director general in 1977-1978.

A Banker in Uruguay

In 1954 Iglesias initiated his career in the private sector as managing director of a bank, the Union de Bancos del Uruguay. From 1962 to 1966 he served as technical director of Uruguay's National Planning Office, where he was responsible for developing and implementing the country's first National Economic and Social Development Plan. Overlapping with his duties at the Planning Office, Iglesias was Uruguay's delegate, from 1964 to 1967, to the Conferences of the Latin American Free Trade Association (LAFTA) and to ECLAC. He was also the representative of his country on the Inter-American Committee on the Alliance for Progress (ICAP).

Iglesias was president of Uruguay's Central Bank from 1966 to 1968, during which time he directed various missions at national and international levels on behalf of his government. During the next three years, from 1968 to 1971, he headed the group of experts who collaborated with Raul Prebisch on an extensive study of Latin America's economic situation, carried out under the auspices of the Inter-American Development Bank. In 1970 he headed a mission to the Venezuelan government agency CORDIPLAN to provide technical advice in regard to planning.

An International Public Official

On March 27, 1972, Iglesias was named executive secretary of the Economic Commission for Latin America and the Caribbean, first with the rank of United Nations Assistant Secretary General, and later with the rank of Under Secretary General. He held his post at ECLAC until February 1985, after which he served as Uruguay's Minister of External Relations from March 1, 1985, until he became president of the Inter-American Development Bank (IDB) on April 1, 1988. While serving as minister he chaired the meeting of ministers convened to launch the Uruguay Round of multilateral negotiations within the framework of the General Agreement on Tariffs and Trade (GATT). At these talks he was labeled ''the star performer'' by the *Financial Times* for saving the negotiations after a 30-hour marathon bargaining session.

He was a member of the Inter-American Committee on the Alliance for Progress' panel of expert advisers. He served as president of the International Society for Development and a member of the North-South Round Table on Energy into the 1990s. He was also a member of the board of trustees of the Institute for Ibero-American Cooperation, of Spain, and in 1982 he was honored with the Prince of Asturias award for Ibero-American cooperation for his contribution towards greater understanding between the peoples of Spain and Latin America and the rest of the international community.

As a dedicated environmentalist, Enrique Iglesias served as senior adviser to the 1972 Conference on the Human Environment in Stockholm, and then as secretary general of the United Nations Conference on New and Renewable Sources of Energy, held in Nairobi, Kenya, from February to August 1981. He was chairman of the United Nations Inter-Agency Group on the Development of Renewable Sources of Energy, as well as chairman of the advisory panel on energy on the Brundtland Commission in 1981. In 1982 he was named by the United Nations Secretary General as special adviser on new and renewable sources of energy to the Director General for Development and International Economic Cooperation. From 1984 to 1986 he chaired the Energy Advisory Panel for the World Commission on Environment and Development (Brundtland Commission). His deep interest in the environment was reflected in the agenda of the Inter-American Development Bank after he assumed his presidency.

Heading the IDB

Iglesias worked hard to create what he called "a big bank" to meet the region's needs. He also tried to streamline the IDB and make it a more "efficient" bank, giving it the flexibility it needed to make a major contribution in the 1990s. Under Iglesias' tenure, the IDB saw drastic cuts in personnel. In addition, he tried to bring the bank into closer association with Bretton Woods institutions.

Iglesias was determined that the IDB make an impact on Latin America's overriding issue, the debt. He wanted to increase the volume of lending and to move into new lending areas. Another issue on the top of his agenda was the environment, an area where Iglesias had plenty of international experience.

In 1994, calling it a model for programs worldwide, the Inter-American Development Bank and Brazilian officials launched a $20-million project to aid Brazil's growing number of neglected, homeless children. The nationwide program was a departure for the bank, which until a few years ago supported only transportation and energy projects. In recent years, the bank had branched into environmental programs, such as sewer construction and the cleanup of Rio's Guanabara Bay.

The biggest achievements of 1995 were Argentine and Mexican resistance to financial crisis, Brazilian stabilization, and growth in the rest of the region, according to the IDB. However, the multilateral organism must confront new challenges for the future: increasing soft loans to the poorest regional nations, funding infrastructure works in the regional blocs and drawing a lesson from the collapse of the Mexican peso in 1994—the so-called "Tequila effect." Iglesias talked of the region's achievements in 1995, but warned that the IDB would be proposing a "controversial" fiscal control proposal in the meeting on controlling capital flight. Iglesias said that the world economic agencies need to pursue policies that are a change "from charity to empowerment." He committed the IDB to some $500 million over the next five years to "the little bancitos." Iglesias said IADB lending had focused on social projects and reform in 1996, emphasizing urban development, public health and education.

Iglesias met with World Bank president James Wolfensohn, the managing director of the International Monetary Fund (IMF), Michel Camdessus, the president, secretary and assistant secretary of CELAM, and the head of the Social Pastoral of Brazilian Bishops, the first joint financial-Catholic gathering convened by the Justice and Peace

Pontifical Council. Iglesias also met with Columbia's new foreign minister, Maria Emma Mejia, in 1996.

In January 1997, the IDB and the Mexican government signed contracts for loan guarantees worth $915 million. More than half of the total was earmarked for social projects including a program of modernization of the labor market. Meanwhile, $365 million dollars was slated for a hydraulic sanitation project in the Mexico. Iglesias expressed his organization's confidence in Mexico, saying, "We have always believed in this country." Iglesias predicted that Mexico would make an economic growth of 5 percent in 1997.

Iglesias is a man of great personal energy, who is said to have to work to relax. He is an aficionado of operas and tries to squeeze in time to pursue this pastime. He is fluent in four languages—English, French, Portuguese, and Italian—in addition to his native Spanish. He is a devout Catholic.

Further Reading

Enrique Iglesias wrote numerous articles and papers on Latin American and Uruguayan economic issues, on such subjects as the capital market, Uruguay's exchange system, the nature and scope of external financing problems, the struggle of multilateralism, and Inter-American Development Bank policies in the 1960s. He was also the author of *Latin America on the Threshold of the 1980s; The Energy Challenge;* and *Development and Equity: the Challenge of the 1980s.* □

St. Ignatius of Antioch

The letters of the Christian bishop St. Ignatius of Antioch (died ca. 115) are an important source of knowledge about the early Church.

Ignatius was overseer (bishop) of the Christians in Antioch in Syria during one of the persecutions that broke out while Trajan was emperor. When Ignatius was arrested, he refused to acknowledge the official gods and, not being a Roman citizen, was sentenced to die in the amphitheater in Rome. The soldiers with whom he traveled to Rome allowed him to visit some of the Christian communities along the way. The letters he sent to these groups before he died reveal many of Christianity's ideals in the early 2d century.

Ignatius was concerned that the Christian community remain united and that it preserve the faith handed down by the Apostles. He saw the pastor of the community, the bishop, as the leader of this unity in faith. "Do nothing without the bishops and presbyters," he wrote. "It is not lawful apart from the bishops either to baptize or to hold a love-feast."

Ignatius's letters also reflected the growing influence of Greek philosophical concerns over the inevitability of death. Ignatius was convinced that Christian baptism brought about a new life in Christ and that this life was eternal unless it was frustrated by sin. Because martyrdom was a way to overcome the sins committed since baptism,

Ignatius wanted to be martyred in order to enter more quickly into eternal life with Christ. He said that if the animals in the amphitheater were not hungry he would urge them on. "Let me be given to the wild beasts, for through them I can attain unto God. I am God's wheat, and I am ground by the wild beasts that I may be found the pure bread of Christ," he wrote to the Christians in Rome.

Some of Ignatius's language had the ring of the Greek mystery religions about it. He called the Eucharist the "mystery" of Christ's body and blood and said it was "the medicine of immortality and the antidote against death." The Eucharist, he wrote, is a spiritual food which strengthens the one who receives it and helps him into eternal life.

Ignatius was an intelligent and articulate leader who would rather die than compromise his faith. The Roman officials saw him as a disruptive influence in an empire which valued the pagan religious rites of Rome as a politically unifying force. Christians have considered Ignatius of Antioch a Father of the Church.

Further Reading

The latest English translation of Ignatius's letters is in James A. Kleist, ed., *The Epistles of St. Clement of Rome and St. Ignatius of Antioch* (1946). Virginia Corwin, *St. Ignatius and Christianity in Antioch* (1960), is a scholarly study of his life, times, and thought. Cyril Charles Richardson, *The Christianity of Ignatius of Antioch* (1935), is helpful for an understanding of the ideas Ignatius expressed in his letters. □

Through the intensive experiences of Manresa and later, Ignatius gradually developed a world view centered on cooperation with Christ and the pope as His vicar in efforts to achieve God's plan in creating and redeeming men. His constant endeavor was to lead men to give greater praise to God through both prayer and apostolic service. Hence arose his phrase, reiterated so often that it became a motto, "For the greater glory of God."

Ignatius reached Jerusalem in 1523 but could not remain because of the enmity between Christians and Turks. He returned to Barcelona and began studies (1524-1526) toward the priesthood. He then studied at the universities of Alcalá (1526-1527), Salamanca (1527), and Paris (1528-1535), where he received the degree of master of arts in April 1534. On the following August 15 he and six companions vowed to live in poverty and chastity and to go to the Holy Land or, should this prove impossible, to put themselves at the apostolic service of the pope. When war prevented passage to Jerusalem in 1537, they accepted a suggestion of Pope Paul III to find their apostolate in Italy.

Ignatius was ordained a priest on June 24, 1537. In Rome in 1539 he and nine companions drew up a "First Sketch" of a new religious order devoted to apostolic service anywhere in the world by means of preaching and any other ministry. On Sept. 27, 1540, Paul III approved this new order and its title, the Society of Jesus. In April 1541 Ignatius was elected its general for a lifelong term.

Chiefly between 1547 and 1550 Ignatius composed his *Constitutions of the Society of Jesus,* a classic both of spiri-

St. Ignatius of Loyola

The Spanish soldier and ecclesiastic St. Ignatius of Loyola (1491-1556) was the founder of the Society of Jesus, or Jesuit order.

Ignatius was born in the castle of Loyola in the Basque province of Guipúzcoa. His real name was Iñigo de Oñaz y Loyola, but from 1537 on he also used the more widely known Ignatius, especially in official documents. From the age of about 15 to 26 he lived at the fortress town of Arévalo as a page of Juan Velázquez de Cuéllar, a treasurer general for Ferdinand the Catholic. After 1516 he participated in military expeditions for the Duke of Nájera. On May 20, 1521, he was wounded in the defense of Pamplona.

During convalescence at Loyola, Ignatius read from the *Life of Christ* by Ludolph of Saxony and from the short lives of saints by Jacobus de Voragine entitled *Legenda aurea.* This resulted in a conversion, whereby he resolved to live as a knight wholly devoted to Christ and to go to the Holy Land. He abandoned Loyola in 1522 and lived for 11 months in austerity and prayer at Manresa. Here he had religious experiences which rank him among the greatest mystics of Christianity, and he composed at least the core of his famous *Spiritual Exercises* (published in 1548).

tual doctrine and of religious law. This work reveals Ignatius's genius as an organizer and administrator. To secure better cooperation in charity, he stressed obedience, but he placed many democratic procedures within the monarchical structure of his order.

From 1537 on Ignatius lived in Rome, engaging in various forms of priestly work. Twelve volumes of his correspondence have been preserved. He founded a chain of schools for the Christian education of youth. Between 1546 and 1556 he opened 33 colleges (3 of them universities) and approved 6 more. He was the first founder of a religious order to make the conducting of schools for lay students a major work prescribed by the Constitutions.

At his death on July 31, 1556, the Society of Jesus had some 1,000 members distributed in 12 provinces. He was declared a saint by Pope Gregory XV on March 12, 1622.

Further Reading

St. Ignatius's dictated autobiography is in González de Cámara, ed., *St. Ignatius' Own Story as Told to Luis González de Cámara,* translated by William J. Young (1956). Paul Dudon, *St. Ignatius of Loyola,* translated by William J. Young (1949), is the most complete and scholarly life of the saint in English. Briefer and reliable is Mary Purcell, *The First Jesuit* (1957). Ignatius's religious experiences are described and analyzed in Joseph de Guibert, *The Jesuits: Their Spiritual Doctrine and Practice* (1964), and in Ignatius's *The Constitutions of the Society of Jesus,* translated with an introduction and a commentary by G. E. Ganss (1970). □

Daisaku Ikeda

Daisaku Ikeda (born 1928), a Japanese Buddhist writer and religious leader, was the third president of the rapidly growing Soka Gakkai, a lay Buddhist organization whose goal was to promote Nichiren Sho-shu, "True" Nichiren Buddhism, worldwide. He founded the Komeito or "Clean Government Party," a successful minority political party in Japan whose goal was to establish a "Buddhist democracy."

Daisaku Ikeda was born in Tokyo, Japan, on January 2, 1928, the son of a seaweed vendor. His formal education ended with graduation from Fuji Junior College. At the age of 19 he became an employee and disciple of Toda Josei. The Japanese government had imprisoned Toda and his mentor, Tsunesaburo Makiguchi, for refusal to participate in the state rites of Shinto and to conform to government restrictions on religion. Upon release a year before Ikeda joined him, Toda began to reconstruct the lay Buddhist religious movement of which Makiguchi was the founder under the name Soka Gakkai, the "Value-Creation Society." On May 3, 1951, Toda became its second president. For 11 years Ikeda received intense training from

Toda and accompanied him on most of his travels. On May 3, 1952, Ikeda married Kaneko Shiraki, by whom he had three sons.

Under Toda's influence Ikeda ascended in the Soka Gakkai organization until he became chief of staff of the Youth Division. During this period of successful, aggressive evangelism by the movement, when allegations of terrorism, coercion, and intimidation were made against it, Ikeda became an aggressive evangelist. Upon Toda's death on April 2, 1958, Ikeda became the general administrator and on May 3, 1960, after a period of factionalism in the movement, Ikeda was appointed its third president. His active presidency, popular personality, and close control over the movement's activities contributed to its phenomenal growth.

One of Soka Gakkai's writers said that "The history of the activities of President Ikeda is no other than the history of the growth of Soka Gakkai." Its founder, Makiguchi, was a geography teacher who with Toda was converted to the relatively small Nichiren Sho-shu, "true Nichiren sect." The sect believed it was the only true group of followers of the Japanese Buddhist prophet Nichiren (1222-1282). In the spirit of Nichiren, it taught that he, not the historical Buddha, is the true Buddha for this last age and that the only acceptable religious acts for this age are recitation of the *daimoku* or name of the *Lotus Sutra* ("Namu myoho renge-kyo") and worship of the sacred diagram, or *gohonzon,* they believe Nichiren had drawn. Soka Gakkai is devoted to the promotion of Nichiren Sho-shu, which it considers the only true religion. Its stated purpose is "to bring peace and happi-

ness to all mankind." With its headquarters at the foot of Mt. Fuji, Soka Gakkai considers pilgrimage to the head temple of Nichiren Sho-shu there, Taisekiji, as an important act of devotion.

Makiguchi died in prison and is considered a martyr. Toda organized the society along military lines and increased the movement's evangelistic fervor through development of the method Nichiren called *shakubuku*, "break and subdue." It included denunciation of rival religions and forceful argumentation to break down the resistance of potential converts. By 1957 Soka Gakkai proclaimed that it had attained its target of 750,000 families months earlier than expected.

Though continuing to maintain the exclusivism of the movement, Ikeda set out to broaden the appeal of Soka Gakkai through better public relations and tempered its open aggressiveness, while still maintaining its goal of *kosen-rufu*, worldwide-dissemination. After accusations of scandal in 1969, he turned the movement's attention to the formation of educational and cultural organizations, founding the Min-on Concert Association and the Oriental Institute of Academic Research in 1962 and the Fuji Art Museum in 1973. He also shifted its emphasis to international affairs and the peace movement.

In the tradition of Nichiren's teaching of *obutsumyogo*, "agreement in purpose of government and Buddhism," on November 17, 1964, Ikeda founded the Komeito, "Clean Government Party," based on the previous success of Soka Gakkai-supported candidates in Japanese elections. Though officially an independent party, the two work closely together. In May 1970 Ikeda announced its separation from Soka Gakkai in response to a public scandal investigation by the Japanese Diet. At the end of 1969 Soka Gakkai and Komeito had been accused of the suppression of the publication of a series of books criticizing the movement. Since then, however, Soka Gakkai-Komeito unity has, in effect, been restored. Komeito remains a minority party, but it has been successful in large metropolitan districts, taking a liberal, neutralist, pacifist, and socialist stance in Japanese politics. In 1978 it joined a more conservative alliance with the majority Liberal Democratic Party and the Democratic Socialist Party.

Ikeda wrote over 100 books and articles concerning "true" Buddhism, its history and the benefits that it can provide which lead to individual happiness and world peace. He was recognized as an honorary citizen of 46 cities in the United States and in 1975 received an honorary doctorate from Moscow State University, followed by honorary degrees from the University of San Marcos (1981), Beijing University (1984) and Fudan University (1984). Also in 1984 Ikeda received the United Nations Peace Prize, again followed by the Kenya Oral Literature Award (1986), the Chinese Peace and Friendship Trophy (1986), and the Shastri Memorial Award (India, 1990). He portrayed Soka Gakkai as a "Third Civilization," a synthesis of East and West and an alternative to East-West power blocks, and under his leadership the movement continued to spread overseas. It claimed more than 10 million adherents world-wide, with 200,000 in the United States in the mid-1980s. He resided in Tokyo.

Ikeda's more recent publications include *The Human Revolution* Vols.I-V (1984); *Life: An Enigma, a Precious Jewel* (1982); *Buddhism and Cosmos* (1986); and *Unlocking the Mysteries of Birth and Death* (1988).

Further Reading

Studies of Soka Gakkai and Ikeda's place in the movement include chapter nine of H. Neill McFarland, *The Rush Hour of the Gods* (1967), and Kiyoaki Murata, *Japan's New Buddhism: An Objective Account of Soka Gakkai* (1969), based primarily on the movement's own publications. One of the polemical works which the movement is alleged to have attempted to suppress is available, Hirotatsu Fujiwara, *I Denounce Soka Gakki* (1970), and one scholarly observer of contemporary religion, Shigeyoshi Murakami, includes the movement in his *Japanese Religion in the Modern Century* (1980).

The U.S. branch of the movement, known as Nichiren Shoshu of America, publishes articles and pamphlets by Ikeda in English. A number of Ikeda's works have been translated into English. See particularly *Lectures on Buddhism* (1962), *The Living Buddha: An Interpretive Biography* (1976), and *Buddhism, the First Millennium* (1977). Readily available is the Oxford University Press publication of a dialogue between Ikeda and Arnold Toynbee, *Choose Life: A Dialogue* (1976). □

Ikhnaton

Ikhnaton (reigned 1379-1362 B.C.) was the tenth pharaoh of the Eighteenth Dynasty of Egypt. His reign was marked by the flourishing of the worship of Aten and by numerous uprisings.

Ikhnaton, son of Amenhotep III (Amenophis III), ascended the throne of Egypt as Amenhotep IV (Amenophis IV). A devotee of the cult of the Aten, or sun disk, the young king soon came into conflict with the priesthood of Amun, one of Egypt's premier gods, and its supporters.

There is evidence that the cult of the sun disk existed in the reign of Thutmose IV (1425-1417 B.C.) and that during the reign of Amenhotep III its importance had grown until it was formally adopted by his son. Basically the cult was monotheistic. It was not anthropomorphic, its manifestation being the disk of the sun, the giver of heat, light, and life. The Aten is represented as the disk from which emanate rays ending in hands holding the sign for "life." Considerable emphasis was laid on *maat,* a word usually rendered "truth," but whose full meaning seems to have been "order" or "reality." While the Aten cult did not embody any complicated theology, at the same time it lacked moral content.

Early in his reign Amenhotep IV proscribed the worship of Amun and other state deities and moved his capital from Thebes to a fresh site on the east bank of the Nile in Middle

Egypt which he named Akhetaten, "the Horizon of the Aten" (now Tell el Amarna). Here, together with his queen, Nefertiti, and his supporters, many of them apparently "new men" taking advantage of the collapse of the old noble class, Amenhotep adopted the new name Ikhnaton (Akhenaten) and devoted himself to the promotion of his new faith.

Ikhnaton found little general support for his ideas, and a number of setbacks toward the end of his 17-year reign obliged him to modify his policies. An apparent disagreement with Nefertiti, together with unrest within the Egyptian Empire, so weakened his position that a rapprochement with the Amun priesthood became necessary, though this may perhaps not have occurred during his lifetime.

Ikhnaton appears to have displayed little interest in foreign affairs and to have done little to maintain the empire created by his predecessors. His inactivity resulted in the rise of subversive movements among the vassal princes of Palestine and Syria and in incursions into friendly areas by hostile forces. Many of the so-called Amarna Letters (discovered in 1887) contain desperate appeals from loyal vassals of the Pharaoh for help against marauding neighbors. After his death the memory of Ikhnaton was abhorred and his name hacked from the monuments.

Further Reading

An excellent general account of Ikhnaton and his times is given in Cyril Aldred, *Akhenaten, Pharaoh of Egypt: A New Study* (1968). For a clear and succinct account of the topography of Akhetaten see J. D. S. Pendlebury, *Tell el-Amarna* (1935). For material on the Aten cult see Jaroslav Černý, *Ancient Egyptian Religion* (1952). Contemporary affairs outside Egypt are discussed in W. F. Albright's chapter, "The Amarna Letters from Palestine: Syria, the Philistines and Phoenicia," in I. E. S. Edwards, C. J. Gadd, and N. G. L. Hammond, eds., *The Cambridge Ancient History*, vol. 2 (rev. ed. 1966). □

Ion Iliescu

The Romanian Communist Party functionary Ion Iliescu (born 1930) rose to full membership on the Central Committee of the party before falling out of favor with Nicolae Ceausescu in the 1970s. Following the collapse of the Ceausescu regime in late 1989, Iliescu was elected president of Romania in May 1990.

Ion Iliescu was born in Oltenita, Romania, on March 3, 1930. His father was a railway worker who was active in the workers'(communist) movement prior to his death, at the age of 45, in the early 1950s. Ion Iliescu pursued advanced studies in the Soviet Union specializing in electrotechnical engineering.

Even before the rise to power of Nicolae Ceausescu in 1965, Iliescu held important posts in the apparatus of the Central Committee of the Romanian Communist Party, the most important being that of deputy chief of the education and health section. In 1965, upon Ceausescu's recommendation, Iliescu, who had been active in the Communist youth movement, was elected secretary of the Union of Communist Youth and also assumed the post of chief of the section of agitation and propaganda of the Central Committee. His career in the Romanian Communist Party reached its zenith in 1968 when he became a full member of the Central Committee.

Association with Ceausescu

Iliescu's close association with Nicolae Ceausescu ended in 1971 when he was removed from the apparatus of the Central Committee following Ceausescu's criticism of Iliescu's liberal attitudes in matters cultural and ideological. It should be noted that the Romanian "cultural revolution" and ensuing neo-Stalinism identified with Ceausescu's "cult of personality" began in 1971 with an attack against policies and attitudes identified with Iliescu and other non-doctrinaire Communist leaders.

Exiled to Iasi and Timisoara where he continued to be active in party affairs, Iliescu was removed from the apparatus a few years later and appointed head of the National Council for Water Resources. His disgrace, apparently due to his continuing opposition to Nicolae Ceausescu's policies, culminated in his appointment as head of a technical publishing house in Bucharest in the late 1970s.

Relatively little is known about Iliescu's activities in the 1980s other than that he was regarded by opponents of the

Ceausescu regime as the most desirable alternative to Ceausescu. Whether he was directly involved in the sequence of events that led to the "revolution" of December 16-22, 1989, the collapse of the Ceausescu regime, and the establishment of the National Salvation Front is somewhat unclear. In any case, he became the head of the Front immediately after the execution of the Nicolae Ceausescu and his wife and was elected president of Romania by an overwhelming majority (about 85 percent) of the voters in May 1990.

The Presidency

As president, Iliescu was subject to severe criticism by political opponents at home and abroad. The primary accusation directed against him was that of being a Communist in ill-fitting democratic clothing. His once close association with Nicolae Ceausescu and the belief that he continued to be "Gorbachev's man" in Romania led to several violent street demonstrations seeking his resignation. Emigre groups influential in the determination of American and Western European policies toward Iliescu tended to equate Iliescu with Ceausescu and the National Salvation Front with the Romanian Communist Party. All of this contributed to continuing political turmoil in post-Communist Romania. These accusations and comparisons, however, seemed baseless, as Iliescu appeared to be committed to democratization and the elimination of all negative aspects of the Ceausescu era. He seemed genuinely committed to the gradual development of a socialist market economy and to respecting the human and political rights inherent in a democratic society.

As president, Iliescu was the first Romanian head of state to participate in the Jewish community's annual commemoration of the Holocaust. In May 1996, Iliescu signed a Treaty of Friendship, Goodneighbourliness and Cooperation with President Zoran Lilic of Yugoslavia. The Treaty will regulate the two countries' inter-state relations until 2016. In a statement to journalists at the close of the Treaty signing ceremony, both Presidents emphasized that the Treaty opened up a new era in the development and strengthening of the traditionally solid relations between Yugoslavia and Romania. Iliescu paid an official visit to Moldova in July 1996 at the invitation of Moldovan President Mircea Snegur. Due to the initiative of Iliescu, Romania and Hungary signed a significant treaty in September, 1996 to end centuries-old disputes and to boost the two nations' chances of joining NATO and the European Union.

1996 Elections

Despite Iliescu's high-profile visits abroad, Romania's domestic situation remained dire. As of 1996, average wages for Romanians were a third of those in other Eastern European states. Iliescu's status as a presidential candidate was controversial because the Romanian constitution limits a president to only to two terms in office. Iliescu was elected to the presidency for the first time in 1990, then won re-election in 1992. He argued successfully in the constitutional court that his first term of office didn't count toward the two-term limit because the constitution was not revised to include this proviso until 1992. Iliescu lost the election to Democratic Convention candidate Emil Constantinescu and peacefully relinquished power.

Further Reading

There is nothing in English by or on Ion Iliescu himself. Pertinent material on the economic, political, and cultural conditions of the time can be found in Daniel N. Nelson, *Romanian Politics in the Ceausescu Era* (1988); Mary Ellen Fischer, *Nicolae Ceausescu: A Study in Political Leadership* (1989); Trond Gilberg, *Nationalism and Communism in Romania: The Rise and Fall of Ceausescu's Personal Dictatorship* (1990), and Edward Behr, *Kiss the Hand You Cannot Bite: The Rise and Fall of Ceausescus* (1991). ☐

Ivan Illich

Theologian, educator, and social critic Ivan Illich (born 1926) sought bridges between cultures and explored the bases of people's views of history and reality.

Ivan Illich was born on September 4, 1926, to Ivan Peter and Ellen Illich in Vienna, Austria. His father came from an aristocratic and Christian family; his mother's family was Jewish. His childhood was spent growing up in the homes of grandparents and wherever his parents might be at the time. His father's career as a diplomat politically protected the Jewish members of his family during the 1930s; yet Ivan was classified as "half-Jew" in 1941 and his family secretly fled from a Hitler-controlled Austria to Italy. In Florence at the age of 15, his father and grandfather having died earlier from natural causes, Ivan began taking care of his mother and younger twin brothers.

He entered the University of Florence where he majored in chemistry. At the age of 24 he graduated from the University of Salzburg with a Ph.D. in history on the work of the popular historian Arnold Toynbee. He prepared for the priesthood at the Gregorian University in Rome and became ordained in 1951. It was here that he met Jacques Maritain, the Catholic philosopher, who was to become his mentor and lifelong friend. Through him, Illich discovered the ideas of Thomas Aquinas and built a Thomistic philosophical foundation for understanding the world.

Stretching the Limits of the Priesthood

In 1951 Illich came to America hoping to study at Princeton University, but his interest quickly changed. On his first day in New York he heard through casual conversations about large numbers of Puerto Ricans migrating into other ethnic neighborhoods. After spending a couple days observing and visiting with them he asked to be assigned to a Puerto Rican parish. In his ministry he sought to make them feel at home in their new country by reinstituting their cultural and religious traditions. He sought to have Spanish materials made available to the children. His popularity among the Puerto Rican community grew and after just five

Awakening People to New Possibilities

Recognizing that Puerto Rico was perceived largely as a U.S. puppet, Illich moved to Cuernavaca, Mexico, in 1961 and established there the Center for Intercultural Documentation. The focus of his work remained unchanged as he sought to establish a bridge linking the two Americas and to train individuals for religious work in Latin America. By the mid-1960s the institute through its research seminars was attracting worldwide individuals concerned with social and economic issues. Illich viewed the center as a place for free, committed, and disciplined intellectual inquiry, yet many participants viewed it as an unstructured forum for political expression. Although still attracting students and economically sound, the center was not accomplishing its original purpose. Therefore, in 1976 it was closed.

The next several years Illich traveled and studied oriental languages and culture with the dream of writing the history of Western ideas in an oriental language. Subsequently, believing the task to be too great, he returned to an old intellectual home, to the study of 12th-century philosophy. Here, while teaching at the University of Marburg in Germany, he sought to find a fulcrum for lifting contemporary people out of their socially-constructed, conventional perspectives and out of a worsening world situation. He sought to enable them to understand how their commonly viewed reality (what is taken for granted or as certain) was historically constructed and can be changed. In the early 1990s Illich taught part of the year at Pennsylvania State University and continued to reside in Cuernavaca, Mexico.

Illich became known as a brilliant satirist and critic of contemporary institutions. In the early 1970s he called for a reexamination of existing social institutions. For example, he argued that schools are a lottery in which everyone invests but few win. As a result of perceived failure, those students who don't succeed in schools are stigmatized and suffer discrimination. In contrast, he proposed to correct this unjust situation by de-schooling society and thereby making it impossible to discriminate on that basis. Later, his thought penetrated to new depths when examining the professions, particularly the medical profession and how it leads individuals to become dependent and to assume less responsibility for their own lives.

In the 1980s Illich's thought shifted and again reached new levels of analysis. He stated that changes in our current situation can be attained if individuals "awaken" to the fact that each person's understanding or perspective of his or her world, a world that each of us takes for granted and as certain, is seen as being formulated and handed down over the centuries. Such conventional perspectives lock individuals into certain solutions and prevent recognition of new ways of living in the world. For example, in his work *ABC: The Alphabetization of the Popular Mind* he shows how our way of thinking has made three shifts throughout time. The first shift that changed our ways of seeing resulted from the introduction of the alphabet. A second shift in our thinking came in the 12th century with the development of the written page as we moved from an oral public and a spoken reality to a written reality and a literacy paradigm. And finally, the computer and word processing have created a

years, in 1956, at age 30 he was made a monsignor and accepted the position of vice-rector of the Catholic University at Ponce in Puerto Rico.

During the decades of the 1950s and 1960s Illich continued his work within the church, yet his commitment often brought him into conflict with those in and outside the church who had different agendas. While in Puerto Rico, and later in Mexico, he threw himself into the study of education and was outspoken in his criticisms of formal schooling. He ridiculed the notion of development in U.S. programs such as the Peace Corps, believing that such volunteer programs damaged not only the people in Latin America but the volunteers themselves. He claimed that the Alliance for Progress was an alliance for the middle classes, and he questioned the motives of missionaries who came to him for further study. He refused to withdraw support from a politician who advocated birth control. He withdrew from his role at the Vatican Council in protest over its political timidity. In essence, he sought de-institutionalization of the church. In 1967 he was summoned to Rome before the Congregation for the Doctrine of the Faith. He refused to answer their questions. Six months later Rome moved against him with documents he claimed were cribbed from U.S. Central Intelligence Agency reports leaked to the Holy See. At that point Illich voluntarily suspended himself from the priesthood, although he never resigned nor was he removed from the priesthood. He insisted that neither his faith, morals, nor theological views were at variance with the gospel and that they were orthodox, even conservative.

new watershed of change in which our thoughts were increasingly arranged more by the logic and efficiency of a technical tool than by the natural meanings embodied in a live discourse and spoken tradition.

Further Reading

An extensive six hour interview titled *Part Moon, Part Travelling Salesman: Conversations with Ivan Illich* was broadcasted by the Canadian Broadcasting Corporation in 1989. Transcripts and this highly informative dialogue can be ordered from Ideas, P.O. Box 6440, Station "A", Montreal, Quebec, H3C 3L4.

A major political article by Francis Duplexis Gray, including biographical information, "Profiles," appeared in the *New Yorker* (1969). A discussion of Illich's writings was in *Contemporary Authors, New Revision Series,* Volume 10. Articles critical of his view included "The 'Deschooling' Controversy Revisited: A Defense of Illich's 'Participatory Socialism,'" by Carl G. Hedman in *Educational Theory* (1979); "Towards a Political Economy of Education: A Radical Critique of Ivan Illich's Deschooling Society" by Herbert Gintis in *Harvard Educational Review* (1972); and "Illich, Kozol, and Rousseau on Public Education," by Jonathan Kozol in *Social Theory and Practice* (1980). A selected list of major works by Illich which trace the development of his thought included: *Celebration of Awareness: A Call for Institutional Revolution,* introduction by Erich Fromm (1970); *De-Schooling Society* (1971); *Tools for Conviviality* (1973); *Medical Nemesis, the Expropriation of Health* (1975); and *ABC: The Alphabetization of the Popular Mind,* with Barry Sanders (1988). □

Alhadji Abubakar Imam

Alhadji Abubakar Imam (1911-1981), Nigerian writer and teacher, was a pioneer in the establishment of modern Hausa literature. The Hausa peoples of northwestern Nigeria and adjacent southern Niger constitute the largest ethnic group in the region. Islamic traditions profoundly influence the Hausa culture

Alhadji Abubakar Imam was born at Kagara, Northern Nigeria, in 1911. After a traditional Arabic education, he enrolled at the Katsina Training College in 1927 to become a teacher.

The Career Years

In 1933, the Translation (later Literature) Bureau in the Hausa province of Zaria announced a competition that led to a dramatic change in the long history of Hausa literature. Composition had traditionally been either oral or in Arabic script, but the publications from Zaria initiated the use of the Roman alphabet for creative works. This marked the beginning of prose fiction as a recognized art form in the land of the Hausa.

Imam won second prize in the competition for *Ruwan Bagaja* (The Water of Cure), a quest story whose hero experiences many adventures on his various travels. While the

book was being printed, Imam left his teaching post and joined the Translation Bureau, where he composed a three-volume collection of tales, *Magana Jari Ce* (The Art of Speech Is a Capital Investment), for which he drew on Arabian, European, and Oriental sources, retelling the stories in typical Hausa narrative style. Thus began Iman's long career devoted to the educational, political, and literary betterment of his people.

In 1939, Imam was appointed editor of a government-sponsored journal, *Gaskiya Ta Fi Kwabo* (Truth Is Worth More than a Penny). This first Hausa newspaper proved very popular, partly because of its vivid writing style, so different from the highly formal and traditional Hausa prose.

In 1943, during a visit to England as a member of a West African press delegation, Imam asked British authorities for more reading materials to educate the Hausa people and as an outlet for public opinion in Northern Nigeria. This led to the formation of the Gaskia Corporation in 1945. Imam became head of its book section in 1951, thus becoming the first Northern Nigerian to be given a senior service post, a status previously reserved for white officials.

A talented and versatile writer, Iman was fluent in Hausa, Arabic, and English. His fame as a Moslem preacher and as a teacher brought about his election to the House of Representatives under the 1951 Nigerian constitution. Although a prominent Hausa poet, Sa'adu Zungur, once called him the "political pilot of Northern Nigeria," Imam gave up political activity in 1954 and devoted himself to improving the civil service and promoting literature in Northern Nigeria.

After pioneering in prose fiction, Imam was one of the first Hausa authors to produce formal stage drama. His nonfiction publications include works on Islam and on Muslim history, a life of the prophet Mohammed, and accounts of his 1943 journey to the United Kingdom and of his pilgrimage to Mecca in 1953.

The Later Years

From 1959 to 1966, Iman was a member of the Public Service Commission of the northern region of Nigeria. Thereafter, the country was plunged into a devastating civil war when the eastern region seceded and called itself the Republic of Biafra. Iman held public service posts over the next several years of military rule, including public service commissioner of the north central state.

By the time Nigeria returned to a peaceful civilian government in 1979, Iman was in ill health. He died at the University of Zaria in 1981. Two years later, Nigeria once again was plunged into a long series of military coups that successfully ended democratic rule.

Further Reading

There is no biography of Imam. Some information on his life is in Sir Bryan Sharwood Smith, *Recollections of British Administration in the Cameroons and Northern Nigeria 1921-1957: "But Always as Friends"* (1969). Brief mention is made in James S. Coleman, *Nigeria: Background to Nationalism* (1958); John P. Mackintosh, *Nigerian Government and Poli-*

tics (1966); and Billy Dudley, *Parties and Politics in Northern Nigeria* (1968). □

Shinichiro Imaoka

Shinichiro Imaoka (1881-1988) was a living legend in Japan who influenced the development of progressive and liberal religion.

Shinichiro Imaoka lived so long and was involved in so many different phases of Japan's emergence in modern life that it was difficult to comprehend his contributions and impossible to compare him with others. At well over 100 years of age he was still healthy, vigorous, and actively influencing educators, progressive religionists, and the general public.

His parents were farmers and Shin Buddhists of Matsue. Born on September 16, 1881, he was named Nobuichiro Imaoka (an unusual rendering of the characters of his name). His signature as the last secretary for the Japan Unitarian Mission was "N. Imaoka." The pronunciation of his personal name was changed to Shinichiro (a more usual rendering) for the convenience of others.

Studying under the famous Professor Aneskai in the department of religious studies at Tokyo Imperial University, he was influenced by the ethics of the New Testament, Quaker mysticism, and the writings of Dean William Inge. He was a member of the second graduating class of Todai in 1906. He then went to Kobe in 1906 as pastor of a Congregational church. A spiritual crisis occurred; he could not convert others from their faith to Christianity. His own theology was found heterodox by an ordination committee, and he resigned and went back to Tokyo. As a part of the youth group of Reverend Danjo Ebina, he met and married Utayo Fukuda in 1907. Her life was not less remarkable than her husband's. She was to walk a path of independence in business and science unique for her times. She received two imperial awards for accomplishments in the telecommunications industry. She died in 1978.

In 1910 Imaoka-sensei met Torajiro Okada, a *seiza* (a form of Zen sitting) master, and began a lifelong practice. Every day Imaoka sat for at least 15 minutes (Buddhists sitting with him often found him a living Buddha, Shintoists a *kami*).

Imaoka pursued further theological studies, attending Harvard University in the United States for four years. After returning to Japan, Imaoka lectured from 1919 to 1936 at Nihon University on the history of religions and the outline of Christianity. In 1925 when he accepted the principalship of Seisoku High School, Seisoku already had a distinguished past. But within 15 years Imaoka had helped turn it into a symbol of academic excellence in private education for all of Japan. In 1940 his school and the academic community honored him for his contribution to education. In 1949 Seisoku followed his leadership and decided to base all the school's activities on the principles of free religion. On the

25th anniversary of his principalship in 1950 the emperor honored him with a blue ribbon award for his service to education, and in 1965 he received the fourth order of merit with the sacred treasure. If any knew beyond his own family, none of his congregation knew in 1980, nor even the scholarly community. Only when his son, daughter, and daughter-in-law begged their father that his life story be shared did these details begin to come out. Imaoka remained at Seisoku High School until 1973.

For 60 years Imaoka worked behind the scenes as an organizer of conferences for religious dialogue, understanding, and mutual cooperation including in 1928 the Great Conference of Japanese Religion, in 1931 the Japan Religious Peace Conference, and in 1963 the Parliament of Religions in Tokyo at the centenary of the birth of Vivekananda. He was one of the founders of the Japan Free Religious Association in 1948 along with Kishimoto and Reverend Akashi Sr., a Japanese Universalist.

For over 70 years Imaoka was a minister. After the dispersal of Japanese Unitarianism into society around 1923 the gathering for spiritual practice or study on Sundays had to be begun again in 1948. Kiitsu Kyokai, the Tokyo Unitarian Church, or more properly the Unity Church, was something new; it was a fellowship for the practice and study of free religion. Its organization made it impossible for it to be anything more than a small gathering.

Imaoka came to teach that free religion was something more than any particular religion. Free religion was not limited to organized religion and has drawn Japanese who were members of the Japanese Unitarian Association to go beyond Unitarianism. Religion was in all of life, including culture, economics, politics, and art. Yet, free religion has its expression in the connectedness of church as community. As Emerson said, there was no fundamental distinction between church and world. All of life was interdependent.

This quiet work was recognized in several ways. In 1972 Meadville Theological Seminary granted him a Doctor of Divinity degree. In 1979 the World Conference on Religion and Peace recognized his leadership with a distinguished founders award, and in 1981 the International Association for Religious Freedom at its congress in Holland presented to his son and daughter-in-law an award for his outstanding contribution to interfaith understanding and cooperation.

In 1985 the Japanese nation was hearing his talks on radio and television. The Japan Free Religious Association published 109 of more than 150 surviving essays. A paperback version emphasizing free religion contained 37 essays. Several Japanese professors began interviewing Imaoka on a continuing basis. Thus, this apostle for free religion will not be forgotten. Imaoka died of pneumonia on April 11, 1988, at the age of 106 years.

Further Reading

There is only one book in English on the life and teachings of Shinichiro Imaoka, George M. Williams, *Liberal Religious Reformation in Japan* (1984). A book of Imaoka's own writings *Jinsel Hyakunen* (Tokyo, 1981) includes four essays in English. The title translates to *Writings for 100 Years*. □

Imhotep

Imhotep (fl. c. 3000 B.C.) was one of world history's most versatile geniuses. Inventor of the pyramid, author of ancient wisdom, architect, high priest, physician, astronomer, and scribe, Imhotep's prodigious talents and vast acquired knowledge had such an effect on his Egyptian contemporaries that he became one of only a handful of individuals of nonroyal birth to be promoted to godhood.

U ntil the late-nineteenth century Egyptologists knew Imhotep, who lived around 3,000 B.C., as a demigod (a mortal with almost divine powers) and then a full deity (or god) of medicine, with numerous temples and a well-organized cult devoted to him between 525 B.C. and 550 A.D. His name was inscribed alongside such powerful deities as Isis and Thoth, but they were purely religious and legendary figures. Until the 1926 discovery at Sakkara of a statue base describing Imhotep as a sculptor and carpenter, a human contemporary of King Zoser of the Third Dynasty, scholars did not believe that a man could achieve such a powerful position among the Egyptian gods.

Second in a Long Line of Architects

Imhotep, or "he who cometh in peace," was born in Ankhtowe, a suburb of Memphis. The month and day of his birth are noted precisely as the sixteenth day of Epiphi, third month of the Egyptian harvest, (corresponding to May 31), but the year is not definitely recorded. It is known that Imhotep was a contemporary of the Pharaoh Zoser (a.k.a. Neterikhet) of the Third Dynasty, but estimates of the era of his reign vary by as much as 300 years, falling between 2980 and 2600 B.C. Imhotep's father, Kanofer, was a distinguished architect who later became known as the beginning of a long line of master builders who contributed to Egyptian works through the reign of King Darius the First in 490 B.C. His mother, Khreduonkh, who probably came from the province of Mendes, is known today for having been deified alongside her son in accordance with Egyptian custom.

Vizier under King Zoser

The office of the vizier in politics was literally described as "supervisor of everything in this entire land," and only the best educated and multifaceted citizen could handle the range of duties associated with serving the Pharaoh so closely. As vizier, Imhotep was chief counsel to Zoser in both religious and practical matters, and he controlled the departments of the Judiciary, Treasury, War, Interior, Agriculture, and the General Executive. The vizier was also believed to have powers beyond those of a mere political figure, and the office was also described as "supervisor of that which Heaven brings, the Earth creates and the Nile brings."

There are no historical records of Imhotep's acts as a political figure, but his wisdom as a religious counsel was widely hailed for ending a terrible famine that afflicted

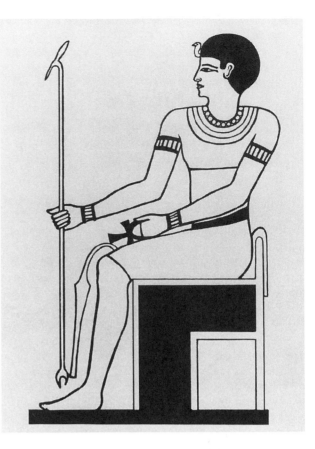

Egypt during seven years of Zoser's reign. It was told that the king was failing in his responsibility to appease the god Khnum, and that his negligence was causing the Nile to fall short of a flood level sufficient to irrigate Egyptian farms. Imhotep, having a vast knowledge of the proper traditions and methods of worship, was able to counsel Zoser on placating the god of the cataract, allowing the Nile to return to its usual flood level. The image of Imhotep as the "bringer of the Nile inundation," found at his temple at Philae, relates directly to those at Memphis, where as a God of Medicine, Imhotep was especially known for the miracle of bringing fertility to the barren.

Architect of the Famous Pyramid at Sakkara

The Step Pyramid at Sakkara is the only of Imhotep's achievements that can still be seen and appreciated today, and its reputation is largely based on his accomplishments as the pyramid's inventor and builder. By far the oldest of the Seven Wonders of the World, this first pyramid— actually only part of a large complex of buildings—was the first structure ever built of cut stone. It took 20 years to complete, and given the newness of the idea and the state of structural science in the Bronze Age, the Macmillan Encyclopedia of Architecture concludes that its construction must have required "all of the initiative and courage of a genius."

The design of the pyramid was inspired by the Egyptian belief that the tomb should "allow the deceased to mingle with the circumpolar stars, thus fulfilling his stellar destiny." Imhotep wanted the tomb to accommodate the Pharaoh's ascent into the heavens. To do this, he planned to improve upon the flat, rectangular mastabas, or built-in benches, which were the traditional tombal structures. About 600 feet north of the original mastaba, where the inner organs of the mummy were kept, Imhotep began the pyramid with another mastaba structure twice the traditional size, approximately 350 feet on the north and south walls by 400 feet on the east and west. The pyramid was raised on top of this structure in five successively smaller steps, or accretion layers, with a passageway on the north side issuing upward within the structure from a sarcophagus chamber (where the stone coffin holding the mummy is kept) 75 feet below ground. The total height of the pyramid and base is just under 200 feet, unimaginably large for a single structure before Imhotep's design.

The project at Sakkara was designed in its entirety as a medium for the deceased to perform the rituals of the jubilee festival, or Hebsed. The complex consisted of many other buildings, as well as ornamental posts some 37 feet high sculpted into drooping leaves, blooms of papyrus, and sedge flower. These carved stone imitations of the images of Hebsed, which was traditionally carried out in buildings made of plant stems, were finished with a bright green ceramic to make them more colorful and lifelike. The Egyptians believed that a sufficient approximation of the real thing would respond by magic for the deceased to the various incantations of the festival.

The protection of the king and his endowment of burial gifts—about 36,000 vessels of alabaster, dolomite, aragonite, and other precious materials—was the other primary function of the burial site. The entire complex, about one-quarter by one-half mile in area, was enclosed within a stone wall about 35 feet high. Of 14 entrance towers projecting from the wall, the doors of 13 were carved imitations, complete with effects for door leaves and a lock. Only two of the buildings, the royal pavilion and the funerary temple where the spirit could perform the liturgies of Hebsed, were actually designed to be entered by the deceased. These were surrounded by dummy buildings filled with sand, gravel and other rubble, also included solely to confuse would-be invaders. As a final measure, the king's treasure was lowered through vertical shafts around the tomb into a long corridor 100 feet below ground. The digging of just this corridor without earth-moving machines of any kind is a phenomenal accomplishment by modern standards.

It is likely that Imhotep was the architect and master builder of many other projects completed during a 40-year period of the Third Dynasty, though none of them compare in size or stylistic influence to the burial site at Sakkara. A graffito, or ink-marking, in the unfinished temple of Zoser's successor, King Sekhemkhet, mentions the "seal-bearer of the king of Lower Egypt, Imhotep." The estimates of Imhotep's death date generally coincide with the fifth year of Sekhemkhet's reign, so it is possible that the abandonment of the project coincided with the death of the master builder. It would not be surprising that no other builder in

Egypt could continue a work begun by the incomparable genius. Imhotep was also the author of an encyclopedia of architecture that was consulted by Egyptian builders for thousands of years after his death. A temple of Imhotep as god of medicine, constructed at Edfu under Ptolemy IX (r. 107-88 B.C.), was recorded to have been built "as specified by the Book of the Order of a Temple, which the chief lector priest Imhotep the Great, son of Ptah, had redacted."

Physician-Magician, God of Medicine

As a god of medicine, Imhotep was beloved as a mediator of everyday problems who could "provide remedies for all diseases," and "give sons to the childless." Members of the cult of Imhotep in the Twenty-sixth and Twenty-seventh Dynasties would pay tribute to the God at his temple just outside Memphis, which also contained halls devoted to the teaching of clinical methods, and to the preservation of the materia medica, papyri detailing the entirety of Egyptian medical knowledge which may actually have originated with Imhotep. His name was often grouped in with such powerful deities as Thoth, God of Wisdom; Isis, the wonder-worker; and Ptah, a healer and the ancient God of Memphis. Although other mortals were deified by the Egyptians, Imhotep is unique for being known by his own name as a god inferior in power only to the chief Sun-God, Re. Imhotep was also a member of the great triad of Memphis, with Ptah, Imhotep's father among the gods, and Sekhmet, a goddess associated with procreation and childbirth.

Science historians do not have the surviving examples of Egyptian medical practices that the pyramids provide the student of architecture. It is a matter of debate today how much of Imhotep's reputation as a curer of disease stems from medical prowess and how much comes from his sage's command of magic and healing rituals. The renowned writer and historian of science, Isaac Asimov, referred to Imhotep as "the first historic equivalent, known by name, of what we would today call a scientist," while the Oxford Companion to Medicine takes the more conservative position that "there is no contemporary evidence of his being a physician." Unfortunately, the papyri of the materia medica have not been recovered, but other medical documents such as the Ebers refer to them as a rich source of scientific knowledge.

Further Reading

Breasted, James Henry, *A History of Egypt from the Earliest Times to the Persian Conquest,* Charles Scribner's Sons, 1912.
Placzek, Adolf K., *Macmillan Encyclopedia of Architects,* Macmillan, 1982, pp. 454-464.
Hurry, Jamieson Boyd, *Imhotep, the Vizier and Physician of King Zoser, and Afterwards the Egyptian God of Medicine,* AMS Press, 1928, 1978.
Walton, John, Paul B. Beeson, and Ronald M. Scott, eds., *The Oxford Companion to Medicine,* Oxford University Press, 1986.
Asimov, Isaac, *Asimov's Biographical Encyclopedia of Science and Technology,* Doubleday, 1982, p. 1.
Great Engineers and Pioneers in Technology, St. Martin's Press, 1981, pp. 9-10. □

William Ralph Inge

William Ralph Inge (1860-1954) was a Church of England clergyman, scholar, social critic, authority on Plotinus and Christian mysticism, and prolific but controversial writer of popular essays and books. He served as dean of St. Paul's Cathedral from 1911 to 1934.

William Inge was born June 6, 1860, at Crayke in the North Riding, Yorkshire. His father was curate of Crayke and later provost of Worcester College, Oxford. Inge was educated at home by his parents until he entered Eton on a scholarship. In 1879 he went up to King's College, Cambridge, where he won numerous scholarships and prizes. He took first class honors in the classical tripos and returned to Eton in 1884, where he served as assistant master for four years.

Academic Career

In 1888 Inge was elected fellow and tutor of Hertford College, Oxford, where he taught the Greek and Latin classics and published learned studies. He did not become a priest until 1892. He was Bampton Lecturer in 1889; the lectures were published as *Christian Mysticism* in 1899, the first of 30 books on religion and social criticism. *Christian Mysticism* was widely read, and it launched Inge's career as an influential writer on religion. The work pioneered a new interest in the study of mysticism, and a number of important works on the subject soon followed, including those of Friedrich von Hügel and Evelyn Underhill.

Inge's study also focussed renewed attention on the place of experience in the religious life. Both of these themes underlined Inge's dissatisfaction with the orthodox seats of religious authority in either an infallible church or an infallible bible. For Inge, the ground of faith resides essentially in the depths of religious experience itself. This was also a central tenet of the turn-of-the-century Anglican Modernism, and Inge became one of its leading spokesmen.

In 1904 Inge left Oxford to become vicar of the fashionable Church of All Saints, Ennismore Gardens. The same year he married Mary Catharine Spooner, daughter of the arch-deacon of Maidstone. Inge was a shy, aloof, melancholy, and irritable man, but his marriage at middle age brought him a measure of freedom from his earlier depression. In 1907 he was elected Lady Margaret's Professor of Divinity at Cambridge and fellow of Jesus College. During his stay in Cambridge he continued his researches on Christian mysticism and resumed his long study of Plotinus and neoplatonism. Books published during this period included *Personal Idealism and Mysticism* (1907) and *Faith and Its Psychology* (1909). His *magnum opus* on Plotinus was the subject of the Gifford Lectures delivered in the University of St. Andrews in 1917 and 1918 and published as *The Philosophy of Plotinus* (2 volumes). Inge's own philosophical sympathies were neoplatonic, and his platonic and idealist convictions carried forward a long tradition in English reli-

gious thought that was sustained through the writings of William Temple. A small book, *Speculum Animae,* published in 1911, the year he was appointed dean of St. Paul's, reveals Inge's personal religion.

Dean of St. Paul's

When Inge was selected for the deanery of St. Paul's by Prime Minister Asquith he joined a succession of distinguished Anglican men of letters, including John Donne, in that position. Some would say that Inge spent more time on his journalistic activity—for a time, two or three articles a week—than on the affairs of St. Paul's. However, he became a celebrated preacher who drew large congregations to the cathedral. Interest in his sermons was due to his outspoken and provocative manner of expression and his genuine independence of mind. His weekly articles for the *Evening Standard* were widely read for a period of 25 years. He was one of the most popular English journalists and was tagged "the gloomy Dean" by the *Daily Mail*—a nickname which stuck—because of his denunciations of current folly and his prophesies of imminent doom. One writer said that, looking out upon the world from the dome of St. Paul's, Dean Inge found it very bad. He attacked optimists of every kind and those who believed in progress, democracy, and socialism. He expressed an antipathy for the Irish, the United States, and especially the Roman Catholic Church. Inge was aristocratic and often showed contempt for the working classes; he seemed incapable of understanding the causes of social unrest. He held social Darwinian views and felt that efforts at social equality meant disaster for civilization. He advocated birth-control and eugenics and served as a member of the council of the Eugenics Society.

Inge wrote a number of books during his tenure at St. Paul's, including *Personal Religion and the Life of Devotion* (1924), *Christian Ethics and Modern Problems* (1930), and *God and the Astronomers* (1934), the most systematic presentation of his idealist metaphysics. He was active for many years in the Modern Churchman's Union and served as its president from 1924 to 1934. These Modernists shared a commitment to unfettered enquiry, to liberal theology, and to a latitudinarian ecclesiology. However, even here Inge's position was unique. Unlike many Modern Churchmen he was an advocate of mysticism, and he was severely critical of the Roman Catholic Modernists, George Tyrrell and Alfred Loisy.

After his retirement from St. Paul's Inge continued to publish popular books, including *The Diary of a Dean* as late as 1949. His last public lecture was in Westminster Abbey in 1951. Inge died on February 16, 1954, at the age of 94. He received many honors during his life. In addition to the Bampton and Gifford Lectures, he was Romanes, Paddock, Rede, and Hibbert lecturer. He received numerous honorary degrees and was an honorary fellow of Hertford College, Oxford, and Jesus College and King's College, Cambridge. He was president of both the Aristotelian Society and the Classical Association. He was elected Fellow of the British Academy in 1921 and received additional honors in 1918 and 1930.

Inge's influence is hard to judge. His work on Plotinus, neoplatonism, and mysticism was influential. He made valuable contributions to the ongoing movement of Anglican Modernism, being one of its chief defenders of theological freedom. His popular books and journalism had an impact at the time, but they have not remained of continuing interest. Nevertheless, they are the work of a prose craftsman of unique mind and literary skill, and Inge deserves a place in the chronicles of English religious prose writing.

Further Reading

In addition to Inge's works mentioned above, the following collections of articles are important: *Outspoken Essays* (1919); *Outspoken Essays,* Second Series (1922); *Lay Thoughts of a Dean* (1926); *More Lay Thoughts of a Dean* (1931); *A Rustic Moralist* (1937); *Our Present Discontents* (1938); and *A Pacifist in Trouble* (1939). Three works on Inge's life and thought are well worth consulting: Sidney Dark, *Five Deans* (1928; reissued, 1969); Adam Fox, *Dean Inge* (1960); Robert M. Helm, *The Gloomy Dean. The Thought of William Ralph Inge* (1962). □

Jan Ingenhousz

The Dutch physician, chemist, and engineer Jan Ingenhousz (1730-1799) is noted for his demonstration of the process of photosynthesis in plants.

Jan Ingenhousz was born on Dec. 8, 1730, in Breda. He studied medicine at the University of Louvain and graduated in 1752. After spending some years in several European capitals in the typical 18th-century tradition, he settled in London in 1779 and worked with the celebrated naturalist John Hunter.

In that year Ingenhousz published his important book, *Experiments upon Vegetables—Discovering Their Great Power of Purifying the Common Air in the Sunshine and of Injuring It in the Shade and at Night.* In this work he anticipated by 2 years Joseph Priestley's discovery of the principles of what is now called photosynthesis, that is, the process by which plants exude oxygen and absorb carbon dioxide, thus purifying the air for animals and man.

Unlike Priestley and other chemists who were working on the characteristics of oxygen from the point of view of chemical philosophy, Ingenhousz was preoccupied by the problem of the fundamental balance in the animal and vegetable kingdoms, and this led him to investigate the mutual interdependence of plants and animals. He introduced the concept that the leaves of plants are great laboratories for cleansing and purifying the air. He also noted that oxygen is emitted by the underside of the leaves and that this is a daylight process, whereas in darkness even plants emit small quantities of carbon dioxide instead of absorbing it. In his reflections at the end of the book, Ingenhousz said, "If these conjectures were well grounded, it would throw a great deal of new light upon the arrangement of the different parts of the globe and the harmony between all its parts would become more conspicuous."

The book was soon translated into many languages and became the foundation of that kind of research which in modern times led to a more basic understanding of the process of photosynthesis; however, his search for the concept of economy or balance in nature was not well understood by his contemporaries. As to the nature and origin of the oxygen which the plant emits, a controversy developed in the 1780s between Ingenhousz and Priestley. Ingenhousz thought that water which plants absorb changes into vegetation and that part of this water is then released as oxygen.

Ingenhousz built electrical machines and invented the plate electric machine. He also wrote a two-volume treatise dealing with problems in medicine which are relevant to the physicist and the medical man, and in a sense it could be said that his basic interest was in what is now called biophysics. Ingenhousz also opposed the theory of subtle electrical fluids and repeated some of the experiments on plant electricity to disprove the accepted view that positive electricity was good for the growth of plants and that negative electricity retarded it.

All of Ingenhousz's scientific work was motivated by a deeply religious attitude and the belief that balance in nature is the best expression of the harmony created by its Author. Ingenhousz died in Wiltshire, England, on Sept. 7, 1799.

Further Reading

Howard S. Reed, *Jan Ingenhousz: Plant Physiologist, with a History of the Discovery of Photosynthesis* (1949), contains a study of Ingenhousz as well as the text of his famous book. □

world, for there was much opposition to freethinkers among the electorate. Thus he missed a career for which many thought him naturally suited. He was able to contribute something to politics, however, by speaking out for candidates in a style of oratory that seemed to cast a spell over his hearers. This skill, his courtroom mastery, and his quite unexceptional personal life enabled him to be appointed attorney general of Illinois from 1867 to 1869.

Ingersoll's lectures on religion and science, combined with discourses on literary and historical subjects, made his Midwestern tours as famous as his law practice. As a delegate to the 1876 Republican convention, he received national attention for his nomination speech in favor of James G. Blaine, whom he dubbed, to the delight of the whole country, the "plumed knight."

Riding the crest of this fame, Ingersoll moved to Washington, D. C., in 1879, hoping to further enlarge his practice and to carry on his religious debate in such lectures as "The Gods," "Some Mistakes of Moses," and "About the Holy Bible." His oratory became legendary, and he was sought out and richly rewarded both by patrons who endorsed his intellectual position and by clients anxious to find legal protection behind the magic of his courtroom presence. Ill health forced his retirement during the presidential campaign of 1896, and he died 3 years later at Dobbs Ferry, N.Y., patriarchal leader of a clan of children, grandchildren, and devoted admirers.

Robert Green Ingersoll

Robert Green Ingersoll (1833-1899), American lawyer and lecturer, was a champion of free thought and an orator of almost magical power.

Robert Ingersoll was the son of a Vermont clergyman and spent his boyhood in a series of parish houses, first in New England, later in the Midwest. The family finally settled in Illinois, where Robert read law. In 1854 he was admitted to the bar at Shawneetown. Three years later he moved to Peoria, where he quickly established a reputation as a superlative trial lawyer. When the Civil War came, he was active in raising a volunteer regiment and in 1861 entered the Union Army as a colonel of the 11th Illinois Cavalry. He acquitted himself well in the Tennessee Valley campaigns, but in December 1862 he was captured, along with large numbers of his men. He was paroled and in June 1863 discharged from the Army.

Returning to Illinois, Ingersoll became a champion of freethinking and a defender of the scientific ideas of Charles Darwin and, later, of T. H. Huxley. Ingersoll proudly claimed to be an "agnostic," a word newly coined, and was known in his day as the "great agnostic." Such an identity effectively prevented his entering the elective political

Further Reading

There are two full-length studies of Ingersoll, both with extensive bibliographies: Clarence H. Cramer, *Royal Bob: The Life of Robert Ingersoll* (1952), is the best of the earlier studies, although not as good as Orvin Prentiss Larson, *American Infidel: Robert G. Ingersoll* (1962). A good account of the intellectual movement to which Ingersoll belonged is in Merle Curti, *The Growth of American Thought* (1943; 3d ed. 1964).

Additional Sources

Smith, Frank, *Robert G. Ingersoll: a life,* Buffalo, N.Y.: Prometheus Books, 1990. ☐

Jean Auguste Dominique Ingres

Jean Auguste Dominique Ingres (1780-1867) was the most important French painter in the neoclassic tradition during the first half of the 19th century and one of the most distinguished draftsmen in the entire history of art.

The first half of the 19th century witnessed a profound shift in the course of Western art, which was dominated largely by French painting. It was a period of transition: new attitudes about painting were pervasive, many of which represented a break with the tradition of Renaissance illusionism and were harbingers of the modern painting forged by Édouard Manet and the impressionists. These new attitudes were present in both neoclassicism and romanticism, the two dominant styles of French painting between 1780 and 1850.

The art of J. A. D. Ingres must be seen within this complex situation: as a student of Jacques Louis David, the first of the neoclassicists, Ingres fashioned himself as the champion of that tradition; yet his work frequently expressed the exotic temperament of the romantics. Likewise, as much as Ingres emulated Raphael and the Renaissance, his art never wholly conformed to pictorial values of that sensibility. Instead, much of its thrust and meaning yields only to the terms of modernism.

Ingres was born on Aug. 29, 1780, in Montauban, where his father, Joseph, was a sculptor of ornamental work. In 1791 Ingres entered the Toulouse Academy and studied history and landscape painting as well as sculpture. In 1797 he moved to Paris to study with David; 2 years later Ingres entered the École des Beaux-Arts. These decisions signaled Ingres's allegiance to both the prevailing public style of his day and the great tradition of classical Renaissance painting in general.

Like nearly every serious artist at the École des Beaux-Arts, Ingres wished to study in Rome, the locus of classical antiquity to which the École philosophically aspired. The opportunity arrived in 1801, when he won the coveted Prix de Rome with the *Envoys from Agamemnon*. Because of

political conditions, however, the stipend for the Prix de Rome did not become available until 1806, and it was not until the end of that year that Ingres finally reached the Eternal City. He spent the next 4 years at the French Academy in Rome. In the words of Walter Friedlaender, "Ingres belonged there—he was a 'southerner,' like Poussin or Claude," the two French masters who had preceded him there more than a century before and had stayed throughout most of their careers.

Years in Rome

Between 1806 and 1820 Ingres produced some of his best-known and most original paintings, including the *Bather of Valpinçon* (1808), *Jupiter and Thetis* (1811), and the *Grande odalisque* (1814). Curiously, the pictures were negatively received when they were shown in the important annual Salon exhibitions in Paris. The criticisms suggested that Ingres's paintings were "Gothic" and "primitive." Although the works show a strong resemblance to Davidian classicism, particularly in their idealized figures, tight sculptural drawing, localized color, painstaking illusionism, and suppression of painterly surface incident, they also seem anticlassical, even romantic. The nudes exhibit a languorous sensuality, an exoticism of setting and mood that is foreign to the neoclassic dicta of clarity and reason.

Moreover, Ingres's figures are frequently characterized by peculiar distortions: torsos are flattened, elongated, and compressed, while arms and legs attach to bodies in ways that are anatomically fantastic—for instance, in the monstrous proportions of the *Grande odalisque* and in the physical impossibility of her left leg in relation to her hip. But these distortions also mark Ingres's complicated relation to Renaissance illusionism and modern abstraction. That is, the images are presented in graphic fashion, as if seen through a window, but they can never be fully explained in this way. Rather, the "distortions" result from what Ingres felt were the demands of the picture surface. When those demands clashed with the demands of visible reality, the latter were forced to yield. To the extent that Ingres's paintings reveal this yielding of illusionism, and this is always a question of degree, his works suggest a gradual breakdown in the Renaissance values he personally revered.

The Portraits

After working in Rome for 14 years, Ingres moved to Florence, a decision that was influenced by Lorenzo Bartolini, a sculptor friend he had met in 1799 in David's studio. Ingres remained in Florence for 4 years. During this period, as well as during the years in Rome—years in which his most ambitious paintings continued to be unsympathetically received in the Parisian Salons—the artist produced numerous portrait paintings and drawings. In this way he supported himself and his wife, Madeleine Chapelle, whom he had married in 1813.

Ingres's portraits are extraordinary examples of the way a graphic language can be made to reveal the presence and uniqueness of the human personality. Superficially they appear cool and aloof, almost repetitious in their taut verisimilitude. But this is not the case. In each portrait Ingres's drawing breathes, expanding and contracting to meet the demands of the personality confronting him. At one moment his line flows quietly, merely suggesting a form; in the next it becomes an agitated arabesque, dramatically enriching an element of body or clothing and serving as a metaphor for human feeling. Moreover, each portrait establishes a unique relationship between sitter and viewer: in some, the linear elements cascade down toward the viewer, inviting access to the sitter's world; in others, severe verticals or horizontals keep the beholder at a distance. Some of his most celebrated portraits are *Madame Rivière* (1805), *Countess of Touron* (1812), *Monsieur Bertin* (1832), and *Madame d'Haussonville* (1840s).

Success in Paris

While he was living in Florence, Ingres completed the *Vow of Louis XIII* (1824) for the Cathedral of his native town of Montauban. He sent it to the Salon of 1824 and, for the first time in almost 2 decades, returned to Paris for the annual exhibition. The painting was an enormous success: the artist received the Cross of the Legion of Honor from Charles X and, just a few months later, was elected a member of the Académie des Beaux-Arts. By the end of 1824 he had opened a Paris studio and had begun to take students. The *Vow of Louis XIII* thus marked a turning point in Ingres's career.

To some historians the huge success of the work has seemed peculiar, largely because it does not appear to be one of the master's most original creations or to mark any decisive stylistic break with works that had been negatively

received at earlier Salons. According to Friedlaender, Ingres's situation at this point must be seen in relation to Eugène Delacroix, the leading exponent of the revolutionary style of romanticism. As he says, "Perhaps it was because in this same Salon of 1824 Delacroix exhibited his *Massacre of Chios* and, needing an upholder of tradition to oppose this revolutionary innovator, the public was happy to find an artist who brought to the conservative point of view such great technical skill and such an irreproachably worthy style."

There is much evidence to substantiate Friedlaender's claim. During their own lifetimes Ingres and Delacroix were viewed (and to some extent viewed themselves) as the leaders of classicism and romanticism and as fierce rivals. That there are many relationships between their respective oeuvres—each combining classicism and romanticism—has become apparent only recently. New studies have thus replaced the simplistic view that the works of the two masters are in clearly opposite camps.

The public success initiated by the *Vow of Louis XIII* continued for Ingres through the next 4 decades. In 1826 the director of the museums of France commissioned him to paint the *Apotheosis of Homer* as a ceiling mural in the Charles X Museum at the Louvre; it was completed the following year. This ambitious composition, which Ingres executed as an easel picture, shows an ideal gathering of the most famous exemplars of classical thought and art, of the history to which Ingres personally aligned himself. In 1829 Ingres was made a professor at the École des Beaux-Arts. In 1832 he became vice president of the École, and in 1833 he became its president for one year. He resigned his professorship in 1851.

Throughout these years Ingres's personal life included very few dramatic events. In 1834 he returned to Rome, where he succeeded Horace Vernet as director of the French Academy. In 1841 Ingres went back to Paris and continued to teach—his fame now brought him a legion of followers—and to produce numerous portraits, including the sensational *Madame d'Haussonville*. His wife died in 1849; he married Delphine Ramel in 1851. Perhaps the most singular event in Ingres's long and tireless career came in 1855 at the Exposition Universelle in Paris. The master was honored with a separate exhibition of his work, a forerunner of the one-man retrospective exhibitions so common today. Yet, even this triumph was tinged with irony because Ingres's archrival, Delacroix, was similarly honored.

Late Work

Ingres died on Jan. 14, 1867, working indefatigably to the end. One of his last great paintings is the *Turkish Bath* (1862-1863). The exotic subject matter, the specific motif of the bather in the foreground whose back is turned to the viewer, and the compellingly abstract, nonillusionistic treatment of the spaces and figures recall works that Ingres had completed almost half a century earlier (for example, the *Bather of Valpinçon*). By themselves these likenesses reveal the remarkable persistence with which Ingres adhered to his personal interpretation of the classical tradition. Even more remarkable, however, is the painting's inherent quality: at the age of 80, Ingres could still draw the human figure with a sensitivity that has few parallels in the entire history of art.

In many ways Ingres was the last member of the neo-classic tradition. By the 1860s the new art of Gustave Courbet, Manet, and the impressionists had already begun to revolutionize the Paris art world, and the Beaux-Arts tradition was becoming sterile and academic. So Ingres had few immediate followers who are remembered today. Nevertheless, the quality and spirit of his work provided an undeniable foundation for the modern art of Manet, Edgar Degas, and other masters of the younger generation.

Further Reading

The two most important monographs on Ingres are Georges Wildenstein, *Ingres* (1954; rev. ed. 1956), and Robert Rosenblum, *Jean-Auguste-Dominique Ingres* (1967). For Ingres's relation to the broader picture of early-19th-century French painting, the crucial study is Walter F. Friedlaender, *David to Delacroix* (1930; trans. 1952).

Additional Sources

Ingres, Jean-Auguste-Dominique, *Ingres,* London: Oresko Books Ltd, 1977.
Rosenblum, Robert, *Jean-Auguste-Dominique Ingres,* New York: H.N. Abrams, 1990. □

George Inness

The American artist George Inness (1825-1894) was primarily a landscape painter, who developed a personal, subjective form of impressionism.

George Inness was born May 1, 1825, near Newburg, N.Y. His family moved in 1829 to Newark, N.J., where Inness was educated and took painting and drawing lessons. In 1841 he worked as a map engraver for a New York firm. He soon gave this up to sketch direct from nature. At the age of 18 he married Delia Miller, who died a few months later. In 1844 he exhibited at the National Academy of Design, and the next year he studied briefly with Régis Gignoux. Inness's earliest pictures show the influence of 17th-century masters such as Claude Lorrain, Gaspard Dughet, and Meindert Hobemma.

In 1847 Inness spent a short time in England and Italy. Three years later he married Elizabeth Hart and spent another 2 years studying and painting in Florence. On returning to New York, he was elected an associate member of the National Academy. Again he returned to Europe, this time to France. Exposure to Camille Corot and the painters of the Barbizon school had a profound effect on Inness's work after 1855. One of his best pictures from this period is the *Lackawanna Valley* (1855), which shows his new breadth of light and atmosphere as well as an openness of composition and a freshness in the handling of paint.

On his return from France, Inness settled in Medfield, Mass., which became the setting for a number of oils painted during the next 5 years. In the early 1860s he

painted in the Adirondacks, Catskills, and Berkshires and also in New Hampshire. He was now in control of his new style, one that allowed him to convey "that subjective mystery of nature with which wherever I went I was filled." Especially appealing were the contrasting moods of nature—sunrise and sunset, calm and storm.

About 1865 Inness met the painter William Page, who introduced him to the teachings of Emanuel Swedenborg. A combination of science and religious mysticism, Swedenborgianism provided Inness with a philosophical basis for his art. Inness was in Rome from 1870 to 1872 and in France for the next 2 years. During this period of travel he systematically refined his manner of composing, use of color, and handling of brushwork, making each as effectively expressive as possible. Many of his Italian paintings have a distinctive decorative flatness and elegant juxtaposition of silhouettes, notably *The Monk* (1873).

In 1875 Inness returned to New York and 3 years later moved to Montclair, N.J., where he painted for most of the rest of his life. His later paintings reveal an increasingly careful sense of design: he mostly relied on dividing his landscapes into foreground and background, with the former subdivided diagonally into approximate halves. Generally, figures and trees are clearly situated within one plane, so that no details are distracting and all design components are harmoniously unified. A typical example is the *Coming Storm* (1878).

Inness spent the summers of the 1880s variously in Connecticut, Nantucket, Mass., and upstate New York. At the end of the decade he traveled to the western and southern United States, Mexico, and Cuba and in the early 1890s to Florida, California, and Canada. His late work is much more subjective and impressionistic, the landscapes appearing less as specific places and more as hazy memory images. In 1894 he visited Paris, Baden, and Munich. He then went to Scotland, where he died suddenly at the little town of Bridge-of-Allan on August 3.

Further Reading

LeRoy Ireland, *The Works of George Inness* (1965), is an indispensable reference work which contains an illustrated *catalogue raisonné,* chronology, list of exhibitions, and complete bibliography, although the prefatory material is short and summary. The fullest published biography is Nicolai Cikovski, *George Inness* (1971). See also George Inness, Jr., *Life, Art, and Letters of George Inness* (1917). □

Harold Adams Innis

The political economist Harold Adams Innis (1894-1952) developed the "staple theory" of Canadian development.

Harold Adams Innis was born in 1894 in Oxford County in southwestern Ontario. His parents, who were strict Baptists, owned a moderately prosperous farm. Harold Innis started his schooling in Sunday school and the local one-room public school, moving on to the nearby Otterville High School and then to Woodstock Collegiate Institute.

In 1913 Innis entered McMaster University, at that time a Baptist college located in Toronto. He took his degree in the spring of 1916 and then, 21 years old, like so many of his friends whose lives were to be turned around by the maelstrom of World War I, he enlisted in the army. The appalling experience of the trenches and the mass slaughter of battles such as Vimy Ridge, where he was wounded, had a profound effect on Innis. As a private at the front he learned to distrust the official view of the war which was sent out from Ottawa and London, and as a Canadian, like many others of his generation, he learned that Canadians would have to interpret their own experiences and that their contribution to the war had given them a right to a new level of independence from Britain.

Returning to Canada, Innis quickly completed an M.A. degree at McMaster and then enrolled in the Ph.D. program at the University of Chicago where he studied with C. W. Wright, F. H. Knight, and J. M. Clark. Innis read and was much influenced by the work of Thorstein Veblen. It was in Chicago that Innis met and fell in love with Mary Quayle, whom he married in 1921.

In 1920 Innis completed his Ph.D. thesis and began teaching in the Department of Political Economy at the University of Toronto. His thesis subject, responding to his resolution to analyze the nature of Canadian society, had been a history of the Canadian Pacific Railway. Working on

the subject as an economist with a keen historical perspective, Innis had come to a fundamentally important conclusion about Canada. The standard view was that the Confederation of 1867, the acquisition and opening up of the west, and the building of the transcontinental Canadian Pacific Railway had created Canada as an act of political will in defiance of geography. But Innis had seen that the railway had re-established an older unity that had been based on water routes. The fur trade had created the first Canadian economy as the Montreal merchants had established trade routes that spread right across the continental hinterland.

Innis' book *The Fur Trade in Canada,* published in 1930, was a landmark in Canadian scholarship. In the conclusion Innis set out the main themes of what became known as the "staple theory" of Canada's development. The Canadian economy, and by extension society and politics, had been formed by the exploitation of a series of resources, the staple products, for export to the countries which had colonized Canada. Canada had developed at the margin of the world economy, exporting raw materials at prices set in an economic system dominated by a succession of center countries. Each staple product—whether cod, fur, wheat, newsprint, or minerals—had its own rhythm of development and brought with it its own pattern of immigration, capital movements, and institutions. Innis went on to explore this perspective in a series of studies and seminal essays—*Cod Fisheries: The History of an International Economy* (1940) and *Essays in Canadian Economic History,* edited by Mary Quayle Innis (1954).

Innis had also seen that ideas flow along trade routes from the center to the margins. He turned his attention increasingly to the study of communications, a subject that was to lead him far from the modern empires to the Greeks, Egyptians, and Babylonians. But Innis also focussed his attention on a contemporary problem in the economics and communications of empire: the process by which Canada had distanced itself from Britain only to be embraced by the United States. This later work was reflected in *Empire and Communications* (1950) and *Changing Concepts of Time* (1952).

In addition to his writing, Innis was active in the creation of institutions to support Canadian scholarship. He remained at the University of Toronto, becoming chairman of the Department of Political Economy and dean of the graduate school. His work was honored by appointment to a fellowship of the Royal Society of Canada and honorary degrees from several universities. He became, as his colleague Donald Creighton said, "Canada's senior academic statesman" in the decade before his death from cancer in 1952.

Further Reading

Additional material can be found in Donald Creighton, *Harold Adams Innis: Portrait of a Scholar* (Toronto, 1957); *Journal of Canadian Studies* (Winter 1977); and William H. Melody, Liora Salter, and Paul Heyer, editors, *Culture, Communication and Dependency* (1981).

Additional Sources

Creighton, Donald Grant, *Harold Adams Innis: portrait of a scholar,* Toronto; Buffalo: University of Toronto Press, 1978.

Havelock, Eric Alfred, *Harold A. Innis: a memoir,* Toronto, Ont.: Harold Innis Foundation, Innis College, University of Toronto, 1982. □

Innocent III

Innocent III (1160-1216), an Italian aristocrat, theologian, and canon lawyer, reigned as pope from 1198 to 1216. His pontificate has customarily been taken to mark the most splendid moment of the medieval papacy.

orn Lothar of Segni, the future pope was the son of Count Thrasimund of Segni. He studied theology at Paris and law at Bologna, the leading medieval centers of these studies, and at about the age of 30 had already attained the rank of cardinal deacon. He owed his elevation to the Sacred College to his uncle, Pope Clement III, but this could not obscure the fact that he was a man of outstanding ability and energy. Not even the temporary eclipse of his fortunes during the pontificate of Celestine III prevented the cardinals from turning to him in January 1198, when that aged and unsuccessful pontiff died. The years of eclipse, indeed, had enhanced rather than diminished Lothar's stature, because they were for him years of literary activity; out of them came the two conventional works which nonetheless attained considerable fame: *De contempt mundi* and *De sacro altaris mysterio.*

Lothar was chosen pope by his fellow cardinals less, it would seem, because they were impressed by the quality of his spirituality than because they saw in him a man of proven strength who could be relied upon to combat the rise of heresy, now for the first time in the Middle Ages a serious threat to the unity of the Church, and to restore the badly damaged political fortunes of the papacy in Italy and elsewhere. As a result, Innocent III expended a great deal of his energy on matters diplomatic and political. The greatest and most enduring achievements of his pontificate lay, nevertheless, in the realm of ecclesiastical government—in his contribution to the development of canon law, his promotion of administrative centralization in the Church, his imaginative encouragement of the Franciscans and Dominicans, and, above all, his convocation and direction of the Fourth Lateran Council (1215).

Conception of the Papacy

An unusually young man at the time of his election to the papacy, Innocent was small and dark and had a commanding presence, a driving dynamic personality, and notable rhetorical gifts which he exploited to the full in expounding and defending his conception of the papal office and responsibilities. It was a lofty conception, well exemplified by a text on which he chose to preach at his consecration: "See, I have set you this day over nations and over kingdoms, to pluck up and to break down, to destroy and to overthrow, to build and to plant" (Jeremiah 1:10).

What this exalted conception meant for Innocent's dealings with the clerical hierarchy and the local churches of Christendom is clear enough. As pope, he was successor to Peter and vicar of Christ, with supreme authority in the Universal Church and the ultimate responsibility for the health of that Church. "Others," he said, "were called to a part of the care, but Peter alone assumed the plenitude of power." Hence his willingness to regard the jurisdictional powers of the bishops as deriving from his own fullness of power; hence, too, his vigorous and wide-ranging judicial activity, his extension of papal rights over episcopal appointments, and his frequent efforts to make the force of his authority felt in the national churches by means of cardinal legates endowed with the broadest of powers.

What Innocent's view of the papal office meant for his relations with temporal rulers is by no means as clear. The formulas in which he couched his claims were undoubtedly often extreme. To Peter was left "not only the Universal Church but the whole world to govern." The pope "set between God and man, lower than God but higher than man . . . judges all and is judged by no one." Innocent claimed, "Just as the moon derives its light from the sun and is indeed lower than it in quantity and quality, in position and in power, so too the royal power derives the splendor of its dignity from the pontifical authority."

On the basis of these and of similar theocratic utterances, some have concluded that Innocent was clearly laying direct claim to the supreme temporal as well as spiritual authority in Christendom, that it was his ambition, in fact, to be nothing less than "lord of the world." Others, however, have noted the disparity between the extremism of such theoretical claims and the caution and scrupulous attention to legality with which he proceeded when he actually did choose to intervene in matters pertaining to the jurisdiction of temporal rulers.

It is true that for Innocent the pope succeeded to the position of Christ, who, like Melchisedech, had been king as well as priest and, as a result, was in some sense possessed of a monarchical authority even in secular matters and over temporal rulers. However, he did not seek to absorb temporal structures of government into ecclesiastical, and he could often defend his intervention in temporal affairs as necessitated by his spiritual responsibilities. Furthermore, his policies in such matters were usually distinguished by a pragmatic rather than a doctrinaire quality.

Political Activity

Matrimonial affairs led to Innocent's intervention in the kingdoms of León, Argon, and France (although in the last case diplomatic considerations also played a role), and a disputed election to the archbishopric of Canterbury led him to intervene in English affairs. King John's refusal to accept Cardinal Stephen Langton, who had been elected to that see after Innocent had invalidated the earlier election, led in 1208 to the imposition of an interdict on England, in 1209 to the King's excommunication, and in 1212 to his deposition and a papal invitation to the French king to invade England. Under this last threat John finally capitulated, accepted Stephen Langton's election, and sought (successfully) to ensure papal support in the future by surrendering and receiving back the kingdoms of England and Ireland as papal fiefs.

In most of these cases Innocent could claim that the need to preserve ecclesiastical discipline dictated his policy, but he could hardly do so in the cases of Portugal, Aragon, and other kingdoms that also became his feudal fiefs. Here he was motivated presumably by the view that he had expressed at the start of his pontificate: "Ecclesiastical liberty is nowhere better cared for than where the Roman church has full power in both temporal and spiritual matters."

Certainly this belief influenced his vigorous efforts to reestablish papal hegemony at Rome and in the affiliated papal territories, where the German emperors Frederick I and Henry VI had done much to extend imperial control at the expense of the papacy. Thus he was able to transfer the feudal allegiance of the city perfect from the emperor to himself, to restore a considerable measure of papal control in the Romagna, and to establish some sort of papal administration for the first time in much of the territory bequeathed to the papacy a century earlier by Countess Matilda of Tuscany.

If Innocent's Italian policy met with a fair degree of success, it did so in part because of the confused conditions prevailing in the empire. Henry VI, already ruler of Germany and large parts of northern Italy, had acquired by marriage the old Norman kingdom of Sicily. His objective to make good his control of all these territories, including the Italian, threatened the papal freedom of action in the future. But Henry VI died 4 months before Innocent became pope, and his widow, Constance, died a few months after, leaving a 3-year-old son, Frederick of Hohenstaufen, under papal guardianship. Although Innocent took his duties as guardian with great seriousness and defended Frederick's rights as king of Sicily, it was clearly in the interest of the papacy permanently to sever the connection between Sicily and the empire. Accordingly, between the years 1198 and 1209, he sought to influence imperial politics by arbitrating between the rival claimants to the imperial succession: Philip of Swabia and Otto of Brunswick, both of them adult relations of Henry VI.

Unable to enforce his claim to arbitrate and later disappointed in the attitude of his own candidate, Otto IV, whom he had crowned emperor after Philip's death, Innocent then compounded the woes of Germany by declaring Otto deposed and finally, in 1213, by throwing his support to the candidacy of Frederick of Hohenstaufen. In return, Frederick pledged not to reunite the German and Sicilian kingdoms, a pledge which he broke in the years after Innocent's death. At the battle of Bouvines in 1214 Frederick was able to make good his claim to be emperor.

Schism, Heresy, and the Crusade

Just as Innocent's imperial policy failed to achieve its ultimate goal, so did his attempts to recover the holy places in Palestine, to revivify the crusading movement, and to bring it once more under papal leadership. His efforts did indeed bring about the Fourth Crusade (1202-1204), but the crusade escaped his control and was diverted into attacking the Christian city of Byzantium, culminating in its capture and the establishment for some decades of a Latin Eastern Empire. The resulting bitterness in the Eastern Orthodox Churches did much to perpetuate the schism between them and the Latin Church, which Innocent himself had longed to terminate.

Comparably questionable results attended Innocent's inauguration of a crusade against the Albigensian heretics in the south of France. Fought with great ferocity and benefiting primarily the northern French nobles and the French monarchy, it succeeded, indeed, in ending the aristocratic protection upon which the survival of the heresy had so largely depended, but it did so at the cost of degrading still further an already degraded crusading ideal.

Ecclesiastical Government

Innocent's sponsorship of the mendicant friars, who set an example of dedicated poverty and preached the Gospel to the poor and neglected, possibly did more to contain the growth of heresy than did his espousal of more violent methods. Here, as with his ecclesiastical government in general, a more positive judgment is appropriate.

He gave immense impetus to the development of canon law (his *Compilation tertia,* issued in 1210, was the first officially promulgated collection of papal laws) and displayed vigor and industry in supervising the administration of the local churches and the centralization of the Church in Rome. These things helped no doubt to spawn the excessive legalism and papal centralization of the later Middle Ages, but they also helped to retard the growth of royal and aristocratic control over the local and national clergy that also became a problem in the later Middle Ages.

Fourth Lateran Council

Regarded by Roman Catholics as an ecumenical council, preceded by 2 years of preparation, and assembled in November 1215 at the Lateran basilica, the Fourth Lateran Council was attended by over 400 bishops, twice as many abbots and priors, and representatives of many secular rulers. So constituted, it was perhaps the greatest of medieval assemblies. Its decrees began with a profession of faith, which, by defining the doctrine of transubstantiation, closed the long medieval dispute about the nature of Christ's presence in the Eucharist.

The Council then endeavored to establish the procedures to be followed in dealing with heresy, requiring all bishops in whose sees the presence of heresy was suspected to hold there an annual inquisition. Another decree, by requiring that all adults confess their sins at least once annually to their own parish priests, buttressed this attempt to establish the responsibility of the local clergy for the elimination of local heresy.

Of related importance were further decrees requiring bishops to ensure the adequate proclamation of the Gospel by appointing suitable priests as diocesan preachers and requiring that an adequately endowed position be set aside at all cathedral and metropolitan churches to support a master charged with the instruction of the diocesan clergy. This last provision was an important one at the time, given the absence of seminaries. Other decrees forbade the foundation of new religious orders; required episcopal supervision and visitation of existing monasteries; sought to eliminate practices by which ecclesiastical positions could become in fact if not in theory hereditary; tried to curtail the trade in relics and the spread of superstitions surrounding them; and attempted by a whole series of disciplinary and administrative regulations to eliminate existing corruptions, to prevent new ones, and to foster a general improvement in the quality of religious life. Of critical importance were those decrees which required the holding of annual provincial councils and which sought to withdraw the clergy from involvement in activities pertaining to secular government.

On July 16, 1216, not long after the close of the Council which was his greatest achievement and a fitting summation to a distinguished career, Innocent suddenly died. Had the reforming legislation of the Fourth Lateran Council been implemented in the years after Innocent's death, many of the corruptions which were to bring the later medieval clergy into disrepute would have been curtailed. Even so, the Council's decrees helped mold the life of the Church for centuries to come.

Further Reading

Some source materials on Innocent III are in *Selected Letters of Pope Innocent III concerning England, 1198-1216,* edited by C. R. Cheney and W. H. Semple (1953). For biographical studies see E. F. Jacob, "Innocent III," in J. B. Bury, ed., *Cambridge Medieval History* (8 vols., 1913-1936); L. Elliott-Binns, *Innocent III* (1931); and Charles Edward Smith, *Innocent III: Church Defender* (1951). For general background see Margaret Deanesly, *A History of the Medieval Church, 590-1500* (1925; 3d ed. 1934); Brian Tierney, *The Crisis of Church and State, 1050-1300* (1964); and Geoffrey Barraclough, *The Medieval Papacy* (1968). □

Ismet Inönü

Ismet Inönü (1884-1973) was a Turkish military man and statesman who became the country's second president and played key roles in Turkey's internal and external political affairs.

Mustafa Ismet (Inönü), known generally in Turkey as Ismet Paşa, was born in Izmir at the time his father, Haji Reşid, was serving in the local judiciary there. His mother Jevriye, of the Temelli family, was an immigrant from Bulgaria. After his graduation from grade school, Inönü entered the preparatory military school in Sivas in eastern Anatolia, from which he went on to the artillery school and was graduated in 1903 as a second lieutenant. Eventually he managed to enter the staff officer's school (*Erkan-i-Harbiye*) in Istanbul, then the Ottoman capital. In this establishment—the institution that produced many of the country's elites—he met and studied with the future leaders of the Young Turks revolution and, especially, of Republican Turkey, including Mustafa Kemal (Atatürk), Kazim Karabekir, Ali Fethi (Okyar), and others.

Early in his career Mustafa Ismet attracted the attention of his superiors, who considered him a cautious organization man, adept at careful planning and with a special eye for detail. These qualities made him an aide much sought after, both by the glory-seeking high-ranking officers and by the more professionally oriented group interested in rejuvenating the army and extricating it from politics. Although he eventually established contact with the members of the secret Union and Progress Association, he did not assume a responsible position in that revolutionary organization. However, after the successful coup of the Union and Progress in 1908 he fought, along with Mustafa Kemal and others, the unsuccessful battle to assume the army's political neutrality.

Successful Military Career

By 1910 Mustafa Ismet had become a *kolaga* (high-ranking captain); he was sent to Yemen to quell the Imam Yahya's rebellion. In 1913, now a staff major, he returned to the army headquarters in Istanbul. One year later he took an eye-opening trip to Europe, visiting Vienna, Berlin, Paris, and Switzerland. Upon his return, he found himself immedi-

ately engulfed in war preparations as a member of the staff of the First Army, commanded by Liman von Sanders, the German officer who represented the kaiser.

During World War I, which the Ottoman state fought on the side of Germany, Mustafa Ismet acquitted himself well on various fronts. It was during a tour of duty on the Russian front (in the Caucasus) in 1917 that he renewed his acquaintanceship with Mustafa Kemal—then serving as regional commander on that front—and became his deputy. The basis for the lifelong friendship between the two men was established. Their widely differing temperaments and personalities were complementary, Mustafa Kemal being a politically oriented military genius capable of broad, visionary planning while Mustafa Ismet had an unparalleled gift for successfully implementing these plans with faithfulness and care. Together the two left an indelible mark on the history of Republican Turkey.

The end of World War I found Mustafa Ismet on the Syrian-Palestinian front where the Ottoman army suffered its final defeat at the hand of the British and was forced to sign the surrender armistice in October 1918. From 1918 to 1920 he occupied various positions in the Istanbul government. Finally he joined the nationalist movement in Anatolia, which had begun as a popular resistance to the invasion of the British, French, and especially the Greeks, but soon, under the command of Mustafa Kemal, became a unified, nationalist-Islamic movement of liberation. The Greek army which had landed in Izmir on May 15, 1919, with the intention of annexing western Anatolia began its march into the interior of Turkey to stamp out the national resistance movement.

Mustafa Ismet was war minister in the cabinet established in Ankara shortly after the British—who occupied Istanbul—had disbanded the duly elected parliament, arresting many of the deputies and forcing many others to flee. Those who fled to Ankara had joined with others, newly elected, to form a populist national assembly that convened on April 23, 1920. The convening of this assembly marked the final break between the monarchy and its supporters in Istanbul and the nationalist movement centered in Ankara. As might be expected, both Mustafa Ismet and Mustafa Kemal were condemned to death, in absentia, by the sultan's government.

At this critical time Mustafa Ismet was placed at the head of the nationalist army and charged with the task of stopping the Greek offensive. This he did in two fateful battles in the winter of 1920-1921 at a site in western Anatolia known as Inönü. When the family name law was enacted in 1934 the surname Inönü was bestowed on him by Mustafa Kemal—now called Atatürk—as a permanent memorial to his feat of leading the young nationalist fighters to their first crucial victory over the Greeks. Ismet Paşa subsequently commanded the troops also in their victory at the battle of Sakarya and in their final defeat of the Greek army in 1922. Then, after the liberation of the country from foreign occupation, Inönü assumed important diplomatic and political responsibilities as the chief Turkish delegate at the peace negotiations in Lausanne, Switzerland. The Lausanne Treaty of 1923 not only established peace between Turkey and the Allies and Greece but also drew the boundaries of the republic.

Establishing a Republic

Atatürk became the first president and Inönü the prime minister of the newly proclaimed republic. Inönü left the premiership for a brief interval but returned to that post on March 3, 1925—in large part in order to enforce stern measures against the rebellion of Seyh Sait—and remained in it until October 25, 1937. Thus most of the major reforms associated with the republic after 1925 were undertaken during Inönü's tenure as premier and as a leading member of the ruling Republican People's Party (RPP). (After the proclamation of the republic, the party added "Republican" to its name.) Inönü obviously followed the instructions of the president during this time, but still he managed to imprint the government with many of his own ideological views and personal characteristics. Socially a conservative, he relied on the bureaucracy to control the economy and society, including the industrialization that started in 1931. He thus unfortunately perpetuated the worst features of the Ottoman bureaucracy that had inhibited the freedom of initiative and kept the economy in stagnation.

In economic matters he proved a failure. His railroad building policy and promotion of monopolistic economic enterprises were two of the better known examples of his flagrant lack of economic know-how. Yet, paradoxical as it may appear, politically speaking Inönü was in favor of a somewhat liberal policy in recognizing the individual's sphere of free activity (but always under the paternalistic eye of the government). Eventually the stagnation of the economy, coupled with the uncontrolled growth of the rigid and increasingly unproductive bureaucracy—which had become both the regime's tool for control and Inönü's main power base—led to a break between him and Atatürk.

In 1937 Inönü was replaced as premier by Celal Bayar. Bayar, who was the head of the private economic-financial group known as the Iş (Labor) Bank, used private enterprise methods and achieved remarkable success. However, the death of Atatürk in 1938 put an end to what appeared to be a liberal economic trend, as Inönü became the president of the republic and the head of the ruling party. He was proclaimed *milli şef* (national chief) and the lifetime head of the Republican People's Party.

During World War II Inönü pursued a policy of neutrality, despite the binding alliance with England and France signed in 1939. This made the Allies wary of Turkey and led to a cooling of relations that in 1944 and 1945 left the country apparently isolated, encouraging the Soviets to demand territory in the north and military bases on the straits. The renewed Soviet expansionism and rising internal dissatisfaction with his regime induced Inönü to seek to align Turkey with the West and to opt for domestic political liberalization. In 1945 and 1946 he made the decision to permit the establishment of opposition political parties and to create the legal framework that lead to the emergence of a pluralist social and political system. The growth of the pluralist socio-economic system was the most profound and continuing revolution experienced by Turkey. Inönü, perhaps by miscalculation, was its architect and must be credited as such, although in the subsequent years he did not hesitate to play a destabilizing role when he found himself in political difficulty.

Political Parties vs. the Military

Inönü and his party were ousted from power in 1950 as a consequence of popular elections. At that time he refused the offer of four army generals to keep him in power by military might, accepting the role as head of the opposition to the victorious Democratic Party of Celal Bayar and Adnan Menderes. However, he had difficulty adjusting to the loss of power and the assumption of a secondary role in Turkish public life. He kept his image of himself and his party as the true masters of the country, the defenders of modernism, entitled by tradition and precedent to decide its ultimate destiny regardless of the electoral wish. It was this attitude that irritated and appeared threatening to the Democratic Party—especially as the army, the press, and the bureaucracy sympathized with Inönü's view. The Democratic Party leadership reacted by trying to silence Inönü and the opposition. The escalating confrontation between the RPP opposition and the ruling party culminated in a successful military coup on May 27, 1960. Democratic Party deputies were arrested and tried wholesale.

From 1961 to 1965 Inönü, again premier, heading during that period three different coalition governments, played a significant role in neutralizing two abortive coups and in achieving a degree of balance between the advocates of free economy and those of expanded statism. After 1965, however, Inönü encouraged the rise of a leftist statist-bureaucratic wing in his own party, supporting Bülent Ecevit, who became party secretary. This policy caused various groups favoring a more liberal economic policy and political pluralism to leave the Republican People's Party. To assume a more populist posture, the RPP gradually abandoned its strident secularism and, eventually, its nationalism and Kemalism. From 1963 until 1969 Inönü regularly supported the radical element of the party against the conservative Kemalists. Until 1969, as the full-fledged chairman and father-figure of the party, he was in full control and still able to chart a fairly cautious policy. Then his position among the younger, radical elements eroded as the party appeared unable to attract young blood and, in fact, found its own young people attracted into the more radical parties of the left.

The military intervention of 1971, caused by a dramatic surge of the left, brought about the open break between Inönü and the radicals in his party. The leftist bureaucratic, statist element headed by Ecevit had adopted increasingly socialist postures. While Inönü opposed the military intervention, he found it expedient to support it publicly; Ecevit, Inönü's protegée, who appeared as the "enfant terrible" of Turkish politics at that time, condemned the military action. Eventually the conflict between Inönü and Ecevit was resolved in the party conventions of 1971 and 1972. Inönü's candidate for the secretariat was defeated by the Ecevit group. Inönü attempted to stop the further ascendancy of the leftist-Marxists by resigning his position as party chairman. His effort proved futile. Bülent Ecevit was elected party chairman and thus was able to chart a course for the Republican People's Party and the country that proved to be disastrous. Ecevit allied himself completely with the Marxists in the party and followed an erratic economic and political course that brought Turkey to the brink of disintegration. The Republican People's Party was eventually shut down by the military after 1980.

Inönü died in 1973 and was buried with great honor in Ankara, close to the tomb of Atatürk, his mentor and friend. In the early 1980s there were some attempts to reassess Inönü's place and role in Turkish history. The new Social Democratic Party functioned as a sort of reincarnated RPP, headed by Ismet Paşa's son Erdal Inönü, a physicist by profession.

Further Reading

There is no single, full-sized book on Inönü in English or French. Most of the available information on him is to be found in general histories of Turkey or the biographies of Atatürk, such as Lord Kinross's *Ataturk: The Birth of A Nation* (1965). For the period of 1940-1959 see Kemal H. Karpat, *Turkey's Politics* (1959). In Turkish literature one may cite, as main sources, Şevket Süreya Aydemir's multi-volume *Ikinci Adam* [Second Man] and Metin Toker's *Inönü ile On Yil* [Ten Years with Inönü] (Toker is Inönü's son-in-law). □

Samuel Insull

Samuel Insull (1859-1938), English-born American entrepreneur, organized a utilities empire in the 1920s valued at over $3 billion.

Samuel Insull was born on Nov. 11, 1859, in London. He attended school until the age of 14, when he became an apprentice clerk. After several jobs he was employed by the London manager for Thomas Edison. When he turned 21, Insull went to the United States, where he worked as Edison's secretary.

Edison liked Insull's stamina and audaciousness, and when the Edison General Electric Company was organized in 1899, Insull was made second vice president in charge of manufacturing and sales. Insull's biggest opportunity came when he took over the Chicago Edison Company, which had at least six competitors in the city. Slowly Insull combined the concerns into Commonwealth-Edison, using business methods which his critics called unfair. However, Insull's success was not due to manipulation alone; he also insisted on improved equipment such as the Curtis turbine, which allowed a wider distribution of electricity. Operating on his own, he expanded his interests into surface and elevated transit lines.

In 1912 Insull organized a conglomerate that became the symbol of "Insullism"—Middle West Utilities. With assets over $2 million, this maze of holding companies served at least 1,718,000 customers from 324 steam plants, 196 hydroelectric generating plants, and 328 ice plants.

During the 1920s Insull continued his pattern of using holding companies to control assets. By 1930 the empire consisted of five systems with assets over $2.5 billion that produced almost one-eighth of the total electric power in the United States.

Insull was recognized as one of the nation's important business leaders and received honorary degrees from several universities. The French government awarded him a knighthood in the Legion of Honor. In politics he supported both major parties as it suited his interests. His most notable philanthropic activities included support for the $20 million Chicago Civic Opera House and a donation of $160,000 to establish the London Temperance Hospital.

Insull's empire was in financial trouble in 1929, when the stock market crash and ensuing Depression sealed its doom. In June 1932 he was removed as executive officer of his companies and left for Paris virtually destitute. He was indicted on charges of fraud and embezzlement but fled to Greece, where he fought extradition. Finally returning to the United States for trial, he was acquitted. He fell into obscurity and died in Paris on July 16, 1938.

Further Reading

Only two books cover Insull's career: M. L. Ramsay is hostile to him in *Pyramids of Power: The Story of Roosevelt, Insull and the Utility Wars* (1937), and Forest McDonald shows sympathy in *Insull* (1962), which is the only full-length biography. □

Tsuyoshi Inukai

Tsuyoshi Inukai (1855-1932) was a Japanese journalist, politician, and statesman. His premiership in 1931-1932 climaxed the trend toward responsible party government, but his assassination by ultranationalists brought this development to a halt.

Tsuyoshi Inukai, whose personal name has alternate readings in Japanese (Ki, Takeshi, Tsuyoki), was born to a samurai of the Niwase *han* (fief) in Okayama Province. His family had traditionally stressed Confucian learning, and he might have ended up a teacher of the classics had not a book on international law aroused his interest in Western learning.

In 1876 Inukai made his way to Tokyo, got a job with the newspaper *Hochi,* and studied political philosophy under Yukichi Fukuzawa. Fukuzawa's support enabled Inukai to found *Tokai,* a financial newspaper, together with Ryohei Toyokawa, who was related to the Mitsubishi; this explains Inukai's close connections with the powerful zaibatsu family throughout his political career.

Inukai first entered politics when Shigenobu Okuma resigned from the government and started the Kaishinto (Progressive party) in 1881. Four years later Inukai ran for the Tokyo City Assembly under its label, and in 1890 he won a seat for Okayama in the Diet, a position he held for the rest of his life.

Inukai's political goal was to break open the narrow political elite to ever wider participation in the decision-making process. His first—short-lived—victory was engineering the coalition Okuma Cabinet of 1889, in which he became minister of education. He accepted the education portfolio in Yamamoto's Cabinet of 1913 on the rationale that, by supporting this Satsuma faction of the ruling oligarchy, he would be weakening Choshu domination. He was accused of being bought off by the elite. To regain his reputation, he struggled to put together the Kato coalition Cabinet of 1924, dedicated to "protecting the constitution" and passing "manhood suffrage." Thereafter, at age 70, he attempted to retire from active politics, but his constituents would not let him, and upon Tanaka's death he was elected president of the Seiyukai party.

After the September 1931 Manchurian incident, which he supported, Inukai was made premier in December. The elder statesman Kimmochi Saionji recommended him in the hope that he could find a diplomatic solution based on his long-time personal connections with Chinese nationalists who had stayed in Japan. As premier, Inukai dissolved the Diet and got the largest party majority in Japanese history, but he still was not able to control the military or get a secret agreement with Chiang Kai-shek before being shot by young army and navy officers in what was known as the "May 15 Affair."

Further Reading

With no biography of Inukai available in English, one must rely on the biographies of others whom he knew well, or else on the more general histories, such as A. Morgan Young, *Japan in Recent Times, 1912-1926* (1929) and *Imperial Japan, 1926-1938* (1938), and Chitoshi Yanaga, *Japan since Perry* (1949). For an overview of the movements of which Inukai was a part see George O. Totten, ed., *Democracy in Prewar Japan: Groundwork or Facade?* (1965). For Inukai's relations with Asian nationalist revolutionaries see Marius B. Jansen, *The Japanese and Sun Yat-sen* (1954). □

Eugène Ionesco

The popular plays of the Franco-Romanian author Eugène Ionesco (1912-1994) protested the dehumanizing effects of modern civilization and depicted the despair of the individual who vainly seeks meaning for his or her existence. He has been called the founder of the *Theater of the Absurd*.

Eugène Ionesco was born on November 26, 1912, in Slatina, Romania, to a French mother and a Romanian father. The following year the family moved to Paris, but soon after he was 12, they returned to Romania. He completed all of his secondary education there and specialized in French at the University of Bucharest. From 1936 to 1938 he taught French in a secondary school in Bucharest. Two years after his marriage in 1936 to Rodica Burileano, he received a grant from the French government to study in France and write a thesis on *Sin and Death in French Poetry Since Baudelaire* . During the war he worked as a proofreader for a Paris publishing house.

Ionesco became a playwright in a roundabout way. While learning English, he was struck by the emptiness of the clichéd language that kept appearing in his phrasebook, and decided to write a play using nonsensical sentences. *The Bald Soprano* (1948) was a comic parody of a play, an "antiplay" as he called it, portraying human life as automatism and language as a senseless fragmentation of sentences. Mr. and Mrs. Smith uttered cliches, while the couple visiting them, the Martins, spoke to each other as though they were strangers until they realized that they shared the same home and child. The dialogue amongst the four eventually disintegrates into meaningless sounds. The idea was that a new vision of reality might occur to audiences if habitual patterns of rational thought were overthrown and presented, not just with arguments about the irrationality (or absurdity) of human existence, but with demonstrations of it. The language theme continued in Ionesco's second play, *The Lesson* (1951), with a professor tutoring a female student in subjects ranging from the logical constructs of mathematics to the less rigorous rules of language. As the language tutoring progresses, the professor became increasingly agitated, and in the end stabbed his student during a discussion of the word "knife." Critics, never at a loss for

words, found that the circular structure of these two plays suggested Ionesco's pessimism.

In later plays, Ionesco used multiplying objects as his metaphor for the absurdity of life. In *The Chairs]* (1952), an elderly couple served as hosts for an audience which would assemble to hear a speaker deliver a message that will save the world. The couple arranged seating for their never-to-arrive guests, and the stage became crowded with chairs. Convinced that their audience had arrived and was seated, the hosts killed themselves, leaving them to hear the speaker who turned out to be a mentally-impaired deaf-mute. In *The Victims of Duty* (1953), coffee cups multiplied, and in *The New Tenant* (1957), the protagonist's apartment became progressively filled with furniture. Critics saw the multiplying objects in these works as suggesting the alienation and loss of identity experienced by people in modern society. Ionesco once remarked that "It's not a certain society that seems ridiculous to me, it's mankind," and rather than "theater of the absurd," he preferred the phrase "theater of derision."

Later in the 1950's, Ionesco wrote several plays featuring a modern-day Everyman named Berenger (Ionesco's self-image). The most famous of these and the one that wrote his name large in English-speaking theater was *Rhinoceros* (1959). In this play, totalitarianism transformed everyone into a savage rhinoceros except Berenger, who thinks about joining them but in the end decided to fight them. The inspiration for the play was Ionesco's reaction to a friend having joined the Nazi party, but its significance was in its denunciation of mindless conformity to a mob mentality. In winning the Jerusalem Prize in 1973 for his entire *oeuvre*, *Rhinoceros* was singled out as "one of the great demonstrations against totalitarianism." Berenger also appeared in *The Killer* (1958), *Exit the King* (1962), and *A Stroll in the Air* (1963).

During the next 20 years Ionesco's predominant theme was the subject of death, in such plays as *Hunger and Thirst* (1964), in which the protagonist (Berenger again) tried to escape death as represented by his wife and child; in *The Killing Game* (1970) an epidemic has taken away the inhabitants of a village. According to one critic, for Ionesco death represented the threat of nothingness, the "quintessence of the Absurd."

Many of Ionesco's plays had a dream-like quality. People can be transformed into animals or change their identity; they walked in the air or continued to grow after death. Ionesco preferred a series of states of consciousness over traditional plots. These dream-like qualities became more prominent in later plays, such as *L'Homme aux Valises* (1975) and *Journey Among the Dead* (1980).

In all, Ionesco wrote 28 plays, some of which have been in constant performance since 1955. He also wrote several volumes of essays, criticism, a novel [*the Hermit* (1972), made into a film called *La Vase,* starring the author himself], and he created illustrations for some of his works as well. During the last 10 years of his life he devoted himself to painting and exhibiting his works.

In the beginning, many critics thought Ionesco's work was obscure, but his plays went on to earn international acclaim. He received many honors during his lifetime, and by 1970 had been elected to *The Academy Francaise*. It was characteristic of the French that Ionesco's death in 1994 was announced by France's Ministry of Culture, rather than by his wife of 58 years or their daughter.

Further Reading

For his personal memoir, see Eugène Ionesco, *Present Past, Past Present* (1997, trans. Helen R Lane). A short work in the Twanye's World Authors Series is Deborah B. Gaensbauer's *Eugène Ionesco Revisited* (1996). See also Nancy Lane, *Understanding Eugène Ionesco* (1994). An older full-length study of Ionesco is Richard N. Coe, *Eugène Ionesco* (1961). A brief biography is available on-line through the Capital PC User Group, Inc. at http://cpcug.org/user/stefan/ionesco.html (July 1997). □

Muhammad Iqbal

Muhammad Iqbal (1877-1938) was an Indian Moslem poet and political philosopher. His fame rests on both his poetry and his formulation of ideas that were influential in the creation of Pakistan.

Muhammad Iqbal was born in Sialkot, Punjab, probably in 1877, although there is some uncertainty about the year of his birth. He graduated from Government College, Lahore, in 1899 with a master's degree in philosophy. He taught there until 1905, while establishing his reputation as an Urdu poet. During this period his poetry expressed an ardent Indian nationalism, but a marked change came over his views between 1905 and 1908, when he was studying for his doctorate at Cambridge University, visiting German universities, and qualifying as a barrister.

The philosophies of Nietzsche and Bergson influenced Iqbal deeply, while he became extremely critical of Western civilization, which he regarded as decadent. He turned to Islam for inspiration and rejected nationalism as a disease of the West. He argued that Moslems must find their destiny through a pan-Islamic movement that ignored national boundaries. He also denounced the mystical trend of Indian Islam, blaming it for weakening the Moslem community and leading to its political downfall. These ideas found vigorous expression in the long poems *Asrar-i-Khudi (The Secrets of the Self)* in 1915 and *Rumuz-i-Bekhudi (The Mysteries of Selflessness)* in 1918. These were written in Persian, not Urdu, presumably to gain his ideas an audience in the Moslem world outside India.

Iqbal was knighted by the British in 1922, and his fame drew him increasingly into public life. Although he was not an active politician, he was elected to the Punjab legislature in 1926, and in 1930 he was made president of the Moslem League. By this time the dream of a pan-Islamic world no longer appealed to him. His statement in his presidential address that the "final destiny" of Indian Moslems was to have a "consolidated Northwest Indian Moslem state" is regarded as one of the earliest expressions of the idea of Pakistan.

Becoming convinced that Moslems were in danger from the Hindu majority if India should become independent, Iqbal gave his powerful support to Mohammad Ali Jinnah as the leader of India's Moslems. In his last years Iqbal returned to Urdu as his poetic medium, publishing *Bal-i-Jibril* (*Gabriel's Wing*) in 1935 and *Zarb-i-Kalim* (*The Rod of Moses*) in 1936. They have been criticized as lacking the energy and inspiration of his early work. He died in Lahore on April 21, 1938.

Further Reading

The most convenient source for a study of Iqbal's religious and political thought is his *The Reconstruction of Religious Thought in Islam* (1934). For translations of Iqbal's major works see R. A. Nicholson, *The Secrets of the Self* (1944); A. J. Arberry, *The Mysteries of Selflessness: A Philosophical Poem* (1953); V. G. Kiernan, *Poems from Iqbal* (1955); and Annemarie Schimmel, *Gabriel's Wing* (1963). Most of these have introductory comments on his style. S. A. Vahid, *Iqbal: His Art and Thought* (1959), discusses most of Iqbal's work. S. M. Ikram, *Modern Muslim India and the Birth of Pakistan, 1858-1951* (1950; rev. ed. 1965), includes a perceptive study of Iqbal.

Additional Sources

Hasan, Masudul, *Life of Iqbal: general account of his life,* Lahore: Ferozsons, 1978.

Hasan, Mumtaz, *Tribute to Iqbal,* Lahore: Iqbal Academy Pakistan, 1982.

Hussain, Riaz, *The politics of Iqbal: a study of his political thoughts and actions,* Lahore: Islamic Book Service, 1977.

Iqbal, Muhammad, Sir, *Mementos of Iqbal,* Lahore: All-Pakistan Islamic Education Congress, 1976.

Munawwar, Muhammad, *Iqbal: poet-philosopher of Islam,* Lahore; Islamic Book Foundation: distributors, al-Marif, 1982.

Qadir, Abdul, Sir, *Iqbal, the great poet of Islam,* Lahore: Sang-e-Meel Publications, 1975.

Tributes to Iqbal, Lahore: Sangemeel Publications, 1977.

Zakaria, Rafiq, *Iqbal: the poet and the politician,* New Delhi, India; New York: Viking, 1993. □

John Ireland

John Ireland (1838-1918), Archbishop of St. Paul, Minn., from 1888 until his death, spoke for liberal Catholics who sought to harmonize Catholicism with American institutions.

J ohn Ireland was born on Sept. 11, 1838, in Kilkenny, Ireland. His family migrated to America in 1849, finally settling in St. Paul, Minn. Ireland attracted the attention of Bishop Joseph Cretin and was sent to France, where he studied under liberal Catholic professors. He returned to America in time to be a chaplain in the Civil War.

Ireland's residence was St. Paul, and for 50 years he was the dominating Catholic influence in the upper Mississippi Valley. His fondest dream was to bring Catholic immigrants out of the tenements of the East to the broad prairies of the West, and he worked in cooperation with the railroads in this colonization enterprise. Although immigrants continued to cluster in the cities, enough of them answered Ireland's appeal to make Minnesota the center of Catholic culture in the Northwest.

A man of energy and decision, Ireland participated in all the great battles racking the Church at this time. Although absolutely loyal to the Pope, he was charged by his conservative enemies with the heresy of "Americanism." Ireland sought to accommodate the American public school system with the Catholic program of parochial schools, though his compromise pleased neither militant Catholics nor militant Protestants. He supported the establishment of the Catholic University of America in 1889, believing that this "age will not take kindly to religious knowledge separated from secular knowledge."

Though Ireland was one of the few Catholic leaders to join the attack on the liquor interests and he upheld labor's right to organize, he was no radical. He was on friendly terms with business tycoons and urged Catholics to get about the business of making money. He exhorted them to participate in American political life, but, unlike his associates, he was an intensely partisan Republican, thereby earning the gratitude of presidents William McKinley and Theodore Roosevelt. A familiar figure in Europe, Ireland was a part-time international diplomat, sent on special missions by both the Pope and the President of the United States.

In 1899 Pope Leo XIII issued a condemnation of "Americanism" in the letter *Testem benevolentiae,* addressed to Cardinal James Gibbons of Baltimore but intended for Ireland as well. Although the church's liberals termed the issue a "phantom heresy," the rebuke was unmistakable and Ireland's voice was muffled. He died in St. Paul on Sept. 25, 1918.

Further Reading

James H. Moynihan, *The Life of Archbishop John Ireland* (1953), is excellent. James P. Shannon, *Catholic Colonization on the Western Frontier* (1957), is invaluable for one aspect of Ireland's career. John Tracy Ellis, *American Catholicism* (1956; 2d ed. 1969), is the best brief treatment of the subject. For the crucial era of Ireland's leadership see two splendid, scholarly works: Thomas T. McAvoy, *The Great Crisis in American Catholic History, 1895-1900* (1957), reprinted as *The Americanist Heresy in Roman Catholicism, 1895-1900* (1963), and Robert D. Cross, *The Emergence of Liberal Catholicism in America* (1958).

Additional Sources

Moynihan, James H., *The life of Archbishop John Ireland,* New York: Arno Press, 1976, 1953.
O'Connell, Marvin Richard, *John Ireland and the American Catholic Church,* St. Paul: Minnesota Historical Society Press, 1988. □

Patricia Ireland

Patricia Ireland (born 1945), who started her career as an airline flight attendant, became a successful corporate lawyer in the mid-1970s but found her true calling as head of the powerful National Organization for Women (NOW), of which Ireland was elected both vice-president and president.

The world of feminist polemics and advocacy is far removed from the middle-class upbringing that Patricia Ireland enjoyed. A child during the 1950s, her youth was relatively uneventful, yet the tumult and tensions of her college years and her early work experiences paved the way for a vastly different lifestyle. Her election to the presidency of the National Organization for Women (NOW) in 1991 represented the culmination of decades of intense political activism on behalf of women's rights.

Middle-Class Upbringing

Patricia Ireland was born in Oak Park, Illinois, on October 19, 1945, to James Ireland and Joan Filipek. She spent her childhood in rural Valparaiso, Indiana, where her father was an engineer and her mother was involved in Planned Parenthood. Patricia's older sister, Kathy, died at age seven in a horseback-riding accident. Patricia, then four and a half, subsequently attributed to this tragedy her ability to cope with difficulty and face challenges with equanimity. Despite the emotional impact of her sister's death, Patricia was, by all accounts, a happy child. She not only made the honor roll in high school but won a school beauty contest as well. She entered DePauw University in 1961, when she was 16.

Fight Against Discrimination

While in college, Patricia became pregnant. She fled to Japan for an abortion, then married for a short time. These events carried her away from a chosen career of teaching, placing her instead on a radically different course. After her marriage Patricia left DePauw University for the University of Tennessee; in 1966 she earned a Bachelor's degree in German. She remained at the university, enrolling in graduate school, and in 1968 married again. After leaving graduate studies, she and her husband went to Miami, Florida, where Ireland became a flight attendant with Pan American World Airways. This detour proved pivotal: her self-assurance, independence, and discomfort with gender stereotypes made it impossible for her to maintain the attitude that the airline required of stewardesses. Her noncompliance with rules brought her, during her initial year there, into direct confrontation with Pan Am. Outraged at the airline's sexist employment policies, Ireland filed action against Pan Am regarding health insurance coverage; she learned that her husband *was not* covered on her dental policy but that wives of Pan Am employees *were* covered. Bringing her concerns to the Dade County chapter of NOW, she received help.

Legal Training

Pan Am reversed its biased dental policy in 1969. This episode marked the beginning of Patricia Ireland's feminist crusade. Realizing that legal action could effect lasting change for women, Ireland entered law school at Florida State University in Tallahassee but kept her Pan Am job. While studying law, Ireland organized fellow classmates formally to protest the use of a biased textbook; she also worked as a volunteer with NOW's Dade County chapter. Earning her degree in 1975 from the University of Miami (to which she had transferred earlier), Ireland was hired by the Miami firm Arky, Freed, Stearns, Watson & Greer. She continued volunteering with NOW, and in 1977 helped mount a challenge to an anti-homosexual referendum in Dade County. Subsequently, Ireland worked to promote Florida's ratification of the Equal Rights Amendment. Although the amendment was defeated nationally in 1982, her efforts led to the ouster of Florida conservative Senator Dick Anderson in his subsequent reelection bid.

NOW Leader

In 1983, Ireland was elected to chair NOW's lesbian rights task force in the Florida chapter where she added her voice to an increasingly powerful lesbian faction within the national organization. In the face of her longtime identification with this issue, Ireland continually spurned the label "lesbian" or "bisexual." She remained low-key about her private affairs, staying married to her second husband while admitting companionship with a woman whose anonymity she strove to protect.

In 1985 Ireland managed Eleanor Smeal's successful campaign for the NOW presidency; two years later Ireland won the vice-presidency, running with firebrand Molly Yard. She founded NOW's Project Stand Up for Women to combat peacefully the efforts of right-wing, anti-abortion advocates. Winning re-election with Yard in 1989, she became acting president of NOW in May 1991 after Yard suffered a stroke. She was named NOW's ninth president in December 1991. As president, she saw NOW membership increase, particularly during the 1991 Senate confirmation hearings of U.S. Supreme Court nominee Judge Clarence Thomas, which involved the alleged sexual harassment of Anita Hill.

Both the organization and its leader endured harsh words from critics who said NOW maintained an overly strident tone and a political stance exclusive of mainstream America. Conversely, Ireland was excoriated by militant feminists who were dismayed by what they saw as her reluctance to declare war on convention. Straddling these perceptions, Ireland nonetheless promoted activism and generated widespread support for women's rights. Organizing the Global Feminist Conference in January 1992, Ireland backed a pro-choice demonstration in Washington, D.C., in April 1992—a show of solidarity attended by nearly one million people.

Putting Ideas Into Words

Ireland's first book *What Women Want* was published in 1996. In the book, she discussed the events in her life that encouraged her to become an advocate for women. She wrote about the struggles of NOW, particularly during their attempt to get the Equal Rights Amendment ratified, and the direction of the organization. She outlined some of the crucial issues facing women today, such as equal pay for work, reproductive freedom, and domestic violence. In addressing the question of what women want, Ireland hoped that her readers would ask themselves the same question. She explained, "When you decide what you want, when you add your own voice to those of other women, when we begin collectively to answer the question of what women want, we become stronger; we become much more determined to get it."

Further Reading

Articles and interviews provide extensive background on this feminist leader. Some sources are the *New York Times Magazine* (March 1, 1992), *Newsweek* (July 22, 1991), and the *National Review* (August 12, 1991).

Additional Sources

Bader, Eleanor J. "*What Women Want* (Book Review)." *The Progressive* 60 (July 1, 1996): 42(2).

Clift, Eleanor. "Patricia Ireland: What NOW?" *Newsweek* (December 16, 1991): 30.

Ireland, Patricia. *What Women Want* New York: Dutton, 1996.

———. "The State of NOW." *Ms.* (July/August 1992): 24-27.

Renwick, Lucille. "NOW Chief Aids Launch of Coalition." *Los Angeles Times,* 24 June 1995.

Selvin, Molly. "Whiplash from Backlash. *What Women Want* by Patricia Ireland (Book Review)." *Los Angeles Times,* 11 August 1996. □

Irene of Athens

An East Roman (Byzantine) empress, Irene of Athens (752-803) convened the Seventh Ecumenical Council and restored the veneration of icons in the Byzantine Empire. Her usurpation of the imperial throne created a theoretical justification for the coronation of Charlemagne.

The first woman ever to hold the throne of the Roman Caesars in her own right, however illegally, the empress Irene was born to an obscure but noble Greek family of Athens. Her beauty alone seems to have gained her the marriage to Leo, son of the Emperor Constantine V Copronymus (740-75). Ruthless and ambitious, she is widely suspected of having poisoned her husband after which she governed the Empire as regent and sole ruler for 22 years. Noted for her liberality, her freeing of prisoners and, above all, for her convening of the Second Council of Nicaea, and for her efforts to restore the veneration of sacred images, Irene was popular among the people despite the irregularity of her conduct of the affairs of state.

Irene came to power as regent for her son (780) in the midst of the iconoclastic controversy which wracked the

Empire for a century (726-87, 815-43). The veneration of sacred images (icons) having grown in intensity and popularity ever since the legalization of Christianity in the fourth century, had developed remarkably in the sixth and seventh centuries, especially encouraged by the emperors of the Heraclid dynasty. It had become so extreme in the East—to the point of bordering on idolatry—that a reaction developed against the practice. To their defenders, the icons were mere representations, visible images of invisible realities, subject to respect and devotion but never to veneration or worship—the position of the Roman Catholic Church to this day.

To the broad masses, however, especially the women, and to the monks who were drawn largely from the ranks of the common people, the line between the images and the sacred reality they were meant to represent was easily blurred. Widely regarded as holy in and of themselves, the icons gradually began to take the place of the idols that Christianity had overthrown. The first assault upon the icons was launched in the Arab Empire, the caliphate, whose ruler Yazid II, supposedly under Jewish influence (the details are very unclear), ordered the icons in Syria to be destroyed. Three years later, the emperor Leo III, never an enemy of images before, suddenly destroyed a major icon and issued an edict against their veneration in 730. When the patriarch of Constantinople, Germanus, showed a lack of sympathy for the emperor's policy, he was deposed the same year, and iconoclasm was firmly pursued despite fierce opposition from the monks.

IRENE OF ATHENS

The chief argument against the creation of images—that the practice violated the second commandment—was easily rejected by iconophiles on the grounds that the biblical injunction referred to images of false gods—idols—and that having revealed himself in the person of Christ and having bestowed His sanctity upon the Virgin and all His saints, the representation of real and tangible personages was valid. A much more complex, intellectual, and refined argument, however, was offered by the Syrian Christian philosopher Mansur, better known as St. John of Damascus, held by both the Catholic and Orthodox churches to have been the last of the Greek "Fathers of the Church." All subsequent arguments of a theological nature in favor of icons were based on his view, namely that the transitory image of the divine—i.e., the icon accessible to the senses—was a necessary link between man's perception of reality and the absolute reality of things divine accessible only to the soul.

There were several sources for the anti-image movement—iconoclasm or "image-smashing," as it came to be known. The biblical injunction and the excesses of veneration observed among the common people, already cited, were two major ones but not the least were the scorn of the Muslims (and Jews) who accused the Byzantines of idolatry, the hostility of the Monophysite Christians of Egypt and Syria who emphasized the unity of the divine—and hence undepictable—nature of Christ, and the hostility of the army with its vast number of Armenian officers and common soldiers whose national church also rejected such holy pictures. On the side of the iconoclasts were also found certain of the Isaurian (actually Syrian) emperors, and, it would appear, the urban mob. On the side of the iconophiles (image-lovers) or iconodules (image-adorers) were the papacy (with suitable cautions), the monks, and the female population. Iconoclasm was especially prevalent in the eastern parts of the Empire; iconophilism in the West. Irene, being an Athenian, was not only a woman but a "westerner" by birth and a devotee of the veneration of the icons who chose to espouse the iconophile cause.

In planning their restoration of icon-worship in the Empire, Irene and her advisors moved with caution, shrewdly awaiting the death of the iconoclastic Paul IV, patriarch of the Imperial Church, before appointing as his replacement the learned Tarasius (784-806). A well-born and highly educated court prelate, skilled in diplomacy, Tarasius was head of the imperial chancellery and de facto prime minister of the Empire. Meanwhile, during the minority of her son, who was only ten when his father died, the empress contented herself with removing iconoclastic generals and other officers, and seeing to it that her husband's five brothers were one by one forced into monasteries to forestall any potential coups. In 785, soon after his elevation, Tarasius invited Pope Hadrian to send delegates to a council, the purpose of which was to reverse the condemnation of the icons issued by the Council of 754.

The first attempt by Irene to convoke the council occurred in Constantinople on May 31, 786, when a conclave attended by the papal delegates was convened in the Church of the Holy Apostles. The council was immediately dispersed by hostile troops recruited by Constantine VI to guard the capital and the papal representatives returned to Sicily, but Irene shrewdly had Constantine's troops shipped to Asia on the pretext of their being sent on a campaign against the Arabs. She then replaced them with Bithynian troops more favorable to her views.

The ecclesiastical gathering was then reconvened in the nearby city of Nicaea, where the First Ecumenical Council had been held nearly 500 years before. Known as the Second Council of Nicaea or the Seventh Ecumenical Council, more than 300 bishops attended this conclave which lasted from September 13 to October 13, 787. Irene managed the council in absentia but when it was clear that her campaign for the restoration of iconolatry had been successful, the attending prelates were brought to Constantinople for the eighth and last session which was held in the capital.

At the end of the deliberations, iconolatry was reestablished, iconoclasts were anathematized, and Constantine VI and his mother were hailed as the new "Constantine and Helena," in reference to the first Christian Roman Emperor and his pious mother. In more far-reaching matters, whenever icons came under attack in the future, those in favor of their use had all the carefully thought out and well-formulated arguments of Nicaea II at their disposal. The council was further hallowed in the minds of the Greeks by the fact that it was to become the last Ecumenical Council recognized by the Greek Church. In the short run, there is no question that the Byzantine government appreciated the support of the monks in favor of iconolatry and, just as they restored the icons, Constantine VI and Irene reversed the policies of Constantine V and Leo III secularizing the enormous monastic estates and limiting the number of monks in the capital.

In dynastic matters, Irene moved as shrewdly as she had done in ecclesiastical affairs. As early as 782, she had arranged for her son, then only 12, to marry Rotrud, daughter of Charlemagne, king of the Franks (786-814), the greatest Western ruler of the age, and had a tutor sent to his capital at Aix-la-Chapelle (Aachen) to teach the German princess Greek and whatever else she might need to know about her future homeland, before her arrival. In 786, however, Charlemagne repudiated this brilliant alliance for reasons that are not clear but which probably concerned the council convened at Nicaea that year without his consultation and his own iconoclast resentment of Irene's well-known iconophile views. In any case, the rupture of the proposed union does not appear to have overly disturbed the empress, who, increasingly ambitious, had good reason not to want a daughter-in-law of such eminent rank. In 788, she arranged for Constantine to marry a certain Maria of Amnia, the daughter of a well-to-do but otherwise obscure family of Paphlagonia (supposedly as the result of a beauty contest held to select the bride). A single daughter was born of this marriage; she eventually reigned as the consort of Michael II (820-829).

For nearly two decades, Irene's power as regent was secure, but as Constantine VI approached manhood, he was determined to rule for himself. Fearing her son's growing independence, Irene pressed too far when she demanded that her own name precede that of his in all public documents. A plot was then hatched to remove Irene from power and have her banished to Sicily, but she learned of this in time and had her son confined in the palace, demanding a direct oath of allegiance to herself from the military. Upon learning of this, the troops of the Armeniac theme (military province) rebelled, secured the liberation of the emperor, and excluded Irene and her entourage of eunuch supporters from the palace.

Once in full power, Constantine embarked on a luckless war against the Bulgars in April 791 and another against the Arabs in October of the same year. Unsuccessful in the field and increasingly unpopular, in January 792, the emperor was rash enough to restore his mother to her former position of authority. Exactly three years later, however, in January 795, Constantine shocked public opinion by repudiating his empress-wife, placing her in a convent, and, on October 7, 796, entering into an irregular marriage with Theodote, one of her ladies-in-waiting. A son was born of this union but, although the patriarch was willing to grant a dispensation for the marriage, this son was considered illegitimate by the monks and the Church at large, and probably would never have reigned even if he had not died in infancy.

Though the monks were furious with Constantine for what they considered his sinful behavior and feared anything that might weaken the authority of the Church which was the basis for their own power, Irene appears to have supported her son's marital escapade precisely to create a reason for removing him from the throne. Though strengthened by a military victory against the Bulgars and on his way to meet the Arabs in battle, Constantine's perennial ineptitude allowed his mother to concoct a clever plot oiled with bribery, involving both civilian and army personnel. When Constantine learned of it, he chose to flee rather than stand his ground.

Captured as he attempted to reach the East, where loyal troops might be secured, he was brought to the palace to the Porphyry Chamber, where he had been born but 27 years before. There, on August 15, 797, he was blinded at his mother's orders, a frequently practiced maneuver that by Byzantine norms rendered a member of the imperial family unfit to reign. Constantine would die shortly after his mutilation, which was probably conducted in such a way as to achieve this result.

With the monks already inimical to him because of his adulterous marriage, he stood as a likely candidate around which the iconoclastic party, now in disarray, might conceivably rally and find a friend and supporter. Irene's ruthlessness and lust for power, hopelessly entwined with her fanatical devotion to the restoration of icons, had overcome all maternal instinct, all human feelings, and all fear of public opinion both at home and abroad. Constantine had to go, and Irene was willing to execute him. In this way, she became the first woman to sit upon the throne established by Augustus over eight centuries before and an all-male preserve until her time.

The overthrow of Constantine VI and seizure of the throne by Irene had grave repercussions that indirectly altered the history of the Western world. As early as 475, the Byzantine Church had been in schism with that of Rome and not until 519 was the patriarch of Constantinople reconciled with the pope. The collapse of Byzantine rule in Rome left the pope free of imperial influence but further alienated the center of the Church from the center of the Empire. The Slavic invasions of Eastern Europe which cut Constantinople from land contact with Rome were followed by the Arab domination of the Mediterranean that made contact by sea increasingly difficult, as well. To these strains were added the hostilities engendered by the iconoclastic controversy which pitted the icon-favoring popes against the iconoclastic emperors for most of the eighth century.

During this period from the fifth through the eighth centuries, the papacy had come to rely increasingly on the support of the Frankish kings, who, after the defeat of the Muslims at Poitiers in 732, could justly be hailed as the defenders of the faith. In any case, Charlemagne, greatest of the Frankish kings and master of a realm that stretched from northern Spain to Poland encompassing France, Germany, Northern Italy, and all Central Europe, was a force to be reckoned with. Although, in theory, the Byzantine Empire was the direct continuation of the Roman Empire of old and it was always recognized that there was but one Empire in the Christian world, the removal of Constantine VI from the throne in 797 and his replacement by his mother constituted a most disturbing turn of events.

While the coup that had cast Constantine from the throne, though illegal, was not without precedent, the placing of a woman on the imperial throne was a thing unheard of in Roman history since the empire had been founded in the first century b.c. The emperor was not a king to be succeeded by his widow or his daughter. Rather, he was the holder of a composite of offices, titles, and positions, including that of commander in chief of the army, all of which had been traditionally held only by men. Since a woman could not legally hold any of these positions (least of all that of commander of the army), the idea of a female emperor was a contradiction in terms.

With Irene on the throne, whatever the circumstances that brought her there, the Pope could legitimately consider the Roman throne to be legally vacant. Thus, it was on Christmas Day, in the year 800, during a visit of Charlemagne to Rome that the pope—undoubtedly with the king's prior knowledge and acquiescence—placed on his head an imperial crown, bestowing upon Charlemagne the title "Holy Roman Emperor" and thereby recognizing his vast realm as the restoration of the Roman Empire in the West.

Charlemagne was astute enough to realize, of course, that Irene's reign would one day end and that he would eventually be faced with an emperor legitimate in Byzantine eyes. He therefore sent emissaries to seek the empress's hand in marriage, apparently with the idea that after the death of the surviving partner one of his own children would succeed them since Irene's only son was dead and she was past childbearing age. Irene consented to this marriage, which accorded well with her ambitions and which would legalize her position, but her fall prevented its conclusion.

Thereafter, until its extinction by Napoleon in 1806, the term "Roman Empire" was used throughout Western Europe to refer to the holdings of the Holy Roman Emperor, whereas, for as long as it lasted (i.e., until the fall of Constantinople to the Turks in 1453), Europeans would refer to the Byzantine state—to the dismay and outrage of its rulers—as the "Empire of the Greeks."

Although it was said of Irene that she had the mind of a man, she was not a competent ruler and much of her reign was dominated by the struggle between her favorite eunuchs. The army was demoralized and alienated by her conduct of affairs; the Arabs invaded Asia Minor as far as Ephesus and ravaged the frontier provinces until peace was obtained by the payment of a large tribute to the caliph, Harun al-Rashid. To curry favor with the masses, Irene reduced some taxes, especially in the capital, and abolished others, moves that were to prove ruinous coupled with the ravages experienced during the Arab invasion. In 802, Irene was finally overthrown by a palace coup led by Nicephorus, her own minister of finance. Realizing that her fall was final, Irene had the intelligence to step aside gracefully thereby perhaps saving herself from physical harm. Despite the dissatisfaction with her rule, however, Irene had many friends, especially among the monks who adored her, and she was allowed to live out the rest of her life in dignified exile on the island of Lesbos where she died in 803.

Irene of Athens was one of the most ruthless, ambitious, and forceful women ever to hold a throne and, in her determination to prevent her son from reigning and her boldness in daring to become the first woman ever to hold the Roman throne, she ranks with Queen Hatshepsut of Egypt and Catherine the Great as a profound breaker with dynastic tradition. Her convocation of the Second Council of Nicaea laid the institutional foundation for the permanent restoration of the icons in the Greek Church and codified the intellectual arguments in favor of the iconophile position. Perhaps most important of all, Irene's usurpation of the throne provided the ideological justification for the coronation of Charlemagne the Great as emperor of the Holy Roman Empire, an institution that was to survive and to trouble Europe until laid to rest by Napoleon. In this way, she changed the course of European history and left a recognizable seal upon it for a millennium after her death.

Further Reading

Canons of the Second Council of Nicaea. Theophanes. *Chronicle.* Translated by H. Turtledove. University of Pennsylvania, 1982.

Anastos, M.V. "Iconoclasm and Imperial Rule 717-842," in *Cambridge Medieval History,* Vol. IV, *The Byzantine Empire, Part I: Byzantium and its Neighbors.* Chapt. III, Cambridge, England, 1966.

Jenkins, Romilly. *Byzantium: the Imperial Centuries a.d. 610-1071.* Random House, 1966.

Ostrogorsky. *The History of the Byzantine State.* Rutgers University Press, 1957.

Vasiliev, A. A. *History of the Byzantine Empire 324-1453.* University of Wisconsin, 1952. ☐

Hipólito Irigoyen

Hipólito Irigoyen (ca. 1850-1933) was an Argentine president. As leader of the Radical party, he united the country behind him in opposition to the land-holding oligarchy; but unable to cope with Argentina's economic problems, he was deposed by Conservatives.

Hipólito Irigoyen received little formal education but was taken under the protection of his uncle Leandro Alem, in whose office he read law. For some years he worked at a variety of jobs, including an instructorship in a girls' school and minor government posts.

In his youth Irigoyen also dabbled in politics on a local level. When Alem organized the Union Civica in 1890 as a protest movement against the dominant rural-based oligarchy, Irigoyen joined the new group. He also followed Alem 2 years later in converting the group, which had originally sought alliances with elements of the old regime to participate in elections, into the Union Civica Radical (Radical Civic Union, UCR), pledged to a policy of electoral abstention so long as fraud and violence were used by the government as the principal determinants of elections.

With Alem's suicide in 1896, Irigoyen succeeded his uncle as the principal leader of the UCR, or Radical party. For 15 years he held the party firmly to the policy of not participating in elections and built up a wide rank-and-file base for the party. Penetrating into even remote parts of the country, Irigoyen and his associated established units of the UCR throughout the nation. The party became the principal spokesman for the burgeoning middle classes and for a considerable segment of the working classes as well.

As the Radical party chief, Irigoyen demanded strict obedience and at times even obeisance from his associates. He kept firm control of the party machinery, although he had few intimates, was a mediocre orator, and only rarely appeared in public. Despite his lack of humor and reticence about public exposure, Irigoyen became vastly admired by his followers because of his modest circumstances—he lived largely from the income from a small property and gave much of his income to charity—and because of his uncompromising fight against the political and economic status quo.

Under President Roque Sáenz Peña, who was elected in 1910, the electoral law was finally changed so as to provide for the secret ballot and the assurance of minority representation in all legislative bodies. As a result, the Radicals began to participate in elections. In 1916 Irigoyen was victorious as his party's first candidate for president.

Irigoyen demonstrated the same character traits in the presidency he had shown in the chieftainship of his party. He ruled with a firm hand, made liberal use of the president's right to oust provincial governors, and made virtually all important decisions of his administration. However, he was unsuccessful in carrying through any basic reforms.

Although he was sympathetic to organized labor, little social legislation was passed during his presidency. Although he was a strong nationalist, his administration took few measures to protect national industry or to weaken Argentine dependence on British markets for its major exports of grain and meat.

In 1922 Irigoyen was succeeded by another Radical, Marcelo T. de Alvear. However, during De Alvear's administration a split developed between the two Radical leaders, and two separate parties emerged, the UCR Personalista, consisting of supporters of Irigoyen, and the UCR Anti-Personalista, made up of backers of De Alvear.

Irigoyen was elected to the presidency once again in 1928, at the expiration of De Alvear's term. However, by this time he was senile, and the corruption on the part of high officials (but not Irigoyen) which had long characterized the Radical governments reached unequaled heights. Finally, Irigoyen was faced with the Great Depression, which he was not able to handle any more effectively than leaders of most other countries.

These circumstances gave right-wing opponents of Irigoyen the opportunity to carry out a coup against him on Sept. 6, 1930, backed by Anti-Personalista Radicals, Conservatives, and dissident Socialists. With his ouster, Irigoyen retired from politics.

Further Reading

There is no full-length biography of Irigoyen in English. However, Robert A. Potash, *The Army and Politics in Argentina* (1969), contains considerable material about him. See also such standard histories of Argentina as Ricardo Levene, *A History of Argentina,* translated and edited by William Spence (1937), and Ysabel F. Rennie, *The Argentine Republic* (1945). □

Kenneth Colin Irving

Kenneth Colin Irving (1899-1992) was an industrialist who built a cluster of interrelated regional businesses into a massive empire that straddled virtually every aspect of his native New Brunswick's economy. He became the "Paul Bunyan of New Brunswick," purportedly one of the wealthiest men in the world by the late 1980s.

Kenneth Colin Irving was born into a fourth-generation Canadian family of Scottish descent on March 14, 1899, at Bouctouche, New Brunswick. While never especially religious in later life, young Irving was clearly stamped by his father James' ardent Presbyterianism, with its emphasis on frugality and hard work. The family capitalized on the strength of the 19th-century maritime economy, sawing timber at their sawmill and purveying dry goods at their local store. Ken displayed an early appetite for work—threshing grain and performing odd jobs—but little enthusiasm for study. After two lackluster years at a university in Nova Scotia, young Irving's jingoism got the better of him and he joined the Royal Flying Corps in 1918, returning home the next year without having seen action.

By the 1920s the 19th-century "wind, water, and wood" glory of the Maritime Provinces' economy was fading; the Irving family sawmill would fail within a decade. At the same time, the region was losing its economic autonomy, as central Canadian capital, technology, and managerial expertise infiltrated the area. Thinly-populated Atlantic Canada lacked the economies of scale and capital pool to independently sustain the growth industries—metalworking and manufacturing—that marked a modern industrial economy. Automobiles were at the heart of such growth. A born tinkerer, Irving was fascinated by the car and in 1920 augmented the faltering family store by grafting a service station onto it. He became an agent for Toronto-based Imperial Oil, the Canadian subsidiary of Standard Oil. He soon added a Ford dealership and repair shop. In 1925 Irving's commitment to expansion was evident in the opening of a service station in Saint John, New Brunswick's leading commercial city.

From the outset Irving sensed that he, like his region, was vulnerable to the whims of outside control. In 1927 he created K.C. Irving Gas & Oil Ltd. and then, in 1929, Irving Oil Ltd. He distanced himself from Imperial, introduced his own brand of gasoline—"Primrose"—and vigorously expanded in the region. Volume sales gave him better leverage over his suppliers; he built bulk storage facilities and struck separate deals with New England suppliers. In 1931 he moved his operations to Saint John, establishing himself in the Golden Ball Building. For the next 60 years the man in the Golden Ball Building would be the most influential factor in the provincial economy.

Two unshakable instincts shaped Irving's entrepreneurship. He believed in "hands-on" control; he distrusted partnerships and maintained tight family ownership and an intrusive presence in the day-to-day management of his enterprises. There was a secretiveness in Irving that would shield his activities from public scrutiny throughout his life; he consequently acquired nicknames—"the Baron of Bouctouche"—that underscored his aloofness. Irving also sensed that success in a region of marginal economic importance was best secured by clustering similar industries, thereby capturing synergies and economies of scale hitherto enjoyed only by large outside corporations such as Ford and Imperial. When later asked the secret of his success, Irving would curtly answer, "Expansion is the thing."

Building an Empire

Expansion began for Irving in the early 1930s when he began to supplement his service station operations with ancillary transportation enterprises—bus manufacture and operation, shipping, and trucking. This transportation net made movement of oil products cheaper and prompted Irving to enter other industries in which transportation loomed large. He reawakened the family's timber traditions by assembling timberlands and venturing into new forestry products. In 1938, for instance, he gained control of Canadian Veneers Ltd., the supplier of high-quality veneer for aircraft production.

Such expansion, coupled with lean management structures, allowed Irving to weather the Great Depression and then to capitalize on the wartime economy. It also put him in an increasingly powerful position in terms of exacting concessions and incentives from the New Brunswick government; Irving's enterprises had become a key ingredient in local growth, and provincial logging legislation, for instance, reflected this fact. Irving's strength in the Maritimes also provided the foundation for expansion into Quebec and Ontario—gas stations and forestry—and south into Maine, where forest lands were acquired.

The postwar boom offered new scope for Irving's strategy of expansion. Newspaper publishing seemed a natural complement to his pulp and paper operations, and beginning in 1944 he began to acquire the leading dailies—the Saint John *Telegraph-Journal,* for instance—of the province. With the newspapers came radio stations and, by the 1960s, television stations. Other expansion projects included a heavy construction company, an ocean towing company, and the purchase of new oil tankers. In the 1950s Irving determined to diminish his dependence on outside suppliers by building an oil refinery in partnership with Standard Oil and through acquisition of the Saint John Drydock Company. He could now take a small part in the international oil trade and, with his own tanker fleet and over 3,000 service stations, had the dominant oil company in the Maritimes. To achieve these gains, Irving was prepared to surrender a degree of control. Partnerships with the American papermaker Kimberly-Clark and with Standard Oil gave him access to capital and larger markets/production runs. Over time, Irving usually managed to buy out his partners.

Irving rounded out his empire in the 1960s and 1970s with more newspapers (e.g., the *Fredericton Gleaner* in 1968), refinery expansion, a deep-water port for supertankers, Cavendish Farms (a food processing conglomerate) in 1979, and the building of naval frigates in Saint John. By the 1980s the Irving companies—some 300 in total—employed 25,000; one out of every 12 New Brunswickers (1986 population 709,000) drew an Irving paycheck. The close-held nature of the Irving empire made valuation of its net worth a tricky proposition, but in 1988 *Forbes* magazine ranked Irving as one of the wealthiest men in the world, with assets of $9 billion in U.S. dollars.

The Family Comes First

Irving's monopoly position in many spheres of the Maritime Provinces' economy and his insistence on tight family control often strained his relations with his workers and with Canadian governments. To many he was the economic savior of the province; to others he was a monopolist, hostile to unions and quick to use his economic clout to influence political decisions. Irving's paternalistic management style bred loyalty in many workers in the Irving "family" of companies; unions had their difficulties penetrating the Irving empire. The dominant market share of the companies also attracted the critical attention of government; from 1971 to 1974 Irving successfully defended his near-monopoly over New Brunswick newspapers against a government charge that his chain operated to the "detriment of the public interest." Irving also battled with large central Canadian corporations (e.g., with Noranda Mines over control of a New Brunswick smelting venture).

In 1971 Irving shifted his legal domicile to Bermuda, a mid-Atlantic tax haven beyond the reach of Canadian authorities. There control of the Irving companies was vested in a new echelon of Bermuda holding companies. Irving California Co. Ltd., for instance, controlled the transshipment of oil destined for his Saint John refinery; the Canadian Government unsuccessfully alleged that this allowed Irving to skim another layer of profit from his trade in oil. In Bermuda, Irving became increasingly reclusive. While remaining intimately involved in his companies' management, he shifted much operational oversight to his three sons, James (born 1928), Arthur (born 1930), and John (born 1932), all from his 1927 marriage to Harriet McNairn, who died in 1976. Each assumed responsibility for a section of the Irving empire (e.g., Arthur for Irving Oil). K.C.'s grandsons were being eased into Irving management. Unlike so many entrepreneurial patriarchs, Irving had engineered a smooth transition of executive control to his heirs.

Irving died on December 13, 1992, in Saint John and was buried in Bermuda. He was survived by his second wife, Winnifred, and by the legacy of what an aggressive strategy of vertical and horizontal integration can achieve in an economy on the margin of North America.

Further Reading

The tight family control of the Irving enterprises and his own abiding secrecy have combined to shield K.C. Irving from definitive scrutiny. He was repeatedly studied from afar by journalists and government regulatory and legal inquiries. Three impressionistic biographies are Russell Hunt and Robert Campbell, *K.C. Irving: The Art of the Industrialist* (1973), John DeMont, *Citizens Irving: K.C. Irving and His Legacy* (1991), and Douglas How and Ralph Costello, *K.C.: The Biography of K.C. Irving* (1993). Study #16 of the *Report of the Royal Commission on Corporate Concentration* (Ottawa, 1978) provides an anatomy of the Irving companies. Numerous journalistic profiles exist (e.g., *Fortune,* October 12, 1987).

Additional Sources

DeMont, John, *Citizens Irving: K.C. Irving and his legacy: the story of Canada's wealthiest family,* Toronto: Doubleday Canada, 1992. □

Washington Irving

Considered the first professional man of letters in the United States, Washington Irving (1783-1859) was influential in the development of the short story form and helped to gain international respect for fledgling American literature.

Following the tradition of the eighteenth-century essay exemplified by the elegant, lightly humorous prose of Joseph Addison and Oliver Goldsmith, Irving created endearing and often satiric short stories and sketches. In his most-acclaimed work, *The Sketch Book of Geoffrey Crayon, Gent.* (1819-20), he wove elements of myth and folklore into narratives, such as "Rip Van Winkle" and "The Legend of Sleepy Hollow," that achieved almost immediate classic status. Although Irving was also renowned in his lifetime for his extensive work in history and biography, it was through his short stories that he most strongly influenced American writing in subsequent generations and introduced a number of now-familiar images and archetypes into the body of the national literature.

Irving was born and raised in New York City, the youngest of eleven children of a prosperous merchant family. A dreamy and ineffectual student, he apprenticed himself in a law office rather than follow his elder brothers to nearby Columbia College. In his free time, he read avidly and wandered when he could in the misty, rolling Hudson River Valley, an area steeped in local folklore and legend that would serve as an inspiration for his later writings.

As a nineteen-year-old, Irving began contributing satirical letters under the pseudonym Jonathan Oldstyle to a newspaper owned by his brother Peter. His first book, *Salmagundi; or, The Whim-Whams and Opinions of Launcelot Langstaff, Esq., and Others* (1807-08), was a collaboration with another brother, William, and their friend James Kirke Paulding. This highly popular collection of

short pieces poked fun at the political, social, and cultural life of the city. Irving enjoyed a second success in 1809 with *A History of New York, from the Beginning of the World to the End of the Dutch Dynasty,* a comical, deliberately inaccurate account of New York's Dutch colonization narrated by the fictitious Diedrich Knickerbocker, a fusty, colorful Dutch-American. His carefree social life and literary successes were shadowed at this time, however, by the death of his fiancee, Matilda Hoffmann, and for the next several years he floundered, wavering between a legal, mercantile, and editorial career. In 1815 he moved to England to work in the failing Liverpool branch of the family import-export business. Within three years the company was bankrupt, and, finding himself at age thirty-five without means of support, Irving decided that he would earn his living by writing. He began recording the impressions, thoughts, and descriptions which, polished and repolished in his meticulous manner, became the pieces that make up *The Sketch Book.* The volume was brought out under the pseudonym of Geoffrey Crayon, who was purportedly a good-natured American roaming Britain on his first trip abroad.

The Sketch Book comprises some thirty parts: about half English sketches, four general travel reminiscences, six literary essays, two descriptions of the American Indian, three essentially unclassifiable pieces, and three short stories: "Rip Van Winkle," "The Legend of Sleepy Hollow," and "The Spectre Bridegroom." Although only the last-named tale is set in Germany, all three stories draw upon the legends of that country. The book was published almost concurrently in the United States and England in

order to escape the piracy to which literary works were vulnerable before international copyright laws, a shrewd move that many subsequent authors copied. The miscellaneous nature of *The Sketch Book* was an innovation that appealed to a broad range of readers; the work received a great deal of attention and sold briskly, and Irving found himself America's first international literary celebrity. In addition, the book's considerable profits allowed Irving to devote himself full-time to writing.

Remaining abroad for more than a decade after the appearance of *The Sketch Book,* Irving wrote steadily, capitalizing on his international success with two subsequent collections of tales and sketches that also appeared under the name Geoffrey Crayon. *Bracebridge Hall; or, the Humorists: A Medley* (1822) centers loosely around a fictitious English clan that Irving had introduced in several of the *Sketch Book* pieces. *Bracebridge Hall* further describes their manners, customs, and habits, and interjects several unrelated short stories, including "The Student from Salamanca" and "The Stout Gentleman." *Tales of a Traveller* (1824) consists entirely of short stories arranged in four categories: European stories, tales of London literary life, accounts of Italian bandits, and narrations by Irving's alterego, Diedrich Knickerbocker. The most enduring of these, according to many critics, are "The German Student," which some consider a significant early example of supernatural fiction, and "The Devil and Tom Walker," a Yankee tale that like "Rip Van Winkle" draws upon myth and legend for characters and incident. After 1824 Irving increasingly turned his attention from fiction and descriptive writing toward history and biography. He lived for several years in Spain, serving as a diplomatic attache to the American legation while writing a life of Christopher Columbus and a history of Granada. During this period he also began gathering material for *The Alhambra* (1832), a vibrantly romantic collection of sketches and tales centered around the Moorish palace in Granada.

Irving served as secretary to the American embassy in London from 1829 until 1832, when he returned to the United States. After receiving warm accolades from the literary and academic communities, he set out on a tour of the rugged western part of the country, which took him as far as Oklahoma. The expedition resulted in three books about the region, notably *A Tour on the Prairies* (1835), which provided easterners with their first description of life out west by a well-known author. Irving eventually settled near Tarrytown, New York, at a small estate on the Hudson River, which he named Sunnyside. Apart from four years in Madrid and Barcelona, which he spent as President John Tyler's minister to Spain, Irving lived there the rest of his life. Among the notable works of his later years is an extensive biography of George Washington, which Irving worked on determinedly, despite ill health, from the early 1850s until a few months before his death in 1859.

The Sketch Book prompted the first widespread critical response to Irving's writings. Reviewers in the United States were generally delighted with the work of their native son, and even English critics, normally hostile in that era to American authors, accorded the book generally favorable—

if somewhat condescending—notice. Among the pieces singled out for praise in the early reviews were most frequently the three short stories, particularly "Rip Van Winkle." Critics found Irving's style pleasingly elegant, fine, and humorous, although some, including Richard Henry Dana, perceived a lack of intellectual content beneath the decorative surface. Dana also observed that in adopting the authorial persona of Geoffrey Crayon—with his prose style modeled after the eighteenth-century essayists—Irving lost the robustness, high color, and comic vigor of his previous incarnations as Jonathan Oldstyle, Launcelot Langstaff, and Diedrich Knickerbocker, an observation that was echoed by later critics. Subsequent "Crayon" works, such as *Bracebridge Hall*, *Tales of a Traveller*, and *The Alhambra*, while generally valued for their prose style, tended to prompt such complaints as that by the Irish author Maria Edgeworth that "the workmanship surpasses the work."

Beginning in the 1950s, however, critics began to explore technical and thematic innovations in Irving's short stories. These include the integration of folklore, myth, and fable into narrative fiction; setting and landscape as a reflection of theme and mood; the expression of the supernatural and use of Gothic elements in some stories; and the tension between imagination and creativity versus materialism and productivity in nineteenth-century America. Many critics read Rip's twenty-year sleep as a rejection of the capitalistic values of his society—ferociously personified by the shrewish Dame Van Winkle—and an embracing of the world of the imagination. Ichabod Crane, too, has been viewed by such critics as Robert Bone as representing the outcast artist-intellectual in American society, although he has been considered, conversely, as a caricature of the acquisitive, scheming Yankee Puritan, a type that Irving lampooned regularly in his early satirical writings.

Today, many critics concur with Fred Lewis Pattee's assertion that the "American short story began in 1819 with Washington Irving." Commentators agree, moreover, that in "Rip Van Winkle" and "The Legend of Sleepy Hollow," Irving established an artistic standard and model for subsequent generations of American short story writers. As George Snell wrote: "It is quite possible to say that Irving unconsciously shaped a principal current in American fiction, whatever may be the relative unimportance of his own work." In their continuing attention to the best of Irving's short fiction, critics affirm that while much of Irving's significance belongs properly to literary history, such stories as "Rip Van Winkle" and "The Legend of Sleepy Hollow" belong to literary art.

Further Reading

Bleiler, E. F., editor, *Supernatural Fiction Writers: Fantasy and Horror 2: A. E. Coppard to Roger Zelazny*, Scribners, 1985, pp. 685-91.
Bowden, Mary Weatherspoon, *Washington Irving*, Twayne, 1981.
Concise Dictionary of American Literary Biography: Colonization to the American Renaissance, 1640-1865, Gale, 1988.
Dictionary of Literary Biography, Gale, Volume 3: *Antebellum Writers in New York and the South*, 1979, Volume 11: *American Humorists, 1800-1950*, 1982, Volume 30: *American His-* *torians, 1607-1865*, 1984, Volume 59: *American Literary Critics and Scholars,1800-1850*, 1987, Volume 73: *American Magazine Journalists 1741-1850*, 1988, Volume 74: *American Short-Story Writers before 1880*, 1988.
Harbert, Earl N., and Robert A. Rees, editor, *Fifteen American Authors before 1900: Bibliographical Essays on Research and Criticism*, University of Wisconsin Press, 1984.
Hedges, William L., *Washington Irving: An American Study, 1802-1832*, Johns Hopkins Press, 1965.
Leary, Lewis, *Washington Irving*, University of Minnesota Press, 1963. □

Heinrich Isaac

Heinrich Isaac (ca. 1450-1517) was a versatile and prolific Flemish composer of both secular and church music. He was one of the greatest masters of High Renaissance music.

Little is known of the early life of Heinrich Isaac. He asserted that he came from Flanders. His birth date is believed to be within a few years of the mid-15th century. He was undoubtedly trained in the Low Countries and remained there until 1484, when Lorenzo de' Medici, impressed by his reputation, invited Isaac to Florence. For 10 years he worked at the principal churches of the city as composer, singer, and choir director.

Isaac was also a composer for the Medici household and taught music to Lorenzo's children. During this decade he composed many carnival songs (now lost) to the poems of his wealthy patron. With the fall of the Medici and their expulsion from Florence (1494), Isaac lost his posts and was obliged to seek employment with the Hapsburgs at Vienna and Innsbruck. He did, however, maintain a house in Florence until his death, partly because he loved the city and partly in deference to his Florentine wife.

In 1496 Emperor Maximilian of Austria appointed Isaac imperial court composer at Vienna, a title he retained for the rest of his life. His church music for the German liturgy as well as his German songs all probably date from this time. As court composer he was required only to furnish the court and chapel with musical compositions; continuous attendance on the monarch was not required, so the composer lived far from Vienna for many years. Maximilian also seems not to have objected to Isaac's composing for other rulers or civic authorities while on the imperial payroll. Isaac received payments from the Elector of Saxony (1497-1500) and wrote music for the Duke of Ferrara (1503-1505). A commission from the German city of Constance in 1508 produced a monumental series of polyphonic Mass Propers (Introits, Alleluias, Sequences, Communions) for feast days celebrated in the city. These pieces, together with other Mass Propers by Isaac, were published posthumously in three volumes as the *Choralis Constantinus* (1550-1555).

In 1512 the Medici returned to Florence, and a year later Giovanni de' Medici, Isaac's former student, ascended the papal throne as Leo X. Isaac thereupon requested papal assistance for reinstatement to his former positions at Florence. When these negotiations were successfully completed in 1514, Isaac journeyed north for release from further obligations to his imperial master. With characteristic magnanimity Emperor Maximilian permitted the composer to return to Florence without loss of salary and, in effect, gave him a pension to enjoy his last days in Italy. Several months after drawing up his final (third) last will and testament, Isaac died in Florence on March 26, 1517.

Isaac's music owes much to the Netherlandish style he learned in his homeland. Among his more conservative traits is a persistent allegiance to the traditional *cantus firmus*. He wrote fewer pieces without a borrowed tune than many contemporaries who were then moving more toward free composition. Among the progressive features of his style is his use of imitation and melodic and rhythmic equality of voice parts. Intricate canons and notational artifices are occasionally found in the Masses, but they almost always serve a musical purpose. Similarly, Isaac's melodic lines may sometimes look intricate and fussy, but they never sound so to the exclusion of their musical interest. That he was a great melodist is shown by his song *Innsbruck ich muss dich lassen,* a tune destined to have a strong influence on the later German song.

Unlike some of his contemporaries, Isaac was equally adept at writing religious and secular music: German, French, and Italian songs; instrumental pieces; Masses for four to six voices and Propers for the entire church year; separate Credos; and motets. He had the rare ability to assimilate different national styles and yet preserve his own idiom.

Further Reading

Isaac's music is discussed in Gustave Reese, *Music in the Renaissance* (1954; rev. ed. 1959), and J. A. Westrup and others, eds., *The New Oxford History of Music,* vol. 3 (1960). For a summary of music in the Renaissance see Paul Henry Lang, *Music in Western Civilization* (1941). □

Jorge Isaacs

Jorge Isaacs (1837-1895) was Colombia's greatest 19th-century novelist. He also was politically active and one of Colombia's first cultural anthropologists.

Jorge Isaacs was born, probably in the city of Cali, on April 1, 1837, the son of a converted English Jew, George Henry Isaacs, and his wife, Manuela Ferrer, a lady well-connected to the elite of the provinces of northwestern Colombia. Jorge was educated in Cali and in Bogotá. Upon the outbreak of the Melo Revolt in 1854, the youthful Isaacs saw service on the Constitutionalist side, and 2 years later he married Felisa González of Cali.

His father's business failure in the late 1850s caused Jorge to seek employment in a variety of public posts and to engage in several unsuccessful business ventures of his

own. Thus, he spent about a year as inspector of the Dagua Road in 1864-1865, a job which permanently damaged his health.

Isaacs wrote poetry (in the romantic genre popular at the time) from an early age and was much applauded for it by the important literary circle, the Mosaico, of Bogotá, which in 1864 brought out the first edition of his verse. Encouraged by this, Isaacs in 1867 published his novel, *María,* in Bogotá. The times were unsettled politically and socially, and the idyllic novel was an almost immediate success in Colombia and in much of Spanish America. Its lyrical evocation of the natural beauties of the valley of the Cauca and its plot of unrequited love combined to fulfill a real need in the Colombian reading public.

Isaacs was a man of strong passions. When, in 1868, he left the Conservative party and joined the Liberals, Isaacs threw himself wholeheartedly into the new cause. He participated actively in politics, and in the Civil War of 1876 he defended his convictions on the battlefield. So profound were his convictions that in 1880 he led a briefly successful armed revolt against the Conservative regime of Antioquia State and justified his actions in *La revolución radical en Antioquia,* today a bibliographic rarity.

His writings brought Isaacs almost no financial reward, and his fervent liberalism, after 1886 (with the establishment of the "Regeneration"), brought only political persecution and ostracism. His last years were spent in poverty. While his reputation justly derives from *María,* Jorge Isaacs should also be remembered as one of Colombia's pioneer cultural anthropologists. His study of the Indian tribes of Magdalena State (1884) is in its own way as much a classic for the student of the Indian cultures of northern Colombia as is his *María* for that of Colombian literature. Leaving a large family, and heavily in debt, Jorge Isaacs died in Ibagué, Tolima Department, on April 17, 1895.

Further Reading

Isaacs has not fared well biographically. He is discussed briefly in Arturo Torres-Rioseco, *The Epic of Latin American Literature* (1942). □

Isabella I

Isabella I (1451-1504) was queen of Castile from 1474 to 1504. She and her husband, Ferdinand V, founded the modern Spanish state.

Born in Madrigal on April 22, 1451, Isabella was the daughter of John II of Castile by his second wife, Isabella of Portugal, and was the half sister of Henry IV, who succeeded to the Castilian throne in 1454. Henry had recognized Isabella as his heir over the claims of his daughter Juana, whose royal paternity was questioned by the King's opponents, but when Isabella married Ferdinand of Aragon in 1469, Henry conferred the succession on Juana.

When Henry died in 1474, Isabella immediately claimed the throne. In the ensuing civil war Juana was supported by a cross section of the great nobles as well as by the Portuguese king, Alfonso V. Alfonso's army was defeated at the battle of Toro in 1476, and he made peace with the Catholic Monarchs (as the pair were styled) in 1479. In that same year Ferdinand succeeded to the throne of Aragon, associating Isabella with his rule in 1481. With Juana sequestered in a convent, the crucial step in the formation of a united Spain had been taken.

Although "Spain" in 1481 was little more than a personal union of the two crowns, and remained so during Isabella's lifetime, the ultimate process of unification was facilitated by the achievements of the Catholic Monarchs, the most significant of which was the reconquest of the Peninsula from the Moorish kingdom of Granada. Begun in 1481, the war lasted until 1492, ending in a complete Spanish victory. Generous peace terms, which allowed the inhabitants to retain their Islamic religion and laws, were soon violated, and, following an abortive Moorish revolt in 1502, adult Moslems who refused Christian baptism were expelled from Spain.

Earlier, in 1492-the same year in which Isabella agreed to subsidize Columbus's first voyage—the Catholic Monarchs had ordered the expulsion of all unbaptized Castilian Jews, nearly 150,000 in all. The Inquisition, established at the Monarchs' behest in 1478, was thus offered a free field to uncover and penalize the backslidings of all remaining "New Christians" (baptized Jews and Moors).

Isabella had five children. The marriage of daughter Catherine of Aragon to Henry VIII of England eventually resulted in the controversy leading to the English Reformation; and the marriage of Joanna (Juana) the Mad to Philip of Burgundy, son of the German emperor Maximilian I, produced a successor to the Spanish crown—Charles I of Spain (Charles V of the Holy Roman Empire). Isabella, who died on Nov. 26, 1504, nearly undid the work of the Catholic Monarchs by leaving the Castilian throne, not to Ferdinand, but to her demented daughter.

Further Reading

One of the best biographical histories of the Catholic Monarchs remains William Prescott, *History of the Reign of Ferdinand and Isabella* (3 vols., 1838; new rev. ed. 1873). A vivid biographical treatment of the royal couple is in Townsend Miller, *The Castles and the Crown: Spain, 1451-1555* (1963). □

Isabella II

Isabella II (1830-1904) was queen of Spain from 1833 to 1868. She was Spain's first true constitutional monarch during a period of growing social and political conflicts.

Born in Madrid on Oct. 10, 1830, Isabella was the daughter of Ferdinand VII of Spain and Maria Cristina of Naples. Her uncle Don Carlos refused to recognize her right to the throne, and after the death of Ferdinand in late 1833 a bitter civil war broke out between the conservative elements, who supported Don Carlos, and the liberal groups, who supported the young princess and her mother, the Queen Regent. The Carlists were defeated in 1839, but the following year Baldomero Espartero, a liberal and the most powerful general in the country, forced Maria Cristina to leave Spain. Isabella remained behind.

Three years later, the conservatives overthrew Espartero and his liberal supporters and on Nov. 8, 1843, had 13-year-old Isabella declared legally of age and crowned queen. Isabella's education had been meager; she could scarcely read and was by all accounts relatively ignorant. But she was highly attractive and utterly charming. Between 1843 and 1868 Isabella reigned but did not rule. During most of this period Spain was governed by a coalition of civilian conservatives and army generals.

On Oct. 10, 1846, Isabella married her cousin Francisco de Asis. Now an attractive 16-year-old, she was generous, friendly, fond of dancing, and amorous, and the timid and effeminate Francisco was a great disappointment to her. On the day after the wedding he moved out of the Queen's quarters, and her first lover, the handsome Gen. Serrano, moved in. He was to be the first of many, until her active sex life (or what an English observer called her "terrible constitutional malady") was the talk of all Europe. Yet she considered herself a devout Catholic and was very much under the

influence of the superstitious and often fanatical nuns and monks who surrounded her at court.

Isabella's scandalous private life, her antiliberalism, and Spain's economic crisis of 1866 brought about a popular revolution in September 1868. Isabella fled to France, and, on June 25, 1870, she abdicated in favor of her son Alfonso XII. He was crowned king of Spain in early 1875, after the republic which had been set up in 1873 was abolished.

In exile Isabella retained her enjoyment of men and fondness for dancing. However, the defeat of Spain in 1898 seems to have broken her spirit; after that year her health began to fail, and on April 19, 1904, she died in her Paris home.

Further Reading

The best biographies of Isabella in English are Peter De Polnay, *A Queen of Spain: Isabel II* (1962), and Ottilie G. Boetzkes, *The Little Queen: Isabella II of Spain* (1966). For a scholarly presentation of the economics and politics of her reign see Raymond Carr, *Spain, 1808-1939* (1966). ☐

Isaiah

Isaiah (active ca. 740-701 B.C.) was a Hebrew prophet. His Hebrew name, Yeshayhu, means "God

is salvation" and alludes to the prophet's major doctrines and teachings.

The son of Amoz, of noble descent, Isaiah lived in Jerusalem. He referred to his wife as the "prophetess" and gave his two sons names symbolic of his prophecies: Shear-Yashub, meaning "a remnant will return," implying a return to the God of Israel, from whom his people were estranged; and Maher-shalal-has-baz, or "quick prey," which may have been intended to serve as a warning to Pekah, the usurper king of Israel, and Rezin, the king of Aram (Syria). They had attacked and besieged Jerusalem (734 B.C.) in an attempt to depose the Judahite king Ahaz, who refused to join them in their alliance against Assyria.

The turning point in Isaiah's life was his call to prophecy in the year of King Uzziah's death (ca. 740 B.C.), which came to Isaiah in a vision in the Temple. To Isaiah the word *kadosh,* or "holy," meant righteousness. To obey God's will was to be just, and Zion would eventually be redeemed in justice.

Historical Context

Isaiah's prophecies can be understood only in the context of the prevailing social conditions. Uzziah's reign (ca. 780-740 B.C.) was one of great prosperity, but Isaiah denounced the ill-gained riches of his people, who oppressed the poor. The richer classes, as often happens, also tended

toward assimilation with their neighbors. In the case of the Judahites this meant the adoption of the idolatrous cults, which were associated with immoral practices.

Judah was situated in a buffer area, surrounded by stronger nations that aspired to overrun its territory or at least to occupy it as a base of operations against neighboring enemies. Judah, moreover, was directly in the path of the rival imperialist giants of that day, Egypt and Assyria. Isaiah opposed alliances with either and urged dependence on the Lord. When Egypt induced Pekah of Israel and Rezin of Aram to join in an alliance against Assyria, Isaiah denounced them as "two tails of smoking firebrands" (Isaiah 7:4). He urged the Judahite king Ahaz (ca. 735-715 B.C.) to rely on God rather than on Tiglathpileser III, to whom Ahaz had given costly gifts to induce him to come to his aid.

Isaiah's prediction that the conspirators would themselves soon be destroyed was realized a few years later, when Damascus, the capital of Aram, was captured in 732 B.C. and Samaria, Israel's capital, in 722 B.C. The involvement of Ahaz with Assyria also had its sinister consequences, for as a result the Assyrian idolatrous cult of the heavenly bodies was introduced into Judea.

King Hezekiah (715-686 B.C.), who succeeded Ahaz, generally heeded the prophet's advice and kept out of political or military entanglements. However, he was swayed by his steward, Shebna, and the court party to join the coalition that revolted against Sennacherib, the Assyrian monarch (705-687 B.C.). Isaiah considered it foolhardy to trust "in the shadow of Egypt" rather than in God. Indeed, the efforts of Egypt to stop Sennacherib proved futile; he conquered the rebellious peoples and invaded Judea.

In his own inscriptions, the Assyrian ruler wrote of having destroyed 46 fortified Judahite towns, deporting their population and capturing Hezekiah. At this crucial juncture the Judean king appealed for counsel to Isaiah, who urged him to have faith in the Lord and not to surrender the city. Before long, Tirhakah, the king of Ethiopia, went to war against Sennacherib, forcing him to move his army from Jerusalem. There a pestilence broke out in his army and destroyed it.

God and the Messiah

Isaiah was fully committed to the idea that God was the author and guide in human history. All nations, moreover, were mere instruments in His hands, and they must serve Him by establishing the rule of justice, righteousness, and peace. This would be achieved only in the "end of days," when all nations would worship the God of Israel, who would teach them His ways.

Isaiah envisioned the glorious future of the world, when the Messiah, God's anointed, a perfect ruler, would bring about an everlasting peace among men. The nations would "beat their swords into plowshares" and would not "learn war any more" (2:4). The Messianic ideal thus gave a spiritual goal to human existence.

Authorship of the Prophecies

The Book of Isaiah is generally believed to include prophecies by several hands. The first part, chapters 1-39, is attributed to Isaiah. Some scholars maintain that the second section encompasses the remainder of the volume, while others claim that it embraces only chapters 40-55, which deal generally with the period of the Babylonian exile. This part of the Book of Isaiah is ascribed to an anonymous prophet, who has been referred to as the Second, or Deutero, Isaiah. Unlike the prophecies of Isaiah ben Amoz, warning of punishment and doom, those of Deutero-Isaiah speak of God's salvation as manifested by Israel's return to Zion and the attainment of universal monotheism (45:22 ff). The reason that scholars believe that the final chapters of the Book of Isaiah (56-66) form a separate division and were composed by another anonymous prophet, designated as Third, or Trito, Isaiah, is that these chapters deal with the problems of the Jewish community after its return to its homeland. This would be around the time of Haggai and Zechariah (ca. 520). The several parts of the Book of Isaiah represent a Hebrew prophecy that attained great heights in human ethics and ideals.

Further Reading

To appreciate Isaiah's message one must read at least portions of the Book of Isaiah in a good standard translation such as the Revised Standard Version (1952) or the Soncino edition (1950). Abraham J. Heschel discusses the mission and the message of the prophet in the chapter "Isaiah, Son of Amoz" in *The Prophets* (1962). He also discusses various aspects of prophecy as well as the Second Isaiah in other portions of this work.

Additional Sources

Hayes, John Haralson, *Isaiah, the eighth century prophet: his times & his preaching,* Nashville: Abingdon Press, 1987.
Ludlow, Victor L., *Isaiah—prophet, seer, and poet,* Salt Lake City, Utah: Deseret Book Co., 1982. □

Christopher Isherwood

Christopher Isherwood (1904-1986) was a British-born American writer who worked in many genres, including fiction, drama, film, travel, and autobiography. He was especially esteemed for his stories about Berlin in the early 1930s.

The son of a career military officer, Christopher Isherwood was born in High Lane, Cheshire, England, on August 26, 1904. He attended the Repton School from 1919 to 1922 and Cambridge University from 1924 to 1925. His university year was significant because it was at Cambridge that he met Wystan Hugh Auden, with whom he later collaborated on several literary projects, and because it was there that he became a practicing homosexual, an orientation which played an important role in his personal and artistic life.

Leaving the university without a degree, Isherwood worked for a year as the secretary to French violinist Andre Mangeot and as a private tutor in London. In his spare hours he worked on his first novel, which was published as *All the Conspirators* in 1928.

Scenes of a Crumbling Germany

In 1929 he went to Germany to visit Auden, who was living there, and was attracted to life in the crumbling Weimar Republic, and particularly to the sexual freedom that existed. As he so succinctly put it in his 1976 book *Christopher and His Kind 1929-1939,* "Berlin meant Boys." He was not long in establishing a liaison with Berthold "Bubi" Szczesny, a bisexual ex-boxer, which lasted until Szczesny was forced to leave the country. Among the young men he met subsequently was one from the working class section of Berlin; he took a room with this boy's family for a time and so became familiar with day-to-day living among the urban proletariat.

At first his stay in Germany was financed through an allowance provided by his only wealthy relative, his uncle Henry Isherwood. His uncle was also homosexual and seemed happy to assist his nephew in the quest for companions. Eventually, however, Uncle Henry stopped his remittances, and Isherwood paid his way by tutoring in English; in this way he met Berliners from the upper classes.

All this provided background for his most successful work, *The Last of Mr. Norris* (1935), *Sally Bowles* (1937), and *Goodbye to Berlin* (1939), all collected under the title

The Berlin Stories in 1945. In these novellas and short stories he presented an in-depth portrait of life in Germany's capital as the republican center collapsed, the Communists tried desperately to stem the rightist tide, and the Nazis came to power.

He began in "A Berlin Diary (Autumn 1930)" with an almost offhand observation about Fráulein Hippi, a student whom the narrator is tutoring in English: "Like everyone else in Berlin, she refers continually to the political situation, but only briefly, with a conventional melancholy. . . . It is quite unreal to her." In "Sally Bowles," he mentioned the closing of two major banks and noted: "One alarmist headline stood out boldly, barred with blood-red ink: 'Everything Collapses'."

In "The Nowaks," about a working class family, he described their neighborhood in this way: "The entrance to the Wassertorstrasse was . . . a bit of old Berlin, daubed with hammers and sickles and Nazi crosses and plastered with tattered bills. . . ." The political pressures are seen increasing in "The Landauers," about a well-to-do Jewish family: "One night in October 1930, about a month after the Elections, there was a big row on the Leipzigerstrasse. Gangs of Nazi toughs turned out to demonstrate against the Jews. They . . . smashed the windows of all the Jewish shops." Finally, in "A Berlin Diary (Winter 1932-33)," the narrator observes: "Schleicher has resigned. Hitler has formed a cabinet. . . . Nobody thinks it can last until the spring."

The Berlin stories were picked up by playwright John van Druten, who was struck by a sentence in "A Berlin Diary (Autumn 1930)": "I am a camera, with its shutter open, quite passive, recording not thinking." He wrote the play *I Am a Camera,* centering on Sally Bowles, of whom Alan Wilde wrote: "Sally's charm is her naíveté, . . . her total capacity for self-deception and self-contradiction, . . . her ability to accommodate herself to each new situation. . . ." *I Am a Camera* in turn became the musical *Cabaret* (1967), with book by Joe Masteroff and lyrics by Fred Ebb, which was produced both on stage and in film.

Isherwood of course became fluent in German and got acquainted, as did Auden, with the expressionist drama of such important figures as Ernst Toller, Georg Kaiser, and Bertolt Brecht. This led the two British artists to collaborate on three expressionist plays: *The Dog Beneath the Skin* (1935), *The Ascent of F6* (1937), and *A Melodrama in Three Acts: On the Frontier* (1938), of which the first two are generally considered the more successful.

Move to the United States

Isherwood and Auden travelled to China in 1938 and in 1939 worked together on *Journey to a War.* In that same year, the year World War II began, both came to America, a move which made them anathema to many Britons. Indeed, even three years later in *Put Out More Flags* novelist Evelyn Waugh, christening them Parsnip and Pimpernell, commented, "What I don't see is how these two can claim to be *contemporary* if they run away from the biggest event in contemporary history."

During World War II Isherwood wrote scripts for Metro-Goldwyn-Mayer, Warner Brothers, and 20th Century

Fox film studios; worked for a year in a refugee center in Haverford, Pennsylvania; and became a resident student of the Vedanta Society of Southern California and co-editor of the group's magazine *Vedanta and the West.*

He became increasingly involved in the Vedantist religion, editing the volumes *Vedanta for the Western World* in 1945 and *Vedanta for Modern Man* in 1951 and writing *An Approach to Vedanta* in 1963, *Ramakrishna and His Disciples* in 1965, and *Essentials of Vedanta* in 1969. He explained its basic tenets in the 1963 work as follows: "We have two selves—an apparent, outer self and an invisible, inner self. The apparent self claims to be an individual and as such, other than all other individuals. . . . The real self is unchanging and immortal."

Isherwood did not confine himself solely to religious writings, however. He authored such novels as *Prater Violet* (1945), *The World in the Evening* (1954), *A Single Man* (1964), and *A Meeting by the River* (1967), which he dramatized in 1972. He also wrote the travel book *The Condor and the Cows* (1949), autobiographical volumes, and the collection of stories, articles, and poems titled *Exhumations* (1966). Additionally, he taught at Los Angeles State University, the University of California at Santa Barbara, and the University of California at Los Angeles and wrote film scripts.

Isherwood's status in modern literature was best summarized by G. K. Hall: "Christopher Isherwood has always been a problem for the critics. An obviously talented writer, he has refused to exploit his artistry for either commercial success or literary status. . . . Isherwood was adjudged a 'promising writer'—a designation that he has not been able to outrun even to this day. It is still a clicheé of Isherwood criticism to say that he never fulfilled his early promise. . . . In any case, five decades of Isherwood criticism present a history of sharply divided opinion."

Isherwood, who became an American citizen in 1946, lived and worked in southern California until his death from cancer January 4, 1986.

Further Reading

Much personal information is in his autobiographical *Christopher and His Kind* (1976). In G. K. Hall's *Christopher Isherwood: A Reference Guide* (1979) the reader will find a comprehensive listing of all works by and about the subject.

Additional Sources

Finney, Brian, *Christopher Isherwood: a critical biography,* New York: Oxford University Press, 1979.

Fryer, Jonathan, *Isherwood,* Garden City, N.Y.: Doubleday, 1978, 1977.

Fryer, Jonathan, *Isherwood: a biography of Christopher Isherwood,* London: New English Library, 1977.

Isherwood, Christopher, *Christopher and his kind, 1929-1939,* London: Eyre Methuen, 1977; New York: Farrar, Straus Giroux, 1976.

Isherwood, Christopher, *My guru and his disciple,* New York, N.Y.: Penguin Books, 1981.

King, Francis Henry, *Christopher Isherwood,* Harlow Eng.: Published for the British Council by Longman Group, 1976.

Lehmann, John, *Christopher Isherwood: a personal memoir,* New York: H. Holt, 1988, 1987. ☐

St. Isidore of Seville

The Spanish cleric and encyclopedist St. Isidore of Seville (560-636) is known for the legacy of ancient culture that he transmitted to the Middle Ages in his chief work, the *Etymologies.*

Isidore was born into a Hispano-Roman family about the time his father, Severianus, brought the family from Cartagena to Seville. The move from Cartagena was probably occasioned by the turmoil caused in Gothic Spain when Emperor Justinian sought to restore imperial power there. However, Visigothic rule survived and flourished. In Seville, Isidore's family became closely involved with the regime. His father died when Isidore was quite young, and he was raised and educated by his older brother, Leander.

Leander became archbishop of Seville and was King Reccared's chief adviser during the Third Council of Toledo (589). This council officially replaced the Arianism of the Visigoths with Roman Catholicism, till then the religion of the subject Hispano-Romans. The many consequent challenges of ecclesiastical administration were taken over by Isidore, who about 599 succeeded Leander as archbishop of Seville. Isidore's main instrument of change was the use of provincial and national Church councils, attended by king and nobility. But more important for posterity was Isidore's concern with religious correctness, which led him to compose *Sententiae* and *Differentiae* (theological textbooks), *De ecclesiasticis officiis* (a liturgical manual), *De viris illustribus* (a bibliography of controversial writings), and his final and most significant work, the *Etymologies.*

The *Etymologies*

Isidore labored over the *Etymologies* from 622 to 633. After his death in 636 it was edited by his student, Braulion. It is an encyclopedic work in 20 books. Books I and II concern the trivium: grammar, rhetoric, and dialectic; Book III, the quadrivium: arithmetic, geometry, astronomy, and music; Book IV, medicine; Book V, history from the Creation to 627 A.D.; Book VI, sacred books and Church offices; Book VII, God, the angels, and the members of the Church; Book VIII, the Church and its heretical opponents; Book IX, languages, peoples, states, and families. Book X is a dictionary. Book XI concerns man; Book XII, zoology; Book XIII, cosmography; Book XIV, geography; Book XV, monuments and means of communication; Book XVI, petrography and mineralogy; Book XVII, agriculture and horticulture; Book XVIII, the army, war, and games; Book XIX, ships, housing, and apparel; and Book XX, alimentation, household arts, and agricultural implements.

Binding together this tour de force in the compilation of knowledge is Isidore's preoccupation with word origins. Each topic is introduced by an examination of its name.

Isidore's assumption is that the understanding of a name is the first step toward the understanding of the thing named. This assumption in turn rests on another: the original givers of names knew the differentiating characteristics of things and wished to have each thing distinguished from every other thing. Isidore is aware of some limitations in his procedure; for example, some names are arbitrarily given, and others are borrowed from languages distinct from Latin and Greek. Nevertheless, he applies his technique throughout in an ingenious but sometimes ridiculous manner.

Obviously the digest of a lifetime of reading, the contents of Isidore's *Etymologies* represent his attempt to write down all that he deemed necessary for a Christian education. Frequently, in the manner of St. Jerome earlier, he is at great pains to establish parallels between the Judeo-Christian culture and classical antiquity. For instance, Isidore finds in the Old Testament a correspondence with the Stoic division of philosophy into physics, ethics, and logic. According to him, Genesis and Ecclesiastes treat of physics, the Proverbs of Solomon of ethics, and the Song of Songs and the Gospels of logic. Also, biblical figures are credited with originating literary genres that were then taken over by the Greeks; for example, Homer borrows the device of the hexameter from Moses. But Isidore often presents philosophical and scientific theories in an objective manner, even when doing so conflicts with his work's religious purpose. For instance, in Book VIII he disparages the atomism of Epicurus because it allowed no role to a providential deity. But in Book XIII he recounts without any similar condemnation the atomic theory of the formation of the world.

To the modern reader Isidore's *Etymologies* seems fragmentary and confused in many places. But this was not the estimation of medieval scholars, and for hundreds of years the work had great popularity. It survived because no other source gave medieval man such a handy treasure of information. In the words of a late medieval reader inscribed on a codex of the *Etymologies:* "This booke is a scoolemaster to those that are wise,/ But not to fond fooles that learning despise,/ A Juwell it is, who liste it to reede,/ Within it are Pearells precious in deede."

Further Reading

A modern edition of the *Etymologies* was made by W. M. Lindsay (2 vols., 1911). Two studies of Isidore are Ernest Brehaut, *An Encyclopedist of the Dark Ages: Isidore of Seville* (1912), and Sister Patrick Jerome Mullins, *The Spiritual Life according to Saint Isidore of Seville* (1940). For general background see the monumental *Cambridge History of Later Greek and Early Medieval Philosophy,* edited by A. H. Armstrong (1967). □

Ismail Pasha

Ismail Pasha (1830-1895) was the charming but spendthrift pasha and khedive of Egypt during the decade prior to British occupation.

I smail Pasha was born in Cairo, the grandson of Mohammed Ali and second son of Ibrahim Pasha. He completed their work in that he bought from the Ottoman sultan the right to the new title of khedive, father-to-son inheritance of the new title for his dynasty, administrative and commercial independence, and relaxation of military restrictions imposed upon Egypt by the European powers in 1841. But Ismail accomplished this at tremendous expense—and it was only the beginning of his financial adventures.

Ismail succeeded Mohammed Said as the ruler of Egypt in 1863, when the American Civil War increased the demand for Egyptian cotton and when the expected profits from the soon to be completed Suez Canal made Egypt seem more prosperous than it actually was. In the euphoria of the 1860s Ismail dreamed of an Egyptian empire in northeast Africa and of Cairo as the Paris on the Nile. He borrowed heavily on Egypt's future and spent lavishly on explorations far up the Nile almost to Lake Victoria for the extension of Egyptian influence, on building many public works such as improved canals and new telegraph lines, and on the modernization of Cairo.

Ismail took a personal interest in the Suez Canal, the concession for which his predecessor had negotiated with a French company. He agreed to pay a huge indemnity equal to half the original capital of the company in order to eliminate the forced labor and other onerous requirements of the initial concession. For the grand opening of the canal in 1869, Ismail lavished over a million dollars on the entertainment of foreign dignitaries.

The close of the American Civil War ended the Egyptian cotton boom, and the Suez Canal did not, at first, earn the expected profits. Ismail resorted to huge loans at ruinous discounts to obtain the funds necessary for his dreams; he further pledged the revenues of the railroads, taxes, and royal lands. In 1875, in desperation, he sold his one remaining investment, his approximately 44 percent of the shares in the Suez Canal Company, to British prime minister Disraeli for £ 4 million.

Bankrupt in 1876 with a 14-fold debt increase to some £ 1 billion since his accession in 1863, Ismail had to accept Anglo-French financial supervision, called the Dual Control. The influx of foreigners during his reign, the special privileges they received via the capitulations, and their obviously increasing influence in Egypt led in the late 1870s to the development of an Egyptian national movement. When Ismail sought to shift the blame from himself to the foreigners for Egypt's financial debacle and when Bismarck threatened German intervention, Great Britain and France succeeded in having the Ottoman sultan depose Ismail in 1879 in favor of his son Tewfik Pasha. Ismail's vainglorious ambitions and gross extravagance had paved the way for the British occupation 3 years after his deposition.

Further Reading

The only biography of Ismail is Pierre Crabitès, *Ismail: The Maligned Khedive* (1933). Mary Rowlatt presents a briefer and not very favorable picture in *Founders of Modern Egypt* (1962). Ismail's ambitions in the Sudan are considered in Richard Hill, *Egypt in the Sudan, 1820-1881* (1959), and in

William B. Hesseltine and Hazel C. Wolf, *The Blue and the Gray on the Nile* (1961), which describes the story of former Civil War officers in Egyptian service. For general background on 19th-century Egypt see John A. Marlowe, *A History of Modern Egypt and Anglo-Egyptian Relations, 1800-1956* (1954; 2d ed. 1965), and Tom Little, *Modern Egypt* (1967). □

Isocrates

Isocrates (436-338 B.C.) was the fourth of the famous 10 Attic Greek orators. Though not an original thinker, he was an exceptional speech writer and teacher who exerted great influence on his contemporaries.

Isocrates was one of five children of Theodorus of Erchia, a flute manufacturer, and his wife Heduto. He received an excellent education along traditional lines but was also acquainted with the new sophistic learning. When the disastrous Peloponnesian War wiped out his father's estate, Isocrates turned to writing forensic speeches for others. He himself did not speak in public or participate directly in politics because of a weak voice and bashfulness.

Isocrates apparently taught rhetoric at Chios and returned to Athens in 403 B.C. In 392 B.C. he founded his famous school, near the Lyceum, which drew students from all over Greece and at which he taught till after 351 B.C. Among his students were the general Timotheus; the historians Theopompus and Ephorus; Nicocles, King of Cyprus; the orators Isaeus, Hyperides, and Lycurgus; and the philosopher Speusippus. The last period of his unusually long and productive life was devoted to writing.

His Works

Though some 60 of Isocrates's works were known to the ancients, only 21 have survived. His style is most remarkable, characterized by pure diction, rhythm, complex structure, and smooth vocabulary, with unusually careful avoidance of dissonance of every kind.

Of the surviving works, six are forensic speeches: *Against Lochites, Aegineticus, Against Euthynus, Trapeziticus, Span of Horses,* and *Callimachus.* Three exhortations, *To Demonicus* and *To Nicocles* (374 B.C.) and *Nicocles* (372 B.C.), treat of ethics and reflect the morality of the times and some of the more advanced ideas of Isocrates. Three works are encomia (epideictic oratory): *Busiris* (391 B.C.), *Helen* (370 B.C.), and *Evagoras* (365 B.C.). The famous *Panathenaicus* (342-339 B.C.), which is educational and political in nature, may also be classified as epideictic.

The six political treatises that involve principally Athenian government and politics are *Panegyricus* (ca. 380 B.C.), *Plataicus* (373 B.C.), *Archidamus* (366 B.C.), *Peace* (355 B.C.), *Areopagiticus* (355 B.C.), and *Philip* (346 B.C.). Nine letters are also extant: to *Dionysius,* to *Philip* (two), to *Antipater,* to *Alexander,* to the *Sons of Jason,* to *Timotheus,* to *Rulers of Mytilene,* and to *Archidamus.* His two educational works are *Against the Sophists* (390 B.C.) and *Antidosis* (355/353 B.C.), in the first case directed against the Sophists and in the second case a defense of his own life and profession.

Thought and Contributions

Isocrates was a firm believer in subordinating the parts to the whole, and in rhetorical composition he looked to the effect of the whole. It is Isocrates who determined the form of rhetorical prose for the ancient Greek and even the Roman world (through Cicero). Though never a politician himself, Isocrates believed that a proper education should equip a person for proper conduct in public as well as private life. Ideas, he believed, were of no value unless they were realized in the actual world.

Described as a pamphleteer and publicist, Isocrates saw himself as molding public opinion and directing political action through his work. For him education was "the cultivation of the art of discourse," which he saw as involving not merely verbal expression but reason, feeling, and imagination.

In politics Isocrates dreamed of a Hellenism that would unite the free Greek states against the common enemy, Persia, but in cultural terms he perceived Hellenism as a brotherhood of culture going beyond all racial boundaries. He clearly saw the East-West conflict rooted in history. In the *Panegyricus* he looked to Athens as the mother of civilization and of free institutions to provide pan-Hellenic leadership; but with the rise of Thebes and a futile appeal to Dionysius of Syracuse in 368 B.C., he desperately appealed to the Spartan king Archidamus in 356 B.C., only to be disappointed.

In his *Address to Philip* it becomes clear that Isocrates had lost all hope that the Greek states would exercise the united action and wisdom that was needed for a united Greece. Isocrates rightly saw that Philip of Macedon was in a position to do this as well as lead an effective force against Persia, and it must be more than a remarkable coincidence that a year after the Battle of Chaeronea (338 B.C.) the Greek states united under Philip against Persia in a way set down in the *Panegyricus* and in the *Address to Philip.*

Further Reading

The most conveniently available edition of Isocrates's works is in the three-volume Loeb Library edition, the first two volumes translated by George Norlin (1928-1929) and the last by La Rue Van Hook (1945). George Kennedy, *The Art of Persuasion in Greece* (1963), is an excellent study that includes a discussion of Isocrates within the history of Greek oratory. Costas M. Proussis' article "The Orator: Isocrates" in Paul Nash, Andreas M. Kazamias, and Henry J. Perkinson, eds., *The Educated Man* (1965), is a fine description of Isocrates's educational ideas. R. C. Jebb, *The Attic Orators from Antiphon to Isaeos* (2 vols., 1876; 2d ed. 1893), is a standard work for the specialist. □

Arata Isozaki

The Japanese architect Arata Isozaki (born 1931) developed a style which reflected both Japanese traditions and Western post-modern and mannerist influences. Isozaki also wrote about architecture and taught in several universities.

Arata Isozaki was born in Oita City, Japan, in 1931. He studied with Kenzo Tange, one of Japan's leading modern architects, at the University of Tokyo from 1950 to 1954. He continued to work for and with Tange as a graduate student at the university and then in the older man's firm from 1954 to 1963. At that point Isozaki established his own practice but did not disassociate himself from his mentor, continuing to design occasionally for Tange into the 1970s. This attitude is in keeping with native Japanese practices that stress collaboration and cooperation, rather than competition, among professionals.

Influences

Nearly all of the leading 20th-century Japanese designers have attempted to synthesize indigenous traditions with Western forms, materials, and technologies. Isozaki's "style" has in fact been a series of modes that have come as a response to these influences. As a young architect he was identified with Metabolism, a movement founded in Japan in 1960. However, Isozaki minimized his connections to this group, seeing the Metabolist style as overly utilitarian in tone. By contrast, in the 1960s, Isozaki's work featured dramatic forms made possible through the employment of steel and concrete but not limited aesthetically by those materials. His designs of branch banks for the Fukuoka Mutual Bank of the mid-1960s are characteristic of this early phase of Isozaki's career. The Oita Branch Bank (1966) is representative of the group: its powerful cantilevered upper stories are more characteristic of his English contemporary James Stirling that of any of his fellow Japanese architects.

In the 1970s Isozaki's architecture became more historical in its orientation, suggesting a connection with the burgeoning post-modern movement of Europe and the United States. His sources included classical Western architects, especially Andrea Palladio, Étienne-Louis Boullée, and Claude-Nicolas Ledoux. These connections Isozaki did acknowledge, and his work of the 1970s represents a mature synthesis of formal, functional, and technical considerations. A representative work of this period is his Fujimi Country Club, Oita City, constructed in 1973, which displays the love of pure form that also characterizes 18th-century French neoclassicism. Another French principle, *architecture parlante* (architecture that bespeaks its function), is also at work at Fujimi: by massing the building in the shape of a question mark, Isozaki commented wittily on his incomprehension of his countrymen's obsession with golf.

Later, his Western influences were decidedly mannerist, with Giulio Romano and Michelangelo replacing the classicists as sources. Isozaki's Tsukuba City Center of 1979-1983, located in Ibaraki, is a complex of buildings clearly indebted to Michelangelo's Campidoglio in Rome, but not at all limited by it. Chosen as project director for this urban development, Isozaki created a design that included large, colorful buildings, a large plaza, and a sunken garden that provides as clear a statement of post-modern aims as any project built in Europe or the United States.

Building Outside Japan

This new-found fascination with what post-modern guru Robert Venturi called "complexity and contradiction" coincided with Isozaki's interest in building outside of his native country. His Los Angeles County Museum of Contemporary Art (1984-1985) may be the best known structure by a Japanese designer in America. Isozaki was, in fact, one of only a handful of Japanese architects to have some impact in the West. In June 1997 the MOMA celebrated its 18th years by honoring 18 individuals, including creator Isozaki.

Isozaki's popularity and prestige as an architect is reflected in the commissions he took throughout the U.S. and Europe. He was a part of a cadre of exclusive architects enlisted by Disney to design buildings throughout the U.S. His creation stands just outside Orlando. The only house he has designed outside of Japan listed for $1.3 million in 1997. Isozaki was one of a team of world-famous architects to design two huge business complexes on Berlin's Potzdamer Platz. He branched out by designing the sets for the Lyon Opera's production of *Madama Butterfly*. Beside the Barcelona Olympic stadium is the Games' most striking structure—the $100-million Sant Jordi sports palace designed by Isozaki for the 1992 Olympics. Its 3,000-ton roof was raised by a dozen hydraulic jacks over a period of 20 days to a height of 45 m. The result is an airy structure whose undulating white roof is pockmarked by 100 transparent bubbles that flood its interior with daylight. When it opened in 1990, 300,000 local people came to view it. Domus, or the House of Man, the interactive science museum in La Coruna, a northern Spanish city 600 km from Madrid. Set on a dramatic rocky site overlooking the Atlantic, the museum is housed in a towering pink-and-gray granite building designed by Isozaki.

Other buildings in the West designed by Isozaki include museums in Nice, Cario, as well as Los Angeles, and Brooklyn (NY), the American Pavilion at the Venice Biennale, and the Palladium discotheque in NY. Charles Jencks, an American critic noted Isozaki has taken the style of the West one step further. By carrying Western concepts to their logical conclusion, Japanese architects introduced new elements. Reyner Banham explains that "it is the marginal minor differences in the thinkable and the customary that ultimately make Japanese architecture a provokingly alien enclave within the body of the world's architecture."

Honors From Japan

Isozaki's excellence was recognized in his native country and around the world. One of the honors he received was the Asahi award, given to individuals who make significant and lasting contributions to Japanese culture. He was also a multiple winner of the Annual Prize awarded by the

Japan Architectural Association. Since the early 1970s there have been several one-man shows honoring Isozaki's work, including a London retrospective (1976).

Nippon Telegraph and Telephone Corporation in Tokyo announced plans for a new gallery, with an opening exhibit by Isozaki called "The Mirage City." In January 1995, a Japanese art and technology center was opened in Krakow, Poland by President Lech Walesa and members of Japan's imperial family, Prince and Princess Takamado. The center, designed in the shape of an ocean wave, was designed free of charge by Isozaki.

Isozaki was a visiting professor at several Japanese and American institutions, including the University of California at Los Angeles, the Rhode Island School of Design, Columbia University, and the University of Hawaii. He also wrote extensively about his architecture and the principles behind it (although, unfortunately, few of these writings have been translated).

Arata Isozaki was instantly recognizable by his distinctive style of dress. He often wore traditional Japanese clothing, and he favored the color black. He appeared on the cover of the *New York Times Magazine* in 1986, dressed in a "dazzlingly" fashionable Issey Miyake creation. By presenting himself as being sartorially distinct from the crowd, Isozaki provided a contemporary parallel to the flamboyant Frank Lloyd Wright, the famous American architect (and admirer of Japanese culture) who continued to affect Victorian dress long after it passed out of style.

Further Reading

An excellent source for background information on recent trends in Japanese architecture is *Contemporary Architecture of Japan: 1958-1984* by Hiroyuki Suzuki, Reyner Banham, and Katsuhiro Kobayashi (1985). This book also contains many fine quality black and white illustrations. For additional general background, see also Udo Kulterman's *New Japanese Architecture* (London: 1960) and *New Directions in Japanese Architecture* by Robin Boyd (1968). For an extended treatment of the architect's work, consult Philip Drew's *The Architecture of Arata Isozaki* (1982). A special issue of *Architectural Design* (London: January 1977) was devoted to Isozaki. A recent review of Isozaki's achievements can be found in Paul Goldberger's article, "Profiles: Arata Isozaki," in *Architectural Digest* (March 1989). The architect wrote extensively about architecture in his native language, but only a few of these writings have been translated into English. These include "About My Method," "A Metaphor Relating with Water," and "Formalism," all published in *The Japan Architect* (1972, 1978, and 1979, respectively). □

Hirobumi Ito

Hirobumi Ito (1841-1909) was a Japanese statesman and one of the younger leaders of the Meiji government. He took primary responsibility for the creation of the constitutional system which governed Japan until 1945.

In the middle of the 19th century, Japan was governed by the Tokugawa shoguns (military dictators, or the *bakufu*). The emperor, though nominally Japan's ruler, had little influence on the government. In virtual isolation from the world since about 1600, a medieval Japan was persuaded by the threat of force by Commodore Matthew C. Perry to open its doors to the West in a series of consular treaties. The shogunate's meek accession to Western demands precipitated a nationalistic reaction, the overthrow of the *bakufu*, and the restoration of the governing power to the emperor.

Hirobumi Ito was born the son of a peasant named Juzo Hayashi on Sept. 2, 1841, in Tokamura, a village in the Choshu domain in western Honshu. His family rose in status when his father was adopted into a low-ranking samurai family.

Loyalist Activities

Ito studied at the private academy of Shoin Yoshida, a fierce advocate of loyalty to the emperor and a critic of the weak response of the *bakufu* to the West. Like many of Yoshida's students, Ito became an ardent imperialist loyalist. In 1859 he went to the capital, Edo (modern Tokyo), where he came into contact with many other young samurai loyalists and participated in such antiforeign demonstrations as an incendiary attack on the British legation.

Ito soon realized that crude antiforeign acts were not a rational policy and that it would be necessary for Japan to adopt the weapons and technology of the West in order to

survive. In 1863, under orders from the lord of Choshu, he sailed for Europe and stayed for nearly a year in London, studying the West at firsthand. In 1864 he received news of Western intentions to send an expedition against Choshu, which had defied the treaties signed by the *bakufu*. Ito rushed back to Japan in a vain attempt to mediate the dispute and to dissuade the Choshu leadership from foolish attempts to defy the foreigners.

Although he roused the ire of more xenophobic loyalists by his efforts, in 1865 he advocated armed resistance to a *bakufu* expedition against Choshu. He also helped to promote the Satsuma-Choshu alliance, which led to the Meiji restoration of 1868.

Early Official Career

As one of the younger members of the new imperial government, Ito had a hand in a wide variety of reforms, including the establishment of a decimal system of currency, the building of a mint at Osaka, the establishment of a banking system, and the building of an internal communication system of telegraphs, railroads, and light-houses.

In 1878 Ito became minister of home affairs and, together with Shigenobu Okuma, one of the leading younger men in the government. However, he disagreed with Okuma on matters of public finance, and believing in the need for caution in constitutional reform, he opposed Okuma's proposal for the immediate establishment of an English-style parliamentary system. In 1881, backed by other officials from Satsuma and Choshu, he succeeded in forcing Okuma out of office. During the next decade Ito became the most powerful and influential leader in the government.

Constitutional Reform

The greatest undertaking of Ito's career began in March 1882, when he departed for Europe to study constitutional systems. He spent most of his time in Berlin and Vienna, learning the technical details and theoretical justification of the German constitutional system. On his return to Japan, he set to work to devise a new political system which would accommodate conservative pressures within the government for an autocratic monarchical system, yet provide a modern and up-to-date alternative to the English model of constitutional government demanded by liberal and radical elements outside the government. He supervised the preparation of laws establishing a new peerage in 1884, a modern cabinet system in 1885, an imperial household ministry in 1886, and a privy council in 1888.

Ito's main achievement was to supervise the drafting of a constitution, which began in 1886 and was finally completed in 1889. A moderate in temperament and political outlook, he aimed at setting up careful checks and balances which would restrain the rasher elements in the political public and yet permit gradual evolution and progress. The document was highly authoritarian in many respects, yet flexible enough to accommodate itself to the exigencies of future political growth and change. The emperor was entrusted with most of the legal powers of the state, and the Cabinet was given most effective powers of decision over

national policy. But at the same time, the constitution, reflecting Ito's concern that the government consult the people, especially on matters of public finance, also provided for a bicameral national diet, the lower house of which was to be popularly elected.

Later Political Career

As the primary author of constitutional government, Ito was the most strongly committed of the late Meiji oligarchs to making his experiment work. He served as premier four times (1885-1888, 1892-1896, 1898, and 1900-1901). At first an advocate of "transcendental government," free from control by the parties in the lower house of the Diet, he gradually realized that, to make the constitution work, compromise with the parties would be necessary. He became persuaded that it would be necessary to form a "national party," loyal to the emperor and committed to national rather than partisan interest, which would control the lower house and support the Cabinet. After an unsuccessful attempt to form such a party in 1892, Ito organized the Seiyukai in 1900. The effort proved only partly successful, and Ito resigned from presidency of the party in 1903 to become president of the Privy Council.

Views on Foreign Affairs

In foreign affairs Ito favored a policy of diplomatic caution backed by military strength. During the 1870s and 1880s he favored compromise with China with respect to the Korea problem. He feared the effects of a more aggressive policy on the attitude of the foreign powers toward the question of treaty revision. By 1894, however, after his foreign minister, Mutsu Munemitsu, had successfully negotiated treaty revisions with the British, Ito as premier led his country into a war with China, which resulted in the acquisition of Formosa (Taiwan) and the Pescadores as Japanese colonies. The war also detached Korea from Chinese influence but left it a target of international rivalry between Japan and Russia. Ito advocated reaching a diplomatic settlement with Russia, offering the Russians paramount control in Manchuria in return for Japanese paramount control in Korea.

Ito ended his career as resident general in Korea from 1905 to 1909. He favored making Korea a Japanese protectorate and encouraging it to undertake a policy of internal reform and Westernization like the one Japan itself had pursued. He resisted demands from Tokyo for annexation but at the same time attempted to suppress separatist movements within Korea. On Oct. 26, 1909, he was assassinated in Harbin Station by three bullets from the gun of a young Korean nationalist.

Further Reading

The only English-language biography of Ito is Kengi Hamada, *Prince Ito* (1936). It is based largely on his complete works, official papers, and reminiscences. A short sketch of his life is in James A. B. Scherer, *Three Meiji Leaders: Ito, Togo, Nogi* (1936).

Additional Sources

Hamada, Kengi, *Prince Ito*. Washington, D.C.: University Publications of America, 1979. □

Agustín de Iturbide

Agustín de Iturbide (1783-1824) was a conservative military leader who won Mexican independence from Spain and then ruled as Emperor Agustín I in 1822-1823.

The Mexican independence movement is distinguished sharply from its counterparts in South America by its two separate phases. The initial revolt, led by Father Miguel Hidalgo, was liberally oriented but went far beyond the South American liberals by its inclusion of the mestizo (mixed-blood) and Indian classes, which gave it an overtone of social revolution. The Creole aristocrats (white American-born individuals of Spanish descent) defeated the rebels but themselves sought independence in a second phase, under the leadership of Agustín de Iturbide.

Early Life and Military Career

Iturbide was born in Valladolid (now Morelia), Mexico, on Sept. 27, 1783, the scion of a wealthy, staunchly Catholic, aristocratic family of Basque descent. He received his education at the seminary in Valladolid and devoted his youth to managing one of his father's haciendas (estates). In 1805 he married Ana María Huarte, daughter of the provincial intendant (governor).

Iturbide received a commission in the royal militia and quickly gained fame for his daring actions during the campaigns against the liberal revolutionaries. Employing imaginative stratagems and stern measures, he acquired a reputation for bravery and harshness, earning several promotions. By 1813 he held the rank of colonel, commanding the Celaya regiment in addition to serving as military commandant of the intendancy of Guanajuato. Two years later he was placed in charge of the Army of the North, whose jurisdiction encompassed the intendancies of Valladolid and Guanajuato.

The "Liberator"

Iturbide was among the young Creole aristocrats who began to contemplate the possibility of separation from Spain in response to an 1820 military revolt which placed Spain under a liberal regime. Iturbide was then commanding royal forces pursuing Vicente Guerrero, one of the few liberal revolutionaries still in the field. The two entered into negotiations, and Guerrero pledged his support to his former adversary.

On Feb. 24, 1821, Iturbide launched his own revolt by issuing the Plan of Iguala, also known as the Triguarantine Plan. His 23-article statement spelled out a conservative program based on three guarantees: religion, independence, and union. These terms indicated that Iturbide was dedicated to preserving the colonial system, merely substituting Creoles for Spaniards in governmental posts. He aspired to constitute Mexico into an independent monarchy, headed by a Bourbon prince, while preserving class and Church privileges.

Execution of Iturbide

Much of the Creole populace rallied to Iturbide's support. When Capt. Gen. Juan O'Donojú arrived to assume his duties as the new Spanish viceroy in Mexico a few months later, he found Iturbide in effective control of the country. Lacking sufficient forces to challenge the Mexican leader's ascendancy, the viceroy proposed negotiations. The resulting Treaty of Cordova confirmed Mexican independence under a Bourbon prince and stipulated that, pending selection of a monarch, Mexico would be governed by a junta headed by Iturbide and including O'Donojú in its membership. Iturbide, the "Liberator," rode triumphantly into Mexico City at the head of his army on his thirty-eighth birthday, Sept. 27, 1821.

Emperor of Mexico

When members of the Spanish royal family spurned the proffered Mexican throne, Creole sentiment turned toward investing Iturbide with the honor. On May 18, 1822, a sergeant in Iturbide's own Celaya regiment launched a "popular" movement to proclaim Iturbide emperor. The Liberator exhibited a proper degree of reluctance, but the next day Congress, with tumultuous crowds of Iturbide's adherents jamming the hall, formally selected him as emperor. Lack of a quorum cast doubt upon the legality of this mandate, but the action had considerable popular support.

Iturbide was crowned Emperor Agustín I on July 21, 1822, amid elaborate pageantry. The new monarch presented an imposing figure in his regal robes. At 5 feet 10 inches, he was taller than his Mexican contemporaries, and his erect, military bearing and aloof, aristocratic manner added to the aura of imperial splendor.

Iturbide devoted considerable effort to creating an elaborate court, attempting to match the magnificence and pomp of European royalty. He also endeavored to secure the traditional prerogatives of the Spanish crown, attempting to assert his right to appoint Church officials as well as civil administrators. Also, even prior to assuming the imperial title, he had initiated preparations for extending Mexican sovereignty southward, and in December 1821 he had dispatched an army to Central America in a futile attempt at annexation.

Iturbide proved to be a tactless ruler, and his regime was characterized by constant disputes with the legislature, which challenged his efforts to concentrate power in his own hands. After imprisoning several of the deputies, the Emperor dissolved Congress on Oct. 31, 1822. Iturbide had already forfeited much of his initial popularity, and a rebellion soon broke out.

On March 19, 1823, Iturbide abdicated and shortly thereafter departed for Europe, where he became alarmed at reports of an impending Spanish expedition against Mexico. Convinced that only he could save his homeland, he offered to ''place his sword'' at the nation's disposal. Interpreting this as an attempt to regain power, the Mexican Congress declared him a traitor and sentenced him to death. Iturbide sailed for Mexico before learning of this decree and was arrested upon landing at Soto la Marina in the province of Tamaulipas. On July 19, 1824, the Liberator of Mexico, thoroughly discredited by his actions while occupying the throne, was executed by a firing squad.

Further Reading

The best work on Iturbide is William Spence Robertson, *Iturbide of Mexico* (1952). For a briefer account see Robertson's *Rise of the Spanish-American Republics, as Told in the Lives of Their Liberators* (1918). □

Ivan III

Ivan III (1440-1505), called Ivan the Great, was grand duke of Moscow from 1462 to 1505. He completed the unification of Russian lands, and his reign marks the beginning of Muscovite Russia.

Born on Jan. 22, 1440, in Moscow, Ivan was the oldest son of Basil II. He was married when he was 12 years old to Princess Maria of Tver. When Basil died in 1462, the 22-year-old Ivan became the grand duke of Moscow without being confirmed by the Mongol Khan. Ivan limited his allegiance to the Golden Horde to the sending of presents instead of regular tribute, finally discontinuing even those. Several Mongol attempts to subjugate the Russians failed, the last one in 1480.

The accomplishment for which Ivan is best known is the consolidation of Muscovite rule. His predecessors had increased Moscow's territory from less than 600 square miles under Ivan II to more than 15,000 square miles at the end of Basil II's reign. It remained for Ivan III to absorb Moscow's old rivals, Novgorod and Tver, and establish virtually a single rule over what had been appanage Russia. Although the circumstances surrounding the acquisitions varied, the results were basically the same: former sovereign or semiautonomous principalities were reduced to the status of provinces of Moscow, while their princes joined the ranks of the service nobility.

Ivan also considered himself the rightful heir to all the former Kievan lands, which in his opinion constituted his lawful patrimony. This presented a challenge to Lithuania, which, following the collapse of Kiev, had expanded into the western and southwestern Russian territories. Thus, much of Ivan's reign was occupied in war against Lithuania. A peace treaty was signed in 1503 by which Lithuania recognized Russian control over parts of the Smolensk and the Polotsk areas and much of Chernigov-Seversk. Another

peace treaty of 1503 ended the war which Moscow had effectively waged against the Livonian Order.

After the death of his first wife, Ivan married Sophia, or Zoë, Paleologue, a Byzantine princess and niece of the last Byzantine emperor, Constantine XI. The marriage was sponsored by the Vatican in hope of bringing Russia under the sway of the Pope and of establishing a broad front against the Turks, a goal that failed. From Ivan's point of view, the marriage fitted well into the general trend of elevating the Muscovite ruler.

Following the marriage, Ivan developed a complicated court ceremonial on the Byzantine model and began to use the title of czar and autocrat. Also during the reign of Ivan and his son, Basil III, Moscow came to be referred to by spokesmen as the Third Rome. Philotheos, a monk from Pskov, developed the idea that Moscow was the true successor to Byzantium and, hence, to Rome.

An impressive building program in Moscow took place under Ivan, directed primarily by Italian artists and craftsmen. New buildings were erected in the Kremlin, and the Kremlin walls were strengthened and furnished with towers and gates. Ivan died on Oct. 27, 1505, and was succeeded by his son, Basil.

Further Reading

The only biography in English of Ivan is J. L. I. Fennell, *Ivan the Great of Moscow* (1961). A good discussion of the Third Rome concept is Nicholas Zernov, *Moscow: The Third Rome* (1937). A firsthand account of the 1486-1506 period is Baron Sigismund von Herberstein, *Notes upon Russia,* translated and edited by R. H. Major (2 vols., 1851-1852). The most thorough study of this period available to the English reader is George Vernadsky and Michael Karpovich, *A History of Russia,* vol. 4 (1959). □

Ivan IV

Ivan IV (1530-1584), known as Ivan the Terrible, was the first Russian sovereign to be crowned czar and to hold czar as his official title in addition to the traditional title of grand duke of Moscow.

The reign of Ivan IV was the culmination of Russian historical developments that began with the rise of Moscow in the early 14th century. The results of these developments were the growth of a unified centralized state governed by an autocracy and the formation of a dominant class of serving gentry, the *pomeshchiki.*

Very little is actually known about Ivan. None of his papers, notes, or correspondence has survived. It is not possible to establish a precise chronology or to give a trustworthy factual account of Ivan's personal life. There are whole successions of years without a single reference to Ivan himself. All that is possible under these circumstances is to make surmises that are more or less in accord with the evidence of the scanty material that has survived.

One of the biggest stumbling blocks to contemporary students of Russian history in understanding Ivan is the epithet accorded him—"the Terrible" or "the Dread." This epithet indicates sadistic and irrational traits in his character, and there is sufficient evidence to make Ivan's reign a study in abnormal psychology. It is said that as a boy he took delight in throwing young animals to their death from high rooftops. He also formed the habit of robbing and beating the people of his capital. There is also the terrible event in 1581, when Ivan, in a fit of anger, lashed out at his 27-year-old son, Ivan Ivanovich, and struck him dead with an iron-pointed staff.

It would, therefore, be foolish to argue that the personality of Ivan IV is irrelevant to an understanding of his reign. It has been shown, in fact, that there was a very real cause for the monstrous aspects of Ivan's personality. A contemporary study of Ivan's skeleton showed that he must have suffered horribly for many years from osteophytes, which virtually fused his spine.

Regency Period

Ivan was born on Aug. 25, 1530, in Moscow. His father was Basil III and his mother Helen Glinsky, a Russian of Lithuanian origin. Ivan was only 3 years old when his father died in 1533. His mother became regent, and the throne rapidly degenerated into a center of wild violence, intrigue, and denunciation as rival boyar families disputed the Glinsky regency. At times they brought their feuds into the Kremlin itself.

Evidence indicates that Ivan was a sensitive, intelligent boy with a remarkably quick and intuitive mind. He became quite aware of all the intrigues around him and of the precariousness of his own position. He was neglected and at times treated with scorn. Apparently, he was even short of food and clothes. This environment, therefore, nourished a hatred for the boyars that revealed itself in Ivan's later policies toward them.

Early Rule

In 1538 Glinsky died suddenly, and years of strife and misrule ensued. In 1547, however, Ivan decided, much to the astonishment of those around him, to be crowned, not as grand prince, but as czar (God's anointed). In the same year Ivan married Anastasia Romanov. The marriage seems to have been a happy one, and when Anastasia died in 1560, deep grief overcame Ivan. Although he married four more times, he was never able to recapture the happiness he had enjoyed with Anastasia.

In 1547 Ivan also appointed the Selected Council, largely dominated by men of modest social standing. He allowed himself to be both directed and restrained by this Council, even agreeing to do nothing without its approval. The period following the Council's creation is generally considered the constructive period of Ivan's reign.

In 1550 Ivan called the first of two *zemskii sobors* (consultative assemblies) to meet during his reign. Although knowledge of the assemblies is fragmentary (some historians even deny that there was an assembly in 1550), they appear not to have been elected but appointed by Ivan himself and to have served in a purely advisory capacity. Approval was given, however, to several of Ivan's projected reforms. In 1552 a reform in local government was instituted. In those areas where the local population could guarantee a fixed amount of state dues to the treasury, officials elected from and by the local inhabitants were given the right to collect taxes in lieu of the old governors, who were abolished in such areas.

The Law Code of 1550 was another important reform of the early part of Ivan's reign. It was concerned primarily with discouraging the use of customary law in the courts, and it introduced the principle of statutory law.

Ivan, a devout churchman, called a church council in 1551. Among other matters, the council considered liturgical questions and passed reforms which tightened and perfected the organization of the Church. Ivan was also concerned with standardizing and organizing the responsibilities and duties of the service class. In 1556 he issued a decree which provided new regulations concerning the length, nature, and form of service which a member of the nobility was expected to render.

Foreign Policy

Among Ivan's military accomplishments was the destruction of the Tatar khanates of Kazan in 1552 and Astrakhan in 1556. Thus, of the three Tatar states in the region of Russia, only the Crimean Tatars remained unconquered by Muscovy. With the addition of Kazan and Astrakhan, Muscovy now extended to the Urals in the east and to the Caspian Sea in the south. Russia also began its expansion to the east beyond the Urals at this time and before Ivan's death had established itself in Siberia. Ivan's ambition to restore to Muscovy the western territories which had been annexed by Lithuania in the 16th century, however, was unrealized.

Another of Ivan's ambitions, contact with the West, was achieved. In 1553 an English sea captain, Richard Chancellor, landed on the Russian shore near the mouth of the Northern Dvina River and made his way to Moscow. Upon his return to England, Chancellor became one of the founders of the Muscovy Company, to which Ivan gave special trade privileges. Although traders of other nations, Dutch and French, began to appear, the English dominated the Russian trade with centers in many Russian towns.

Later Years

Despite governmental improvements at home and successes abroad, the constructive or early period of Ivan's rule was not to endure. He broke with his Selected Council, turned against many of his former advisers, and introduced a reign of terror against the boyars. The major turning point came in 1560, when Anastasia died quite suddenly. Convinced that his advisers, backed by the boyars, had caused her death, Ivan condemned them and turned against the nobility. In 1564 he abandoned Moscow. What his intentions were is not clear, although he threatened to abdicate and denounced the boyars for their greed and treachery. Confused and frightened, the people of Moscow begged the Czar to return and rule over them. His eventual agreement to return was dependent upon two basic conditions: the creation of a territorial and political subdivision—the *oprichnina*—to be managed entirely at the discretion of the Czar; and Ivan's right to punish traitors and wrongdoers, executing them when necessary and confiscating their possessions.

The area encompassed by the *oprichnina* was a large one, constituting about one-half of the existing Muscovite state. It also included most of the wealthy towns, trading routes, and cultivated areas and was, therefore, a stronghold of wealthy old boyar families. Ivan's establishment of his rule over the area necessarily involved, then, displacement (and destruction) of the major boyar families in Russia. This task fell to his special bodyguards, a select group known as the *oprichniki* .

In 1584 Ivan's health began to fail. As portents of death came to obsess him, he called on witches and soothsayers to aid him, but to no avail. The end came on March 18, 1584. In a final testament he willed his kingdom to Feodor, his oldest surviving son. Although the transition from Ivan to Feodor was relatively easy and quiet, Muscovy itself was, according to most observers, on the verge of anarchy.

Further Reading

There are several biographies of Ivan in English. The best is probably K. Waliszewski, *Ivan the Terrible* (trans. 1904). Robert Wipper justifies Ivan's actions in *Ivan Grozny* (trans., 3d ed. 1947). Other biographies include Stephen Graham, *Ivan the Terrible: Life of Ivan IV of Russia* (1933), and A. M.

Kurbsky, *Prince A. M. Kurbsky's History of Ivan IV,* edited and translated by J. L. I. Fennell (1965). For a vivid self-portrait of Ivan as well as a justification of his actions see *The Correspondence between Prince A. M. Kurbsky and Tsar Ivan IV of Russia, 1564-79* , edited and translated by J. L. I. Fennell (1955). A contemporary account of Ivan's Russia is Giles Fletcher, *Of the Rus Commonwealth,* edited by Albert J. Schmidt (1966). British trade with Russia can be studied in T. S. Willan, *The Early History of the Russia Company, 1553-1603* (1956). □

Charles Edward Ives

American composer Charles Edward Ives (1874-1954) was an experimental and boldly original pioneer in musical expression. Recognition of his forceful, often eccentric genius came late in his life and much more fully after his death.

Born in Danbury, Conn., on Oct. 20, 1874, of an old New England family, Charles Ives really lived two lives: an outward, tradition-bound public life as an insurance executive, and an inward, musical, and reflective life full of paradoxical and revolutionary ideas.

As a student, Ives was essentially involved in law and business administration programs. However, he received solid musical training, first under his father, who had been a bandleader in the Civil War and, later, at Yale University, under Horatio Parker (a then respected, now nearly forgotten composer and teacher). Musically daring from the first, Ives shocked Parker with some of his student essays. Yet Parker was impressed by, and generally encouraged, his maverick pupil. Ives graduated from Yale in 1898. A skilled organist during his student days and early years in business, Ives often earned spending money by playing at church services. He also sometimes conducted bands at vaudeville houses, a fact that may explain his later use in serious compositions of the small, odd groups of instruments such as he had encountered in nightly changing vaudeville orchestras.

In 1906 Ives began a career in the insurance business, and his Yankee shrewdness eventually made him a near millionaire. Mainly preoccupied with his business and, later, with health just poor enough to force him to retire, he was a musician much like a "weekend painter." Music remained his avocation. Sometimes this "hobby" was used to make private jokes: his scribbled, sometimes nearly undecipherable manuscripts occasionally contain rude marginal comments about everything from music and philosophy to notes on personal friends. For the most part, however, he was quite serious. Friends reported that he probably did not expect his spare-time musical creations to become accepted eventually as masterpieces; yet he did work at some of his compositions as if they might attain such status someday.

Working in the Dark

The musical environment in late-19th-century America, when Ives began composing, was conservative, cold, and retrogressive, still attached to the nearly exhausted European romantic tradition. Most of Ives's music was composed between 1896 and 1916, with short bursts of production after that. He worked alone, often in what he felt was a mysterious, unexplored darkness; paradoxically, he wrote knowingly, quietly, but with a determined seriousness. Though working outside the musical activity of his time, he never faltered in his creative spontaneity and passion for finding his own way. He possessed extraordinary musical intuition as well as a kind of visionary power. Though he sometimes wrote traditional pieces, he mostly experimented with new musical procedures, and works completed before he was 20 years old presaged techniques introduced into the mainstream of music by other composers 2 and 3 decades later.

For the most part, Ives's works remained unknown to other musicians for many years after their composition. Nevertheless, the few bits and pieces that reached other composers worked a real, if mostly oblique, effect upon their own creations. American composers who early knew some of Ives's experiments included Henry Cowell, Aaron Copland, and John Cage; foreign composers included Carlos Chávez, Benjamin Britten, and Edgard Varèse. Ives was a prophet, however, rather than the founder of a "school." Though his ideas had impact on others, he could not be followed in any traditional sense, since he lived in a musical and philosophical world of his own which could not be imitated. He disdained to explain the whys and wherefores of his increasingly unusual work, quoting Henry Thoreau: "I desire to speak to men in their waking moments . . . for I am convinced that I cannot exaggerate enough even to lay a foundation for true expression."

Musical "Inventions"

By the 1920s Ives had experimented with (or, as one critic has said, "invented") practically every important musical innovation that would still be influential 50 years later. Thus, far in advance of contemporary compositional styles, Ives pioneered with techniques such as atonality, polymetric patterns, polyharmonic and polytonal particulars, quarter tones, microtones, tone clusters, and tone-rows. (These were not unlike the techniques that formed the basis of the twelve-tone serialism composer Arnold Schoenberg was working out in the early 1920s.) Ives's early experiments were akin to (and perhaps had some influence on) the mid-20th-century music of the tapesichord and even multidirectional music (written for music-making groups of varying sizes, sometimes calling for several conductors conducting independently but at the same time).

Mixed with Ives's formal innovations were his special "Americana" accents: the bittersweet seasoning of old American hymn tunes, banal parlor songs, and barbershop quartet songs of far-gone yesterdays which he called up in quotation or in sincerely fond remembrance; fragments of songs by Stephen Foster; sounds of minstrel shows; patriotic tunes; reminiscences of scores by Johannes Brahms and other classical composers; and native American ragtime. All of these bits and pieces were snipped and stitched together, sometimes expertly, sometimes crudely, almost always with mesmerizing effect. Sometimes in an Ives piece the listener can hear an old tune (such as "Columbia, the Gem of the Ocean" or "Bringing in the Sheaves") emerging from what seems a background either of accompaniment or of clashing competition. Occasionally, the elements simply combine with great beauty.

Ives's varied, empirical inventions blended eventually into something that could be called a definite style. This was characterized by a complex texture (often deliberately "muddy") and simple melodic shapes, mixed with zig-zagging ultrachromatic twists, free-swinging harmony and counterpoint, and something like a "jargon" of rhythms.

His Accomplishment

In all, Ives wrote a staggeringly large amount of music: four symphonies (though his *Three Orchestral Sets* and the *Holidays Symphony*—the latter consisting of the four separate works *Washington's Birthday, Decoration Day, The 4th of July,* and *Thanksgiving,* played in that order—bring that number to eight); numerous large and small orchestral and chamber works; two finger-breaking, sprawling piano sonatas (the second interestingly subtitled *Concord, Mass., 1840-1860,* its first movement entitled "Emerson"; its second, "Hawthorne"; its third, "The Alcotts"; its last, "Thoreau"); four violin sonatas (the last bearing the subtitle *Children's Day at the Camp Meeting*); nearly 200 songs;

many choral pieces; and short solo piano or organ works. It is almost impossible to fix accurate completion dates to most of these compositions; some were worked at on and off over a period of years.

During most of his life Ives was treated simply as a musical eccentric or a sort of "prophet without honor." Fortunately, he lived just long enough to see his work begin to be accepted. His Third Symphony won the Pulitzer Prize in 1947. His influence upon younger creative musicians has increased since his death on May 19, 1954, in New York City.

Further Reading

Perhaps the best book on Ives is Henry and Sidney Cowell, *Charles Ives and His Music* (1955), a warm portrait by two musically knowledgeable friends. The book is not overly technical and offers many anecdotes, as well as penetrating comments on Ives's music. There is considerable material on Ives in such works on contemporary music as Peter Yates, *Twentieth Century Music* (1967).

Additional Sources

Block, Geoffrey Holden, *Charles Ives, a bio-bibliography,* New York: Greenwood Press, 1988.

Burkholder, J. Peter (James Peter), *Charles Ives, the ideas behind the music,* New Haven: Yale University Press, 1985.

Cowell, Henry, *Charles Ives and his music,* New York: Da Capo Press, 1983.

Feder, Stuart, *Charles Ives, "my father's song": a psychoanalytic biography,* New Haven: Yale University Press, 1992.

Perlis, Vivian, *Charles Ives remembered: an oral history,* New York: Da Capo Press, 1994.

Rossiter, Frank R., *Charles Ives and his America,* New York: Liveright, 1975.

Sive, Helen R., *Music's Connecticut Yankee: an introduction to the life and music of Charles Ives,* New York: Atheneum, 1977.

Swafford, Jan, *Charles Ives: a life with music,* New York: W.W. Norton, 1996.

Wooldridge, David, *From the steeples and mountains; a study of Charles Ives,* New York, Knopf, 1974. □

Tomomi Iwakura

The Japanese statesman Tomomi Iwakura (1825-1883) played a key role in bringing about the Meiji restoration of 1868 and is best known as the leader of a mission of government leaders to the West.

Tomomi Iwakura was born into the family of a lower-ranking court noble on Sept. 15, 1825, in Kyoto. Adopted into the Iwakura family in 1837, he began his career as a court chamberlain. In the late 1850s he rose to prominence as a leader of the antiforeign element at the court, helping to resist efforts of the *bakufu* (military government) to secure imperial approval for the commercial treaty negotiated with the United States. In spite of his relatively low rank, Iwakura became a personal confidant and adviser of Emperor Komei because of his devotion to the cause of restoring the Emperor to power. Iwakura favored a moderate policy of "union between court and *bakufu*," advocating in 1861 a marriage between Princess Kazunomiya, the Emperor's sister, and the incumbent shogun, Iemochi Tokugawa.

By the mid-1860s Iwakura had become impatient with the failure of the *bakufu* to cooperate honestly with the court and began to establish contacts with loyalist samurai from the Satsuma domain. He urged the Emperor to rescind the powers of the shogun and call an assembly of the domain lords, hoping for a unified national regime, under the Emperor, capable of resisting foreign pressure and undertaking internal reform. In December 1867, cooperating with Toshimichi Okubo, Iwakura helped engineer the overthrow of the shogun and the formal restoration of full executive authority to the Meiji emperor.

Iwakura occupied a leading role in the new imperial government. During 1872-1873 he headed a diplomatic mission to the Western nations, composed of men like Okubo, Koin Kido, and Hirobumi Ito, as well as a host of lesser officials and technical experts. The mission intended to renegotiate the "unequal treaties" and to investigate conditions in the West at firsthand. It was unsuccessful in achieving its first purpose, but it did leave the leaders of the new government with a concrete appreciation of Western military and economic strength.

After returning to Japan Iwakura led the opposition to an expedition against Korea proposed by Takamori Saigo and others. Together with Okubo, he argued that the country was too weak to undertake a foreign military expedition and that priority should be given to internal consolidation. Although his views triumphed, he was seriously wounded by would-be assassins in January 1876 for his role in the decision.

After Okubo's death in 1878, Iwakura became the most authoritative senior figure in the government until his death on July 20, 1883. Iwakura was highly conservative in outlook; his most important achievement was to advocate the establishment of a new constitutional order on the Prussian model: the promulgation of a constitution by the emperor, the vesting of most state powers in the imperial institution, and the assignment of a weak role to the popularly elected legislature.

Further Reading

Robert A. Wilson, *Genesis of the Meiji Government in Japan* (1957), discusses Iwakura and his leadership role in overthrowing the ruling Tokugawa family. Rachel F. Wall, *Japan's Century* (1964), offers a brief but good historical background, including the era of Iwakura's activities. For a fuller historical discussion see John K. Fairbank and others, *East Asia: The Modern Transformation* (1965). □

Alija Izetbegovic

Alija Izetbegovic (born 1926), a lawyer, businessman, and writer, founded the Muslim-based Party for Democratic Action in 1989. He became head of the eight-member presidency of the Republic of Bosnia-Herzegovina in 1990.

Alija Izetbegovic was born in Bosanski Samac on August 8, 1926, into a well-to-do and devout Muslim family. Little is known about his early years. The Izetbegovic family moved to Sarajevo in 1928, where young Alija received all of his education. In 1943 he graduated from Sarajevo's First Real Gymnasium for Boys. For the next three years Izetbegovic attended the agricultural school but left it to study law. He received his law degree from the University of Sarajevo in 1956. Izetbegovic spent most of his career as a lawyer as legal adviser to two large public corporations in Sarajevo.

Izetbegovic was married, but virtually nothing is known about his wife and her background. They have two daughters and one son. The older daughter, Lejla, was a mathematician. The younger, Sabina, taught French and English and worked as her father's translator. The son, Bakir, was a trained architect, but headed Izetbegovic's security force. In the 1993-1994 civil war Bakir commanded a brigade of special forces, code named "Delta," that included some mujaheddins.

Young Activist Designated Radical

Izetbegovic went to jail for the first time in Marshal Tito's Yugoslavia in 1946, when he and a group of Bosnian

Muslim intellectuals organized a Muslim antithesis to Tito's secular Marxist program and named it "Young Muslims." The end result was that he and 12 other radical Muslims were arrested and charged with "associating for the purpose of hostile activity and jeopardizing the constitutional order" and for "acting from the standpoint of Islamic fundamentalism and Muslim nationalism." Although tried and sentenced to three years of imprisonment, he was soon released as a first offender.

The second brush with the law was more serious and came as a result of his authorship of *The Islamic Declaration: A Programme for the Islamization of Muslims and the Muslim Peoples* (1970, reprinted 1990). The work recalls nostalgically the greatness of the Ottoman Empire and urges Muslims to return to life as prescribed by the Koran. Izetbegovic also wrote *Islam Between East and West* (1976) and *Problems of Islamic Revival* (1981).

It was *The Islamic Declaration,* however, that caused the greatest splash. Not only did Izetbegovic condemn the modernist reformers in several Islamic countries, he virtually declared war on everything non-Islamic when he asserted the incompatibility of Islam with non-Islamic religions. "There can be neither peace nor coexistence between the Islamic religion and non-Islamic political and social institutions," said Izetbegovic. Serbs and Croats pointed to such statements when explaining why they resisted living in an unitary state dominated by Izetbegovic and his party. Izetbegovic, however, continued to advocate what he called "a citizens' state" of ethnic and religious equals. Bosnian Serbs and Croats asserted that he never

renounced a single word in his "Declaration" and declined as consistently to comment on it when asked. Izetbegovic's supporters noted that the work never directly refers to Bosnia, and characterized it as a consideration of the place of Islam in the modern world. Later he told a news correspondent, "Our home is in Europe and not in any fundamentalist state. My aim is to have an independent, democratic republic which conforms to European standards."

Communist Yugoslavia also did not take lightly a second publication, *Islam Between East and West,* but addressed it only after Tito's death in 1980. In 1983 Izetbegovic was tried for Muslim nationalism and sedition and sentenced to 14 years of imprisonment. He was released from Foca prison, however, in November 1988 after five years and eight months of imprisonment. Undaunted, only a year later Izetbegovic gave impetus to the creation of a Muslim political party, which soon became the Party for Democratic Action. He spoke of creating an ethnically and culturally diverse environment in Bosnia-Herzegovina. He was its first and only president.

Withstood War—Again

At the first democratic multi-party elections in the Republic of Bosnia-Herzegovina, in November 1990, Izetbegovic (at age 65) was elected to the republic's eight-member presidency, a remnant of Tito's concept of collective leadership that, some argue, made Yugoslavia virtually ungovernable. On December 20, 1990, the presidency appointed him its president.

In 1991 the loosely organized nation of Yugoslavia fell apart. Slovenia, Croatia, and Macedonia declared independence, followed by Bosnia-Herzegovina the following year. But fierce fighting erupted almost immediately—Serbs against Croats, Bosnian Serbs and Bosnian Croats against Muslim Bosnians. Despite repeated peace efforts, the bloody civil war—fought almost exclusively within the 1991 boundaries of Bosnia-Herzegovina—dragged on well into 1994. Of the conflict's main leaders, Izetbegovic was blamed least for the war's ethnically motivated atrocities against the civilian population.

A small, soft-spoken man of pleasant demeanor, Izetbegovic did not betray the shrewd politician he was. In spite of his radical politico-religious writings that suggested strong fundamentalist leanings and the $93,000 King Faisal Fund Prize (1993) he received for "services rendered to Islam," Izetbegovic was able to convince the West, especially the U.S. leadership, that he was indeed a moderate. This in spite of a close relationship he developed with Iran's leaders. From 1991 to 1994 one of the Bosnian Muslims' big-three—President Izetbegovic, Vice President Ganic, or Prime Minister Silajdzic—visited Iran at least once every month. A result of this relationship was that Iran provided arms to the Bosnian Muslims in spite of the United Nations' embargo. In addition, mujaheddins Iran recruited entered Bosnia-Herzegovina to fight against Croats and Serbs.

Reluctant Participant in Just Accord

Critics believe that Izetbegovic was allowed to renege on several agreements he signed with Bosnian Croats and Bosnian Serbs, designed to end the civil war. He rejected the concept of three ethnic states tied together in a loose confederation, favoring instead a unitary Bosnia-Herzegovina. In the fall of 1995 Izetbegovic and his military/political enemies, Milosevic of Serbia and Tudjman of Croatia, were persuaded by an exasperated international community to participate in peace talks at Wright-Patterson Air Force Base near Dayton, Ohio—the fourth Bosnian peace initiative since 1992. After three weeks of on-again-off-again talks, they grudgingly agreed to end the war. A NATO-led peace keeping force, Implementation Force (IFOR) was charged with maintaining the cease fire.

The cornerstone of the agreement was to be free elections held the following year with the objective of reunifying Bosnia. Yet as the date neared, opposition candidates had been able to make little progress. Karadzic, military leader of Bosnian Serbs and one of the most-wanted criminals on The Hague's list, could not participate in elections, but was clearly in charge of candidates from the Serb Democratic Party (SDS). The parties of the other two factions, Izetbegovic's Party of Democratic Action (SDA) and Zubak's Croatian Democratic Union (HDZ) demonstrated similar holds on their electorates. As many predicted, the September 14, 1996 election returned to power the very people who had taken Bosnia-Herzegovina to war. The vote split along ethnic lines; each candidate won a majority of votes in areas they controlled. The three separatists were to share a tripartite presidency, as ratified by the Dayton accord. Having the greatest number of votes, Izetbegovic became the first to head the tripartite. Leadership would rotate thereafter to govern the uneasy peace.

Izetbegovic's role in history and Bosnia-Herzegovina's fratricidal civil war has yet to be evaluated. Future generations must decide whether he was a hero and the father of the Bosnian Muslim nation or an ambitious politician who rejected peace through compromise and helped destroy his own dream of a united multinational and multi cultural Bosnia-Herzegovina.

Further Reading

Numerous books have been written about the Balkan war, including: *Balkan Tragedy: Chaos and Dissolution After the Cold War* by Susan L. Woodward; *Balkan Odyssey* by David Owen; *Yugosalvia: Death Of A Nation* by Laura Silber and Allan Little; and *The Last Days of Yugoslavia* by Borisav Jovic.

There was virtually no information available in English about Alija Izetbegovic as an official or private person. The two books he wrote, *The Islamic Declaration* (Sarajevo, 1970; reprinted 1990) and *Islam Between East and West* (1976) were informative with respect to Izetbegovic's religious and political thinking. Both have been translated into English but are not widely available. Most helpful on the political situation was a paper dated September 1, 1992, by the House Republican Research Committee on Terrorism and Unconventional Warfare titled "Iran's European Springboard?" The authors are Yossef Bodansky and Vaugn S. Forrest. Two books on the area provided good background to the 1990s warfare: Noel Malcolm, *Bosnia: A Short History* (1993) and Robert Kaplan, *Balkan Ghosts: A Journey Through History* (1993).

Among the magazine, newspaper articles and reports, the following are useful and informative: Judy Dempsey, "Man in the News: Former Rebel with a Pacifist Cause," *Financial Times* (March 7, 1992); Mervyn Hiskett, "Islam and Bosnia," *Salisbury Review* (June 1993); and Julia Preston, "Bosnia's Muslims Say the U.S. Let Them Down on Peace Plan," *The Washington Post* (March 11, 1993). □

J

Kareem Abdul Jabbar

Kareem Abdul Jabbar (born 1947), formerly Ferdinand Lewis Alcindor, Jr. was one of the greatest basketball players to play the game at the high school, college, and professional ranks.

Kareem Abdul Jabbar was born Ferdinand Lewis Alcindor, Jr., on April 16, 1947, in New York City, the only child of Ferdinand and Cora Alcindor. He grew up in middle-class circumstances in Inwood, an upper Manhattan neighborhood. A Roman Catholic, he attended the St. Jude's parish elementary school, where he excelled in baseball, swimming, and ice skating. His height began to increase dramatically, and his characteristic self-consciousness led him to seek refuge on the basketball court. By the time he completed eighth grade, Jabbar's height had rocketed to six feet, six inches and he played basketball exclusively.

Already a local basketball legend, Jabbar was heavily recruited by many of the local New York preparatory schools. He chose Power Memorial Academy, and his six foot, eight inch height gave Coach Jack Donohue no alternative but to place him on the varsity squad, a rarity for a ninth grader. He spent the year building his coordination. As a sophomore averaging 19 points per game, Jabbar led his team to 27 straight victories en route to the 1963 New York City Catholic High School championship. Power Memorial's unbeaten streak continued the following year, as Jabbar averaged 26 points a game and led Power to another City Catholic High School championship. As a senior he averaged 33 points per game, and although Power's unbeaten streak of 71 games was snapped by DeMatha High

School of Hyattsville, Maryland, they again won the New York City Catholic High School championship by going undefeated the rest of the season.

With the college offers as abundant as the publicity, Jabbar heeded the advice of notable African Americans such as Arthur Ashe, Jackie Robinson, and then Undersecretary of the United Nations Ralph Bunche and elected to accept the scholarship from the University of California at Los Angeles (UCLA). A conscientious student, he enrolled at UCLA in the fall of 1965 believing that there would be a strong balance between sports and academics there.

Although freshmen were ineligible to play varsity sports at the time, Jabbar gave Coach John Wooden a preview of his forthcoming dominance by leading the freshman team to an easy 75-60 victory over the varsity team that had already won the National Collegiate Athletic Association (NCAA) basketball championship in two of the preceding three seasons. In his first varsity game, Jabbar scored 56 points against California. Along with guards Mike Warren and Lucious Allen and forwards Kenny Heitz and Lynn Shackelford, Jabbar led UCLA to a perfect 26-0 season. The UCLA Bruins again won the national championship in 1967, beating Dayton in the final game.

Jabbar spurned a one-million dollar offer to sign with the Harlem Globetrotters after the 1967 season. In spite of the fact that he was a sensitive individual and somewhat of a loner, Jabbar was also extremely mature for his age and able to cope with constant media attention. He became a history major and enjoyed reading and music. His awareness of racial prejudice was strong, and he became a follower of the teachings of Malcolm X, who stressed pride among African American people. He entered his junior year somewhat jaded, disappointed at the lack of social awareness he saw

in many Californians. However, he was also on the threshold of even greater basketball accomplishments.

Although the 1967-1968 basketball season brought with it many more triumphs for Jabbar and the UCLA Bruins, Houston University handed UCLA their first loss after 47 consecutive victories. The 55,000 fans at the Houston Astrodome who witnessed the 69-68 defeat saw Jabbar's six-foot, nine-inch nemesis, Elvin Hayes, score 39 points in college basketball's most exciting spectacle to that point. The UCLA team gained sweet revenge against the Cougars in the NCAA championship semi-final that year, scoring a lopsided 101-69 victory. They defeated North Carolina in the final game, to win the NCAA championship again in 1968.

UCLA also won the NCAA championship in 1969, losing only once along the way to Southern California. Jabbar's totals in three years of varsity play were a phenomenal 88 wins in 90 games, three straight NCAA championships, three straight years as the tournament's most valuable player, and a career average of 26 points per game on a .639 shooting percentage. Many called him the greatest collegiate player ever.

Jabbar graduated from UCLA in 1969 and was the National Basketball Association's (NBA's) first draft choice, selected by the Milwaukee Bucks. He joined the Bucks reluctantly, but settled in to become the 1970 NBA Rookie of the Year. Following the 1970 season, he changed his name to Kareem Abdul Jabbar and professed his membership in the Hanafi Muslim sect of the Islamic religion. In

1971, Jabbar led the Bucks to the NBA championship and was named the NBA's league's most valuable player.

In the four seasons that followed, Jabbar perfected his trademark sky-hook and was named the NBA's most valuable player in the 1972 and 1974 seasons. In 1975, he was traded to the Los Angeles Lakers and earned even more accolades. He led the Lakers to NBA championships in 1980 and 1982 and was the NBA's most valuable player in 1976 and 1980.

Jabbar became one of the NBA's most prolific players and served as a positive representative for the league. He was named to the All-Star team every year, including his rookie season. An eloquent individual, Jabbar came out of an introverted phase to make numerous television show appearances and commercials. He also appeared in cameo roles in movies such as Bruce Lee's *Enter the Dragon* (1971), *The Fish That Saved Pittsburgh* (1979), and *Airplane* (1980).

During the 1984 season, Jabbar became the NBA's all-time scoring leader, eclipsing the record of 31,419 points set by Wilt Chamberlain, and capped things off by leading the Lakers to yet another NBA championship in the 1984-1985 season. The following season, he broke the record of 1,303 games played in the NBA.

Jabbar officially retired from the sport of basketball after the 1989-1990 season. He continued to remain very active following his retirement. In 1990, he penned yet another autobiography titled *Kareem* (an earlier one titled *Giant Steps* appeared in 1983). *Black Profiles in Courage: A Legacy of African American Achievement* was co-authored by Jabbar and Alan Steinberg, and released in 1996. In 1991, Jabbar traveled to Saudi Arabia to play basketball for an exhibition team entertaining troops involved in Operation Desert Storm. Jabbar also appeared in the Stephen King television mini-series *The Stand* in 1994. He has continued working as a producer and developer for motion pictures and television.

Jabbar was named one of President Bill Clinton's *The Great Ones* for National Sports Awards and was inducted into the Basketball Hall of Fame in 1995.

Further Reading

An interesting account of Jabbar's early years of basketball is provided in *Giant of the NBA* (1972) by Robert Jackson. Jabbar, a self-confessed enigmatic individual, set the record straight in his autobiographical *Giant Steps* (1983). Paul Deegan's *Kareem Abdul-Jabbar* (1974) is a biography for children, and *Kareem, Basketball Great* (1975), by Arnold Hano, is a biography through the eyes of a sports fan. For more information, see Helen Borrello, *Kareem Abdul-Jabbar* (1995). Many of the best in-depth accounts about him are provided in the many years of coverage and attention given him by *Sports Illustrated* magazine. □

Jaber Al-Ahmad Al-Jaber Al-Sabah

Shaykh Jaber Al-Ahmad Al-Jaber Al-Sabah (born 1926) ruled Kuwait as the amir after the death of Shaykh Sabah Al-Salem Al-Sabah on December 31, 1977. His nation was attacked and overrun by Iraqi military forces on August 2, 1990. The amir fled to Saudi Arabia, returning in March 1991 when U.N. armies liberated Kuwait.

Born in 1926, Shaykh Jaber was the third son of the former ruler of Kuwait, Shaykh Ahmad Al-Jaber Al-Sabah. As a young boy Shaykh Jaber received his preliminary education at Al-Mubarakiya School, the first school to open in Kuwait. He was subsequently tutored privately in religion, Arabic literature, English, and the basic sciences. At the age of 23 Shaykh Jaber began his career in public service by holding the post of director of public security for the Ahmadi region, and in 1962 he became the first minister of finance and economy for Kuwait. In 1965 he moved closer to the seat of power, being appointed prime minister, and in mid-1966, by Amiri decree, he was named crown prince and heir apparent. Shaykh Jaber became the 13th amir of Kuwait on December 31, 1977. In 1991 Shaykh Jaber also held the position of chairman of the Kuwait Fund for Arab Economic Development and the Kuwait Fund for the Advancement of Science. He chaired the World Islamic Conference, which was held in Kuwait in 1988.

Foreign Relations

Shaykh Jaber's rule was especially challenging as he had to deal with immediate external threats, mainly the Iranian revolution of 1978-1979 and the subsequent Iran-Iraq war, which lasted from 1980 to 1988, and their repercussions on internal development within Kuwait and relations between Kuwait and the world community. Not only was Kuwait threatened because of its physical proximity to the battle zone, but it was also susceptible to the exportation of the Iranian revolution into its own borders. Approximately 30 percent of Kuwaitis are Shiite Muslims sharing a strong affinity with neighboring Iran and with the spirit and substance of the Iranian revolution. At the same time, Kuwaitis are Arabs and thus had reason to side with Iraq in the war against a common Persian enemy. Throughout these turbulent years, with war going on literally next door to Kuwait, the amir managed to appease both sides (or at least not to antagonize them) and to maintain an official policy of neutrality. While secretly giving financial assistance to Iraq, he avoided direct confrontation with Iran. This was especially difficult considering that numerous terrorist activities in Kuwait, including an attempt at the amir's life, were blamed on pro-Iranian Kuwaiti Shiites.

Iranian threats to navigation in the Persian Gulf led Kuwait to ask for help from its regional neighbors in the Gulf Cooperation Council with whom it had a joint security pact. When that effort proved fruitless, Kuwait resorted to the U.N. Security Council for help to keep this international waterway open and safe from Iranian attacks. The result was the reflagging of all ships with the American flag. To avoid antagonizing its neighbors, Kuwait announced that its agreement with the United States was a purely commercial one and did not involve joint security commitments with the United States. Although successful during the Iran-Iraq war, the amir's shrewd political maneuvering—or lack of it—did not save his country from an Iraqi invasion on August 2, 1990.

Internal Affairs

Like his predecessors, Shaykh Jaber had an uneasy relationship with the Kuwaiti parliament, the National Assembly (N.A.). Nevertheless, he managed not to alienate the Kuwaiti opposition, led by the leading merchant families of Kuwait. This is evidenced by the fact that the opposition stood in firm support of the amir and the ruling family, Al-Sabah, and refused to cooperate with the Iraqis during the 1990 Iraqi invasion of Kuwait. When Shaykh Jaber came to power, the N.A. had already been dissolved (in 1976). Responding to petitions calling for the N.A. to resume, Shaykh Jaber called for general elections in 1981. Astute government maneuvering, however, resulted in a N.A. dominated by 24 members (out of a total of 50) of bedouin background and strong loyalty to the Al-Sabah. Nevertheless, the N.A. continued to challenge the Al-Sabahs' discretion in matters of national concern.

In August 1982, after the disastrous fall of the unofficial Kuwaiti stock market, Souk Al-Manakh, the N.A. officially accused members of the Al-Sabah family of using their influence to make huge personal profits during the market's existence. The N.A. also objected to the government's handling of the financial crisis resulting from the stock market crash. Huge personal debts were paid out of public funds, eventually costing the government approximately $90 billion. After the 1985 election, which brought major opposition leaders back into office, this tension between the Al-Sabah and the N.A. reached a high point. The new N.A. called for the resignation of the minister of interior and minister of oil, both of the Al-Sabah family, blaming them for the economic and security problems in the country. After the Cabinet resigned, Shaykh Jaber challenged the Assembly's new leadership by forming a new Cabinet and including in it the same figures that had been implicated in the Souk Al-Manakh scandal. Furthermore, to reinforce his personal and the Al-Sabahs' ultimate power in the country, he dissolved the N.A. indefinitely, suspended the constitution, and imposed press censorship. Only in 1990 were elections for the N.A. allowed again (the voting franchise limited to men who can trace their Kuwaiti roots back to 1920 or earlier). In this way Shaykh Jaber was able to reassert for himself and the Al-Sabah family their dominating position in the country.

During his rule, Shaykh Jaber continued to practice the government's traditionally paternal relations with its citizens. A big portion of the oil revenues was transferred to the private sector through current expenditures (including social allowances and price subsidies), land purchases, and capital expenditures in development projects. Also, the government's stepping in to save the "small" investors in the stock market crash of 1982 is another example of this calculated benevolence. Here again, the old system of personal governing prevailed over the institutions of a modern state. In this way the amir managed to maintain the support and loyalty of his people, which was crucial in maintaining national unity in the face of Iraqi aggression.

When the amir returned from the safety of Saudi Arabia, where he had fled during the Iraqi invasion, to a liberated Kuwait in March 1991 he found a devastated land. Almost all of the 700 oil wells burned fiercely, set ablaze by retreating Iraqis. (It was one of the great manmade disasters of the 20th century). Reconstruction of Kuwait was estimated to cost from $60 to $100 billion, spent over several years' time. When the restoration of basic services moved slowly and there were no steps to liberalize the government, murmurs of popular discontent were heard, probably the most expressed dissatisfaction in the 300 years of rule by the Al-Sabah family. The discontent increased when the amir announced on June 2, 1991, that there would be no elections until late 1992. Meanwhile, Crown Prince Saad Abdullah Al-Sabah seemed to be in charge of day-to-day administration.

Kuwait paid the final installment of its $16.5 billion (Operation Desert Storm) debt to the United States in December 1991. It appeared that the amir was prepared to totally rely on the United States for protection.

Further Reading

There is no full biography of Jaber Al-Sabah. Information on the amir, the Al-Sabah family, and Kuwait can be found in R. S. Zahlan, *The Making of the Modern Gulf States* (1989); Richard Johns, "Trouble for Kuwait," *World Press Review* (May 1980); Jacqueline S. Ismael, *Kuwait: Social Change in Historical Perspective* (1982); John Barnes, "Kuwait Rolls the Dice for High Stakes," *U.S. News and World Report* (August 3, 1987); and Milton Viorst, "A Reporter At Large: Out of the Desert," *New Yorker* (May 16, 1988). An article discussing Kuwait's condition after the Persian Gulf War appeared in *Time*, January 27, 1992. A variety of information about Kuwait is available on the internet. To access the Ministry of Information, Kuwait Information Office in Washington D.C., visit http://www.kuwait.info.nw.dc.us (August 6, 1997). □

Jabir ibn Hayyan

Jabir ibn Hayyan (active latter 8th century), called Geber by Europeans, was reputedly the father of Moslem alchemy and chemistry.

It seems clear that there was a real person called Jabir ibn Hayyan about whom we know little except that he lived in al-Kufa, an important city of Abbasid Iraq, and that he had the reputation for skill in alchemy. There exists a vast body of Arabic writings attributed to this Jabir which could not possibly have been written by someone living in the late 8th century because the bulk of Greek scientific and alchemical works had not been translated at that time; Arabic scientific terminology had not even been coined. The earliest biography of Jabir is contained in Ibn al-Nadim's *Fihrist,* a monumental bibliography compiled in 988; the author of the *Fihrist* is partially aware of such discrepancies but insists that Jabir was a historical personage.

Attributions to Jabir

Scholarship has shown that there was a sizable corpus of alchemical works attributed impossibly to the historical Jabir. The first references to these works by Jabir appear in the latter half of the 10th century. The corpus contains a great percentage of what medieval Islam knew of the scientific knowledge of the ancients, viewed through Islamic spectacles, and it appears impossible that the 9th- or 10th-century Jabir could have been a single man, however industrious. The Islamic point of view from which this encyclopedic collection of late Hellenistic science is viewed in the works of Jabir is an extremely heterodox one, and this is doubtless the reason for assigning its authorship to a long-deceased but actual Jabir of the 8th century.

Jabir's science of *al-kimiya,* from which Arabic word both "alchemy" and "chemistry" stem, was based upon the Hellenistic idea that all metals are fundamentally the same substance, but with varying impurities. The main object of alchemy was to discover a method which would transmute the base metals into the purest form of metal, gold; this could be done by means of a supposed substance called "red sulfur" by the Moslems and "the philosophers' stone" by Europeans. In the process of searching for red sulfur, Jabir and other Moslem alchemists developed a great many sound facts and processes which formed some of the basic building blocks for the science of chemistry.

In terms of practical methods evolved by Jabir and set forth in the almost 100 works ascribed to him, we are indebted to Moslem alchemy for methods of distillation, evaporation, crystallization, filtration, and sublimation. Methods of producing a considerable number of chemical substances are described: nitric acid, sulfuric acid, mercury oxide, lead acetate, and others.

Further Reading

None of Jabir's works has been translated into English, but E. J. Holmyard, *Alchemy* (1957), is useful. See also "The Time of Jabir ibn Hayyan" in George Sarton, *Introduction to the History of Science,* vol. 1 (1927). □

Vladimir Evgenevich Jabotinsky

Vladimir Evgenevich Jabotinsky (1880-1940) led the Revisionist Zionist party. He fought for a Jewish state extending on both sides of the Jordan River.

Vladimir Jabotinsky was born on Oct. 18, 1880, in Odessa, the Jewish cultural center of southern Russia. He received his elementary and secondary education in Russian schools and showed special gifts in languages and literature. He learned Russian, English, German, Spanish, French, Italian, Polish, Latin, Greek, Hebrew, and Yiddish. He started his literary career at the age of 18 as a foreign correspondent of *Odessky Listok* in Bern and Rome. In 1901 he returned to Russia and, after the 1903 pogrom in Kishinev, became an active member of the Zionist movement. Under his influence Jewish defense groups started to organize in Russia to avoid repetition of the earlier pogroms. In 1904 he was a delegate to the Sixth Zionist Congress, and in 1906 he was active in the conference of Russian Jewry at Helsinki. In 1909 he represented the Executive of the World Zionist Organization in Constantinople to establish contact with a new Turkish regime. With his mission completed in 1910, he returned to Russia and devoted himself to the fight against assimilation and for Hebrew as the language of instruction in Jewish schools.

When World War I started, Jabotinsky was in western Europe as a correspondent of *Russkiya Vyedomosti.* In opposition to the official Zionist leaders, who remained neutral, he insisted on active Jewish participation in the Allied conquest of Palestine. As a result of his agitation, the first Jewish military unit, the Zion Mule Corps, was accepted by the British and sent to the Gallipoli front. In 1917 Jabotinsky succeeded in forming three Jewish battalions, which were sent to Palestine and participated, as the Jewish Legion, in the conquest of Palestine.

With the establishment of the British administration in Palestine, in 1920 Jabotinsky directed underground Jewish activity against Arab rioters. He was sentenced by the British authorities to 15 years at hard labor; the sentence was commuted to a year, however, and he was banished from Palestine. In 1921 Jabotinsky joined the Executive of the World Zionist Organization. In opposition to Chaim Weizmann, Jabotinsky demanded a militant Jewish stand against the British policy in Palestine and the Churchill White Paper. He resigned in 1923 from the Executive and devoted himself entirely to the organization of the Union of the Revisionist Zionists, whose goal was transformation of Palestine, by unlimited immigration, into a Jewish state. Becoming convinced that the Executive was destroying Zionism, he later left the World Zionist Organization; the majority of the Revisionists followed him and organized the New Zionist Organization in 1935. He settled in London, where he fought against the partition plan of the Peel Commission of Palestine, against compromise with the mandatory authorities, and against the policy of self-restraint of the Haganah in the face of growing Arab violence.

At the beginning of World War II, Jabotinsky went to the United States, where he was active on behalf of the Jewish communities under Hitler. He died suddenly on Aug. 3, 1940. He was buried in New York but, according to his wishes, his body was later buried in Israel.

In addition to being a statesman, Jabotinsky was also a linguist, orator, editor, and journalist. He wrote several books, among them *War and the Jew,* in which he claimed that the only solution for the Jewish problem is the liquidation of the Jewish communities outside Palestine and mass immigration to Palestine.

Further Reading

A full-length study of Jabotinsky is Joseph B. Schechtman, *The Vladimir Jabotinsky Story* (2 vols., 1956-1961).

Additional Sources

Katz, Shmuel, *Lone wolf: a biography of Vladimir Jabotinsky,* New York: Barricade Books, 1995.

Nedava, Joseph, *Vladimir Jabotinsky, the man and his struggles,* Tel Aviv: Jabotinsky Institute of Israel, 1986.

Schechtman, Joseph B., *The life and times of Vladimar Jabotinsky,* Silver Spring, MD: Eshel Books, 1986. □

Andrew Jackson

Andrew Jackson (1767-1845), seventh president of the United States, symbolized the democratic advances of his time. His actions strengthened the power of the presidential office in American government.

When Andrew Jackson emerged on the national scene, the United States was undergoing profound social and economic changes as the new, postrevolutionary generation pushed forward in search of material gain and political power. Jackson was a classic example of the self-made man who rose from a log cabin to the White House, and he came to represent the aspirations of the ordinary citizen struggling to achieve wealth and status. He symbolized the "rise of the common man." So total was his identification with this period of American history that the years between 1828 and 1848 are frequently designated the "Age of Jackson."

Andrew Jackson was born on March 15, 1767, in Waxhaw country, which straddles North and South Carolina. His father, who died shortly before Andrew's birth, had come with his wife to America from Ireland in 1765. Andrew attended several academies in the Waxhaw settlement, but his education was spotty and he never developed a taste for learning.

After the outbreak of the American Revolution, Jackson, barely 13 years old, served as an orderly to Col. William Richardson. Following one engagement, Jackson and his brother were captured by the British and taken to a prison camp. When Jackson refused to clean an officer's boots, the officer slashed him with a sword, leaving a permanent scar on his forehead and left hand. Jackson was the only member of his family to survive the war, and it is generally believed that his harsh, adventuresome, early life developed his strong, aggressive qualities of leadership, his violent temper, and his need for intense loyalty from friends.

After the war Jackson drifted from one occupation to another and from one relative to another. He squandered a small inheritance and for a time lived a wild, undisciplined life that gave free rein to his passionate nature. He developed lifelong interests in horse racing and cock-fighting and frequently indulged in outrageous practical jokes. Standing just over 6 feet tall, with long, sharp, bony features lighted by intense blue eyes, Jackson presented an imposing figure that gave every impression of a will and need to command.

After learning the saddler's trade, Jackson tried schoolteaching for a season or two, then left in 1784 for Salisbury, N. C., where he studied law in a local office. Three years later, licensed to practice law in North Carolina, he migrated to the western district that eventually became Tennessee. Appointed public prosecutor for the district, he took up residence in Nashville. A successful prosecutor and lawyer, he was particularly useful to creditors who had trouble collecting debts. Since money was scarce in the West, he accepted land in payment for his services and within 10 years became one of the most important landowners in Tennessee. Unfortunately his speculations in land failed, and he spiraled deeply into debt, a misadventure that left him with lasting monetary prejudices. He came to condemn credit because it encouraged speculation and indebtedness. He distrusted the note-issuing, credit-producing aspects of banking and abhorred paper money. He regarded hard money—specie—as the only legitimate means by which honest men could engage in business transactions.

While Jackson was emerging as an important citizen by virtue of his land holdings, he also achieved social status by marrying Rachel Donelson, the daughter of one of the region's original settlers. The Jacksons had no children of their own, but they adopted one of Rachel's nephews and named him Andrew Jackson, Jr.

When Congress created the Southwest Territory in 1790, Jackson was appointed an attorney general for the Mero District and judge advocate of the Davidson County militia. In 1796 the northern portion of the territory held a constitutional convention to petition Congress for admission as a state to the Union. Jackson attended the convention as a delegate from his county. Although he played a modest part in the proceedings, one tradition does credit him with suggesting the name of the state: Tennessee, derived from the name of a Cherokee Indian chief.

In 1796, with the admission of Tennessee as the sixteenth state of the Union, Jackson was elected to its sole seat in the U.S. House of Representatives. His voting record revealed strong nationalistic tendencies. The following year he was elected U.S. senator but he soon resigned to become judge of the Superior Court of Tennessee. His decisions as judge were described by one man as "short, untechnical, unlearned, sometimes ungrammatical, and generally right." He resigned from the bench in 1804 to devote himself exclusively to his plantation, where he later built a graceful mansion called the "Hermitage," and to his other business enterprises, including boatbuilding, horse breeding, and storekeeping.

Military Career

By the beginning of the War of 1812, Jackson had achieved the rank of major general of the Tennessee militia. He and his militia were directed to subdue the Creek Indians in Alabama who had massacred white settlers at Ft. Mims. At the Battle of Horseshoe Bend (1814) Jackson inflicted such a decisive defeat that the Creek's power to wage war was permanently broken. During this engagement Jackson's men acknowledged his toughness and indomitable will by calling him "Old Hickory."

When the U.S. government heard rumors of an impending British penetration of the South through one of the ports on the Gulf of Mexico, Jackson was ordered to block the invasion. Supposing that New Orleans was the likeliest point of attack, he established a triple line of defense south of the city. After several minor skirmishes and an artillery bombardment, the British attacked in force on Jan. 8, 1815, and were decisively defeated. Over 2,000 British soldiers, including their commanding general, perished in the battle, while only 13 Americans were killed. It was a stupendous victory. Jackson became a national hero overnight, for he had infused Americans with confidence in their ability to defend their new liberty.

Florida Territory

When the war ended, Jackson returned to his plantation. However, he soon resumed military duty to subdue Indian raids along the southern frontier emanating from Spanish Florida. In a series of rapid moves he invaded Florida, subdued the Seminole Indians, extinguished Spanish authority, and executed two British subjects for inciting Indian attacks. Despite an international furor over this invasion, President James Monroe defended Jackson's actions and prevailed upon Spain to sell Florida to the United States for $5 million. Jackson served as governor of the Florida Territory briefly, but he was highhanded, was antagonistic to the Spanish, and tried to exercise absolute authority. He quit in disgust after serving only a few months.

These exploits served to increase Jackson's popularity throughout the country, alerting his friends in Tennessee to the possibility of making him a presidential candidate. First, he was elected to the U.S. Senate in October 1823. Then, the following year four candidates sought the presidency, each representing a different section of the country: Jackson of Tennessee, William H. Crawford of Georgia, John Quincy Adams of Massachusetts, and Henry Clay of Kentucky. In the election Jackson won the highest plurality of popular and electoral votes, but because he did not have the constitutionally mandated majority of electoral votes, the issue of selecting the president went to the House of Representatives. Here, on the first ballot, John Quincy Adams was chosen president. Adams's subsequent selection of Clay as his secretary of state convinced Jackson that a "bargain" had been concluded between the two to "fix" the election and cheat him of the presidency. For the next 4 years Jackson's friends battered the Adams administration with the accusation of a "corrupt bargain." In the election of 1828 Jackson won an overwhelming victory. During the campaign Martin Van Buren of New York and John C. Cal-

houn of South Carolina joined forces behind Jackson, and out of this coalition emerged the Democratic party. Supporters of Adams and Clay were now called National Republicans.

"Old Hickory" as President

Jackson's presidential inauguration demonstrated the beginning of a new political age as thousands of people swarmed into Washington to witness the outdoor inauguration, then poured through the White House to congratulate their hero, nearly wrecking the building in the process. Jackson appointed many second-rate men to his Cabinet, with the exception of Martin Van Buren, his secretary of state.

An initial estrangement between Jackson and his vice president, John C. Calhoun, soon grew worse because of their obvious disagreement over the important constitutional question of the nature of the Union. During a Senate debate between Daniel Webster of Massachusetts and Robert Y. Hayne of South Carolina, Hayne articulated Calhoun's doctrine of nullification (that is, the right of a state to nullify any objectionable Federal law). Although Jackson was politically conservative and a strong advocate of states' rights, he was also intensely nationalistic, and he regarded nullification as an abomination. At a dinner commemorating Thomas Jefferson's birthday, Jackson found the opportunity to express his feelings. When called upon to deliver a toast, he is said to have looked straight at Calhoun and said, "Our Federal Union. It must be preserved."

The final break between Jackson and Calhoun occurred when it was disclosed that, earlier, as secretary of war in James Monroe's Cabinet, Calhoun had sought to censure Jackson for his invasion of Florida. In self-defense, Calhoun gave his side of the controversy in a newspaper statement and ended by arguing that Van Buren had deliberately sought his downfall in order to eliminate him as a presidential rival. Van Buren there-upon resigned from the Cabinet, thus forcing the resignation of the remaining members, which gave Jackson the opportunity of reconstituting his Cabinet and ridding himself of Calhoun's friends. Later, however, when Jackson made Van Buren U.S. minister to Great Britain, confirmation of this appointment resulted in a tie vote in the Senate, and Calhoun, as vice president, gained a measure of revenge by voting against it. This action prompted Jackson to insist on Van Buren as his vice-presidential running mate in the next election.

Bank War

The presidential contest of 1832 involved not only personal vindication for Van Buren but also the important political issue of the national bank. The issue developed because of Jackson's prejudice against paper money and banks and because of his contention that the Second Bank of the United States (established in 1816) was not only unconstitutional but had failed to establish a sound and uniform currency. Moreover, he suspected the Bank of improper interference in the political process. Jackson had informed the Bank's president, Nicholas Biddle, of his displeasure in his first message to Congress back in December 1829. Following this, Biddle, at the urging of Henry Clay and other

National Republicans, asked Congress for a recharter of the Bank 4 years before it came due. In this way the issue could be submitted to the people during the 1832 election if Jackson blocked the recharter.

Although the bank bill passed Congress rather handily, Jackson vetoed it in a strong message that lamented how "the rich and powerful too often bend the acts of government to their selfish purposes." This veto message broadened presidential power because it went beyond strictly constitutional reasons in faulting the bill. By citing social, political, and economic reasons, Jackson went beyond what all his predecessors had considered the limit of the presidential veto power.

In the 1832 election Henry Clay, running against Jackson on the bank issue, was decisively defeated. Jackson interpreted his reelection as a mandate to destroy the Bank of the United States. He therefore directed his secretary of the Treasury to remove Federal deposits and place them in selected state banks (called pet banks). Biddle counterattacked by a severe contraction of credit that produced a brief financial panic during the winter of 1833/1834. But Jackson held his ground, Biddle was finally forced to relax the pressure, and the Bank of the United States eventually collapsed. With the dispersal of government money among state banks and, later, with the distribution of surplus Federal funds to individual states, the nation entered a period of steep inflation. Jackson unsuccessfully tried to halt the inflation by issuing the Specie Circular (1836), which directed specie payments in the purchase of public land.

At the beginning of his second term, Jackson informed Congress of his intention to pay off the national debt. This goal was achieved on Jan. 1, 1835, thanks to income the Federal government received from land sales and tariff revenues. Jackson also advocated a policy of "rotation" with respect to Federal offices. In a democratic country, he declared, "no one man has any more intrinsic right to official station than another." He was accused of inaugurating the spoils system, but this was unfair for, actually, he removed only a modest number of officeholders. Jackson also advocated moving Native Americans west of the Mississippi River as the most humane policy the government could pursue in dealing with the Native American problem. Consequently he signed over 90 treaties with various tribes, in which lands owned by Native Americans within the existing states were exchanged for new lands in the open West. Jackson's veto of the Maysville Road Bill as an unwarranted exercise of Federal authority was widely interpreted as an expression of his opposition to Federal aid for public works.

Nullification Ordinance

Jackson also sought to modify tariff rates because they provoked sectional controversy. The North advocated high protective rates, but the South considered them a way of subsidizing northern manufacturers at the expense of southern and western purchasers. With the passage of the Tariff of 1832, South Carolina reacted violently by invoking Calhoun's doctrine of nullification. At a special convention in November 1832, South Carolina adopted the Ordinance of Nullification, declaring the tariffs of 1828 and 1832 null and

void and warning the Federal government that if force were used to execute the law, the state would secede from the Union. In response to this threat, Jackson issued the Proclamation to the People of South Carolina that blended warning with entreaty, demand with understanding. "The laws of the United States must be executed," he said. "Those who told you that you might peaceably prevent their execution deceived you. . . . Disunion by armed force is *treason*."

Meanwhile a compromise tariff was hurried through Congress to reduce the rates schedule over a 10-year period, while another bill was passed giving Jackson permission to use the military to force South Carolina to obey the laws. The state chose to accept the compromise tariff and repealed its nullification ordinance, thereby averting a national crisis. Jackson's actions during the controversy were masterful. Through the careful use of presidential powers, by rallying the public to his side, alerting the military, and offering compromise while preparing for possible hostilities, he preserved the Union and upheld the supremacy of Federal law.

Foreign Affairs

Jackson also exercised forceful leadership in his relations with foreign nations, and he scored a number of notable diplomatic victories. He obtained favorable treaties with Turkey, Cochin China, and Siam (the first United States treaties with Asiatic powers), and he was also able to reopen American trade with the British West Indies. Furthermore, he forced France into agreeing to pay the debts owed to American citizens for the destruction of American property during the Napoleonic Wars. However, when the French chamber of deputies failed to appropriate the money to pay the debt, Jackson asked Congress to permit reprisals against French property in the United States. The French interpreted this as a deliberate insult, and for a time war between the two countries seemed unavoidable. The French demanded an apology, which Jackson refused to give, although in a message to Congress he denied any intention "to menace or insult" the French government. France chose to accept Jackson's disclaimer as an apology and forthwith paid the debt; thus hostilities were avoided.

At the end of his two terms in office, having participated in the inauguration of his successor, Martin Van Buren, Jackson retired to his plantation. He continued to keep his hand in national politics until his death on June 8, 1845.

Further Reading

The most scholarly, but not the most interesting, study of Jackson's life is John Spencer Bassett, *The Life of Andrew Jackson* (2 vols., 1911; new ed. 1916). More colorful is Marquis James, *The Life of Andrew Jackson* (1938), but its analysis of Jackson's character is superficial. James Parton, *Life of Andrew Jackson* (3 vols., 1860), is old but extremely valuable, particularly since it was researched among many people who actually knew Jackson. A brief biography is Robert V. Remini, *Andrew Jackson* (1966).

Arthur M. Schlesinger, Jr., is generally sympathetic to Jackson in *The Age of Jackson* (1945), while Glyndon G. Van Deusen in *The Jacksonian Era* (1959) and Edward Pessen in *Jacksonian*

America (1969) are more critical. See also Harold Coffin Syrett, *Andrew Jackson: His Contributions to the American Tradition* (1953), and Leonard D. White, *The Jacksonians: A Study in Administrative History, 1829-1861* (1954). For the elections of 1828 and 1832 see Arthur M. Schlesinger, Jr., ed., *History of American Presidential Elections,* vol. 1 (1971). □

Helen Hunt Jackson

Helen Hunt Jackson (1830-1885) was an American author of fiction whose most famous novel, *Ramona,* dramatized the plight of California's Indians.

Helen Hunt Jackson was born Helen Marie Fiske on Oct. 15, 1830, in Amherst, Mass. Her father taught Latin, Greek, and philosophy at Amherst College. After her mother died of tuberculosis in 1844, an aunt cared for Helen and her younger sister. To recover from his grief and improve his health—he too suffered from tuberculosis—Professor Fiske sailed for the Near East in 1846. He died in Jerusalem in 1847.

In 1852 Helen met and married Lt. Edward Hunt of the Coast Survey Department. The son born in 1853 lived only 11 months. Another son, Warren ("Rennie"), was born in 1855. In 1863 her husband, by this time a major in the Navy Department, died while testing a submarine device he had developed. Yet another blow fell: Rennie died in 1865.

Hunt expressed her grief in poems that she sent to the *New York Evening Post* over the signatures "Marah" and later "H.H." She was encouraged in her writing by Thomas W. Higginson, who was always anxious to help female writers and gave important encouragement to Hunt's lifelong friend Emily Dickinson. While Hunt traveled in Europe (1868-1870), Higginson arranged publication in magazines and newspapers of the sketches she sent back. Her first book, *Verses* (1870), was well received, as were *Bits of Travel* (1872) and *Bits of Talk about Home Matters* (1873), collections of her periodical sketches. In 1871 she began publishing short stories in *Scribner's Magazine* under the name "Saxe Holm."

In 1872 Hunt traveled to California. The next year, while in Colorado Springs, she met William Sharpless Jackson, a banker and leading citizen of that community. They married in October 1875, and Colorado Springs became her home.

Saxe Holm's Stories had been published in 1873 (second series 1878). Helen Hunt Jackson's first novel, *Mercy Philbrick's Choice* (1876), was widely circulated. Two years later she published another volume, *A Masque of Poets.*

Jackson's interest in the conditions of the western Indians resulted in *A Century of Dishonor* (1881), a thoroughly researched exposé of the injustices Indians had suffered. She was subsequently appointed by the U.S. government as special commissioner to investigate the conditions of Mission Indians. When she realized that amelioration by official means was unlikely, she turned from report writing to fiction. She pleaded for justice for Indians in her novel *Ramona* (1884), though the book owed its enduring popularity more to its romantic than to its propagandistic aspects. Jackson died on Aug. 12, 1885.

Further Reading

Ruth Odell, *Helen Hunt Jackson, H.H.* (1939), was the first, and remains the only, reliable biography. For light on her relationship with Emily Dickinson see Thomas H. Johnson, *Emily Dickinson: An Interpretative Biography* (1955), and David Higgins, *Portrait of Emily Dickinson, the Poet and Her Prose* (1967). □

Henry Martin Jackson

An influential U.S. senator for 30 years, Henry Martin Jackson (1912-1983) was an ardent proponent of an anti-Soviet foreign policy. He championed increased defense spending and a more activist U.S. international role.

Henry Jackson was born in Everett, Washington, on May 31, 1912, the youngest of five children. His parents had immigrated to the United States from Norway in the late 19th century, eventually settling in the Puget Sound area of Washington. Jackson's father, Peter, was a building contractor and a long-time officer in the local plasterers' union; his devoutly religious mother, Marine, was instrumental in forming a local Norwegian Lutheran church in Everett and had selected his middle name to honor Martin Luther. Nicknamed "Scoop" when a teenager by an older sister after a popular comic strip character, Jackson carried this nickname through his adult life. Somewhat radical in his youth (having joined the Democratic Socialist League for Industrial Democracy while in college), Jackson gradually moved rightward from ardent New Dealer in the 1940s to neoconservative by the 1980s.

An ambitious but not outstanding student, Jackson earned his bachelor's and law school degrees from the University of Washington, working his way through college. After graduating from law school in 1935, he established his own law practice in Everett. Three years later he won election as prosecuting attorney of Snohomish County. Earning the reputation of a crusading and principled prosecutor through a series of dramatic cases involving organized prostitution, slot machine operations, and bootlegging, Jackson won promotion to the Congress in 1940 when the incumbent Democratic congressman Mon Wallgren sought election to the U.S. Senate.

A member of the House from 1941 through 1952, Jackson was a New Deal Democrat in domestic policy. In contrast to his postwar foreign policy views, Jackson at first followed the isolationist sentiments of his congressional district, opposing Roosevelt's Lend Lease Bill in early 1941. Then, in the aftermath of Pearl Harbor, Jackson emerged as one of the most vocal anti-Japanese spokesmen on Capitol

Hill. An unsuccessful candidate for a naval commission, Jackson volunteered for the draft in 1943 but was recalled (as were other congressmen) on Roosevelt's orders after five months of service.

Jackson's congressional career was undistinguished, as he authored no substantive legislation and was identified with no major policy initiative. A cautious politician, Jackson instead took pains to service the needs of his constituents. This prosaic commitment was underscored by his various committee assignments (merchant marine and fisheries, Indian affairs, wildlife resources, small business, civil service, and appropriations). This record of solid service ultimately benefited Jackson when in 1952 he successfully challenged the incumbent but vulnerable Republican senator Harry Cain, who had won election in the Republican landslide of 1946.

As a senator, Jackson continued to work to promote the interests of his state and rose to prominence as a member of the Interior (becoming chairman in 1963) and Armed Services committees, supporting respectively the timber and aircraft industries of the state. In a career marked by an absence of legislative initiative, Jackson was instrumental in securing congressional passage of the National Environmental Policy Act of 1969, which created the Environmental Protection Agency (EPA). An ardent proponent of military spending and a leading spokesman for an anti-Soviet foreign policy, Jackson first raised in 1955 the false issue of a "missile gap" when criticizing the Eisenhower administration's efforts to reduce defense spending. (Democratic presidential candidate John F. Kennedy later adopted this issue in the 1960 campaign.) By 1960 Jackson had gained a reputation within the Senate as an expert on national security policy through his chairmanship of the Armed Services Subcommittees on National Policy Making and on National Security Staffing and Operations. Earlier, in 1954, he had gained limited nationwide exposure for his cautious criticisms of Senator Joseph McCarthy's conduct as chairman of the Senate Permanent Investigations Subcommittee, of which Jackson was a junior member.

A close friend and political associate of Senator John F. Kennedy, Jackson was rumored to have been under consideration as Kennedy's running mate in 1960 but was bypassed when the Democratic presidential nominee instead chose Lyndon Baines Johnson. Jackson, however, served at Kennedy's request as chairman of the Democratic National Committee for the duration of the presidential campaign.

Despite the election of a Democratic administration, Jackson did not mute his criticisms of presidential foreign and defense policies. Between 1961 and 1963 he dissented from President Kennedy's various policy initiatives to defuse the tensions attendant to the Cold War: in 1961 he opposed the creation of the Arms Control and Disarmament Agency; in 1962 in a highly publicized speech he denounced the value of the United Nations; and in 1963 he initially opposed the test ban treaty (although he voted for the treaty after exacting certain concessions from the administration).

Throughout the 1960s and 1970s, Jackson emerged as a leading supporter of U.S. involvement in the Vietnam War, as an opponent of detente with the Soviet Union, and as a proponent of increased defense spending. At a time when American liberals divided sharply over the Vietnam War and had come to reassess the tenets of the policy of containment, Jackson remained a leading spokesman of a militant anti-Soviet policy. Because of this record, Richard Nixon, following his election to the presidency in 1968, offered Jackson the post of secretary of defense. Unwilling to abandon his own base in the Senate and his prospects for gaining the Democratic presidential nomination, Jackson turned down this proffered appointment. In 1972 and again in 1976 Jackson was an unsuccessful candidate for the Democratic presidential nomination. Never a serious contender in 1972, Jackson was considered one of the front-running candidates in 1976 (and did win the Massachusetts and New York primaries), although his candidacy collapsed before the Democratic National Convention met in New York.

As a senator in the 1970s Jackson remained skeptical of President Nixon's efforts at detente with the Soviet Union—opposing the Strategic Arms Control Talks (SALT) in 1972—but emerged as a champion of Israel and of normalizing relations with the Peoples Republic of China. So long as detente and fears of another Vietnam remained popular issues, Jackson found himself outside the mainstream of national politics. His political influence soared again as the political climate shifted rightward following the Iranian and Afghanistan crises of 1979 and 1980 and with the election to the presidency of former California Governor Ronald Reagan.

A bachelor for most of his congressional career, Jackson married late at the age of 49. He met his wife, Helen Hardin (the daughter of the president of American Gypsum and at the time on the staff of fellow Democratic Senator Clinton Anderson), in January 1961. Married in December 1961 in Albuquerque, New Mexico, Helen and Henry Jackson became parents of two children, Anna Marie and Peter Hardin. On September 1, 1983, Jackson died in Everett, Washington, of a burst blood vessel. Apparently in excellent health, the senator had just returned from a two-week trip to the Peoples Republic of China and, earlier on the day of his death, convened a press conference to denounce the Soviet Union for shooting down a South Korean commercial jet.

Further Reading

There is no good biography of Henry Jackson's life and Senate career, although there are two journalistic studies: Peter Ognibene, *Scoop: The Life and Politics of Henry M. Jackson* (1975) and William Prochnau and Richard Larsen, *A Certain Democrat: Senator Henry M. Jackson, A Political Biography* (1972). Readers might also consult the biographical sketches in *The New York Times,* September 3, 1983, and in Eleanora Schoenebaum (editor), *Political Profiles: The Nixon/Ford Years,* volume 5, (1979).

Additional Sources

Memorial services held in the Senate and House of Representatives of the United States, together with tributes presented in eulogy of Henry M. Jackson, late a senator from Washington, Ninety-eighth Congress, first session, Washington: U.S. G.P.O., 1983. □

Jesse Louis Jackson

Civil rights leader Rev. Jesse Louis Jackson (born 1941), the most successful African American presidential candidate in U.S. history, received over three million votes in the 1984 election.

Jesse Louis Jackson was born on October 18, 1941, in Greenville, South Carolina, a city beset with the problems of racial segregation. From birth, Jackson faced his own personal brand of discrimination. As a young girl his mother, Helen Burns, became pregnant by her married next-door neighbor, Noah Robinson. The young boy was shunned and taunted by his neighbors and school classmates for being "a nobody who had no daddy." Instead of letting this adversity defeat him, Jackson developed his exceptional drive and understanding of those who are oppressed. His mother eventually married and became a successful hairdresser while his stepfather, a postal employee, adopted Jackson in 1957. With helpful advice from his maternal grandmother and his own desire to succeed, Jackson overcame his numerous childhood insecurities, finishing tenth in his high school class, even though he was actively involved in sports. His academic and athletic background earned Jackson a football scholarship at the University of Illinois in Chicago. Jackson, eager to get away from the Southern racial climate, traveled north only to find both open and covert discrimination at the university and in other parts of the city.

After several semesters Jackson decided to leave the University of Illinois, return to the South, and attend North Carolina Agricultural and Technical College (A&T) in Greensboro, an institution for African American students. Jackson again proved himself an able scholar and athlete. When his popularity on the campus led to his victory as student body president, Jackson did not take the responsibility lightly. As a college senior, he became a civil rights leader. Although he was not in Greensboro when the four African American freshman from A&T staged their famous Woolworth's sit-in in February 1960—the action which launched sit-down demonstrations throughout the South—Jackson actively encouraged his fellow students to continue their protests against racial injustice by staging repeated demonstrations and boycotts. Much of the open discrimination in the South fell before the onslaught of these student demonstrations.

Civil Rights Movement

In the spring of 1968 many of SCLC's officers—including Jackson—were drawn away from other civil rights protests by the Memphis, Tennessee, garbage collectors' strike. The situation in that city was especially tense because many African Americans who professed to be tired of passive resistance were willing and ready to fight. Tragically, King, in his attempt to prevent racial violence in that city, met a violent death by an assassin's bullet while standing on the balcony of his hotel room on April 4, 1968.

son relentlessly spoke out against racism, militarism and the class divisions in American. He became a household name throughout the nation with his slogan "I Am Somebody".

By the mid 1970's, Jackson was a national figure. He realized that many of the problems plaguing the African American community stemmed from drug abuse and teen pregnancy and not simply economic deprivation. In 1976, Jackson created the PUSH-Excel, a program aimed at motivating children and teens to succeed. A fiery orator, Jackson traveled from city to city delivering his message of personal responsibility and self-worth to students: "You're not a man because you can kill somebody. You are not a man because you can make a baby . . . You're a man only if you can raise a baby, protect a baby and provide for a baby."

Jackson's support in the African American community allowed him to influence both local and national elections. Possibly the most important campaign in which he was involved was the election victory of the first African American mayor of Chicago, Harold Washington, in 1983. Washington's victory was attributed in part to Jackson's ability to convince over 100,000 African Americans, many of them youths, to register to vote. Jackson would also use his charisma to garner new voters during his 1984 campaign for the Democratic presidential nomination.

The Rainbow Coalition

Jackson's debut on the international scene occurred when President Jimmy Carter approved his visit to South Africa. Jackson attracted huge crowds at his rallies where he denounced apartheid, South Africa's oppressive system that prevented the black majority population from enjoying the rights and privileges of the white minority. Later in 1979, he toured the Middle East where he embraced Yassar Arafat, the then-exiled Palestinian leader. Jackson's embrace of a man considered a terrorist by the American government created yet another controversy. The result of these international excursions caused Jackson's fame and popularity to grow within the African American community.

As the 1980's began, Jackson moderated many of his political positions. He was no longer the flamboyant young man wearing long hair and gold medallions, but a more conservative, mature figure seeking ways to reform the Democratic party from within. He continued to advocate his "rainbow coalition" as a way for all Americans to improve the country.

After growing increasingly disenchanted with the existing political scene, Jackson decided that he would campaign against Walter Mondale and Gary Hart in the 1984 Democratic presidential primaries. His campaign centered on a platform of social programs for the poor and the disabled, alleviation of taxes for the poor, increased voting rights, effective affirmative action initiatives for the hiring of women and minorities, and improved civil rights for African Americans, poor whites, immigrants, homosexuals, Native Americans, and women. Jackson also took a stand on many world issues. He called for increased aid to African nations and more consideration of the rights of Arabs. His support for Arab nations and African American Muslims provoked much criticism, especially from Jewish voters. In early 1984,

Some controversy surrounds the moments just after King was wounded. Jackson claimed on national television that he was the last person to talk to King and that he had held the dying leader in his arms, getting blood all over his shirt. The other men present unanimously agreed that this was not true, that Jackson had been in the parking lot facing King when he was shot and had neither climbed the steps to the balcony afterward nor gone to the hospital with King. Whatever the truth of the matter, Jackson's appearance on national television the next day with his bloodied turtleneck jersey vaulted him into national prominence. The image of Jackson and his bloody shirt brought the horror of the assassination into American homes. Jackson's ego, stirring oratory and charismatic presence caused the media to anoint him and not Ralph Abernathy, King's successor. Many observers believe that at this point, Jackson determined to become heir to King's position as the nation's foremost African American leader. In 1971, Jackson was suspended from the SCLC after its leaders claimed that he was using the organization to further his own personal agenda.

Operation PUSH

After his suspension from the SCLC, Jackson founded Operation PUSH (People United to Save Humanity), an organization which essentially continued the work of Operation Breadbasket without SCLC's sponsorship. Standing in front of a picture of Dr. King, Jackson promised to begin "a rainbow coalition of blacks and whites gathered together to push for a greater share of economic and political power for all poor people in America." Throughout the decade, Jack-

Jackson used his popularity in the Arab world to obtain the release of an American pilot, Lt. Robert Goodman, who had been shot down over Lebanon.

When he returned home, Jackson concentrated on securing the African American vote for his candidacy. He did not receive support from most senior African American politicians, who felt that Jackson's candidacy would cause disunity within the Democratic camp and benefit the Republicans. However, many poor African Americans enthusiastically supported him. Jackson received 3.5 million votes, and possibly 2 million of those voters were newly registered. He carried 60 congressional districts on a budget of less than $3 million. Although many Americans, both black and white, were decidedly opposed to Jackson, he earned grudging respect because his campaign fared better than most people had expected. When Jackson conceded defeat at the 1984 Democratic National Convention, much of America listened respectfully to his address. Although his campaign was unsuccessful, Jackson's powerful presence had broken new ground and involved more African Americans in the political process.

After the 1984 election, Jackson devoted his time between working for Operation PUSH in Chicago and his new National Rainbow Coalition in Washington DC. This national coalition was designed to be a force for reform within the Democratic party. It also provided Jackson with a platform from which to mount his 1988 presidential bid. Jackson's campaign received a much broader base of support than in 1984. His polished delivery, quick wit, and campaign experience helped him to gain many new supporters. Among the seven serious contenders for the Democratic nomination, Jackson finished second to Massachusetts Governor Michael Dukakis.

In 1990, Jackson was named one of two "shadow senators" to Congress from Washington DC to press for the district's statehood. Although the idea fizzled, it helped to keep Jackson in the public eye. In 1992, Jackson backed Democratic candidate Bill Clinton during the presidential campaign. He used his influence to urge African American voters to support Clinton. These efforts helped Clinton to win the election and return a Democrat to the White House for the first time in 12 years.

Critics often accuse Jackson of simply being a cheerleader of causes, a person who favors style over substance. Despite his unflagging energy and devotion to his causes, many felt that he was devoted only to his own self-aggrandizement. "This is the long-term pattern of Jackson's politics. He has always sought to operate and be recognized as a political insider, as a leader without portfolio or without accountability to any constituency that he claims to represent" wrote political critic Adolph Reed Jr. in the *Progressive*. "PUSH ran as a simple extension of his will and he has sought to ensure that the Rainbow Coalition would be the same kind of rubber stamp, a letterhead and front for his mercurial ambition."

Despite the criticism he has faced, Jackson continues to advocate for the rights of the downtrodden and challenge others to move beyond adversity. In 1995, Jackson wrote in *Essence* magazine, "People who are victimized may not be responsible for being down, but they must be responsible for getting up. Slave masters don't retire; people who are enslaved change their minds and choose to join the abolitionist struggle . . . .Change has always been led by those whose spirits were bigger than their circumstances . . . I do have hope. We have seen significant victories during the last 25 years."

Further Reading

Jackson's autobiography, *Straight from the Heart,* was published in 1987. There are a number of biographies of Jackson and several analytical studies of his presidential campaign. Two are Barbara A. Reynolds' sympathetic biography entitled *Jesse Jackson: America's David* (1985) and a critical work written by Thomas Landess and Richard Quinn, *Jesse Jackson and the Politics of Race* (1985). Several other biographies are Adolph L. Reed, *The Jesse Jackson Phenomenon,* a somewhat negative portrait (1986); Shield D. Collins, *From Melting Pot to Rainbow Coalition* (1986); and a children's book by Warren J. Halliburton, *The Picture Life of Jesse Jackson* (1984). Other works include *Jesse: The Life and Pilgrimage of Jesse Jackson;* James Haskins, *I Am Somebody! A Biography of Jesse Jackson,* and *Political Parties and Elections in the United States Vol. 1,* edited by L. Sandy Maisel. □

Maynard Holbrook Jackson Jr.

A lawyer by training, Maynard Holbrook Jackson, Jr. (born 1938), was the first African American to be elected mayor of Atlanta, Georgia (1973-1981 and 1989-1993), and the first to serve as chief executive of any major Southern city.

Born in Dallas, Texas, on March 23, 1938, the third of six children, Maynard Holbrook Jackson, Jr., was considered to be a member of the "Black aristocracy." His father, Maynard Jackson, Sr., was a Baptist minister and his mother, Irene (Dobbs) Jackson, was a college language teacher with a doctorate in French. When Maynard Jr. was age seven, his family moved to Atlanta, Georgia, where his father took over as pastor of the Friendship Baptist Church. Young Maynard considered becoming a clergyman but then enrolled at Morehouse College in Atlanta as an early admissions scholar and earned a BA degree in political science and history in 1956.

After graduation from college, Jackson worked a number of different jobs, including a stint at the Ohio State Bureau of Unemployment Compensation and selling encyclopedias. He enrolled in law school at North Carolina Central University, where he received a JD degree *cum laude* in 1964. He returned to Atlanta and worked for the National Labor Relations Board as an attorney, passed his bar exams in 1965, and two years later joined a public interest, low-income legal service which he eventually managed. He soon married Valerie Richardson Jackson and became the father of four daughters and a son.

Inspired by Martin Luther King, Jr.'s Death

Jackson claimed that Martin Luther King Jr.'s death in 1968 prompted him, to enter politics for the first time. He ran for the United States Senate seat held by Southern powerhouse Herman Talmadge. Acting on a spur-of-the-moment impulse, Maynard filed only minutes before the deadline on June 5, 1968, with $3,000 he had borrowed to pay the filing fee. During the campaign, Jackson's populist appeals brought unexpected support from poor white farmers, but African American voters did not support him automatically. Although he was defeated by Talmadge by a three to one margin, Jackson had won a majority in Atlanta.

Carefully planning his campaign for vice-mayor of Atlanta in 1969, Jackson did not take the African American vote for granted and campaigned tirelessly, appearing in African American churches every Sunday until election day. He also appealed for the white vote and won about one-third of it, and that, along with 99 percent of the African American vote, brought him victory. He was sworn in January 5, 1970, as Atlanta's first African American vice-mayor. In that position, Jackson worked hard at establishing a constituency to support his forthcoming bid for mayor.

In spring 1973, Jackson entered a multi-candidate race for mayor where his toughest opponent proved to be the incumbent, Sam Massell, a certified liberal and the city's first Jewish mayor. The campaign turned into a rough, no-holds-barred affair that went into a runoff election. Race became a central issue during the campaign, with both candidates openly appealing to their racial core constituencies. Jackson emerged the victor, garnering 59 percent of the vote.

In the Mayor's Office

Under a new charter which enhanced the mayor's power, Atlanta's first African American mayor, Maynard Jackson, assumed office in January 1974 and brought in an outside administrator to reorganize city departments. Administration was centralized and new planning districts were established with enhanced neighborhood and citizen input. Jackson provoked his first major racial crisis in May 1974 when he attempted to fire the incumbent white police chief, John Inman. Atlanta's growing crime problem and charges of racial insensitivity toward African Americans prompted Jackson's decision. The firing increased racial tensions within the city and detracted from Atlanta's proud motto: "too busy to hate." Another controversy followed in August 1974 when Mayor Jackson appointed a college crony and African American activist to become public safety commissioner. The new commissioner, A. Reginald Eaves, lacked police experience and created a great deal of controversy when he appointed an ex-convict as his personal secretary and began a system of quota promotions and hiring in the police department, which many decried as "reverse discrimination." Despite the outcry Eaves remained in his post and, by the spring of 1976, Atlanta experienced a drop in crime rates. However, Jackson was forced to fire Eaves after a police exam cheating scandal was uncovered.

Jackson continued to press for vigorous affirmative action programs and set-asides for African Americans on publicly-funded public works, which often brought him into conflict with the downtown business community. Despite criticism, most of Jackson's public projects, including a new airport, were completed on schedule, and by his second term Jackson had reconciled with Atlanta's business elite. Meanwhile, African American businesses and minorities were obtaining more than 30 percent of the city's contracts, which benefited the growing black middle class.

Barred by the city charter from serving more than two consecutive terms, Jackson left office. He established an Atlanta branch office for a Chicago law firm that was strategically positioned for public business. As a bond lawyer with political savvy, Jackson attracted politically-connected business from many African American mayors and, in the process, enriched himself and his political contacts.

A Third Campaign

In 1989, Jackson announced his intention to seek a third term as mayor of Atlanta. Running against a talented literature professor at Spelman College, and county commissioner Michael L. Lomax, Jackson's florid rhetoric and political reputation proved to be decisive. Unable to overcome a 34 percent point deficit in the polls, Lomax withdrew from the race. Although both major candidates were African Americans, Lomax had become identified as the "white" candidate and Jackson the "Black" candidate, a decidedly comfortable position in a city where nearly two thirds of the population was African American. As Jackson was cruising toward the October 3rd nonpartisan election, a former city councilman and Black militant, Hosea Williams, emerged late in the campaign to challenge Jackson. Williams's candidacy gained little support, however, and Jackson coasted to victory, capturing an overwhelming 79 percent of the vote. As one of the losing candidate's strategists put it: "Maynard Jackson is god in this town, and how do you run against god?"

In January 1990, Jackson began his new term of office by promising to follow former Mayor Andrew Young's footsteps and to work "hand-in-glove with our business community." Cognizant of criticism of his predecessor's overly pro-business slant, Jackson promised to devote more attention to the neighborhoods and the problems of the poor. The mayor's popularity increased when he helped to secure Atlanta's selection as the site of the 1996 Summer Olympic Games. He also formed an organization to assist students who were academic underachievers to help them develop leadership, critical thinking and self-esteem skills.

Considered a shoo-in for a fourth term as mayor, Jackson surprised supporters in 1993 by declining to run again, citing the effects of a heart-bypass operation. After leaving the mayor's office, Jackson conducted a $12.3 million bond sale for a city-backed apartment project and secured a lease to operate a restaurant and bar at Hartsfield International Airport. Jackson's firm, Atlanta-based Jackson Securities Inc., was named one of the top five black investment companies by *Black Enterprise* magazine in 1996. As chief executive of the company, Jackson was the lead manager for $337 million worth of securities issues and co-manager for $2 billion worth of securities issues.

Further Reading

For general information on Maynard Jackson, see "mayor's file," City Hall, Atlanta, Georgia. For politics, see "Michael Lomax," *Governing* (June 1988); "Tomorrow is still another day," *Economist* (May 6, 1989); and R. Smothers, "Atlanta Mayoral Candidate Drops Out" (August 9, 1989); "Styles in Conflict in Atlanta Mayor Race" (July 24, 1989); "Maynard Jackson Wins in Atlanta" (October 5, 1989); and Peter Applebome, "Atlanta As Mayor Returns. . . ." (January 7, 1990), all in *New York Times*. See also Clarence N. Stone, *Regime Politics Governing Atlanta, 1946-1988* (1989). ☐

Michael Joe Jackson

One of the most popular singers in history was Michael Joe Jackson (born 1958). A performer since he was five years old, he was one of the few child stars ever to achieve greater success as an adult than as a child. Through his record albums and music videos he created an image imitated by his millions of fans, whose style of dressing and dancing was instantly recognizable all over the world.

Michael Jackson was born in Gary, Indiana, on August 29, 1958, the fifth of nine children. He was raised in a family that listened to music constantly and sang continuously, and regarded music as a ticket to success. Jackson's father ran a crane at a steel plant, but he dreamed of becoming a successful rhythm and blues musician. This dream eluded him, but relentlessly drove him to promote the careers of his children. The fact that he had marginal success with a group of his own caused him to attempt to exert control over his children's careers even after they were adults. The struggle for the control of the musical destiny of the Jackson family was a constant source of turmoil.

The Jackson 5 Is Born

The Jackson children were taught the gentler aspects of music by their mother, Katherine, who sang folk songs and spirituals to them. The boys sang along with her, and their joyful harmonizing took on a life of its own when the boys formed a family band that became a success at amateur shows and talent contests throughout the Midwest. From the age of five, Michael's amazing talent asserted itself; his dancing and stage presence caused him to become the focus of the group. The fame and popularity of the group spread until they were booked at the Apollo Theater in New York City's Harlem. While performing at the Apollo in 1968, they were discovered by Motown recording artist Gladys Knight and pianist Billy Taylor. Later that year Diana Ross, who would become a crucial figure in Michael Jackson's life and career, became associated with the boys dur-

ing a "Soul Weekend" in Gary, Indiana. With the support of Ross, the Jacksons signed a contract with Motown Records. Berry Gordy, the legendary Motown mogul, became the caretaker of the Jacksons' careers, which he nurtured zealously. As the lead singer, Michael took his brothers to the top of the charts with the group known as the Jackson 5.

Destined for Solo Stardom

Almost immediately, Gordy recognized Michael's special appeal and released solo albums of the child. These solo albums sold as well as those of the Jackson 5. Two years later, in 1970, the Jackson 5 were topping the charts and riding a wave of youth adulation with such hits as "ABC," "The Love You Save," and "I'll Be There," each selling over one million copies. However, the longer the Jackson 5 existed, the more apparent Michael's importance to the group's success became. The group managed to survive his voice change and a bitter break with Motown Records in 1976. The squabbles among the siblings and between them and their father might well have caused Jackson to withdraw from his family, even as he continued to live with his mother.

Having been successful in his appearances in a television variety show and as an animated cartoon character, it was not surprising to Jackson's fans that his appearance in the musical film The Wiz (1978) was the only distinguished aspect of this African American version of The Wizard of Oz. He sang the only hit to emerge from its soundtrack album ("Ease On Down the Road") in a duet with the film's star, Diana Ross. His success as the Scarecrow may also be seen as a preview of what was to come in his videos, for Jackson seemed to care most about dancing. He dedicated his autobiography to Fred Astaire, and its title, Moonwalk, refers to a dance that he popularized.

Emergence of a Pop Icon

Jackson's work in The Wiz was also notable in that it introduced Jackson to producer Quincy Jones, who arranged and conducted the film's score. In 1979, Jackson and Jones collaborated on Jackson's solo album Off the Wall. The album sold ten million copies and earned critical praise. In 1982, Jackson and Jones again collaborated on the blockbuster Thriller album. Thriller fully established Jackson as a solo performer and his trio of hit songs from the album—"Beat It," "Billie Jean," and "Thriller"—made him the major pop icon of the early 1980s. Jackson was also notable as a crossover performer. The spectacular success of the Thriller album and video enabled him to break the color barrier of album-oriented radio stations and the powerful music video channel, MTV. By 1983, Jackson had established himself as the single most popular entertainer in America.

Although Jackson's next two albums, Bad (1987) and Dangerous (1991), did not produce the phenomenal results of Thriller, Jackson remained in the entertainment spotlight throughout the 1980s and into the 1990s. In 1993, he was presented with the "Living Legend Award" at the Grammys and the Humanitarian of the Year trophy at the Soul Train awards. He also involved himself in many philanthropic

efforts. In 1985, he reunited with Quincy Jones, this time on the vocal arrangement for USA for Africa's "We Are the World" to raise funds for the impoverished in Africa. In 1992, Jackson founded "Heal the World" to aid children and the environment.

Rocked By Scandal

Despite Jackson's popularity and philanthropic efforts, he became the subject of a major scandal. In 1993, a 13-year-old boy accused Jackson of sexually abusing him at the star's Neverland ranch. Jackson settled out of court, while always maintaining his innocence. The scandal cost Jackson his endorsement contract with Pepsi and a film deal. His sexual preference was called into question and his public image was severely damaged.

In 1995, Jackson was again the subject of scandal following the release of his new album HIStory: Past, Present, and Future, Book I. One of the songs on the album, "They Don't Care About Us", seemed to contain anti-Semitic lyrics. Jackson publicly apologized and changed the lyrics. He told the Associated Press that the song was supposed to "say no to racism, anti-Semitism, and stereotyping." He wrote a letter to Rabbi Marvin Hier, dean of the Simon Wiesenthal Center for Holocaust Studies, who had protested the lyrics, stating that "my choice of words may have unintentionally hurt the very people I wanted to stand in solidarity with. I apologize to anyone I might have hurt." Hier replied, "It's the ambiguity I'm concerned of when it [the song] reaches 20 million buyers around the world."

Marriage and Fatherhood

In May of 1994, Jackson stunned the world when he married Lisa Marie Presley, daughter of the late rock legend Elvis Presley, at a private ceremony in the Dominican Republic. Many critics of Jackson speculated that the marriage was an attempt to improve his public image. In August of 1996, Jackson and Presley divorced. Many of Jackson's fans were shocked when he announced, in November of 1996, that he was to be a father. The child's mother was Debbie Rowe, a long-time friend of Jackson. They married later that month in Sydney, Australia. On February 13, 1997, their son, Prince Michael Jackson, Jr., was born at Cedars-Sinai Medical Center in Los Angeles.

Despite the demands of fatherhood, Jackson continued to keep a busy schedule during 1997. He and his brothers were inducted into the Rock and Roll Hall of Fame in Cleveland, Ohio on May 6, 1997. He also attended the showing of his 40-minute musical Ghosts at the Cannes film festival on May 8, 1997. Another album, Blood on the Dance Floor: HIStory in the Mix, containing re-mixes of songs from HIStory plus five new songs, was released on May 29, 1997. The album received good reviews from both the New York Times and Rolling Stone, although the New York Times preferred the new songs, calling the re-mixes the "least interesting" music on the CD. Village Voice reviewer Armond White said of the new material, "His singing . . . has never been so tormented, or audacious". As the 20th century draws to a close, it seems likely that the world will continue to be fascinated by the talent and career of Michael Jackson.

Further Reading

Moonwalk (1988), Jackson's autobiography, is as good as any of the other books about him, perhaps better because it gives the reader insight into Jackson's "Peter Pan" image of himself; Dave Marsh, *Trapped: Michael Jackson and the Crossover Dream* (1985) is a most peculiar book. The author is highly critical of almost every aspect of Jackson's career and personality, yet he attempts to apologize to Jackson through open letters from himself to his subject. George Nelson, *The Michael Jackson Story* (1987) is a workman-like treatment of the basic biographical material. Jackson continued to be a mainstay of gossip columnists and was frequently featured in all sorts of periodicals from tabloids to newsweeklies in the 1990s. J. Randy Taraborrelli, *Michael Jackson: The Magic and the Madness* (1991) is a large (640 pages) unauthorized biography. A review of *HIStory* is in *Rolling Stone* (August 10, 1995). An interview with Jackson and Jackson-Presley is in *Jet* (July 3, 1995). □

Reginald Martinez Jackson

Baseball great Reggie Jackson (born 1946) was inducted into the Hall of Fame in 1993. Placed sixth on the all-time list for home runs, he also held the Major League record for strikeouts.

Former professional baseball player and Hall of Fame inductee Reggie Jackson's hard hitting, fleet footed style helped him lead two teams to five World Championships in only seven years. Called "the most theatrical baseball player of the last quarter century," by writer Mike Lupica in *Esquire,* Jackson made headlines with his egomaniacal remarks, hot temper, and flamboyant manner.

Reginald Martinez Jackson was born on May 18, 1946 in Wyncote, Pennsylvania. One of six children of African American and Spanish descent, he moved at an early age with two of his siblings to live with his divorced father in Cheltenham, Pennsylvania. His father, a once semi-pro baseball player in the Negro leagues who made a living running a small tailoring and dry cleaning business, encouraged his talented son in sports. By the time Jackson entered his senior year at Cheltenham High School he was an all star athlete: in track he ran the 100 yard dash in 9.7 seconds; on the football team he played halfback; in basketball he was a unparalleled player; and in baseball as a lefty player, he pitched three no-hitters and batted .550.

Jackson always felt he would be a professional athlete; the difficult part was deciding between football and baseball. College scholarships poured in and he ended up accepting a scholarship form Arizona State University in Tempe. In his sophomore year he was a receiver on the football team, and was chosen to the All-American first team in baseball. His outstanding performance on the baseball team caught the attention of Charles O. Finley, owner of the Kansas City Athletics, who offered Jackson, a

$95,000 bonus. Unable to refuse, he left college after his sophomore year and entered the world of professional baseball.

In 1966, Jackson was the second pick in the amateur draft. The New York Mets having the first pick chose another player, Steve Chilcott. Jackson played with the Kansas City Athletics farm teams for one and a half seasons. At the end of the 1967 season, he was called up to join the team in Kansas City, and in 1968 moved with the Athletics to their new home in Oakland, California.

In his first full season in the majors, he hit 29 home runs, and drove in another 74 runs. But he also made a dozen outfield errors and struck out a near record-breaking 171 times. The following season, in 1969, he again held a record number of strikeouts with 142, but hit a fantastic 47 home runs and led the American League in scoring 123 runs. Jackson credits then vice-president of the Athletics and Joe DiMaggio, the Hall-of-Fame center fielder of the New York Yankees, with developing his skills as a hitter.

The end of that glorious season was followed by a slump. The progressive pressures of trying to keep up with his own home run pace and the beginning of the eventual breakdown of his marriage to Jenni, his Mexican-American wife, contributed to his temporary decline. Further, he failed to negotiate successfully with Finley for a high increase in pay. The sour salary negotiations got the following season off to a bad start. Known for his hot temper, Jackson squabbled with teammates in the clubhouse, fought with Finley and often, after striking out, threw his bat in a rage. His average and his homers dropped and his continued poor performance caused him to be benched for a portion of that season.

In the Winter of 1970-71 he went to Santurce, Puerto Rico to work under an old idol, Frank Robinson. Robinson, a veteran player-manager, helped Jackson to ease up on himself and to put his own game into perspective. When he returned to the Athletics in Oakland he no longer felt the burdensome need to carry the team or to pressure himself for a hit every time he came to bat. Robinson's invaluable tutoring also helped him to cultivate his aggressive playing style while keeping his temper in check.

The following season saw him bouncing back to his high level of performance. Jackson helped lead the Athletics to the American League Eastern Division Title in 1971 with 32 home runs. But the Baltimore Orioles took the pennant at the playoffs. In 1972 the Athletics won the Western Division Title. In the playoffs, the Athletics beat the Detroit Tigers, with Jackson sliding into home plate to score the winning run in the final game. Tragically, during his slide he incurred an injury, a torn hamstring muscle, which forced him to sit out of the World Series. But as Jackson watched, the Athletics reigned victorious over the Cincinnati Reds.

Voted the American League's Most Valuable Player (MVP) in 1973, Jackson batted .293 and led the leagues in 32 home runs. That year the Atheltics defeated Baltimore to win the pennant. The team went on to win the World Championship over the New York Mets, with Jackson batting .310, driving in six runs, and hitting two home runs in the seventh game. Leading the league in runs, he was chosen MVP in the World Series. As sensational as the 1973 series was, it was not without its dark cloud. Anonymous death threats were sent to the Oakland office warning that Jackson would be killed if he played in the Championship games. During the playoffs and the World Series Jackson was under constant guard from both private and FBI agents. In the end, seemingly nothing resulted from the threats.

The Athletics won their fourth American League pennant in 1974, with Jackson hitting 29 homers for the season, and went on to defeat the Los Angeles Dodgers for their third straight World Series Championship. Finally, in 1975, after winning the American League Western Division Title and losing the pennant to the Boston Red Sox, Jackson, who had hit more homers and struck out more often than anyone on the team, ended his nine year stint with the Oakland Athletics. After unsuccessful contract negotiations, Finley traded Jackson to the Baltimore Orioles on April 2, 1976. The end of that season found Jackson a free agent, signed on with the New York Yankees for $300,000, and a five year contract, when Baltimore could not agree with Jackson's long term contract demands.

As a member of the New York Yankees, Jackson's ego and temper flared. He referred to himself as "the straw that stirs the drink," according to *Jet* magazine in a January 25, 1993 article. His comments and behavior antagonized his peers. Once again Jackson fought with teammates, his manager, Billy Martin, and the team owner, George Steinbrenner. And once again he led his team to the World Championship. The night of October 18, 1977 was one of Jackson's greatest triumphs. In the final game of the World Series, he hit three consecutive home runs, drove in five runs and brought the Yankees to victory over the Dodgers, winning 8-4. He had hit a Series record-breaking five home runs. "Maybe now, for at least this one night, I can feel like a real superstar," he was quoted in the *Lincoln Library of Sports Champions*. According to an article in *New York* written by Mike Lupica, Jackson had amazed himself on the day of the final game when during batting practice he hit 20 balls out of 40 into the seats. Amazingly enough, he had three more left to hit that night. He was named MVP of the World Series that fall and ended the season with 32 homers, 110 runs batted in (RBIs) and a .286 batting average.

Jackson followed that spectacular season with a second Series win against the Dodgers in 1978. He scored two runs, eight RBIs and batted .391. That year the first Reggie! chocolate candy bar appeared lasting only a short while as public interest waned. His walloping World Series hitting earned him the title "Mr. October," as he could always be counted on to pull his team to victory in a clinch.

1980 proved to be another fine season as Jackson hit a career high of .300 with 41 home runs and 111 RBIs. The Yankees won the American League pennant in 1981. In keeping with his fashion of coming through for the team, he hit his tenth and final Series home run that year. The California Angels signed Jackson on in 1982, and in a stunning achievement he reached the 500-homer plateau in 1984. Before retiring in 1987, he rejoined the Oakland Athletics for one last season. He was placed sixth on the all-time major leagues career home run list with 563 home runs during his 21 year baseball career. After retiring, Jackson worked briefly as a sports broadcaster for the Angels before moving on to coach for the Athletics. Dissatisfied with his coaching responsibilities he took a job with the Upper Deck Company handling sales of trading cards and sports collectibles.

The crowning achievement of his career came on August 1, 1993 when Reggie Jackson became the 216th inductee into the Baseball Hall of Fame—the only player to be so honored in that year. On his plaque he chose to be shown in the Yankee stripes, the uniform he found most fitting. Speaking of New York in the January issue of *Jet*, he said, "I feel this is the place that's really claimed me." His plaque lists him as sixth on the all-time list, ahead of such greats as Mickey Mantle, Ted Williams, and Lou Gehrig. His remarkable achievements run to both extremes: ten World Series home runs; five World Championships; 11 American League Championships with three different teams; and holding the major league record for lifetime strikeouts at 2,597. "Strung together, that's five years." Jackson quipped in Michael Angeli's article, "for five years I never touched the ball." At the induction, a passionate and eloquent Jackson spoke of the game he loved and his debt to the first Black Major League players, Jackie Robinson and Larry Doby. Quoting Lou Gehrig he ended by calling himself "the luckiest man on the face of the earth," as noted in *Jet*, August 16, 1993. The Yankees retired his number 44 baseball uniform and the Reggie! bar was reintroduced the year of Jackson's induction, packaged with a specially designed Reggie baseball card put out by Upper Deck.

During the Summer of 1993, George Steinbrenner announced that his former ballplayer was returning to the club in the capacity of special assistant and advisor to the Yankees general partners. Jackson continued his work in California for the trading card company and was made director of new buisness at a California-based computer company for which he was already a spokesman. However, Jackson still took on the added responsibility of evaluating players for the team, returning to New York one week out of each month. Given his celebrity status Jackson felt his presence was an asset to the ball club. Speaking of his fans to Mike Lupica in *Esquire* he noted, "If I walked out there right now, I could still stop the . . . place cold."

Jackson was emphatically disinterested in a career in sports broadcasting for the future. "I don't want to rip players," he stated in Angeli's article. "I don't want to talk on the air condescendingly about players. I know what it's like to try . . . and look like a bum." But he was open to the possibility of coaching for the Yankees down the road. "Never say never," he told Lupica. Going on to talk about his role with the ball club in the Angeli article, Jackson stated, "I'm very happy doing what I'm doing. I'm about as high as I can get here in this company without owning it. . . . I got it all."

Further Reading

Esquire, June 1993, pp. 69-71.
Jet, January 25, 1993, p. 46; May 1993, p. 47; August 16, 1993, p. 51; September 6, 1993, p. 51.
New York, April 19, 1993, pp. 158-160.
New Yorker, August 2, 1993, pp. 40-41.
Sports Illustrated, August 2, 1993, pp. 58-64. □

Robert Houghwout Jackson

Robert Houghwout Jackson (1892-1954) was an associate justice of the U.S. Supreme Court and chief American prosecutor at the Nuremberg war trials.

Robert H. Jackson was born on Feb. 13, 1892, in Spring Creek, Pa. He spent a year at the Albany Law School, apprenticed with a local lawyer, and was admitted to the bar in 1913. He set up practice in Jamestown, N.Y.

A passionate Democrat, Jackson supported New York's governor Franklin Roosevelt. After Roosevelt's election to the U.S. presidency in 1932, Jackson went to Washington to serve as general counsel of the Bureau of Internal Revenue. After serving as assistant attorney general in charge of the Tax Division of the Department of Justice, and then as head of the Antitrust Division, he was named solicitor general in 1938. In 1940 he became attorney general and in 1941 took his oath as associate justice of the Supreme Court.

During Jackson's tenure one of the chief public issues was the role and power of the Supreme Court. In his book *The Struggle for Judicial Supremacy* (1941) Jackson castigated the Court's willingness to establish itself as a superlegislature over the decisions of the popularly elected Congress and president; he called for a more restrained role. With some notable exceptions, Jackson continued this argument throughout his years on the Court. In one of his first major opinions, in 1942, the Federal government was granted extremely broad powers of economic regulation under the interstate commerce clause of the Constitution. Concerning the nation's economy, supremacy was placed firmly in the hands of Congress.

Devoted to civil liberties, Jackson worked to determine how the Court could protect unpopular minorities against persecution and oppression by inflamed majority rule. In 1943 he delivered an opinion for the Court upholding the constitutional right of Jehovah's Witnesses (a religious group) to refuse to salute the American flag. Toward the end of his life, however, he joined Justice Felix Frankfurter in thinking that the Court should play a relatively minor role in protecting civil liberties. In his posthumous *The Supreme Court in the American System of Government* (1955), Jackson attacked the civil libertarian views of his colleagues Hugo Black and William O. Douglas.

Justice Jackson left the Court for a year in 1945-1946 to serve as the chief United States prosecutor at the Nuremberg war trials in Germany. Two books by him came out of this experience: *The Case against the Nazi War Criminals*

(1946) and *The Nuremberg Case* (1947). He died on Oct. 9, 1954, in Washington.

Further Reading

There is no scholarly biography of Jackson. Eugene C. Gerhart, *America's Advocate: Robert H. Jackson* (1958), is useful but biased in Jackson's favor. *Dispassionate Justice: A Synthesis of the Judicial Opinions of Robert H. Jackson,* edited by Glendon Schubert (1969), contains an interesting introduction. □

Shirley Ann Jackson

Shirley Ann Jackson (born 1946), a theoretical physicist, was the first African American woman to earn a Ph.D. at MIT. In 1995, President Bill Clinton appointed her as chairwoman of the Nuclear Regulatory Commission. During her tenure, Jackson has instituted massive crackdowns on the nuclear power industry's violations.

S hirley Ann Jackson is a theoretical physicist who has spent her career researching and teaching about particle physics —the branch of physics which uses theories and mathematics to predict the existence of subatomic particles and the forces that bind them together. She was the first African American woman to receive a Ph.D. from the Massachusetts Institute of Technology (MIT), and she spent many years conducting research at AT & T Bell Laboratories. She was named professor of physics at Rutgers University in 1991 and is the recipient of many honors, scholarships, and grants.

Jackson was born on August 5, 1946, in Washington, DC. Her parents, Beatrice and George Jackson, strongly valued education and encouraged her in school. Her father spurred on her interest in science by helping her with projects for her science classes. At Roosevelt High School, Jackson attended accelerated programs in both math and science, and she graduated in 1964 as valedictorian. Jackson began classes at MIT that same year, one of fewer than twenty African American students and the only one studying theoretical physics. While a student she did volunteer work at Boston City Hospital and tutored students at the Roxbury YMCA. She earned her bachelors degree in 1968, writing her thesis on solid-state physics, a subject then in the forefront of theoretical physics.

Although accepted at Brown, Harvard, and the University of Chicago, Jackson decided to stay at MIT for her doctoral work, because she wanted to encourage more African American students to attend the institution. She worked on elementary particle theory for her Ph.D., which she completed in 1973. Her research was directed by James Young, the first African American tenured full professor in MIT's physics department. Jackson's thesis, ''The Study of a Multiperipheral Model with Continued Cross-Channel Uni-

tarity,'' was subsequently published in the *Annals of Physics* in 1975.

Jackson's area of interest in physics is the study of the subatomic particles found within atoms, the tiny units of which all matter is made. Subatomic particles, which are usually very unstable and short-lived, can be studied in several ways. One method is using a particle accelerator, a device in which nuclei are accelerated to high speeds and then collided with a target to separate them into subatomic particles. Another way of studying them is by detecting their movements using certain kinds of nonconducting solids. When some solids are exposed to high-energy particles, the crystal lattice structure of the atoms is distorted, and this phenomenon leaves marks or tracks that can be seen with an electron microscope. Photographs of the tracks are then enhanced, and by examining these photographs physicists like Jackson can make predictions about what kinds of particles have caused the marks.

As a postdoctoral student of subatomic particles during the 1970s, Jackson studied and conducted research at a number of prestigious physics laboratories in both the United States and Europe. Her first position was as research associate at the Fermi National Accelerator Laboratory in Batavia, Illinois (known as Fermilab) where she studied hadrons—medium to large subatomic particles that include baryons and mesons. In 1974 she became visiting scientist at the accelerator lab at the European Center for Nuclear Research (CERN) in Switzerland. There she explored theories of strongly interacting elementary particles. In 1976 and 1977, she both lectured in physics at the Stanford Linear

Accelerator Center and became a visiting scientist at the Aspen Center for Physics.

Jackson joined the Theoretical Physics Research Department at AT & T Bell Laboratories in 1976. The research projects at this facility are designed to examine the properties of various materials in an effort to discover useful applications. In 1978, Jackson became part of the Scattering and Low Energy Physics Research Department, then in 1988 she moved to the Solid State and Quantum Physics Research Department. At Bell Labs, Jackson explored theories of charge density waves and the reactions of neutrinos, one type of subatomic particle. In her research, Jackson has made contributions to the knowledge of such areas as charged density waves in layered compounds, polaronic aspects of electrons in the surface of liquid helium films, and optical and electronic properties of semiconductor strained-layer superlattices. On these topics and others she has prepared or collaborated on over 100 scientific articles.

Jackson has received many scholarships, including the Martin Marietta Aircraft Company Scholarship and Fellowship, the Prince Hall Masons Scholarship, the National Science Foundation Traineeship, and a Ford Foundation Advanced Study Fellowship. She has been elected to the American Physical Society and selected a CIBA-GEIGY Exceptional Black Scientist. In 1985, Governor Thomas Kean appointed her to the New Jersey Commission on Science and Technology. Then in the early 1990s, Governor James Florio awarded her the Thomas Alva Edison Science Award for her contributions to physics and for the promotion of science. Jackson is an active voice in numerous committees of the National Academy of Sciences, the American Association for the Advancement of Science, and the National Science Foundation, where her aim has been to actively promote women in science. Her most recent assignment came in 1995, when she was appointed head of the Nuclear Regulatory Commission by President Bill Clinton.

Jackson is very involved in university life at Rutgers University, where in addition to being professor of physics she is also on the board of trustees. She is a lifetime member of the MIT Board of Trustees and was formerly a trustee of Lincoln University. She is also involved in civic organizations that promote community resources and developing enterprises. She is married and has one son.

Further Reading

Carwell, Hattie, *Blacks in Science: Astrophysicist to Zoologist,* Exposition Press, 1977, p. 60.
Notable Black American Women, Gale, 1992, pp. 565–566.
Blacks in Science and Medicine, Hemisphere, 1990, p. 130. □

Thomas Jonathan Jackson

The American Thomas Jonathan "Stonewall" Jackson (1824-1863) was a Confederate hero and one of the outstanding Civil War generals.

Thomas Jackson was born on Jan. 21, 1824, at Clarksburg, Va. After the deaths of his father in 1826 and his mother in 1831, he was raised by his uncle. He went to local schools and then attended the U.S. Military Academy (1842-1846), graduating in time to join the 1st Artillery Regiment as a brevet second lieutenant in the Mexican War. Following service at the siege of Veracruz and at Cerro Gordo, he became a second lieutenant and transferred to a light field battery. While engaged in the fighting around Mexico City, Jackson received promotion to first lieutenant and later won brevets to captain and major.

Military Instructor

After the Mexican War, Jackson served at Ft. Columbus and at Ft. Hamilton. In 1851 he accepted a position as professor of philosophy and artillery tactics at Virginia Military Institute, where he proved a dedicated but inept instructor.

On Aug. 4, 1853, Jackson married Elinor Junkin of Lexington, Va., who died, with her baby, in childbirth in October 1854. After a tour of Europe in 1856, he married Mary Anna Morrison; they had a daughter. In December 1859 he commanded the cadet artillery at the hanging of abolitionist John Brown. He voted for John C. Breckinridge, the presidential candidate of the Southern Democrats in 1860, but hoped the Union would not be dissolved.

First Bull Run

When Virginia seceded from the Union in April 1861, Jackson traveled to Richmond with the cadet corps. The state government immediately commissioned him a colonel and sent him to Harpers Ferry. There he relinquished command to Joseph E. Johnston and became a brigade commander and brigadier general. At the First Battle of Bull Run on July 21, when Jackson's brigade reinforced the Confederate left to stem the Union attack, Gen. Bernard E. Bee rallied his men with the words, "There is Jackson standing like a stone wall." The Confederates drove back the Union advance, and Jackson won a new name.

Shenandoah Valley Campaigns

In October 1861 Jackson became a major general, and in November he received command of the Shenandoah Valley district of Virginia. On March 23 his attack on the Federal army at Kernstown forced the diversion of troops intended to reinforce the Union army moving against Richmond.

Jackson attacked an enemy force at McDowell in May 1862 and then struck another Union army at Front Royal, driving it back to the Potomac. He withdrew and fought off converging Union armies at Cross Keys and at Port Republic. Thus, with 16,000 men he had diverted 60,000 Federal troops from the Richmond campaign.

Seven Days Battles

Jackson then joined his forces with those of Gen. Robert E. Lee outside Richmond and began the Seven Days Battles to defend the Confederate capital against Gen. George McClellan's army. Tired and unfamiliar with the country, Jackson moved slowly and failed to flank the enemy position at Beaver Dam Creek. His troops did participate in the successful attack at Gaines's Mill on June 27 and pursued the Union army to White Oak Swamp. There, because of personal fatigue, he again failed to press the Union retreat as expected. Some of his men were among those repulsed at Malvern Hill on July 1.

Second Bull Run

In mid-July of 1862 Lee detached Jackson and his men to meet the advance of a new Union army under Gen. John Pope in northern Virginia. At Cedar Run on August 9 Jackson defeated part of that command. He led his force around the Union right flank and destroyed its supply base at Manassas on August 27. He then withdrew to Groveton, where he held off attacks while waiting for Lee. When Lee had reunited his forces, Jackson's men joined in a successful counterattack that drove the Union army from the field in the Second Battle of Bull Run on June 30.

Harpers Ferry, Sharpsburg, Fredericksburg

In September 1862 Lee advanced into Maryland and sent Jackson ahead with five divisions to capture the Union garrison of 11,000 men at Harpers Ferry. Jackson surrounded the town, which surrendered on September 15, then hurried north to help Lee beat off Union attacks at Sharpsburg on September 17. Lee withdrew into Virginia after the battle to recruit and reorganize his army. In October, Jackson received promotion to lieutenant general and became commander of the new 2d Corps.

In November 1862 the Confederate army moved east to meet a Union advance at Fredericksburg, Va. Lee placed his troops on the hills south of the town, with Jackson's corps on the right. On December 13 Gen. Ambrose Burnside attacked across the Rappahannock River with two columns, one aimed at Jackson's position. Though Burnside broke through a gap between two Confederate brigades, reinforcements drove the attackers back to the river. The entire Union assault was repulsed with heavy losses.

Chancellorsville and Mortal Injury

In late April 1863 Gen. Joseph Hooker decided to turn the Confederate left flank by crossing the Rappahannock River above Fredericksburg, while part of Lee's 1st Corps had been diverted to southern Virginia and North Carolina. Lee sent Jackson's corps around the Union position at Chancellorsville to strike it from the rear. Late in the afternoon of May 2, Jackson launched an attack that routed the Union right wing and drove it back almost to Chancellorsville. As Jackson returned with his staff from scouting Union lines, his left arm was broken by shots from his own men who mistook the riders for Union troops. The arm required amputation before Jackson was removed south to Guiney's Station, Va., for rest and recovery. There he developed pneumonia and died on May 10, 1863.

Stonewall Jackson was a masterful military strategist. He campaigned with aggressiveness and audacity; he moved rapidly; he was tenacious in defense and pursuit. His victories made him a hero in the Confederacy and won him the accolades of military historians, who consider him among America's greatest generals.

Further Reading

The most detailed analysis of Jackson's personal life and military campaigns is Lenoir Chambers, *Stonewall Jackson* (2 vols., 1959). The best one-volume biography is Frank E. Vandiver, *Mighty Stonewall* (1957). Of the older biographies, two are most useful: one by Jackson's chief of staff (in early 1862), Robert L. Dabney, *Life and Campaigns of Lieut.-Gen. Thomas J. Jackson* (2 vols., 1864-1866); the other by a British army officer, G. F. R. Henderson, *Stonewall Jackson and the American Civil War* (2 vols., 1898). □

John Edward Jacob

During his term as president of the National Urban League, John E. Jacob (born 1934) pushed for the social and economic progress of African Americans and other minority groups.

"America will become a second-rate power unless we undertake policies to insure that our neglected minority population gets the education, housing, health care and job skills they need to help America compete successfully in a global economy," John E. Jacob, president of the National Urban League, told Martin Tolchin in the *New York Times.* Reiterated in his annual address to the organization, titled "The State of Black America," Jacob's efforts are often controversial; he repeatedly attacks what he views as the indifference of the American political system to the plight of the disadvantaged. During the 1980s, he called for the withdrawal of billions of dollars from the military budget to be used for training minorities to become skilled laborers. Jacob commented to Ari L. Goldman in the *New York Times,* "America has only one hope of entering the 21st century as a world power and a global economic force. That is its ability to achieve racial parity and to make full use of the African Americans and minorities it has so long rejected."

Born December 16, 1934, in Trout, Louisiana, Jacob is the son of Baptist minister Emory Jacob and his wife Claudia. Emory eventually moved the family to Houston, Texas, where he worked in carpentry and construction to supplement the small income he received from the church. "I grew up so poor," Jacob recalled to Luix Overbea in the *Christian Science Monitor.* "Two rooms and a kitchen for seven people. No gas. No electricity. We did our homework by the light of a kerosene lamp and bathed in a washtub in the kitchen." He told Jacqueline Trescott in the *Washington Post* that his parents' "very rigid middle-class standards,"

including "southern Baptist principles—no drinking, no dancing, no card playing, no movies on Sunday," saved the family from the "syndrome of poverty." "The overriding principle," Jacob related to Trescott, "was 'Do unto others as you would have them do unto you. . . . ' You had to do well in school; you had to work. I can never remember not working. You could not create any problems for anybody, at any time. So we grew up straight, upright, good, well-mannered, smart poor kids."

In 1957 Jacob received a bachelor's degree in economics from Howard University in Washington, D.C.; an E. E. Worthing scholarship made college possible. After spending a brief period in the U.S. Army where he achieved the rank of second lieutenant, he returned to Washington. His first job, as a post office clerk, was secured several months later with the intervention of the office of Senator Lyndon B. Johnson. Jacob experienced frustration that his employment opportunities were limited because of his race. "I hated the work [in the post office]," he told Trescott. "I went to work mad, I came home mad."

Two years of postal work preceded Jacob's employment as a public assistance caseworker with the Baltimore Department of Public Welfare in 1960, a position he held while pursuing his masters degree in social work at Howard University. During his five years with the department, Jacob was made child welfare supervisor, a post he considered his most difficult. He explained to Trescott that when taking a child from a parent, you "just have to hope you are right, that what you are doing is right for the child and the parent, at least for the child." In 1965, two years after Jacob completed his masters degree, he was appointed director of education and youth incentives at the Washington Urban League.

Established Leader in His Field

After the turbulent summer of 1967, when racial tensions resulted in urban riots across the United States, Jacob oversaw the creation of Project Alert in the nation's capitol. Rioting in Washington was confined to one day, and 34 persons were arrested for disruptive acts, including arson and looting. The Washington Urban League responded by becoming a liaison for the community; youths from the ghetto were recruited as leaders to bring slum residents' problems to the League, which then directed families to appropriate social services. By 1968, when Jacob was named acting executive director of the Washington Urban League, he led his organization's participation in several other development programs, including the Ford Foundation-funded Operation Equality and the government-funded Project Enable (Education and Neighborhood Action for a Better Living Environment).

During the 1970s, Jacob served as the head of several levels of the National Urban League, including director of community organizing and training for the League's eastern region and director of the San Diego Urban League. In 1975, he returned to the east coast as president of the Washington Urban League and in 1979 was appointed executive vice-president of the National Urban League. The League was renowned for its passage of progressive acts against racial discrimination throughout the 1970s, particularly the 1972 federal Employment Opportunity Act. The Supreme Court upheld the legality of the organization's affirmative action programs, which required those corporations seeking federal contracts to integrate their workforce under specific guidelines involving racial quotas for hiring and promotions.

When National Urban League chief executive Vernon Jordan, was seriously injured in an assassination attempt in 1980, Jacob became acting chief executive of the League. Jordan retired in 1982, and Jacob was subsequently elected to the presidency of the organization by unanimous vote. By this time, the politics of the country had changed under Republican President Ronald Reagan, who was opposed to affirmative action and mandatory busing of school children to desegregate public schools. Under the Reagan administration, several policies, including cutbacks in federal social programs, increased the strain on the financially beleaguered National Urban League. Jacob was outspoken in his objections to the administration, citing in particular its appointment of a conservative majority to the Civil Rights Commission; the result, he felt, would be a weakening of the agencies that protected civil rights. The 1980s also marked the Supreme Court ruling that valid employment seniority systems take precedence over the protection of minority jobs in *Firefighters v. Stotts*. Additionally, suits filed by the Justice Department against public employers who used the affirmative action tactics of quotas and specific numerical goals increased significantly. Jacob responded by joining other civil rights groups in their boycott of the hearings on employment quotas by the Civil Rights Commission.

Called for Domestic Marshall Plan

During the early 1980s, Jacob formulated a new philosophy for the National Urban League that was similar to the 1947 Marshall Plan initiated by the United States to assist the recovery of European nations after World War II. Aid was sought from private sectors to facilitate entry-level job training programs, and Jacob proposed the League give direct assistance from its own resources to poverty-stricken minorities and whites, including housing and job placement. In addition, he suggested the federal government institute full employment through substantial public works and job training programs, and he joined other civil rights groups in supporting economic boycotts against private industry to induce corporate funding for developing markets and jobs for racial minorities.

Jacob is an adherent of self-help, particularly as advocated by black churches, civil rights and social welfare agencies, and community-led groups. He outlined various strategies—tutoring and counseling to raise Scholastic Aptitude Test (SAT) scores, a comprehensive teenage pregnancy prevention plan, and a male responsibility program for fatherhood and parenthood—for addressing contributing factors to the cycle of poverty in black America. Key issues he cited were the plight of unwed, adolescent mothers who often dropped out of school and entered welfare roles, the nearly half of all black households headed by single women, and black victims of black crime. Jacob added

voter registration, education, and drug control to the League's agenda of top priorities, issues to be addressed through the nineties. "What has distinguished us organizationally, is that in addition to our civil rights portfolio," Jacob told *Ebony*, "we have always been a direct service organization." Reasoning that blacks should attack their internal problems themselves, he pointed out in *Ebony* that the Reagan years "may wind up being a blessing." Jacob reckoned, "As a people, we must remember that we are not as weak as we have allowed ourselves to be painted and we are not as strong as we *can* be."

During the presidency of George Bush—in the late 1980s and early 1990s—Jacob persisted in advocating an Urban Marshall Plan. Inspired by the lessening of tensions between the Eastern and Western worlds, he proposed that funding for the $50 billion project to train minority workers be transferred from the military budget. Although Bush declined an invitation to address the National Urban League when he was campaigning for the presidency, Jacob was encouraged by Bush's civil rights record in Congress. In 1989, Jacob praised Bush's administration to Julie Johnson in the *New York Times* for the "fresh winds of openness it has brought to our Government." When Bush was receptive to Jacob's domestic Marshall Plan proposals, Jacob welcomed dialogue with the new administration, but Bush's veto of the Civil Rights Act of 1990 soon soured the relationship. In the 1990s, Jacob faced repeated resistance to affirmative action in the courts and legislature, where conservative politicians, white and black, spurned government intervention programs in favor of self-reliance.

Warned of Economic Suicide

While acknowledging that self-reliance is a factor in social reform, Jacob postulates that self-help alone will not deter racial discrimination against blacks and other minorities. He asserts that government funding is necessary to provide fair competition at work and school and argues that the costs are justified to produce skilled laborers, capable of global competition. "Job discrimination is not only a civil rights issue—it's a form of economic suicide," Jacob remarked to Goldman, expressing his hope that the American work force will admit more Hispanics, women immigrants, and African-Americans.

Winner of numerous honorary degrees and social service awards, Jacob, as head of the National Urban League, oversees the operations of one of the largest black organizations in the country. The League—founded by black social worker George Edmund Hayes and white philanthropist Ruth Standish Baldwin in 1910 as the Committee on Urban Conditions among Negroes—began as an organization aiding black laborers from the South who migrated to northern urban areas at the beginning of the twentieth century. In 1911 the Committee combined with two other groups under the appellation the National League on Urban Conditions among Negroes. The National Urban League, an abbreviation of the original League's name, became the organization's designation when affiliates were chartered. Over the decades, the League has grown to encompass a national staff of more than 30,000 salaried workers and non-salaried volunteers and a national governing board made up of 60 trustees chosen from various fields, including churches, corporations, universities, youth groups, labor unions, and civic organizations. Funding from businesses, individuals, and nonprofit organizations, including the United Way, provides the large sum of money required to operate the National Urban League and its affiliates.

A longtime proponent of change, Jacob revealed his aspirations for American society in an address delivered at a conference on public policy and African-Americans. As quoted in *Vital Speeches,* the activist reminded the forum of the words of the late Episcopal Bishop of Washington, John Walker, who said, "It is God's will that we live together in peace. It's God's will that we grow beyond our racial animosities and that we must commit ourselves to continue that work." Jacob added, "That strikes me as a credo that will serve us well as we go about our business today, tomorrow and into eternity."

New Challenges Ahead

Jacob decided to announce his retirement in 1993 from the National Urban League. He stayed on as president and CEO of the organization until 1994 when accepting the position of executive vice president of Anheuser-Busch. His new responsibilities include working on the company's marketing strategies in minority and foreign markets and educating the public about Anheuser's other companies and theme parks.

Further Reading

"Climbing Jacob's New Ladder." *Black Enterprise,* September 1994, pp. 128-31.
Christian Science Monitor, July 19, 1985; July 22, 1986; January 15, 1987; July 31, 1987; August 2, 1988.
Ebony, March 1982; July 1989; August 1990.
Jet, February 6, 1984; February 10, 1986; February 1, 1988; August 22, 1988; October 18, 1993.
Newsweek, May 7, 1984; January 28, 1985.
New York Times, December 8, 1981; July 28, 1985; July 23, 1987; January 25, 1989; August 7, 1989; January 10, 1990; July 30, 1990; June 4, 1991.
Time, May 14, 1984; May 27, 1991.
USA Today, November 1988; March 1991.
Vital Speeches, October 19, 1989; January 15, 1990; May 1, 1991.
Washington Post, January 19, 1982. □

Abraham and Mary Putnam Jacobi

Abraham (1830-1919) and Mary Putnam (1834-1906) Jacobi, husband and wife, were foreign-born American physicians and humanitarians who greatly improved medical care in the United States.

Abraham Jacobi was born into a poverty-stricken family in Westphalia, Germany. With work and sacrifice, he was able to begin studying medicine at the University of Greifswald in 1848. He continued at the University of Göttingen but received his medical degree from the University of Bonn in 1851. Involved in the revolutionary movement in Germany in 1848, he was a friend of Karl Marx; his outspoken support led to imprisonment, but he escaped to England, where he tried unsuccessfully to establish a practice. In 1853 Jacobi arrived in Boston. He finally settled in New York City.

First American Pediatrician

Jacobi had always been concerned about diseases of infants and children. In 1857 he became a lecturer on the pathology of infancy and childhood at the College of Physicians and Surgeons. In 1860 he was appointed to the first chair of pediatrics at the New York Medical College. There he opened the first free clinic for children. In 1865 he held the chair of diseases of children in the medical department of the University of the City of New York. In 1870 he returned to the College of Physicians and Surgeons, where he taught for 32 years.

Pioneer Woman Physician

Mary Corinna Putnam, the daughter of publisher George Putnam, was born in London and at the age of 5 went to New York City with her family. She was an intelli-

Abraham Jacobi

gent young woman with a zeal for learning. Those who knew her were not surprised when she decided to become a physician and to confront the almost unanimous prejudice against admitting women into the profession. She graduated in 1863 from the New York College of Pharmacy and in 1864 from the Woman's Medical College in Philadelphia.

Putnam went to Paris in 1866 and unsuccessfully attempted to enroll at the famous École de Médecine, which did not admit women. She remained in Paris studying in less well-known schools and writing articles for American journals and newspapers. In January 1868 she was admitted by special permission of the minister of public instruction to a course of lectures in the École. A few months later she was allowed to matriculate and finally took her degree in medicine in 1871 with highest honors.

Putnam returned to New York City and began teaching in the Women's Medical College of the New York Infirmary, just opened by Dr. Elizabeth Blackwell and her surgeon sister, Dr. Emily Blackwell. At the same time she practiced medicine among the poor in the slums. When she applied for membership in the Medical Society of the County of New York, it was fortunate that an idealist, Abraham Jacobi, was president. She married the pediatrician in 1873, and they had two children. Her ability to diagnose and her insistence on the highest standards ranked her, with her husband, among America's great physicians.

Humanitarians and Reformers

The humanitarian concerns of the Jacobis were an important part of their lives. While other physicians were telling tuberculosis patients in the stifling slums to sleep with their heads resting on the fire escapes, Abraham Jacobi was asking why the slums must be tolerated. He joined Carl Schurz in calling for civil service reform, and his wife in advocating birth control. Mary Jacobi sought to obliterate myths and prejudices about women and urged women to show by study and scholarship that they were not inferior in scientific matters. She and the Blackwells were basically opposed to "separate but equal" medical schools and closed their own college as soon as Cornell University opened its doors to women.

Mary Jacobi's literary ability brought her Harvard's coveted Boyleston Prize (1876) for *The Question of Rest for Women during Menstruation*. The essay argued against the myth of incapacitation during the menses. Her humanitarianism led her to defend Native and African Americans and consumers. In 1894 she delivered a forceful address, which later became the book *Common Sense Applied to Woman Suffrage*.

In 1894 Abraham Jacobi was invited to assume the chair of pediatrics at the University of Berlin. He declined this honor, giving as his reason his firm belief in democracy. He was honored widely and was twice elected president of the American Pediatric Society and was president for one term of the Association of American Physicians, the New York Academy of Medicine, and the American Medical Association.

Mary Jacobi wrote close to 100 medical articles, as well as *The Value of Life, Physiological Notes on Primary Education and the Study of Language,* and *Stories and Sketches;* she also edited her husband's *Infant Diet.* She died of what she rightly diagnosed as a brain tumor in 1906.

Abraham Jacobi's eminence in American medicine made all the more tragic the fire at his home that burned his life's records, including diaries, notes, and letters, when he was in his 80s. He died in 1919. His writings were numerous; most were gathered in *Collectanea Jacobi* by William J. Robinson (1909). He had helped found the *American Journal of Obstetrics* in 1862. His monographs include *The Intestinal Diseases of Infancy and Children* (1887), and *The Therapeutics of Infancy and Childhood* (1896), which went through several editions.

Further Reading

For a good popular work on Abraham and Mary Putnam Jacobi see Rhoda Truax, *The Doctors Jacobi* (1952). Useful studies are *Life and Letters of Mary Putnam Jacobi,* edited by Ruth Putnam (1925), and *Mary Putnam Jacobi, M.D.: A Pathfinder in Medicine, with Selections from Her Writings and a Complete Bibliography,* edited by the Women's Medical Association of New York City (1925). □

Friedrich Heinrich Jacobi

Friedrich Heinrich Jacobi (1743-1819), a German philosopher of the Enlightenment, emphasized the philosophic dimensions of feeling and faith in opposition to the claims of pure reason.

On Jan. 25, 1743, F. H. Jacobi was born in Düsseldorf, the son of a wealthy sugar manufacturer. He prepared at Geneva for a business career and succeeded his father as head of the firm from 1764 to 1772. Friedrich retired in favor of a political career, first as a member of the governing council of two duchies and eventually as privy counselor to the Bavarian court. His household became an important center of German literature.

With his older brother, Johann Georg (1740-1814), a well-known romantic poet, Jacobi edited a journal and wrote several philosophical novels inspired by his studies of Jean Jacques Rousseau, C. A. Helvétius, and the 3d Earl of Shaftesbury. Jacobi's activities brought him into personal and literary contact with most of the central thinkers and writers of the German Enlightenment, including Gotthold Ephraim Lessing, Moses Mendelssohn, and J. W. von Goethe. In 1804 he became president of the Academy of Sciences in Munich, where he remained until his death on March 10, 1819.

The point of departure for Jacobi's thought is the antinomy, or seeming contradiction, between realism and idealism. Baruch Spinoza was a dogmatic realist who drew out the logical consequences of the traditional definition of substance as that which is the cause of itself. According to this view, there could be only one substance, an infinite

eternal being of which the world of nature is only a partial but determinate modification. The meaning of Spinoza's pantheism, or the identification of God with nature, was a subject of other disputes throughout the 19th century. Jacobi sided with those who thought that Spinoza was, in fact, an atheist who had reduced God to a logical, mathematical, and mechanistic concept of nature. Other writers and philosophers such as Johann Georg Hamann, Johann Gottfried von Herder, Lessing, and Mendelssohn held that Spinoza was the first religious thinker to seriously develop the philosophic dimensions of the concept of an infinite being. Largely through Jacobi's instigation the major figures of the Enlightenment produced an extensive literature of books, inquiries, and couterinquiries about Spinoza.

Jacobi saw in Spinoza the elimination of real subjectivity and in the philosophy of Immanuel Kant an opposite "nihilism of objects." Kant was the first to raise the critical question of how subjective consciousness arrives at a knowledge of things, and he concluded that ultimately we can know of things "only what we have placed in them." Thus for Kant, human experience is simply the appearance of the way things seem and are thought about according to the subjective conditions of the mind. Objects as things-in-themselves are unknowable.

The point of these criticisms was to show that if reason begins with objects it is unable to account for subjectivity and a subjective perspective annihilates objectivity. The conclusion which Jacobi drew was that the enterprise of human reason itself rests on faith. Man's immediate certainty that there are real objects, which produce passive sensations, rests on faith. And if the concept of objective nature depends on faith, then man's feelings and intuitions of freedom, moral principles, and religious certainties need not defer to rational skepticism.

Further Reading

Friedrich Heinrich Jacobis Werke, 6 vols. (1812-1825), has never been translated. The only secondary source available in English is Alexander W. Crawford, *The Philosophy of F. H. Jacobi* (1905). For general background see Frederick J. Copleston, *A History of Philosophy,* vol. 6: *Wolff to Kant* (1964).

Additional Sources

Hegel, Georg Wilhelm Friedrich, *Faith & knowledge,* Albany: State University of New York Press, 1977. □

Harriet A. Jacobs

Harriet A. Jacobs (1823–1897) was a slave who decided she must run away in order to protect her children from harsh treatment by their owners.

Delilah Horniblow was a slave to Margaret Horniblow in the town of Edenton, North Carolina, just as Delilah's mother, Molly, had been for much of her life. In the early 1800s, slaves could not be officially married without the permission of their masters, so the marriage of Delilah to the carpenter Daniel Jacobs, a slave on a neighboring plantation owned by Dr. Andrew Knox, is not recorded. Nevertheless, Daniel and Delilah had two children together. In the autumn of 1813, Harriet Ann was born, followed two years later by John.

Harriet was just six years old when her mother died. There must have been no thought of sending her to live with her father; he was, after all, the property of another master. So Harriet went to live in the home of her late mother's (and therefore her own) master. Margaret Horniblow was a kind master—so kind that Harriet did not realize until her mother died that she herself had been born into slavery. For a few years, Harriet stayed with Horniblow, who taught her to sew, read, and spell.

Property of the Norcoms

In 1825, twelve-year-old Harriet's life took a turn for the worse. Margaret Horniblow died and left Harriet and her brother to her niece, Mary Norcom. Because Mary was a child and still lived at home, this essentially made Harriet the property of Mary's father, Dr. James Norcom. Harriet and her brother became house slaves for the doctor.

Grandmother Molly

Harriet's grandmother, Molly, was more fortunate. When her owner, Elizabeth Horniblow, died, Molly, along with her son Mark, was sold to Hannah Pritchard, an aunt of the Horniblows. Just four months later, Mrs. Pritchard gave

Molly her freedom. In a short time, Jacobs's grandmother had earned enough from her cooking to buy the freedom of her son. Fortunately for Jacobs and her brother, the two free relatives moved into a house not far from that of the Norcoms. Jacobs could sometimes visit her grandmother, and the family remained in contact.

Unwanted advances

The Norcom house was not a pleasant one. Mrs. Norcom distrusted her husband, and for good reason. Dr. Norcom pursued other women, and soon began to make advances toward Jacobs. Suspicious, Mrs. Norcom took out her fears in threats and abuses on the innocent slaves. By the time Jacobs was sixteen, Norcom's advances and the abuse from his wife had become unbearable. Perhaps thinking that Norcom would leave her alone if she began having an affair with another man, Jacobs took up with one of the doctor's white neighbors, Samuel Sawyer, and became pregnant. When the suspicious Mrs. Norcom learned the news, she threatened Jacobs, prompting the doctor to send her off to live with her grandmother. It was there that Jacobs's son, Joseph, was born.

The Nat Turner affair

Jacobs and her son were living with Molly when the Nat Turner incident took place in Virginia in 1831. Turner and some other slaves had staged a rebellion in which white slave owners and their families were killed. More than fifty slaves joined the rampage. By the time white farmers could gather a militia to stop the uprising, the rebels had killed fifty-five whites.

The event alarmed the white southerners, who armed themselves and proceeded to terrorize blacks, free or slave. The news of the Nat Turner Rebellion reached Edenton early in 1832, just after white men had held their annual muster, a yearly show of the militia to demonstrate its strength. Now it was announced that a second muster would be held and men came into town from all over the territory. Poor whites who were hired to search for signs of rebellion among the blacks tore through black family homes looking for weapons or signs that the blacks might join Turner's Rebellion. A band broke into Molly's house, threatened Jacobs and the others, and tore up everything in the house in search of any sign that the residents should be punished.

For two weeks whites roved the streets and spread into the farmland outside the town. Blacks suspected of plotting to join the rebellion were whipped and otherwise tortured. A black minister was taken off to be shot after a few bits of gunshot were found in his house. Black men from the farmlands were bound and tied to the saddles of horsemen who forced them to run to the jail yard in town. Black homes and black churches were destroyed. Eventually, calmer whites restored peace and innocent blacks who had been held in prison were released. Black slaves were returned to their owners, and the black community began to recover.

"Breaking" Jacobs

In 1833, Jacobs was still carrying on an affair with Samuel Sawyer and her daughter Louisa was born. Soon after, Dr. Norcom again began making sexual demands on Jacobs. By 1835, the doctor had become so aggravated by her refusals that he sent her to be a slave on his nearby plantation. Forced to leave her son with her grandmother so that he could recover from an illness, Jacobs joined about fifty other slaves on the estate. Norcom planned to send her son to the plantation as soon as possible. In the meantime, however, Jacobs was to be punished for her failure to submit to his advances. Norcom's son, who was master at the new plantation, would "break her" and train her son and daughter to be slaves worthy of being sold. In Jacobs's words: "I heard Mr. [Norcom] say to a neighbor, ''I've got her down here, and I'll soon take the town notions out of her head. My father is partly to blame for her nonsense. He ought to have broke her in long ago.''

Plantation slavery

Jacobs was committed to making the best of the situation. Assigned the task of getting the house ready for young Mr. Norcom's new bride, she performed her assignments faithfully even when daughter Louisa had to remain unattended in the kitchen for long periods of time. Still, Jacobs worried about Louisa each time she saw a child of one of the slaves knocked out of the way or beaten for being too near the master. She worried also about her own well being when she saw that the mothers of these children had been so thoroughly whipped, physically and in spirit, that they raised no protest over the brutality to their children.

One day about noon, Louisa, who was feeling ill, disappeared from her place near a window of the room in which her mother was working. Jacobs went in search of the child and found her sound asleep in the cool space below the house, where earlier that day a large snake had been seen. The worried mother decided to send her child away for safe keeping. The next day, Louisa was put in a cart carrying shingles to town. She would remain with her great-grandmother until she was strong again. Norcom protested that he should have been asked for permission to do this, but he allowed Louisa to leave. At two years old, she was of no use to him.

The treatment of slaves

Jacobs was treated differently from most slaves on the plantation. During the first six weeks of her stay, as she prepared every room and every bit of furniture for the coming of the new Mrs. Norcom, she saw other slaves being treated much more harshly than she. In the fields, men, women, and children frequently were beaten for the slightest offense—beaten until, as Jacobs described it, pools of blood surrounded their feet. Because permanently scarred slaves brought lower prices on the trading block, brine, or salted water, often would be poured over the open flesh to make the wounds heal more rapidly.

Slave managers controlled every action on the plantation. On the Norcom plantation these overseers gave each male slave a weekly allotment of three pounds of meat, a peck (about eight quarts) of corn, and some herring. Women received half as much meat, and children over twelve and a half received half the allowance of the women.

Jacobs did not sleep in the huts arranged for the slaves, but rather, in the "great house." The young Mr. Norcom was beginning to have ideas like those of his father. Mrs. Norcom agreed to have Jacobs in the house but refused to allow her a bed. Instead, Jacobs had to sleep on the floor. She was willing to endure this treatment for the safety of her children. But when she learned that the owners were planning to bring her children back to the plantation to be "broken in" with the idea of selling them, Jacobs realized she had to take action. Her own children were being used to force her to submit to Norcom and his son. She felt she had no choice but to run away.

Jacobs knew the risks she would encounter as a runaway slave. Her uncle Joseph had been so mistreated by his owner that he had knocked the man down and run away. Upon his capture, he was chained, jailed for six months, and then sold to an owner in far-off New York. Other runaways who had been captured had not fared so well as her uncle. Yet Jacobs reasoned that her children would be of less interest to the Norcoms if she was not there. So one dark night in 1835, she fled from the plantation and hid in the home of a friend.

The search begins

When the Norcoms learned of Jacobs's disappearance, they started a search. Unable to find her, Dr. Norcom took his anger out on Jacobs's relatives. Jacobs's Aunt Berry, her brother, and her children were all put in jail. Samuel Sawyer, perhaps troubled by the thought of his young children chained up in jail, arranged through a slave trader to buy the children and John. Sawyer then sent the children to live with Jacobs's grandmother, Molly.

Meanwhile, the Norcoms continued searching through the homes of Jacobs's friends. Her hiding place became unsafe for her and for the friend who sheltered her, so Jacobs's uncle arranged for her to steal out of the house at night and hide in a swamp. It was infested with mosquitos and snakes, but Jacobs judged it the better of two evils and bravely stayed there. For the moment, she was free of the Norcoms.

Her freedom was threatened, however, when a snake bit her. With her leg swollen and infected and with no way to treat the bite, it became necessary for Jacobs to move to another hiding place. Fortunately, Harriet's uncle Mark had been preparing for this. He had cut a carefully hidden hole in the ceiling of Molly's pantry. Above the hole was a small space between the pantry ceiling and the shingles of the roof.

Jacobs's family waited until dark one night to help Jacobs escape the swamp and take up permanent residence in the attic of Molly's house. Equipped with only a blanket and water, Jacobs settled into the cramped space, which allowed for neither sitting nor standing, nor for stretching out and rolling over comfortably.

The seven-year exile

Jacobs remained in this small space below the roof for seven years. Mark and Molly brought her food and talked with her at night when everyone else was asleep. On a few occasions Jacobs was lowered to sit with them in the dark pantry for brief moments, but all the while, the air was tense with the fear that Norcom would discover her hiding place. His home was just around the corner and his office a short distance away in the next block. He often passed by Molly's house on his way to work.

Jacobs sometimes saw Norcom through a small hole she had carved out between the rafters with a piece of metal. This tiny opening to the outside world brought a little air into the sometimes hot, sometimes cold and damp space. She could see a little of the street and Molly's yard through this hole. To make matters worse, she could see Joseph and Louisa playing in the yard and hear the grumblings and threats of the doctor as he passed them. Jacobs did not dare let her children know where she was; if she did, the truth might be forced out of them and everyone would suffer. (Later, Joseph remarked that he knew that she was there but did not dare tell anyone about it.)

Years passed with Jacobs stuck in her prison. Conditions in the small cell were nearly unbearable. Mosquitos pestered her, mice scurried around her, and rain drenched her, but Mark was afraid to fix the holes in the roof lest she be seen from the street. Cramped into her small cell, she began to lose strength in her legs. Still she felt that she was better off here than living as Dr. Norcom's slave. Finally, in 1842, after seven years, an opportunity came to leave her hiding place. One of her uncle's friends found a sea captain who was willing, for a fee, to take Jacobs to New York.

Runaway

Although Molly knew the conditions were gradually taking her granddaughter's health and strength, she urged Jacobs not to go. North Carolina runaways were subject to severe punishment if caught—chains, whippings (as many as 100 lashes or more), and even branding. One North Carolina owner ran an advertisement for his runaway, describing her as "burnt . . . with a hot iron on the left side of her face; I tried to make the letter M" (Stampp, p. 188). Some disgruntled owners offered a reward for the capture of a runaway, and would add more to that reward if the slave was returned dead. It was not uncommon to track runaways with dogs, which were sometimes not restrained from mauling the slave when he or she was found.

Jacobs knew that Norcom had already hired slave hunters to search for her in the North. While in the attic, Jacobs had written some letters to Norcom, and the family arranged for their delivery from New York. Her purpose was to distract the doctor from too close a search of the Horniblow house. Norcom had followed up on these letters at least once with a trip to New York to find her. If she really fled to the North, she would face the threat of slave hunters as well. Besides the constant threat of being caught, she would have to figure out a way to earn a living there. Knowing that she would be hunted, Jacobs still decided to go, convinced that her children would be better off if she could be free of Dr.

Norcom. At the last minute she disguised herself and went with her new friend to meet the boat.

Northward bound

Just before she left, Jacobs finally spoke to Joseph and Louisa, whom she had peeped at and heard below her for those long years but had not dared to involve in her criminal act of running away from slavery. It was during their brief meeting that she learned that Joseph had known her whereabouts for several years. He had heard her cough but had carefully kept the secret, often leading visitors away from his mother's corner of the house for fear that another cough would expose her hiding place.

New York

Jacobs arrived in New York in 1842 and was fortunate in her search for a job. She found work with the Willis family as nurse to their new baby daughter. She continued even after the death of Mary Willis and traveled with the family to England as caretaker of the Willises young daughter. All the while, Jacobs was sure that Sawyer, the father of her children, would free them now that he was their owner. He never did. John gained his freedom by running away, but her own children remained slaves.

Meanwhile, the younger Norcom died and his wife remarried. She wanted the slave property she believed she owned and made repeated attempts to capture Jacobs and her children, who had by that time joined her in New York. Whenever she heard a rumor about slave hunters or one of Mrs. Norcom's visits to New York, Jacobs would move to Boston, Massachusetts or some other distant place until the crisis passed. She was always on her guard.

Hunted or freed?

The year 1850 was an eventful one. The new Fugitive Slave Law encouraged bounty hunters to search northern cities for runaways, so it was more dangerous than ever for an escaped slave in the North. Meanwhile, Jacobs's family support was fading. She had not dared to contact her grandmother or John, and Joseph had headed out to the California gold mines. John and Joseph left her life forever, later moving to Australia to pursue their search for gold. Fortunately, her former employer, Mr. Willis, remarried and now he and his wife, Cornelia, wanted Jacobs to care for their baby. Cornelia proved to be as kind as the first Mrs. Willis.

At the end of the year, old Dr. Norcom died. His daughter, Mary Matilda, now had official legal ownership of Jacobs and the two children. She and her husband, Daniel Messmore, made several attempts to capture the family. In 1852, Messmore again returned to New York to find Jacobs, but without success. Cornelia had arranged for her to escape to Massachusetts once again. Frustrated, Messmore put the capture and disposal of Jacobs into the hands of a slave hunter.

Cornelia had often spoken of buying Jacobs's freedom, and Jacobs had as often protested being bought. But, with a slave hunter on the chase, Cornelia felt she had to act. She offered the slave hunter $300 for Jacobs and her two children. It was a small sum, but better than nothing, and the

slave hunter grudgingly accepted. In late 1852, Jacobs and her children were finally set free.

Antislavery work

For the rest of her life, Jacobs and Louisa worked actively in the antislavery movement. This work resulted in Jacobs writing her autobiography, which was published in England under the title *The Deeper Wrong*. In 1862 and 1863 Jacobs was in Washington, D.C., to help with relief work for runaway slaves.

When the Emancipation Act was passed in 1863, Jacobs and Louisa were living in Alexandria, Virginia, where they were distributing clothing and teaching health care. Then, with the surrender of General Robert E. Lee in 1865, Jacobs at last was free to return to Edenton, carrying relief supplies to the place where she had been imprisoned in a house that was now her own.

After a trip to England to raise money for an orphanage in Savannah, Georgia, Jacobs settled in Cambridge, Massachusetts, to operate a boarding house. She lived to see Louisa help organze the National Association of Colored Women in Washington. There, on March 7, 1897, Harriet Jacobs died.

Further Reading

Holland, Patricia G., and Milton Meltzer, eds., *The Collected Correspondence of Lydia Maria Child, 1817-1880,* Millwood, New York: Kraus Microform, 1980.

Jacobs, Harriet A., *Incidents in the Life of a Slave Girl Written by Herself,* Self-published, 1862. Cambridge: Harvard University Press, 1987.

Stampp, Kenneth M., *The Peculiar Institution: Slavery in Ante-Bellum South,* New York: Vintage Books, 1964. □

Jens Peter Jacobsen

The works of the Danish author Jens Peter Jacobsen (1847-1885) were the first in Danish literature to interpret man naturalistically.

Jens Peter Jacobsen was born at Thisted on April 7, 1847. For many years he was torn between science and literature, and he struggled all his life with a strong tendency to dream, an important theme in his writings. In 1873 he won a university gold medal for a scientific dissertation. His articles on Charles Darwin and his translations of *Origin of Species* and *Descent of Man* did much to spread Darwin's theories in Scandinavia. Parallel with his scientific work, he wrote poetry. In the early 1870s he became an influential member of the circle around Georg Brandes, who was beginning his agitation for a modern, realistic literature based on European models.

Jacobsen made his debut in 1872 with the story "Mogens," a controversial departure in Danish literature. Man is seen, for the first time, as an animal governed biologically like all other animals, rather than by forces—ideals—

outside himself. In 1873, full of plans for new scientific and literary work, Jacobsen was stricken with tuberculosis and told that he did not have long to live. He abandoned his scientific plans and devoted his last 12 years to literature, producing under the most difficult conditions two remarkable novels and a handful of poems and stories, a small production that yet ranks with the most original and enduring works in Danish literature.

Marie Grubbe (1876) is Denmark's first genuinely naturalistic novel. Jacobsen interprets his heroine, a historical person, in terms of her heredity and environment, showing with exquisite subtlety how these forces and her unconscious and semiconscious impulses determine her behavior. Jacobsen's technique, appropriate to the new view of man, is the literary equivalent of impressionism in painting.

Jacobsen's second novel, *Niels Lyhne* (1880), also a psychological novel, is a deeply personal study of a man living in a period of transition when a deistic view of life is succumbing to a naturalistic one. Niels is intellectually able to abandon the old views, but emotionally he fails, since he cannot find a new philosophy to give meaning to his life. The shadow of Jacobsen's own end is upon *Niels Lyhne,* and the central character (soon to become a common type in Scandinavian literature) is too deeply split, trapped in his biological prison, to realize his ambitions.

Jacobsen's novels and the best of his stories have had an important influence on Scandinavian literature for their penetrating psychology, their themes, and their style, which lift them out of the times in which they were written. Jacobsen died on April 30, 1885, at the age of 38.

Further Reading

Jacobsen's life and work are discussed in Alrik Gustafson, *Six Scandinavian Novelists* (1940; 2d ed. 1966), and Philip M. Mitchell, *A History of Danish Literature* (1957). ☐

Jacopone da Todi

The religious fervor of the Italian poet and mystic Jacopone da Todi (ca. 1236-1306) found expression in his "Laudario," a collection of personal religious poetry unique in early Italian literature.

Few facts are known concerning the life of Jacopone da Todi. He was born in Todi of the noble Benedetti family. By profession he was an attorney. His wife is said to have been Vanna di Bernardino di Guidone; according to tradition she shared her husband's worldly life until she died about 1268 in the collapse of a building during a dancing feast. Jacopone found that she was wearing a hair shirt under her festive dress, and this discovery determined his conversion to a religious life. For 10 years he lived in seclusion as a penitent before joining the Franciscan order. At the time, the order was divided in a struggle between the Conventuals, who favored a relaxed monastic rule, and the Spirituals, who strove for strict adherence to the original rule of absolute poverty. Jacopone was a strong advocate for the latter group.

Jacopone wrote several *laude* on the corruption of the Franciscan order. (The sacred ballad, or *lauda,* was a form popularized in 13th-century Umbria by confraternities of laymen devoted to public penitence and spiritual singing.) Another group of poems accuses the Church of corruption.

In 1294, a poor hermit, Pier da Morrone, became Pope Celestine V. Jacopone expressed his confidence in Celestine and went with a delegation to the Pope to request a special disposition for the Spirituals. The Pope granted them some autonomy within the Franciscan order as "poor hermits of Celestine." Jacopone's *laude* exalting poverty may belong to this period.

Celestine V was soon succeeded by Boniface VIII (December 1294), who revoked the disposition in favor of the Spirituals. Together with other Franciscans and some prelates, particularly the cardinals Jacopo and Pietro Colonna, protectors of the Spirituals, Jacopone signed a manifesto at Lunghezza (May 10, 1297) that declared Celestine's abdication and the election of Boniface invalid. Boniface excommunicated the rebels, and Cardinal Colonna withdrew to Palestrina with his supporters, including Jacopone. In September 1298 the papal militia occupied Palestrina, and Jacopone was imprisoned.

During his imprisonment Jacopone wrote of his own wretched state, offering all his troubles to God, his "tavern keeper." Jacopone was absolved from excommunication and released from prison by Boniface's successor, Benedict XI. He spent his last 3 years in his native Umbria at the convent of S. Lorenzo in Collazzone, where he died, probably on Christmas Day, 1306.

Jacopone wrote close to a hundred *laude.* They express his psychological and spiritual reflections, contempt for the world, horror of sin, and an impetuous love for God. His style is always energetic, sometimes crude, and starkly realistic. Many of his *laude* are in dialogue form; one of the most beautiful is *Il pianto della Madonna.*

Further Reading

Evelyn Underhill, *Jacopone da Todi, Poet and Mystic, 1228-1306: A Spiritual Biography* (1919), is the only full-length study of Jacopone da Todi in English. Eugenio Donadoni, *A History of Italian Literature,* vol. 1 (trans. 1969), is recommended for general background. ☐

Michael Philip Jagger

Michael Philip Jagger (born 1944) was the lyricist and lead singer for the world's most enduring rock 'n' roll band, the Rolling Stones.

Michael Philip Jagger was born in Dartford, Kent, England, on July 26, 1944, one of two sons of Eva and Joe Jagger. As a student at Dartford Grammar School Jagger had varied interests that included sports, history, American rock 'n' roll music, and especially the rhythm and blues music that had spawned rock 'n' roll. His favorite and most influential musicians were Muddy Waters, Chuck Berry, Bo Diddley, and Fats Domino. An excellent student, Jagger graduated from Dartford in 1962 and traveled to London to attend the London School of Economics on a government grant.

On a London train, Jagger recognized Keith Richard, a childhood Dartford acquaintance who played guitar and was studying art in London. They discovered that they shared an interest in music and decided to start a band. The third member, Brian Jones, was found at a Soho pub, and the three moved to a Chelsea flat to form their band. Their first performance was at the Marquee, a small London jazz club. Before their gig, they chose the name "The Rolling Stones" from Muddy Waters's song "The Rolling Stone Blues." Drummer Charlie Watts and bassist Bill Wyman completed the band, and they struggled for a year's time playing in mostly working-class London barrooms. Their first big break came in 1963 when they played at the Crawdaddy Club in Richmond, outside London. Their audience was a college crowd, and it was this age group, along with the even younger "teeny-boppers," that propelled them to fame and fortune. By the end of 1964 they had

Mick Jagger (pointing)

released three albums through Decca Records, were the most popular band in England, and were, at least for that year, more popular than the Beatles.

The Rolling Stones reached two milestones in the summer of 1965 with their first international hit single, "Satisfaction." First, it marked the beginning of their great American popularity, as it was number one on the American charts for six consecutive weeks. Second, it marked the emergence of Jagger and Richard as rock 'n' roll composers. While they had previously echoed the music of their mentors, they had now developed their own creative individual sound—that of a gutsy, hard-driving derivative of rhythm and blues. The sound was distinctively new, yet well-rooted in Black American music. From the *December's Children* album (1966) came "Get Off My Cloud," followed by "Paint It Black" from *Aftermath* (1966), and then "Let's Spend the Night Together" and "Ruby Tuesday" from *Between the Buttons* (1966).

At the core of the Rolling Stones was the harsh-voiced Jagger with his daring, racy, and raucous lyrics. Just as significant was his stage presence. Bedecked in tights, large belts, loose shirts, long scarves, and an occasional cape, Jagger pranced, preened, and strutted his slender frame about the stage. America first witnessed these theatrics briefly in 1964 and later in the group's major US tours in 1965 and 1966. As the Beatles became beloved, so too did the Rolling Stones, but in a completely different fashion. The Beatles, though long-haired and clothed in the "mod" fashions, had the good guys image, while the shaggy-haired Jagger and his ragged crew were branded as the bad boys of rock 'n' roll. Their rebellious young fans served to heighten that image.

The bad boy, evil reputation caught up with the group in 1967, and those that scorned them—including a hostile press—reveled as Jagger, Richard, and Jones received stiff prison sentences for a relatively mild drug offense that consisted of possession of "pep pills" from Italy. The convictions were overturned by a higher court, but new dissension problems faced the group. Their concerts stopped briefly, and a commercial low point was reached with their 1967 album, *Their Satanic Majesties Request,* an attempt at psychedelic music that was universally panned. This nadir was short-lived, however, as the group bounced back in 1968 with their best artistic efforts. The *Beggars Banquet* album featured "Street Fightin' Man" and Jagger's famous essay on world history from the viewpoint of Satan, "Sympathy for the Devil." *Let It Bleed* soon followed, with the Jagger/Richard masterpieces "Gimme Shelter" and "You Can't Always Get What You Want." Also released in 1968 was Jagger's imaginary biography—and Rolling Stone trademark—"Jumping Jack Flash." Off-stage Jagger had become a connoisseur of art and expensive cars.

Upon the heels of success came tragedy, when the dissension-causing Brian Jones was dropped from the group in June 1969 and his drug difficulties caused his drowning death a month later. Mick Taylor was hired in his stead, and the release of "Honky Tonk Woman" (1969) set the stage for the Stones' successful American concert tour in the fall of 1969. Their final tour stop was at Altamont Speedway near

San Francisco, a fateful one, as the infamous Hell's Angels motorcycle gang, hired as bodyguards, beat fans until one was stabbed to death. This scene was captured on film in *Gimme Shelter* (1970), and it fueled and typified the criticism Jagger had received about inciting his audiences. Indeed, many of his concerts had been accompanied by violence, and Jagger decided to keep the group away from the United States, an exile that lasted for almost two years. During this time Jagger married Bianca Perez Morena de Macais, a model from Nicaragua, in 1971. His daughter Jade was born later that same year.

Jagger returned triumphantly to America in the summer of 1972 on a widely celebrated concert tour that earned Jagger vindication from the media. The group had outlasted the Beatles despite its problems, and their critically acclaimed *Exile on Main Street* album (1972) was the first of many more albums and singles released throughout and beyond the decade. These included *Sticky Fingers* (1973) with "Brown Sugar" topping the charts; *Goat's Head Soup* (1973) with the number one single "Angie"; *It's Only Rock and Roll* (1974); *Some Girls* (1978); *Tattoo You* (1981) with "Start Me Up" and "Waiting on a Friend"; *Under Cover of the Night* (1983) and *Dirty Work.*

Jagger and Bianca divorced in 1980 after twelve years of marriage. Jagger was involved with Texas-born model Jerry Hall, with whom he has had three children and finally married in 1990. Despite tabloid gossip, the couple were still married and expecting their fourth child in 1997. At the helm of the world's most enduring rock 'n' roll band, it was fitting that Jagger, clad in his usual stage garb, gave the most rousing performance of the record-setting Live Aid concert telethon before 92,000 fans in Philadelphia's John F. Kennedy Stadium and a worldwide television audience estimated at over one billion in 1985.

In 1981, the Rolling Stones were one of the first bands to accept corporate sponsorship (from Jovan Perfumes). Now a common occurrence, the band was criticized for "selling out" and, in fact, released two disappointing albums: *Undercover* (1983) and *Dirty Work* was released, Jagger and guitarist Keith Richards split up as a result of their ongoing struggle for creative control of the band. Jagger began a solo career and released *She's the Boss* (1985) and *Primitive Cool* (1987) to lukewarm reviews.

In 1989, Jagger and Richards not only resolved their differences, but re-grouped the band, were inducted into the Rock and Roll Hall of Fame in Cleveland, OH, released their first hit album, *Steel Wheels* in a decade, and went on tour for the first time in seven years.

In 1993, Jagger turned fifty and became a grandparent (his daughter Jade, by Bianca Jagger, gave birth to a daughter). The Rolling Stones were still together after thirty years. They signed to Virgin Records for $30 million. Jagger released his third solo album *Wandering Spirit* to good reviews and, despite replacing the retired Bill Wyman on bass with Darryl Jones, the Stones released *Voodoo Lounge* to critical acclaim. The album was said to be "the best Stones LP of the past two decades," by Jas Obrecht of *Guitar Player* magazine (October 1994) and compared to *Exile on Main*

Street and *Beggar's Banquet.* The band went on a world tour to support the album—their first US tour in thirty years.

Along with Stones guitarist Ron Wood and blues virtuoso Willie Dixon, Jagger released a predominantly acoustic album—*Stripped* in 1995, re-working such songs as Bob Dylan's "Like a Rolling Stone," "Shine a Light" from *Exile on Main Street,* "The Spider and the Fly" and "Love in Vain."

Jagger started his own film company, Jagged Edge, in 1996 and has been devoting his time to film projects and his family while working on new Stones material.

Further Reading

Mick Jagger was not a man of mystery but simply an extremely creative entertainer as well as an imaginative and excellent lyricist. Anthony Scaduto's biography *Mick Jagger* (1974) is mediocre at best and attempts to create a mystery about a man who was simply well-educated and brilliant. Jagger was also the subject of *Jagger Unauthorized* (1993): a revealing and, at times, embarrassing biography by Kate Meyers. The various rock music encyclopedias, especially *The Illustrated Encyclopedia of Rock* (1978) by Nick Logan and Bob Woffinden, are informative. Most elucidating is Mick Jagger's autobiography, *Mick Jagger In His Own Words* (1982) and interviews.

Additional Sources

"The Rolling Stones at 50," *Maclean's,* Feb. 15, 1993. "Mick Jagger," *Esquire,* April 1993. □

Jahangir

Jahangir (1569-1627), the fourth Mughal Emperor of India and patron of the arts, ruled for 22 years.

J ahangir was an amicable, liberal Muslim—an emperor who loved painting, architecture, and the fine arts. A successful and benevolent ruler, he cherished the well-being of his Indian subjects, revered both Hindu and Muslim saints, and improved social conditions without interfering with customs. But Jahangir was not without military ambitions. A capable soldier, he dreamt of conquering Transoxiana, the seat of the government of the early Timurids.

Jahangir was a child of many prayers—the eldest son of Akbar, one of the most notable rulers in Islamic history, and his Rajput wife Jodh Bai. The boy was brought up with all possible care and affection and when he grew up, arrangements were made for his education at the new capital, Fatehpur-Sikri. Expert tutors taught the prince Persian, Turki, Arabic, Hindi, arithmetic, history, and geography, but he was most influenced by Abdur Rahim Khan Khana, a versatile genius, soldier, and successful diplomat. Under his guidance, Prince Salim (Jahangir) also mastered the technique of composing verses.

Anxious For The Throne

In compliance with the time, the prince was also given training in civil and military administration. During the Kabul expedition of 1581, he was placed in charge of a regiment of troops and subsequently conducted independent military expeditions. In 1585, he was elevated to the rank of an army officer, commanding 12,000 men. Unfortunately, he was familiar with wine at an early age and became addicted to the good life. He was also impatient. An estrangement developed between father and son due to the prince's scheming ambition to succeed to his father's throne without the customary death of his father. When Akbar was persuaded by his favorite courtier Abul Fazl to develop a brotherhood of "seekers" who viewed the emperor as divinely inspired and hailed him with the phrase *allahu akbar,* in 1602 the prince had Abul Fazl murdered. Akbar was so depressed by the death of his friend that he did not appear in public for three days. But there was no other reliable successor. Desperate to keep the dynasty alive, in 1605, a dying Akbar (from poisoning traceable to the prince) reluctantly had his imperial turban placed on the head of his eldest son.

A week later, Salim succeeded to the throne at Agra at the age of 36, assuming the name Nur-ud-din Muhammad Jahangir. But he was soon disturbed by the impatience of his own eldest son, Khusrau. When Prince Khusrau's troops were defeated by the imperial forces near Jullunder, the captive prince suffered total humiliation; Janhagir had his son ride along a street lined with the impaled bodies of his

Jahangir Mohammed Selim (with walking stick)

recent supporters. Khusrau had neither the capacity to organize a successful revolt nor moral and material support of any influential party in the state, and the people had no desire to have him as their ruler. Jahangir then turned to Sikh Guru Arjun, who had given money to the rebellious Khusrau, and fined him for his offence. But Guru Arjun refused to pay. Though the Sikh was subjected to torture until he died, evidence shows that the Sikh religious leaders suffered only when they interfered in politics. Jahangir did not persecute the Sikhs out of hand.

In fact, Jahangir was determined to dispense justice fairly. One of his earliest orders was the setting up of a "chain of justice" made of gold. Anyone who failed to secure justice might pull the end outside the Agra fort in order to draw the attention of the emperor so that the latter might redress his grievances.

Internal disturbances in India prompted the Shah of Persia to make a bid for the fortress of Kandahar. Owing to its strategic and commercial importance, the fort was a bone of contention between Persia and India during the middle ages. After the death of the second Mughal ruler Humayun, it was given to Shah Husain Mirza by the Persian emperor. Though Akbar had recovered it in 1594, it had again passed into Persian hands. Three attempts were made to recapture the fortress, but the Mughal armies were unsuccessful. These repeated failures had diminished the prestige of the Empire.

Jahangir Gains Territories And Erects
Statues And Mosques

In pursuance of his father's policy of imperialism, Jahangir aimed at the conquest of the entire country. In 1605, he sent his second son to reduce Rana Amar Singh, a Hindu ruler, to submission. It was not easy to conquer the great fort of Chittor. In 1608, the Emperor sent another force. Eventually a treaty of peace was signed in 1615. Because the Rana recognized the suzerainty of Jahangir, the Mughal emperor restored all his territory, including Chittor. Jahangir's treaty is a landmark in the history of the relations between Mewar and Delhi. No ruler of the Sishodia dynasty had ever before openly professed allegiance to a Mughal ruler and a long-drawn struggle came to an end. Subsequently, Jahangir placed two lifesize marble statues of the Rana and his son in the gardens of his palace at Agra. By granting generous terms and adopting a conciliatory policy, Jahangir secured Mewar's loyalty for the empire which lasted until his grandson's (Emperor Aurangzeb) policy alienated Rana Raj Singh.

Jahangir's Deccan policy was a continuation of that of Akbar's which, following ancient Hindu traditions, treated the north and south as indivisible parts of one country. It was the emperor's desire to annex Ahmadnagar and, if possible, the two remaining independent states of Bijapur and Golkunda. Jahangir placed his son, Prince Khurram, in command of his army in 1613 and ordered him to lead a number of campaigns against Rajput forces in Mewar and Kanga, and the Deccani sultanates of Ahmadnagar, Bijapur, and Golkonda. The long siege of Kanga was brought to a successful end in 1629. This was the most notable military achievement of Jahangir's reign, prompting him to visit the place of conquest and build mosques there.

The complete success of the Mughal army over the forces of Ahmadnagar was not possible, however, owing in part to the strength of the Deccan kingdom and in part to the inferiority of Mughal weapons. Not only did Ahmadnagar defy the Mughal advance, but successful opposition came from an able Abyssinian named Malik Ambar, a former slave, who prepared for a war by training the mountaineers of Maharasthra in guerrilla tactics (later perfected by the great Hindu ruler Shivaji to the despair of Emperor Aurangzeb). When the Mughals had partial success in 1616, Prince Khurram was rewarded by Jahangir with the title of Shah Jahan ("King of the World"). But the Deccan was far from conquered.

Wife And Son Vie For Power

The most important development in the first half of Jahangir's reign had been the rise of his favorite wife Nur Jahan ("Light of the World") and the emergence of this third son Khurram (whose mother was a Rajput princess). Nur Jahan was a lady of great energy and many talents. Because of her, Persian poets and artists, architects, and musicians flocked to the Mughal court at Agra. She became an effective political power in India. But Shah Jahan was the leading contender for his father's mantle, and Nur Jahan resented his growing influence.

Nur Mahal's first step was simply to persuade the suggestible Jahangir that Shah Jahan should leave court, get away from the center of affairs, and return to military service against rival kings in the Deccan. Shah Jahan accepted the commission in ill grace, and took with him Khusrau, who had remained popular despite his rebellion and had a strong claim to the throne. Hearing that Jahangir's health was worsening and that his death was imminent, Shah Jahan's first act was to kill this brother, who would otherwise have become the center of a rival faction.

In 1623, Shah Jahan marched in open rebellion toward Agra. At Nur Mahal's behest an imperial army set out to track down Shah Jahan's forces, but the shrewd prince evaded his pursuers rather than meet them at a military disadvantage. The rebellious Shah Jahan was chased around southeast India for three years before finally agreeing to return to his father's fold.

Meanwhile, Jahangir held an impressive court. For one thing, he was fond of religious discourse. Sir Thomas Roe of England would testify that the Emperor accorded equal welcome to Christians, Jews, and Muslims. Once again, Hindu festivals like Rakhi, Dasahra, etc., were allowed to be celebrated. Because of his father, Jahangir had come in contact with the Jesuits at an early age and treated them with great courtesy. He was too good a Muslim and too proud a Mughal, however, to convert to Christianity as they had hoped. The veneration he showed to the paintings of Jesus and Mary was due to his passion for works of art. Though in the spirit of the times there were incidents of fanaticism, for the most part Jahangir followed the policy of Akbar in showing general tolerance for Christianity and contributing large sums for the erection of churches.

Soon the Jesuit mission at the Mughal court assumed the character and functions of an embassy with the intention of outplaying the English and furthering the interests of the Portuguese. But Portuguese power, owing to its contempt for orientals, was already on the decline. The English seized the opportunity and made a significant impression on Jahangir. English trade was then secured.

In 1608, Captain William Hawkins arrived with a letter from James I of England. Though the emperor was impressed, the Portuguese effectively prevented Hawkins from gaining any tangible success from his mission. In 1615, came the aforementioned Sir Thomas Roe, England's first official ambassador to India, who tried to secure from the Mughal ruler a trade agreement for the young East India Company. The Portuguese had a head start in the lucrative business of exporting calicoes and indigo from India, and the Dutch also were ahead of the English. Though Roe failed to enter into any agreement with Jahangir, he secured some privileges for the English trading company that made it a factor in Indian politics. Roe's accounts provide valuable insight into the royal court.

A notable military success of Jahangir's reign was the capture of the strong fortress of Kangra in the northeast Punjab on November 16, 1620. But this event, which Jahangir found cause for exultation, was quickly followed by disasters and rebellions which continued until he died. Alienated by the intrigues of his wife Nur Jahan, his son Shah Jahan rose in rebellion against him. Facing Persian pressure from the northwest and the defection of Shah Jahan within the heart of the empire, Jahangir's situation was grave. Though Shah Jahan's rebellion ended in futility, it caused substantial damage to the empire.

Reign An Era Of Family Strife And Notable Architecture

Jahangir's reign was noted for architectural works. When his chief minister Itimad-ud-daulah died in 1622, his daughter, the powerful Nur Jahan, commissioned the construction in white marble of his exquisite tomb at Agra which was finished in 1628. Unlike the much larger Taj Mahal, with which it ranked in quality, the appeal of the tomb depended on its decoration. It looked like a brilliant casket, bejewelled with various styles of inlay. Its two major innovations—the extensive use of white marble as a material and inlay as a decorative motif—were to become the distinguishing features of the greatest period of Mughal architecture.

The high quality of both paintings and coins during Jahangir's reign was a direct result of the emperor's personal interest. Having grown up at Fatehpur-Sikri in the busy days of Akbar's studio, he was a keen student of technique and claimed to be able to tell which master had painted the eye and eyebrow in a face and which the rest of the portrait. In addition, he seems to have invented and commissioned from his artists a new style of political allegory in art which, however self-congratulatory and vain, provided some of the most magnificent paintings of the period. One such picture claims to celebrate a new spirit of peace with his Persian neighbor, Shah Abbas.

Toward the end of Jahangir's reign, Nur Jahan took a more active role in the government and appointed her politically adroit brother, Asaf Khan, as the premier of the realm. In 1626, brother and sister decided to attack the powerful Mahabat Khan. An Afghan by birth, Mahabat Khan realized the precarious situation and so marched north with 5,000 Rajput troops toward the imperial camp on the bank of the Jhelum. As Jahangir and Nur Jahan traveled to Kabul, Mahabat Khan took the emperor prisoner. Though Jahangir managed to escape with the help of a clever scheme by Nur Jahan, Mahabat Khan then joined forces with Shah Jahan. The prince was now stronger than ever.

A shaken emperor turned north to the only place where he now found solace. For several years, he had made an almost annual journey to Kashmir. There, he had found a natural paradise, but he and his court had done much to make it an artificial one. The Mughal gardens, which are one of the main glories of Srinagar, are the direct result of his enthusiasm. The Shalimar Bagh, built by Jahangir, is distinguished by a series of pavilions on carved pillars, surrounded by pools with seats which can only be reached by stepping stones.

When Jahangir died in October on 1627 in a village at the foot of the Kashmir hills, Asaf Khan betrayed his sister by backing his son-in-law, Shah Jahan. Informed by Asaf's courier of his father's death, Shah Jahan rushed north to claim his throne, reaching the capital in 1628. Nur Jahan was pensioned off and went to live in solitude in Lahore until she died in 1645.

While some European historians consider Jahangir as a fickle-minded tyrant, Indian authors regard him as a just and noble ruler. Most writers now agree that he was a highly educated and cultured man. His autobiography is a testimony of his interest in subjects like botany and zoology. Among the notable buildings renovated by him, Akbar's tomb at Sikandra is the most remarkable. He altered its design and partly rebuilt it. Under his patronage, a great mosque was built in Lahore; it rivals the grand mosque in Delhi, built by his son, Shah Jahan.

But he did not possess the high idealism and genius of Akbar. The administrative machinery of his father was allowed to remain untouched. The vakil (chief minister) remained the highest dignitary next to the emperor. A liberal ruler, he made no departure from his father's policy of admitting Hindus to higher public services. On the whole, Jahangir was a successful ruler and his people were well off. Agriculture, industries, and commerce flourished. Jahangir's diary is brimming with his ideas for promoting social justice and administrative efficiency, and in most cases he tried to follow or outdo the liberal ideas of his father, but he was less successful in putting them into effect.

Further Reading

Gascoigne, Bamber. *The Great Moghuls*. Harper, 1971.

Majumdar, R. C., H. C. Raychaudhuri, and Kalikinkar Datta. *An Advanced History of India*. St. Martin's Press, 1965.

Sastri, K. A. Nilakanta and G. Srinivasachari. *Advanced History of India*. Calcutta: Allied Publishers Private Ltd., 1970.

Wolpert, Stanley. *A New History of India*. Oxford University Press, 1977.

Jahangir. *Memoirs of The Emperor Jahangueir*. London: Printed for the Oriental Translation Committee, 1829.

Srivastava, Ashirbadilal. *The History of India*. Agra: Shiva Lal Agarwala & Co., Ltd, 1964. □

Helmut Jahn

The buildings of German-American architect Helmut Jahn (born 1940) dramatically combine the modernist, glass-skinned style of Mies van der Rohe with traditional architectural imagery. Always mindful of energy and cost efficiency, and yet convinced that buildings should enjoy a variety of colors, patterns, and textures, Jahn created technologically advanced structures that had widespread appeal.

Helmut Jahn was born in Nuremberg, Germany, in 1940. His father, William Anton Jahn, served in the German army during World War II. He spent a year as a prisoner of war in Philadelphia, Pennsylvania, in the United States. After the war, William Jahn returned to his career as a primary school teacher, a profession that he hoped young Helmut would pursue. His son, however, showed an aptitude for drawing and decided to become an architect, a decision that may have been inspired by his growing up among the war-ravaged buildings of his country. In 1965, Jahn received a diploma in architecture from a technical high school in Munich. With the help of a Rotary Club scholarship, he emigrated to the United States in 1966 and began postgraduate work in architecture at the Illinois Institute of Technology (IIT). Here Jahn was thoroughly imbued with the work of Mies van der Rohe, the German architect who designed the campus of IIT and left the school with a strong tradition of modernist design. While at IIT, Jahn studied with the structural engineer Fazlur Khan, whose discoveries about wind shear resistance made possible the construction of the Sears Tower in Chicago, the world's tallest building.

Early Career

In 1967 Jahn entered the prestigious Chicago firm of C. F. Murphy and Associates. Working initially as an assistant to Gene Summers, Jahn spent much of his early tenure with the firm on the design of the huge McCormick Place convention center in Chicago. Within six years Jahn was promoted to director of planning and design.

Soon thereafter he began the first major project he could call his own, the Kemper Arena in Kansas City. Completed in 1974, the arena was the first of Jahn's so-called "mat" buildings, which were characterized by their low, flat profile and high-tech appearance. The most dramatic aspect of the arena was the roof, which was suspended over the building by three giant trusses, an idea perhaps inspired by Mies' Crown Hall at IIT. The structural supports for the

building were left uncovered, inside and out, as were all the pipes, ductwork, and other mechanical components. Built in great haste, and of cheaper materials than the architect wanted, the roof of the arena collapsed during a wind storm in 1979. Nevertheless, the building won some prestigious awards and established Jahn as a flexible and reliable designer.

Energy-Conscious Architect

With the onset of the energy crisis in the mid 1970s, Jahn turned his attention toward designing structures that were energy efficient. For the Auraria Library in Denver (1975), he provided external blinds to prevent too much direct sunlight from entering during the summer. The blinds were angled to admit what warming sunlight is available during the winter. Similar louvers were employed in Jahn's Program Support Facility building for the Argonne (Illinois) National Laboratories (1978-1982). This building was shaped like a truncated disk, sporting three rows of ribbon windows facing north. The shape reduced the building's heat loss during the winter and facilitated the entry of indirect northern light, thereby reducing the amount of energy needed to artificially illuminate the structure. Another of Jahn's mat buildings, the St. Mary's Athletic Facility in South Bend, Indiana (1977), was sunk well into the ground and surrounded by an earth berm. This not only decreased the scale of the huge gymnasium (making it more compatible with the other low-profile buildings around it), but significantly improved its ability to retain heat.

Reaching New Heights

In the late 1970s Jahn secured some major urban commissions that caused him to move from mat buildings to skyscrapers. In so doing, the architect was able to demonstrate a sensitivity to urban context often lacking in modern architecture. In his Chicago Board of Trade Addition (1978-1982), for instance, Jahn visually united the addition to the original 1930 Board of Trade Building by employing setbacks, a hipped roof, and a vertical window arrangement that echo features of the older building. Inside are curved lines and scallop-shaped ornaments that recall the Art Deco style of the 1930s. The architect's respect for history appears even in his most modernistic of urban structures, the State of Illinois Center in Chicago (1979-1985), which has a curved facade and a glazed atrium that connects it with the classical tradition of elegant, domed administrative centers.

Jahn's love of curves and setbacks executed in glass resulted in some of the most dramatic skyscraper designs of the last quarter of the twentieth century, including One Liberty Place in Philadelphia (1987) and Park Avenue Tower in New York City (1986). In such buildings Jahn, like Mies before him, employed rich materials and colors to delight the eye: terrazzo floors, marble walls, black plastic laminate elevators with aluminum stripes, pink ceilings. Taking his buildings well beyond their mere functional requirements, Jahn used his architecture to make a statement. He said, "I don't think there's anything wrong in using a building to connote achievement and a certain commercial power. I think that's the way architecture has been used historically. Great statesmen, great emperors, great dictators always build great buildings."

International Acclaim

The 1990s saw a decline in building in the United States so Jahn stayed busy with foreign projects. Two of these, the Kurfurstendamm office building in Berlin, Germany and the Munich Order Center, also in Germany, won prestigious awards in 1995 from the American Institute of Arts. In the second half of the 1990s, Jahn's focus seemed to return to the United States. His works were included in the U.S. entry to the sixth Venice Architecture Biennale, which featured the architecture of Disney. In 1997, Jahn entered two major architectural competitions, one for a new campus center at the Illinois Institute of Technology, and the other for the Coliseum on Columbus Circle in New York City.

Jahn himself could be described as a flamboyant personality. He wore fashionably long hair and expensive Italian suits, drove a Porsche, skied in Aspen, went scuba diving in Australia, and sailed in the Chicago-to-Mackinac Island yacht race. This side of his life, though, was tempered with long hours in his Chicago offices. In 1981, he was made a principal in the firm of Murphy/Jahn, becoming president and chief executive officer two years later. The winner of some of the most prestigious awards in his profession, Jahn also served as a visiting professor of architecture at both Harvard (1981) and Yale (1983). Married to Deborah Lampe in 1970, Jahn had one son.

Further Reading

The best single book on Jahn is Nory Miller's *Helmut Jahn* (1986). This volume contains a complete bibliography and includes some outstanding photographs and drawings; reviews of Jahn's work appear in Mark Michael Leonhart, "Helmut Jahn: The Building of a Legend," *New Art Examiner* 15 (November 1987); and Jim Murphy, "To Be Continued (New Buildings and Projects by Helmut Jahn)," *Progressive Architecture* 71 (March 1990); Jahn himself did not write much, but one of the best interviews with him can be found in Barbarlee Diamonstein, ed., *American Architecture Now II* (1985).

Additional Sources

Dickerson, Maria. "Disney Architecture to be Shown at Exhibit." *Los Angeles Times,* 3 September 1996.

Kamin, Blair. "ITT Going Worldwide for Design of Center." *Chicago Tribune,* 1997.

———. "Urban Dressing: Projects by Chicago Architects Sweep Up Prestigious National Design Awards." *Chicago Tribune,* 28 November 1995.

———. "The Sky's the Limit: Designers Honor Chicago Architects' Best Buildings." *Chicago Tribune,* 24 September 1995.

Muschamp, Herbert. "Worthy of a World Capital." *The New York Times,* 19 January 1997.

Rechtenwald, William. "Thirsty Tiger Uses Wind to Win Mac." *Chicago Tribune,* 18 July 1995. □

Ja Ja of Opobo

JaJa of Opobo (ca. 1820–1891) was a political and military strategist, brought to the Bonny Kingdom as a slave, who was perhaps the most troublesome thorn in the flesh of 19th-century British imperial ambition in southern Nigeria.

The story of Ja Ja recounts a man of servile status hurdling intimidating odds to attain wealth and power, and founding in the latter half of the 19th century the most prosperous city-state in the Delta area of Nigeria. Information regarding his parentage and early childhood, derived from uncertain and speculative oral tradition, is scanty and unsatisfactory. According to informed guesstimates, Ja Ja was born in 1820 or 1821, in the lineage of Umuduruoha of Amaigbo village group in the heartland of Igboland, Southeastern Nigeria. He was sold into slavery in the Niger Delta under circumstances which are far from clear. One version of the oral traditions says that he was sold because, as a baby, he cut the upper teeth first, an abominable phenomenon in traditional Igbo society. Another version claims that he was captured and sold by his father's enemy. Regardless, he was bought by Chief Iganipughuma Allison of Bonny, by far the most powerful city-state on the Atlantic coast of Southeastern Nigeria before the rise of Opobo.

To follow the Ja Ja story or, indeed, revolution, an explanatory note is necessary. Until the end of the 19th century, the Delta communities played a crucial role in European and American trade with Nigeria. Acting as middlemen, these communities carried into the interior markets the trade goods of European and American supercargoes stationed on the coast and brought back in exchange the export produce of the hinterland, basically palm oil. As the Delta is dominated by saline swamps and crisscrossed by a labyrinth of creeks and rivers, the canoe was indispensable for trade.

The Delta society was organized in Canoe Houses. A Canoe House was the pivot of social organization and also, notes K.O. Dike, "a cooperative trading unit and a local government institution." It was usually composed of a wealthy merchant (its founder), his family, and numerous slaves owned by him. A prosperous house could comprise several thousand members, both free and bonded, owning hundreds of trade canoes. In this intensely competitive society, leadership by merit—not by birth or ascriptions—was necessary if a house was to make headway in the turbulent, cut-throat competition that existed between houses. Any person with the charisma and proven ability, even if of servile birth, could rise to the leadership of a house, but could never become king. Ja Ja would achieve this, and much more.

Finding young Ja Ja too headstrong for his liking, Chief Allison made a gift of him to his friend, Madu, a chief of the Anna Pepple House, one of the two houses of the royal family (the other being the Manilla Pepple House). Ja Ja was slotted into the lowest rung of the Bonny slave society ladder, that of an imported slave, distinct from that of someone who was of slave parentage but born in the Delta.

As a youth, he worked as a paddler on his owner's great trade canoes, traveling to and from the inland markets. Quite early, he demonstrated exceptional abilities and business acumen, quickly identified with the Ijo custom of the Delta, and won the hearts of the local people as well as those of the European supercargoes. It was unusual for a slave of his status to make the transition from canoe paddling to trading, but Ja Ja—through his honesty, business sense, and amiability—soon became prosperous.

For a long while, Ja Ja turned his back on Bonny politics, concentrating his immense energies on accumulating wealth through trade, the single most important criterion to power in the Delta. At the time, Bonny politics were volatile as a result of the irreconcilable and acrimonious contest for supremacy between the Manilla Pepple House and the Anna Pepple House to which Ja Ja belonged. Coincidentally, both houses were led by remarkable characters of Igbo slave origins—Oko Jumbo of the Manilla House and Madu (after him Alali his son) of the Anna House.

In 1863, Alali died, bequeathing to his house a frightening debt of between £10,000 and £15,000 owed to European supercargoes. Fearing bankruptcy, all of the eligible chiefs of the house declined nomination to head it. It was therefore a great relief when Ja Ja accepted to fill the void. With characteristic energy, he proceeded to put his house in order by reorganizing its finances. Conscious that the palm-oil markets in the hinterland and the wealth of the European trading community on the coast constituted the pivot of the Delta economy, he ingratiated himself with both sides. In a matter of two years, he had liquidated the debt left behind by his predecessor and launched his house on the path of prosperity. When less prosperous and insolvent houses sought incorporation into the Anna House, Ja Ja gradually absorbed one house after another.

By 1867, his remarkable success had become common knowledge throughout Bonny. The British consul to the area, Sir Richard Burton, had cause to remark that although Ja Ja was the "son of an unknown bush man," he had become "the most influential man and greatest trader in the [Imo] River." Predicted Burton: "In a short time he will either be shot or he will beat down all his rivals."

Burton's words proved prophetic. Ja Ja's successes incurred the jealousy of opponents who feared that, if left unchecked, his house might incorporate most of the houses in Bonny and thereby dominate its political and economic arena. Oko Jumbo, his bitterest opponent, was determined that such a prospect would never materialize.

Meanwhile, two developments occurred in Bonny, serving to harden existing jealousies. First, in 1864, Christianity was introduced into the city-state, further polarizing the society. While the Manilla House welcomed the Christians with a warm embrace, the Anna House was opposed to the exotic religion. Not surprisingly, the missionaries sided with the Manilla House against the Anna House. Second, in 1865, King William Pepple died and, with this, the contest for the throne between the two royal houses took on a monstrous posture.

Three years later, in 1868, Bonny was ravaged by fire, and the Anna House was the worst hit. In the discomfiture of his opponent, Oko Jumbo saw his opportunity. Knowing that the fire had all but critically crippled Ja Ja's house, he sought every means to provoke an open conflict. On the other side, Ja Ja did everything to avoid such a conflict, but, as Dike states, "Oko Jumbo's eagerness to catch his powerful enemy unprepared prevailed."

On September 13, 1869, heavy fighting erupted between the two royal houses. Outmatched in men and armament, though not in strategy, Ja Ja pulled out of Bonny, accepted defeat, and sued for peace with a suddenness that surprised both his adversaries and the European supercargoes. Peace palaver commenced and dragged on for weeks under the auspices of the British consul. This was exactly what Ja Ja planned for. It soon became doubtful if the victors were not indeed the vanquished.

Ja Ja had sued for peace in order to gain time to retreat from Bonny with his supporters with little or no loss in men and armament. A master strategist, he relocated in the Andoni country away from the seaboard at a strategic point at the mouth of the Imo river, the highway of trade between the coastal communities and the palm-oil rich Kwa Iboe and Igbo country. There, he survived the initial problems of a virgin settlement as well as incessant attacks of his Bonny enemies.

In 1870, feeling reasonably secure, Ja Ja proclaimed the independence of his settlement which he named Opobo, after Opubu the Great, the illustrious king of Bonny and founder of Anna House who had died in 1830. As Dike writes:

[I]t is characteristic of the man that he had not only a sense of the occasion but of history. . . . Kingship was impossible of attainment for anyone of slave origins in Bonny. Instead he sought another land where he could give full scope to his boundless energies.

Long before the war of 1869, Ja Ja had been carefully planning to found his own state. The war merely provided him with the occasion to implement his design.

In naming his new territory Opobo, Ja Ja was appealing to the nostalgia and historical consciousness of his followers while giving them the impression that he was truly the heir of the celebrated king. That this impression was widespread and accepted by most Bonny citizens may be judged from the fact that of the 18 houses in Bonny, 14 followed Ja Ja to Opobo.

To no avail, the British consul tried to coerce Ja Ja to come back to Bonny. Against the admonition of the consul, and in the face of Bonny's displeasure, many British firms began to trade openly with Opobo while others transferred their depots there. By May of 1870, the Ja Ja revolution had driven the death-knell on Bonny's economy. British firms anchoring there are said to have lost an estimated £100,000 of trade by mid-1870. The city-state fell from grace to grass as Opobo, flourishing on its ashes, became in Ofonagoro's words, "the most important trade center in the Oil Rivers," and Ja Ja became "the greatest African living in the east of modern Nigeria."

For 18 years, Ja Ja ruled his kingdom with firmness and remarkable sagacity. He strengthened his relations with the hinterland palm-oil producers through judicious marriages and blood covenants which bound the parties into ritual kingship. He armed his traders with modern weapons for their own defense and that of the state. He thus monopolized trade with the palm-oil producers and punished severely any community that tried to trade directly with the European supercargoes.

In 1873, the British recognized him as king of independent Opobo, and Ja Ja reciprocated by sending a contingent of his soldiers to help the British in their war against the Ashanti kingdom in the Gold Coast (now Ghana). Queen Victoria expressed her gratitude in 1875 by awarding him a sword of honor. It seemed a honeymoon had developed between Opobo and Britain.

Ja Ja's reign has been described as a striking instance of selective modernization. He retained most of the sociopolitical and cultural institutions of Bonny, such as the house system, and stuck steadfastly to the religion of his fathers, arguing that Christianity was a serious ferment of societal destabilization. While recognizing the value of Western education and literacy, he objected to its religious component. Thus, he sent his two sons to school in Scotland but insisted they acquire only secular education. He established a secular school in Opobo and employed an African-American, Emma White, to run it. An Englishman who visited Opobo in 1885 stated that the standard of the pupils in the school compared quite favorably with that of English children of the same age.

The honeymoon between Ja Ja and the British turned out to be meteoric: the ultimate ambitions of the two ran at cross-purposes. Ja Ja guarded his independence jealously, had a tight grip on the interior markets and confined British traders to Opobo, away from these markets. He made sure that the traders paid their *comeys* (customs and trade duties) as and when due.

But in the 1880s, the clouds of British imperialism were closing in menacingly on Opobo, the overthrow of indigenous sovereignties having been initiated by John Beecroft, the first British consul to Nigeria (1849-54). British imperialism had begun to assert itself forcefully; British officials on the spot were increasingly ignoring indigenous authorities, while British traders had begun to insist on trading directly with the hinterland palm-oil producers. Ja Ja tackled these formidable problems judiciously and with restraint.

In July 1884, fearing German intrusion in the Delta, the British consul, Edward Hewett, rushed to the area, foisting treaties of protection on the indigenous sovereignties. With a veiled threat from a man-of-war, Ja Ja too was stampeded into placing his kingdom under British protection. But unlike the other African monarchs, this was not before he had sought explanation for the word "protectorate," and had been assured by the consul that his independence would not be compromised. Hewett wrote to Ja Ja informing him, *inter alia* (among other things), that:

> the queen does not want to take your country or your markets, but at the same time she is anxious that no other nation should take them. She undertakes . . . [to] leave your country still under your government; she has no wish to disturb your rule.

At Ja Ja's insistence, a clause providing for free trade in his kingdom was struck off before he agreed to sign the treaty.

The following year, European powers entered into the Treaty of Berlin which set the stage for the scramble and partition of Africa among themselves, without regard to the wishes of Africans. The treaty provided for free navigation on River Niger and other rivers, such as the Imo, linked to it. On the basis of this, the British consul asserted that British firms were within their rights to trade directly in the interior palm-oil markets. That same year, 1885, Britain proclaimed the Oil Rivers Protectorate, which included Ja Ja's territory. Sending a delegation to the British secretary of states for the colonies to protest these actions by right of the treaty of 1884, Ja Ja's protest fell on deaf ears. A man of his word, he was shocked at Britain reneging on her pledge.

Worse times were yet to come as political problems were compounded by economic dispute. The 1880s witnessed a severe trade depression that ruined some of the European firms trading in the Delta and threatened the survival of others. The surviving firms responded to the situation in two ways. First, they reached an agreement among themselves, though not with complete unanimity, to offer low prices for produce. Second, they claimed the right to go directly to the interior markets in order to sidestep the coastal middlemen and reduce the handling cost of produce.

As would be expected, Ja Ja objected to these maneuvers and proceeded to ship his own produce directly to Europe. The British consul directed the European firms not to pay *comey* to Ja Ja anymore, arguing that in shipping his produce directly to Europe, he had forfeited his right to receive the payment. Once again, Ja Ja sent a delegation to Britain to protest the consul and the traders' action. Once again, this was to no avail.

Under a threat of naval bombardment, Ja Ja signed an agreement with the British consul in July 1887 to allow free trade in his territory. By now, he knew that Britain's imperial ambition was growing rapidly, and he began transferring his resources further into the Igbo hinterland, his birthplace. But as Elizabeth Isichei points out, "he was confronted with a situation where courage and foresight were ultimately in vain."

Harry Johnston, acting vice-consul, a young hothead anxious to advance his colonial career, imagined that Ja Ja would be a perfect stepping-stone to attain his ambition. Arriving at Opobo on a man-of-war, Johnston invited Ja Ja for a discussion on how to resolve the points of friction between Opobo and the British traders and officials. Suspicious of Johnston's real intentions, Ja Ja initially turned down the invitation but was lured to accept with a promise of safe return after the meeting. Said Johnston:

> I hereby assure you that whether you accept or reject my proposals tomorrow, no restrictions will be put on you—you will be free to go as soon as you have heard my message.

But again the British reneged on their pledge: Ja Ja would not return to his kingdom alive. Once on board the warship *Goshawk,* Johnston confronted him with a deportation order or the complete destruction of Opobo. Nearly 18 years to the day when he pulled out of Bonny, Ja Ja was deported to the Gold Coast, tried, and declared guilty of actions inimical to Britain's interest. Still afraid of his charm and influence on the Gold Coast, even in captivity, Johnston saw to it that he was deported to the West Indies, at St. Vincent Island.

With the exit of Ja Ja, the most formidable obstacle to Britain's imperial ambition in Southeastern Nigeria had been removed. But the circumstances of his removal left a sour taste in certain British mouths. Lord Salisbury, British prime minister, could not help criticizing Johnston, noting that in other places Ja Ja's deportation would be called "kidnapping." Michael Crowder describes the event as "one of the shabbiest incidents in the history of Britain's relations with West Africa." Among the indigenous population, it left a deep and lasting scar of suspicion of Britain's good faith and, for a long time, trade in the area all but ceased.

In exile, Ja Ja is said to have borne himself with kingly dignity. He made repeated appeals to Britain to allow him to return to Opobo. In 1891, his request was granted, belatedly as it turned out: Ja Ja died on the Island of Teneriffe en route to Opobo, the kingdom built with his sweat and devotion.

His people gladly paid the cost of repatriating his body and spent a fortune celebrating his royal funeral.

Today, an imposing statue of Ja Ja stands in the center of Opobo with the inscription:

A king in title and in deed. Always just and generous.

Further Reading

Burn, Alarn. *History of Nigeria.* George Allen & Unwin, 1929.
Dike, Kenneth O. *Trade and Politics in the Niger Delta, 1830-1885.* Oxford University Press, 1956.
Isichei, Elizabeth. *A History of the Igbo People.* Macmillan, 1976.
Ogonagoro, Walter I. *Trade and Imperialism in Southern Nigeria, 1881-1929.* Nok Publishers, 1979. □

James I

James I (1566-1625) reigned as king of England from 1603 to 1625. As James VI, he was king of Scotland from 1567 to 1625.

The son of Mary Stuart, reigning queen of Scotland, and (presumably) her husband, Lord Darnley, James I was born in Edinburgh Castle on June 19, 1566. His mother's subsequent indiscretions forced her to renounce her title in her son's favor in 1567.

The infant king was placed in the trust of the Earl of Mar, a zealous Protestant, who was a firm believer in the value of education and discipline. The King's tutors, George Buchanan and Peter Young, were stern taskmasters, but James proved an apt pupil. By the age of 8 he was fluent in French, Latin, and reasonably conversant in English. But he received no instruction in the "courtly arts." James's sense of humor never outgrew the primitive, his language was coarse and vulgar, and his manner was most distinctly unregal.

In 1571 the regent, Lennox (James's paternal grandfather), was killed by the Marians, and he was then succeeded by the harsh Earl of Morton. In 1578 James was kidnaped by two of the Marians, Atholl and Argyle, only to be rescued within the month.

The two Catholic superpowers, France and Spain, both sought to influence developments in Scotland. From France came James's cousin, the corrupt Esmé Stuart, ostensibly to win James to the side of the house of Guise and the Catholic faith. The young king was completely smitten by this adventurer, and he gave him lands, income, and the title of Earl and then Duke of Lennox.

The new duke soon encompassed the downfall and execution of the regent, Morton. His influence over the King seemed paramount, and James's Protestant subjects vented their fears for the King's moral and religious state. In fact, the influence of Lennox and his equally corrupt accomplices seems to have been greatest in the field of politics—James completely turned from the basically democratic ideas espoused by his early tutors and began to think in terms of absolute monarchy.

In 1582 James was taken into custody at Ruthven Castle, and Lennox was driven from the country. Within a year the King had escaped from his new captors, but he succeeded merely in placing himself under the tutelage of Lennox's most aggressive companion, the Earl of Arran, who soon took over the actual running of the state.

Personal Rule

Egged on by Arran, James attacked the Presbyterian Church, and in 1584 he forced himself to be recognized as head of the Church. James's ambition to be king of England was matched by his need for English money; despite the attack on his favorite, Arran, the alliance with England was maintained. When his mother let herself be drawn into outright treason, James did little to prevent her execution in 1587.

James then turned his attention to dynastic (and romantic) matters, and he began his courtship of Anne of Denmark. The King, newly come of age, sailed after his bride, to the joy of his subjects. He married her in Norway, where severe weather had compelled her to remain. Six months later the royal couple returned to Scotland.

By 1592 the feuds between Lord Bothwell and the Catholic lords had reduced James to a virtual fugitive, pursued by one side and then the other. By 1593 Bothwell had made James his captive—to the praise of the Presbyterians and Elizabeth, who both feared the influence of the Catholic Earl of Huntly. Bothwell, however, had overplayed his hand—James talked his way to freedom, and with the aid of the middle classes he proceeded against the man who had not merely held him a prisoner but had also sought his life through witchcraft and the black arts.

Bothwell, now desperate, allied himself with Huntly, Errol, and Angus. The result was the destruction of the Catholic earls as well as Bothwell. By the end of 1594 the position of the monarchy seemed exceptionally secure.

James's sense of security was heightened by another event of 1594—the birth of a son and heir, Henry Frederick. Entrusted to the care of the Dowager Countess of Mar, the young prince symbolized James's coming of age.

During the next 4 years James continued to consolidate his position. His finances were restored by the efforts of the "Octavians," and when the Catholic earls returned to Scotland they seemed a much chastened lot. Their return led to an excess of emotion on the part of the most zealous of the Presbyterians, and this in turn allowed the King to proceed against them and to further advance the episcopal form of ecclesiastical polity. His ideas on church-state relations, on the attitude of subjects toward their king, and on the nature of divine right appeared in print in 1598 in *The Trew Law of Free Monarchies.* Within 2 years James had further refined his ideas in his most important work, *Basilikon Doron* (written for the edification of the young Henry).

King of England

James also accepted the advice offered by Robert Cecil, Elizabeth's most astute minister, to abandon his harebrained plots with Catholics and Protestants alike and to adopt a respectful and calm tone toward the aging queen. On Mar. 24, 1603, only 8 hours after Elizabeth's death, James was proclaimed king in London.

In a sense, the events of the first 2 years of James's reign in England serve to "set the stage" for the growing conflicts that marked the remainder of his 22 years on the throne. James had decisions to make in the areas of foreign policy, domestic religion, finance, and, in the broadest sense, in the field of governmental theory. In each of these areas, and in the matter of his northern kingdom and his royal favorites, he came into conflict with the English Parliament—especially with the House of Commons. James's great failure as an English king stemmed from his inability at first to perceive wherein the English assembly differed from the Scottish Parliament, and from his unwillingness to accept the differences when at last he became aware of them.

Especially in matters of secular domestic policies, James's first year on the English throne led to his asserting what he considered to be his "rightful" role in the government and in the constitution. Thus, in the first session of his first Parliament (1604), the King's speeches about his prerogative and the privileges that he had granted Parliament led that body to draft the "Apology of the Commons," in which the Commons equated their rights with those of all Englishmen. The Commons had suddenly assumed a new role. During James's first Parliament, which lasted until 1610, the opposition to him was sporadic and relatively uncoordinated. It tended to center on the figure of James's heir, Henry, who was given his own household at the age of 9.

Affairs of Church and State

The harsh treatment to which he had been subjected by some of his ministers of the Presbyterian Church as a youth, and the disruptive, highly antimonarchical bias of the Church, led James to support an episcopal church—a church that moreover acknowledged him as its head. Indeed, James's instincts seemed to incline him toward a very highly ritualized form of worship, and he seemed at first disposed to move toward a more lenient position regarding Roman Catholicism. Whatever his real feelings on this issue might have been, the discovery of a Catholic conspiracy led by Guy Fawkes to blow up the royal family—and Parliament as well—robbed him of any initiative in dealing with the Catholics as a group. He was forced to bow to the harsh measures adopted by Parliament; his subsequent efforts to relieve the disabilities imposed on Catholics only made Parliament suspect his motives.

Suspicion clouded James's relations with Parliament over several other issues as well. His attempts to unite England and Scotland as one kingdom were thwarted; his meddling in the dealings of his common-law courts led him to quarrel with his own chief justice, Sir Edward Coke, and to espouse a more extreme view of his own prerogative; his arbitrary raising of customs duties further outraged the Com-

mons; finally, his untoward fondness for a succession of worthless favorites (Scottish and English alike) annoyed Parliament, irked Prince Henry, and irritated Queen Anne.

Always impecunious, and without a trace of thrift, James maintained finances that were a source of embarrassment and of weakness. By 1610, amidst mutual recriminations and with the financial crisis unabated, James's first Parliament came to an end.

With Parliament in abeyance, government rested in the hands of James's favorite of the moment, Robert Carr, Earl of Somerset, and Carr's pro-Spanish in-laws, the Howards. Carr's implication in a scandalous murder trial, the death of Henry Howard, leader of the Spanish faction, and the emergence of a new favorite, George Villiers, seemed to undercut the Spanish party, but this eclipse was only temporary; the more the King seemed to incline toward Spain, the more he alienated his more substantial subjects. This mutual mistrust found expression in the "Addled Parliament" of 1614. For 2 months neither Commons nor King would concede a point to the other, and finally, despite his growing need for money, James dissolved his unruly legislature.

In his desperation, James now turned for help to Don Diego Sarmiento, the Spanish ambassador. His poverty really afforded him no choice, but his subjects saw this as further proof of duplicity. James began to consider a Spanish bride for Prince Charles, who had succeeded his late brother as Prince of Wales—a most unpopular project, but one which endured for more than a decade. Sarmiento encouraged the King but demanded substantial concessions that would have been impossible for James to meet.

Thirty Years War

The year 1616 saw the new favorite, Villiers (raised to the peerage as Baron, Viscount, Earl, Marquis, and finally, Duke of Buckingham), secure his position at court and become the focus of royal government. By 1618 he had destroyed the Howard family, and his power seemed to be complete. Buckingham's rise and his arrogance led to a quarrel with Prince Charles. James reconciled the two young men, and they soon became the best of friends.

By 1618, too, James's health was failing. He was badly crippled by gout and by attacks of kidney stones, and he clearly was no longer as alert mentally as he had been. It was precisely at this unfortunate moment that he was called upon to meet the greatest challenge of his reign: the outbreak of the Thirty Years War.

James's potential reasons for action were immediate, urgent, personal, and obvious—the conflict revolved around his son-in-law, daughter, and grandchildren. On a broader level, the very existence of the reformed faith was in danger. Despite the virtually unanimous urging of his subjects, favorite, and son for an aggressive foreign policy, James vacillated, hesitated, and ultimately to his disgrace appeared to abandon his own family and to attempt an alliance with their enemies. That James sought to use Spanish friendship to aid his son-in-law's cause was neither apparent nor sensible to his subjects. When, in 1620, Spain invaded the Palatinate itself, even James was roused to anger.

Royal anger, to be effective, needed money, and money could only come from a Parliament. Reluctantly, against the advice of Buckingham (who had become pro-Spanish), James summoned Parliament in 1621. At first, despite James's habitual sermonizing to the Commons, things seemed to go well. Money was voted, and while the King refused to allow Parliament to discuss matters of foreign policy, he made no overt move to keep them from overhauling domestic affairs. By the end of the first session, Commons and King were closer together than they had been for years.

Spanish blandishments dissipated this goodwill, and when, during November and December 1620, the Commons refused to vote supplies blindly but insisted on presenting their views on foreign policy, the King was furious. He denied virtually all of Parliament's privileges, and when the Commons responded with a mild protestation, he dissolved Parliament.

Final Years and Death

The gulf between James and his subjects, indeed between the Crown and the nation, was now total. Morally as well as financially, James was bankrupt. He was also wholly dependent upon the goodwill of Spain, or so he thought.

As James grew senile, he lost control not only over his country but over his son and his favorite as well. Charles and Buckingham exposed themselves, their King, and their country to ridicule by their hasty and futile pursuit of the Spanish Infanta.

James's last Parliament was no more peaceful than his first had been. Again King and Commons clashed over prerogative and privilege, but now the Commons was joined by the Lords, and the King's harsh strictures were explained away by his own chief minister and his heir. In the end, the King, and not Parliament, gave way, and England's long flirtation with Spain was at an end.

James's end came soon after; always in poor health, he died on March 27, 1625. He left behind an empty treasury, a malcontented Parliament, and a son who would succeed him peaceably—for a while.

Further Reading

The best modern biography of James is David Harris Willson, *King James VI and I* (1956), which provides a lucid and balanced picture of the age as well as an insightful study of the King. David Mathew, *James I* (1967), is episodic and far less satisfactory. James's early life is recounted in Caroline Bingham, *The Making of a King: The Early Years of James VI and I* (1968). Other biographical works include Thomas Finlayson Henderson, *James I and VI* (1904), and William Lloyd McElwee, *The Wisest Fool in Christendom: The Reign of King James I and VI* (1958). James figures prominently in Godfrey Davies, *The Early Stuarts* (1937; corrected repr. 1952), and G. P. V. Akrigg, *Jacobean Pageant* (1962). Documents dealing with James's view of the monarchy and with his clashes with the courts and Parliament are in J. P. Kenyon, *The Stuart Constitution, 1603-1688: Documents and Commentary* (1966). Wallace Notestein, *The English People on the Eve of Colonization* (1954), is a readable and scholarly study of the period.

Additional Sources

Bergeron, David Moore, *Royal family, royal lovers: King James of England and Scotland,* Columbia: University of Missouri Press, 1991.

Bingham, Caroline, *James I of England,* London: Weidenfeld and Nicolson, 1981.

Durston, Christopher, *James I,* London; New York: Routledge, 1993.

Finsten, Jill, *Isaac Oliver, art at the courts of Elizabeth I and James I,* New York: Garland Pub., 1981.

Fraser, Antonia, *King James, VI of Scotland, I of England,* London: Weidenfeld and Nicolson, 1994.

Houston, S. J., *James I,* London; New York: Longman, 1995.

Lee, Maurice, *Great Britain's Solomon: James VI and I in his three kingdoms,* Urbana: University of Illinois Press, 1990.

McElwee, William Lloyd, *The wisest fool in Christendom; the reign of King James I and V,* Westport, Conn., Greenwood Press 1974, 1958. □

James I

James I (1394-1437) was king of Scotland from 1406 to 1437. Although he was an English captive for more than half his years as king, his reign was one of the most vigorous in medieval Scottish history.

When James I was born, his father, Robert III, already rather elderly and feeble, had been reigning for 4 years but was strongly under the influence of his brother, the Earl of Fife (later Duke of Albany). James's life falls into three convenient periods: his boyhood in Scotland during the troubled reign of Robert III, the years of his captivity, and his personal rule. The young James was not brought up as heir apparent, for he had an older brother, David, Duke of Rothesay. But Rothesay, whose scandalous living had brought him many enemies, was bested in a power struggle with his uncle Albany and died shortly (and mysteriously) after being imprisoned in 1402. This thrust James into the midst of the factiousness and intrigue that characterize this period of ambitious nobles and weak monarchs in Scottish history.

English Captivity

In 1406 King Robert sent James to Scotland's ally the king of France, probably so that the boy would be out of Albany's reach; but the ship was intercepted off the English coast, and James soon found himself a prisoner of the king of England, Henry IV. The news of the prince's capture is said to have caused the death of Robert III within a few weeks, and Albany, as regent for the new prisoner-king, was in no hurry to arrange for the release of his nephew. In fact, James spent over 18 years in captivity in comfortable conditions and everywhere recognized as king of Scotland, but a prisoner nonetheless. During these years James was moved about frequently, from the Tower of London to Windsor and elsewhere in England. Henry V took him to the siege of Melun in France in 1420 (in the hope, unsuccessful, that

James's presence would detach some Scottish mercenary captains from the French army).

The unexpected death of Henry V and the troubled minority situation that ensued in the English government gave James an opportunity to intensify the negotiations for his release, which had became a real possibility in Scotland since the death of Albany in 1420. James was finally released in 1424, following a treaty that provided for a large ransom, suspension of Scottish military aid to France, and an English wife for James (Joan Beaufort, daughter of the Earl of Somerset and great-granddaughter of Edward III).

His Reign

After being solemnly crowned at Scone in May 1424, James initiated vigorous steps to try to tighten up the government of the country and to strengthen the monarchy. Strongly worded acts of Parliament provided for more stringent enforcement of law and maintenance of order, and a strong effort was made to restore the royal finances. At the same time, many important government offices were taken away from the great nobility and given to men James could trust. Apparently these measures aroused opposition, for several of the leading nobles were executed in 1425. Another means of controlling the nobility was by sending certain of their numbers to England to serve as the required hostages until the King's ransom was wholly paid (which it never was).

James's assertion of the powers of the central government was generally popular with other elements of the kingdom, if not with the nobility; and his reign is noteworthy for advances in the structure of Parliament and for reform in the law courts. His efforts both to concentrate governmental powers in the royal courts and to improve the financial position of the throne led also to laws limiting clerical appeals to the papacy and restricting payments from the Scottish Church to the papacy.

Despite James's marriage to an English noblewoman and the promise to suspend aid to France, the King's foreign policy remained basically pro-French and anti-English, especially in the latter years of the reign. In 1428 an engagement had been arranged between James's 2-year-old daughter Margaret and the 5-year-old dauphin Louis (the future Louis XI), son of Charles VII of France. The marriage took place in 1436, and in the same year war was resumed with England.

Though the last years of James's reign are somewhat obscure, it is clear that his efforts to secure effective royal government aroused bitter hostility among some of the nobility (a feeling highly aggravated by James's acquisitiveness in seizing the lands of inimical nobles). A conspiracy was formed to put the Earl of Atholl (the surviving son of Robert II's second marriage) on the throne, and James was murdered by Sir Robert Graham and others on Feb. 20, 1437. The conspirators' hopes were not fulfilled; they were hunted down and executed, and the crown passed to James II, the 6-year-old son of James I and Queen Joan.

James remains a notable Scottish hero, renowned alike for his efforts at good government and for the romantic aspects of his life. He is almost certainly the author of the *King's Quair* (that is, the King's Book), celebrating his love for Joan (or Jane) Beaufort in some 200 Chaucerian stanzas. The ascription of three other poems to him is dubious. He was fond of good living (some of his ransom money was diverted to buy jewels for the royal person) and was described by Aeneas Sylvius (the future Pope Pius II) as Quadratus, or foursquare.

Further Reading

The standard life of James is E. W. M. Balfour-Melville, *James I: King of Scots, 1406-1437* (1936). Historical background for the period is in William Croft Dickinson, *A New History of Scotland,* vol. 1 (1961; 2d rev. ed. 1965). □

James II

James II (1633-1701) was king of England, Scotland, and Ireland from 1685 to 1688. Britain's last Stuart and last Catholic monarch, he granted religious minorities the right to worship. He was deposed by the Glorious Revolution.

Since the Declaration of Rights of 1689 charged him with attempting to "subvert and extirpate the Protestant religion and the laws and liberties of the kingdom," James II has traditionally been treated as a would-be tyrant by older historians. Recent writers have pointed out that his failures were more personal than political. In 1679, in lofty concept of his office, James stated that "the monarchy, . . . I thank God, yet has had no dependency on parliaments nor on nothing but God alone." And within the strict letter of the constitution, James was not wrong. James's Catholicism, to which he was converted about 1670, is viewed as a major impediment, for in its cause he committed most of his excesses.

Born in October 1633, the second son of Charles I, James was created Duke of York at baptism. He mastered the rudiments of soldiering and seamanship. He emulated his older brother, Charles II, to the point of matching him in number of mistresses. However, he turned increasingly to religion in his later years.

After his father's execution in 1649, James wandered into foreign military service during the Commonwealth period (1649-1660). With the restoration of the Stuarts, he served his brother as lord high admiral, administered colonies in Africa and New York, and fought at sea in two wars against Holland, in 1665 and 1672.

After his conversion to Catholicism, James's religion, his pro-French policies, and his antiparliamentarian sentiments attracted the hostilities of the emerging Whig party. The Test Act (1673), which deprived Catholics of government office, was aimed largely at James. Though he resigned from the Admiralty, the Whigs hounded him between 1679 and 1681 with the Exclusion Bill, designed to remove him totally from the succession to the throne.

Charles crushed this opposition and reinstated James in the Admiralty and the Council in 1682.

In February 1685 James became king upon his brother's death and began a troubled reign of nearly 4 years. The Monmouth Rebellion (1685), led by his illegitimate nephew, was put down so severely by Judge Jeffreys that James's popularity was impaired. He attempted to master opposition by controlling local elections, expelling Protestant university officials and replacing them with Catholics, reviving the Anglican Church's High Commission, which removed the critical bishop of London, and maintaining a standing army outside London. While granting toleration to Catholics and to Protestant Dissenters, he did so by decree and not by parliamentary statute. When the archbishop of Canterbury refused to promulgate the decree, he and six bishops were arrested in June 1688. The occasion caused even passive observers to resent James's autocracy, and when a few ardent opponents summoned William of Orange, James's son-in-law, to save England's "religion, liberties and properties" by invasion, most of the nation willingly allowed the so-called Glorious Revolution to run its course. James fled England in December 1688, never to return.

Louis XIV gave asylum to James. Until July 1690 French military and naval units aided the efforts of James's English supporters, the Jacobites (from the Latin *Jacobus*, James), in Ireland, but at the battle of the Boyne River (July 1, 1690) James was defeated. Upon his return to France, James withdrew from active leadership of his own cause, demoralized still further by Louis's recognition of William and Mary's legitimate rule in the Treaty of Ryswick (1697). He died in September 1701.

Two marriages, to Anne Hyde (1660) and to Mary of Modena (1673), produced 15 children; two of James's daughters later became queens of England, and a son became the "Old Pretender" of the Jacobite cause.

Further Reading

The only reliable biography of James is Francis C. Turner, *James II* (1948). The best study of his reign is David Ogg, *England in the Reigns of James II and William III* (1955).

Additional Sources

Ashley, Maurice, *James II,* Minneapolis: University of Minnesota Press, 1977.
Miller, John, *James II: a study in kingship,* Hove: Wayland, 1978.
Trevor, Meriol, *The shadow of a crown: the life story of James II of England and VII of Scotland,* London: Constable, 1988. □

James III

James III (1451-1488) was king of Scotland from 1460 to 1488. His reign marked perhaps the weakest point of the Scottish monarchy.

James III came to the throne suddenly in 1460, when his father, James II, was killed by the back-firing of a siege gun. The queen mother, Mary of Gueldres, tended to favor the Yorkist side in the English dynastic stuggles (often called the Wars of the Roses), but her influence was contested by that of James Kennedy, Bishop of St. Andrews, who favored the Lancastrian cause and arranged that King Henry VI of England and his queen flee to Scotland after their disastrous loss at Towton in 1461. This meant that Edward IV, the new English (Yorkist) king, would regard the monarchy of the young James as something to be overthrown if possible. For the moment, however, a truce was made with England.

The regency proceeded well enough until the death of Bishop Kennedy in 1465. The King then fell under the influence of his tutor, Sir Alexander Boyd, governor of Edinburgh Castle, and a party of minor nobility headed by the Boyds seized the young king and kept control of affairs in the kingdom for some 3 years. Robert, Lord Boyd, now leader of the regency, arranged for James a marriage with Margaret, daughter of Christian I of Denmark. This marriage, in 1468, had far-reaching effects for Scotland, for Margaret's dowry was the Orkney and Shetland islands, which until then had been under the control of the Scandinavian kingdom. But, more immediately, while the Boyds had been away arranging the marriage, their enemies had plotted their downfall, and their power was broken in November 1469.

James was now old enough to rule personally, but he was not a great success. Many of the older nobility resented his preference for men of low rank as his intimate coun-

selors and his fondness for the arts rather than for fighting. Parliament frequently exhorted him to maintain order more vigorously. Even within his own family there was trouble, for James had two ambitious and disloyal younger brothers, the Duke of Albany and the Earl of Mar. Mar was arrested in 1479 (having been accused of witchcraft) and died soon thereafter. Albany escaped from captivity and allied himself with Edward IV, who was prepared to support him against James. An English army invaded Scotland, but suddenly James and Albany were reconciled. However, Albany's plotting continued, and he was finally banished, narrowly escaping to France in 1484.

A new and even more serious conspiracy arose among many of the Lowlands nobility in 1488, and in a battle at Sauchieburn near the celebrated field of Bannockburn the royal army was defeated. The King himself, having been carried away from the battle, was discovered and killed by a rebel soldier. His eldest son, who was the nominal head of the rebels, succeeded him on the throne as James IV and in his reign did much to reverse the unfortunate characteristics which had marred that of his father.

Further Reading

For information on James see general histories of Scotland, especially William Croft Dickinson, *A New History of Scotland,* vol. 1 (1961; 2d rev. ed. 1965).

Additional Sources

Macdougall, Norman, *James III, a political study,* Edinburgh: J. Donald Publishers; Atlantic Highlands, NJ, USA: Exclusive distribution in the U.S. and Canada by Humanities Press, 1982. □

Daniel James Jr.

Daniel "Chappie" James, Jr. (1920-1978) was the first African American man to become a four star general in the history of the U.S. military.

Daniel "Chappie" James was born in Pensacola, Florida, in 1920, the last of 17 children. His father was a laborer and his mother a teacher who conducted a school for African American youths in the backyard of the James' home. James' mother was diligent about preparing her offspring and her students to confront racial prejudice. She emphasized that they should strive for academic excellence in order to demonstrate that the African American was inferior to none. She believed that if blacks performed well, whites would acknowledge their achievements and racial discrimination would gradually end. She encouraged her students with her "eleventh" commandment, "Thou shalt never quit."

Together James' parents imbued him with a desire to succeed, the gift of laughter, and a sense of freedom and fair play. All of these characteristics would prove invaluable to him in his career as a leader of men. James was popular and reasonably successful in high school. He planned to go to

Tuskegee Institute but feared that his plans would fail when his father died before he graduated from high school. However, his mother and older brothers and sisters assured him that they would help him pay his tuition and fees.

James' interests wavered among music, drama, and football, but he was unswerving in his desire to become a military pilot. While he was growing up in Pensacola he often observed flights at a nearby naval air base and dreamed about flying a plane himself. Many of his friends laughed at the idea of an African American youth becoming a pilot—something that was almost unheard of at the time—but James had been taught to firmly believe in himself and his capabilities.

When James enrolled at Tuskegee in 1937, he was over six feet tall and considered quite handsome by many of the coeds. James led his fellow students into a variety of escapades during his undergraduate years, but in his senior year he pushed the school's administrators too far and they expelled him. In 1969, after almost 30 years passed, Tuskegee awarded James a bachelor of science degree based on the numerous credit hours he had earned during his military career.

Pilot Training

James' expulsion proved to be a blessing in disguise. A civilian pilot training program had been established at Tuskegee and young men were being actively recruited. The training school for the Tuskegee airmen was an experimental program designed to determine the ability of African

American men to perform satisfactorily as pilots. James qualified for training and embarked on the very career he had dreamed about. He not only learned how to fly but began to teach other trainees. James subsequently enlisted in the Army Air Force and was commissioned as a second lieutenant in 1943.

Because the armed forces were rigidly segregated by race, African American officers and enlisted men often faced tense racial situations in military and civilian life. When James was assigned to Selfridge Field in Michigan he found that African American officers were humiliated in a number of ways, including their exclusion from the officer's club. The military was legally obligated to provide separate but equal facilities for blacks and whites. Since this racial policy proved to be costly, military commanders often failed to provide equal facilities for African Americans. Dissatisfaction among African American officers and enlisted men, coupled with the expense of segregation, prompted President Harry Truman to declare it illegal in 1948.

Combat Pilot

James flew 101 combat missions during the Korean War and 78 missions in North Vietnam while he was stationed in Thailand. After his tour in Southeast Asia, James was named vice commander of the 33rd Tactical Fighter Wing at Elgin Air Force Base in Florida. One of his most challenging assignments, however, was the command of the 7272nd Flying Training Wing at Wheelus Air Force Base in Libya. The time James spent in Libya—from fall 1969 until spring 1970—was critical because General Muammar Gaddafi, who had led a successful coup d'etat against Libyan King Idris in September 1969, wanted the Americans out immediately. After the United States decided to evacuate, James directed the operation.

Air Force General

In December 1969 James learned that he had been nominated by President Richard M. Nixon to be promoted to the rank of brigadier general. His next assignment was in the Pentagon Public Affairs Office. In this position he travelled around the country speaking to various groups, including dissatisfied African American servicemen, high school and college students, and the wives of U.S. soldiers in Vietnam who were either missing in action or prisoners of war. He attempted to combat both anti-Vietnam War sentiment and racial antipathy by cogently stating the necessity for unity and patriotism. James, who had been promoted to lieutenant general in 1973, became a four star general in 1975 and was assigned to be the commander-in-chief of North American Air Defense (NORAD), the primary defense system for the United States and Canada. After successfully serving in this position for several years, James retired in 1978. Within several weeks of his retirement he died of a heart ailment.

Further Reading

James R. McGovern has written a biography of James entitled *Black Eagle, General Daniel "Chappie" James, Jr.* (1985).

Carolyn Dubose wrote "Chappie James, A New Role for an Old Warrior," for the October 1970 *Ebony* magazine.

Two helpful general studies about Blacks in the military are Richard M. Dalfiume, *Desegregation of the U.S. Armed Forces: Fighting on Two Fronts, 1939-1953* (1969) and Morris J. MacGregor, Jr., *Integration of the Armed Forces, 1940-1965* (1981).

Additional Sources

Phelps, J. Alfred, *Chappie: America's first Black four-star general: the life and times of Daniel James, Jr.,* Novato, CA: Presidio, 1992. □

Henry James

The American author Henry James (1843-1916) was one of the major novelists of the late 19th and early 20th centuries. His works deal largely with the impact of Europe and its society on Americans.

Henry James, the son of a theologian and the brother of the philosopher William James, was born on April 15, 1843, at Washington Place in New York City. His childhood was spent in the city and in Albany and then, between the ages of 12 and 17, in Europe. He was privately tutored in London, Geneva, and Paris. His American education began at school in Newport, R.I. James entered Harvard Law School in 1862, leaving after a year. In 1864 his family settled in Boston and then in Cambridge. That same year he published his first story and early reviews.

James's frequent appearances in the *Atlantic Monthly* began in 1865. Four years later he traveled again in England, France, and Italy, returning to Cambridge in 1870 and publishing his first novel, *Watch and Ward*. It concerned American life in a specifically American setting, the upper-class world of Boston, its suburbs, and Newport. At the age of 29 James was again in Europe, spending a summer in Paris and most of 1873 in Rome, where he began *Roderick Hudson*. For a year in New York City he was part of the literary world of the era. His criticism appeared in 1874 and 1875 in the *Nation* and the *North American Review*. Also in 1875, *Transatlantic Sketches, A Passionate Pilgrim,* and *Roderick Hudson* appeared. *Transatlantic Sketches* is a travel book, as is *A Passionate Pilgrim,* which anticipates the theme of the European impact on what James repeatedly identified as the "American state of Innocence." *Roderick Hudson* is fiction on the same theme, a response to the colony of American expatriates James knew in Rome.

His Expatriation

James's disengagement from America was a long process; he wrote: "I saw my parents homesick, as I conceived, for the ancient order, and distressed and inconvenienced by many of the more immediate features of the modern, as the modern pressed about us, and since their theory of a better living was from an early time that we should renew the question of the ancient on the very first possibility I simply grew greater in the faith that somehow to manage that would constitute success in life." Living in Paris during 1876, James wrote *The American*. At the time, he knew Ivan Turgenev, Gustave Flaubert, Edmond de Goncourt, Émile Zola, and others. His expatriation was complete by the end of that year, when he settled in London.

The impact of his short novel *Daisy Miller* (1879) brought James fame in Europe and the United States; it was his first popular success. He explained the novel this way: "The whole idea of the story is the little tragedy of a light, thin, natural, unsuspecting creature being sacrificed as it were to a social rumpus that went on quite over her head and to which she stood in no measurable relation. To deepen the effect, I have made it go over her mother's head as well." James repeated the same effect, and intention, in several other novels and stories. In *The Portrait of a Lady,* for example, the effect is similar but more intricate. James mentioned his "Americano-European legends" as one of the central impulses of his work.

Between 1879 and 1882 James produced his first major series of novels. They were *The Europeans, Washington Square, Confidence,* and *The Portrait of a Lady*. Of the four, only *Washington Square* is about American life. By 1886 a 14-volume collection of his novels and tales was published. He wrote *The Bostonians* and *The Princess Casamassima* in 1886 while living in a flat in De Vere Gardens in London. Both are social dramas. "The Aspern Papers," the short novel *The Reverberator,* and "A London Life" appeared the following year. *The Tragic Muse,* one of his most ambitious novels, was serialized in the *Atlantic Monthly* in 1890.

James then entered a 5-year period in which he concentrated on writing drama. *The American* was produced as a play in London by Edward Compton. The effort ended in 1895, when he was jeered at the opening of his play *Guy Domville* at St. James's Theatre in London. He abandoned the stage. Almost never revived, his plays are included in two volumes, *Theatricals* and *Theatricals: Second Series*.

Later Career

A bachelor, James settled in Lamb House, Rye, in 1898, and continued his 20-year "siege" of English life and society. His schedule of concentrated work during the day and of relaxation at night produced in 1898 *The Two Magics,* a collection of stories that includes his novella "The Turn of the Screw" and the short novel *In the Cage.* What is frequently identified as his third and best phase began the following year with *The Awkward Age,* and between 1899 and 1904 he wrote *The Sacred Fount, The Wings of the Dove, The Ambassadors,* and *The Golden Bowl.* James himself described *The Ambassadors* as the "best 'all round'" of his novels. In his early, middle, and later periods he relied explicitly on "devices" and the "grammar" of fiction, on "point of view," "scene," "dramatizing," selection of incidents, structure, and perspective. It was through technique that he isolated values, and he insisted that the primary values were "truth" and "life."

In September 1904 James returned to the United States after a 20-year absence, passing the fall with his brother William in New Hampshire and, later, revisiting New York City. After a year of lecturing he returned to Lamb House in England and began revising his fiction and writing the critical prefaces to the definitive New York edition of his work. During 1909 he suffered from a long nervous illness and produced a series of stories that appeared as *The Finer Grain.* He was in New Hampshire when William died after a long illness. Before returning to England in 1911, he received an honorary degree from Harvard; he received another from Oxford the following year.

James's autobiographical memoirs, *A Small Boy and Others* and *Notes of a Son and Brother,* were completed shortly before the outbreak of World War I. The war's disruption greatly disturbed him. He began war work in various hospitals, writing for war charities and aiding Belgian refugees. On July 26, 1915, James was naturalized as a British subject. Later in the year his last illness, a stroke and pneumonia, began. Before his death on Feb. 28, 1916, he received the Order of Merit from King George V. The funeral services were in Chelsea Old Church, London, and his ashes were buried in the family plot in Cambridge, Mass.

Further Reading

Critical and biographical material on James is extensive. The definitive biography is Leon Edel, *Henry James* (5 vols., 1953-1972). Other biographies are Van Wyck Brooks, *The Pilgrimage of Henry James* (1925), an early and influential book, and Quentin Anderson, *The American Henry James* (1957). F. W. Dupee, *Henry James* (1951; 2d ed. rev. 1956), is a critical biography. Millicent Bell, *Edith Wharton and Henry James: The Story of Their Friendship* (1965), contains correspondence of James to Mrs. Wharton and considerable biographi-

cal material. Oscar Cargill, *The Novels of Henry James* (1961), is an articulate introduction to his writing. Important critical studies of James are Joseph Warren Beach, *The Method of Henry James* (1918; rev. ed. 1954), and F. O. Matthiessen, *Henry James: The Major Phase* (1944). See also Christof Wegelin, *The Image of Europe in Henry James* (1958). Roger Gard, ed., *Henry James: The Critical Heritage* (1968), is a collection of reviews and articles on James and is useful in viewing responses to James's work from the late 19th to the early 20th century. □

Jesse Woodson James

American outlaw Jesse Woodson James (1847-1882) was a colorful bandit whose escapades made him a legendary figure of the Wild West.

Jesse James was born near Kearney, Mo., on Sept. 5, 1847, the son of a Baptist minister. Little is known about Jesse's childhood except that his father left the family in 1850 to minister to the gold prospectors in California and died soon after his arrival there. The three James children grew up on a Missouri farm with a stepfather.

As slave owners with origins in Kentucky, James's entire family were Southern sympathizers. So, during the Civil War, he joined the Confederate guerrilla band known as Quantrill's Raiders in 1863 or 1864. Returning to Missouri in 1865, Jesse and his brother Frank found that, although the Civil War was officially over, Missourians were still belligerent. In 1866 the James brothers joined forces with the Younger brothers to form an outlaw band.

For 16 years Jesse James and his gang robbed trains and banks in Missouri, Kentucky, and the midwestern states. Killings accompanied these activities, and James was hunted by the law. Of necessity, he was always on the run. His daring exploits during these years captured the imagination of the public, and all sorts of legends sprung up about him.

On April 23, 1874, occurred the one documented event in James's life: he married Zerelda, or Zee, Mimms near Kearney, Mo. In time they had two children.

The most famous bank robbery attempted by the James-Younger band was at the First National Bank of Northfield, Minn., on Sept. 7, 1876. The bank clerk, who refused to open the safe, was savagely murdered; then the gang tried to escape. In the shoot-out that followed, two of the band were killed. A posse captured the three Younger brothers. Jesse and Frank James, both wounded, escaped. After they recovered, they continued robbing and killing sporadically.

Finally the governor of Missouri offered a $10,000 reward for the capture of the James brothers. At this time Jesse was living with his family in St. Joseph, Mo., under the name of Thomas Howard. Robert and Charles Ford, youthful recruits in the outlaw band, were staying for a few days with the James family. Robert had been in contact with authorities about the reward for several weeks. On April 3, 1882, when Jesse put his guns down to climb on a chair to

straighten a picture, Robert Ford shot him in the back of the head and killed him. Soon after, Frank James turned himself in.

Further Reading

A conscientious effort to ferret out the facts on James is William A. Settle, Jr., *Jesse James Was His Name; or, Fact and Fiction concerning the Careers of the Notorious James Brothers of Missouri* (1966). It is well researched and interestingly written. Another good treatment, fairly accurate and thorough but not dealing with the legends, is Carl W. Breihan, *The Complete and Authentic Life of Jesse James* (1953).

Additional Sources

Brant, Marley, *Outlaws: the illustrated history of the James-Younger gang,* Washington, DC: Elliott & Clark Pub., 1996.

Breihan, Carl W., *The escapades of Frank and Jesse James,* New York: F. Fell Publishers, 1974.

Breihan, Carl W., *The man who shot Jesse James,* South Brunswick N.J.: A. S. Barnes, 1979.

Breihan, Carl W., *Saga of Jesse James,* Caldwell, Idaho: Caxton Printers, 1991.

Dyer, Robert, *Jesse James and the Civil War in Missouri,* Columbia: University of Missouri Press, 1994.

James, Stella F. (Stella Frances), *In the shadow of Jesse James,* Thousand Oaks, CA, USA: Revolver Press, 1990, 1989.

Love, Robertus, *The rise and fall of Jesse James,* Lincoln: University of Nebraska Press, 1990.

Newmans, Evans, *The true story of the notorious Jesse James,* Hicksville, N.Y.: Exposition Press, 1976. □

P. D. James

The British author P(hyllis) D(orothy) James (born 1920) wrote in the tradition of the British crime storyteller, but her extensive explorations of relationships, motivations, and meanings of justice classified her, in the opinion of some, as a novelist.

P. D. James—Queen of Crime, Mistress of Murder, OBE (Order of the British Empire), baroness, and grandmother—was born Phyllis Dorothy James on August 3, 1920, in Oxford, England, the oldest of three children. Her parents, Sidney Victor, a tax official, and Dorothy May (Hone) James, moved the family to Cambridge, where James attended the Cambridge High School for Girls. One of this century's foremost crime novelists had to leave school at age 16 to work in a tax office, followed by a stint as assistant stage manager for the Festival Theatre in Cambridge. (Her own play *A Private Treason* was staged in 1985 in London's West End.)

During World War II she worked as a Red Cross nurse and for the Ministry of Food. On August 8, 1941, she married Ernest Connor Bantry White of the Royal Army Medical Corps, and in 1942 and 1944 gave birth to their daughters, Claire and Jane. When White returned from the war in 1945, he was suffering from schizophrenia and frequently had to be hospitalized.. He was unemployable, leaving her to provide for their family until his death in 1964. So James studied hospital administration, and from 1949 to 1968 she served as administrative assistant with the North West Regional Hospital Board in London.

First Novel

She would be in her early forties before her first novel, *Cover Her Face,* was published in 1962. By that time both personal and professional experience and contacts had nurtured her knowledge and powers of observation and reflection. These informed both her depiction of police detection and her portrayal of characters drawn within a given social ambience.

Cover Her Face was followed during this period by *A Mind to Murder* and *Unnatural Causes.* She co-authored with Thomas A. Critchley *The Maul and the Pear Tree,* a recounting of a real life murder from the annals of 19th-century London.

Not until 1979 would she devote herself to full-time authorship. In 1968, she qualified—via open exam—for civil service in the Home Office, rising from her initial appointment (1968) with the Department of Home Affairs, London, to senior civil servant in the Crime Department (1972-1979). Additionally, her various public service roles included that of magistrate. James's work experience is reflected in her novels, providing convincing backgrounds for both the medical establishment and police procedure. The settings of four of her mysteries are in medicine-related facilities: a psychiatric clinic in *A Mind to Murder* (1962), a nurses' training school in *Shroud for a Nightingale* (1971), a

private home for the disabled in *The Black Tower* (1975), and a forensic science laboratory in *Death of an Expert Witness* (1977). In all these novels she is just as interested in dissecting the relationships among people living in closed communities as she is in the conventions of the mystery genre. She is often inspired by a sense of place, as in *Devices and Desires* (1989), with its bleak landscape dominated by a nuclear power station.

On the one hand, James wrote in the tradition of the British crime storyteller as represented by such authors as Dorothy L. Sayers, Agatha Christie, Margery Allingham, Ngaio Marsh, and Josephine Tey—what Marilyn Stasio, in the *New York Times* for October 9, 1988, refers to as the "polite mystery." (Her Adam Dalgliesh has joined Lord Peter Wimsey, Miss Marple, Hercule Poirot, and Albert Campion on television. Her *Original Sin* was also adapted for the television series *Mystery!*).

On the other hand, she probed for motivations; explored relationships between even relatively minor characters and within individual characters; raised complex questions about guilt and innocence, about the adequacy and ultimate justice of legal assumptions and processes, about religion; and explored the resonance of setting of significant landmarks, of the individual's tellingly personal surroundings. Frequently in her settings she confronts an extensive Past with a not always appreciative and usually clumsily adapting Present; her characters, too, have resonant pasts.

Experimentation With the Mystery Form

James's work is distinguished not only for the consistent quality of plot, setting, and character, but for her increasing experimentation with the mystery form. Her first novel, *Cover Her Face* (1962), is a classic "locked-room" puzzle, set in a British country house, complete with a confrontation of all the suspects at the end. *Innocent Blood* (1980) departs from the form almost entirely because the search is not to find the murderer but to find the natural mother of a child adopted at birth. In the brilliantly complex *A Taste for Death* (1986), an unlikely pair of companions stumble upon an unlikely pair of murder victims in an anteroom of an imaginary London cathedral. The situation allows James to deal with questions of privilege, politics, aesthetics, and theology. *The Children of Men* (1993) leans toward science fiction, using as its premise a global disease that blocks all future births. Such complexity and depth led her, in the opinion of some, out of the classification of crime genre author into that of, simply, novelist. James herself admitted to using the detective story format to comment on men, women, and society and to having first viewed writing a mystery as practice toward her ambition of writing a novel. She later came to view her detective stories as "novels, too," and told Julian Symons (*New York Times,* October 5, 1986) that she would, should it become necessary, "sacrifice . . . the detective element" to the requirement of the novel.

Some critics are dismayed by her concern with the psychology of her characters, especially when it has more to do with presenting a well-rounded character and exploring the ramifications of crime among even tangential characters than with forwarding the basic detective story puzzle and solution. They criticize her for violating the purity of the genre, for delaying plot progress, and for dissipating reader interest. Yet the qualities condemned by one group are prized by another as evidence of the maturing into true literary status of a subgenre. Her many honors include the Crime Writers' Association's gold and silver daggers.

In her 13th novel, *Original Sin,* a ruthless book publisher is found asphyxiated by gas, with the head of the office mascot—a snake nicknamed Hissing Sid—stuffed in his forever-silenced mouth. Another ill-fated publishing figure meets her end in the lapping waters of the Thames River—her body kept anchored by the shoulder strap of her pocketbook.

Main Characters

The James canon of novels, with the exception of *Innocent Blood* (1980), involves either Adam Dalgliesh or Cordelia Gray, a struggling young private detective introduced in *An Unsuitable Job for a Woman* (1972). In addition to the individual mysteries, the Dalgliesh and Gray biographies, tantalizingly interwoven, unfold from book to book.

Dalgliesh, who is also a published poet, has risen from chief inspector to commander of the Special Squad, newly formed in *A Taste for Death* (1986). Sensitive, respected though not always liked by colleagues, he is a man shadowed by grief—the death in childbirth of his wife and, shortly afterward, of their infant son. The only son of an

Anglican clergyman, he is no longer a believer yet seems haunted by that forsaken heritage. This is not simply a matter of the occasional case involving a respected clergyman from his youth—as in *The Black Tower* (1975) and the short story "Great-Aunt Allie's Flypapers" (1979)—nor even the religious experience of Paul Berowne in *Taste.* Repeatedly detection discloses sympathetic perpetrators, unsympathetic victims, disruption in the lives of all—kith, kin, and bystanders—necessarily caught up in the investigation. Complexities of justice are exposed to which law does not reach but for which, he acknowledges, Christian theology provides a solution. Yet, for all its limitations, law is necessary to the safety of society.

Cordelia Gray is similarly troubled and, in *Unsuitable Job,* helps a killer escape. The daughter of an atheistic father so cause-committed as to be somewhat negligent of his motherless daughter's rearing, she has been educated in a Roman Catholic school. One of the major influences on her life, in addition to Bernie Pryde, from whom she inherited Pryde's Detective Agency and through whom she has been instructed in detection according to Dalgliesh, is Sister Perpetua.

James herself was troubled by the increasing violence and insecurity of contemporary society and, while professing to be a devout Anglican, was not sure that she believed in the after-life where Christians are urged to look for totally satisfying justice.

Reader speculation as to whether Dalgliesh and Gray would marry led James to declare that, for the sake of the unity and quality of their respective novels (Gray's second book, *The Skull Beneath the Skin,* appeared in 1982), she had no such plans for them. However, she deliberately avoided making the statement an absolute negative and continued to weave references to one into the other's novels. She trailed the possibility of Dalgliesh's remarriage—to Deborah Riscoe—through earlier books; the situation by 1990, however, differed both in Gray's stature and in Dalgliesh's circumstances, updated in *Devices and Desires* (1989).

James also published a number of short stories in such mystery collections as *Winter's Crimes, Ellery Queen's Murder Menu,* and *Ellery Queen's Masters of Mystery.*

P. D. James, the much honored author who, like her detective Cordelia Gray, has known the pinch of a budget, lived comfortably in London. She was awarded the Order of the British Empire (OBE) in 1983 and made a baroness on the Queen's New Year's Honors List (1991). James was made a member of the governor's board of the BBC maintaining that writers should be involved with the outside world. James was also named the Baroness James of Holland Park (her London neighborhood) in 1991 and was made a Commander of the British Empire in 1992.

Further Reading

Two books are available on James: *P. D. James* by Richard B. Gidez (1986); and *P. D. James* by Norma Siebenheller (1981); SueEllen Campbell discusses "The Detective Heroine and the Death of her Hero: Dorothy Sayers to P. D. James" in *Modern Fiction Studies* 29 (Autumn 1983); in the same volume ap-

pears Erlene Hubly's "The Formula Challenged: The Novels of P. D. James"; Patricia A. Ward treats of "Moral Ambiguities and the Crime Novels of P. D. James" in *Christian Century* 101 (May 16, 1984); and M. Cannon discusses James' particular brand of crime in "Mistress of Malice Domestic" in the *New York Times Book Review* for April 27, 1980; P. D. James herself, in *Murder Ink,* has written "House Calls: The Doctor Detective Round-up." ☐

William James

The American philosopher and psychologist William James (1842-1910) is considered America's major philosopher and one of the great psychologists of all times.

Member of an illustrious family which included his younger brother, the novelist Henry James, William James was born in New York and reared there and in Europe by adoring parents. The family went repeatedly for long and intimate visits to the great cultural centers of England, France, Switzerland, Germany, and Italy. William's cosmopolitanism went deep; when in Europe he always felt eager to be home again, and when in America he was homesick for Europe.

James's Education

James was equally interested in art (he almost became a painter), in literature, in philosophy, and in science (he made a visit as a field naturalist under Louis Agassiz to the Amazon and achieved broad science training and a medical degree at Harvard in 1869). In these same years he was studying philosophy and physiology, notably in Germany, where he attended lectures and saw the laboratory work of such great leaders as Hermann von Helmholtz and Rudolf Virchow. But James was also drawn very vigorously into the pioneering intellectual adventures of the America of the mid-19th century, notably its new religious movement.

As an ardent evolutionist, William James saw many ways in which the mind could be fruitfully regarded as the organ of primary adaptation to the environment, in a full Darwinian sense, and how all its functions—whether cognitive, emotional, or impulsive—could be viewed in evolutionary terms. This conception drew him to a philosophy which later he was to call pragmatism; it constitutes one of the major bridges between his psychology and his philosophy.

Despite his eager and strenuous ways, as shown in his mountain rambles with his brother Henry, James was not strong, and in the 1860s and early 1870s he was subject to ill health, which included much depression and doubt of his own worth. During this period, however, he read the French philosopher Charles Bernard Renouvier on the problem of the freedom of the will and came suddenly and firmly to the conviction that he could, by his own act of free will, make himself a well man. His own life and the testimony of the family bear out the profundity of this experience.

William James (right)

James's appointment to a junior teaching position at Harvard in 1872 set him on a new professional track. He was to teach anatomy and physiology to undergraduate students, and he soon set up a small psychological laboratory, emphasizing the fact that it was not a classical "mental philosophy" that he was to teach but a physiological and experimental science. It is plain from his letters to his brother that he was already thinking of himself as committed to the new laboratory approach to psychology. This does not, however, mean that he was willing to relinquish any of his other manifold interests. He was soon publishing original and brilliant articles in the professional journals of psychology and philosophy. He married Alice Gibbens in 1878.

Principles of Psychology

Also in 1878 James began writing a comprehensive treatise and textbook, *Principles of Psychology,* the two volumes of which, intended for 1880, finally appeared in 1890. This extraordinary treatise brought him worldwide response and has continued everywhere to be regarded as one of the few great comprehensive treatises that modern psychology has produced.

Five of the chapters are worthy of special note: (1) The chapter dealing with "habit," considered as a prime factor so deeply organized within one as to make each one the creature of a system of inbuilt ways of thinking, feeling, and

acting. (2) "Emotion," the subjective or inner aspect of the "coarser" organic physiological responses to stress situations, such as fear and rage, with a place also provided for the subtler emotions, entering into the intellectual and esthetic life. (3) The "consciousness of self," the various ways in which one knows one's self and the aspects of one's own individuality that are most precious to one. (4) The "stream of thought," the complex, dynamic, ever-changing world of subjectivity in which there is no firmly fixed invariant part, no unalterable unit, except that each person is always aware that it is his *own* continuous past, present, and anticipated future. (5) The "will." The very long and rich chapter on the will provides for many "types of decision" and for the experience of effort when "we ourselves incline the beam." An empirical psychology must accept as a reality the experience of making an effortful decision; this leaves the ultimate philosophical question of the nature of such freedom as a problem beyond the scope of scientific psychology as such.

James's treatment indeed is embedded in the context of a lifetime preoccupation with the nature of freedom. James recurred to this problem in other writings again and again. In his lecture "The Will to Believe," he argued that spontaneous and free decisions may initiate a new path through life, and the will does, in fact, implement beliefs; the "will to believe," instead of being intellectually disreputable, may engender beliefs which are creative. He made clear the basic differentiation to be made between "hard determinism," or fatalism, and "soft determinism," in which persons are part of the causal texture of reality, products of real forces, and in turn forces which create new realities. Soft determinism is still determinism, but it gives the freedom to act in terms of what one is. This is still to be distinguished from the kind of freedom represented by a belief in undetermined action.

Not only was the *Principles of Psychology* universally acclaimed, but James, as teacher, dynamically taught a generation concerned with psychology and its relation to life. The playwright and poet Gertrude Stein, for example, was a Radcliffe-Harvard student of James, who put the notion of the "stream of thought" or "stream of consciousness" to work in American letters. Many of his lectures, both at Harvard and elsewhere, became landmarks of the era of social confrontation, notably "The Moral Equivalent of War," in which he pleaded for warlike intensities in devotion to nonwarlike social struggles.

During the last decade of the 19th century and the first decade of the 20th, James was plainly moving away from the new "experimental psychology" of the university laboratories to the world of personal, subjective, philosophically challenging problems, such as the perennial problem of whether there is really any truth independent of the working principles which are known to be effective in one's own action (pragmatism). These questions were being raised in new form by many, notably Charles Peirce, and James himself offered the term pragmatism as "a new name for some old ways of thinking." During the last years of his life he was constantly asked to explain and develop pragmatism, and it became a major American way of thinking.

Lectures on Philosophy

Very great indeed was the impact of James's extraordinary lectures delivered at Edinburgh in 1901 under the title "The Varieties of Religious Experience." This is regarded by many as the first great, insightful application of psychology to the study of the religious life. Insisting that the religious experience of "individual men in their solitude" must be studied independently of medical preconceptions, he distinguished between the "religion of healthymindedness" and the "sick soul." James showed how a wider and deeper range of sensitivity, often shown by the sick soul, may lead to meaningful experiences of deep change or conversion and to states of ecstasy and self-renewal.

The concluding lectures were given to the psychology of mystical experience as represented in the mystical tradition of such men as Plotinus and of modern men, Eastern and Western, who were speaking and writing of "cosmic consciousness." To James it appeared that the message of mystical experience, the "windows" into experience which it offered, could well be absolute and compelling for the individual, though, of course, not compelling to the outside observer or analyst who has not had such experiences. Here he stressed the importance of many "altered states of consciousness." (He himself studied nitrous oxide intoxication and was keenly interested in the new drug experiences of the day as well as in a variety of trance and hypnotic states: a person's present mode of consciousness is only one from among many "states of consciousness that exist.")

James strongly supported "mental healing." He went to the Boston State House to protest the attempt of many physicians to require non medical practitioners to take a type of medical examination as a qualification for practice; he insisted that no one can really tell by what means the sick are healed. He had himself, shortly before that time, sought help from a "healer" and remained entirely empirical regarding the question of gains in health due to unorthodox sources.

Psychical Research

In the same empirical spirit James pursued throughout his life many types of psychological phenomena rejected by official science, such as apparitions, hauntings, and spiritualist trance mediumship. In 1884 he discovered Mrs. L. E. Piper, who, in the sittings given to his wife and his wife's mother, had referred to information which they were positive Piper could not have acquired through any normal channel. In his own sittings, equally convincing evidence was given, and many of James's professional friends, both in the United States and in Britain, had similar experiences which entirely convinced them of the reality of her powers, which, at the very least, included telepathy from distant persons. He took the initiative in organizing an American counterpart to the Society for Psychical Research, which had just been launched in London in 1882. He made firsthand studies of the powers of other clairvoyants whose work was drawn to his attention. In a much-quoted essay, "What Psychical Research Has Accomplished," he asserted that telepathy, as represented by Piper's experiences, constituted a true breakthrough into a world of vast scientific importance. Her powers pointed to a new kind of reality. Regarding the spiritualist conviction that survival of death was established through such research, he remained uncertain.

James was also profoundly impressed by the current French studies of "subconscious ideas." Pierre Janet, for example, had apparently shown that in deep hypnotic trance a man may act upon ideas which have been planted in his mind, though he is plainly not conscious at the time. He gave much attention likewise to dreaming, to hypnotic consciousness, and to multiple personality. He felt that Sigmund Freud was one of those to whom the future belonged. In his last years his emphasis was not on rounding out a system of ideas but in gaining new varieties of experience. His expression "radical empiricism" is his fortunate summary of a whole approach to life. He was empirical in the sense of looking always for the quality of immediate experience and remaining loyal to this first reality, as against the abstractions which seek an "absolute," an approach characteristic of much of the German, British, and American philosophy of his era. He was radical in the sense that he wanted to find the very roots of reality in the nature of experience itself. Faith healing, psychical research, and the stream of consciousness were all to be embraced for the same reason: they offered realities which were incapable of being rationally ruled out of their right to exist. So, too, the "pluralistic universe" of which he wrote in the last years, when pragmatism was everywhere being discussed, was a loosely articulated collection of separate parts, each aspect of which must be respected although a philosophically unified system cannot be created from it.

Further Reading

James's correspondence was edited by his son, Henry James, *The Letters of William James* (1920). Robert C. LeClair edited *The Letters of William James and Theodore Flournoy* (1966). The two indispensable works for studying James are Ralph Barton Perry, *The Thought and Character of William James* (2 vols., 1935), and Gay Wilson Allen, *William James: A Biography* (1967). Also useful are Edward C. Moore, *William James* (1965), and Bernard P. Brennan, *William James* (1968). For a discussion of William, his brother Henry, and his father Henry, Sr., see C. Hartley Grattan, *The Three Jameses: A Family of Minds* (1932).

Additional Sources

Bjork, Daniel W., *The compromised scientist: William James in the Development of American psychology,* New York: Columbia University Press, 1983.

Bjork, Daniel W., *William James: the center of his vision,* New York: Columbia University Press, 1988.

Feinstein, Howard M., *Becoming William James,* Ithaca, N.Y.: Cornell University Press, 1984.

Lewis, R. W. B. (Richard Warrington Baldwin), *The Jameses: a family narrative,* New York: Anchor Books, 1993.

Weissbourd, Katherine, *Growing up in the James family: Henry James, Sr., as son and father,* Ann Arbor, Mich.: UMI Research Press, 1985.

William James remembered, Lincoln, NE: University of Nebraska Press, 1996. □

Sir Leander Starr Jameson

Sir Leander Starr Jameson (1853-1917) was a British administrator and South African statesman. He played an important role in the colonization of Rhodesia (now Zimbabwe) and is known largely for his leadership of the abortive raid on Johannesburg.

Leander Jameson was born in Edinburgh on Feb. 3, 1853, and trained as a physician at the university medical college. He sailed for South Africa in 1878 and set up practice in Kimberley, where he met and became close friends with Cecil Rhodes, who wanted to establish a British colony stretching from the Cape of Good Hope to Cairo. Jameson performed several missions for Rhodes which eventually led to the founding of the colony of Rhodesia (now Zimbabwe).

The discovery of gold on the Witwatersrand had attracted large numbers of foreigners (mainly British) to Johannesburg, and these clamored for political rights to secure their economic interests. When their efforts failed, crisis followed crisis until some of them organized rifle clubs and threatened to use military force to ensure respect for their wishes.

Jameson, who had become administrator of Rhodesia, sympathized with the reformers. He believed that events in Johannesburg called for a military solution. In Rhodesia he had organized the company's police and volunteers into a fighting unit.

Some of the reformers, who included mining magnates and leaders in the business community, wanted Rhodes, then prime minister of the Cape Colony, to intervene and unite the Boer republics and the British colonies. They planned a revolt which, Jameson was led to believe, would be the signal for him to march into the Transvaal and overthrow the Boer government.

Jameson's Raid

Differences on the wisdom of a military as against a political solution, the design of the flag, and other issues forced the reformers to reconsider their plans. They asked Jameson not to march on Johannesburg until they gave him the signal. He was impatient with their wavering, and on Dec. 29, 1895, he started on the march to Johannesburg with 470 mounted men. He had covered two-thirds of the journey when the British high commissioner ordered him not to enter Boer territory. Believing that the reformers would rebel on hearing that he was on Transvaal soil, he ignored the high commissioner's instructions. The Boers converged on him, and he surrendered at Doornkop on Jan. 2, 1896.

After his arrest and release in Pretoria, Jameson returned to England, where he was tried for organizing an illegal expedition into the territory of a friendly state and sentenced to 15 months without hard labor. His health broke down in Holloway Prison. On his release he returned to South Africa, where he worked with Rhodes on the plan to link Cape Town and Cairo by telegraph.

Jameson's friends persuaded him that entering politics would enable him to accelerate movement toward union. He was elected to the Cape Parliament in 1900 and was prime minister from 1904 to 1908. He was made a baronet in 1911 and became chairman of the British South Africa Company in 1913. He died on Nov. 26, 1917.

Further Reading

The comprehensive biography of Jameson is the detailed work by Ian Colvin, *The Life of Jameson* (2 vols., 1922). Two books on Jameson's raid into the Boer territory are Hugh Marshall Hole, *The Jameson Raid* (1930), a full account of all the participants, and Jean Van Der Poel, *The Jameson Raid* (1951), which emphasizes the significance of the raid in the context of an emerging South African union. John Eric Sidney Green, *Rhodes Goes North* (1936), deals with Cecil Rhodes's role in the raid and its milieu. □

Jami

Jami (1414-1492) is usually described as the last of the great classical Persian poets. He was a mystic and a member of the Nakshibandi Sufi order, an influence vital to understand when reading his poetry.

Maulana Nur al-Din Abd al-Rahman, called Jami, was born in the district of Djam in the province of Herat in what is today Afghanistan. His father came from the district of Dasht around Isfahan, and thus the first *takhallus* (poetical name) Jami adopted was Dashti. This he later changed to Jami.

Early in his life Jami was given to a strong interest in mysticism. Contrary to what one might expect, this was quite natural for intellectuals in his day. Mysticism was popular during the time Jami lived, because life in general was in such turmoil. Thus Jami became a follower of the disciple who had succeeded the great saint Baha al-Din Nakshiband, the founder of the mystical Sufi order of Nakshibandis. This was to affect his later writings by means of philosophical innuendo.

The great portion of Jami's life was spent in Herat. He was not a great traveler, like Sadi or Rumi. Apart from two pilgrimages, one to Meshed in Persia and another to the Hejaz in 1472 with a side trip to Baghdad, Damascus, and Tabriz, he stayed at home and lived a quiet, introspective life. It is said that in his later years, after his writings were completed, he suffered from senility and eventually went mad.

The type of work Jami produced is considerable and varied. It is typified by a depth and variety of knowledge and a finely honed mastery of diction and style. Although he wrote a great deal of prose, it is for his poetry that he is known mainly. He used the theme of the court epic to great benefit as had his predecessor Firdausi. Most famous of these are his stories "Salaman and Absal," "Yusuf and Zulaikha," and "Laila and Majnun." These are three of the seven long tales that make up his famous literary series called *The Seven Stars of the Great Bear*. All of these works appear on first observation to be love stories of young couples. But when considering the serious nature of Jami's mysticism, it is realized that in fact these works are meant to be read as object lessons for teaching pupils a unique Sufi way to approach God. Like many of his contemporaries, Jami must be read on many philosophical levels.

In the field of lyric poetry he wrote late in life three diwans (collections of poetry): *Beginning of Youth* (1479), *Central Part of the Chain* (1489), and *Close of Life* (1491). Finally he wrote in prose the *Baharistan,* an imitation of Sadi's *Gulistan,* and the *Zephyrs of Intimacy,* a compendium of biographies of many Sufi saints.

Thus it may be said of Jami that he brought a fresh, subtle, and graceful style to his writing. His theme was usually on a philosophical-level, pantheistic mysticism. He deserves comparison with the greatest of the Sufi poets. His death in Herat marked the passing of the last great mystical Persian poet.

Further Reading

Jami is represented in English translation in James Kritzeck, ed., *Anthology of Islamic Literature* (1964). The best biographical sources are Edward G. Browne, *A History of Persian Literature under Tartar Dominion, A.D. 1265-1502* (1920), and Jan Rypka, *History of Iranian Literature,* edited by Karl Jahn (1956; trans. 1968). There is also a useful introduction by F. Hadland Davis in his translation of poems by Jami, *The Persian Mystics: Jami* (1908). For a comprehensive discussion of the Sufi thought of Jami see A. J. Arberry, *Sufism: An Account of the Mystics of Islam* (1950), and Idries Shah, *The Sufis* (1964). □

Leoš Janáček

The Czech composer Leoš Janáček (1854-1928) was one of the most important opera composers of the first half of the 20th century.

Leoš Janáček, one of 14 children, was born in an obscure village in Moravia, where his father was an impoverished schoolteacher and church organist. Leoš was sent as a choirboy to the St. Augustine Abbey, Brno, at the age of 10, where he received a rudimentary musical education and learned to play the organ. With the help of a patron, he went to Prague in 1874 to enter the organ school with the intention of becoming an organist and church choir director. His interest in composition grew, and study at the conservatories in Leipzig and Vienna followed. By the time he was 25, he had acquired a solid technique, although he had not written any compositions of consequence.

In 1875 Janáček returned to Brno, where he spent the rest of his life. He worked indefatigably to make this provincial city into a musical center. He conducted choirs, established a symphony orchestra, and founded an organ school to train church musicians. Frank and impolitic, he alienated himself from the musical establishment in Prague, and thus his recognition as a composer was delayed.

Janáček became interested in collecting folk songs and in studying the relationships between language and music. He wrote down, in musical notation, sentences and expressions he heard, and he was fascinated with animal sounds.

Not until he was almost 50 did Janáček achieve musical maturity in his opera *Jenufa* (1903). First produced in Brno, it eventually received performances in Prague, Vienna (in German), cities in Germany, and New York City at the Metropolitan Opera in 1924. The last 20 years of his life were very fruitful and filled with honors. His operas *Kata Kabanova* (1921), *The Cunning Little Fox* (1924), *The Makropolous Case* (1925), and *The House of the Dead* (1928) were widely performed in the post-World War II period.

Janáček's opera texts show a wide variety of types, from the animal fairy-tale atmosphere of *The Cunning Little Fox* to the gloom of Fyodor Dostoevsky's *House of the Dead.* *Jenufa* and *Kata Kabanova* are in the tradition of verismo, that is, realistic, opera: they are stories of simple, rural people involved in violent emotional experiences. The outstanding traits of these operas are the vividness of emotional expression and the avoidance of typically operatic conventions. The melodic lines proceed in lines close to speech, while the orchestra uses leitmotivs in a free manner. All the operas, no matter how different in subject, express the composer's compassion for the human condition.

Janáček also wrote a number of important instrumental compositions. These include two String Quartets (1923, 1928), *Taras Bulba* for orchestra (1924), the *Suite for Wind Instruments* (1924), and numerous songs and piano pieces. His *Glagolitic (Slavonic) Mass* (1927) achieved international recognition.

Further Reading

Hans Hollander, *Leoš Janáček: His Life and Work* (trans. 1963), is a sympathetic study of the man and his music. See also Rosa Newmarch, *The Music of Czechoslovakia* (1942), and Jaroslav Šeda, *Leoš Janáček* (trans. 1956).

Additional Sources

Horsbrugh, Ian, *Leoš Janáček, the field that prospered,* Newton Abbot: David & Charles; New York: Scribner's, 1981.

Janáček, Leoš, *Janáček, leaves from his life,* New York: Taplinger Pub. Co., 1982.

Susskind, Charles, *Janáček and Brod,* New Haven: Yale University Press, 1985.

Vogel, Jaroslav, *Leoš Janáček, a biography,* London: Orbis Pub., 1981. □

Pierre Marie Félix Janet

Pierre Marie Félix Janet (1859-1947) was a French psychologist particularly well known for his work on psychopathology and psychotherapy.

B orn in Paris on May 28, 1859, Pierre Janet spent his childhood and youth in that city. His bent for natural sciences led him to pursue studies in physiology at the Sorbonne at the same time that he was studying philosophy, for which he received a master's degree in 1882. Janet then left Paris for Le Havre and for 7 years taught philosophy there in the lycée.

Janet, however, wanted to study medicine and at the hospital of Le Havre began to do research in hypnosis, using the well-known medium Léonie. Through these studies, the first of this sort, Janet came into contact with Jean Martin Charcot, but after reading Charcot and Hippolyte Bernheim he thought these investigators did not sufficiently take into consideration the psychological factors involved in neurotic phenomena. This forced Janet to undertake a deep psychological study of the neuroses, in particular of hysterical neurosis.

In his doctoral thesis in 1889 entitled "L'Automatisme psychologique" (Psychological Automatism), Janet devised an inventory of the manifestations of automatic activities, thinking that it would help him in studying the "elementary forms of sensibility and conscience." At the age of 30 he returned to Paris, and Charcot appointed him director of the laboratory of pathological psychology at the Salpêtrière hospital. Janet completed his medical studies, and in 1893 he published his medical dissertation entitled "The Mental State of Hysterics."

Janet was by temperament a naturalist, and during all his life he improved his herbarium. He had the same acquisitive attitude toward mental patients, from whom he collected thousands of precise and detailed observations. However, in his books he attempted to give a more theoretical and depth interpretation of a few particular cases. From 1902 until 1934 he taught at the Collège de France.

Janet's works are numerous, and many of his writings have been translated into English. Among his books one can cite *Névroses et idées fixes* (1902); *Les Obsessions et la psychasténie* (1903); *The Major Symptoms of Hysteria* (1907, symposium undertaken in the United States); *Les Médications psychologiques* (1919); *De l'angoisse à l'extase* (1926); *Les Débuts de l'intelligence* (1935); and *L'Intelligence avant le langage* (1936).

Janet characterized his dynamic psychology as being a psychology of conduct, accepting the schema of a psychology of behavior while integrating in his schema conscious processes acting as regulators of action. Janet's work has often been compared to the work of Freud, and his influence has been great in both North and South America.

Well after Janet had retired, he continued to teach and to give conferences, manifesting a great vitality until the time of his death on Feb. 23, 1947.

Further Reading

Janet's autobiography is in Carl Murchison and others, *A History of Psychology in Autobiography* (4 vols., 1930-1952). See also Benjamin B. Wolman, ed., *Historical Roots of Contemporary Psychology* (1968). □

Cornelis Jansen

The Dutch Roman Catholic theologian Cornelis Jansen (1585-1638) wrote an interpretation of St. Augustine's teachings on original sin and grace. Although condemned by the Church, his teachings, known as Jansenism, had an enormous impact.

C ornelis Jansen was born near Leerdam, Holland, and he received his early education in Leerdam and Utrecht. In 1602 he went to the Catholic University of Louvain in the Spanish part of the Netherlands (now Belgium). Soon he was introduced to the theology of Michael Baius, a former master of divinity at the same university. Baius's doctrine on grace and original sin had been condemned in 1567, but the battle continued between his Augustinian supporters and the Jesuits (led by Leonard Lessius). The young student's sympathies were all with the Augustinians.

In 1604 Jansen fell ill and went to live in Paris, where he became more and more intimate with a fellow student of his Louvain days, Jean Duvergier de Hauranne, the future Abbé de St-Cyran, who later would be the most ardent and political defender of his theology. In 1612 both went to live in Bayonne, where Jansen first directed a diocesan college but soon withdrew entirely from the active life in order to devote all his time to the study of St. Augustine. In 1617 he returned to Louvain, where he became headmaster of a university college. During the following years his ideas reached full maturity. Although some of his views came quite close to Calvinism, he strongly opposed the Protestant churches which, he felt, had no legal status outside the Catholic community. By 1630 Jansen had become a controversial theology professor whose development was followed with a great deal of distrust in Rome and Madrid. In 1636 he was appointed bishop of Ieper in West Flanders, where he died 18 months later, possibly from the plague.

Major Work

Jansen's lifework, *Augustinus,* was published posthumously at Louvain in 1640 despite the strong opposition of the Jesuits. The book contains the entire doctrine that came to be called Jansenism and that was to exercise an enormous influence upon the Catholic life of France, of the Low Countries, and, via the Irish clergy trained in Flanders, of America. The three-volume study claims to be an interpretation of Augustine's thought on original justice, sin, predestination, and grace. Jansen's synthesis was undoubtedly based upon Augustine's anti-Pelagian writings, all of which he had read 30 times. The first part is devoted entirely to the history of Pelagianism, a doctrine which in various ways upheld the thesis that man needs no other grace to be saved than that of his own efforts.

In the second and third parts Jansen stated his own controversial interpretation of Augustine. He held that man had been created in a state of original justice, free from concupiscence. Although man needed divine grace to do good, this grace was required by human nature itself and could therefore not be considered gratuitous. After the Fall, which consisted in, and was transmitted through, concupiscence, man lost his freedom. The original grace is no longer sufficient for salvation. Man's "freedom" can efficaciously be restored only by a grace that helps him overcome his irresistible inclination toward evil and that predetermines him to do good. There is no place for human merit in the process of salvation: all depends on God's undeserved, efficacious grace.

Jansen's theory leads him directly to predestinarianism. God does not confer his sufficient grace to all men, nor did Christ die for the salvation of all. Yet, contrary to Calvinist doctrine, Jansen teaches that faith alone is not sufficient for man's justification: cooperation through good works is essential, even though for the elect this cooperation itself is assured through God's grace.

In 1642 Pope Urban VIII condemned *Augustinus* mainly on grounds of its appearance without the previous approval then required for all publications on grace. A more specific condemnation of five theses found in *Augustinus* was made by Innocent X in 1653. One of the most confusing episodes in the dogmatic history of the Catholic Church followed, with Jansenists admitting that the censured theses were unacceptable but denying that they were to be found in *Augustinus*. Innocent's successor, Alexander VII, tried to cut the knot by declaring that the pope had the right to decide whether a de jure pronouncement applies to a de facto situation, and then formally applied the previous condemnation. Later a written submission of the Jansenist leaders was required. The movement, however, remained strong in France through the first half of the 18th century under the intellectual guidance of Henri Arnauld and Blaise Pascal, and later of Pasquier Quesnel.

Further Reading

The standard work on Jansen in English remains Nigel J. Abercrombie, *The Origins of Jansenism* (1936), which contains an analysis of *Augustinus* and an extensive bibliography. ☐

Emile Jaques-Dalcroze

Emile Jaques-Dalcroze (1865-1950) was a Swiss teacher and composer known for developing eurhythmics, an approach to music education involving whole body movement.

Born July 6, 1865, Emile-Henri Jaques was the only son of Jules-Louis and Julie Jaques, a French-Swiss couple living in Vienna, where his father represented Swiss clockmakers. Emile and his sister were introduced as children to concerts, theater, opera, and piano lessons. After the family moved to Geneva Emile studied at the Conservatoire de Musique (1877-1883) and continued his professional training in Paris and Vienna (1884-1891) with Talbot, Fauré, Lavignac, Marmontel, Lussy, Graedener, Prosnitz, Fuchs, and Bruckner. He worked one season as a conductor at the Théatre des Nouveautés in Algiers, where North African music stimulated his interest in the connections of human movement and rhythm.

Emile Jaques began to compose seriously during his early 20s and soon changed his name to the more distinctive Jaques-Dalcroze, perhaps to avoid confusion with a French composer famous for his polkas. His extensive works included music for orchestra, chamber orchestra, and piano; music dramas; operas; choral works; some 1,700 songs; and many books relating to teaching.

In 1892 Jaques-Dalcroze was named a professor at the Conservatoire de Musique de Genève, where he remained until 1910. During the 1890s he searched for better ways to help his students hear accurately and respond spontaneously. "Rhythmic gymnastics," as Jaques-Dalcroze called his special movement work, offered many new ways to move and make music with the original instrument, the human body. Working from the basics of singing, breathing, walking, and beating time, Jaques-Dalcroze and his early students eventually explored more adventurous possibilities of connecting music and movement. Lunging, skipping, pulling a partner, carrying an imaginary weight, making a cannon—these called for timing, strength, greater use of the body in space, imagination, awareness of form, and/or cooperation with other people.

Many exercises in the method were based on walking, which Jaques-Dalcroze took to be the natural breakdown of time into equal parts. For example, students might be told to walk around the room following the music which he would improvise at the keyboard, responding directly to the beat and to changes in speed and dynamics. Students would thus become aware of how they had to adjust the length of their steps and how they needed to control their use of energy and body weight. Other typical activities included quick reactions such as starting or stopping on command and walking twice as fast or twice as slow. Another basic practice was the walking or stepping out of rhythmic patterns. The teacher would play a musical example. After listening carefully, the students would immediately repeat it, matching their steps exactly to the sequence of short and long notes they perceived. Work to develop the sense of measure or bartime was developed from the standard arm gestures of conducting. Experienced students could beat regular bartime with their arms while simultaneously stepping rhythmic patterns.

Breathing was understood by Jaques-Dalcroze to be a natural source of dynamics and phrasing. He created many exercises to help students feel how they could shape the flow and energy of breathing. Ideas to encourage the sense of phrasing also included contrasting light and heavy steps, using a real or imagined resistance such as stretching an elastic, or taking turns moving with a partner or in groups. This work led to "realizations" of more complex forms such as inventions, fugues, and rondos. Sometimes students even created "plastic counterpoint," or movement independent of, but related to, its music. Jaques-Dalcroze saw the new work of solo dancers such as Loie Fuller and Isadora Duncan, who inspired him and confirmed his own experiments between 1900 and 1910. Like Duncan, Jaques-Dalcroze explored movement through deep research into the natural movements of breathing, walking, lunging, running, skipping, and jumping.

Jaques-Dalcroze made his work known by giving lecture-demonstrations and publishing the *Méthode Jaques-Dalcroze* (1906), which appeared in both French and German editions. From 1910 to 1914 he directed the Bildungsanstalt Jaques-Dalcroze, a training college built to support his work at Hellerau near Dresden, Germany. Hundreds of teachers and professional students were attracted to this forward-looking school, which offered solfège (ear training), rhythmic gymnastics, keyboard improvisation, *plastique* (advanced music-movement study), music theory and practice, Swedish gymnastics, dance, and anatomy.

The Hellerau school festivals of 1912 and 1913 included a student version of Gluck's *Orpheus,* based on the new movement principles of Jaques-Dalcroze and using the new architectural theater designs and lighting concepts of Adolphe Appia. Among the faculty and students of Hellerau were people who became prominent in music, dance, theater, and many other fields. Many helped to spread the Jaques-Dalcroze method by teaching in conservatories and schools throughout Europe and North America. The method came to be known in English as *eurhythmics,* which means good or right rhythm. The early exercises were continually renewed and elaborated, however, so that eurhythmics has always been developing and is, in fact, still a vital method.

During World War I Jaques-Dalcroze established his own school in Geneva, the Institut Jaques-Dalcroze, where he taught until shortly before his death on July 1, 1950. The institute, now state-supported, serves today as an international center of this approach to music education. Professional training programs are also currently available in a number of other countries. Thousands of people have had contact with the Jaques-Dalcroze method, which has had widespread influence in 20th-century teaching of music and dance.

Jaques-Dalcroze increased understanding of the sources of music and movement in the human body. For nearly 60 years he was an inspiring, imaginative master, whose musicianship and personality helped to form many outstanding teachers and artists. Beyond the circle of his students and associates, his writings stimulated a broad public.

Further Reading

The best sources of information on Jaques-Dalcroze are in French. However, his two most influential books are available in translation: *Rhythm, Music and Education* (1921) and *Eurhythmics, Art and Education* (1930). □

Randall Jarrell

Randall Jarrell (1914-1965), poet and critic, was one of the most versatile American men of letters during the two decades immediately after World War II.

Randall Jarrell was born June 6, 1914, in Nashville, Tennessee, but spent most of his early years on the West Coast, in Long Beach and Hollywood, California. His troubled, lonely childhood is reflected in some of his most vivid poems. When he was 11 his parents separated, and he lived for a time with his father's parents before joining his mother back in Nashville. He took business courses in high school, but as a student at Vanderbilt he came under the influence of John Crowe Ransom, with Allen Tate and Robert Penn Warren one of the leaders of an earlier Southern poetry renaissance in the 1920s and 1930s.

Jarrell's early poetry was largely shaped by a continuing relationship with Ransom. He took bachelor's and master's degrees at Vanderbilt, and in 1937 followed Ransom to Kenyon College where they both taught English. Jarrell's early poems appeared in the *American Review* and *Southern Review,* and also in the *Kenyon Review,* founded by Ransom. During the years before World War II Jarrell had rich association with a number of young writers who also gained recognition later, such as the poet Robert Lowell and the fiction writer Peter Taylor.

Jarrell served in the U.S. Air Force during much of World War II. Ironically, he owed much of his reputation with the general public to his war poems: "Eighth Air Force," "Losses," and most especially "The Death of the Ball Turret Gunner," one of the most famous short poems to come out of this conflict:

From my mother's sleep I fell into the State,
And I hunched in its belly till my wet fur froze.
Six miles from earth, loosed from its dream of life
I woke to black flak and the nightmare fighters.
When I died they washed me out of the turret with
   a hose.

Actually, Jarrell had been washed out of flight training and spent most of the war on the ground in Illinois and Arizona.

In the two decades after World War II, Jarrell did most of his writing in an academic setting. After a short appointment at the University of Texas, he spent most of the last 18 years of his life as a professor of English at the Women's College of the University of North Carolina, in Greensboro. His greatest influence on American letters and in the lives of younger poets was exercised during this period. He was always encouraging and generous in his support of these writers. Two official positions enhanced this influence: poetry consultant of the Library of Congress and chancellor of

the Academy of American Poets. Jarrell was also the recipient of two Guggenheim fellowships. In this fruitful period he became respected as much for his criticism as for his poetry, serving at various times as poetry editor or critic for *Nation, Partisan Review,* and the *Yale Review.*

Jarrell also made one notable contribution to the newly important academic novel with *Pictures from an Institution* (1954). This is a satire of a "progressive" college and closely observed feuding among faculty and administration described with wit and epigrammatic characterization.

Writing about his own poetry, Jarrell was characteristically modest. "I have tried to make my poems plain, and most of them are plain enough; but I wish they were more difficult because I had known more." If they are plain they are often deeply meaningful, more resonant and complex than may at first appear. His most common themes, in addition to the "knowing yet innocent" child's view of the world and the horror of war, are the energies of art and the banalities of postwar American consumerism. The materialist way of life is scathingly anatomized in a series of satirical poems, one of the best of which is "The Woman at the Washington Zoo" (1960).

Jarrell's idiomatic poetry was written to be listened to, joining the popular style of the 1960s and younger poets such as Allen Ginsberg and Gregory Corso. But Jarrell's work is much more disciplined, his persona more varied, than that of the Beat School. He was a gifted prosodist, equally at ease with free and traditional verse forms, and he wrote vivid modern versions of such established forms as

the sestina. Also, he could effectively combine different poetic modes. A fine fusion of person portrait with social satire is to be found in "In Montecito" (1963).

In the historical context of Anglo-American poetry Jarrell's work echoes back to the dramatic monologues of Robert Browning, through the war poetry of Wilfred Owen, presaging, ultimately, the last confessional poems of his friend Robert Lowell. Although Jarrell is not a Sylvia Plath-like confessional poet, late in his life he became more directly personal in "The Lost World" and "Thinking about the Lost World" (1965).

There are still other facets of Jarrell's expression. He translated works by Rilke, E. Morike, and Tristan Corbiere and was working on a translation of Goethe's *Faust* at the time of his death. He also wrote highly successful children's books, among which are *The Bat Poet* (1964) and *The Animal Family* (1965). In his quiet way he was a Renaissance person, a versatile "man of letters in the European sense, with real verve, imagination and uniqueness" (Robert Lowell). This still evolving career was cut short when Jarrell was struck and killed by an auto in Greensboro, North Carolina, on October 14, 1965.

Further Reading

Jarrell's works include, among others, *The Complete Poems* (1969). His books of criticism include: *Poetry and the Age* (1953); *A Sad Heart at the Supermarket* (1962); and *The Third Book of Criticism* (1971). *Randall Jarrell: 1914-1965* (1967) is a book of personal reminiscences edited by Robert Lowell, Peter Taylor, and Robert Penn Warren. Suzanne Ferguson's *The Poetry of Randall Jarrell* (1971) is a comprehensive critical assessment. Twenty years after his death his widow, Mary Jarrell, edited *Randall Jarrell's Letters: An Autobiographical and Literary Selection* (1985).

Additional Sources

Jarrell, Randall, *Randall Jarrell's letters: an autobiographical and literary selection,* Boston: Houghton Mifflin, 1985.
Meyers, Jeffrey, *Manic power: Robert Lowell and his circle,* London; New York: Macmillan London, 1987.
Pritchard, William H., *Randall Jarrell: a literary life,* New York: Farrar, Straus and Giroux, 1990. ☐

Wojciech Witold Jaruzelski

A career soldier, General Wojciech Witold Jaruzelski (born 1923) became Poland's head of state in 1981. After reaching a historic compromise with the Solidarity trade unions he took the presidency in 1989 but resigned 18 months later.

Wojciech Jaruzelski was born in Kurów near Pulawy in the Lublin province on July 6, 1923. The son of a Polish landed gentry family, his origins can scarcely be called proletarian, as he came from interwar Poland's social elite. His father was said to have served in the cavalry, the prestige arm of the interwar Polish army. His family's ties to eastern Poland and its social milieu made him one of the last major Polish political figures to originate from the Kresy, the Russo-Polish borderlands.

Little is known of Jaruzelski's early years except that he was educated at a Catholic boarding school near Warsaw that was highly regarded as an establishment school. World War II, however, would prove more formative to Jaruzelski's life. Deported with his family to the interior of the Soviet Union in 1939 or 1940, Jaruzelski was its only surviving member. His odyssey ended in Soviet Central Asia, where he was put to work in the Karaganda coal mines.

While living in the uncertain world of the Polish deportee, Jaruzelski made an ideological conversion that was to lead him eventually back to Poland. By 1943 he arrived in Ryazan, a hundred miles south of Moscow, where he attended Officers School for a Soviet-sponsored Polish army. Upon graduation he joined the First Polish Army and participated in the Soviet drive to Berlin. His wartime service took in the liberation of Warsaw as well as battles on the Baltic, and the Odra and Elbe rivers. Clearly considered reliable, Jaruzelski furthered his combat experience in the postwar suppression of the anticommunist underground in Poland between 1945 and 1947.

Jaruzelski's rapid military and political advancement in postwar Peoples' Poland indicated that he had been singled out as a high-flyer. He attended the Senior Infantry School in 1947 and the General Staff Academy in Warsaw in 1948-1951. He formally joined the Polish Workers' Party (Communist Party) in 1947, and its successor, the Polish United Workers' Party (PUWP), in 1948. In 1956 he became the youngest brigadier general in the Polish army and a year later was given command of the 12th Motorized Division, a post he held until 1960. Promoted to division general, he moved from an operational command to head the Main Political Administration (MPA) of the army (1960-1965). Two years later he acquired the additional post of deputy minister of defense (1962-1968) and in 1965 moved from the MPA to become chief of the general staff (1965-1968). In what would appear to be a culmination of his career, he was promoted to general of arms and became minister of defense in March 1968.

Jaruzelski's parallel advancement in the PUWP belied his growing political importance. He entered the party's Central Committee in 1964 and the Politburo in 1970. It was only in the late 1960s and early 1970s that Jaruzelski began to emerge as a political personality. He sanctioned the use of Polish troops in the Warsaw Pact invasion of Czechoslovakia in 1968 but reportedly opposed the use of deadly force by the army against protesting workers in 1970 and again in 1976. From these episodes comes the perhaps apocryphal story that he told his Politburo colleagues: "Polish soldiers will not fire on Polish workers." If true, the statement reflected as much Jaruzelski's realistic assessment of the limitations of employing Poland's conscript army against the civil population as any political objections he may have harbored about resolving worker unrest by force.

The birth of the Solidarity trade union in August 1980 presented the most fundamental challenge to Communist rule in Poland's cycle of political crises. The disintegration of PUWP authority and Soviet pressure for a decisive resolution of the crisis propelled Jaruzelski and the military to the fore of Polish politics. Representing the only cohesive political group within the ruling Communist establishment, almost by default the task of "saving socialism" fell on Jaruzelski's shoulders. He quickly added a number of pivotal government and party positions to his defense minister's portfolio: premier (February 1981) and first secretary of the party (October 1981).

Jaruzelski's policy toward Solidarity, when viewed with hindsight, represented a curious mixture of dialogue and threats. He apparently sought agreement in talks held with Lech Walesa, Solidarity's leader, and the Polish Catholic primate, Jozef Glemp, in November 1981 while earlier, in March, a security service operation in Bydgoszcz had the trappings of an abortive crackdown. Caught as he was between domestic political and economic demands and Brezhnev's orthodox rule in the Soviet Union, however, his options were far more limited. He had to find a Polish solution for eliminating Solidarity and reestablishing party rule.

Jaruzelski's answer to his political dilemmas was the declaration of martial law on December 13, 1981. For his decision to impose martial law, he was alternately criticized for being a Soviet stooge or praised as a patriot saving the country from Soviet intervention. Overnight, he demolished Solidarity with the mass internment of its leading elements. Public support for the organization was gradually broken through the remorseless deployment of the ZOMO riot po-

lice. On Poland's wry political joke circuit, it earned Jaruzelski the nickname of "General Zomosa." Martial law not only meant the eclipse of Solidarity but also the decoupling of the PUWP from the political process. Jaruzelski ran the country through an "old boy" network of generals and political officers. It was the communist world's first, and perhaps only, example of military rule usurping party authority.

In the decade following the imposition of martial law, Jaruzelski was firmly in control of Poland's politics. He launched a program of "normalization" that attempted to rebuild the Communist Party, repress the opposition, and restore the health of the Polish economy. After the official lifting of martial law he attempted to impose his program on the country. By 1986, however, normalization was failing on all fronts: the PUWP remained factionalized and demoralized; underground Solidarity survived and succeeded in politicizing Polish society (despite continual oppression); and the Polish economy steadily declined.

The failures of normalization and the coming to power of Mikhail Gorbachev in the Soviet Union paved the way for the most dramatic U-turn in the career of Jaruzelski. With his regime's authority measurably eroding and the Kremlin veto over Polish internal affairs discarded by Gorbachev, Jaruzelski decided to reach an accommodation with the opposition. In late 1988, preliminary contacts with the opposition paved the way for formal talks. In the new year, events moved rapidly: in January 1989 Solidarity was relegalized; in April the government reached the historic Round Table agreement which cleared the way for partially free elections; and the June balloting confirmed support for Solidarity and indicated the near complete lack of support for the Communist Party.

Under the Round Table agreement, the Polish presidency was strengthened with a view to Jaruzelski occupying the position until the five-year transition to full democracy ran its course. On June 4, 1989, he was elected to the post by a majority of one vote in the Polish parliament. The Round Table agreement, however, quickened the pace of political change both in Poland and in Eastern Europe. By August, Tadeusz Mazowiecki became Poland's first non-Communist prime minister since World War II, sparking an East European revolution that swept aside nearly a half-century of Communist rule in the region.

Taking advantage of the continued ferment for democratic reforms, Walesa now pressed for repeal of the Round Table agreements and for holding a popular election for president. Jaruzelski set late November 1990 for such an election. When Walesa announced his candidacy Jaruzelski chose to resign and participate in an orderly transfer of power.

In the early 1990s Jaruzelski wrote a book titled *Martial Law*. During a book signing in 1994, a farmer threw a stome at him from close range. He suffered a broken jawbone from the incident.

In November 1996 the Polish parliament voted not to charge him for imposing martial law in 1991. Jaruzelski insisted that his action of imposing martial law kept the Russians from invading. In an opinion poll, 54% of Poles surveyed agreed with his decision.

Further Reading

Details concerning Jaruzelski's career can be obtained from the following sources: Ewa Celt, "Wojciech Jaruzelski: A Prime Minister in Uniform," Radio Free Europe Background Report/72, March 13, 1981; Michael T. Kaufman, "The Importance of General Jaruzelski," *The New York Times Magazine* (December 9, 1984); and Andrew A. Michta, *Red Eagle: The Army in Polish Politics, 1944-1988* (1990). See also *Time* magazine (October 24, 1994 and November 4, 1996). □

Karl Jaspers

The German philosopher Karl Jaspers (1883-1969) wrote important works on psychopathology, systematic philosophy, and historical interpretation.

Karl Jaspers was born in Oldenburg, close to the North Sea coast, on Feb. 23, 1883. His father was a prosperous bank director. After graduation from the gymnasium in Oldenburg, Jaspers studied at Heidelberg, Munich, Berlin, and Göttingen.

Though he lived to be 86, Jaspers's health was always fragile. From early childhood he suffered from bronchiectasis with cardiac decompensation. This required him to organize his limited energies with great care. Yet he accomplished much teaching and writing under these limitations and was helped greatly, particularly in his writing, by his wife, Gertrud Mayer, whom he married in 1910.

In 1909 Jaspers received the degree of doctor of medicine and began to specialize in psychiatry. For 7 years thereafter he worked in the psychiatric clinic attached to the university hospital in Heidelberg. It was here that Jaspers began to work out a classification of basic personality types. This work, influenced further by discussions with his friend Max Weber and by the latter's theory of ideal types, culminated in Jaspers's first major work, *General Psychopathology* (1913). With this work Jaspers acquired a position on the psychology faculty at Heidelberg.

In this first major work Jaspers discovered one of the essential themes of his thought: "Man is always more than what he knows, or can know, about himself." From Immanuel Kant, Jaspers learned that man, the source of all objective inquiries, cannot himself be known—in his entirety—through objective inquiry. All scientific views on man are limited and partial. But, following Søren Kierkegaard, Jaspers began to develop a way of describing what lies behind these objective inquiries—the unique individual, or, as he called it, *Existenz*.

In his next major work, *The Psychology of World Conceptions* (1919), Jaspers explored the range of fundamental world views, in relation to which individual men find their own identity. He also began to explore those "boundary situations" in life that force individuals to face up to the

These opinions were put to a severe test after the Nazis came to power. Always critical of Nazism, Jaspers was forced to retire in 1937 and forbidden to publish in 1938. His wife, who was Jewish, was under constant threat, and the couple had already been scheduled for deportation to a death camp when the U.S. army entered Heidelberg in April 1945.

Jaspers took a chair of philosophy at Basel in 1949 and spent the next 2 decades writing on such topical questions as German guilt, demythologizing the Gospels, and the atom bomb, in addition to large-scale historical works. He died after a stroke on Feb. 26, 1969, in Basel.

Further Reading

The fundamental book for approaching Jaspers is *The Philosophy of Karl Jaspers,* edited by Paul Arthur Schilpp (1957). It contains a lengthy "Philosophical Autobiography" by Jaspers and two dozen important descriptive and critical essays on his philosophy, together with his replies and a bibliography complete to early 1957. Charles F. Wallraff, *Karl Jaspers: An Introduction to His Philosophy* (1970), is useful.

Additional Sources

Ehrlich, Leonard H., *Karl Jaspers: philosophy as faith,* Amherst: University of Massachusetts Press, 1975. □

meaning of their unique existence. These include the awareness of one's sexuality; suffering and conflict; shame, betrayal, and guilt; and the death of loved ones and the awareness of one's own death. In this way Jaspers brought to the fore that concentration on the individual self and its experiences that has come to be the distinguishing mark of existentialism. In 1921 he was given a chair in philosophy at Heidelberg.

Jaspers himself always placed alongside the emphasis on subjectivity an equal emphasis on shared reason in all its forms, particularly in the sciences. The philosophical task is first to come to grips with the basic modes of objectifying reason, then to understand the forms and methods by which the objectifications are made, and finally to relate these forms to the human subjectivity from which they arise. Philosophical thought then rises to the "encompassing," the ultimate reality that contains both the objects and the acts of thinking within itself.

In the works of his maturity, *Philosophy* (3 vols., 1932), *Philosophical Logic* (1947), and *Philosophical Faith* (1948), Jaspers develops a view of philosophy as a never-ending search for this total vision. No such vision is or can be complete and final. Supporting the limited attempts is a philosophical faith in truth and communication which preserves the thinker from dogmatism and intolerance of other attempts. Jaspers's philosophical faith also maintains that man, finding himself dependent and inadequate, is open to a transcendence that grounds and supports his existence and maintains his freedom.

Jean Jaurès

Jean Jaurès (1859-1914), the greatest of the modern French Socialists, played a key role in the unification of the Socialist movement and in the struggle to prevent World War I.

On Sept. 3, 1859, Jean Jaurès was born at Castres, Tarn, into a lower-middle-class family. After studies there, he attended the lycée Louis-le-Grand in Paris. His intellect and articulateness won him first place in the 1878 entrance competition for the prestigious École Normale Supérieure, from which he graduated with a philosophy degree in 1881. While teaching at the lycée of Albi and then at the University of Toulouse, he became involved in politics.

In 1885 Jaurès was elected to the Chamber of Deputies from the Tarn as a moderate, unaffiliated republican. In the Chamber he worked for social welfare legislation and spoke vigorously against Gen. Boulanger. Defeated in 1889, he returned to teaching at Toulouse. His studies and his contact with the workers, especially the miners of Carmaux, whom he aided during the strike of 1892, led Jaurès to socialism.

Running on the platform of the Marxist French Workers' party, Jaurès was returned to the Chamber in January 1893, principally through the support of the Carmaux miners. Both within and without the Chamber he now emerged as one of the most effective spokesmen for the Socialist cause. His appeal was not limited to the working class; indeed, he was particularly effective with the petty

bourgeoisie and the intelligentsia, who were impressed by his stand during the Dreyfus Affair, when he insisted that socialism stood for justice for every individual, regardless of class.

At the same time Jaurès was working to unify the Socialist movement, a role for which his eclectic formation, moralism, preference for synthesis over doctrinal purity, and conciliatory temperament well fitted him. The dogmatists, like Marxist leader Jules Guesde, distrusted him; but because he was the Socialists' most effective parliamentarian and most widely respected figure, they needed him. The first effort at federation (1899) broke down, largely over the entry of Socialist Alexandre Millerand into the ministry.

Jaurès defended ministerial participation under certain circumstances in a democratic regime, but this view was definitively rejected by the Second International (International Working Men's Association) in 1904. His decision to yield the point made possible the unification of French socialism in 1905, and his newspaper, *Humanité,* became the principal organ of the new party. Unification also forced him to abandon his leading role in the coalition which sustained the anticlerical ministry of J. L. E. Combes and to remain for the rest of his career an opposition leader.

The shadow of the coming war brought forth his greatest effort, to prevent France from causing conflict, to use the International to dissuade the powers, and to appeal to the common sense of mankind, but the forces for war were much stronger. His effort, mistakenly construed as

unpatriotic, aroused bitter hatred that led to his assassination on July 31, 1914.

Further Reading

The best book on Jaurès in any language is Harvey Goldberg, *The Life of Jean Jaurès* (1962), a sympathetic, scholarly, and well-written treatment. Two older, briefer works worth reading are Harold R. Weinstein, *Jean Jaurès: A Study of Patriotism in the French Socialist Movement* (1936), and J. Hampden Jackson, *Jean Jaurès: His Life and Work* (1943). □

Sir Dauda Kairaba Jawara

Sir Dauda Kairaba Jawara (born 1924) led his nation of the Gambia to independence and became its first president. Until a military coup in 1994, this veterinary surgeon brought years of stable parliamentary democracy to Africa's smallest republic.

Dauda Jawara was born into a Moslem Mandingo family at Barajally, MacCarthy Island Division, in the Gambian Protectorate, a British colony. He was educated in a local Moslem primary institution and at the Methodist Boys' Grammar School. From 1945 to 1947 Jawara was a trainee nurse in the Gambia Medical Department.

Medical School

Awarded a veterinary scholarship, Jawara spent a year studying science at Achimoto College in the Gold Coast (now Ghana). After passing his intermediate bachelor of science examination, he entered the University of Glasgow and graduated from the Royal College of Veterinary Surgeons in 1953. Jawara was president of the African Students' Union during his years in Scotland.

Upon his return to Africa as his country's first veterinarian, Jawara worked up-country for a short while before joining the government veterinary service in January 1954. In 1958, a year after earning a diploma in tropical veterinary medicine from Glasgow, he became the colony's principal veterinary officer, a post he held until February 1960.

Disturbed by the unequal development between his native Mandingo tribal area and the capital city of Bathurst, he joined the Protectorate People's Party in 1959. By December he was in charge of the organization, which changed its name to the People's Progressive Party.

Jawara resigned his government post to contest the May 1960 elections, in which he won a seat in the House of Representatives. Appointed minister of education (1960-1961) by the British, he spent part of that time in London as a member of a finance delegation.

When Pierre Saar N'Jie, leader of the opposition United Party, was appointed first chief minister of the colony in 1961, Jawara resigned from the government. In the next elections, the People's Progressive Party won the majority of House seats, and Jawara was called on to form a government. He thus became Gambia's first premier. When the Gambia achieved independence, on February 18, 1965, he became the prime minister of this smallest African nation. Located on the western coast and containing only 4,127 square miles, the Gambia is a 30-mile-wide strip of land surrounded on three sides by Senegal. Jawara negotiated the Defense and Foreign Representation Agreement, which placed an independent Gambia within the protection of Senegal's foreign affairs.

Sir David

Jawara was knighted by Queen Elizabeth II in 1966. He had become a Christian in 1955 and was known as "David" thereafter, but he returned to his Moslem faith in 1965. His wife, the former Augusta Mahoney, an Aku trained in nursing in Britain, campaigned with her husband each time he ran for reelection, urging women to become actively interested in politics. The Jawaras had five children.

When an April 1970 referendum changed the Gambia's status to a republic, Jawara became the country's first president. He headed one of Africa's most stable and successful parliamentary democracies until, after 24 years in power, he was brought down by a bloodless military coup.

Further Reading

Harry A. Gailey, Jr., *A History of the Gambia* (1964), discusses Jawara's political career; an informal study of Gambia and its politics is Berkeley Rice, *Enter Gambia: The Birth of an Improbable Nation* (1967). □

Alexej von Jawlensky

The Russian painter Alexej von Jawlensky (1864-1941) was one of the important contributors to Expressionism, to which he added a meditative, or inward reflective, component of unique power.

Born March 13, 1864 (old calendar), on the noble family's estate near Torschok in Russia, Jawlensky was the son of a colonel and was himself destined to become an officer. While still attending cadet school he discovered the arts, and by obtaining a transfer as a young lieutenant to St. Petersburg, he was able to study at the Academy of Fine Arts and under the important Russian realist painter Ilya Repin (called the Russian Courbet). There he met the painter Marianna von Werefkin, the daughter of a general, who was to devote a large part of her life to encouraging and furthering Jawlensky's career as an artist. In 1896, by then a captain, he left the service and moved with Werefkin and Helen Nesnakomoff (her servant and later Jawlensky's wife and mother of his son Andrej) as well as two other painter friends to Munich to attend the private art school of Anton Azbé. Here he met and began a lifelong friendship with Wassily Kandinsky, who was to become one of the founders of abstract (non-objective) painting.

Extended travels in Europe and especially through France introduced Jawlensky to modern art developments. He met Henri Matisse (in 1907 he worked for a while in Matisse's studio), the symbolist painters Paul Sérusier and Jan Verkade (later to become monk Willibrord in the artistically important monastery of Beuron), as well as the Fauvist Kees van Dongen, among others. After his return to Munich he met Paul Klee and Franz Marc and joined them and Kandinsky in the most avant-garde artist group in southern Germany, the *Neue Künstler Vereinigung München* (New Artist Association Munich). Kandinsky's long time friend Gabriele Münter, Alfred Kubin, Adolf Erbslöh, the Russian Bechtjeleff, and others belonged to his circle, in which Werefkin played an important intellectual role.

With the beginning of World War I, Jawlensky as a Russian had to leave Germany, settling in Switzerland. In 1916 he met Emmy (whom he called Galka) Scheyer, who became his student and shortly thereafter his impresario, organizing exhibitions of his works in Germany. In 1924 she formed the "Blue Four" consisting of Jawlensky, Kandinsky, Klee, and Lyonel Feininger to introduce the works of these artists to the United States; she organized—primarily in California—a number of exhibits, gave lectures, and represented the artists until her death in 1945. In 1921 Jawlensky had moved to Wiesbaden in Germany and, his friendship with Werefkin broken, had married Helen Nesnakomoff in 1922. In 1929 he began to suffer from arthritis which forced him to paint with both hands since he could no longer hold a brush; he was unable to paint at all after 1937. His art was declared "degenerate" by the Nazis in 1937 and 72 of his works were confiscated from collections of German museums. Jawlensky died on March 15, 1941.

Jawlensky's life work contained only three themes: still lifes, landscapes, and portraits. Convinced that the visual representation of inner experiences is the goal of the arts, he consistently sought a synthesis between the external world and the experience of the inner world of the artist. Painting in strong colors, he abbreviated the natural forms until his landscapes became colorful visions and his still lifes manifestations of serene spaces. During his time in Switzerland he painted a series of abstracted landscapes which he called "Songs without words," indicating that not an objective reproduction of natural vision but an invocation of feelings created by the natural settings was intended. Having studied the works of van Gogh and Matisse, Gauguin and Cezanne and familiar with the works of the symbolist painters as well as with Cubism and Fauvism, Jawlensky created his own forms, which were strong-colored expressions of his emotions and of his spiritual strivings and convictions.

Today he is primarily famous for the large number of portraits, which by 1916 were reduced to heads and which after 1918 became abstractions of faces. In the last form a harmonious U-form on the lower part provides the base while mouth, eyes, and forehead furnish a horizontal structure and the nose divides as a vertical the face into a lighter and a darker side. The eyebrows provide a gentle bow, and the face appears to look inwards with closed eyes. In the last works, often called "Meditations," nose, eyes, mouth, and forehead form a Greek cross with one small speck of light centered on the forehead, reminding the viewer of the sign of wisdom found on Byzantine and Russian icons of the Virgin Mary. Although consistently counted among the Expressionists, Jawlensky is the only artist to have created a meditative art: this was his unique contribution to modern art.

Further Reading

Two portfolios of lithographs were published: in 1919 a portfolio of eight lithographs of nudes and in 1922 a portfolio of heads. Clemens Weiler's monograph containing the oeuvre catalogue (Cologne, 1959) and his assessment *Heads/Faces/Meditations* (in English, 1970) are the most comprehensive studies. Weiler's 1970 work contains Jawlensky's memoirs as dictated to Lisa Kümmel. Mela Escherich (Wiesbaden, 1934), Ewald Rathke (Hanau, 1968), and Jürgen Schulze (Cologne, 1970) are important monographs. There are three important studies of Marianna von Werefkin: Clemens Weiler edited the "Letters to an Unknown, 1890-1905," which she wrote in the earlier times of her relationship with Jawlensky; Jelena Hahl-Koch wrote her dissertation on Marianna von Werefkin and the Russian Symbolism (Munich 1967); and Konrad Federer was the editor of a monograph on the artist. For the history of the "Blue Four" see the exhibition catalogues of the Leonard Hutton Gallery, New York (1984) and of the Norton Simon Museum of Art at Pasadena, which owns the Galka Scheyer Collection. □

Leon Jaworski

Leon Jaworski (1905–1982) was an independent prosecutor whose investigation into the Watergate affair eventually brought down the Nixon White House.

When in November 1973 the Nixon administration appointed Leon Jaworski special prosecutor in the Watergate case, many suspected that he was a Nixon crony, bent on obstructing the legal issues in the case and absolving the Nixon administration of wrongdoing. Nixon had already fired the previous Watergate special prosecutor, Harvard law professor Archibald Cox, precisely because of his insistence on pursuit of the truth in the case no matter which administration officials— including the president—were hurt. Jaworski seemed comfortable with those whose political conduct may have left them vulnerable. He successfully defended Lyndon Johnson against vote-rigging charges following the congressional elections of 1948; won another electoral case for Johnson in 1960; and was associated by many with fellow Texan John Connally, whose close ties to Nixon were well known. Yet Jaworski kept Cox's staff, continued his investigation of corruption in the Nixon administration, and subpoenaed the White House for Watergate tapes and documents— evidence that ultimately brought down the Nixon presidency. Leon Jaworski was every bit as high-minded and unbiased in pursuing the truth as had been Cox.

Background and Career

Like Cox, Jaworski was an achiever whose hard work and intelligence brought him wealth and influence. Son of a Polish father and Austrian mother who immigrated to Waco, Texas, Jaworski grew up poor but earned a reputation as an outstanding student. He graduated from high school at fifteen and went on to Baylor University, where he supplemented his scholarship by correcting papers for seventeen cents an hour. At sixteen he was admitted to the Baylor University Law School; at eighteen he graduated first in his class and became the youngest person admitted to the Texas bar in 1924. Jaworski returned to Waco and began his law career representing bootleggers and moonshiners. He lost a sensational case against a black client accused of murdering a white couple in 1929, but at a time when lynching was still common in Texas, Jaworski's defense gained him statewide attention and a position with the Houston firm of Fulbright, Cooker, Freeman and Bates. By age twenty-nine he was a full partner and the confidant of some of Texas's most powerful and influential businessmen. Jaworski served as a colonel in the army during World War II and henceforth would be nicknamed "Colonel" by friends and subordinates. After the war he became chief of the war crimes trial section of the Judge Advocate General's Corps, later recounting his experiences prosecuting Nazi criminals in a memoir, *Fifteen Years After* (1961). Returning to the United States, he renewed his law practice in Houston, becoming a senior partner in the Fulbright firm in 1946.

Democratic Counsel

During the 1950s and 1960s Jaworski extended his contacts among Texan business and political interests, becoming a close associate of Lyndon Johnson and an influential figure in the Democratic party. From 1962 to 1965 he worked for Archibald Cox and Robert Kennedy, pressing contempt charges against Mississippi governor Ross Barnett for his failure to comply with school desegregation orders. Later he served on the Warren Commission investigating the assassination of John Kennedy, and on President Johnson's crime and violence commissions. By the 1970s Jaworski had also built his law firm into largest in the country. It was famous for its egalitarianism—his was the first law firm in the Houston area to hire Jews, blacks, and women. From July 1971 to July 1972 Jaworski served as president of the American Bar Association, notable, given his future role, for his concern over "errant lawyers," who possessed "vanishing respect for law."

Special Prosecutor

Especially after the firing of Cox, Jaworski understood the politically tenuous nature of his job as special prosecutor. His position required that he collect evidence in the Watergate case, present it to grand juries, and prosecute wrongdoing, but not appear partisan or vindictive. Jaworski's judicious temperament and patient amassing of evidence insulated him from any partisan charges. To demonstrate his independence from the White House which appointed him, Jaworski retained Cox's staff of lawyers and broadened the scope of their investigations to include not only events connected to the Watergate break-in and cover-up but also illegal contributions to the Nixon reelection campaign. Ultimately, like Cox, Jaworski found himself at odds with the Nixon administration over the Watergate tapes, which Jaworski sought to review for evidence but which Nixon refused to surrender. As had Cox, Jaworski rejected the Nixon administration's claims to "executive privilege" and compromise proposals wherein the White House provided transcripts of the tapes instead of the tapes themselves. In the spring of 1974 he subpoenaed the administration for sixty-four tapes, but the White House refused to comply. Jaworski took his case to the Supreme Court. On 24 July 1974 the Supreme Court ruled, eight to zero, that Nixon must turn over the tapes, including the famous 23 June 1972 "smoking gun" tape, which proved that Nixon personally ordered his subordinates to obstruct justice. Sixteen days later Nixon became the first president in American history to resign the office.

Prosecuting Nixon

Jaworski had not taken the job as special prosecutor in order to bring down Nixon. On the contrary, he consistently operated with deference to and respect for the president, suggesting, for example, a compromise regarding the delivery of Watergate tapes, which Nixon rejected. He also refused to expand his powers beyond their limits, failing, while Nixon was still a sitting president, to indict Nixon for obstruction of justice, because he believed it to be beyond his power. Jaworski believed that it was a constitutional requirement that Congress prosecute the president. With Nixon's resignation, that dilemma was lifted, and Jaworski moved to prosecute Nixon as he had his fellow Watergate conspirators. President Ford's pardon of Nixon ended his efforts. On 25 October 1974 Jaworski returned to Houston. Under the third special Watergate prosecutor, Henry S. Ruth, Jr., White House officials John Mitchell, John Ehrlichman, H. R. Haldeman, and Robert Mardian were found guilty of conspiracy to obstruct justice. Judge John Sirica sentenced Mitchell, Haldeman, and Ehrlichman to two and a half to eight years in prison; Mardian was sentenced to ten months to three years. Twenty-seven corporate executives and lawyers were found guilty of campaign violations, but only three received prison sentences. Jaworski had not taken an active role in thes prosecutions. His importance was symbolic: stepping into the role of special prosecutor after its independence had been called into question, Jaworski proved that the special-prosecutor's office could be both impartial and rigorous—setting the stage for more extensive investigations by special prosecutors in the future.

Further Reading

James Doyle, *Not Above the Law: The Battles of Watergate Prosecutors Cox and Jaworski* (New York: Morrow, 1977). □

John Jay

John Jay (1745-1829), American diplomat and politician, guided American foreign policy from the end of the Revolution until George Washington's first administration was under way. Jay headed the U.S. Supreme Court during its formative years.

Long accustomed to a colonial status, Americans were ill-prepared to negotiate with foreign powers after the Revolution. The handful of men with diplomatic skill who emerged worked from a difficult position as the new nation experienced crises of credit and unity. John Jay's tenacity helped him survive the sectional battles and placed him in the inner councils of the Federalist party. Inclined to favor northern interests, he worked in a trying atmosphere until the Constitutional Convention of 1787 set a firmer tone for both domestic and diplomatic concerns. Jay's treaty with England, though highly controversial, probably avoided war. As chief justice, he gave the Supreme Court a national approach under the new Constitution.

John Jay was born on Dec. 12, 1745, in New York; he was the eighth child in a wealthy merchant family. Descended from French-Dutch stock and reared in the Huguenot tradition, Jay had few of the sentimental ties with England that made some Americans ambivalent in their allegiance after 1765. He graduated from King's College (later Columbia University) and trained in the law by a 5-year apprenticeship.

Admitted to the bar in 1768, Jay was briefly in partnership with Robert R. Livingston. Before 1774 Jay served on a royal commission formed to settle a boundary dispute between New York and a neighboring state, thus gaining his first experience as a negotiator. As a member of the "Moot Club" in New York, he associated with the lawyers who led the resistance movement against England a few years later. He married the beautiful and ambitious Sarah Livingston, daughter of William Livingston, on April 28, 1774.

Coming of Revolution

Almost before his honeymoon was over, Jay was serving on the New York Committee of Fifty-one, organized to control local anti-British measures. The committee manifesto, reportedly drafted by Jay, urging a convocation of deputies from all the Colonies to aid Boston and seek a "security of our common rights," led to the First Continental Congress. The cautious tone of the manifesto, however, brought some criticism from more militant groups that favored immediate boycott of British goods.

The Congress began Sept. 4, 1774; as Jay saw it, the Colonies were bound to try negotiations, to suspend commerce with Great Britain if these failed, and to go to war only when all other methods proved futile. Prudent to the point of timidity, Jay favored the narrowly defeated Galloway Plan of reconciliation. In Congress, Jay won a reputation as a skillful writer and moderate Whig, qualities that bore him into the New York Convention of 1775 and back to the Second Continental Congress. Meanwhile, the

first battles of the Revolution at Lexington-Concord made discussion of a peaceful solution academic.

Jay's capacity for hard work brought him into the vortex of the congressional struggle. He served on the committee that drafted the July 6 declaration justifying armed resistance against England, but he also worked for one last attempt at reconciliation. By November 1775 he was on a secret congressional committee charged with engendering friendship abroad.

In May 1776, upon his return to New York, Jay cautiously supported a motion that disavowed any declaration favoring independence from Great Britain. However, the votes of his colleagues back in Philadelphia compelled Jay to submerge his views and work for independence.

President of the Continental Congress

In 1777 Jay took a leading part in drafting the New York constitution, an essentially conservative document peppered with Jay's concept of justice and blended with the mercantile spirit of the Dutch-Huguenot merchants. Jay himself became chief justice of New York in the transition government, but because of wartime circumstances the court functioned in desultory fashion. In 1778 he was chosen president of the Continental Congress. While Congress tottered on the verge of bankruptcy, many private citizens made paper fortunes in land dealings and mercantile speculations. Jay wrote Washington that there was "as much intrigue in this State House as in the Vatican, but as little secrecy as in a boarding-school." On Aug. 10, 1779, Jay resigned as chief justice of New York, and on Oct. 1 he left the Congress to resume his law practice.

Instead of returning to private life, however, Jay was appointed minister to Spain in October 1779. He was instructed to seek a commercial treaty with Charles III which would establish American rights to Mississippi navigation and to secure a sizable loan. The Spanish court withheld formal recognition (possibly because of its own colonial interests), and Jay ended his mission in May 1782 on a note of failure.

Sectional jealousy had made the negotiations with Spain difficult, for New England congressmen were eager to trade away navigation rights on the Mississippi provided their fisheries gained a Spanish market. Jay showed little sympathy for the Kentuckians, who insisted that they needed a waterway to market their products, and ultimately their anger brought into focus the conflict of interests between the North and South. Jay found the Spanish ministry too arrogant to negotiate anyway, and he journeyed to Paris in June 1782 for the preliminary peace negotiations then in motion. Suspicious of French motives, Jay led the American commissioners in Paris to sign a separate agreement with England, in violation of their instructions from Congress. The French were not pleased.

Secretary of Foreign Affairs

Jay declined posts as minister to both France and Great Britain, but Congress would not permit him to retire from public service. In July 1784 he was appointed secretary of foreign affairs, although New York had also elected him to serve in Congress. Jay resigned the congressional seat and took the foreign affairs assignment.

Jay's immediate concerns as foreign secretary were the British occupation of western posts (in defiance of a treaty) and the festering Mississippi problem. Jay made indiscreet remarks supporting British complaints that they would hold the forts until prewar debts were paid, and the Spanish emissary, Diego de Gardoqui, reported that Jay was "a very self-centered man" with a vain and domineering wife. The Spanish emissary had instructions that permitted negotiation of a treaty that would have pleased the North because it promised hard cash for fish but would have kept the gateway to the West closed. The gift of a prized stallion from Charles III to Jay may have been only incidental; at any rate, Jay decided to recommend concessions which the Spaniards believed would restrict America's western expansion.

Jay explained the commercial treaty to Congress in August but did not mention the military alliance Gardoqui also sought. Congress, voting along sectional lines, approved the pact, but by less than the required two-thirds majority. Tempers on both sides were heated, and the matter was unresolved when the Constitution was sent to the states for ratification.

The Federalists

Though not a delegate to the Constitutional Convention, Jay was to be an outspoken supporter of its handiwork. He joined Alexander Hamilton and James Madison in supplying articles for New York newspapers in support of the Constitution under the pen name "Publius." Of these *Federalist* papers, Jay wrote Publius 2, 3, 4, 5, and 63. He might have contributed more but for an injury received in the "Doctor's Riot" of April 1788.

Jay recovered in time to write *An Address to the People of New York,* which pointed out the unique dangers inherent in New York's failure to ratify the Constitution. Such a prospect was likely, as a 2-to-1 Antifederalist majority had been elected to go to the state ratifying convention scheduled for June. Jay himself was a delegate from New York and, with Hamilton, worked a political miracle: the convention voted for ratification by a slender majority. The Federalist victory was tempered by instructions to Jay to prepare a circular letter to all the states seeking a second constitutional convention. Though some Federalists feared that this device would create trouble, its effect was dissipated by the general goodwill apparent in the winter of 1788/1789.

Supreme Court

In the interim period Jay continued to serve as foreign secretary to the expiring Continental Congress, more as a caretaker than a policy maker. American relations with France had remained generally on an excellent footing, but Jay's policy toward the Barbary pirates was ineffective. Jay served as acting secretary of state until Thomas Jefferson returned from France and assumed the office in March 1790. Meanwhile, George Washington had prevailed on Jay to accept the position of chief justice of the Supreme Court. Jay held this office until 1796 and presided over several fundamental cases.

While still chief justice, Jay undertook negotiations to end Anglo-American differences stemming from irritating events that had followed their 1783 peace treaty. Known to history as Jay's Treaty, the new document bore Jay's signature, but it was chiefly the work of Alexander Hamilton, whose advice and information leaks allowed the British diplomats to move confidently. Jay became a special envoy at Washington's request. He left for England in 1794 and signed a treaty with Lord Grenville that gained a British promise to evacuate western posts and negotiate boundaries but made considerable concessions to British creditors and to the British concept of neutrality. France interpreted the treaty as a direct rebuff, and its hostile reception in America strengthened the rising opposition to Washington's government by followers of Thomas Jefferson. The treaty was ratified by the Senate after a stormy debate.

Meanwhile, Jay had been elected governor of New York. Four years earlier Jay had won the popular vote for governor, but a legislative board had nullified his election. His victory in 1795 was clear-cut, however, and Jay gave up his Court position to serve in his last public office. His administration (1795-1801) was conservative and consolidating, marked by a refusal in 1800 to rig an election at Hamilton's suggestion. After two terms Jay announced his retirement and declined the offer to resume his old place on the Supreme Court. Within a year after his long-delayed return to Bedford, N.Y., Jay's wife (who had seven children) died. But for this, Jay's long retreat from public life bore out his repeated expectations of a pleasant "domestic life in rural leisure passed." He died on May 7, 1829, at Bedford.

Further Reading

Frank Monaghan, *John Jay* (1935), is readable but uncritical. A good short account is in Samuel Flagg Bemis, ed., *The American Secretaries of State,* vol. 1 (1927). Also valuable is Bemis's *Jay's Treaty* (1923; rev. ed. 1962). See also Henry P. Johnston, ed., *Correspondence and Public Papers of John Jay* (4 vols., 1890-1893).

Additional Sources

Johnson, Herbert Alan, *John Jay, colonial lawyer,* New York: Garland Pub., 1989.

McLean, Jennifer P., *The Jays of Bedford: the story of five generations of the Jay family who lived in the John Jay Homestead,* Katonah, N.Y.: Friends of John Jay Homestead, 1984.

Pellew, George, *John Jay,* New York: Chelsea House, 1980. □

William Jay

American reformer William Jay (1789-1858) was an abolitionist whose prestige and understanding of constitutional law gave vital support to the cause.

William Jay was born in New York City on June 11, 1789. His father was the illustrious statesman John Jay. Young Jay attended Yale College and studied law but gave up the profession because of weak eyes. He then devoted himself to philanthropic causes and to writing. His life was dominated by love of family, devout and evangelical Episcopalianism, and patriotism. In 1810 he helped organize the American Bible Society and often wrote on the duty of churchmen to support just causes.

An early adopter of abolitionist principles, in 1818 Jay was appointed a judge of Westchester County, a position he retained until 1843, when the governor conceded to proslavery pressure and refused to reappoint him. Jay saw putting limits on slavery territory as a primary target for abolitionists. In 1826 he aided the successful movement to help Gilbert Horton, a free African American, who had been arrested as a fugitive slave in Washington, D.C. Jay also sponsored a petition for the abolition of slavery in the District of Columbia that became a major abolitionist cause.

Jay also took up conservative causes, including temperance, education, and Sabbath observance. In 1833 he published a biography of his father. The next year he wrote one of his most influential books, *Inquiry into the Character and Tendency of the American Colonization and American Anti-slavery Societies*. Widely used, the book did severe harm to the movement to create colonies for Negroes in Africa, which had been considered a gradual and painless means of ending slavery.

Jay added many influential writings to the abolitionist cause and during the 1840s was thought of as a presidential figure by political abolitionists. However, Jay himself doubted the value of political action. By 1853, when his

Miscellaneous Writings on Slavery was issued, other political forces dominated the scene.

Jay was also an ardent pacifist. His major pacifist works were *War and Peace: The Evils of the First, with a Plan for Securing the Last* (1842) and *Review of the Causes and Consequences of the Mexican War* (1849). The earlier pamphlet, in which he advanced arguments favoring mediation and arbitration in peace efforts, was influential in peace congresses abroad and during peace negotiations following the Crimean War. It was recalled during the Hague Peace Conference of 1899 and reprinted in 1917 as a contribution to pacifist thinking in that period.

On Oct. 14, 1858, Jay died. African American abolitionist Frederick Douglass, eulogizing Jay, said that "he was our wise counsellor, our fine friend, and our liberal benefactor."

Further Reading

The only study of Jay is Bayard Tuckerman, *William Jay and the Constitutional Movement for the Abolition of Slavery* (1894), which has a preface by Jay's son John Jay. □

Junius Richard Jayewardene

Junius Richard Jayewardene (1906-1996) was a leader of the nationalist movement in Ceylon (now Sri Lanka) who served in a variety of cabinet positions in the decades after independence. In 1977, he became prime minister, and then president, of Sri Lanka.

Junius Richard Jayewardene, eldest in a family of 11 children, was born September 17, 1906, in Colombo, Ceylon (now Sri Lanka). His father was a judge of the Ceylon Supreme Court, and JR, as he was popularly known in his country, became a lawyer after attaining a distinguished academic record in the Colombo Law College.

Jayewardene did not practice law for long, however. He became an activist in the Ceylon National Congress (CNC), which provided the organizational platform for Ceylon's nationalist movement (the island was officially renamed Sri Lanka in 1972). Drawing inspiration from the non-violent freedom movement of the Indian National Congress (INC) under the Mahatma Gandhi's leadership in nearby India, JR soon became the effective spokesman for the CNC's younger generation of leadership. He became CNC secretary in 1939, and held that position until 1947 when Ceylon became a dominion in the British Commonwealth.

Jayewardene made his parliamentary debut in 1943. After that, JR's political career had its ups and downs. In the first general election, in 1947, the CNC regrouped itself as the United National Party (UNP) to accommodate those who had been outside the congress and won the largest number of seats in the House of Representatives. UNP

leader D. S. Senanayake was called upon to form the government. Senanayake chose Jayewardene to be his finance minister. And when independence was heralded on February 4, 1948, the UNP regime became the legatee of the new state.

The life of the parliament ended in 1952. By then D. S. Senanayake had passed away, leaving the mantle of UNP leadership to his son, Dudley Senanayake. Dudley and JR had worked closely together in the CNC, and JR continued as finance minister when the UNP was again returned to power in the newly formed parliament.

In his second term as finance minister JR found himself confronted with external constraints. The plantation-based economy depended solely on tea and rubber exports for revenues and Sri Lanka imported virtually all its food. JR found himself compelled to cut drastically the subsidies on rice and flour when export earnings from rubber fell sharply.

This led to food riots, finally forcing Senanayake to resign as prime minister. His successor, Sir John Kotelawala, retained JR in his cabinet as minister for food and agriculture, a portfolio he held until the general elections of 1956. In the elections, marked by a resurgence of the Sinhalese-Buddhist forces, the Sri Lanka Freedom Party (SLFP) won the elections and the UNP suffered a shattering defeat.

Jayewardene applied himself to the difficult task of rebuilding a party that had become identified with the Western-oriented elite, against which the electorate had revolted. It was a measure of JR's success that in the elections of 1965 the UNP was returned to power. In the new UNP government JR became the parliamentary secretary for defense and external affairs with a protocol ranking him next to Dudley Senanayake, who had again become prime minister.

In the general elections of 1970, dissatisfied with the pace of economic growth, the electorate voted overwhelmingly for the opposition and the SLFP was back in power under Sirimavo Bandaranaike. The SLFP and its leftist allies had won 116 seats. The UNP won only 17 in a house of 151.

As he had done earlier while in opposition, JR's principal task was to reorganize the party. His relations with Dudley Senanayake became somewhat strained because of differences over the party's role, but their long association and friendship did not rupture. With Dudley's death in 1973, JR was the unanimous choice for the UNP presidency. Earlier he had been the party's treasurer, secretary, and vice-president. Alongside his varied political and organizational experience, his position as the top UNP leader left him free to effect his socio-economic and political ideas. The opportunity soon came when in the general election of 1977 the UNP emerged with 140 seats in a House of 168. The SLFP won just eight seats and its leftist allies none.

Within months of assuming the highest office, as he neared age 70, Prime Minister Jayewardene's UNP regime geared itself to draw a new constitution modeled on the French system, with the president being both the head of the state and of the government. JR was sworn in as the first executive president under the new constitution, with con-

current duties as premier and president. In the presidential election of October 1982 (scheduled originally for February 1984 and advanced at his own initiative) JR won with a convincing majority. By then, JR was cherishing a new nickname: "the Old Fox."

The Jayewardene regime began its task with a set of bold socio-economic initiatives. Broadly speaking, JR's economic policies were based on principles of a free market economy with the state providing infrastructural facilities for private investment, similar to the Singapore model.

However, the politico-economic activities of the JR regime were adversely affected and marred by ethnic strife between the majority Buddhist Sinhalese, of which Jayewardene was a member, and the minority Hindu Tamils. After simmering a number of years, the antagonism erupted into a near holocaust in July 1983, engulfing the country. This spate of violence and counter-violence seriously set back JR's vision of a Dharmishtha Society—a society based on the principles of justice and equity—in Sri Lanka.

JR retired in 1989. By the time of his death seven years later, Sri Lanka's top office was held by Chandrika Kumaratunga, daughter of his old political foe, Sirimavo Bandaranaike. The nation's ethnic strife was unsettled, but JR's free market initiatives remained in place.

Further Reading

A one-volume biography, *J.R. Jayewardene,* by K.M. De Silva, was published in 1997; *The Break-Up of Sri Lanka* (1988) is Canadian professor A. Jeyaratnam Wilson's account of his mediation efforts between Jayewardene and Tamil rebels. Jayewardene's extensive writings are available in English as well as Sinhalese; also of note are: *Buddhist Essays* (Colombo, 1942); *Buddhism and Marxism* (Colombo, 1950); *Selected Speeches: 1944-1973* (Colombo, 1974); *A New Path* (Colombo, 1978); and *Tolerance, Nonaggression and Mutual Respect* (Colombo, 1979). □

Jean de Meun

The French author Jean de Meun (ca. 1240-1305) wrote the second, and longer, part of the "Romance of the Rose." His work is noted for its erudition and encyclopedic spirit.

Jean de Meun, also known as Jean Chopinel or Clopinel, was born in Meun-sur-Loire, the general region of Guillaume de Lorris, to whose *Romance of the Rose* he added 17,722 lines between 1269 and 1278. Afterward he translated Vegetius's *Military Art,* Boethius's *Consolation of Philosophy,* the *Letters of Abelard and Heloise,* Ailred's *Spiritual Friendship,* and Giraldus's *Topography of Ireland* and wrote at least two original works in verse: *The Testament of Jean de Meun* and *The Codicil of Master Jean de Meun.* He died in a comfortable house near the University of Paris, where he may have had some academic connection.

In Jean's continuation of the *Romance of the Rose,* Reason tries to dissuade the lover, but the god of Love later reproaches the lover for lending an ear to Reason. In the course of the lover's turmoil he has occasion to reflect, among other things, that possessions are burdens, that charity and justice are by no means equal, that power and virtue never go together, and that, even in destroying, Nature carries on her struggle against death. At last Love organizes an assault on the prison of the rose, depending on False Appearance for military success. The attack succeeds, and the lover receives the rose.

A résumé of many pages would be hopelessly inadequate, for Jean discourses on innumerable matters and draws from a great variety of sources, including the Bible, Plato, Aristotle, Livy, Virgil, Ovid, Horace, Juvenal, St. Augustine, Boethius, Roger Bacon, John of Salisbury, Alain de Lille, and Andreas Capellanus. Sometimes he reminds us of the scholastics, sometimes of the humanists, and often, with his interest in mining and alchemy, of the medieval scientist-philosopher.

In contrast with Guillaume de Lorris, Jean is bourgeois, extremely learned, realistic, a satirist, and a representative of another generation. Anticlerical and antimilitary, he is clear and eloquent, with didactic instincts that keep him from being negative; it is not surprising that he has been called the ''Voltaire of the Middle Ages.'' Jean's antifeminism shows a curious crossing of the traditions of the fabliaux and of St. Jerome; in fact, there are precious few aspects of medieval life and thought which are not found in Jean's part of the *Romance of the Rose.*

Further Reading

A study of Jean de Meun is Dorothy Marie Ralph, *Jean de Meun: The Voltaire of the Middle Ages* (1940). □

Sir James Hopwood Jeans

The English mathematician, physicist, and astronomer Sir James Hopwood Jeans (1877-1946) made important contributions to the development of quantum theory and to theoretical astrophysics, especially to the theory of stellar structure.

On Sept. 11, 1877, James Jeans was born in Ormskirk, Lancashire, the son of a parliamentary journalist. He was brought up in a strict, very religious Victorian home atmosphere. A precocious child, he was reading by age 4 and had a remarkable ability to memorize numbers. At an early age he also became interested in physics, as well as in mechanical devices, especially clocks—the subject of a short book he wrote at age 9.

In 1897 Jeans entered Trinity College, Cambridge, and in 1903 received his master's degree. In 1904 he was appointed university lecturer in mathematics at Cambridge; and in 1906, at the very early age of 28, he was elected a fellow of the Royal Society—all this in spite of the fact that during 1902-1903 tuberculosis of the joints forced him to go to several sanatoriums. During his illness, from which he completely recovered, he wrote his first book, *The Dynamical Theory of Gases.*

Jeans taught applied mathematics at Princeton University, N.J., from 1905 to 1909. He returned to Cambridge as Stokes lecturer in 1910 but 2 years later relinquished the position and thereafter devoted full time to research and writing.

In 1907 Jeans married Charlotte Tiffany Mitchell; she died in 1934, leaving one daughter. The following year he married Suzanne Hock, a concert organist, with whom Jeans wrote his very popular and informative book *Science and Music* (1938). They had two sons and a daughter.

In the first period of his scientific life (1901-1914), Jeans's interests were centered mainly on the kinetic theory of gases and the theory of radiation, especially applied to the new quantum theory of Max Planck and others. Through a vigorous interchange of ideas, Lord Rayleigh and Jeans, in 1905, separately derived what later came to be called the Rayleigh-Jeans law. Despite the fact that this law implied a failure of classical theory when applied to blackbody radiation, Jeans, during the ensuing years, repeatedly attempted to sustain classical theory instead of accepting quantum theory. Only after Henri Poincaré's 1912 paper on the quantum theory did Jeans become convinced. Two years later Jeans wrote a brief but comprehensive *Report on Radiation and the Quantum Theory,* which, after World War I, was extremely influential in convincing physicists of the importance of the new quantum ideas.

During the war years Jeans experienced his finest hour as a scientist—now a theoretical astrophysicist. His researches on stellar structure were most significant, especially his proof that a rotating incompressible mass will, with increasing rotational velocity, first become pearshaped and then cataclysmically fission into two parts (one model for a single star evolving into a double-star system). This and other important results, including a tidal encounter nebular hypothesis that replaced the classical Kant-Laplace nebular hypothesis, were published in his 1919 Adams Prize essay, *Problems of Cosmogony and Stellar Dynamics.*

The next decade of Jeans's life (1918-1928) was marked by a rather sharp decrease in his reputation as a theoretical astrophysicist. Already, in 1917, he had a famous debate with Arthur S. Eddington on stellar structure and, though not really apparent at the time, Jeans by and large emerged the loser. In 1929 Jeans turned to popular science writing, especially in astronomy, and soon became very successful. His *Universe around Us* ushered in a series of eight books between 1929 and 1942. All are stimulating expositions, though they suffer in one degree or another from presenting the results of scientific research a bit too dogmatically, thereby giving a distorted picture of such research in progress.

Jeans was awarded numerous honorary degrees and professional offices. He was knighted in 1928 and won the coveted Order of Merit in 1939. He was a modest and unassuming man and a devoted father. Jeans died on Sept. 16, 1946, at his home in Dorking, Surrey.

Further Reading

A study of Jeans is E. A. Milne, *Sir James Jeans* (1952). Milne also wrote a short obituary notice of Jeans in *Biographical Memoirs of the Fellows of the Royal Society, 1945-1948,* vol. 5 (1947). There is a bibliography of Jeans's writings in both of these works. □

John Robinson Jeffers

American poet John Robinson Jeffers (1887-1962) glorified the stern beauties of nature. He saw the human race as doomed and often utilized Greek myths to emphasize man's tragic position in the universe.

Robinson Jeffers was born on Jan. 10, 1887, in Pittsburgh, Pa., where his father taught at Western Theological Seminary. Young Jeffers rejected his father's belief in God but retained the Calvinistic sense of man as depraved and damned. Jeffers was reading Greek by the age of 5, and he attended boarding schools in Switzerland and Germany. He received a bachelor of arts degree in 1905 from Occidental College. He undertook graduate study in the sciences at several universities, studying medicine at the University of California. In 1912 an inheritance freed him to concentrate exclusively on writing poetry.

After his marriage in 1914, Jeffers settled in Carmel, Calif., where he built a stone tower on a lonely cliff overlooking the Pacific Ocean and began to write. Though his earliest published poems were conventional romantic celebrations of nature, in *Tamar and Other Poems* (1924) he found his voice in celebrating the supremacy of the inhuman. In *Dear Judas and Other Poems* (1929) he presented Christ as traitor because he trapped men into believing in love rather than urging them to seek annihilation. Jeffers's reading of Oswald Spengler's *The Decline of the West* and Friedrich Nietzsche's ideas on the death of God, while speculating on the implications of his own scientific studies, probably accounts for the shift in his beliefs. He considered life a tragic "accident" in a universe designed for the subhuman and the inanimate.

In *The Double Axe and Other Poems* (1948) Jeffers viewed World War II in Spenglerian terms. Though his philosophy of "inhumanism" was increasingly unacceptable to the postwar generation, his best work proclaimed a kind of dignity in man's inevitable defeat. Critical interest in Jeffers's poetry has waned in recent years, but a few of his best poems, such as "Apology for Bad Dreams," "To the Stone-cutters," "Shine, Perishing Republic," and "Roan Stallion," continue to be admired.

Jeffers's free adaptation of Euripides's *Medea* (1946) was an immediate sensation when produced on Broadway. He published some 19 volumes of poetry and drama. His last volumes were *Hungerfield and Other Poems* (1954) and the posthumous *The Beginning and the End* (1963) and *Selected Poems* (1965). He wrote primarily in free verse,

relying mainly on direct statement and rhetoric to set his forms. Jeffers died in Carmel on Jan. 10, 1962.

Further Reading

A full-length biography is Frederic Ives Carpenter, *Robinson Jeffers* (1962). There are sections on Jeffers in Hyatt H. Waggoner, *The Heel of Elohim: Science and Values in Modern American Poetry* (1950) and *American Poets, from the Puritans to the Present* (1968).

Additional Sources

Adamic, Louis, *Robinson Jeffers: a portrait,* Covelo, Calif.: Carolyn and James Robertson, 1983.

Karman, James, *Robinson Jeffers: poet of California,* Brownsville, OR: Story Line Press, 1995.

Luhan, Mabel Dodge, *Una and Robin,* Berkeley: Friends of the Bancroft Library, University of California, 1976.

Ritchie, Ward, *I remember Robinson Jeffers,* Los Angeles: Zamorano Club, 1978.

Ritchie, Ward, *Jeffers: some recollections of Robinson Jeffers,* Laguna Beach, Calif.: Laguna Verde Imprenta, 1977.

Robinson Jeffers, poet, 1887-1987: a centennial exhibition, Los Angeles: Occidental College, 1987. □

Joseph Jefferson

American actor Joseph Jefferson (1829-1905) is remembered chiefly for his characterization of Rip Van Winkle. He was one of America's best comic actors.

J oseph Jefferson was born on Feb. 20, 1829. His great-grandfather had been an actor in England; his grandfather, who went to America in 1795, became one of the country's leading actors; his father had been an itinerant actor. Young Joseph was destined to outshine them all.

Jefferson had his debut at the age of 4, when comedian Thomas Rice painted his face black and carried him on stage in a large bag, and the two then danced and sang "Jim Crow." As a youth, Jefferson barnstormed the West and South. His father died in 1842, but the family continued touring. Jefferson followed the armies in the Mexican War and did a stint acting and tending bar in Matamoros.

Then Jefferson returned to Philadelphia to join his half brother, Charles Burke, at the Arch Street Theater. From Burke, Jefferson learned the art of comedy. Jefferson first appeared in New York City in 1849; but it was not until 1857 that, as a member of Laura Keene's celebrated company, he gained a national reputation playing in *Our American Cousin.* He was also outstanding as Dr. Pangloss in *The Heir at Law* and as Caleb Plummer in Dion Boucicault's *The Cricket on the Hearth.* But it was as Rip Van Winkle that he became famous. He first played this role in 1859 in the version used previously by Burke.

When his wife, actress Margaret Lockyer, died in 1861, Jefferson took to the road again. After a while, he sailed to Australia and New Zealand, going to London in 1865. He commissioned Boucicault to prepare a new version of *Rip Van Winkle,* and it was an immediate success, playing 170 performances in London. The success was repeated in America, and Jefferson played this role for the rest of his life, continuing to change and re-create his characterization.

Jefferson married Sarah Warren, a distant cousin, in 1867. In addition to remaining popular and continuing to act until a year before his death, as the years passed he became more and more respected in and out of the profession. He was also a landscape painter of some merit and a gifted writer. His autobiography, though chronologically vague, is witty, contains many insights into the arts of acting and playwriting, and indicates his philosophy of life.

Jefferson asserted that in the role of Rip Van Winkle he hoped to create a character in whom laughter and tears were closely allied, also saying that he played best with a cool head and a warm heart. Though some critics have had reservations about Jefferson's scope, all would agree that he was a great comic actor. He died on Jan. 23, 1905.

Further Reading

Perhaps the best book on Jefferson is the unreliable *Autobiography of Joseph Jefferson* (1890). More accurate is William Winter, *The Life and Art of Joseph Jefferson* (1894). Eugénie Paul Jefferson, *Recollections of Joseph Jefferson* (1909), is also helpful. □

Thomas Jefferson

American philosopher and statesman Thomas Jefferson (1743-1826) was the third president of the United States. A man of broad interests and activity, he exerted an immense influence on the political and intellectual life of the new nation.

Thomas Jefferson was born at Shadwell, Va., on April 13, 1743. His father had been among the earliest settlers in this wilderness country, and his position of leadership descended to his eldest son, together with 5,000 acres of land.

Jefferson became one of the best-educated Americans of his time. At the age of 17 he entered the College of William and Mary, where he got exciting first glimpses of "the expansion of science, and of the system of things in which we are placed." Nature destined him to be a scientist, he often said; but there was no opportunity for a scientific career in Virginia, and he took the path of the law, studying it under the tutelage of George With as a branch of the history of mankind. He read widely in the law, in the sciences, and in both ancient and modern history, philosophy, and literature. Jefferson was admitted to the bar in 1767; his successful practice led to a wide circle of influence and to cultivated intellectual habits that would prove remarkably creative in statesmanship. When the onrush of the American Revolution forced him to abandon practice in 1774, he turned these legal skills to the rebel cause.

Jefferson's public career began in 1769, when he served as a representative in the Virginia House of Burgesses. About this time, too, he began building Monticello, the lovely home perched on a densely wooded summit that became a lifelong obsession. He learned architecture from books, above all from the Renaissance Italian Andrea Palladio. Yet Monticello, like the many other buildings Jefferson designed over the years, was a uniquely personal creation. Dissatisfied with the first version, completed in 12 years, Jefferson later rebuilt it. Monticello assumed its ultimate form about the time he retired from the presidency.

His Philosophy

Jefferson rose to fame in the councils of the American Revolution. Insofar as the Revolution was a philosophical event, he was its most articulate spokesman, having absorbed the thought of the 18th-century Enlightenment. He believed in a beneficent natural order in the moral as in the physical world, freedom of inquiry in all things, and man's inherent capacity for justice and happiness, and he had faith in reason, improvement, and progress.

Jefferson's political thought would become the quintessence of Enlightenment liberalism, though it had roots in English law and government. The tradition of the English constitution gave concreteness to American patriot claims, even a color of legality to revolution itself, that no other modern revolutionaries have possessed. Jefferson used the libertarian elements of the English legal tradition for ideo-

logical combat with the mother country. He also separated the principles of English liberty from their corrupted forms in the empire of George III and identified these principles with nascent American ideals. In challenging the oppressions of the empire, Americans like Jefferson came to recognize their claims to an independent nationality.

Jefferson's most important contribution to the revolutionary debate was *A Summary View of the Rights of British America* (1774). He argued that Americans, as sons of expatriate Englishmen, possessed the same natural rights to govern themselves as their Saxon ancestors had exercised when they migrated to England from Germany. Only with the reign of George III had the violations of American rights proved to be "a deliberate, systematical plan of reducing us to slavery." Though the logic of his argument pointed to independence, Jefferson instead set forth the theory of an empire of equal self-governing states under a common king and appealed to George III to rule accordingly.

Declaration of Independence

The Revolution had begun when Jefferson took his seat in the Second Continental Congress, at Philadelphia, in June 1775. He brought to the Congress, as John Adams recalled, "a reputation for literature, science, and a happy talent for composition." It was chiefly as a legislative draftsman that he would make his mark. His great work was the Declaration of Independence. In June 1776 he was surprised to find himself at the head of the committee to prepare this paper. He submitted a rough draft to Adams and Benjamin Franklin, two of the committee, who suggested only minor changes, revised it to Jefferson's satisfaction, and sent it to Congress. Congress debated it line by line for 2 1/2 days. Though many changes were made, the Declaration that emerged on July 4 bore the unmistakable stamp of Jefferson. It possessed that "peculiar felicity of expression" for which he was noted.

The Declaration of Independence crisply set forth the bill of particular grievances against the reigning sovereign and compressed a whole cosmology, a political philosophy, and a national creed in one paragraph. The truths declared to be "self-evident" were not new; as Jefferson later said, his purpose was "not to find out new principles, or new arguments . . . , but to place before mankind the common sense of the subject." But here, for the first time in history, these truths were laid at the foundation of a nation. Natural equality, the inalienable rights of man, the sovereignty of the people, the right of revolution—these principles endowed the American Revolution with high purpose united to a theory of government.

In Virginia

Jefferson returned to Virginia and to his seat in the reconstituted legislature. A constitution had been adopted for the commonwealth, but it was distressingly less democratic than the one Jefferson had drafted and dispatched to Williamsburg. He sought now to achieve liberal reforms by ordinary legislation. Most of these were contained in his comprehensive Revision of the Laws. Although the code was never enacted in entirety, the legislature went over the bills one by one. Of first importance was the Statute for Religious Freedom. Enacted in 1786, the statute climaxed the long campaign for separation of church and state in Virginia. Though Jefferson was responsible for the abolition of property laws that were merely relics of feudalism, his bill for the reform of Virginia's barbarous criminal code failed, and for the sake of expediency he withheld his plan for gradual emancipation of the slaves. Jefferson was sickened by the defeat of his Bill for the More General Diffusion of Knowledge. A landmark in the history of education, it proposed a complete system of public education, with elementary schools available to all, the gifted to be educated according to their ability.

Jefferson became Virginia's governor in June 1779. The Revolutionary War had entered a new phase. The British decision to "unravel the thread of rebellion from the southward" would, if successful, have made Virginia the crucial battleground. Jefferson struggled against enormous odds to aid the southern army. He was also handicapped by the weakness of his office under the constitution and by his personal aversion to anything bordering on dictatorial rule.

Early in 1781 the British invaded Virginia from the coast, slashed through to Richmond, and put the government to flight. Jefferson acted with more vigor than before, still to no avail. In May, Gen. Charles Cornwallis marched his army into Virginia. The government moved to safer quarters at Charlottesville. The Redcoats followed, and 2 days after his term of office expired but before a successor could be chosen, Jefferson was chased from Monticello. The General Assembly resolved to inquire into Jefferson's conduct, and months after the British surrender at Yorktown, he attended the legislature on this business. But no inquiry was held, the Assembly instead voting him resolution of thanks for his services.

Nevertheless, wounded by the criticism, Jefferson resolved to quit public service. A series of personal misfortunes, culminating in his wife's death in September 1782, plunged him into gloom. Yet her death finally returned him to his destiny. The idealized life he had sought in his family, farms, and books was suddenly out of reach. That November he eagerly accepted congressional appointment to the peace commission in Paris. He never sailed, however, and wound up in Congress instead.

During his retirement Jefferson had written his only book, *Note on the State of Virginia*. The inquiry had begun simply, but it grew as Jefferson worked. He finally published the manuscript in a private edition in Paris (1785). Viewed in the light of 18th-century knowledge, the book is work of natural and civil history, uniquely interesting as a guide to Jefferson's mind and to his native country. He expressed opinions on a variety of subjects, from cascades and caverns to constitutions and slavery. An early expression of American nationalism, the book acted as a catalyst in several fields of intellectual activity. It also ensured Jefferson a scientific and literary reputation on two continents.

Service in Congress

In Congress from November 1783 to the following May, Jefferson laid the foundations of national policy in several areas. His proposed decimal system of coinage was adopted. He drafted the first ordinance of government for the western territory, wherein free and equal republican states would be created out of the wilderness; and his land ordinance, adopted with certain changes in 1785, projected the rectilinear survey system of the American West.

Jefferson also took a leading part in formulating foreign policy. The American economy rested on foreign commerce and navigation. Cut adrift from the British mercantile system, Congress had pursued free trade to open foreign markets, but only France had been receptive. The matter became urgent in 1783-1784. Jefferson helped reformulate a liberal commercial policy, and in 1784 he was appointed to a three-man commission (with Adams and Franklin) to negotiate treaties of commerce with the European powers.

Minister to France

In Paris, Jefferson's first business was the treaty commission; in 1785 he succeeded Franklin as minister to France. The commission soon expired, and Jefferson focused his commercial diplomacy on France. In his opinion, France offered imposing political support for the United States in Europe as well as an entering wedge for the free commercial system on which American wealth and power depended. Louis XVI's foreign minister seemed well disposed, and influential men in the French capital were ardent friends of the American Revolution. Jefferson won valuable concessions for American commerce; however, because France realized few benefits in return, Britain maintained its economic ascendancy.

His duties left Jefferson time to haunt bookstores, frequent fashionable salons, and indulge his appetite for art, music, and theater. He toured the south of France and Italy, England, and the Rhineland. He interpreted the New World to the Old. Some of this activity had profound effects. For instance, his collaboration with a French architect in the design of the classical Roman Capitol of Virginia inaugurated the classical revival in American architecture.

About Europe generally, Jefferson expressed ambivalent feelings. But on balance, the more he saw of Europe, the dearer his own country became. "My God!" he exclaimed. "How little do my countrymen know what precious blessings they are in possession of, and which no other people on earth enjoy. I confess I had no idea of it myself. . . ."

Secretary of State

On Jefferson's return to America in 1789, President Washington prevailed upon him to become secretary of state. For the next 3 years he was chiefly engaged in fruitless negotiations with the European powers. With Spain he sought to fix the southern United States boundary and secure free navigation of the Mississippi River through Spanish territory to the Gulf of Mexico. With Britain he sought removal of English troops from the Northwest and settlement of issues left over from the peace treaty. In this encounter he was frustrated by the secretary of the Treasury, Alexander Hamilton, whose ascendancy in the government also checked Jefferson's and James Madison's efforts for commercial discrimination against Britain and freer trade with France. In Jefferson's opinion, Hamilton's fiscal system turned on British trade, credit, and power, while his own system turned on commercial liberation, friendship with France, and the success of the French Revolution. Hamilton's measures would enrich the few at the expense of the many, excite speculation and fraud, concentrate enormous power in the Treasury, and break down the restraints of the Constitution. To combat these tendencies, Jefferson associated himself with the incipient party opposition in Congress.

Developing Political Parties

As the party division deepened, Jefferson was denounced by the Federalists as the "generalissimo" of the Republican party, a role he neither possessed nor coveted but, finally, could not escape. When war erupted between France and Britain in 1793, the contrary dispositions of the parties toward these nations threatened American peace. Jefferson attempted to use American neutrality to force concessions from Britain and to improve cooperation between the embattled republics of the Atlantic world. In this he was embarrassed by Edmond Genet, the French minister to the United States, and finally had to abandon him altogether. The deterioration of Franco-American relations did irreparable damage to Jefferson's political system.

Jefferson resigned his post at the end of 1793, again determined to quit public life. But in 1796 the Republicans made him their presidential candidate against John Adams. Losing by three electoral votes, Jefferson became vice president. When the "XYZ affair" threatened to plunge the United States into war with France in 1798, Jefferson clung to the hope of peace and, in the developing war hysteria, rallied the Republicans around him. Enactment of the Alien and Sedition Laws convinced him that the Federalists aimed to annihilate the Republicans and that the Republicans' only salvation lay in political intervention by the state authorities. On this basis he drafted the Kentucky Resolutions of 1798, in which he elaborated the theory of the Union as a compact among the several states, declared the Alien and Sedition Laws unconstitutional, and prescribed the remedy of state "nullification" for such assumptions of power by the central government. Kentucky did not endorse this specific doctrine, but the defense of civil liberties was now joined to the defense of state rights. Though the celebrated resolutions did not force a change of policy, by contributing to the rising public clamor against the administration they achieved their political purpose.

President of the United States

Republicans doubled their efforts to elect the "man of the people" in the unusually bitter campaign of 1800. Jefferson topped Adams in the electoral vote. But because his running mate, Aaron Burr, received an equal number of votes, the final decision went to the House of Representatives. Only after 36 ballots was Jefferson elected.

Jefferson became president on March 4, 1801, in the new national capital, Washington, D.C. His inaugural address—a political touchstone for a century or longer—brilliantly summed up the Republican creed and appealed for the restoration of harmony and affection. "We have called by different names brethren of the same principle. We are all republicans: we are all federalists." Jefferson extended the hand of friendship to the Federalists and, although Federalists monopolized the Federal offices, he attempted to limit his removals of them. Even after party pressures forced him to revise this strategy, moderation characterized his course.

Reform was the order of the day. Working effectively with Congress, Jefferson restored freedom of the press; lowered the residency period of the law of naturalization to 5 years; scaled down the Army and Navy (despite a war against Barbary piracy); repealed the partisan Judiciary Act of 1801; abolished all internal taxes, together with a host of revenue offices; and began the planned retirement of the debt. The Jeffersonian reformation was bottomed on fiscal policy; by reducing the means and powers of government, it sought to further peace, equality, and individual freedom.

The President's greatest triumph—and his greatest defeat—came in foreign affairs. Spain's cession of Louisiana and the port of New Orleans to France in 1800 posed a serious threat to American security, especially to the aspirations of the West. Jefferson skillfully negotiated this crisis. With the Louisiana Purchase (1803), America gained an uncharted domain of some 800,000 square miles, doubling its size, for $11,250,000. Even before the treaty was signed, Jefferson planned an expedition to explore this country. The Lewis and Clark expedition, like the Louisiana Purchase, was a spectacular consummation of Jefferson's western vision.

Easily reelected in 1804, Jefferson soon encountered foreign and domestic troubles. His relations with Congress degenerated as Republicans quarreled among themselves. Especially damaging was the insurgency of John Randolph, formerly Republican leader in the House. And former vice president Aaron Burr mounted an insurgency in the West; but Jefferson crushed this and, with difficulty, maintained control of Congress. The turbulence of the Napoleonic Wars, with American ships and seamen ravaged in the neutral trade, proved too difficult. France was not blameless, but Britain was the chief aggressor.

Finally there appeared to be no escape from war except by withdrawing from the oceans. In December 1807 the President proposed, and Congress enacted, a total embargo on America's seagoing commerce. More than an alternative to war, the embargo was a test of the power of commercial coercion in international disputes. On the whole, it was effectively enforced, but it failed to bring Britain or France to justice, and the mounting costs at home led to its repeal by Congress in the waning hours of Jefferson's presidency.

Active Retirement

In retirement Jefferson became the "Sage of Monticello," the most revered—by some the most hated—among the remaining Revolutionary founders. He maintained a large correspondence and intellectual pursuits on a broad front. Unfinished business from the Revolution drew his attention, such as revision of the Virginia constitution and gradual emancipation of slaves. But the former would come only after his death, and the failure of the latter would justify his worst fears. He revived his general plan of public education. Again the legislature rejected it, approving, however, a major part, the state university. Jefferson was the master planner of the University of Virginia in all its parts, from the grounds and buildings to the curriculum, faculty, and rules of governance. He died at Monticello on the fiftieth anniversary of American independence, July 4, 1826.

Further Reading

There are several editions of Jefferson's writings: *The Writings of Thomas Jefferson,* edited by Paul Leicester Ford (10 vols., 1892-1899); *The Writings of Thomas Jefferson,* edited by Andrew A. Lipscomb and Albert Ellery Bergh (20 vols. in 10; 1905); and *Papers,* edited by Julian P. Boyd and others (17 vols., 1950-1965). The Boyd work, though complete only to November 1790, is the best edition; a good companion piece is *The Family Letters of Thomas Jefferson,* edited by Edwin Morris Betts and James Adam Bear, Jr. (1966).
The major biography is Dumas Malone, *Jefferson and His Time* (4 vols., 1948-1970), complete to 1805 and still in process. Less comprehensive is Merrill D. Peterson, *Thomas Jefferson and the New Nation* (1970). Accounts of Jefferson's elections are given in Arthur M. Schlesinger, Jr., ed., *History of American Presidential Elections* (4 vols., 1971). Jefferson as president is brilliantly, if not quite fairly, portrayed in the first four volumes of Henry Adams, *History of the United States of America during the Administrations of Jefferson and Madison* (9 vols., 1889-1891).
Other studies of Jefferson's life and thought include Fiske Kimball, *Thomas Jefferson: Architect* (1916); Roy J. Honeywell, *The Educational Work of Thomas Jefferson* (1931); Adrienne Koch, *The Philosophy of Thomas Jefferson* (1943); Karl Leh-

man, *Thomas Jefferson: American Humanist* (1947); Daniel J. Boorstin, *The Lost World of Thomas Jefferson* (1948); Edwin T. Martin, *Thomas Jefferson: Scientist* (1952); Caleb Perry Patterson, *The Constitutional Principles of Thomas Jefferson* (1953); Phillips Russell, *Jefferson: Champion of the Free Mind* (1956); and Merrill D. Peterson, *The Jefferson Image in the American Mind* (1960). Merrill D. Peterson, ed., *Thomas Jefferson: A Profile* (1967), collects essays by historians of Jefferson's era as well as modern ones. Jonathan Daniels, *Ordeal of Ambition: Jefferson, Hamilton, Burr* (1970), an account of the intertwining political careers of these three, is part biography and part history. □

Sir Harold Jeffreys

British mathematician, astronomer, geophysicist, and philosopher Sir Harold Jeffreys (1891-1989) was one of the great original applied-mathematical thinkers of the 20th century. He is noted for his wide variety of scientific contributions.

Harold Jeffreys was born on April 22, 1891, in Durham, England. He graduated from Durham University and then carried out research in chemistry and photography. He won major prizes at the University of Cambridge, from which he graduated in 1917, in mathematics, astronomy, and geophysics. At Cambridge he was a lecturer in mathematics, reader in geophysics, and Plumian professor of astronomy and experimental philosophy from 1946 to his retirement in 1958. In 1940 he married Bertha Swirles, a talented mathematician and a fellow of Girton College, Cambridge.

Scientific Contributions

The contributions for which Jeffreys is noted cover a wide range of fields. Much of his interest centered on the solar system and the theory of geophysics, fields in which progress demands the use of evidence and techniques from a variety of other fields, for example, statistical techniques and mathematical methods. It was characteristic of Jeffreys that when he found it necessary to refer to fields outside of astronomy and geophysics, he usually made important contributions to those fields as well. Noted examples are to be found in his books on the theory of probability, scientific inference, operational calculus, Cartesian tensors, and asymptotic approximations, as well as in a large treatise on the methods of mathematical physics written jointly with his wife. All of these works contain much original material inspired by the needs of his work in astronomy and geophysics. Additionally, he made significant contributions to the general theory of dynamics, aerodynamics, meteorology, relativity theory, and plant ecology.

To Jeffreys's credit are a number of outstanding achievements in astronomy and geophysics. In 1923, Jeffries calculated the surface temperatures of the four large outer planets—Jupiter, Saturn, Uranus, and Neptune—to be more than 100° below zero Centigrade. This was in sharp

conflict with the then-prevailing view that these outer planets were red-hot. His findings were later verified by direct observation and led to a complete revision of theories on the composition and structure of the outer planets.

Using observations on the earth's bodily tides, Jeffreys, in 1926, gave the first quantitative estimate of the rigidity of the earth's core and established that most of the core is probably molten. He was the senior author of tables produced during 1930-1940, giving the travel times of earthquake waves through the interior of the earth. Since 1940 these tables have been used as the standard in calculating the epicenters and origin times of the world's earthquakes for the International Seismological Summary. Jeffreys also contributed notably to theories of seismic wave propagation, of mutations of the earth's axis, on mountain building, on convection currents inside the earth, on tidal problems, on the figure of the earth and the moon, and a theory on the internal structures of other terrestrial planets.

Knighted for his outstanding contributions to the scientific community in 1953, Jeffreys spent his career at Cambridge until his retirement in 1958. He died in Durham on March 18, 1989.

Further Reading

For references to Jeffreys and for background see Ruth Moore, *The Earth We Live On* (1956). □

John Rushworth Jellicoe

The English admiral John Rushworth Jellicoe, 1st Earl Jellicoe (1859-1935), was commander in chief of the British Grand Fleet during the first half of World War I.

Born on Dec. 5, 1859, at Southampton, John Jellicoe was the heir to a long naval tradition. Before he was 13 years old, Jellicoe was in the navy training to be an officer, and 2 years later he was a midshipman on a 2 1/2-year cruise of the sailing vessel *New-castle*. In 1877 he was with the fleet at the Dardanelles during the Russo-Turkish War and, as the result of his excellent record there, was sent to the Royal Naval College at Greenwich.

Until 1898 Jellicoe was assigned to various posts, including gunnery and torpedo schools and sea duty. He became closely associated with the naval reforms and innovations of John French. In 1898 he was sent to East Asian waters as chief of staff to Adm. Seymour. There he was largely responsible for setting up the Chinese village of Weihaiwei as a British naval station. He later went as the leader of an international force that tried unsuccessfully to relieve Peking during the Boxer Rebellion. He was assigned to the Admiralty in 1905 and given charge of naval ordnance.

In 1910, when his tour at the Admiralty was over, Jellicoe, then a vice admiral, was given command of the Atlantic fleet; in this position he was able to direct the new dreadnought-class battleships at sea. In 1912 he was back at the Admiralty as second sea lord. The prewar crisis moved rapidly toward its climax, and Jellicoe was assigned on Aug. 4, 1914, when Britain entered the war, to be commander in chief of the British Grand Fleet.

At the end of May 1916 the German High Seas Fleet challenged the Grand Fleet, resulting in the war's only great naval action, the Battle of Jutland. Both sides lost heavily, but the German fleet escaped destruction by slipping back safely to its bases. As commander in chief, Jellicoe had won a great strategic victory, for the German fleet never came out to fight again, but the government and public opinion demanded his removal for failure to crush the German fleet completely. In November 1916 Jellicoe was transferred to the Admiralty as first sea lord and remained in that post about a year.

After the war Jellicoe returned to service to tour the empire and assess its naval defenses before going to New Zealand as governor general (1920-1924). Jellicoe was made a viscount in 1918 and an earl in 1925. After 10 years of active retirement he died on Nov. 20, 1935. Jellicoe was married and had one son and five daughters.

Further Reading

The best full-scale biography of Jellicoe is A. Temple Patterson, *Jellicoe* (1969). The older standard work is Sir R. H. Bacon, *The Life of John Rushworth, Earl Jellicoe* (1936).

Additional Sources

Winton, John, *Jellicoe,* London: Joseph, 1981. □

Mae C. Jemison

Mae C. Jemison (born 1956), the first African American woman to be selected for NASA's astronaut training program, was also the first American American woman to travel in space.

Mae C. Jemison had received two undergraduate degrees and a medical degree, had served two years as a Peace Corps medical officer in West Africa, and was selected to join the National Aeronautics and Space Administration's astronaut training program, all before her thirtieth birthday. Her eight-day space flight aboard the space shuttle *Endeavour* in 1992 established Jemison as the United States' first female African American space traveler.

Mae Carol Jemison was born on October 17, 1956, in Decatur, Alabama, the youngest child of Charlie Jemison, a roofer and carpenter, and Dorothy (Green) Jemison, an elementary school teacher. Her sister, Ada Jemison Bullock, became a child psychiatrist, and her brother, Charles Jemison, is a real estate broker. The family moved to Chicago, Illinois, when Jemison was three to take advantage of

better educational opportunities there, and it is that city that she calls her hometown. Throughout her early school years, her parents were supportive and encouraging of her talents and abilities, and Jemison spent considerable time in her school library reading about all aspects of science, especially astronomy. During her time at Morgan Park High School, she became convinced she wanted to pursue a career in biomedical engineering, and when she graduated in 1973 as a consistent honor student, she entered Stanford University on a National Achievement Scholarship.

At Stanford, Jemison pursued a dual major and in 1977 received a B.S. in chemical engineering and a B.A. in African and Afro-American Studies. As she had been in high school, Jemison was very involved in extracurricular activities including dance and theater productions, and served as head of the Black Student Union. Upon graduation, she entered Cornell University Medical College to work toward a medical degree. During her years there, she found time to expand her horizons by visiting and studying in Cuba and Kenya and working at a Cambodian refugee camp in Thailand. When she obtained her M.D. in 1981, she interned at Los Angeles County/University of Southern California Medical Center and later worked as a general practitioner. For the next two and a half years, she was the area Peace Corps medical officer for Sierra Leone and Liberia where she also taught and did medical research. Following her return to the U.S. in 1985, she made a career change and decided to follow a dream she had nurtured for a long time. In October of that year she applied for admission to NASA's astronaut training program. The *Challenger* disaster of January 1986

delayed the selection process, but when she reapplied a year later, Jemison was one of the fifteen candidates chosen from a field of about two thousand.

When Jemison was chosen on June 4, 1987, she became the first African American woman ever admitted into the astronaut training program. After more than a year of training, she became an astronaut with the title of science-mission specialist, a job which would make her responsible for conducting crew-related scientific experiments on the space shuttle. On September 12, 1992, Jemison finally flew into space with six other astronauts aboard the *Endeavour* on mission STS–47. During her eight days in space, she conducted experiments on weightlessness and motion sickness on the crew and herself. Altogether, she spent slightly over 190 hours in space before returning to Earth on September 20. Following her historic flight, Jemison noted that society should recognize how much both women and members of other minority groups can contribute if given the opportunity.

In recognition of her accomplishments, Jemison received several honorary doctorates, the 1988 *Essence* Science and Technology Award, the *Ebony* Black Achievement Award in 1992, and a Montgomery Fellowship from Dartmouth College in 1993, and was named Gamma Sigma Gamma Woman of the Year in 1990. Also in 1992, an alternative public school in Detroit, Michigan—the Mae C. Jemison Academy—was named after her. Jemison is a member of the American Medical Association, the American Chemical Society, the American Association for the Advancement of Science, and served on the Board of Directors of the World Sickle Cell Foundation from 1990 to 1992. She is also an advisory committee member of the American Express Geography Competition and an honorary board member of the Center for the Prevention of Childhood Malnutrition. After leaving the astronaut corps in March 1993, she accepted a teaching fellowship at Dartmouth and also established the Jemison Group, a company that seeks to research, develop, and market advanced technologies.

Further Reading

Hawthorne, Douglas B., *Men and Women of Space,* Univelt, 1992, pp. 357–359.
Smith, Jessie Carney, editor, *Notable Black American Women,* Gale, 1992, pp. 571–573. □

Roy Harris Jenkins

Roy Harris Jenkins (born 1920), British Labour politician and author, was a leading member of the cabinet before becoming president of the European Community and later a founder of the Social Democratic Party.

Roy Jenkins was born on November 11, 1920, the son of Arthur Jenkins, a Welsh miner who became an officer of his union and later a Labour member of Parliament. Roy was educated at Abersychan Grammar School and Balliol College, Oxford, where he took first class honors in politics, philosophy, and economics in 1941, having already been active in student politics and debate. He served in the Royal Artillery from 1942 to 1946, rising to captain in 1944.

Even before he was demobilized Jenkins entered politics, contesting the seat for Solihull unsuccessfully in the general election of 1945. He filled in the years 1946 to 1948 working for the Industrial and Commercial Financial Corporation. In 1948 Jenkins obtained his seat in Parliament after winning a by-election for Central Southwark; from 1950 to 1976 he sat for Stechford, Birmingham. He held office only briefly under Prime Minister Clement Attlee, in 1949-1950 as parliamentary private secretary to the secretary for Commonwealth relations. He early showed his interest in European union, serving as a United Kingdom delegate to the Council of Europe from 1955 to 1957. He belonged to the moderate side of the Labour Party; and was Fabian Society chairman from 1957 to 1958.

When the Labour Party was out of power, Jenkins occasionally held directorships or consultantships for various businesses; he also served on the boards of the Society of Authors and the British Film Institute. He was himself an author of some repute, publishing a history of the parliamentary crisis of 1911, *Mr. Balfour's Poodle,* in 1954; biographies of Sir Charles Dilke (1958) and Herbert Asquith

(1964); and numerous books on politics—15 titles in all, plus his autobiography (1991). His wife, Jennifer Morris, whom he married in 1945, was active in the historical preservation movement and was chairwoman of the Historic Buildings Council from 1975 to 1984. They had two sons and one daughter.

When Labour returned to power in 1964, Jenkins entered Harold Wilson's cabinet as minister for aviation. Hitherto known as a party intellectual and debater, he showed himself in office to be an excellent administrator and was promoted in 1965 to home secretary, roughly equivalent to being U.S. attorney general and HUD secretary. Both as a backbencher and as home secretary Jenkins was instrumental in ending capital punishment and literary censorship and easing divorce and abortion laws. He moved up to chancellor of the exchequer in 1967. Here he distinguished himself by devaluing the pound—a measure he had supported earlier—and courageously retrenching spending and raising taxes. In the controversy over wage and price control which divided the Labour Party in 1969, Jenkins supported Prime Minister Wilson. In the general election of 1970, Labour was defeated, despite an economic upturn to which Jenkins' measures may have contributed. He lost his office but became deputy leader of the party in opposition.

Seemingly on the way to the party leadership and perhaps the prime ministry, Jenkins' career was sidetracked by his commitment to Europe and the Common Market, which Britain joined in 1972. When the Labour Party insisted on holding a referendum on British entry, Jenkins resigned as deputy leader. The referendum was held in 1975, after Labour had regained power. Though again holding cabinet office, Jenkins, as president of "Britain in Europe," led the pro-Common Market campaign, which triumphed.

When Labour returned to office in the general elections of 1974, Jenkins joined Harold Wilson's second ministry, once again as home secretary. Wilson's abrupt decision to retire in March 1976 opened a contest for the succession. Jenkins was a candidate, but he proved to have little support in the party. In the first ballot of the Labour members of Parliament, Jenkins came in third; he eventually dropped out, his votes mostly going to the winner, James Callaghan. Jenkins continued as home secretary, but he was glad to accept election, when Britain's turn came round, as president of the European Commission, the executive branch of the Common Market. A devoted Europeanist, Jenkins served as "President of Europe" from 1977 to 1981, holding a position of much prestige though limited power. Honors poured in on him from many countries.

Returning to British politics in 1981, Jenkins was dismayed by the leftward drift of his Labour Party, again out of office, and the absence of a credible opposition to Margaret Thatcher's Tory government. He became the senior leader in the formation of a centrist third party, the Social Democratic Party, drawing support mainly from disillusioned Labourites and agreeing to cooperate for electoral purposes with the small Liberal Party as the "Alliance." Jenkins contested the Warrington seat, unsuccessfully but credibly, in 1981. He was elected for Glasgow Hillhead in 1982 and became the first leader of the Social Democratic

Party in Parliament. But in the general election of 1983, Margaret Thatcher, fresh from her Falklands victory, overwhelmed all opposition. Jenkins kept his seat, but he was ousted from the leadership of his small parliamentary party by the younger David Owen. Seven years after its founding, the new party collapsed without getting near power.

Soon after his parliamentary career ended, Jenkins, the coal miner's son, was elected chancellor of Oxford University and was named a peer. He also continued to write, and to proselytize for internationalist views.

Further Reading

As one would expect from a professional writer, Jenkins's autobiography, *A Life at the Center: Memoirs of a Radical Reformer* (1993), was a cut above most political memoirs. A Jenkins biography, *Roy Jenkins,* was published in 1983 just as the S.D.P. experiment was under way. Jenkins also was discussed in general works on the history or politics of the period, of which the best is Alfred F. Havighurst, *Britain in Transition* (1979). □

Edward Jenner

The English physician Edward Jenner (1749-1823) introduced vaccination against smallpox and thus laid the foundation of modern concepts of immunology.

Edward Jenner was born on May 17, 1749, in the village of Berkeley in Gloucestershire. At 8 his schooling began at Wooton-under-Edge and was continued in Cirencester. At 13 he was apprenticed to Daniel Ludlow, a surgeon, in Sodbury. In 1770 Jenner went to London to study with the renowned surgeon, anatomist, and naturalist John Hunter, returning to his native Berkeley in 1773.

Jenner had been interested in nature as a child, and this interest expanded under Hunter's guidance. For example, in 1771 the young physician arranged the zoological specimens gathered during Capt. James Cook's voyage of discovery to the Pacific. His thorough work led to his being recommended for the position of naturalist on the second Cook voyage, but he declined in favor of a medical career. Jenner aided in Hunter's zoological studies in many ways during his few years in London and then from Berkeley. Hunter's experimental methods, insistence on exact observation, and general encouragement are reflected in this work in natural history but are especially apparent in Jenner's introduction of vaccination.

In Eastern countries the practice of inoculation against smallpox with matter taken from a smallpox pustule was common. This practice was introduced into England in the early 18th century. Although such inoculation aided in the prevention of the dreaded and widespread disease, it was dangerous. There was a common story among farmers that if a person contracted a relatively mild and harmless disease of cattle called cowpox, immunity to smallpox would result.

Further Reading

W. R. Le Fanu, *A Bio-bibliography of Edward Jenner, 1749-1823* (1951), is a chronological accounting of Jenner's publications. The comprehensive study of Jenner's life and work is John Baron, *The Life of Edward Jenner* (2 vols., 1838), which is based on the manuscripts and publications of Jenner and contains his correspondence. Louis H. Roddis is indebted to Baron's work in *Edward Jenner and the Discovery of Smallpox Vaccination* (1930), which, although brief, gives a feeling of the man. □

Robert Yewdall Jennings

A British judge, Sir Robert Yewdall Jennings (born 1913) was appointed to the International Court of Justice in 1982 and re-appointed in 1991, becoming president of the court.

Robert Yewdall Jennings capped a long and distinguished legal career in Great Britain when he was selected in February 1991 to sit as presiding judge of the International Court of Justice at The Hague in the Netherlands. Chosen for a term of nine years, not to expire until the year 2000, Chief Justice Jennings was given the opportunity to promote the rule of law in world affairs on the threshold of the 21st century.

Legal Training

The future justice was born on October 19, 1913, at Idle in the Yorkshire district of England. Attending Belle Vue grammar school in Bradford, he impressed his teachers sufficiently to be accepted to Downing College at Cambridge University, where he received both an M.A. and an LL.B. degree. Determined upon a legal career, he went on to advanced studies in the United States. Chosen as a Joseph Hodges Choate fellow from 1936 to 1937, he attended Harvard Law School, but returned to England when given an appointment as assistant lecturer in law at the London School of Economics. Prospects for academic contemplation were disrupted, however, by the outbreak of war in Europe.

Jennings saw military service in the British Army through World War II, being a member of the Intelligence Corps from 1940 to 1946. Even so, this did not prevent him from being called to the Bar of Lincoln's Inn in 1943. Once demobilized, he promptly resumed his teaching duties at the London School of Economics, where he was a lecturer until 1955. At the age of 42 his career took a major step forward with the appointment as professor of international law at Cambridge University, which continued until 1981, when he was chosen to be a justice on the 15-member International Court of Justice, after winning approval of both the United Nations' General Assembly and Security Council.

Jenner first heard this story while apprenticed to Ludlow, and when he went to London he discussed the possibilities of such immunity at length with Hunter. Hunter encouraged him to make further observations and experiments, and when Jenner returned to Berkeley he continued his observations for many years until he was fully convinced that cowpox did, in fact, confer immunity to smallpox. On May 14, 1796, he vaccinated a young boy with cowpox material taken from a pustule on the hand of a dairymaid who had contracted the disease from a cow. The boy suffered the usual mild symptoms of cowpox and quickly recovered. A few weeks later the boy was inoculated with smallpox matter and suffered no ill effects.

In June 1798 Jenner published *An Inquiry into the Causes and Effects of the Variolae Vaccinae, a Disease Discovered in Some of the Western Counties of England, Particularly in Gloucestershire, and Known by the Name of the Cowpox*. In 1799 *Further Observations on the Variolae Vaccinae or Cowpox* appeared and, in 1800, *A Continuation of Facts and Observations Relative to the Variolae Vaccinae, or Cowpox*. The reception of Jenner's ideas was a little slow, but official recognition came from the British government in 1800. For the rest of his life Jenner worked consistently for the establishment of vaccination. These years were marred only by the death in 1815 of his wife, Catherine Kingscote Jenner, whom he had married in 1788. Jenner died of a cerebral hemorrhage in Berkeley on Jan. 26, 1823.

Academic Successes

During those interim years Jennings earned a reputation for scholarship and legal acumen. While at Cambridge he also doubled as a reader in international law to the Inns of Court Council of Legal Education (1959-1970), and over the course of several decades was a fellow (beginning 1939), senior tutor (1949-1955), honorary fellow (1982), and sometime president of Jesus College, Cambridge. A long-time member of the Oxford and Cambridge United University Club, he was awarded honorary doctor of jurisprudence degrees from the universities of Hull (1987), Saarland (1988), and La Sapienza in Rome (1990). Upon his appointment to the international tribunal Robert Jennings was awarded a knighthood in 1982, having been made a queen's counsel already in 1969 and an honorary bencher of Lincoln's Inn (1970).

International Experience

Sir Robert Jennings' list of earlier professional accomplishments included being legal consultant at various times to a number of governments, among them Argentina, Bangladesh, Brunei, Canada, Sharjah (part of the United Arab Emirates), Sudan, and Venezuela. In this capacity he was involved in several landmark international legal cases as counsel in the *Rio Ecuentro, Begal Channel,* Franco-British *Continental Shelf Delimitation,* and Dubai-Sharjah *Frontier Delimitation* arbitrations; and he appeared as counsel before the International Court of Justice (I.C.J.) in the *Continental Shelf* (*Tunisia/Libyan Arab Jamahiriya*) case. Prior to his appointment to the I.C.J. itself, Sir Robert had been judge *ad hoc* on the European Court of Human Rights in *X* vs. *United Kingdom* (1982); after 1982 he was also a member of the Permanent Court of Arbitration.

Publications and Affiliations

This familiarity with both the institutions and codes of international law was further enriched by Jennings' diverse professional work. For example, he authored various books, articles, and monographs that were circulated within the international community of legal scholars. As recently as 1995, he published an article in the *American Journal of International Law* to celebrate the 50th anniversary of the I.C.J. In addition, as early as 1967, he visited The Hague, where he gave the general course on principles of international law at the Academy of International Law. Justice Jennings had a long affiliation with the Institute of International Law, advancing from associate (1957) to member (1967), vice-president (1979), president (1981), and honorary member (1985). He was also an honorary life member of the American Society of International Law. In addition, at one time he was public international law editor (1957-1959) of the *International and Comparative Law Quarterly,* going from there to the *British Year Book of International Law,* first as co-editor in 1959 and then as senior editor from 1974 to 1982. His two principal book publications were *The Acquisition of Territory* (1963) and a textbook, *General Course on International Law* (1967).

Retirement

Though Jennings' term on the I.C.J. would not expire until February 5, 2000, the judge announced his retirement in 1995 when he was 81 years old. He was replaced by Rosalyn Higgins of Britain, who was the first woman to be elected to the World Court. Despite his retirement, Jennings continued to play an active role in international legal matters. In January of 1997, he headed an arbitration panel to settle a territorial dispute between Yemem and Eritrea.

Further Reading

There is little published material on the personal life of Sir Robert Jennings. For his writings see the titles mentioned in the text.

Additional Sources

Goodman, Anthony. "Italian Jurist Elected to World Court." *Reuters Ltd.,* 21 June 1995.

Jennings, Robert Y. "The International Court of Justice after Fifty Years." *American Journal of International Law* 89 (July 1995): 493-505.

Wallis, William. "Briton Elected World Court's First Woman Judge." *Reuters Ltd.,* 12 July 1995.

"Yeman-Eritrea Dispute Goes to Arbitration." *Reuters Ltd.,* 14 January 1997. □

Jeremiah

Jeremiah (active late 7th-early 6th century B.C.) was one of the four major Jewish prophets. A priest from Anathoth, Israel, he is the reputed author of the Book of Jeremiah.

The dates of Jeremiah's birth and death are not known. It is known that he began his preaching either in the thirteenth year of King Josiah of Judah (626 B.C.) or at the accession of King Jehoiakim of Judah (608). He preached and taught for over 40 years, so his death must have taken place sometime in the first half of the 6th century B.C., probably between 580 and 560 B.C.

The entire background of Jeremiah's life and the words ascribed to him are permeated with the sense of disaster and disintegration which Judaism and Jews underwent in the 6th century B.C. The northern portion of Palestine, the kingdom of Israel, fell to the Assyrians in 622 B.C. A similar fate threatened the south, the kingdom of Judah, with its capital city of Jerusalem. The Assyrians were conquered by the Babylonians. The latter invaded Judea and captured Jerusalem in 587 B.C. A year later the Babylonians destroyed the First Temple, ended the kingdom of Judah, and deported the Jews (the Babylonian Captivity). Many Jews, among them Jeremiah, fled to Egypt for safety. As far as is known, however, Jeremiah died violently, perhaps by crucifixion, perhaps by the sword.

Not all of the writings ascribed to Jeremiah are considered by modern scholars to be really his. In fact, it is not certain that he ever actually wrote a line. It seems more

likely that he dictated much of his material to an assistant or secretary called Baruch. Baruch made two collections of Jeremiah's words, one toward the end of the 7th century B.C. (605-600) and one toward the end of the prophet's life. Baruch added some materials of his own, and there were some later additions. Jewish tradition also ascribes the Book of Lamentations and the Book of Kings to Jeremiah.

Jeremiah's words and pronouncements are directly concerned with the febrile political maneuvering between 605 and 586 B.C. and with the Babylonian Captivity. His early message was simple: unless both king and people reformed their morals and returned to the true worship of God as taught by Moses, Jerusalem would be destroyed and its people killed or exiled. Jeremiah's general message was that temple and priesthood and kingship were of no avail if the heart of man was not clean from idolatry, from lies, and from deception of all kinds. His novel contribution as a prophet was his claim that God would replace the Old Covenant with the Israelites by a new covenant. Peculiarly, this new covenant was not to be restricted to Jews but was to include all the world. Jeremiah taught a universalist creed which would embrace all people.

Further Reading

Useful works on Jeremiah include Terrot R. Glover, *The Pilgrim: Essays on Religion* (1921); John Skinner, *Prophecy and Religion: Studies in the Life of Jeremiah* (1922); Adam C. Welch, *Jeremiah, His Time and His Work* (1928); James P. Hyatt and S. R. Hopper, eds., "The Book of Jeremiah," in George A.

Battrick, gen. ed., *The Interpreter's Bible* (1956); and James P. Hyatt, *Jeremiah: Prophet of Courage and Hope* (1958). □

Jeroboam I

Jeroboam I was the first king (reigned ca. 931-ca. 910 B.C.) of the independent northern kingdom of Israel. As a result of his successful rebellion against Rehoboam, the Hebrew nation was divided into the kingdoms of Israel and Judah.

An Ephraimite and the son of Nebat, Jeroboam was of humble origin. He served as the prefect of a forced-labor contingent engaged in constructing fortifications around Jerusalem, Solomon's capital city, as well as numerous buildings on Mt. Zion, the most important and magnificent of which was the Holy Temple. The northern tribes chafed under the yoke of oppressive taxes and compulsory labor imposed by King Solomon. Led by Jeroboam, they plotted a revolt against the King. When it failed, Jeroboam fled to Egypt, where he was given asylum by Shishak, the reigning pharaoh, who saw in the revolt an opportunity to weaken a strong neighbor.

On the death of Solomon and the accession of his son Rehoboam, Jeroboam returned from exile and headed a delegation of the northern tribes that petitioned the new king to redress their grievances. Rehoboam responded by threatening to inflict upon the people even heavier burdens than his father had. The 10 tribes then seceded from the formerly united kingdom and established their own under Jeroboam, whom they elected their king. The northern kingdom of Israel, or as it was sometimes called, Ephraim, after Jeroboam's tribe, never reunited with the southern kingdom, known as Judah, which consisted only of that tribe and the tribe of Benjamin.

Frequent clashes occurred between Judah and Israel during the reign of Rehoboam, who could not accept the loss of the larger part of his father's kingdom; though the prophet Ahijah had announced that the division was divinely decreed. Jeroboam on his part fortified his capital, Schechem, against the king of Judah. At one time the pharaoh Shishak aided the kingdom of Israel to prevent its conquest by Rehoboam and a consequent reunion of the two kingdoms. Shishak, of course, was concerned not with defending Israel but with keeping it apart from Judah.

To divert his subjects from the Temple of Jerusalem, Jeroboam established two central shrines in the northern kingdom, Bethel, near the boundary between the two kingdoms, and Dan in the north. At each site Jeroboam set up a heathen cult centered on a gilded calf, reminiscent of the golden calf the Israelites had worshiped on their way from Egypt. In appointing the priests for these shrines, he disregarded the time-honored rights of the tribe of Levi to the priesthood. These and other acts alienated the prophets of Yahweh from Jeroboam, and they denounced him. The

Bible, in fact, describes Jeroboam not only as a sinner but also as one who caused others to sin.

Further Reading

The biblical account of Jeroboam is in 1 Kings and 2 Chronicles. Harry M. Orlinsky, *Ancient Israel* (1954; 3d ed. 1965), and John Bright, *A History of Israel* (1959), discuss Jeroboam. □

St. Jerome

St. Jerome (ca. 345-420) was an early Christian biblical scholar. The official Latin Bible of the Roman Catholic Church, the Vulgate, is largely the product of his labors of translation and revision.

Born in territory now in northwest Yugoslavia, Jerome studied rhetoric as a youth at Rome in preparation for a career in law, which he did not pursue. The 2 decades from his early 20s were a period of much travel and temporary settlement. After a journey to the German city of Trier, he stopped for a time at Aquileia, in Italy, and there became a member of circle of young Christian intellectuals sharing a common commitment to the ascetic life. He had already formed his two consuming interests: scriptural studies and the pursuit of Christian asceticism. In Syria from about 374, for 4 or 5 years he lived as a recluse in the desert, beginning there his study of Hebrew. Finding that life not entirely compatible, he journeyed in 379 to Constantinople, where he was a student of Gregory of Nazianzus; and there also he undertook the translation from Greek into Latin of homilies by Origen, that eminent biblical scholar much admired by Jerome.

For 3 years from 382 Jerome was at Rome, serving as secretary to Pope Damasus. At the Pope's suggestion, he undertook a complete revision of the Latin Gospels of the New Testament, the aim of which was to replace older, varying, and inaccurate versions with a uniform one based on the best available Greek manuscripts. At Rome also he took every opportunity to commend the life of ascetic renunciation, particularly among wealthy and aristocratic ladies, among whom he had a notable following. The death of Damasus in 384 led to Jerome's departure from Rome, and in the company of a group of ascetic enthusiasts he made a pilgrimage to the monastic centers of Palestine and Egypt.

From 386 to the end of his life Jerome was settled in Bethlehem. There he presided over a monastery endowed by the wealthy Paula, who herself presided nearby over a sister foundation for women. Jerome's most significant accomplishment in his 34 years at Bethlehem was his translation of the Old Testament from the original Hebrew into Latin. It was an act of scholarly courage, arousing in his lifetime the criticism of many (including Augustine) who were wedded to the traditional Greek Old Testament as the basis for Latin translations. Of much less credit to Jerome in these years was his role in a number of vitriolic controversies; in the most unfortunate of these he aligned himself with

implacable foes of that teacher, then dead a century and a half, from whom Jerome had learned so much—Origen.

Further Reading

A variety of opinions on Jerome are in F. X. Murphy, ed., *A Monument to Saint Jerome* (1952), a symposium of essays by a number of scholars on various aspects of Jerome's life and significance. David S. Wiesen, *St. Jerome as a Satirist: A Study in Christian Latin Thought and Letters* (1949), deals with Jerome's writings. See also Jean Steinmann, *Saint Jerome and His Times* (1959).

Additional Sources

Kelly, J. N. D. (John Norman Davidson), *Jerome: his life, writings, and controversies,* New York: Harper & Row, 1975.

Warmington, William, *A moderate defence of the oath of allegiance, 1612,* Ilkley etc.: Scolar Press, 1975. □

George Jessel

George Jessel (1898-1981) was a screen, stage, radio, and television actor and comedian. He was also a film director, composer, and screenwriter.

George Jessel was born in New York City on April 3, 1898, the son of Joseph Jessel, a playwright, and Charlotte Schwartz. As a child he sang at his grandfather's lodge meetings, and when his father became ill he left school to sing on the streets for money. His first professional work (1909) was as one of the members of the Imperial Trio who provided singing accompaniment to silent films in a Nickelodeon.

In 1910 Jessel became a part of Gus Edwards' "Boys and Girls," a popular vaudeville touring show. He left Edwards in 1914 to form his own act with Lou Edwards, "Two Patches from a Crazy Quilt." This act took him to London, where he toured for several years and also appeared at the prestigious Victoria Palace. Upon his return to the United States in 1919 he appeared in *Gaieties* and then wrote, produced, and acted in *The Troubles of 1920*. The success of this production led him to do a sequel, *The Troubles of 1921*, which included his popular songs "Oh How I Laugh When I Think How I Cried About You" and "I'm Satisfied To Be My Mother's Baby."

In 1922 Jessel wrote and produced a solo act called *George Jessel's Troubles*. This show introduced the beginnings of what was to be his acting trademark—conversations with his "mother." His classic monologue routine started with Jessel talking on the phone to his mother, assuring her that he knew nothing about the missing money or the cookies missing from the house. In *Passing Show of 1923* the act was expanded to include a mother on the stage, replying as he tried to make up excuses. Jessel continued to develop this role over the years, which be-

came known as "Hello Mama." The act exemplified George Jessel's style—light banter with a sentimental twist and ethnic Jewish humor.

In 1925 Jessel landed the part of Jack Robin in *The Jazz Singer*. Although this role was not comic, it became his most popular theater role, which he performed over 1,000 times. It tells the story of a rabbi's son who yearns for the stage yet gives up his career to return home to his family. Jessel was praised for his poignancy in the role. The play became more famous for its film adaptation with Al Jolson in the leading role. According to Jessel, he passed up the opportunity to star in the film because the ending was changed—the performer did not return to his home in the movie, he remained on the stage.

In 1928 he played the part of Eddie Rosen in *War Song*, the story of a Jewish song writer who ends up on the front lines in World War I. In 1930 he appeared in Billy Rose's *Sweet and Low* with the famous comedienne Fanny Brice. He followed this with *Box of Tricks* (1931), for which he wrote the lyrics, music, and sketches; designed the sets and costumes; and also acted. In the same year he reunited with Eddie Cantor, a close friend with whom he had worked in vaudeville, to do the Cantor-Jessel show at the Palace (an old vaudeville theater). An enormous success, the show was held over for six weeks.

Jessel's stage producing work included *High Kickers* (1941) and *Showtime* (1942). Both of these shows were about the old vaudeville days, and *Showtime*, due to its success, was heralded as being responsible for vaudeville's return to the legitimate theater.

Jessel's first movie came in 1911, when he made a test film with Eddie Cantor directed by Thomas Edison. His real film career started in 1926 when he made *Private Izzy Murphy*. He also appeared in *Lucky Boy*, for which he wrote the dialogue and which featured a Jessel song favorite, "My Mother's Eyes." Other film credits include *Love, Live and Laugh, Ginsburg the Great*, and *Happy Days*. Modern audiences may know him best for his appearance in the 1967 film *Valley of the Dolls*. Jessel also produced many films, including *The Life of Haym Solomon* (1937), *The Dolly Sisters* (1945), and *Tonight We Sing* (1953).

George Jessel began his radio career in 1938 with *Jessel's Jamboree*, and he also was host on radio of *George Jessel's Celebrity Program* (1940) and *The George Jessel Show* (1958). He hosted two television shows, *George Jessel's Show Business* and *Here Come the Stars*.

In 1965, after a long absence from the stage, Jessel returned to tour in cabaret shows with Sophie Tucker and Ted Lewis. He spent a good deal of the 1960s entertaining the troops in Vietnam, which he also did in 1972 and 1973 at bases in England and Germany. In 1972 he gave a solo performance at Carnegie Hall to packed houses and in 1975 the multi-talented man did a U.S. tour of *That Wonderful World of Vaudeville*.

In addition to acting, producing, and radio/television work, Jessel made many recordings for which he was praised for his "rich, vibrant, baritone voice." He also wrote several books, including *Talking to Mother* (a series of com-

ic telephone conversations); *We Have With Us Tonight* (after dinner speeches); his autobiography, *So Help Me* (1943); and *The World I Lived In* (1975).

George Jessel was named Toastmaster General of the United States by President Franklin D. Roosevelt for his over 300 after-dinner speeches in support of political, humanist, and social causes. A fervent supporter of Jewish and Israeli causes, he was the vice president of the Jewish Theater Guild and received the Man of the Year Award of the Beverley Hills B'nai Brith in 1975. He also was made honorary member of the U.S. Air Force in 1952 and received the 1969 Jean Hersholt Humanitarian Award from the Academy of Motion Pictures of Arts and Sciences.

George Jessel had four wives and one daughter, Jerilyn, from his third marriage. He died of a heart attack on May 23, 1981, shortly after appearing in the award winning film *Reds* (1981).

Further Reading

Biographies of George Jessel are included in *The Vaudevillians* (1981) by Anthony Slide and in *Who's Who in the Theatre,* 17th Edition (1981), edited by Ian Herbert. A description of Jessel's performance at the Palace can be found in Marian Spitzer's *The Palace* (1969). Jessel's book *The World I Lived In* (1975) updated his earlier autobiography *So Help Me* (1943). ☐

Jesus ben Sira

The Jewish sage and author Jesus ben Sira (born ca. 170 B.C.), or Sirach, is the reputed author of the wisdom book commonly called Ecclesiasticus.

According to the Hebrew text of Ecclesiasticus, the author's full name was Simeon ben Jeshua ben Elazar ben Sira. The Greek text, however, and most of the Christian sources refer to him as Jesus, the Greek equivalent of the Hebrew Joshua. In the prologue to his Greek version, Jesus Ben Sira's grandson dates his translation from the Hebrew into Greek at a time calculated to be 132-131 B.C. From this it is surmised that the original Hebrew text was written about 4 decades earlier, making it the oldest book of the Apocrypha. In Hebrew the volume was called *Hokhmat Ben Sira* (The Wisdom of Ben Sira). In Greek the work is known as *Ecclesiasticus* (The Preacher). It is similar in form and content to the Hebrew Book of Proverbs and to Ecclesiastes.

The Wisdom of Ben Sira is divided into eight sections, each of which begins with a poem of praise to wisdom and the wise. The last portion, consisting of chapters 44-49 and headed "Praise to the Patriarchs of the World," extols the biblical heroes, while the ensuing chapter (50) is devoted to Simeon, son of Jochanon, probably Simon the Just (ca. 3d century B.C.). The final chapter of the book (51) appears to be a sort of epilogue that contains several psalms and hymns of thanks to God, who had saved the author from death,

evidently from some plot or false charge. The book ends with an exhortation to love and acquire wisdom.

Jesus Ben Sira apparently lived in Jerusalem during most of his life and belonged to the intellectual aristocracy. The object of his book was to teach people to live wisely, intelligently, and morally. The author's accent is on moderation in all aspects of life. He also offers advice on a person's attitude toward the rich and the poor, the righteous and the wicked, the wise and the foolish, the creditor and the borrower, the sick and the physician. Like the Book of Proverbs, this work stresses that fear of the Lord is the beginning and end of wisdom. The highest wisdom is, accordingly, to obey the Divine Will and the Torah, Jewish doctrine and law.

The Wisdom of Ben Sira is included in the Old Testament Apocrypha, though in the Septuagint it is part of the Canon. Unlike other books of the Apocrypha, "Ben Sira," a popular work, exerted a considerable influence on subsequent Jewish literature and on medieval moralist works. Many of Jesus Ben Sira's aphorisms found their way into the Talmud; his sayings are also quoted in the New Testament. The original Hebrew version of this work was preserved for a longer period than the other Apocrypha books—until about the time of Saadia ben Joseph (died 942). It was lost for centuries, but in 1897 Professor Solomon Schechter discovered a number of fragments of the work in the storeroom of the Old Cairo Synagogue. Almost two-thirds of the original was eventually recovered.

Further Reading

An English version of "The Wisdom of Ben Sira," along with commentary, is available in R. H. Charles, ed., *Apocrypha and Pseudepigrapha,* vol. 1 (1913). The brief sketch of Jesus ben Sira in Meyer Waxman, *A History of Jewish Literature,* vols. 1 and 4 (1960), provides helpful background and orientation. ☐

Jesus of Nazareth

Jesus of Nazareth (ca. 4 B.C.-A.D. 29), also known as Jesus Christ, was the central personality and founder of the Christian faith.

It is likely that Jesus was born not later than 4 B.C., the year of King Herod's death. Jesus' crucifixion was probably in A.D. 29 or 30. (The term Christ is actually a title, not a proper name; it comes from the Greek *Christos,* meaning the anointed one; in the Bible it is the Greek equivalent for the Hebrew word Messiah.) Information about Jesus is in some ways scant, in other ways plentiful. Although such ancient historians as Tacitus and Suetonius mention him, as does the Jewish Talmud, the only detailed information comes from the New Testament. There are a few other ancient accounts of Jesus' life, called Apocryphal Gospels because of their poor historical reliability; and in 1946 a Gospel of Thomas, actually a collection of sayings attributed to Jesus, was discovered in Upper Egypt. But none of these sources adds significantly to the New Testament. The letters of Paul are the earliest biblical records that tell about Jesus. But the four Gospels by Matthew, Mark, Luke, and John, although written later, used sources that in some cases go back very close to the time of Jesus.

Early Years

Jesus first came to general attention at the time of his baptism, just prior to his public ministry. He was known to those around him as a carpenter of Nazareth, a town in Galilee, and as the son of Joseph (John 6:42). Matthew and Luke report that Jesus was born in Bethlehem, a town near Jerusalem, famous in Jewish history as the city of David. They further report that he was miraculously born to the Virgin Mary, although they both curiously trace his Davidic ancestry through Joseph, to whom Mary was betrothed.

Little is known of Jesus' childhood and youth. But about the year A.D. 28 or 29 his life interacted with the career of John the Baptist, a stormy prophet-preacher who emerged from the wilderness and called on the people to repent and be baptized. A controversial character, he was soon jailed and killed by Herod Antipas, the puppet ruler of Galilee under the Roman Empire. Jesus heard John's preaching and joined the crowds for baptism in the Jordan River. Following his baptism Jesus went into the desert for prayer and meditation.

It is clear that Jesus had some consciousness of a divine calling, and in the desert he thought through its meaning. The Gospels report that he was tempted there by Satan as to

what kind of leader Jesus would choose to be—a miracle worker, a benefactor who would bring people what they wanted, a king wielding great power. Jesus accepted a harder and less popular mission, that of the herald of the kingdom of God.

Galilean Ministry

Returning from the desert, Jesus began preaching and teaching in Galilee. His initial proclamation was similar to John's: "The time is fulfilled, and the kingdom of God is at hand; repent, and believe in the gospel" (Mark 1:15; Revised Standard Version). This message was both frightening and hopeful. It told people not to cling to the past, that God would overthrow old institutions and ways of life for a wonderful new future. This future would be especially welcomed by the poor, the powerless, the peacemakers. It would be threatening to the rich, the powerful, the cruel, and the unjust.

Jesus attracted 12 disciples to follow him. They were mainly fishermen and common workers. Of the 12 it seems that Peter, James, and John were closest to Jesus. Peter's home in Capernaum, a city on the Sea of Galilee, became a headquarters from which Jesus and the disciples moved out into the countryside. Sometimes he talked to large crowds. Then he might withdraw with the 12 to teach only them. Or he might go off by himself for long periods of prayer. On one occasion he sent out the disciples, two by two, to spread the message of God's kingdom.

The Miracles

The records concerning Jesus report many miracles. Through the years there have been great disagreements about these reports. For centuries most people in civilizations influenced by the Bible not only believed literally in the miracles but took them as proofs that Jesus had a supernatural power. Then, in an age of rationalism and skepticism, men often doubted the miracles and denounced the reports as fraudulent.

Today, partly because of psychosomatic medicine and therapy, people are more likely to believe in the possibilities of faith healing. The Bible candidly reports that on some occasions, when people had no faith, Jesus could do no mighty works. People were especially skeptical in his hometown, where they had known him as a boy (Mark 6:1-6). However, usually the Gospels report the healings as signs of the power of God and His coming kingdom.

Teachings of Jesus

Jesus taught people in small groups or large gatherings; his sayings are reported in friendly conversations or in arguments with those who challenged him. At times he made a particularly vivid comment in the midst of a dramatic incident.

The starting point of his message, as already noted, was the announcement of the coming of the kingdom of God. Since this kingdom was neither a geographical area nor a system of government, it might be better to translate the phrase as "God's reign."

The rest of Jesus' teaching followed from this message about the reign of God. At times he taught in stories or parables that described the kingdom or the behavior of people who acknowledged God's reign. Perhaps the most famous of his many parables are those of the Prodigal Son and the Good Samaritan. At times he pronounced ethical commandments detailing the demands upon men of a loving and righteous God. At times Jesus taught his disciples to pray: the words that he gave them in the Lord's Prayer are often used today.

Jesus' teaching was a subtle teaching, and often it was directed to the needs of a particular person in a specific time and place. Therefore almost any summary can be challenged by statements of Jesus that point in an opposite direction. One way to explore the dynamics of his teachings is to investigate some of its paradoxes. Five are worth mentioning here.

First, Jesus combined an utter trust in God with a brute realism about the world. On the one hand, he told men not to be anxious about life's problems, because God knows their needs and will look out for them. So if men trust God and seek His kingdom, God will look out for the rest of their needs. Yet, on the other hand, Jesus knew well that life can be tough and painful. He asked men to give up families and fortunes, to accept persecution out of faithfulness to him, thus promising them a hard life.

Second, Jesus taught both ethical rigor and forgiveness. He demanded of men more than any other prophet or teacher had asked. He criticized the sentimentalists who call him "Lord, Lord" but do not obey him, and he told men that, if they are to enter God's kingdom, their righteousness must exceed that of the scribes and Pharisees, who made exceedingly conscientious efforts to obey God's laws. He told men not to be angry or contemptuous with others, not to lust after women, and not to seek revenge but to love their enemies. Yet this same Jesus understood human weakness. He was known as a friend of sinners who warned men not to make judgments of others whom they consider sinful. He forgave men their sins and told about a God who seeks to save sinners.

Third, Jesus represented a kind of practicality that offends the overly spiritual-minded; but he also espoused an expectation of a future world (God's reign) that will make the attractions of this world unimportant. As a worldly man, he wanted to relieve hunger and sickness. He wanted no escape from responsibility into worship. He taught that sometimes a man would better leave church and go to undo the wrongs he has done.

But with this attention to the world was coupled the recognition that men are foolish to seek security and happiness in wealth or possessions. They would do better to give away their riches and to accept persecution. Jesus promised—or warned—that God's reign will reverse many of the values of this world.

Fourth, Jesus paradoxically combined love and peace with conflict. His followers called him the Prince of Peace, because he sought to reconcile men to God and each other. He summed up all the commandments in two: love for God and love for men. He refused to retaliate against those who had harmed him but urged his followers to forgive endlessly—not simply seven times but seventy times seven. Yet he was not, as some have called him, "gentle Jesus, meek and mild"; he attacked evil fearlessly, even in the highest places.

Fifth, Jesus promised joy, freedom, and exuberant life; yet he expected sacrifice and self-denial. He warned men not to follow him unless they were ready to suffer. But he told people to rejoice in the wonders of God's reign, to celebrate the abundant life that he brings.

Views of His Contemporaries

To some people Jesus was a teacher or rabbi. The healing ministry did not necessarily change that conception of him, because other rabbis were known as healers. But Jesus was a teacher of peculiar power, and he was sometimes thought to be a prophet.

Jesus certainly was a herald of the kingdom of God. But then a question arises: was he simply talking about God and his reign, or did he have some special relationship to that kingdom? Those who heard Jesus were frequently perplexed. In some ways he was a modest, even humble man. Instead of making claims for himself or accepting admiration, he turned people's thoughts from himself to God. But at other times he asked immense loyalty of his disciples. And he astonished people by challenging time-honored authority—even the authority of the Bible—with his new teachings. He was so audacious as to forgive sins, although men said that only God could do that.

There was also the question whether it was possible that Jesus was the Messiah. For generations some of the Jewish people had hoped that God would send a king, an heir of the great King David of past history, who would undo the oppression that the Jews suffered, would reestablish the glorious old kingdom, and would bring justice. Some expected even more—that a divine savior would come and inaugurate a radical transformation of life.

Various reports in the New Testament lead to various possible conclusions. Today some scholars think that Jesus never claimed to be the Messiah. Others feel that he clearly did. But there was one occurrence that is especially interesting. Once, in the neighborhood of Caesarea Philippi, a city north of the Sea of Galilee (Mark 8:27-30), Jesus asked his disciples, "Who do men say that I am?" They gave various answers: John the Baptist, Elijah, or another of the prophets. Then Jesus asked, "But who do you say that I am?" And Peter answered, "You are the Christ [Messiah]." Jesus' answer was curious, for "He charged them to tell no one about him."

Why, if he accepted the designation, did he want it kept a secret? One persuasive answer often given is that Jesus was radically revising the traditional idea of the Messiah. If the people thought he was the promised Messiah, they would demand that he live up to their expectations. He had no intention of becoming a conquering king who would overthrow Rome.

Jesus, who knew the Old Testament well, had read the Messianic prophecies. He had also read the poems of the suffering servant in Second Isaiah, the unknown prophet whose writings are now in Isaiah, chapters 40-55. These tell of a servant of God and man, someone despised and rejected, who would bear the cost of the sins of others and bring healing to them. It may be that Jesus combined in his own mind the roles of the Messiah and the suffering servant. The undeniable fact is that his life and character were of such a sort that they convinced his followers he was the Messiah who, through his suffering love, could bring men a new experience of foregiveness and new possibilities for human and social life.

Passion Week

Soon after Peter's confession Jesus led his disciples to Jerusalem in an atmosphere of gathering crisis. On the day now known as Palm Sunday he entered the city, while his disciples and the crowds hailed him as the Son of David, who came in the name of the Lord. The next day Jesus went to the Temple and drove out the money changers and those who sold pigeons for sacrifices, accusing them of turning "a house of prayer" into a "den of robbers." This act was a direct challenge to the small group of priests who were in charge of the Temple, and they clearly resented it. During the following days he entered into controversies with the priests and authoritative teachers of religion. Their anger led them to plot to get rid of him, but they hesitated to do anything in the daytime, since many people were gathered for the feast of Passover.

On Thursday night Jesus had a meal with his disciples. This meal is now reenacted by Christians in the Lord's Supper, the Mass, or the Holy Communion. After the meal Jesus went to the Garden of Gethsemane, where he prayed alone. His prayer shows that he expected a conflict, that he still hoped that he might avoid suffering, but that he expected to do God's will. There into the garden one of his disciples, Judas Iscariot, led the priests and the temple soldiers, who seized Jesus.

That same night Jesus' captors took him to a trial before the temple court, the Sanhedrin. Several evidences indicate that this was an illegal trial, but the Sanhedrin declared that Jesus was a blasphemer deserving death. Since at that time only the Roman overlords could carry out a death sentence, the priests took Jesus to Pilate, the Roman governor of Judea.

Pilate apparently was reluctant to condemn Jesus, since it was doubtful that Jesus had disobeyed any Roman laws. But as the ruler of a conquered province, Pilate was suspicious of any mass movements that might become rebellions. And he also preferred to keep the religious leaders of the subjugated people as friendly as possible. Jesus, as a radical intruder into the conventional system, and believing that obedience to God sometimes required defiance of human authority, represented a threat to both the Sanhedrin and the Romans. Pilate thus ordered the crucifixion of Jesus. Roman soldiers beat him, put a crown of thorns on his head, and mocked him as a fraudulent king. Then they took him to the hill Golgotha ("the Skull"), or Calvary, and killed him as an insurrectionist. Pilate ordered a sign placed above his head: "King of the Jews." Among the "seven last words," or sayings, from the cross are two quotations from Jewish

psalms, "My God, my God, why hast thou forsaken me?" (Psalms 22:1) and "Into thy hands I commit my spirit" (Psalms 31:5); and the especially memorable "Father, forgive them; for they know not what they do" (Luke 23:34). That same day (now known as Good Friday) Jesus was buried in a cavelike tomb.

The Resurrection

On Sunday morning (now celebrated as Easter), the Gospels report, Jesus rose from the dead and met his disciples. Others immediately rejected the claim of the resurrection, and the controversy has continued through the centuries.

The New Testament states very clearly that the risen Christ did not appear to everybody. "God ... made him manifest; not to all the people but to us who were chosen by God as witnesses, who ate and drank with him after he rose from the dead" (Acts 10:40-41). Among those who saw Jesus were Cephas (Peter), the 12 disciples, "more than five hundred brethren at one time," James, "all the apostles," and finally Paul. Other records tell of appearances to Mary Magdalene and other women and of a variety of meetings with the disciples both in the Jerusalem area and in Galilee. The four Gospels all say that the tomb of Jesus was empty on Easter morning, but Paul never mentions the empty tomb. None of the records ever tells of an appearance of the risen Christ to anyone who had not been a follower of Jesus or (like Paul) had not been deeply disturbed by him.

The evidence is very clear that the followers of Jesus were absolutely convinced of his resurrection. The experience of the risen Jesus was so overwhelming that it turned their despair into courage. Even though it might have been easier, and certainly would have been safer, to regard Jesus as dead, the disciples spread the conviction that he had risen, and they persisted in telling their story at the cost of persecution and death. Furthermore they were sure that their experiences of Jesus were not private visions; rather, as in the statement quoted above, they "ate and drank with him." The faith in the resurrection (and later the ascension) of Jesus, despite differences in interpretation and detail, is a major reason for the rise and propagation of the Christian faith.

Further Reading

There are thousands of books about Jesus, written for many purposes and from many points of view. Those mentioned here are only a few of the most reputable works using the methods of modern historical scholarship. Although many scholars doubt, on the basis of the sources, that an objective biography of Jesus can be written, several noteworthy attempts should be mentioned. Vincent Taylor, *The Life and Ministry of Jesus* (1955), is a direct, narrative account. Two longer books that give more space to the analysis of sources are Maurice Goguel, *The Life of Jesus,* translated by Olive Wyon (1933), and Charles Guignebert, *Jesus,* translated by S. H. Hooke (1935). A very readable biography by a distinguished American scholar is Edgar J. Goodspeed, *A Life of Jesus* (1950).

More frequent than biographies among contemporary scholars are efforts to interpret the sources in their meaning for modern man's belief in Jesus. Probably the most notable such Protestant effort is Gunther Bornkamm, *Jesus of Nazareth,* translated by Irene and Fraser McLuskey with James M. Robinson (1960). A distinguished Roman Catholic work is Yves Congar, *Jesus Christ,* translated by Luke O'Neill (1966). Joseph Klausner, *Jesus of Nazareth: His Life, Times, and Teaching,* translated by Herbert Danby (1925), is a scholarly study written by a Jewish historian. Sholem Asch, an American Jew, in *The Nazarene,* translated by Maurice Samuel (1939), wrote a novel about Jesus that is both imaginative and scholarly.

The most important sources for all these works are the letters of Paul and the Gospels of the New Testament. Matthew, Mark, and Luke are known as Synoptic Gospels because they parallel each other in many respects, although each has its own point of view. The fourth Gospel, John, has a different structure and a more highly articulated theological position. □

William Stanley Jevons

The English economist, logician, and statistician William Stanley Jevons (1835-1882) did pioneering work in marginalist economics, index numbers of prices, and economic fluctuations.

The son of a merchant, W. S. Jevons was born in Liverpool on Sept. 1, 1835. At age 15 he went to secondary school in London and then to the University of London. His excellent record in chemistry led to an offer as assayer to the Royal Mint in Sydney, Australia. While there, from 1854 to 1859, he read widely and showed increasing concern for social problems. On his return to England, he resumed his studies, receiving the bachelor's and master's degrees from the University of London.

Jevons taught at Owens College, Manchester, from 1863 to 1876, when he became professor of political economy at University College, London. He resigned in 1880 to devote all of his energies to writing. He married Harriet Ann Taylor, daughter of the founder of the *Manchester Guardian,* in 1867. Despite ill health, his accomplishments, before he drowned at the age of 46, were highly impressive. However, he did not receive the recognition which the originality and quality of his work merited.

Two scholarly papers presented in 1862 foreshadowed Jevons's later work on the mathematical theory of economics and on business fluctuations. His first important publication, *A Serious Fall in the Value of Gold* (1863), was followed by Pure Logic (1864), *The Coal Question* (1865), *Elementary Lessons in Logic* (1870), *The Theory of Political Economy* (1871), *Principles of Science* (2 vols., 1874 and 1877), *Money and the Mechanism of Exchange* (1875), and *The State in Relation to Labour* (1882). At the time of his death he was working on *Principles of Economics;* it was published in incomplete form in 1905 and does not represent what would have been the full fruition of his thought.

Jevons was a utilitarian, treating economics as a calculus of pleasure and pain. The degree of utility of a commodity is some continuous mathematical function of the quantity available. The more one has, the less the utility of

the additional unit. Here was the solution of the paradox that had troubled classical economists as well as Karl Marx—diamonds bring a higher price than water, even though water seems more useful. The marginal utility of a gallon of water is slight because much other water is available. The labor theory of value no longer ruled. But labor as a cost of production influences the quantity supplied and thereby affects the final degree of utility of amounts offered on the market.

Jevons found the economic theory of David Ricardo and John Stuart Mill, that value rests upon cost of production, to be unacceptable, but he did not succeed in getting wide acceptance of his own advances in economic theory. As a writer on practical problems of the time and on issues of social reform, however, he received considerable recognition for his work on applied economics and statistics: fluctuations of prices, business crises, and money and banking. Jevons developed concepts of market processes and economic equilibrium, using diagrams of the general type familiar to students of economics. He was a free-trader, doubting the effectiveness of trade unionism to raise the earnings of labor, and placed hope in cooperation.

Further Reading

Letters and Journal of W. S. Jevons was edited by his wife (1886). E. W. Eckard, *Economics of W. S. Jevons* (1940), includes a biography as well as a description of Jevons's theories.

Additional Sources

Peart, Sandra, *The economics of W.S. Jevons,* New York: Routledge, 1996. □

Sarah Orne Jewett

The American Sarah Orne Jewett (1849-1909) was a regional novelist whose work depicted Maine settings and personalities.

Sarah Orne Jewett was born in the village of South Berwick, Maine, on Sept. 3, 1849. Because she suffered from arthritis and could not attend school regularly, her formal education at Berwick Academy was intermittent. Her father, a distinguished obstetrician, encouraged her to read widely in his library, and she accompanied him on his visits to patients in the countryside. She read the major English and European writers and also important American authors, such as Emerson, Lowell, and Harriet Beecher Stowe. Talks with her father about the country and the seacoast and about his patients' lives and characters, and talks with the patients in their homes saturated the budding author with firsthand information. Her adoration of her father was so strong, apparently, that it prevented her from ever falling in love.

Jewett's first story was published in 1868, when she was 19, and the next year another story initiated her long association with the *Atlantic Monthly* and other prestigious magazines. William Dean Howells, an editor of the *Atlantic,* encouraged her to collect several sketches and connect them with a fictional framework. These became the novel *Deephaven* (1877). Outstanding collections of stories and sketches followed: *Old Friends and New* (1879), *Country By-ways* (1881), *A White Heron and Other Stories* (1886), and *A Native of Winby and Other Tales* (1893). At intervals Jewett wrote successful books for children, including *Play Days* (1878), *The Story of the Normans* (1887), and *Betty Leicester* (1890). Her novels included *A Country Doctor* (1884), *A Marsh Island* (1885), and the book generally considered to be her masterpiece, *The Country of Pointed Firs* (1896).

Jewett's best fiction portrayed the area surrounding and including the town of her birth and childhood, a home to which she always returned after her wide-ranging travels and where she died on June 24, 1909. "My local attachments," she wrote, "are stronger than any cat's that ever mewed." In the state of Maine the end of the importance of clipper ships had led to the abandonment of shipyards and wharves. Villages much like South Berwick were almost deserted by the men and by the young of both sexes, leaving as inhabitants mostly older women. Jewett wrote about this dying world and the isolated or the elderly who find deep meanings in local customs and private experiences. She wrote realistically but gently, creating what many critics regard as the best fictional narratives to come out of New England during a period when regional writing flourished there.

Further Reading

Letters of Sarah Orne Jewett was edited by Annie Fields, a close friend (1911), and *Sarah Orne Jewett Letters* by Richard Cary (1956). There are two illuminating critical studies: Francis Otto Matthiessen, *Sarah Orne Jewett* (1929), and Richard Cary, *Sarah Orne Jewett* (1962).

Additional Sources

Blanchard, Paula, *Sarah Orne Jewett: her world and her work,* Reading, Mass.: Addison-Wesley Pub. Co., 1994.
Keyworth, C. L. (Cynthia L.), *Master smart woman: a portrait of Sarah Orne Jewett: based on the film by Jane Morrison in collaboration with Peter Namuth,* Unity, Me.: North Country Press, 1988. □

Jiang Qing

Jiang Qing (1914–1991) was a Chinese Revolutionary. "The Gang of Four" was the name given to Jiang Qing, wife of Mao Zedong, and her three allies, Zhang Chunqiao, Yao Wenyuan, and Wang Hongwen, who led the attack on traditional Chinese culture during the Great Proletarian Cultural Revolution in the People's Republic of China; Jiang Qing

attempted to succeed her husband as the leader of China.

Wang Hongwen. Name variations: Wang Hung-wen. Born in northeastern China's Jilin province in 1934; died of a liver ailment at age 58 in August 1992; son of poor peasants. Little is known of the family life or early history of the other two members of "The Gang": Zhang Chunqiao (Chang Ch'un-ch'iao) was born in 1918; Yao Wenyuan was born in 1934.

Jiang Qing, the leader of The Gang of Four, was born in Tsucheng (Zuzheng) in Shantung (Shandong) province, China, in March of 1914. At the time of her birth, her father Li Te-wen was 60 years old. A poor man who frequently drank, he beat Jiang's mother, a concubine who was almost 30 years younger and deserted the family when Jiang was about six years old; her mother may have been forced into prostitution by poverty during Jiang Qing's youth. The difficulty of her early years taught Jiang Qing to hate the traditional Chinese society in which men wielded absolute power over their wives and families. It also taught her the rules of survival.

The China into which Jiang Qing was born was in turmoil. The Manchu-Qing (Ch'ing) dynasty had fallen in 1912. The Chinese emperor was briefly replaced by a Republican form of government led by Sun Yat-sen, then militarists seized power and China fell into the chaos of the Warlord years.

In Jiang's youth, women were forbidden to engage in public life. The few women in Chinese history who had real political power—such as Empress Lu, wife of the Han emperor Liu Bang (r. 220-195 b.c.), Empress Wu of the great Tang era (a.d. 618-907), and the famed Empress Dowager Cixi (Tz'u-hsi; 1835-1908)—were condemned as power-hungry opportunists. Though not initially interested in politics, Jiang Qing later studied the careers of these women, encouraging a reevaluation of their place in Chinese history.

But where young Chinese girls were shut out from the political world of men, the lively world of culture was open to them. In Jiang's early years, Chinese culture was in an absolute ferment. Many Chinese believed that their tradition had failed to keep pace with modern history because the culture itself was inadequate. Chinese of the early 20th century measured their country against the Western powers, and against modernizing Japan, in which they saw advances in modern industry, science, and education. But China was then no more than a prize to be fought over, as Western and Japanese colonialism tore at the country's very vitals. Parts of Shantung province where Jiang Qing was born, for example, had been a colonial holding first of Germany, then— following the German defeat in World War I—of Japan. Russia had held parts of north China before the Bolshevik Revolution, England held parts of the Yangtze valley, and France held parts of south China. Great cities like Shanghai and Guangzhou (Canton) were directly controlled by foreigners.

As a young girl, Jiang Qing was tall and thin. Though she suffered from a number of serious ailments, she always had a high level of nervous energy. She entered school briefly in her home town, only to be looked down upon for her poverty and family background. She fought with other students, resisted her teachers, and was soon expelled. At about age ten, she and her mother returned to her maternal grandparents' home, where Jiang Qing once again entered school and was this time more successful, avoiding the temptation to lash out. In 1926 or 1927, she followed her mother to the large port city of Tientsin (Tianjin). Her mother became less important to her, and she was soon living on her own in this new and fascinating city.

One of the few traditional outlets for unsettled youth in China had been the world of the theater. Both rich and poor loved to watch the traditional Chinese operas. The impact of the West had also introduced Western theater, and then film. Touring with a theatrical troupe in Shantung, Jiang Qing matured early and by the age of 14 was frequently taken as much older.

After returning briefly to her grandparents' home in 1929, at 15, she joined the provincial Experimental Arts Academy, where she was exposed to a variety of theatrical genre and a much wider range of roles; she knew that theater would be her life. While at the academy, which was quartered in an old Confucian temple, an event occurred that illustrated both her courage and rebellious nature. In an unused room of the temple, there was a large altar to Confucius, the sage whose thought formed the basis of traditional Chinese culture. The male students dared each other to enter the room at night, climb up on the statue, and take off its ceremonial headdress. But no student dared to seize the headdress until Jiang Qing did so. Ross Terrill, in *The White-boned Demon,* cites one of the event's witnesses:

> After that, she was unforgettable. It *amazed* us that a girl had done that. We men were really too frightened to do it and it never crossed our minds that one of the girls would do it—it was *Confucius* himself, after all. But that girl just went and *did* it. She was a shocker, she made storms, she drew attention to herself.

In 1930, Jiang Qing married a merchant named Fei but found marriage too confining and soon divorced him. She then left for Qingdao (Tsingtao), the very Europeanized city of the province which had long been occupied by Germany. There she took a step that was very natural for a youth in her position and joined the Communist party, formed in 1921. One of the founding members was Jiang Qing's future husband Mao Zedong (Tse-tung).

Chinese who were alarmed by Western encroachments, and discouraged by the state of their own nation and its traditional culture, were attracted by the Bolshevik Revolution in Russia which had been a backward, agrarian, monarchical state much like their own traditional society. In China, the members of the demimonde worlds of art, literature, and theater were much attracted by both traditional and revolutionary Russian and Soviet models in those fields.

Jiang Qing fell in love with another member of the radical groups, Yu Qiwei. In those unsettled times, living together was taken as "marriage" by Chinese society, and so Yu is regarded as Jiang Qing's second husband. She was not yet 18. In 1933, Yu was arrested for radical activities and, upon his release, left Qingdao and Jiang Qing.

The same year, Jiang Qing moved to Shanghai, then the center of banking and trade as well as Western cultural influences. She again linked up with radical groups, working with them while playing a series of minor theatrical roles.

Disturbed by the slow development of her career in theater, she traveled briefly to Peking (Beijing), the capital of China, where she was detained as a suspected leftist. Though quickly released, in 1934 she was jailed for a period of three to eight months. Later, concerned about her image as a former actress turned wife of Mao Zedong, she would take care to expunge much of this early history from the record. Basic facts, such as how long she spent in prison, then became controversial. Whereas Jiang Qing claimed eight months to establish her *bona fides* as a radical activist, others said three, minimizing her contributions and painting her an opportunist who used her beauty and sexuality to rise through a series of liaisons with men like her earlier husbands and Mao himself.

Regardless of her actual time in prison, upon her release Jiang Qing returned to Shanghai. From the standpoint of young people like Jiang, one of the few benefits of Western colonialism was the culture that accompanied it to China. Grasping for clues as to how the West had become so advanced, many Chinese youths eagerly read everything from the West they could find. One of the major influences

on the nascent modern culture of China were the works of the writer Henrik Ibsen, and particularly his play "The Doll's House." Nora, the hero of this play, was presented as a modern woman who wished to lead her own life and the role became the most attractive of all the parts in Western plays and films which deluged China to the onset of the Second World War. In Shanghai, Jiang Qing won the coveted role and played Nora for many performances to outstanding reviews. Jiang Qing and others would later deprecate her talent as an actress, describing her as no better than "second-rate," but her Nora was superb. As one critic, cited by Ross Terrill said, "[In the Shanghai theater,] 1935 was the year of 'Nora.'" The following year, she began acting in films and soon married an influential Shanghai critic, Tang Na (Dang Na).

As an actress, she was, once again, controversial. Not only were her films suspect for their leftist leanings, but her personal life was publicly linked with the volatile lives of other actors and actresses. When she left Tang Na, he publicly threatened to commit suicide. For personal and political reasons, she left Shanghai for the Communist base at Yenan (Yan'an).

In 1937, the struggle with Japan for control over China became a shooting war, bringing together two disparate Chinese political groups—the Communist party and the Nationalist party. The Nationalists, known as the KMT from their Chinese name (Kuo Min Tang), were the actual, if relatively powerless, government of China. In 1927, the KMT had driven the Communists underground, but under the threat from Japan the two groups agreed to cooperate. This cooperation was, in fact, little more than an armed truce, frequently violated. Yenan became the central base of the Communists when survivors of the KMT's attempt to destroy them wound up there in 1935. On this epochal retreat, known as the "Long March," Mao Zedong became the leader of the Party.

Jiang Qing arrived in Yenan in August of 1937. By the summer of 1938, she was living with Mao and carrying his child, a daughter to be named Li Na. Mao, like Jiang Qing, had already been married three times, and he had accumulated at least six children; Jiang Qing would raise some of them as her own. As a mother, she was said to have been busy and uninvolved; certainly, she was never close to her own child, and was later said to have viewed Mao's other children as rivals to her own status and that of Li Na. But in Yenan, Jiang Qing was apparently a model and modest wife. She played the hostess for Mao when visiting with foreign dignitaries, American diplomats, and newspaper reporters, along with writers such as Edgar Snow, whose classic work *Red Star over China* is the best source on life in Yenan. Because Mao had several love affairs in Yenan and had recently broken with his third wife, Ho Tzu-chen, evidently party leaders had insisted that Mao and Jiang Qing could marry only if she foreswore open political activity.

The unexpectedly quick collapse of the Japanese, following the use of the atomic bombs in August of 1945, was soon followed by renewed civil war in China. Weakened by decades of war and its own corruption, the KMT fell quickly. In October of 1949, Mao Zedong proclaimed the founding of the People's Republic of China, making Jiang Qing the wife of the head of the country.

For some time, Jiang Qing lived quietly as Mao tried to guide the infant communist state forward. After some years of attempting to follow Soviet Russian models, Mao grew impatient with the slow progress of China and, in 1957, launched a series of campaigns known as the "Great Leap Forward," which were intended to promote rapid growth. The Great Leap was disastrous and other Party leaders soon began to reduce Mao's power. Disturbed by this, and by changes which were occurring in Soviet communism, it seemed to Mao that a general phenomenon—which he referred to as "Revisionism"—was occurring in both China and the Soviet Union. Revisionism was said to occur when revolutions ran their courses and later generations of leaders proved cautious, seeking to institutionalize a revolution rather than carry it forward.

Mao's analysis of this phenomenon was complimented by Jiang Qing's interest in Chinese culture. She blamed traditional culture for Revisionism, saying that because people still followed cultural models in opera, theater, music, and film, the traditional Chinese values were reasserting themselves. Whether Mao was following her lead, or whether Jiang Qing was seizing the opportunity to establish independent political power for herself is unclear, and unimportant. The two of them shared a common perspective on the importance of culture.

Beginning in 1962, Mao turned to examine culture in a systematic fashion and Jiang Qing scrutinized the many traditional plays and operas. She decided that they were revisionist and created new ones to provide models for revolutionaries to follow. In Shanghai, she linked up with two local political leaders, Zhang Chunqiao and Yao Wenyuan. Jiang Qing had known Zhang Chunqiao earlier in the leftist world of the 1930s. He had become the head of the Communist party in Shanghai, and like Mao, was very interested in such theoretical issues as Revisionism. Yao, an important writer, was the son of a prominent business family. Jiang drew both of them into her clique. Mao was shut out of the political and intellectual life of Peking, and turned to the Party and cultural apparatus in Shanghai to get his perspective heard. This put Jiang Qing on center stage.

In 1966, Mao and Jiang launched their attack on Chinese culture, upon Mao's political enemies, and, many said, upon Jiang Qing's personal enemies. Called the "Great Proletarian Cultural Revolution," this attack was an all-encompassing event whose precise causes and parameters are even now only partially understood. When Mao was excluded from Party circles, he recruited the alienated youth of China, known as "Red Guard" to "Smash the Four Olds," and to attack both traditional culture and the party. Jiang Qing staged revolutionary operas, met with Red Guard groups, spoke to the army where she had a strong position, and represented Mao in all phases of the movement.

The Great Proletarian Cultural Revolution became violent, and many wrongs were done as noted political and cultural figures were attacked for alleged wrongdoings. Jiang Qing used her new political power to avenge herself upon many who had slighted her in the past, going back to

the conflicts of her youthful career as an actress in Shanghai. Some of her victims died in prison. Finally, the violence became so divisive that even Mao knew it had to be stopped. By 1967, the extremist phase was over.

An undercurrent to the Cultural Revolution was fed by widespread awareness that Mao was old and ill. It was apparent that he would soon die, and that somebody would succeed him. Jiang Qing felt that she, who had been at Mao's side for 40 years, was his proper heir. The conservative group which had opposed the Great Proletarian Revolution's excesses was led by Deng Xiaoping (Teng Hsiao-p'ing) , who became Jiang Qing's chief adversary.

Working with her allies, Zhang Chunqiao and Yao Wenyuan, in Shanghai, Jiang Qing added another, Wang Hongwen (Hung-wen), a young firebrand who had distinguished himself in the Cultural Revolution. Worried about the fight to succeed him, Mao at one point warned Jiang Qing, "Don't become a Gang of Four," a caution against becoming an isolated group within the government. The group used their control over cultural and propaganda channels to attack their enemies in an increasingly frenzied fashion, as it became apparent that Mao was dying, leaving them little time to establish Jiang as successor.

On September 9, 1976, when Mao died, Jiang Qing and her allies strove to move troops into position and create a documentary record that demonstrated Mao's desire for Jiang Qing to succeed him. But she had angered too many people, and the conventions against women in power were too strong. Deng Xiaoping and his clique came together behind a benign, temporary successor to Mao, Hua Guofeng (Hua Kuo-feng), and Jiang Qing was arrested. By 1980, Deng had established his own power, and she and the others went on trial for crimes committed during the Cultural Revolution. Because Deng and his supporters did not dare attack Mao directly, they blamed the Cultural Revolution on individuals like the "Gang of Four."

At the trial, Zhang Chunqiao stood mute, refusing to dignify the attack against him by speaking. Wang Hongwen, seeking leniency, cooperated eagerly, confessing to crimes which he had not committed. Jiang Qing, typically, took the offensive. Her position held much truth: that Mao had been behind the Cultural Revolution and had not been duped by others. "I was Mao's dog; I bit whom he said to bite."

All of the Gang were given long sentences (Yao Wenyuan was given 20 years; Wang Hongwen was sentenced to life; and Zhang Chunqiao's death sentence was commuted to life in prison). Jiang Qing's was initially a death sentence, commuted for two years to see if she "reformed." Steadfastly refusing to recant, she spent the next decade in prison. In 1991, it was announced that she had committed suicide on May 14.

Like all powerful women in Chinese society, Jiang Qing's life and role is impossible to extricate from the tangled threads which make up that society itself. Women had never had a legitimate political role, and the only way they could achieve power was by means defined as illegitimate: by going outside the system or by manipulating powerful men. Jiang Qing was an ambitious, talented, and resourceful woman who seized every opportunity to rise. In doing so, she caused a great deal of suffering, but her role in life was to smash "with a big hammer" at that culture which attempted to hold her back.

Further Reading

Snow, Edgar. *Red Star over China*. Random House, 1938.
Terrill, Ross. *The White-boned Demon*. William Morrow, 1984.
Witke, Roxanne. *Comrade Chiang Ch'ing*. Little Brown, 1977.
Chin, Steven S. K. *The Gang of Four*. University of Hong Kong, 1977.
Hsin, Chi. *The Case of the Gang of Four*. Hong Kong: Cosmos Books, 1977.
Lotta, Raymond, ed. *And Mao Makes 5*. Banner Press, 1978. □

Jiang Zemin

Hand-picked by Deng Xiaoping to be built up as China's future leader, Jiang Zemin (born 1927) became general secretary of the Chinese Communist Party Central Committee in 1989.

Jiang Zemin was born in July 1926 in Yangzhou city, Jiangsu Province, a small town on the banks of the Chang River west of Shanghai. After one of his uncles joined the then-outlawed Communist party and was killed in combat, his biological father offered him for adoption to the surviving family members so that they would have an heir to continue the Shinquing's bloodline. Jiang joined the Chinese Communist Party (CCP) in 1946 and graduated from the electrical machinery department of Jiaotong University in Shanghai the following year.

After the Communists took over power in China in 1949, Jiang assumed several positions in Shanghai: CCP committee secretary and first deputy director of the Yimin No. 1 Foodstuffs Factory; first deputy director of the Shanghai Soap Factory; and chief of the electrical machinery section of the Shanghai No. 2 Designing Division of the First Ministry of Machine-Building Industry.

In 1955 Jiang was sent to work as a trainee at the Stalin Automobile Factory in Moscow. After returning to China the following year, his career advanced steadily as an engineer and a technocrat under the First Ministry of Machine-Building Industry. From 1971 to 1979 he was appointed deputy director, later director, of the Foreign Affairs Bureau under the same ministry.

He moved into a new field of work (import and export) in August 1980 and became vice-minister of the State Foreign Investment Commission in March 1981. His job changed in May 1982 as he was appointed vice-minister of electronics industry. Later that year he was elected a member of the CCP Central Committee at the 12th Party Congress. In June 1983 he was promoted to minister of electronics industry and in September 1984 he was concurrently appointed the deputy head of the Leading Group for Electronics Industry under the state council. After 1985 Jiang's career was boosted as he returned to Shanghai as its deputy party secretary, later secretary and mayor. In 1987 he entered the Politburo at the 13th CCP Congress.

Positions under Deng Xiaoping

In June 1989, in the aftermath of the Beijing massacre, Jiang was chosen elder statesman by Deng Xiaoping to succeed the disgraced Zhao Ziyang as the general secretary of the CCP. In November 1989 Jiang also took over the chairmanship of the Central Military Commission when Deng stepped down. Like Deng Xiaoping, Jiang advocated economic reform, but he was also a conservative insofar as political reform was concerned. As mayor of Shanghai, Jiang initiated and implemented a series of economic reforms. For example, Shanghai was the first city in China to auction land-use rights, even though such a measure clearly violates the Communist dogma. Jiang was quite responsive to foreign investors' concerns, and hence won praise from them. Nevertheless, during the 1989 pro-democracy movement, he brusquely dismissed Qin Benli from the post of the editor-in-chief of *The World Herald*, a Shanghai publication well known for its outspoken and candid criticism of the regime's policies as well as economic and political conditions in China; the pretext was that the paper published a long article deviating from the CCP's line. Jiang's action and his skillful handling of student protests in Shanghai, where few students were killed, enhanced his political career.

After Jiang became party general secretary, he faithfully followed the new party line. For example, he blamed hostile external forces for China's domestic political turmoil in the late 1980s. In the 1989 National Day address, which was a required reading for all Chinese, Jiang asserted that the international reactionary forces "adopt political, economic, and cultural means to infiltrate and influence socialist countries, exploiting their temporary difficulties and reforms. They support and buy over so-called 'dissidents' through whom they foster blind worship of the Western world and propagate the political and economic patterns, sense of values, decadent ideas and lifestyle of the Western capitalist world. . . . They fabricate rumors, provoke incidents, plot turmoil, and engage in subversive activities against socialist countries." Likewise, he put a renewed emphasis on "redness" over expertise in selecting and promoting party officials. He was prominently quoted in a *People's Daily* front-page commentary on June 24, 1990, as saying, "In choosing people, in assigning people, in educating people, we must take a revolutionary outlook as the prerequisite to insure that party and government leaders at every level are loyal to Marxism."

After Deng Xiaoping

In spite of Deng Xiaoping's efforts to build him up as China's future leader, Jiang may end up as another transitional leadership figure like Zhao Ziyang and Hu Yaobang before him. Xiaoping officially retired in 1989, the same year of the Tiananmen Square massacre. Jiang did not have a base of support within the party or the army, and in 1990 still lacked leadership stature. Capitalistic ventures undertaken since the 1980s have emphasized economic class disparity. The widening class gap is only agitated by the constant inflation. *Tokyo Business Today* reported that the Chinese Central Committee's commission on general measures for maintenance of social order notes 1.67 million disturbances in rural farming villages. These disturbances resulted in more that 8,000 deaths and rising ill will between farmers and government. Concurrently, urban areas are experiencing increased crime and revolutionary groups have sprung up. In the autumn of 1994, a militant group placed explosives on train tracks, derailing a train carrying troops from China's 13th Army. The explosion killed 170 and injured 190. Moreover, China's relationship with the rest of the world grows increasingly strained with widespread reports of human rights abuses, including prison labor and political imprisoning.

In April 1996, in an attempt to reestablish law and order, Jiang launched an anticrime drive, known as "Strike Hard" (Yanda in Chinese). Within six months Strike Hard had resulted in more than 160,000 arrests and more than 1,000 executions. Though many were critical of the initiative, the government claimed that it was well received by the Chinese citizens who were alarmed by the rising crime statistics. Jiang is also known for reclaiming Hong Kong and attempting to convince Taiwan to follow.

Further Reading

Additional information on Jiang Zemin can be found in Parris H. Chang, "The Power Game in Beijing" in *The World & I* (October, 1989). Lee Feigon, *China Rising: The Meaning of Tiananmen* (1990) is an eyewitness report as well as a scholarly analysis of the 1989 military assault on Chinese students. Yi Mu and Mark V. Thompson (both are pseudonyms), *Crisis at Tiananmen: Reform and Reality in Modern China* (1990), report what the CCP leaders were thinking and doing during the 1989 events. □

Juan Ramón Jiménez

The Spanish symbolist poet Juan Ramón Jiménez (1881-1958) was one of his country's greatest writers. His influence on the succeeding generation of writers was profound.

Juan Ramón Jiménez was born in Moguer in Andalusia on Dec. 24, 1881. After early training in a Jesuit school, he was sent to study law in Seville; he chose, however, to study literature, especially romantic poets. In 1900 Jiménez went to Madrid, carrying an ample collection of his early poems, finally published under the delicate titles *Ninfeas* and *Almas de violeta*. At this time he suffered a mental breakdown, spending months in clinics in France and in Madrid. In spite of his condition, Jiménez helped to found and direct the literary journal *Helios* and continued to write poetry. His expressive titles indicate accurately the type of poetry he was writing: *Arias tristes* (1903), *Jardines lejanos* (1905), *Pastorales* (1905).

In 1905 Jiménez returned to Moguer and spent 6 tranquil years writing the same kind of poetry: *Elejlas, Baladas de primavera, La soledad sonora*. Essentially this poetry is impressionistic, with a stylized backdrop of nature in pastel colors (rose, white, mauve). The tone is generally one of languid melancholy; the form is elegant, aristocratic, and musical. Even at this stage, however, Jiménez's imagery is focused toward sublimation of human emotions. In his early maturity this tendency toward sublimation becomes pronounced, especially in the fine book *Sonetos espirituales* (1915).

In 1916 Jiménez went to the United States and married Zenobia Camprubi. On this trip the poet composed his important book in the symbolist manner, *Diario de un poeta reciencasado*, which is an elaborate projection of two basic symbols, the sea and the sky. Back in Madrid, in the following years Jiménez gradually withdrew from participation in the real world to concentrate upon his poetry. He created four major books: *Eternidades* (1917), *Piedra y cielo* (1918), *Poesía* (1923), and *Belleza* (1923). By this time he was writing a pure poetry of intellectual tone reduced to essential symbol and stripped of all anecdote and verbal music.

At the outbreak of the Spanish Civil War, Jiménez (never interested in politics) went again to the United States and began a late career (followed by many other exiles) of teaching and lecturing for brief periods. Although his poetic creation slackened somewhat in the 1930s, in the 1940s he enjoyed a final burst of inspiration. As a result of a boat trip to Argentina, Jiménez, again moved by the symbol of the sea, wrote what he considered his final major work, *Dios deseado y deseante* (1949). This book projects the resolution of themes Jiménez had been pursuing all his career. His

was the organizing of Indian Moslems to demand a separate state, which culminated in the creation of Pakistan, the world's largest Islamic state.

Mohammad Ali Jinnah was born in Karachi, probably on Dec. 25, 1876, although the day is uncertain. His family were merchants and members of the Khoja sect of Moslems. He went to England in 1892 to study law, and after his return in 1896 he practiced in Bombay. He joined the Indian National Congress, giving his support to the moderate faction led by Gopal Krishna Gokhale, whom he greatly admired. Jinnah was also a member of the Moslem League, and he worked for greater Hindu-Moslem unity. He broke with the Congress in 1920 with the advent to leadership of Mahatma Gandhi, whose methods he deplored as unconstitutional and as based on an appeal to the mob. Jinnah's attempts to work with the Moslem League were so frustrating, however, that he concluded its leaders were either "flunkeys of the British or camp followers of the Congress" and went to England in 1931 to take up a law practice there.

In 1934 Jinnah was persuaded to return to India by the changes brought about in the political situation by the proposals for the new constitution, which resulted in the India Act of 1935. Convinced that Moslems would become second-rate citizens in a political society dominated by the votes of the Hindu majority, he succeeded in revitalizing the Moslem League as an effective political organization after

first period was esthetic, his second intellectual; in his final period, a religious one, he expressed his neomystical union with his God both "desired and desiring." In all these periods the poet is seeking a perfection of his soul, what he calls a "unique, just and universal consciousness of beauty."

Jiménez also wrote significant prose in his long career. In 1917 he published *Platero y yo* (*Platero and I*), a poetic, melancholy, Franciscan book that has become a classic, especially for children. He also wrote *Españoles de tres mundos,* short and sometimes biting portraits of his contemporaries.

In 1956, just at the time his beloved Zenobia lay dying, Jiménez received the Nobel Prize in literature for his lyrical poetry. He died in San Juan, Puerto Rico, on May 29, 1958.

Further Reading

For the poetry of Jiménez see *Three Hundred Poems, 1903-1953,* translated by Eloise Roach (1962). Two fine English studies of his poetry are Paul R. Olson, *Circle of Paradox: Time and Essence in the Poetry of Juan Ramón Jiménez* (1967), and Leo R. Cole, *The Religious Instinct in the Poetry of Juan Ramón Jiménez* (1967). □

Mohammad Ali Jinnah

Mohammad Ali Jinnah (1876-1948) was the first governor general of Pakistan. His great achievement

the elections in 1937, in which the Indian National Congress had won large majorities.

Jinnah's success was particularly striking as he had few of the characteristics of a popular politician. A friend described him as "tall and stately, formal and fastidious, aloof and imperious of manner," and he had few personal friends. His first wife, a child bride, had died when he was a student, and his second wife, who was a Parsi and half his age, separated from him in 1928. She died in 1929. His only close personal contacts after this seem to have been his daughter and later his sister, Fatima.

Jinnah's energy, integrity, and relentless logic made him the spokesman of Indian Moslems, earning him the title Quaid-i-Azam, "supreme leader." By 1945, when Indian independence was imminent, neither the British government nor the Indian National Congress could find a political solution for India without Jinnah's agreement. His insistence that Hindus and Moslems constituted two separate nations became the central fact of all discussions, and the partition of India on Aug. 15, 1947, into India and Pakistan was the fruit of his argument that Moslems must have their own homeland.

Jinnah was the first governor general of Pakistan, and while the office in other parts of the British Commonwealth was ceremonial, his enormous popularity and skill made his authority virtually absolute. He tackled the many problems facing the new nation with zeal, but he was already worn out by the long struggles. He died on Sept. 11, 1948, leaving to his successors the task of consolidating the nation he had done so much to create.

Further Reading

Jinnah's views are in Jamil-ud-Din Ahmad, ed., *Speeches and Writings of Mr. Jinnah* (2 vols., 6th ed. 1960-1964), and S. S. Pirzada, ed., *Quaid-i-Azam Jinnah's Correspondence* (2d rev. ed. 1966). Hector Bolitho, *Jinnah: Creator of Pakistan* (1954), provides biographical details. Jinnah's political role is examined in Khalid B. Sayeed, *Pakistan: The Formative Phase, 1857-1948* (2d ed. 1968).

Additional Sources

Wolpert, Stanley A., *Jinnah of Pakistan,* New York: Oxford University Press, 1984. □

Joachim of Fiore

The Italian mystic Joachim of Fiore (ca. 1132-1202) developed a philosophy of history based on his interpretation of the Trinity.

Joachim was born at Celico near Cosenza in Calabria. While on a pilgrimage to the Holy Land, he decided to enter the monastic life. Returning to Sicily, he entered the Cistercian abbey of Sambucina. At the Cistercian monastery of Corazzo Joachim was ordained a priest in 1168 and elected abbot in 1177.

Preferring a solitary life of meditation and writing, about 1185 Joachim retired to the Benedictine monastery of Casamari, where he began to write his commentary on the Book of Revelation. In 1191 he left the Cistercian order and moved to Fiore (Flora), in Calabria, where he founded a hermitage and later, as disciples were attracted, a monastery. This group, eventually organized into the order of San Giovanni in Fiore, was a strict, reformed branch of the Cistercians; it was approved in 1196, and its members came to be known as the Florensians.

In his later years Joachim came increasingly to feel that he possessed special insights into Christian Scriptures and doctrine and was perhaps subject to a special revelation. Through the encouragement of Pope Innocent III, Joachim wrote down his interpretations and visions and submitted them to the papacy for consideration and approval shortly before his death in 1202. Although Joachim had no intention of disseminating heretical doctrines, ideas drawn from his writings influenced heterodox thinkers and caused problems for the Church and society for the next 200 years.

Joachim's thought centers on his concept of the Trinity and its implications for the understanding of human history. In his *Liber figurarum* and in several other works, Joachim divided history into two dispensations, or eras: the dispensation of the Old Testament, or former covenant, which culminated in the first coming of Christ, and the second dispensation, or new covenant, of the Christian Church, which would culminate in the second coming of Christ. Joachim believed that he was living near the end of his second age and that only two generations remained before the second advent of Christ.

A slightly different view of history was extracted from Joachim's writings after his death. According to the view with which his name increasingly became associated, history is divided into three periods, the ages of the Father, Son, and Holy Spirit, each of the first two being composed of 42 generations. The third age, which was supposed to dawn about 1260, was to be the age of the Spirit, an age of love, liberty, and freedom in which the principal institution in the world would be monasticism and in which the visible, hierarchical structure of the Catholic Church would be superseded by the Spiritual Church.

One such eschatological movement that founded its doctrine in the writings of Joachim was led by the Franciscan Gerardo of Borgo San Donnino, who was condemned along with the teaching of Joachim in 1256 by Pope Alexander IV. However, the ideas of Joachim, especially the concept of a golden age of the Spirit and the threefold division of history, remained influential in Western thought from the 13th century on.

Further Reading

Major works on Joachim are in German. In English, a popular treatment of medieval heterodox movements that includes Joachim is Norman Cohn, *The Pursuit of the Millennium* (1957).

Additional Sources

Bett, Henry, *Joachim of Flora,* Merrick, N.Y.: Richwood Pub. Co., 1976. ☐

Joan of Arc

The French national heroine Joan of Arc (c. 1412-1431) led a troop of French soldiers and served as a temporary focus of French resistance to English occupation in the last phase of the Hundred Years War.

The life of Joan of Arc must be considered against the background of the later stages of the Hundred Years War (1339-1453). The war, which had begun in 1339 and continued intermittently till the 1380s, had caused severe hardship in France. In 1392 the insanity of the French king, Charles VI, had provided the opportunity for two aristocratic factions to struggle for control of the King and kingdom. The leader of one of these, John the Fearless, Duke of Burgundy, finally assumed control, and both factions appealed for help to England. Henry V of England invaded France on the Burgundian side in 1415 and inflicted a shattering defeat upon the French at Agincourt in the same year. The English and Burgundians entered Paris in 1418, and the murder of John the Fearless in 1419 strengthened Burgundian hatred for the Armagnac faction.

In 1420 Charles VI, Henry V, and Philip the Good of Burgundy agreed to the Treaty of Troyes, according to which Henry was to act as regent for the mad Charles VI, marry Charles's daughter, and inherit the throne of France on Charles's death. The treaty thus disinherited Charles VI's son, the Dauphin Charles (later Charles VII). Charles VI also implied that the Dauphin was illegitimate. In 1422 both Henry V and Charles VI died, leaving Henry VI, the infant son of Henry, as king of both kingdoms. Henry VI, through his regent, the Duke of Bedford, ruled uncontested in Normandy and the Île-deFrance. The Duke of Burgundy followed an independent policy in the territories he was assembling to the north and east of France. The Dauphin was reduced to holding the south of France, threatened with Anglo-Burgundian invasion, and taunted with the title "King of Bourges," from which city he ineffectively ruled what was left of his kingdom. He was in perpetual fear that the key city of Orléans, the gateway to his lands, might be captured by the English. In the autumn of 1428 the English laid siege to Orléans. Charles, dominated by the infamous favorite Georges de la Tremoille, naturally apathetic, and lacking in men and money, could do nothing. By the spring of 1429 the city appeared about to fall and with it the hopes of Charles VII.

Early Life

Joan was born to a peasant family in Domrémy, a small town near Vaucouleurs, the last town in the east still loyal to Charles VII. "As long as I lived at home," she said at her trial in 1431, "I worked at common tasks about the house, going but seldom afield with our sheep and other cattle. I learned to sew and spin: I fear no woman in Rouen at sewing and spinning."

Some time in 1425 Joan began to have visions— "When I was thirteen, I had a voice from God to help me govern myself." The voice was that of St. Michael, who, with St. Catherine and St. Margaret, "told me of the pitiful state of France, and told me that I must go to succor the King of France." Joan twice went to Robert de Baudricourt, the captain of Vaucouleurs, asking for an escort to Charles VII at Chinon. The third time she was granted an escort, and she set out in February 1429, arriving 11 days later at Chinon. She was immediately examined for orthodoxy and 2 days later was allowed to see the King.

A contemporary described her: "This Maid . . . has a virile bearing, speaks little, shows an admirable prudence in all her words. She has a pretty, woman's voice, eats little, drinks very little wine; she enjoys riding a horse and takes pleasure in fine arms, greatly likes the company of noble fighting men, detests numerous assemblies and meetings, readily sheds copious tears, has a cheerful face. . ." Joan appears to have been robust, with darkbrown hair, and, as one historian succinctly remarked, "in the excitement which raised her up from earth to heaven, she retained her solid common sense and a clear sense of reality." She was also persuasive. In April 1429 Charles VII sent her to Orléans as captain of a troop of men—not as leader of all his forces. With the Duke d'Alençon and Jean, the Bastard of Orléans (later Count of Dunois), Joan relieved the city, thus removing the greatest immediate threat to Charles and for the first time in his reign allowing him a military triumph.

Her Mission

Although Charles VII appears to have accepted Joan's mission—after having had her examined several times at Chinon and at the University of Poitiers—his attitude toward her, on the whole, is ambiguous. He followed her pressing advice to use the respite provided by the relief of Orléans to proceed to his coronation at Reims, thereby becoming king in the eyes of all men. After a series of victorious battles and sieges on the way, Charles VII was crowned at Reims on July 18, 1429. Joan was at his side and occupied a prominent place in the ceremonies following the coronation. From the spring of 1429 to the spring of 1430, Charles and his advisers wavered on the course of the war. The choices were those of negotiation, particularly with the Duke of Burgundy, or taking the military offensive against English positions, particularly Paris. Joan favored the second course, but an attack upon Paris in September 1429 failed, and Charles VII entered into a treaty with Burgundy that committed him to virtual inaction. From September 1429 to the early months of 1430, Joan appears to have been kept inactive by the royal court, finally moving to the defense of the town of Compiègne in May 1430. During a skirmish outside the town's walls against the Burgundians, Joan was cut off and captured. She was a rich prize. The Burgundians turned Joan over to the English, who prepared to try her for heresy. Charles VII could do nothing.

The Trial

Joan's trial was held in three parts. Technically it was an ecclesiastical trial for heresy, and Joan's judges were Pierre Cauchon, the bishop of Beauvais, and Jean Lemaitre, vicar of the inquisitor of France; both were aided by a large number of theologians and lawyers who sat as a kind of consulting and advising jury. From January to the end of March, the court investigated Joan's "case" and interrogated witnesses. The trial itself lasted from April to nearly the end of May and ended with Joan's abjuration. The trial was both an ecclesiastical one and a political one (because Joan was kept in an English prison rather than in that of the archbishop of Rouen and because the English continually intervened in the trial). Joan was charged with witchcraft and fraud, tested by being asked complicated theological questions, and finally condemned on the grounds of persisting in wearing male clothing, a technical offense against the authority of the Church. Joan's answers throughout the trial reveal her presence of mind, humility, wit, and good sense. Apparently Joan and her accusers differed about the nature of her abjuration, and 2 days after she signed it, she recanted. The third phase of her trial began on May 28. This time she was tried as a relapsed heretic, conviction of which meant "release" to the "secular arm"; that is, she would be turned over to the English to be burned. Joan was convicted of being a relapsed heretic, and she was burned at the stake in the marketplace of Rouen on May 30, 1431.

Rehabilitation and Later Legend

From 1450 to 1456, first under the impetus of Charles VII, then under that of Joan's mother, and finally under that of the Inquisition, a reinvestigation of Joan's trial and condemnation was undertaken by ecclesiastical lawyers. On July 7, 1456, the commission declared Joan's trial null and void, thereby freeing Joan from the taint of heresy. The Joan of Arc legend, however, did not gather momentum, and then only intermittently, until the 17th century. The 19th and 20th centuries were really, as a historian has called them, "the centuries of the Maid." In spite of her legend, Joan was not canonized until May 16, 1920.

Further Reading

There is an immense literature about Joan of Arc, most of it fanciful and inaccurate. Some of it, however, is great literature in its own right: for example, George Bernard Shaw's play, *Saint Joan,* or Jules Michelet's *Joan of Arc,* translated by Albert Guerard (1957). There is no standard English or French biography which is entirely reliable. Therefore, the best source concerning Joan's career is the text of her trial and rehabilitation proceedings. Full texts were published by J. Quicherat in French. The choice English works have been built around extracts from these texts; the best of these is Regine Pernoud, *Joan of Arc* (1959; trans. 1964). A shorter work, consisting only of extracts from the trial materials, is Willard R. Trask, *Joan of Arc: Self Portrait* (1936). Joan's place in 15th-century France is described by Edouard Perroy, *The Hundred Years War* (1945; trans. 1951), and Alice Buchan, *Joan of Arc and the Recovery of France* (1948). A careful analysis of the sources concerning Joan and a brief description of her later reputation are in Charles W. Lightbody, *The Judgements of Joan* (1960). □

Steven Jobs

Computer designer and corporate executive Steven Jobs (born 1955) is cofounder of Apple Computers. With his vision of affordable personal computers, he launched one of the largest industries of the past decades while still in his early twenties and remains one of the most inventive and energetic minds in American technology.

Born in 1955, Steven Jobs was adopted shortly thereafter by a California couple, Paul and Clara Jobs. Jobs showed an early interest in electronics and gadgetry. As a high school student, he boldly asked William Hewlett, co-founder and president of the Hewlett-Packard computer firm, for some parts he needed to complete a class project. Hewlett was impressed enough to give Jobs the parts and offer him a summer internship at Hewlett-Packard.

Dropped Out of College

After graduating from high school in 1972, Jobs attended Reed College in Portland, Oregon, for two years before dropping out, partly to ease his family's financial burden and partly to find himself. He hoped to visit India and study eastern spiritualism, but lacking necessary funds, went to work part-time for Atari Computers. He was able to save enough money to finance a trip to India in the summer of 1974. While there, he practiced meditation, studied eastern culture and religion, and even shaved his head. But by the fall, he became ill with dysentery and was forced to return to the United States.

For a short time, Jobs lived in a California commune but soon became disenchanted with the lifestyle. In 1975, he began associating with a group of computer aficionados known as the Homebrew Computer Club. One member, a technical whiz named Steve Wosniak, whom Jobs had first met at Hewlett-Packard, was trying to build a small computer. Jobs became fascinated with the marketing potential of such a computer, and in 1976 he and Wosniak formed their own company. The team was content to sell circuit boards designed by Wosniak until the computer prototype was complete. That same year, Wosniak succeeded in designing a small computer, and using Jobs's parents' garage, the two men worked to refine and market the product.

Cofounded Apple Computer Co.

Jobs saw a huge gap in the existing computer market, as no product was targeted for home use. Wosniak improved his initial computer while Jobs lined up investors and bank financing. Marketing manager A. C. Markkula eventually invested $250,000 and became an equal partner in the Apple Computer Company. With new capital, Jobs and

Wosniak refined the prototype. The redesigned computer—christened the "Apple II"—hit the market in 1977, with impressive first year sales of $2.7 million. In one of the most phenomenal cases of corporate growth in U.S. history, the company's sales grew to $200 million within three years. Jobs and Wosniak had opened an entirely new market, that of personal computers, bringing the computational speed of business systems into people's homes and beginning a new era in information processing.

By 1980, the personal computer era was well underway. Apple was forced to continually improve its products to remain ahead in a growing marketplace. Competitors such as Radio Shack, Commodore, and IBM were gaining sales from Apple's market. In 1980, Apple introduced the Apple III computer, and improved version of the Apple II, but the new model suffered technical and marketing problems. It was withdrawn from the market, but was later reworked and reintroduced.

Jobs continued to be the marketing force behind Apple. He admitted that mistakes were made with the Apple III, but looked for innovative ways to meet new and existing consumer needs. Early in 1983, Jobs unveiled Lisa, another new computer, aimed this time at business executives. Lisa was designed for people possessing minimal computer experience. The model did not sell well, however, because of its high price and increased competition from IBM personal computers. By 1983, it was estimated that Apple lost half of its market share to IBM.

Macintosh falls, Jobs resigns

Faced with a declining market share, Apple introduced the Macintosh in 1984. In designing the model, Jobs apparently paid more attention to appearances than function. Although the Macintosh had "user-friendly" software and on-screen displays, Jobs failed to equip it with either a letter-quality printer or a hard disk drive. Lacking these features, the Macintosh did not sell well to businesses. The failure of the Macintosh signalled the beginning of Jobs's downfall at Apple Computer Company. In 1985, following a highly publicized showdown at Apple, Jobs resigned from the company he had founded, though he retained his title as chairman of its board of directors.

It was not long before Steve Jobs resurfaced, however. Soon after leaving Apple, he hired some of his former employees to begin a new computer company. The company was called NeXT, and Jobs invested $7 million of his own money to get it started. For three years, Jobs and his employees worked to produce the first NeXT computer, which was aimed at the educational market. Late in 1988, the NeXT computer was introduced at a large gala event in San Francisco. Initial reactions were generally good; the product was user-friendly, with very fast processing speed, excellent graphics displays, and an outstanding sound system. Other innovations included an optical disk drive instead of floppy disks, and a special sound chip to provide the fidelity of a compact disc. Judging from initial reactions, many critics were convinced that Steve Jobs had brought another revolutionary product to American consumers.

Despite the warm reception, however, the NeXT machine never caught on. It was too costly, had a black-and-white screen, and couldn't be linked to other computers or run common software, Joseph Nocera wrote in a biting profile of Jobs in *Gentleman's Quarterly.* Nocera argued that Jobs's charisma and persuasive charm duped his employees, the press, and Jobs himself into believing he could not fail—despite strong evidence to the contrary. "Jobs started NeXT with an unshakable faith in his own press clips, in which his mistakes were always overlooked while his supposed triumphs were always wildly oversold," Nocera wrote.

Nocera said he also fell victim to the Jobs myth when he visited NeXT in 1986. He witnessed Jobs brutalize employees who worshipped him, obsess over mindless details, and indulge his expensive tastes—yet Nocera reported none of the contradictions. "The point is," he wrote in 1993, "my willingness to be seduced by Steve Jobs caused me to miss what I was seeing with my own eyes. Even in 1986, the evidence strongly suggested that lightning was not going to strike twice. The incongruities were too severe, the dreams too farfetched. . . . You'd ask the people at NeXT how, exactly, their computer was going to change the world and they would lapse into gobbledygook; they really had no idea what they were trying to accomplish with this new machine."

Bought Pixar, Made *Toy Story*

NeXT was not, however, the end of Steve Jobs. Lightning, indeed, struck a second time. In 1986, Jobs paid filmmaker George Lucas $10 million for a small firm called Pixar that specialized in computer animation. "Over the next six years Jobs poured another $40 million of his own money into the company . . . as it set out to make the first-ever computer-animated feature film," *Time* magazine reported in February 1996. That film was *Toy Story,* a huge box office hit. Pixar's initial public stock offering was an enormous success. The share price climbed dramatically, and Jobs's 80 percent stake in Pixar suddenly was worth $1 billion.

"Jobs makes the point that Pixar, like other (initial public offering) overnight successes, was really anything but an overnight success," said the *Time* article. "'The things I've done in my life have required a lot of years of work before they took off,' he says. He and Wosniak started work on Apple in 1975. 'So it was really six years of work before we went public. And Pixar has been 10 years. . . . The thing that drives me and my colleagues . . . is that you see something very compelling to you, and you don't quite know how to get it, but you know, sometimes intuitively, it's within your grasp. And it's worth putting in years of your life to make it come into existence.'"

In December of 1996, Apple announced that it was purchasing Next Software for over $400 million. Jobs returned to Apple as a part-time consultant to CEO Gilbert Amelio. The following year, in August, Apple entered into a partnership with archrival Microsoft, in which the two companies, according to the *New York Times,* "agreed to cooperate on several sales and technology fronts." The alliance was an unprecedented one for the industry, but analysts predicted that Microsoft's support will ultimately save Apple, a company that had in the late 1990s come to serve a much more niche market than Microsoft. "We want to let go of this notion that for Apple to win, Microsoft has to lose," Jobs said. In September of 1997, Jobs was named interim CEO of Apple while a replacement for the ousted Amelio was sought.

Further Reading

Butcher, Lee, *Accidental Millionaire: The Rise and Fall of Steven Jobs at Apple Computer,* Paragon House, 1987.
Young, Jeffrey S., *Steve Jobs: The Journey Is the Reward,* Scott, Foresman, 1988.
Esquire, December, 1986, pp. 84-101.
Fortune, February 20, 1984, pp. 86-88.
Gentleman's Quarterly, October 1993, pp. 105-111.
Newsweek, January 30, 1984, pp. 54-57; September 30, 1985, pp. 46-50; October 24, 1988, pp. 46-51.
Rolling Stone, April 4, 1996, pp. 51 + .
Time, February 15, 1982, pp. 40-41; January 3, 1983, pp. 25-27; January 30, 1984, pp. 68- 69; February 19, 1996, pp. 43-47.
Business Week March 17, 1997, pp. 116. ☐

Joseph Jacques Césaire Joffre

The French marshal Joseph Jacques Césaire Joffre (1852-1931) was supreme commander of French armies in World War I until the end of 1916.

Born on Jan. 12, 1852, at Rivesaltes in the eastern Pyrenees, Joseph Joffre graduated from the college of Perpignan with high honors in mathematics and then entered the École Polytechnique in Paris. In the Franco-Prussian War he served in the army during the defense of Paris; afterward he resumed his education and in 1872 entered the engineering corps of the army. He worked on the fortifications of Paris and at the age of 24 was promoted to captain.

The death of his first wife led Joffre to request transfer to Indochina. He took part in the occupation of Formosa in 1885 and served for 3 years as chief of engineers at Hanoi. In 1892 he was sent to Senegal to build a railway, and in 1894 he led the successful attack on Timbuktu. Transferred to Madagascar in 1897, Joffre constructed the naval base of Diégo-Suarez and was subsequently made colonel.

Returning to France, Joffre won rapid promotion, becoming major general in 1905. In 1911, amidst the outcry after the second Moroccan crisis for unity of military command, Joffre was appointed to the combined functions of vice president of the Higher Council of War and chief of the general staff of the army. Under his auspices the Higher Council of War prepared Plan XVII, a campaign plan for possible war against Germany. Joffre believed that victory depended on preparedness and that national resources,

illuminates the political strife that eventually resulted in Joffre's loss of command. □

Robert Joffrey

Dancer and choreographer Robert (1930-1988) Joffrey's trailblazing Joffrey Ballet, which he created in the 1960s, continues to be one of the most popular and respected dance troupes.

A dancer and choreographer, Robert Joffrey stormed onto the American ballet scene with his first company in 1953. Never intending to become a professional dancer, Joffrey turned simple medical advice into a phenomenal career. He elevated ballet, the "conservative" art form, to new heights that were never thought of or attempted before including the production of one of the first rock ballets. Joffrey viewed ballet as not only a theatrical art form, but an art form that was forever evolving. Operating from this credo, Robert Joffrey created one of the most respected and best-known ballet companies of the 1960s. Even after Joffrey's death in 1988, the reputation and ability of his company continues to amaze viewers of all ages.

Dancer Realized

Robert Joffrey was born in Seattle, Washington, on December 24, 1930, to an Afghan father and an Italian mother. He was given the name of Abdullah Jaffa Anver Bey Khan. During his childhood, Joffrey experienced multiple bouts with various illnesses, most notably asthma. He was confirmed as suffering from chronic asthma in his youth by his family's doctor. Based on the advice of his physician, Joffrey took to dancing. The doctor believed that the breathing exercises taught to the children would help alleviate some of Joffrey's asthmatic conditions thereby making the task of breathing a little easier and his overall childhood a little better.

Formal Study and Instruction

At the age of 12, Joffrey began serious study of dance under the auspices of Mary Ann Wells. Through her guidance and care Joffrey began to excel at dance. He performed locally on several occasions throughout his teens and even presented a solo recital of his own choreography in 1948. When Robert Joffrey turned 18, he traveled to New York City where he enrolled and began study at the School of American Ballet. Additionally, Joffrey studied under Alexandra Fedoroua. Joffrey studied modern dance techniques under May O' Donnell and Gertrude Shurr. Joffrey made his professional dance debut with Roland Petit's Ballets de Paris during that troupe's 1949-1950 New York season. Shortly after, Joffrey was invited to perform in O'Donnell's troupe between 1950 and 1953. Joffrey performed as a soloist in the troupe, Miss O'Donnell's, during the 1953 season of "American Dance" at the Alvin Theater in New York. Even while dancing under the guidance and protection of these greats, Joffrey longed to establish his own company. Joffrey

brain power, and moral energy had to be oriented and organized in advance toward victory.

At the beginning of World War I, Joffre assumed command of all French armies, and on Dec. 2, 1915, this was reconfirmed by granting him the title of commander in chief. France hailed Joffre as a hero after his victory in the Battle of the Marne in September 1914, but disillusionment with the failures of 1915 encouraged attacks by Joffre's rivals and enemies. A dispute arose over the fortifications of Verdun between Joffre and the minister of war, Joseph Galliéni. When those defenses, still incomplete, failed to hold fully the German offensive in February 1916, a further confrontation between the two resulted in Galliéni's resignation. However, dissatisfaction with Joffre's management continued and grew, strengthened by the poor success of the Somme offensive and concern over the Germans' Verdun offensive. Therefore, in December 1916 Joffre was replaced by Gen. Robert Georges Nivelle.

Joffre remained in Paris as technical adviser to the government and was given the title of marshal of France. In December 1918 he was elected to the French Academy. Joffre spent his last years preparing his memoirs; he died on January 3, 1931.

Further Reading

Joffre's account of the Timbuktu expedition is *My March to Timbuktu* (1915). A contemporary evaluation of his career is in Charles Dawbarn, *Joffre and His Army* (1916). Jere C. King, *Generals and Politicians: Conflict between France's High Command, Parliament and Government, 1914-1918* (1951),

knew his ambitions lied there since the companies he worked with were either too restrictive or conservative in their approach to ballet. He continued, however, to study and master a variety of styles knowing that a successful company was dependent on successful dancers and an extensive repertoire of dances.

Student Becomes Teacher

During his early years, Joffrey earned a well-deserved reputation as not only a skilled dancer but an excellent teacher. He taught his students not only the dance technique but the interpretation as well. Between 1950 and 1955, Joffrey served as a faculty member at the High School of Performing Arts in New York City. He also served on the board and faculty of the American Ballet Theater School. Joffrey used his skills as a teacher to produce his first ballet. *Persephone,* Joffrey's first ballet, was produced utilizing students of the High School of Performing Arts. He also used the students to assist him in the production of his next two ballets as well. *Persephone,* was staged for the Choreographer's Workshop Program in 1952. His next two ballets, *Scaramouche* and *Umpateedle* were given in 1953 at Jacob's Pillow in Lee, Massachusetts, under the auspices of the Workshop as well. Joffrey's reputation as a consummate and creative professional was growing rapidly.

Professional Beginnings

Finally in 1953 Joffrey realized his long held dream. The Robert Joffrey Ballet Concert was formed in 1953 and first appeared at the YM-YWCA in New York City. Joffrey premiered two new ballets on that occasion, *Pas des Deesses* and *Le Bal Masque.* The ballet company was well-received. In 1955 his company was invited back and again Joffrey used the opportunity to premiere another grouping of ballets. The two ballets premiered on that occasion were *Harpsichord Concerto* and *Pierrot Lunaire.* During these years, Joffrey undertook a variety of choreography assignments. One such assignment included the summer series at the Seattle Aquatheater from 1954 to 1956. Between 1957 and 1962, Joffrey became the resident choreographer for the New York City Opera. Additionally, Joffrey staged dances for the NBC-TV Opera Theater in 1956, 1957, and 1958. Joffrey accomplished all this besides his already heavy teaching load. However, Joffrey realized in order to keep his fledgling company afloat financially, this work was necessary. Joffrey launched his company to tour with six dancers, one of whom was longtime friend, co-founder and associate director, Gerald Arpino, and a borrowed station wagon in 1956. The group immediately set out on a 23 United States city tour. The music they used was prerecorded by another dancer in the group who also played the piano. A crowning achievement for Robert Joffrey and his company came just one year earlier in 1955. Joffrey had attracted enough media and dance world attention to become the first American choreographer invited to stage his works for the prestigious Ballet Lambert in England. Joffrey performed *Pas des Deesses* and *Persephone* while exhibiting there.

National Recognition and Sponsorship

The spring of 1962 brought changing fortune to Joffrey's company. He had renamed his company the Robert Joffrey Ballet and had already completed six national tours with no external financial assistance. Joffrey knew that he had to obtain money from some source as creativity could not be stifled due to lack of resources. His company had now grown to 38 members including a small orchestra. The ballet owned a repertoire of 21 ballets including some by the American choreographers Todd Bolender and Job Sanders. Perhaps the biggest change of fortune for the company came when they were taken under the wing of a wealthy arts patron, Rebekah Harkness Kean. Along with the Harkness Foundation which was founded by Mrs. Kean in 1959 to help American dance, Robert Joffrey was now able to freely work on his first love, choreography and dance. The Harkness Foundation also sponsored Jerome Robbins's Ballet USA which was an African tour by Pearl Primus as well as the late summer seasons of dance in Central Park's Delacorte Theater. The sponsorship and generosity of the Harkness relationship toward Joffrey and his company resulted in great things. They were invited to spend the summer of 1962 in the Harkness estate at Watch Hill, Rhode Island. Six choreographers—Joffrey, Arpino, Nault, Donald Saddler, Brian MacDonald, and Alvin Ailey created a variety of works during that summer. All dances were then previewed that fall and those which were deemed a success were added to Joffrey's company's repertoire complete with set and costumes courtesy of the Harkness Foundation. Additionally Joffrey's company toured the Middle East and Southeast Asia sponsored in part by the President's Special International Program for Cultural Presentations. His company was able to do work such as this due to ties within the Foundation. Upon concluding a second summer at Watch Hill, the company appeared in a Ballet Gala program at the Harkness Dance Festival in Central Park.

In October of 1963, Joffrey's company was invited to perform at the White House by invitation of President John F. Kennedy. Shortly after, the company began a two-month tour of the Soviet Union sponsored in part by the State Department and the Harkness Foundation. This tour took the company to Moscow Leningrad, Donetsk, Kiev, and Kharkov. They were extremely well received up to the point of a 20 minute standing ovation after their debut in Leningrad. Unfortunately, for Joffrey's ballet though, the return to the United States meant significant changes.

End of Good Fortune

The Joffrey Ballet began a ten-week American tour once they returned to the United States. Near the end of the tour, March 16, 1964, came the news that stunned not only the dance world, but Joffrey's company as well. Rebekah Harkness announced that the Foundation was allocating more than one million dollars for the creation of the Harkness Ballet. Joffrey told the press that he was given an "ultimatum" to change the company's name while he retained artistic control. It was never clear as to how much control he would actually have let alone if he was really in real control over the direction of the company. Joffrey refused to rename his company and as a result he and his company were plunged into poverty. After two years, the relationship with the Harkness Foundation was over. This separation was crippling to the company. Most of the costumes, sets, and scores were owned by the Harkness Foundation even though they were created by Joffrey and his staff. Additionally, many of Joffrey's dancers were still under contract with the Foundation so it made performing for Joffrey's company very difficult, even impossible. Without equipment and dancers the Joffrey Ballet was all but finished.

Rebuilding a Career

Unlike other choreographers of his time, Joffrey possessed a certain resiliency and set about to re-build his company. By September of 1964 the Foundation for American Dance was chartered as a nonprofit, tax-exempt organization to support Joffrey's company. It was headed by a friend of Joffrey's who also served as the business manager during the Harkness years. The foundation immediately secured an emergency grant for thirty-five thousand dollars from the Ford Foundation. The re-organized company appeared at the June 1965 White House Festival of the Arts and then made its public debut in August at Jacob's Pillow. Additionally, Joffrey's company earned the opportunity to become the ballet in residence at the New York City Center when the New York City Ballet moved to the Lincoln Center of the Performing Arts. Though the financial troubles had not ended for Joffrey and his company, but the ballet's renewed eminence and prestige attracted help from important sources including a twenty-five thousand dollar grant from the New York State Council on the Arts which enable

the company to revive the 1932 antiwar masterpiece, *The Green Table,* by Kurt Joss. Additionally, the Ford Foundation provided a three year grant worth $500,000.

Death of a Dancer

Despite the setbacks and his extensive list of duties including artistic director of the City Center Joffrey Ballet and director of the American Ballet Center, Joffrey still found the time to enjoy leisure activities such as skiing and mountain climbing. Robert Joffrey also taught master classes, gave lecture-demonstrations and judged at master regional ballet festivals. He also pioneered the "crossover" ballet which included the rock classic ballet, *Astarte,* in 1967, and *Deuce Coupe,* in 1973. *Deuce Coupe* was developed in part with the modern dance choreographer Twyla Tharp. Joffrey also created *Rememberances* in 1973, *Beautiful Dreamer* in 1975, and *Postcards* in 1980. Robert Joffrey and his company have won many awards including those from the National Academy of Dance Masters at Chicago and from the Dance Masters of America. Robert Joffrey passed away on March 25, 1988, in New York due to ARC-Aids Related Complexes. These included liver and kidney aliments which resulted ultimately in respiratory arrest. However before passing on, Joffrey was able to prove his dictum that "ballet does not belong in the rarified realm of esoteric art, but . . . is a living, evolving form which is part of the 'theater' in its most comprehensive sense." The Joffrey Ballet, by which it is now known, has become one of America's major ballet companies. The company still performs annually based in both New York and Los Angeles. In true dedication, the company continues to pay tribute to their founder and dreamer, the remarkable Robert Joffrey. A man who, whatever the circumstances, never let the fire of his dreams become extinguished.

Further Reading

Holder, Christian, "A Rock Classic," in *Dance Magazine,* Vol. 68, August 1994, p. 28.
Hlibok, Bruce, *Silent Dancer,* Messner, 1981.
Solway, Diane, *A Dance Against Time,* Pocket Books, 1994. □

St. Isaac Jogues

St. Isaac Jogues (1607-1646), French Jesuit priest and martyr, was a missionary among the North American Indians.

Isaac Jogues was born in Orléans. He entered the Jesuit novitiate at 17 and became a priest in 1636. He went immediately to Canada as a missionary and from Quebec was sent to the Huron Missions on Georgian Bay. Later he proselytized among the so-called Tobacco Nation (the Petuns) south of the Hurons but failed to make any religious impression on them.

In 1642 Jogues returned to Quebec. In August he left again for the Georgian Missions with a party of Hurons and two French lay missionaries. At Lake Saint Peter they were attacked and captured by an Iroquois war party, which took them south to the Iroquois villages in present-day New York State. All underwent torture on the way; Jogues had his hands mutilated and fire applied to his body; he was near death several times but managed to struggle on. He was held captive from late 1642 to late 1643, undergoing constant ill treatment but never losing a chance to perform baptisms—frequently by stealth. The Indians had not the slightest understanding of Jogues's ceremony, and later he said that he had no idea why they refrained from killing him.

Jogues, now a slave, accompanied a group of Mohawks to the Dutch village of Rensselaerswyck (later Rensselaer, N. Y.), where the Indians traded for firearms. The governor of the town and a Protestant minister, who both spoke French, befriended Jogues and planned for his escape aboard a ship bound for New Amsterdam. This proved impossible, but the minister managed to keep Jogues with them until the governor of New Netherland arranged for the priest's ransom and transfer to New Amsterdam. Jogues sailed in a Dutch ship to Falmouth, England, and from there traveled to France, arriving on Christmas Day 1643.

Jogues was given a warm reception by the French Jesuits, who had already learned something of his captivity. The queen mother (Anne of Austria) and the ladies of the French court knelt to kiss his mutilated hands. Though those with physical deformities are barred from performing mass, Pope Urban VIII granted Jogues a special dispensation. In the spring of 1644 he departed again for Canada with no intention of returning to the Mohawks. However, he was persuaded in 1646 to head a government mission to them.

Because he came in lay dress and because the Mohawks for the moment wished peace with France, he suffered no injury.

Later that year the Jesuit mission superior asked Jogues to return to the dangerous post to continue his missionary work. He made his departure with a premonition of death, and on October 18 he was murdered by the Mohawks, who had always thought him a practitioner of evil magic.

Jogues was beatified by Pope Pius XI in 1925 and canonized by him in 1930. Jogues had accomplished little as a missionary, but his religious zeal and unflinching courage fully justified sainthood.

Further Reading

An old but still excellent account of Jogues is Francis Parkman, *The Jesuits in North America in the Seventeenth Century* (1867; 2 vols., 1897). There are two 20th-century biographies by American Jesuits: Francis Talbot, *Saint among Savages: The Life of Isaac Jogues* (1935), is a well-documented work; Glenn D. Kittler's briefer *Saint in the Wilderness: The Story of St. Isaac Jogues* (1965) is worthwhile, though Kittler apparently describes imagined incidents.

Additional Sources

Jogues, Isaac, Saint, *Narrative of a captivity among the Mohawk Indians,* New York: Garland Pub., 1977.
Shea, John Dawson Gilmary, *Perils of the ocean and wilderness,* New York: Garland Pub., 1976. □

Johanan ben Zakkai

The Jewish teacher Johanan ben Zakkai (active ca. A.D. 70) was the leading expounder of Jewish law of his time. He founded an important academy at Yavneh.

Johanan ben Zakkai was the youngest among the numerous disciples of the great Hillel and also of Hillel's opponent Shammai. It therefore appears that Johanan was born about 15 B.C. He evidently lived to a ripe old age, for he survived the destruction of the Holy Temple in Jerusalem (A.D. 70). Tradition speaks of his span of life as 120 years. His brilliant mind and diligence enabled him to become conversant with every field of Jewish learning.

Johanan ben Zakkai was a member of the Great Sanhedrin in Jerusalem, the assembly of 71 ordained scholars that functioned both as supreme court and as a legislature. In that body, Johanan, a Pharisee, often debated his Saducean colleagues on issues of Jewish law. While in Jerusalem, he also presided over an important yeshiva. Johanan foresaw that the Jews could not be victorious in their desperate struggle against Rome; he was determined, however, that Judaism should not perish even if the Jewish state and the Temple were destroyed.

While Jerusalem was under siege, Johanan was unable to receive permission to leave the city. He therefore had his pupils carry him out of Jerusalem in a coffin, presumably for burial. Once outside the city, Johanan went to see Vespasian and asked the Roman general to spare the town of Yavneh on the Mediterranean coast, together with its scholars. According to a Talmudic tradition, Johanan predicted to Vespasian that he would soon be chosen emperor, and when this came true, Vespasian granted the rabbi his requests. This was a turning point in Jewish history, for in this unimportant town of Yavneh, Johanan established an academy that had immense influence.

Johanan was not formally designated as Nasi, prince or head of the Sanhedrin, probably because he was not a descendant of Hillel or of Davidic stock, as Hillel was. He nonetheless assumed the duties of this office and the title of Rabban, meaning "our master," which was commonly attached to the rank of Nasi. Yavneh replaced Jerusalem as the new seat of a reconstituted Sanhedrin, which reestablished its authority and became a means of reuniting Jewry.

With the Temple gone, a substitute was necessary for the sacrificial cult. The aged Johanan suggested that the Temple worship be replaced by benevolent deeds; under his influence, the synagogue and house of study replaced the Temple. The important principle was thus established that Judaism does not depend for its existence on land or sanctuary but rather on the preservation of the Jewish spiritual heritage—the Torah and its teachings. This principle played a vital role in the survival of Judaism in the Diaspora.

True to the ideals of his master Hillel, Rabban Johanan advocated peace among men and nations. He was scrupulously ethical in all his dealings and behavior. He taught that the best character attribute a man could possess is a good heart, which he believed included all other virtues. His lofty attitudes and doctrines made Rabban Johanan ben Zakkai the most revered teacher of his times.

Further Reading

Jacob Neusner, *A Life of Rabbi Johanan ben Zakkai* (1960), is a good general study with a bibliography. The sage and his work are discussed in "Disciples of the Wise" in Louis Ginsberg, *Students, Scholars and Saints* (repr. 1945). A good sketch of Johanan ben Zakkai's work at Yavneh is in chapter 7 in George Foote Moore, *Judaism in the First Centuries of the Christian Era*, vol. 1 (1927). A historical account is in Heinrich Graetz, *History of the Jews*, vol. 2, translated by Henrietta Szold (repr. 1940). □

Johannes IV

Johannes IV (1836-1889) was an Ethiopian emperor who thwarted Egyptian, Italian, and Sudanese attempts to overrun Ethiopia and took important steps to unify the country.

Johannes IV was born in the northern Ethiopian region of Tigre with the baptismal name of Kassa. After inheriting his father's position of nobility in 1867, Kassa declared himself the independent king of Tigre. Two years later, when Takle Giorgis II, the reigning Ethiopian emperor, taunted Kassa into battle, the Tigrean king easily defeated and imprisoned the hapless emperor. Armed with the guns, ammunition, and military supplies abandoned earlier by a British expeditionary force, Kassa so built up his position that on Jan. 21, 1872, he was crowned emperor, taking the throne name of Johannes (John), after the writer of the Book of Revelation.

The opening of the Suez Canal in 1869, the Egyptian revival under Khedive Ismail, and shadowy Egyptian claims to portions of the Red Sea shore combined to pose a potential threat to Ethiopia. In 1875, however, the Egyptian forces that attempted an invasion were nearly annihilated by Emperor Johannes, who forced their immediate evacuation from Ethiopia. He then turned to internal problems.

Struggle against Invaders

The Emperor's main rival, Menilek of Shoa, was defeated after a short and decisive campaign in 1878 but was forced to pay little more than ceremonial homage to the Emperor. Throughout his reign, in fact, Johannes IV was willing to acknowledge the local rights of tributary kings, such as Menilek, provided they recognized his senior status. He later applied this pragmatic policy to areas of western Ethiopia in an attempt to modify the tradition of separatist feudal chieftains.

Throughout the 1880s Johannes was preoccupied with powers bent on territorial aggrandizement at Ethiopian expense: Italy in the Red Sea region and the revivalist Islamic state of the Mahdi in the Sudan. The Italians had purchased the important entrepôts of Assab and Massawa positioned dangerously near Ethiopian boundaries. When Johannes's efforts to negotiate with the Italians were marred by delays and diplomatic insults, the Emperor was eventually forced to attack the invaders, and in January 1887 ten thousand Ethiopian soldiers under Commander Ras Alula defeated an Italian force at Dogali. Johannes tried to arouse the entire nation against Italy, but local interests, especially those of Menilek, apparently prevented immediate action. Angered but not deterred, the cautious emperor then temporarily postponed his attack on the Italian main force.

Meanwhile the victories of the Mahdist state in the west posed a threat that also demanded immediate attention. Johannes sent a deputation to the area to arrange peace and to estimate the strength of the dervish forces. Though his position was difficult, he concluded in late 1888 that a military advance was imperative, hoping that a "final" victory over the Mahdi would leave him free to deal with the Italians and the recalcitrant Menilek. The Ethiopian army assaulted dervish fortifications and inflicted heavy losses on the Moslems, but on the verge of a brilliant victory Emperor Johannes was mortally wounded. As the news spread, the army faltered, withdrew, and finally scattered. Before his death on March 10, 1889, Johannes had tried to acknowledge his son Ras Mangasha as his successor, but the more powerful and influential Menilek of Shoa was proclaimed emperor.

Evaluation of His Reign

Emperor Johannes IV was a fervent Christian considered just and fair by most subjects. While some historians tend to view his reign as one marked by growing disunity, Johannes actually operated within the existing feudal structure, reached agreements with obviously localized leaders, and thereby contributed to a growing sense of interdependence between the provinces, particularly in certain struggles against foreign powers. This development was clearly important in repelling the attacks of Egypt and the Mahdist state and in keeping Italy at bay. That Ethiopia alone in Africa retained its independence in the European "scramble" for the continent must be attributed to the military skills of its generals and the diplomatic skills of its emperors. Menilek II's national victory over the Italians in 1896 assured Ethiopian independence, but the efforts of his predecessor, Johannes IV, to unify the country provided the bases for critical alliances that made the later national effort possible.

Further Reading

Although there is no biography of Johannes, aspects of his reign are examined in Thomas E. Marston, *Britain's Imperial Role in the Red Sea Area, 1800-78* (1961); Richard Greenfield, *Ethiopia: A New Political History* (1965); and the chapter by Harold Marcus in L. Gann and P. Duignan, *The History of Colonialism in Africa* (1969). Edward Ullendorff, *The Ethiopians* (1960), remains an excellent introduction to Ethiopian culture, while Donald Levine, *Wax and Gold* (1965), provides a perceptive anthropological account of Amhara society in Ethiopia. □

sented as one of the leaders of the Jerusalemite followers of Jesus. In the Acts, John testifies to Jesus with Peter and James. He goes to Samaria with Peter to confirm new converts (Acts 8:14, 25). When Paul is converted, he submits his orthodoxy to John, Peter, and James (Galatians 2:1-10).

It is not known how John ended his life. Some traditions claim that he was martyred. Others claim he died at a ripe old age. Tradition from the 2d century claimed that John died and was buried at Ephesus.

Considerable doubt, particularly by modern scholars, has been thrown on the identity of John as the author of the Fourth Gospel. Some claim that John, the son of Zebedee, is not the same as the author of the Gospel, the Book of Revelation, and the three Letters. It is certain that the Fourth Gospel was written a considerable time later than the other three Gospels. The Gospels speak of the "disciple whom Jesus loved"; it was long assumed that this was John, but the Gospel never identifies this disciple by name. Doubt has also been created by some scholars who have concluded that the three Letters were not written by the author of the Fourth Gospel.

Tradition relates that John was banished to the Greek island of Patmos during the persecution initiated by the Roman emperor Domitian (reigned A.D. 81-96). Here, it is said, John wrote the Book of Revelation. The Fourth Gospel apparently was composed sometime between A.D. 85 and 95.

St. John

St. John (active 1st century A.D.), one of the 12 Apostles chosen by Jesus, is traditionally considered the author of the Fourth Gospel, of the Book of Revelation, and of three Letters, or Epistles, bearing his name.

The son of Zebedee and Salome, John was born in Galilee, probably between A.D. 10 and 15. His father was a fisherman, a trade which John was plying when he met and joined Jesus (Mark 5:37). His mother joined the women who served the followers of Jesus (Mark 15:40-41; 16:1). His brother James also followed Jesus. Jesus nicknamed both brothers Boanerges, meaning in Aramaic "sons of thunder" (Mark 3:17), a reference to their rather fiery attitude to Jesus.

John and James, together with Peter, are presented throughout the Gospels as the most closely associated with Jesus of all his followers. John, with Peter and James, witnesses Jesus' supernatural communication with Moses and Elias on Mt. Tabor; he is present in the Garden of Gethsemane the night before Jesus dies. When all others leave the dying Jesus, John remains, and Jesus entrusts his mother, Mary, to John's care. After the death of Jesus, John is pre-

Further Reading

Works dealing with John include E. F. Scott, *The Fourth Gospel* (2d ed. 1930); Wilbert F. Howard, *Christianity according to St. John* (1943); Charles H. Dodd, *The Interpretation of the Fourth Gospel* (1953); and Aileen E. Guilding, *The Fourth Gospel and Jewish Worship: A Study of the Relation of St. John's Gospel to the Ancient Jewish Lectionary System* (1960).

☐

John

John (1167-1216) was king of England from 1199 to 1216. The Magna Carta, or Great Charter, was issued during his reign.

Born on Dec. 24, 1167, John was the youngest son of King Henry II and Eleanor of Aquitaine. When Henry first assigned provinces to his sons, John received no share, hence his nickname "Lackland." He grew up among family feuds, rebellion, and treachery. During his formative years, his mother was his father's prisoner, and his brothers quarreled with their father and among themselves and allied with the most dangerous enemy of their house, the king of France. In 1176 John was betrothed to Isabella, the richly endowed coheiress of the Earl of Gloucester; a year later Henry made him lord of Ireland. John repaid Henry's affection by joining his brother Richard and Philip II of France against him in 1189; his treachery was the final blow to his sick and defeated father.

When Richard the Lion-Hearted became king (1189) and was preparing to go on crusade, he made lavish grants to John in England and made him Count of Mortain, in Normandy, but excluded him from any share in the government. John was ambitious; he tried by every means to obtain power and recognition as Richard's heir, at least in England. He put himself at the head of the opposition to Richard's chancellor, William Longchamp, Bishop of Ely, and forced him out of the country but failed to bring over the Council of Regency to his treacherous designs. Richard's return resulted in his total discomfiture, but he eventually regained the King's favor and most of his property.

Loss of Normandy

On Richard's death (April 6, 1199) John was accepted in Normandy and England. He was crowned king at Westminster on May 27, Ascension Day. But Anjou, Maine, and Brittany declared for Arthur, son of his older brother Geoffrey, who had died in 1186. Philip of France, as overlord, claimed to have the power to adjudicate matters concerning the French fiefs; in May 1200 at Le Goulet he recognized John as heir to all Richard's lands in return for substantial concessions and an exceptionally large payment as "relief."

Shortly afterward, his first childless marriage having been annulled, John married Isabella, daughter of Adhémar, Count of Angoulême. His position in France was still precarious; Arthur, as a rival claimant, was a focus for rebellion in Anjou and Poitou. In 1201, in the course of a renewed dispute with John, members of the important family of Lusignan appealed against him to the court of King Philip. John dared not appear; his French fiefs were therefore declared to be forfeit, and Philip set out with an army to enforce the sentence. John captured Arthur, who was murdered, possibly by John himself (April 1203), but he could not oppose King Philip's advance. By July 1204 Normandy, which with short intervals had been united to England since 1066, was in the hands of the king of France.

Dispute with the Church

In July 1205 John lost one of his best advisers, Hubert Walter, Archbishop of Canterbury. As new archbishop, the monks of Canterbury chose first their subprior and then the King's nominee; Pope Innocent III rejected both and arranged the election of the learned Englishman Cardinal Stephen Langton. John declared that his customary rights had been infringed; he refused to admit Langton and seized the property of the monks. The Pope laid an interdict on England from March 24, 1208, and in November 1209 John was declared excommunicate (but not deposed, as is sometimes stated). He responded by seizing the property of the clergy and monks, who had to buy it back, and by keeping abbeys and bishoprics vacant.

Neither interdict nor excommunication seriously disrupted the government of England, but heavy taxes and capricious treatment of certain barons caused an alarming conspiracy against John in 1212, and he learned that the king of France was preparing an invasion. This dangerous situation led him to negotiate with the Pope. By a cunning stroke he turned this formidable opponent into his protector. In May 1213, having agreed to accept Langton, he made over England and Ireland to the Roman Church, to receive them back as fiefs on payment of an annual tribute.

Magna Carta

John now prepared a counterattack on King Philip. In 1214, in league with the emperor Otto and Philip's enemies in the Low Countries, he led an army into Poitou and Anjou. He had some success, but Philip's decisive victory over Otto and John's other allies at Bouvines (July 27, 1214) destroyed his hope of recovering Anjou and Normandy. This defeat reacted on his prestige at home, where he had already alienated powerful barons. In January 1215 John received demands for reform and promised to reply after Easter. Meanwhile, both sides gathered their forces, and both complained to the King's overlord, the Pope. But the Pope's attempts at peacemaking, heavily biased in favor of the King, only exacerbated the dispute.

In April 1215 John heard that a large group of barons had met in arms at Brackley and had renounced their fealty; on May 17 they were admitted to London. Negotiations went on for several weeks, but the King was temporarily outmaneuvered and was forced to restore lands and castles to his opponents. At the same time, he made more general promises of new reforms and of the observance of old customs in a comprehensive charter (Magna Carta) dated June 15, 1215, at Runnymede, between Windsor and Staines. The charter as a whole deserves its ancient reputation as a landmark in the struggle to secure government without oppression, efficiency without tyranny. Many of its clauses were designed to control the arbitrary behavior of the King and his officials; many others concerned the administration of justice. Two clauses (39 and 40) were of great importance in later times: the King promised not to act against free men except by judgment of their peers or the law of the land and never to sell, delay, or deny justice.

These promises were mostly unexceptionable and were the result of negotiations in which the King's advisers had hammered out terms with the rebels. Unfortunately, a "security clause" appended to the charter, imposed by the more extreme faction, made it unworkable. John was forced to authorize a committee of 25 barons to enforce the terms, even against himself, and to approve a general oath taking throughout the country in support of the 25. No medieval king could submit to such coercion; John claimed that his oath to observe the charter had been extracted by force and fear, and on these grounds the Pope immediately annulled it.

Compromise was now impossible. Civil war broke out in earnest later in the summer, and the rebels, their temporary military superiority reduced by the skill of the King and the efforts of his supporters, now adopted the aim of the extremists, the substitution of another king. Louis, son and heir of King Philip of France, was invited to claim the throne. Louis arrived in May 1216 and at first had some success, but again John recovered his position with the help of loyal barons and foreign mercenaries. His sudden death

at Newark on Oct. 19, 1216, robbed him of victory. He was buried at his own request next to St. Wulfstan in Worcester Cathedral. His death did indeed make the reconciliation of the rebels easier; within a year Louis retired from England, and the country settled down to the long minority of John's young son King Henry III.

Despite its stormy close, John's reign saw important developments in royal administration. There were experiments in methods of taxation and reforms of the Exchequer. The Chancery organized more elaborate and complete records than any contemporary state. The courts of Common Pleas and King's Bench became distinct, and better procedures were evolved for dealing with different types of action. Municipal self-consciousness was stimulated by the grant of royal charters to many towns and by increased trade.

Because of the loss of Normandy, the King and the aristocracy spent more time in England and identified themselves with English life and institutions; thus a long step was taken toward the formation of a unified English people.

Further Reading

Excellent for the general reader is W. L. Warren, *King John* (1961). Sidney Painter, *The Reign of King John* (1949), was intended as the first part of a large-scale study. J. C. Holt, *Magna Carta* (1965), supersedes earlier books on that subject. A. L. Poole, *From Domesday Book to Magna Carta* (1951; 2d ed. 1955), describes John's reign in England. There is a good short account of John's activities in France by F. M. Powicke in *The Cambridge Medieval History*, vol. 6 (1929). John's relations with the Church and the Pope are illustrated in *Selected Letters of Pope Innocent III concerning England*, edited and translated by C. R. Cheney and W. H. Semple (1953). □

John II

John II (1319-1364) was king of France from 1350 to 1364. Stubborn and greedy, he refused to heed good advice, and his reign was marked by social and economic crises.

The son of Philip VI of France and Jeanne of Burgundy, at the age of 13 John was married to Bonne of Luxemburg. He began his military career in 1340, as the commander of royal military forces in Hainaut. In 1341 he was his father's lieutenant in Brittany, and in 1344 he held the same office in Languedoc.

Shortly after his coronation in 1350, John II began the round of banquets, festivals, and tournaments that characterized his reign, and he continued the recently established French royal tradition of lavishly dispensing artistic patronage. His ill-considered attachment to favorites, however, created hostility among the higher nobility, and his employment of men in high public office who exploited their power for private gain contributed substantially to the crisis of public finance that culminated in the 1350s, a point of economic crisis for all of Christendom.

John's inability or unwillingness to deal with political crises diplomatically alienated his powerful cousin and rival Charles (the Bad) of Navarre, who remained John's most dangerous subject throughout his reign. In 1355 the war with the king of England, later called the Hundred Years War (1339-1453), resumed. John sustained a stunning defeat by Edward the Black Prince at Poitiers on Sept. 19, 1356. Captured by the English, he was taken in 1357 to England as a prisoner until his enormous ransom could be paid.

John's misrule had created a social and economic crisis in France. As early as 1351 the coinage, for example, had to be debased, and his humiliation and disaster at Poitiers inspired a revolutionary faction of the Estates General to make strong demands for reform upon the regent, John's son Charles, later King Charles V. From 1356 to 1358 these demands and the later uprising known as the Jacquerie threatened France with political and social chaos. By 1359, however, Charles had managed to restore some public order, and in 1360 he signed the Treaty of Brétigny, which set John's ransom at an impossibly high figure, and promised to give hostages to the English until the ransom was paid.

John returned to France to resume his governance and raise his ransom, but with little success or good judgment in either project. In 1363 one of his sons escaped from the English, to whom he had been given as a hostage for his father. John II returned voluntarily to England to finish his own captivity. He died in England in April 1364.

Although John's reign failed to guide France in its quarrel with England or forestall its economic and social crisis, it did witness the beginning of a standing army, the regularization of extraordinary taxation, the patronage of the arts, and, in spite of John's repeated personal failures, the immense, politically creative prestige of the king of France.

Further Reading

There is no adequate biography of John in English. The best and most recent discussion of John's reign and its contemporary background is in Kenneth Fowler, *The Age of Plantagenet and Valois* (1967). A lengthier discussion is in E. Perroy, *The Hundred Years War* (1945; trans. 1951). The contemporary view of John's reign is in Jean Froissart, *The Chronicles of England, France, and Spain* (many editions). □

John III

John III (1629-1696), King of Poland, also called John Sobieski, saved the country from Turkish and Tatar invasions, becoming the hero of Europe by raising the siege of Vienna in 1683.

John, or Jan, Sobieski was born at Olesko near Lvov, Poland, on Aug. 17, 1629, the eldest son of Jakób Sobieski, commander of the Cracow fortress. He began his education at home, continued it at Cracow, and completed it with a tour of Germany, Holland, France, and England. His powerful physique and keen intelligence quickly earned him the reputation of a good soldier, and his amorous exploits proclaimed him an extraordinarily successful lover. Typical of the arrogant and unruly Polish aristocracy, he pursued his own fortunes, often at the expense of his country. He firmly opposed the non-Christian Tatars and Turks, serving in wars against the Cossacks and Tatars, and became commander in chief of all Polish forces in 1668.

Much of his political ambition he owed to his wife, Maria Kazimiera d'Arquien, whom he married in 1665. Tied by her connections to the pro-French faction in the Polish Diet, Sobieski plotted to overthrow the weak king, Michael Wisniowiecki, in 1669. His plot discovered, Sobieski redeemed himself in a brilliant campaign against the Turks, culminating in the victory of Khotin on Nov. 11, 1673.

At the moment of Sobieski's triumph, King Michael died. The victorious general hurried to Warsaw seeking the throne; with a force of 6,000 veterans he overawed the elective Diet and was proclaimed king in 1674. He immediately began clearing Poland of Turks and Tatars, a task accomplished before his triumphant coronation at Cracow on Feb. 2, 1676.

In 1682 John III overcame his distrust of the Hapsburgs and, against the wishes of French supporters, allied with Austria against the Turks. Cooperating with Duke Charles of Lorraine, his former rival for the Polish throne, he led the combined imperial and Polish forces at the battle of the Kahlenberg on Sept. 12, 1683, crushing the Turkish armies besieging Vienna. It was Sobieski's finest hour; he was hailed as a hero throughout Europe.

After Sobieski's campaigns to conquer the Danubian province of Moldavia failed, he returned to Poland in 1690 in broken health. Bitterness and humiliation filled his last years as he tried to secure the royal succession for his ambitious but inept and treacherous son Jakób. Poland's aristocratic constitution, which could turn any conspiracy into an occasion for civil war, frustrated his efforts to create a strong hereditary kingdom, opening the way for foreign intervention in Polish affairs. Although Poland's most popular monarch, Sobieski failed, as others had, to overcome the disruptive power of his own noble caste. He died on June 17, 1696, leaving the Polish throne a pawn of European power politics.

Further Reading

There is a wide literature on John Sobieski in many languages. The best scholarly biographies are by O. Laskowski, *Sobieski, King of Poland* (1944), and O. Forst de Battaglia, whose original German work appears in a much-condensed English version in the first volume of the *Cambridge History of Poland* (1947). J. B. Morton, *Sobieski, King of Poland* (1932), is a popularized account. □

John XXIII

John XXIII (1881-1963) was pope from 1958 to 1963. He convoked the Second Vatican Council, thus launching a renewal in the Roman Catholic Church and inaugurating a new era in its history.

The future pope was born Angelo Giuseppe Roncalli at Sotto il Monte (Bergamo), Italy, on Nov. 25, 1881, the third child and eldest son in the family of 13 born to Giovanni Battista and Marianna Giulia (Mazzola) Roncalli. The boy's forebears for several generations had been tenant farmers on an estate, and even when he reigned in the Vatican, his brothers were still engaged in eking a plain livelihood out of the hard and unfriendly Bergamo soil.

The simple piety of Italian peasants was the most important element in the life of the Roncallis and led Angelo, following elementary education, to enter the diocesan minor seminary in Bergamo at the age of 12. His studies for the priesthood continued at the Seminario Romano ("Apollinare") in Rome but were interrupted for a year of volunteer service in the Italian army. He was ordained on Aug. 10, 1904, and shortly thereafter was named secretary to the new bishop of Bergamo, Count Giacomo Radini-Tedeschi.

The latter was an extremely vigorous, farseeing prelate deeply concerned about social reforms, and the young Father Roncalli, during the 9 years that he served him, gained invaluable knowledge and experience in the problems of the working class and the poor. Simultaneously he taught patrology and Church history in the Bergamo seminary. Radini-Tedeschi died in August 1914, just as World War I was breaking out, and since his successor was a man of quite different temperament, Roncalli decided to enlist. He served first in the medical corps and later as a lieutenant in the chaplains' corps.

At the war's end Pope Benedict XV, who as a close friend of Radini-Tedeschi had come to know Roncalli, asked him to handle the arrangements for the 1920 Eucharistic Congress in Bergamo; and it was undoubtedly as a result of the way in which he organized this event that a year later he was made director of the Italian Society for the Propagation of the Faith. This was a delicate assignment since it involved not only modernizing the society but detaching responsibility from numerous regional directors and centralizing administration in Rome. He remained in this post for 4 years, until Pius XI appointed him apostolic visitor to Bulgaria. For this it was desirable that he hold a higher ecclesiastical rank, and he was named titular archbishop of Areopolis and consecrated to the episcopate on March 19, 1925.

Diplomatic Career

This was the beginning of a diplomatic career which was to last for almost 30 years and take Roncalli to many

European countries. In Bulgaria, since the state religion was Orthodox, his presence was resented by both government and Orthodox Church authorities. Yet he managed to provide spiritual leadership for the 40,000 Latin-rite and 4,000 Eastern-rite Catholics scattered thinly among the population. In 1934 he was named apostolic delegate to Turkey and Greece, where his position was, if possible, even more precarious. The Turkish government of Kemal Atatük was aggressively antireligious, but Roncalli, by personal charm and diplomatic finesse, managed to be on friendly terms with authorities.

During World War II, Istanbul, as the capital of a neutral power, was a hotbed of intrigue and espionage, and Roncalli provided the Holy See with much valuable information gleaned from personal contacts as well as official connections. He was instrumental in helping many Jewish refugees fleeing from central Europe through his friendship with the German ambassador to Turkey, Franz von Papen. In Greece his efforts were less successful, since he was of the same nationality as the occupying troops; but here, too, he worked hard to provide food, shelter, and safety for many thousands of refugees.

In 1944, following the liberation of France, Pius XII named Roncalli papal nuncio to that country. The position was even more difficult and challenging than his earlier ones, since the nation was split by many bitter political and religious divisions resulting from the period of occupation and resistance. Roncalli labored patiently and skillfully to repair them, maintaining cordial relations with the governments that came and went in rapid succession. Among other things he was instrumental in securing government subsidies for pupils in private schools, and he viewed with sympathy the "workerpriest" movement.

On Jan. 12, 1953, Pius XII elevated Roncalli to the Sacred College of Cardinals, and on Jan. 15, in accordance with long-standing tradition, he received his red hat from President Vincent Auriol in the Élysée Palace. On that same day he was named patriarch of Venice and took possession of his new see on March 15. This enabled him to be at last what he had always wanted to be, a "shepherd of souls"; and during his years in Venice he was a vigorous and much-loved prelate, visiting all the parishes in his diocese and creating 30 new ones. He erected a new minor seminary, initiated various forms of Catholic Action, and showed special concern for the poor.

Pius XII died on Oct. 9, 1958, and on Oct. 25 Roncalli entered the conclave which was to choose a successor. He was himself elected 3 days later and took the name John XXIII, the first pope to bear this name since 1334.

His Pontificate

John XXIII was 76 years old when he came to the papal throne, and his age—plus the fact that he was not widely known—led many persons to assume that he would simply be a transitional or "caretaker" pope. Inevitably his reign was brief, but in terms of its significance and its effects upon religious and world history it was perhaps the most important pontificate since the Middle Ages.

Much of this significance stemmed, naturally, from the train of events which he set in motion during the 5 years of his reign, but much of it also lay in his unique personality. Previous popes had usually been remote and austere figures; from the very outset John endeared himself to the whole world by his warmth, humor, and easy approachability. He had an impatience with empty traditionalism and often astonished his aides by the forthright way in which he cut through meaningless formalities.

For example, it had always been customary for the pope to dine alone; within a week after his election John announced that he could find nothing in either Revelation or canon law that required such a thing and that henceforth, when the mood was upon him, he would have guests in to dinner. He became the first pope in 200 years to attend the theater by having T. S. Eliot's *Murder in the Cathedral* performed before him in the papal apartments. He literally horrified Vatican officials and the Italian government by having his chauffeur drive him unannounced and unescorted through the streets of Rome. He visited—sometimes at very short notice-hospitals, nursing homes, and even prisons. (It is said that when he declared his intention of paying a Christmas visit to Rome's Regina Coeli prison, one of his aides protested that there was simply no protocol for such a thing, and the Pope replied," Well, then, make some!")

The conclave that had elected Pope John had been reduced to 52 cardinals, of whom 12 were more than 80 years old; one of his first acts was a consistory (Dec. 15, 1958) at which he elevated 23 prelates to the Sacred College, including many younger and more vigorous men. By so doing he broke the rule, established in 1586 by Sixtus V, limiting the number of cardinals to 70 and also gave the College much wider geographical representation than it had known until that time. In three subsequent consistories he expanded the membership to 87, its highest figure to that date.

But the most momentous act of his pontificate was, of course, his decision to call an ecumenical council of the Universal Church, the first since 1870 and only the twenty-first in the Church's 2,000-year history.

Following the definition of papal infallibility at Vatican I, it had been assumed in many quarters that there would never again be need for a council. Pope John's motive in calling one was, as he said, to bring about a renewal—a "new Pentecost"—in the life of the Church, to adapt its organization and teaching to the needs of the modern world, and to have as its more far-reaching goal the eventual unity of all Christians. The term which he used to describe what he had in mind—and which was to become a kind of keynote for the Council in the years that followed—was *aggiornamento,* an Italian word literally meaning "bringing up to date."

In addition to the frequent and demanding general audiences, Pope John met with many outstanding world figures. Among those received at the Vatican during his reign were Queen Elizabeth II of England, U.S. president Dwight D. Eisenhower, Mrs. Jacqueline Kennedy, the Shah of Iran, and—in a move which surprised many—Alexei Adzhubei, son-in-law of Soviet premier Nikita Khrushchev and editor of the Russian newspaper *Izvestia*. This last reception appeared part of a gradual relaxation of the hitherto implacable hostility between the Church and communism, at least one practical result of which was the release of the Ukrainian archbishop Josyf Slipyi, who had been imprisoned for years in Siberia by Soviet authorities.

International tensions and the crises generated by "hot" and "cold" wars also greatly preoccupied the Pontiff. In September 1961 he issued an urgent appeal to the heads of the governments involved in the threatening Berlin crisis. He endeavored to mediate between the French government and the revolutionaries in the Algerian crisis of June 1962. He made an especially fervent appeal to President John F. Kennedy and Premier Khrushchev during the Cuban missile crisis of October 1962. It was undoubtedly in recognition of his untiring efforts to bring about world peace that the International Balzan Committee awarded him its Peace Prize in 1962.

Second Vatican Council

After 3 1/2 years of intensive preparation, the Second Vatican Council convened in St. Peter's on Oct. 11, 1962. In his memorable opening address Pope John declared that its purpose, unlike that of many previous councils, was not to condemn error but rather to study more deeply the truths of Catholic teaching and to offer those truths to the modern world in a language that would be meaningful and relevant to it. "The substance of the ancient doctrine of the deposit of faith," he said," is one thing, and the way in which it is presented is another." And he emphatically disagreed with the "prophets of gloom" who saw the modern world as heading toward disaster. During the Council's first session, which lasted from Oct. 11 to Dec. 8, 1962, Pope John took care that its members should work in an atmosphere of complete freedom.

But Pope John was not destined to see the end of the Council which he had started. Even while the first session was in progress, it became evident that he was not in good health, but only those closest to him were aware—as he himself was—that he was suffering from a gastric cancer which, because of his great age, was considered by the doctors to be inoperable. During the following months his condition gradually worsened, and much of the time he was in great pain. He appeared at his window overlooking St. Peter's Square for the last time on May 23, 1963. Shortly thereafter he was confined to bed, and during the next few days he sank rapidly. At one point he did rally enough to talk to members of his family and to tell his physician, "My bags are packed and I am ready, very ready, to go." He passed quietly away on June 3, 1963, mourned as perhaps no other figure in world history had been and was interred in the crypt of St. Peter's 4 days later. On Nov. 18, 1965, his successor, Paul VI, announced that beatification procedures had been initiated for him as well as for Pius XII.

Pope John and Christian Unity

One of the most notable features of Pope John's reign was the great advance in ecumenical relations between the Catholic Church and other religious bodies. He envisioned Christian unity as one of the ultimate goals of the Council, and one of the bodies that he set up for the Council's work was the Secretariat for Promoting Christian Unity, under the chairmanship of the Jesuit cardinal Augustinus Bea. This body was subsequently raised to the dignity of a full commission. Large numbers of Protestant and Orthodox clergy were invited as observers to the Council. Pope John met with them on a number of occasions and—as with everyone else—completely won them over by his warmth, simplicity, and openness of manner. In December 1960 he received at the Vatican the archbishop of Canterbury, Geoffrey Francis Fisher—the first meeting ever held between a Roman pope and an Anglican primate. A year later, in November 1961, history was made again when for the first time the Catholic Church was represented at a meeting of the World Council of Churches: Bea's office sent five official priestobservers to the Third General Assembly in New Delhi.

Pope John's ecumenical efforts, however, were not confined to Protestantism. Catholic theologians met with members of the Orthodox Church for discussions at Rhodes in August 1959, and the Holy See sent envoys to Patriarch Athenagoras of Constantinople in June 1961. And he showed equal consideration to those of the Jewish faith: one of his acts, seemingly trivial but actually bearing immense significance, was his directive to remove from the centuries-old Good Friday liturgy its reference to the "perfidious Jews."

His Encyclicals

Pope John issued eight encyclicals during his reign, and at lest two deserve to be ranked with the most important documents of Church history. These are *Mater et Magistra* (Mother and Teacher), issued May 15, 1961, and *Pacem in terris* (Peace on Earth), dated April 11, 1963.

Mater et Magistra restated the social teaching of the Church as set forth in Leo XIII's *Rerum novarum* and Pius XI's *Quadragesimo anno* but greatly amplified it in the light of later developments and problems. Among other things, the Pontiff pointed out the right that all classes have to benefit from technological advances and stressed the obligation of large and wealthy nations to assist underdeveloped ones. It was perhaps natural that the son of a poor farming family should lay special emphasis on the necessity for improved agricultural methods in still backward countries.

Pacem in terris was unique among papal encyclicals in being the first one ever addressed not just to Catholics but " to all men of good will." Pope John enumerated the rights of the human person—to life, to respect, to freedom, to an education, to be informed, and numerous others—and dwelt at length on the obligations of the citizen to the state and of states to their citizens and to each other. He pleaded for the banning of nuclear weapons and an end to the arms race. Pointing out that the problems of modern times could not be solved unilaterally, he expressed hope that the United Nations would prove an ever more effective instrument for mutual cooperation among nations and for the preservation of world peace.

His Importance

John XXIII, the son of simple Italian peasants, never lost either the simplicity or the humility that were part of his origins. It was precisely these qualities, indeed, that made him so unique in his times. Unlike his predecessor and successor, he was not a scholar or a theologian (though he was a highly cultured man with a profound knowledge of history, a love for literature, art, and music, and a fluency in many languages); but he had an intuitive understanding of people and problems that enabled him to deal with them in way that scholars perhaps could not have done. It is no exaggeration but a literal truth to say that he loved everyone, and that this in turn caused everyone to love him.

In an age largely given over to secularism, he not only increased the prestige of the papacy but also restored the importance and relevance of religion to a degree that few would have thought possible. By concentrating on what unites men rather than on what divides them, he took the first steps toward the eventual unity of all Christians. When he was elected, many thought that his pontificate would be a transitional one, and in a sense this was true. The transition, however, was not merely from one pope to another, but also and especially from an old to a new era of religious history.

Further Reading

A primary source is Pope John's own *The Journal of a Soul* (1965; trans. 1965). Among the biographies of Pope John are Paul Christopher Perrotta, *Pope John XXIII: His Life and Character* (1959); Aradi Zsolt, *Pope John XXIII* (1959); and Alden Hatch, *A Man Named John* (1963). Other works on him are Francis X. Murphy, *Pope John XXIII Comes to the Vatican* (1959), and E. E. Y. Hales, *Pope John and His Revolution* (1965).

Additional Sources

Bonnot, Bernard R., *Pope John XXIII: an astute, pastoral leader,* New York: Alba House, 1979.

Hebblethwaite, Peter, *John XXIII, pope of the council,* London: G. Chapman, 1984.

Hebblethwaite, Peter, *Pope John XXIII, shepherd of the modern world,* Garden City, N.Y.: Doubleday, 1985.

John XXIII, Pope, *Journal of a soul,* Garden City, N.Y.: Image Books, 1980.

Johnson, Paul, *Pope John XXII,* Boston, Little, Brown 1974.

Zizola, Giancarlo, *The utopia of Pope John XXIII,* Maryknoll, N.Y.: Orbis Books, 1978. □

St. John Chrysostom

The Christian preacher St. John Chrysostom (ca. 347-407) was bishop of Constantinople. A renowned orator, he earned the epithet Chrysostom, or "golden-mouthed," and is a Father of the Church.

Born at Antioch in Syria, John studied there as a young man with eminent teachers of rhetoric, philosophy, and theology. Adopting the life of Christian asceticism, he practiced austerities so severe as a desert recluse that his health collapsed, forcing him to return to his native city about age 33.

At Antioch, John was ordained deacon in 381 and presbyter 5 years later. As preacher, he drew the enthusiastic approval both of his bishop and of the Christian laity. His sermons are notable for their attention to the historical meaning of Scripture as opposed to allegorical interpretation, for their concern with practical moral application, and for their pungent thrusts against the loose morality of a city nominally Christian.

The fame of John's preaching spread to Constantinople, capital city of the empire. In late 397 he was virtually kidnaped and taken by military escort to Constantinople, where under pressure from figures in government and Church he reluctantly agreed to be consecrated bishop of that city. The ascetic and outspoken bishop was, tragically, not a sufficiently astute tactician to save himself from downfall. His personal simplicity of life, his determination toward moral reform of the clergy, and his caustic comments on the follies and vices of life at the court created enemies, the most powerful of whom was the scheming empress Eudoxia. She found a convenient ally in Theophilus, Bishop of Alexandria, who had long harbored resentment over John's elevation to the bishopric of Constantinople.

John was providing sympathetic shelter in Constantinople to four monks, known from their stature as the Tall Brothers, who were enthusiasts for the teachings of Origen and who had been expelled from Egypt by Theophilus. Arriving in Constantinople ostensibly to defend his expulsion of the Tall Brothers, Theophilus gathered 36 bishops hostile to John at a synod in the Palace of the Oak at Chalcedon, across the straits from the capital. There in 403 John was condemned in absentia on charges which included sponsoring heretical teachings of Origen and making treasonable statements about the Empress.

The synod was followed by an edict of banishment from the Emperor, which in spite of a temporary recall led to John's exile in 404 to a tiny village in distant Armenia. His continuing wide influence through correspondence from his place of exile prompted the government to order that he be marched on foot to a more remote and desolate place on the Black Sea. The hardships of the march killed him in September 407, before he reached his destination. A new emperor, Theodosius II, penitent for the injustice perpetrated by his parents, had John's body transported back to Constantinople in 438.

Further Reading

The standard work on St. John Chrysostom is C. Baur, *John Chrysostom and His Time* (trans., 2 vols., 1959-1960), which is very detailed and supplies complete bibliographical data. A shorter treatment is Donald Attwater, *St. John Chrysostom: Pastor and Preacher* (1959). See also the Reverend William Richard Stephens, *Saint Chrysostom: His Life and Times* (1872). □

River, to govern nearly half of the effective territory of Brazil at that time. Captivated by the beauty of Brazil, the governor general put to work some 46 scholars, scientists, and artists to study and to depict the land. He was representative of a curiosity the Dutch displayed toward the tropics, a curiosity which the Iberians hitherto had lacked. That curiosity prompted the Dutch to make the first and for a long time the only scientific study of the tropics. Albert Eckhout and Frans Post painted magnificent canvases portraying the Dutch colony. Willem Piso studied tropical diseases and their remedies. Georg Marcgraf made collections of fauna, flora, and rocks. The Dutch maintained an aviary as well as zoological and botanical gardens. The first European astronomical observatory and meteorological station in the New World were built by the Dutch in Brazil.

Economic matters quite naturally commanded much of John Maurice's attention as well. In an endeavor to avoid monoculture, he tried to make the colony self-supporting in foodstuffs. By reducing taxes and providing liberal credit terms to planters to rebuild ruined sugar mills and to buy slaves, he rehabilitated the sugar industry, which was well on its way to recovery from the ravages of fighting when he left. The Dutch profited from the most productive sugar-producing region in the world during the first half of the 16th century.

With genuine sadness John Maurice returned to Europe in 1644. He fought again in the Thirty Years War. In 1647 the elector of Brandenburg named Maurice governor of Cleves. He died in Cleves on Nov. 20, 1679.

John Maurice of Nassau

John Maurice of Nassau (1604-1679) was a Dutch military officer whose rise to power paralleled Dutch ascendancy in the Atlantic; his years as governor general of Netherlands Brazil marked the apogee of Dutch authority in South America.

John Maurice, who bore the title Count of Nassau-Siegen, was born on June 17, 1604, in the family castle at Dillenberg, Germany, scion of a famous European family. He received a thorough Calvinist education at Herborn, Basel, and Geneva. As early as 1620 he took up arms with the Protestants in the Thirty Years War; by 1626 he reached the rank of captain, and 3 years later he was promoted to colonel. Meanwhile, Dutch power was spreading through the North and South Atlantic. In 1630 Dutch arms triumphed in Recife, and the Dutch West India Company seized northeastern Brazil. From that powerful company, John Maurice accepted the post of governor general of Netherlands Brazil in 1636 and disembarked in Recife, its capital, on Jan. 23, 1637.

John Maurice presided over the most fruitful years of Dutch occupation, 1637-1644. He successfully expanded Dutch occupation from Maranhão to the São Francisco

Further Reading

Information on the life of John Maurice is in Pieter Geyl, *The Netherlands Divided, 1609-1648* (trans. 1936) and *Orange and Stuart* (1939; trans. 1969), and in Nina Brown Baker, *William the Silent* (1947). □

St. John of Damascus

The Syrian theologian St. John of Damascus (ca. 680-ca. 750) opposed the Byzantine emperor in the controversy over religious images. He is considered the greatest medieval theologian of the Eastern Church.

Little is known of the early life of St. John of Damascus. He was born and raised in Damascus a half century after the Moslems began to rule Syria. His father, an important official in the court of the Caliph, was allowed to practice the Christian religion. When John took over his father's position at court, he was familiar with both Islam and Christianity. John eventually left the service of the Caliph to seek the solitude of a monk's life and entered the monastery of St. Sabas near Jerusalem. Soon his reputation for holiness and intelligence made him a popular and respected preacher in the city of Jerusalem. Because of his background at court and his common sense, a number of bishops came to the monastery to seek his advice. John was loved and respected by those who came in contact with him.

The Byzantine emperor Leo III, the Isaurian, issued in 726 a decree forbidding images in churches. John, the learned theologian and articulate preacher, quickly entered the controversy. Leo had ordered that all statues and pictures of religious subjects be removed from the churches because he felt they were close to idolatry. The Church officials of Constantinople protested strongly, and many of the people, aided by the monks, resisted vigorously when the Emperor's soldiers came to remove the statues from the churches.

From his position of relative security in Moslem territory, John wrote and spoke freely against the iconoclasts, the "image breakers," as those who supported the Emperor came to be known. His reasoning was so clear and forceful that his tracts became the principal weapons of those who opposed the Emperor. John argued that if God himself became flesh, then material things cannot be evil and are not to be rejected as aids to religious feeling. Images, he said, are the books of the unlearned, lifting them up from the symbol to that which the symbol points to. In 787, long after John's death, the Seventh Ecumenical Council, meeting in Constantinople, ended the controversy by decreeing that images be restored to the churches.

John's most important work is the *Fountain of Knowledge,* presenting a closely reasoned system of theology based on the Scriptures and Church Fathers. It had wide influence in the Middle Ages in western Europe.

Further Reading

St. John's *Writings* (1958), translated by Frederic H. Chase, includes the principal works and a biographical introduction. Herbert Packenham-Walsh, *Lights and Shades of Christendom to A.D. 1000* (1936), includes a chapter on John and the iconoclastic controversy. See also Francis Patrick Cassidy, *Molders of the Medieval Mind: The Influence of the Fathers of the Church on the Medieval Schoolmen* (1944); Henry Daniel-Rops, *The Church in the Dark Ages* (1950; trans. 1959); and William Ragsdale Cannon, *History of Christianity in the Middle Ages: From the Fall of Rome to the Fall of Constantinople* (1960). □

John of Gaunt

The English soldier-statesman John of Gaunt (1340-1399), 5th Duke of Lancaster, played an active part in military and political affairs.

Born in March 1340, John of Gaunt was the fourth son of Edward III and received his name from his birthplace, Ghent. He was created Earl of Richmond in September 1342. Trained in military skills, at the age of 19 he took part in an expedition to France, and on May 19, 1359, he married Blanche, younger daughter and coheiress of Henry of Lancaster. Through this marriage he was created Earl of Derby in April 1362 and in November Duke of Lancaster.

For the next years Lancaster was active in various military campaigns, serving under his brother Edward the Black Prince in Spain in 1367, as captain of Calais 2 years later, and in 1371 as lieutenant of Aquitaine. After the death of his first wife in September 1369, he married Constance of Castile in 1372, surrendered his title of Earl of Richmond, and assumed the title of king of Castile.

Upon his return to England Lancaster took an active part in politics as head of the court party that was opposed by the "Good Parliament" of 1376. At the same time he supported John Wyclif and protected him from the Londoners at the Council of London the following year. With the accession of Richard II in 1377, Lancaster had great influence at court, advising on the French war, serving on the Scottish border and making a truce there in 1380, and serving on several commissions the following year to deal with the rebellion of 1381 and the reform of the royal household.

Lancaster continued to serve Richard II in other roles: negotiating peace with France and dealing with the Scottish border. But in 1385 he fought with the King and, though reconciled, continued to serve as a mediator between the King and his opponents. In 1388 he was made lieutenant of Guienne and in 1390 Duke of Aquitaine, but he failed to have the latter claim recognized. After he married his daughter Catherine to Henry of Castile, he gave up the claims to the kingship of that country, and after effecting a reconciliation between the Duke of Gloucester and Richard, Lancaster retired from active politics. With the death of

his second wife, in 1396 he married Catherine Swynford. He died in early February, 1399.

After Lancaster's death Richard seized his estates, which caused Lancaster's son, Henry of Bolingbroke, to claim the throne as Henry IV. The children of his last marriage, known as the Beauforts by patent in 1397, were the line through which Henry Tudor (Henry VII) claimed the throne.

Further Reading

The standard biography of John of Gaunt is Sydney Armitage-Smith, *John of Gaunt* (1905; repr. 1964). Information on the period can be found in Sir James H. Ramsay, *Genesis of Lancaster* (1913), and May McKisack, *The Fourteenth Century* (1959). ☐

John of Leiden

The Dutch Anabaptist John of Leiden (1509-1536) led the Anabaptist attempt to establish by force a "kingdom of God" in Münster, Germany. His excesses unfairly discredited all Anabaptists in the eyes of contemporaries and of succeeding generations.

Also known as Jan Beuckels or Bockelszoon, John was born in a village near Leiden. He practiced various occupations, including those of tailor, merchant, and innkeeper. In November 1533, having been baptized by John Matthys of Haarlem, John became a follower of Anabaptism. He grew quite active in this religious movement and was sent by John Matthys to various parts of the Netherlands as an apostle for this faith. His views at that time were the conventional and generally peaceful Anabaptist ones of the need for the faithful to pray and await the coming of the kingdom of God. But he gradually abandoned those principles in favor of calling the faithful to use the sword against all unbelievers in order to establish the kingdom of God on earth.

In January 1534 John of Leiden took up residence in the episcopal city of Münster in Westphalia, Germany, near the Dutch border. Although he was very active in the revolt that overthrew the bishop and city council, it was John Matthys, who had arrived in Münster in February 1534, who took over power and began the establishment of the kingdom of God. Under his direction, Münster was purged of the "godless," or nonbelievers, and communism of goods, based on biblical texts, was introduced. Matthys, however, was killed in April 1534, and John then replaced him as the new Anabaptist leader in Münster, gaining supreme power by July 1534. Although he effectively coordinated the defense of the city against the army of the bishop of Münster, who had laid siege to the city, his ambition and fanaticism soon led him into more radical behavior. In July 1534 he introduced polygamy, a step that created much opposition. In order to maintain his position, he became increasingly ruthless in the exercise of his power. In September he had himself crowned king of the New Jerusalem. After this, John lived in an increasingly unreal world, parading around Münster in lavish regal costumes and promising his followers to lead them miraculously to the defeat of the besieging army. He managed, however, to keep the city from falling to the episcopal army until June 25, 1535.

John of Leiden was then arrested, sentenced to death, and executed with horrible tortures on Jan. 22, 1536. His brief reign had tragic consequences for Anabaptism, since contemporaries identified all Anabaptists with the radical variety in Münster. Such an identification led to a constant persecution of Anabaptists by Lutherans, Calvinists, and Catholics.

Further Reading

For a brief account in English relating John of Leiden's role in the Münster affair see Cornelius Krahn, *Dutch Anabaptism: Origin, Spread, Life, and Thought, 1450-1600* (1968). See also Ernest Belfort Bax, *Rise and Fall of the Anabaptists* (1903; repr. 1966), and John Christian Wenger, *Even unto Death: The Heroic Witness of the Sixteenth-century Anabaptists* (1961). ☐

John of Piano Carpini

The Italian traveler and Franciscan monk John of Piano Carpini (ca. 1180-1252) journeyed across central Asia and was the first European to write a detailed account of the Mongol Empire.

John was born in Umbria, probably at Pian' di Carpini (now Piano della Magione). He was attracted by the preaching of Francis of Assisi, and by 1220 he was a member of Francis's order. Friar John's practical sense and his capacity for long and hard work soon led him to be placed in charge of Franciscan efforts in other parts of Europe, and for several years he was superior of the order in Germany.

In 1241 the Mongols, or Tatars, came across Russia and invaded eastern Europe, causing great destruction in Poland, Hungary, and parts of Germany. Four years later Pope Innocent IV decided to send a formal protest to them. He chose Friar John, in his mid-60s but still vigorous and determined, for the mission.

John and two companions set out from Lyons on Easter Sunday 1245. They crossed Germany and Poland and were allowed to go to the camp of the western commander of the Mongols on the shores of the Volga River in Russia. After explaining his mission, John was allowed to proceed to Mongolia. On Easter Sunday 1246 the three friars began a long and difficult journey across central Asia, their bodies tightly bandaged to protect against the hardships of their ride. They reached Karakorum in eastern Asia, center of the Mongol kingdom, on July 22, making the trip of 3,000 miles in just 106 days.

A month after they arrived, the friars witnessed the formal installation of Genghis Khan's grandson as the new emperor, and it was to him they presented the Pope's message. The Khan sent them back with a brief reply in which he completely dismissed the Pope's protest and asserted that he would continue to act as the scourge of God against Christian Europe. The three left the Khan's court in November and returned through the harsh winter months, taking more than twice as long as they had to journey to the Mongol kingdom. When they reached Kiev in western Russia on June 9, 1247, they were greeted by the Christian community as men risen from the dead.

After making his report to the Pope at Lyons, John wrote a long, clear, clam book about the Mongols. This work, which provided the Middle Ages with the first authoritative account of the mysterious people from the East, still ranks among the finest journals of exploration. Nearly 70, John was made bishop of Antivari in Dalmatia and continued his diplomatic missions until his death on Aug. 1, 1252.

Further Reading

The best English translation of John's description of the Mongols is in *The Mongol Mission: Narratives and Letters of the Franciscan Missionaries in Mongolia and China in the Thirteenth and Fourteenth Centuries,* edited by Christopher H. Dawson (1955). An account of his journey and its importance is in Willem van Ruysbroek's 13th-century *The Journey of William of Rubruck . . . with Two Accounts of the Earlier Journey of John of Pian de Carpini,* translated and edited by William Woodville Rockhill (1900). More recent works which discuss John are Donald F. Lach, *Asia in the Making of Europe* (1 vol. in 2, 1965), and R. A. Skelton, Thomas E. Marston, and George D. Painter, *The Vinland Map and Tartar Relation* (1965). □

John of Salisbury

The English bishop and humanist John of Salisbury (c. 1115-1180) is generally considered to have been the most cultured man of his day. He associated with great scholars, rulers, and churchmen, and his writings testify to the wide scope of his interests.

John was born in Old Sarum near Salisbury. In 1136 he began a career as student and then scholar in the schools of Paris (where he studied with Peter Abelard) and Chartres, then the center of humanistic studies of the arts and of the Latin classics. He became proficient in rhetoric, literary analysis, logic, and law, both ecclesiastical and Roman.

In 1148 John probably entered the service of Theobald, Archbishop of Canterbury, where he remained until 1150, when he went to Rome to assume a post of uncertain nature in the Papal Curia. From 1153 or 1154 he was again at Canterbury, as Theobald's private secretary. In 1159 John completed his first major work, *Policraticus,* or *Statesman's Book. Policraticus* was the first medieval study of the state and the prince; John's analyses of the conduct of good and bad princes testify to his understanding of the new power attained by centralized authority in the 12th century, thanks to the end of the Viking invasions and the development of stable feudal relationships.

The *Metalogicon,* written shortly after *Policraticus,* is a work of educational theory, assessing the role of the arts and defending them against narrow-minded critics. John utilized in *Metalogicon* the newly discovered works of Aristotle, which would dominate education in the following century.

About this time (1162), Thomas Becket, whom John had befriended while Becket was still chancellor of England, succeeded Theobald as archbishop. John sided with Becket in his controversy with Henry II of England and in 1164 went into voluntary exile because of his views. Early in 1170 he returned to England and was present at Becket's martyrdom on December 29. While in exile, he had written the *Historia pontificalis* (probably begun in 1164; *Papal History*), an unfinished but fascinating account of the papal court during the years 1148-1152.

John remained at Canterbury, at work on an unfinished biography of Becket, until 1176, when he was elected bishop of Chartres, an office he held until his death on Oct. 25, 1180. Charitable, honest, and reasonable, he appears in all his works as a model Christian humanist.

Further Reading

The source of most information about John is his letters, a collection of which, edited and translated by W. J. Millor and S. J. and H. E. Butler, was revised by C. N. L. Brooke (1955). The best introduction to John is the biography by C. C. J. Webb, *John of Salisbury* (1932). Hans Liebeschütz, *Medieval Humanism in the Life and Writings of John of Salisbury* (1950), provides the intellectual context for John's career. ☐

St. John of the Cross

The Spanish Carmelite St. John of the Cross (1542-1591) is the most important mystical writer in the Catholic tradition. He also played a leading role in the 16th-century reform of the Carmelites.

Juan de Yepes, later St. John of the Cross, was born at Fontiveros. His father died when Juan was 2 years old and left the family of three children penniless. After they all moved to Medina del Campo, the boy tried several trades without success. Excellent at school, he continued his studies at the Jesuit college in Medina. In 1563 he became a novice at the monastery of St. Ana in Medina. His superiors sent him to the University of Salamanca, where he was ordained a priest in 1567.

In 1568 the reformer and mystic Theresa visited John's monastery of Medina to discuss the possibility of including male monasteries in her reform of the Carmelite order. Both John and the prior of the house went over to the Primitive Rule, and John was the first friar to enter the first foundation, Duruelo. After some short stays in Pastrana and Alcalá, John joined Theresa as confessor in the unreformed Carmelite convent of Ávila, of which she had become prioress. During this period they stayed in constant spiritual contact, in which John was Theresa's director as well as her spiritual son.

Meanwhile, the opposition between Discalced (reformed) and Calced Carmelites, which had existed from the beginning, took on alarming proportions. In 1575 John was abducted and imprisoned by the Calced friars. He was set free at the request of the papal nuncio. But the same occurred again in 1577, and this time he had to escape. For safety he stayed in remote places in Andalusia. During those years of obscurity he wrote most of his mystical works.

After the two branches of the order were finally split, John remained in the south but regained status as vicar provincial. It was only toward the end of his life, in 1588, that he returned to Castile as prior of the house of Segovia and as councilor of the provincial. Because of his disagreement with the radical, innovative provincial, he was soon removed from office and sent back to Andalusia, where he died after an excruciating agony in 1591. He was canonized in 1726 and pronounced a Doctor of the Church in 1926.

His Works

The work of St. John consists of poetry and of mystical commentaries that he wrote on some of his poems. Best known are *The Spiritual Canticle, The Living Flame of Love, The Dark Night of the Soul,* and *Ascent of Mount Carmel* (the last two works comment on the same poem). It is not easy to define the nature of those commentaries since they are at once didactic (often in a scholastic way) and obscurely symbolic. The traditional division of spiritual life into the three ways of purgation, illumination, and union provides the basic framework for all John's treatises. Yet the order of succession appears clearly only in *The Spiritual Canticle.* In *The Ascent of Mount Carmel* and *The Dark Night of the Soul,* the process of spiritual life is considered mainly from the purgative point of view: to reach the union of light the soul must pass through the night of purification. Yet in this purifying night John also includes the illumination of faith and even the union with God. The soul can be fully purified only in the highest mystical states. The three ways, then, must not be considered as definitive stages of a rectilinear succession. Their nature is cyclical; that is, they appear at each level of the mystical life.

The Ascent of Mount Carmel deals primarily with the early stages of spiritual life, the *active* purification of the senses (Book I) and of the spirit (intellect, memory, and will, Books II-III). The *passive* purgation is described in *The Dark Night of the Soul.* Here also the purgation of the senses (Book I) is distinguished from that of the spirit (Book II). The union with God is treated explicitly in *The Spiritual Canticle* and *The Living Flame of Love.*

Aside from being the most important Christian mystical writer, John is one of the greatest poets in the Spanish language. His prose has been influential on the development of the literary language of his culture.

Further Reading

The best-known English translation of St. John's works is Edgar Allison Peers, *The Complete Works of St. John of the Cross* (3 vols., 1934-1935). Several recent translations of the poems, all entitled *The Poems of Saint John of the Cross,* are by Willis Barnstone (1968), which includes a good bibliography; by Roy Campbell (1951), which is perhaps less felicitous than Barnstone's rendering; and by John Frederick Nims (1968), which is faithful to the originals, includes the Spanish text, and provides an introduction by Robert Graves. The classic biography is Gabriele di Santa Maria Maddalena, *St. John of the Cross* (trans. 1946). Other studies include Edgar Allison Peers, *Spirit of Flame* (1943); Robert Sencourt, *Carmelite and Poet* (1944); and Leon Cristiani, *St. John of the Cross* (trans. 1962). Interpretive and critical discussions are in Edgar Allison Peers, *Studies in the Spanish Mystics* (3 vols., 1927-1960), and E. W. Trueman Dicken, *The Crucible of Love* (1963).

Additional Sources

Cumpiano, Marion, *Saint John of the Cross and the dark night of FW,* Colchester, Essex: Wake Newsletter Press, 1983.

Hardy, Richard P., *God speaks in the night: the life, times, and teaching of St. John of the Cross,* Washington, D.C.: ICS Publications, 1991.

Peers, E. Allison (Edgar Allison), *Spirit of flame: a study of St. John of the Cross,* Philadelphia: R. West, 1978. ☐

John Paul I

John Paul I (1912-1978) was pope only from August 26 to September 28, 1978, the shortest term in modern times.

The future 262nd pope of the Roman Catholic Church was born Albino Luciani in the town of Canale d'Agordo in mountainous northeastern Italy on October 17, 1912. Unlike his predecessor Paul VI who came from a well-to-do family, Luciani's parents were very poor (his mother was a scullery maid and his father was an itinerant stonemason). In fact, his younger brother Edoardo told reporters at the time of Albino's election as pope that as children they both had had to go without shoes half the year. Albino did well in school and by the fourth grade had determined that he wanted to be a priest. He began his seminary studies at Feltre, Italy, when he was 11, studied at the major seminary at Belluno, and was ordained a priest on July 7, 1935. During the summers of his student years he would return home to work in the fields.

Luciani's first assignments were to parish duties in his home area. From 1937 to 1947, however, he taught at the major seminary in Belluno, while earning a doctorate in theology at the Gregorian University in Rome with a dissertation on the controversial 19th-century Italian theologian Antonio Rosmini. From 1948 to 1952 he was in charge of religious education for the diocese of Belluno, and one of his biggest successes was publishing a popular little book called *Catechisi in Briciole* (*Catechetical Crumbs*). His next assignment was as vicar general (administrator) of the diocese of Belluno, during which time he opposed the priest-worker movement—the first of what proved to be numerous conservative stands.

In 1958 Pope John XXIII named Luciani bishop of Vittorio Veneto in northern Italy. The new bishop's first crisis was a local scandal in which two priests of his diocese had swindled tens of thousands of dollars from contributions of the laity. Luciani made restitution for the theft and laid the foundations of a fine reputation for honesty and directness. His pastoral style was to make the rounds of his parishes on a bicycle, and he downplayed the rings, jewels, and ceremonial splendor that his office could command.

The Second Vatican Council (1962-1965) had a considerable influence on Bishop Luciani, for it forced him to develop somewhat beyond his instinctive conservatism. He was slow to accept the collegiality (greater play given to the role of bishops) that seemed to be detracting from the absolute authority of the pope, and he opposed efforts to stress the church's role in promoting social reform. He also opposed moves by German and Dutch bishops to drop celibacy as a requirement for the priesthood and to admit women as priests. Still, he stayed in contact with progressive bishops and won a reputation for being more affable than the typical staunch conservative. Another important experience came when he was appointed to Pope Paul VI's international commission that studied the possibility of changing the church's traditionally negative stand on artificial birth control. Luciani himself thought change possible, but when the pope's 1968 encyclical *Humanae Vitae* reasserted the traditional prohibitions he fell in line behind the pope's stance.

In 1969 Paul VI appointed Luciani archbishop and patriarch of Venice (an auspicious appointment, because two 20th-century popes, Pius X and John XXIII, had headed the Venetian patriarchate prior to their election). In Venice he continued his policy of simplifying the bishop's lifestyle and trying to serve the poor. He also attacked the immorality of the Venetian film festival, efforts of priests to involve themselves in politics, governmental moves to repeal Italy's strict laws on divorce, and the growing strength of the Italian Communist Party.

Luciani, now a cardinal, was elected pope in 1978, three weeks after the death of Paul VI. Most commentators considered him a good political choice: Italian, yet not identified with the Curia (the Church's administrative arm); conservative, yet possessed of good relations with liberals and leaders of third-world dioceses. The press quickly dubbed him "the smiling pope" because of his manifest joy and good nature. In appearance the new pope seemed frail. He wore his hair closely cropped, peered out from under heavy brows through rather strong glasses, and had a large broken nose. His voice tended to crack; his hands moved when he spoke; and he suffered from rheumatism. In addition, he had been operated on for gallstones and eye problems. (Since birth his health had been frail.)

The pope's intelligence, along with his warm smile, simplicity, and dedication to the poor, led many to hope for a return to the style of Pope John XXIII. Paul VI had worked tirelessly for peace and justice, yet toward the end of his pontificate he had seemed almost crushed by controversies within the Church, especially those stemming from the debates over birth control and priestly celibacy. The new pope seemed likely to continue Paul's policies, but many hoped he would seem more at ease personally and be able to show greater flexibility. His best known writings, a series of imaginary letters to famous historical figures collected under the title *Illustrissimi* (a literary salutation), revealed a man who loved literature and who himself could write well. When he addressed such luminaries of the past as Sir Walter Scott and Mark Twain, Luciani expressed a wideranging humanism. His letter to the English novelist Charles Dickens, for example, praised the attacks on the oppressors of the poor that Dickens' works carried. It seemed possible, even likely, therefore, that humanism, simplicity, and concern for the poor would be hallmarks of the new pope's leadership. Although Luciani ate sparingly, he smoked and enjoyed a glass of wine—traits that further humanized him and suggested a man at home in God's world.

All of this was rendered idle speculation, however, for the pope suddenly and shockingly died in his sleep on September 28, 1978, having been officially installed less than a month. Once again the cardinals had to troop to Rome for a papal election, and their choice of Karol Wojtyla, a Pole, quickly put the brief rule of John Paul I in the shade. Wojtyla took the name John Paul II in honor of his two immediate predecessors, Paul VI and John Paul I. Like them, he pledged himself to implement the reforms and teachings of the Second Vatican Council. The first impressions of people knowledgeable about Vatican affairs were that he was chosen for his conservative doctrinal stands and for his considerable experience in dealing with Communists. As he proved increasingly rigid on infra-church matters, commentators again speculated from time to time on what "the smiling Pope" might have done differently.

Further Reading

The best view of Pope John Paul I comes from his own book *Illustrissimi: Letters from Pope John Paul I* (1978). The future pope wrote to both past saints and pagans, letting their literary works stimulate his reflections on faith and life. Most of the other treatments of John Paul I either concentrate on his death or treat him as part of the Roman Catholic Church's amazing changes from the time of Pope Pius XII, through the time of Pope John XXIII and the Second Vatican Council, to the pontificates of the two men who flanked him, Pope Paul VI and Pope John Paul II. See, for example, Andrew M. Greeley, *The Making of the Popes 1978* (1979) and Gordon Thomas and Max Morganwitts, *Pontiff* (1983). Good brief sketches of John Paul I were published by *Newsweek* and *TIME* in their editions for September 11, 1978.

Additional Sources

Hebblethwaite, Peter, *The year of three popes,* London: Collins, 1978.
O'Mahony, T. P., *The new pope: the election, the man, and the future,* Dublin: Villa Books, 1978. □

and in 1958 he was consecrated auxiliary bishop of Krakow. In 1962, upon the death of Archbishop Baziak, Wojtyla became the vicar capitular or administrative head, and in 1964 he became archbishop of Krakow. Paul VI made him a cardinal on May 29, 1967, in good part because of the fine impression he had made during the Second Vatican Council (1962-1965).

Dealing with Communist Poland

In Poland Bishop Wojtyla, along with his patron Cardinal Wyszynski of Warsaw, was a rallying point for anti-Communist religious people. The bishop tended to show himself more flexible than the hard-line cardinal, and constantly his patriotism kept him from supporting any movements against the government that would do the people or the land more harm than good. The Communist government came to look upon him as a formidable foe, for he was an attractive public figure: handsome, strong, a good speaker, and a penetrating intellectual. First as bishop and then as archbishop and cardinal, Wojtyla fought for the Church's rights to full religious practice and expression of opinion.

During the Second Vatican Council he had contributed to the Catholic Church's broadened appreciation of religious liberty, and he impressed many of the Church's princes as a strong leader with first-hand experience of what Communist rule could mean. In fact, in 1976 Pope Paul VI invited the then Cardinal Wojtyla to preach the annual Lenten Retreat to the pope himself and members of the Curia that work in Rome as the pope's right arm. (These

John Paul II

Karol Wojtyla (born 1920), cardinal of Krakow, Poland, was elected the 263rd pope in 1978, the first ever of Slavic extraction.

Karol Wojtyla was born May 18, 1920, in Wadowice, Poland, the second child of Karol Wojtyla, Sr., an army sergeant, and Emilia (Kaczorowska) Wojtyla. His mother died when he was nine. His only sibling, a much older brother Edmund (a physician), died four years later; and Karol Senior died in 1942. These sorrows of early family life, along with the hard times that Poland experienced both prior to World War II and throughout it, were bound to give an intelligent young man cause for sober reflection. In 1939, under the Nazi occupation, he enrolled at Jagiellonian University in Krakow, and shortly thereafter he began secret studies for the priesthood. Publicly, however, he worked as a laborer in a quarry and a chemical factory.

After World War II, upon ordination to the priesthood on November 1, 1946, Wojtyla did pastoral work with Polish refugees in France and then did graduate studies at the Angelicum University in Rome run by the Dominicans. When he returned from these studies to his native Poland, Wojtyla was assigned to parish work and soon became well-known for his successes in youth ministry. He was then assigned to teach ethics at the Catholic University of Lublin,

sermons were published in English under the title *Sign of Contradiction* in 1979.)

When Pope Paul VI died in August 1978, and then scarcely a month later his successor, Pope John Paul I, died unexpectedly, the stage was set for a more dramatic occurrence. On October 16, 1978, on their eighth ballot, the cardinals assembled in Rome for the papal election chose Karol Wojtyla as the first non-Italian pope in 455 years and the first Slavic pope ever. The new pope, who chose the name John Paul II in honor of his immediate predecessors (John XXIII, Paul VI, and John Paul I), quickly showed himself to be a charismatic figure. From his student years in Rome he retained fluent Italian, and his powerful figure (5'10'', 175 lbs.), so greatly contrasting with the frail Paul VI, radiated strength. Speculation was rife about what sort of pontiff he would prove to be, all the more so since his election had caught the "pope-watchers" off-guard. In their bones they had become so used to Italian popes that a non-Italian seemed a practical impossibility.

Early Years as Pope

Pope John Paul II plunged into a whirlwind of activity from which he scarcely rested. In January 1979 he made his first trip abroad to Latin America. He also discouraged priests and nuns—the most visible representatives of the hierarchical church—from direct or full-time political activities. For example, he ordered the American Jesuit priest, Father Robert Drinan, who had been a congressman from Massachusetts for ten years, to resign his office.

The crowds who greeted the pope in Latin America exceeded all expectations, but the atmosphere of his return to his native Poland less than six months later was even more emotional. For nine days in June of 1979 he walked in the midst of Eastern Europeans, symbolizing their Christian roots and a culture that greatly predated the more recent invasions of either Communists or Nazis. The Polish government understandably was uneasy, if not embarrassed, but there was little they could do in the light of the pope's status as a national hero. At the end of September 1979 the pope flew first to Ireland and then to the United States, bringing his message of justice, peace, and the rightness of traditional Catholic morality.

After these early trips Pope John Paul II consolidated his reputation as the most travelled pope of all history. He met with the archbishop of Canterbury, head of the Anglican Church; with German Lutherans who stand in the tradition of the Protestant Reformation; and with Africans and Asians—all on their own soil (which he usually kissed when he deplaned). The personal danger in these trips was brought home to the world on May 13, 1981, when the pope was shot in Rome by a Muslim fanatic reputed to be in the employ of the Bulgarian Communist government. Not long after his return to nearly customary vigor he began planning for future trips, telling his aides that his life belonged to God and the people much more than to himself.

The Pope as Teacher

Pope John Paul II's first encyclical (a papal letter addressed to the bishops of the church or to a specific group or country), *Redemptor Hominis* (*Redeemer of Man,* came in March 1979, only five months after his election. It was a rather general and not wholly cogent piece that clearly expresses the pope's conviction that the redemption offered in Christ is the center of human history. (In apparent contrast to many of his predecessors, John Paul II wrote his own encyclicals, producing longhand drafts in Polish that were then translated into Latin and Italian.) The second encyclical, *Dives in Misericordia* (*Rich in Mercy*), appeared in December of 1980. Its theme was the mercy of God and the need for human beings to treat one another mercifully, going beyond strict justice to the love and compassion that human suffering ought to create.

The third encyclical, *Laborem Exercens* (*Performing Work*), was delayed by the pope's shooting but finally appeared in September of 1981. Because of the tense contemporary situation in Poland, where the labor union Solidarity was standing off against the Communist government, the encyclical's references to "solidarity" (between the pope or Christian teaching and working people) was read as a sign of the pope's awareness that what he was saying applied "in spades" to his native land.

Apart from the reference to Poland, this third encyclical made the deepest impression because it was a strong statement in the tradition of the "social encyclicals" of the recent popes. *Laborem Exercens* made it clear that the pope, for all his anti-Communism, is no friend of traditional capitalism. Moreover, the pope echoed the traditional Christian teaching that the goods of the earth come from the Creator God and are for all the earth's people. He affirmed the basic rights of working people to a fair wage, decent housing, good education, health care, and the like, which his predecessors had affirmed.

A Man of Firm Beliefs

John Paul II continued to be absolutely opposed to abortion, to allow only "natural" methods of birth control (which in fact have become considerably more sophisticated), to condemn homosexual activity (which he distinguished from being a homosexual), and to forbid even serious discussions of women's ordination to the priesthood.

On his trips abroad, especially those to Africa and Latin America, the pope puzzled both commentators and theologians by, on the one hand, manifesting a great interest in and support for the world-wide diversity of Roman Catholicism and, on the other hand, seeming to be inflexible in the face of demands for more local autonomy (in liturgical matters and tribal mores, for example).

By the mid-1980s, Pope John Paul II was considered a brilliant linguist, a devoted churchman, a charismatic leader, and an intriguing blend of conservatism and progressivism. On matters outside the Church, especially those of world-wide peace and economic justice, he had almost radical ideas for change and manifested great compassion for the world's starving and suffering peoples. On matters inside the Church, especially the explosive matter of the rights and roles of women, he apparently had no willingness to put the axe to the root and break up old structures or patterns of thought that many find unjust. He continued to impose his own traditional beliefs on a church that seemed to want more diversity in many areas.

In his many travels John Paul II continued to press toward his goal of advancing international consciousness on two ethical fronts: socio-economic justice and personal sexual restraint. Visits to Chile, Argentina, Poland, and the United States in 1987 stressed these points.

The millennial celebration of the introduction of Christianity to Russia in 1988 furnished the occasion for renewed attention to Catholic-Orthodox relations. Most commentators ranked the pope's 1988 encyclical *Sollicitudo Rei Socialis* on social justice as one of his most substantial documents. It threaded a middle ground between capitalist and socialist positions, arguing for both proper economic development and placing the needs of the poor over the wants of the wealthy.

Key events of 1989 included a protest by German Catholic theologians against Vatican control, a bitter controversy in Poland about a Carmelite monastery at Aushwitz, pressure for more religious freedom for Catholics in the Baltic nations, a visit of Soviet President Mikhail Gorbachev to the pope in Rome, and discussions with the Archbishop of Canterbury about Catholic-Anglican relations (which the Anglican consideration of ordaining women to the priesthood had complicated). The major papal visits were to Africa, Scandinavia, South Korea, Indonesia, and East Timor, an area fraught with Catholic-Muslim tensions.

Pope Confronted "New World Order"

Catholic-Orthodox relations absorbed the pope in 1990, as events moved swiftly in the Soviet Union. Protests within the theological community continued to accuse the Vatican of heavy-handedness in doctrinal matters. Rumors circulated that the pope was ill, but he traveled to Czechoslovakia, Mexico, and Africa, on the last trip confronting the growing epidemic of AIDS. The 1991 encyclical *Centesimus Annus,* along with the pope's statements on the Gulf War, made him a critic of the "new world order" based on democratic capitalism being proposed by American President George Bush.

The pope ran a synod in Rome in 1992 to focus the church on the new situation in Europe, where the breakup of the Soviet Union was changing many relationships. Catholic-Orthodox and Catholic-Anglican relations dragged along, making any easy estimate of the pope's "ecumenical" ambitions impossible. The Vatican proceeded with its plan for a universal catechism that might unify basic instruction in faith throughout the church. In July the pope had a serious operation for the removal of a precancerous intestinal tumor and appeared to recover well.

No Compromise on Moral Issues

During 1993 John Paul II had to confront the pedophilia crisis that had developed in the United States, where numerous priests were accused of having abused children and the church was accused of ignoring it or covering it up.

Against that backdrop he brought to an international youth convention in Denver a stern message of traditional sexual morality, including not only opposition to abortion but also opposition to contraception. In October he published a large encyclical on moral issues, *Veritatis Splendor* (The Resplendence of Truth), the burden of which was that the Christian moral life demanded heroism; certain traditional teachings never change; some acts (genocide, abuse of the innocent) are intrinsically evil; and recent technical developments in moral theology casting doubt on such traditional positions are unacceptable.

Pope Embraced the People

This prolific pope departed from his customary encyclical, or papal letter, in 1994 to publish a book, *Crossing the Threshold of Hope,* which became an international bestseller. John Paul II reached out to the masses, the public responded, and *Time* magazine named him the Man of the Year. The book received wide critical acclaim for addressing today's major theological concerns, and further established John Paul as a great intellect and teacher of our time. As the year progressed, the pope's general health improved and he recovered from a fall that occurred earlier in the year.

Long known for being dedicated to social justice, John Paul issued a strong message in his 1995 encyclical entitled, *Evangelism Vitae* or *Gospel of Life.* He confronted the issues of abortion, assisted suicide, and capital punishment making a plea to Roman Catholics to "resist crimes which no human law can claim to legitimize." He spoke out invoking the full teaching authority of the church to declare abortion and euthanasia always evil, and denouncing the moral climate of affluent western nations. He referred to an "eclipse of conscience" in the name of individual freedom pursued by many. A second encyclical entitled *Ut Unum Sint* or *That They May Be One* was released in 1995. In this letter, for the first time in Church history, he acknowledged and apologized for past sins and errors committed in the name of the Church. Admitting painful things have been done that harmed Christian unity, he accepted responsibility and asked for forgiveness in the hope that Christians could have "patient dialogue." The pope also carried out a demanding travel schedule, beginning the year by going to Australia, followed by a trip to Bosnia, and in the fall visiting several cities in the United States. While in New York City, he addressed the United Nations General Assembly during its 50th anniversary ceremonies.

Church business claimed John Paul's attention in 1996. Several major changes were instituted at his urging; for instance, he ruled that the next pope will be elected by an absolute majority. Analysts said such a change could discourage compromise and consensus in the selection of future popes. Although John Paul himself was a compromise candidate, some believed this was an intentional move to ensure succession by another conservative pope.

As the millennium neared, John Paul reiterated that his mission was to usher the Church into the twenty-first century. His legacy was already long, having been hailed for reinvigorating young people's interest in religion, lauded for his role in bringing about the demise of communism in his native Poland and the former Soviet Union, and credited for reaching out to the peoples—and religions—of the world. He was the first modern pope to enter a synagogue or to visit an Islamic country.

Further Reading

The pope's own writings don't reveal as much about the man himself as one might expect, yet certainly they area good place to begin. The pope's views of the Second Vatican Council may be gleaned from his commentary on the documents *Sources of Renewal* (1980). Representative speeches from his first journey to Latin America are available in *John Paul II in Mexico* (London, 1979). Works by Andre Frossard *Be Not Afraid* (1984) and Mary G. Durkin *Feast of Love* (1983) give his views, respectively, on matters of general faith and matters of sexual love. Finally, a fascinating (but unreliable) account of the pope's life is Antoni Gronowicz's *God's Broker* (1984).

Additional information on Pope John Paul II can be found in David Willey's *God's Politician: Pope John Paul II, the Catholic Church and the New World Order* (1993). A related volume is Gene Burns' *The Frontiers of Catholicism: The Politics of Ideology in a Liberal World* (1993).*His Holiness: John Paul II and the Hidden History of Our Time* shows how the pope's influence goes far beyond the church by Carl Bernstein and Marco Politi (1994). *Pope John Paul II: The Biography* by Tad Szulc (1995) can also be consulted for good information. □

St. John the Baptist

St. John the Baptist (4? B.C.-31? A.D.) is important in Christian tradition as the forerunner of the Messiah, Jesus of Nazareth.

The two ancient sources that speak of John are the Gospels and the *Antiquities* of the Jewish historian Josephus Flavius. John was the son of the priest Zachariah and of Elizabeth, and the cousin of Mary, the mother of Jesus. He was born in Palestinian hill country about 4 B.C. Little is known of his early years. The Gospels state that his birth and name were foretold by God to his father and that his conception was miraculous because his mother, Elizabeth, was beyond childbearing age. He spent his early years "in the desert," according to the Gospel; this phrase is almost a technical term in Qumran literature for the place where the Jewish sectaries lived together near the Dead Sea.

As an adult, John appeared on the banks of the river Jordan sometime during the reign of Herod Antipas (ca. 21 B.C.-A.D. 39). Since Jesus was put to death sometime between A.D. 29 and 31, and since he and John met at the beginning of Jesus' public life, it can be assumed that John started his own public ministry sometime in the mid-20s of the 1st century A.D.

According to the sources, John was a reforming zealot. He preached an imminent catastrophe of divine punishment; he castigated hypocrisy, demanded repentance, and announced the imminent coming of the Messiah. Many of the elements of John's doctrine resemble some teachings of the Qumran sectaries as noted in the Dead Sea Scrolls, particularly his antiestablishment attitude, his insistence on imminent divine punishment for sinners, and his preaching of a kingdom of God that would soon be established. John furthermore insisted that all who repented of their sins should come to him and go through a rite of washing or baptizing; hence he was called the Baptist.

Two major events marked John's career. First was the baptism of Jesus (Matthew 3:13-17; Mark 1:9-11; Luke 3:21-22; John 1:29-34). Jesus came and, being baptized by John, was recognized by him as the son of God. The second event concerned king Herod, who had dismissed his first wife, the daughter of King Aretas, and had married Herodias, the wife of his brother. John denounced this act. Herod, fearing that John's preaching might provoke retributive action by Aretas, imprisoned John in the fortress of Machaerus. The Gospels relate that Herodias, wounded in her pride, prevailed on Herod through the charms of her daughter, Salome, to have John beheaded. He died sometime between A.D. 26 and 31. The Christian churches commemorate the event on August 29 of each year.

Further Reading

The best books on John the Baptist have been written in the light of the Dead Sea Scrolls. Recommended are Carl Hermann Kraeling, *John the Baptist* (1951), and Matthew Black, *The Scrolls and Christian Origins* (1961). □

Augustus Edwin John

The Welsh painter Augustus Edwin John (1878-1961) was the leading British portraitist of his period and a brilliant draftsman.

Augustus John was born on Jan. 4, 1878, in Tenby, Pembrokeshire, and studied art at the Slade School in London. The Slade placed great emphasis on draftsmanship, and John soon attracted attention by the vitality and accomplishment of his drawings. His painting technique, which was slower to develop, at first revealed his attempt to combine the tradition of dark-toned impressionism current among artists of the New English Art Club with something of the grandeur of Rembrandt and other Old Masters, but gradually John began to work with brighter colors and a more simplified composition. This tendency reached its peak about 1911-1914 in a series of small, brilliantly colored paintings executed in North Wales, the majority of which showed figures (usually his second wife, Dorelia, and one or more of their children) in a setting of lakes and mountains.

Influenced perhaps by contemporary movements like the Celtic revival, John was greatly attracted to Irish tinkers, Normandy fisherfolk, and above all the gypsies, whose language he learned and with whom he camped. Being himself a rebel against convention, he felt great sympathy for people who lived independent, undisciplined lives in close contact with nature, and he expressed this in a series of drawings and large-scale decorative figure paintings, almost all of which remained at the project stage or were left unfinished. These works usually showed Dorelia and their children or gypsies and tinkers posed in a wild outdoor setting.

Although he continued throughout his life to paint occasional nude studies, flower paintings, landscapes, and figure compositions, John became increasingly involved with portraiture, which forms the main body of his work. His most successful portraits, rendered with spontaneous, flamboyant directness, are of his family and of writer and artist friends, including William Butler Yeats and George Bernard Shaw. In his commissioned portraits of society figures, if the face and personality had little to interest him, John would often have recourse to mannerisms such as large liquid eyes and elongated chins and necks.

John's method of painting depended to a great extent on improvisation and on preserving the freshness and immediacy of the sketch. He took little interest in the more radical developments of 20th-century art, and by the time of his death on October 31, 1961, in Fordingbridge, Hampshire, his work had somewhat lost touch with the most vital currents of his day.

Further Reading

John wrote two books of memoirs: *Chiaroscuro: Fragments of Autobiography* (1952) and the posthumous *Finishing Touches,* edited by Daniel George (1964). The best book on John is John Rothenstein, *Augustus John* (1944).

Additional Sources

Easton, Malcolm, *Augustus John,* London: H.M.S.O., 1975.

Holroyd, Michael, *Augustus John: a biography,* Harmondsworth; New York etc.: Penguin, 1976.

Holroyd, Michael, *Augustus John: the new biography,* New York: Farrar, Straus and Giroux, 1996.

John, Augustus, *Autobiography of Augustus John,* London: Cape, 1975. □

Jasper Johns

Jasper Johns (born 1930), American painter and sculptor, helped break the hold of abstract expressionism on modern American art and cleared the way for pop art. Versatile in several different artistic fields, he has given the world sculptures, lithographs, and prints, as well as paintings.

Jasper Johns was born in Augusta, Georgia, in the middle of the Great Depression, to Jean Riley Johns and her husband, Jasper, Sr. He was a year old when his mother left his alcoholic father. Shortly afterwards, he had yet another upset when his mother found herself unable to support him and left him with her father in Allendale, South Carolina. He was nine years old when he lost his grandfather, and thereafter, he was shuttled back and forth between his mother and various relatives on his father's side.

In Search of Focus

After graduating from high school in 1946, Johns drifted without noticeable focus for some time. He spent a desultory three semesters at the University of South Carolina, then moved on to New York, where he entered a commercial art school in 1949. Here he stayed until 1951, dropping out when told that his work did not merit a scholarship for which he had applied, but that it would nevertheless be granted to him on grounds of need. Completely on his own, he worked first as a messenger, then as a shipping clerk, and finally, after entering college for just one day, he got a job as a clerk in the Marlboro Bookstore.

In 1954, he was introduced to Robert Rauchenberg, an artist five years older than he was, and the two of them soon became firm friends. Both set up studios in the same building, and both supported themselves by doing collages, drawings and paintings for window displays used by luxury stores such as Tiffany and Bonwit Teller.

A Developing Artist

For the first time in his life, Johns was supporting himself with his art. This change from part-time painting and part-time clerking represented a profound change in the way he viewed his own profession and his own future. "Before, whenever anybody asked me what I did, I said I was going to become an artist," he told Michael Crichton, the author of his biography. "Finally, I decided that I could be going to become an artist forever, all my life. I decided to stop *becoming* and to *be* an artist." He was, in essence,

reinventing himself, and as always when drastic measures are undertaken, there was both good and bad in his approach. One of the first things he did was to rip up and destroy every piece of his early work.. Fortunately, four paintings survived this action to give art-lovers an idea of his early creative years.

He began to develop a definite discipline and a method all his own. Intensely interested in experimentation, he learned to work with "encaustic" a method which combines pigments and hot wax before they are applied to the surface of a painting. Plaster casts of different types also began to appear on various paintings. The works most commonly associated with this period were his paintings of flags and of targets. The subjects he chose were oftentimes objects which are often seen, but are usually too commonplace to be closely noticed. Then, he proceeded to give them individuality by adding encaustic textures and other elements which both enhanced and lessened their familiarity at the same time.

In 1955, his painting *Green Target* was exhibited in the Jewish Museum as a part of the *Artists of the New York School: Second Generation* show. But this was not the only place Johns' paintings were to be seen. Along with other artists supplying pictures and drawings for Bonwit Teller's displays, he was invited to show two of his flag paintings in their windows. Johns had the first of many one-man shows in 1958. Paintings of flags, numbers and targets abounded, and all were sold, three of them to New York's Museum of Modern Art.

The year 1958 was noteworthy also for his first sculptures, called,*Flashlight* and *Lightbulb I*. But perhaps one of the year's most enduring achievements was a painting called *Three Flags,* which would be sold to the Whitney Museum in 1980 for the sum of $1 million.

Dada in Development

In 1959 Johns met the artist Marcel Duchamp for the first time. Duchamp, forty seven years Johns' senior, had long been one of the art world's most influential figures. He was a proponent of the school known as Dada, which, before dying out in 1923, had sought to destroy preconceived notions of what was or was not artistically acceptable. Duchamp himself had contributed to the movement, largely by depicting what he called "ready-mades," (utilitarian articles such as snow shovels and bottle racks) signing the resulting pictures, and presenting the result as objects of art rather than objects made for everyday use.

This was an idea that Johns embraced and modified. Like Duchamp he embellished his paintings with "devices," but shied away from Duchamp's spontaneity by making complex arrangements of the objects he used. His *Painted Bronze* consisting of a Savarin coffee can filled with paint brushes, is a perfect example of his careful arrangement.

By the middle of the 1970s, these ideas were joined by a technique called crosshatching. Johns was inspired to try this method after an automobile trip to the Hamptons, during which he saw a car covered with marks flash past in the opposite direction. Adapting it to his own purposes, he began to use it to convey a sense of something swiftly glimpsed, then turned into art.

By this time, Jasper Johns was well-known, and was expanding his interests to embrace new fields.

In 1967, for instance, he became artistic advisor to the Merce Cunningham Dance Company, for which he designed sets, costumes, and occasionally, posters. Cunningham's ballet *Second Hand,* produced in 1980, was just one work bearing the mark of Johns' creativity. Characteristically, he crystallized his experiences on canvas, with a picture called *Dancers on a Plane,* which he completed in 1980.

Another new direction was collaboration in the field of book illustration. In 1973 he started to create 33 etchings for a collection of short stories called *Foirades/Fizzles,* written by Nobel Prize winner Samuel Beckett. Unfortunately, as Johns biographer Richard Francis remarks, though the collection appeared on schedule in 1976 the two men could not compromise on interpretation. Despite their commonly held bleak view of life, the resulting work leaned more towards two parallel works, rather than one seamless one created by two artists working in unison.

The Legendary Jasper Johns

Over the years, the stylistic changes showing Jasper Johns' development as an artist have been seen by the public in so many exhibitions that they have been listed on a CD-ROM. Some of these have been retrospectives, in which the galleries responsible have tried to obtain works from each of his periods, so that earlier and later works can be compared and contrasted. In October 1996, the Museum of Modern Art held a Jasper Johns retrospective that stirred great interest in the art world. Occupying two floors of the museum, the exhibition featured 225 works arranged chronologically.

Johns rarely granted interviews. One friend, who remained anonymous, told the magazineVanity Fair, " . . . he's terrified he might let slip something personal." This is why Johns was so incensed at the appearance of Jill Johnston's 1996 biography, *Privileged Information* . Currently a former friend who has known Johns for some 30 years, Johnston amazed Johns with her interpretation of some of his paintings, which she saw as coded references to his lonely childhood lurking behind the locked gate of his reticence. Because he believed her interpretations of his works to be inaccurate, as well as presumptuous, he forbade publisher Thames & Hudson to reproduce any of his paintings for the book. As always, his motto remained "privacy above all."

Further Reading

Max Kozloff, *Jasper Johns* (1968), is the largest and most recent monograph on the art of Johns; the catalog of the 1964 Jewish Museum exhibition has a fine essay by Alan Solomon. Leo Steinberg, *Jasper Johns* (1963), is a brief study; Mario Amaya, *Pop Art . . . and After* (1966), is recommended for general background.

Additional Sources

Crichton, Michael, *Jasper Johns,* Harry N. Abrams, 1977.
Francis, Richard, *Johns* Abbeville Modern Masters, 1983.
Johnston, Jill, *Jasper Johns: Privileged Information.*
Art in America, April, 1997.
Vanity Fair, September, 1996. □

Alvin Saunders Johnson

American economist and editor Alvin Saunders Johnson (1874-1971), as director of the New School for Social Research, established the graduate faculty of political and social science.

A son of a Danish immigrant farmer, Alvin Johnson was born on December 18, 1874, in Homer, northeastern Nebraska. His pioneer upbringing did not prevent him from learning enough Greek and Latin at home to be admitted to a premedical course at the University of Nebraska. He graduated from the university in 1897 and enlisted in the military service during the Spanish-American War. After an honorable discharge, he began his graduate studies at Columbia University. He received his doctorate in economics in 1902 and subsequently taught at Columbia, Cornell, and Stanford universities and at the universities of Nebraska and Chicago.

In 1917 Johnson became editor of the *New Republic,* a prominent liberal periodical. He remained editor until 1923, when he assumed the directorship of the New School for Social Research in New York City. It was there, during the 1930s, that he provided a haven for refugee scholars from Nazi Germany and created, in the graduate faculty of political and social science, a center for social research of international renown. While at the New School, Johnson accepted the position of associate editor of the *Encyclopedia of the Social Sciences,* which became a monument to scholarship in the social sciences and remained the standard reference work in its field for many years.

In both his academic and private lives, Johnson demonstrated his concern for members of minority groups discriminated against or persecuted at home and abroad. In 1944 he drafted the Ives-Quinn Law for the New York Legislature. This statute was enacted to penalize discrimination against Jews and African Americans.

In 1945 Johnson retired from his post at the New School and also stopped actively participating in political and educational affairs. He remained, however, an indefatigable raconteur and continued to publish works of fiction, as well as an autobiography. He received many accolades during his lifetime for his scholarship, his courageous defense of academic freedom, and his support for refugee scholars. He was given honorary doctorates from Brandeis University and the University of Nebraska and from foreign universities, including Brussels, Algiers, and Heidelberg. Johnson died on June 7, 1971, in Upper Nyack, N.Y.

Further Reading

Johnson's autobiography, *Pioneer's Progress,* was published in 1952. His career as an economist is well covered in Joseph Dorfman, *The Economic Mind in American Civilization* (5 vols., 1946-1959). For an account of Johnson's role in setting up the "university in exile" see Laura Fermi, *Illustrious Immigrants: The Intellectual Migration from Europe, 1930-41* (1968). □

Andrew Johnson

Andrew Johnson (1808-1875), seventeenth president of the United States, was the only president ever to be impeached.

Andrew Johnson was born on Dec. 29, 1808, in Raleigh, N.C. After serving an apprenticeship with a tailor, he moved to Greeneville, Tenn., where he opened a tailor shop in 1826. Johnson laboriously taught himself to read and write with the help of Eliza McCardle, whom he married in 1827. His business prospered, and Johnson entered the rough-and-tumble world of politics, becoming a formidable stump speaker.

A Jacksonian Democrat, Johnson moved up through local elective offices to U.S. senator in 1857. In the Senate he crusaded for a homestead law and was bitter when the South blocked its passage. Yet he supported Jefferson Davis's demand for a congressional guarantee of slave property in the territories and in 1860 backed the proslavery presidential candidate.

When the Southern states began seceding, however, Johnson was the only senator from the Confederate states to remain in Congress. In 1862 President Abraham Lincoln appointed him military governor of partly reconquered Tennessee with instructions to begin restoring the state to the Union. Johnson did a good job under trying circumstances. Converted by the Civil War to an antislavery position, he set in motion the machinery for a constitutional convention that abolished slavery in Tennessee (January 1865).

Accident President

In 1864 the Republicans, hoping to attract support from Unionist Democrats, nominated Johnson for vice president. When Lincoln was assassinated in 1865, heavy responsibilities fell upon Johnson. The new president indicated that he would impose severe punishment on "traitors," but his actual policy during 1865 was surprisingly lenient. He extended amnesty to all but the most prominent and wealthy Confederates and provided for the election (by white voters only) of delegates to the conventions to draw up new Southern state constitutions. Subsequently, Johnson granted thousands of pardons to Southerners exempted from the general amnesty.

Under their new constitutions the Southern states elected several prominent Confederates to high office. Some of the states passed "black codes" restricting the rights of freed slaves to a level little better than slavery. Republicans in Congress grew alarmed and feared that the South would regain by Johnson's leniency much of what it had lost in war; they sought a settlement that would provide Federal protection for freedmen and restrict the power of former Confederates. Congress passed a civil rights bill and a Freedmen's Bureau bill in 1866, but Johnson vetoed both. Congress sent the 14th Amendment to the states for ratification, but Johnson influenced Southern states to reject it.

Impeachment Proceedings

Johnson's belief that "the people" supported his policies should have been shaken by the 1866 congressional elections, which gave the Republicans an overwhelming mandate. Nevertheless, he continued to force Congress to pass every Reconstruction measure over his veto. He tried to weaken enforcement of Reconstruction laws by appointing conservative commanders for some Southern military districts.

An exasperated and vengeful House of Representatives finally impeached Johnson on Feb. 25, 1868. The ostensible grounds were technical transgressions; in reality he was impeached for resisting Congress's will on vital national issues. At Johnson's trial before the Senate, his lawyers proved that he had committed no constitutional crimes or misdemeanors; the verdict for conviction fell one vote short of the necessary two-thirds majority. Johnson served out his term as a powerless president.

Six years later, in 1875, Johnson was elected to the U.S. Senate by Tennessee. However, he suffered a paralytic attack and died on July 31.

Further Reading

Pro-Johnson biographies include Robert W. Winston, *Andrew Johnson* (1928); Lloyd Paul Stryker, *Andrew Johnson* (1929); George F. Milton, *The Age of Hate: Andrew Johnson and the Radicals* (1930); and Howard K. Beale, *The Critical Year: A Study of Andrew Johnson and Reconstruction* (1930). Recent scholarship is critical of Johnson; see Eric L. McKitrick, *Andrew Johnson and Reconstruction* (1960); LaWanda Cox and John H. Cox, *Politics, Principle, and Prejudice, 1865-66* (1963); and William R. Brock, *An American Crisis: Congress and Reconstruction, 1865-1867* (1963). A collection of essays that attempts balanced appraisal is Eric L. McKitrick, ed., *Andrew Johnson: A Profile* (1969). □

Betsey Johnson

Betsey Johnson (born ca. 1941), dress designer for the young and young-at-heart, set fashion trends during four decades.

Fashion designer Betsey Johnson, with her red hair and perpetual ear-to-ear grin, was a colorful burst of energy in the fashion world. She first exploded onto the style scene in the swinging 1960s, a turbulent time when fashion designers were considered stuffy, pretentious, and totally out-of-touch with the growing wave of street-inspired chic and the unmistakable influence of British rock and roll on American youth culture.

During this decade, Johnson helped launch the American fashion revolution with her space age silvery sci-fi dresses, see-through plastic shifts with discreet stick-on cover-ups, a "noise dress" with metal grommets at the hem that went clink-clank when the wearer moved, elephant bell-bottoms, and 14-inch metal micro-miniskirts. In those years her designs were worn by style setters such as actresses Julie Christie and Brigitte Bardot, model Twiggy, and first lady Jackie Kennedy. Over the ensuing decades Johnson continued to be an energetic leader in fashion design. As Susie Billingsley of *Vogue* magazine wrote: "She got on the street fashion wagon before anyone. She's always been way ahead of what's hip."

Born in Wethersfield, Connecticut, Johnson graduated from Syracuse University *magna cum laude* in 1964. She landed a coveted position as a guest editor at *Mademoiselle,* a young women's fashion and lifestyle magazine. The short-term guest editorship led her to a permanent position in the magazine's art department. Soon she was sent by the magazine to London in the heyday of the Beatles, bell-bottoms, and belly-baring knit tops. There Carnaby Street was the eye of the style storm. Johnson was so inspired that when she returned to New York she began designing wacky wear for New York's clothing boutique, Paraphernalia.

She pioneered the now commonplace use of avant garde fabrics: car interior lining and shower curtain dresses. She imported a wool pinstripe material used for the original New York Yankee's baseball uniform for her "gangster suits." In the 1970s Johnson designed slip dresses, drop-waist ballerina dresses, double knit A-line minis, and "nutsy artsy" embroidered sweaters for the Alley Cat clothing line, then for her own New York shop, Betsey Bunky Nini.

She married Velvet Underground bassist John Cale but they divorced in 1969. For three years she was involved with a sculptor, a relationship that produced her daughter, Lulu, later her top runway and print model. In the 1980s she married again."

In the 1990s, most of her clothes, available in large department stores and her more than 20 U.S. boutiques from sexy South Beach in Miami, Florida, to the ever-so-staid capital, Washington, D.C., sold for under $150. Her young and young-at-heart customers search her out, and they are fashionably faithful. Polly Mellen of *Allure* magazine said: "Her clothes are fun, female, flirty, slightly aggressive and teasing. Her fashion shows are always witty, fun and slightly shoddy. But in the showroom, the clothes are real and the prices right." Johnson self-deprecatingly said: "I've never had a new or brilliant idea. I just like to make things. The truth is, fashion doesn't really change all that much. I'm still doing the same things now that I was back then."

Maybe. But they are all interesting variations on her theme. Johnson ships out dozens of new styles every month to her U.S. boutiques. In 1991, she launched a new division called "Luxe," which drew from her background in dance. The more expensive line was designed to complement the skirts and leggings that had been her trademark. In1992 she launched her sweetly sexy swimwear collection of push-up bras, bikinis with petticoats, and skirts in black lace, ging-ham, madras, and velvet, all priced affordably from $35 to $75. She also unleashed a line of clunky funky women's shoes. And her 1993 line of menswear looked tailor-made for all modernday Robin Hoods: velvet capes and tunics, hooded monk robes, forest and mead-hued caftans, and paisley leggings. That year also brought her own fragrance, a light floral scent of lilies and mimosas. Forever evolving, Johnson introduced a new "Ultra" collection featuring bet-ter fabrics and more elaborate styling and priced up to $500 in 1996.

Johnson was always her own fitting model: "Small top, big bottom, that's my shape. And I think it's the shape of most women." Long known for her short, tight, "boy-friend getting dresses," she also acknowledged: "Since AIDS, ev-eryone's pulling back and clothing is getting much more reserved and more romantic."

Part of Johnson's success was her ability to sniff the winds and sense the social and subsequent style and silhou-ette changes. She started with the British Invasion of Amer-ica style, hopped on the early 1980s punk bandwagon with safety pins and ripped T-shirts, and kept current with the 1990s rave, grunge, medieval, and deconstructionist fash-ion movements, all of which began on the streets and in music clubs haunted by disenfranchised youth.

Johnson clearly understood her place in a woman's closet, telling *The Atlanta Journal and Constitution* in 1995, "I'm usually the sparkle in a closet full of conservative clothes. Either that or my customer has a closet full of my clothes and a few conservative suits from Calvin Klein. I think you've got to give a girl what's missing from her closet. If something jazzy, tacky or sexy is what's missing, I provide it."

As 1995 brought the advent of youthful baby-doll and empire-waist dresses, Johnson explained the trend by say-ing, "After grunge, girls wanted to wear things that were very feminine. Something deep down said, 'Is there a girl inside me?'" She simply says: "I've stopped aging in my work 25 years ago."Perhaps it is just that sense of wonder, openness, and a bizarre sense of humor that keeps this over-50 designer in touch with the youthful trends of today.

Further Reading

For further information on Betsey Johnson and the fashion indus-try see *Fairchild Dictionary of Fashion* (1988); *McDowell's Directory of 20th Century Fashion* (1987); *NY Fashion: The Evolution of American Style* by Caroline Rennolds Milbank (1989); *Women of Fashion: Twentieth Century Designers* by Valerie Steele (1991); and *Contemporary Designers* (2nd ed. 1990) edited by Ann Lee Morgan. □

Charles Spurgeon Johnson

African American educator and sociologist Charles Spurgeon Johnson (1893-1956) gave outstanding leadership to Fisk University and conducted impor-tant research on human relations and the problems of blacks in America.

Charles Spurgeon Johnson was born on July 24, 1893, in Bristol, Va., the son of a Baptist minister. His father's books on philosophy, history, and reli-gion were sources of inspiration. He completed college at Virginia Union University in 1917, having been a student leader. Johnson received his bachelor of philosophy degree from the University of Chicago and pursued graduate work in sociology there. He married Marie Burgette in 1920; they had four children.

Johnson's distinguished and extraordinarily productive career as a sociologist began when he organized the De-partment of Research and Investigation of the Chicago Ur-ban League in 1917. He was a member of the Committee on Race Relations, which reported on the Chicago race riot of 1919 in *The Negro in Chicago* (1922). In 1920, as director of research and investigation for the New York Urban League, he established the magazine *Opportunity,* a leading periodical during the "Harlem Renaissance" that inspired many young blacks. In 1928, he went to head Fisk Univer-sity's sociology department; with unmatched vision, he made it internationally famous. He was president of Fisk from 1947 to 1956.

Meanwhile, Johnson published books, articles, book reviews, pamphlets, and chapters in books. His research and writing centered on African American life and culture and on race relations. Among his most outstanding books are *The Negro in American Civilization* (1930), *The Shadow of the Plantation* (1934), *A Preface to Racial Understanding* (1936), *The Negro College Graduate* (1938), *Growing Up in the Black Belt* (1941), *Patterns of Segregation* (1943), *To Stem This Tide* (1943), and *Into the Mainstream* (1947).

Johnson's profound grasp of sociology was recognized in his numerous positions: as member, International Commission of the League of Nations; secretary, Commission on Negro Housing of President Herbert Hoover's Conference on Homebuilding and Home Ownership; member, President Franklin D. Roosevelt's Committee on Farm Tenancy; member, White House Conference on Children in a Democracy; president, Southern Sociological Society; one of 10 American delegates to the first session of the United Nations Educational, Scientific, and Cultural Organization; one of 20 educators sent to Japan in 1946 to reorganize the educational system; and member, Conference on Science, Religion, and Philosophy. From 1944 to 1950 Johnson was director of race relations of the American Missionary Association of the Congregational and Christian Churches. In 1948 he served as a delegate to the World Council of Churches Assembly. He also lectured widely in America and Scandinavia.

In addition to the Harmon Award (1930) and the University of Chicago Alumni Citation for distinguished public service (1945), Johnson received honorary degrees from Virginia Union, Howard, Columbia, Harvard, and Lincoln universities, from Central State College, and from the University of Glasgow, Scotland. He died on October 27, 1956.

Further Reading

A short autobiography of Johnson is in Louis Finkelstein, ed., *American Spiritual Autobiographies: Fifteen Self-Portraits* (1948). An account of him is in W.S. Robinson, *Historical Negro Biographies* (1968). Edwin R. Embree, *13 against the Odds* (1944), contains a chapter on Johnson.

Additional Sources

Robbins, Richard, *Sidelines activist: Charles S. Johnson and the struggle for civil rights,* Jackson: University Press of Mississippi, 1996. ☐

Earvin Johnson Jr.

Joining the Los Angeles Lakers of the National Basketball Association in 1979, Earvin "Magic" Johnson, Jr. (born 1959) became one of basketball's most popular stars.

In November 1991, Magic Johnson stunned the sportsworld with his announcement that he was infected with the human immune deficiency virus (HIV), the virus that causes the disease acquired immune deficiency syndrome (AIDS). Johnson announced that he was retiring from professional basketball but returned in 1992 and again in 1996. He turned his enthusiasm and leadership skills to business. Among his successes, he developed movie theaters and shopping malls in poor and neglected sections of large cities where no one else would invest.

Johnson was born in 1959 in Lansing, Michigan. He first played organized basketball at Everett High School. In 1977 Johnson and the Everett team won the Michigan state high school championship. Johnson then attended Michigan State University. As a sophomore, he averaged 17.1 points per game and was named an All-American. In 1979 Michigan State won the national collegiate championship by defeating Indiana State University, a team led by future Boston Celtics star Larry Bird. Johnson scored 24 points and was chosen Most Valuable Player (MVP).

Johnson was selected first in the 1979 National Basketball Association (NBA) draft by the Los Angeles Lakers. In his first game for the Lakers he scored 26 points. He then became the first rookie to start in an NBA All-Star game. The Lakers won the 1979-1980 Pacific Division title and went on to play the Philadelphia 76ers for the championship. The Lakers defeated the 76ers for the NBA title, and Johnson

Earvin Johnson (no. 32)

became the youngest player ever to be named MVP of the playoffs.

Transformed Lakers into Champions

At 6 feet 9 inches, Johnson became the first big man to dominate play at point guard, a position usually reserved for smaller players. His passing, dribbling skills, and ballhandling technique won him the nickname "Magic." His magnetic personality made him one of the most popular players in the league.

During the 1981-1982 season Laker head coach Paul Westhead designed an offense that focused around center Kareem Abdul-Jabbar. The change upset Johnson, and he asked to be traded, a move that angered some Laker fans who felt that Johnson was selfish. Westhead was replaced by Pat Riley, who stressed the role of the point guard in his offense. Under Riley, Johnson matured into one of the best all-around players in the league. In his first season with Riley, Johnson had more than 700 rebounds and 700 assists, the first player since Wilt Chamberlain to do so. Johnson was again named MVP of the playoffs.

In 1985 the Lakers won their third NBA title, defeating the Boston Celtics and Larry Bird. The sports media liked to refer to the matchup between Bird and Johnson, but Johnson was a guard and Bird a forward. During that same season, Johnson averaged 23.9 points per game, 5 points above his career average. That season he became the first guard in league history to be voted MVP of the regular season. In 1987 the Lakers again defeated the Celtics for the championship, and Johnson was named MVP of the series.

During his 12 years with the Lakers beginning in 1979, John's team went to the playoffs eight times and won five championship titles. Johnson was chosen playoff MVP three times. He was a 12-time All-Star and the 1990 All-Star games' MVP. He scored a total of 17,239 points in 874 games, averaging 19.7 per game. He displayed his defensive skills by pulling down 6,376 rebounds and making 1,698 steals. During the 1990-1991 season he broke Oscar Robertson's assist record with 9,888, finishing the season with a total of 9,921. Not surprisingly, in October 1996, he was named one of the 50 greatest players in the history of the NBA.

Retires after Contracting AIDS

In November 1991, during a routine physical examination for an insurance policy, Johnson found out that he was a carrier of the HIV virus. Johnson admitted that his lifestyle as a sports celebrity included extensive heterosexual promiscuity. However, he never suspected that he might contact HIV, which he thought was limited to homosexual men. The Lakers team physician advised Johnson to quit basketball immediately in order to safeguard his threatened immune system. Johnson shared his discovery with the other players on the Laker team, then announced to the American people that he was HIV-positive.

Johnson's admission stunned his fans. Overnight the likeable player became a spokesman for AIDS awareness. "I want [kids] to understand that safe sex is the way to go, Johnson told *People*. Sometimes we think only gay people

can get it [HIV], or that it's not going to happen to me. Here I am. And I'm saying it can happen to anybody, even Magic Johnson." President George Bush appointed Johnson to the National Commission on AIDS, but he resigned to protest what he considered to be the president's lack of support for AIDS research. Johnson continued to speak out and literally raised millions for research to combat the disease. He founded the Magic Johnson Foundation for HIV/AIDS education and coauthored *What You Can Do To Prevent AIDS*.

Retirement, Return, Retirement, and Return

In January 1992, two months after he had retired, Johnson was among the leaders in voting for the 1992 NBA All-Star game. He came out of retirement to play in the game, scoring 25 points, with nine assists, in 29 minutes. There was little surprise when Johnson was named the game's MVP.

In the summer of 1992, Johnson went to Barcelona, Spain, as a member of the United States' basketball team in the 25th Summer Olympics. Dubbed the "Dream Team," by sports journalists, the American entry also included NBA stars Michael Jordan, Larry Bird, John Stockton, Patrick Ewing, Karl Malone, Clyde Drexler, David Robinson, Charles Barkley, Scottie Pippen, Chris Mullen, and Duke University's Christian Laettner. The Dream Team easily won the gold medal. Fans were saddened, however, because they believed that the careers of both Magic Johnson and Larry Bird were over.

But Magic hoped that he still could have a future in basketball. He announced his return to the NBA shortly before the 1992 season began, but only played in five preseason games before retiring for the second time. Johnson cited the other players' concerns about the possibility of being infected while playing and his desire to stay healthy for his family.

Johnson remained active in the basketball world. He purchased five percent of the Lakers, and he formed a charitable—but competitive—basketball team that played exhibition games around the world. He became a vice-president in the Lakers organization and took over as interim head coach of the team for the last part of the 1992-93 season.

But Johnson really preferred playing to coaching. At the beginning of 1996, the rumors of his return proved to be true. Magic Johnson came back to the L. A. Lakers, this time as a power forward and not a point guard. By May 1996, however, Johnson, once again announced his retirement—this time for good. He had discovered that the current players on the team did not idolize him and would not give the ball exclusively to him.

Successful Business Ventures

Johnson showed the same all-star success as an entrepreneur. Like other star athletes, Johnson endorsed products, licensed use of his name, and gave corporate speeches for big fees. He led his Magic Johnson All-Stars round the world, playing exhibition games against foreign basketball teams for substantial profits. Since he lived in L.A, it was only natural for him to get involved in entertainment, possibly as host of of a late night talk show.

However, in a move less typical of a sports star, Johnson also became personally involved in large-scale property development. Among his successes were movie complexes and shopping centers in inner-city areas where no one else wanted to invest. In June 1995, Johnson partnered with Sony to open the 12-screen Magic Theatres multiplex in a predominantly black section of Los Angeles. The project became one of the top grossing movie outlets in America and helped boost sales and occupancy at the mall in which it was located. In 1997, Johnson opened another movie complex in southwest Atlanta. Magic movie marquees were under construction in Houston and Cleveland, and Johnson announced plans for 14 new multiplexes in 10 other cities. His company, Johnson Development went on to buy entire shopping centers in poor communties in Las Vegas and Los Angeles.

Johnson earned goodwill for helping spiff up and bringing jobs to the inner cities. His ventures also brought him great personal wealth. *Time* quoted him as saying "It's important to help the community, but the number one goal here is to make money. This is not charity."

Johnson's personal involvement in business affairs got its impetus early in his hoop career. He realized he had signed away his talents for too low a salary. And he also witnessed the fleecing of fellow Laker Kareem Abdul-Jabbar, who lost millions to unscrupulous financial advisers. In the mid-1980s, Johnson dumped his own advisers and demanded monthly statements from his new ones. By 1996, he had a net worth of more than $100 million.

Living with HIV

In September 1991, just before he learned he had HIV, Johnson wed longtime friend Earletha "Cookie" Kelly. The couple had a son in 1993 and adopted a daughter in 1995. Johnson also has a son from a previous relationship who spends the summers with him. Ever optimistic, Johnson believed that the right combination of medicine, diet, and exercise would help him to survive until a cure for AIDS was found.

Johnson's physicians announced in early 1997 that the AIDS virus in his body had been reduced to undetectable levels. They attributed the improvement to the use of powerful drugs, including protese inhibitors. His wife Cookie gave the credit to God stating, "The Lord has definitely healed Earvin. Doctors think it's the medicine. We claim it in the name of Jesus." The Johnsons attended the West Angles Church of God in Christ, to which he donated $5 million in 1995.

Further Reading

Two early biographies, *Magic* with Richard Levin (1983) and *Magic's Touch* with Roy S. Johnson (1989) are interesting but were written before the devastating discovery that ended Johnson's career. An important and well written biography is *Magic Johnson: My Life* (1992). Deeply moving, the book contains a message to young persons that shows Johnson's

sincere concern for them. For more about the Olympic "Dream Team" readers should see *The Golden Boys* by Cameron Smith (1992).

Also see Blatt, Howard, *Magic! Against the Odds* (Pocket Books, 1996); "The Magic and the Money," *Forbes,* December 16, 1996, p. 264-266; and Monroe, Sylvester, "Post-game show," *Time,* March 17, 1997, p. 38-39. ☐

Guy Benton Johnson

Guy Benton Johnson (1901-1991) was a sociologist, social anthropologist, and archaeologist. He was a distinguished student of black culture in the rural South and a pioneer white southern advocate of racial equality.

Guy B. Johnson was born in Caddo Mills, Texas, where he grew up on a farm. He took degrees in sociology from Baylor University (A.B., 1921), the University of Chicago (M.A., 1922), and the University of North Carolina at Chapel Hill (Ph.D., 1927). In 1936-1937 he did postdoctoral study in anthropology at Chicago and Yale.

After teaching a year each at Ohio Wesleyan University and Baylor College for Women (now Mary-Hardin Baylor), Johnson was recruited to North Carolina as a research assistant in Howard W. Odum's new Institute for Research in Social Science in 1924, which he never left for long. He taught at Chapel Hill from 1927 until he retired as Kenan Professor of Sociology and Anthropology in 1969. He held visiting professorships at Louisiana State University, Peabody College, Earlham College, the University of Hawaii, and Rhodes University (Grahamstown, South Africa).

Along with Odum, Rupert B. Vance, Katharine Jocher, and others, Johnson was one of the remarkable group who put Chapel Hill sociology on the map in the 1920s and 1930s. He also taught the university's first anthropology courses. While his main writings were on southern Black folk culture and U.S. race relations, his interests and accomplishments were broad. He wrote about musicology and contemporary Africa and was co-founder of the Archaeological Society of North Carolina in 1933 and its president from 1941 to 1943. As a staff researcher in the early 1940s, he analyzed many of the data that went into Gunnar Myrdal's monumental study of American race relations, *An American Dilemma* (1944). He was coeditor of Social Forces, a major sociological journal, from 1961 to 1969.

Johnson's most notable scholarly contributions were his studies of southern rural black culture, done early in his career. In *Folk Culture on St. Helena Island* (1929) he analyzed the Gullah dialect of English spoken by blacks on that isolated South Carolina island and, in sophisticated technical detail, the musical structure of the spirituals they sang to support a new interpretation of black folk culture. He argued that neither the dialect nor the music had many characteristics brought to America by slaves from Africa. Rather, he wrote, they were somewhat-altered versions of the dialect and music of lower-class whites, with a small amount of African influence on the kinds of changes the blacks had made.

Johnson's thesis may seem tame today, but it stirred up heated controversy then. It offended nearly everyone who was interested in the subject. Leading anthropologists had argued that much of American black culture consisted of "African survivals," and attacked Johnson for disagreeing with them. Some Black intellectuals did not like what they saw as a denial that Blacks were capable of inventing their own culture, though Johnson had taken pains to show that the Black versions of many cultural patterns were more intellectually complex than the original white versions. Most of all, racist whites were upset by the notion that white and black cultures had been blended; they wanted both the cultures and the people kept separate. Johnson neither backed off nor counterattacked. He let the evidence in his book speak for itself.

In the 1930s Johnson turned his attention to current race relations. From then on, he was best known as a tireless and influential worker for racial equality. He wrote articles advocating equality and analyzing the harm done to African Americans by discrimination. He was active in organizations dedicated to equality. From 1944 to 1947 he was executive director of the Southern Regional Council, a biracial organization working for interracial cooperation throughout the South. He was a trustee of Howard University from 1937 to 1974, a trustee of the Phelps-Stokes Fund from 1948 to 1975, and at various times an officer of the North Carolina Council on Human Relations.

He was not a civil rights "activist." He did not help organize demonstrations, civil disobedience, or other forms of mass protest that became the chief weapons of the civil rights movement of the 1950s and 1960s. He aimed his message at white professionals such as journalists and clergymen. He tried to persuade them to say in public that segregation was wrong and to cooperate with African American professionals in efforts to influence community officials. For this moderate, conciliatory approach he was later criticized by African American activists and white liberals; but he knew that the leaders of mass activism would have to be African American. When the civil rights movement flowered, he was an approving spectator, not a participant, but his work had helped pave the way. Simply advocating racial equality took courage in the South of the 1930s. There was organized pressure on the University of North Carolina to fire Johnson. (The university ignored it.) He got hate mail, including death threats. None of this slowed him down, or speeded him up either; he just went about his work, teaching, doing scholarly research, and writing the truth as he saw it.

In recognition of his research and service, Johnson received the Anisfield Award for Research in Race Relations in 1937 and the Catholic Committee of the South Award for Work in Human Relations in 1948. In 1975 the University of North Carolina at Chapel Hill honored him and his wife, Guion Griffis Johnson, a noted historian, with Distinguished Alumnus awards. The Southern Sociological Society elected him its president for 1953-1954, and in 1987 inscribed his name on its Roll of Honor.

Johnson's analyses of race relations reflected optimism tempered by realism. From 1920s population data showing a vast migration of southern blacks to northern city ghettos and a continuing high birth rate among the blacks who had moved, he predicted that militant black nationalism would grow alongside blacks' demands for integration into the mainstream of society; but he also predicted that black separatist movements would have little effect on the pace or nature of desegregation. In 1953, a year before the Supreme Court mandated the desegregation of schools, he wrote: "Anyone who thinks that the transition from segregation to racial coeducation can be made without problems . . . is a fool. Anyone who thinks the transition means the end of civilization is a fool. The operation may be serious, but the patient will recover. And when he recovers and looks back over his experience, he may say, 'Well, it wasn't half as bad as I thought it would be.'" History has borne out these forecasts.

Further Reading

Besides many articles and book chapters, Johnson published seven books: *The Negro and His Songs* (with Howard W. Odum, 1925), *Negro Workaday Songs* (with Odum, 1926), *Folk Culture on St. Helena Island* (1929), *John Henry: Tracking Down a Negro Legend* (1930), *Encyclopedia of the Negro,* Preparatory Volume (with W.E.B. DuBois, 1944), *Folk, Region, and Society: Selected Papers of Howard W. Odum* (edited with commentary, with Katharine Jocher, George L. Simpson, Jr., and Rupert B. Vance, 1964), and *Research in Service to Society: The First Fifty Years of the Institute for Research in Social Science* (with Guion Griffis Johnson, 1980). This last-named book, a history of the research center founded by Odum at Chapel Hill, gives many facts about Johnson's academic career, especially about his research projects. Discussions of Johnson's relations with his mentor Odum and of his strong influence on the thinking of southern social scientists and intellectuals about blacks and black-white relations appear at various points in Daniel Joseph Singal, *The War Within: From Victorian to Modernist Thought in the South, 1919-1945* (1982). □

Hiram Warren Johnson

Hiram Warren Johnson (1866-1945), American politician, was a reform governor of California. As a U.S. senator, he was a leading spokesman for isolationism in international affairs.

Hiram Johnson was born in Sacramento, Calif., on Sept. 2, 1866. After finishing high school, he worked in his father's law office for a year. He entered the University of California in 1884. He left school in 1886 to marry and once again studied law in his father's office, where he became a partner in 1888. After disagreements with his conservative father over political issues, he moved to San Francisco and opened a law office in 1902.

Johnson's swift rise in politics began in 1906, when he became a prosecuting attorney in San Francisco's graft trials and won the conviction of a party boss. A critic of corporate influence in California politics, Johnson was selected by Progressive Republicans as their gubernatorial candidate in 1910.

As governor, Johnson organized his followers for aggressive reform. Under his leadership his adherents pushed many Progressive ideas through the legislature: a public utilities commission, a railroad commission, a conservation commission, women's suffrage, workingmen's compensation, restrictions on child labor, and direct primary elections.

In 1912 Johnson supported Theodore Roosevelt over incumbent William Howard Taft for the Republican presidential nomination. When Roosevelt bolted the party, Johnson accepted the vice-presidential nomination of Roosevelt's Progressive party. The ticket lost, but that it carried California testified to the strength of Johnson's reform organization. In 1914 Johnson ran for governor again as a Progressive. His legislative record, which included some conservative measures (notably the Alien Land Law of 1913 directed against resident Japanese in California), sufficed to reelect him without Republican endorsement. In 1916, however, he successfully sought the Republican nomination for senator and returned to leadership in that party.

As U.S. senator from 1917 until 1945, Johnson took Progressive positions on domestic issues but was an isolationist in foreign affairs and helped defeat President Woodrow Wilson's League of Nations proposal. He bolted the Republican party in 1932 and 1936 to endorse Franklin Roosevelt and the New Deal. However, his support for Roosevelt's domestic policies was matched by his hostility to the administration's proposals for American membership on the World Court, reciprocal trade agreements, and a peacetime draft. He also opposed Roosevelt's campaigning for a third term. During World War II he voted against American membership in the United Nations. Although Johnson had been an outstanding Progressive governor, by the time of his death on Aug. 6, 1945, his views on foreign affairs made him part of an outdated isolationist minority in Congress.

Further Reading

Materials on Johnson's career after he entered the Senate are not readily available. For a scholarly account of his years as governor see George E. Mowry, *The California Progressives* (1951), and Spencer C. Olin, Jr., *California's Prodigal Sons: Hiram Johnson and the Progressives, 1911-1917* (1968).

Additional Sources

Weatherson, Michael A., *Hiram Johnson: a bio-bibliography*, New York: Greenwood Press, 1988.
Weatherson, Michael A., *Hiram Johnson: political revivalist*, Lanham: University Press of America, 1995. □

Jack Johnson

Jack Johnson (1878?-1946) became the first black heavyweight champion after winning the crown from Tommy Burns in Sydney, Australia on December 26, 1908. As a result of this victory, he became the center of a bitter racial controversy with the American public clamoring for the former white champion, Jim Jeffries, to come out of retirement and recapture the crown.

Jack Johnson, who became the first black heavyweight boxing champion in the world in 1908, was the preeminent American sports personality of his era, a man whose success in the ring spurred a worldwide search, tinged with bigotry, for a "Great White Hope" to defeat him. Handsome, successful, and personable, Johnson was known as much for his exploits outside of the ring as for his boxing skills. He married three white women in a time when such interracial unions resulted in denunciations of him from the floor of the United States Congress. He made big money, spent it lavishly, and lived grandly. And in doing so he gained admirers and detractors all over the world and became, quite simply, one of the best known men of the early twentieth century.

Johnson's autobiography, *Jack Johnson, In the Ring and Out*, remains the key source for information about his early life. In it he writes, "I am astounded when I realize that there are few men in any period of the world's history, who have led a more varied or intense existence than I." Like Muhammad Ali after him, Johnson was not shy about promoting himself or his exploits. Little is known of his early family life; Johnson writes that his three sisters and one brother had little effect on his life. His father was a janitor who was also known to have preached in local churches. He appears to have been closest to his mother, Tiny Johnson, and talks with pride of buying her a house with some of the purses he collected in his long boxing career.

When he was only 12 years old Johnson determined to leave his hometown of Galveston, Texas, and see the world, especially New York City. But getting to the city was difficult. He jumped a freight train, but was discovered, beaten, and thrown off. He jumped a boat, but ended up in Key West and worked as a fisherman. Finally, he hopped a freighter, worked as a cook on board, and reached New York. From there he went to Boston, where he worked in a stable, then hightailed it back to Galveston, where he became a dockworker at the age of 13.

Fought to Survive

Of his co-workers on the Texas waterfront, Johnson wrote, "To them, fighting was one of the important functions of existence. They fought upon every occasion and on any pretext. . . . Although I was one of the youngest in this rough and aggressive group, I had to do my share of fighting." After a series of street fights in Galveston, Johnson went to Dallas where he started to train as a boxer. Returning to Galveston, he began fighting his first series of bouts.

After whipping a man named Pierson—known throughout Galveston as the toughest man in town—Johnson's reputation was firmly fixed. And he had a new nickname, one that he would carry throughout his life, "Lil' Arthur."

Johnson soon outgrew Galveston; he had fought every tough guy in town. So he travelled to Springfield, Illinois, and then to Chicago, fighting in hastily arranged bouts for food and lodging. He was 17 years old when he fought a man named "Klondike" and lost. Johnson claimed that the loss marked the time when he decided he could make a living as a fighter. From Chicago, he went to New York by way of Pittsburgh, fighting all the while. Then it was back to Texas, across the South, and finally out to Denver where he traveled about with a group of other boxers, taking on all comers in all weight classes.

Johnson had been married to a black woman, Mary Austin, since 1898, but in Colorado their marriage broke up, sending Johnson into a state of depression. They had a brief reconciliation, but Johnson writes in his autobiography that the troubles he had with women "led me to forswear colored women and to determine that my lot henceforth would be cast only with white women." In a United States where Jim Crow was the law of the land, that decision would get him into a great deal of trouble. In fact, after Johnson's marriage to the white woman, Etta Duryea, in 1911, a Georgia Congressman, Seaborn Roddenberry, was so incensed he tried to get passed a constitutional amendment banning racial intermarriage. His bill died.

Back in Colorado, Johnson continued to fight while serving as camp cook for the traveling stable of boxers. Eventually he moved west, won the world's light heavyweight championship from a boxer named George Gardiner and began to set his sights on the heavyweight championship of the world. That would prove to be an elusive goal. By the end of 1906, Johnson had fought in 56 official fights and lost only two. But no one would give him a shot at the title. "I had demonstrated my strength, speed and skill, but still faced many obstacles, the principle one of which was the customary prejudice because of my race," he wrote. To win the championship, he had to defeat the reigning champ, Tommy Burns, so Johnson began a two-year quest to get that match.

Champion of the World

Johnson fought in Australia and England and began to generate a worldwide following. The press began to criticize Burns for avoiding Johnson. Finally the fight was set for December 26, 1908, in Sydney, Australia. Thirty thousand people attended the bout; the purse was $35,000, of which only $5,000 went to Johnson. In another concession to get the bout underway, Johnson had to agree to let Burns's manager referee the fight. Even under that manifestly unfair condition Johnson won; the police stopped the fight in the 14th round and Johnson was declared champ.

"A new champion had arrived and that new champion was Jack Johnson," he wrote in his autobiography. "I had attained my life's ambition. The little Galveston colored boy had defeated the world's champion boxer and, for the first and only time in history, a black man held one of the greatest honors which exists in the field of sports and athletics—an honor for which white men had contested many times and which they held as a dear and most desirable one. . . . To me it was not a racial triumph, but there were those who were to take this view of the situation, and almost immediately a great hue and cry went up because a colored man was holding the championship."

Thus began the era of the "Great White Hope," the name given to the white man who could take the championship belt away from Johnson. Johnson wrote that he "regretted" the racial aspect of the search for a new contender but that he was willing to take on anyone, no matter their color. While the search went on, Johnson fought a few minor bouts and engaged in his second career: that of music hall performer. Throughout his professional life, Johnson was booked on the vaudeville and lecture circuit, singing and dancing, telling stories and giving boxing exhibitions. He performed across the United States and in Europe.

But the life of the stage was not what the public expected of Johnson. They expected him to fight and a good number of them, especially whites upset with Johnson's rich living style and his dating of white women, expected him to be "put in his place" by a white fighter. The ultimate White Hope was Jim Jeffries, the retired heavyweight champ. When Jeffries retired he had anointed Burns as his replacement. With Burns thoroughly beaten by Johnson, the pressure was on Jeffries to come out of retirement and defend the title, and his race. One of the prime movers behind the White Hope search was the novelist Jack London. In an *Ebony* magazine article about the Johnson-Jeffries bout, London is quoted as writing after the Burns fight, "But one thing now remains. Jim Jeffries must now emerge from his Alfalfa farm and remove that golden smile from Jack Johnson's face. Jeff, it's up to you. The White Man must be rescued!"

Finally, Jeffries agreed to come out of retirement. The fight was originally set for California, but the governor there intervened and banned the match. The match was then set for Reno, Nevada, on July 4, 1910. When they climbed into the ring, the 32-year-old Johnson was a trim 208 pounds, while the 35-year-old Jeffries weighed 230 pounds. At 2:45 pm the fight began in front of tens of thousands of people who had gathered under the hot sun. In the weeks preceding the fight, editorial writers had warned that a Johnson victory would give blacks the wrong ideas: that African Americans might get it into their heads to rebel against oppression with their fists like Johnson. There was fear of rioting no matter which way the fight decision went.

According to *Ebony*, crowds around the world gathered outside of telegraph offices to hear updates of the fight taking place in Reno. The fight itself was, by all accounts, a great one. Jeffries was known for his famous crouch, a bent-over way of boxing. But Johnson neutralized this strategy quickly and landed numerous blows to Jeffries' face. He also taunted the ex-champ, saying, "Let me see what you've got," or "Do something." Johnson recalled in his autobiography, "I recall that occasionally I took time during the exchange of these blows to suggest to telegraph operators what to tell their newspapers." Johnson was "trash talking"

before it became fashionable and while some saw his words as evidence that he was in total control of the match, others—mainly whites—never forgave him for it.

In the *New York Times,* in an article that appeared the day after Johnson died in 1946, sports columnist Arthur Daley had little good to say about Johnson. He called Johnson's taunting of Jeffries an example of Johnson's "inherent meanness" and he talked about the "the stain that Lil' Arthur left on boxing and on his race." It seems that few people could forgive Johnson for what he had done in Reno that hot July day in 1910, when he knocked Jeffries out in the 15th round. In doing so, Johnson collected $60,000, as well as picture rights and bonuses that brought his total take to $120,000, a good sized sum in those days.

The predictions of violence in America came true: race riots erupted in many cities. Whites and blacks engaged in shoot outs and fistfights. As for Johnson, he took to the road to fulfill theatrical contracts, and when he had made some good money doing that, he traveled to London and Paris with his wife, Etta Duryea, who he had married in 1909. Johnson's vanity is evident when he describes his London trip, which occurred during the coronation of King George V: "Despite the fact that the King and his coronation were the center of attention, when my car traveled along London streets and it was announced that I was in sight, the attention of the crowds was turned upon me, and as long as I was in view the coronation ceremonies were forgotten while crowds milled and struggled for a glance at me."

When Johnson returned to the states, he opened a cabaret in Chicago. All races were welcome in his club. After about a year in Chicago, in September of 1912, Johnson's wife Etta committed suicide by shooting herself in the head. It was a great blow to the champ and his interest in boxing and business waned.

Exiled and a Questionable Defeat

Two months later Johnson would face an even greater personal challenge. He was arrested for violating the Mann Act, the statute prohibiting the transportation of women across state lines for unlawful purposes. The woman in question was Belle Schreiber, an old acquaintance of Johnson's. The problem with the charge is that Johnson and Schreiber were an item before the Mann Act became law in June of 1910. "It was a rank frame up," Johnson recalled in his memoirs. "The charges were based upon a law that was not in effect at the time Belle and I had been together, and legally was not operative against me."

That did not stop the courts from finding Johnson guilty in May of 1913, nor did it keep the judge from imposing a sentence of one year and one day in prison, and a fine of $1,000. In the meantime, Johnson had married Lucille Cameron, his 18-year-old white secretary. When the verdict was handed down, Johnson arranged for he and his wife to travel to Canada and, from there, to Paris. For the next seven years, Johnson was an exile from the United States, living in Europe, Mexico, and South America. His lifestyle overseas was lavish, and his exploits, including bullfighting, racing cars, performing on stage, and boxing, continued to receive worldwide attention. While in exile, his mother died, an event which saddened him very much.

On April 5, 1915, Johnson fought Jess Willard in Havana, Cuba. Willard won the bout, and the championship from Johnson, but Johnson would always claim that he threw the fight. He said that he was promised that he could return to the United States and avoid his year-and-a-day jail term if he would give up the championship to Willard, the latest in a line of White Hopes. Whether Johnson did indeed throw the fight, or whether he just got beat, has been a point of contention for many boxing observers since the fight ended by a knockout in the 26th round. "I could have disposed of him long before the final round," Johnson wrote of Willard. John Lardner in *Newsweek* recalled that Willard described his victory by saying, "I hit him [Johnson] a good uppercut." But Lardner goes on to write, "Very few people outside of Willard believe this, and maybe Jess doesn't either."

Whether fixed or fair, the bout cost Johnson the championship and did not end his exile. He wandered the globe for five more years before giving himself up to U.S. authorities in 1920. He served eight months in Leavenworth prison and became the physical director of the inmates, supervising track meets, baseball games, and fight training. While behind bars he continued to track his business interests and he used the time to think long and hard about the prison experience. Johnson came to believe that prison was good for the hardened criminal. But for the man who erred slightly in life, prison does nothing more than to arouse bitterness, Johnson felt. In any event, when he was released from Leavenworth, Johnson was met at the prison gates by a marching band and a horde of friends.

By 1921, Johnson had ended his exile, paid his debt to society, and began a new series of theatrical engagements. In 1924 he and his third wife were divorced and Johnson returned to boxing. He soon won a unanimous decision over a fighter named Homer Smith of Kalamazoo, Michigan. Two years later, at age 48, he beat a 24-year-old boxer named Pat Lester in Mexico.

In his autobiography, Johnson wrote, "I have always been an ardent motorist." He had cars when people were still riding bicycles and horses. Following his release from prison, the only run-ins with the law Johnson had came when he was behind the wheel of a car driving too fast. Five times cars rolled on top of Johnson and five times he survived. The sixth time he was not so lucky. According to the *New York Times* report of his death, Johnson was driving on Highway 1 near Raleigh, North Carolina, on June 10, 1946, when he lost control of his car, which hit a light pole and overturned. He died three hours later.

In the years before his death, Johnson had lectured at Hubert's Museum on Forty Second Street in New York. It was a seedy job that his friends and observers said allowed the great ex-champ to earn "bread and beer money." His last years were made enjoyable by his marriage to Irene Pineau in 1925. Johnson called her his true love.

The *Times* called Johnson, "One of the craftiest boxers known to the ring, recognized by many as one of the five outstanding heavyweight champions of all time." Johnson,

who was cocky, confident, and talented, would not have disagreed. But as John Lardner wrote in *Newsweek* after Johnson died, the champ's interest in how he would be remembered ranged beyond boxing. "Whatever you write about me," Lardner remembered Johnson telling him, "Just please remember that I'm a man, and a good one."

Further Reading

Johnson, Jack, *Jack Johnson, In the Ring and Out,* Proteus Publishing, 1977.
Ebony, April 1994, pp. 86-98.
Newsweek, June 24, 1946, p. 90.
New York Times, June 11, 1946, p. 1; June 12, 1946, p. 20. □

James Weldon Johnson

African American man of letters James Weldon Johnson (1871-1938) was also a teacher, politician, and lawyer. He is best known for his novel, *The Autobiography of an Ex-Colored Man,* and a book of poems, *God's Trombones.*

On June 17, 1871, James Weldon Johnson was born in Jacksonville, Fla. His father, a restaurant headwaiter, was entirely self-taught; his mother was a musician and school teacher. After taking his bachelor of arts degree at Atlanta University in 1894, Johnson taught in the public school for blacks in Jacksonville. Meanwhile he studied law and helped establish the first daily African American newspaper in his native city.

In 1898 Johnson joined his older brother, J. Rosamond Johnson, in New York City. Collaborating with his brother, a skilled musician, he wrote such hits as "Tell Me, Dusky Maiden," "Nobody's Looking but the Owl and the Moon," and "Oh, Didn't He Ramble." Some of Johnson's early poetry was published in the *Century* and the *Bookman.* He took his master of arts degree from Atlanta University in 1904.

Returning from a European theatrical tour in 1904, Johnson joined Theodore Roosevelt's successful presidential campaign and was rewarded with the appointment as U.S. consul at Puerto Cabello, Venezuela, in 1907. Two years later he went to Nicaragua in this same capacity. There he wrote his only novel, *The Autobiography of an Ex-Colored Man.* First published in 1912, the book established Johnson's concern with the social problems that beset black people and his commitment to finding solutions. He had married Grace Nail in 1910.

In 1916 Johnson joined the staff of the National Association for the Advancement of Colored People (NAACP) and, becoming general secretary in 1920, continued there until 1930. He was a militant crusader for black Americans, demanding political and cultural equality. Though his fight for congressional passage of the Dyer Antilynching Bill was unsuccessful, it stirred the South to action to abolish lynching.

Johnson's *Fifty Years and Other Poems* was published in 1917, and in 1920 a book on politics, *Self-determining Haiti,* appeared. He presented the *Book of American Negro Poetry* in 1922. This was a pioneering anthology, like his *Book of American Negro Spirituals,* which, with piano arrangements by his brother, appeared in 1925. (The two volumes had their ninth printing in 1964). But the book that brought him national attention as a poet was *God's Trombones: Seven Negro Sermons in Verse* (1927). Here Johnson broke new literary ground by discarding Negro dialect, employing instead the "native idiom of Negro speech" without distortion. *Black Manhattan,* a kind of memoir, was published in 1930, the year Johnson became professor of creative literature at Fisk University in Nashville, Tenn. He was also visiting professor of creative literature at New York University from 1934 until his death. His autobiography, *Along This Way* (1933), went through eight printings in 10 years. His last book, *St. Peter Relates an Incident* (1935), is a poetic satire on race prejudice.

Johnson won the W. E. B. Du Bois Prize for Negro literature in 1934, the Spingarn Medal twice, and the Harmon Award for distinguished achievement. He died in an automobile accident on June 26, 1938. In 1950 the James Weldon Johnson Memorial Collection of Negro Arts and Letters was founded in the Yale University Library.

Further Reading

Along This Way: The Autobiography of James Weldon Johnson (1933) is the best factual source. Johnson's *Black Manhattan* (1930) gives additional material. Sterling A. Brown, Arthur P.

Davis, and Ulysses Lee, *Negro Caravan* (1940), and James A. Emanuel and Theodore Gross, eds., *Dark Symphony: Negro Literature in America* (1968), contain brief critical treatment. More extensive treatment is in Saunders Redding, *To Make a Poet Black* (1939).

Additional Sources

Egypt, Ophelia Settle, *James Weldon Johnson,* New York, Crowell 1974.

Johnson, James Weldon, *Along this way: the autobiography of James Weldon Johnson,* New York, N.Y., U.S.A.: Penguin Books, 1990. □

Sir John Johnson

Sir John Johnson (1742-1830), American loyalist leader, engaged in military activities on the New York frontier during the American Revolution and was later a leader of the Tory refugees in Canada.

John Johnson was born in the Mohawk Valley, N.Y., the son of Sir William Johnson, a British colonial official. With his father's backing, John became a captain in the New York militia and fought during Chief Pontiac's rebellion. Sir William's prestige also accounted for John's being knighted during a visit to England in 1765. On his father's death, he inherited the title of baronet, lands estimated as high as 200,000 acres, and significant influence with the surrounding Indians and the British government.

Like his father, Sir John Johnson supported British authority along the frontier. In 1775, at the beginning of the American Revolution, Johnson began gathering ammunition and recruiting supporters. When threatened with force by Gen. Philip Schuyler, Johnson agreed to disarm his men, and when it became apparent that he would soon be arrested, he fled to Canada. He was promptly commissioned a lieutenant colonel in the British provincial forces and began raising a force of loyalist rangers.

Johnson marched with the British officer Barry St. Leger against Ft. Stanwix in 1777. But while St. Leger's men were successfully repulsing an American relief force at Oriskany, Johnson and his rangers were routed by a sortie from within Ft. Stanwix. Later, Johnson participated in Indian affairs and led a series of raids into the Mohawk Valley.

Whatever the limited value of his military activities during the Revolution, Johnson retained his prestige among British officials. Based in Canada, he was commissioned as Indian superintendent in 1782. He was compensated for the loss of his property in New York by grants of land and substantial cash payments. When the Revolution was over, he was given the task of explaining the consequences of the terms of the peace treaty to England's Iroquois Indian allies. He also supervised the settlement of loyalist refugees along the St. Lawrence River and remained active in Indian and loyalist matters. His notoriety as a leader of British and Indian raiding parties along the frontier ensured that he would never be allowed to return from Canadian exile to

New York. He lived on—relatively wealthy and still influential—in Montreal, dying at the age of 88.

Further Reading

There are numerous studies of Sir William Johnson which illuminate the early life of his son, John; perhaps the best is Arthur Pound and Richard E. Day, *Johnson of the Mohawks* (1930). For New York border warfare in general and Sir John Johnson's role in it see Howard Swiggett, *War out of Niagara: Walter Butler and the Tory Rangers* (1933).

Additional Sources

MacLachlan, Alan J., *John Johnson (1742-1830)*, Toronto: Dundurn Press, c1977. □

John Harold Johnson

John Harold Johnson (born 1918), an African American entrepreneur, turned a five hundred dollar loan into a multimillion-dollar business empire and became one of the richest men in the United States. He headed the most prosperous and powerful African American publishing company with such titles as *Ebony, Jet, Ebony Man, EM, Ebony Jr.,* as part of his journalistic successes.

John H. Johnson was born in Arkansas City, Arkansas, on January 19, 1918. When he was six years old, his father died, so Johnson was raised by his mother and stepfather. He attended an overcrowded and segregated elementary school. Such was his love of learning, he repeated the eighth grade rather than discontinue his education, since there was no public high school for African Americans in his community. After a visit with his mother to the Chicago World's Fair, they decided that opportunities in the North were more plentiful than in the South. Facing poverty on every side in Arkansas during the Great Depression, the family made the move to Chicago, Illinois, in 1933 to try to find work and for Johnson to continue his education. Johnson entered DuSable High School while his mother and step-father scoured the city for jobs during the day. He looked for work after school and during the summer. Their attempts were un-rewarded. His mother was not even able to find any domestic work, the work that was generally available when all else failed. To support themselves the family applied for welfare, which they received for two years until Johnson's stepfather was finally able to obtain a position with the Works Projects Administration (WPA) and Johnson himself secured a job with the National Youth Administration.

Johnson endured much teasing and taunting at his high school for his ragged clothes and country ways. This only fueled his already formidable determination to "make something of himself." Johnson's high school career was distinguished by the leadership qualities he demonstrated as student council president and as editor of the school news-

paper and class yearbook. After he graduated in 1936, he was offered a tuition scholarship to the University of Chicago, but he thought he would have to decline it, because he could not figure out a way to pay for expenses other than tuition. Because of his achievements in high school, Johnson was invited to speak at dinner held by the Urban League. When the president of the Supreme Life Insurance Company, Harry Pace, heard Johnson's speech, he was so impressed with the young man that he offered Johnson a job so that he would be able to use the scholarship,

Johnson began as an office boy at Supreme Life and within two years had become Pace's assistant. His duties included preparing a monthly digest of newspaper articles. Johnson began to wonder if other people in the community might not enjoy the same type of service. He conceived of a publication patterned after *Reader's Digest*. His work at Supreme also gave him the opportunity to see the day-to-day operations of an African American-owned business and fostered his dream of starting a business of his own.

Once the idea of *Negro Digest* occurred to him, it began to seem like a "black gold mine," Johnson stated in his autobiography *Succeeding against the Odds*. Johnson remained enthusiastic even though he was discouraged on all sides from doing so. Only his mother, a woman with biblical faith and deep religious convictions, as well as a powerful belief in her son, supported his vision and allowed him to use her furniture as collateral for a $500 loan. He used this loan to publish the first edition of *Negro Digest* in 1942.

Johnson had a problem with distribution until he teamed up with Joseph Levy a magazine distributor who was impressed with him. Levy provided valuable marketing tips and opened the doors that allowed the new digest to reach newsstands in other urban centers. Within six months circulation had reached 50,000. This publication covered African American history, literature, arts, and cultural issues. After several decades of publication its name was changed to *Black World*.

Although that publication achieved some success and at its height had a circulation of more than 100,000, it could not be compared with Johnson's subsequent publication, *Ebony* magazine, which was so popular that its initial run of 25,000 copies easily sold out. The articles in *Ebony*, which were designed to look like those in *LIFE* or *Look* magazines, emphasized the achievements of successful African American. Photo essays about current events and articles about race relations were also included in the magazine. Initially focused on the rich and famous in the African American community, Johnson expanded the reporting to include issues such as "the white problem in America," African American militancy, crimes by African Americans against African Americans, civil rights legislation, freedom rides and marches, and other aspects of segregation and discrimination. Trained historians were recruited for the magazine's staff so that the contributions of African American Americans to the history of the United States could be adequately documented. African American models were used in the magazine's advertisements and a conscious effort was made to portray positive aspects of African American life and culture. Everything in the magazine was addressed to the African American consumer. Johnson maintained that *Ebony*'s success was due to the positive image of African Americans that it offered.

In 1950, Johnson launched *Tan* magazine - a true confessions type magazine and in 1951, *Jet* - a weekly news digest. Later publications included *African American Stars* and *Ebony Jr.*—a children's magazine. Although all of the magazines achieved a measure of success, none was able to compete with *Ebony*, which in its 40th year of publication had a circulation of 2,300,000 and was the primary reason that Johnson was considered one of the 400 richest individuals in the United States. In 1972, he was named publisher of the year by the major magazine publishers in the United States.

Johnson expanded his business interests to areas other than his magazines. He became chairperson and chief executive officer of the Supreme Life Insurance Company, where he had begun as part-time office boy. He developed a line of cosmetics, purchased three radio stations, and started a book publishing company, and a television production company. He served on the board of directors of several major businesses, such as the Greyhound Corporation, and received numerous honors and awards for his achievements, including the National Association for the Advancement of Colored People's Spingarn Medal in 1966 for his contributions in the area of race relations.

In 1993, Johnson published his autobiography wherein he states "if it could happen to a Black boy from Arkansas it could happen to anyone" This publication celebrated the 50th anniversary of his publishing company.

In 1995, Johnson received the Communication Award for Communication on the occasion of Ebony magazine's 50th anniversary. Alfred C. Sykes, the chairman of the Center for Communication and president of Hearst Media Technology said "Mr. Johnson is a role model for many young people today, an example of how hard work, commitment and belief in oneself can lead to outstanding achievement. He rose from disadvantaged circumstances to achieve success in both business and national service during a time when great obstacles were placed in his path."

Because of his influential position in the African American community, Johnson was invited by the U.S. government to participate in several international missions. In 1959, he accompanied the vice president of the United States on a mission to Russia and Poland. He was appointed special ambassador to represent the United States at the independence ceremonies in the Ivory Coast in 1961 and in Kenya in 1963. Over the years Johnson had devoted a portion of several issues of *Ebony* to articles relating to African independence movements, but in August 1976 he dedicated an entire special issue to the subject "Africa, the Continent of the Future."

In 1996, President Bill Clinton bestowed the Presidential Medal of Freedom on Johnson and in 1997 Johnson was inducted into the Junior Achievement National Business Hall of Fame.

Further Reading

Johnson's autobiography *Succeeding Against the Odds* was published in 1989; biographical materials also appear in all of his publications *Ebony, Jet, Black World,;* other articles have appeared in *Black Enterprise, Chicago Tribune, Forbes, Fortune. Newsweek, LA Times, New York Post, Time, Printer's Ink,* and *Ebony Negro Almanac* (1976); some information about him is available in *The Shaping of African American America* (1975) by Lerone Bennett, Jr.; and in *African American Capitalism, Strategy for Business in the Ghetto* (1969) by Theodore L. Cross. □

Jonathan Eastman Johnson

The American painter Jonathan Eastman Johnson (1824-1906) excelled at genre paintings of life in America during the 1860s and 1870s. He also drew and painted many portraits.

Eastman Johnson was born in August 1824 at Lovell, Maine. His family soon moved to nearby Fryeburg. He spent his youth in Augusta, the capital, for his father was Maine's secretary of state. At the age of 15 Johnson left home to work in a dry-goods store in New Hampshire. Because of his interest in drawing, he worked for a year in a lithographic shop in Boston. In 1842 he returned to Augusta and began making and selling crayon portraits at modest prices. Successful, he drew portraits in Cambridge, Mass., and Newport, R.I., and in 1845 he moved to Washington, D.C., where within a year he had drawn such famous people as Daniel Webster and Dolly Madison. In 1846 he moved to Boston at the invitation of Henry Wadsworth Longfellow, whose portrait he drew, as well as those of Longfellow's family and friends. He remained in Boston for 3 years.

It was not until 1848 that Johnson made his first oil painting, a portrait of his grandmother. The following year he went to Europe to improve his art. He studied for 2 years at the Royal Academy in Düsseldorf, Germany. After a brief visit to France and Italy, Johnson spent 3 1/2 years at The Hague, Holland, where he made a close study of Dutch 17th-century painting, particularly Rembrandt. Known in The Hague as the "American Rembrandt," he was offered, but refused, the post of court painter.

Intent on portraying American subjects, Johnson returned to America in 1855. Shortly afterward, while visiting a sister in Wisconsin, he made paintings of American Indians. In 1859 in Washington, D.C., he made his first large genre painting, titled *Life in the South* (today called *Old Kentucky Home*). This won him acclaim and election to the National Academy in New York.

During the Civil War, Johnson followed the Union Army, sketching subjects for genre paintings, the most famous of which is the *Wounded Drummer Boy*. During the next 2 decades he spent much of his time painting New Englanders of all ages at work and at play. It is for these that he is now famous.

At Fryeburg, Johnson made many informal oil sketches around a sugar-making camp. In the early 1870s he visited Nantucket, where he painted a group of old men sitting around a stove (*Nantucket School of Philosophy*) and the large *Corn Husking Bee*. At Kennebunkport, Maine, he painted a group of intimate little pictures of his family that are among his best works.

As the demand for his genre paintings decreased, Johnson's popularity as a portraitist increased, and after 1880 he painted few genre subjects. For the most part his commissioned portraits, though they brought him wealth, are dark and dull. Toward the end of his life he made three brief trips to Europe. He died in New York City on April 5, 1906.

Further Reading

John I.H. Baur, *An American Genre Painter: Eastman Johnson, 1824-1906* (1940), the catalog for the 1940 Johnson exhibition at the Brooklyn Museum, contains a brief life of the artist, illustrations of some of his work, and a listing of located and unlocated works. Since 1940, additional works have been located. Patricia Hills, *Eastman Johnson,* is the catalog of the 1972 Johnson exhibition held at the Whitney Museum of American Art, New York City. □

Lyndon Baines Johnson

As the thirty-sixth president of the United States, Lyndon Baines Johnson (1908-1973) created new programs in health, education, human rights, and conservation and attacked the crushing 20th-century problems of urban blight and poverty with what he called the "War on Poverty."

Most commentators account Lyndon Johnson as one of America's most experienced and politically skilled presidents. He sponsored a flood of new legislation designed to better the quality of life among the disadvantaged and the dispossessed of the nation. In foreign policy he set about to strengthen regional arrangements of power so that new and small nations might develop their own form of political society without fear of intrusion from their more powerful neighbors. He inherited an American commitment in South Vietnam, and his determination to preserve the independence of that beleaguered country led to virulent attacks and, finally, his momentous decision not to seek reelection.

Lyndon Johnson was born on Aug. 27, 1908, near Johnson City, Texas, the small community founded by his forebears. Life was hard and plain in the Texas hill country at this time. Johnson's father struggled to raise his two sons and three daughters. His mother was a gentle woman, who encouraged her children to love books and gave them a sense of duty and responsibility. Johnson graduated from Southwest State Teachers College in San Marcos, Tex., with a bachelor of science degree, having combined his studies with a job teaching Mexican-American children.

Johnson's early teaching assignments were at Pearsall, Tex., and in the Houston high schools. In 1931, politics beckoned. He went to Washington, D.C., as secretary to Texas congressman Richard Kleberg. Almost immediately Johnson's talent for attracting affection and respect became visible. He was elected Speaker of the "Little Congress," an assembly of congressional secretaries on Capitol Hill.

On Nov. 17, 1934, an event occurred which Johnson always described as the most notable triumph of his life: he married Claudia (Lady Bird) Taylor of Karnak, Texas. She became his partner, confidant, and counselor, and from her, Johnson drew strength and love and reserves of support that never faltered.

Johnson's ultimate destiny was beginning to take shape. At age 27, he was already exhibiting his characteristic traits of energy, intellect, and tenacity when he resigned as a congressional secretary in 1935 to become the Texas director of the National Youth Administration. The origins of the later Johnson can be located in his conduct of this office; he surrounded himself with bright, young men and invested his duties with a 24-hour torrent of activity.

Rising through Congress

In 1937, the congressman from Texas's Tenth District died suddenly. When a special election was called to select a successor, Johnson hesitated only slightly. His wife provided campaign funds from her inheritance, and Johnson leaped into a race crowded with eight opponents. The only candidate to support President Franklin Roosevelt's court-

packing plan, he did so with such vigor that the eyes of the nation were drawn to the outcome, and none watched it with more intensity than Roosevelt himself. To the amazement of political veterans, the 28-year-old Johnson won the race.

President Roosevelt, in Texas on a fishing trip, was so elated that he invited Johnson to accompany him back to Washington, D.C. Thus, Johnson became his personal protégé. With the aid of the powerful House Speaker Sam Rayburn of Texas and the continuing support of the President, Johnson was brought into the councils of ruling establishmentarians of the House of Representatives.

In 1941, Johnson entered another special election, this time for a Senate seat made vacant by a death. Texans were surprised by the campaign he launched by helicopter. Nearly every community watched the tall, smiling Johnson alight from his helicopter. In a bitter campaign Johnson lost by 1,311 votes to that bizarre political phenomenon Governor W. Lee ("Pass the Biscuits Pappy") O'Daniel.

There was little time for Johnson to lick his wounds. That December he became the first member of Congress to enter active military duty. He joined the Navy and in 1942 received the Silver Star for gallantry in a bombing mission over New Guinea. When President Roosevelt ordered all congressmen back to the capital in 1942, Johnson reentered the House.

In 1948, Johnson's restless quest for higher office was finally successful. In a savagely fought senatorial campaign, he defeated a former governor of Texas by a celebrated margin of 87 votes. The elders of the Senate soon recognized that Johnson was no ordinary rookie senator. He did his homework, was knowledgable on every item that confronted the Senate, and was in instant command of all the nuances and subtleties of every important piece of legislation.

In January 1951, just 3 years into his first term, Johnson was elevated to Democratic "whip" (assistant minority leader). Regarding his age and tenure, no similar selection had ever been made in the history of the Senate. In 1953, when the post of minority leader in the Senate opened up Democratic senators without hesitation chose Johnson to take charge. With the congressional elections of 1954, the Democrats took command of both houses. And with this new alignment, Johnson again set a record as the youngest man ever to become majority leader.

The Johnson legend of leadership now became visible to the nation. Not since the early days of the republic had one man assumed such clear direction over the course and affairs of the Senate. Operating his office around the clock, intimately aware of all that transpired, and firmly fixed in his intent and design, Johnson was the "complete Senate leader." Now one voice spoke for the Democrats, as Johnson became the "second most powerful man in Washington, D.C."

The habits of work and discipline that would later confound the nation when Johnson became president were now on display in the Senate chamber. He handled the Senate with confidence and skill. The Republican opposition found it impossible to outflank this majority leader; legislation opposed by Johnson rarely found acceptance by the Senate. He encouraged new, young senators and found coveted spots for them on important committees.

Johnson led the first civil rights bill in 82 years through the Senate. He guided to final victory the first space legislation in the National Aeronautics and Space Act of 1958. In 1958, designated by President Dwight Eisenhower to represent the United States at the United Nations, he presented the resolution calling for the peaceful exploration of outer space. He exposed wastes in defense procurement during the Korean War and conducted defense hearings that were a model of accuracy and dispassionate scrutiny.

In 1960, Johnson briefly opposed John F. Kennedy for the Democratic presidential nomination; then Kennedy electrified the country by choosing Johnson as his vice-presidential running mate. While some Kennedy supporters grumbled, experts later agreed that Johnson's relentless campaigning in Texas and throughout the South had provided Kennedy with his winning margin.

Serving as Vice President

As vice-president, Johnson had important assignments. One of his principal tasks was the burgeoning space program, which was overshadowed by Russian triumphs with *Sputnik* and subsequent innovations that put the United States in an inferior role. Regarding civil rights, as chairman of the Equal Employment Opportunity forces, Johnson surprised many critics by putting uncompromising pressure on American industry. At the President's request, he made fact-finding trips to Berlin and to the Far East.

On Nov. 22, 1963, President Kennedy was assassinated in Dallas. Aboard the plane *Air Force One* at Love Field in Dallas, Johnson took the presidential oath of office on November 23. Giving orders to take off seconds later, the new president flew back to Washington to take command of the government, while the nation grieved for its fallen leader.

Filling the Presidency

Five days after taking office, President Johnson appeared before a joint session of the Congress. Speaking with firmness and controlled passion, he pledged "we shall continue." Important legislation submitted by President Kennedy to the Congress, currently bottled up and seemingly stymied in various committees of both houses, was met by Johnson's deliberate and concentrated action. The new president—meeting round the clock with staff, Cabinet, and congressmen—unbuckled key legislation, so that within a few short months the tax cut and the civil rights bills were passed by Congress and signed by the President.

Six months after assuming the presidency, Johnson announced his concept of the "Great Society." The areas he considered vital were health and education; the whole complex of the urban society, with its accompanying ills of ghettos, pollution, housing, and transportation; civil rights; and conservation.

Johnson took his innovative domestic programs to the nation in the election of 1964. Meanwhile, the American involvement in Vietnam, sanctioned by three presidents, became an issue. Senator Barry Goldwater chastised Johnson for his liberal approach to domestic problems and suggested a massive step-up in the bombing of North Vietnam. Johnson traversed the nation and convinced it that his leadership was of such caliber that the voters could not afford to drive him from office. He won by a margin of almost 16 million votes, more than 61 percent of the total vote, the widest margin in totals and percentage of any presidential election in American history.

Administration Achievements

Barely pausing, the President, reinforced by this clear mandate, began a legislative program which was rivaled in scope and form only by Franklin Roosevelt's New Deal a generation earlier. Between 1965 and 1968 more than 207 landmark bills were passed by the Congress.

In education, Johnson's administration tripled expenditures. By the end of 1968, 1.5 million students were receiving Federal aid to help them gain their college degrees; over 10 million people learned new skills through vocational education; and 19,000 school districts received special help under the Elementary and Secondary Education Act. More than 600,000 disabled citizens were trained through vocational rehabilitation programs. Head Start and other preschool programs brought specific assistance to more than 2 million children.

In the area of health, Johnson's administration increased Federal expenditures from $4 billion to $14 billion in 4 years. More than 20 million Americans were covered by Medicare, and more than 7 million received its benefits. About 31 million children were vaccinated against four severe diseases, reducing by 50 percent the number of children who suffered from these diseases, and more than 3 million children received health care under Medicaid in one year. Some 286 community mental health centers were built. More than 390,000 mothers and 680,000 infants received care through the Maternal and Child Health programs. Some 460,000 handicapped children were treated under the Crippled Children's Program.

Fighting poverty, the Johnson administration lifted more than 6,000,000 Americans out of the poverty depths. Over 100,000 young men and women completed Job Corps training; 2.2 million needy Americans were helped under the Food Stamp Program; school children benefited from the School Milk and School Lunch programs.

In the area of human and civil rights, the Voting Rights Act was passed in 1965, and within 3 years nearly 1 million Negroes registered to vote in the South. More than 98 percent of all the nation's hospitals agreed to provide services without discrimination. More than 28 percent of all Negro families by 1968 earned about $7,000 a year, doubling the 1960 figure. Some 35 percent more Negroes found professional, technical, and managerial jobs between 1964 and 1968.

In housing, in 4 years the Johnson administration generated the construction of 5.5 million new homes. Direct

Federal expenditures for housing and community development increased from $635 million to nearly $3 billion. Two million families received Federal Housing Administration improvement loans. Federal assistance provided housing for 215,000 families earning less than $7,000 a year. Nearly $427 million was spent for water and sewage facilities in small towns. More than 3.5 million rural citizens benefited from economic opportunity loans, farm operation and emergency loans, and watershed and rural housing loans.

Most importantly, the Johnson administration presided over the longest upward curve of prosperity in the history of the nation. More than 85 months of unrivaled economic growth marked this as the strongest era of national prosperity. The average weekly wage of factory workers rose 18 percent in 4 years. Over 9 million additional workers were brought under minimum-wage protection. Total employment, increased by 7.5 million workers, added up to 75 million; the unemployment rate dropped to its lowest point in more than a decade.

In foreign affairs, where risk and confrontation stretched a perilous tightrope throughout the Johnson years, the President made significant achievements. In the Western Hemisphere, at Punta del Este, Uruguay, the Latin American nations agreed to a common market for the continent. Normal relations with Panama were restored and a new canal treaty negotiated. In Cyprus, at the brink of war, the President's special emissaries knitted a settlement that staved off conflict. A rebellion in the Congo, which would have had ugly repercussions throughout the continent, was put down with American aid in the form of transport planes. In the Dominican Republic, an incipient Communist threat was challenged by an overwhelming show of American force, with Latin American allies. Amid tangled criticism from sections of the press and some Latin American nations, the President persevered in the Dominican Republic, where democratic government and free elections were restored and U.S. troops promptly withdrawn.

An outer-space treaty was negotiated with the Soviet Union and a nuclear nonproliferation treaty was formulated and agreed to in Geneva. In June 1967 the President met with Premier Alexei Kosygin of the Soviet Union. Meanwhile, the North Atlantic Treaty Organization was successfully realigned after France withdrew, and the vast Western European alliance was restructured and strengthened.

It was the troubled Southeast Asian problem in South Vietnam to which Johnson devoted long, tormented hours. Presidents Truman, Eisenhower, and Kennedy had declared that the security of the United States was involved in deterring aggression in South Vietnam from an intruding Communist government from the North. However, there was much disagreement in the United States over this venture; some critics claimed the Vietnam war was a civil one, an insurrection, and not an invasion. When Johnson first became chief executive, 16,000 American troops were in Vietnam as advisers and combat instructors. In 1965 the United States decided to increase its military support of South Vietnam and authorized commitment of more American troops. By 1968 there was considerable disaffection over the Asian policy, and many critics in and out of the

Congress determined to force the Johnson administration to shrink its commitment and withdraw U.S. troops.

Beginning in April 1965 with the President's speech at Johns Hopkins University, in which he set forth the American policy of reconstruction of the area and the promulgation of the Asian Development Bank as an instrument of peace building, the Johnson administration attempted to negotiate with a seemingly intransigent North Vietnam, whose troops were infiltrating into the South in increasing numbers. A 37-day bombing pause in December 1965 raised hopes for negotiation, but lack of response from the North Vietnamese blotted this out, and the bombing resumed.

Assaulted by fierce and growing criticism, yet determined to fix some course of action which would diminish the war and commence serious peace talks, the President startled the nation and the world on March 31, 1968, by renouncing his claim to renomination for the presidency. Johnson said that he believed that the necessity for finding a structure of peaceful negotiation was so important that even his own political fortunes must not be allowed to stand in its way. Therefore, he stated, he would not seek renomination, so he could spend the rest of his days in the presidency searching for negotiation without any political taint marring a possible response from the enemy.

On May 11, 1968, it was announced that peace talks would indeed begin in Paris, and in November 1968 the President declared that all bombing of North Vietnam would cease.

Johnson retired to his ranch near San Antonio, Texas, where he took a keen interest in the care and sale of his cattle, while nursing a serious heart ailment.

The tragic Vietnam War was in its last days in January, 1973 when a period of mourning was declared to mark the death of President Harry S Truman. Shortly after it began, it also marked the death of Lyndon B. Johnson.

On the afternoon of January 22, 1973, Johnson suffered a heart attack while lying down to take a nap. He was flown to a hospital by his Secret Service agents, but was pronounced dead on arrival at 4:33 pm. His body lay in state first at the Johnson Library in Austin, Texas, then, as is usual for American presidents, in the rotunda of the Capitol in Washington, D.C. until his burial on his beloved ranch.

Johnson's Influence

While historians search the record and evaluate its significance, there seems little doubt that Lyndon Johnson's impress on the form and quality of life in the United States will be seen to be large. In the fields of health, education, civil rights, conservation, and the problem of the elderly, his legislative achievements have left their clear mark. His insistence that the pledges of the four preceding presidents be upheld in Southeast Asia is a subject for debate. But it must be argued that his peace-keeping efforts in the Middle East, in the Near East, in Africa, and in Latin America were forceful, remedial, and worthy of praise; the results have proved his policies' merits.

Johnson belongs in the tradition of the "strong president"; he dominated the government with his energy and personality and invested his office with intimate knowledge of all government business. He was the target of intense and sometimes virulent criticism, just as all strong American presidents have found themselves ceaselessly and bitterly attacked.

Further Reading

Johnson's *The Vantage Point* (1971) presents his own perspectives on his White House years. There is not yet an authoritative or comprehensive biography of Johnson. Boothe Mooney, *The Lyndon Johnson Story* (1956; rev. ed. 1964); and Clarke Newlon, *LBJ: The Man from Johnson City* (1964; rev. ed. 1966), are journalistic; Sam Houston Johnson, *My Brother Lyndon,* edited by Enrique Hank Lopez, is a superficial and undocumented account by the President's brother. Aspects of Johnson's life and presidency are treated in William S. White, *Citadel: The Story of the U.S. Senate* (1957); and *The Professional: Lyndon B Johnson* (1964); Michael Amrine, *This Awesome Challenge: A Hundred Days of Lyndon Johnson* (1964); Rebekah Baines Johnson, *A Family Album,* edited by John S. Moursund (1965); Charles Roberts, *LBJ's Inner Circle* (1965); Theodore H. White, *The Making of the President* (1965); Rowland Evans and Robert Novak, *Lyndon B. Johnson, The Exercise of Power: A Political Biography* (1966); Philip Geyelin, *Lyndon B. Johnson and the World* (1966); Jim Bishop, *A Day in the Life of President Johnson* (1967); James Deakin, *Lyndon Johnson's Credibility Gap* (1968); Hugh Sidney, *A Very Personal Presidency: Lyndon Johnson in the White House* (1968); Tom Wicker, *JFK and LBJ: The Influence of Personality upon Politics* (1968); and Eric F. Goldman, *The Tragedy of Lyndon Johnson* (1969); Lady Bird Johnson, *White House Diary* (1970), is a record of the Johnson presidency as experienced by his wife; for the mid-century political background see James L. Sundquist, *Politics and Policy: The Eisenhower, Kennedy, and Johnson Years* (1968). □

Marietta Louise Pierce Johnson

Marietta Louise Pierce Johnson (1864-1938), founder and 30-year teacher of an Alabama experimental school, made herself a pioneer in the progressive education movement.

Marietta Louise Pierce Johnson was born in St. Paul, Minnesota, daughter of Clarence D. and Rhoda Matilda (Morton) Pierce. Her early education was in public schools in Minnesota, and even as a young girl in school she dreamed of becoming a teacher herself. On her graduation from the State Normal School (now St. Cloud State College) in 1885 she did become a teacher, and in time a distinguished one. Within a few years she had taught every grade in the elementary school and had also had some high school teaching experience. In 1890 she was appointed a supervisor of student teachers on the faculty first of the St. Paul Teachers' Training School (1890-1892), then at the State Teachers Colleges at

Moorhead (1892-1895) and at Mankato (1896-1899). As a supervising "critic teacher" she observed students in practice teaching, gave special instruction in pedagogy, and on occasion would take over a class to demonstrate her ideas. She is remembered in these years as an inspiring and creative teacher, full of new ideas on schooling.

In June 1897 she was married to John Franklin Johnson, and they became the parents of two children. The Johnsons spent the winter of 1903 at Fairhope, Alabama, a small community on the eastern shore of Mobile Bay that had been founded some years earlier by followers of Henry George's single-tax theory. In this somewhat utopian community Marietta Johnson was invited to open an experimental school to explore some of her educational ideas. Her new ideas on schooling owed much to the early writings of John Dewey and specifically to Nathan Oppenheim's book *The Development of the Child.* As an educational theorist she was in broad terms the heir of the child-centered romanticism of Jean-Jacques Rousseau. She accepted the opportunity with enthusiasm and in 1907 moved permanently to Fairhope to found the School of Organic Education which she served as director until 1938.

Beginning with six students the first day, the Organic School, as it came to be called, enrolled in time as many as 200 each year. With parent and community support and Johnson's tireless fundraising, the school received no public funds but was always tuition free to its students. It was called "organic" in that the central aim of the school was to "minister to the health of the body, develop the finest mental grasp, and preserve the sincerity and unself-consciousness of the emotional life." That is, the child was seen always as a "unit organism" in order for schooling to promote the growth of the whole child. In Johnson's view, education and growth were identical.

The curriculum organization and the life of the Organic School were carefully informal. All grades, marks, promotions, and reports were thought to create only tensions of self-consciousness and were therefore omitted entirely. Students were judged only in terms of their individual abilities and hence extrinsic rewards were eliminated in favor of the intrinsic satisfactions of learning and growth. The measures of success of students, and indeed of the entire school, were to be based on creativity, spontaneity, interest, and sincerity in their lives.

The school was divided into six divisions beginning with a kindergarten for children under age six and reaching through high school and college preparatory studies. Based on the Rousseauan (and later Deweyan) idea that formal studies should emerge from the child's awakening intrinsic interests, instruction in reading and writing were delayed as long as possible, certainly no sooner than age eight. Throughout the grades there was always strong emphasis on creative expression; on crafts, music, dance, and imaginative drama; and on trips and visits ranging over the countryside. In the later grades came the shift to more formal studies, from nature study to biological sciences, and so on. The high school was fully accredited; its graduates entered colleges on certificate, where they appeared to do well.

Commenting on the possible influence of her experimental school on American education in general, Johnson late in her life wrote, "It is very thrilling to contemplate what society might be in a few years. . . . No examinations, no tests, no failures, no rewards, no self-consciousness; the development of sincerity, the freedom of children to live their lives straight out, no double motives, children never subjected to the temptation to cheat, even to appear to know when they do not know; the development of fundamental sincerity, which is the basis of all morality." The principles of the Organic School in Johnson's view could be the basis for the transformation of public education and of American society.

Johnson's vision of a new education, based as it was on her Organic School experiment, took on national prominence with the publication in 1915 of the Deweys' *Schools of Tomorrow*. John Dewey and his daughter Evelyn after visiting and studying the school wrote extensively and glowingly about the experiment in this widely read survey of innovative schools in America. The Johnson school along with the others reviewed as *Schools of Tomorrow* helped form the base for the emerging theories of progressive education. Marietta Johnson herself was one of the leading spirits in the founding of the Progressive Education Association in the years following World War I and remained throughout her life an inspiration to that organization. In her later years she was honored by the association as a permanent honorary vice-president. Ever a crusader, Johnson established a second Organic School following the Fairhope model in Greenwich, Connecticut, and by the late 1920s she was dividing her time between Alabama and New England. She also was active over the years in conducting summer schools for parents, teachers, and children in Greenwich (1913-1916 and 1919-1921) and in Fairhope (1917 and 1918). Her best account of the Fairhope experiment and her statement of the principles of Organic Education are contained in her book *Youth in a World of Men*, published in 1929.

At the time of her death in 1938 Marietta Johnson was honored as one of the founding forces of the progressive education movement and as particularly influential in the child-centered schools organized in following years by such theorists as Margaret Naumburg and A.S. Neill. Her child-centered vision of education continues to inspire and stimulate new ideas in schooling.

Further Reading

Additional information on the work of Marietta Johnson can be found in Lawrence A. Cremin, *The Transformation of the School: Progressivism in American Education, 1876-1957* (1962); John Dewey and Evelyn Dewey, *Schools of Tomorrow* (1915); and "Marietta Johnson and Fairhope," in *Progressive Education* (February 1939). □

Philip Johnson

Philip Johnson (born 1906) was an American architectural critic and historian and a practicing archi-
tect. His buildings are characterized by formal elegance.

B orn in Cleveland, Ohio, on July 8, 1906, Philip Johnson attended Harvard College, majoring in the classics. There, in 1927, he was introduced to the modern movement in architecture through the writings of Henry-Russell Hitchcock.

Johnson began his career as an architectural critic and historian in 1931, when he became director of the architectural department at the newly formed Museum of Modern Art in New York. That year he and Hitchcock mounted the first International Exhibition of Architecture, showing the work of such major modern figures as Le Corbusier, Walter Gropius, and Ludwig Mies van der Rohe. With Hitchcock he published *The International Style* (1931), which not only defined the esthetic qualities of the new style but also gave it a name.

During the 1930s and 1940s, in his role as museum director and in his writings (he wrote the first monograph on the work of Mies van der Rohe in English in 1947), Johnson remained a leading American advocate of the International Style. But by 1940 Johnson decided to shift from propagandist to practitioner. He entered the Harvard Graduate School of Design and studied under Marcel Breuer.

In 1949 Johnson designed his own home in New Canaan, Conn., following closely Mies's principle of the glass box in which the steel skeletal structure is exposed. But

while Mies's work often conveys a feeling of austerity, Johnson's glass house seems romantic—an effect achieved by placing the building in a parklike setting. His other homes of this period which have a similar quality are the Hogson House (1951) and the Wiley House (1953), both in New Caanan.

By 1954, Johnson was beginning to move away from the dictums of Mies's architectural theory, although he collaborated with his mentor on the design for the Seagram Building in New York City (1958). In his design for the Kneses Tifereth Israel Synagogue, Port Chester, N.Y., Johnson introduced certain non-International Style elements—for example, an elliptical entrance hall and butterfly vaulting on the interior ceilings. During the 1960s Johnson turned more to historical motifs as the means of individualizing his buildings. In contrast to the stark lines of his earlier Munson-Williams-Proctor Institute (1957-1960) in Utica, N.Y., he utilized clear historical allusion in the Byzantine domes which top the Art Gallery at Dumbarton Oaks, Washington, D.C. (1962-1964). An interest in classical forms is evident in his use of colonnades in the Sheldon Art Gallery at the University of Nebraska (1964) and the New York State Theater in New York City (1963).

Johnson maintained his interest in the Museum of Modern Art and designed an addition to the building in 1964. The same year he exploited new technological techniques in the structure of his daring New York State Pavilion at the New York World's Fair. In some of his later designs (for example, the Kline Tower at Yale University) Johnson showed—through his use of texture and color on the exterior surfaces—how far he had come from the earlier Miesian style toward a more robust, individualized idiom.

His later more significant works include the New York State Theater, Lincoln Center (1964) as well as New York City's American Telephone and Telegraph Company Building (1978-1984). Even into his nineties, his thoughts about style continued to evolve and he continued to be a presence in the world of architecture.

Further Reading

Schulze, Franz, *Philip Johnson: Life and Work* (1994)
Blake, Peter, *Philip Johnson* (1996)
Johnson, Philip, et al, *Philip Johnson: The Architect in His Own Words Vol 1* (1994)
Kipnis, Jeffrey and Kipuis, Jeff, *Philip Johnson Recent Work* (1996) □

Samuel Johnson

Samuel Johnson (1696-1772), American clergyman and educator, was the first Anglican minister in Connecticut and first president of King's College, later Columbia University.

Samuel Johnson was born in Guilford, Conn., on Oct. 14, 1696. His father was a deacon. A precocious student, Samuel acquired a fondness for Hebrew at the age of 6. He was unable to enter grammar school until the age of 11, but at 14 he was admitted to the Collegiate School (now Yale) at Saybrook, Conn. Even before graduating in 1714, he began teaching school at Guilford. When Yale moved to New Haven in 1716, he was made a tutor. For the first 2 years he taught the three lower classes alone, introducing students to the works of two prominent Englishmen—philosopher John Locke and scientist and philosopher Isaac Newton.

However, Johnson's relations with his students were unhappy. A student contingent presented a petition complaining of the "Public Expositions & Disputations & Managements of the Tutors"; Johnson was singled out as the worst. Although the Yale Corporation found him guiltless, he tendered his resignation in September 1719 and accepted a call to the pulpit of neighboring West Haven.

Johnson continued to use the growing resources of the Yale library, which had recently acquired the latest English works, including several volumes of liberal Anglican theology. He read and discussed these works with his classmate Daniel Browne and with Yale's new president, Timothy Cutler, and the three developed doubts concerning the validity of the "Congregational Way." In September 1722 the three men announced their misgivings at commencement, launching the "Great Apostasy." Soon after, they sailed to England, where they obtained Anglican ordination. A year later Johnson returned to Stratford, Conn., as the first Anglican minister to the colony and remained the only one for 3 years. On Sept. 23, 1725, he married Charity Nicoll, a widow, and became guardian of her two sons.

The work of propagating and defending the Anglican persuasion in New England consumed 30 years of Johnson's life. As the acknowledged intellectual and ecclesiastical leader of the movement, he was asked to become the head of the new King's College in New York City in 1753. In 1754 he moved his family to New York and began a decade as president of the college.

In a colonial culture of rampant denominationalism, King's College was chartered as a nonsectarian institution with a mixed board of trustees. The only Anglican requirements were that the president always be of the Church of England and that the daily prayers be conducted from the Book of Common Prayer. On Sundays the students attended the church of their choice.

The enrollment was small—only eight boys graduated in the first class of 1758—and the fees were the highest in the Colonies. The boys' median age at entrance was 15, and the attrition rate was high. But this was fertile ground for Johnson. As he advertised in the *New York Gazette* in 1754, "the chief thing that is aimed at in this college is to teach and engage the children to know God in Jesus Christ, and to love and serve Him in all sobriety, godliness, and righteousness of life, with a perfect heart, and a willing mind."

Johnson taught the first-year class himself so that he might "carry them through the New Testament in its Greek original, and not only make them understand the words but the things, explaining all difficult passages, and giving them a clear understanding of the whole scheme of Christianity." And he ensured that his graduates would have a greater understanding of the "New Philosophy" than he had by devoting three-fourths of the sophomore and junior class curriculum to mathematics and science.

Unfortunately Johnson's personality and probably his well-known disparagement of colonial culture robbed him of success. "He did not figure greatly as a president," wrote President Ezra Stiles of Yale, "but it does not seem to have been for want of Learning. Dr. Johnson was an excellent Classical Scholar—he had few equals in *Latin, Greek* and *Hebrew*. He was good at the Sciences, easy and communicative, was eminent in Moral Philosophy," as he demonstrated in his book *Elementa philosophica* (1752). Nevertheless, Stiles concluded, "Some Geniuses, with half the Observation and Reading of Dr. Johnson, would make ten times greater Men."

When Johnson's second wife died of smallpox in 1763—a previous outbreak had carried off his first wife, son, and stepdaughter—he lost the heart to continue and retired to his parish in Stratford. He died on Jan. 6, 1772.

Further Reading

Herbert and Carol Schneider edited *Samuel Johnson, President of King's College: His Career and Writings* (4 vols., 1929). Johnson's work as president of King's College is recounted in Horace Coon, *Columbia: Colossus on the Hudson* (1947). His importance as a philosopher is ably discussed in Robert Clifton Whittemore, *Makers of the American Mind* (1964).

Additional Sources

Carroll, Peter N., *The other Samuel Johnson: a psychohistory of early New England,* Rutherford N.J.: Fairleigh Dickinson University Press, 1978. □

Samuel Johnson

The writings of the English author and lexicographer Samuel Johnson (1709-1784) express a profound reverence for the past modified by an energetic independence of mind. The mid-18th century in England is often called the Age of Johnson.

Samuel Johnson was born in Litchfield, Staffordshire, on Sept. 18, 1709. His father was a bookseller—first successful, later a failure—and Johnson, whom Adam Smith described as the best-read man he had ever known, owed much of his education to the fact that he grew up in a bookstore. Though he lived to old age, from infancy Johnson was plagued by illness. He was afflicted with scrofula, smallpox, and partial deafness and blindness. One of his first memories was of being taken to London, where he was touched by Queen Anne, the touch of the sovereign then thought to be a cure for scrofula.

Johnson was educated at the Litchfield Grammar School, where he learned Latin and Greek under the threat of the rod. He later studied with a clergyman in a nearby village from whom he learned a lesson always central to his thinking—that, if one is to master any subject, one must first discover its general principles, or, as Johnson put it, "but grasp the Trunk hard only, and you will shake all the Branches." In 1728-1729 Johnson spent 14 months at Pembroke College, Oxford. He was poor, embarrassed by his poverty, and he could not complete the work for a degree. While at Oxford, Johnson became confirmed in his belief in Christianity and the Anglican Church, a belief to which he held throughout a life often troubled by religious doubts. His father died in 1731, and Johnson halfheartedly supported himself with academic odd jobs. In 1735 he married Mrs. Elizabeth Porter, a widow some 20 years older than he. Though Johnson's references to his "Tetty" were affectionate, the 17 years of their childless marriage were probably not very happy. Still casting about for a way to make a living, Johnson opened a boarding school. He had only three pupils, one of them being David Garrick— eventually to become the greatest actor of his day. In 1737 Johnson went to London to make a career as a man of letters.

Making His Name

Once in London, Johnson began to work for Edward Cave, the editor of the *Gentleman's Magazine*. Parliament did not then permit stenographic reports of its debates, and Cave published a column called "Debates in the Senate of

Lilliput''—the name is taken, of course, from the first book of Jonathan Swift's *Gulliver's Travels*—for which Johnson, among others, wrote re-creations of actual parliamentary speeches. Years later, when someone quoted to him from a speech by William Pitt the Elder, Johnson remarked, ''That speech I wrote in a garret in Exeter Street.''

Johnson worked at a variety of other literary tasks. He published two ''imitations'' of the Roman satirist Juvenal, *London, a Poem* (1738) and *The Vanity of Human Wishes* (1749), transposing the language and situations of the classical originals into those of his own day. In 1744 Johnson published a biography of his friend Richard Savage. A neurotic liar and sponger and a failed writer, Savage had been one of Johnson's friends when they were both down and out, and to such early friends Johnson was always loyal. The *Life of Savage* is a sympathetic study of a complex and initially unsympathetic man. In 1749 Johnson completed his rather lifeless tragedy in blank verse *Irene*; it was produced by Garrick and earned Johnson £300.

In the early 1750s Johnson, writing usually at the rate of two essays a week, published two series of periodical essays—*The Rambler* (1750-1752) and *The Adventurer* (1753-1754). The essays take various forms—allegories, sketches of representative human types, literary criticism, lay sermons. Johnson constantly lived in the presence of the literature of the past, and his essays refer to the classics as if they were the work of his contemporaries. He has a satirist's eye for discrepancies and contradictions in human life, yet he is always in search of the central and universal, for whatever is unchanging in man's experience. His prose is elaborate and richly orchestrated, and he seems to have tried to enlarge the language of moral philosophy by using scientific and technical terms.

Johnson's interest in specialized vocabularies can be easily explained. In 1746 he had, with the help of six assistants, begun work on a dictionary of the English language. The project was finally completed in 1755. Johnson had originally tried to interest Lord Chesterfield in becoming patron for this vast project, but he did little to help Johnson until help was no longer needed. Johnson wrote Chesterfield a public letter in which he declared the author's independence of noble patronage. Johnson's *Dictionary* is probably the most personal work of its kind that will ever be compiled; though Johnson received help from others, it was not the work of a committee. His own definition of *lexicographer* was a ''writer of dictionaries; a harmless drudge,'' yet the work bears his personal stamp: it is notable for the precision of its definitions, for its appreciation of the paramount importance of metaphor in use of language, and for its examples, which draw on Johnson's reading in 200 years of English literature.

Johnson's *Rasselas, Prince of Abissinia* appeared in 1759, the year of the publication of Voltaire's *Candide*, a work which it somewhat resembles. Both are moral fables concerned with an innocent young man's search for the secret of happiness. The young Prince Rasselas, accompanied by his sister and the philosopher Imlac, leaves his home in the Happy Valley and interviews men of different kinds in the hope of discovering how life may best be lived.

Disillusioned at last, Rasselas returns to his old home. Though Johnson was given to fits of idleness, he could at other times work with great facility; he wrote *Rasselas* in the evenings of one week to pay for the expenses of his mother's funeral. The work was immediately successful; six editions appeared during Johnson's lifetime and also a number of translations.

Years of Success and Fame

In 1762 Johnson, though he had been anti-Hanoverian in his politics, accepted a pension of £300 a year from George III. A year later he met James Boswell, the 22-year-old son of a Scottish judge. Boswell became Johnson's devoted companion; he observed him closely, made notes on his conversation, and eventually wrote the great biography of his hero. Boswell's Johnson is a formidable and yet endearing figure: bulky, personally untidy, given to many eccentricities and compulsions, in conversation often contentious and even pugnacious, a man of great kindness who delighted in society but was also the victim of frequent black moods and periods of religious disquiet. In 1773 Boswell persuaded Johnson, who pretended a stronger dislike of the Scots than he actually felt, to join him in a tour of Scotland, and there are records of the trip made by both men—Johnson's *A Journey to the Western Islands of Scotland* (1775) and Boswell's journal.

In 1764 Johnson and the painter Joshua Reynolds founded a club whose members eventually numbered some of the most eminent men of the time; they included the writer Oliver Goldsmith, Johnson's old pupil David Garrick, the economist Adam Smith, the historian Edward Gibbon, and the politicians Edmund Burke and Charles James Fox. In 1765 Johnson met Mr. and Mrs. Henry Thrale. He was a well-to-do brewer, and in the Thrales' home Johnson found a refuge from the solitude which had oppressed him since his wife's death in 1752. In 1765 Johnson published an eight-volume edition of the works of Shakespeare; in his ''Preface'' Johnson praises Shakespeare for his fidelity to nature and defends him against the charge that his failure to observe the three classical unities was a limitation on his achievement.

Last Years

Johnson's last great literary enterprise, a work in 10 volumes, was completed in his seventy-second year; it is the *Prefaces, Biographical and Critical, to the Works of the English Poets,* better known as the *Lives of the Poets.* It is a series of biographical and critical studies of 52 English poets, the earliest being Abraham Cowley; it is a magisterial revaluation of the course of English poetry from the early 17th century until his own time by a man whose taste had been formed by the poetry of John Dryden and Alexander Pope and who was thus in varying degrees out of sympathy with the metaphysicals and John Milton, as he was with the more ''advanced'' writers of his own time. Even when he deals with writers whom he does not much like, Johnson shows his genius for precise definition and for laying down fairly the terms of a critical argument.

Johnson's last years were saddened by the death of his old friend Dr. Robert Levett (to whom he addressed a beautiful short elegy), by the death of Thrale, and by a quarrel with Mrs. Thrale, who had remarried with what seemed to Johnson indecorous haste. In his last illness Johnson, always an amateur physician, made notes on the progress of his own disease. He died on Dec. 13, 1784, in his house in London, and he was buried in Westminster Abbey.

Further Reading

The Yale Edition of the Works of Samuel Johnson, edited by Edward L. McAdam, Jr., and others (9 vols., 1958-1971, and still in progress), will eventually supersede all earlier editions. The Letters of Samuel Johnson was edited by R. W. Chapman (3 vols., 1952). The Poems of Samuel Johnson was edited by David Nichol Smith and Edward L. McAdam, Jr. (1941). The best edition of Lives of the Poets is by George B. Hill (3 vols., 1905). A convenient one-volume edition of James Boswell's Life of Johnson was edited by Robert William Chapman (1953). Joseph Wood Krutch, Samuel Johnson (1944), is a reliable modern biography. James Lowry Clifford, Young Sam Johnson (1955), is an account of Johnson's life before he met Boswell.

Critical studies particularly recommended are Walter Jackson Bate, The Achievement of Samuel Johnson (1955), and Matthew J. C. Hodgart, Samuel Johnson and His Times (1962). Aspects of Johnson's career and thought are examined in Donald Johnson Greene, The Politics of Samuel Johnson (1960); Maurice J. Quinlan, Samuel Johnson: A Layman's Religion (1964); Arieh Sachs, Passionate Intelligence: Imagination and Reason in the Work of Samuel Johnson (1967); Paul Kent Alkon, Samuel Johnson and Moral Discipline (1967); and Paul Fussell, Samuel Johnson and the Life of Writing (1971). A useful guide to the literature on Johnson is James Lowry Clifford and Donald J. Greene, Samuel Johnson: A Survey and Bibliography of Critical Studies (1951; rev. ed. 1970). □

Tom Loftin Johnson

American entrepreneur and politician Tom Loftin Johnson (1854-1911) made a fortune from his inventions and investments, then began a second, distinguished career as a reform congressman and mayor.

Tom L. Johnson was born at Blue Spring, Ky., on July 18, 1854. During the Civil War his family experienced hard times, and he received little formal education. Young Johnson made his way by selling newspapers, and his earnings enabled the family to move to Louisville, Ky., just after the war. While still a teenager, he began working for the streetcar company of family friends. He quickly worked his way up from office boy to superintendent.

Johnson invented the first fare box for coins, and his earnings from this, plus loans from friends, gave him enough capital at the age of 22 to buy controlling interest in an Indianapolis streetcar company. In 1879 Johnson boldly bought into a Cleveland streetcar line. This venture made him a business rival of Mark Hanna, who later became his political rival as well. Johnson prospered and soon was able to increase his streetcar holdings. He also invented an improved streetcar rail and built steel mills to produce his inventions. By the late 1890s he was a millionaire.

Though he had made his fortune in business, Johnson began to turn against capitalism. He had read Henry George's Progress and Poverty, a powerful critique of America's economic system, and after meeting George in 1885, he became a spokesman for George's tax reform ideas. At George's urging Johnson ran for the U.S. Congress from Ohio, losing twice, but winning in 1890 and 1892. In Congress, Johnson was a free-trade Democrat who opposed the protective tariff, which he saw as another form of economic privilege.

By 1900 Johnson's conversion to reform was complete. He sold all his streetcar and manufacturing interests and was elected mayor of Cleveland in 1901 as a reform Democrat. His program of municipal home rule, regulation of streetcar monopolies, and municipal ownership of public utilities attracted bright young progressives to his administration. He built an efficient political organization, which was as effective as many orthodox city "machines" but did not resort to traditional machine practices of bribery and patronage.

During Johnson's four terms as mayor (1901-1909), he fought the political bosses successfully and modernized the city through scientific management of public works, nonpartisan administration of many city bureaus, and extension of social services. He was a remarkable organizer and an outstanding figure of the early Progressive movement. He died on April 10, 1911.

Further Reading

Johnson's autobiography, My Story, edited by Elizabeth J. Hauser (1913), provides the best overview of his career. Frederick C. Howe, The Confessions of a Reformer (1925), is by an admiring associate. Carl Lorenz, Tom L. Johnson: Mayor of Cleveland (1911), is more critical. A balanced assessment of Johnson is in Hoyt Landon Warner's scholarly Progressivism in Ohio, 1897-1917 (1964).

Additional Sources

Johnson, Tom Loftin, My story, Kent, Ohio: Kent State University Press, 1993.

Murdock, Eugene C., Tom Johnson of Cleveland, Dayton, Ohio: Wright State University Press, 1993. □

Virginia E. Johnson

Virginia E. Johnson (born 1925) is a researcher in human sexuality. With her then-husband, William H. Masters, she cowrote Human Sexual Response in 1966.

n collaboration with Dr. William Howell Masters, psychologist and sex therapist Virginia E. Johnson pioneered the study of human sexuality under laboratory conditions. She and Masters published the results of their study as a book entitled *Human Sexual Response* in 1966, causing an immediate sensation. As part of her work at the Reproductive Biology Research Foundation in St. Louis and later at the Masters and Johnson Institute, she counseled many clients and taught sex therapy to many professional practitioners.

Johnson was born Virginia Eshelman on February 11, 1925, in Springfield, Missouri, to Hershel Eshelman, a farmer, and Edna (Evans) Eshelman. The elder of two children, she began school in Palo Alto, California, where her family had moved in 1930. When they returned to Missouri three years later, she was ahead of her school peers and skipped several grades. She studied piano and voice, and read extensively. She entered Drury College in Springfield in 1941. After her freshman year, she was hired to work in the state insurance office, a job she held for four years. Her mother, a republican state committeewoman, introduced her to many elected officials, and Johnson often sang for them at meetings. These performances led to a job as a country music singer for radio station KWTO in Springfield, where her stage name was Virginia Gibson. She studied at the University of Missouri and later at the Kansas City Conservatory of Music. In 1947, she became a business writer for the St. Louis *Daily Record*. She also worked briefly on the marketing staff of KMOX- TV, leaving that position in 1951.

In the early 1940s she married a Missouri politician, but the marriage lasted only two days. Her marriage to an attorney many years her senior also ended in divorce. On June 13, 1950, she married George V. Johnson, an engineering student and leader of a dance band. She sang with the band until the birth of her two children, Scott Forstall and Lisa Evans. In 1956, the Johnsons divorced.

In 1956, contemplating a return to college for a degree in sociology, Johnson applied for a job at the Washington University employment office. William Howell Masters, associate professor of clinical obstetrics and gynecology, had requested an assistant to interview volunteers for a research project. He personally chose Johnson, who fitted the need for an outgoing, intelligent, mature woman who was preferably a mother. Johnson began work on January 2, 1957, as a research associate, but soon advanced to research instructor.

Gathering scientific data by means of electroencephalography, electrocardiography, and the use of color monitors, Masters and Johnson measured and analyzed 694 volunteers. They were careful to protect the privacy of their subjects, who were photographed in various modes of sexual stimulation. In addition to a description of the four stages of sexual arousal, other valuable information was gained from the photographs, including evidence of the failure of some contraceptives, the discovery of a vaginal secretion in some women that prevents conception, and the observation that sexual enjoyment need not decrease with age. In 1964, Masters and Johnson created the non-profit Reproductive Biology Research Foundation in St. Louis and began treating couples for sexual problems. Originally listed as a research associate, Johnson became assistant director of the Foundation in 1969 and co-director in 1973.

In 1966, Masters and Johnson released their book *Human Sexual Response,* in which they detailed the results of their studies. Although the book was written in dry, clinical terms and intended for medical professionals, its titillating subject matter made it front-page news and a runaway best seller, with over 300,000 volumes distributed by 1970. While some reviewers accused the team of dehumanizing and scientizing sex, overall professional and critical response was positive.

At Johnson's suggestion, the two researchers went on the lecture circuit to discuss their findings and appeared on such television programs as NBC's *Today* show and ABC's *Stage '67.* Their book and their public appearances heightened public interest in sex therapy, and a long list of clients developed. Couples referred to their clinic would spend two weeks in intensive therapy and have periodic follow-ups for five years. In a second book, *Human Sexual Inadequacy,* published in 1970, Masters and Johnson discuss the possibility that sex problems are more cultural than physiological or psychological. In 1975, they wrote *The Pleasure Bond: A New Look at Sexuality and Commitment,* which differs from previous volumes in that it was written for the average reader. This book describes total commitment and fidelity to the partner as the basis for an enduring sexual bond. To expand counseling, Masters and Johnson trained dual-sex therapy teams and conducted regular workshops for college teachers, marriage counselors, and other professionals.

After the release of this second book, Masters divorced his first wife and married Johnson on January 7, 1971, in Fayetteville, Arkansas. They continued their work at the Reproductive Biology Research Foundation, and in 1973 founded the Masters and Johnson Institute. Johnson was co-director of the institute, running the everyday business, and Masters concentrated on scientific work. Johnson, who never received a college degree, was widely recognized along with Masters for her contributions to human sexuality research. Together they received several awards, including the Sex Education and Therapists Award in 1978 and Biomedical Research Award of the World Sexology Association in 1979.

In 1981, the team sold their lab and moved to another location in St. Louis, where they had a staff of twenty-five and a long waiting list of clients. Their book *Homosexuality in Perspective,* released shortly before the move, documents their research on gay and lesbian sexual practice and homosexual sexual problems and their work with "gender-confused" individuals who sought a "cure" for their homosexuality. One of their most controversial conclusions from their ten-year study of eighty-four men and women was their conviction that homosexuality is primarily not physical, emotional, or genetic, but a learned behavior. Some reviewers hailed the team's claims of success in "converting" homosexuals. Others, however, observed that the handpicked individuals who participated in the study were not a representative sample; moreover, they challenged the team's assumption that heterosexual performance alone was an accurate indicator of a changed sexual preference.

The institute had many associates who assisted in research and writing. Robert Kolodny, an M.D. interested in sexually transmitted diseases, coauthored the book *Crisis: Heterosexual Behavior in the Age of AIDS* with Masters and Johnson in 1988. The book, commented Stephen Fried in *Vanity Fair,* "was politically incorrect in the extreme": it predicted a large-scale outbreak of the virus in the heterosexual community and, in a chapter meant to document how little was known of the AIDS virus, suggested that it might be possible to catch it from a toilet seat. Several prominent members of the medical community questioned the study, and many accused the authors of sowing hysteria. Adverse publicity hurt the team, who were distressed because they felt the medical community had turned against them. The number of therapy clients at the institute declined.

The board of the institute was quietly dissolved and William Young, Johnson's son-in-law, became acting director. Johnson went into semi-retirement. On February 19, 1992, Young announced that after twenty-one years of marriage, Masters and Johnson were filing for divorce because of differences about goals relating to work and retirement. Following the divorce, Johnson took most of the institute's records with her and is continuing her work independently.

Further Reading

Robinson, Paul, *The Modernization of Sex: Havelock Ellis, Albert Kinsey, William Masters, and Virginia Johnson,* Cornell University Press, 1988.

Duberman, Martin Bauml, review of, *Homosexuality in Perspective, New Republic,* June 16, 1979, pp. 24–31.

Fried, Stephen, "The New Sexperts," in *Vanity Fair,* December 1992, p. 132.

"Repairing the Conjugal Bed," in *Time,* March 25, 1970. □

Sir William Johnson

British colonial administrator Sir William Johnson (1715-1774) was an important intermediary between England and the Indians in North America.

William Johnson was born at Smithtown, County Meath, Ireland. He came to New York about 1738 to supervise the lands along the Mohawk River belonging to his uncle. There he either married or took as a mistress Catherine Weisberg, who bore him a son and a daughter.

Johnson gained influence with the Indians and in 1745, at the outbreak of king George's War, he kept the Iroquois from allying with the French. The following year he was appointed a colonel and given responsibility for Indian affairs. In February 1748 Johnson was given command of 14 companies of militia raised for the defense of the New York frontier, and on May 1 he was commissioned as colonel for the Albany County militia regiment.

In April 1750 Johnson was appointed to the Council of New York, a position he held for the rest of his life. Five years later, in the French and Indian War, he received a commission for "sole Management & direction of the Affairs of the Six Nations of Iroquois & their Allies." As a major general, with 2,000 militia and 200 Indians, he defeated the French and Indians forces at Crown Point in September 1755. Although failing to take Crown Point, Johnson built a fort and won acclaim for blunting the French threat.

In November 1755 Johnson was made a baronet and appointed superintendent of Indian affairs for the Northern Department. For the next 3 years he concerned himself with Indian affairs and the defense of the northern frontier. He commanded the column that captured Ft. Niagara on July 25, 1759, and participated in Gen. Jeffery Amherst's successful expedition against French Montreal.

Johnson next undertook the organization of new tribes under his jurisdiction and in 1763 was able to put down the conspiracy of Chief Pontiac. In the Treaty of Ft. Stanwix (November 1768) he persuaded the Indians to give up their claims to lands in New York, Pennsylvania, and Virginia. He was successful in preventing the Iroquois from joining the Shawnees at the outbreak of Lord Dunmore's War in 1774.

Johnson was a member of the American Philosophical Society and of the Society for the Promotion of Arts, an organization devoted to the development of agriculture. After the death of his first wife he took a niece of a Mohawk chief as a housekeeper; she bore him three children. Later, by his common-law wife, the sister of another Mohawk chief, he had eight children. He died on July 11, 1774.

Further Reading

The best biography of Johnson is Arthur Pound and Richard E. Day, *Johnson of the Mohawks* (1930). Still useful are William L. Stone, *The Life and Times of Sir William Johnson, Bart.* (1865); William Elliot Griffis, *Sir William Johnson and the Six Nations* (1891); and Augustus C. Buell, *Sir William Johnson* (1903).

Additional Sources

Flexner, James Thomas, *Lord of the Mohawks: a biography of Sir William Johnson,* Boston: Little, Brown, 1979.

Flexner, James Thomas, *Mohawk baronet: a biography of Sir William Johnson,* Syracuse, N.Y.: Syracuse University Press, 1989, 1979.

Igneri, David S., *Sir William Johnson: the man and his influence,* New York: Rivercross Pub., 1994.

Rowles, Catharine Bryant, *Tomahawks to hatpins,* Lakemont, N.Y.: North Country Books, 1975.

Simms, Jeptha Root, *Trappers of New York: or, A biography of Nicholas Stoner and Nathaniel Foster: together with anecdotes of other celebated hunters, and some account of Sir William Johnson, and his style of living,* Harrison, N.Y.: Harbor Hill Books, 1980.

Powell, Richard J., *Homecoming: the art and life of William H. Johnson,* Washington, D.C.: National Museum of American Art, Smithsonian Institution; New York: Rizzoli, 1991. □

William H. Johnson

Living and working abroad for many years, the African American painter William H. Johnson (1901-1970) is best known for his style of colorful, neo-folk depictions of the black experience.

William Henry Johnson was born in Florence, South Carolina, in 1901. As a young boy Johnson drew frequently, mainly copying comic strips, between odd jobs. At 17 Johnson left South Carolina to pursue a career as a newspaper cartoonist in New York. By 1921 he was admitted to New York's School of National Academy of Design. At the academy Professor Charles W. Hawthorne guided the talented Johnson and provided him with employment to fund his studies. Johnson also worked in George Luks' studio in exchange for painting lessons.

Recognized as having tremendous potential, Johnson was encouraged to study abroad. Like African American artist Henry O. Tanner, Johnson sought professional recognition and racial acceptance overseas. In 1926 Johnson sailed for Paris. In Paris his art was influenced by such popular modern movements as Post-Impressionism and Expressionism. Specifically, his works drew from the styles of Paul Cezanne (French, 1839-1906) and Chaim Soutine

(Lithuanian, 1894-1943). Aspects of a tumultuous, Expressionist style were evident in Johnson's landscapes such as *Cagnes sur Mer* (1928-1929).

After nearly two years in France, the young artist visited New York where he again met George Luks. Impressed with Johnson's artistic progress, Luks nominated him for the prestigious Harmon Award, and with his support Johnson's work received recognition in the city's art community. While in America, Johnson also returned to his childhood home where his style took an important turn. Using friends and family as subjects, Johnson started to document the daily activities of Florence, South Carolina. A painting from this period, *Girl in Green Dress* (1930), demonstrated Johnson's direct style and ability to capture expression.

Painting in Europe and New York

Confident from his American trip, Johnson returned to France with the promise of a successful career. Johnson also looked forward to a reunion with Danish textile artist Holcha Krake, with whom he had begun a relationship. Soon after his arrival in Europe, they married. The couple resided in the resort town of Kerteminde, Denmark, where Johnson painted many landscapes. Many of these works recalled paintings of his wife's friend Oskar Kokoschka (Austrian, 1886-1980). Kokoschka's sinuous lines and thick pigment were prominent elements of Johnson's work *Tiled Rooftops, Denmark* (1931).

The Johnsons continued to create art and travel extensively. After a trip to Tunisia, the Johnsons moved to Norway

in 1935. Once again Johnson's style changed as he abandoned Kokoschka's distortions and remembered his South Carolina trip where young subjects became a theme. Johnson returned to child models as he approached his mature style in works such as *Girl in a Red Dress* (1936). In 1937 Johnson completed one of the finest works of his oeuvre, *Self Portrait with Pipe*. This regal self-portrait in a smoking jacket commanded recognition for Johnson based on its dynamic brushstrokes, striking color, and captivating expression.

By the end of the 1930s Johnson, like many in Europe, found the events in Germany as well as rumors of a Nazi invasion of Denmark gravely unsettling. The threat of world war was the catalyst for the Johnsons' move to the United States in 1938. William H. Johnson arrived in New York and quickly became active in the city's art scene. New York, a refuge for many European artists during the war, became the art center of the world. Johnson's return to the United States presented him with opportunities to once more "paint his own people."

With a new teaching job at the Harlem Community Art Center through the government-sponsored Works Progress Administration (WPA) program, Johnson produced paintings of African Americans from his studies of European art and African sculpture. His knowledge of European modernism and primitive forms was instrumental in establishing Johnson's style. By 1940 his paintings concentrated solely on African-American subjects and were executed in a direct manner referring to American folk art.

Johnson's depictions of African-American urban life, such as *Cafe* (1939-1940) and *Street Musicians* (1940), were well received by New York's diverse population. Johnson was also known for his portraits of celebrities including singer Marian Anderson, boxer Joe Louis, and scenes from the Savoy Ballroom.

A trip to South Carolina resulted in the production of Johnson's signature folk art works including *Farm Couple at Work* (1940), *Sowing* (1940), and *Going to Church* (1940-1941), as he then applied his command of color and direct style to Black subjects of the rural south. These paintings showed the culmination of his training and talent. Boasting a bright palette and abstract features, Johnson's mature compositions were attributed to his exposure to modern French painters and study of African tribal sculpture.

As World War II raged on, Johnson abandoned the carefree New York subjects and moral southern life in favor of combat scenes. He participated in the national art competition to promote war awareness with works such as *Station Stop, Red Cross Ambulance* (1942) and *Killed in Action* (1942).

Johnson's compassion was evident through his World War II paintings, but he also painted suffering in his "Breakdown" series. In this series Johnson's subjects cope with life's difficulties and setbacks. *The Honeymooners* (1940-1941) and *Breakdown with Flat Tire* (1940-1941) are works with subjects based on automotive problems and their symbolic reference to overcoming life's hardships.

Following the "Breakdown" series, Johnson concentrated on upbeat themes of America's swing culture. The Jitterbug dance craze was of special interest to American artists as evidenced by Johnson's abstract compositions such as *Jitterbugs* that captured the free-spirited energy of America's cities in the 1940s.

During this productive period, tragedy struck. Fire raged through the Johnsons' Greenwich Village apartment, but this was only one of the difficulties which Johnson faced in 1943. In that same year the Harlem riots ignited racial tensions and changed Johnson's paintings of the city. The socially conscious work *Moon over Harlem* (1943-1944) chronicled the aftermath of an urban dispute and the mistreatment and prejudice directed toward African Americans.

The uprising paralleled Johnson's personal struggle as his beloved wife battled cancer. As a result Johnson's paintings dealt with religious subjects. Maintaining his African-American heritage, Johnson created a series of religious works tied to the Black folk art tradition, including *Mount Calvary* (1944) and *Climbing Jacob's Ladder* (1944).

Home to South Carolina

Following Holcha's death Johnson went home to South Carolina. He quietly immortalized family members in *Mom Alice* (1944), *L'il Sis* (1944), and *Little Girl in Green* (1944). After completing a great body of portraits, Johnson returned to New York and concentrated on subjects documenting African American historical events. He promoted African American history through portraits of important figures in the struggle for equality, including Harriet Tubman, John Brown, and Abraham Lincoln.

While Johnson painted the rise of African Americans, his own life began to deteriorate. After a final trip to Denmark, he settled in New York where his wife's death, racism, and economic hardship took their toll. These events resulted in a mental breakdown, and from the late 1940s until his death in 1970 Johnson was institutionalized. He stopped painting completely after 1949.

Although his later years were riddled with mental instability, William H. Johnson's contribution to American art remains monumental. He was responsible for the introduction of various aspects of European modernism into American art. He played an integral role in creating opportunities and acceptance for other African American artists. Through his paintings he documented his heritage while simultaneously depicting urban and rural America at mid-century. From the southern homestead to the Savoy Ballroom, William H. Johnson's unique brand of neo-folk art drew from European modernism and traditional African forms to spark a new movement in modern American painting.

Further Reading

The most thorough and inclusive works on the career of William H. Johnson are exhibition catalogues: *Homecoming: The Art and Life of William H. Johnson* (1991) and *William H. Johnson: 1901-1970* (1971) by Adelyn Breeskin. For examinations of African American art within its cultural context, see Mary Schmidt Campbell, *Harlem Renaissance: Art of Black Amer-*

ica (1987); and *Flash of the Spirit: African and Afro-American Art and Philosophy* (1983). □

Henry Hamilton Johnston

Henry Hamilton Johnston (1858-1927), or Sir Harry Johnston, was an English administrator, explorer, naturalist, painter, and author. He helped to explore Africa, to govern its subject peoples, and to make scholarly sense of the continent's complexity.

Henry Johnston was born in London on June 12, 1858, the eldest of 12 children of Esther and John Johnston, a wealthy and well-traveled insurance company director. Henry discovered his aptitude for drawing, painting, and languages at an early age and, before he was out of his teens, had attracted the attention of the London Zoological Society and the Royal College of Surgeons. For a time he pursued the study of languages at King's College, University of London, but in 1875 became a pupil of painting at the Royal Academy.

In 1878 Johnston began painting in France, and during the next 2 years his paintings began to be hung in the academy. He also illustrated for the Zoological Society, and his studies of birds and animals appeared in *The Field,* a leading natural-history periodical. In late 1879 Johnston went to Tunis to paint. He spent the better part of the next 2 years there and in Algiers. He grew artistically and learned to feel comfortable in, and knowledgeable about, a Moslem culture. Even more important, Johnston was swept up in the tide of European imperialism; he was prepared emotionally and intellectually for an intensely political career as one of England's far-flung proconsuls.

Travels in Africa

In 1882 Johnston accompanied the Earl of Mayo, an enthusiastic amateur zoologist and adventurer, on a hunting expedition through Angola. In preparing for this voyage Johnston, reading in the British Museum, developed a lifelong interest in the problems associated with classifying the Bantu tongues.

During 1882-1883 Johnston traveled in western and southern Angola, first with Lord Mayo and then with Africans, and throughout a large section of the Congo. The meeting of explorer Henry Stanley near the mouth of the Congo fed Johnston's ambition and joined him mentally to the great age of exploration. Yet Johnston's published account of his experiences in the Congo, *The River Congo* (1884), discusses politics little. Like so many of Johnston's books, it is a supremely illustrated travel narrative of lasting historical, ethnographical, and botanical value.

With the publication of his book and a number of articles in British periodicals, Johnston achieved a degree of recognition as an Africanist and explorer. In 1884 he was called to the Foreign Office for confidential discussions about the activities of Belgium's King Léopold in the Congo.

The same year he was asked by the British Association and the Royal Geographical Society to visit Kilimanjaro in East Africa and there collect alpine equatorial flora. The results of this journey were significant botanically and linguistically. *The Kilimanjaro Expedition,* again with his own magnificent illustrations, appeared in 1886.

Civil Service Career

By late 1885 Johnston was on his way to the Bight of Biafra as vice-consul for the Oil Rivers and the Cameroons. He was Britain's overlord in the area. When King Ja Ja, the celebrated palm oil merchant of Opobo, proved antagonistic to the success of British traders, Johnston tricked and then forcibly ousted him. Johnston encouraged and perpetrated a number of similar acts of gunboat diplomacy on behalf of British imperialist expansion before returning home in 1888.

From 1889 to 1896 Johnston, as Her Majesty's commissioner and consul general for Mozambique and the Nyasa districts, created the nucleus of modern Malawi and personally articulated and directed the development of British energies in the trans-Zambezian regions of Central Africa. First in partnership with Cecil Rhodes and later with the help of Alfred Sharpe, Johnston's successor and the first governor of Nyasaland, he subdued the opposition of Africans to the white incursion, fought off the Portuguese, who claimed the region, and encouraged white settlement and agriculture.

After marrying Winifred Irby in 1896, Johnston was appointed consul general in Tunis. During the 2 years he spent there, his scholarly inclinations became more pronounced. He published *British Central Africa* (1897), the important record of his first proconsulship, and readied the first edition of what, in the second edition of 1913, became *The Colonization of Africa.*

From 1899 to 1901 Johnston created the basis of modern Uganda. Although the protectorate had been in existence for 7 years, he, as special commissioner and commander in chief, arranged the settlement of internal difficulties known as the Uganda Agreement. Johnston gave the Ganda, the dominant people in the southern sector of the country, considerable political and territorial advantages over the other hierarchically organized peoples of the protectorate.

For the remainder of his life, Johnston turned his energies to writing and scholarship. He completed a two-volume report on his last mission, *The Uganda Protectorate* (1902); wrote *British Mammals* (1903) and *The Nile Quest* (1903); after visits there, the two-volume *Liberia* (1906); a two-volume study of an influential Protestant missionary, *George Grenfell and the Congo* (1908); and the remarkably prescient *The Negro and the New World* (1910), a volume personally encouraged by President Theodore Roosevelt and based on a journey to the West Indies and the United States. Between 1919 and 1924, in addition to *The Story of My Life* (1923), he published six novels. His major work during this last phase of his life was the two-volume *Comparative Study of the Bantu and Semi-Bantu Languages* (1919, 1922), a taxonomic work of lasting, if now exceedingly controversial, value. Johnston died in 1927 near Worksop in Nottinghamshire.

Further Reading

In addition to Johnston's autobiography, there is a biography by his brother, Alex Johnston, *The Life and Letters of Sir Harry Johnston* (1929). The standard work is Roland Oliver, *Sir Harry Johnston and the Scramble for Africa* (1957). □

Joseph Eggleston Johnston

Joseph Eggleston Johnston (1807-1891) had a distinguished career in the U.S. Army before becoming an important Confederate general.

Joseph E. Johnston was born into a prominent family of Prince Edward County, Va. He enrolled at West Point in 1825 and, except for a brief interlude as a civil engineer, remained in military service until 1865. In 1845 he married Lydia McLane, the daughter of a diplomat and U.S. Cabinet officer. Johnston was a member of Gen. Winfield Scott's expedition against Mexico City during the Mexican War and was made brevet colonel in 1848. In 1860 he became quartermaster general of the U.S. Army.

When Virginia seceded from the Union, Johnston resigned from the Army and accepted a commission as a brigadier general in the Confederate service. When the Union army advanced toward Bull Run, he marched to cover Confederate troops at Manassas, thus making possible a Confederate victory. He was subsequently promoted to full general. In spring 1862 he marched to Yorktown to confront Union forces that were preparing to advance on Richmond. Although Confederate president Jefferson Davis believed that Johnston should defend his position as long as possible, Johnston disagreed and fell back on Richmond, leaving behind irreplaceable heavy artillery. He attacked the enemy army before Richmond on May 31, 1862, but poor planning and execution resulted in a drawn battle. Johnston was severely wounded and forced to retire temporarily.

Johnston's first assignment after his recovery was to coordinate the movements of Confederate forces in Mississippi and Tennessee. He complained that this arrangement was unworkable, and in fact he accomplished little. When the Union general Ulysses S. Grant crossed the Mississippi and moved against Vicksburg, Johnston went to take field command. Because one of Johnston's commanders disobeyed orders, both an army and Vicksburg were lost on July 4, 1863.

Despite the loss of Vicksburg, Davis chose Johnston to command the Army of Tennessee in 1863. He opposed Gen. William T. Sherman, who advanced on Atlanta in May 1864. Johnston retreated adroitly in the fact of heavy odds, but by July he had reached the outskirts of Atlanta. Davis relieved him of command on July 17, after Johnston refused to say whether or not he would abandon the city without a

fight. He was recalled to active duty in February 1865 but was forced to surrender to Sherman's vastly superior forces that April.

After the war Johnston engaged in various pursuits, serving one term in Congress, writing his memoirs, and continuing his feud with Jefferson Davis. His last employment was as commissioner of railroads under President Grover Cleveland.

Further Reading

A scholarly and sympathetic biography of Johnston is Gilbert E. Govan and James W. Livingood, *A Different Valor* (1956). See also Robert M. Hughes, *General Johnston* (1893).

Additional Sources

Johnston, Joseph E. (Joseph Eggleston), 1807-1891, *Narrative of military operations during the Civil War,* New York, N.Y.: Da Capo Press, 1990.

Symonds, Craig L., *Joseph E. Johnston: a Civil War biography,* New York: Norton, 1992. □

Joshua Johnston

Though questions about his identity and whether or not certain works should be attributed to him remain, Joshua Johnston (1765-1830) is considered to

be the first African American portrait artist of distinction.

Joshua Johnston may or may not have been the first African American artist of distinction, and conflicting evidence about his identity, race, and work continue to exist. Many unsigned late eighteenth-century and early-nineteenth century family portraits are attributed to him. Nonetheless, a man in post-colonial Baltimore named Joshua Johnson or Johnston was listed in directories of the time and who, on at least two occasions, advertised himself as a portraitist. This man has since been assigned credit for a body of work and is universally included in histories of African-American art.

The "Brass Tacks" Artist

The existence of Joshua Johnston was first suggested by J. Hall Pleasants, a retired doctor and a nationally recognized expert on Colonial artists from Maryland. In the 1940s, Pleasants began investigating long-circulating stories among prominent Maryland society that a slave had painted the portraits of several of their ancestors. The story had been passed down for several generations without any documentation. Many families said the painter had been black. According to one story, the slave had belonged to a well known artist of the period, and that his name was William Johnson. Pleasants searched old directories of Baltimore, and although he didn't find any William Johnsons, he did find an 1817 listing for Joshua Johnston, described as a portrait painter in the section for "free householders of colour."

This information further piqued Pleasant's curiosity, since he thought he had known of all the painters of that period. Pleasants eventually concluded that Johnston was most likely the painter of a series of portraits that were stylistically similar, of which the artist had never been identified. Previously, the painter was referred to simply as the "brass tacks artist" because his paintings often featured furniture upholstered with brass tacks.

Portrait Featured in *Life* Magazine

Over the next several years, Pleasants identified 34 paintings he felt could be attributed to Johnston, and in 1942 he published an article in the *Maryland Historical Magazine* called, "Joshua Johnston, the First Black American Portrait Painter?" In 1940, *Life* magazine sparked furthered interest in Johnston when it published a portrait attributed to him. The publicity from that article led to the discovery of four more paintings believed to be Johnston's.

In 1948, the Peale Museum in Baltimore held an exhibition of 23 paintings attributed to Johnston, and by the time of Pleasant's death in 1957, he had "identified" 50 paintings done by the artist. Over the next two decades, the mystery of Joshua Johnston continued, and in 1973 an auction in Washington sold three paintings assigned to Johnston for $31,000. The high prices were a result of the belief that Johnston was black, making the works historically significant. In Baltimore, a prominent art historian and friend of

Pleasants wrote an essay published in the *Baltimore Evening Sun* challenging anyone to prove that either Johnston was black or that he was, in fact, the artist of these works. Three years later, half of this challenge was answered: documentary evidence revealed that Johnston actually did paint the works attributed to him.

Race Remains a Mystery

The proof came with the discovery of a will from Mrs. Thomas Everette, the wife of a wealthy Baltimore businessman, who had a family portrait done by the brass tacks artist. In her will, she left the painting to her daughter, claiming that it had been painted by J. Johnson. With this documentation, art historians were able to establish which works of the Johnston canon were stylistically similar enough to be his. While the Everette will established that the brass tacks artist was Joshua Johnston, it did nothing to establish his race, which remains a mystery.

In the mid-1980s, the Abby Aldrich Rockefeller Folk Art Center began a major study of the issue of Johnston's race. Running the study was Carolyn Weekely, the curator of the center. Her study focused on the family stories that had first interested Pleasants nearly four decades earlier. The Weekely study focused on the idea that Johnston was West Indian. This theory would explain the racial ambiguity from the Baltimore directories that Pleasants had first uncovered. In one, Joshua Johnston is listed as a "free householder of colour." Yet in an 1800 census, Johnston is listed as a free white householder and that his household consisted of his immediate family and, importantly, a free black. An obvious conclusion would be that Johnston, if he was in fact black, was so light skinned that he could pass for white, and at times did. This further supports the West Indies theory, because in the West Indies, racial inter-mixing was far more common than in colonial America.

Employed by an Abolitionist

The study never uncovered any definitive documentation as to Johnston's race, but it did raise some interesting new possibilities, the most significant of which was that Johnston was a French-speaking slave inherited as a young boy by Charles Wilson Peale, a prominent Baltimore portraitist and outspoken abolitionist. According to this theory, for which there is almost no documentation, Peale may have inherited the young Johnston from his brother-in-law and employed him as his assistant. As such, Johnston would have been exposed to the art of portraiture as it was practiced at the time. The Weekely study went to great lengths to show that Johnston's style was very much similar to that of Peale's. This theory has detractors, though, who point out that Peales kept extensive diaries and never once mentioned a Joshua Johnston or any artist apprentice.

Adding to the Johnston mystery is that he managed to pass unknown into history in the first place. There is no mention of him by any of the many Baltimore artists of the time, about which a great deal is known. Pleasants himself knew nothing of Johnston, and he was the greatest living expert on Colonial Maryland artists. Had he not been a portrait artist, this anonymity might be explainable, but painting portraits is a socially oriented art; it is often mentioned, and requires, that an artist be well known among a wide circle of people. Surely, if Johnston had been a black man, mention of this would have been made by someone. Of course, research in this area has been limited to a very few studies and it is hoped that in the future the truth about Joshua Johnston can be uncovered.

Further Reading

Bearden, Romare, *A History of African American Artists, from 1792 to the present,* Pantheon Books, 1993.

Fine, Elsa Honig, "A Search for Identity," in *The Afro-American Artists,* Hacker Art Books, 1982.

Samella, Lewis, *Art: African American,* Harcourt Brace Jovanovich, 1978. ☐

Jean de Joinville

The French nobleman and author Jean de Joinville (1224-1317) is known for his *Life of Saint Louis,* a chronicle that furnishes intimate glimpses of King Louis IX.

Jean de Joinville was born in the second half of 1224 or the first months of 1225 and became lord of Joinville and seneschal of Champagne at an early age. He was 17 when he attended with his overlord, the poet Thibaut de Champagne, the feast at Saumur in 1241. When Louis IX left on the Seventh Crusade, Joinville dutifully followed him to Egypt and Palestine and fought there, but he had little enthusiasm for military action. After the taking of Damiette in 1249, the only real success of the whole expedition, Joinville and the King were taken prisoners and shared certain perils until they were released by ransom. In 1254 Joinville was back home, occupying himself with administrative duties. When Louis set off for the Eighth Crusade, Joinville begged off on the grounds that his duty was to protect his people at home.

About 1305 Jeanne de Navarre asked Joinville to write his memoirs of Louis, but she was long dead by the time the old gentleman had dictated his *Livre des saintes paroles et des bons faiz nostre roy saint Looys* (*Life of Saint Louis*), dedicated in 1309 to the Dauphin. The events recorded are recalled with remarkable accuracy and clarity; the visual effects are outstanding.

The *Life of Saint Louis,* written with no idea of publication, is perhaps the most personal series of reminiscences that have come down from Louis's century. Unlike the more formal histories, this little book is subjective. The first part is concerned with the exemplary integrity and virtue of its subject. The second contains a sympathetic account of his career from his birth (1214) and coronation (1226), emphasizing naturally the Seventh Crusade with a frankness that includes the King's fears and reveals a rather ill-conducted campaign. The last chapters tell of Louis's second crusade, his illness and death (1270), and Joinville's participation in the canonical inquiries that led to the canonization of Louis.

Joinville's other writings include a devout commentary on the Credo, which shows considerable scriptural knowledge, a pious epitaph on his forebears, and a few letters.

Further Reading

The best English translations of Joinville's major works are Joan Evans, *The History of Saint Louis* (1938), a literal though archaized version, and René Hague, *The Life of Saint Louis* (1955), a faithful rendition. For general historical background see Robert Fawtier, *The Capetian Kings of France: Monarchy and Nation, 987-1328* (1942; trans. 1960). ☐

Irène Joliot-Curie

Irène Joliot-Curie (1897-1956), with husband Frédéric, studied artificial radioactivity and contributed to the discovery of the neutron. They won a Nobel Prize for chemistry.

Irène Joliot-Curie, elder daughter of famed scientists Marie and Pierre Curie, won a Nobel Prize in chemistry in 1935 for the discovery, with her husband Frédéric Joliot-Curie, of artificial radioactivity . She began her scientific career as a research assistant at the Radium Institute in Paris, an institute founded by her parents, and soon succeeded her mother as its research director. It was at the Institute where she met her husband and lifelong collaborator, Frédéric Joliot. They usually published their findings under the combined form of their last names, Joliot-Curie.

Born on September 12, 1897, in Paris to Nobel laureates Marie and Pierre Curie, Irène Curie had a rather extraordinary childhood, growing up in the company of brilliant scientists. Her mother, the former Marie Sklodowska and her father, Pierre Curie, had been married in 1895 and had become dedicated physicists, experimenting with radioactivity in their laboratory. Marie Curie was on the threshold of discovering radium when little Irène, or "my little Queen" as her mother called her, was only a few months old. As Irène grew into a precocious, yet shy child, she was very possessive of her mother who was often preoccupied with her experiments. If, after a long day at the laboratory, the little Queen greeted her exhausted mother with demands for fruit, Marie Curie would turn right around and walk to the market to get her daughter fruit. Upon her father Pierre Curie's untimely accidental death in 1908, Irène was then more influenced by her paternal grandfather, Eugene Curie. It was her grandfather who taught young Irène botany and natural history as they spent summers in the country. The elder Curie was also somewhat of a political radical and atheist, and it was he who helped shape Irène's leftist sentiment and disdain for organized religion.

Curie's education was quite remarkable. Marie Curie made sure Irène and her younger sister, Eve Denise (born in 1904), did their physical as well as mental exercises each day. The girls had a governess for a time, but because Madame Curie was not satisfied with the available schools, she organized a teaching cooperative in which children of

the professors from Paris' famed Sorbonne came to the laboratory for their lessons. Madame Curie taught physics, and other of her famous colleagues taught math, chemistry, language and sculpture. Soon Irène became the star pupil as she excelled in physics and chemistry. After only two years, however, when Irène was 14, the cooperative folded and Irène enrolled in a private school, the College Sevigne, and soon earned her degree. Summers were spent at the beach or in the mountains, sometimes in the company of such notables as Albert Einstein and his son. Irène then enrolled at the Sorbonne to study for a diploma in nursing.

During World War I, Madame Curie went to the front where she used new X-ray equipment to treat soldiers. Irène soon trained to use the same equipment and worked with her mother and later on her own. Irène, who was shy and rather antisocial in nature, grew to be calm and steadfast in the face of danger. At age 21, she became her mother's assistant at the Radium Institute. She also became quite adept at using the Wilson cloud chamber, a device which makes otherwise invisible atomic particles visible by the trails of water droplets left in their wake.

In the early 1920s, after a jubilant tour of the United States with her mother and sister, Irène Curie began to make her mark in the laboratory. Working with Fernand Holweck, chief of staff at the Institute, she performed several experiments on radium resulting in her first paper in 1921. By 1925 she completed her doctoral thesis on the emission of alpha rays from polonium, an element that her parents had discovered. Many colleagues in the lab, including her future husband, thought her to be much like her father in her almost instinctive ability to use laboratory instruments. Frédéric was several years younger than Irène and untrained in the use of the equipment. When she was called upon to teach him about radioactivity, Irène started out in a rather brusque manner, but soon the two began taking long country walks. They married in 1926 and decided to use the combined name Joliot-Curie to honor her notable scientific heritage.

After their marriage, Irène and Frédéric Joliot-Curie began doing their research together, signing all their scientific papers jointly even after Irène was named chief of the laboratory in 1932. After reading about the experiments of German scientists Walther Bothe and Hans Becker, their attention focused on nuclear physics, a field yet in its infancy. Only at the turn of the century had scientists discovered that atoms contain a central core or nucleus made up of positively charged particles called protons. Outside the nucleus are negatively charged particles called electrons. Irène's parents had done their work on radioactivity, a phenomenon which occurs when the nuclei of certain elements release particles or emit energy. Some emissions are called alpha particles which are relatively large particles resembling the nucleus of a helium atom and thus contain two positive charges. In their Nobel Prize-winning work, the elder Curies had discovered that some elements, the radioactive elements, emit particles on a regular, predictable basis.

Irène Joliot-Curie had in her laboratory one of the largest supplies of radioactive materials in the world, namely polonium, a radioactive element discovered by her parents. The polonium emitted alpha particles which Irène and Frédéric used to bombard different elements. In 1933 they used alpha particles to bombard aluminum nuclei. What they produced was radioactive phosphorus. Aluminum usually has 13 protons in its nuclei, but when bombarded with alpha particles which contain two positive charges each, the protons were added to the nucleus, forming a nucleus of phosphorus, the element with 15 protons. The phosphorus produced is different from naturally-occurring phosphorus because it is radioactive and is known as a radioactive isotope.

The two researchers used their alpha bombardment technique on other elements, finding that when a nucleus of a particular element combined with an alpha particle, it would transform that element into another, radioactive element with a higher number of protons in its nucleus. What Irène and Frédéric Joliot-Curie had done was to create artificial radioactivity. They announced this breakthrough to the Academy of Sciences in January of 1934.

The Joliot-Curies' discovery was of great significance not only for its pure science, but for its many applications. Since the 1930s many more radioactive isotopes have been produced and used as radioactive trace elements in medical diagnoses as well as in countless experiments. The success of the technique encouraged other scientists to experiment with the releasing the power of the nucleus.

It was a bittersweet time for Irène Joliot-Curie. An overjoyed but ailing Marie Curie knew that her daughter was headed for great recognition but died in July of that year from leukemia caused by the many years of radiation exposure. Several months later the Joliot-Curies were informed of the Nobel Prize. Although they were nuclear physicists, the pair received an award in chemistry because of their discovery's impact in that area.

After winning the Nobel Prize, Irène and Frédéric were the recipients of many honorary degrees and named officers of the Legion of Honor. But all these accolades made little impact on Irène who preferred spending her free time reading poetry or swimming, sailing, skiing or hiking. As her children Helene and Pierre grew, she became more interested in social movements and politics. An atheist and political leftist, Irène also took up the cause of woman's suffrage. She served as undersecretary of state in Leon Blum's Popular Front government in 1936 and then was elected professor at the Sorbonne in 1937.

Continuing her work in physics during the late 1930s, Irène Joliot-Curie experimented with bombarding uranium nuclei with neutrons. With her collaborator Pavle Savitch, she showed that uranium could be broken down into other radioactive elements. Her seminal experiment paved the way for another physicist, Otto Hahn, to prove that uranium bombarded with neutrons can be made to split into two atoms of comparable mass. This phenomenon, named fission, is the foundation for the practical applications of nuclear energy—the generation of nuclear power and the atom bomb.

During the early part of World War II, Irène continued her research in Paris although her husband Frédéric had gone underground. They were both part of the French Resistance movement and by 1944, Irène and her children fled France for Switzerland. After the war she was appointed director of the Radium Institute and was also a commissioner for the French atomic energy project. She put in long days in the laboratory and continued to lecture and present papers on radioactivity although her health was slowly deteriorating. Her husband Frédéric, a member of the Communist Party since 1942, was removed from his post as head of the French Atomic Energy Commission in 1950. After that time, the two became outspoken on the use of nuclear energy for the cause of peace. Irène was a member of the World Peace Council and made several trips to the Soviet Union. It was the height of the Cold War and because of her politics, Irène was shunned by the American Chemical Society when she applied for membership in 1954. Her final contribution to physics came as she helped plan a large particle accelerator and laboratory at Orsay, south of Paris in 1955. Her health worsened and on March 17, 1956, Irène Joliot-Curie died as her mother had before her, of leukemia resulting from a lifetime of exposure to radiation.

Further Reading

Opfell, Olga S., *The Lady Laureates: Women Who Have Won the Nobel Prize,* Scarecrow, 1978.

Pflaum, Rosalynd, *Grand Obsession: Madame Curie and Her World,* Doubleday, 1989. □

Jean Frédéric Joliot-Curie

The French physicist Jean Frédéric Joliot-Curie (1900-1958) discovered artificial radioactivity and the emission of neutrons in nuclear fission.

Frédéric Joliot was born in Paris on March 19, 1900, the youngest of six children whose father had served in the militia of the Paris Commune 30 years earlier. While a student of Paul Langevin at the School of Physics and Chemistry in Paris, he received in 1925 an assistantship at the laboratory of the Radium Institute of Marie Curie, the discoverer of radioactivity. There he met and the next year married Irène Curie, the elder daughter of Madame Curie, who pursued her research at her mother's laboratory, and added his wife's surname to his own.

The union of Irène and Frédéric constituted in the history of science an outstanding example of husband-wife teamwork. Among the 26 papers published jointly by the Joliot-Curies during the first 10 years of their partnership was the 1932 paper announcing a penetrating radiation from beryllium when bombarded with alpha rays. In a 1934 paper they disclosed their greatest discovery, the artificial production of radioactive elements. They achieved this by bombarding certain light elements, such as aluminum, boron, and magnesium, with alpha radiation. The significance of this discovery was that it allowed scientists to study more systematically the patterns of nuclear transformations. For this achievement they received the Nobel Prize in chemistry in 1935.

Two years later Joliot-Curie, as newly appointed professor at the Collège de France, launched the development of a research center in nuclear physics. He and his collaborators established for the first time that approximately three fast neutrons were produced when a uranium atom was fissioned by slow neutrons. From this they concluded shortly afterward that a chain reaction in uranium was a distinct possibility.

After World War II Joliot-Curie's scientific activity largely concerned the reorganization of French atomic and nuclear research. At his recommendation the French government set up the Commissariat à l'Énergie Atomique, on which Joliot-Curie served as high commissioner. He had to resign from this post in 1950 because of his most vocal advocacy of the aims and policies of the French Communist party, of which he had been a member since 1942. His last 8 years were spent in directing research at the Centre National de la Recherche Scientifique and at the Collège de France, where during his tenure he offered 13 different courses in advanced physics. Upon the death of his wife in 1956, Joliot-Curie succeeded her as the director of the Curie Laboratory of the Radium Institute. His last contribution to the cause of French science, a new and large nuclear research center at Orsay, had just become operational when he died in Paris on Aug. 14, 1958.

Further Reading

The most accessible though highly partisan account of Joliot-Curie's life and work in English is Pierre Biquard, *Frédéric Joliot-Curie* (trans. 1965). Shorter, but scientifically informative, is the biographical essay by P. M. S. Blackett in *Biographical Memoirs of Fellows of the Royal Society*, vol. 6 (1960). □

Louis Jolliet

Louis Jolliet (1645-1700) was a Canadian explorer, musician, hydrographer, fur trader, and teacher. The most famous exploit in the career of this multifaceted man was the exploration of the Mississippi River in 1673.

The exact birth date of Louis Jolliet is unknown. He was baptized on Sept. 21, 1645, at the parish church of Quebec. In 1656 he entered the Jesuit college in Quebec City and began classical studies which, it was expected, would lead eventually to the priesthood. He took minor orders in the summer of 1662. During this early period of his life Jolliet became an accomplished musician, the first organist of the Cathedral of Quebec, where he played for many years.

Jolliet apparently lost his desire for the life of a religious and withdrew from the seminary in 1667. After a year in France, Jolliet determined to enter the fur trade, that magnet of the youth of New France, and began his career in the west. Two years later, the Comte de Frontenac, the new governor, authorized Jolliet to undertake an exploration of the Mississippi.

This mysterious river was already well, if imprecisely, known to many through contacts with the Indians. It was hoped that it would lead to the "Southern Sea" and the long-sought passage to China. Jolliet's precise mission was to discover into what body of water the Mississippi River emptied. The government did not underwrite the venture. It was to be profitably financed, hopefully, by a group of private individuals whose return would come from the fur trade. Following his instructions, Jolliet proceeded to Michilimackinac to join forces with Father Jacques Marquette, who had been ordered to accompany the expedition. Part of the group would remain at this settlement to engage in the fur trade.

Exploration of the Mississippi

In May 1673 Jolliet, Marquette, and five others set out on their great adventure. They followed the Fox and Wisconsin rivers to the Mississippi. During the journey southward past the confluence of the Missouri and then the Ohio, they marveled at the unfamiliar scenery and the exotic birds. The little group halted at the Arkansas River and went no further, deterred by their suspicion of the Indians and fear of the Spanish.

It was clear, however, that the river flowed into the Gulf of Mexico and that the legendary route to the "Southern

Sea'' was not the Mississippi. The arduous trip upriver was accomplished without incident, and Jolliet passed the winter of 1673/1674 at Michilimackinac completing his log and maps. He set out in the spring for Quebec, but his canoe capsized when nearly home, and the precious map and logbook were lost (a duplicate set left at Sainte-Marie was destroyed by fire).

After his return from the west, Jolliet married in 1675 and engaged in commerce and the fur trade along the north shore of the St. Lawrence River. Four years later he was off on another mission, this time to Hudson Bay. He became quite convinced that if the English were left in uncontested control of the bay, they would soon dominate the whole fur trade of Canada. Jolliet then obtained Anticosti Island in the Gulf of St. Lawrence and for several years became a prosperous merchant.

Jolliet's last important expedition was undertaken in 1694, when he charted the coast of Labrador far to the north but returned disappointed with the meager prospects for trade in the area. At the age of 49, after another trip to France, Jolliet began a new career as a teacher at the Jesuit college. In 1697 he was appointed to fill the office of hydrographer and produced many excellent navigation maps of the St. Lawrence River and Gulf. He died sometime during the summer of 1700.

Further Reading

Almost all the studies of Jolliet are in French. The best book in English is Jean Delanglez, *Life and Voyages of Louis Jolliet, 1645-1700* (1948). □

Jewish man, but eventually Harry Jolson and Palmer took over the comedy and Al Jolson sang. Jolson was best on the stage when he was alone, when he could be spontaneous and not under the pressure of delivering lines. In this manner he could really relate to the audience he loved so much to please.

In order to develop his singing abilities Jolson left his brother's group and spent several years in San Francisco playing in small clubs. One day he decided he must liven up his act, and he went on stage in blackface and sang ''Rosey My Posey'' in Southern style. The makeup and his unique musical interpretation brought a sensitivity to the act that elicited three encores from the audience. Al Jolson's style was born.

In 1909 he was given a job as one of the minstrels in Dockstader's *Minstrel Show,* a successful touring production. It was here that Arthur Klein, who became his agent, spotted Jolson and convinced the powerful Broadway producer, Lee Shubert, to put him in his new show, *La Belle Paree* (1911). On March 20, 1911, the blackface singer went on stage and sang ''I Want a Girl Just Like the Girl That Married Dear Old Dad.'' He was an instant hit. Jolson's singing and stage manner were different from anything the audience had seen. He took a song and applied to it a loose jazz/ragtime rhythm (this type of music had not yet been popularized). He wore blackface and rolled his eyes with a mischievous grin on his face. He also appealed to the emotions of the audience with his sentimental song deliveries interpolated with ad libbed dialogue.

Al Jolson

Al Jolson (1886-1950) was a vaudeville, theater, and radio singing performer and a film actor.

Al Jolson (Asa Yoelson) was born on May 6, 1886, in Srednike, Lithuania. Jolson's family immigrated to the United States in 1894. Several factors in Jolson's youth were to influence his career, including his religious Jewish upbringing, the death of his mother when he was ten, and his father's tradition-steeped profession of cantor. Jolson may have acquired a love of singing from his father, but he did not want to use his voice in the synagogue. Instead, he and his brother Harry sang on street corners to earn money. Jolson also attended the theater whenever possible and discovered a deep desire to become a performer.

In 1900 Jolson left Washington, D.C., for New York. His first job on the stage was in Israel Zangwill's *Children of the Ghetto,* in which he played one of the mob. He also sang in a circus sideshow and finally teamed up with his brother to play vaudeville. They toured as Jolson/Palmer/Jolson (Palmer, a paraplegic, was the third member of the team) with an act called *The Hebrew and the Cadet.* At first Al Jolson played the straight man to his brother's comic

Although Jolson did not receive star billing until 1914 in *Dancing Around,* the audiences clearly came to see *him.* The Shuberts knew this and signed Jolson for a seven year contract at the Winter Garden on Broadway. He played to overflowing houses in such shows as *Vera Violetta* (1911), *The Honeymoon Express* (1913), *Robinson Crusoe, Jr.* (1916), *Sinbad* (1918), and *Bombo* (1921). In most of these Jolson had no set script and no scheduled list of songs. He would come out on stage after the final act and talk to the audience and sing what pleased him. After each song he delighted the audiences with his standard retort, "You ain't heard nothing yet."

Jolson's renditions of songs were sung by people throughout the country, and he became known for songs like "Sonny Boy," "Swanee" (with this song Jolson introduced the composer George Gershwin), and most particularly "My Mammy." In "Mammy" the performer would go down on one knee with his hands in front of him as if in prayer. With tears in his eyes he would speak to "mother," telling her he'd "walk a million miles" just to see her. At the end he would get up and sing the last chorus with his hands spread wide and his face tilted upwards. After he introduced this song he was billed as "the greatest entertainer of all time." To his adoring audiences this was the truth.

Jolson's intense need to be constantly at work led him to do a six week tour of his own one-man show, in which he established the format for solo performance; then a vaudeville tour; a Sunday theater series for performers; and finally—Hollywood. On October 6, 1927, Warner Brothers presented the world's first talking-picture feature, *The Jazz Singer.* The story of Jakie Rabinowitz, the rabbi's son who turned actor against the wishes of his father, became a sensation and remains a motion picture classic. It starred Al Jolson. People came to associate the movie with Jolson's own life, a myth that he encouraged and had even contributed to early in his career with songs like "Mammy." This myth of the lonely man who had given up everything for the public was necessary for him—it was indeed reflected in his need for the audience's love.

Despite the overwhelming popularity of this film and its sequel, *The Singing Fool* (1928), Jolson did not succeed in film. He made several films afterwards, but his ultimate gift was his personal appeal to an audience. He was too big for the camera and could not convey his personality by way of screen. His career, in general, declined in the 1930s—sentimentality was out and the audiences sought after a different type of singing.

Jolson filled his time by performing on radio and entertaining the troops in World War II. (He also did this in the early days of the Korean War.) He was a politically involved man, and he campaigned for several presidents by singing at rallies.

In 1946 Columbia Pictures presented *The Al Jolson Story,* in which Larry Parks impersonated Jolson and Jolson sang. The film was a fantasized version of his life and an immediate success. In 1949 they presented a sequel, *Jolson Sings Again,* another smash hit. These films not only brought the singer's career back to its heights but also immortalized this unique performer.

Jolson was married four times (his third wife was the actress Ruby Keeler), and he had three children. Al Jolson died of heart failure on October 24, 1950, the night before a planned radio taping with Bing Crosby.

Further Reading

Al Jolson: You Ain't Heard Nothin' Yet! by Robert Ober-first (1980) is a biography/dramatization of the central aspects of Jolson's work and personal life, with pictures. Jolson is listed in *Who's Who In The Theatre* (1939), edited by John Parker, and in *Famous Actors and Actresses on the American Stage,* Volume I (1975), by William C. Young. The latter book includes reviews of his work. Recordings of Al Jolson's songs and performances are still available. □

Chief Joseph Leabua Jonathan

Chief Joseph Leabua Jonathan (1914-1987) was the first prime minister of independent Lesotho. For 20 years beginning in 1966, until he was ousted in a military coup, Jonathan struggled to maintain a good-neighbor status despite the racial policies of the Republic of South Africa, which completely surrounds his small country.

Leabua Jonathan was born on Oct. 30, 1914, the son of a minor hereditary chief and the great grandson of Moshesh, founder of Basutoland (now Lesotho). A Protestant, Jonathan was educated in the mission school at Leribe. He converted to Catholicism as an adult.

Basutoland, then as now, lies in southern Africa completely surrounded by the Republic of South Africa. Until the early 1990s, South Africa was governed by the racist policy of apartheid, or strict and total separation of the races. As such, South African policies had a major impact upon Basutoland. In 1934, Jonathan followed the traditional young Basuto's economic path by going to work in the gold mines of South Africa's Rand. Returning home in 1937, he gained experience in the administration of the Paramount Chief Regent and rose within a year from clerk to the presidency of the Basuto courts and assessor to the judicial commissioner.

Early Political Experience

Jonathan served in the National Council before acquiring a chief's place there. As adviser to the Paramount Regent, he earned a reputation as a popular progressive leader duly respectful of tradition. He also served on the Panel of 18, the council's constitutional reform committee.

In 1959, Jonathan founded and subsequently led the Basuto National Party (BNP), whose slogan stressed better economic conditions at home and a good-neighbor policy toward South Africa. Despite financial support and campaign management by Catholic priests, the BNP fared poorly. Jonathan himself was defeated but entered the Legislative Council as a nominated member. There, he turned his attention to such injustices as the plight of the Indian community, land tenure, and women's rights. Beginning in 1962, he served on the committee to write a new constitution.

Turmoil Over Independence

Preindependence elections of 1965 heightened tensions over relations with South Africa. The BNP's moderate stand, as well as its willingness to accept financial support from private South African companies, led to the belief that Jonathan was ruled by the leadership in that country.

Jonathan was defeated, but his party won a slim majority. The deputy BNP leader became interim prime minister until Jonathan could contest a vacated and safe party seat. He then served as prime minister and minister of external affairs, first for independent Basutoland and then for the independent Kingdom of Lesotho (Oct. 4, 1966).

In the January 1970 elections, a serious crisis developed again as the opposition demanded more independence from South Africa. With returns still incomplete, the opposition claimed victory. Jonathan declared a state emergency, suspended the constitution, and arrested his opponents. He also exiled the king for campaigning in violation of his constitutional role. "I have seized power and I am not ashamed of it," he said, leveling a pro-Communist charge against his opponents. More than 150 people died in the riotous months that followed. Jonathan then called for a national coalition, with the opposition in the minor role, to write a new constitution. Calm returned when the Basutoland Congress party agreed.

Military Takeover

For the next few years, Jonathan walked a narrow path between cooperation with South Africa and criticism of its policy of apartheid. But by the early 1980s, opposition was building in the country over his autocratic rule. There was renewed hostility when Jonathan permitted China, the then Soviet Union, and North Korea to open embassies in Lesotho in 1982.

South Africa imposed a blockade on the small country on Jan. 1, 1986. This was the beginning of the end of Jonathan's government. It toppled in a military coup just 20 days later. Chief Leabua Jonathan died in 1987. Military rule ended in 1994 and constitutional government of the kingdom was restored.

Further Reading

Biographical information on Jonathan and background material on Lesotho are in Jack Helpern, *South Africa's Hostages* (1965); and Richard P. Stevens, *Lesotho, Botswana, and Swaziland* (1967). □

Ernest Alfred Jones

The British psychologist Ernest Alfred Jones (1879-1958) championed the cause of psychoanalysis from its early days, becoming one of its most active leaders and supporters.

Born in Gowerton, Glamorgan, Wales, on Jan. 1, 1879, Ernest Jones attended Swansea Grammar School, University College at Cardiff, University College Hospital, and the University of London, where he obtained his undergraduate and medical degrees. He went on to earn a doctorate at Cambridge University.

While studying neurology and psychiatry at the University of Munich, Jones encountered the writings of Sigmund Freud. Engaging in the practice of clinical psychiatry, Jones discovered a need for deeper understanding of the patient's mind. Only psychoanalysis, he found, could fill this need.

In 1905 Jones began practicing psychoanalysis. An unfortunate incident, which caused his dismissal from a London hospital, proved to be a blessing in disguise. In 1908 he moved to Toronto, Canada, where with the help of Sir William Osler he became a professor of psychiatry and director of the Clinic for Nervous Disorders. That same year Jones published his masterful "Rationalization in Every Day Life" in the *Journal of Abnormal Psychology*. In this article he instituted the term "rationalization," which then became known as one of the several "psychic mechanisms" by means of which mental life is better explained.

Jones made frequent trips to the United States, lecturing and proselytizing for the new science of the unconscious. In Boston he met the eminent New England neurologist J. J. Putnam and converted him to psychoanalysis. On May 9, 1911, the American Psychoanalytic Association was founded with Putnam as president and Jones as secretary.

Jones's *Papers on Psychoanalysis* (1912), revised and republished many times, was the first systematic presentation of psychoanalysis in England. This book contained not only a didactic exposition of the principles of psychoanalysis for the student but suggestive and stimulating ideas for the researcher as well. In 1913 Jones returned to England, and during World War I he trained doctors to a recognition of the psychogenic causation of disease. He founded the British Psychoanalytic Society and continued as honorary president of the International Psychoanalytic Association.

In 1947 Jones began work on *Sigmund Freud: Life and Work,* a comprehensive and definitive biography. It appeared in three volumes (1953-1957) and covers the years of Freud's life chronologically.

One of the few major subjects on which Jones disagreed with Freud was the nature of death. Jones felt that death was simply the end of individual life, not the fulfillment of an inner instinct. Jones died in London on Feb. 11, 1958.

Further Reading

Jones's *Free Associations: Memories of a Psychoanalyst* (1959) is an informal and readable autobiography published a year after his death. Dieter Wyss, *Depth Psychology: A Critical History* (trans. 1966), contains the section "The British Group and Its Most Important Representatives," which includes Jones. Clarence P. Oberndorf in *A History of Psychoanalysis* (1953) discusses Jones's relationship to the psychoanalytic movement. See also Henri F. Ellenberger, *The Discovery of the Unconscious* (1970).

Additional Sources

Jones, Ernest, *Free associations: memories of a psycho-analyst,* New Brunswick, U.S.A.: Transaction Publishers, 1990. □

Fay Jones

American architect Fay Jones (born 1921) carried the principles of his mentor Frank Lloyd Wright into his own work, primarily private residences and small religious structures. His most famous work is the Thorncrown Chapel (1980) at Eureka Springs, Arkansas. In 1997, he was commissioned to build a multi-million dollar chapel on the campus of Chapman University in California.

Euine Fay Jones was born January 31, 1921, in Pine Bluff, Arkansas. His family later settled in El Dorado. As a child, he once built an elaborate treehouse, something that perhaps inspired some treetop residences built as a mature architect. As a youth he was impressed with a film about architect Frank Lloyd Wright's Johnson's Wax Headquarters at Racine, Wisconsin.

Because there was no school of architecture in the state at the time, Jones first studied engineering at the University of Arkansas in Fayetteville. Following service in the Navy during World War II, he returned to the university where there a new program in architecture was offered; Jones was one of the first to graduate (in 1950) with a degree in the subject.

In 1949 a serendipitous meeting between the young student Jones and the great master Wright took place at an American Institute of Architects annual convention in Houston. Jones later described his meeting with Wright: "All of a sudden the doors popped open and out walked Frank Lloyd Wright, putting on his cape, with his cane and porkpie hat . . . We threw ourselves back to give him plenty of room to walk by but he walked up and said, 'My name's Frank Lloyd Wright, I'm an architect.' " Although a brief encounter, it led to further developments in the coming decade.

Jones attended Rice University on a fellowship and then taught architecture at the University of Oklahoma in Norman (1951-1953), where he was associated with Bruce Goff. A visit from Wright to the university led to an invitation for Jones to visit Taliesin West in Arizona during the spring of 1953, and then to spend the following summer at Taliesin East in Wisconsin. Jones subsequently made shorter trips to visit with Wright until the latter's death in 1959.

In 1953 Jones returned to Fayetteville to teach in the architecture program. Much of his energy in the following decades was devoted to teaching design and architectural history. In 1955, he designed his own house, and there soon followed several commissions by faculty at the university for homes. In the 1960s and 1970s Jones was building residences at the rate of one to four per year, most in Fayetteville or northwest Arkansas, but also some in surrounding states.

Chapel Was Crowning Achievement

Although some of these houses received national awards from the American Institute of Architects (AIA), it was not until the Thorncrown Chapel was built that Jones was widely recognized as a significant 20th-century architect. The AIA considered that building one of the best of the 1980s, and its success led to commissions for additional small religious buildings and more residences in following years.

The Thorncrown Chapel was designed as a place of quiet retreat near Eureka Springs, a busy tourist mecca. Made of wood and glass, it harmonizes with its isolated environment. The surrounding forest and the sky overhead can be seen through its glass; it is a place where the outside is inside. The floor is stone, and metal is used for some details. A small building (24 by 60 by 48 feet), it is nevertheless a dramatic space. Jones' emphasis on natural materials, and his making the outdoor setting a part of the interior experience are characteristics found in Wright's work, in which organic forms tie together different spaces. It cost only $150,000 to build and seats 115.

Thorncrown Chapel proved to be such a popular site for weddings and worship services that its role as a place of contemplation was threatened. Jones was then commissioned to design the Thorncrown Worship Center (1989) nearby. It is a larger building designed for more formal functions but, like its sister building, uses natural materials, and its open ends allow the Ozark mountain scenery to become part of the interior experience.

In a radio interview in 1994, Jones said there is a religion to his architecture. "I like to think of myself as being concerned with a higher order of things and probably the clearest manifestation we have of some higher order in the universe is wheat we see in nature and what we feel in nature."

The success of the Thorncrown Chapel led to other commissions for similar small religious structures. They include the Mildred B. Cooper Memorial Chapel (1988) in Bella Vista, Arkansas, which features steel beams fashioned in gothic arches; and the brick and wood Marty Leonard Community Chapel (1990) at the Lena Pope Home, Fort Worth, Texas. Both the Pinecote Pavilion for the Crosby Arboretum near Picayune, Mississippi (1987), and the tiny Pine Eagle chapel at a Boy Scout camp near Wiggins, Mississippi, seem to float above the water and with their openness and airiness recall Japanese pavilions. This similarity is again reminiscent of Wright's interest in oriental architecture and its relationship to surrounding nature.

In 1997, it was announced that Chapman University in Orange County, California, would build a new chapel designed by Jones at the center of the campus and it would be called the Wallace All Faiths Chapel.

Work Noted for Craftsmanship

He has had residential commissions in more than a dozen states from Massachusetss to Michigan. Jones' houses emphasize natural materials, a close relationship to the landscape, and easy movement from one space into another. Normally light fixtures and cabinetry are especially designed for the interiors. Fountains, skylights, hearths and fireplaces, and large windows are found in Jones' interiors, and a concern for craftsmanship is evident in the details.

Jones once said, "I felt I was somewhat outside the pale" in terms of contemporary architecture. That he limited his practice to small-scale structures and spent much of his career in the classroom, kept him from full recognition of his talent until late in life. He might be considered a regionalist in the sense that his architecture is so sympathetic to the terrain and stresses simple and natural forms. Nevertheless, the sophistication of forms and shapes found in his structures reveal his training and learning. Appropriately in an era of pluralism and acceptance of many ways of building, Fay Jones has been recognized as a significant creative figure working quietly and consistently in the foothills of the Ozarks.

Further Reading

Robert Adams Ivy, Jr.'s *Fay Jones* (1992) offers a succinct discussion of the architect and a number of his works are beautifully illustrated. Included is a complete bibliography, which can direct the reader to numerous articles in such publications as *House Beautiful, Architectural Digest, Progressive Architecture, Architectural Record,* and *L'Architettura.* An article by Michael Ryan on the architect in *Parade* magazine (January 17, 1993) provides a good general introduction. Also, Robert T. Packard's *Encyclopedia of American Architecture* (2nd edition) (1995). □

Inigo Jones

The English architect and designer Inigo Jones (1573-1652) was the most talented native artist in England in the first half of the 17th century. He was responsible for introducing Italian Renaissance architecture into England.

Inigo Jones was born in London on July 15, 1573. Little is known of his early life and education, but between 1596/1597 and 1605 he traveled on the Continent and spent some years in Italy. In and around Venice and Vicenza he observed the buildings of Andrea Palladio, one of the major architects of the Late Renaissance, whose theories and designs had a profound effect on him.

During this period Jones may have worked for a time for King Christian of Denmark. In 1609 Jones traveled in France, and in 1613-1614 he toured the Continent, spending most of the time in Italy. During this Italian sojourn Jones undertook a professional study of Palladio's architecture and architectural theories.

In 1615 James I appointed Jones surveyor of the King's works, an important position, which was essentially that of chief architect to the Crown. He also held this position under Charles I until 1642, when the outbreak of the civil war disrupted court life.

Court Masques

During the reigns of both monarchs Jones designed and produced court masques, elaborate theatrical festivals which were common at courts on the Continent, especially in Italy. Ben Jonson often wrote scripts for the masques, and between 1605 and 1640 Jones worked on at least 25 of these productions. James I's queen, Anne of Denmark, was devoted to lavish entertainment and to the masques, and the tradition was continued in the reign of Charles I.

The masques, in which the sovereigns and courtiers participated, were dazzling spectacles organized around allegorical or mythological themes; they involved music, ballet, and spoken parts and required fantastic costumes, complex stage machinery, and brilliant stage settings. Hundreds of Jones's drawings for the costumes and stage designs are extant, none of which would have been possible without his knowledge of Italian art and draftsmanship. The

masques allowed him to exercise an imaginative fantasy which rarely appears in the sobriety of his architectural designs.

His Architecture

Jones was the first professional architect in England in the modern sense of the term, and he turned English architecture from its essentially medieval Gothic and Tudor traditions into the mainstream of the Italian Renaissance manner. He designed many architectural projects, some of them vast in scale; but of the buildings actually executed from his designs only seven remain, most of them in an altered or restored state.

The earliest of Jones's surviving buildings is the Queen's House at Greenwich, a project he undertook for Queen Anne in 1616. The lower floor was completed at the time the Queen died in 1619. Work then stopped but was resumed in 1630 for Queen Henrietta Maria, Charles I's wife, and was completed in 1635. The building is marked by a symmetrical plan, simplicity of classical detail, harmonious proportions, and severe purity of line, all elements that reflected Italian Renaissance sources and constituted an architectural revelation to the English.

The building now most associated with Jones is the Banqueting House at Whitehall (1619-1622). Intended to serve as a setting for state functions, it is a sophisticated manipulation of Italian classical elements and owes much to Palladio. The main facade consists of seven bays and two stories gracefully unified in an elegant, rational pattern of classical columns and pilasters, lightly rusticated stone, discreetly carved ornamentation, and a delicate contrast of textures. The interior is one large double-cube room; its classical severity contrasts dramatically with the richly baroque ceiling containing paintings by Peter Paul Rubens that were installed in 1635.

The Queen's Chapel, Marlborough Gate, completed in 1627, has a coffered barrel vault derived from imperial Roman architecture; it was Jones's first design for a church and the first church structure in England in the classical style. In 1631 he became associated with a city planning project in the Covent Garden district of London and designed St. Paul's Church there. The church, which still exists in a restored condition, is in the form of an austere classical temple with a deep portico and severe Tuscan columns. Between 1634 and 1642 Jones was occupied with extensive restoration of the old St. Paul's Cathedral (now destroyed), which he fronted with a giant classical portico of 10 Corinthian columns. From about 1638 Jones was involved in preparing designs for a vast baroque palace projected by Charles I, but it was not realized.

In 1642 the conflict between Parliament and King erupted in open warfare which swept away the elegant Cavalier court of Charles I, and Jones's world disappeared with it. His last important work was undertaken in 1649, when he and John Webb, who had been his assistant for many years, provided designs for the Double-and Single-Cube Rooms at Wilton House. The architectural decoration of this splendidly proportioned suite of rooms is essentially French in character; the cream-colored walls are decorated with a rich variety of carved and gilded moldings and ornaments to create an effect both opulent and disciplined. Jones died in London on June 21, 1652, the same year that Wilton House was completed.

Further Reading

The most recent work on Jones is Sir John Summerson, *Inigo Jones* (1966). An older but still useful study is J. Alfred Gotch, *Inigo Jones* (1928). For an excellent analysis of Jones's place in the history of English architecture see Sir John Summerson, *Architecture in Britain, 1530-1830* (1954; 5th ed. 1969). Margaret Whinney and Oliver Millar, *English Art, 1625-1714* (1957), is valuable for placing Jones within the context of 17th-century English art in general. J. Lees-Milne, *The Age of Inigo Jones* (1953), is a useful examination of the artist against the historical background of his period. □

James Earl Jones

Award-winning actor James Earl Jones (born 1931) has acted on television, stage, and screen. He is, perhaps, best known for his sonorous bass voice.

Some people know him as one of the nation's finest stage actors, an artist who tackles the works of such playwrights as William Shakespeare and Eugene O'Neill. Others know his sonorous bass voice as the most menacing aspect of the evil Darth Vader in the blockbuster film *Star Wars.* Still others recognize him as a television star who brings depths of humanity to cliched character parts. James Earl Jones fits all these descriptions, and more: for more than 30 years he has been one of the most esteemed actors in the United States.

Jones has worked steadily for decades in a market that supplies little hope to black performers. Having first established himself as a serious dramatic actor, he has never balked at the so-called "low brow" pursuits of television and popular film. His resume includes *Othello* as well as television episodes of *Tarzan.* He has been laden with Tony, Emmy, and Obie awards, and yet he can be heard as the voice announcing "This is CNN" for Cable News Network. With film appearances ranging from the classic *Dr. Strangelove* to the forgettable *Conan, the Barbarian,* Jones admitted in the *Saturday Review* that he takes roles to surprise people—including himself. "Because I have a varied career, and I've not typecast myself, nobody knows what I'm going to do next. They don't know if I'm going to drop 20 pounds and play an athlete. They don't know whether I'm ready to be a good guy or a bad guy."

Whatever Jones plays—villain or hero—he infuses each role with "enormous talent, range, courage, taste, [and] sensitivity," in the words of a *Newsweek* correspondent. During a career that began in the late 1950s, James Earl Jones has struggled to define himself not as a black actor, but simply as an actor. In an effort to resist stereotypes, he has opted for maximum variety, but each new part bears his particular, memorable stamp. In *Newsweek,* Jack

Kroll called Jones "the embodiment of the living paradox that informs all great acting: his powerful persona is at once intimate and apart, friendly and heroic. He's right there in the room with you, but he's also in your mind, an electrifying double presence that only the strongest actors can create."

A Traumatic Boyhood

The only child of Robert Earl and Ruth Connolly Jones, James Earl Jones was born in Arkabutla, Mississippi, on his maternal grandfather's farm. Before his son's birth, James's father left the family to pursue a career as a prize fighter and later as an actor. Ruth Jones soon followed suit when she found tailoring work that kept her separated from her son for long periods of time. Born during the Great Depression, in 1931, Jones remarked in *Newsweek* that he realizes economic circumstances forced his parents apart. Still, he said, the abandonment hurt him deeply. "No matter how old the character I play," he concluded, "those deep childhood memories, those furies, will come out. I understand this."

Living on his grandparents' farm, Jones was afforded a measure of security. As a youngster he hunted, fished, and performed various farm chores. He also attended church, where he watched his grandmother's emotional displays of holy rapture. "There was a strong evangelistic aspect to her religion, and when she went to church and felt the spirit, she ended up behaving like a holy roller," Jones recalled in the *Saturday Review.* "There wasn't much touching in the family, but there was emotion."

Eventually Jones's grandparents formally adopted him, and took him north to rural Michigan. Jones acknowledged in *Newsweek* that the move north helped him to escape "a certain self-castration" common among Southern blacks at the time, but he did not adjust easily to his new surroundings. He developed a stutter and eventually found communication so difficult that at certain periods during grammar school he could talk only to himself or his immediate family. The problem followed him to high school, where one of his English teachers suggested he memorize speeches and enter oratorical contests. It seemed an unlikely way to cure a stutter, but it worked for Jones. Slowly, wrote Michelle Green in the *Saturday Review,* Jones "became such a skilled speaker that he began besting his voluble opponents."

Acting Beat out Other Careers

Jones attended the University of Michigan on a full scholarship, intending to study medicine. At first he took acting classes simply as a sideline, but he soon switched his major to theater. When he was 21 years old, and a junior at Michigan, he traveled east to New York City to meet his father. They had only spoken briefly on the telephone several times. The relationship was strained by the long years without communication, but Jones's father encouraged him to pursue a career in theater; James graduated from Michigan in 1953 with a bachelor's degree in drama.

The U.S. Army, specifically the Reserve Officers' Training Corps (ROTC), recruited Jones in 1953 for two years of compulsory service. He spent much of his stint in a rigorous ranger training program in the Colorado mountains and was set to reenlist in 1955 when his commanding officer suggested that he taste civilian life before making a long-term commitment to the armed services. So Jones moved to New York City and enrolled in further acting classes. Two things helped ease his decision: he knew he could return to the army if he did not find success as an actor, and his tuition at the American Theater Wing was paid for by the Army's G.I. Bill.

Jones lived with his father for a time, and the two supplemented their meager acting incomes by polishing floors in Off-Broadway theaters. In 1957 the younger Jones earned his first professional role in an Off-Broadway production of *Wedding in Japan*. He was rarely out of work after that, but his salary during the last years of the 1950s averaged $45 a week. He made ends meet by renting a cold-water flat on the Lower East Side. Even as a journeyman actor, Jones proved willing to try any role, no matter how small. In 1959 he began a long tenure with the New York Shakespeare Festival, carrying a spear in *Henry V*. Before long he was given more prominent roles, culminating in his 1963 performance as the lead in *Othello*—one of a staggering 13 plays he appeared in that year.

Fame Assured by The Great White Hope

Othello ran for a year Off-Broadway with Jones in the lead. The actor also found time to do television spots and to make one film appearance—as the bombardier in Stanley Kubrick's dark comedy *Dr. Strangelove*. In the mid-1960s Jones began augmenting his theater work with television parts. He took cameo roles in shows such as *The Defenders* and *East Side/West Side*, and he became the first black man to take a continuing role on a daytime serial when he portrayed a doctor on *As The World Turns*. The big break for Jones, though, came during a period when he was touring Europe as the lead in Eugene O'Neill's *The Emperor Jones*.

A copy of a play titled *The Great White Hope* landed in Jones's lap in 1967. A dramatization of the life of boxing champion Jack Johnson, *The Great White Hope* was slated for a possible Broadway run. Jones wanted the part desperately. He began to train at gymnasiums in order to build his muscles, working with boxing managers and watching old footage of Johnson's fights. He was ultimately awarded the part, and the show opened on Broadway on October 3, 1968.

The Great White Hope was a success, and its reception propelled Jones to stardom. "Fourteen years of good hard acting work, including more Shakespeare than most British actors attempt, have gone into the making of James Earl Jones," wrote a *Newsweek* reviewer who also concluded that "only an actor with the bigness and power of Jones" could make such a play work. Jones won a Tony Award for his contribution to *The Great White Hope,* and he was nominated for an Academy Award in 1970 when the play was made into a motion picture.

The instant celebrity brought Jones a new awareness of his limitations. The actor told *TV Guide* that his work in *The Great White Hope* did not prove to be the career boost he thought it would. "I thought with the Oscar nomination that several projects would be waiting for me immediately," he

continued in *TV Guide*. "But then projects—very viable ones close to getting go-aheads—caved in under racism's insanity." One of those projects was a life story of civil rights activist Malcolm X, a version of which was finally scheduled for release by filmmaker Spike Lee in 1992.

Working for Love and Money

Jones returned to the stage, appearing in *Hamlet* in 1972, *King Lear* in 1973, and *Of Mice and Men* in 1974. He also performed in a series of minor films, including *The Man* and *The Bingo Long Traveling All-Stars and Motor Kings*. Jones's most notable movie role of the 1970s and early 1980s, though, was one in which only his voice was used. He gave a memorable level of malevolence to the half-man, half-machine villain Darth Vader in all three *Star Wars* films.

In 1982 Jones appeared on Broadway as Othello to standing ovations. He also portrayed the villain in the film *Conan, the Barbarian*. To critics who faulted him for taking roles in substandard films, Jones had a simple reply: movies and television pay well, theater does not. "I can't afford to take a vacation unless I do some commercials when I'm in New York," he pointed out in the *Saturday Review*. "Money goes fast, and you can't get along doing only stage work. I've never minded doing commercials. . . . Commercials can be very exciting." In 1991 Jones lent himself to a string of TV ads for the Bell Atlantic Yellow Pages, his first on-air product endorsement.

Jones's work in the late 1980s and early 1990s was as varied as his early career. He played an enigmatic writer in the 1990 hit film *Field of Dreams*, a CIA chief in the 1992 screen adaptation of Tom Clancy's novel *Patriot Games,,* and a judge in the 1994 film *Sommersby*. On televison he starred as an ex-convict private investigator in the award-winning series *Gabriel's Fire* and, in 1995, as a widowed police officer in the series *Under One Roof*. Not neglecting his onstage work, he earned yet another Tony Award in 1988 for his portrayal of a disenchanted Negro League baseball player in August Wilson's play *Fences*. Jones explained in the *Los Angeles Times* that he has taken so many minor film roles and so much television work simply because he likes to work. "Just as, on stage, I waited years for a role like Jack [Johnson] in *Great White Hope,* or a role like Troy in *Fences,* you do the same thing in movies," he said. "Unless you are among that handful of exceptions, the stars who have projects lined up, you don't wait, at least I didn't want to wait. . . . I don't, think I've done many films that counted. What I'm getting at, rather than waiting for that wonderful role in a movie, I take 'off' jobs."

To quote *Los Angeles Times* correspondent David Wallace, those "off jobs" are often "memorable only for [Jones's] commanding presence [or] for the brevity of his appearance." That situation would change, however; in 1990 Jones announced that his age and health were forcing him to curtail his work in live theater. "After six months in a play, the fatigue factor begins to affect the quality of a performance," the actor conceded in the *Los Angeles Times*. "The audiences might not know it, but I do. My thing is serious drama, and usually the lead character has a heavy load to carry. I find that after six months, if you get four out of eight shows a week that work perfectly the way you want, you're lucky." Jones stressed that he did not plan to retire from the theater completely, but rather to cut back his live work in favor of other projects.

A shelf full of awards to his credit and contributions to every sort of mass media notwithstanding, James Earl Jones remains a modest man with a sense of adventure about his career. He and his second wife, actress Cecilia Hart, have one son, and Jones told the *Los Angeles Times* that he guards against appearing heroic to his child. "When I go home nobody is saying, 'Hi, can I have your autograph?' I'm me, that's reality. I'm an actor. That's something you do, not something you are, and I want my son to have a sense of reality." Looking toward the future, Jones sees no lack of opportunities in show business. "There are lots of wonderful cameos and a lot of good lead roles out there," he concluded in the *Los Angeles Times.* "There are a lot of things I can do."

In 1995, Jones played Neb Langston in the CBS drama *Under One Roof.* Langston is a retired police officer who is raising a foster child. In early 1996, Jones starred opposite Richard Harris in the apartheid movie *Cry, Beloved Country.* Jones plays the role of a preacher whose son is arrested for the murder of a prominent white man.

Further Reading

Chicago Tribune, May 26, 1990; May 5, 1991.
Ebony, April 1965; June 1969.
Los Angeles Times, September 2, 1990; August 26, 1991; September 26, 1991.
Newsweek, October 21, 1968; April 6, 1987.
Saturday Review, February 1982.
Time, April 6, 1987.
TV Guide, October 27, 1990.
Variety, September 23, 1991. □

John Paul Jones

John Paul Jones (1747-1792), American Revolutionary War officer, was a great fighting sailor and a national hero.

Like any master mariner in the 18th century, John Paul Jones was in the fullest sense the captain of his ship. He ruled by authority as well as by skill and personality. The rigging, the navigation, the ordnance, and the internal discipline were all his concerns. He was a proud man, slight and wiry, intellectually alert, and as tough with rowdy seamen as he was suave and urbane with Parisian women.

Becoming a Mariner

Born in Scotland as John Paul, he was a seafarer by the age of 12. He turned up in Virginia and took the surname Jones, for disguise, after killing a mutinous sailor in self-defense in 1773. Because he was already a veteran merchant captain, the Continental Congress commissioned him

a lieutenant in 1775 and promoted him to captain the next year. Cruising as far north as Nova Scotia, he took more than 25 prizes in 1776.

It was in the European area, however, that Jones won lasting acclaim. In 1777 he sailed to France in the *Ranger,* and in Paris he found American diplomat Benjamin Franklin sympathetic to his strategic objectives: hit-and-run attacks on the enemy's defenseless places and abduction of a prominent person to compel the British government to exchange American seamen rotting in English jails. If this master of a single cruiser was scarcely able to alter the course of the war, he was able to bring the impact of the struggle home to the enemy's civilian population. Early in 1778 Jones sailed boldly into the Irish Sea and also assaulted the port of Whitehaven, Scotland—not since 1667 had a British seaport suffered such humiliation; a second raid on St. Mary's Isle failed to bag Lord Selkirk as a hostage, for Selkirk was away from home.

Battling the *Serapis*

France became America's ally, but Jones had to be satisfied with a good deal less than he had hoped for in men and ships. With an old, clumsy vessel renamed *Bon Homme Richard* (in honor of Franklin) as his flagship, in the summer of 1779 Jones led a small squadron around the coasts of Ireland and Scotland, taking several small prizes. Then, off the chalk cliffs of Flamborough Head on September 23, he fell in with a large British convoy from the Baltic, escorted by the *Serapis* (50 guns) and the *Scarborough* (20 guns).

The most spectacular naval episode of the Revolution followed—a duel between the decrepit *Bon Homme Richard* and the *Serapis,* a sturdy, new, copper-bottomed frigate. After each captain, in standard tactical fashion, sought unsuccessfully to get across his opponent's bow to deliver a broadside, Jones managed to lash his ship to the *Serapis* in order to grapple and board. Jones's sharpshooters soon drove the enemy from the *Serapis*'s deck with their rain of musket and grenade fire, but below the deck the enemy cannon roared on, wrecking the *Bon Homme Richard*'s topsides. The English captain's nerve gave way when his main mast began to tremble, and he struck his colors. Jones abandoned the sinking *Richard,* took over the *Serapis,* and along with the *Scarborough,* which had fallen to his other vessels, sailed to Holland.

Back in France, Jones was the toast of Paris. His personal life seems to have scandalized John Adams, who was shocked at Jones's suggestion that the taking of a French mistress was an excellent way to learn the language. Whatever his personal life, Jones's naval conquests were over.

Postwar Life

Most of Jones's postwar life was spent in Europe. He made a final visit to the United States in 1787, when Congress unanimously voted to award him a gold medal for his outstanding services. He was the only naval officer of the American Revolution so honored. Soon afterward he accepted a commission in the Russian navy and was put in command of a Black Sea squadron with the rank of rear admiral. That rank, which he had eagerly but unsuccessfully sought in America, was the bait that had lured him to Russia. He fought in the Linman campaign against the Turks, but the jealousies and intrigues of rival officers limited his effectiveness, and in 1790 he returned to Paris.

In 1792 U.S. Secretary of State Thomas Jefferson wrote to tell him that President George Washington had appointed Jones a commissioner to negotiate with Algiers for peace and the release of imprisoned American citizens. Jones, whose last years were pathetic, never lived to receive the letter. With few friends because he was a colossal egotist, Jones saw his health steadily decline before his death on July 18, 1792. He was buried in Paris. His remains were finally found in 1905 and brought to Annapolis, Md., where they are entombed in the crypt of the Naval Academy chapel.

Further Reading

Most biographies of Jones are filled with myth and misinformation; the first to set the record straight is Lincoln Lorenz, *John Paul Jones* (1943). But the character of the master mariner is best seen in Samuel E. Morison's Pulitzer Prize-winning *John Paul Jones* (1959), a magnificent book by a distinguished sailor-historian. Recommended for general historical background are Gardner W. Allen, *A Naval History of the American Revolution* (2 vols., 1913), and Alfred Thayer Mahan, *The Major Operations of the Navies in the American War of Independence* (1913). □

Mary Harris Jones

Mary Harris "Mother" Jones (1830-1930) was an Irish immigrant who devoted her life to improving conditions of the working class. A vagabond agitator, she worked primarily among miners, supporting their strikes and urging them to unionize.

The early years of Mary Harris Jones are obscured by lack of records and her own inconsistencies in reporting her history. She was born in 1830 (some historians argue that 1843 is the accurate date) to Irish parents who migrated to America when she was a child. She graduated from normal school in Toronto, taught in public and parochial schools in Canada and the United States, and practiced the trade of dressmaking in Chicago. She took a teaching job in Memphis, Tennessee, where she met and married George E. Jones, an iron moulder, in 1861. Six years later, she lost her husband and four children to a yellow fever epidemic.

Jones returned to Chicago and dressmaking. Made homeless by the Great Fire of 1871, she began to attend meetings of the Knights of Labor. There she developed her commitment to rectifying inhumane working conditions, and she began a life-long friendship with Terrence V. Powderly, who led the Knights from 1879 to 1893. Jones's particular contribution was to mobilize workers and to publicize their plight, which she did with her forceful personality and her flamboyant and salty oratory. Without a home, she went from town to town, from strike to strike, staying in hotels, in the homes of sympathizers, or in jails. When asked where she lived, she replied, "Wherever there is a fight."

Mother Jones worked on behalf of workers in the railroad, steel, copper, brewing, garment, and textile industries. She was particularly appalled by child labor, and in 1903 she marched with a group of adult and child textile workers from Philadelphia to President Theodore Roosevelt's home at Oyster Bay, New York, in a public demonstration against the evils of child labor. But she worked most prominently and persistently among the coal miners of West Virginia and Colorado. At times the United Mine Workers paid her a salary, though she was often at odds with its leadership. The miners themselves adored her and called her "Mother."

Jones's own courage and willingness to risk arrest, jail, and violence served powerfully to inspire the miners. She also exhorted women to support strikes, and she developed the tactic of organizing miners' wives, armed with mops and brooms, to demonstrate and to keep strikebreakers from entering the mines. While she encouraged militance among women in mining families, she held traditional ideas about women. Jones sometimes joined in labor activism with working women, but she did not believe that women should work outside the home. She publicly opposed women's suffrage, in part because its supporters were mostly privileged women and because it would co-opt working-class women and divert them from economic issues. She said, "You don't need the vote to raise hell."

A pragmatic socialist who on occasion supported Democratic candidates, Jones was more interested in immediate reforms than in long-range socialist goals. She helped to found the Social Democratic Party in 1898 and the Industrial Workers of the World in 1905, but she never lived easily in any organization and frequently clashed with leaders and associates. She served in the defense of various radicals, including Western Federation of Miners' leaders Bill Haywood, George Moyer, and George Pettibone; California socialist Tom Mooney; and Mexican rebels who were imprisoned in the United States.

Jones continued to be active past 1920 when, by her count then, she was in her nineties. She spent most of her last decade at the Washington, D.C., home of the Powderlys. On May 1, 1930, the American Federation of Labor staged celebrations of her birth in major cities, which Jones addressed by radio. Though ill, she enjoyed visits by reporters and hundreds of well-wishers. She died on November 30. As she had wished, Mother Jones was buried in the Miners' Cemetery in Mt. Olive, Illinois, near the graves of miners killed in the labor strife at Virden in 1898.

Further Reading

Jones published her autobiography in 1925, but *Autobiography of Mother Jones* (paper edition, 1969), contains major gaps and inaccuracies. Dale Fetherling, *Mother Jones, The Miners' Angel: A Portrait* (1974) provides the fullest account of her life; the much briefer *Mother Jones, Woman Organizer; and Her Relations with Miners' Wives, Working Women, and the Suffrage Women* (1976) examines her life from an interesting

angle. The magazine *Mother Jones* continued to publish in the 1980s, retaining some of the activism of its namesake. □

Quincy Delight Jones Jr.

A resume for Quincy Delight Jones, Jr. (born 1933), would read like a run-on sentence with too many hyphens: musician-composer-arranger-producer-film and television executive, just to name a few. He propelled not only his own stardom, but that of Michael Jackson, Oprah Winfrey, James Ingram, Donna Summer—again, just to name a few. For more than four decades, Jones left a permanent, unique mark on the world of entertainment.

Quincy Delight Jones, Jr., was born on the south side of Chicago on March 14, 1933. His parents divorced soon after his younger brother, Lloyd, was born, and the Jones boys were raised by their father, a carpenter, and his new wife. She had three children of her own, and three more with Quincy Jones, Sr. His birth mother, Sarah Jones, was in and out of mental health facilities, and it wasn't until his adult life that Quincy was able to enjoy a close relationship with her.

When Jones was 10 years old his family moved to Bremerton, Washington. The Seattle suburb was alive with World War II sailors on their way to the Pacific; the nightlife and its music were the backdrop for Quincy's early teens. Three years later he met a 15-year-old musician named Ray Charles. The two formed a combo and played in local clubs and weddings, and soon Jones was composing and arranging for the group. After high school and a scholarship at Boston's Berklee College of Music, Quincy was introduced to the life of a musician on the road, a road which started in New York and went around the world. He toured with Dizzy Gillespie in 1956, Lionel Hampton in 1957, and then made his base in Paris. He studied with Nadia Boulanger and Olivier Messiaen, was musical director at Barclay Disques, wrote for Harry Arnold's Swedish All-Stars in Stockholm, and directed the music for Harold Arlen's production "Free and Easy," which toured Europe for three months, ending in early 1960.

After a financially unsuccessful tour of the United States with a big band made up of 18 musicians from "Free and Easy," Jones served as musical director at Mercury Records in New York. He became the first African American executive in a white-owned record company in 1964 when he was promoted to vice-president at Mercury. At the company he produced albums, sat in on recording sessions with the orchestra, and wrote arrangements for artists at Mercury as well as other labels. Jones wrote for Sammy Davis, Jr., Andy Williams, Sarah Vaughan, Peggy Lee, and Aretha Franklin, as well as arranged and conducted *It Might As Well Be Swing*, an album featuring Frank Sinatra and the Count Basie Band.

In 1969 Jones signed a contract as a recording artist with Herb Alpert's A&M Records, and Quincy's first album with that label, *Walking in Space,* won a Grammy for best jazz instrumental album of 1969. Quincy Jones was later nominated for 67 Grammys, and had won 25 going into 1997.

His first foray into Hollywood—another crossing of a racial barrier—came when he composed the score for *The Pawnbroker,* a 1965 film by Sidney Lumet. Two films released in 1967 featured music by Jones: *In Cold Blood* and *In the Heat of the Night.* Both scores won enough votes to be nominated for Academy Awards. Jones was advised not to "compete with himself," so he went with *In Cold Blood* and it was the other film that ended up winning the Oscars. It didn't stop him from going on to write the music for over 52 films.

Television, as well, has featured the music of Quincy Jones, starting in 1971 with theme songs for "Ironside," "Sanford and Son," and "The Bill Cosby Show" (the first one). In 1973 Jones co-produced "Duke Ellington, We Love You Madly," a special for CBS, featuring Peggy Lee, Aretha Franklin, Count Basie, Joe Williams, Sarah Vaughan, and a 48-piece orchestra conducted by Jones. The special was a project of the Institute for Black American Music, a foundation formed by Jones, Isaac Hayes, Roberta Flack, and other musicians with the intention of promoting recognition of the African American contribution to American music. Jones also wrote the score for the widely acclaimed 1977 television mini-series "Roots."

Burned out from producing film score after film score, Jones stopped working for Hollywood in 1973 to explore his own pop music career as a vocalist. His singing debut was with Valerie Simpson on an album called *You've Got It Bad, Girl.* The title song from the album stayed at the top of the charts for most of the summer of 1973. Jones's next album was an even bigger hit. *Body Heat,* released in the summer of 1974, contained the hit songs "Soul Saga," "Everything Must Change," and "If I Ever Lose This Heaven." The album remained within the top five on the charts for over six months and sold over a million copies.

In 1974 Jones suffered two aneurysms two months apart. He nearly died, but after a six-month recuperation he was back at work, touring and recording with a 15-member band. *Mellow Madness* was the first album by the new band, which included songs by George and Louis Johnson, Otis Smith, and Stevie Wonder ("My Cherie Amour").

His 1980 album, *The Dude,* featured a host of talent directed by Jones, earned 12 Grammy nominations, and won five awards. At the same time *The Dude* was released, Jones signed a deal with Warner Brothers Records creating his own label, Quest. It took Jones almost ten years to make his next album, *Back on the Block.* During that time he was focused on producing hit albums for other artists such as Donna Summer, Frank Sinatra, and James Ingram. In 1983 Michael Jackson recorded a Quincy Jones production, and at 40 million copies *Thriller* is still the best-selling album of all time. Quincy Jones also has the best-selling single of all time to his credit: the all-star choir on "We Are the World." Another triumph for Jones in the mid-1980s was his production of *The Color Purple,* the film adaptation of Alice Walker's novel, which featured the Oscar-nominated, debut film performance of Oprah Winfrey.

Jones's projects in the early 1990s included continuing work on an ongoing, mammoth project for which he'd been gathering material for decades, "The Evolution of Black Music." He was back in television, as well, with the Quincy Jones Entertainment Company producing the NBC situation comedy "Fresh Prince of Bel Air," as well as a weekly syndicated talk show hosted by Jones's friend the Rev. Jesse Jackson. Quincy Jones was also working on a film biography of the Black Russian poet Alexander Pushkin. The film was a co-production with Soviet filmmakers. Quincy Jones Broadcasting and Time Warner bought a New Orleans television station, WNOL, which Jones was to oversee.

The personal life of Quincy Jones was strained because of the pace of his professional endeavors. He was married and divorced three times (his latest wife was actress Peggy Lipton), and his six children have only recently been able to spend time with and come to know their father. The 1990 documentary "Listen Up: The Lives of Quincy Jones," produced by Courtney Sale Ross, contains poignant scenes in which Quincy confronts his difficult childhood, his mentally ill mother, and his strained past with his children. The film also contains testimonials from Frank Sinatra, Ella Fitzgerald, Michael Jackson, Miles Davis, Stephen Spielberg, Barbara Streisand, Oprah Winfrey, Ray Charles, Billy Eckstine, and others. They talk about an obsessed genius, a workaholic, and a man with a creative brilliance that has touched virtually every facet of popular entertainment since 1950.

In 1993 Jones announced that he was starting a magazine called *Vibe*. The magazine has been well received as an African American music journal. The album Jones released in 1995 was *Q's Jook Joint*. The album combined the talents of many of Quincy Jones's counterparts such as Stevie Wonder, Ray Charles, Sonny Bono and many others. The album was a celebration of his 50 years within the music industry. In 1996 Jones released an instrumental album entitled *Cocktail Mix*.

Further Reading

Two excellent in-depth and insightful interviews with Quincy Jones are in *The New York Times Magazine* (November 18, 1990) and *The Washington Post Style* section (October 6, 1990); Jones is the cover story of the October 22, 1990, issue of *Jet*. □

Robert Edmond Jones

Robert Edmond Jones (1887-1954) designed scenes for the theater that were simple and conducive to a more complete and coherent collaboration between the director and the designer. His work provided the foundation for the whole present day tradition of scene design in the United States.

Robert Edmond Jones was born on December 12, 1887, in the township of Milton, New Hampshire, roughly halfway between Portland and Portsmouth, in a house built by his great grandfather Levi Jones. He was the second child born to Fred and Emma Jane Cowell Jones.

Robert began taking violin lessons at the age of nine and eventually played in the Harvard Pierian Sodality Orchestra, but even as a child he had decided that he wanted to become an artist. He graduated from Nute High School in Milton in 1905 and entered Harvard University the following fall. While at Harvard, Jones pursued a liberal arts curriculum and graduated *cum laude* in 1910. It was during this time that he was enrolled in the famous drama course taught by George Pierce Baker. It must have been a great disappointment to Jones that he was not chosen to be one of the select group known as the "Baker's Dozen" who were regularly invited to the professor's house in the evenings.

After graduation Jones stayed at Harvard for two more years as a graduate assistant and later as an instructor in the Department of Fine Arts. In 1912 he went to New York for a series of small jobs and a brief period as a costume designer on the staff of Comstock and Gest. Feeling a need for a larger frame of reference, he formed The Robert Edmond Jones Transportation and Development Company and, thanks to the contributions of friends such as John Reed and Kenneth Macgowan, went to Europe.

In 1913 Jones was in Florence seeking in vain to be admitted to the art school of Gordon Craig, the English scene designer. While in Italy Jones produced a design for Shelley's *The Cenci* that won high praise by the New York critics during a later showing. It was a "conceptual" approach that clearly foretold his future greatness. He then spent a year in informal study and observation at Max Reinhardt's Deutsches Theatre in Berlin. While he was working there on a production of the *The Merchant of Venice* World War I erupted, and Jones was forced to return to New York early in November of 1914. However, after working with Reinhardt and his two principal designers, Ernst Stern and Emil Orlik, Jones was bringing back to America the concept of "The New Stagecraft."

Once back in New York he wasted no time and by the ninth of November had mounted an exhibition of stage designs, including that of *The Merchant of Venice*. The show was held in a vacant Fifth Avenue store, and it was this exhibit that brought Jones to the attention of Arthur Hopkins. Hopkins quickly hired Jones to design his production of Anatole France's *The Man Who Married a Dumb Wife*, directed by Harley Granville-Barker. The show, which opened January 27, 1915, was successful and not only marked the beginning of a long collaboration between Hopkins and Jones, but proved to be a pivotal point in American stage design. The simplicity and style of Jones's design clearly broke the "realistic" tradition of scenic design and pointed the way to a more complete and coherent collaboration between the director and the designer.

It was also during this time that Jones "improvised a setting" for *The Glittering Gate.* This was the first production of the Washington Square Players, a group that later became the Theatre Guild. The next 19 years proved to be exceptionally productive for Jones. In his association with Hopkins he designed sets (and usually costumes as well) for 39 productions, many of which became hallmarks of American design (*Hamlet* and *Richard III* with John Barrymore, *Macbeth* with Lionel Barrymore). In 1916, in collaboration with Joseph Urban, Jones designed *Caliban by the Yellow Sands* for the New York Shakespeare Tercentenary Celebration. At the very least, this "community masque" must be considered a monumental production for its extensive use of outdoor lighting and over 3,000 costumes.

Jones's directing credits began with a modest production of *Simon the Cyrenian* for the Colored Players, an early all-Black company. Soon, however, he was directing, designing, and producing for the Experimental Theatre in Provincetown, Massachusetts. This was an extension of the Provincetown Playhouse organized by himself, Eugene O'Neill, and Kenneth Macgowan. Jones returned to Europe in 1922 and along with Macgowan produced the book *Continental Stagecraft.* A few years later—in 1925—he published a collection of his designs under the title *Drawings for the Theatre.*

In 1932 he was appointed art director for the Radio City Music Hall, and as such was responsible for its inaugural program on December 27; however, his resignation was announced by January 9 of 1933. In the summer of 1933 he married Margaret Huston Carrington.

Hollywood beckoned, and in 1934 Jones did the "color designs" for the film *Becky Sharp.* He had previously done work on a short film called *La Cucaracha* which was released in 1934. His only other film work was *The Dancing Pirate,* which carried the credit "Designed by Robert Edmond Jones."

Returning to the "legitimate" theater, Jones continued to produce, direct, design, and write. Perhaps his most famous written work is *The Dramatic Imagination,* published in 1941. This collection of essays defined an understanding and respect for the art of the theater that was as relevant over 40 years later as at the time it was written.

Although Jones's last significant design is generally considered to be *Lute Song,* which opened in 1946, his influence continued to grow through the work of his apprentices, such as Jo Mielziner and Donald Oenslager, for many years. Mordecai Gorelik (another of his students) summed it up: "He was the founder of the whole present day tradition of scene design in the United States."

In the late 1940s Jones's health began to fail, and although he continued to design and write into the 1950s, his work was clearly restricted. In 1953 he retired to the Jones farm in New Hampshire, where he died on Thanksgiving Day, 1954.

Further Reading

Books by Jones include *Towards a New Theater* (1952); *The Dramatic Imagination* (1941); *Drawings for the Theatre*

(1925); and *Continental Stagecraft* (1922), written with Kenneth Macgowan. See also Ralph Pendleton, editor, *The Theatre of Robert Edmond Jones* (1958), and Lee Simonson, *The Stage Is Set* (1932). □

Robert Tyre Jones

Golf great Robert Tyre Jones (1902-1971) won his first match, a neighborhood tournament for kids, when he was only six years old. He went on from there to become America's greatest golfer.

Bobby Jones was born March 17, 1902, in Atlanta, Georgia. By the time he was 12 he was the Georgia state champion, and in 1921 he became the youngest member of the U.S. Walker Cup team when it journeyed to England. Between 1923 and 1930 he won five U.S. amateur titles, four U.S. Opens, three British Opens, and one British amateur title. He won the "Grand Slam"— four separate tournaments consisting of amateur and professional championships in the United States and England—in 1930. Meanwhile he earned a law degree from Emory University, following degrees from what is now Georgia Tech and from Harvard University.

After 1930 Jones gave up his amateur standing and made a series of instructional films. He practiced law, and in 1934 he founded the "Masters Tournament," a yearly event held in Augusta, Georgia, at the Augusta National Golf Club, which he had helped establish.

A spinal injury suffered in 1948 made it increasingly difficult for him to move about, but Jones continued to make yearly visits to the Masters to drape the green jacket, symbol of the event, around the shoulders of the winner.

In 1948 Bobby Jones was granted the "freedom of the burgh" of St. Andrew's, Scotland, traditional birthplace of the game of golf and one of the world's most famous courses. The only other American to have been granted that honor was Benjamin Franklin.

When he died on December 18, 1971, he was known as the greatest player who ever lived. Good looking and well educated, he was the personification of the all-American boy.

Further Reading

No book about golf would be complete without considerable space devoted to Bobby Jones. The reader needs only to pick up a book about golf to read more about Bobby Jones. His biography, *Golf Is My Game,* was published in 1960. □

Samuel Milton Jones

Samuel Milton Jones (1846-1904), American manufacturer and political reformer, was noted for his

enlightened labor policies and progressive political crusades.

Samuel Jones was born Aug. 8, 1846, near Beddgelert, Caernarvonshire, Wales. His parents immigrated to an upstate New York farm when he was 3. After only a few years of school he started working at the age of 10. He left home 4 years later, worked at various manual jobs, and was employed finally in the oil fields in Titusville, Pa. By 1870 he had begun to acquire wells of his own, and in 1885 he moved to Lima, Ohio, where he struck even richer wells. He invented several improved oil-drilling devices and in 1894 established the Acme Sucker Rod Company of Toledo to manufacture oil-well machinery.

Jones's business success did not harden him to the lot of underprivileged men. Instead, he earned the nickname "Golden Rule" Jones for running his factory on Christian and humanitarian precepts. Although he opened it in a depression year, he raised his men's pay. He also instituted an 8-hour day, a 48-hour week, a week's vacation with pay, a 5 percent bonus at Christmas, lunches at cost in the Golden Rule Dining Room, and cooperative health insurance—all of which were progressive workmen's benefits in the 1890s. Jones felt responsible for his employees' social awakening and brought in guest lecturers at his own expense. Even paychecks were accompanied by homilies on applied Christianity written by Jones.

In 1897 Jones, a Republican, was elected mayor of Toledo, Ohio. He tried to make Toledo a model city. He established an 8-hour day in the police and water departments; expanded municipal services to include playgrounds, golf links, kindergartens, and free concerts; and attacked the police courts for what he believed was their unfairness to social outcasts and poorer citizens. These ideas seemed radical and dangerously eccentric to many Toledo residents, but Jones was reelected in 1899, 1901, and 1903.

A dispute with the state Republican leadership in 1899 prompted Jones to run without party affiliation in every election thereafter. This was a fitting departure for a man whose personal style was more educational and evangelical than political in a partisan sense. Jones died in office on July 12, 1904, one of the most widely respected civic leaders of his time.

Further Reading

Jones produced two statements of his philosophy: *The New Right: A Plea for Fair Play through a More Just Social Order* (1899), which contains autobiographical material on his early life, and *Letters of Love and Labor* (2 vols., 1900-1901). Jones's protégé, Brand Whitlock, wrote an admiring assessment of him in *Forty Years of It* (1914). Hoyt Landon Warner, *Progressivism in Ohio, 1897-1917* (1964), and Jack Tager, *The Intellectual as Urban Reformer: Brand Whitlock and the Progressive Movement* (1968), contain useful sketches of Jones's career. □

Ben Jonson

The English playwright and poet Ben Jonson (1572-1637) is best known for his satiric comedies. An immensely learned man with an irascible and domineering personality, he was, next to Shakespeare, the greatest dramatic genius of the English Renaissance.

Ben Jonson was probably born in or near London, about a month after the death of his clergyman father. He received his formal education at Westminster School, where he studied under the renowned scholar William Camden. He did not continue his schooling, probably because his stepfather forced him to engage in the more practical business of bricklaying. He spent a brief period as a soldier in Flanders and sometime between 1592 and 1595 he was married.

Early Career

English literature, and particularly the drama, had already entered its golden age when Ben Jonson began his career. Jonson's special contribution to this remarkably exuberant age was his strong sense of artistic form and control. Although an accomplished scholar, he had an unusual appreciation of the colloquial speech habits of the unlettered, which he used with marked effect in many of his plays.

Jonson began his theatrical career as a strolling player in the provinces. By 1597 he was in London, the center of dramatic activity, and had begun writing plays for the theatrical manager Philip Henslowe. In what is probably his first piece of dramatic writing. *The Isle of Dogs,* Jonson ran afoul of the law. The play (which has not survived) was judged to be a "lewd" work containing "seditious and slanderous matter," and Jonson was imprisoned. In 1598 he was in more serious trouble. Having killed a fellow actor in a duel, he escaped hanging only by claiming right of clergy—that is, by reciting a few words of Latin commonly known as "neck-verse."

In the same year Jonson's first major work, *Every Man in His Humour,* was performed by the Lord Chamberlain's Men, with Shakespeare taking the lead role. This play stands as a model of the "comedy of humors," in which each character's behavior is dictated by a dominating whim or affectation. It is also a very cleverly constructed play.

Jonson's next major play, *Every Man out of His Humour,* appeared in 1599 or early 1600, followed closely by *Cynthia's Revels* (1601) and *Poetaster* (1601). These three "comical satires" represent Jonson's contribution to the so-called war of the theaters—a short-lived feud between rival theatrical companies involving Thomas Dekker, John Marston, and perhaps other playwrights in addition to Jonson himself. After this brief but heated skirmish, Jonson turned his energies to what he clearly regarded as one of his most important works, *Sejanus His Fall,* which eventually appeared in 1603. This rigidly classical tragedy was admired by some of Jonson's learned contemporaries, but the

great majority of playgoers considered it a pedantic bore. Jonson's only other surviving tragedy, *Catiline His Conspiracy* (1611), met with a similar fate.

By 1604, before he had written his most enduring works, Jonson had become known as the foremost writer of masques in England. These highly refined allegorical spectacles were designed for courtly audiences, and as a rule members of noble or royal families took part in the performances. Jonson continued writing masques throughout his career, frequently in cooperation with the famous architect Inigo Jones, who designed the stage sets and machinery.

Major Works

Jonson's dramatic genius was fully revealed for the first time in *Volpone, or the Fox* (1606), a brilliant satiric comedy which Jonson claimed was "fully penned" in 5 weeks. It was favorably received not only by London theatergoers but by more sophisticated audiences at Oxford and Cambridge.

Volpone contains Jonson's harshest and most unremitting criticism of human vice. All the principal figures are named (in Italian) after animals suggestive of their characters: for example, Volpone, the cunning fox, and Voltore, the ravenous vulture. The main action turns on Volpone's clever scheme to cheat those who are as greedy as he but not nearly so clever. With the help of his servant Mosca, he pretends to be deathly ill; each of the dupes, encouraged to believe that he may be designated heir to Volpone's fortune, tries to win his favor by presenting him with gifts. Volpone is too clever for his own good, however, and is finally betrayed by Mosca and exposed to the magistrates of Venice. The punishment imposed on him (and on the self-seeking dupes as well) is unusually severe for a comedy; in fact, there is almost nothing in *Volpone* which provokes laughter.

The satire of Jonson's next three comedies is more indulgent. *Epicoene, or the Silent Woman* (1609) is an elaborate intrigue built around a farcical character with an insane hatred of noise. The principal intriguer, Sir Dauphine Eugenie, tricks his noise-hating uncle Morose into marrying a woman Morose believes to be docile and quiet. She, however, turns out to be an extremely talkative person with a horde of equally talkative friends. After tormenting his uncle and in effect forcing him into a public declaration of his folly, Sir Dauphine reveals that Morose's voluble wife is actually a boy disguised as a woman.

In *The Alchemist* (1610) the characters are activated more by vice than folly—particularly the vices of hypocrisy and greed. Jonson's treatment of such characters, however, is less harsh than it was in *Volpone,* and their punishment consists largely in their humiliating self-exposure. *Bartholomew Fair* (1614), unlike Jonson's other comic masterpieces, does not rely on complicated intrigue and deception. Its relatively thin plot is little more than an excuse for parading an enormously rich and varied collection of unusual characters.

Later Years

After *Bartholomew Fair,* Jonson's dramatic powers suffered a decline. His major achievements were solidified by the appearance of his *Works* in a carefully prepared folio volume published in 1616. Although he continued writing plays for another 15 years, most of these efforts have been dismissed as "dotages." He remained nonetheless an impressive and respected figure, especially in literary and intellectual circles. In 1619, for example, he was awarded an honorary degree from Oxford. He was also idolized by a group comprising younger poets and playwrights who styled themselves the "tribe of Ben."

It is from this last phase of Jonson's dramatic career that much of the information about his personal life and character comes. One major source of information is the record of conversations with Jonson kept by the Scottish poet Drummond of Hawthornden. In the summer of 1618 Jonson took a walking tour to Scotland, in the course of which he spent a few days with Drummond. His host concluded that Jonson was "a great lover and praiser of himself, a contemner and scorner of others, given rather to lose a friend than a jest; jealous of every word and action of those about him, especially after drink, which is one of the elements in which he liveth; . . . oppressed with fancy, which hath ever mastered his reason." This somewhat unflattering portrait accords reasonably well with the personality that reveals itself indirectly in Jonson's plays.

Jonson's nondramatic writings include a grammar of English (printed in 1640), a miscellaneous collection of notes and reflections on various authors entitled *Timber, or Discoveries* (also printed in 1640), and a large number of poems, almost all of them written in response to particular events in the poet's experience. Most of his poetry was written in short lyric forms, which he handled with great skill. His lyric style tends to be simple and unadorned yet highly polished, as in the epigram on the death of his first daughter, which begins "Here lies to each her parents ruth,/ Mary, the daughter of their youth."

After the death of King James I in 1625, Jonson suffered a number of setbacks. His talents as a masque writer were not fully appreciated by the new king, and as a result Jonson was frequently short of money. He was paralyzed in 1628 and confined for the remainder of his life to his home in Westminster. He evidently continued his scholarly study of the classics, which had occupied him throughout his active life. He died on Aug. 6, 1637. In recognition of his stature as the foremost man of letters of his age, he was buried with great ceremony in Westminster Abbey.

Further Reading

The standard biography of Jonson is C. H. Herford and Percy Simpson, *Ben Jonson: The Man and His Work* (1925), which constitutes the first 2 volumes of an 11-volume edition of Jonson's works completed in 1952. The following works contain detailed criticism of most of Jonson's plays: Edward B. Partridge, *The Broken Compass: A Study of the Major Comedies of Ben Jonson* (1958); Jonas A. Barish, *Ben Jonson and the Language of Prose Comedy* (1960); and Robert E. Knoll, *Ben Jonson's Plays: An Introduction* (1964). Useful background studies are L. C. Knights, *Drama and Society in the Age of Jonson* (1937); Thomas Marc Parrott and Robert H. Ball, *A Short View of Elizabethan Drama* (1943; rev. ed. 1958); Madeleine Doran, *Endeavors of Art: A Study of Form in Eliza-bethan Drama* (1954); and Muriel Clara Bradbrook, *The Growth and Structure of Elizabethan Comedy* (1955). □

Scott Joplin

While Scott Joplin (1868-1917) is most noted for developing ragtime music, he also wrote music for ballet and opera.

As Johann Strauss is to the waltz and John Philip Sousa is to the march, so is Scott Joplin to ragtime: its guru, chief champion, the figure most closely associated with its composition. It was Joplin's short, hard-driving melodies—and the syncopated backbone he furnished them—that helped define the musical parameters of ragtime, a style that gave voice to the African American experience during the late 19th and early 20th centuries. According to David W. Eagle in the liner notes to *Scott Joplin: Greatest Hits,* "Ragtime, a type of written piano music, . . . was actually a hybrid of European and African musical traditions" consisting of "folk melodies (usually of black origin) and commercial music from minstrel shows . . . overlaid on West African cross-rhythms."

Sadly, for all his accomplishments in putting a new musical form on the map, Joplin spent his final years madly obsessed with a fruitless crusade to enter, if not conquer, another arena: opera, the staid, classical venue accepted by a white community that had for so long ridiculed ragtime as cheap, vulgar, and facile black music.

Many of the details of Joplin's life, like much of his music, have been lost to history. He was born November 24, 1868, in Texarkana, a small city straddling the border of Texas and Arkansas. Joplin's father, Giles, was a railroad laborer who was born into slavery and obtained his freedom five years before his son's birth. Florence Givens Joplin was a freeborn black woman who worked as a laundress and cared for her children. Like many in the black community, the Joplins saw in music a rewarding tool of expression, and the talented family was sought out to perform at weddings, funerals, and parties.

Scott, whose first foray into the world of scales and half notes came on the guitar, discovered a richer lyrical agent in his neighbor's piano. At first, Giles Joplin was concerned that music would sidetrack his son from a solid, wage-earning trade, but he soon saw the clear inventive genius in Scott, who, by the time he was 11, was playing and improvising with unbelievable smoothness. A local German musician, similarly entranced with Scott Joplin's gift, gave the boy free lessons, teaching him the works of European composers, as well as the nuts and bolts of musical theory and harmony.

Articulated Black Experience

In a move not uncommon for young blacks at the time, Joplin left home in his early teens, working as an itinerant pianist at honky-tonks and salons of the Midwest, South,

and Southwest. Although some revisionist historians have placed the birth of ragtime at the feet of white composers, such as Irving Berlin, who published "Alexander's Ragtime Band" in 1911, the true origin of the music was to be found in these low rent musical halls. In explaining the black roots of the musical form, Rudi Blesh and Harriet Janis wrote in *They All Played Ragtime,* "Piano ragtime was developed by the Negro from folk melodies and from the syncopations of the plantation banjos. As it grew, it carried its basic principle of displaced accents played against a regular meter to a very high degree of elaboration." The signature fast and frenetic pace of ragtime reflected the jubilant side of the black experience—compared with the melancholy-heavy blues—and the music became, according to Blesh and Janis, America's "most original artistic creation."

In 1893 Joplin played cornet with a band at the World's Columbian Exposition in Chicago, where musicians from throughout the country displayed for one another the regional variations of ragtime and where Joplin was encouraged by pianist Otis Saunders to write down his original compositions. Joplin left Chicago leading a male vocal octet, the repertoire of which included plantation medleys, popular songs of the day, and his own compositions. Ironically, Joplin questioned the staying power of ragtime, and his first two published pieces, "A Picture of Her Face" and "Please Say You Will," were conventional, sentimental, waltz songs.

After touring, Joplin settled in Sedalia, Missouri, which would later become known as the "Cradle of Classic Ragtime." Joplin attended music classes at the George R.

Smith College for Negroes, played with local bands, and taught piano and composition to other ragtime composers, most notably Arthur Marshall and Scott Hayden. This nurturing side would forever buoy Joplin's reputation within the musical community. In several cases, to help the careers of his lesser known contemporaries, Joplin lent his big-money name to their compositions.

In 1899 Joplin issued his first piano rags, "Original Rags" and "Maple Leaf Rag," the latter named for a social club where he often played. A white music publisher, John Stark, had heard Joplin playing the "Maple Leaf" and, though he was concerned that its technical difficulty exceeded even the grasp of its composer, he gave Joplin a $50 advance and a royalty contract that would bring Joplin one cent per copy sold. Such an arrangement was a wild departure from the norm, which netted composers no royalties and advances rarely surpassing $25. According to Peter Gammond in his book *Scott Joplin and the Ragtime Era,* Joplin said after he had finished this tune, "One day the 'Maple Leaf' will make me King of Ragtime Composers." Although only about 400 copies were sold in the first year, it had sold nearly half a million copies by the end of 1909.

Made Ragtime Premier Musical Trend

With this financial cushion, Joplin was able to stop playing at the clubs and devote all his time to composition and teaching. Joplin's prolific output, including "Peacherine Rag," "A Breeze from Alabama," "Elite Syncopations," and "The Entertainer," made ragtime the premier musical trend of the time, with Joplin the ingenious trendsetter. His compositions—glossed over by some shallow-minded white critics as the so-called "music of brothels"—showcased his keen understanding of inner voices, chromatic harmonies, and the rich interrelationships of melody and rhythm. William J. Schafer and Johannes Riedel wrote in *The Art of Ragtime: Form and Meaning of an Original Black American Art:* "The secret of Joplin's ragtime is the subtle balance of polarities, continuity, and repetition of melody and rhythm, much the same combination of energy and lyricism as in the marches of his contemporary, John Philip Sousa."

Despite his material successes and the regal status bestowed on him by ragtime composers and aficionados, Joplin could not easily brush off the disparaging accent the white world gave the term "rag"; such condescension, according to Joplin, was a transparent means of discrediting the black music as an artless form of folk entertainment. He gave his compositions elegant names, such as "The Chrysanthemum" and "Heliotrope Bouquet," capturing the lyrical mood and seriousness of classical music. To educate the advanced music student about the intricacies of ragtime, Joplin wrote a series of études, *The School of Ragtime: Six Exercises for Piano,* published in 1908, when schools promising the quick learning of the music were popping up across the country. John Rublowsky, writing in *Black Music in America,* quoted Joplin's preface to the series: "Syncopations are no indication of light or trashy music, and to shy bricks at 'hateful ragtime' no longer passes for musical culture. To assist the amateur players in giving the

'Joplin Rags' that weird and intoxicating effect intended by the composer is the object of this work.''

But Joplin was not satisfied with the composition of unconnected, short pieces, and his wish to explore the cultural context and functions of ragtime—in short, to explain the deeper meaning of ragtime to the white world—led to his *Rag Time Dance*. Published in 1902, it was conceived as a sort of ragtime ballet, combining folk dances of the period choreographed by Joplin, and a narrative written by him. Unable to find financial backers, Joplin put up his own money for an ensemble production of the piece. Although *The Rag Time Dance* proved Joplin's ability to write in extended, musical themes, it did not have the unifying and didactic effects for which he had hoped.

Undeterred and still courting the kind of exposure he believed his music needed, Joplin penned the first ragtime opera, *A Guest of Honor*. Unfortunately, the opera, which was performed once in a test rehearsal to gauge public sentiment, was never published and was lost. It was apparently Joplin's most inventive musical exercise, but, like *The Rag Time Dance,* its reception was a major disappointment to him. Blesh and Janis wrote, ''The fate of *A Guest of Honor* is the story of what might have been, for the time was right for syncopated opera. It was certainly time for the romantic-costume idea of light opera as epitomized by the sentimentalities of Victor Herbert to be superseded by something more American, and there is no doubt that America itself was ready for it and that Joplin was the man equipped to write it.''

Penned Opera, Suffered Disappointment

But this would be not be the last, nor the most consuming of Joplin's failures. Ever driven to push his own musical limits and to break the shackles in which he believed the white world had bound him, Joplin spent the final years of his life composing and maneuvering to produce a full-fledged opera. *Treemonisha* is a fable, a folk story about an orphaned girl (the title character), who, by virtue of having an education, is chosen to raise her people above ignorance, superstition, and conjuration to enlightenment. In *Treemonisha,* Joplin found a forum for the exploration of history and politics, a piece that would never allow the seriousness of his music and of his intellect to be questioned.

With words, choreography, and music by Joplin, *Treemonisha* was not a ragtime opera, but instead a complex work borrowing the phraseology and themes of some of the popular music of the day: Gilbert and Sullivan's sentimental show music, spirituals, plantation songs, brass band marches, and barber shop harmonies. Schafer and Riedel wrote that *Treemonisha* was Joplin's ''greatest accomplishment as a composer,'' and that it, having been composed two decades before George Gershwin's *Porgy and Bess,* served as ''the first demonstrably great American opera, for it speaks a genuine American musical idiom within the conventional forms of Western opera.''

The world at that time, however, was not ready for Joplin's operatic alchemy, in some respects because Joplin's name, so closely associated with ragtime, had begun to fade from the popular mind as ragtime became absorbed by the derivative white tunes of Tin Pan Alley. There was a threadbare performance of *Treemonisha* in 1915, but without scenery, orchestra, costumes, or lighting, the piece that had been at the center of his musical and intellectual life for more than five years came across as thin and unconvincing. Some writers have suggested that when Joplin died in 1917, he did so brokenhearted, shattered that his entry into the most socially redeeming class of music—opera—had been a bust. ''The death certificate said that he had died of 'dementia paralytica-cerebral' which had partly been brought on by syphilis,'' Gammond wrote, ''but it didn't add that it had been hastened by a violent addiction to *Treemonisha.*''

Though Joplin died well after he had reached the heights of his popularity, his contributions to music, particularly in the popularization of an originally black musical form, have never been in question. The mesmerizing interplay of rhythm and melody influenced European composers Claude Debussy and Antonín Dvorák, and ragtime enjoyed a brief revival in the 1970s, when the film *The Sting,* starring Paul Newman and Robert Redford and featuring Joplin's song ''The Entertainer,'' reintroduced music lovers to Joplin's playful brilliance.

''The genius of Joplin was twofold,'' attested Blesh and Janis, ''the tyrannical creative urge and the vision. With the first alone, even had he been, perhaps, the greatest of all the ragtime players, his most perfectly constructed pieces, unscored, would today be one with all the others, lost with a lost time. But his vision was the sculptor's, molding transitory vision into stone's indestructibility. He was at once the one who makes and the one who saves. Through the labor of this one 'homeless itinerant' the vast outcry of a whole dark generation can go on sounding as long as any music will sound.''

Further Reading

Blesh, Rudi, and Harriet Janis, *They All Played Ragtime,* Oak Publications, 1971.
Gammond, Peter, *Scott Joplin and the Ragtime Era,* St. Martin's, 1975.
Rublowsky, John, *Black Music in America,* Basic Books, 1971.
Schafer, William J., and Johannes Riedel, *The Art of Ragtime: Form and Meaning of an Original Black American Art,* Louisiana State University Press, 1973.
New York Times, December 1, 1991.
Additional information for this profile was taken from liner notes by David W. Eagle to *Scott Joplin: Greatest Hits,* RCA Victor, 1991. □

Jacob Jordaens

Jacob Jordaens (1593-1678) was a Flemish painter of prodigious energy and lively imagination. He is one of the outstanding masters of the school of Antwerp.

Jacob Jordaens was born in Antwerp. At the age of 14 he was apprenticed to Adam van Noort, who had been one of Peter Paul Rubens's masters. In 1615 Jordaens was admitted as a master into the Guild of St. Luke. The earliest dated extant work is an *Adoration of the Shepherds,* which was painted in 1616, the year he married Van Noort's daughter. Unlike Rubens and Anthony Van Dyck, Jordaens did not make the journey to Italy which was regarded in his day as essential for all ambitious young painters. Indeed, except for a visit to Holland in 1661, his entire life was passed in the southern Netherlands.

The influences that shaped the art of the young Jordaens are plainly visible in the *Daughters of Cecrops* (1617). The impress of Rubens reveals itself in the heavy, fleshy nudes and the brilliant coloring. The realistic details and the strong side lighting, on the other hand, are derived from the Italian painter Caravaggio, whose influence reached Jordaens only indirectly, through certain Flemish artists who had visited Rome and become imitators of his style.

Mature Works

During the period 1620-1640 Jordaens produced most of the works which established his reputation as an artist of genius. In 1628, when the Augustinians of Antwerp required three altarpieces for their church, they gave the commissions to Rubens, Van Dyck, and Jordaens. Jordaens's subject was the *Martyrdom of St. Apollonia,* and he made of it a spectacular, if somewhat overcrowded, composition. At this time his inventiveness began to express itself in the creation

of new genre subjects, which he repeated with variations in numerous canvases. Among the earliest is *The Peasant and the Satyr,* a series of illustrations for Aesop's fable. Equally well known are his boisterous scenes of family feasts, such as *The King Drinks,* and the many pictures of *As the Old Sang, So the Young Pipe,* from the Flemish proverb, which are full of comic and trenchant observations.

When applied to biblical subjects, Jordaens's homely realism sometimes overshadows the religious narrative: even in the 17th century his painting *St. Peter Finding the Coin in the Fish's Mouth* was described as the "Antwerp Ferry" because of the prominence given to a boat crowded with people and animals. The artist's delight in interpreting mythological subjects in a spirit of parody is exemplified by his *Nurture of Jupiter,* in which the god is depicted as a squealing infant, crying for his milk.

When, during the 1630s, Rubens found himself faced with monumental projects requiring many assistants, Jordaens became one of his principal collaborators. At the time of the entry of the cardinal infante Ferdinand into Antwerp in 1635, when the streets were filled with lavish baroque decorations, Jordaens executed several large canvases from Rubens's designs. He performed a similar service a few years later by assisting Rubens in the execution of the vast cycle of pictures for the Torre de la Parada, Philip IV's hunting lodge in Spain.

Jordaens was given the lion's share in the decoration of the Huis ten Bosch near The Hague in Holland. His chief painting for this project was the *Triumph of Prince Frederick Henry* (1652).

Late Works

In his later years Jordaens forsook the Roman Church to become a Calvinist, and Protestant Communion services were frequently held at his house. He continued, nevertheless, to paint devotional pictures for Catholic patrons, and his conversion to the Reformed Church seems to have caused him no difficulties. One of his largest and most impressive late religious works is *Christ among the Doctors* (1663), in which the amusing characterizations of the scribes and Pharisees listening to the child Jesus form a striking contrast to the dry and sober classicism of the composition as a whole.

Jordaens died at the age of 85. He was buried in the Calvinist churchyard at Putte just over the Dutch border north of Antwerp.

Further Reading

The most informative book on Jordaens in English is Max Rooses, *Jacob Jordaens: His Life and Work,* translated by E.C. Broers (1908), which presents a detailed and reliable account of the artist's career, with supporting documents and copious illustrations. The excellent chapter on Jordaens in H. Gerson and E.H. ter Kuile, *Art and Architecture in Belgium, 1600-1800* (1960), summarizes the more recent scholarly investigations and offers a sound assessment of the artist and his work. A useful supplement is the catalog by Michael Jaffé of the Jordaens exhibition held at the National Gallery of Canada (1968-1969).

Additional Sources

Hulst, Roger Adolf d', *Jacob Jordaens,* Ithaca, N.Y.: Cornell University Press, 1982. □

Barbara Charline Jordan

Attorney Barbara Charline Jordan (1936-1996), who served in the U.S. House of Representatives from 1972 to 1976, was a prominent member of the House Judiciary Committee when it held President Richard M. Nixon's impeachment hearings.

Barbara Jordan was born in Houston, Texas, to parents with strong convictions about the behavior of their three daughters. Jordan's father, a Baptist preacher, was probably the most important influence in her life. He valued God, the Bible, his family, good music, and the spoken and written word. Although the Jordans were poor, their lot was not very different from that of other African Americans in the Houston area. Jordan's parents made every effort to provide adequately for her and her sisters and to shield them from the detrimental effects of the racially segregated society in which they lived by regularly exposing them to the most positive aspects of their own African American community. They attended schools and churches led by prominent members of the African American community and conducted their business with African American-owned establishments. It was Jordan's parents who made contact with the white world when it was necessary.

All of the Jordan girls played musical instruments, and two of them decided that they wanted to become music teachers. Barbara, however, was more ambitious. She was not sure what she wanted to do, but she knew she wanted to achieve something great. Her father had taught her that race and poverty had nothing to do with her brain power or her ability to achieve lofty goals if she had the drive to work for them.

Young Jordan Decides To Become a Lawyer

At first Jordan thought about being a pharmacist, but as she researched that profession, she noted that she had never heard of a famous pharmacist and, consequently, she decided to abandon that field. When a African American female lawyer from Chicago, Edith Sampson (who later became a judge), visited Jordan's high school on "career day," Jordan was so impressed with her that she made a definite decision about her life work. That evening she announced to her parents that she wanted to be a lawyer. Jordan's mother was reluctant about her daughter's choice—after all, African American women lawyers were a rarity in the South—but her father supported her, reassuring her that she could excel in any endeavor.

Money was certainly an important consideration when Jordan was choosing a college. After many family conferences, she decided to enroll at Texas Southern University (TSU), an inexpensive school for African American students, in order to save money for law school. At TSU Jordan, already a skilled orator, joined the debating team. In a bout with Harvard University debators, the TSU team, with Jordan at the helm, was jubilant when the match ended in a tie. After Jordan graduated *magna cum laude* from TSU in 1956 she went to Boston University Law School. She was an excellent and extremely disciplined student who often worked long into the night. Because her family made tremendous financial sacrifices to pay for her education, Jordan did not want to disappoint them in any way. She graduated in 1959 and in the same year passed both the Massachusetts and Texas bar examinations.

Early Practice and Senate Years

After she returned to Houston in 1959 Jordan began her law practice on her parents' dining room table. When she was finally able to convince friends and neighbors that she was indeed a competent attorney her clientele grew, enabling her to open an office downtown. Since the civil rights movement was in full swing by the time Jordan had established herself, she decided that she might be able to do her part in the unweaving of the web of segregation laws by becoming a member of the Texas State House of Representatives. She waged two unsuccessful campaigns, one in 1962 and another in 1964, on a shoestring budget. Although she lost both elections, she was gaining popularity.

When the lines of Houston's voting districts were redrawn, Jordan found that most of those who had voted for her were united in a single district. She decided to run for the Texas Senate in 1966 and won. She was the first African American woman ever to be elected to the Texas Senate and the first African American person to serve since the Reconstruction period. In 1972, after six years in the Texas Senate, where she sponsored important labor legislation, Jordan decided to run for the U.S. House of Representatives. She was not the first African American woman to be seated in the U. S. Congress; that honor went to Shirley Chisholm of New York, who had been elected in 1968. She was, however, the first African American woman from the South.

Service as Member of House Judiciary Committee

Jordan was particularly interested in becoming a member of the House Judiciary Committee. A word from a man she admired—former President Lyndon B. Johnson—helped to bring that desire to fruition. Thus, when the difficult question of President Richard M. Nixon's collusion in the Watergate Hotel burglary in an effort to secure his 1972 election victory was brought before the Judiciary Committee, Jordan was among its members.

The committee, seeking evidence to determine whether Nixon had committed an impeachable offense, commanded so much public attention that its hearings were televised. The viewing audience was interested in the questions raised by all of the committee members, but it was Barbara Jordan, who riveted the attention of the viewers with her oratorical ability, clarity of presentation, and thorough knowledge of constitutional issues. As more and more damaging information was uncovered, it seemed that President Nixon's impeachment was inevitable. Before the committee made its final decision, Nixon resigned on August 9, 1974, the first president in U. S. history to do so. The televised impeachment hearings catapulted Jordan to national fame.

Jordan As Teacher and Orator

Jordan did not seek reelection after her second term. Part of her reason for leaving politics was that she was suffering poor health due to leukemia and multiple sclerosis, which eventually caused her to rely on a wheelchair or a walker. Her ill health did not keep her from many honorable accomplishments in her later years, however. She held several teaching positions, including professor at the Lyndon Baines Johnson School of Public Affairs in Houston, Texas, where her ethics course was so popular that students entered a lottery to enroll. In 1976, she became the first African American selected to deliver the keynote address at a national convention of the Democratic Party. She was the keynote speaker again in 1992 for the Democratic Convention which nominated Bill Clinton. Jordan was such a skilled and respected lecturer and speaker that in 1985 she was named Best Living Orator.

President Clinton appointed her to the U.S. Commission on Immigration Reform in 1994. Here Jordan denounced hostility toward immigrants, and opposed a plan which would deny automatic citizenship to children of immigrants born in this country. That same year she received the Medal of Freedom from President Clinton. Jordan died on January 17, 1996 in Austin, Texas from viral pnemonia caused by complications from leukemia. President Johnson's widow, Lady Bird Johnson was quoted in *Jet* in February 1996, saying, "I feel a stabbing sense of loss at the passing of a good friend."

Further Reading

There are several biographies of Jordan available, including her own *Barbara Jordan, A Self Portrait* (1979); James Haskins, *Barbara Jordan* (1977); Ira Bryant, *Barbara Charline Jordan* (1977); Linda Jacobs, *Barbara Jordan* (1978); and Naurice Roberts, *Barbara Jordan, the Great Lady from Texas* (1984); also, "Barbara Jordan, former congresswoman and educator dies at 59 in Austin, Texas," *Jet*, February 5, 1996; and "Jordan's rules," from *The New Republic*, February 12, 1996, vol. 214, no. 7. □

David Starr Jordan

David Starr Jordan (1851-1931), American scientist and university administrator, distinguished himself as a teacher of biology, an ichthyologist, and an influential college president.

David Starr Jordan was born in Gainesville, N.Y., on Jan. 19, 1851. In 1869 he entered Cornell University and was awarded both his bachelor of arts and master of arts degrees 3 years later. He served as instructor in botany in Lombard University, Galesburg, Ill., in 1872-1873, and the following year he was principal of the Appleton Collegiate Institute in Wisconsin. After attending a school of science established by the famous scientist Louis Agassiz, Jordan became professor of natural history at Northwestern Christian College (later Butler University) in 1875. He received a medical degree in 1875 and 3 years later a doctorate in philosophy.

In 1879 Jordan became chairman of the department of natural sciences at Indiana University, where he distinguished himself as a teacher of organic evolution and bionomics. His research in ichthyology resulted in numerous publications, of which the most famous is *Synopsis of Fishes of North America* (1882).

Jordan became president of Indiana University in 1885 and during his 6 years in office instituted the concept of a major field of academic study for college students. In 1891 he became president of Stanford University and served in this position until 1913, when he became chancellor. Jordan's speeches and writings gained him a place among the great leaders in American higher education. His recognition of the need and importance of students' selecting their own subjects for study from the total range of the university program led to the introduction of the elective system at Stanford.

Many of Jordan's critical and scholarly assessments of higher education are contained in *The Voice of the Scholar*. This book consists of addresses delivered on such subjects as "The Personality of the University," "The University and the Common Man," "The Woman and the University," "The University of the United States," and "College Spirit."

Jordan held numerous important positions as an ichthyologist. He was assistant to the U.S. Fish Commission, head of the American commission to study the fur seals in the Bering Sea, and member of the International Commission for Fisheries. He was also chief director of the World Peace Congress and one of the original trustees of the Carnegie Foundation. He died Sept. 19, 1931, having served as chancellor emeritus of Stanford for 15 years.

Further Reading

A carefully written, detailed account of Jordan's life and work is his own *The Days of a Man* (2 vols., 1922). A biography, as well as an exposition of Jordan's social and political ideas, is in Edward McNall Burns, *David Starr Jordan* (1953). For his role as university president see Orrin Leslie Elliott, *Stanford University: The First Twenty-five Years* (1937).

Additional Sources

Moran, Hugh Anderson, *David Starr Jordan, his spirit and decision of character*, Palo Alto, Calif., Daily Press, 1969. □

June Jordan

The Jamaican American poet June Jordan (born 1936) explored multicultural and multiracial reality, feminism, and Third World activism in her many poems. She was also politically active in revolutionary movements in the Third World.

June Jordan was born in Harlem on July 9, 1936, to Jamaican immigrants, Granville Ivanhoe and Mildred Jordan, who had left rural Jamaica in search of American prosperity. In 1942 the Jordans moved to Bedford-Stuyvesant in Brooklyn where Jordan was raised in a home that was optimistic about America and middle-class in its aspirations. Her father was a postal worker, her mother a nurse, and one of her aunts the first African American principal in the New York public school system. The Jordans belonged to the Episcopal Church, and Jordan completed the last three years of high school at Northfield School for Girls, a religious preparatory school in Massachusetts.

As a young girl, Jordan's struggle to define herself as a female, African American person, and poet was both hampered and nurtured by the cultural ambivalences of her Jamaican American home. She had often violent disagreements with her parents. Growing up in Brooklyn, she survived physical abuse from her father starting at age 2. Yet she insists he had the greatest influence on her. An African American nationalist, he taught her how to fight using boxing, chairs and knives. "I got away any way I could," Jordan said. "I had the idea that to protect yourself, you try to hurt whatever is out there. I think of myself as my father's daughter." Her mother, who committed suicide when Jordan was an adolescent, never tried to intervene in their fights, she said. "At this point I'm far more forgiving of my father than my mother."

Jordan found the all-white environment of Northfield School crippling to her sense of identity and her urge to express her own reality in poetry.

Jordan entered Barnard College in 1953 but left New York in 1955 for Chicago after marrying Michael Meyer, a white student at Columbia University. While Meyer pursued a graduate degree at the University of Chicago, Jordan resumed her undergraduate career and struggled to cope with the tensions of an environment hostile to her interracial marriage. Back in New York, a year later, Jordan re-entered Barnard but ultimately chose to sacrifice her college education to raise her son Christopher and to support her husband's pursuit of a graduate degree. She wrote freelance articles under the name June Meyer, wrote speeches for James Farmer of the Congress of Racial Equality (CORE), worked in city planning and in social programs for youth, and even served as a film assistant to the noted documentary filmmaker Frederick Wiseman, who was filming *The Cool World,* a portrait of Harlem.

First Book Publication

Her first book-length publication was *Who Look At Me* (1969), a series of poetic fragments about Black identity in white America interspersed with paintings in the tradition of Langston Hughes' *The Sweet Flypaper of Life* (1955), whose text alternated with the photographs of Roy de Carava. Jordan's book ends with the lines: "Who see the roof and corners of my pride / to be (as you are) free? / WHO LOOK AT ME?"

Jordan published early poems in *Negro Digest* and *Black World,* the journals out of which grew the nationalistic Black Aesthetic movement of the 1960s, but she felt the Black Arts movement was "too narrow." Her second volume, *Some Changes* (1971), includes poems reminiscent of the Black poetry of the 1960s, such as "Okay 'Negroes'" and "What Would I Do White." It also contains intense personal reflections, vivid domestic portraits such as "The Wedding" and "Uncle Bullboy," and historical poems that redefine America through a focus on its multicultural and multiracial reality, such as "47,000 Windows."

Subsequent volumes of poetry continued to explore these themes and reflected Jordan's increasing interest in feminism and her radical belief in the need for the Third World to combat Western domination. Her feminism reveals itself strongly in poems such as "Case in Point," which describes being raped, and "1978," a feminist statement of solidarity with all women (*Passion,* 1980). Jordan supported the Sandinistas of Nicaragua, the Palestinian struggle, and the South African fight against apartheid in both her writing and political activism. Although she called for violence in such poems as "I Must Become a Menace to My Enemies" in *Things I Do in the Dark* (1981), she also perceived herself

as an American poet in the tradition of Walt Whitman, who she felt lost his deserved prominence in the American poetic tradition because of his all-encompassing vision of a multicultural, multiracial America and because of his life as an outsider, homosexual, and bohemian.

Her Many Works

Other books of poetry include *New Day: Poems of Exile and Return* (1974), *I Love You* (1975), *The Things I Do in the Dark* (1977), *Things I Do in the Dark: Selected Poems 1954-1977* (1981), *Passion: New Poems, 1977-1980* (1980), *Living Room, New Poems: 1980-1984* (1985), and *Naming Our Own Destiny: New and Selected Poems* (1989). Her strength as an essayist is reflected in *Civil Wars, Selected Essays: 1963-1980* (1981), *On Call: New Political Essays: 1981-1985* (1986), and *Moving Towards Home: Political Essays* (1989).

Jordan's interest in children is reflected in *The Voice of the Children* (1970), an edited collection that grew out of a creative workshop for Black and Hispanic children, and poems for young people, such as *Dry Victories* (1972), *Fannie Lou Hamer* (1972), *New Life: New Room* (1975), and *Kimako's Story* (1981). She wrote a novel for young adults entitled *His Own Where,* which was nominated for a National Book Award in 1971.

Jordan wrote and produced three plays: *In the Spirit of Sojourner Truth* (1971), *For the Arrow that Flies by Day* (1981), and *Bang Bang Uber Alles,* a musical in collaboration with the composer Adrienne Torfin. The last, which targeted racial hate groups, was picketed by the Ku Klux Klan. Jordan wrote the libretto for "I Was Looking at the Ceiling and Then I Saw the Sky"—an unusual song-play about social issues in Los Angeles told in popular song with composer John Adams, and director Peter Sellars.

Later Work

She also brings her analysis to bear on events that have captured the national stage in *Technical Difficulties: African American Notes on the State of the Union* (1995). "America in Confrontation With Democracy" looks at the reasons behind Jesse Jackson's failed 1988 presidential campaign. Jordan examines the Clarence Thomas/Anita Hill hearings in "Can I Get a Witness," where she condemns Hill's enemies. "To be a Black woman in this savage country: Is that to be nothing and no one revered and defended and given our help and our gratitude?" she writes. Other topics Jordan explored in "Technical Difficulties" included the legacy of Martin Luther King Jr.; the poverty of American education; the fall of Mike Tyson; and the Rodney King verdict and the Los Angeles riots.

In addition to her essay collection, Jordan released a book of poems. The book is a serious, intense, poetry collection. Jordan rewrites and stretches the definition of love. She is not subtle or afraid of the full range of passion that these four letters encompass. She writes as a confident woman, a poet for whom words are precious tears caught in one's palm. Through her provocative and vivid imagery, she invites the reader to celebrate everyday pleasures that are transformed into extraordinary feelings as a result of being in love.

Touchstone (1995) is a collection of essays and previously unpublished musings, first issued in 1980. The final essay was written when Jimmy Carter worked in the Oval Office. Yet the writing remains amazingly fresh, a testimony to the strength of Jordan's convictions, and the intractability of segregation and ignorance in this country. Whether she's writing letters, magazine articles or speeches, Jordan pours herself into the issue at hand, which could be police brutality, neglect of New York City schoolchildren or Zora Neale Hurston's overlooked status as a writer. Jordan's think pieces contain a vision of current events wide enough to contain history, and that gives them shelf life long after their use-by dates.

Overall, Jordan is probably best known for her strident poems decrying the unjust murder of black youths by police throughout New York. Underlying the angry tone of those poems about police brutality, is the love Jordan feels for her people. Jordan has never shown that she fears undressing in public. Evidenced in her poignant, poetic essay, "Many Rivers to Cross," Jordan traces her remarkable journey from being a recently divorced single parent, confronted by unemployment and her mother's suicide, to a woman who relinquishes weakness. In other essays and poems about being raped, June Jordan repeatedly shares deeply personal pains; she renders herself vulnerable so that others may garner strength and stand bravely assured, determined to survive the storm.

Jordan was awarded a Prix de Rome in environmental design to write and live in Rome, in 1970 after being nominated by R. Buckminster Fuller. Jordan taught at City College in New York, Connecticut College, Sarah Lawrence College, Yale University, and State University of New York, and Stony Brook, Long Island, where she taught for many years. She was a professor of African American studies at the University of California (Berkeley) in 1997.

Further Reading

For more biographical information, see Jordan's *Civil Wars* (1981); Alexis Deveaux, "Creating Soul Food," in *Essence* (April 1981); and *The Dictionary of Literary Biography: Afro-American Dramatists and Prose Writers after* 1955 (volume 38); further critical analysis can be found in Peter Erickson, "June Jordan," in *Black Sister II: Poetry by Black American Women, 1746-1980* (1981), edited by Erlene Stetson; and Erickson, "The Love Poetry of June Jordan" in *Callaloo* (Winter 1986). ☐

Louis Jordan

Louis (1908-1975) Jordan's jazz-based boogie shuf-fle rhythms laid the foundation for rhythm and blues, modern electric blues, and rockabilly music.

At the height of his career, in the 1940s, bandleader and alto saxophonist Louis Jordan scored 18 Number One hit records. In the tradition of Louis Armstrong and Fats Waller, Jordan exhibited a brilliant sense of showmanship that, as music critic Leonard Feather explained in his book *The Jazz Years,* brought audiences first-rate entertainment "without any loss of musical integrity." Against the backdrop of house parties, fish fries, and corner grills, Jordan performed songs that appealed to millions of black *and* white listeners. Able to "straddle the fence" between these two audiences, Jordan emerged as one of the first successful crossover artists of American popular music.

Born on July 8, 1908, in Brinkley, Arkansas, Jordan was the son of Jim Jordan, a bandleader and music teacher. Under the tutelage of his father, Jordan began studying clarinet at age seven. After spotting a saxophone in a music store window, however, he "ran errands all over Brinkley" until he could raise the money to purchase the instrument. While on summer vacation at the age of 15, Jordan landed his first gig, with Ruby "Tuna Boy" Williams's Belvedere Orchestra, at the Green Gables in Hot Springs, Arkansas. His first professional engagement was with Fat Chappelle's Rabbit Foot Minstrels, playing clarinet and dancing throughout the South. At Arkansas Baptist College in Little Rock, Jordan majored in music and played on the school baseball team. After school he played local dates with Jimmy Pryor's Imperial Serenaders.

Moving to Philadelphia in 1930, Jordan worked with trumpeter Charlie Gaines's orchestra and tuba player Jim Winters's band. Two years later, Jordan traveled to New

York with Gaines's group, where he took part in a recording session with pianist Clarence Williams's band. In New York he briefly worked with the bands of Kaiser Marshall and drummer Joe Marshall. His most important job, though, came in 1936 when he joined drummer Chick Webb's orchestra—a 13-piece ensemble that featured singer Ella Fitzgerald. A small, "hunch-backed" man whose physical deformity nonetheless failed to hinder his inventive drumming talent, Webb hired Jordan as a singer, sideman, and announcer. In 1937 Jordan recorded his first vocal with Webb's band, a song titled "Gee, But You're Swell." During his stint with Webb Jordan developed his skills as a frontman. "Louis would go out and just break up the show," recalled former bandmember Garvin Bushell in his autobiography *Jazz From the Beginning.* "Nobody could follow him."

In the summer of 1938, Jordan left Webb's orchestra to form his own, nine-piece, band; although Jordan enjoyed performing as part of large jazz ensembles, he embarked on a career as a bandleader and more general entertainer. "I wanted to play for the people, for millions, not just a few hep cats," explained Jordan in Arnold Shaw's *Honkers and Shouters.* Billing himself as "Bert Williams," Jordan played shows at the Elk's Rendezvous at 44 Lenox Avenue, in Harlem. His long residency at the club eventually prompted him to name his group the Elk's Rendezvous Band. After playing various club dates on 52nd Street, he booked his band at proms and dances at Yale University and Amherst College. In 1939, this group recorded several sides for the Decca label.

That December, after changing the name of his band to the Tympany Five, Jordan reduced the size of the unit to six members (later it would number seven or eight). Invited to open for the Mills Brothers at the Capitol Theater in Chicago, Jordan played a ten-minute spot during the intermission between the featured performances. In no time, Jordan's energetic stage presence began to draw larger crowds than the headline acts, so Capitol's management decided to lengthen his performance to half an hour.

But the real turning point in Jordan's career came when he performed at a small "beer joint" called the Fox Head Tavern in Cedar Rapids, Iowa. Distanced from the demanding crowds of Chicago and New York, Jordan found he was freer to experiment with new material. At the Fox Head he assembled a large repertoire of blues and novelty songs. On his return to the Capitol Theater, Jordan became a sensation. In January of 1942 he hit the charts with a rendition of the blues standard "I'm Gonna Move to the Outskirts of Town."

From 1942 Jordan was rarely absent from the *Harlem Hit Parade.* Over the following ten years he recorded more than 54 rhythm-and- blues best-sellers. Material for his band came from a number of black and white songwriters. As Jordan's manager, Berle Adams, told *Honkers and Shouters* author Shaw, "When we found something we liked, an arrangement would be made up, and we'd play it on one-nighters. The songs the public asked for again and again were the songs we recorded." Jordan soon produced a stream of hits, including "What's the Use of Getting Sober (When You're Gonna Get Drunk Again)," "Five Guys Named Moe," and "G.I. Jive," a boogie number intended for the entertainment of troops fighting in World War II.

Aside from the universal appeal of his material, the key to Jordan's success lay in his tight organization and the use of talented arrangers such as pianists Wild Bill Davis and Bill Dogget. Though he exhibited a casual manner, Jordan was a serious bandleader who demanded that his outfit be well dressed and thoroughly rehearsed. In *An Autobiography of Black Jazz,* saxophonist Eddie Johnson described how Jordan's penchant for "neatness" led him to require his band to "look right even down to their shoes." Jordan furnished bandmembers with six or seven uniforms, which displayed a post-zoot-suit style with multicolor designs.

In the mid-1940s, Jordan's Tympany Five drew thousands of listeners to white nightclubs and black theaters. Traveling by car caravan, the band toured constantly, playing shows at venues like Billy Berg's Swing Club in Hollywood, the Oriental Theatre in Chicago, the Apollo in Harlem, and the Paradise Theatre in Detroit. In black movie houses, Jordan's releases were featured in film shorts, many of which became so popular that the regular features often received second billing. Around this time Jordan also appeared in several motion pictures, including *Meet Miss Bobby Socks, Swing Parade of 1946,* and *Beware,* which was advertised as "the first truly great all-colored musical feature."

After World War II, when the big bands began to disappear, Jordan's small combo continued to find commercial success. "With my little band, I did everything they did with a big band. I made the blues jump," Jordan explained in *Honkers and Shouters.* The band became so popular, in fact, that Jordan toured with such sought-after opening acts as Dinah Washington, Ruth Brown, Sarah Vaughn, and Sister Rosetta Tharpe. Following his 1945 million-seller "Caldonia," Jordan and the Tympany Five continued to score hits, among them "Beware Brother Beware," "Boogie Woogie Blue Plate," "Nobody Here But Us Chickens," and "Open the Door Richard," a song adapted from a black vaudeville comedy routine popularized during the 1930s and '40s. In 1950, Jordan recorded a cover version of "(I'll be Glad When You're Dead) You Rascal You" with trumpeter-singer Louis Armstrong.

The following year Jordan changed course, disbanding the Tympany Five and forming a 16-piece big band. But this group did not live up to the sound or favor of the earlier unit. On leaving the Decca label in 1954, Jordan largely lost the steady stream of material, sidemen, and producers that had helped him maintain his national celebrity. Determined to keep up with the burgeoning rhythm and blues market, however, he signed with West Coast-based Aladdin Records. But after failing to score commercially, he moved to RCA's Victor X subsidiary. In the meanwhile, Jordan had recorded for more than a dozen labels in the U.S., including Mercury, Warwick, Tangerine, Pzazz, and Blue Spectrum. Despite his persistence, Jordan faced a new record-buying public dominated by teenagers who demanded rock 'n' roll lyrics, idol images, and heavy back-beat rhythms.

Health problems eventually forced Jordan to retire from one-night stands, which required that he drive hundreds of miles across the country. In 1946 he bought a home in Phoenix, Arizona, where he stayed for 18 years; he moved to Los Angeles in the early 1960s. During this period he devoted his time to playing occasional month-long engagements in Phoenix, Las Vegas, and New York. On a tour of England in 1962, Jordan performed and recorded with the Chris Barbers band. Two years later, he reformed the Tympany Five to appear at show lounges and music festivals. His performances in the Near East in 1967 and 1968 received enthusiastic responses. At the 1973 Newport Jazz Festival, too, crowds gave him a warm reception.

In October of 1974, Jordan suffered a heart attack while performing in Sparks, Nevada. After entering St. Mary's Hospital in Reno, he returned home to Los Angeles, where he died on February 4, 1975. His body was flown to St. Louis for burial at Mt. Olive Cemetery.

In 1987 Jordan was inducted into the Rock and Roll Hall of Fame. Though many had forgotten his contributions to popular music over the intervening years, this honor paid tribute to one of the performers most responsible for the development of rhythm and blues and rock and roll. As trumpeter Dizzy Gillespie related in his autobiography *To Be or Not to Bop*, " Rock n' roll had been with us a long time" and "Louis Jordan had been playing it long before Elvis Presley." Jordan helped shape the careers of rock and roll pioneers Chuck Berry, Fats Domino, Bill Haley, and countless others, though his music would later become obscured by evolving trends. In 1990 Jordan's work was celebrated in the hit stage production *Five Guys Named Moe*, a rollicking look at a man whose "whole theory of life" was to make audiences "smile or laugh." With the many reissues of Jordan's music on compact disc, one need only listen to realize the lasting sincerity of his commitment.

Further Reading

Bushell, Garvin, *Jazz From the Beginning: As Told to Mark Tucker*, University of Michigan Press, 1988.

Chilton, John, *Let the Good Times Roll: The Story of Louis Jordan and His Music*, University of Michigan Press, 1994.

Feather, Leonard, *The Jazz Years: Earwitness to an Era*, Quartet Books, 1989.

(With Al Fraser) Gillespie, Dizzy, *To Be or Not to Bop: Memoirs*, Doubleday, 1979.

Rusch, Robert D., *Jazztalk: The Cadence of Interviews*, Lyle Stuart Inc., 1984.

Shaw, Arnold, *Honkers and Shouters: The Golden Years of Rhythm and Blues*, Collier, 1978.

Simon, George T., *The Big Bands*, Schirmer, 1981.

Tosches, Nick, *Unsung Heroes of Rock n' Roll*, Scribner's, 1984.

Travis, Dempsey J., *An Autobiography of Black Jazz*, Urban Research Institute, 1983.

Down Beat, March 27, 1975.

Newsweek, April 20, 1992.

Pulse!, November 1992.

Variety, November 1990.

Additional information for this profile was obtained from liner notes by Peter Grendysa to *Just Say Moe! Mo' of the Best of Louis Jordan*, Rhino Records, 1992. □

Michael Jordan

Basketball superstar Michael Jordan (born 1963) was one of the most successful, popular, and wealthy athletes in college, Olympic, and professional sports history.

Michael Jordan was born on February 17, 1963. He did not make the high school basketball team as a sophomore in his native Wilmington, North Carolina, but did make the team as a junior. After high school he accepted a basketball scholarship to the University of North Carolina where he played under head coach Dean Smith. In his first season at Carolina he became only the second Tarheel player to start every game as a freshman and was named Atlantic Coast Conference (ACC) Rookie of the Year (1982). In his freshman year he played on the ACC championship team and made the clutch jump shot that beat Georgetown University for the championship of the National Collegiate Athletic Association (NCAA). He led the ACC in scoring as a sophomore in the 1982-1983 season and as a junior in the 1983-1984 season. The *Sporting News* named him college player of the year in 1983 and again in 1984. He left North Carolina after his junior year and was drafted by the Chicago Bulls of the National Basketball Association (NBA) as the third overall pick of the 1984 draft, behind standouts Hakeem Olajuwon and Charles Barkley. Before joining the Bulls, Jordan was a member of the Summer 1984 United States Olympic basketball team that easily won the gold medal in Los Angeles, California.

Air Jordan Was Born

When Jordan was drafted by the Chicago Bulls they were a lackluster team, seldom drawing not much more than 6,000 fans to a home game. Jordan quickly turned that around. His style of play and fierce spirit of competition reminded sportswriters and fans of Julius Erving, who had dominated play during the 1970s. Jordan's incredible leaping ability and hang time thrilled fans in arenas around the league. As a rookie in his first season he was named to the All-Star team and was later named the league's Rookie of the Year (1985).

A broken foot sidelined him for 64 games during the 1985-1986 season, but he returned in rare form, scoring 49 points against the Boston Celtics in the first game of the playoffs and 63 in the second game, an NBA record. The 1986-1987 season was again one of individual successes, and Jordan started in the All-Star game after receiving a record 1.5 million votes. He became the first player since Wilt Chamberlain to score 3,000 points in a single season. Jordan enjoyed personal success, but Chicago did not advance beyond the first round of the playoffs until 1988, when they defeated the Cleveland Cavaliers. The Bulls were then eliminated in the semi-final round by the Detroit Pistons. During the season Jordan had concentrated on improving his other basketball skills to the point where he was named Defensive Player of the Year (1988). He was also named the league's Most Valuable Player (MVP) and be-

straight title. Then, unexpectedly, tragedy struck. Jordan's father, James, was murdered by two men during a robbery attempt. Jordan was grief stricken, and that, combined with increasing media scrutiny over his gambling, left him feeling depleted and disenchanted with his life as a basketball superstar. Stating that he had nothing left to accomplish, he announced his retirement from professional basketball in October. By all accounts Jordan handled the personal tragedy of his father's death with great dignity. And while he felt the joy and challenge was gone from basketball, nothing could diminish what he had accomplished: three consecutive NBA titles, three regular season MVP awards, three playoff MVP titles, member of the All-Star team every year that he was in the league, and seven consecutive scoring titles. In just nine seasons he had become the Bulls all-time scoring leader.

In 1994 Jordan changed sports and joined the Chicago White Sox minor league baseball team. Professionally, the next 17 months proved to be mediocre at best, but the experience and time away from basketball provided a much needed respite and opportunity to regain his passion for basketball.

The Road Back Was a Slam Dunk

It had been a long time since anyone who knew Jordan thought—or dared ask—could he cut it. But when he returned to the Chicago Bulls during the 1994-1995 regular season, people wondered, "Could he do it again?"He played well, but inconsistently and so did the Bulls. The team was defeated in the playoffs by the Orlando Magic. After a summer of playing basketball during breaks from filming the movie *Space Jam,* he returned with fierce determination to prove any skeptic that he had what it took to get back on top. The 1995-1996 season was built on the type of playing on which records are made—the team finished the regular season 72-10, an NBA record that topped the 1971-1972 record established by the Los Angeles Lakers, and Jordan, with his shooting rhythm back, earned his eighth scoring title. He also became the tenth NBA player to score 25,000 career points, second only to Wilt Chamberlain in the number of games it took. The Bulls, with the Jordan, Pippen, and Dennis Rodman super combo, went on to win their fourth NBA championship in the decade, overpowering the Seattle Supersonics in six games. It was a moment few who watched will ever forget, as Jordan sank to his knees, head bent over the winning ball, in an emotional moment of bittersweet victory and deep sadness. The game had been played on Father's Day, exactly three years after his father's murder. It was the kind of moment both Jordans would have relished sharing.

The defending champions encountered a tougher playing field during the 1996-1997 season, but entered the playoffs as expected. Sheer determination took the Bulls to their fifth NBA championship. Illness, injury, and at times wavering mental focus plagued the team. In the fifth game Jordan almost single handedly delivered the winning score, despite suffering from a stomach virus.

Jordan's other professional life as businessman and celebrity endorser was never off track. He co-starred with

came the first player to lead the league in both scoring and steals. He was again named the MVP in that year's All-Star game.

The Bulls' management knew that they had a superstar in Michael Jordan, but they knew as well that they did not have a championship team. By adding such players as center Bill Cartwright, Horace Grant, and John Paxon to complement Jordan's skills they created a strong team that won the 1991 title by defeating the Los Angeles Lakers. When the Bulls defeated the Portland Trail Blazers for the NBA championship in 1992, they became the first back-to-back winners since the Boston Celtics during the 1960s, who won eight straight championships.

In 1992 Jordan joined NBA stars Magic Johnson, Larry Bird, John Stockton, Patrick Ewing, Karl Malone, Clyde Drexler, David Robinson, Charles Barkley, Scottie Pippen, Chris Mullin, and Duke University's Christian Laettner to form the "Dream Team" that participated in the 25th Summer Olympic Games in Barcelona, Spain. The Olympic Committee had voted to lift the ban on professional athletes participating in the games. The team easily won the gold medal, winning their eight games by a 43.7 average margin of victory, scoring more than 100 points in each game.

1993—Personal Trials and Triumphs

In 1993, after a grueling semi-final playoff series with the New York Knicks, the Bulls met the Phoenix Suns for the NBA championship. When it was over, Jordan was again playoff MVP and Chicago had an unprecedented third

Bugs Bunny and the Loony Tunes gang in the live action/animation film, *Space Jam.* Megabuck endorsements for companies such as Nike and Wheaties, as well as his own golf company and branded products such as Michael Jordan cologne, which reportedly sold 1,500,000 bottles in the first two months on the market, made Jordan a multimillionaire. In 1997 Jordan was ranked the world's highest paid athlete, with a $30 million contract—the largest one-year salary in sports history—and approximately $40 million a year in endorsement fees.

To top off his stellar professional resume, Jordan was regarded as an all around nice guy with moral courage, poise, *and* personal charisma. He credited his family and faith for his success. As the twentieth century came to a close, this African-American hero was a cultural and sports icon around the world.

Further Reading

Hang Time, Jordan's biography, written with Bob Greene (Doubleday, 1992) and *Rare Air: Michael on Michael,* edited by Mark Vancil (Collins Publishers, San Francisco, 1993) are good general accounts of his life through 1992. *Taking to the Air: The Rise of Michael Jordan* by Jim Naughton (Warner Books, 1992) and *Hang Time: Days and Dreams with Michael Jordan* by Bob Greene (1992) are both good general biographies. For a critical look at Jordan see *The Jordan Rules* by Sam Smith (1992). For more on the Olympic "Dream Team" see *The Golden Boys* by Cameron Stauth (1992). See also *Second Coming: The Strange Odyssey of Michael Jordan— from Courtside to Home Plate and Back Again* by Sam Smith (HarperCollins, 1995). □

classes at the University of Georgia. (Charlayne Hunter-Gault later became a newscaster on public television.)

Shortly after the university was desegregated, Jordan left private practice and devoted full time to work in the civil rights movement. In 1962 he was appointed Georgia field director for the National Association for the Advancement of Colored People (NAACP), leading a boycott of Augusta, Georgia, merchants who refused to serve African Americans. After four years as NAACP field director, Jordan in 1966 became director of the Southern Regional Council's Voter Education Project. The project sponsored voter registration campaigns in 11 southern states and conducted seminars, workshops, and conferences for candidates and office holders. After four years, Jordan took a six-month appointment as a fellow at the Kennedy Institute of Politics at Harvard and then, in 1970, became executive director of the United Negro College Fund. When Whitney Young, executive director of the National Urban League, died in 1972 Jordan was appointed his successor.

As director of the league, Jordan continued its emphasis on African American uplift through training, employment, and social service programs, but the organization also began to emphasize research and advocacy as part of its thrust toward implementing promises of the 1960s civil rights reforms. For example, during Jordan's administration the league developed a highly regarded research and information dissemination capability, including a policy journal— *The Urban League Review*—and the annual *State of Black America* reports. *The State of Black America,* issued each January to coincide with the president's State of the Union

Vernon Jordan

An American civil rights leader, Vernon Jordan (born 1935) was executive director of the National Urban League from 1972 to 1982 and later one of the few African American partners in a major law firm in the United States.

Vernon E. Jordan was born August 15, 1935, in Atlanta, Georgia. His father was a mail clerk in the U.S. Army and his mother ran a local catering service. Jordan was educated in the Atlanta public schools and graduated from DePauw University in 1957. For his legal training Jordan attended the Howard University Law School where he received the *J.D.* in 1960.

Jordan then returned to Atlanta to practice law. Almost immediately he became involved in a landmark civil rights case of the era. Jordan and two other Atlanta attorneys sued the University of Georgia for failing to admit African American students. The suit, on behalf of Hamilton Holmes and Charlayne Hunter, resulted in a federal court order directing their admission. Jordan received national attention in 1961 when he escorted Hunter through a violent mob of whites as she became the first African American student to attend

address, became a principal source of systematic data on the African American condition in the United States and an important resource for identifying African American policy perspectives.

During his tenure at the League Jordan was recognized as a leading African American spokesman, writing a weekly syndicated column, lecturing, and appearing on national television interview programs. A frequent adviser to government, corporate, and labor leaders, Jordan also was frequently appointed to presidential advisory boards and commissions.

In May of 1980 Jordan was shot in the back and wounded by a lone gunman waiting in ambush outside a Fort Wayne, Indiana, motel. Although Joseph Paul Franklin, an avowed white racist, was charged in the shooting, he denied involvement and was acquitted. Fourteen years later, awaiting trial on other charges, Franklin admitted he had shot Jordan.

Shortly after recovering from the attempted assassination, Jordan resigned as director of the Urban League and became a partner in the Washington, D.C., offices of the Dallas-based firm of Akin, Gump, Strauss, Hauer and Feld, and began serving on the boards of directors of nine major American corporations. From the vantage point of his influential law firm Jordan continued to be an important behind-the-scenes operative and advocate for civil rights interests. The 1992 election of Jordan's longtime friend Bill Clinton, after 12 years of Republican presidencies, propelled Jordan to more influence.

Further Reading

Jordan's life and career are profiled in Karen DeWitt's "Vernon Jordan: Urbane Urban League" in *Washington Post* (July 28, 1977); and in Robert Meyers, "Vernon Jordan: Using Old Contacts in a New Setting" in *National Law Journal* (October 3, 1983); a lengthy *New York Times* analysis (July 14, 1996) discusses Jordan's uncommon position and power within civil rights, corporate and government circles. □

Joseph

The American Indian Joseph (ca. 1840-1904), a Nez Percé chief, fought to preserve his homeland and did much to awaken the conscience of America to the plight of Native Americans.

Joseph was born in the Wallowa Valley of northeastern Oregon. In 1871, upon the death of his father, he assumed leadership of the nontreaty Nez Percé. White settlers coveted the traditional homeland of these Native Americans, and Joseph, seeking confirmation of Nez Percé territorial rights, met with Federal commissioners to discuss a spurious treaty in which the Indians had supposedly ceded their land to the U.S. government. The commissioners were disconcerted by Joseph, who stood 6 feet tall, was amicable but firm, and spoke with amazing eloquence.

Despite the obvious fraudulence of the old treaty, President Ulysses S. Grant opened the Nez Percé lands to settlement and ordered the Native Americans onto reservations. White settlers moved onto the land and committed atrocities against the Indians. Against his will, Joseph was forced by his tribesmen to fight. Pressed hard by Gen. Oliver Otis Howard's forces, Joseph was convinced that he could not win and began a lengthy withdrawal toward Canada. Pursued by Howard and harassed by many small detachments, Joseph fled toward Canada and thrilled the nation, whose sympathies were with the Native Americans.

During the fall of 1877 Joseph led his 500 followers into Montana. In the fighting he showed rare military genius and great humanity; he refused to make war on women and children, bought his supplies when possible, and allowed no mutilation of bodies. On October 1, as the Nez Percé paused to rest at the Bear Paw Mountains just 30 miles from Canada, they were surprised by Col. N. A. Miles with approximately 600 soldiers. With only 87 warriors, Joseph chose to fight. He would not abandon the children, the women, and the aged. After a 5-day siege, however, he said to Miles and his followers: "It is cold and we have no blankets. The little children are freezing to death. . . . Hear me, my chiefs. I am tired; my heart is sick and sad. From where the sun now stands, I will fight no more forever."

The 431 remaining Nez Percé were taken to Kansas and subsequently to the Indian Territory (Oklahoma). There so many of them sickened and died that an aroused American public demanded action. Chief Joseph was moved to Colville Reservation in Washington, along with 150 of his

followers; the others were returned to Oregon. Joseph made many pleas to be returned to his tribal homeland, but he died on Sept. 21, 1904, and was buried on the Colville Reservation.

Further Reading

The best of the many biographies of Joseph is Merrill D. Beal, *I Will Fight No More Forever: Chief Joseph and the Nez Percé War* (1963). Other interesting works include Helen Howard and Dan McGrath, *War Chief Joseph* (1941; published in 1965 as *Saga of Chief Joseph*), and Lucullus McWhorter, *Hear Me, My Chiefs,* edited by Ruth Bordin (1952). □

Joseph II

Joseph II (1741-1790) was Holy Roman emperor from 1765 to 1790. He is one of the best examples of Europe's enlightened despots.

Born in Vienna on March 13, 1741, the first son of Maria Theresa, Archduchess of Austria, and Francis Stephen of Lorraine, Grand Duke of Tuscany, Joseph achieved his first triumph merely by being born a boy. A year earlier, as Joseph's grandfather Charles VI left no male heirs, Maria Theresa had succeeded to the hereditary dominions of the house of Hapsburg. Her succession, challenged by Frederick II of Prussia, had unleashed a general European war (War of the Austrian Succession), and the fact that Maria Theresa had previously given birth to three daughters had raised further questions about the succession.

The War of the Austrian Succession cost the house of Austria one of its richest provinces, Silesia, a loss confirmed in the Seven Years War (1756-1763). Maria Theresa and her chief ministers were determined first to recover that province and later to compensate themselves somehow for its loss. Both of these aims required a general overhaul of the monarchy's inadequate armed forces, which in turn would require a general overhaul of the machinery of state in order to raise the necessary funds. Joseph was educated with these considerations in mind.

By the time he had reached the age of 20, with a high forehead, piercing blue eyes, a Roman nose, pouting lips, and a somewhat receding chin, Joseph had learned his lessons rather too well. In 1761 he submitted to his mother a memorandum proposing a general reform of the state that suggested a general centralization so pervasive that it not only would have done away with all of the remaining powers of the provincial estates but also would have overridden most of the national differences of the widespread dominions of the house of Austria. He was politely told to tend to his business. Meanwhile, he had married Isabella of Bourbon Parma in 1760; in 1762 she gave birth to a daughter, Maria Theresa; a year later Isabella died, a blow from which Joseph was never to recover. Although, for reasons of state, he entered into a second marriage, with Josepha of Bavaria, he treated her with disdain, and when she died in 1767, he refused to consider a third marriage. The death of his daughter in 1768 confirmed him in his growing misanthropy and finished the job of making him a compulsive worker.

Early Reign

In 1765 Joseph's father, who had with his wife's backing been elected Holy Roman emperor in 1742, died. Joseph was duly elected to succeed him in that dignity. His position was now an anomaly. His father, in spite of his high-sounding title, had been essentially a prince consort; Maria Theresa had given him no share in the administration of her dominions. Joseph was unwilling to play such a passive role. His mother now granted him the title of coregent, but it soon became clear that it too was an empty one. For the next 15 years Joseph would complain that he was unable to initiate what he regarded as necessary reforms.

The Empress did turn over to Joseph prime responsibility for the conduct of foreign affairs. In 1772, in the wake of a joint Prussian-Russian initiative, the kingdom of Poland was partitioned. Maria Theresa was reluctant to participate in what she regarded as a blatantly immoral action, but Joseph insisted and Austria received the southern Polish province of Galicia. In 1778 Joseph attempted to take advantage of the fact that the ruling family of Bavaria, the house of Wittelsbach, had died out. Pressing some rather doubtful Hapsburg claims to the succession, he sent in Austrian troops. This action provided an opportunity for Frederick II of Prussia to pose as the defender of German liberties by declaring war on Austria. As neither side was anxious for a major war, operations soon degenerated into a desultory war of maneuver, contemptuously dubbed the "Potato War" by participants, who spent more time in digging up fields for food than in fighting. The Treaty of Teschen (1779) gave Austria insignificant territorial gains.

Enactment of Reforms

In 1780 Maria Theresa died, and Joseph, who now became sole ruler of all the Hapsburg dominions as well as emperor, was in the position of implementing the program of changes he had long desired. The reforms that Joseph now introduced had, with few exceptions, been under consideration in his mother's reign and were organically related to policies formulated under her. At any rate, the Josephinian reforms addressed themselves broadly to the inequities of the old regime.

In 1781 Joseph abolished serfdom, although the Austrian peasantry still was left with serious financial and work obligations. In the same year an edict of toleration lifted the Protestant and Greek Orthodox subjects of the monarchy to a condition of near equality. The next year the Jews of Austria also were granted a measure of toleration. The dominant position of the Catholic Church was further undermined by the creation of the Commission on Spiritual Affairs, which came perilously close to establishing secular control over the Church. At the same time Joseph ordered the dissolution of the majority of the monasteries in Austria. These events moved Pope Pius VI to take the unprecedented step of traveling to Vienna, but Joseph refused to give way on any question of substance, and Pius returned to Rome empty-handed.

In 1783 Joseph commuted the robot, the work obligation owed by the Austrian peasants to the noble owners of the land, to money payments, an action that led to untold difficulties. In order to assess the amount due by the peasants accurately, it was necessary to survey and register all land holdings. But, as the nobility had traditionally concealed a portion of its holdings in order to escape taxation, it now began to oppose Joseph in earnest and could do so more easily, for the Emperor had all but abolished censorship. In 1786 he did away with the restrictive craft guilds, a reform which was designed to create a distinct economic advantage but which added considerably to the number of Joseph's enemies. Finally, in 1789, Joseph abolished the robot entirely.

These reforms, striking as they did at the economic advantage enjoyed by the privileged orders, would have been difficult to enforce under ideal circumstances. As it was, Joseph's peculiar conduct of foreign policy in the 1780s did not contribute to the strength of his position. In 1784 he had tried to acquire Bavaria once more, this time in exchange for the Austrian Netherlands. Frederick II managed to block the scheme once more, this time by representing himself as the leader of the League of German Princes, dedicated to the maintenance of the status quo. Far worse, in 1787, as the result of an alliance recently concluded with Russia, Joseph involved Austria in a war with the Ottoman Empire. It was meant to be a joint venture with the Russians, but they were involved in a separate campaign against Sweden and left him to his own devices. The result

was a military fiasco that brought on painful losses of territory and ruined Joseph's health. Concurrently his subjects in the Netherlands, resenting his attempts to enforce his ecclesiastical reforms there, rose in rebellion. Hungary, with the support of Prussian agents, was threatening secession. In 1790 Joseph was forced to repeal his reforms for Hungary. On Feb. 20, 1790, he died.

Further Reading

In English, the most recent biographies of Joseph are Saul K. Padover, *The Revolutionary Emperor: Joseph II of Austria* (1934; rev. ed. 1967), and Paul P. Bernard, *Joseph II* (1968). See also Edith M. Link, *The Emancipation of the Austrian Peasant, 1740-1798* (1949).

Additional Sources

Beales, Derek Edward Dawson, *Joseph II*, Cambridge Cambridgeshre; New York: Cambridge University Press, 1987.

Blanning, T. C. W., *Joseph II*, London; New York: Longman, 1994. □

Josephus Flavius

Josephus Flavius (ca. 37-100) was a Jewish historian, diplomat, and military leader, and the sole source of information concerning numerous events in the final centuries of the Jewish state.

According to his own account, Josephus was born to an aristocratic, priestly family in Jerusalem. He was well educated in Judaism and in the Greek disciplines. At the age of 16 he became interested in the principal Jewish sects of his time and lived 3 years in the wilderness with a hermit, probably an Essene. At 19 Josephus became a Pharisee. At 26 he went on a mission to Rome and succeeded in securing the release from prison of several Judean priests. He came home impressed with the grandeur and might of Rome, only to find that the Jewish revolt had started.

Josephus was appointed governor of Galilee with responsibility for its defense. After his defeat at Jotapata, he escaped but later surrendered to the Romans. They treated him well, largely because his prediction that Vespasian would become emperor came true (69). Formerly known as Joseph ben Mattathias, Josephus took the Emperor's family name, Flavius. He was an eyewitness to the siege and fall of Jerusalem, after which he returned to Rome, where Vespasian granted him Roman citizenship and a pension. Subsequently, Josephus devoted himself to writing.

His Writings

Only four of Josephus's works are extant. His earliest volume, *The Jewish Wars,* probably written in his native Aramaic, was lost. It was apparently intended to discourage the Babylonian Jews and other peoples from joining in the Parthian War against Rome. Its present Greek version (79), consisting of seven books, fixes responsibility for the up-

rising against Rome solely on the Zealots. Josephus takes occasion to praise his patrons, Vespasian and Titus, and indicates that Titus did not order the Temple burned.

Josephus's *Antiquities of the Jews* (ca. 93), in 20 volumes, outlines the history of the Jews from creation to the revolt. Its laudation of John the Baptist, Jesus, and James is deemed to be a 3d-century interpolation by a Christian. Josephus also refers to the conversion to Judaism of the royal family of Adiabne in the 1st century B.C. His autobiographic *Vita,* or "Life" (ca. 93-100), was originally appended to the second edition of the *Antiquities.* In a section of this work Josephus attempts to refute the charge of disloyalty lodged against him, especially by the rival Jewish historian Justus of Tiberias (ca. 65).

There are numerous discrepancies in the accounts between the *Wars* and the *Antiquities.* These works, however, are a principal source of information about the Jewish sects: the Sadducees, Pharisees, and Essenes. Josephus's history also sets the stage for the Dead Sea Scrolls and the excavations at Masada, the site of the last Jewish stand (73). The latter archeological findings proved the accuracy of Josephus's description.

In *Against Apion* (ca. 93), Josephus refutes the malicious anti-Jewish slanders circulated by Apion and others. He defends and extols the Mosaic law and Jewish ethics. Josephus's writings are generally apologetic in nature. The Talmud, however, ignores him. His works were preserved by the medieval Church, chiefly for the references to Chris-

tianity and also because they deal with the early Christian period.

Further Reading

The writings of Josephus were translated into English by Henry St. John Thackeray and Ralph Marcus in the Loeb Classical Library (1926-1958). A splendid study of Josephus is in G.A. Williamson, *The World of Josephus* (1964). Thackeray's *Josephus: The Man and the Historian* (1929) is excellent. The life and works of Josephus are also treated in Norman Bentwich, *Josephus* (1914). Yigael Yadin, *Masada: Herod's Fortress and the Zealots' Last Stand* (trans. 1966), is a beautifully illustrated account of the archeological discoveries at Masada.

Additional Sources

Bentwich, Norman De Mattos, *Josephus,* Philadelphia: R. West, 1978.

Hadas-Lebel, Mireille, *Flavius Josephus: eyewitness to Rome's first-century conquest of Judea,* New York: Macmillan Pub. Co.; Toronto: Maxwell Macmillan Canada; New York: Maxwell Macmillan International, 1993. □

Josquin des Prez

The Franco-Flemish composer Josquin des Prez (ca. 1440-1521) developed a personal style by adding to the northern, contrapuntal idiom the text-oriented chordal writing of Italian masters. His works were described as models of the "perfect art."

The birth date and birthplace of Josquin des Prez are unknown, and until recently even the spelling of his name was conjectural. If the Milanese archives from 1459 to 1472 that refer to the "biscantor" (singer) "Juschino de Frantia" concern the composer, he must have been born about 1440, or 10 years before the hitherto-accepted date. A travel document of 1479 describes him as "Joschino picardo," and he is identified as "belga veromanduus" in an early-16th-century manuscript. Both remarks indicate that he was born on Burgundian territory, then ruled by Philip the Good. The discovery of an acrostic "Josquin des Prez" in a poem, *Illibata Dei virgo,* presumably written by the composer himself, has settled the spelling of his name.

All that is known about the composer's early training is a remark by Claude Hémeré, writing over 100 years after Josquin's death, that he studied music at the collegiate church of St-Quentin. Despite the epitaph for the composer Johannes Ockeghem, in which Josquin (among others) is asked to lament his "good father" ("perdu avez vostre bon père"), the assumption of a teacher-student relationship between the two is not warranted.

Years in Italy

The earliest report about Josquin is an archival document of 1459 from Milan Cathedral, where he was employed as a singer. He remained in the choir until 1472, when his name disappeared from the rolls. He sang in the chapel choir of the dukes of Milan from 1474 until at least 1479. Where Josquin was until 1486, when he was listed in the papal choir in Rome, is not known. He stayed in Rome until 1494 and perhaps even later. The chapel files for the years 1494-1501 are lost, but the absence of his name in the lists of 1501 indicates he departed before that date.

Josquin worked for Ascanio, Cardinal Sforza, the youngest brother of his former Milanese employer, in Rome probably between 1490 and 1493. At least two Italian *frottole, El grillo* and *In te, Domine* by "Josquin Dascanio" (Josquin [singer] of Ascanio), date from this period. Both pieces, written in the chordal style Josquin learned in Italy, contain allusions to the parsimoniousness of his employer.

His Service to Patrons

From 1501 to 1503 Josquin was at Blois with King Louis XII of France. Compositions from this time include the chanson *Adieu mes amours* with the biting verse "Vivrai-je du vent si l'argent du roi ne vient pas souvent?" and a motet, *Memor esto,* in which the composer reminds the monarch of a forgotten promise. An instrumental fanfare, *Vive le roi,* and a humorous work with a single tenor note for the King to sing along on also probably date from these years.

Despite this activity in France, much evidence suggests that Josquin was "on loan" to the French king from his Italian employer, Ercole d'Este, Duke of Ferrara. Relations between the composer and the duke can be traced to 1499, but only in 1501 is there proof of a contractual agreement between them. In a letter believed to date from 1502, an agent of the duke, signing himself "Gian," describes for Ercole his impressions of Josquin des Prez and Heinrich Isaac, both under consideration for the position of choir conductor. The writer recommends Isaac as more flexible, industrious, and engaging and less expensive, but he does give the palm to Josquin in one respect: talent as a composer. For Ercole of Ferrara this was sufficient, and Josquin was appointed to the coveted post.

Leaving the French court, then at Lyons, on April 17, 1503, Josquin journeyed to Ferrara, where he remained until after the duke's death 2 years later. Among the master's most important works composed during this time are the motets *Salve regina* and *Miserere mei Deus* and the celebrated *Missa Hercules Dux Ferrariae.*

Return Home

Josquin passed the rest of his life in his native land. Famous throughout the Continent in his old age, compatriots and foreigners alike requested musical works from him. In 1507 he set to music the verses *Plus nulz regretz* of the poet Jean Lemaire de Belges, written to celebrate a treaty between Flanders and England. In 1515 he wrote a beautiful five-voice *De profundis* for the funeral of his former patron Louis XII. As late as 1520 Josquin composed "aucunes chanssons nouvelles" for the young monarch Charles V, nephew of his last patron, Marguerite of Austria, regent of the Netherlands. This intelligent and talented woman especially admired the composer and appointed him provost of the collegiate church of Notre Dame at Condé-sur-l'Escaut.

Josquin's death date is inscribed in a 17th-century volume of Flemish grave inscriptions. Marguerite ordered a monument and portrait of the composer erected in the church of St-Gudule in Brussels; the portrait has long since disappeared, but a woodcut made of it by Petrus Opmeer in 1611 exists.

Josquin's fame during and after his lifetime resulted in many spurious works that carry his name. Scribes and publishers often attributed works to him through ignorance or deceit. At present 20 Masses, about 90 motets, and 70 secular works (including 10 for instruments) are assumed to be genuine.

The Masses

Of the 20 Masses, 17 were published during the composer's lifetime. Among the 9 works probably written before Josquin left Milan (ca. 1479) are the *Missa L'ami Baudichon* and *Missa Ad fugam.* In the *Missa L'ami Baudichon* he stresses long duets, emphasizes the upper voices, and generally avoids imitation, all of which point to the model of Guillaume Dufay. The *Missa Ad fugam,* on the other hand, is a canonic work that owes much to the *Missa Prolationum* of Ockeghem. In these as well as several other Masses of his early period, Josquin uses ostinato and sequences, and he manipulates the *cantus firmus* through rhythmic proportions—all for structural purposes.

Between 1486 and 1505 Josquin devised even more elaborate techniques. Most celebrated is his *Missa L'homme armé super voces musicales,* in which the "L'homme armé" tune is repeated for each movement on a different step of the scale. In the *Missa Hercules Dux Ferrariae,* he contrived a *cantus firmus* by replacing the vowels in his patron's name and title with their scale equivalents, that is, "Re ut re ut re fa mi re." It is also believed that the vowels in the opening words of the poem *Lassa far a mi* furnish the pitches of the *cantus firmus* in the *Missa La sol fa re mi.*

Josquin's last three Masses, *Da pacem, De beata Virgine,* and *Pange lingua,* all differ from one another in some respect. For the *Missa Da pacem* Josquin at times retains the sustained-note *cantus firmus* and canonic writing of earlier works, while he completely abandons the cyclic tenor in the *Missa De beata Virgine.* In the *Missa Pange lingua* he avoids canonic obscurities and a sustained-note *cantus firmus* for a paraphrase of the borrowed tune that moves from voice to voice by means of imitation. What distinguishes these Masses from earlier compositions, however, is the close relation between music and text.

The Motets

Josquin's motets represent him at his best. By setting texts rarely touched by his predecessors or contemporaries (psalms, Gospel verses), he opened up new possibilities for musicians. By having the motet text generate melodic motives and thereby replace in function the traditional *cantus firmus,* he made the motet the harbinger of a new style.

From most evidence it appears that Josquin turned to the writing of motets somewhat late in his career but composed them in large numbers after he turned away from the

Mass. The earliest motets, *Illibata Dei virgo* and *Ut Phoebi radiis,* are built on a solmization tenor in which the vowels of specific words ("Ma ria") are assigned equivalent degrees of the scale (la, mi, la).

In Josquin's famed motet *Ave Maria . . . virgo serena,* probably composed in his middle (Roman) period, he consistently uses imitation. For each of several lines or phrases, he creates a unique musical motive that is imitated by each voice in turn. Sometimes a phrase is set to a pair of counterpointing voices that are in turn imitated by a second pair. For variety, chordal sections emphasizing the text alternate with those in imitation. A few motets like *Domine Jesu Christe* and *Qui velatus facie fuisti* are wholly chordal, but Josquin prefers, as in his *Ave Maria,* to alternate chordal with linear writing.

The text is underscored syntactically and symbolically in other prominent works such as the *Miserere mei Deus,* in which the tenor unceasingly repeats an ostinato phrase. Similarly, the repetition of the opening words at the close of the motet *Memor esto verbi tui* illustrates the composer's awareness of the text as an equal partner with the music.

Secular Works

Several of Josquin's secular songs match the high level of the motets. In his early period the composer wrote bitextual chansons with two French voice parts supported by a Latin contratenor, as well as French chansons for three and four voices in such traditional *formes fixes* as the ballade, rondeau, and virelai. In his middle and late periods he wrote many chansons for five and six parts with canon in two or more voices. To replace the old ballade, rondeau, and virelai, Josquin devised new formal structures in his songs *Faulte d'argent* (ABA), *Basiez moy* (ABB'C), and *Incessament livré* (AABBC). The few chordal *frottole* that are extant (such as *El grillo* and *In te, Domine*) reveal Josquin's full command of the Italian secular style, a style that influenced the Masses and motets of his later years.

Although other masters of Josquin's generation wrote much music of high quality, not one, with the possible exception of Heinrich Isaac, reached his level. Josquin's reputation was unequaled in the early 16th century, and he was considered the composer of the "Ars perfecta" or perfect art, to which nothing could be added or taken away. His "humanizing" of music from a branch of mathematics to a synthesis in which music and word were equals was to be the signpost for succeeding generations.

Further Reading

Gustave Reese, *Music in the Renaissance* (1954; rev. ed. 1959), discusses Josquin and his works. Additional information is in the *New Oxford History of Music,* vol. 3 (1960). ☐

James Prescott Joule

The English physicist James Prescott Joule (1818-1889) proved that mechanical and thermal energies are interconvertible on a fixed basis, and thus he established the great principle of conservation of energy.

On Dec. 24, 1818, James Joule was born at Salford near Manchester, the second of the five children of a wealthy brewery owner. A rather frail boy, he received his early education at home. In 1839, in the laboratory in his home, he began his studies of electrical motor efficiency, which ultimately led to his development of the mechanical theory of heat. In connection with this work he became one of the first to realize the necessity for standard units in electricity and to advocate establishing them.

In the course of his efficiency experiments Joule made his first discovery—now known as Joule's law: the heating of a conductor depends upon its resistance and the square of the current passing through it. He presented this important generalization in a paper, "On the Production of Heat by Voltaic Electricity," before the Royal Society in London in 1840.

Joule's study of the interrelation of heat and electrical energy may have stimulated his study of the relationship between heat and mechanical work. His approach was direct: he used the mechanical energy provided by falling weights to heat water by stirring it and made precise measurements of the heat produced and the energy lost by these weights. The results provided the first value of the mechanical equivalent of heat, corresponding to a temperature increase of 1°F of 1 pound of water for the expenditure of 838

foot-pounds of work. The apparent simplicity of Joule's experiment is quite misleading, for enormous experimental skill, great care, and limitless patience were needed to get repeatable results; experts regard his work as demonstrating exceptional skill.

Joule presented the results of these mechanical work experiments in a paper, "On the Calorific Effects of Magneto-electricity and on the Mechanical Value of Heat," which he read at the meeting of the British Association in 1843, but no notice was taken of them. During the next 6 years, using variations in procedure, he continued his measurements and consistently substantiated his first results. His reports continued to be overlooked until 1847, when they came to the attention of William Thomson (later Lord Kelvin). He realized their significance, and through his efforts Joule finally got an attentive hearing of his work in 1849, when his paper "On the Mechanical Equivalent of Heat" was read to, and accepted for publication by, the Royal Society. His only other notable work, done with Thomson, led to the discovery of the so-called Joule-Thomson effect in 1862.

Joule remained an isolated amateur scientist for most of his life. After the death of his wife and young daughter in 1853, he lived in relative seclusion. Beginning about 1872 his health deteriorated. He died at his home in Sale, Cheshire, on Oct. 11, 1889.

Further Reading

James G. Crowther gives an excellent treatment of Joule in his *British Scientists of the Nineteenth Century* (1935). Alexander Wood, *Joule and the Study of Energy* (1925), merits reading.

Additional Sources

Cardwell, D. S. L. (Donald Stephen Lowell), *James Joule: a biography,* Manchester; New York: Manchester University Press; New York: Distributed exclusively in the USA and Canada by St. Martin's Press, 1989.

Cardwell, D. S. L. (Donald Stephen Lowell), *James P. Joule,* Manchester, Manchester (97 Grovenor St., Manchester (M1 7HF)): North Western Museum of Science and Industry, 1978. □

Benjamin Jowett

The English educator and Greek scholar Benjamin Jowett (1817-1893) is famous for his translation of the dialogues of Plato and for his academic reforms at Oxford.

Benjamin Jowett was born on April 15, 1817, at Camberwell, London. He was educated at St. Paul's School and Balliol College. In 1838, while still an undergraduate, he achieved the unusual distinction of being elected a fellow of Balliol. He received his bachelor's degree in 1839 and his master's in 1842, and in the same year he was ordained a deacon in the Anglican Church and appointed to a tutorship in the college. In 1845 he became a priest.

In his summers Jowett traveled on the Continent, making the acquaintance of leading German scholars. At that time he was fascinated with the philosophy of Hegel. He was especially attracted by Hegel's published lectures on the history of philosophy. By 1848 Jowett had also become a student of Plato and was lecturing on political economy. In the 1850s he was engaged in university reform, favoring the entry of more poor students, and in the reform of the Indian civil service.

However, Jowett's chief interest during this period was theology. His commentary on the Epistles of St. Paul (1855) is regarded as a landmark in the history of liberal theology. He argues that since St. Paul's thoughts transcended his power of expression, his meaning must be determined by the context rather than from a strictly grammatical and syntactical analysis of the words, a position which offended not only the more conservative theologians but also the leading philologists of the age. Despite the condemnations of conservative churchmen, Jowett was appointed in the same year to the prestigious regius professorship of Greek at Oxford.

Jowett began a series of lectures on Plato's *Republic* and on the fragments of the early Greek philosophers, the tremendous success of which greatly stimulated Greek scholarship throughout and beyond the university. In the following 10 years Jowett fell under even greater suspicion for his heterodox theological views. The publication of his essay "On the Interpretation of Scripture" caused an uproar in the Anglican Church and led to Jowett's civil trial for heresy, with the prosecution eventually being dropped.

From 1860 to 1870 Jowett accomplished a prodigious amount of work. He sponsored various administrative reforms in the university which relaxed the harsh student regulations, inspired reform of curriculums, and added to the physical plant. He was also influential in introducing reforms of elementary and secondary education throughout England, and in his own administration as master of Balliol he stressed teaching above research. In 1871 he published his famous four-volume translation of the *Dialogues of Plato;* a revised edition of five volumes appeared in 1875. He also published a two-volume translation of Thucydides's *History* (1881).

Jowett was vice-chancellor of Oxford from 1882 to 1886. Despite administrative preoccupations, he put out a translation of Aristotle's *Politics* with notes, but without the introductory essays which he did not live to finish. The strain of this enormous amount of work led to an illness in 1887 from which he never fully recovered. Nevertheless, he was able to put out a third revised edition of Plato in 1892 and to continue work on an edition of the *Republic,* upon which he had then labored 30 years and which was published posthumously. Jowett's view of Plato's thought, which is one of the leading interpretations, was that no unified or comprehensive systematic philosophy exists in Plato, that his view changes in different dialogues, and that in some no definite conclusion is ever reached. It was therefore better to treat each dialogue separately.

Jowett died on Oct. 1, 1893. Through his own work and through his pupils he exerted a lasting influence on scholarship. He was largely responsible for the influential movement known as Oxford idealism (English Hegelianism).

Further Reading

Primary sources on Jowett are his *Letters* (1899) and selections of his letters in Evelyn Abbott and Lewis Campbell, *Jowett's Life and Letters* (2 vols., 1897). Studies of Jowett include L. A. Tollemache, *Benjamin Jowett: Master of Balliol College* (1895); Leslie Stephen, *Studies of a Biographer* (1898); and Geoffrey Cust Faber, *Jowett: A Portrait with a Background* (1957). For relevant background see Wilfrid P. Ward, *W. G. Ward and the Oxford Movement* (1889). □

James Joyce

The fiction of the Irish author James Joyce (1882-1941) is characterized by experiments with language, symbolism, and use of the narrative techniques of interior monologue and stream of consciousness.

The modern symbolic novel owes much of its complexity to James Joyce. His intellectualism and his grasp of a wide range of philosophy, theology, and foreign languages enabled him to stretch the English language to its limits (and, some critics believe, beyond them in *Finnegans Wake*). The trial of his novel *Ulysses* on charges of obscenity and its subsequent exoneration marked a breakthrough in the limitations previously placed by social convention upon the subject matter and language of the modern English novel.

James Joyce was born on Feb. 2, 1882, in Rathgar, a suburb of Dublin. His father, John, an amateur actor and popular tenor, was employed first in a Dublin distillery, then as tax collector for the city of Dublin. His mother, Mary Jane Murray Joyce, was a gifted pianist. Endowed with a fine tenor voice and a love for music (he once entered a singing competition against the noted Irish tenor John McCormack), James Joyce was described by his brother Stanislaus as tall, thin, and loose-jointed, with "a distinguished appearance and bearing." In spite of 10 major operations to save his sight, he was almost blind at the time of his death. He often wore a black patch over his left eye and dressed in somber colors, although his friends remember him as witty and gay in company.

Joyce was educated entirely in Jesuit schools in Ireland: Clongowes Wood College in County Kildare, Belvedere College in Dublin, and University College, where he excelled in philosophy and languages (he mastered Norwegian in order to read Henrik Ibsen's plays in the original). After his graduation in 1902, he left Ireland in a self-imposed exile that lasted for the rest of his life. He returned briefly in 1903 for his mother's last illness but left for Paris in 1904 after her death, taking with him Nora Barnacle, his future wife. Until 1915 he taught English in Trieste, then moved to Zurich with his wife and two children. In 1920

they settled in Paris, living in virtual poverty even after the successful publication of *Ulysses* in 1922. The intervention of literary friends such as Ezra Pound secured for Joyce some much-needed financial assistance from the British government.

Although his fame rests upon his fiction, Joyce's first published work was a volume of 36 lyric poems, *Chamber Music* (1907). His *Collected Poems* (including *Poems Penyeach* and *Ecce Puer*) appeared in 1938. Much of his fiction is lyrical and autobiographical in nature and shows the influence of his musical studies, his discipline as a poet, and his Jesuit training. Even though he cut himself off from his country, his family, and his Church, these three (Ireland, father, and Roman Catholicism) are the basis upon which he structured his art. The city of Dublin, in particular, provided Joyce with a universal symbol; for him the heart of Dublin was "the heart of all the cities of the world," a means of showing that "in the particular is contained the universal."

Early Fiction

Dubliners (1914) is a collection of 15 short stories completed in 1904 but delayed in publication because of censorship problems, which arose from a suspected slur against the reigning monarch, Edward VII. Joyce himself described their style as one of "scrupulous meanness" and said they were written "to betray the soul of that . . . paralysis which many consider a city." His characters are drawn in naturalistic detail, which at first aroused the anger of many readers. Among various devices such as symbolism, motifs (paralysis, death, isolation, failure of love), mythic journeys, and quests for a symbolic grail which is never there, Joyce employs his literary invention, the epiphany; this is a religious term he used to describe the symbolic dimension of common things—fragments of conversation or bits of music—moments of sudden spiritual manifestation in which the "soul" of the thing or the experience "leaps to us from the vestment of its appearance."

In the final story, considered one of Joyce's best, "The Dead," Gabriel Conroy, a careful and studious man surrounded by doting aunts and material comforts, discovers to his surprise that his wife has had a romantic love affair with a passionate young man who died for love of her. The story ends with snow falling softly over Ireland and the universe, an ambiguous symbol which could mean either life-giving moisture and preservation or the coldness of moral and spiritual death.

A Portrait of the Artist as a Young Man (1916) is a semi-autobiographical novel of adolescence, or *Bildungsroman* (development novel). A sensitive and artistic young man, Stephen Dedalus is shaped by his environment but at the same time rebels against it. He rejects his father, family, and religion, and, like Joyce, decides at the novel's close to leave Ireland. He states as the reason for his exile his mission "to forge in the smithy of my soul the uncreated conscience of my race." The hero's symbolic name is drawn from Ovid's Dedalus, the artificer who made wings on which his son flew too near the sun, melting their wax and causing him to plunge into the sea.

For Joyce and others after him, Dedalus became a symbol for the artist, and the hero, Stephen, appears again in *Ulysses* (1922). Joyce's portrait of the artist in adolescence is like a painting, showing the hero in his immaturity, still seeking his identity. His major flaw, the failure to love, is shown by Stephen's isolation, his inability to immerse himself in life. The hero's declaration, "I will not serve," links him with another soaring figure, Lucifer, whose sin of pride also precluded the possibility of love, which for Joyce (always doctrinally orthodox) represented the greatest of all the Christian virtues and the most humanizing.

Ulysses

Ulysses (1922), generally considered Joyce's most mature work, is patterned on Homer's *Odyssey*. Each of the 18 chapters corresponds loosely with an episode in the Greek epic, but there are echoes of Joyce's other models, Dante's *Inferno* and Goethe's *Faust,* among other sources. The action takes place in a single day, June 16, 1904 (still observed as "Bloomsday" in many countries), on which the Irish Jew, Leopold Bloom (Ulysses), walks or rides through the streets of Dublin after leaving his wife, Molly (Penelope), at home in bed.

Through the stream-of-consciousness technique, Joyce permits the reader to enter the consciousness of Bloom and perceive the chaos of fragmentary conversations, physical sensations, and memories which register there. Underlying the surface action is the mythic quest of Leopold for a son to replace the child he and Molly have lost. He finds instead Stephen Dedalus (Telemachus), who, having rejected his family and faith, is in need of a father. At each of their chance encounters during the day, the mythic quest becomes more evident. The two are finally united when Bloom rescues the drunken Stephen from unsavory companions and the police; they share a symbolic communion over cups of hot chocolate in Bloom's home, a promise of future involvement for Stephen with Leopold, his spiritual "father," and Molly, the earth mother, who, with her paramours, represents fleshly involvement in the experience of life. Joyce's technical innovations (particularly his extensive use of stream of consciousness), his experiments with form, and his unusually frank subject matter and language made *Ulysses* an important milestone in the development of the modern novel.

Finnegans Wake

Finnegans Wake (1939) is the most difficult of all Joyce's works. The novel has no evident narrative or plot and relies upon sound, rhythm of language, and verbal puns to present a surface beneath which meanings lurk. Considered a novel by most critics, it has been called a poem by some, a nightmare by others. Joyce called his final book a "nightmaze." It concerns the events of a Dublin night, in contrast to *Ulysses,* which deals with a Dublin day.

The submerged plot centers upon a male character, H. C. Earwicker, the genial host of a Dublin pub, his wife, and their children, particularly the twins, Kevin and Jerry. Joyce once again employs myth in a more complex pattern than ever before, associating Dublin with the fallen paradise and the hero with a long séries of heroes beginning with Adam; he associates him also with a geographic landmark in Dublin, the Hill of Howth. His wife, Anna Livia Plurabelle, is associated with the river Liffey and with various female figures from history and legend. Snatches of Irish and universal history are blended with realistic details of world history and geography.

Working in the metamorphic tradition of Ovid, Joyce causes his characters to undergo a dazzling series of transformations. The hero, H. C. E. (his nickname, "Here Comes Everybody," indicates an Everyman figure), becomes successively Adam, Humpty Dumpty, Ibsen's Master Builder (all of whom underwent a fall of some kind in literature), Christ, King Arthur, the Duke of Wellington (all of whom are associated with rising). Mrs. Earwicker becomes Eve, the Virgin Mary, Queen Guinevere, Napoleon's Josephine, and other feminine characters (her initials, A. L. P., designate her as the alpha figure, the feminine principle and initiator of life). The twins become rival principles, Shem and Shaun, extrovert and introvert, representing opposing facets of their father's character; they merge into all the rival "brothers" of literature and history—Cain and Abel, Jacob and Esau, Peter and Paul, Michael and Lucifer—and their quarreling gives rise to the famous battles of myth and cyclic history.

Geographic places around Dublin also take on symbolic significance; for example, the noted Dublin garden, Phoenix Park, becomes the Garden of Eden. The difficulties arising from the complicated symbolism and linguistic structure of verbal puns and double meanings become more complex with Joyce's introduction of unfamiliar foreign words which may have two, three, or more meanings in the various languages with which he was familiar (including Danish and Eskimo). Examples may be seen in the compression of Matthew, Mark, Luke, and John, the writers of the New Testament Gospels, into "Mamalujo"; the Garden of Eden appears in one of its many doubles in modern Ireland as "Edenberry, Dubblen, W.C."

Beneath the puzzling verbal surface of *Finnegans Wake* lie themes which have been the concern of traditional writers and philosophers of all ages—the process of renewal through division of opposites, rising and falling, the one in the many, permanence and change, and the dialectic emergence of truth from the opposition of antithetical ideas. Not unexpectedly, *Finnegans Wake* was not well received by the reading public, and Joyce was forced to seek financial help from friends after its publication. With the outbreak of World War II, he and his family fled, on borrowed money, from France to Switzerland, leaving a daughter in a sanatorium in occupied France. Joyce died in Zurich on Jan. 13, 1941.

Further Reading

Herbert Gorman's early biography of Joyce, *James Joyce* (1939), is still useful but has been superseded by the definitive work of Richard Ellmann, *James Joyce* (1959). Two good studies of Joyce's life and work are William York Tindall, *James Joyce: His Way of Interpreting the Modern World* (1950) and *A Reader's Guide to James Joyce* (1959), which gives brief introductory notes to each of the major works in turn. Other informative introductory studies include Harry Levin, *James Joyce: A Critical Introduction* (1941; rev. ed. 1960); Marvin Magalaner, *Joyce, the Man, the Work, the Reputation* (1956); and A. Walton Litz, *James Joyce* (1966).

On specific novels, Stuart Gilbert, *James Joyce's Ulysses* (1930; rev. ed. 1952), is still the standard work on the Homeric structure of *Ulysses,* and Frank Budgen, *James Joyce and the Making of Ulysses* (1934), supplies additional background on the novel. Joseph Campbell and Henry Morton Robinson, *A Skeleton Key to Finnegans Wake* (1944), was the best of many "keys" to the novel until the appearance of William York Tindall, *A Reader's Guide to Finnegans Wake* (1969). Useful background on the period as it relates to Joyce can be found in Patricia Hutchins, *James Joyce's Dublin* (1950); William York Tindall, *The Joyce Country* (1960); and Chester G. Anderson, *James Joyce and His World* (1967). □

Sister Juana Inés de la Cruz

Sister Juana Inés de la Cruz (1651-1695) was a Mexican nun renowned for her phenomenal knowledge of the arts and sciences of her day, her devotion to scientific inquiry, and her lyric poetry.

Sister (or Sor) Juana Inés de la Cruz was born Juana Inés de Abasje Y Ramirez de Santillana on the Hacienda of Nepantla of respectable although unmarried parents. She was placed in the custody of her maternal grandfather. By the time she was 3, she had learned to read. At 8 she wrote a respectable short Eucharistic drama. At about the same time she moved to Mexico City to live with relatives,

where she soon learned enough Latin to write excellent verse in that language.

Juana's talents came to the attention of the vicereine, who named her maid-in-waiting in the viceregal court. Here Juana's intellectual and literary capacities continued to develop, along with an equally precocious physical beauty which devastated the young men of Mexico's high society.

Monastic Life

Ultimately, Juana found the worldly life not to her taste. In 1667 she joined the ascetic Order of Discalced (barefoot) Carmelites in Mexico City, motivated, perhaps, less by religious convictions than by her need for a sanctuary in which to pursue her intellectual and literary interests. The rigorous existence of the Carmelites brought on a severe illness and forced her to change to the less demanding Jeronymite order, in which she spent the rest of her life.

Surrounded by her library of some 4,000 books and her musical and scientific instruments, Sister Juana continued to develop and refine her knowledge of theology, philosophy, astronomy, mathematics, literature, painting, and music. She corresponded with the best minds of Mexico and Europe and was a friend of savants in the viceregal capital.

Sister Juana wrote morality plays, Christmas carols, allegorical essays, worldly three-act comedies, and, above all, love lyrics, which were her greatest source of fame. The meter and rhyme of her poetry varied, and the style of her writings was florid, ornate, and obscure, as dictated by the prevailing baroque fashion. Yet beneath these artificialities,

her work reveals a profound and subtle intellect as well as a spirit deeply troubled by internal tensions and pressures from her external environment. Sister Juana was torn between intellectuality and emotionality; her interests placed her at odds with a value system which for women condoned only marriage, childbirth, and religiosity; her emphasis on secular knowledge conflicted with her status as a bride of Christ; her insistence on rational inquiry challenged sanctified scholastic modes of thought resting on revealed truth.

Sister Juana's social and intellectual deviancy inevitably generated hostility among her monastic associates and opprobrium from her ecclesiastical superiors. Criticism reached a climax in 1690 in the form of a letter from the bishop of Puebla, posing as "Sister Philotea," which admonished her for neglecting religious literature. In her "Reply to Sister Philotea," written the following year, Sister Juana vigorously defended her interests and methods of inquiry. Nevertheless, hurt by such criticisms and perhaps burdened by feelings of guilt, she abjectly reaffirmed her faith in 1694, renounced the world, disposed of her books and instruments, and devoted herself to penance and mortification of the flesh. She died the following year while ministering to sisters stricken by an epidemic.

Despite her great literary talent, modern scholars tend to place greater emphasis on the variety of Sister Juana's intellectual accomplishments. Her passionate devotion to knowledge and her insistence on rational methods of inquiry place her above all contemporary Mexican savants, except perhaps Don Carlos de Sigüenza y Góngora, and identify her as a precursor of the 18th century Enlightenment.

Further Reading

There are no major studies in English of Sister Juana. Useful introductions to her life and work, however, are in Arturo Torres-Rioseco, *New World Literature: Tradition and Revolt in Latin America* (1949), and in Irving A. Leonard, *Baroque Times in Old Mexico* (1959). □

Juan Carlos I

Juan Carlos I (born 1938), proclaimed king of Spain on November 22, 1975, played an instrumental role in the transformation of his nation from a dictatorship to a constitutional monarchy.

Juan Carlos Víctor María de Borbón y Borbón was born in the Anglo-American Hospital in Rome, Italy, on January 5, 1938. His grandfather, Alfonso XIII, had been king of Spain from 1902 to 1931, after which Spain became a republic. With the emergence of Francisco Franco's fascist dictatorship in 1939, the father of Juan Carlos, Don Juan de Borbón y Brattenberg, became a pretender to the Spanish throne and a hostile critic of Franco's regime, which endured until 1975.

Juan Carlos' early years were spent in exile in Rome, Lausanne, Switzerland, and Estoril, Portugal. He did not set foot on Spanish soil until Franco summoned him to "supervise" his education. After completing his high school education in 1955, Juan Carlos studied at Spain's military academy, naval college, and general air academy. Later in life his strong background and contacts in the armed forces would help save a fledgling constitutional monarchy from an attempted military coup. After military training Juan Carlos began his studies at Madrid University. In the 1960s, he augmented his education with training at a number of public administration agencies: the Ministry of Public Works, Ministry of Agriculture, Ministry of Finance, Ministry of Justice, Ministry of the Interior, and Ministry of Commerce.

In 1961, the future king announced his engagement to Princess Sofia of Greece, and they were married the following year in Athens. Three children, one boy and two girls, were subsequently born to the royal couple. Princess Sofia's background was in many ways similar to that of her husband. She had spent part of her childhood in Egypt and in South Africa and had studied in Germany. She held a diploma in pediatrics, had a keen interest in archaeology and classical music, and became fluent in Greek, Spanish, English, German, and French.

In 1969 General Franco made an announcement important of Juan Carlos and to the nation's future. Franco declared that after his retirement or death Juan Carlos, and

Juan Carlos I (left)

not Don Carlos (the father of Juan Carlos), would become king. When Franco fell ill in the summer of 1974, Juan Carlos became Spain's acting head of state. Franco died in November of 1975, and Juan Carlos was proclaimed king in a ceremony in the Cortes, the Spanish parliament. King Juan Carlos declared: "The Monarchy can and must be effective as a political system if it is able to maintain a just and true balance of powers, and if it is rooted in the real life of the Spanish people." Thus began the change to a constitutional monarchy.

Until the time of Franco's death, little was known about the political convictions of Juan Carlos. Yet, following his ascendancy he retained the loyalty of the military and Franco supporters while providing Spain with a peaceful transition to a political democracy. The new king asked Carlos Arias Navarro (Franco's prime minister) to remain in office, but eventually appointed Adolfo Suárez, a man often identified as a loyal follower of Franco but who turned out to be a cryptodemocrat, to be his prime minister. Political collaboration between Juan Carlos and Suárez led to the Law of Political Reform, passed by the Cortes in November 1976. This new law ended dictatorship and called for a new bicameral legislature, elected through universal suffrage. A month later the same law was submitted to the people in a referendum. It won approval by 94 percent of the voters.

In 1977, the king and Suárez began moving Spain closer to a true political democracy. Political parties (including the socialist and communist parties) were once again legalized; the right to strike was recognized; and the organization of free trade unions was permitted. Then, on June 15, 1977, more than 18 million people—79 percent of the electorate—went to the polls to elect a 350-member lower house, known as the Congress. The major winners were the center-right coalition, represented by the Democratic Center Union (UCD) with 34.8 percent of the vote, and the Spanish Socialist Workers' Party (PSOE) with 29.4 percent. A sub-committee of the newly elected Congress produced a constitution that provided Spain with a constitutional monarchy. Under the new constitution, approved by the Cortes in October 1978 and by a national referendum in December, legislative power was vested in a bicameral Cortes, while the king was "the head of state and symbol of its unity and permanence." The constitution vested executive authority in the prime minister, but the king sanctions and promulgates laws and is commander-in-chief of the armed forces. Furthermore, the king, after consulting with representatives of the political parties, nominates a candidate for prime minister, who must win a vote of confidence in the Congress of Deputies. On December 27, 1978, Juan Carlos, before the Cortes, sanctioned the new constitution.

Besides overseeing the transition from dictatorship to constitutional government, Juan Carlos personally intervened in matters of state and saved the new government from a right-wing military coup in 1981. On February 23, 1981, a group of military conspirators stormed the Cortes while it was voting on a new prime minister. Although the conspirators intended to set up an authoritarian monarchy under the protection of the armed forces, the plan failed because Juan Carlos refused to engage in the attempted coup. Throughout the night of February 23 the king worked to rally loyal military officers by telephone; and at 1 a.m. on February 24 he addressed the nation pleading for calm and trust, assuring his people that the constitution would be honored. Within hours the coup was over. The king had saved the Spanish experiment with political democracy.

After the abortive coup of 1981, Juan Carlos' Spain witnessed several key political developments. First, in 1982 the electorate voted the Spanish Socialist Workers' party, headed by Felipe González, into power. Secondly, in the summer of 1985 the king made an official visit to France where he and President Mitterrand signed an historic accord pledging economic, political, and military cooperation between the two nations. Thirdly, on January 1, 1986, Spain entered the European Economic Community, a development that it hoped would aid the modernization of the Spanish economy and further stabilize the nation's political system. Fourthly, in March of 1986 Spanish voters went to the polls in a referendum and elected to remain in NATO, a position that the new socialist government favored because of the technological, economic, and political benefits to be gained from membership in the Atlantic alliance. Before the socialist victory in 1982 socialist leader González had opposed Spain's tie to NATO. Thus, Spain owes its re-entry into the European community and its return to democracy in large part to Juan Carlos' direction and moderation.

Spain's central government maintains authority in a complex relationship with 16 "autonomous" regions, including Catalonia, home of the Basque separatist movement. When Catalan activists attempted to turn the 1992 Barcelona Olympic Games into a political embarrassment for the Madrid government and for Juan Carlos, the king defused the potential crisis and engendered warmer feelings between Barcelona and Madrid than had existed in years. At the opening ceremonies he said a few words in the Catalan language, attended many events, and watched as his son, Prince Felipe, carried the Spanish flag into the stadium.

Further Reading

Juan Carlos of Spain: Self-Made Monarch was published in 1996; two other readable and comprehensive works that examine the political transition in Spain under Juan Carlos are E. Ramón Arango's *Spain: From Repression to Renewal* (1985); and David Gilmour's *The Transition of Spain: From Franco to the Constitutional Monarchy* (1985); also Stanley Payne, editor, *Politics and Society in Twentieth-Century Spain* (1976). □

Benito Juárez

Benito Juárez (1806-1872) was a Mexican statesman and resistance leader against the French. After defeating the Austrian would-be emperor Maximilian, Juárez instituted numerous liberal reforms as president.

By 1850 Mexico seemed on the verge of total collapse. Thirty years of violence had left the treasury bankrupt, communications disrupted, and the population demoralized. Two factions, defining themselves as Conservatives and Liberals, constantly fought over the control of the state and its shrinking revenues. The Conservatives, representing the large landholders, the Church, the professional army, and the large cities, tried to make Mexico into a highly centralized state based upon the institutions and ideology of the colonial period. The Liberals, who represented small merchants, some intellectuals, political leaders in rural areas, and the small ranchers of the west and south, stood for a federal system, the abolishment of colonial prerogatives, land distribution, and a constitutional democracy based upon the ideals of Jean Jacques Rousseau and Thomas Jefferson.

Benito Juárez was born in the small Zapotec Indian village of San Pablo Guelatao, Oaxaca, on March 21, 1806. His parents, poor peasants, died when he was 3 years old. Juárez then lived with his grandparents and later with an uncle. He worked with his uncle until he was 13, when he left for the city of Oaxaca; at this time he could not yet speak Spanish.

His Education

In Oaxaca, Juárez worked with Don Antonio Salanueva, a bookbinder, who took a strong liking to the young Indian boy, became his godparent, and to all intents and purposes adopted him. Helped by Salanueva and a

local teacher, Juárez learned to read and write. In 1827 he graduated from the Seminary of Santa Cruz.

In 1828, despite Salanueva's wishes that he take on the priesthood, Juárez entered the Oaxaca Institute of Arts and Sciences to study law. The curriculum proved the perfect stimulus for the rebellious and ambitious former seminarian. In 1831 he qualified to enter a local law office, but as the legal profession was already overcrowded, he began a second career as an antiestablishment Liberal politician.

Early Career

In 1831 Juárez entered politics as an elected alderman on the Oaxacan town council. In 1835 the city elected him as a Liberal deputy to the federal legislature. He carried forward his legal career, often serving as a representative of impoverished Indian communities in their struggles to protect their landholdings. Incorruptible and intelligent, he was one of Oaxaca's leading lawyers.

During the Conservative domination of Mexico between 1836 and 1846, Juárez largely avoided elective office but often accepted professional and political appointments from the Conservative state authorities. In 1841 the state government appointed him a federal court judge, a post in which he served with distinction. His local standing had increased through his marriage to Margarita Mazza, the daughter of one of Oaxaca's wealthiest Creole families.

Juárez served as secretary to the state's Conservative governor and as a member of the local assembly. He showed his liberalism by resigning the judgeship because of unwillingness to prosecute those who refused to pay clerical tithes, but the state government soon reinstated him.

Governor of Oaxaca

In 1846 the Liberal party, led by former president Valentín Gómez Farías, took power throughout Mexico. Despite his Conservative connections, Juárez became again a Liberal federal deputy. In 1847-1848, during the debacle of Mexico's war with the United States, he became Oaxaca's acting governor and then elected governor.

Juárez curbed corruption and built roads, public buildings, and schools. He reorganized the state national guard, and when he left office in 1852, a respectable surplus remained in the state treasury. His state government became renowned throughout Mexico for its honesty, public spirit, and constructiveness. In 1852 Juárez became director of the Institute of Arts and Sciences. He also again served as a lawyer, often helping the poor.

In 1853 the Conservative party, led by the brilliant Lucas Alamán, seized power by a barracks coup. One of the revolt's leaders, and its inevitable president, was Antonio López de Santa Ana, the unscrupulous Creole general who had frequently dominated Mexico during the previous 20 years. Seeking to consolidate power, Santa Ana immediately exiled the leaders of the Liberal party.

Exile and Revolutionary

Government troops arrested Juárez without warning and then sent him into exile. He lived first in Havana and then in New Orleans. In the early 1850s the future Liberal leaders of Mexico, including Ignacio Comonfort, José María Mata, and Melchor Ocampo, formed a revolutionary junta in New Orleans and began to plan the reforms with which they hoped to rebuild their shattered nation.

In Mexico, Santa Ana had run the country into further bankruptcy. Disgruntled Liberals, led by Juan Álvarez, a hero of the war for independence, launched a revolt known as the Revolution of Ayutla. Juárez offered his services to Álvarez's rebel army. Santa Ana's government collapsed with a minimum of fighting, and the Liberals again assumed power with Álvarez as president. In October 1855 he named Juárez minister of justice.

Juárez immediately began to implement some of his reform ideas: the Ley Juárez (Juárez Law, Nov. 23, 1855) reorganized the judicial system, but most important, it abolished the right to separate courts for the military and the clergy. In January 1856 Juárez again became governor of Oaxaca, where he reestablished the Institute of Arts and Sciences and promulgated the New Liberal Constitution of 1857.

The voluntary retirement of Juan Álvarez in 1857 ended the Liberal hopes for a peaceful transformation of Mexico. The ensuing period (1857-1860), known as the Three Year War, proved to be one of the most bloody and wasteful in Mexican history. Armies defining themselves often arbitrarily as Conservative or Liberal roamed the countryside looting and burning. The economy was again halted; Mexico, bankrupt and divided, tempted foreign intervention.

The only positive result of these years was the emergence of Juárez as the undisputed leader of the Liberal party. He served as minister of government and later as president of Mexico's Supreme Court under Ignacio Comonfort. In 1858 Comonfort resigned; Juárez traveled northward, organizing the divided Liberal party. The departure of Comonfort had left Juárez as Supreme Court president, the legal executive power in Mexico. Simultaneously the Conservatives had named one of their own number the president of Mexico, repealed the laws of reform, and sent their troops northward to exterminate Liberal resistance. Beset by fractious allies and mutinous troops, Juárez fled to Veracruz.

For 3 years Juárez and the Liberals held Veracruz while the Conservatives held Mexico City. The Church helped the Conservatives with money, troops, and moral persuasion. The angered Liberals reacted in 1859 by promulgating drastic anticlerical laws, confiscating all ecclesiastical property, except buildings, without compensation. The same year Melchor Ocampo signed the infamous Maclane-Ocampo Treaty, selling more of Mexico to the United States (this was rejected by the U.S. Senate) for badly needed funds to prosecute the war.

After 2 years of defeat, the reorganized Liberal armies under Santos Degollado, Porfirio Díaz, and Jesús González Ortega took Mexico City. The Conservative armies disinte-grated, and their leaders went into exile. Leonardo Márquez, leading Conservative general, held out as a guerrilla, but the Liberals were firmly in control. In 1860 the Mexican people elected Juárez president.

President and Reformer

Juárez acted determinedly to carry out national reconstruction. He exiled the archbishop of Mexico, five bishops, and the Spanish ambassador, all of whom had aided the Conservative cause. The new government strictly enforced the anticlerical codes of the constitution, seizing for the nation Church lands and monastic buildings. Juárez's program was ambitious, but he had staggering problems. The government, seeking to develop a large agrarian middle class, tried to distribute the lands to those working them.

However, the Liberals needed money to pay the army bureaucracy and the national debt. Pressed for funds, public officials allowed these lands to go to those who could pay for them immediately, mostly rich speculators and foreigners. The land reform did not create a large yeoman class but instead allowed secular individuals to monopolize the large former Church estates and to gain control of Indian communal lands, also abolished by the reform laws and the Constitution of 1857.

The same financial exigencies which forced the government to curtail its ambitious land reform program caused it in 1862 to declare a 2-year suspension of the external debt. This gave England, France, and Spain the excuse to intervene in Mexico. The English and Spanish soon withdrew, but the French emperor, Louis Napoleon, attempted to establish a client Mexican empire under the Austrian archduke Maximilian. Aided by small Conservative forces, the French took Mexico City in 1863, forcing Juárez to flee.

Fight against a Foreign Usurper

The years 1864 to 1867 determined the future of Mexico and the Liberal reforms. Juárez refused to serve in an imperial cabinet. He retreated north with his cabinet and a small bodyguard in his famous black coach. The imperialists controlled the cities, but the countryside remained in a state of insurrection. Faced with mounting costs in men and money and the rise of Prussia, the French withdrew from Mexico.

In 1867 the empire collapsed. The Liberal forces captured Maximilian and his main Mexican adherents in Querétaro. In June 1867 Juárez ordered the Emperor's execution despite worldwide pleas for clemency. Always a strict legalist, Juárez would not countermand the courtmartial; he saw the execution as a firm warning to other foreign conquerors.

In 1867 the Mexican people again elected Juárez president. His first act was to arbitrarily dismiss without pension two-thirds of the 90,000-man Liberal army, many of whom either became bandits or joined the subsequent rebellions of Porfirio Díaz. Juárez accomplished much in the remaining 4 years of his life. The government began to build railroads and schools; the military budget was cut; and the Church was stripped of its large landholdings. Most important, Mexico had its first effective government, based upon the Constitution of 1857, which guaranteed free speech, free press, right of assembly, and the abolishment of special legal privileges.

On the negative side, Juárez refused to delegate authority and insisted, despite much opposition, upon his own reelection in 1871. He obviously sincerely believed that he alone could govern Mexico, but many now saw him as a dictator. Furthermore, he had failed to abolish internal tariffs or to curb large secular landholdings. In 1871 his army crushed the revolt of Porfirio Díaz, but the Liberal party had split into irreconcilable factions. On July 18, 1872, the President died at his desk.

Juárez had many failings, but he was one of the greatest Mexican executives. He fought for and established a liberal constitution and stubbornly saved the country from foreign domination, although he did little to help the rural proletariat.

Further Reading

There is a great deal of material on Juárez in English. The best works are Ralph Roeder, *Juárez and His Mexico* (2 vols., 1947), and Walter V. Scholes, *Mexican Politics during the Juárez Regime, 1855-1872* (1957). For background consult Henry Bamford Parkes, *A History of Mexico* (1938; 3d ed. 1960), and Hudson Strode, *Timeless Mexico* (1944). A brilliant discussion of the Liberal ideology is Charles A. Hale, *Mexican Liberalism in the Age of Mora, 1821-1853* (1968). See also Wilfrid Hardy Callcott, *Church and State in Mexico, 1822-1857* (1926), and Richard A. Johnson, *The Mexican Revolution of Ayutla, 1854-1855* (1939). □

Judah I

The Jewish scholar Judah I (ca. 135-ca. 220), also called Judah Ha-Nasi, was head of the Sanhedrin and edited the Mishnah, a collection of the Oral Law.

The son and successor of Rabban Simeon, Judah received his Jewish training at his father's home at Usha and at the academies of Akiba ben Joseph's disciples. He also received a broad secular schooling in foreign languages, particularly Greek. However, Judah favored Hebrew and made it the language of his household.

Shortly after his father died (ca. 170), Judah succeeded him to the powerful office of Nasi, or head of the Sanhedrin. Judah was known for his great learning and was commonly called Rabbi, or master par excellence. He was also called Ha-Nasi, or the Prince. He was a wealthy man who gave of his riches and conducted his office with great dignity.

Not long after he assumed his post, Judah was compelled by a devastating plague of locusts and other hardships to move from Usha to Bet Shearim, another town in Galilee. He also transferred his academy there. Later, because of illness, he went to Sepphoris, north of Nazareth, where he spent the last 17 years of his life.

Judah was concerned with retaining Palestine as the spiritual center of Diaspora Jewry. He therefore limited ordination to scholars who agreed to remain there. For this reason, the eminent sage Abba Arika (the Tall), who later founded the great yeshiva at Sura in Babylonia, received only partial ordination.

Judah associated freely with colleagues and pupils and extolled the dignity of labor. The path that one should choose in life, he urged, should be a source of honor to the individual as well as to mankind. Judah's unselfishness, teachings, and meritorious conduct earned for him the appellation of Ha-Kadosh, the Saint.

Although Judah aspired to establish his office as the supreme authority in Judaism, he did not succeed in doing so. However, his Mishnah, or compilation of the Oral Law, achieved this objective. The Oral Law was a body of oral tradition; it consisted of explanations and amplifications of the written, or scriptural, text. Since the days of Hillel (died A.D. 10) and his contemporary Shammai, attempts had been made to arrange systematically the confused and growing mass of oral laws. At Yavneh, in the days of Gamaliel II (ca. 80-115), an effort was made to resolve the disputes between the schools of Hillel and Shammai in order to produce a unified and undisputed version of the Oral Law. Akiba ben Joseph (died ca. 135) arranged these Halakahs, or Oral Laws, in a logical system, thereby laying the groundwork of Judah's Mishnah. Judah prepared a standard and authoritative version. Unlike the existing collections of the Oral Law, that of Rabbi was composite in nature and included laws and traditions expounded by him as well as other Tannaim (Mishnaic teachers).

The compendium prepared by Judah was a momentous work that required over a half century of labor and was completed about 217. Judah generally assembled the ritual regulations in separate volumes. Because of his personal prestige and authority as the titular head of Jewry, Judah's Mishnah became the norm. Some 148 scholars are mentioned in Rabbi's Mishnah by name, but many more contributed to it anonymously.

The Mishnah was not a code, strictly speaking, because it contained nonlegal as well as legal matter. It has been spoken of as a legal digest. Though Jews generally spoke Aramaic at the time, the language of the Mishnah is Hebrew, couched in a concise, lucid style. It appears that Judah's Mishnah was not completed entirely by him, for it contains insertions by authorities of the following generation.

Judah's Mishnah soon became a text for students and a guide and reference work for scholars and rabbis. It provided the foundation and structure for the work of the next generation of teachers, known as Amoraim, or discoursers or expounders of the Mishnah, who continued the work of the Tannaim. Several centuries later (ca. 600), the Amoraim produced the Gemara. The Mishnah and the Gemara together constitute the Talmud.

Further Reading

To understand the Oral Law, the reader should peruse Herbert Danby's excellent English translation of the Mishna (1933).

Recommended for background material and orientation is George Foote Moore, *Judaism in the First Centuries of the Christian Era,* vol. 1 (1927). A good treatment of the work of Judah Ha-Nasi and his colleagues is presented in Judah Goldin, "Period of the Talmud," in the first volume of Louis Finkelstein, ed., *The Jews* (1949; 2d ed. 1955). For a general background sketch of the Halakahs see the essay "The Significance of the Halacha for Jewish History" in Louis Ginsberg, *On Jewish Law and Lore* (1955). □

Judah Halevi

The Spanish Hebrew poet and religious thinker Judah Halevi (ca. 1085-ca. 1150) taught that God had revealed Himself primarily through the people of Israel.

Few definite facts are known about Judah Halevi. He was born in Toledo, Castile, to a family of means. A gifted youth, he received his Jewish training in the school of the famous Talmudist Isaac Alfasi. He also had a secular education in Greek and Arabic philosophy, the poetic arts, and medicine. Halevi was not happy in the medical profession; he found fulfillment, however, in his poetry, in which he expressed his true genius and gift. He employed the forms and structure of Arabic poetry in his Hebrew verse. Halevi's verse is replete with graphic symbolism and simile, embroidered with biblical idioms and allusions. It may be divided in three main classes: secular, religious, and national.

The first half of his life Halevi seems to have spent in lightheartedness and gaiety, the enjoyment of nature, friends, love, and wine. This is reflected in the mood of his earlier secular verse. As he grew older, however, and he saw the destruction of the Spanish Jewish communities in the *reconquista,* the struggle for the reconquest of Spain by the Christians from the Moslems, his outlook became more somber. His people's suffering in the course of the Crusades, when entire Jewish communities were completely destroyed, also contributed to his change of mood.

Aside from the physical extermination Halevi's people suffered, there were ravages from within. Jewish intellectuals in his day were falling prey to Greek rationalism and philosophy, which challenged and weakened their faith. These conditions are reflected in his religious poetry, which is characterized by a deep and often mystic yearning and love of God. The tragedy of his people, too, is given voice in his national poems, in which he depicts the past glory of Zion and his pain and sorrow at its desolation, as well as his hopes for its restoration. Many of Halevi's religious and national poems have been preserved in the Jewish liturgy.

To counter the influence of philosophy on his generation, Halevi wrote *Kitab al-Khazari* in Arabic to reach a wide audience, particularly among the enlightened. It was translated by Judah ibn Tibbon into Hebrew. The *Sefer ha-Kuzari* (or the *Kuzari*), as it is called in Hebrew, is still one of the most popular classics in Judaism. It is written in dialogue and employs the historical and romantic theme of the conversion to Judaism early in the 8th century of the heathen king of the Khazars, a Tatar tribe on the Volga. Before his conversion, the King called in a rabbi, a Christian theologian, a Moslem scholar, and an Aristotelian philosopher, who expounded the merits of their respective religious beliefs.

Unlike earlier Jewish philosophers, Halevi was not concerned in demonstrating that Judaism conforms to the tenets of rationalism, but rather in proving its excellency and its superiority over its two daughter religions, Christianity and Islam. Halevi argues that the God of Judaism requires no rational proof of His existence since He has manifested Himself in history through the people of Israel. Israel is therefore "the heart of the nations," for like the heart, which sends blood to other parts of the body, Israel supplies the world with ethical and spiritual nourishment. In Messianic times, however, all nations will attain Israel's spiritual level.

The language of Jewish prophecy is Hebrew, and its most favored site is the Holy Land. Halevi therefore left his only daughter and grandchild, his family, friends, and possessions, to make a pilgrimage to Jerusalem. According to legend, he was kneeling at the Wailing Wall when a galloping Arab horseman rode him down and crushed him to death.

Further Reading

The Selected Poems of Judah Halevi comprises Halevi's original Hebrew verses, well translated and annotated by Nina Salaman (1946). A translation of the *Kuzari,* with an introduction by Henry Slonimsky (1964), is available in paperback. Rudolf Kayser, *The Life and Time of Jehudah Halevi,* was translated from the German by Frank Gaynor (1949). An article entitled "Judah Halevi," written by Jacob S. Minkin, is included in Simon Noveck, ed., *Great Jewish Personalities in Ancient and Medieval Times* (1959).

Additional Sources

Silman, Yochanan, *Philosopher and prophet: Judah Halevi, the Kuzari, and the evolution of his thought,* Albany: State University of New York Press, 1995. □

Theodore Dehone Judah

Theodore Dehone Judah (1826-1863), American engineer and railroad promoter, developed the plans that led to construction of the first transcontinental railroad.

Theodore Judah was born in Bridgeport, Conn., where his father was an Episcopal minister, but the family moved to Troy, N.Y., while he was still young. He attended the Rensselaer Polytechnic Institute, the first private engineering school in the world. After graduation he took a job helping build the Troy and Schenectady Railroad. Then, in rapid succession, he worked for three other railroads, planned and built the Niagara Gorge Railroad, helped build the Erie Canal, and erected a large bridge in Vermont.

Following the example of a brother who had gone to California in the gold rush of 1849, Judah went west in 1854, shortly after marrying. Two years earlier a group of California promoters had conceived of a railroad from Sacramento, where ships arrived from San Francisco, up to the gold country in the Sierra Nevada foothills. Judah was hired as chief engineer of the project, and the line was completed to its terminus at Folsom, Calif., 22 miles away, in 1856. Almost immediately the company wanted to extend the line into the mountains, but a general business depression made this impossible.

Judah left the railroad shortly before its completion and spent the next 3 years working at various engineering tasks connected with projected railroads in California. During these years he nurtured his dream of building a railroad across the mountains and eastward. In the spring of 1859 he made his third trip to Washington, D.C., hoping at last to persuade Congress to allocate Federal aid for a transcontinental railroad. Throughout the 1850s Pacific Railroad surveys had been made of the three potential routes (northern, central, and southern), but strong sectional rivalries prevented any one route from being selected.

Judah continued his promotional efforts and took a prominent part in the Pacific Railroad Convention of 1859. In 1860 his announcement that he had discovered a practical route through the forbidding Sierra Nevada enhanced the prospect of congressional action. In the following year he succeeded in bringing together the group of men—Collis P. Huntington, Leland Stanford, Mark Hopkins, and Charles Crocker—who would eventually build the Central Pacific Railroad. On July 1, 1862, with Southern opposition removed by the ongoing Civil War, Congress passed an act to aid the construction of the transcontinental railroad.

But Judah did not live to see the road completed. Disagreements arose with the Huntington group, and they offered to buy Judah out for $100,000. He died on Nov. 2, 1863, from typhoid fever contracted while crossing the Isthmus of Panama on his way back to New York.

Further Reading

There is no full-length biography of Judah. Some information on him is in Lucius Beebe, *The Central Pacific and the Southern Pacific Railroads* (1963). □

Judas Maccabeus

Judas Maccabeus (died 160 B.C.) was the leader of a Jewish revolt against the repressive policies of Antiochus IV Epiphanes, the king of Syria.

Third son of Mattathias, the Hasmonean priest of Modin, Judas received the added name Maccabeus, generally believed to mean "Hammerer," because of the hammer blows dealt by Judas and his small and poorly equipped guerrilla bands of Jewish patriots against the well-equipped and well-trained Syrian army. The Syrians had been sent by Antiochus IV Epiphanes to Judea to suppress Judaism and supplant it with Greek paganism. This marked the first recorded war for religious freedom.

Judas, a remarkable strategist, succeeded by means of surprise attacks, ambush, and quick mobility of his forces in defeating a succession of Syrian generals. After several years of conflict Judas drove out his foes from Jerusalem, except for the garrison in the citadel of Acra. Judas then proceeded with a group of faithful priests to cleanse the Temple of its pagan gods and restore the Sanctuary. On the twenty-fifth of the Jewish month of Kislev, 165 B.C., the golden menorah was rekindled, and the Temple was solemnly rededicated. Chanukah ("Dedication"), as the festival was called, is still celebrated each year for 8 days with the kindling of lights in commemoration of this event.

Antiochus died in 163. Judas ventured to attack the Acra citadel. Lysias, who had assumed the regency, counterattacked and defeated Judas at Bet Zecharia (162). Judas retreated to the Temple Mount but could not hold out because of an acute food shortage.

Lysias, however, needed a respite as well to deal with Philip, the regent appointed by Antiochus before his death. He therefore agreed to a peace (162) in which the Jews received complete freedom of worship. Lysias defeated Philip, only to be overthrown by Demetrius, the true heir to the Syrian throne. Demetrius appointed Alcimus (Jakim), a Hellenist, as high priest, a choice the Hasidim (Pietists) might have accepted since he was of priestly descent.

Alcimus's treacherous assassination of 60 priests, however, led Judas to continue to fight for political independence to secure his people's religious liberty. Demetrius dispatched Nicanor, a trusted general, with a strong force against Judas (161). Nicanor was defeated in several encounters and died in the battle of Adassa, in which Judas scored a brilliant victory. The triumphal day, the thirteenth of Adar, was ordained as an annual festival.

Judas solicited help from Rome, but before it could come, a new general, Bacchides, attacked him at Elesea with a formidable force. Judas's soldiers lost courage and fled, leaving their leader with only 800 men. They were completely routed, and Judas fell in battle (160). The conflict against foreign rule, however, was continued intermittently for a period of almost 3 centuries.

Further Reading

Sidney Tedesche and Solomon Zeitlin, *First Book of the Maccabees and Second Book of Maccabees* (1950-1954), are translations from the Greek originals of these works. Elias Bickerman, *The Maccabees* (1935; trans. 1947), presents an illuminating discussion of the adjustment of Judaism to Hellenism. Victor Tcherikover, *Hellenistic Civilization and the Jews* (trans. 1959), is the English version of a Hebrew work which examines the influence of Hellenistic culture on the

Jews in Judea and the Diaspora. Norman Bentwich, *Helle-nism* (1919), sketches the impact of the various branches of Hellenistic thought on Judaism.

Additional Sources

Bar-Kochva, Bezalel, *Judas Maccabaeus: the Jewish struggle against the Seleucids,* Cambridge Cambridgeshire; New York: Cambridge University Press, 1989.

Healy, Mark, *Judas Maccabeus: rebel of Israel,* Poole, Dorset: Firebird Books; New York, NY: Distributed in the United States by Sterling Pub. Co., 1989. □

Charles Hubbard Judd

Charles Hubbard Judd (1873-1946), a psychologist and education reformer, was an exponent of the science of education. Under his leadership the University of Chicago became a recognized center for the scientific study of education and of American schools.

Charles Hubbard Judd was born on February 20, 1873, in Bareilly, India. His parents, Charles Wesley Judd and Sarah (Hubbard) Judd, were Methodist missionaries, and in 1879, when Judd was six years old, the family returned to the United States. Upon graduation from high school Judd attended Wesleyan University in Connecticut, receiving the A.B. degree in 1894. He next entered graduate work at the University of Leipzig in Germany, where he studied psychology under the renowned Wilhelm Wundt. Judd completed his Ph.D. degree in 1896, after only two years of study and when he was 23 years old. Wundt's scientific study of psychology made a lasting impression on Judd, who became a tireless advocate of the scientific approach in American psychology and education. Judd later translated Wundt's *Outlines of Psychology* into English (1907), a work that helped further scientific psychology in the United States.

Judd's career may be divided into two main phases. The first phase, from 1896 to 1909, was in psychological research and teaching. The second phase, from 1909 on, was in university administration and professional education. Throughout his career, Judd was a prolific writer and editor. Upon his return from Germany in 1896 he was appointed to the position of instructor in psychology at Wesleyan University, which he held until 1898. Over the next several years he rapidly rose through the ranks, first as professor of psychology at New York University and then as professor of psychology and pedagogy at the University of Cincinnati.

In 1902, Judd went to Yale University as an instructor because he wanted to become involved in the psychological research going on at that institution. Although Judd was, in effect, starting out at the bottom again, he was promoted to assistant professor by 1904 and to full professor and director of the Yale Psychological Laboratory by 1907. The Yale years were productive ones for Judd. Not only did he

translate Wundt's *Outlines* during that time, but he also published *Genetic Psychology for Teachers* (1903), *General Introduction to Psychology* (1907), and *Psychological Laboratory Equipment and Methods* (1907). In addition, he edited several monograph supplements of the *Psychological Review* and several important studies from the Yale Psychological Laboratory.

Move to the University of Chicago

Judd's productivity did not go unnoticed, and in 1909 he was invited to the University of Chicago as professor and chairman of the Department of Education, a post he held until his retirement in 1938. This second phase of his career—in professional education—did not mean that he left psychology completely. He continued to publish in the field, and from 1920 to 1925 he also served as the chairman of the Department of Psychology. Yet, education became his central focus, and his research and publications became more specifically involved in the psychology and science of education.

Part of Judd's interest in the University of Chicago was precipitated by the educational reform movement then sweeping the country. Progressive education had long been connected with the university, particularly with John Dewey's work. The progressive focus had to some extent followed Dewey, who left Chicago in 1904 for New York's Columbia University and Teachers College, but when Judd arrived he continued the university's pattern of a socially involved professoriate.

Judd spoke out against the individualistic or "child centered" progressives who wanted to make the learner the center of the curriculum. While the learner's psychological state, capacities, and sense experience are important, Judd argued, many, if not most, educational objectives relate to developing the learner's social consciousness. For example, language is an extremely important part of social consciousness, but it is not so much the expression of an individual's instinct as it is the product of centuries of cooperative social experience. The importance of language for the individual is obvious, but language is also of supreme social importance. It helps individuals relate to each other, binds groups together in a community, and enables cooperative human endeavor to occur. If the potential to use language is a part of the original equipment of individuals, language itself is learned in the give and take of social life. Thus, a supremely important objective of education is to provide learners with a command of language that enlarges their individual and collective social experience.

The Science of Education

The emphasis on the social nature of education was connected with what was perhaps Judd's single most important reform effort. This was the development of the science of education, a topic to which he devoted a number of publications, including *Measuring the Work of the Public Schools* (1916) and *Introduction to the Scientific Study of Education* (1918). Just as he thought psychology should move from introspection to the scientific method, so too should education. Education is conducted through social life and its institutional configurations, he reasoned, and the key to teasing out the proper paths in education is to study scientifically how institutions influence mankind. In what was perhaps his most important book, *The Psychology of Social Institutions* (1926, 1974), he stated, "It is the duty of science to go beyond introspection and to set up a system of explanations which will make clear the true nature of institutional control over men's minds and lives."

Under Judd, the University of Chicago became the leading center for the scientific study of education in the United States. In his leadership position as the chairman of the Department of Education, Judd surrounded himself with a faculty, many of whom had been his former students, devoted to the science of education. The department attracted students who spread the scientific approach to the public schools, educational policy-making bodies, and other universities. In addition, Judd continued to produce numerous papers, articles, and books, and he served as editor of the *Elementary School Journal* and the *School Review,* through which his ideas were further disseminated. He put many of his ideas into practice by conducting school surveys in St. Louis, Missouri; Grand Rapids, Michigan; and Denver, Colorado. He was also a team member on the New York Rural School Survey in 1921.

Involved in Many Areas

His reform penchant also launched him into heavy involvement in professional societies and philanthropic endeavors. For a number of years he served on the Board of Trustees of the Julius Rosenwald Fund, a philanthropic foundation devoted to the social and educational advancement of African Americans. He was a fellow in the American Association for the Advancement of Science and a member of the Social Science Research Council and held membership in the National Education Association, Phi Beta Kappa, Delta Kappa Epsilon, and the University Club of Chicago. He was a member and officer of the American Psychological Association (president, 1909); the National Society of College Teachers of Education (president, 1911, 1915); the North Central Association of Colleges and Secondary Schools (president, 1923); and the American Council on Education (chairman, 1929-1930).

With respect to his teaching, Judd was confident, forceful, and persuasive. Tall, with a neatly trimmed beard and piercing blue eyes, he presented a striking physical appearance. He had a voice of unusual carrying quality, which he used for dramatic effect in his lectures, bringing forth moods of irony, ridicule, or humor. He exhibited an extraordinary command of language and placed great emphasis on the importance of language in education and mental development. Precision of thought and expression were hallmarks of his teaching, and his clear exposition of ideas made him popular with students. While he was at Yale, the undergraduates voted him "best lecturer in the College."

Judd's many contributions were recognized by honorary degrees from Yale (1907), Miami University (1909), Wesleyan University (1913), the State University of Iowa (1923), Colorado College (1923), and the University of Louisville (1937). He was also honored by the University of Chicago when it changed the name of the Graduate Education Building to the Charles Hubbard Judd Building in 1946.

Judd was married twice, first to Ella (Compte) Judd in 1898. They had one daughter, Dorothy. Ella died in 1935, and Judd remarried in 1937 to Mary (Diehl) Judd, who survived him at his death on July 18, 1946.

Further Reading

Biographical sketches on Charles Hubbard Judd may be found in *The National Encyclopedia of American Biography,* Vol. 42 (1967) and in *The Biographical Dictionary of American Educators,* Vol. II (1978). His obituary in the *New York Times* (July 19, 1946), is also informative. An excellent article by a former student is "Reflections on the Personality and Professional Leadership of Charles Hubbard Judd," by Frank N. Freeman, in *The Elementary School Journal* (January 1947). Recommended additional readings of Judd's own works include *Education and Social Progress* (1934), *Educational Psychology* (1939), and his last major publication, *Teaching and the Evolution of Civilization* (1946). □

Donald Judd

American sculptor and art writer Donald Judd (1928-1994) was best known as a major practitioner of and spokesman for Minimalism in the 1960s. His works, or "specific objects," display an overall sense of wholeness and clarity and reiterate the belief that art and idea are inseparable.

Donald Judd was born in Excelsior Springs, Missouri, on June 3, 1928. By the time he had graduated from high school his family had lived in Omaha, Kansas City, Des Moines, Dallas, Philadelphia, and Westwood, New Jersey. Judd served in the U.S. Army in Korea from 1946 to 1947. In 1953 he settled in New York City, where he maintained a studio into the 1980s. In 1964 Judd married Margaret Hughan Finch. They had two children, Flavin Starbuck and Rainer Yingling.

Upon his return from Korea Judd spent a short time studying at the Art Students League in New York. From 1948 to 1949 he was enrolled at the College of William and Mary in Williamsburg, Virginia, and from 1949 to 1953 he studied at Columbia University and at the Art Students League concurrently. Judd's area of concentration at Columbia was philosophy, with particular emphasis on empiricism and pragmatism. He graduated, *cum laude,* in 1953 with a Bachelor of Science. Judd received a Masters in Art History from Columbia in 1962, having majored in the Renaissance and the contemporary arts. Beginning in 1953 he taught, off and on, at such diverse institutions as the Christadora Home and the Police Athletic League (1953), the Allen Stevenson School (1957-1961), the Brooklyn Institute of the Arts and Sciences (1962-1964), Dartmouth College (1966), and Yale University (1967).

In 1959, partially in an attempt to support his artmaking, Judd began his career as a critic and art writer. He served as a reviewer for *Art News* in 1959 and that same year moved to *Arts Magazine,* where he asserted that painting was "finished," and where he continued as a contributing editor until 1965. In 1965 he also wrote reviews for *Art International.* Judd's writings are compressed and concrete and have been compared to his mature sculpture. His undergraduate interest in philosophy remains evident, as does his graduate work in art history. Judd is considered to have been one of the major spokespersons for the Minimalists in the 1960s, a period in American art when concept and art object were firmly melded. He was particularly praised for his successful integration of the artist's perspective with that of the critic and art thinker.

Donald Judd began his art-making career as a painter in the late 1950s and early 1960s, when Abstract Expressionism was still the prevalent force in the New York art world. For Judd, and for many other artists of his generation, works that reflected gesture and/or the artist's physical or emotional state were no longer viable. Judd preferred to have his art reflect a set of decisions intrinsic to the individual work itself. Although he attempted to eliminate such devices as spatial illusion and reference to figure or movement from his painting, in the end he still found the very relationship between picture field and support to be object unspecific. Seeking to resolve such problems, Judd began working in three dimensions around 1962. His first works of this period were reliefs and, soon after, pieces built for the floor. As the result of his initial attempts to translate field and support into real space, he began to work with boxes, a form which was to become the signature of his mature work. By 1963 he began to produce his long wall boxes, which served as a source for his series of progressions—structures which depend upon mathematical systems and thereby avoid reference to composition. Judd, who had been painting his works with industrial pigments, first made use of industrial fabrications in metal in 1964. By 1970 Judd began designing site specific pieces and by 1972 larger scale outdoor works which reflected their surroundings.

Judd was viewed as an advocate of objective sculpture and non-relational art. His decision to attempt to do away with compositional effects was based on his belief that composition carried with it all the structures and values of the European tradition. Judd linked composition to rationalism, and he preferred to think of himself as an antirationalist. In his works—which always affirm their aesthetic purpose—the artist-repeatedly insisted that the whole is more important than the parts.

Judd's sculpture, usually untitled, is identified with the collection within which it is housed. His works, or "specific objects," are included in numerous private collections and in the permanent holdings of a host of such major public institutions as the Museum of Modern Art, the Whitney, the Guggenheim, the Hirshhorn, the Art Institute of Chicago, the San Francisco Museum of Modern Art, and the National Gallery of Canada. Special note should be made of the following from the extensive list of Judd's exhibitions. After Judd's first and only one-man show as a painter, in 1957, he decided not to show his two-dimensional work again. He exhibited his first "relief in three dimensions" at the Brook-

lyn Museum in 1962, and in 1963 his sculpture was included in the first of a series of Green Gallery Exhibitions (New York). In 1966 Leo Castelli, who remained Judd's dealer into the 1980s, presented the first of many Judd exhibitions at the Castelli Gallery (New York), a show composed exclusively of industrially manufactured metal pieces. In 1968 the Whitney Museum of American Art mounted a Judd retrospective, as did the National Gallery of Canada in 1975.

In his later years, he designed furniture and redesigned several buildings in and around Marfa, Texas, where he maintained one of his homes. At his death, he was designing a fountain and a railroad station facade in Switzerland, where he also maintained a residence.

Further Reading

Donald Judd: Complete Writings 1959-1975 (1975); offers an overview of this important aspect of Judd's career; the catalogue for the 1978 Whitney retrospective, *Don Judd* by William Aggee, also provides access to selected writings by the artist; *Minimal Art: A Critical Anthology,* Gregory Battcock, ed. (1968), contains an interview with Judd; *Icons and Images of the Sixties* by Nicolas and Elena Calas (1971); *Donald Judd,* the catalogue of the exhibition at the National Gallery of Canada (1975), includes an essay by Roberta Smith, a catalogue raisonne, a list of exhibitions, and a selective bibliography. □

Adoniram Judson

Adoniram Judson (1788-1850), Baptist missionary, was the first American clergyman to devote himself to Christianizing Burma.

Adoniram Judson was born in Malden, Mass., on Aug. 9, 1788. His father, a Congregationalist minister, encouraged Adoniram's ambitions, and he was pressed toward intellectual excellence by his forceful mother as well. He entered the sophomore class of Brown University at the age of 16. Graduating first in his class in 1807, he taught school at Plymouth while preparing *The Young Lady's Arithmetic and Elements of English Grammar.* In 1808, uncertain about a permanent vocation, he began a short tour of the North. He entered Andover Seminary in 1808 but did not announce his ministerial intentions until 1809.

Influenced by contemporary romantic sentiments for preaching to the heathen, Judson joined other youthful seminarians in forming the American Board of Commissioners for Foreign Missions (1810). In 1811 the board dispatched him to seek joint missionary action with the London Missionary Society. The ship on which Judson sailed was captured by a French vessel, and only after 6 weeks' confinement in France did he reach London. On his return to Boston he convinced the board to proceed without British aid.

Though censured for rashness, Judson and his new bride, Ann Hasseltine, received permission to locate in India. Soon after arrival, the Judsons announced their conversion to the Baptist faith and severed connections with the board. Judson gained support from the American Baptist Missionary Union, which had been formed in response to his activities in India.

The hostility of the British East India Company forced Judson to establish his missionary headquarters in neighboring Rangoon. An able linguist, he translated Scriptures and wrote tracts in Burmese. After 7 months' imprisonment during the Anglo-Burmese War of 1824, he successfully urged the Burmese king to negotiate his domain's dismemberment in the interests of peace. After Mrs. Judson's death in 1826, he moved to Moulmein in British (Lower) Burma (now Myanmar) but never succeeded in posting missions in the native sectors. An interest in Catholic ascetic mysticism temporarily clouded his reputation among American Protestants.

Sarah Hall Boardman, widow of a fellow missionary, became Judson's second wife. Several months after her death in 1845, he married Emily Chubbuck. In his last 4 years at Moulmein, Judson completed his *Dictionary, English and Burmese*. He died at sea on April 12, 1850. His contemporaries considered Judson one of America's greatest missionary leaders, and his colorful adventures, publicized in press and pulpit, helped stimulate the missionary spirit in Protestant America.

Further Reading

The standard work on Judson is Francis Wayland, *A Memoir of the Life and Labors of the Rev. Adoniram Judson, D.D.* (2 vols., 1853). See also Edward Judson, *The Life of Adoniram Judson* (1883); Stacy R. Warburton, *Eastward! The Story of Adoniram Judson* (1937); and Courtney Anderson, *To the Golden Shore: The Life of Adoniram Judson* (1956).

Additional Sources

Anderson, Courtney, *To the Golden Shore: the life of Adoniram Judson,* Valley Forge: Judson Press, 1987.
McElrath, William N., *To be the first: adventures of Adoniram Judson, America's first foreign missionary,* Nashville: Broadman Press, 1976. □

Julian

The Roman emperor Julian (331-363), or Flavius Claudius Julianus, tried to turn the Roman world from Christianity to a reformed paganism and thus earned the sobriquet "the Apostate."

Julian was born at Constantinople, the son of Julius Constantius, half brother of Constantine the Great. When Constantine died in 337, nearly all his relatives except his three sons were killed, and Julian and his half brother Constantius Gallus were spared because of their extreme youth. The boys were confined to a castle in Cappadocia, where they lived until 351, and were given a monkish education. Julian idealized the ancient Hellenic world and was attracted by Greek literature and philosophy; he despised what he considered the falsity and hypocrisy of Christianity.

By 351 Constantius II was Constantine's sole surviving son, and he brought Gallus out of retirement and made him the administrator of the East. Julian remained in retirement, but when Gallus proved to be cruel and incompetent and was executed, Julian was summoned to the court in Milan to free himself of suspicion of treasonable involvement with his half brother. Exonerated, he went to Athens to pursue his philosophical studies. By 355, however, Constantius again found the problems of empire too much for a single person. He recalled Julian from his studies, gave him the title of Caesar (successor-designate), married him to Helena, the Emperor's sister, and sent him to Gaul to protect it from the Germans.

The Soldier

In Gaul, Julian proved unexpectedly successful and popular. Constantius surrounded him with spies and aides, who often hindered Julian's work, but he rapidly became a competent general and drove the Germans out of Gaul and beyond the Rhine. Further, he rejected the financial policies of Constantius's ministers, which called for increasing levies on the Gauls. Instead, he insisted on a firm but honest administration of the current system. In 5 years he managed

syncretization of pantheism, sun worship, and philosophy. He did not persecute the Christians, but he ordered them to restore the temples they had destroyed and removed from their clergy their special privileges and subsidies. He naturally gave preference to pagans in his own service; and his numerous celebrations of religious sacrifices provided quantities of meat for the soldiers, who seem to have enjoyed this turn of affairs. By protecting the Jews and by allowing freedom of expression to the various heretical Christian groups, he weakened the Church, for the Christians were thereby encouraged to destroy themselves with their interminable theological squabbles.

In 362 Julian amassed an army of 65,000 with which to continue the Persian War. In March 363 he marched down the Euphrates to the Persian capital of Ctesiphon and defeated the Persian army. But the victory was not decisive, and the enemy harassed his troops as he marched north to join a supporting force. In one of these battles, on June 26, 363, he was mortally wounded.

The Writer

Julian was a prolific writer, and 8 of his orations, 73 genuine letters, a criticism of the emperors from Caesar onward, a satire on the people of Antioch, and various fragments and epigrams are extant. Julian's style is somewhat pedantic, but his letters are interesting, for they reveal the ideal condition toward which he was trying to direct the pagan church.

Julian was far superior to his contemporaries as an emperor and as a man. His rule was just and humane. What the effect on the Christian Church would have been had he enjoyed a long reign is disputed. But contemporaries noted that many gladly returned to paganism, especially those who had recently converted for political purposes.

Further Reading

The Works of Emperor Julian was translated for the Loeb Classical Library by Wilmer Cave Wright (3 vols., 1913-1923). Francis A. Ridley, *Julian the Apostate and the Rise of Christianity* (1937), places him in the setting of the totalitarian state and Universal Church. Another useful study is Giuseppe Ricciotti, *Julian the Apostate* (trans. 1960).

Additional Sources

Bowersock, G. W., *Julian the Apostate,* London: Duckworth, 1978. □

to reduce the tax rate by better than two-thirds, yet providing sufficient funds for government operations.

Julian's successes and his popularity with soldiers and civilians apparently aroused Constantius's suspicion. He was engaged in a campaign against the Persians and used this as a subterfuge to weaken Julian. He ordered Julian to dispatch to him the flower of his Gallic army. But many soldiers were local recruits and unwilling to serve so far from their homelands. Further, they suspected that this was a first step by Constantius to accord to Julian the same fate as Gallus. The soldiers therefore mutinied and proclaimed Julian emperor. After fruitless refusals, Julian was forced to accede, though he attempted to placate Constantius with apologies and explanations. Constantius headed west to dispute Julian's position but died in Cilicia in November 361. Julian thereupon entered Constantinople the following month as sole emperor.

Emperor and Reformer

Julian remained in Constantinople 5 months, instituting for the whole empire many of the reforms he had effected in Gaul. He cut to the bone the multitude of court functionaries, drastically reduced the national spy system, and encouraged home rule by the municipalities of the empire by restoring public property to them and strengthening the local councils to administer them.

The most dramatic of Julian's reforms concerned religion. Upon his elevation to power, he at once acknowledged his own religious beliefs, which amounted to a

Juliana

Princess Juliana of the Netherlands (born 1909) reigned as queen from 1948 to 1980. Despite repeated troubles in her personal and public life, she held the respect and affection of the Dutch people during the country's difficult recovery from the devastation of World War II.

orn at The Hague on April 30, 1909, Juliana was the only child of Queen Wilhelmina of the Netherlands and her husband, Prince Henry of Mecklenburg-Schwerin. She was educated at home and at the University of Leiden, where instead of the usual degree she received an honorary doctorate upon completion of her studies; with characteristic candor, she felt it was a sham because she had not really earned it. She married a German nobleman, Prince Bernhard of Lippe-Biesterfeld, in 1937; in accepting Dutch nationality he firmly turned his back on his native country and its regime. This change from German to Dutch—although Bernhard never wholly shed his German accent when he spoke Dutch—became of crucial importance with the Nazi invasion of the Netherlands on May 10, 1940. Juliana and Bernhard, along with their children, Beatrix (born January 31, 1938) and Irene (born August 5, 1939), accompanied Queen Wilhelmina in a danger-filled escape across the North Sea to England.

A month later Juliana took her daughters to greater safety in Canada, where she resided for the duration of the war, with frequent visits to the United States and to Dutch colonies in the Caribbean and Surinam. Bernhard, who remained in Britain, took a leading part in the formation of a Dutch army-in-exile, visiting Juliana in Canada for the first time a year later. Another daughter, Margriet, was born in Ottawa on January 19, 1943.

In April 1945 Juliana returned to a just-liberated Netherlands, taking an active part in the rehabilitation of the country after five years of occupation, destruction, and hunger. A fourth daughter, Marijke (who later took the name Christine), was born on February 18, 1947; she suffered from near-blindness because Juliana had caught German measles (rubella) during her pregnancy. Juliana sought a cure from a faith-healer named Geert Hofmans, but the improvement in the child's eyesight over the next decade came from skilled medical treatment; nonetheless, the princess, who was deeply religious, continued her intimacy with Hofmans, a mystic and pacifist. This association led to reported tension with her husband and with the Dutch government until she finally broke with Hofmans in 1956.

Another crisis in relations with the government arose in 1964 when Princess Irene became a secret convert to Roman Catholicism, outraging many Dutch Protestants. (Although there is no state religion in the Netherlands, the reigning House had traditionally been Protestant since the 16th century.) She then wed Prince Carlos Hugo of Bourbon-Parma, a Carlist pretender to the throne of Spain. Because she had not obtained prior approval of her marriage by the States General (parliament) as required by the Dutch constitution, Irene lost her place in the succession to the Dutch throne. Deeply disturbed and angered, Juliana had sought to prevent the marriage by personal intervention without consultation with the cabinet, but was finally persuaded to refrain from flying to Spain to confront her daughter. They were later reconciled, and the marriage ended in divorce years later.

Even greater difficulties developed over the years. When Beatrix married a German diplomat, Claus von Amsberg, in 1966 there were wide protests and rioting because the bridegroom had served in the German army during World War II. Perhaps the most severe blow, however, was the disclosure in 1976 that Prince Bernhard was implicated in a bribery scandal with Lockheed, the American aircraft company. Censure of the prince by an official commission of inquiry brought talk of a possible abdication by the queen, but it was averted when Bernhard resigned all his positions in the armed forces and in private business.

Despite all these troubles, Juliana if anything strengthened the personal respect and affection in which she was held by the large majority of the Dutch people. She always displayed her deep concern for their welfare, as during the disastrous floods that struck Zeeland and southern Holland provinces in 1953. In strictly political matters, she hewed tightly to her constitutional role without the occasional impatience which her mother had displayed. Even political parties in principle committed to republicanism, such as the Labor party, did not see her as an enemy but as "one of us" across party lines; her closest friend in political life was the Labor premier William Drees. The comedian Wim Kan, in a famous quip, said he favored a republic but only if Juliana became its first president. She broke with the tradition of a royal house separated by ceremony and etiquette from the nation at large. She enjoyed riding her bicycle in public with the same dignity and grace that mark Dutch women who continue to travel about by cycle until well advanced in age. As queen, she presided over the post-war transformation of the country into a prosperous, technically developed land with an elaborate social welfare system.

In 1980, after the return of political calm, Juliana stepped down from the throne amid general acclaim, although there were disturbances during the inauguration ceremonies for her successor, Queen Beatrix. She received the title of princess and continued to be active in work of social welfare.

Further Reading

There was little available in English on Queen Juliana personally. Alden Hatch, *Bernhard, Prince of the Netherlands* (1962), emphasized the role of her husband, which was put in a favorable light; published when the reign was only half over, many important episodes are missing. Ivo Schöffer, *A Short History of the Netherlands* (2nd edition, 1973) was a thoughtful and informative sketch of general Dutch history by a distinguished historian. Richard de Burnchurch, *An Outline of Dutch History* (1981) may also be consulted. S. J. Eldenburgh *et al.*, *Elite Images of Dutch Politics: Accommodation and Conflict* (1981); Arend Lijphart, *The Politics of Accommodation: Pluralism and Democracy in the Netherlands* (1968); and Richard T. Griffiths, editor, *The Economy and Politics of the Netherlands Since 1945* (1980) all gave a deeper understanding of Dutch politics and society in the postwar period. W. Hoffman, *Queen Juliana: The Story of the Richest Woman in the World* (1979) provided a journalistic account with emphasis on the sensational. □

Julian of Norwich

Julian of Norwich (1342-c 1416) was the most important English mystic of the 14th century. Her spirituality is strongly Trinitarian and basically Neoplatonic.

In her *Revelations of Divine Love* Julian relates that in May 1373, when she was 30 years old, she suffered a serious illness. After she had been administered extreme unction, she received 16 revelations within the span of a few hours. When she wrote her *Revelations,* she was a recluse at Norwich, supported by the Benedictine convent of Carrow. Anchorite seclusion was a rather common form of life in 14th-century England among Christians with high spiritual aspirations. A woman of little formal education—she calls herself "unlettered"—Julian writes in a beautifully simple style and shows a solid grasp of traditional theology.

Julian's revelations, a mixture of imaginary and intellectual visions, bear all the characteristics of true mysticism. According to her, her visions came in fulfillment of three petitions of her youth: to have in mind the Passion of Christ, to have a critical bodily sickness at 30 years of age, and to receive the wounds of "true contrition," "genuine compassion," and "sincere longing for God." The revelations consist mostly of visions of the crucified Christ occasioned by the sight of a crucifix which the priest had left at her bedside. But through the Passion, Julian is led to intellectual visions of the Trinity and of the universe as it exists in God. Thus she is confronted by the teachings of sin and damnation, which she finds hard to reconcile with God's grace in Christ. Nevertheless the accepts the traditional Church doctrine of the existence of an eternal rejection. Yet on the sinfulness of those who will be saved she hedges: "In every soul to be saved is a godly will that has never consented to sin, in the past or in the future. Just as there is an animal will in our lower nature that does not will what is good, so there is a godly will in our higher part, which by its basic goodness never wills what is evil, but only what is good." Obviously she finds herself unable to accept that divine goodness could ever allow the elect to be truly sinful. Her fundamental outlook is optimistic. The Lord tells her: "All shall be well," and "You will see for yourself that all manner of thing shall be well."

Little is known of Julian's later years, not even the date of her death. She is last referred to as a living person in a will dated 1416. Apparently even during her life she enjoyed a certain renown, for people came from afar to see and consult her.

Further Reading

There are two versions of the *Revelations,* one much longer than the other. It is not known whether the short one is merely an excerpt from the older one or whether it is the first authentic report on which Julian elaborated in the longer version. A critical edition is being prepared by Sister Anna Maria Reynolds and James Walsh. Meanwhile, a modernized edition of the short version is *A Shewing of God's Love* (1958) by Anna

Maria Reynolds. Several modern translations of the longer version, under the title *Revelations of Divine Love,* are by Roger Hudleston (1927), James Walsh (1961), Anchoret Juliana (1966), and Clifton Wolters (1966). Important studies of Julian are Paul Molinari, *Julian of Norwich: The Teaching of a 14th Century English Mystic* (1958), and James Walsh, ed., *Pre-Reformation English Spirituality* (1966). □

The Julias of Rome

Julia Domna, Julia Maesa, Julia Soaemias, and Julia Mammaea were empresses of the so-called Severan Dynasty who guided Rome through its last good days before the plague, civil war, barbarian attacks, and famine of the third-century crisis. Julia Domna was the wife of ruler Serevus and was considered an intellect in her time. Her influence became more prominent after her husband's death, during her son's reign.

While Julia Domna spent much of her husband's reign in political eclipse, her influence was felt again during her son's regime. Her sister Julia Maesa revived the Severan dynasty by taking the ruthless actions necessary to place first one grandson and then another on the throne. Her actions staved off the type of civil war that would nearly destroy Rome a generation later, brought Roman jurisprudence to its height, and completed the integration of the eastern and western parts of the Mediterranean world, thereby contributing to the survival of *Romanitas.* Whereas Maesa's daughter Julia Soaemias lacked her mother's political acumen, her other daughter Julia Mammaea might well have proved a worthy successor as a power behind the throne, had not the army refused her leadership, killing her along with her son and thereby inaugurating the third-century Crisis.

Julia Domna and Julia Maesa were daughters of the high priest of Baal at Emesa. Since Emesa had originally been a kingdom ruled by its high priest, even 200 years after its incorporation into the Roman Empire, the high priest of Baal was wealthy and influential. His children would have expected to marry into the richest local families or to contract marriages with other eastern, princely lines. Septimius Severus, an ambitious young senator from Africa, might well have met both daughters at affairs for the local social elite when he commanded a legion in Syria in 179. Julia Domna was about ten at the time, Maesa about 15. Seven years later, when his first wife died, Severus sought Domna's hand. Maesa may have been less attractive to him, she may have already married, or perhaps the following story reported in the ancient sources was indeed true. Supposedly, Domna's horoscope had earlier been cast, predicting she would marry the ruler of the world. Perhaps an astrologer did flatter her with such a reading, and perhaps the superstitious Severus had heard the accompanying local gossip.

Marriage to the 42-year-old Severus meant that the teenage Domna had to leave her family in Emesa and join him on a series of provincial assignments that were necessary for a man hoping to rise in the imperial service. First, she was taken to Lugdunum in Gaul at the other end of the Roman world, where she bore her first son Caracalla. A year later in 189, her second son Geta was born in Sicily. It was probably a relief to the family when the emperor Commodus, who had become suspicious of Severus's ambition, was assassinated in 192. The proclamation of Severus's friend Pertinax as emperor was also surely welcome.

At their new post on the Danube, Domna and Severus received word that the Praetorian Guard back in Rome had killed the disciplinarian Pertinax and auctioned off the empire to the highest bidder—the fabulously wealthy Didius Julianus. Promptly expressing their horror, the Danubian legions declared Severus emperor. As they were not the only legions to so express their esteem for their commander, brutal civil war followed. Predictably, Parthian princelings took advantage of Roman disorder, causing trouble on the borders as well as in areas demanding Severus's attention. Domna accompanied him even into the barren gulleys of Mesopotamia, acquiring the first of many honorific titles: Mother of the Camp. Domna's travels presumably led her to meet many new people with different customs and beliefs, providing experiences that perhaps contributed to her later participation in an intellectual circle.

Unfortunately for the family, Plautianus, Severus's friend from boyhood and his commander of the Praetorian Guard, began undermining Domna's marriage. He may have envied her influence or, as Caracalla insisted, simply aspired to seizing power for himself. In any case, when the civil wars and their travels ended, Domna did not enjoy the fruits of victory in Rome because Plautianus's false accusations of adultery had destroyed Severus's trust in her. She continued to live in the palace with her husband and sons to avoid public scandal, and in 204 was accorded prominence unprecedented for an empress in the Secular Games. This was a rare event, held only once every 110 years. Domna presided as Augusta over a special ceremonial gathering of women—drawn primarily from the most powerful senatorial families—which included her sister Julia Maesa.

Largely excluded from political influence during her time in Rome, Domna encouraged various intellectuals of the day. While some later scholars have questioned the significance of her circle, the first emperor Augustus had set the precedent for exercising literary patronage to rally scholars and artists around a new dynasty, and no contemporary would have been surprised by her activities. Philostratus, author of the *Life of Apollonius* which would later prove so influential, was a good friend; Aelian collected stories of exotic (or even fantastic) animals like the manticore and made his contribution to later European folklore; Galen's medical books remained supreme until the later medieval period; even the multitalented Apuleius, best known for the novel *The Golden Ass,* might have been associated with the group. The vitally important historian and senator Dio

Cassius was a close associate of the family, and presumably part of the circle—however critical he was of some of its members later, when it was safe.

Though Plautianus's self-serving plots were finally exposed and he was killed, Domna could not have enjoyed the last few years of her husband's reign without wondering what was to come. Her sons had never been friends, and the prospect of having an empire to quarrel over did nothing for their relationship. In an action that offered a solution to the problem of overambitious prefects of the Praetorian Guard while also attributing new importance to legal theory, Severus, for his part, appointed the great legal scholar Papinian—perhaps a member of Domna's circle—to head the guard. The classical Roman law which had such an overwhelming influence on later European, and even Latin American, history is the product of Papinian and Ulpian, about whom more will shortly be said.

Domna Refuses To Divide the Empire

Domna accompanied Severus on what would prove to be his final trip to Britain. When he died there in 211, his final words to their sons were: "Keep peace between yourselves." Their hostility, of course, intensified. According to Herodian, their mother brought them together at one conference with high-ranking senatorial advisors, but no one could see any solution short of cutting the Empire in two. Domna refused to countenance any such measure, responding: "Do you intend to divide your mother's body between you too?" The idea was dropped, rather ironically, considering that later ages would be driven to even finer subdivisions.

Had Domna foreseen the horrible outcome, she might well have agreed to the division. In 212, persuading her that he was ready for a reconciliation with his brother, Caracalla begged that they meet quietly and affectionately in the family chambers without the distractions of attendants. Though ancient sources differ as to whether Caracalla reserved the pleasure of stabbing his brother for himself or had planted assassins to do it, they all agree that Geta died in his mother's lap, drenching her with his blood. Nor was Domna even permitted to outwardly mourn her son's death. Dio, a trustworthy source in this instance, writes: "She was compelled to rejoice and laugh as though at some great fortune, so closely were all her words, gestures, and changes of color observed.

It is true that Domna was raised to even higher honors during Caracalla's sole reign and that she virtually served as regent in his absence, but that does not mean that she was insensitive or capable of being bribed with grants of power. Turton, who is often more imaginative than scholarly, put it well for once, commenting, "She was a woman of great strength of mind, who refused to let personal feeling impair her political judgment." Having refused to countenance the destruction of the Empire as a unit, she was dedicated to providing it with the best government her power could allow.

But in 217 she lost everything. Caracalla was assassinated, and she was sent back to Emesa to live in seclusion with her sister Julia Maesa. Then only in her mid-40s, she had lost both her children to violent deaths; had seen the destruction, she believed, of everything for which she and Severus had fought; and had only hostility, and perhaps even death, to look forward to at the hands of the new emperor, Macrinus. Some of the ancient sources claim that she missed the exercise of power and influence, and it probably is true that she did not mourn Caracalla as a beloved son. Nonetheless, Domna must have seen in his death the destruction of the hopes of many, including the hope for continued peace and stability. Undoubtedly victim to bitterness and depression described in the sources, she was also afflicted with breast cancer. Refusing food, she starved herself to death.

Her sister Julia Maesa was by then a wealthy widow. Her husband's career and fortune had prospered with his brother-in-law's elevation to rule, and her grandson, Bassianus, later called Elagabalus, had inherited his grandfather's position of high priest of Baal. As his grandmother, Maesa could therefore draw on the ages-old treasury of the great temple. Why should a nobody like Macrinus be allowed to usurp the imperial power? She knew that Caracalla had been popular with the troops in the region. Maesa began spreading rumors that her widowed daughter Julia Soaemias had had an affair with Caracalla, and that her son Elagabalus was also Caracalla's natural son. Helping the cause of such rumors, Macrinus proceeded to alienate senate, people, and army in a series of errors.

Maesa next enlisted Gannys, Elagabalus's tutor and Soaemias's long-time lover, in her scheme. Maesa, Gannys, Soaemias, Elagabalus, Maesa's other daughter Julia Mammaea, and her small son Alexianus all entered a camp of a friendly legion and were effusively welcomed. Though Mammaea's husband was caught on his way and killed by Macrinus's forces, the soldiers proved unwilling to enthusiastically fight other Romans in his name. The young Elagabalus did in fact resemble Caracalla and, having been togged out to strengthen the resemblance, his appearance won over many. In the final confrontation on the battlefield, a determined charge by the Praetorian Guard almost broke the ranks of Maesa's forces, but she and Soaemias jumped down from their chariot in the rear and ran forward to rally the men to stand their ground. When Macrinus's troops discovered that he had fled the scene, they promptly changed sides, and the war was won.

Maesa's Grandson Defies Her

Elagabalus, however, was not mature enough to be emperor, and his first impression on the Romans was disastrous. Maesa could stage rebellions, finance and stage-manage ceremonies to impress and win popular support, but she could not get her rebellious adolescent grandson to wear his toga. Having earlier lived with her sister in Rome, Maesa knew that Elagabalus's heavily made-up face and exotic priestly garb would strike the Romans as combining the worst of effeminacy and eccentricity. But she simply could not convince him that a Roman emperor should look Roman. Thumbing his nose at his grandmother, Elagabalus had a high-camp portrait done and sent it to Rome with instructions that it be hung in the senate. Finally, Gannys

was stabbed to death by guards during an argument with Elagabalus. What should have been a triumphant entrance into Rome was significantly tarnished as a result of Elagabalus's outrageous conduct. The sources do not record that Soaemias shared her mother's disquiet nor that she joined Maesa in trying to get Elagabalus to behave with some propriety. Presumably she did not know Rome or Romans as well, or perhaps the ancient sources assessed her correctly as the most flighty member of the family.

Sill, Roman government continued essentially unaffected since it was Maesa who went into the senate, not Elagabalus, who took no interest in anything except Baal and debauchery. Nonetheless, he still threw money around, was generally offensive, and engaged in open corruption with the distribution of horrors and offices. Knowing perfectly well how many emperors had been assassinated in the previous half-century, and what had happened to their families, Maesa must have been quick to see the solution close at hand.

Mammaea's son Alexianus was a precocious little boy who honored his grandmother and mother. Like her aunt Julia Domna, Mammaea was more philosophically inclined and more interested in providing good government than her sister Julia Soaemias. Although some have believed that Maesa hoped Elagabalus could peacefully be persuaded to resign in favor of Alexianus, so that he could devote himself exclusively to his priesthood and sensuality, she almost certainly decided early that Elagabalus would have to be removed. Rumors were spread that Alexianus too was Caracalla's natural son.

Elagabalus, however, was not stupid and knew that once he adopted Alexianus as his grandmother wished, he was expendable. Maesa argued that his almost exclusive homosexuality made it vital for him to adopt an heir to provide for succession, but Elagabalus kept putting it off. Finally, liking and trusting Alexianus as much as everyone else, Elagabalus gave in and adopted him. Then, growing uneasy, he started trying to promote his mother politically, presumably as a counterweight to his grandmother. He sent Alexianus's tutor, the distinguished legal scholar Ulpian, into exile, an action which only cost him more credibility with the senate, as did an abortive assassination plot against Alexianus.

All too late, Soaemias began telling her son to appear for ceremonies appropriately garbed in a toga. She could not, however, make him act with dignity when he got there. The Praetorian Guard became convinced, perhaps correctly, that there was another attempt under way against Alexianus. Modern historians have taken positions ranging from the belief that Elagabalus's ensuing murder at the hands of the Praetorian Guard was a shock to Maesa, who had hoped to prevent it, to the assertion that she had planned all along to eliminate both mother and son. The truth is likely in between. Maesa might well have considered Elagabalus unsalvageable but hoped to get Soaemias out of the predicament. Dio, however, blamed her daughter Mammaea for the final riot in the Praetorian camp in 222, claiming that she had become openly hostile to her sister Soaemias. In any case, Soaemias did not run; on the contrary, she tried shielding her son with her body and died with him. Their corpses were stripped and dragged through the streets.

Mammaea's Son Named Emperor

Mammaea was certainly a different kind of woman than her sister had been. Whereas Soaemias had acquired a shady reputation—although it may well have been exaggerated—Mammaea was known as puritanical. She had always wanted to acquire the best tutors for Alexianus, now Alexander Severus, but after the adoption she had been openly grooming him to be a philosopher king, of the sort Plato wanted to produce. At 13 he had been taught to maintain a dignified public bearing in deliberate contrast with the appearance of his cousin. Though the senate confirmed him, it exacted its price from Maesa and Mammaea. Women could no longer enter the senate. They would have to consult a special advisory group of senators even when a full meeting of the senate was not possible or appropriate. Maesa and Mammaea showed no signs of resenting these measures; they may even have appreciated more genuine involvement in government by the senate. Ulpian was appointed Praetorian Prefect, with lasting consequences for the blossoming of the classical period of Roman law and for the legal traditions of Europe and its colonies.

Unfortunately, Maesa died, probably still in her 50s, just three years later. If she had lived, subsequent tragedies might have been avoided, and the course of European history might have been much different. Though undoubtedly well-meaning (perhaps the most well-meaning of all the women in the family), Mammaea never had the iron will and ruthlessness of her mother and her presence did not evoke the respect that Maesa's had. Ulpian's discipline was uncongenial to the Praetorian Guard, and, in a drunken riot, they pursued him into the royal chambers, where they killed him in the presence of Mammaea and her son Alexander Severus. Even Dio Cassius feared assassination. Mammaea shared Ulpian's devotion to fiscal responsibility, which did nothing for her popularity. Nonetheless, the reign of the popular boy with his comparatively reserved, honest mother seemed later like the last moments of sunshine before the storm.

Had the Romans been left to their own devices, a son of Alexander Severus might have inherited the throne. As it was, Severus's defeat of the Parthians had unleashed a resurgent Persian Empire to overrun the eastern borders. Alexander Severus was only 21 when he and his mother, who was just 40, had to go east to fight a major war. Alexander became sick, and the troops began to think him weak while resenting the suffering they endured in the desert for an expedition aborted through what they believed to be his lack of strength.

The same troops were brought to meet a new threat on the Rhine, the second major wave of Germans who would eventually overwhelm the imperial defenses on the north. A counteroffensive was largely successful but not followed up aggressively as the troops wanted. With his popularity among the troops eroded, and given his reputation for clinging to his mother's skirts, Alexander could not help but

appear weak. Malcontents began gathering around a Thracian giant called Maximinus, and one day some of Alexander's troops proclaimed Maximinus emperor. A personal appeal to the assembled troops brought cries that he was a "money-grubbing milktoast." Running to his mother's tent, Alexander found comfort from Mammaea until the assassins came for them both.

In actuality, the Roman Empire had been governed by Syrian princesses of the priestly house of Baal from the time when Caracalla had begun losing interest in civil affairs in about 213 until the death of Alexander Severus in 234. In that way, these two decades were a strange interlude in Roman history; it would be untrue, however, to call it an unhappy one. The dynasty was not responsible for the revival of a brilliantly led Persian Empire, nor for the mass movement of peoples out of central Asia which was just starting to drive the German tribes into the Rhine and Danube frontiers. Subsequent centuries showed that men with military experience were often defeated by these intractable problems. The Julias left Rome's greatest legacy to Europe: classical Roman law of the golden age of Papinian and Ulpian.

Further Reading

Balsdon, J. P. V. D. *Roman Women.* Barnes and Noble, 1962.
Birley, Anthony R. *Septimius Severus: The African Emperor.* Yale University Press, 1972.
Cleve, Robert L. "Some Male Relatives of the Severan Women," in *Historia.* Vol. 37, 1988.
Turton, Godfrey. *The Syrian Princesses.* Cassell, 1974.
Dio Cassius. *Dio's Roman History.* Vol. IX, Putnam, 1927.
Herodian. Vols. I-II. Harvard University Press, 1969.
The Scriptores Historiae Augustae. Vols. I-II. Harvard University Press, 1959. □

Julius II

Julius II (1443-1513), who was pope from 1503 to 1513, was a noted Renaissance patron of the arts. A warrior pope, he failed to bring Italy under papal control. His costly concern with the arts and politics alienated northern Europe and helped pave the way for the Reformation.

Giuliano della Rovere, who became Pope Julius II, was born in December 1443 in Albissola near Savona, Italy. He was elevated to the cardinalate in December 1471 by his uncle Pope Sixtus IV. Giuliano rapidly became an influential member of the College of Cardinals and servant to both Sixtus IV and his successor, Innocent VIII. In 1492 Innocent VIII died, and Cardinal della Rovere was considered Innocent's logical successor. However, because of the greater wealth of the Spaniard Cardinal (Rodrigo) Borgia to purchase votes, the College of Cardinals elected Borgia, and he assumed the title Alexander VI.

The Borgias were vassals of Ferdinand of Aragon, and during Alexander's reign Giuliano resented this foreign influence in Italy and also opposed Alexander's nepotism. Because of his opposition to the Pope, Giuliano underwent much hardship. During most of Alexander's pontificate Giuliano felt it safer to absent himself from Rome.

Alexander VI died in August 1503, and his elderly successor, Pius III, died in October. In November Giuliano was elected pope and assumed the title Julius II.

First Conflicts

From the start of his pontificate it became clear that Julius intended to make the papacy the dominant political and military force in Italy and to drive all rivals of papal authority out of the peninsula. In 1503 there were three rivals to papal authority. The first was Cesare Borgia, the son of Alexander VI and conqueror of the richest of the Papal States, the Romagna, in northern Italy. The other rivals were Venice and France. France controlled several important cities in northern Italy, among them Florence and Pavia.

In 1504 Julius confiscated the landholdings of Cesare Borgia in Italy and ordered his arrest. In the absence of Cesare Borgia and his military forces in the Romagna, Venice occupied the area, including the cities of Rimini, Faenza, Forli, and Cesena. Julius knew the defeat of this second rival to papal authority would require force of arms. In order to raise the money necessary to equip an army, Julius ordered the Dominicans in Germany to sell indulgences. In 1505 Julius marched out of Rome with a small army.

En route to the Romagna, Julius captured the cities of Perugia and Bologna in 1506. Julius then led his troops into Cesena and Forli, which had been evacuated by the Venetians in the face of a threat by Julius to lay an interdict upon Venice. However, Venice adamantly refused to evacuate Faenza and Rimini. Meanwhile, in 1507 the Genoese revolted against their overlord, Piero Soderini, ruler of Florence and a political puppet of France. The French believed Julius had engineered the revolt in order to force their withdrawal from Italy, and the French king, Louis XII, dispatched an army to smash the insurrection. This threat forced Julius to abandon his campaign against Venice and return to Rome.

The enmity between Louis XII and Julius increased when the Holy Roman emperor Maximilian I announced his intention of journeying to Rome in order to be crowned by the Pope. Louis XII feared that Julius had invited the Germans into Italy to participate in another effort to drive France from the peninsula. Since the Venetians also felt threatened by what they believed to be a papal-German alliance, France and Venice formed an alliance. In 1508 war broke out between the Germans and the Franco-Venetian alliance, and before the end of the year the alliance defeated the Germans.

League of Cambrai

Because of its assistance in this war, France expected to receive territory in northern Italy from Venice, but Venice relinquished no lands. Louis XII also realized Julius had not invited Maximilian into Italy. France, therefore, abandoned its alliance with the Venetians.

Julius took advantage of the Venetian isolation and created the military League of Cambrai to drive Venice from Faenza and Rimini. France and a number of independent city-states in northern Italy joined the league. Maximilian joined in order to revenge his defeat and win back territory in northern Italy which he had lost to the Venetians. Spain, which controlled the kingdom of Naples, also participated in order to drive the Venetians from Adriatic seaports which they held in that kingdom. In 1509 Julius placed an interdict on Venice, and the League of Cambrai declared war on the city-state.

Venice suffered a number of disastrous defeats on land and sea. The French insisted upon the total destruction of Venice as a power in Italy. But this would have upset the balance of power in northern Italy and would have removed a major obstacle to French domination of that area. Therefore, in 1510 Julius negotiated a separate peace with Venice. By the terms of the settlement, Venice surrendered the Romagna to the Pope, the Apulian seaports to the Spanish, and most of its possessions in northern Italy to the other members of the League of Cambrai. Because of this separate peace the members of the League of Cambrai ended hostilities against Venice. Thus, Julius saved the republic of Venice from annihilation.

War with France

Julius now had to deal with the final threat to papal supremacy in Italy, the French. In August 1510 Louis XII called all French prelates to a synod at Orléans. Here, Louis declared that papal authority extended only over spiritual matters. He proclaimed his right as a prince and protector of the Church on earth to call a council in order to punish a worldly pope such as Julius and reform the Church. Louis thus hoped to frighten Julius into abandoning his plans to drive France from Italy.

In 1511 Louis XII issued the call for a Church council. By May a small number of cardinals had gathered at Pisa. Louis promised these cardinals rich rewards for their participation. Support for the council also came from Germany, where the 16th-century voices of reform assailed the worldliness of a papacy which seemed more concerned with Italian politics than with religion. The Germans resented the financial burdens placed upon them by the Pope in order to pay for his wars in Italy.

In the face of disaster Julius acted with characteristic audacity. He issued the call for Western Christendom to gather in ecumenical council at the Lateran Basilica in Rome. This bold action won for Julius the religious and political support of the Spanish and the English. These powers, along with the Swiss and the Venetians, in 1511 joined Julius in the Holy League. In fear of this new military alliance, Louis XII withdrew his support of the schismatic Council of Pisa, and at the beginning of 1512 the council ended in failure.

In June 1512 the Holy League attacked the French in northern Italy. The Swiss captured the French-controlled city of Pavia, and the Spanish captured Florence. By the end of the summer the league drove the French out of Italy.

The defeat of the French was a Pyrrhic victory for Julius, for now the Spanish were in control of much of northern Italy. Julius began preparing new alliances to drive them from Italy. But the energy expended through long years of warfare and in manipulating the complicated balance of power in Italy physically and mentally overtaxed Julius. On February 21, 1513, Julius II died.

During his pontificate Julius hired the costly services of the greatest artists of the Renaissance to embellish the papal apartments. Above the protests of most of Western Christendom he ordered the demolition of the ancient and crumbling Basilica of St. Peter. He hired the services of the architect Donato Bramante, who designed and began the construction of the present Basilica. Julius hired Michelangelo to design and execute a tomb for the Pontiff and to decorate the ceiling of the Sistine Chapel. All of this and his wars and political escapades in Italy, Julius financed in large part by the sale of ecclesiastical offices and indulgences in northern Europe.

Further Reading

The best account in English of Julius II is still that contained in Ludwig Pastor, *The History of the Popes: From the Close of the Middle Ages* (trans., 40 vols., 1938-1968).

Additional Sources

Shaw, Christine, *Julius II, the warrior pope,* Oxford, UK; Cambridge, Mass., USA: Blackwell 1993. □

Kamal Jumblatt

Kamal Jumblatt (1917-1977) was a distinguished ideologue and Druze leader in Lebanese politics who was considered the father of the contemporary Left in Lebanon despite his feudal background.

K amal Jumblatt was born in Mukhtarah, Lebanon, in 1917. He was the only son of Fuad and Nazirah Jumblatt. His ancestors were the Kurdish Janbuladhs who converted to the Druze faith and were in control of an expansive feudal entity in northern Syria. In the 17th century they established themselves among their Druze Tanukh and Manid kin in southeastern Lebanon, by which time their surname had evolved into Jounblatt (written Jumblatt). A lawyer by training, Jumblatt was involuntarily diverted into politics in 1943 after serving for one year as an apprentice lawyer with francophile ex-president Emile Edde's law firm.

Jumblatt considered his political career a diversion from his calling as a searcher for knowledge in history and the humanities. In the 1960s he taught history and politics at the Lebanese University and often lectured at all leading institutions of higher learning in Lebanon. His ideological orientation was a product of diverse intellectual influences coming from West and East. He matured into a mixture of French socialism, Hindu pacifism, and Druze traditionalism. In addition, Jumblatt inherited from his family prestige, wealth, and status, as well as a past full of power feuds between the Jumblatts, their Druze Yazbaki adversaries, and the ruling families of feudal Lebanon and their modern successors: the Ottoman Mutasarrifs and Maronite presidents. Jumblatt's desire to transform the Lebanese system and avenge the "wrong" done to his ancestors and his deep interest in Hinduism and adoration of the socialism and humanism of Teilhard de Chardin and Alexis Carrel are said to have been the main sources of the two dimensions of the duality that bedeviled him—that is, his feudal background and his humanist-socialist drive for reform. Jumblatt did not want to escape from his primordial heritage, yet always strove to live up to his intellectual universalism.

Kamal was hardly 26 and totally subsumed by his interest in the humanities when he was cast into the leadership of his Druze community after the death of his uncle Hikmat Jumblatt in 1943. He was caught unprepared and became a politician "by chance." Between then and 1977 he led an active political life in his own right, serving continuously as a member of parliament and leader of a parliamentary bloc, with a short interruption between 1957 and 1960. He was appointed cabinet minister seven times between 1946 and 1970. Jumblatt was in the opposition even when he, or those he deputized, were in government. Whenever he took office he did so with the intention of utilizing the uniquely Lebanese institution of built-in opposition to discreetly promote his political programs and reinforce his influence. His clout in presidential elections earned him the label "king-maker."

Despite overwhelming indications—ranging from his education to his mother's political closeness to French au-

thorities—that Jumblatt was groomed to be yet another pro-French politician, soon after his election in 1943 he backed the struggle for independence from France. He gradually became a leading advocate of socialism, decolonization, and non-alignment. Jumblatt derived influence from nurturing an ever-growing number of political groups clamoring for reform. In 1949 he launched the Progressive Socialist party (PSP), which gradually shrunk from an indigenous socialist-humanist movement into a predominantly Druze political association. In 1951 he was instrumental in establishing the Socialist National Front, which played a central role in forcing the resignation of President Bishara al-Khoury in 1952. When the front succeeded in putting one of its members, Camile Chamoun, in the presidency, the reform plank Chamoun was willing to adopt did not quench Jumblatt's thirst; the front dissipated.

This experience was a turning point in Kamal Jumblatt's political life. Frustrated with the gradualist approach of his allies, he set out on a course to destroy the consociational system of government engineered by the National Pact of 1943 after having earlier described it as a "free" and "tolerant" system of "consultation and democracy" and "a great attempt to coordinate and harmonize the relationship between Christianity and Islam." By 1958 Jumblatt was not only willing to participate in a war against the regime, but was one of the engineers of that war.

Beginning in the mid-1960s his allies were openly the radicals, including the Communists, Nasserites, and Arab nationalist groups. The new alliance, labeled the Front of Progressive parties and National Forces, evolved into the National Movement after the mid-1970s. In the same vein, Jumblatt championed the Palestine cause for a national homeland and went into open alliance with the Palestine Liberation Organization (PLO) against the government after 1967. As minister of interior in 1970 he licensed the Communist party of Lebanon and the Syrian Nationalist Social party, and in 1972 he accepted the general secretariat of the multi-national Front for the Support of the Palestine Resistance. For the qualitative change in his political conduct Jumblatt earned the Lenin Peace Prize and the Order of Lenin from the Soviet government.

When war broke out in Lebanon in 1975 Jumblatt warned that "revolution is knocking at the door" and that it would not relent until the "decadent system is gone forever." In its place he proposed an Interim Program for Democratic Reform designed by the National Movement and calling for sweeping changes, including the abolishment of political sectarianism, restructuring the army, reinforcing democratic representation and augmenting the influence of parliament within the structure of power, and introducing "socio-economic democracy." This revolutionary course and his alliance with the radicals and the PLO, as well as his rejection of a Syrian-sponsored program for constitutional reform in February 1976, put him on a collision course with Damascus which was catastrophic for his career. Succumbing to Syrian pressure, the PLO grudgingly moved away from a badly defeated Jumblatt. On March 16, 1977, Kamal Jumblatt was assassinated while on the way to his home village, Mukhtarah in the Shouf region. His assassin's identity was not determined.

Kamal Jumblatt attended French schools throughout his academic career. He went to the Lazarist School in Ayntourah, Lebanon, for his pre-college education. In 1936 he went to Paris where he pursued his interest in the humanities in the Sorbonne. Prospect of World War II prematurely brought him back to Lebanon in 1938, where he joined the Universite Saint Joseph in Beirut and obtained a law degree in 1942. He continued his self-education in the humanities throughout his life. He was proficient in numerous foreign languages, regularly travelled to Europe and the East, practiced meditation, and was a vegetarian. Jumblatt was married to May Shakib Arslan in 1948. They separated soon after they had their first and only son, Walid, who took over leadership of the Druze during Lebanon's devastating military conflicts that ran through most of the 1980s.

Further Reading

Most of Jumblatt's own writings are in Arabic. Whatever is attributed to him in a foreign language appeared in French: *Pour un Socialisme Plus Humain* (n.d.), *Pour Le Liban* (1978), and *Les Travailleurs et Les Artistes* (1979). Valuable information about him can be found in Michael Suleiman, *Political Parties in Lebanon* (1967); Michael Hudson, *The Precarious Republic* (1968); Majid Khadduri, *Arab Contemporaries* (1973); "Interview with Kamal Jumblatt," *Monday Morning* (No. 249, 1977); *Who's Who i n Lebanon* (1973-1974); and the English-language international press, April 1976 and March 17, 1977. □

Abu al-Qasim ibn Muhammad al Junayd

Abu al-Qasim ibn Muhammad al-Junayd (ca. 830-910) was one of the great early mystics, or Sufis, of Islam. He laid the groundwork for "sober" mysticism in contrast to that of "God-intoxicated" Sufis like al-Hallaj.

Al-Junayd lived and died in Baghdad, although his family had come originally from western Persia. He studied law and the Traditions of the prophet Mohammed, after having learned the Koran by heart. Later he studied mysticism under the guidance of his uncle, a famous Sufi. It is clear that al-Junayd's sound training in the orthodox Moslem sciences greatly influenced his mystical career and restrained him from the antinomian excesses which many other Sufis indulged in and which gave Sufism a bad name among the more orthodox.

After a period of training with his uncle, al-Junayd began to attract disciples and initiated many into his understanding of the path to mystical experience of God. He was always prudent in his teaching, however, and maintained that mystic knowledge was not intended for the average person. Late in his life there came a period of general persecution of Sufis in Baghdad, but he managed to avoid serious trouble with the authorities by maintaining that he was merely a jurist, for which he had a sound reputation.

While it is well established by scholars that the Neoplatonic philosophy of Plotinus was studied by later Moslem mystics, there is also evidence that al-Junayd may have been exposed to Neoplatonic ideas, despite the fact that such works as Porphyry's so-called *Theology of Aristotle* had been translated into Arabic only a generation earlier. There is no evidence that al-Junayd had actually read Plotinus or his pupil Porphyry—simply a rather striking parallelism in thought. This parallelism exists in the doctrines concerning the soul and mystical experiences. With regard to the idea of God, however, al-Junayd is as orthodox a Moslem as could be conceived: God is the Creator, active, omnipresent, nearer to man than his own neck vein. This contrasts sharply with the remote, inactive "One" of Plotinus.

Other analogous ideas in Plotinus and al-Junayd are the notions that mystical experiences are for an elect few, that to follow the path to such experiences requires a skilled guide, and that the aftereffects of mystical experiences are beneficial and sublimely sober. Such ideas, kept within bound by the basic sobriety of al-Junayd and by his firm grounding in the Moslem disciplines of Koran study and Tradition, led his much more ecstatic pupil al-Hallaj to utter provocative statements about his own mystical experiences, which eventually led to al-Hallaj's execution for blasphemy, one of the rare instances in Islam of such a punishment.

Further Reading

A work on al-Junayd is Ali Hassan Abdel-Kader, *The Life, Personality and Writings of al-Junayd* (1962). □

Carl Gustav Jung

The Swiss psychologist and psychiatrist Carl Gustav Jung (1875-1961) was a founder of modern depth psychology.

Carl Jung was born on July 26, 1875, in Kesswil, the son of a Protestant clergyman. When he was 4, the family moved to Basel. As he grew older, his keen interest in biology, zoology, paleontology, philosophy, and the history of religion made the choice of a career quite difficult. However, he finally decided on medicine, which he studied at the University of Basel (1895-1900). He received his medical degree from the University of Zurich in 1902. Later he studied psychology in Paris.

In 1903 Jung married Emma Rauschenbach, his loyal companion and scientific collaborator until her death in 1955. The couple had five children. They lived in Küsnacht on the Lake of Zurich, where Jung died on June 6, 1961.

Jung began his professional career in 1900 as an assistant to Eugen Bleuler at the psychiatric clinic of the University of Zurich. During these years of his internship, Jung, with a few associates, worked out the so-called association experiment. This is a method of testing used to reveal affectively significant groups of ideas in the unconscious region of the psyche. They usually have a disturbing influence, promoting anxieties and unadapted emotions which are not under the control of the person concerned. Jung coined the term "complexes" for their designation.

Association with Freud

When Jung read Sigmund Freud's *Interpretation of Dreams,* he found his own ideas and observations to be essentially confirmed and furthered. He sent his publication *Studies in Word Association* (1904) to Freud, and this was the beginning of their collaboration and friendship, which lasted from 1907 to 1913. Jung was eager to explore the secrets of the unconscious psyche expressed by dreaming, fantasies, myths, fairy tales, superstition, and occultism. But Freud had already worked out his theories about the underlying cause of every psychoneurosis and also his doctrine that all the expressions of the unconscious are hidden wish fulfillments. Jung felt more and more that these theories were scientific presumptions which did not do full justice to the rich expressions of unconscious psychic life. For him the unconscious not only is a disturbing factor causing psychic illnesses but also is fundamentally the seed of man's creativeness and the roots of human consciousness. With such ideas Jung came increasingly into conflict with Freud, who regarded Jung's ideas as unscientific. Jung accused Freud of dogmatism; Freud and his followers reproached Jung for mysticism.

Topology and Archetypes

His break with Freud caused Jung much distress. Thrown back upon himself, he began a deepened self-analysis in order to gain all the integrity and firmness for his own quest into the dark labyrinth of the unconscious psyche. During the years from 1913 to 1921 Jung published only three important papers: "Two Essays on Analytical Psychology" (1916, 1917) and "Psychological Types" (1921). The "Two Essays" provided the basic ideas from which his later work sprang. He described his research on psychological typology (extro- and introversion, thinking, feeling, sensation, and intuition as psychic functions) and expressed the idea that it is the "personal equation" which, often unconsciously but in accordance with one's own typology, influences the approach of an individual toward the outer and inner world. Especially in psychology, it is impossible for an observer to be completely objective, because his observation depends on subjective, personal presuppositions. This insight made Jung suspicious of any dogmatism.

Next to his typology, Jung's main contribution was his discovery that man's fantasy life, like the instincts, has a certain structure. There must be imperceptible energetic centers in the unconscious which regulate instinctual behavior and spontaneous imagination. Thus emerge the dominants of the collective unconscious, or the archetypes. Spontaneous dreams exist which show an astonishing resemblance to ancient mythological or fairy-tale motifs that are usually unknown to the dreamer. To Jung this meant that archetypal manifestations belong to man in all ages; they are the expression of man's basic psychic nature. Modern civilized man has built a rational superstructure and repressed his dependence on his archetypal nature—hence the feeling of self-estrangement, which is the cause of many neurotic sufferings.

In order to study archetypal patterns and processes, Jung visited so-called primitive tribes. He lived among the Pueblo Indians of New Mexico and Arizona in 1924/1925 and among the inhabitants of Mt. Elgon in Kenya during 1925/1926. He later visited Egypt and India. To Jung, the religious symbols and phenomenology of Buddhism and Hinduism and the teachings of Zen Buddhism and Confucianism all expressed differentiated experiences on the way to man's inner world, a world which was badly neglected by Western civilization. Jung also searched for traditions in Western culture which compensated for its one-sided extroverted development toward rationalism and technology. He found these traditions in Gnosticism, Christian mysticism, and, above all, alchemy. For Jung, the weird alchemical texts were astonishing symbolic expressions for the human experience of the processes in the unconscious. Some of his major works are deep and lucid psychological interpretations of alchemical writings, showing their living significance for understanding dreams and the hidden motifs of neurotic and mental disorders.

Process of Individuation

Of prime importance to Jung was the biography of the stages of inner development and of the maturation of the personality, which he termed the "process of individuation." He described a strong impulse from the unconscious to guide the individual toward its specific, most complete uniqueness. This achievement is a lifelong task of trial and error and of confronting and integrating contents of the unconscious. It consists in an ever-increasing self-knowledge and in "becoming what you are." But individuation also includes social responsibility, which is a great step on the way to self-realization.

Jung lived for his explorations, his writings, and his psychological practice, which he had to give up in 1944 due to a severe heart attack. His academic appointments during the course of his career included the professorship of medical psychology at the University of Basel and the titular professorship of philosophy from 1933 until 1942 on the faculty of philosophical and political sciences of the Federal Institute of Technology in Zurich. In 1948 he founded the C. G. Jung Institute in Zurich. Honorary doctorates were conferred on him by many important universities all over the world.

Further Reading

Jung's writings are being assembled in the 18-volume *Collected Works* (1953—). Studies of Jung's life and work include Gerhard Adler, *Studies in Analytical Psychology* (1948); Frieda Fordham, *An Introduction to Jung's Psychology* (1953); Ira Progoff, *Jung's Psychology and Its Social Meaning* (1953); Richard I. Evans, *Conversations with Carl Jung* (1964); E. A. Bennett, *What Jung Really Said* (1967); and Aniela Jaffé, *From the Life and Work of C. G. Jung* (1970). □

Leo Jung

The rabbi Leo Jung (1892-1987) provided practical and theological leadership to American Orthodox Judaism, helping it become more dignified and responsive to the needs of contemporary Jews while retaining traditional rabbinical values and laws.

When Leo Jung (born June 20, 1892, in Ungarisch Brod in Moravia) first came to the United States in 1920 he was charged with hypocrisy. Americans could not believe that an intellectual rabbi, who spoke in elegant English and whose approach to Judaism was sophisticated and modern, could be truly Orthodox. After more than 60 years that mistake (ludicrous even in its own day) was unthinkable; by the 1980s American Jewish Orthodoxy itself demonstrated a dignity, intellectualism, and responsiveness to modernity that resulted in no small measure from the work of Jung.

A Life Dedicated to Orthodox Judaism

Jung was educated in both secular German studies and in traditional Hebraica by a father who understood the challenges of the modern world and who was totally committed to Jewish tradition. By 1910 Jung had graduated his gymnasium *summa cum laude* and matriculated at Vienna University while pursuing training at Orthodox Yeshivot as well. From 1911 to 1914 he was in Berlin studying at the Hildesheimer Rabbinical Seminary and gleaning secular scholarship from various German universities, including the University of Berlin and Geissen University, in which he pursued doctoral studies with a thesis on the concept of God in Anglo-Saxon philosophy.

The outbreak of World War I prevented completion of this course of study. From 1914 to 1920 he was in England studying at Cambridge (1916-1919) and earning both a bachelor's and a master's degree, obtaining three rabbinical ordinations, and beginning his practical rabbinical work. In 1920 he returned briefly to Germany to gain a definitive rabbinical ordination from the Hildesheimer Seminary. Both his intellectual training and personal qualities were evident in the variety of his achievements in England.

From his first years as rabbi of Congregation Kenesset Israel in Cleveland, Ohio, he began pioneer work transforming American Orthodox Judaism. He fought for decorum in worship and for improved Jewish education, creating a movement directed at the needs of Orthodox Jewish youth. In 1922 he left Cleveland to become spiritual leader of the New York Jewish Center, where he remained as rabbi for 50 years, becoming emeritus rabbi upon his retirement in 1976. His concern for practical issues led him to head the Beth Jacob Movement for the Religious Education of Women, to chair the New York State Government Advisory Board on Kosher Law Enforcement from 1935 to 1965, and to accept chairmanship of the cultural committee of the American Joint Distribution Committee, beginning in 1940, working for the good of European Jews. In that capacity he helped bring more than 9,000 refugees to the United States. Although associated with the Agudath Israel group within Jewish Orthodoxy, he resigned in 1929 to protest its anti-Zionist stance.

Jung's sensitivity to pressing issues of his day was reflected in his academic and professional work. His approach to worship emphasized meeting modern esthetic standards while remaining true to traditional regulations. He championed an atmosphere of decorum, dignity, and sanctity in the Orthodox Jewish synagogue. At the same time he spoke out against the insularity of many Orthodox rabbinical leaders and castigated Jewish intellectuals who rejected the Judaic tradition without fully knowing its content. He was sensitive to the changing needs of the American Jewish community, speaking out on behalf of Orthodoxy, offering critical analysis on such questions as Jewish intermarriage, proselytism and conversion, love and family life, and business ethics. His academic interests focused on ethics, which he taught at Yeshiva University for more than 40 years beginning in 1931. He became professor emeritus upon his retirement in 1968. He also taught at the university's Stern College for Women, where he introduced a course in ethics in 1956.

Writings on Everyday Problems

Jung's writings display an engaging and wide-ranging competence. He wrote or edited more than 31 books. His most ambitious task, beginning in 1928, was to serve as editor of the Jewish Library, to which he also contributed original essays. Jung was the only American contributor to the prestigious Soncino translation of the Babylonian Talmud (the foundation of rabbinical Jewish law and thought). He was not an ivory tower academic. Constantly aware of contemporary needs, he wrote in response to critical questions of Jewish life. The observance of Jewish law and the problems of living as an Orthodox Jew in a secular environment were dealt with seriously, sympathetically, but always from the perspective of a committed traditional Jew. He taught it was more important to "judaize" the modern world than to modernize Judaism—an approach mirroring that of the German Jewish thinker Samson Raphael Hirsch, whose influence Jung acknowledged.

Theologically Jung confronted the problem of evil, whether experienced as the trauma of Jewish history and particularly the Nazi Holocaust, or in personal tragedy. He contended that misery was not an argument against God but rather a challenge for human beings, that free will is not only a blessing but also a demand. Jung believed the Torah, Jewish teaching, is a way of peace and truth, but that human evil perverts it and engenders sorrow and distress. Jung's ability to listen sympathetically to those in pain could bring them slowly to recognize the enduring and eternal presence of God and the value of Jewish tradition amid their distress.

Jung's most impressive work involved Jewish ethics. His moral writings are not abstract and distant. He wrote about such subjects as business ethics, the needs of the poor, and interhuman obligations. A collection of his writings—*Between Man and Man*—has been revised and expanded a number of times and translated into Hebrew. The title demonstrates his practical concerns with human relationships. Daily acts of kindness no less than dramatic deeds are considered acts of self-sacrifice.

The Hebrew term for such sacrifice is *kiddush hashem* —the sanctification of God's name. Jung wrote at length on the meaning of holiness (*kedushah*) and of the love of God and others. His theoretical exposition of sanctification, both in ritual and ethics, is persuasive: the purpose of being a human is to bring God into the world and make the world more holy. His essays on Jewish ethics as a means of sanctification provided a fitting foundation for his practical and educational efforts.

Despite his age and his emeritus status, Jung remained active at the Jewish Center in Manhattan until his death in 1987.

Further Reading

A useful sketch of Jung the man and the religious leader is found in Nima H. Alderblum's essay "Leo Jung" included in *The Leo Jung Jubilee Volume,* edited by Menahem M. Kasher, et al. (1962). Jung's autobiography, *The Path of a Pioneer* (London, 1981), provided important information and insight about his life and character as well as about the struggles involved in being a modern Orthodox Jewish leader. The most recent dialogue on Jung's legacy can be found in *Reverence, Righteousness and Rahamanut: Essays in Memory of Rabbi Dr. Leo Jung,* edited by Jacob J. Schacter (Baltimore, 1996). □

tihumanistic and indeed totalitarian cast. Analogies with fascistic doctrines may be easily discerned in these works that define freedom as total identification with the mass will. But Jünger was not a member of the Nazi party; a group with which he had connections, the National Bolsheviks, was broken up by the Gestapo in 1937. He himself, however, was protected by his high military friends.

Jünger's novel *Auf den Marmorklippen* (1939; *On the Marble Cliffs*), his best-known work, shows an evolution of attitude and is generally regarded as an allegorical critique of Hitlerism and of the totalitarian state. The book appeared in December 1939 and was suddenly banned in the spring of 1940. *Auf den Marmorklippen* portrays the violence with which a peaceful culture, reflected in the secluded lives of two practicing botanists, is overrun and destroyed by the hordes of a tyrant known as the Head Forester. The language is highly colored, recondite, strange, and brutal. The apostrophe of "Spirit," of science and humanism, which seems to be the message of the book, is perhaps somewhat belied by the exultancy with which the violence is described.

Jünger served in the German army once more, from 1939 to 1944. His subsequent novels, *Heliopolis* (1949) and *Gläserne Bienen* (1957; *Glass Bees*), restate the central issue of the conflict between reason and instinct, contemplation and action. He also published several volumes of essays and diaries.

Ernst Jünger

The German author Ernst Jünger (born 1895) was one of the most original and influential German writers and intellectuals of the 20th century.

Ernst Jünger was born on March 29, 1895, in Heidelberg, the son of a druggist. At the age of 16 he ran away from school and enlisted in the Foreign Legion. Extricated by his family, he volunteered for war service in 1914; wounded 14 times, he was decorated in 1918. Subsequently Jünger studied botany and zoology at Leipzig and Naples. His war experience and his scientific experience are the two poles of his life, his subject matter, and his vocabulary and imagery.

Jünger first wrote a series of essentially autobiographical war diaries, *In Stahlgewittern* (1920; *In Storms of Steel*), *Der Kampf als inneres Erlebnis* (1922; *Battle as Inner Experience*), *Das Wäldchen 125* (1925; *Wood 125*), and *Feuer und Blut* (1926; *Fire and Blood*). He blends stark realism— indeed brutality—of detail with a language that is often intoxicated, highly stylized, or apodictic; he glorifies the primacy of instinctual life and imputes to Western democracy "the metaphysics of the restaurant-car."

Involved in politics in the late 1920s, in 1931 Jünger published *Die totale Mobilmachung* (*Total Mobilization*) and in 1932 *Der Arbeiter* (*The Worker*). His concept of the total mobilization of society and his view of the worker as a mere integer in a technological world have an an-

Further Reading

Joseph Peter Stern, *Ernst Jünger* (1953), is an excellent, penetrating analysis of Jünger's strengths and weaknesses. Good short discussions may also be found in Jethro Bithell, *Modern German Literature* (1939; 3d ed. 1959), and in H. M. Waidson, *The Modern German Novel* (1959). □

Ernest Just

Ernest Just (1883-1941) was a prominent African American biologist who was noted for his contributions to marine biology.

Ernest Everett Just was born on August 14, 1883, in Charleston, South Carolina. He had a rough childhood; his father died when he was very young, leaving his mother to fend for herself and her family. He was educated by his mother until the age of 13, when he entered the Colored Normal, Industrial, Agricultural and Mechanical College. He received a Licentiate of Instruction that permitted him to teach in the black public schools of South Carolina.

The prospects for advancement in the school system were small, however, and Just wanted to continue his education. He thus obtained a scholarship to attend the Kimball Union Academy in Vermont, where he was the only African American in a group of 170 students. There he received a broad education, and he was able to continue his schooling at Dartmouth, where he won a degree in biology with a minor in history in 1907. Just soon obtained a teaching position at Howard University, the most prestigious African American institution in the country at the time. He helped to develop the science curriculum there, largely by teaching zoology and setting up laboratories.

Determined to pursue the same type of career that a white man would have in science, Just started spending his summers as research assistant at the famed Marine Biology Laboratory in Woods Hole, Massachusetts. There he worked under Frank Lillie, the head of the Zoology Department of the University of Chicago. Lillie helped him enroll "in absentia" in the Ph.D. program at the University of Chicago, and after considerable delay, due mostly to his teaching responsibilities at Howard, he received his Ph.D. in 1916, becoming one of the first African Americans to do so.

Throughout his life Just had problems obtaining funding for his work, partly because of racial discrimination and partly due to the general lack of funding for science during the Great Depression of the 1930s. He continued to teach on and off at Howard for the remainder of his life. He also went to Europe several times, having achieved greater recognition there than in his own country. Just preferred Europe to the United States. In 1938 he went to France with the intention of staying for good. In the middle of 1940, however, the Nazis drove him out, and he was forced to return to Washington, D.C., where he died on October 27, 1941.

During the earlier stages of his career Just was primarily concerned with collecting a mass of verifiable data on marine eggs. He concentrated on some of the fundamental problems of cell biology, and in particular dealt with the problem of parthenogenesis, or the ability of certain types of eggs to reproduce without sperm. He developed a precise and much respected style of experimentation and was considered an authority on experimentation with marine invertebrates. He wrote a number of well-received articles on experimental methods that was later collected in a volume entitled *Basic Methods for Experiments on Eggs of Marine Animals* (1939).

Once Just became an established scientist with a worldwide reputation he started concentrating on a theory that had been brewing in his mind for several years. He theorized that the outer part of the cell (the cortical cytoplasm) was more significant in vital life processes than had been previously recognized. He thought, in fact, that it was a crucial link between an animal and its environment. One way he used to show this was by showing that the fertilization of an egg was independent of how mature it was and that the cytoplasm thus became important in the fertilization process.

While in France, Just wrote a book with Hedwig Schnetzler, his second wife and research assistant, entitled *The Biology of the Cell Surface* (1939). He explained this theory, along with many of his past scientific achievements, in this book. He also categorized biological experimentation and claimed that it fell into three categories: experiments done on living systems, those done on killed living systems, and those done on nonliving systems. He showed the importance of the purity of the system being tested, which was an aspect that had not been emphasized enough by most biologists. Finally, the book was also somewhat of a philosophical treatise, endeavoring to answer the question "what is life?"

Just was also known for his work on cell morphology (the form and the changes in form of a cell), and in particular cell division, the process by which living cells reproduce themselves. Because of his problems with funding, with certain members of the American scientific community, and with racial discrimination, Just was never able to undertake a major research project. However, the accumulation of his work is important to the field of marine biology. His achievements were particularly significant and encouraging to the African American scientists that succeeded him.

Further Reading

The complete story of Ernest Just's life—both the personal and the professional aspects of it—is presented in the biography by Kenneth R. Manning, *Black Apollo of Science: the Life of Ernest Everett Just* (1983). □

Justinian I

Justinian I (ca. 482-565) was Byzantine emperor from 527 to 565. Ruling in a transitional epoch, he was both a conscious steward of the past and a pragmatic innovator.

The Roman Empire in the 4th century was an all-Mediterranean Christian state with an Eastern focus. But in the 5th century it was shattered by internal dissensions and eroded by barbarian attacks. Various Germanic tribes dismantled the Western provinces and established their own regional kingdoms, such as those of the Visigoths in Spain, the Vandals in North Africa, the Franks in Gaul, and the Ostrogoths in Italy. As recognized upholders of the continuing Roman imperial tradition, the Eastern line of emperors in Constantinople survived barbarian dangers, thanks to the richer resources of the Eastern provinces. But they faced internal strife, regional unrest, and sectarian religious controversy in these provinces. Subsequent developments in the 7th century would make the Eastern provinces into what we call the "Byzantine" Empire, with a more distinct Greek character. But in the 6th century Justinian could still see his mission as a Latin one, requiring him to restore the Christian Roman world of the past.

Rise to Power

Justinian was born Flavius Petrus Sabbatius in the Macedonian Balkans; his parents were of Latin-speaking Thracian-Illyrian peasant background. All we know of his youth is that he was taken under the wing of his uncle Justin, who brought him to Constantinople for an education. The youth adopted the name Justinianus out of gratitude. Fol-

lowing thorough schooling, which left him with a particular taste for theology, Justinian was further aided by his uncle to rapid advancement in the army.

When the childless Anastasius I died in 518, Justin was unexpectedly made emperor, at age 66, as Justin I. Outmaneuvering rivals, Justinian rose to ever higher positions, becoming Caesar in 525 and finally being made coemperor and successor in early 527. It was also at this time that Justinian arranged to marry Theodora, thereby acquiring an important helpmate and also giving his age one of its most striking personalities.

When Justin I died on Aug. 1, 527, Justinian and Theodora succeeded without contest. During the first 4 years the mounting burden of governmental expenses made the regime oppressive and unpopular, while Justinian's autocracy provoked the old senatorial aristocracy. The so-called Nika Riots of Jan. 13-18, 532, which began as rioting among the circus factions of the Hippodrome, amplified into demands for changes in governmental policies and were finally converted by aristocratic opportunism into an effort to dethrone Justinian. The Emperor rallied his troops under some loyal generals, like Belisarius, and had them massacre the rioters. The mob broken, Justinian punished the conspirators, thus crushing both popular and aristocratic opposition for the time being.

External Policies

The bulk of Justinian's era was marked by war, partly sought, partly unsought. The unwanted war, which he had inherited, was with Sassanid Persia, the empire's one fully civilized neighbor. The accession of a new Persian king, Chosroes (Khosrow) I, in 531 made peace possible, and while the "Perpetual Peace" negotiated in 532 cost Justinian a veiled obligation to pay tribute, it freed him for his projects of territorial reconquest in the West. Jealous of Justinian's subsequent successes, however, Chosroes broke the peace in 540 by invading Syria-Palestine and devastating Antioch. Still committed in the West, Justinian was plunged into new war with Persia for almost all of his remaining reign. Only in 562 was the Fifty-year Peace agreed upon, requiring even heavier tribute payments to Persia.

By contrast, Justinian's wars in the West were part of his grand design. Justinian never considered himself merely an Eastern emperor, and his empire had never officially accepted the loss of its territory, which always remained legally Roman and subject to eventual recovery. Thus, the Germanic successor states in the West were regarded as temporary interlopers, and their rulers as Arian Christians, therefore heretics. As Roman emperor, Justinian was obligated to liberate these lands and restore them to imperial rule.

Because the Franks were so distant and were not Arian heretics, Justinian made no hostile plans against them. Visigothic Spain was virtually ignored until late in the reconquest program; only in 550 was a small force sent to Spain.

The two primary targets were Vandal North Africa and Ostrogothic Italy. The Vandal kingdom was quickly destroyed by Justinian's brilliant general Belisarius in 533-534. Two years later operations were begun against Italy. Belisarius eventually negotiated a settlement with the Ostrogoths in 540, but this was only short-lived. An Ostrogothic resurgence threatened to undo this work, and so Belisarius was restored to command in Italy. But Justinian supported him so inadequately that the war drifted indecisively until the Emperor then gave fuller backing to a new commander, Narses, who defeated the Ostrogoths decisively in two battles during 552. Further campaigning completed the pacification of Italy. Nevertheless, the region had been brutally ravaged by endless warfare that had shattered its prosperity and had left it exposed to renewed German invasion by the Lombards only a few years after Justinian's death. Nor was North Africa free of prolonged war; despite the rapid Vandal collapse, the unruly Berber tribes of the hills tied imperial forces down for decades. In both sectors, the expected rapid reannexation turned into interminable war, which continuously drained the empire's manpower and money.

Justinian's foreign relations were not entirely warlike. Anxious to free the empire's commercial life from dependency on Persian middlemen, he sought new trade routes, and his cooperation with the Christian kingdom of Abyssinia realized this aim briefly. But as his wars else-where strained his resources, Justinian relied increasingly upon diplomacy as a substitute for strength. The Balkan provinces suffered the most for this juggling. Denuded of adequate defenses, they were left exposed to new marauders, such as

the Hunnic tribes and the vanguard of the Slavs, soon to be joined by the Asiatic Avars.

Internal Policies

To fill public needs neglected by previous regimes and to leave his own stamp upon the scene, Justinian built lavishly in all parts of his empire: fortresses and works of regional defense, structures of public utility and practical function, buildings for urban adornment, and, above all, churches and monasteries. Among his greatest buildings was his reconstruction of the Temple of the Holy Wisdom, or Sancta (Hagia) Sophia, in Constantinople, one of the supreme monuments of all Christian architecture.

Equally ambitious to leave institutional monuments, Justinian initiated a total overhauling of the empire's legal system. In the Corpus Juris Civilis his commissioners assembled a systematic exposition of the basic legal texts and the essential interpretational literature that summed up the great heritage of Roman law and preserved it for transmission to later generations. Less glorious, however, was the more practical side of his own legislative record. Justinian issued decrees on all aspects of his society's life. His goal was the noble one of a just government, but as the costs of his undertakings mounted, he was obliged to sacrifice it to the more urgent needs for immediate money and to allow his government to become ruthlessly oppressive.

Justinian was anxious to end religious disunity within the empire. The chief theological issue of his day was the persisting Monophysite rejection of the decisions of the Council of Chalcedon (451) regarding the natures of Christ. Since the Monophysite religious dissent was linked with regional unrest, especially in Syria-Palestine and Egypt, the problem had wide political implications. Justinian repeatedly sought to end the dissension, either by some compromise formula or device or by arbitrary pressures. His policies alternated between extremes of conciliation and persecution. At Justinian's behest, the Fifth Ecumenical Council met (553) to ratify some of his measures. Yet, for all his exertions, a resolution of the issues seemed even less attainable at the end of his reign than at the beginning.

Later Years

During 542-543 the worst plague before the 14th-century Black Death ravaged the Mediterranean world, leaving the population depleted for generations. Theodora's death of cancer in 548 was a cruel personal loss to Justinian. The deteriorating Balkan defenses exposed even the capital to dangerous barbarian attacks. Religious strife, economic ruin, popular disaffection—all reached new peaks. As a result, Justinian's death on Nov. 14, 565, was greeted with popular rejoicing.

Further Reading

The chief contemporary historian of Justinian's age was Procopius of Caesarea, whose complete works were translated by H. B. Dewing for the Loeb Classical Library series (7 vols., 1914-1940). The fullest account of Justinian's reign in English is John B. Bury, *History of the Later Roman Empire from the Death of Theodosius I to the Death of Justinian,* vol. 1

(1923). John W. Barker, *Justinian and the Later Roman Empire* (1966), puts the reign within the context of the 3d-8th centuries. Percy N. Ure, *Justinian and His Age* (1951), is a provocative short account from a classicist's point of view. Robert Browning, *Justinian and Theodora* (1971), is a lively narrative, richly illustrated.

Glanville Downey, *Constantinople in the Age of Justinian* (1960), gives a lively picture of the period, while the same author's paperback, *The Late Roman Empire* (1969), is a concise digest that includes a discussion of Justinian's era. Aleksandr A. Vasiliev, *Justin the First: An Introduction to the Epoch of Justinian the Great* (1950), is the indispensable introduction to Justinian's reign. Valuable information on Justinian's era is in Arnold H. M. Jones's massive *The Later Roman Empire, 284-602: A Social, Economic and Administrative Survey* (2 vols., 1964). Also useful is William Gordon Holmes, *The Age of Justinian and Theodora: A History of the Sixth Century A.D.* (2 vols., 1905-1907; 2d ed. 1912). □

St. Justin Martyr

St. Justin Martyr (ca. 100-ca. 165) is the first Christian apologist of non-Jewish heritage whose writings have survived.

Justin was born near the site of modern Nablus, Israel, of parents who practiced the Roman religion. By 132 he had become a Christian and had studied philosophy at Greek schools. He then traveled and spoke about the Christian religion, entering into violent controversies with non-Christians (Romans, Greeks, and Jews). He finally established himself in Rome, where he taught and composed his books.

Of Justin's writings only a portion survive: his two *Apologies* and his *Dialogus*. These works, however, preserve his method of explaining Christianity to new or possible converts and his method of argument in controversy. Justin was well grounded in Greek philosophy and Greco-Roman mythology. He adapted Platonism to suit his doctrinal and apologist functions, and he translated the Platonic doctrine of the Logos into a new form—the *logos spermatikos*. Logos was God's message of salvation for men. Justin held that fragments and pieces of Christianity were to be found, like seeds, in the religions and in the thinkers preceding Christianity but that only Jesus had given the full revelation of the Logos. He knew Judaism well and had a thorough knowledge of Latin and Greek literature. Many of his concepts and terms are derived from the Stoics of his day.

Justin's method of explaining Christianity follows a pattern. He first tackles the objections of non-Christians that Christians are atheists or seditious revolutionaries plotting the overthrow of the Roman state. He then illustrates the preeminence of Christianity by describing its ethicomoral code and its doctrine. He also compares these with the dogmas of the Greco-Roman religion; and he describes the way in which Christian worship, prayer, and way of life differ from the Roman way and thus demonstrates the truth and beauty of Christianity.

In his controversies, Justin sets up a straw man, Trypho, who speaks for Greco-Roman religion. The tone is anti-Jewish. Justin holds that Christianity eliminated the need for Judaism. From Judaism he derived a millenarist theory (there will be a final period, 1,000 years in length, of prosperity and peace before the end of the world). He condemned Judaism because, he said, Christianity had inherited all that was valuable, religiously, doctrinally, and messianically, in Judaism. Thus Judaism as a religion had been evacuated of all meaning and value. This became common doctrine in the Christian Church and persisted into the 20th century.

Scholars find the writings of Justin very informative about Christianity at the beginning of the 2d century. He knew the Gospels of Matthew, Mark, Luke, and John. He described the prevalent Christian worship, which included the essential elements of the modern Mass, and he stated that sections of the Gospels and the Jewish prophets were read at liturgical gatherings. His other source of importance is that he constitutes some sort of bridge between the early Judeo-Christianity of the first Christians in Palestine and the Western type of Christianity that became dominant about the 4th century. He died by execution between 163 and 167. It is said that his opponents denounced him to the authorities as seditious.

Further Reading

A scholarly yet readable study is the work by Leslie William Barnard, *Justin Martyr: His Life and Thought* (1967), the first major work on Justin Martyr since the 1920s. Archibald Robertson, *The Origins of Christianity* (1954; rev. ed. 1962), devotes a chapter to Justin Martyr. Also useful is Henry Chadwick, *Early Christian Thought and the Classical Tradition* (1966). □

Agustin Pedro Justo

Agustin Pedro Justo (1876-1943) was an Argentine general and president who instituted vigorous antidepression measures in the 1930s and favored the democracies during World War II.

B orn in Concepción del Uruguay, Entre Ríos, on Feb. 26, 1876, Agustin Pedro Justo was the son of Agustin P. Justo, who had been a congressional deputy and governor of Corrientes Province, and Otilia Rolón Justo. After being deposed in 1871, Governor Justo moved to Entre Ríos and later to Buenos Aires.

Young Justo's military career began in 1888, when he entered the Colegio Militar, the national military academy. He graduated in 1892 as a sublieutenant; later he served in the Colegio as a mathematics professor (1904-1915) and as director (1915-1922), rising to the rank of colonel. As President Marcelo Alvear's war minister (1922-1928), he completely reorganized and reequipped the army, thereby earning lasting favor with politically active officers.

The 1929 Depression soon led to military revolts, and Justo joined former military associates in overthrowing the aged president, Hipólito Irigoyen, in 1930. Gen. José Félix Uriburu served as provisional president until 1932, when conservatives elected Justo to that office. During the worsening economic crisis of 1933, Justo reacted to a radical conspiracy by arresting Irigoyen for 2 months. Local election frauds and violence aggravated the tense political situation, and by 1935 radicals controlled the Chamber of Deputies.

An honest and vigorous executive, Justo fought the Depression with remedial economic legislation and a public works program. These measures slightly improved the economy but did not satisfy radical opponents or increase his popularity.

In international affairs Justo's capable foreign minister, Carlos Saavedra Lamas, helped to end the Chaco War between Peru and Bolivia. A trade agreement with Great Britain guaranteed Argentine beef a market in return for concessions to British investors. With a world war threatening, Justo reactivated Argentine participation in the League of Nations, and Buenos Aires hosted the 1936 Pan American Conference, which Franklin D. Roosevelt attended in an effort to promote hemispheric solidarity against aggressor nations.

Before Justo quietly relinquished the presidency in 1938, his son's death in an airplane accident aroused some public sympathy. After touring Europe, Justo reentered politics. When the European war broke out in 1939, he supported the Allies and offered his personal services to Brazil after that country declared war on the Axis in 1942. He was considered a serious presidential candidate for the coming elections, when he died suddenly in Buenos Aires on Jan. 11, 1943. Although a conservative, Justo had opposed the forces of repression and aggression at home and abroad. Throughout his life he was respected as an intellectual and bibliophile.

Further Reading

International affairs during Justo's administration are reviewed in Harold F. Peterson, *Argentina and the United States, 1810-1960* (1964). For Argentina's political and economic affairs see James R. Scobie, *Argentina: A City and a Nation* (1964). □

Filippo Juvara

Filippo Juvara (1678-1736), the greatest Italian architect of the 18th century, was an immensely imaginative and prolific designer.

Filippo Juvara was born in Messina, Sicily, on March 27, 1678, the son of a silversmith. In Messina he would have seen the buildings of Guarino Guarini, but at this stage of his career he was probably equally influenced by the exuberant fantasy associated with his father's trade and his Sicilian background, so that it is not surprising to find him practicing as a stage designer in later years.

In 1703 or 1704 Juvara went to Rome and began to work under Carlo Fontana, the most celebrated architectural teacher of the age. Fontana is said to have told Juvara to forget everything he had ever learned and to start all over again: this may well be true, since Fontana's late baroque style was much more classical than the—presumably riotous—fantasy of Juvara's imagination at that time.

From 1708 to 1714 Juvara worked in Rome for Cardinal Ottoboni as a stage designer and architect. Juvara's early architectural style is obscure, but a sketchbook dating from the decade he spent in Rome is evidence of his inventiveness. All his life he designed ornament and decoration in a rich and exuberant style, but the classical discipline he learned from Fontana provided an effective restraint.

In 1714 Juvara returned to Sicily to design a royal palace for Victor Amadeus II of Savoy, who had just become king of Sicily, but within a few months he was established as the royal architect in Turin. Juvara did an immense amount of work in Turin in a short time, including the planning of two quarters of the city and the designing of four royal residences, palaces for individual nobles, and five churches.

Juvara traveled to Portugal in 1719-1720, designing a royal palace at Mafra and other buildings, and to London and Paris in 1720. In 1735 he went to Madrid to design another royal palace; he died there, suddenly, on Jan. 31 or Feb. 1, 1736.

Juvara's Palazzo Madama in Turin (1718-1721) is a splendid combination of the traditional Italian palace type with the regal elements of Versailles, the object of every prince's envy at that time. The Palazzo Madama contains a superb staircase hall, unusual in Italy, but a feature of Versailles. His huge royal hunting lodge at Stupinigi near Turin (1729-1733) also shows French influence.

The architect's masterpiece is the church and monastery of La Superga (1716/1717-1731), set high on a mountain overlooking Turin with a stupendous view of the Alps. This was a votive offering from the King and is therefore richly decorated. The combination of the huge dome set between two towers (perhaps a reminiscence of Francesco Borromini's S. Agnese in Rome and Christopher Wren's St. Paul's in London) and the long, low buildings of the monastery gives a picturesque outline to the whole and is very close to similar scenic compositions in the monasteries at Melk, Austria, and Einsiedeln, Switzerland, which are almost exactly contemporary.

Further Reading

The best account of Juvara's work is in Rudolf Wittkower, *Art and Architecture in Italy, 1600-1750* (1958; 2d rev. ed. 1965). □

Juvenal

Juvenal (died c. 127), or Decimus Junius Juvenalis, was the greatest of the Roman satirists. His bitter and rhetorical denunciations of Roman society, presented in a series of vivid pictures of Roman life, inspired all later satirists.

The life of Juvenal coincided with one of the most eventful periods of Roman history, one in which the weaknesses and failures of the government and the corruption and decadence of society were especially grave and evident. In reaction to this, Juvenal molded a new kind of satire, and he was able to impose it by his example on posterity.

An Undocumented Life

Juvenal was apparently almost completely unread between his own lifetime and the 4th century, when an attempt seems to have been made to compile his biography. This work, of which we have traces in over a dozen medieval biographies, seems to have been derived mainly from (occasionally misunderstood) passages in his works. As a result, the facts of his life are almost singularly lacking in certainty.

Juvenal was apparently born at Aquinum, a town in Latium. He spoke of himself as middle-aged in his first satire (the satires seem to be arranged in at least roughly chronological order), written shortly after 100; and in Satire XIII, the first satire of his last book, he refers to Juncus (consul in 127) as the recent consul. According to the medieval biographies, he lived to be over 80; if he was born about 50, this would fit the facts well enough, but it is only a guess.

We know nothing certain about Juvenal's life and activities before he started writing his satires. An inscription found at Aquinum tells of a dedication to Ceres by a——nius Juvenalis who was a military tribune, held high public office in Aquinum, and was a priest of the deified Vespasian. But the inscription may refer not to the poet but to some other member of the family, and the date is uncertain.

Martial knew Juvenal and calls him "eloquent" in the 90s, suggesting, as do the general tone of his poems and the vividness of his bleak picture of the teacher's life, that Juvenal may have been a rhetorician, although it might refer to his having been an advocate. He was certainly poor and knew the miseries of a client intimately; if Satire XI was written from personal experience, late in life he acquired a modest farm at Tibur (Tivoli) and a small house in Rome. Juvenal's references to the great figures of the day do not seem to imply familiarity.

According to the tradition of some very late ancient writers, Juvenal was banished because of the anger of an actor, the Emperor's favorite (supposedly at some lines in Satire VII). The time and place of exile are uncertain because of the conflicting evidence handed down to us.

His Satires

Juvenal's 16 satires were apparently issued in 5 separate books. The first book, written sometime after 100, consists of Satires I-V and contains savage attacks on the city of Rome and the physical dangers and discomforts of life there, which were accompanied by social corruption and sexual degeneration. Book I is characterized by a greater scope and generality of attack and less use of specific virtues and vices to serve as the focus of the exposition than are any of the later books.

The first satire is programmatic. In Rome, he declares, "it is difficult *not* to write satire . . . even if nature does not allow you to write verse, your indignation will write it for you." A brilliant series of pictures of disgusting parvenus, forgers, poisoners, informers, and fortune hunters is adduced as demonstration, and Juvenal angrily declares that money, obtained by whatever shameful or evil means might come to hand, is alone honored and "honesty is praised and freezes." Never have selfish luxury and cringing, dependent poverty been so prevalent or been accompanied by so much vice. But it is no longer safe to make personal attacks on great sinners, as it was in the time of Lucilius, and so, to avoid a horrible death, one must limit oneself to attacking the dead.

This Juvenal proceeds to do: when he is not using traditional type names, his attacks are on figures of the age of Domitian and Nero. For this he has often been accused of cowardice and irrelevance, but Juvenal clearly intended an oblique attack against the rich and powerful of his own time, whose practices and morals could hardly have changed very greatly from what they were under Nero and Domitian.

The other charge often made against him, that his indignation is as frequently spent with as much force against relatively harmless breaches of current standards of behavior as against the gravest crimes and grossest immoralities, can be answered as well. First, the outrage of the average man (which Juvenal always purports to be) is often as much exercised against, for example, harmless eccentricities of dress and personal appearance as against the darkest crimes and corruptions of the day. Second, the Stoic doctrine that the good man was totally good, and the evil completely evil, with no intermediate position being possible, had a great influence on Juvenal's thought. These attacks on minor breaches usually occur at the climax of one particular line of invective, where they can serve as wry, half-humorous anticlimaxes, thus pointing up the weaknesses and hypocrisies of conventional morality (like Mark Twain's young man who, after thefts and murders, gradually "sank" to lying, swearing, and breaking the Sabbath).

The second satire is a violent and explicit attack on the hypocrisy of those who pretend to be pillars of morality, yet are deep in vice and are thus worse than open offenders. Satire III was paraphrased by Samuel Johnson in his "London": it is an attack on the city of Rome, where wealth is everything and "poverty makes a man ridiculous" and subjects him to many annoyances, troubles, and dangers.

The fourth satire is a satirical account of the calling of a council of state by the tyrant Domitian—to discuss how to cook a giant turbot with which he had been presented. Its picture of the gathering of the councilors, frightened by the sudden, unexplained summons, each either compromised or sinister and evil in his own way, is unforgettable. Satire V is an indignant account of a client dining with his patron and being subjected to indignities by the servants and eating cheap food while his host dines luxuriously, all so that the patron can amuse himself at the discomfiture of his guest.

Satire VI, a separate book in itself, written after 115, is by far the longest satire and is often considered Juvenal's masterpiece. It scathingly attacks women, their vanities and affectations.

Satire VII is an account of the miseries which the writer and teacher of literature must endure. It opens with the anticipation of brighter prospects under the patronage of a new emperor who was interested in literature and so is probably to be dated shortly after the accession of Hadrian in 117. The eighth satire is on the subject of the superiority of virtue to noble birth and contains interesting pictures of the evil and degenerate aristocracy. Satire IX, one of the most amusing of the satires, is generally neglected because of the obscenity of its subject matter.

With the fourth book, critics have generally felt that a weakening of the satirical force becomes evident. Thereafter, the subjects and illustrations seem chosen less from life than from literature. No decline in excellence, however, can be noted in the tenth satire, paraphrased in Dr. Johnson's "Vanity of Human Wishes." Its subject is the foolishness of human desires, illustrated by brilliant vignettes, derived from history and mythology, on the evil ends to which great political power, eloquence, military glory, long life, and beauty have led their possessors. At the end he answers the question "What, then, should men pray for?" with the famous phrase "mens sana in corpore sano"—"a sound mind in a sound body."

The eleventh satire is a contrast between the extravagant follies of contemporary gourmandise and ancient austerities at the table and is couched in the form of an invitation to dinner at the satirist's humble farm at Tibur, where rustic simplicity will mark the fare. The twelfth satire consists of congratulations to a friend on his escape from a shipwreck, with observations on the distinction between true and false friendship.

The incomplete, final, fifth book consists of Satire XIII, written shortly after 127, which attempts to console a friend who has been cheated of some money by telling him that the true punishment for crime is a guilty conscience; XIV, on the influence of parental example in teaching their children to sin, which is linked to a long sermon on avarice; XV, a horrified account of a murder and cannibalism as the result of a feud between two Egyptian towns; and XVI, a fragment apparently originally intended to be part of a long satire on the military life.

General Characteristics and Influence

Juvenal was little read until a revival of interest in the 4th century, probably first in the circle of Servius, to whom

Juvenal's allusiveness and occasional obscurity gave ample field for the exercise of their learning and who appreciated the rhetorical style of his invective and the mastery of his Virgilian hexameters. The pagan poet Claudian and the Christian poets Ausonius and Prudentius imitated him.

After the revival of learning under Charlemagne, Juvenal became popular, and he was one of the most widely read Latin authors during the Middle Ages. To the medieval reader, he was primarily an ethical writer: his memorable phrases (some of which are still familiar, for instance, ''rara avis,'' ''bread and circuses,'' ''Who will guard the guards themselves?'') were prized, and his moral indignation was respected and admired. He is referred to by Geoffrey Chaucer, among others.

Juvenal's influence continued during and after the Renaissance, when he began to be read more for his style and his pictures of Roman life than as a moral handbook. Shakespeare refers to a passage by him in *Hamlet,* and Nicholas Boileau uses him as a model. In the 18th century John Dryden (who translated him) and Alexander Pope are permeated by the Juvenalian spirit, and Byron refers to him and clearly knew his work well.

Further Reading

The introductions to various (partial) editions of Juvenal's works in English are valuable, especially those of James D. Duff, *Saturae XIV: Fourteen Satires of Juvenal* (3d ed. by Michael Coffey, 1971, omitting Satires II and IX), and John E. B. Mayor, *Thirteen Satires of Juvenal* (5th ed., 2 vols., 1900-1901; repr. 1966, omitting Satires II, VI, and IX). Translations of Juvenal's works are *The Satires of Juvenal,* translated by Rolfe Humphries (1958), the most vivid, racy, and poetic rendering available in English; *Juvenal: Satires,* translated by Jerome Mazzaro (1965), with an introduction and explanatory notes; and *Juvenal: The Sixteen Satires,* translated with an introduction and notes by Peter Green (1967), which is faithful to the original Latin.

The standard work on Juvenal in English is Gilbert Highet, *Juvenal the Satirist* (1954), although the objection is usually made that Highet places too much reliance on the satires as a source for Juvenal's life. Good older appreciations of Juvenal are in H. E. Butler, *Post-Augustan Poetry from Seneca to Juvenal* (1909), and the two works of J. Wight Duff, *A Literary History of Rome in the Silver Age: From Tiberius to Hadrian* (1927; 3d ed., edited by A. M. Duff, 1964) and *Roman Satire: Its Outlook on Social Life* (1936). See also Inez Gertrude Scott, *The Grand Style in the Satires of Juvenal* (1927). □

K

Dmitri Kabalevsky

The Soviet composer, pianist, and conductor Dmitri Kabalevsky (1904-1987) was an important figure in the musical life of the Soviet Union. His compositions for children are among his best known and most successful works.

Dmitri Kabalevsky was born in St. Petersburg on December 30, 1904. In 1918 his family moved to Moscow, where he enrolled at the Scriabin Musical Institute. There he received formal instruction in music and piano. When he was only in his mid-teens he began giving piano lessons and composing simple pieces for his students. After leaving the institute in 1922 he continued to study intermittently with V. Selivanov (his piano teacher at the institute), taught piano, and played for silent movies.

In 1925 he entered the Moscow Conservatory, where he studied piano with Goldenweiser and composition with Catoire and, later, Miaskovsky. He began teaching composition at the conservatory in 1932 and was made a full professor in 1939. During these years he wrote his first major works and also served as senior editor at Muzgiz, the state-owned music publishing house. After he joined the Communist Party in 1940, he became a prominent personality in Soviet musical life and held important administrative positions in the musical establishment, including various offices in the Union of Soviet Composers, editor of *Sovetskaia Muzyka* (the official organ of the Union of Soviet Composers), head of the music department of the Soviet Radio Committee, and head of the music section of the Institute of Arts History in the Academy of Sciences. He was honored with the Order of Merit in 1940; with the Stalin

Prize three times—in 1946 for his Second String Quartet, in 1949 for his Violin Concerto, and in 1951 for his opera *The Taras Family*—and with the Order of Lenin in 1965.

As a spokesperson for official musical policy he frequently appeared on television, addressed factory and farm workers, wrote articles for domestic and foreign newspapers and journals, presented awards, and led delegations. In 1959 he was part of a small group of Soviet composers who visited the United States.

Kabalevsky composed operas, ballets, choral works, incidental music for plays and radio productions, film music, four symphonies, a number of concertos, chamber music, songs, and piano pieces. Of these works, the best known in the West are the overture to his opera *Colas Breugnon, The Comedians,* a suite for small orchestra, his *Second Symphony,* the Violin Concerto, the Sonatina in C Major, and other piano works for children.

Kabalevsky, like other Soviet composers whose training and creative work began after the revolution, subscribed to the Soviet aesthetic theory that works of art should reflect political and social ideology. Many of his compositions extol the goals and aspirations of the Soviet Union and its people and commemorate important events in Soviet life and history. In the *First Symphony* (1932), dedicated to the revolution on its 15th anniversary, the music of the first movement with its funereal passages for double-bass, cello, and bassoon represents the Russian people under the Czarist regime, while that of the second and final movement, based on a folk theme, celebrates the people's rebellion and victory. The *Third Symphony* ("Requiem") was composed on the tenth anniversary of Lenin's death. The *Requiem* (1963) for solo voices, chorus, and orchestra was written in memory of the fallen Soviet heroes of World War II. His opera *Colas Breugnon* describes the life and world

Preludes for Piano (1943) he based each prelude on a folk song.

Kabalevsky maintained a life-long interest in young people both as composer and teacher. His tuneful, direct, buoyant style seems particularly well suited to the composition of children's pieces. He wrote songs, choral ensembles, and piano pieces for children. The three concertos—for violin (1948), cello (1948-1949), and piano (1952)—dedicated to "youth" and meant to be played by young musicians are full of vitality and joy. These works are a significant contribution to the repertory of children's music and represent one of Kabalevsky's most valued accomplishments. The U.S.S.R. reported his death on February 18, 1987.

Further Reading

Chapters on Kabalevsky may be found in the following books: James Bakst, *A History of Russian-Soviet Music* (1962, 1966); Stanley Dale Krebs, *Soviet Composers and the Development of Soviet Music* (1970); and Gerald Abraham, *Eight Soviet Composers* (1943).
In Boris Schwarz, *Music and Musical Life in Soviet Russia 1917-1970* (1972) references to Kabalevsky are made throughout the book. In Lyudmila Polyakova, *Soviet Music* (no date; translated by Xenia Danko), published in the Soviet Union, there is a brief discussion of Kabalevsky's music. □

Clements Kadalie

Clements Kadalie (ca. 1896-1951) was South Africa's first black national trade union leader. He headed the Industrial and Commercial Worker's Union (ICU) from its inception in 1919 until his resignation as national secretary in 1929. The meteoric rise of Kadalie and the ICU signalled the emergence of South Africa's black proletariat as a potential challenger to entrenched white domination of the established economic and political order.

Kadalie achieved prominence in the nascent South African black trade union movement with only limited experience as a worker and even less as a resident of South Africa. A grandson of Chiweyu, a paramount chief of the Tonga of Nyasaland, Kadalie was born in or shortly before 1896 near the Bandawe mission station. Educated by Church of Scotland missionaries, Kadalie completed teacher training in 1912. After a short stint of primary school teaching, Kadalie in early 1915 joined the stream of Nyasalanders seeking employment in neighboring southern African states. Working for several months in Portuguese Mozambique, Kadalie continued to Southern Rhodesia, where he held a variety of clerical posts from 1915 to 1918 before moving to Cape Town. Through a chance encounter with a white socialist Kadalie was drawn into organizing work at a time when trade unions were mushrooming among black workers in many of South Africa's burgeoning

view of a 16th-century Burgundian craftsman. Romain Rolland, the author of the novel on which the opera was based, intended his book to be "without politics, without metaphysics . . . ," but Kabalevsky and his librettist V. Bragin emphasize the social conflict between the craftsman and the feudal Duke and superimpose modern proletarian ideas on the story. Another opera, *The Taras Family,* deals with the struggle of partisan fighters against the invading Nazis in World War II.

After initially striking out on a modernistic musical path in early works such as the set of songs to words by Aleksandr Blok (1927) and the First Piano Concerto (1928), Kabalevsky settled into an essentially conservative style that changed little throughout his career. He was strongly influenced by the Russian romantic tradition of Tchaikovsky, Mussorgsky, and Borodin. His music is extroverted, charming, engaging, but not profound or challenging—characteristics that make it easily accessible and appealing to a wide audience. He utilized classical forms, traditional harmony (sparked by chromaticism and dissonance), broad lyrical melodies, and energetic rhythms. His scores tend to be transparent rather than thick-textured. The folk element plays an important part in his works. He incorporated folk material either by direct quotation of folk songs or by writing melodies that have a folk-like flavor. While working on *Colas Breugnon* he made a study of French folk songs. A number of the scenes in the opera have a folk flavor, but only two brief themes are taken directly from Burgundian tunes. In his Violin Concerto he used a popular Ukrainian folk song for the second theme of the first movement, and in the 24 cities. At a meeting of dockworkers in Cape Town in January 1919 the ICU was formed; Kadalie, a resident of less than a year who spoke no South African language other than English, was elected secretary.

Catapulted into local and national visibility at the end of 1919 by leadership of a partially successful strike of Cape Town dockworkers and his subsequently successful effort to block his deportation, Kadalie by the end of 1921 had gained sufficiently broad support to be elected secretary of the national ICU which linked black trade unions in the Cape Providence and the Orange Free State. Under Kadalie's leadership the ICU continued to expand, becoming a focal point for national politics in 1924 when Kadalie, acting in the well established tradition of Africans bargaining for influence through exercise of their franchise as voters in the Cape Providence, urged Africans to vote for the Afrikaner Nationalist Party of General J.M.B. Hertzog.

Betrayed when the successful Nationalist-Labor coalition government made "civilized labor" its policy, Kadalie switched to criticism and concentration upon trade union organizing. ICU branches were established in the industrial heartland of the Witwatersrand, as well as in the port of Durban. Over the opposition of Cape Town members, ICU headquarters were shifted to Johannesburg in 1926, and the ICU began to find a wellspring of support among agricultural workers in Natal and the Orange Free State. By 1927 the ICU was claiming membership of 100,000, well above that of the established white trade unions. Alarmed white farmers and politicians reacted by calling for action to curb the ICU.

The explosive growth of the ICU also attracted attention from the government's opponents. Following a 1924 policy shift away from white workers, the small multiracial Communist Party offered support and began to recruit ICU members into its ranks. Initially Kadalie welcomed cooperation with the Communists, but when Communists began to criticize his policies from within the ICU he sought and obtained majority support for the expulsion of party members from the ICU executive committee at the end of 1926; subsequently, in 1927, Communists were banned from membership in the ICU.

The ouster of the Communists was warmly received by white liberals in Johannesburg and Durban who had also offered assistance in the mid-1920s. Through their good offices Kadalie in 1927 was able to realize his longstanding goal of travelling to Europe to gain recognition and support for the ICU as representative of the country's black workers. Although denied official recognition by the International Labor Organization, Kadalie was cordially received by European social democrats and trade unionists. Through extensive discussions with Arthur Creech-Jones, Fenner Brockway, and other contacts within the British labor movement, Kadalie obtained the promise of a British adviser who would aid the ICU to establish itself efficiently upon the model of a European trade union.

Kadalie returned home in late 1927 amidst a rising crescendo of calls by whites for government repression. Within the ICU organization he found bitter antagonisms, precipitated by charges of financial malpractice. In 1928

large branches in Natal and the Orange Free State seceded, and the arrival of William Ballinger, the long awaited British adviser, only accentuated controversy in debates over the need for internal reorganization and the proper role for whites in the ICU. Resigning, and then unsuccessfully returning as national secretary in early 1929, Kadalie failed to staunch the accelerating collapse of the national ICU. As leader of a rump Independent ICU he reestablished a base of support in East London, where he organized a local general strike in 1930 for which he served a two-month jail term. Through the 1930s and 1940s he intermittently sought to reassert himself nationally, but without success. He remained a respected community leader in East London, where he died in 1951.

Although Kadalie spoke publicly only in English, he was able to mobilize thousands of black workers, urban and rural, into the country's first nationwide labor movement. Few immediate advances were realized and no national black trade union organization was consolidated as a legacy for the subsequent generation of trade unionists in the 1930s and 1940s. Yet unquestionably Kadalie coalesced the imagination of South Africa's new black wage earners into a movement whose scope was previously unequalled.

Further Reading

Kadalie's autobiography, *My Life and the ICU* (London, 1970), is the best source of information on his life and work. Other sources include Edward Roux, *Time Longer than Rope* (London, 1948); P. L. Wickens, *The Industrial and Commercial Worker's Union of Africa* (Cape Town, 1978); and Sheridan W. Johns, III, "Trade Union, Political Pressure Group, or Mass Movement? The Industrial and Commercial Worker's Union of Africa," in Robert I. Rotberg and Ali A. Mazuri (editors), *Protest and Power in Black Africa* (1970). □

János Kádár

Hungarian statesman and premier János Kádár (born 1912) played a key role in his country's transition to a pro-Communist regime following the uprising of 1956. He was impressive in steering a middle course between total obedience to, and total independence from, the Soviet Union until the Hungarian economy faltered and he was removed from party power shortly before his death in 1989.

J ános Kádár (original name János Csermanik) was born on May 25, 1912, in a small Hungarian village south of Lake Balaton, the largest lake in central Europe. After attending the village school, he was apprenticed to a toolmaker and was trained as a skilled mechanic.

Under Communist Influence

Kádár began his political career at the age of 19 when he became a member of Hungary's then illegal Communist party in 1931. Said the *New York Times* in an article in 1956

(October 26), "It was in the harsh conditions of underground work before and during World War II that he came to political maturity." Over the next 12 years, he was arrested several times for illegal party activities. In 1942, he was admitted to the Central Committee of the party and in 1945 to the power-holding Politburo. During World War II he gained hero status for his resistance against the Germans. At one point he was captured by the Nazis, but managed to escape.

Like many other Eastern European Communists, Kádár found it difficult to come to terms with the harsh brand of communism advocated by Russian leader Josef Stalin. Although he seemed destined for high honors when he was named Hungary's minister of the interior in 1948, increasingly, he was found wanting by the Stalinists. In 1950, he was dismissed from both his government post and the party. He was imprisoned the following year and not released until 1954, in the thaw that followed Stalin's death.

Hungarian Uprising

Through the years, the Communists had steadily been gaining power in Hungary. On October 23, 1956, a demonstration led by students and intellectuals began the Hungarian revolt against communism and the presence of Soviet troops in the country. As the revolt spread, Communist leaders returned "liberal" Communist Imre Nagy to power to quell the uprising. Kádár joined the short-lived Nagy government, but deserted it when Communist troops took over the country on November 4. Supposedly, Kádár had long been in contact with Soviet leaders, and it is said that

he entered the capital city of Budapest riding on a Russian tank.

A New Hungary

The new government under Premier János Kádár, under Russian auspices, was announced in 1958. He also served as premier from 1961 to 1965. Kádár pledged an "independent and sovereign" Hungary that would preserve Communist achievements of the past 12 years but also improve the living standard of the Hungarian people.

It was a tall order. The new premier did allow some limited freedom of expression, eased political spying tactics, and permitted greater political tolerance in cultural spheres. But Soviet troops remained and so did the unrest. Hungarians fought Soviet tanks with bare hands. Thousands were killed and more thousands fled their homeland.

In all important matters, Kádár supported Soviet policies. In 1968, Hungarian troops helped to suppress the revolution in Czechoslovakia (now the Czech Republic and Slovakia). As the unrest continued and ties with the Soviet Union remained, Kádár reorganized his government in an attempt to improve the failing economy. As he introduced a partial profit motive into the country, Hungary became the most properous nation in eastern Europe.

The Fall of Kádár

After years of walking a tightrope between Communist and democratic policies, Kádár could do no more. The pace of reform slowed and the economy stagnated. Finally, the Soviet Union had had enough. Kádár was removed as general secretary of the Hungarian Communist party in 1988 and given instead the largely ceremonial post of party president. Even that was taken away in May 1989 when he was also removed from the Central Committee. The man who played such a key role in Hungary's transition died two months later in Budapest, on July 6, 1989.

A secretive man who shunned social life—for instance, his wife never appeared at Budapest parties in the postwar years—Kádár was described by *Time* in 1956 as a man with "rough proletarian manners." An article in *Life* in 1957 characterized him as "dark, mysterious, and primitive."

Further Reading

Kádár's speeches and interviews were published in English as *On the Road to Socialism* (1965); some information on him appears in two books by Paul E. Zinner, *National Communism and Popular Revolt in Eastern Europe* (1956) and *Revolution in Hungary* (1962), and in Bennett Kovrig, *The Hungarian People's Republic* (1970). □

Franz Kafka

The Czech-born German novelist and short-story writer Franz Kafka (1883-1924) presented the experience of man's utter isolation. In his works man

finds himself in a labyrinth which he will never understand.

F ranz Kafka was born July 3, 1883, the eldest of six children of a middle-class merchant who had come from southern Bohemia to the beautiful old city of Prague, its capital, then a part of the Austro-Hungarian Empire. He grew up as a member of a minority (the Jewish community) within a minority (the German-speaking population) at a time when there was little or no communication between these two groups or with the predominantly Czech-speaking citizens of Prague. When he failed to be accepted by either group, he sank into bitterness, distrust, insecurity, and hatred. Although he acquired early in life a thorough knowledge of Czech and a deep understanding of its literature, the gap remained, and this alienation was reflected in his writing, most notably in the protagonists of his stories, who were for the most part outcasts constantly asking, "Where do I belong?" or "Where does man belong?"

An even greater source of frustration for Kafka was his domineering father, a powerful, robust, imposing man, successful in his business, who considered his son a weakling and unfit for life. His childhood and youth were overshadowed by this conflict with his father, whom he respected, even admired, and at the same time feared and subconsciously hated. Kafka later transformed this total lack of communication into the relationship between God-Father and man in his literary production.

Kafka attended only German schools: from 1893 to 1901 the most severe grammar school, the Deutsches Staatsgymnasium in the Old Town Square, and from 1901 to 1906 the Karl Ferdinand University of Prague. He started out in German literature but changed in his second semester to the study of law. In June 1906 he graduated with a degree of doctor of jurisprudence. Even as a youngster, Kafka must have wanted to write. For his parents' birthdays he would compose little plays, which were performed at home by his three younger sisters, while he himself acted as stage manager. The lonely boy was an avid reader and became deeply influenced by the works of Goethe, Pascal, Flaubert, and Kierkegaard.

Early Works

In October 1906 Kafka started to practice at the criminal court and later at the civil court in Prague, while serving as an interne in the office of an attorney in order to gain some practical experience. In early 1908 he joined the staff of the Workmen's Compensation Division of the Austrian government, in a semigovernmental post which he held until his retirement for reasons of ill health in July 1922. Here he came to know the suffering of the underprivileged workmen and wrote his first published work, "Conversation with a Beggar" and "Conversation with a Drunkard," two sections from *Die Beschreibung eines Kampfes* (*Description of a Struggle*). In 1909 these two pieces were published by Franz Blei in his journal, *Hyperion.*

Kafka's first collection of stories was published in 1913 under the title *Betrachtung* (*Contemplation*). These sketches are polished, light impressions based on observation of life in and around Prague. Preoccupied with problems of reality and appearance, they reveal his objective realism based on urban middle-class life. The book is dedicated "To M. B.," that is, Max Brod, who had been his closest friend since their first meeting as university students in 1902.

In September 1912 Kafka met a young Jewish girl from Berlin, Felice Bauer, with whom he fell in love—an affair which was to have far-reaching consequences for all his future work. The immediate result was an artistic breakthrough: he composed in a single sitting, on the night of September 22/23, the story *Das Urteil* (*The Verdict*), dedicated to his future fiancée, Felice, and published the following year in Brod's annual, *Arcadia.* The story contains all the elements normally associated with Kafka's world, the most disorderly universe ever presented by a major artist. The judgment is passed by a bedridden, authoritarian father on his conscientious but guilt-haunted son, who obediently commits suicide. In this story Kafka successfully blends the disparate aspects of his writing—fantasy, realism, speculation, and psychological insight—into a new unity.

Kafka's next work, completed in May 1913, was the story *Der Heizer* (*The Stoker*), later incorporated in his fragmentary novel *Amerika* and awarded in 1915 the Fontane Prize, his first public recognition.

Early in 1913 Kafka became unofficially engaged to Felice in Berlin, but by the end of the summer he had broken all his ties, sending a long letter to her father with the explanation that his daughter could never find happiness in marriage to a man like himself whose sole interest in life was literature. The engagement, nevertheless, was officially announced in June 1914, only to be dissolved 6 weeks later.

Major Novellas

The year 1913 saw the publication of Kafka's best-known story about the man degraded to an animal, *Die Verwandlung* (*The Metamorphosis*). By means of an *unerhörte Begebenheit* (outrageous event), Kafka creates for his reader a world of psychotic delusion which his narrative art preserves as a reality in its own right: "When Gregor Samsa woke one morning from restless dreams, he found himself transformed in his bed into a monstrous insect." In spite of Gregor's gallant efforts to master his new situation, he dies.

One of Kafka's most frightening stories is the novella *In der Strafkolonie* (*In the Penal Colony*), written in 1914. In spite of this literary output, Kafka maintained his position in Prague and his relations with Felice Bauer until the end of 1917, when he found that he had tuberculosis. The stories written during the war years, from 1916 to 1918, were published in 1919 in a collection dedicated to his father and entitled *Der Landarzt* (*The Country Doctor*), and the following year, in October, *Die neue Rundschau* published his story *Ein Hungerkünstler* (*The Hunger Artist*). Again, as in *Die Verwandlung*, it is the outsiders, however sensitive and gifted, who succumb, whereas the healthy realists survive in the struggle for existence. *Ein Hungerkünstler* became the title story for the last book published during the author's lifetime, a collection of four delicate stories that appeared in 1923.

One of Kafka's most important writings is the 100-page letter to his father, written in November 1919 as an attempt to clarify his conscience before his father and to assert his final independence of the latter's authority. "Dearest Father," it begins, "you once asked me why I maintain that I am afraid of you. As usual, I did not know how to answer you, partly because of this very fear I have of you, and partly because the explanation of this fear involves so many details that, when I am talking, I can't keep half of them together." There follows a detailed analysis of the relationship between father and son, essentially a short autobiography, emphasizing the years of his childhood.

His Novels

Kafka's three great novel fragments, *Amerika, Der Prozes* (*The Trial*), and *Das Schloss* (*The Castle*), might have been lost to the world altogether had it not been for the courage of Max Brod, who edited them posthumously, ignoring his friend's request to destroy all of his unpublished manuscripts.

The first of them, begun in 1912 and originally referred to by Kafka as *Der Verschollene* (The Man Who Disappeared), was published in 1927 under the title *Amerika*. The book, which may be considered a *Bildungsroman*, or novel of education (in the tradition of Goethe's *Wilhelm Meister*), recounts the adventures of Karl Rossmann, who, banished by his father because he was seduced by a servant girl, emigrates to America. Perhaps his "love affair," in which he

was the passive party, explains Karl's vague sense of guilt, a feeling from which most of Kafka's heroes suffer.

The anonymous hero of Kafka's next novel fragment, *The Trial*, which was begun in 1914 and published in 1925, is suddenly arrested and accused of a crime, the nature of which is never explained. Put before a mysterious court, he is finally condemned to death and executed on the eve of his thirty-first birthday. Though he does not understand his fate, he accepts the trial and follows the orders of the court conscientiously. Kafka shows man to be awakened to the consciousness of original sin: all men are condemned to death in this world in which there is no justice. Joseph K., the protagonist, has only one basic guilt: that he is a human being, a mortal who, by ordinary civil standards, would undoubtedly be considered innocent. The book, therefore, is a parable of an average man in a state of crisis, and of his defeat.

The third and longest novel fragment is *The Castle*, begun in 1918 and published in 1926. The anonymous hero tries in vain to gain access to a mysterious castle—somehow symbolizing security—in which a supreme master dwells. Again and again he seeks to settle in the village belonging to the castle, but his every attempt to be accepted as a recognized citizen of the village community is thwarted. In one of his aphorisms about his own work, Kafka once said that all of his parables or metaphors were intended to convey the message "that the incomprehensible cannot be comprehended."

During the years 1920 to 1922, when he was working on *The Castle*, Kafka's health was badly threatened, and he was forced to take sick leave for cures in Meran and the Tatra Mountains. In the summer of 1923 Kafka and his sister Olga were vacationing in Müritz on the Baltic when he met a 19-year-old girl, Dora Dymant, an employee of the Berlin Jewish People's Home. He fell deeply in love with her. She remained with him until the end, and under her influence he finally cut all ties with his family and managed to live with her in Berlin. For the first time he was happy, independent at last in spite of parental objections. Kafka left Prague at the end of July 1923 and moved to Berlin-Steglitz, where he wrote his last, comparatively happy story, "The Little Woman," returning to Prague only 3 months before his death on June 3, 1924.

Further Reading

The basic biography of Kafka was written by his closest friend, Max Brod, *Franz Kafka: A Biography* (trans. 1947); it is available in a second, enlarged edition (1960) with good illustrations. A welcome supplement, again by a friend, comprises the notes written after each discussion with Kafka by Gustav Janouch, *Conversations with Kafka: Notes and Reminiscences* (trans. 1953); rev. ed., trans. by Goronwy Rees, 1971).
The greatest authority on Kafka in the United States is Heinz Politzer, whose monograph, *Franz Kafka: Parable and Paradox* (1962), is the standard critical interpretation. The best contemporary critical opinion is in Ronald D. Gray, ed., *Kafka: A Collection of Critical Essays* (1962). The many Kafka studies include Angel Flores, ed., *The Kafka Problem* (1946); Paul Goodman, *Kafka's Prayer* (1947); Charles Neider, *The Frozen Sea: A Study of Franz Kafka* (1948); Angel Flores and Homer Swander, *Franz Kafka Today* (1958); Peter Heller,

Dialectics and Nihilism: Essays on Lessing, Nietzsche, Mann and Kafka (1966); R. M. Albérès and Pierre de Boisdeffre, *Kafka: The Torment of Man* (trans. 1968); Michel Carrouges, *Kafka versus Kafka* (trans. 1968); Wilhelm Emrich, *Franz Kafka: A Critical Study of His Writings* (trans. 1968); and Martin Greenberg, *The Terror of Art: Kafka and Modern Literature* (1968). ☐

Frida Kahlo

Frida Kahlo (1907-1954) was a Mexican painter often associated with the European Surrealists as well as with her husband, Mexican muralist Diego Rivera. She was noted for her intense autobiographical paintings.

Frida Kahlo, was born in Coyoàcán, a suburb of Mexico City, in 1907, the daughter of a German-Jewish photographer and an Indian-Spanish mother. Despite her European background, Kahlo identified all her life with New World, Mexican heritage, dressing in native clothing wherever she travelled. Injured in a bus accident at the age of 15, Kahlo was disabled for life. After numerous operations to correct her spinal and internal injuries, she eventually became an invalid prior to her death at the age of 47. Like her husband, the muralist Diego Rivera, Kahlo maintained a life-long commitment to leftist politics, and in the 1930s she accompanied him on several trips to the United States where he was commissioned to do murals in New York, Detroit, and San Francisco. The most controversial of these was a mural for Rockefeller Center which was cancelled because it included a portrait of Lenin that Rivera refused to remove. Kahlo died in Mexico City in 1954.

Unlike Rivera's murals, which were grandiose and filled with political ideology, Kahlo's work was intimate, personal, and in the tradition of easel painting. Usually autobiographical, she painted the events of her life with symbolic elements and situations, creating a dreamlike reality, frighteningly real but fantastic and magical. One painting, *Broken Column* (1944), shows the artist against a bleak desert landscape with her flesh cut away to reveal a cracked classical column in place of her spine, a painful record of her life-long struggle with the psychological and physical aftermath of her accident. Another, *The Wounded Deer* (1946), shows Kahlo as a deer with her own human head, shot full of arrows in a mysteriously forlorn forest with a body of water in the background. She painted many self-portraits throughout her life.

Kahlo incorporated elements of Mexican folk art into her paintings. Thematic content often takes precedence over a fidelity to realism, and the scale of things represents symbolic relationships rather than physical ones. Reoccurring themes of earthly suffering and the redemptive cycle of nature reflect the mixture of Spanish Catholicism and Indian religion prominent in Mexican culture. Kahlo's color, while naturalistic, is flat and dramatic.

The French Surrealist poet Andre Breton, who lived for a while in Mexico, claimed Kahlo as a Surrealist. She bristled at this association with artists living thousands of miles away and working with psychoanalytic theories of the subconscious. She claimed, "Breton thought I was a Surrealist but I wasn't. I never painted dreams. I painted my own reality." She did, however, show at the Julian Levy Gallery in New York, known for showing Surrealism, and she travelled to Paris at Breton's urging to show her work.

Early in her life her work and reputation as an artist were overshadowed by her relationship to Rivera, who was older and famous before they met. She also seemed conflicted by her sense of duty to him as a wife. In the late 1930s she asserted her independence from him, and in 1939 they were divorced, only to be remarried a short time later. This event served as an important theme in her work of the period. In contrast to Rivera, who was relatively wealthy from his work, Kahlo had great difficulties supporting herself from the sale of her paintings.

Together they led a flamboyant life in Mexico and during their trips to the United States. They were at the center of Mexican cultural life in the 1920s and 1930s when Mexican artists and intellectuals were rediscovering their own heritage and rejecting European ties. This desire for a Mexican art came in part from an interest in leftist politics. Kahlo was a life-time member of the Communist Party, which believed that art should serve the Mexican masses rather than a European elite. Unlike Rivera, Kahlo was not a muralist, but later in her life, when she was asked to teach in an important state art school, she organized teams of students to execute public works.

During her life Frida Kahlo received more recognition as a painter in the United States than in Mexico. She was included in several important group exhibitions, including "Twenty Centuries of Mexican Art" at the Museum of Modern Art and a show of women artists at Peggy Guggenheim's Art of This Century Gallery in New York. Her first one-person show in Mexico at the Galeria Arte Contemporaneo occurred only one year before her death and in part because her death was anticipated. After her death in 1954 her reputation grew in Mexico and diminished in the United States, a time when communists and their sympathizers were discredited. Diego Rivera himself is less known in the United States now than in the 1930s.

Like many prominent women artists of her generation, such as Louise Nevelson and Georgia O'Keefe, Frida Kahlo's art was individualistic and stood apart from mainstream work. They were often overlooked by critics and historians because they were women and outsiders and because their art was difficult to fit into movements and categories. Kahlo has received increased attention since the 1970s as objections to her politics have softened and as interest grows about the role of women artists and intellectuals in history. Concepts of modernism are also being expanded to encompass an uninterrupted strain of figurative art throughout the 20th century, into which Kahlo's painting smoothly fits. Frida Kahlo was the subject of major retrospective exhibitions in the United States in 1978-1979 and in 1983 and in England in 1982.

Further Reading

Hayden Herrera published *Frida: A Biography of Frida Kahlo* (1983), an extensive work that focuses on her life. Her painting is discussed more historically and critically in Whitney Chadwick's *Women Artists and the Surrealist Movement* (1985), which focuses on women artists who worked within Surrealist circles but were seldom recorded in its history. □

Albert Kahn

Architech Albert Kahn (1869–1942) has been called the father of the modern American factory. The factories that he designed for many Detroit manufacturers were known for their streamlined forms and functionalities.

Detroit-based architect Albert Kahn has been called the father of the modern American factory. By the 1920s Detroit had become the center of the flourishing U.S. automobile industry, and Kahn provided what he described as "beautiful factories"—streamlined and functional—for many of the great Detroit manufacturers. Packard, Chrysler, General Motors, and Ford were among his clients, as were giants in such worldwide industries as food, textiles, chemicals, and business machines. During

the early 1930s Kahn helped establish factories and engineering education in the Soviet Union; later in the 1930s and in the first years of World War II he developed plants for the construction of tanks and military aircraft. Throughout his career he also designed notable nonindustrial structures: the Detroit Athletic club, office buildings for General Motors and Fisher, the Hill Auditorium and Clements Library at the University of Michigan, and handsome private homes for such Grosse Pointe auto magnates as H. E. Dodge and Edsel Ford. But it is for his more than two thousand factories that Albert Kahn is remembered.

Life

Kahn, the oldest son of an itinerant rabbi, was born in Germany but spent his early childhood in Luxembourg. In 1880 the family immigrated to Detroit, where young Kahn did not attend school but instead worked at odd jobs and took free Sunday-morning art lessons from sculptor Julius Melchers. Discovering that his pupil was color-blind, Melchers recommended that he take up architecture instead of art and in 1885 helped him earn an apprentice position with the Detroit firm of Mason and Rice. Kahn proved an apt student of design and in 1890 won a scholarship that allowed him to travel for a year in Europe, where he met and became friends with another young architect, Henry Bacon. Returning to Detroit, Kahn rose to the position of chief designer with Mason and Rice. He refused an offer to replace Frank Lloyd Wright in Louis Sullivan's firm during the early 1890s, instead remaining with Mason and Rice until 1896. In that year he married Ernestine Krolik and set up an

architectural partnership with two colleagues from Mason and Rice. By 1902 Kahn had established his own practice, which grew during the next forty years to a company of nearly four hundred people.

Early Industrial Accomplishments

Kahn's first significant industrial commission came from Henry B. Joy, manager of the Packard Motor Car Company, who asked him to design a ten-building production plant in Detroit. Completed between 1903 and 1905, the project included nine conventional buildings and a tenth constructed of reinforced concrete, a material that had rarely been used before in factory construction. In 1908 Henry Ford had introduced the Model T, and late that year Ford contracted with Kahn to design a factory that would place all aspects of the auto's production under a single roof. This Highland Park construction (1909-1914) combined reinforced concrete with large, steel-framed windows, thus providing improved lighting and ventilation for assembly-line workers. Through this project Kahn and Ford established a long and mutually beneficial relationship: both were energetic, inventive, self-educated men who sought innovative but practical solutions to problems in the workplace.

River Rouge

In early 1918 Ford asked Kahn to design and construct a single-building production plant for the Eagle Submarine Chaser, which Ford wanted to produce as part of the U.S. war effort. In fourteen weeks Kahn erected a huge, one-story, steel-framed, lavishly windowed structure on a new two-thousand-acre Ford site on the Rouge River near Detroit. After the war the building was converted to a Model T body shop, and its site became the nucleus of Ford's expanding empire. Between 1922 and 1926 Kahn constructed at River Rouge a complex of innovative factory buildings, including the Glass Plant (1922), the Motor Assembly Building (1924-1925), and the Open Hearth Building (1925). In most cases these one-story structures incorporated steel frames, windowed walls, roofs with monitors (raised sections containing additional windows or louvers), and interior planning built around assembly-line organizational systems. Clean and attractive, River Rouge was America's first truly modern industrial complex because its design and construction fully expressed the architecture of utility.

Later Career

Following the stock-market crash in October 1929, automobile production radically declined, but Kahn and his company remained busy renovating plants so that they could produce vehicles in the most economical way possible. Between 1929 and 1932 he also directed the construction of 521 factories and the training of more than four thousand engineers in the Soviet Union as part of the Soviets' First Five-Year Plan of industrialization. By 1937 Kahn's firm was performing nearly one-fifth of all architect-designed factory construction in the United States. And as World War II approached he developed Ford's giant Willow Run bomber plant (1941-1943), the Glenn Martin Assembly

Building and its additions (1937-1941) for the manufacture of other military aircraft, and the Chrysler Tank Arsenal (1941), all models of modern design. In the course of his career Albert Kahn seized the opportunity—and the responsibility—to transform the architecture of American industry. Toward the end of his life he recalled, with obvious satisfaction and with tongue firmly in cheek: "When I began, the real architects would design only museums, cathedrals, capitols, monuments. The office boy was considered good enough to do factory buildings. I'm still that office boy designing factories. I have no dignity to be impaired."

Further Reading

Architectural Forum, 69 (August 1938): 87-142.
Grant Hildebrand, *The Architecture of Albert Kahn* (Cambridge, Mass.: MIT Press, 1974). □

Louis I. Kahn

Louis I. Kahn (1901-1974) was one of the most significant and influential American architects from the 1950s until his death. His work represents a profound search for the very meaning of architecture.

L ouis I. Kahn was born February 20, 1901, in Estonia on the island of Saaremaa. His face was severely burned as a child, resulting in lifelong scars. His Jewish family immigrated to America in 1905 and settled in Philadelphia, where Louis was raised in poverty. A precocious artist and musician in high school, Kahn was inspired to become an architect during an architectural history course he took his senior year. He studied architecture at the University of Pennsylvania in Philadelphia (1920-1924), where the Classical tradition in architecture was taught by Paul Philippe Cret, a graduate of the École des Beaux-Arts in Paris. This would prove to have a significant influence on his later career.

Kahn became a renowned architect only late in his life, after a long period of maturation. After graduating in 1924 he worked for a number of architects, including his former teacher Cret. The Classically-trained Kahn began to develop an appreciation for the emerging architecture of the International Style through his contacts with such Philadelphia architects as Oscar Stonorov and George Howe, both of whom Kahn was associated with in private practice during the 1940s. He especially respected the architecture and writings of the modern master Le Corbusier. Like Le Corbusier, Kahn was drawn to the ancient architecture of the Mediterranean. He made his first trip to Europe in 1928-1929, and in 1950-1951 was a resident at the American Academy in Rome. The timeless, monumental grandeur of ancient Greek, Roman, and Near Eastern ruins was often suggested in his later buildings.

Kahn's rise to prominence began in 1948-1957 when he was a professor at Yale University. In 1957 he returned to

architecture in its clarification and expression of functions (once more through "served" and "servant" spaces), honest use of materials, and use of advanced structural systems (precast-prestressed concrete). Yet Kahn was striving for something more. Despite the requisite emphasis on technology in such a commission, he was just as concerned with the human side of the scientists, both as a scholarly community and as independent researchers. Also, his use of picturesque "servant" towers clad in brick provided a visual link with the older and more traditional buildings nearby.

Kahn had thoroughly absorbed his sources. He was able to unite characteristics of modern architecture with those of historical architecture, which he knew well from his Beaux-Arts training. By extending the potential of modern architecture toward a new stability and inner security, while responding to the architecture of the past, Kahn became a pivotal figure in the history of architecture during the 1960s and 1970s.

In the Salk Institute for Biological Studies (1959-1965) at La Jolla, California, the laboratory buildings are grouped with Classical formality around a central court, the west end of which is open to a spectacular view of the Pacific Ocean. In the world of modern architecture, then dominated by glass boxes, Kahn was searching for a meaningful monumentality. Walls and voids, rather than glass and transparency, dominate. The exposed concrete of the structure was cast with such refinement that it almost ascends to the level of a precious material. Kahn was attempting to rethink all aspects of his architecture, as if he was at the very beginning of architecture.

Kahn was a great maker of rooms. He felt that a room worthy of the name should clearly exhibit its structure and be animated by the presence of natural light. With spare and economical materials he was able to create a very special, naturally lit inner space for the meeting room of the First Unitarian Church (1959-1967) in Rochester, New York. His supreme expression of the importance of natural light within architecture was his museums, particularly the Kimbell Art Museum (1966-1972) in Fort Worth, Texas, with its skylights running the length of the building's vaults, and the Yale Center for British Art (1969-1977) in New Haven, Connecticut, with its sky-lit top floor and the two grand interior courts bringing natural light down into the building.

To Kahn a city was a place of "assembled institutions." He made several unexecuted proposals for modifying and rebuilding his own Philadelphia. His greatest opportunity to build on a large scale was the Capital Complex for Dacca, Bangladesh (originally planned as a second capital for Pakistan), begun in 1962. The central assembly hall of this problem-laden commission was completed in 1984, a decade after Kahn's death. In his monumental use of basic geometric forms for this complex he approached the character of the ancient ruins he so admired. In the Third World he had begun to build works that truly appeared to be emerging from the very "beginnings" of architecture.

At the peak of his creativity, yet overworked and financially troubled, Kahn died in his early seventies in a New York train station after a trip to India. It is possible to consider him the most significant American architect of the

the University of Pennsylvania and taught there until his death. Kahn was a highly respected and influential teacher. His exploratory, questioning attitudes probed in a poetic manner the inner meaning of architecture. For Kahn, the designing of buildings went well beyond just fulfilling utilitarian needs. He searched for "beginnings" and wanted to discover what a particular building "wants to be." In creating a building Kahn first sought to understand its "Form," or inner essence, which he considered to be "unmeasurable." Once the "Form" was conceived, it was then subjected to the realities of the "measurable" through "Design." In a successful final product, Kahn believed, the original "Form" can still be strongly felt.

Kahn was entering his fifties when he built his first major design, the Yale University Art Gallery (1951-1953) in New Haven, Connecticut. In this building the open lofts of the galleries are "served" by an inner "servant" core containing such services as stairs and an elevator. The ceiling of each gallery is a concrete space frame (with a pattern of tetrahedrons) which allows the mechanical services to spread horizontally without intruding into the gallery. Kahn was beginning to distinguish between primary, human-oriented spaces and the necessary, but secondary, support spaces. He first crystallized his approach to "served" and "servant" spaces in his modest, but critically important, Trenton Bath House (1955-1956) in New Jersey.

Kahn emerged as a major figure in architecture with his Richards Medical Research Building (1957-1961) at the University of Pennsylvania. This work can be interpreted as a summary of the positive accomplishments of modern

20th century since Frank Lloyd Wright. Before his death in 1974 he received a gold medal from the American Institute of Architects in 1971 and a royal gold medal from the Royal Institute of British Architects in 1972.

Further Reading

Two good introductions to the architecture and philosophy of Kahn are John Lobell, *Between Silence and Light: Spirit in the Architecture of Louis I. Kahn* (1979), and Romaldo Giurgola and Jaimini Mehta, *Louis I. Kahn* (1975). For more extensive coverage see Heinz Ronner, Sharad Jhaveri, and Alessandro Vasella, *Louis I. Kahn: Complete Works, 1935-74* (1977), and Alexandra Tyng, *Beginnings: Louis I. Kahn's Philosophy of Architecture* (1984). An important early book on Kahn is Vincent Scully, Jr., *Louis I. Kahn* (1962). *18 years with Architect Louis I. Kahn* (1975) by August E. Komendant was written by a structural engineer who often worked with Kahn. An extensive interview with Kahn can be found in John W. Cook and Heinrich Klotz, *Conversations with Architects* (1973). □

Kaifu Toshiki

On August 8, 1989, Kaifu Toshiki (born 1931) was elected the 14th president of the Liberal Democratic Party (LDP) and, next day, the 76th prime minister of Japan since the cabinet system was instituted in the country in 1885. Despite much popular support Kaifu was abandoned by his party and left office in October 1991.

K aifu Toshiki was born on January 2, 1931, in Nagoya City. His father owned and managed the oldest photography studio in the city. The studio had been founded by Kaifu's grandfather. After finishing a local primary school, Kaifu attended Tokai Middle School in the same city, then enrolled in the special two-year law course at Chuo University in Tokyo, which he completed in 1951. The next year he was admitted to the night school program in the law faculty of Waseda University as a junior and graduated from the program with the Bachelor of Arts degree in 1954.

While at the middle school, but especially at Chuo and Waseda universities, Kaifu developed a keen interest in competitive oratory, an extracurricular activity among high school and college students that dates back to the turn of the century. He began to participate in speech contests in middle school and while at Chuo University won the Prime Minister's Cup in an annual Kanto regional intercollegiate contest. By the time he arrived at the Waseda campus and joined its Oratorical Society in 1952, he was well known among fellow student orators as a "genius speaker," a reputation he proved himself to be amply deserving by, for example, leading the Waseda team to victory in 1953 "with unequaled sophistry and double-talk," as one of the judges at the contest is said to have remarked. In that same year he was elected a deputy secretary of the society.

Founded in 1902, Waseda's original Oratorical Society was disbanded in 1929 under the pressure of the increasingly conservative and nationalistic university administration. When re-established after Japan's defeat in World War II, the organization with the same name was a much more conservative organization than its prewar predecessor. By the early 1950s, when Kaifu joined it, it had become a staunchly anti-Communist rightwing campus organization, a part of the national alliance of rightist student groups, the League for the Democratization of the Student Movement. Kaifu's relationships with it and with its other alumni were to have important impacts on his subsequent life and career.

More immediately important for Kaifu's subsequent career was his encounter with Kono Kinsho, a Reform Party member of the lower house and a longtime ally of Miki Takeo, who led the small Cooperative Party in the early 1950s but subsequently joined the LDP and became its president and Japan's prime minister in 1974. When Kaifu enrolled in Waseda's law faculty in 1952, he visited Kono, who represented the Nagoya constituency where Kaifu's family lived. Kono offered the smooth-talking young compatriot the job of a live-in staffer. For the next six years, until Kono died in 1958, Kaifu kept the job, initially to earn a stipend with free board and room that put him through Waseda and, subsequently, to receive the veteran representative's hands-on training for a political career. Over this period they developed a close personal relationship; Kaifu learned from his physically handicapped mentor—not only about politics and elections, but also about such virtues as courage, perseverance, sincerity, and compassion.

At the 1954 Oratorical Society's party for graduating seniors, Kaifu told his audience that someday he was going to run for a Diet seat and eventually become prime minister. He did not wait very long before he could prove that he had meant what he said on that occasion. Kono suddenly died in March 1958, and his widow, Takako, ran for his seat and won it. She served, however, only a brief two-year term before she passed her seat, and the entire local campaign machine she had inherited from her late husband, on to Kaifu in the 1960 general election. At the age of 29, Kaifu was the youngest winner in that election. He was subsequently reelected to the lower house nine times before he was elected the LDP's top leader, and Japan's, 29 years later.

Upon his election to the lower house, Kaifu joined the Miki faction of LDP Diet members. Almost immediately Kaifu became one of Miki's most favored and trusted confidants. After the faction's reins passed to Komoto Toshio upon Miki's retirement in 1980, Kaifu stayed with the faction. His uninterrupted record of reelections in the subsequent lower house elections made him by the early 1980s a senior member of the faction and one of the most promising potential successors to the aging Komoto.

Kaifu's close relationship with Miki and the fact that the faction had few members helped Kaifu rise quickly to a leadership position in the Komoto faction. The faction's minor group status, however, also seriously handicapped Kaifu's position among his fellow LDP Diet members at large.

In the period between his first election to the lower house in 1960 and his election to the LDP presidency in 1989, Kaifu served at the LDP headquarters in various positions, but none of the party's Big Three positions—i.e., secretary-general, the General Council chair, and the Policy Research Council chair. Moreover, he held only one notable parliamentary position during the same period, i.e., the chair of the lower house's House Management Committee. Finally, he served in the mid 1970s as deputy chief cabinet secretary during Miki's prime ministership and twice as minister of education, first in Fukuda Takeo's cabinet in the mid 1970s and then in Nakasone Yasuhiro's cabinet in the mid 1980s. He thus never held any of the major cabinet portfolios, such as Finance, Foreign Affairs, and International Trade and Industry.

Kaifu's lackluster career record prior to his election to the top party and government position in 1989 partly reflected the limitations of his ability and competence as a legislator. Unlike many of his fellow LDP Diet members, especially those with bureaucratic backgrounds, Kaifu had no proven and outstanding expertise in any particular policy area except education. Even in that area he was not a specialist by training but became a leader largely because it was dominated by alumni of Waseda's Oratorical Society. More importantly, however, Kaifu's record reflected the minor group status of the faction to which he belonged.

Keenly aware of this handicap, Kaifu sought to make friends in other factions, especially the largest and most influential one once led by Tanaka Kakuei and later by Takeshita Noboru. For one thing, Takeshita was another Waseda graduate. For another, Takeshita was director of the LDP Youth Bureau and Kaifu's boss when, following his election to the lower house in 1960, Kaifu served in his first party post as head of the Youth and Student Department in that bureau. In 1977 he joined, with a dozen other LDP Diet members, a group of up-and-coming conservative politicians, businessmen, and scholars called the Free Society Study Association that was set up by Tanaka's deputy, Takeshita, and Abe Shintaro, with the help of Sony's Morita Akio and Suntory's Saji Keizo. At that time Kaifu's involvement provoked a rare rebuke from Miki, who was Tanaka's archenemy. After Komoto took over from Miki in 1980 and Takeshita from Tanaka in 1985, however, the relationship between the two factions significantly improved, and by 1989 Kaifu had become known as a closet Takeshita faction member.

Takeshita served as LDP president and prime minister for one and a half years, from late 1987 to mid 1989, before he was forced to resign by a stock-for-political-favor (Recruit/Cosmos Company) scandal involving not only himself but, directly or indirectly, virtually all other top LDP leaders. His immediate successor, Uno Sosuke, served only two months before he, too, was forced to resign by another scandal, involving this time a paid mistress. In the search for Uno's successor, Kaifu was a candidate preferred by three major factions led, respectively, by Takeshita, Abe, and Nakasone, as well as by his own Komoto faction, mainly because all prominent leaders of the three allied factions were involved in the Recruit scandal. In an election held by

an assembly of all LDP Diet members on August 8, 1989, Kaifu easily beat two opponents, and became the new LDP president. At 58, he was the second youngest LDP president and prime minister in postwar Japan, next only to Tanaka, who had been four years younger when he was elected to those posts in 1972.

The circumstances of Kaifu's election, combined with his relatively lackluster history and the inferior position of his faction, led many observers to call him Takeshita's puppet and predict his fall from power within a few months. But he survived into the 1990s, successfully handling several controversial policy issues. The substantial number and influence of Waseda alumni among LDP Diet members—in 1989, 56 out of 413—did help. However in late 1991 Kaifu lost the support of the LDP forcing him from office. Kiichi Miyazawa became the new party head October 27 and premier a week later.

Despite his loss of power, Kaifu remained influential and in the spotlight. In 1994, he was the president of the New Frontier Party (NFP), a party formed from the merger of nine political parties. However, misguided moves by Kaifu in 1995 led the party to choose another candidate to lead them in early 1996.

Further Reading

For additional information on Kaifu and Japanese politics see Richard J. Samuels, "Japan in 1989," *Asian Survey* (January 1990). See also Toshiki Kaifu, "Japan's Vision," *Foreign Policy* (Fall 1990); *Financial Times* (January 13, 1994 and December 12, 1994); *Nikkei Weekly (Japan)* (October 16, 1995); and *Far Eastern Economic Review* (January 11, 1996). □

Georg Kaiser

The German playwright Georg Kaiser (1878-1945) was the most gifted and prolific dramatist of the expressionist school. Extremely skillful and inventive, he did more than any other writer, except perhaps Brecht, to transform German theater in the 20th century.

Georg Kaiser was born on Nov. 25, 1878, in Magdeburg, the son of a businessman. He himself entered business and worked from 1898 to 1901 in Buenos Aires. Then, during years of ill health and unemployment, he turned to writing plays—*Rektor Kleist* (1905) and *Die jüdische Witwe* (1911; *The Jewish Widow*) —but attained wide recognition only with *Die Bürger von Calais* (1913; *The Burghers of Calais*). This play, ostensibly historical, dramatizes Jean Froissart's tale of the six Calais burghers who were to be surrendered to the English king so that he would spare the city. The play illustrates Kaiser's faith in the emergence of a "New Man," a truly altruistic human being. Kaiser is a great formalist, and *The Burghers* is a finely chiseled drama full of splendid diction—a series of carefully composed and patterned tableaux.

Von Morgens bis Mitternachts (1916; *From Morn till Midnight*), an equally famous play, depicts a sequence of stages in the evolution of a man, a bank cashier, through the course of a single day that he begins with a theft. The trilogy *Die Koralle* (1917; *The Coral*), *Gas I* (1918), and *Gas II* (1920) is perhaps Kaiser's greatest achievement. *The Coral* portrays the spiritual transformation of a billionaire who attempts to escape his conscience by exchanging his identity for that of his secretary and double, whom he kills. In *Gas I* Kaiser shifts the emphasis to society and its regeneration; the billionaire's son is destroyed by those very workers at the gas plant whom he would save from enslavement to machines. *Gas II* is a futuristic play in which the world appears totally mechanized and man is the permanent victim of machines and war.

In his many plays Kaiser returns again and again to the same themes: hostility to war, militarism, and industrialism; fear of dehumanization; yearning for spiritual regeneration. Later, such dramas as *Rosamunde Floris* (1937) stress the need for sacrifice and love. During the 1930s and 1940s Kaiser's work becomes even more intense and inward. Constantly innovative, he was experimenting at the end of his career with ''Greek'' plays in iambic verse (*Zweimal Amphitryon, Pygmalion,* and *Bellerophon,* published posthumously in 1948) that again assert the need for love and devotion to truth in a vicious world. Kaiser left Germany in 1938 and died in Ascona, Switzerland, in 1945.

Further Reading

The standard work in English on Kaiser is B. J. Kenworthy, *Georg Kaiser* (1957), an extremely thorough and informative study. There is an excellent chapter on Kaiser in Walter H. Sokel, *The Writer In Extremis* (1959). A useful general introduction may be found in Hugh F. Garten, *Modern German Drama* (1959). For background material see Richard Samuel and R. Hinton Thomas, *Expressionism in German Life, Literature, and the Theatre, 1910-1924* (1939). □

Henry John Kaiser

Henry John Kaiser (1882-1967), American industrialist, was the driving force behind the expansion of his small construction firm into an industrial corporation with assets exceeding $2.7 billion.

Henry J. Kaiser was born on May 9, 1882, in Sprout Brook, N.Y. He left school at the age of 13 to work, and in 1906 he moved to the West Coast. Sales jobs led him into the construction business, and in 1914 he formed a road-paving firm, which pioneered in the use of heavy construction machinery. His boundless energy, imagination, and optimism were reflected in his company's reputation for speed, efficiency, and economy.

In 1927 a $20-million Cuban road-building contract helped forge the expansion of Kaiser's firm. Four years later he joined with several other large contractors to build the Hoover, Bonneville, and Grand Coulee dams; he also ex-

panded into sand and gravel and cement production. When the United States entered World War II, he decided to apply his company's construction skills to shipbuilding. By 1945 the company had built 1,490 vessels, establishing new records for speed. During this period Kaiser built the first integrated steel plant on the West Coast, a factory which supplied material for his wartime manufacturing.

In 1944 Kaiser began looking forward to the postwar period. He predicted needs for housing, medical care, and transportation and began working to fill them. He expanded his cement and steel operations; began manufacturing aluminum, gypsum, and appliances and other household products; and built 10,000 houses. His most ambitious project, undertaken with Joseph W. Frazer, was the manufacture of automobiles, which Kaiser approached with his customary boldness and imagination. However, postwar and Korean War shortages, under-capitalization, and the disadvantages of being a new entrant in the automotive industry caused his company's failure. It sustained a $111,188,000 loss, although the Kaiser Jeep division survived.

One of Kaiser's proudest achievements of this period was his medical care plan, begun for employees in 1942 and made public in 1945. This became the largest privately sponsored health plan in the world.

In 1954 Kaiser began a new building project in Hawaii, after a visit there had revealed great opportunities for his undiminished desire to build. From that time on he left the day-to-day control of the rest of his enterprises to his son. Kaiser himself remained in the islands, supervising the con-

struction of a hotel, hospitals, plants, housing developments, and a $350,000,000 "dream" city called Hawaii Kai. He died in Honolulu on Aug. 24, 1967, at the age of 85.

Further Reading

The Kaiser Story, published by Kaiser Industries Corporation in 1968, offers a fairly detailed, if nonanalytic, account of his career and the growth and development of his companies.

Additional Sources

Foster, Mark S., *Henry J. Kaiser: builder in the modern American West,* Austin: University of Texas Press, 1989.

Heiner, Albert P., *Henry J. Kaiser, American empire builder: an insider's view,* New York: P. Lang, 1989. □

David Kalakaua

David Kalakaua (1836–1891) was a Hawaiian King who was a staunch supporter of native Hawaiian civil rights. His opposition to the white business community led to a rebellion forcing him to sign a new constitution relinqushing his powers as head of state.

David Kalakaua ruled Hawaii as its king from 1874 to 1891, a period of significant change in the land's internal political makeup and its relationship with the United States. A supporter of the rights of the native peoples of the Hawaiian islands, the monarch frequently clashed with the powerful *haole* (a term used for people who are not natives of Hawaii) business community during his reign. The animosity between the two camps, which was exacerbated by Kalakaua's sometimes questionable use of his power, resulted in a white-led rebellion in 1887. A few days later, Kalakaua was forced to sign a new constitution that stripped him of his power, relegating him to figurehead status.

Kalakaua made his first bid for Hawaii's throne in 1873. The Hawaiian legislature, comprised largely of native Hawaiians and *haoles* qualified by wealth or land-ownership to be either electors or elected representatives in the legislature, was presented with two choices: Kalakaua, who ran on a campaign slogan of "Hawaii for Hawaiians," a sentiment that did not endear him to the islands' white power brokers, and William C. Lunalilo. Lunalilo won easily, but he died a year later, leaving no successor. Another election was held to determine Hawaii's monarch. Buoyed by the support of the influential Walter Murray Gibson, Kalakaua was victorious in the 1874 election.

The triumphant Kalakaua toured the islands, stopping in every district to affirm his primary goals. "To the planters, he affirmed that his primary goal was the advance of commerce and agriculture, and that he was about to go in person to the United States to push for a reciprocity treaty. To his own people, he promised renewal of Hawaiian culture and the restoration of their franchise," wrote Ruth M.

Tabrah in *Hawaii: A Bicentennial History.* The proposed reciprocity treaty with America was important for both sides. Hawaii knew that a trade agreement with the giant United States would significantly boost its domestic economy. America, meanwhile, wanted to prevent Hawaii from developing close commercial or political ties to any other nations (such as Britain). Ralph Kuykendall reported in *The Hawaiian Kingdom* that American minister to Hawaii Henry Peirce successfully argued that a treaty with Kalakaua's kingdom would hold the islands "with hooks of steel in the interests of the United States, and . . . result finally in their annexation to the United States."

Consummation of the 1875 treaty helped Kalakaua's popularity in Hawaii in some respects, but the king lost the support of the white business community for various reasons. Many of his ministerial appointments, for instance, went to native Hawaiians, a reflection of the king's consistent loyalty to his core constituency. They also loathed Gibson, Kalakaua's premier, whom they viewed as a traitor. Kalakaua's white opposition grew increasingly frustrated with their lack of power, and their rhetoric grew increasingly bigoted in tone as their anger grew. "Attempts to build a strong political party of opposition ran into the dismal fact that Kalakaua and Gibson controlled too many votes," wrote Gavan Daws in *Shoal of Time: A History of the Hawaiian Islands.* "In 1880 a slate of Independents was drawn up, but after six years Reform had not got very far. The king still dominated the legislature."

During the 1880s other events further alarmed the *haoles* . Kalakaua's decision to throw an expensive coronation ceremony in 1883 (nine years after first ascending to the throne) angered many, and they disagreed with the government's tentative steps toward universal suffrage, but of greater consequence was his decision to welcome increasing numbers of foreigners (especially Chinese and Japanese people) to the islands. In 1883 a government representative delivered a speech in Tokyo in which he declared that "His Majesty Kalakaua believes that the Japanese and Hawaiian spring from one cognate race and this enhances his love for you," reported Kuykendall. "Hawaii holds out her loving hand and heart to Japan and desires that your people may come and cast in their lots with ours and repeople our Island Home with a race which may blend with ours and produce a new and vigorous nation." Thousands of Japanese families accepted Kalakaua's offer, to the chagrin of white landowners and businessmen who feared further loss of influence.

Early in 1887, a *haole*-dominated organization called the Hawaiian League formed in opposition to Kalakaua and Gibson. Shortly after its formation, "a splendid scandal, just what the League wanted, burst about the head of the king," remarked Daws. Kalakaua had accepted a big payment from a Chinese businessman to secure a government license for opium imports, only to award the license to another Chinese businessman without returning the money to the first individual. News of this scandal gave the League the excuse it needed to move. They detained Gibson, and armed members of the League patrolled Honolulu's streets. Kalakaua knew that his largely ceremonial royal forces were outmatched, so he called on the governments of Britain, America, and other nations for aid. Instead, "they urged him to yield to the demands of the league in order to preserve the peace of his kingdom," said Tabrah. "On July 6, he signed the constitution that relegated him to a figurehead and that imposed a fairly high property ownership qualification on those running for the new legislature." This new constitution, which came to be known as the Bayonet Constitution, marked the end of Hawaii's kingdom.

The Hawaiian League proceeded to dismantle many of Kalakaua's programs. Two years later, Kalakaua retired to Waikiki, his health failing. He made a final visit to the United States, where he was given a warm welcome. "A title was a title, and (the Americans) enjoyed him as a personality," said Tabrah. "He died there in San Francisco after a final whirl of being adulated, feted, and given the fond aloha of American friends." □

Kalidasa

Kalidasa (active late 4th-early 5th century) was classical India's master poet and dramatist. He demonstrated the expressive and suggestive heights of which the Sanskrit language is capable and revealed the very essence of an entire civilization.

Nothing is known with certainty about the life of Kalidasa. Clearly later than the great Buddhist poet Asvaghosha (1st century), Kalidasa was celebrated as a major literary figure in the first half of the 7th century (the Aihole inscription, 634). The scholarly consensus outside India is that Kalidasa flourished in the time of Chandragupta II (reigned 380-413). A traditional Indian view would have it that he adorned Vikramaditya's court in the 1st century B.C. Although he was especially fond of the Gupta capital city, Ujjain (about 30 miles north of Indore in west-central India), there is no proof that he was born there. Kalidasa was a devotee of Siva, but there is no trace of sectarian narrowness in his writings.

Just as it is impossible to write Kalidasa's biography, it is impossible to establish the order in which his works were composed or to show development therein. Six major works are important. The epic poem *Kumarasambhava* (*Birth of Kumara;* Kumara, the Prince, was the war-god son of Siva) boldly recounts the divine romance that led to the birth of Siva's son. Another epic poem, the *Raghuvamsa*, praises the origins and life of Rama. The cantos devoted to Rama show Kalidasa's brilliant condensation and modulation of the Valmiki *Ramayana*. A comparison of the two poets is inevitable, and Kalidasa does not suffer. His Rama exhibits a depth of near-tragic heroism unparalleled in Sanskrit literature.

The lyric "elegy" *Meghaduta* (*Cloud Messenger*) is a short but striking work displaying another dimension of Kalidasa's genius. This masterpiece tells of an exiled demidivinity who, in his anguish for the well-being of his bride, commissions a monsoon thunderhead to carry news of his safety to her in the north. This work is the fount of an enormously productive genre in Sanskrit and related Indic literatures. (The *Meghaduta* alone drew 45 commentaries, more than any other Sanskrit composition.)

As love stories, Kalidasa's three dramas are not unusual, but the author's control of dialogue, situation, and detail is masterly. Though the *Malavikagnimitra* is assumed to be the earliest of Kalidasa's dramas, it is not an immature work. It is less satisfying than the other two because of its story. The *Vikramorvasiya*'s theme of the love of the human king and the divine nymph has greater potential for high pathos and even tragedy, and, for the most part, Kalidasa again takes advantage of the subject matter. The king's love-madness in Act IV is depicted with unsurpassed lyric brilliance. Some critics have been offended that the play carries beyond the "natural tragic climax" to a happy ending; but it is in the poetry that its true grandeur lies.

Sakuntala in the *Abhijnanasakuntalam* is India's most famous heroine. The prototype is found in the *Mahabharata*, but the great Sakuntala is the creature of Kalidasa. This drama is justly the most renowned of Kalidasa's, for here poetry and drama become indissolubly one. There is order, delicacy, serenity, cohesion, and balance. It is appropriate that this was the literary work that first introduced India to Europe in modern times. All that Sanskritic culture was, its celebration of the real, and its conception of itself were epitomized in this drama fashioned by the culture's greatest spokesman and poet.

Further Reading

There are many translations of Kalidasa's works. The most convenient is *Kalidasa: Shakuntala and Other Writings*, translated by Arthur W. Ryder (1912). The complete translation of the *Meghaduta*, with accompanying Sanskrit text, is Franklin and Eleanor Edgerton, *The Cloud Messenger* (1964). The famous translation of the *Sakuntala* by Sir William Jones (1796) is a classic. Various arguments concerning the dates of Kalidasa and other biographical points are examined critically in Arthur Berriedale Keith's two works, *The Sanskrit Drama in Its Origin, Development, Theory and Practice* (1924) and *A History of Sanskrit Literature* (1928), whose critical commentary on the poetry and drama is still of interest. An excellent essay is the chapter on Kalidasa in Surendra N. Dasgupta and S. K. De, *A History of Sanskrit Literature*, vol. 1 (1962), which also includes other valuable material on Kalidasa. ☐

Kumaraswami Kamaraj

Political leader Kumaraswami Kamaraj (1903-1975) rose from the next-to-lowest rung in the caste system of India to become president of the all-powerful Congress party.

He was known simply as Kamaraj, now used as his surname. The low caste Nadars were rising in importance when Kamaraj was born on July 15, 1903, in the southern Madras town of Virudunagar, India. His father, who died when Kamaraj was six, was a coconut merchant. The boy had only six years of schooling when he dropped out to work in his uncle's cloth shop.

A Political Journey

At 17 Kamaraj joined the nationalist movement and soon became the chief lieutenant of Madras Congress leader Sundaresa Satyamurti. His steps up the political ladder include: national Congress Committee in 1931, secretary of the state party in 1935, and member of the Madras Legislative Assembly in 1937 and 1946 and of the Constituent Assembly in 1947. In addition, he was state party president from 1939 to 1954, when he replaced the urbane national leader C. Rajagopalachari, a top-caste Brahmin, as chief minister of Madras.

In 1963 Kamaraj began to devote full time to strengthening the state party. He feared the rise of the Dravida Munnetra Kazagham (DMK), a regional group that threatened to lead Madras out of the national union. His resignation to Jawaharlal Nehru stimulated what came to be known as the Kamaraj Plan, which called for officials to resign to devote time to reorganizing the Congress party at the grassroots level. Kamaraj was made president of the party and his act was interpreted in the selfless sacrifice tradition of Mahatma Gandhi.

When Nehru died in 1964, Kamaraj engineered the selection of Lal Bahadur Shastri as prime minister. The state-level Congress leaders crucial to the transition were dubbed the "syndicate." A second term as Congress president followed. After Shastri's death in 1966, Kamaraj arranged the selection of Indira Gandhi as prime minister.

Waning Power

Kamaraj's political influence began to descend in 1967 when he was defeated for a seat in Parliament, and the DMK, now respectable, captured control of the Madras government. An increasingly independent Indira Gandhi continued as prime minister, and a conflict ensued between the government and Kamaraj's group. The party formally split in 1969 with Kamaraj as part of the old guard that tried, unsuccessfully, to remove Gandhi from power. In the same year Kamaraj was elected to Parliament in a by-election and began to rebuild his Madras base.

Although Kamaraj was fluent only in the Tamil language, with English or Hindi being the power tongues of India, his political skills and the timing of crucial events combined to make him a respected national leader. His own low-caste birth helped him to bring others of comparable social order into the Congress fold. Kamaraj devoted himself to the affairs of his home state of Madras until his death there on Oct. 2, 1975.

Further Reading

Kamaraj: A Study (1967) by V. K. Narasimhan. Robert L. Hardgrave, Jr.'s *The Nadars of Tamilnad* (1969) is an excellent study of the rise of Kamaraj's caste. ☐

Kamehameha I

Kamehameha I (ca. 1758-1819), first king of the Hawaiian Islands, conquered and united the islands. He became a statesman who knew how to keep the best of the old ways while adopting the best of the new.

Born in Kohala, Hawaii, of a family of high chiefs, Kamehameha learned the chiefly arts at the court of his uncle Kalaniopuu, ruler of the island of Hawaii. When Capt. James Cook visited Hawaii in 1778, his lieutenant wrote that the young warrior had "as savage a face as I ever saw" but his disposition was "good natured and humorous."

After his uncle's death in 1782, Kamehameha led a group of rebellious chiefs in civil war. By 1790 he controlled much of the island of Hawaii. He added to his staff two English seamen, John Young and Isaac Davis, who knew about muskets and cannon. With their advice he won victories on the islands of Maui, Molokai, and Lanai. He then went back to Hawaii to put down an uprising by a chief, Keoua. Ashes and fumes from a sudden eruption of a volcano killed about a third of Keoua's warriors. The survivors took this as a sign that the volcano goddess favored Kamehameha.

In 1795 Kamehameha completed his conquest of Maui, Molokai, and Lanai and invaded Oahu, where during the climactic battle many of the enemy were driven to their death over the Nuuanu cliffs. With this victory he gained control of all the islands except Kauai and Niihau, which yielded in 1810 without a fight.

Kamehameha organized the government in the period of peace after 1795 and centralized power in his own hands. While entering into friendly and profitable relations with foreigners, he kept the ways of his ancestors. As a leader in restoring the islands, he urged his people to work and to grow food. They said of him, "He is a farmer, a fisherman, a maker of cloth, a provider for the needy, and a father to the fatherless."

Kamehameha died at Kailua, Kona, on the island of Hawaii. The funeral was in the traditional Hawaiian style, except that no human sacrifice was offered. His bones were carefully hidden, and it is said that only the stars know Kamehameha's final resting place. His favorite wife, Kaahumanu, became a prime minister and a regent of the kingdom after his death. By another wife, Keopuolani, he had two sons who ruled as Kamehameha II and Kamehameha III.

Further Reading

The most reliable account of Kamehameha I is in Ralph S. Kuykendall, *The Hawaiian Kingdom, 1778-1854: Foundation and Transformation* (1938). Two other useful works are Herbert H. Gowen, *Napoleon of the Pacific: Kamehameha the Great* (1919), and James T. Pole, *Hawaii's First King* (1959). Gavan Daws, *Shoal of Time: A History of the Hawaiian Islands* (1968), has an accurate, well-written chapter on Kamehameha.

Additional Sources

Gowen, Herbert H. (Herbert Henry), *The Napoleon of the Pacific: Kamehameha the Great,* New York: AMS Press, 1977.
Judd, Walter F., *Kamehameha,* Norfolk Island, Australia: Island Heritage, 1976. □

Kamehameha III

Kamehameha III (ca. 1814-1854), king of the Hawaiian Islands for 30 years, reigned longer than any Hawaiian ruler. He gave his people a constitution and reformed the land laws.

Kamehameha III, son of Kamehameha I, was born at Keauhou, Hawaii. He became king in 1825 after his brother, Kamehameha II, died in England. Kaahumanu, who had been the favorite wife of Kamehameha I, served as regent until her death in 1832. She had become a devout Protestant, and after her death Kamehameha III was torn between Hawaiian ways and the ways of the Protestant missionaries from New England. After a few years of rebellious dissipation, he became one of Hawaii's great kings. In 1837 he took Kalama as his queen. Their two children died in infancy.

During the reign of Kamehameha III, Protestantism became practically a state religion. Repression of Catholics led in 1839 to troubles with France, which regarded itself as protector of Catholics in the Pacific. Kamehameha III proclaimed religious tolerance, and this became a fact long before the end of his reign.

With Kamehameha's encouragement, the missionaries helped Hawaii make one of the greatest advances in literacy in modern times. Government support of common schools began in 1840. By midcentury most of the population was literate in Hawaiian, and English had become the language of business.

In 1840 Kamehameha proclaimed Hawaii's first constitution. Its preamble included an earlier bill of rights that began, "God hath made of one blood all nations of men." For the first time commoners were chosen to sit in council with the chiefs. An even more liberal constitution in 1852 gave the vote to all male citizens. Three acts after 1845 created an executive ministry, reformed the judiciary, and created a land commission. In a far-reaching reform, land was divided among the chiefs, the king, and the government. By 1850 commoners and foreigners could own land outright.

A serious threat to Hawaii's independence came in 1843. Lord (George) Paulet forced Kamehameha to cede the islands to Great Britain. But 5 months later Adm. Richard Thomas revoked the cession. Kamehameha then uttered the words that have become the motto of Hawaii: "The life of the land is preserved in righteousness."

After a French attack on Honolulu in 1849, Hawaii obtained new treaties with Great Britain and the United States. During Kamehameha III's reign British influence declined, while American influence increased. A movement toward annexation by the United States ended with the King's death.

Further Reading

Most of Ralph S. Kuykendall, *The Hawaiian Kingdom, 1778-1854: Foundation and Transformation* (1938), concerns Kamehameha III and is the most comprehensive account. For an accurate and interesting account see chapters 3 and 4 of Gavan Daws, *Shoal of Time: A History of the Hawaiian Islands* (1968). ☐

Lev Borisovich Kamenev

The Russian politician Lev Borisovich Kamenev (1883-1936) was a leader of the prerevolutionary Social Democratic movement, as well as major official in the Soviet government and Communist party after 1917.

Lev Kamenev, whose family name was Rosenfeld, was born in Moscow, the son of a skilled laborer. He completed his secondary schooling in the Georgian town of Tiflis, where he apparently first came into contact with members of the Russian Social Democratic revolutionary movement. Kamenev's attempt to continue his education at Moscow University was punctuated by his participation in political discussion groups and demonstrations and, finally, in his arrest (1902). It was at this time that he emigrated briefly to western Europe, where he met and formed a lasting attachment to V. I. Lenin and other future Bolshevik leaders. After this, Kamenev's life took on a pattern familiar in the careers of many Russian revolutionaries—arrest, escape or release, followed by renewed work in the revolutionary movement, followed by fresh difficulties with authorities.

Kamenev, like many of his colleagues, was in prison at the outbreak of the Russian Revolution of March 1917. After he obtained release through a general amnesty, Kamenev began working in the Soviet (or representative council) of Workers' and Soldiers' Deputies of Petrograd. His expectation of failure of the revolution placed him in direct opposition to Lenin. In response to Lenin's urging that the Bolsheviks should seize and hold political power, Kamenev argued for caution regarding the issue of seizure of power and for a postrevolutionary coalition government composed of all socialist parties. In spite of his publicly proclaimed doubt of the outcome, he continued to work with the party throughout the revolutionary and postrevolutionary period. Thus, he became first chairman of the revolutionary Central Executive of Soviets (1917) and, later, chairman of the Council of Peoples' Commissars (1919). In addition, he was a member (1919-1925) of the Politburo (executive committee) of the party and held dominant positions in the local party apparatus of the city of Moscow.

When Lenin died in 1924, no single personality immediately succeeded to his position of leadership. Instead, a triumvirate of leaders, Grigori Zinoviev, Joseph Stalin, and Kamenev, combined to prevent the strongest individual claimant, Leon Trotsky, from succeeding to power. In the ensuing struggle, Stalin gradually increased his following and his real power. By late 1925 Stalin had begun to ease Kamenev out of his formal positions in the party and state bureaucracies. By 1926-1927 Kamenev held the relatively insignificant position of ambassador to Italy. This was followed by exclusion, readmission, and, again, exclusion from the party (1927-1932), and in 1935 he was arrested for "moral complicity" in the assassination of one of Stalin's strongest supporters, Sergei Kirov. In 1936 he was rearraigned on charges of treason. In the first of the "show trials" of the Great Purge, Kamenev was found guilty of treason and shot.

Further Reading

Kamenev is discussed in various studies of the early history of the Soviet Union. A useful study of the October Revolution is Robert V. Daniels, *Red October: The Bolshevik Revolution of 1917* (1967). Kamenev's character and career are covered in Isaac Deutscher's superb study of Trotsky, *The Prophet Armed: Trotsky, 1879-1921* (1954), *The Prophet Unarmed: Trotsky, 1921-1929* (1959), and *The Prophet Outcast: Trotsky, 1929-1940* (1963). Background material on Kamenev's general role in the party is in Leonard B. Schapiro, *The Communist Party of the Soviet Union* (1960). □

Heike Kamerlingh Onnes

Heike Kamerlingh Onnes (1853-1926) won the Nobel Prize in physics for his work with liquefied helium.

Heike Kamerlingh Onnes was a Dutch experimental physicist distinguished for his work in the field of low-temperature physics. He was the first scientist to succeed in liquefying helium, a breakthrough which yielded a previously unattainable degree of cold. This accomplishment won him the 1913 Nobel Prize in physics, in addition to numerous other awards. He is also credited with the discovery of superconductivity—that is, the complete disappearance of electrical resistance in various metals at temperatures approaching absolute zero.

Kamerlingh Onnes was born in Groningen, the Netherlands, on September 21, 1853. His father owned a tile factory, and both his parents were strict, imbuing Kamerlingh Onnes and his brothers with an understanding of the value of hard work and perseverance. He was initially educated at Groningen High School under J. M. van Bemmelan, and in 1870 he enrolled in the physics program at the University of Groningen. The following year he submitted an essay on vapor density and won first prize in a contest sponsored by the University of Utrecht. In October 1871, Kamerlingh Onnes transferred to the University of

Heidelberg in Germany, where he was taught by the eminent German chemist Robert Wilhelm Bunsen. He was one of only two students allowed to work in the private laboratory of German physicist Gustav Robert Kirchhoff. In April 1873, he returned to the University of Groningen, where he spent the next five years studying for his doctorate.

In 1878, Kamerlingh Onnes moved to Delft Polytechnic where he became an assistant to the professor of physics there. In 1879 he travelled to Groningen to defend his thesis, entitled "New Proof of the Earth's Rotation." He was awarded his physics doctorate *magna cum laude*. At Delft Polytechnic, Kamerlingh Onnes composed a paper on the general theory of fluids from the perspective of kinetic theory. He soon realized though that such a general theory of the nature of fluids required accurate measurements of volume, pressure, and temperature over as wide a range of values as possible. To this end, he turned his attention to the problem of attaining and maintaining very low temperatures.

In 1882, at the age of twenty-nine, Kamerlingh Onnes accepted Holland's first chair in experimental physics at Leiden University. He also became the director of the laboratory there, where he was able to pursue his interest in low-temperature physics, also known as cryogenics. A dedicated experimentalist, Kamerlingh Onnes declared in his inaugural address: "I should like to write 'through measuring is knowing' as a motto above each physics laboratory." He would spend the rest of his career at Leiden. During the next forty-two years, he established it as the undisputed world headquarters of low-temperature research.

When Kamerlingh Onnes began his pioneering work, cryogenic physics was a relatively unknown science. Before him, the liquefaction of gases at very low temperatures was considered an end in itself, but Kamerlingh Onnes was interested in low-temperature physics in order to gather experimental evidence about the atomic nature of matter. When he set out to cool gases such as oxygen, hydrogen, and helium to extremely low temperatures, there were three means at his disposal. A cooling effect due to the rapid evaporation of a liquid had been discovered in 1877 by the Swiss physicist R. P. Pictet. That same year, the French physicist L. P. Cailletet had achieved low temperatures when he was able to cool oxygen by the application of intense pressure. The final method was based on the 1850 discovery by J. P. Joules and W. Thomson (Lord Kelvin) that when a gas under pressure is released through very small openings, its temperature is lowered by an amount that depends on the nature of the gas. In Munich in 1895, Carl Linde constructed an apparatus that made use of the so-called Joule-Thomson effect; gas was put under pressure and repeatedly forced into a coil of tubes that also acted as a heat exchanger. This was known as the regenerative process. The amount of liquid gas produced by all of these means was, however, negligible.

In trying to achieve very low temperatures, Kamerlingh Onnes employed a combination of Pictet's and Linde's methods. His first objective was to liquefy oxygen—the creation of a bath of liquid oxygen being necessary for the liquefaction of other gases, particularly hydrogen.

Kamerlingh Onnes vaporized oxygen, then liquefied it, and then forced it under pressure into a closed, circulating system. The system was bathed in gases that had achieved progressively lower temperatures than the circulating oxygen. This methodology proved successful and Kamerlingh Onnes was able to produce about fourteen liters of liquid air an hour.

The production of liquid helium and liquid hydrogen proved more difficult than the production of liquid air. Kamerlingh Onnes theorized that if he could begin from a point of normal pressure and liquefy oxygen by the application of immense pressure, then it would be possible to liquefy hydrogen, starting with the temperature of liquid oxygen. In 1892, he was midway through this painstaking process when the Scottish chemist and physicist James Dewar succeeded in liquefying oxygen using a modified form of Pictet's cascade method. The process yielded about a pint of liquid oxygen.

One practical advantage of Dewar's achievement was that Kamerlingh Onnes now had a source of cold with which to attempt to liquefy helium. He believed that if he started out from the freezing point of hydrogen—the lowest temperature to which it was possible to cool it—he could thereby liquefy helium using Linde's regenerative process. Kamerlingh Onnes constructed a system with a jacket of liquid hydrogen; the liquid hydrogen evaporated, which cooled the helium, and then the helium was forced under pressure through a small aperture which cooled it further, liquefying some of it. He then compressed the helium in a refrigerator, where it passed through an elaborate circuit surrounded by circuits of liquid hydrogen, which were themselves surrounded by liquid air, which were in turn surrounded by a flask in which warmed alcohol circulated.

In 1908, Kamerlingh Onnes finally succeeded in the long-elusive goal of liquefying helium. At first, he and his colleagues did not even notice what they had achieved: the liquid helium was colorless, and it was not until the circuit was almost full that they realized what had finally appeared before them. The accomplishment meant that a previously unattainable degree of cold was now at their disposal. Liquid helium was found to have a temperature of −268.8 degrees Celsius, only about four degrees above absolute zero—absolute zero being a hypothetical temperature characterized by a complete absence of heat and equivalent to about −273.15 degrees Celsius or −459.67 degrees Fahrenheit. Kamerlingh Onnes now set out to solidify the liquid helium in order to reach even lower temperatures, and in 1910, by boiling liquid helium under reduced pressure, he reached just over one degree above absolute zero.

Kamerlingh Onnes used these temperatures to extend the range of his research into the properties of substances at low temperatures, and the results of these investigations were published regularly in English as "Communications from the Physical Laboratory at Leiden." In 1911, Kamerlingh Onnes made yet another breakthrough when he discovered superconductivity, the complete disappearance of electrical resistance in various metals at temperatures approaching absolute zero. He also discovered that the

superconductor effect can be negated without changing the temperature by the application of a magnetic field.

Kamerlingh Onnes and his team remained preoccupied with the challenge of crystallizing helium. Their experiments yielded some intriguing if baffling results. In 1911, they found that the density of liquid helium peaked at a temperature of 2.2 degrees Kelvin. When the various physical properties of liquid helium were measured, Kamerlingh Onnes discovered strange behavior in the helium in and around this temperature. Above 2.2 Kelvin it was violently agitated, but at or below this temperature it seemed to lose its dynamic qualities. Kamerlingh Onnes was unable to explain this phenomenon. This was because he was attempting to understand it in terms of the classical laws of physics, but the behavior of liquid helium at these temperatures, unbeknownst to him, obeys the laws of quantum mechanics. Kamerlingh Onnes simply did not have the tools at his disposal to account for his findings. In the end, he and his colleagues put them down to some fault in their methodology and published only "definite and reliable" values for temperatures above 2.2 Kelvin, the position of the inexplicable maximum of the density of liquid helium.

Although he had yet to achieve absolute zero, in 1913 Kamerlingh Onnes was awarded the Nobel Prize for physics for his investigations into the properties of matter at low temperatures leading to the discovery of liquid helium. By 1921, Kamerlingh Onnes came within a degree of reaching absolute zero, and for the next three years he relentlessly pursued his quest. In 1926, he came across further peculiarities in the behavior of helium at 2.2 degrees Kelvin. This time Kamerlingh Onnes did not dismiss his findings as due to technical faults but began to seriously consider the possibility that some kind of fundamental change in helium occurred at this temperature. Unfortunately, although he was on the right track, Kamerlingh Onnes did not live long enough to resolve the mystery. His successor at Leiden, W. H. Keesom, came to the conclusion that helium above and below 2.2 degrees Kelvin is in fact two separate liquids, differing in fundamental ways. Keesom also completed another aspect of Kamerlingh Onnes' work: he succeeded in obtaining solid helium by cooling the liquid to about −272 degrees Celsius under pressure.

Kamerlingh Onnes was widely recognized for his work in low-temperature physics, and he received a number of awards in addition to the Nobel Prize. In 1904, he received the first of many distinctions when he was created Chevalier of the Order of the Netherlands Lion. In that same year, which was the twenty-fifth anniversary of his doctorate, his students and colleagues at Leiden issued a *Gedenkboek*, a survey of the work carried out at the laboratory from 1882 to 1904. A second *Gedenkboek* was issued in 1922, commemorating Kamerlingh Onnes' forty-year tenure as professor of experimental physics at Leiden. In 1912, he was awarded the Royal Society of London's Rumford Medal, and four years later the society made him a foreign member. In 1923, he was elevated from Chevalier to Commander of the Netherlands Lion. Despite being known by his friends as "the gentleman of absolute zero," Kamerlingh Onnes died at Leiden on February 21, 1926, without ever having achieved it (German chemist Walther Nernst proved it was impossible to reach absolute zero in an experimental setting when he articulated the Third Law of Thermodynamics in 1905). That same year, he was posthumously elected a Corresponding Member of the Prussian Academy of Sciences in Berlin.

Further Reading

Klein, Martin J., *Paul Ehrenfest: The Making of a Theoretical Physicist,* North-Holland Publishing Co., 1970.
Livanova, Anna Landau, *A Great Physicist and Teacher,* Pergamon Press, 1980. □

Kammu

Kammu (737-806) was the fiftieth emperor of Japan. A wise and effective ruler, he reigned for 25 years and laid the foundation for the prosperity of the Heian period. The Heian Shrine is dedicated to his spirit.

Kammu was born Yamabe, a son of Emperor Konin. Because his mother was a naturalized Japanese, it appeared unlikely that Yamabe would ascend the throne. He was, however, designated the heir apparent at the age of 35 and was enthroned at the age of 44. The reign of this rare, efficient ruler was marked inter alia by the move of the capital from Nara to Kyoto, the subjugation of the Ezo (Ainu) in northern Japan, and introduction of reforms in administration.

Move of the Capital

In 784 Emperor Kammu decided to leave Heijo, or Nara, largely to escape what had become the oppressive influence of the great Buddhist monasteries and temples that ringed Nara. The favors bestowed upon the great monasteries by many emperors preceding Kammu and the leading noble houses served to so increase the economic and political power of the Buddhist establishments that the authority of the imperial house appeared to be endangered. It is also probable that Kammu concluded from the history of previous decades that reforms he had in mind could not be carried out unless there was a complete change of atmosphere. Kammu was a Confucian by training and as such was opposed to encroachment of political power by the Buddhist clergy.

The court was first moved to a place called Nagaoka, but work was begun on the new capital in Kyoto early in 793. The Emperor moved into his new palaces in 794, but work on other buildings continued for some years more. This was the city styled Heian-kyo, the "Capital of Peace and Tranquility." It was built on the same lines as the Chinese capital at Ch'ang-an under the Sui dynasty.

The seven great monasteries of Nara were left behind. Emperor Kammu also issued an edict which was intended to cut down the building of new Buddhist edifices, to limit entries into the monastic order, and to prevent the sale or donation of land to religious institutions.

Pacification Campaigns

Kammu ruled firmly, relying upon his own judgment. It is generally agreed that the power and prestige of the throne were at their highest during his reign. In order to expand the effective rule by the imperial house into regions inhabited by the aboriginal settlers, the Ezo, or the Ainu, a number of military expeditions were launched during the reign of Kammu.

In 791, for instance, a new commander was appointed and given the title of Seito Taishi, or "Envoy for the Pacification of the East." In a series of military campaigns, the expeditionary forces were able to expand the pacified areas considerably. So important was this task of subjugation in the eyes of the court that the new title of Sei-i Tai-Shogun, or "Barbarian-quelling Generalissimo," was created, and this was sought by the highest military officers of the land for the next thousand years.

During these military campaigns, Kammu ordered the intensification of the manufacture of armors and arms not only by artisans of the capital but also by those of the local areas. This tended to encourage the development of handicraft in many parts of Japan. He also paid keen attention to local administration. The *chokushiden,* or rice fields opened with imperial sanction, were also initiated during Kammu's reign. These tax-free rice fields, when opened from wastelands, belonged to the imperial court—enriching the imperial treasury. Emperor Kammu died in the spring of 806 at the age of 69.

Further Reading

A fine background to the move of the capital and some political developments under Kammu at the very beginning of the Heian period are in Sir George Sansom, *A History of Japan,* vol. 1 (1958). An intelligent discussion of Buddhist imprints on the transitional era between the Nara and Heian periods is in Ryusaku Tsunoda and others, eds., *Sources of Japanese Tradition* (1958). For general background on early Japan, including the reign of Kammu, see Edwin O. Reischauer and John K. Fairbank, *A History of East Asian Civilization,* vol. 1 (1960). □

Wassily Kandinsky

The Russian painter and graphic artist Wassily Kandinsky (1866-1944) was one of the great masters of modern art and the outstanding representative of pure abstract painting that dominated the first half of the 20th century.

Wassily Kandinsky produced his early work in Russia, his mature and most revolutionary work in Germany, and his later work in France. He invented a language of abstract forms with which he replaced the forms of nature. His ultimate intention was to mirror the universe in his visionary world. He felt that painting possessed the same power as music and that sign, line, and color ought to correspond to the vibrations of the human soul.

Kandinsky was born on Dec. 4, 1866, in Moscow; his father was a tea merchant. When he was 5 the family moved to Odessa. The young Kandinsky drew, wrote poems, and played the piano and the cello. Between 1886 and 1892 he studied law and economics at the University of Moscow. In 1889, as a member of an ethnographic mission to the Vologda district, he was highly impressed by the interior decorations of the village houses. In 1893 he accepted a position on the law faculty of the university.

Beginnings as an Artist

Only in 1896, when he was 30 years old, did Kandinsky decide to become an artist. Of importance for his artistic development was the exhibition of French impressionists in Moscow in 1895, particularly the works of Claude Monet. In Monet's paintings the subject matter played a secondary role to color. Reality and fairy tale intermixed—that was the secret of Kandinsky's early work, which was based on folk art, and it remained so even later although more intellectualized.

Between 1897 and 1899 Kandinsky attended the Azbé School of Painting in Munich, and in 1900 he was a pupil of Franz von Stuck. In 1901 Kandinsky founded the artists'

group Phalanx and taught at their private art school. The following year he met the painter Gabriele Münter, with whom he lived until 1916. The works of his Phalanx period, from 1901 to 1904, are in the Jugendstil. In 1903 Kandinsky traveled to Venice, Odessa, and Moscow; in 1904 to Holland and Tunisia; in 1906 to Odessa and Rapallo. From 1905 on he was a member of the Salon d'Automne and the Salon des Indépendants. He spent 1906-1907 in Sèvres near Paris. He exhibited with the Brücke (Bridge) artists in Dresden and returned to Munich in 1908.

Kandinsky's early impressionist-inspired paintings and those of his Jugendstil period are strong in color, and color continued to dominate in his landscapes of Murnau, where he bought a house in 1909 (for example, *Railway at Murnau,* 1909-1910). He was one of the founders of the Neue Künstlervereinigung (New Artists' Associaton) in Munich in 1909, of which he became the chairman.

First Abstract Art

The year 1910 was crucial for Kandinsky and for world art. Kandinsky produced his first abstract watercolor, in which all elements of representation and association seem to have disappeared; he also wrote *Über das Geistige in der Kunst* (1912; *Concerning the Spiritual in Art*), the first theorization of a nonobjective form of art ever elaborated by an artist and his most influential treatise. He met Franz Marc in 1910, and in 1911, after a trip to Russia, he met Paul Klee, Jean Arp, and August Macke. Kandinsky and Marc founded the Blaue Reiter (Blue Rider) group in Munich in 1911 and exhibited with them. A second exhibition followed in 1912, and the *Almanach Blauer Reiter* was published. The exhibition was repeated in the Sturm Gallery in Berlin, for which a special Kandinsky album was issued.

In 1913 Kandinsky produced a series of color lithographs and prose poems *Klänge* (*Sounds*) and took part in the first Herbstsalon (Autumn Exhibition). The Blaue Reiter disbanded in 1914. In his early abstract works vehement linear strokes are combined with powerful patches of color, as in *Composition V* (1911) and *With the Black Arch* (1912).

Return to Russia

When World War I broke out, Kandinsky returned to Russia. In 1917 he married Nina Andreewsky. During the Russian Revolution the artist occupied an important post at the Commissariat of Popular Culture and at the Academy in Moscow. He organized 22 museums and became the director of the Museum of Pictorial Culture. In 1920 he was appointed professor at the University of Moscow. The following year he founded the Academy of Arts and Sciences and became its vice president. When, at the end of that year, the Soviet attitude to art changed, Kandinsky left Russia.

Years in Germany and France

In 1922 Kandinsky became a professor at the Bauhaus in Weimar. Together with Klee, Alexei von Jawlensky, and Lyonel Feininger he founded the Blaue Vier (Blue Four) group in 1924. When, in 1925, the Bauhaus moved to Dessau, Kandinsky moved with it. In 1926 he published the principles of his teaching in *Punkt und Linie zur Fläche*

(*Point and Line to Plane*). His art from about 1920 to 1924 has been defined as his architectural period. The shapes are more precise than before; there are points, straight or broken lines, single or in bunches, and snakelike, radiating segments of circles; the color is cooler, more subdued, with occasional outbursts of earlier expressionist tonality. This period is exemplified in *Composition VIII* (1923). From 1925 to 1927 he emphasized circles in his paintings, as can be seen in *Several Circles* (1926).

Kandinsky became a German citizen in 1928, and the same year he designed sets for Modest Mussorgsky's *Pictures from an Exhibition* for the Dessau Theater. In 1929 Kandinsky held his first one-man show in Paris and traveled to Belgium and the French Riviera. In 1930 he had another exhibition in Paris. For the large architectural exhibition in Berlin of 1931 he produced wall decorations. When the Bauhaus was closed in 1932, Kandinsky moved to Berlin, and the following year he left for Paris.

Kandinsky's romantic, or concrete, period, from 1927 to 1933, in which his use of pictorial signs was abundant and his color was softer, is exemplified in *Between the Light* (1931). It led to the last phase of his art, that spent in France, which was an intellectual synthesis of his previous strivings.

Kandinsky settled in Neuilly-sur-Seine near Paris. He met Joan Miró, Robert Delaunay, and Piet Mondrian, and a friendship developed with Antoine Pevsner, Arp, and Alberto Magnelli. In 1939 Kandinsky became a French citizen. He died on Dec. 13, 1944, in Neuilly-sur-Seine. The paintings of his Paris period have a Russian splendor of color, a richness of formal invention, and a delightful humor, as in *Composition X* (1939), *Sky Blue* (1940), and *Reciprocal Accord* (1942).

Further Reading

Kandinsky's views are in his *Concerning the Spiritual in Art, and Painting in Particular* (1912; trans. 1947). The most comprehensive study of Kandinsky is Will Grohmann, *Wassily Kandinsky: Life and Work* (trans. 1958). Max Bill, *Wassily Kandinsky* (1951), with articles by various contributors, contains important biographical and art-historical data. Paul Overy, *Kandinsky: The Language of the Eye* (1969), applies Gestalt psychological and philosophical viewpoints to the assessment of Kandinsky's art. □

various cities where he was working, but each time he was forced to quit because of poverty. About the turn of the century, he lost his leg in a railway accident and had to give up his arduous jobs as a laborer.

Kane supported himself, in part, by painting freight cars and doing the lettering on the sides. Later he colored photograph enlargements. Often, he would use photographs as the original stimulus for some of his paintings. When he first began to paint, he submitted, as originals, paintings done right over enlarged photographs without knowing that this was unethical. In 1924 he submitted a painting to the Pittsburgh Carnegie Exhibition, but it was rejected, partly because it had been based closely upon a photograph.

About 1915 Kane began painting subjects based on his memories of Scotland and his impressions of the region about Pittsburgh. This work is marked by bright colors, a feeling for pattern, and a naiveté of handling in which sophisticated devices such as perspective and modeling are not attempted. His paintings are imbued with an attitude of affection for the people and places pictured.

One of Kane's most memorable paintings is his selfportrait (1929). The work shows the artist half-length, nude from the waist up, staring fixedly ahead at the spectator. He flexes his muscles, his fists meeting at the waist, his elbows jutting to the sides. The rigidity of the pose and the almost absolute symmetry of the design, with three concentric arches above the head, create a hieratic image of tension and power.

Recognition came to Kane late in life. With the support of another painter, who was a member of the jury of the Carnegie Exhibition, he began to be exhibited. In 1927 he was accepted in the Carnegie Exhibition, and his first one-man show was held in 1931, when he was over 70 years old. In 1936 his first one-man show abroad was held posthumously in London.

Further Reading

John Kane, Painter, edited by Leon A. Arkus (1971), reprints the artist's autobiography; it also includes a *catalogue raisonné*. Sidney Janis, *They Taught Themselves: American Primitive Painters of the Twentieth Century* (1942), contains quotations from Kane and some biographical material on him. □

John Kane

John Kane (1860-1934) was a Scottish-born American primitive painter who specialized in landscapes and scenes of the industrial environment in and around Pittsburgh, Pa.

John Kane was born in West Calder, Scotland, and as a teen-ager worked in the coal mines. After he arrived in America in 1879, he again worked as a miner and also as a street paver, carpenter, house painter, and lumber cutter. He settled in Pittsburgh and by 1890 had begun to draw in his spare time. He started attending art classes in the

Paul Kane

Paul Kane (1810-1871) was a Canadian painter and writer. His works form a unique record of the appearance and customs of the Indians of western Canada in the middle of the 19th century.

Paul Kane was born on Sept. 3, 1810, at Mallow, County Cork, Ireland. His father, a soldier turned wine and spirit merchant, took him to York (Toronto) when he was 8, and it was here that young Paul had his first introduction to art, from Thomas Drury, the drawing master of the grammar school. From 1826 to 1830 Kane worked in a furniture factory in Cobourg, Ontario, and painted portraits of the local citizens in his spare time. In 1836 he set off on 9 years of wandering, during which time he supported himself by his wits and his brush. His travels first took him south through the United States to New Orleans; from there he sailed for Marseilles in 1841 and after that across Europe and briefly to the eastern Mediterranean and North Africa. By the time he returned to Toronto in 1845, he had decided on his life's work and had acquired the necessary skill to carry it out.

A Vanishing Culture

Recalling his early years, Kane wrote: "I had been accustomed to see hundreds of Indians about my native village, then Little York, muddy and dirty, just struggling into existence. . . . But the face of the red man is now no longer seen . . . and those who would see the aborigines of their country in their original state . . . must travel far through the pathless forest to find them." He therefore resolved to devote his talents to painting "a series of pictures illustrative of the North American Indians and scenery." In this decision he may have been influenced by the example of the American George Catlin, who had been painting the western Indians since 1832 and had published a book on the subject in 1841. In any case, Kane had prepared himself for his task by copying Old Masters in the museums of Florence and Rome.

Kane's first expedition among the Indians, in the summer of 1845, took him no farther west than Lake Michigan, but, armed with his first sketches of encampments on Manitoulin Island and on the Fox River, he persuaded Sir George Simpson, governor of the Hudson's Bay Company, to let him accompany the fur brigades across Canada the following spring. In the course of the next 2 years he traveled from one trading post to another by canoe, on horseback, and by sleigh and dog team as far as Vancouver Island, sketching the Indians in oils and watercolors and collecting artifacts as he went.

Major Works

Returning to Toronto in the autumn of 1848, Kane began the series of 100 canvases, now in the Royal Ontario Museum, commissioned by his patron, George William Allan. Kane also painted a dozen pictures for Sir George Simpson and another 12 for the Canadian legislature, 11 of which are now in the National Gallery of Canada. In these products of the studio the artist's European training comes out in the academic poses of the figures and the subdued coloring of the landscape. In contrast to them, the original sketches have a freshness of composition and vividness of color akin to the open-air studies of John Constable and Camille Corot.

In 1858 Kane revisited London to arrange for the publication of his journal, *Wanderings of an Artist among the Indians of North America*. In his pocket he carried letters of introduction from Sir George Simpson, who may also have arranged for 12 of Kane's pictures to be shown to Queen Victoria. In 1866 blindness forced Kane to abandon his

plans for further painting and publication. He died in Toronto on Feb. 20, 1871.

Further Reading

Kane's own book, *Wanderings of an Artist among the Indians of North America: From Canada to Vancouver's Island and Oregon through the Hudson's Bay Company's Territory and Back Again* (1859), is the major source of information about him. The revised edition, published by the Radisson Society in 1925, contains additional biographical detail, and this material is reproduced in a new, revised edition of 1968. A short monograph is Albert H. Robson, *Paul Kane* (1938). J. Russell Harper, ed., *Paul Kane's Frontier* (1971), contains a biography, a reprinting of the first edition of *Wanderings of an Artist,* and a *catalogue raisonné* of all Kane's known works.

Additional Sources

Benham, Mary Lile, *Paul Kane,* Don Mills, Ont.: Fitzhenry & Whiteside, 1977. □

K'ang-hsi

The Chinese emperor K'ang-hsi (1654-1722) was a man of enormous personal vitality and exceptional administrative and military ability. He was one of the greatest emperors of the Ch'ing period.

B orn on May 4, 1654, K'ang-hsi was the third son of the sickly and weak emperor Shun-chih (reigned 1643-1661). K'ang-hsi's mother, who died in 1663, came from a family in southern Manchuria which had served under the Manchus since the early 17th century. As a youth, he was raised outside the imperial palace in the care of his grandmother, the dowager empress Hsiao-chuang and the mother of Shun-chih. Here K'ang-hsi received his tutoring, learning the Manchu language and acquiring enough ability in Chinese to deal efficiently with state documents. While still a child, K'ang-hsi suffered an attack of smallpox, leaving his face pockmarked, but also elevating his chances to become emperor since he was thereafter considered to be immune to that disease.

Accession and Regency

On Feb. 5, 1661, K'ang-hsi's father died and the 6-year-old boy was declared emperor of China. He was not to gain full control of the government, however, until 1669. In the meantime, four Manchu statesmen, led by the ambitious Oboi, forged Shun-chih's "Imperial Will" and thus took over as regents for the child emperor. Oboi and his coregents sought to reverse many of Shun-chih's policies, which they felt favored Chinese officials instead of Manchu officials. They relied primarily on Manchu bureaucrats for advice, while often disregarding Chinese officials and cutting back on the number of civil service examination degrees which would be granted to Chinese. They ousted the eunuchs and Buddhists who had been close associates of Shun-chih and persecuted several Jesuit missionaries who had received favorable treatment from him. In the provinces Oboi and his colleagues ruthlessly suppressed anti-Manchu sentiments.

Although K'ang-hsi was formally declared head of state in 1667, Oboi continued to dominate the court at Peking by rallying a faction to support his power-hungry policies. After 2 years of infighting, K'ang-hsi, then 15 years old, gained the support of several high officials who purged the Oboi faction, imprisoned the powerful regent, and finally placed the Emperor in a position of control. Confronted with a variety of perplexing domestic and foreign problems, K'ang-hsi boldly set forth in 1669 to resolve them in his characteristically vigorous fashion.

Conciliatory Moves

One of his most serious dilemmas was Chinese hatred for the Manchu regime, a hatred which had been intensified by the blatantly anti-Chinese actions during the Oboi regency. In 1670 K'ang-hsi began his campaign to win Chinese support by issuing his famous Sacred Edict (*sheng-yü*). The Sacred Edict consisted of 16 moral maxims admonishing the people to be filial toward their parents, to be frugal in their everyday lives, and to respect education and scholarship. K'ang-hsi was thus creating a self-image of the traditional Chinese benevolent emperor concerned for the well-being and morals of his flock. In 1679 K'ang-hsi announced a special civil service examination (*po-hsüeh*), in which eminent scholars who had formerly refused to serve the Manchus and who had remained loyal to the defunct Ming dynasty would be permitted to compete. Showing exceptional sensitivity to the feelings of the loyalist scholars, K'ang-hsi also declared that the successful candidates in this examination would be permitted to work on an official history of their beloved Ming dynasty.

K'ang-hsi was also cognizant of the Chinese belief that the emperor was the "first scholar of the realm," and thus he paid special attention to the patronization of scholarship. Among the more famous works compiled under his reign were the "K'ang-hsi Dictionary" (*K'ang-hsi tzu-tien*) and the "Complete Poems of the T'ang Dynasty" (*Ch'üan T'ang shih*). Many painters and calligraphers were invited to K'ang-hsi's court in Peking; one of them, Wang Yüan-ch'i, painted a scroll over 300 feet long in honor of the Emperor's sixtieth birthday.

K'ang-hsi also was very tolerant in dealing with the Jesuit missionaries, who had been persecuted under his regents. Jesuits were placed in charge of the Imperial Board of Astronomy, and they assisted the court in astronomical observations and in mathematical calculations. Jesuit fathers also directed a huge project to map the Chinese Empire, using modern Western techniques of cartography. In 1705 K'ang-hsi issued an "Edict of Toleration" concerning the Jesuits, one of whom had cured him of malaria by administering quinine.

Consolidation of the Empire

But the Emperor also had a tough side to his personality, which was particularly evident in his role as commander in chief. In the early 1670s K'ang-hsi decided to suppress several former Chinese allies of the Manchus who had been reluctant to relinquish their positions as feudatory princes in South China. The most famous of these princes was Wu San-kuei, who, after offering the Manchus invaluable military assistance in 1644-1662, developed his own independent regime covering much of southwestern and central China. During the 1660s Wu began to appoint his own officials, levy his own taxes, and increase his already substantial army.

In 1673 K'ang-hsi, ignoring the advice of some of his cautious colleagues, precipitated the Rebellion of the Three Feudatories by indicating that he was willing to accept the retirement of one of the feudatory princes. A long and dangerous period of battle ensued which threw all of China south of the Yangtze River into civil war. At one point in 1674 it appeared that Wu San-kuei had the advantage, but he failed to press northward across the Yangtze and eventually died of dysentery in 1678.

After his successful operation against the feudatories, K'ang-hsi boldly committed imperial troops to a series of spectacular campaigns along the frontiers of China. Since the early years of the Ch'ing dynasty, the southeastern coast of China had been prey to the attacks of a large army and navy who refused to accept the Manchu government. Originally led by the colorful pirate Coxinga, these renegades retreated to Taiwan in the 1660s under the command of Coxinga's son.

While the Ch'ing were occupied with the suppression of the feudatories in the 1670s, these rebels sailed from Taiwan to the mainland and forced K'ang-hsi to use some of his best troops against them. By 1680 they had retreated from the China coast, but they still remained a potential threat in their island refuge of Taiwan. Once again K'ang-hsi took the offensive. He developed a large fleet and ordered it to sail for Taiwan in 1683. After a number of battles on the rough seas in the Taiwan Straits, the Manchu forces overwhelmed remnants of Coxinga's band, and Taiwan fell under Ch'ing control, where it remained until China's defeat in the Sino-Japanese War in 1895.

Turning his attention to the northern frontiers, K'ang-hsi became alarmed at the growth of a Russian threat along the Amur River in northern Manchuria. Groups of Russian Cossacks, who had been a constant menace in the Amur region in the early years of the Ch'ing, began to launch new expeditions in search of game, loot, and settlement sites. In the early 1680s K'ang-hsi sent a strong contingent of troops to northern Manchuria, where they clashed with Russian forces in 1685-1686, driving the Russians into Siberia.

The Russians rallied and began a new offensive, and the Sino-Russian encounters of the 1680s might have reached enormous proportions had not K'ang-hsi and the Russian regent, Sophia, agreed to negotiations. Russian and Ch'ing envoys met at the town of Nerchinsk, where, with Jesuit missionaries serving as intermediaries and interpreters, several months of heated bargaining ensued. Finally, in 1689, in the Treaty of Nerchinsk the Russians agreed to recognize all territory south of the Amur as belonging to the Ch'ing. A subsequent agreement (Treaty of Kiakhta, 1727) brought all of Mongolia into Ch'ing hands in return for regular Russian trade along the northern Mongolian frontier.

Threat from the West

A key reason why K'ang-hsi and the Russian court were willing to negotiate in the 1680s was the rise of a large western Mongolian tribal confederation which threatened both Russia and China. A dynamic leader of the western Mongols had emerged, Galdan, and by the time of the Treaty of Nerchinsk he had gained allegiance throughout western Mongolia, had obtained considerable support from Tibet, where he had been educated as a lama in his youth, and had marched his armies deep into western Mongolia (to within 400 miles of Nerchinsk itself).

In 1696 K'ang-hsi made a counterattack. Personally leading some 80,000 troops, he rapidly crushed Galdan's Mongol armies, and Galdan himself died in the following year (perhaps by suicide). K'ang-hsi had thus extended the Ch'ing frontiers as far west as Hami and had laid the framework for the final conquest of Chinese Turkistan in the 1750s.

Personal Administration

Although K'ang-hsi's tough side is seen perhaps most clearly in his military operations, his domestic policies were also colored by a considerable dose of forcefulness. In order to bypass the slow and formalized system of transmitting official reports, K'ang-hsi allowed a select few provincial officials to send secret reports (*tsou-che*) by rapid horse express directly to the Emperor himself. Another of K'ang-hsi's techniques was to station trusted personal servants from his imperial household staff (bondservants) in key posts about the empire.

One of K'ang-hsi's bondservants, Ts'ao Yin, provided the Emperor a great service by overseeing lucrative government monopolies on textiles and salt and by sending him regular secret reports about local developments. K'ang-hsi also went on six southern tours, in the provinces south of Peking, in order to personally inspect his realm. Although these tours were highly formal affairs, involving hundreds of attendants, advisers, and bodyguards, K'ang-hsi is reported to have spent at least some of his time chatting with the common people about the crops and local affairs. On his tours K'ang-hsi paid special attention to the dikes on the Yellow River and the navigability of the Grand Canal; and on one occasion he publically berated the director general of river conservancy for negligence on the basis of his observations during a tour.

In spite of the fact that K'ang-hsi patronized Chinese art and literature (he even spent some leisure evenings on his tours reading the Chinese classics), he retained a great fondness for the martial traditions of the Manchus and revered the Manchu homeland. As early as 1668, K'ang-hsi prohibited Chinese emigration to Manchuria, largely because he did not want Chinese to dilute the ethnic and cultural purity of the homeland. He went on several hunting expeditions in Manchuria, taking with him thousands of troops. Rejecting the usual comforts provided for an emperor, he slept in a simple tent and often sat outdoors in cold and rain while cooking venison.

K'ang-hsi was a competent archer and enjoyed displaying his prowess with the bow while riding horseback. After 1683, when the domestic military problems had been largely resolved, K'ang-hsi began spending his summers in the southern Manchurian city of Jehol to the north of the Great Wall of China. In the early 18th century, as his age began to inhibit his enjoyment of the rugged hunting trips, he ordered the construction of a summer palace at Jehol for himself and his entourage.

Personally a frugal individual, K'ang-hsi endeavored to keep government expenditures to a minimum in spite of the costly military operations of the late 17th century. By systematizing the provincial financial reports and by cutting down on expenditures at the capital, particularly those in the imperial household, K'ang-hsi managed to accumulate a surplus in the imperial treasury. Because of these measures K'ang-hsi was able to reduce taxes. In 1712 he decreed that the per capita tax (*ting*) would be permanently frozen at the current level. Since during the 18th century the land tax and the per capita tax were gradually merged into one tax-paying unit, K'ang-hsi's decision had the effect of maintaining a relatively fixed rate for these traditional sources of dynastic revenue throughout the Ch'ing dynasty. The average Chinese peasant of this period, in fact, may well have been better off than his counterpart in the West or in Japan during the same period.

Political Factionalism at Court

In political affairs K'ang-hsi diligently sought to select responsible and loyal officials for important posts. In general, K'ang-hsi was quite successful in this respect, and cases of government corruption were considerable less frequent than in the late Ming period and in the 19th century. Nevertheless, court factions, greatly feared by the Ch'ing emperors, emerged in the reign of K'ang-hsi.

Several high officials, among them many Chinese and Manchus who had been close associates of K'ang-hsi during his perilous rise to power in the 1660s, banded together in a series of shifting factional alliances. The primary motive behind such factions seems to have been political power and prestige for one's family and associates. K'ang-hsi spent considerable effort trying to eliminate court factions by reprimanding their leaders and in some cases degrading and even dismissing members of cliques.

The most flagrant case of factionalism and perhaps the most disappointing aspect of K'ang-hsi's career concerned his second son and heir apparent, Yin-jeng (1674-1725). Yin-jeng's mother, Empress Hsiao-ch'eng, who had married K'ang-hsi when the Emperor was only 11 years old, died in giving birth to Yin-jeng. Perhaps in remembrance of Hsiao-ch'eng, K'ang-hsi designated the child heir apparent and personally taught him how to read. As Yin-jeng matured, K'ang-hsi devoted special attention to his education, selecting outstanding tutors, and assuring that he became a competent horseman and archer.

Unfortunately Yin-jeng began to associate with ambitious courtiers, and it was reported to K'ang-hsi that his son was engaging in immoral practices. Even the great Manchu official Songgotu, brother of Empress Hsiaoch'eng, developed overly close relations with Yin-jeng. Consequently, K'ang-hsi imprisoned Songgotu and executed a number of other officials who sought to use the heir apparent for their own ends. Eventually K'ang-hsi turned on Yin-jeng himself. Declaring that his son was insolent, that he was immoral and extravagant, and that he had plotted regicide, K'ang-hsi placed Yin-jeng in perpetual confinement in 1712 and refused to name another heir apparent.

After 1715 the Emperor's health declined rapidly and, perhaps suffering a stroke, he found it impossible to read and write. After several years of illness, he died in Peking on Dec. 20, 1722. Almost immediately after K'ang-hsi's death, his fourth son, Yin-chen, declared himself emperor with the support of the commandant of the Peking gendarmerie. It is entirely possible that K'ang-hsi did not want Yin-chen to succeed him, and it is remotely possible that Yin-chen murdered his ailing father in order to take the throne.

In spite of the fact that K'ang-hsi's reign ended on such a gloomy note, it was of paramount importance in the consolidation of Manchu rule in China. In almost every respect, militarily, politically, economically, and culturally, his reign laid the foundations for China's splendid 18th century.

Further Reading

The standard biography of K'ang-hsi is in Arthur W. Hummel, ed., *Eminent Chinese of the Ch'ing Period, 1644-1912* (2 vols., 1943-1944). An excellent monograph that deals with several aspects of K'ang-hsi's life and personality is Jonathan D. Spence, *Ts'ao Yin and the K'ang-hsi Emperor: Bondservant and Master* (1966). □

K'ang Yu-wei

K'ang Yu-wei (1858-1927) was one of the most prominent scholars of modern China, particularly famous for his radical reinterpretations of Confucianism and for his role as the Emperor's adviser during the abortive Hundred Days Reform movement of 1898.

In the late 19th century the helplessness of China in the face of the imperialist powers was becoming increasingly difficult to ignore. Chinese literati, who in midcentury had been supremely confident of the superiority of China's traditional ways, were becoming aware in the 1880s and 1890s that their nation's political institutions and economic system must be reformed if China were to avoid becoming a colony of the Europeans.

K'ang Yu-wei was born near Canton to a scholarly and locally prominent family on March 19, 1858. Like his father and grandfather, K'ang prepared for a bureaucratic career by studying the Confucian classics in preparation for the civil service examinations. He passed the first series of

examinations, but in 1876 he failed the provincial examinations. K'ang thereupon began 3 years of study under the scholar Chu Tz'uch'i. It was under Chu's tutelage that K'ang adopted an eclectic approach to the various schools of interpretation of the Confucian classics. In particular, K'ang learned to search for the ultimate truths in the words of Confucius himself, rather than in latter-day commentaries.

Early Intellectual Development

The period of study with Chu Tz'u-ch'i ended in late 1878, when K'ang experienced an emotional crisis. He suddenly sensed that his preoccupation with pedantic Confucian learning was suffocating his intellectual talents. He shut himself into his room and sat in solitary meditation, causing his friends to think he had gone mad. This retreat from the world ended after he suddenly received mystical enlightenment. "I perceived suddenly," he wrote later, "that I was in an all-pervading unity with Heaven, Earth, and all things. I beheld myself as a sage and laughed for joy. But thinking of the sufferings of mankind I suddenly wept in sorrow."

Now believing himself a sage destined "to set in order all under Heaven," K'ang broadened his studies to include governmental organization and political geography; he also read extensively in Mahayana Buddhism. Curious about the Western nations, he visited Hong Kong in 1879 and in 1882 toured the foreign concessions in Shanghai. Greatly impressed by the cleanliness and orderliness in these cities, he realized that the Europeans were different from the "barbarians" of Chinese antiquity. And in 1882 he began

seriously studying the West through the relatively meager literature on the subject then available in Chinese.

"New Text" Interpretation

Between 1888 and 1890 K'ang acquired a new insight into the Confucian classics that was to provide the basis for his mature philosophy. He became convinced that the orthodox and officially sanctioned version of the classics had in large part been forged during the ascendancy of the usurper Wang Mang (ruled A.D. 8-23). Instead of these "Old Text" versions, K'ang favored the "New Text" versions—which had once been the basis of the Confucian orthodoxy during the Former Han Dynasty—probably because they could be more easily put to the service of a political reform movement.

Making selective use of the New Text interpretations, K'ang now wrote two of his most important books. In *The Forged Classics of the Wang Mang Period* (1891), he mobilized evidence to demonstrate that the orthodox texts of the classics were not authentic. And in *Confucius as a Reformer* (1897), he argued that Confucius was the real author of the classics—Confucius's statement that he was not the author but merely the transmitter of the teachings of the ancient sages had been Confucius's stratagem to win acceptance for his own teachings. K'ang therefore insisted that Confucius had been a reformer who believed that institutions had to be adapted to altered circumstances. K'ang's conclusion was that Confucius, had he been alive in the 1890s, would also have advocated the reform of the existing political and economic order.

K'ang Yu-wei opened a school in Canton in 1891, and many of the students, like Liang Ch'i-ch'ao, were in later years his most avid partisans. The course of study at the school contained K'ang's own interpretations of Confucianism but included also the study of the West, mathematics, music, and even military drill.

In 1893 K'ang passed the second, or provincial, civil service examinations, and in 1895 he succeeded in the highest, or metropolitan, examinations in Peking. He was thereupon appointed a secretary second-class in the Board of Works and might have pursued a normal bureaucratic career had he not in the same year, at the age of 37, burst upon the national political stage.

Reform Activity

In April 1895 the Treaty of Shimonoseki, ending the Sino-Japanese War, was signed. The terms of the treaty were humiliating and damaging to China, and K'ang Yu-wei, together with Liang Ch'i-ch'ao, drafted a petition urging the court to disavow the treaty. They acquired the signatures of nearly 1,300 scholars. The petition had no effect on the outcome of the peace settlement; but K'ang, undaunted, quickly sent two memorials to the Emperor proposing extensive governmental, educational, and economic reforms. When these memorials similarly failed of acceptance by the court, K'ang turned his energies to organizational and propaganda work, hoping thereby to broaden interest in reform among the literati.

The most notable of several reform societies with which K'ang associated himself between 1895 and 1898 was the Ch'iang-hsüeh hui (Society for the Study of National Strengthening). This was organized in August 1895 and won the support of numerous eminent officials, such as Chang Chih-tung and Yüan Shih-k'ai. The successes of this reform society frightened powerful conservative officials, and the Ch'iang-hsüeh hui was banned in early 1896.

During 1897 and early 1898 the foreign powers were staking out "spheres of influence" in China, and the partitioning of the country by the imperialists seemed imminent. This renewed threat inspired K'ang Yu-wei to new reform endeavors. He formed several new societies, most prominent of which was the Pao-kuo hui (Society for the Preservation of the Nation). This organization was founded in April 1898 with the avowed goal of saving "the nation, the race, and the Confucian teaching." He also submitted a succession of reform memorials to Emperor Kuang-hsü. The Emperor had now also become convinced of the need for reform, and in January 1898 he commanded K'ang to elaborate his reform proposals. K'ang also wrote two short books for the Emperor, one on Peter the Great of Russia and one on the Japanese Meiji restoration, and these reportedly strengthened the Emperor's determination to modernize the nation.

On June 12, 1898, Kuang-hsü issued a momentous edict proclaiming a new national policy of "reform and self-strengthening." Four days later K'ang was called for an imperial audience. And for the next 3 months the Emperor, much under K'ang's influence, issued a series of decrees designed to revamp the creaking dynastic system.

The reform movement was cut short by the dowager empress Tz'u-hsi and her conservative supporters on Sept. 21, 1898. But K'ang, forewarned by the emperor, had left Peking for Shanghai the previous day, and he subsequently escaped to Hong Kong in a British gunboat.

Exile and Later Career

For the next 14 years K'ang—with a price on his head—lived the life of a fugitive and exile. His political activities, however, continued. Fearing that Kuang-hsü's life was in danger and that the restoration of power to the Emperor represented China's only hope of national salvation, K'ang founded the Pao-huang hui (Society to Protect the Emperor) in July 1899. This organization had branches among Chinese living in Japan, Southeast Asia, Latin America, Canada, and the United States.

During the first decade of the 20th century, K'ang wrote several scholarly commentaries on the classics and also some vehement denunciations of the anti-Manchu revolutionaries. He also traveled in India, Europe, and the United States—gaining a familiarity with Western culture that, paradoxically, lessened his admiration for the West and increased his appreciation for the traditional culture of China.

Following the establishment of the Chinese Republic in 1912, K'ang Yu-wei never became wholly reconciled to the revolutionary overthrow of the Confucian monarchy. He ardently supported the brief restoration of the Ch'ing dynasty in 1917 by Chang Hsün and, as late as 1923, was still seeking support among such warlords as Wu P'ei-fu for his plan of reviving the Ch'ing dynasty and implanting Confucianism as the officially sanctioned religion. By the time K'ang died on March 31, 1927, most Chinese intellectuals dismissed him as a hopeless relic of the past.

K'ang's Utopian Vision

K'ang adhered consistently to a philosophy of evolutionary change. According to his "Doctrine of the Three Ages," mankind had progressed inexorably from the primitive Age of Disorder to the Age of Approaching Peace and would culminate in the Age of Universal Peace. In K'ang's view, human nature was improving steadily with the progression of history; human institutions must similarly evolve so that they exactly suit the needs of man at every stage of his historical ascent. K'ang thought that the world, in his day, had reached the Age of Approaching Peace, for which the appropriate political institution was constitutional monarchy, and that the final Age of Universal Peace (in which a republican form of government would exist) would be realized only in the distant future. K'ang, then, actually viewed republicanism as the ideal form of government. But he opposed it in 1912 because he thought China and human nature were unprepared for that ideal.

As a practical reformer, K'ang Yu-wei always remained a convinced—if unorthodox—Confucian. As a utopian thinker, however, he transcended Confucianism, displaying an astounding independence of Chinese cultural values. This appears in his most famous book, *Ta-t'ung shu* (The Grand Unity), which is one of the outstanding works in world utopian literature. Essentially, this work is a description of K'ang's vision of the world order as it would exist during the Age of Universal Peace. K'ang envisaged that political boundaries would be abolished; government would consist of small self-ruling communities which would send representatives to a world parliament. The family system would disappear: men and women could freely change partners each year, and children would be reared in public nurseries and schools. The economy would be highly industrialized; all property would be owned communally; and social, sexual, and racial distinctions would be entirely abolished. In this utopia, laws and courts would be unnecessary, for mankind would have learned to live together in perfect harmony.

K'ang had conceived the basic ideas for the *Ta-t'ung shu* as early as 1885, although he did not complete the book until 1902, while living in India. He dared not publish the work, however, for he thought the public was unprepared for its radical ideas, and to disclose them prematurely would be "to consign mankind to a vast deluge or ravening beasts." K'ang finally relented to the persistent entreaties of his students, and in 1913 Books I and II (which contained only a statement of his general principles and political ideals) appeared in print. The rest of the work, containing the more controversial social ideals, was not published until 1935, 8 years after his death.

K'ang Yu-wei was a brilliant thinker, his reinterpretations of Confucianism assuring him of lasting fame in Chinese intellectual history. His reform organizations and publications in the 1890s had a lasting influence on the course of Chinese political development. He was, however, a man of monumental egotism and arrogance, and although he derived many of his ideas and political programs from his teachers and predecessors, he seldom deigned to recognize his intellectual debts.

Further Reading

K'ang Yu-wei's chronological autobiography, together with a number of essays interpreting aspects of his thought, are in an edition by K'ang's grandson, Professor Jung-pang Lo, *K'ang Yu-wei: A Biography and a Symposium* (1967). Laurence G. Thompson translated a portion of K'ang's utopian vision under the title *Ta T'ung Shu: The One-world Philosophy of K'ang Yu-wei* (1958), which also contains a useful introduction to K'ang's life and thought.

Additional Sources

A modern China and a new world: K'ang Yu-wei, reformer and utopian, 1858-1927, Seattle: University of Washington Press, 1975. □

Kanishka

Kushan ruler Kanishka (flourished c. 78-c. 103 A.D.) controlled an empire covering most of India, Iran, and central Asia in the first and second centuries. With his conversion to and official support of Mahayana Buddhism, the religion underwent a period of substantial growth, gaining converts throughout the Kushan realm, including parts of China. This growth was attended by a blossoming of Buddhist iconography, sculpture, and architecture.

Kanishka was the greatest ruler of the Kushan Empire, a realm that covered much of present-day India, Pakistan, Iran and other parts of central Asia and China during the first and second centuries. Under his influence, the developing religious philosophy of Mahayana Buddhism was spread to areas of central Asia and China and gained a prominent following in the areas under his control. A supporter of the arts who embraced ideas from the many peoples of his region, Kanishka also helped bring about a new era of sculpture that combined Buddhist themes with representational approaches adopted from other cultures, particularly the Roman Empire.

Almost no biographical information on Kanishka exists; what is known is primarily drawn from legends and archaeological artifacts originating during his rule. Modern scholars debate even the exact dates of his reign. For many years Kanishka was generally accepted to have flourished during the years 78 A.D. to 103 A.D., but some more recent arguments have placed him between 128 A.D. and 151 A.D. The Kushan empire was already a powerful force when he became its leader. The Kushan people had originated from a central Asian region that was the site of extensive migrations of numerous ethnic groups. Around 130 B.C., the Kushans were one of about five central Asian nomadic tribes that conquered the region of Bactria, which is now part of northern Afghanistan. Here the Kushans absorbed the Greek and Indian cultural influences that had developed in Bactria. The tribe eventually became the most powerful group in the area, and under the Kushan ruler Kujula Kadphises I, the various tribes were unified. Eventually, the Kushans moved east, adopting the Hindu Kush region of northwestern India as their home. Beginning with the rule of Kujula Kadphises, and continuing through the reign of his son, Wima Kadphises II, and then Kanishka, the Kushans gained control of a large part of India. This was a notable feat, as the area was historically unstable due to the feuding of a number of states.

Controlled Vast Empire

It has been suggested that Kanishka may not have been of the same lineage as the Kadphises rulers. Various theories propose that he may have been a successful invader from a northern region, such as Khotan in Sinkiang, or that he may have been a leader of an Indian state who emerged victorious from a power struggle after the demise of the Kadphises line. Once he assumed power, Kanishka instituted a system of co-rule, sharing his authority with a man named Vashishka, who was probably his son or brother. Control of his huge empire was maintained by instituting a number of local governments headed by provincial governors (satraps), district officers (meridareks), and military governors (strategoi) appointed by Kanishka. Like many royal rulers, Kanishka claimed a divine heritage. This is reflected in the many titles he adopted from a number of cultures, including King of Kings,'' Great King,'' "Son of Heaven," and "Emperor." It is also evident in the Kushan practice of deifying emperors and dedicating temples to them after their death.

Under Kanishka, the Kushan empire reached its greatest heights. The center of the region was the upper Indus and Ganges river valleys in what is now Iran and India; its capital was the city of Purushapura, now the city of Peshawar in Pakistan. Kushan holdings in central Asia gave them control of a number of major trade routes and ports, and traders were charged significant fees to transport goods through these routes. The kingdom's economy thrived on the money brought in by foreign trade, creating a prosperous urban society filled with merchants and guilds. The Kushans were also enriched by the new ideas and artistic influences that they gained from their interactions with other cultures ranging as far as the Roman Empire in the west to China in the east.

Supported Growth of Mahayana Buddhism

Kanishka himself seems to have embodied the strong, yet tolerant and diverse Kushan culture. As depicted in sculpture and on coins of the period, he presented a forceful image; one statue of him in Mathura portrays him in the costume of a warrior. But he also took an eclectic interest in religion and the arts, as can be seen by the variety of deities that appear on his coins. Eventually, like many other Kushan people, Kanishka came to favor Buddhism, probably due to the fact that in the caste system of Hinduism, the Kushans would have held a rather low position. The Mahayana form of Buddhism was just developing at this time, and by his official support of the religion it enjoyed a rich period of growth. By providing resources for Buddhist practitioners to educate others in the faith, particularly through the spread of religious iconography, Mahayana Buddhism spread throughout central Asia and into China. Acting under Kanishka's authority, the Sarvastivadin monks, supporters of the new Mahayana Buddhism, held a religious council in which a series of Buddhist canonical writings was drafted. This work also helped to establish the fledgling denomination.

Kanishka's religious policies, combined with artistic influences arriving from the western Greco-Roman and Iranian cultures resulted in the development of a new trend in sculpture that represented Buddhist themes in a more naturalistic, popular style. The emperor was also responsible for some impressive architectural accomplishments. In Peshawar he oversaw the construction of a 638-foot tall Buddhist shrine. The building, which was known across Asia for its magnificence, was composed of a five-stage base, a second section comprised of a 13-story structure of carved wood, and the crowning detail of an iron column decorated with umbrellas of gilded copper. Kanishka is reputed to have been an enthusiastic patron of scholarship and the arts who brought scientists and writers to his court.

There is no available information about the death of Kanishka. A relic casket bearing an inscription of Kanishka, however, was found early in the twentieth century and now resides at the museum in Peshawar. Despite the dearth of concrete information, the effects of Kanishka's rule are evident in the cultural and religious history of India, China, and central Asia. The spread of Mahayana Buddhism that was made possible by his support provided a strong base for the religion. In addition, this development also affected the retention of Hinduism by many Indian people, who considered Kanishka and his religion to be a foreign presence. Research will probably never reveal a complete picture of Kanishka's life, but the numerous artistic and architectural artifacts surviving from his reign testify to his recognition of the value of the ideas and traditions of a multitude of cultures.

Further Reading

Basham, Arthur L., *Papers on the Date of Kanishka,* E. J. Brill (Leiden, Netherlands), 1968.

Davids, T. W. Rhys, *Buddhist India,* T. Fisher Unwin (London), 1903.

Majumdar, R. C., *The History and Culture of the Indian People,* Volume 2: *The Age of Imperial Unity,* 5th ed., Bhartiya Vidya Bhavan (Bombay, India), 1980.

Warder, A. K., *Indian Buddhism,* Motilal Banarsidass (Delhi, India), 1970. □

Immanuel Kant

The major works of the German philosopher Immanuel Kant (1724-1804) offer an analysis of speculative and moral reason and the faculty of human judgment. He exerted an immense influence on the intellectual movements of the 19th and 20th centuries.

The fourth of nine children of Johann Georg and Anna Regina Kant, Immanuel Kant was born in the town of Königsberg on April 22, 1724. Johann Kant was a harness maker, and the large family lived in modest circumstances. The family belonged to a Protestant sect of Pietists, and a concern for religion touched every aspect of their lives. Although Kant became critical of formal religion, he continued to admire the "praiseworthy conduct" of Pietists. Kant's elementary education was taken at Saint George's Hospital School and then at the Collegium Fredericianum, a Pietist school, where he remained from 1732 until 1740.

In 1740 Kant entered the University of Königsberg. Under the influence of a young instructor, Martin Knutzen, Kant became interested in philosophy, mathematics, and the natural sciences. Through the use of Knutzen's private library, Kant grew familiar with the philosophy of Christian Wolff, who had systematized the rationalism of Leibniz. Kant accepted the rationalism of Leibniz and Wolff and the natural philosophy of Newton until a chance reading of David Hume aroused him from his "dogmatic slumbers."

The death of Kant's father in 1746 left him without income. He became a private tutor for 7 years in order to acquire the means and leisure to begin an academic career. During this period Kant published several papers dealing with scientific questions. The most important was the "General Natural History and Theory of the Heavens" in 1755. In this work Kant postulated the origin of the solar system as a result of the gravitational interaction of atoms. This theory anticipated Laplace's hypothesis (1796) by more than 40 years. In the same year Kant presented a Latin treatise, "On Fire", to qualify for the doctoral degree.

Kant spent the next 15 years (1755-1770) as a nonsalaried lecturer whose fees were derived entirely from the students who attended his lectures. In order to live he lectured between 26 and 28 hours a week on metaphysics, logic, mathematics, physics, and physical geography. Despite this enormous teaching burden, Kant continued to publish papers on various topics. He finally achieved a professorship at Königsberg in 1770.

Critique of Pure Reason

For the next decade Kant published almost nothing. But at the age of 57 he published the first edition of the *Critique of Pure Reason* (1781; 2d ed. 1787). This enormous work, one of the most important and difficult books in Western thought, attempts to resolve the contradictions inherent in perception and conception as explained by the rationalists and empiricists.

On the level of experience, Kant saw the inherent difficulties in the "representative theory of perception." Our percepts, or intuitions of things, are not themselves objects but rather images or re-presentations. Since these perceptual images are the only evidence for an external, physical world, it can be asked how faithfully mental images represent physical objects. On the level of conception, mathematical, scientific, and metaphysical judgments make predictions about the connections and consequences of events. As these judgments tell us about the past, present, and future, they cannot be derived from our immediate experience. Some events, however, can be experienced as conforming to these universal and necessary laws; hence, these judgments are more than mere definitions. The aim of the critique is to explain how experience and reason interact in perception and understanding.

Philosophers had long recognized two kinds of judgment. The first is *analytic,* which is the product of the analysis or definition of concepts. All analytic propositions are reducible to statements of identity, that is, they define what a thing is. For example, a triangle is a three-sided figure universally (always) and necessarily (could not be otherwise) by definition. As such, all analytic judgments are true a priori, or independent of experience. The content and form of the second type of judgment is exactly the reverse. *Synthetic* propositions expand or amplify our knowledge, but these judgments are a posteriori, or derived from experience.

Kant's position is that of the first thinker to posit the problem of pure reason correctly by isolating a third order of judgment. Consider the following propositions: 10 times 2 is 20; every event has a cause; the universe is created. As universal and necessary, all three judgments are a priori but also, according to Kant, synthetic, in that they extend our knowledge of reality. Thus the fundamental propositions of mathematics, science, and metaphysics are synthetic a priori, and the question that the *Critique of Pure Reason* poses is not an analysis of whether there is such knowledge but a methodology of *how* "understanding and reason can know apart from experience."

The solution to this problem is Kant's "Copernican Revolution." Until Copernicus hypothesized that the sun was the center of the universe and the earth in its rotation, science had assumed the earth was the center of the universe. Just so, argues Kant, philosophers have attempted and failed to prove that our perceptions and judgments are true because they correspond to objects. "We must therefore make trial whether we may not have more success . . . if we suppose that objects must conform to our knowledge." This radical proposal means that the mind constitutes the way the world appears and the way in which the world is thought about.

But, unlike later idealists, Kant does not say that the mind creates objects but only the conditions under which objects are perceived and understood. According to Kant, "we can know a priori of things only what we ourselves put into them." The attempt to preserve a realist orientation leads Kant to distinguish between the appearances of things (*phenomena*), as conditioned by the subjective forms of intuition, and the categories of the understanding and things-in-themselves (*noumena*). In brief, mathematics and science are true because they are derived from the ways in which the mind conditions its percepts and concepts, and metaphysics is an illusion because it claims to tell us about things as they really are. But since the mind constitutes the appearances and their intelligibility, we can never know noumenal reality (as it exists apart from mind) with any certainty. Although Kant considers the denial of metaphysics inconsequential because it has consisted only of "mock combats" in which no victory was ever gained, he is at some pains to establish that the restriction of pure reason to the limits of sensibility does not preclude a practical knowledge of morality and religion. In fact, the limitation of pure reason makes such faith more positive.

The first critique attempts to reconcile the conflict between rationalism and empiricism over the role of experience. Kant's ingenuity is to suggest that both parties are correct but one-sided, that is, "though all knowledge begins with experience it does not follow that it arises out of experience." Kant attempts to isolate the a priori element in the various parts of knowledge: intuition, which Kant calls esthetic, understanding, or analytic and speculative reason, or dialectic. He calls his method "transcendental" as opposed to formal or material logic, and by this he means only the manner, or mode, in which we perceive, understand, or think.

The problem of the transcendental esthetic can be seen in the term "a priori intuition." That is, what does the mind tell us about experience prior to having experience. Kant argues that if one eliminates the content of any possible intuition, space and time remain as the a priori forms, or ways, in which the mind can perceive. As a priori forms of any possible experience, space and time are subjective conditions or limitations of human sensibility. But as the universal and necessary conditions without which there will be no experience, these forms are empirical conditions of appearances, or *phenomena*. Thus, for Kant, space and time are "transcendentally ideal" and "empirically real" as subjective conditions and objective, constitutive principles of intuition. In brief, this is Kant's resolution of the scientific debate between the adherents of Newton's concept of absolute space and time and Leibniz's relational view. Kant is saying that space and time are absolute conditions for human experience even though there may be nonspatial and nontemporal entities that are unknown.

This argument provides an answer to how synthetic a priori judgments in mathematics are possible. These judgments are universal and necessary, and yet they apply to and yield new knowledge about experience. The principle of Kant's explanation may be expressed as follows: whatever is true of a condition is a priori true of the conditioned. Space and time are the conditions for all possible perceptions. And Euclidean geometry and arithmetic are true of space and time. Therefore, arithmetic and geometry are a priori valid for all possible appearances.

A weak analogy with eyeglasses will explain the drift of Kant's thinking. If I cannot see anything without the glasses, they are my subjective limitation since there may be things which are not perceivable. But the glasses are also objective conditions for the possibility of anything appearing to me. And whatevers true of this condition—such as their being tinted—will be true a priori of whatever can be seen but not necessarily of whatever can be. The point of Kant's radical proposal is that human experience may be just that— exclusively human—but that it is valid of appearances since space and time are the a priori and empirical conditions of every possible perception.

A similar explanation of the working of human understanding presented a great difficulty occasioned by the seeming impossibility of specifying the forms of thinking in other than an arbitrary and chance manner. Eventually Kant discovered a "transcendental clue" in the traditional forms of logical judgment enumerated by Aristotle. The question raised is why are there only 12 forms of judgment? Kant argued that each form of possible judgment was related to a thought form that he called an a priori category of the understanding. Thus, again, there is a form and content division such that, if one thinks, there are only certain ways in which one can make judgments about the quantity, quality, relation, and modality of objects. In human understanding, as the name implies, experience is made to stand underneath and be organized by the categories. Experience is given as conditioned by space and time, a category is superimposed by the mind, and the resulting synthesis produces human knowing. This complicated process of synthesis is unified by the ego and aided by the imagination, which associates particular percepts with appropriate universal concepts. As in the case of perception, Kant's efforts are directed toward reconciling the claims of both rationalism and empiricism. Concepts of themselves are empty logical forms, and percepts, alone, are blind; it is only in their synthesis that understanding, or knowing, takes place.

This development commits Kant to the position that science is knowing and metaphysics is false, speculative thinking. Knowing is confirmed by experience as above, but the categories can be extended beyond space and time, and they, then, function as ideas of pure reason. Since metaphysics claims to speak about things as they are rather than as they appear, such pure thinking must justify itself without appeal to experience. But that is just the difficulty when one asks questions about the unconditioned reality of the self, world, or God!

It is not that reason is incapable of producing arguments, but rather that there are equally valid arguments that contradict one another, and experience is unable to resolve these "antinomies," or seeming contradictions. For example, we know that the universe is either created or eternal, and we can think both of these alternatives through; but the spatiotemporal world of experience would be the same in either instance; and so while the mind can think about these problems, it can never know the answers to the questions that it raises. The only exception to this rule occurs in what Kant calls the "dynamical antinomies" concerning the dilemmas of necessity or freedom and atheism or theism. Here Kant suggests that in the realms of morality and religion one can entertain the possibility that while necessity and determinism are true of *phenomena,* freedom and God are true of *noumena.* Thus, one could live in a universe that is physically determined and still believe in human freedom.

Later Works

In 1783 Kant restated the main outlines of his first critique in a brief, analytic form in the *Prolegomena to Any Future Metaphysics.* In 1785 he presented an early view of the practical aspects of reason in *Fundamental Principles of the Metaphysic of Morals.* In 1788 he published the *Critique of Practical Reason.*

While theoretical reason is concerned with cognition, practical reason is concerned with will, or self-determination. There is only one human reason, but after it decides what it can know, it must determine how it shall act. In the analytic of practical reason Kant attempts to isolate the a priori element in morality. The notion that happiness is the end of life is purely subjective, and every empirical morality is arbitrary.

Thus the freedom of the will, which is only a speculative possibility for pure reason, becomes the practical necessity of determining how one shall lead his life. And the fundamental, rational principle of a free morality is some universal and necessary law to which a man commits himself. This principle is called by Kant the "Categorical Imperative," which states that a man should obligate himself to act so that any one of his actions could be made into a universal law binding all mankind. The dignity of man consists in the freedom to overcome inclination and private interest in order to obligate oneself to the duty of performing the good for its own sake. In examining the consequences of man's freedom, Kant insists that practical reason postulates the immortality of the soul and the existence of God as the conditions for true freedom.

In 1790 Kant completed his third critique, which attempts to draw these conflicting tensions together. In pure reason the mind produces constitutive principles of *phenomena,* and in practical reason the mind produces regulative principles of noumenal reality. The *Critique of Judgment* attempts to connect the concepts of nature with the concepts of freedom. The reflective or teleological judgment of finality, which is derived from our esthetic feelings about the fittingness of things, mediates between our cognition and our will. This judgment neither constitutes nature like the understanding nor legislates action like practical reason, but it does enable us to think of the "purposiveness" of nature as a realm of ends that are in harmony with universal laws.

Although Kant continued writing until shortly before his death, the "critical works" are the source of his influence. Only a life of extraordinary self-discipline enabled him to accomplish his task. He was barely 5 feet tall and extremely thin, and his health was never robust. He attributed his longevity to an invariable routine. Rising at five, he drank tea and smoked his daily pipe and meditated for an hour. From six to seven he prepared his lectures and taught from seven to nine in his own home. He worked in his study until one. He invited friends for long dinners, which lasted often until four. After his one daily meal he walked between four and five so punctually that people were said to set their watches on his passing. He continued to write or read until he retired at ten. Toward the end of his life he became increasingly antisocial and bitter over the growing loss of his memory and capacity for work. Kant became totally blind and finally died on Feb. 12, 1804.

Further Reading

There is no standard edition in English, but virtually all of Kant's major works are available in various paperback editions. The field of general and critical studies is rich. Basic accounts of Kant's critique are Herbert James Paton, *Kant's Metaphysic of Experience* (2 vols., 1936); Heinrick Cassirer, *A Commentary on Kant's Critique of Judgment* (1938); A. C. Ewing, *A Commentary on Kant's Critique of Pure Reason* (1938); Lewis White Beck, *A Commentary on Kant's Critique of Practical Reason* (1960); Norman Kemp Smith, *A Commentary to Kant's Critique of Pure Reason* (2d ed. 1962); and S. Körner, *Kant* (1964), which is one of the best general works available. Specialized studies include Paul Arthur Schlipp, *Kant's Precritical Ethics* (2d ed. 1960); Martin Heidegger, *Kant and the Problem of Metaphysics,* translated by James S. Churchill (1962); Robert Paul Wolff, *Kant's Theory of Mental Activity* (1963); and P. F. Strawson, *The Bounds of Sense* (1966). □

Kao-tsung

Kao-tsung (1107-1187) was a Chinese emperor. After the Sung dynasty lost the North, he continued Sung rule in the South and became the first emperor of the Southern Sung.

As the ninth son of Emperor Hui-tsung (1082-1135) and child of a concubine, the Lady Wei, the future emperor Kao-tsung would not normally have risen to the throne, but after Emperor Ch'in-tsung (1100-1161) and the abdicated Hui-tsung were taken prisoner, he ascended the throne in what was then the Southern capital. The Sung forces, confronting Chin (Jürchen) armies as well as widespread rebellion in the South, were unable to hold their position, and still in the first year of his reign, Kao-tsung had to flee farther south.

A low point in Kao-tsung's career came in 1129, when the generals Miao Fu and Liu Cheng-yen succeeded in deposing him for 28 days before they were defeated by loyal forces under Chang Chün and Han Shih-chung. But even then the Emperor's future was still precarious. He had to resume his flight in the face of a Chin offensive and, in 1130, took refuge in some islands off the southeast coast of China. Then, during the 1130s, the tide of war turned: under the command of Chang Chün, Han Shih-chung, and the famous Yüeh Fei, the Sung armies suppressed the rebellions in the South and not only stopped the Chin but even carried the war to the North.

Kao-tsung has been much criticized for rejecting the arguments of Yüeh Fei and other advocates of continuing the war until China was reunified. Aware of the dangers of such a policy, which might well have led to the preponderance of the generals, the Emperor preferred to support the peace plans of Ch'in Kuei, which resulted in the treaty of 1141.

In 1138 Kao-tsung decided on Hangchow as the new capital and thus contributed to the greatness of this scenic city, which even after the fall of the Southern Sung elicited the admiration of Marco Polo. The Emperor further demonstrated his good taste as well as his love for the arts by reestablishing the Painting Academy, where many of the artists who had served his father once again enjoyed imperial patronage. His reign also saw the restoration of the university. Various measures for economic rehabilitation and fiscal reform, including a land survey, the equalization of taxes and establishment of new taxes, the restoration of war-damaged fields, and the issuance of paper money, were undertaken during his reign.

In 1161 war broke out again between the Sung and the Chin, but the peace of 1165, although somewhat milder, was basically similar to that of 1141. By then Kao-tsung himself had abdicated. Retiring with him was Empress Wu, a remarkable, strong-willed lady who outlived the Emperor and rendered a final service to the dynasty when, in 1194, she effected the abdication of the mentally incapacitated Emperor Kuang-tsung and his succession by Emperor Ning-tsung.

Further Reading

General background on Kao-tsung is in Kenneth S. Latourette, *The Chinese: Their History and Culture* (1934; 4th ed. 1964); René Grousset, *The Rise and Splendour of the Chinese Empire* (trans. 1953); and Edwin O. Reischauer and John K. Fairbank, *History of East Asian Civilization*, vol. 1: *The Great Tradition* (1958). For information on Hangchow see Jacques Gernet, *Daily Life in China on the Eve of the Mongol Invasion, 1250-1276* (1959; trans. 1962). □

Pyotr Leonidovich Kapitsa

The Soviet physicist Pyotr Leonidovich Kapitsa (1894-1984) made notable contributions to knowledge of atomic structures and to understanding the behavior of matter in strong magnetic fields and at extremely low temperatures.

Pyotr Kapitsa was born on July 8, 1894, in Kronstadt near St. Petersburg (Leningrad) and was raised in Tsaritsyn (Volgograd). He obtained his education in the physical sciences and engineering at the high school of Kronstadt and at the Polytechnic Institute of Petrograd (St. Petersburg), from which he graduated in 1918. The following year he became a lecturer at the Polytechnic Institute. He published six papers between 1916 and 1921, which clearly reveal his wide-ranging interests and his skillful and ingenious experimentation.

On the recommendation of a colleague and the personal intercession of a well-known Russian writer, Kapitsa was able to leave the country in 1921 as a member of a scientific mission representing the Soviet Academy of Sciences. In July of that year Kapitsa met Ernest Rutherford, impressed him favorably, and was invited to work in the Cavendish Laboratory at Cambridge, England. Preferring to continue his studies of physics under Rutherford, Kapitsa temporarily suspended his activities with the scientific mission.

Cambridge Period

From 1921 until 1934 the Cavendish Laboratory was Kapitsa's home. The professional respect that Kapitsa and Rutherford initially displayed toward each other matured into an enduring and warm friendship. After a year's activity in the Cavendish Laboratory, Kapitsa was impressed with the English commitment to individualism in scientific research and to insistence of obtaining results; he believed that the Soviet physicists would benefit more by following the English pattern instead of the German model.

Kapitsa's early experiments in the Cavendish Laboratory were in nuclear physics. He constructed a microradiometer, an instrument capable of measuring the energy of the rays emitted by radium, and was able to

determine the loss of energy of a beam of alpha particles as it passed through air and carbon dioxide gas. After 3 1/2 months of investigating alpha particles, Kapitsa was excited when he managed to produce the first photograph of three distorted tracks of alpha particles in a strong magnetic field.

Another area requiring Kapitsa's engineering ability was cryogenics. When he turned to low-temperature physics, the Royal Society Mond Laboratory was built for him and others interested in the pioneering areas of physics. The Mond Laboratory officially opened on Feb. 3, 1933, and Kapitsa was its first director. It was here that he constructed a helium liquefier capable of producing 2 liters of helium an hour; this cryogenic apparatus made possible experiments at extremely low temperatures.

Stalin's Captive Physicist

Kapitsa and his wife traveled to the Soviet Union (Russia) several times, but in the fall of 1934 their exit visas were unexpectedly canceled. The following year Kapitsa and Stalin came to a reconciliation resulting in Kapitsa's being appointed director of the Institute of Physical Problems, part of the U.S.S.R. Academy of Sciences, founded on Dec. 28, 1934; in negotiations for the acquisition of his equipment at the Mond Laboratory; and in reuniting Kapitsa and his wife with their two children.

The Institute of Physical Problems was purposely designed to enable Kapitsa to continue his work with strong magnetic fields and low temperatures. In 1937 he began a series of experiments with helium II, whose thermal con-

ductivity is 3 million times greater than normal helium (helium I) and about a million times greater than copper. A consequence of his study was the discovery of the phenomenon of superfluidity, whereby atoms move among each other without friction. However, World War II interrupted his investigations; he returned to the field of nuclear physics, experimented with uranium, built instruments for the study of cosmic rays, and delivered scientific lectures before the command staff of the Red Army.

There was speculation in 1945-1946 that Kapitsa was working on the Soviet atomic bomb, but he consistently and vigorously denied this. Late in 1946 his name vanished from public view, and secrecy surrounded his work. He was under house arrest in Zvenigorod, a suburb of Moscow, from 1946 until the death of Stalin in 1953, for refusing to cooperate with Soviet authorities on projects to improve atomic military capability. During this period of restriction Kapitsa produced papers dealing with heat transfer, the problem of the wave flow of thin viscous fluid layers, the problem of determining the effect of airflow on a flowing liquid, and a study on the dynamic stability of a moving pendulum with a vibrating suspension. It is now becoming evident that Kapitsa and his collaborators had done some remarkable theoretical work in the area of high-power electronics between 1946 and 1955; the monographs in this field began to appear after 1961. For example, Kapitsa and his colleagues considered the possibility of constructing generators, such as the plane magnetron, for producing ultrahigh frequencies which could be used for the transmission of electrical energy in waveguides.

In 1978, Kapitsa received a share of the Nobel prize for his work in low temperature physics. He died in Moscow on April 8, 1984.

Outlook and Philosophy

In many respects Kapitsa was more British than Russian in his approach to science, believing that it should be free to question and probe, that it should be buttressed by experimentation, and that it should be unfettered by political ideologies. In the article "Theory, Experiment, Practice" (1962), Kapitsa castigated the divergence between Soviet theoretical and experimental physicists, the ignorant application of dialectical materialism to science by Marxist philosophers who know little about science, and the general divorcement between theory and practice in Soviet science. In another piece he insisted that science is an international enterprise and that international cooperation and contact are a necessity if science is to progress.

Respecting the future course of science, Kapitsa discussed in "The Future of Science" (1962) the tremendous challenge mankind faces in the conquest of outer space. He foresaw the use of nuclear energy to power space vehicles, the use of outer space for the disposal of dangerous radioactive waste products, and the easing of population pressure on earth through colonization of other planets. Turning to biology, Kapitsa believed that genetics can be extremely valuable if scientists can produce desired mutations.

Of special interest were Kapitsa's views on the social sciences. It was his opinion that the social sciences are at the same level of historical development that the natural sciences were during the Middle Ages, which in part explains the wide chasm between the natural and the social sciences; it is only with the emergence of the science of man's higher nervous activity that the social sciences have finally been provided with an empirical base. Being a man of peace, Kapitsa pleaded that the social sciences be developed intensively in order to create a social system of states that would make war impossible.

Further Reading

Kedrov, Fedor B. *Kapitza: Life and Discoveries (Outstanding Soviet Scientists)* (1986); Boag, J.W. *Kapitza in Cambridge and Moscow: Life and Letters of a Russian Physicist* (1990); Badash, Lawrence *Kapitza, Rutherford and the Kremlin* (1985). □

Mordecai Menahem Kaplan

Mordecai Menahem Kaplan (1881-1983), American Jewish theologian and educator, was the founder and leader of the Reconstructionist movement in American Judaism.

Mordecai Kaplan was born on June 11, 1881, in Swenziany, Lithuania, and emigrated to the United States in 1889. He took his bachelor of arts degree at the City College of New York in 1900 and his master of arts at Columbia University, New York City, in 1902, the same year he was ordained a rabbi by the Jewish Theological Seminary. In 1908 he married Lena Rubin.

Kaplan served in the rabbinate for a number of years. Most of his career, however, was devoted to education and theology. From 1910 until 1963, he taught at the Jewish Theological Seminary, becoming principal of its teachers' institute in 1909, dean in 1931, and dean emeritus in 1947. He also taught at the Graduate School for Jewish Social Work (1925-1937), Columbia University (1932-1944), and Hebrew University (1937-1939).

Reconstructionist Movement

Kaplan is best known for his role as founder and leader of the Reconstructionist movement in Judaism. In 1922 he founded the Society for the Advancement of Judaism. The society, especially through its journals, provided a forum for the dissemination of Kaplan's views. In 1940 the Jewish Reconstructionist Foundation was established and assumed responsibility for the publication of the *Reconstructionist,* whose editorial board Kaplan headed until 1959.

Mordecai Kaplan developed the philosophy of the Reconstructionist movement over many years. His first major work on the subject was *Judaism as a Civilization: Toward a Reconstruction of American-Jewish Life* (1934). Among his other important books are *Judaism in Transition* (1936); *The Meaning of God in Modern Jewish Religion* (1937); *The Future of the American Jew* (1948); *A New Zionism* (1955);

Questions Jews Ask; Reconstructionist Answers (1956); *Judaism without Supernaturalism: The Only Alternative to Orthodoxy and Secularism* (1958); *The Greater Judaism in the Making: A Study of the Modern Evolution of Judaism* (1960); *The Purpose and Meaning of Jewish Existence: A People in the Image of God* (1964); and *Not So Random Thoughts* (1966). Kaplan was also coeditor of *Sabbath Prayer Book* (1945), which denied the literal accuracy of the biblical text. As such, the Union of Orthodox Rabbis of the United States and Canada declared his theories unacceptable.

Kaplan's philosophy contends that the survival of Judaism is dependent upon its "reconstruction," that is, its adaptation to the changing conditions of the modern world, especially to nationalism and naturalism. He viewed Judaism as an evolving civilization and the Jewish religion as its highest expression of the idea of the greatest good. In Kaplan's theology, the land of Israel is central to the continued development of Judaism as a civilization, and Zionism is the means to the spiritual unification of world Jewry. Kaplan was responsible for the revision of Jewish liturgy to meet the needs—as seen by the Reconstructionist philosophy—of contemporary Jewish life.

Kaplan retired in 1963. His last published work was *The Religion of Ethical Nationhood: Judaism's Contribution to World Peace* (1970). He died in New York City on Nov. 8, 1983.

Further Reading

For a bibliography of Kaplan's writings consult, *Mordecai M. Kaplan Jubilee Volume* (2 vols., 1953)Moshe Davis, ed; *Mordecai Kaplan: An Evaluation* (1952). Ira Eisenstein and Eugene Kohn, eds.; *Encyclopedia of Judaica* □

Wolfgang Kapp

The German nationalist politician Wolfgang Kapp (1858-1922) led a putsch in March 1920, an abortive rightist-military coup.

Wolfgang Kapp was born in New York City on July 24, 1858, the son of a lawyer-politician. Returning to Germany in 1870, the young Kapp earned a doctorate of law and entered the Prussian civil service in 1886. A hardworking bureaucrat, he advanced through the ranks of district magistrate in 1891 and councilor in the Prussian Ministry of Agriculture in 1900 until he was appointed director general of the East Prussian Land Bank in Königsberg in 1906, a position he held until his putsch in 1920.

A partisan of the ultra nationalist Pan-German League, Kapp emerged during World War I as a determined foe of a negotiated peace and campaigned bitterly against the moderate chancellor Theobald von Bethmann Hollweg and the Reichstag (parliamentary) Peace Resolution of 1917 in two violent pamphlets. In September 1917, with Adm. Alfred von Tirpitz and others, he founded the ultranationalist German Fatherland party. From February until November 1918 he held a mandate in the Reichstag.

Outraged by the revolution of 1918-1919, Kapp reorganized his party with the support of several disenchanted army officers and freebooters under the new name of Nationale Vereinigung (Alliance for National Unity) in July 1919. Together with the Berlin army group commander Gen. Walther von Lüttwitz, he staged the so-called Kapp Putsch against the republican government of Friedrich Ebert and Gustav Bauer in March 1920. Kapp and Lüttwitz used the rebellion of the elite Marine Brigade Ehrhardt—which under Lüttwitz's command was defying a government order that they disband—to march on Berlin, seize the government buildings, and declare the republican government deposed on March 13. Kapp took over the chancellorship, Lüttwitz the Ministry of Defense. Lacking active army support, however, the putschists were unable to carry on the business of government in the face of general popular distrust and an effective general strike called by the labor unions at the request of the fleeing government in Stuttgart.

Kapp and Lüttwitz fled on the morning of March 17, making their way to Sweden the following day. Although its duration was brief, the putsch left the republic severely shaken and faced with new unrest in the industrial areas of the Ruhr and Saxony as well as several important power readjustments in the central and state governments. Kapp returned to Germany in May 1922 to stand trial but died in custody on June 12.

Further Reading

For general information on Kapp see Robert G. L. Waite, *Vanguard of Nazism: The Free Corps Movement in Postwar Germany, 1918-1923* (1952), and Walther H. Kaufmann, *Monarchism in the Weimar Republic* (1953). □

Jacobus Cornelis Kapteyn

The Dutch astronomer Jacobus Cornelis Kapteyn (1851-1922) founded a unique astronomical data analysis laboratory, helped compile a monumental star catalog, discovered the two star streams, and constructed a model of our galaxy.

Jacobus Kapteyn was born on Jan. 19, 1851, in Barneveld. At 18 he entered the University of Utrecht and 6 years later obtained his doctorate in physics. He became a professional astronomer somewhat accidentally: just as he received his doctoral degree, the position of observer at the Leiden Observatory became vacant. He applied and obtained it, a decisive event in his life, for it appears likely that it was during his subsequent 3 years at Leiden that he resolved to try to understand the structure of the universe. In 1878 he became professor of astronomy, calculus of probabilities, and theoretical mechanics at the University of Groningen. The following year he married Catharina E. Kalshoven; they had three children.

The University of Groningen had no observatory, and for years Kapteyn unsuccessfully attempted to secure funds to establish one. However, he found a unique solution to the problem: in 1896 he established at Groningen not an observatory but a laboratory, where stellar photographs taken elsewhere could be analyzed. In 1903, after several years at a temporary location, his laboratory found a permanent home in the mineralogical laboratory of the university; it is now known as the Astronomical Laboratory Kapteyn.

In 1885 Kapteyn took upon himself a prodigious task: he offered to help David Gill measure and reduce the photographs Gill had taken of the southern sky from his observatory at the Cape of Good Hope. The project took 14 years. The resulting star catalog contained almost a half million entries; this work alone would have put generations of astronomers in Kapteyn's debt.

By 1889 Kapteyn had developed new methods for determining stellar parallaxes, or distances. This work soon evolved into studies on stellar proper motions, and by 1896 he found indications that, contrary to accepted belief, stars do not move about at random in space. By 1904-1905 he had proof that they do not. He discovered, by photographically sampling limited portions of the night sky—a technique that made him the founder of modern statistical astronomy—that stars tend to move in two diametrically opposed directions in our galaxy, the Milky Way, toward the constellations Orion and Scutum. His discovery of these two "star streams" was one of the most significant astronomical discoveries ever made.

While it was not until much later that a correct explanation of the star streams was offered, it was immediately obvious to Kapteyn that it was of the greatest importance for understanding the structure of the universe. Accordingly, in 1906 he proposed the Kapteyn Plan of Selected Areas for enlisting the help of astronomers throughout the world to determine the apparent magnitudes, parallaxes, spectral types, proper motions, and radial velocities of as many stars as possible in over 200 patches of sky. On the basis of the results he proposed a model of our galaxy, now known as the Kapteyn universe. The solar system was pictured to be nearly centrally embedded in a dense, almost ellipsoidal, concentration of stars which thinned out rapidly a few thousand light-years (a relatively small distance in astronomy) away from the center.

Between 1908 and 1914 Kapteyn was a research associate at Mt. Wilson Observatory in southern California during the summers. He died in Amsterdam on June 18, 1922.

Further Reading

A. Van Maanen's obituary of Kapteyn is in the *Annual Reports of the Smithsonian Institution* (1923). General accounts of some of Kapteyn's contributions are in Hector MacPherson, *Makers of Astronomy* (1933), and Otto Struve and Velta Zebergs, *Astronomy of the 20th Century* (1962).

Additional Sources

The life and works of J. C. Kapteyn, Dordrecht; Boston: Kluwer Academic, 1993. □

Radovan Karadzic

Radovan Karadzic (born 1945), the leader of the Bosnian Serbs, pursued a course of "ethnic cleansing" as he struggled to gain independence from the Muslim-controlled Bosnian government in the former Yugoslavia. He has been indicted by the World Court in The Hague for his actions.

Radovan Karadzic, leader of the Bosnian Serb faction in the war-torn former Yugoslavia, has been called a man guilty of war crimes, the "Butcher of Bosnia," and a world-class terrorist. His political opponents have called him a "black-shirt Fascist," and compared him to former Soviet leader Joseph Stalin. His program of "ethnic cleansing," which has resulted in the death of more than 200,000 Muslim opponents and the displacement of an estimated one million more—in addition to the systematic rapes of thousands of Muslim women by Serb troops—has sickened world observers. The *New York Times* has claimed that he is "surely one of Europe's most endangered men," who should include a bullet-proof vest in his wardrobe if he does not already own one. And *New Perspectives Quarterly*

introduced an interview with Karadzic by opining that his political philosophy seems to be, "Do genocide unto them before they can do it unto you." All in all, Karadzic is not a well-loved man.

Although roundly criticized inside and outside of his country, Karadzic has the one quality possessed by almost every successful politician: he has endured. He has more guns and a bigger army than anyone else in the midst of an extremely chaotic situation, and because of that essential fact, governments have been forced to swallow hard and deal with him. In fact, as 1995 began, Karadzic was ignoring United Nations and United States diplomats and calling most of his own shots in determining the course of the Bosnian civil war.

His Background

Not much about the early life of Karadzic is known. He was born in Montenegro, which became one of Yugoslavia's six autonomous republics in 1945. In the early 1960s he relocated to Sarajevo to attend the university and ended up in a literary circle of poets and dissidents. Karadzic was educated as a psychiatrist but has always had an abiding love of literature and poetry. He studied both psychiatry and poetry in a year of graduate studies at Columbia University in New York City during 1974 and 1975. According to an interview in the *New York Times,* he especially likes Walt Whitman's "Leaves of Grass."

While in Sarajevo, Karadzic met and married another psychiatrist, his wife Lilyan, and they have a son and a

daughter. Although he must have been aware of ethnic strife from his years in the hills of Montenegrin, he and his wife's family lived together in an apartment building in Sarajevo with Muslims, Serbs, Croats, and Croat-Hungarians. As Samantha Power pointed out in *U.S. News and World Report,* "It remains a metaphor for the Sarajevo spirit of coexistence: Even though Karadzic himself has been saying for years that Bosnia's three nations 'cannot live together,' all but Karadzic and his Serb in-laws still reside at [the building]."

Karadzic's daughter, Sonja, was identified in a scathing *New Yorker* editorial against Karadzic as his current main buffer against an increasingly hostile international press corps. "Only journalists who have produced favorable reports on her father and his followers are allowed into the territory under Serb control," editorialist Anna Husarska wrote in December of 1994. "Others are simply turned back at the border-control checkpoints. Thus, the outside world has largely ceased to hear about all the atrocities committed in the Bosnian Serbs' holy war of conquest."

Hatred of Moslems

As a psychiatrist, Karadzic worked mainly in state hospitals and focused primarily on patients with neuroses, especially paranoia. Some observers have noted that many of his political pronouncements—which the *Washington Post* diplomatically noted seem to be "misstatements of fact"—often are meant to instill fear and a measure of paranoia in his listeners. "He has dredged up old stories of massacres of Serbs by Croats and Muslims, playing on old fears," the *Boston Globe* reported. "Some of the charges are bizarre—that the Muslims, for example, are sending out subliminal messages on Sarajevo television telling Muslims to attack Serbs and destroy Serb cultural monuments." The *New York Times* noted of Karadzic's probing into paranoia and his current political stances, "The irony is unmistakable, since what has driven the Serbs' offensive in Bosnia has been the deeply rooted anxieties of Balkan history."

The *New York Times* summed up Karadzic's and the Serbian point of view in a 1992 article. The paper reported, "A two-hour conversation with Mr. Karadzic, as with almost everybody caught up in Yugoslavia's disintegration, is a bumpy ride through Balkan history: the 500-year Turkish occupation, Europe's betrayal of Bosnia's Serbs at the Congress of Vienna in 1878, the devastating Serb losses in World War I, the genocide by Croatan fascists in World War II. All this has driven a Serb conviction that their survival could be assured only by a "Greater Serbia," or at least by a pan-Slavic state, Yugoslavia, in which Serbs could dominate."

Greater Serbia

That background serves as a foundation for the war that broke out in April of 1992 in what was once Yugoslavia. When Bosnia declared its independence, fighting began. The bordering state of Serbia has supported Serbs within Bosnia—the Bosnian Serbs that Karadzic leads. The Croats and Muslims formed an alliance to counter the much better armed Serbian aggressors. According to well-publicized

census data, before the fighting began, Serbs in Bosnia comprised about 31 percent of the population. Muslims accounted for 41 percent, and Croats for 17 percent. By the beginning of 1995, Serbian-backed forces controlled about 70 percent of the territory in Bosnia. The *New York Times* said of that 70 percent: "A horseshoe-shaped chunk of land, it was identified by Serbian nationalists and military planners in the years before the war as territory that would be seized and eventually annexed to Serbia if Yugoslavia fell apart after the collapse of Communism across Eastern Europe in 1989. . . . Similar maps have been drawn up since the late 19th Century as part of the nationalist dream of a 'Greater Serbia' in which all Serbs could live under Serbian rule."

Karadzic obviously has strong Serbian nationalist leanings. The *Boston Globe* quoted a high-level diplomat just weeks after the fighting broke out in 1992. "Democracy is not exactly triumphant," the diplomat noted of the Yugoslav situation. "It's more like a new brand of national socialism—fascism. That is what Karadzic embodies. And that is what is worrying."

His Image

However much his critics deplore him, Karadzic has generated an element of interest among those observers who are required to chart his political comings and goings. He is described as possessing a level of sophistication that one would expect to find in a well-educated medical man. He is "nattily dressed," often surrounded by bodyguards, and often to be found holding court in posh European hotels. And no description of Karadzic is complete without mention of his long flowing hair, or his thick clumps of eyebrows. The *Washington Post* once described Karadzic as "a robust bear of a man [who] talks as much as a traveling salesman."

Of course, at various times during the three-year-old conflict, which Karadzic has had a great role in prolonging, descriptions of him have been much harsher. Former U.S. Secretary of State Lawrence Eagleburger pointed out in 1992 that Karadzic was a possible war criminal because of the ethnic cleansing policy he promulgated. In fact, when Karadzic traveled to the United Nations in February of 1993 for yet another round of peace talks to resolve the conflict, there was talk of denying him a visa to enter the United States. Five Republican senators signed a letter asking that Karadzic be denied the visa. The Clinton Administration, arguing that Karadzic should be allowed to visit the United Nations, nonetheless had reservations; a State Department spokesman was quoted in the *New York Times* as saying, "We continue to believe that this man has things that he has to answer for."

Ethnic Cleansing

Foremost among those "things" is the well-documented Bosnian Serb policy of eliminating Muslims from Serbian occupied land within Bosnia. Karadzic is generally viewed to have been handpicked for his position by Serbian leader Slobodan Milosevic. Together, the two Serb leaders have waged an ethnic cleansing campaign that has been denounced by the world community. Anthony Lewis wrote in a 1993 *New York Times* column, "The phrase 'ethnic cleansing' was actually invented by the Serbs for their operations in Bosnia. And everyone knows what it has meant: the murder of 150,000 Muslims [since increased to about 250,000] and the expulsion of more than one million from their towns and villages. There is no secret about any of this except to the willfully blind. . . . Serbian soldiers themselves have described the systematic rape of Muslim women."

In a November, 1993 article, the *New York Times* reported that Karadzic appeared "pallid and nervous, particularly when asked about assertions by Western governments that he and his fellow leaders will have to answer for war crimes that Serbian troops are accused of committing." Karadzic's long-standing response to those charges is that the Bosnian Serbs are merely protecting themselves from Muslim aggression. "I regret every life that has been lost," he told the *New York Times*, "But it is not the Serbs' fault." He has argued that allowing the Muslims to gain control of Bosnia will result in an Islamic foothold in Europe and the expansion of Islamic "fundamentalism." And he has stated, quite simply, in a *New York Times* article, "History has proven it. . . . It is impossible for Serbs to live together with other peoples in a unitary state."

Partition of Bosnia

Karadzic has always called for a partition of Bosnia into three parts, each controlled by a rival faction. He has said he would be willing to give up some of the territory his forces seized in order to get a Serb-controlled government in one of the partitions. Not everyone believes that. The latest peace plan—in late 1994—had the country divided up into two portions, with the Muslim-Croats controlling 51 percent and the Serbs 49 percent. The Bosnians accepted it; the Serbs rejected it. When U.N. Secretary General Boutros Boutros-Ghali traveled to Sarajevo in November of 1994 to meet with Karadzic, the Bosnian Serb leader refused to meet him at the airport. Boutros-Ghali, quoted in the *New York Times*, said Karadzic's snub "projected a bad image on his policy, on his attitude and even his personality." Karadzic did not seem to care. "As for the Americans," the *New Yorker* opined, "Karadzic has learned that when they start to get bellicose it is enough to whisper 'Vietnam.' The word alone seems to scare them witless."

The U.S. government did try to put pressure on Karadzic by applying the squeeze to Serbia and Milosevic. The United States figured that since it was not going to commit any military power to stop the fighting in Bosnia, it could put pressure on the Bosnian Serbs by applying economic sanctions to their suppliers—Serbia. But Milosevic refused to meet with a U.S. ambassador in February of 1995, further hurting the chances for peace. This came even though there had been a reported rift between Milosevic and his protege, Karadzic.

The relationship between Milosevic and Karadzic is often compared to that between Frankenstein and his monster, according to the *New York Times*. "Mr. Milosevic plucked Dr. Karadzic from obscurity several years ago and helped engineer his rise, but now finds he cannot control the figure he helped create." But the rift between the two men was characterized in other quarters as a ruse, set up merely to placate the United States and to get the United States to stop putting pressure on Serbia.

In late March of 1995, Karadzic made an offer of peace that surprised many observers, since he seemed to hold the upper hand in the fighting. Bosnian Serb forces were faced with a lack of fuel to power their army and Karadzic was seen as ready to make concessions. But the *Christian Science Monitor* quoted an anonymous Western diplomat as saying, "Now Karadzic is the peacemaker? I don't trust him." And in late April, the United Nations-sponsored International Criminal Tribunal for the former Yugoslavia formally named Karadzic as a suspected war criminal and asked that Bosnian leaders allow it to bring its own charges against the leader in order to prevent him from being tried twice—at the tribunal and in Bosnia.

The tribunal indicted Karadzic on charges of genocide, other civilian-directed offenses, and crimes carried out by subordinates, including murder, rape, and torture. The general commander of the Bosnian Serb Army, Ratko Mladic, was also indicted. Karadzic flaunted the Dayton peace accord, drafted in 1995 by world leaders to end the war in Bosnia. One of the agreement's provisions called for him to relinquish power and hold elections, which he refused to do until the United States threatened economic sanctions. It is speculated that although he has claimed that he has stepped down, he will continue to pull the strings. If he continues his hold, perhaps military force will eventually be necessary, according to the *New York Times*, returning the threat of more conflict in the already ravaged land.

Biljana Plavsic eventually replaced Karadzic as Bosnian Serb president. However, she found herself locked in a power struggle with Karadzic's allies and fearing for her life ever since her outspoken attacks on the former president and threats to arrest Karadzic and his supporters for rampant corruption. Bosnian Serb ultra-nationalists loyal to Karadzic expelled Plavsic from the ruling Serb Democratic party in July 1997, demanding she step down from office. In response, she dissolved parliament and called for new elections on September 1, 1997, but Karadzic loyalists refused to recognize her decision and said they would continue to hold parliamentary sessions.

Further Reading

Boston Globe, April 25, 1992, p. 2.
Christian Science Monitor, March 27, 1995, p. 6.
Detroit Free Press, April 24, 1995. p. 5A; April 27, 1995, p. 5A.
Los Angeles Times, May 17, 1993, p. A1; March 3, 1994, p. A11.
New Perspectives Quarterly, fall 1992, p. 47.
New Statesman & Society, June 2, 1995, pp. 14-16.
New Yorker, December 26, 1994/January 2, 1995 (double issue), p. 7.
New York Times, May 17, 1992, Sec. 4, p. 7; February 3, 1993, p. A8; March 5, 1993, p. A8; March 24, 1993, p. A3; May 19, 1993, p. A10; October 29, 1993, p. A8; November 14, 1993, p. 1; July 22, 1994, p. A3; August 11, 1994, p. A10; December 1, 1994, p. 1; February 3, 1995, p. A12; April 13, 1995, p. 1; November 3, 1995, pp. A1, A12; June 3, 1996, pp. A1, A4.
U.S. News & World Report, July 24, 1995, p. 26.

Washington Post, November 10, 1992, p. A24; August 19, 1993, p. A24.

CNN Interactive June 25, 1997, "http://cnn.com/WORLD/europe/9707/24/RB002732.reut.html."

Additional information for this profile was obtained from the New York Times Web site, May 17, 1996, and May 21, 1996.

□

Constantine Karamanlis

Constantine Karamanlis (born 1907) sustained an active career in Greek politics for 48 years. He was elected member of Parliament 12 times, governed the country as prime minister for 14 years (1955-1963; 1974-1980), and later was twice elected president, leaving office for the last time in 1995 at age 88.

Constantine Karamanlis ranks among the most prominent political figures of 20th-century Greece. He was born on March 8, 1907, in the small town of Proti, near Serres, in Eastern Macedonia. His father, a teacher and later a tobacco grower, was known for his patriotic feelings and involvement in the struggle over Macedonia, at that time under Turkish rule. Karamanlis' political philosophy was shaped by the impact of the Macedonian struggle, the Balkan Wars, and World War I on the peoples of northern Greece; the sharply divisive Greek politics during World War I between the Royalists and the Venizelists, usually referred to as the "great schism"; and the instability of Greek political and social life in the interwar years. This philosophy can be described as a commitment to an orderly democratic process made possible through constructive reforms aimed at improving social and economic conditions and ensuring political stability and continuity. He gradually emerged as a conservative Western-type reformer with a definite vision of the needs and aspirations of modern Greece. He served Greece at crucial historical periods and ultimately made it a member of the European Community.

Education and Early Political Career

Karamanlis received his primary education in his home town of Proti and his high school education in Serres and Athens. After finishing law school at the University of Athens, he did his military service and in 1930 embarked on a successful law career in Serres. There he also began his political career when in 1935, at the age of 28, was elected to Parliament. The Metaxas dictatorship (with which he refused to cooperate), World War II, the German occupation of Greece, and the bitter civil war that followed slowed or modified his political plans. For most of this period he remained a reflective observer.

Karamanlis was reelected to Parliament in 1946 by the Populist Party, and from this time on he became increasingly involved in committees dealing with both domestic and foreign matters. In 1946 he went to the United States as a member of a mission that secured badly needed American aid for the postwar reconstruction of Greece. Later that year he was appointed minister of labor, a position which was later expanded to include agriculture, and in 1948 he became minister of transportation.

After the end of the civil war Karamanlis became indefatigably involved in Greek politics, especially after joining the Greek Rally directed by General Papagos. When the Greek Rally asserted its position in the November 1952 elections, Karamanlis was appointed minister of public works, a position he held until 1955 and after 1954 simultaneously with that of the ministry of transportation. This was a crucial appointment, enabling him to set the foundation of the economic reconstruction of Greece which many foreign observers described as the Greek miracle. In essence, the reconstruction included the building of better roads and an efficient communications system, irrigation, hydroelectric dams, electrification, the development of new industry, decentralization of industry, and, finally, the rapid growth of tourism and related services and industries. The experiences of this decade (1945-1955) sharpened Karamanlis' political acumen, contributed to his enhanced visibility at home and abroad, and earned him a reputation as an efficient, and clearly pro-Western, political figure. Thus, when General Papagos died in October 1955, King Paul asked Karamanlis to form a new government.

Prime Minister (1955-1963)

For nearly a decade Karamanlis dominated Greek politics as prime minister and gained in popularity as evidenced by the results of the 1958 and 1961 elections. On January 4, 1956, he organized a new party, the National Radical Union (ERE), which reflected his own ideological position. He then informed the Greek people that on the basis of his experiences and research, he believed that Greece could transform itself and that the Greek people could change their fate. In his opening speech in Parliament he had already outlined his main objectives in domestic and foreign matters: to reform public life and modernize the national economy and to deal with the thorny Cyprus problem caused by the Greek Cypriots' desire for independence from British colonial rule and enosis (union) with Greece.

It was an enormous task with impressive results in some areas. At home there was a stabilization of the currency, development of new industry, and increased agricultural and industrial production. The living standards of Greek farmers and workers doubled, and the per capita income rose from $305 in 1955 to $565 in 1963, an increase of 85.2 percent in eight years. Generally this was a period of political stability and economic growth, even though it was marred by allegations of fraud in the 1961 elections, the assassination of Gregory Lambrakis, and conflict with the royal family, especially Queen Frederika. These incidents affected his plans for constitutional reforms through which he had hoped the executive would acquire more power.

The Cyprus problem haunted him, contributing to the deterioration of relations between Greece and Turkey and weakening the NATO alliance to which both Greece and Turkey belonged. Still, Karamanlis used his prestige to support the Cypriot struggle for independent statehood with

Great Britain, Greece, and Turkey as guarantor powers through the signing of the Zurich Agreement in 1959. He believed that the idea of the Union of Cyprus with Greece should at best be postponed. Thus Cyprus remained an irritant for the rest of his political career.

His term as prime minister was interrupted in 1963 when disagreements with young King Constantine and pressures from the opposition party of the veteran politician George Papandreou compelled him to resign and leave the country to avoid a new schism or a civil war. He moved to Paris where he lived for the next 11 years studying and observing Greek politics. He was saddened but not surprised by the events that led to the overthrow of the king and establishment of the military dictatorship in Athens (1967-1974). He criticized the junta but did not participate in any overt attempts to overthrow it. This was in keeping with his style of not participating in politics if there was not a legitimate political mechanism through which to act.

Prime Minister (1974-1980); President (1980-1985, 1990-1995)

After the fall of the Athens military regime, precipitated by the Cyprus crisis of July 1974, an invited Karamanlis returned to Greece as a political messiah and helped the country make a bloodless transition from dictatorship to democracy highlighted by the Constitutional Charter of 1975 and strict guarantees for democratic institutions. Karamanlis had by now reached full political maturity and great prestige. Under the banner of his party, renamed or reformed as the New Democracy, Karamanlis again dominated the political scene, acting with tolerance and confidence. The deposed military dictators were sent to jail, the Communist Party of Greece was legally recognized, and the question of the nature of the regime which had pestered Greek politics for over half a century was settled by a plebiscite at the expense of the royal house.

Even though the transition from dictatorship to democracy was a relatively smooth process, the last years of Karamanlis' political life were tense. The matter of education and other old social issues were articulated in a new context by critics fond of identifying Karamanlis with the "Old Order" dependent on the NATO Alliance, especially the United States. Despite inflation the economy improved and per capita income almost doubled from 1974 to 1979. And, despite his pro-Westernism, one of the distinctive characteristics of his foreign policy during this period was the Greek rapprochement with the Balkan countries, a new phenomenon in postwar Greek foreign policy.

Karamanlis was understandably disappointed with the turn of events over the Cyprus problem in July 1974 which led to the coup against President Makarios, the Turkish invasion, and the de facto partition of the island—all seemingly with U.S. consent. Though these events contributed directly to the fall of the military regime in Athens and to Karamanlis' return to active Greek politics, he chose not to go to war with Turkey over the issue. This, too, was in keeping with his style of assessing realities correctly and his faith in the negotiating process.

Although he disapproved of U.S. policy toward Greece during this period, he nevertheless remained firmly within the Western camp, seeking at the same time to strengthen Greece's self-reliance. This self-reliance, he felt, could be pursued best within the context of a united Europe. From the beginning of his career as prime minister, Karamanlis envisaged Greece as part of Europe and, as a believer in the "European Idea," he worked hard to have Greece included among the European communities. Thanks to his efforts, Greece became the tenth member of the European Economic Community on January 1, 1981.

Karamanlis pursued the same ideals and practices after he became president of Greece in March 1980, a post he held until his resignation on March 10, 1985, and for another five years beginning in 1990. Amid the constantly shifting tides of Greek politics, he remained a hero in retirement, enjoying a respect and recognition not frequently accorded Greek politicians. Europeans expressed their admiration and respect for him with such awards as the Charlemagne and Schumann prizes for his effort on behalf of the European Community. He was also honored with the golden medal of the European Parliament and with the highest medal of the Sorbonne and the Universities of Paris.

In 1997, ailing and in his 90th year, he saw his nephew and namesake, Costas Karamanlis, elected as leader of the bickering New Democracy party, with an eye toward recapturing power from the Socialists in a turn-of-the-century election.

Further Reading

Because of Karamanlis' centrality in modern Greek politics, almost every book of history or politics that deals with postwar Greece includes discussion or appreciable references to his work as a statesman. A good introduction is Richard Clogg, *A Short History of Modern Greece* (1974), and the much more detailed description of the Greek political system during the 1950s and 1960s by Keith Legg, *Politics in Modern Greece* (1969). The most accessible biography of Karamanlis is the sympathetic account by C. M. Woodhouse, *Karamanlis: The Restorer of Greek Democracy* (1982) and the same author's *The Rise and Fall of the Greek Colonels* (1985), which makes special references to Karamanlis' stay in Paris during the military dictatorship. □

Nikolai Mikhailovich Karamzin

The Russian journalist, historian, and author Nikolai Mikhailovich Karamzin (1766-1826) was a founder of 19th-century Russian imperial conservatism and a pioneer national historian.

N ikolai Karamzin was born on Dec. 1 (Old Style), 1766, on the provincial estate of his father at the village of Mikhailovka, Orenburg district. He was educated at home and was ready by his fourteenth year for advanced study in Moscow. After a period of drifting, he settled into the intellectual life of the city. He wrote poetry and several novels, including *Poor Liza*. He joined the active Masonic movement and was close to the liberal circle of the famous writer and publisher Nikolai Novikov.

In 1789-1790 Karamzin traveled to Berlin, Leipzig, Geneva, Paris, and London. On his return to Russia he launched his journalistic career by publishing in the *Moscow Journal,* which he also edited, his "Letters of a Russian Traveler," a landmark in his intellectual development. Like most of his literary efforts, the "Letters" were sentimental and romantic in the style of Laurence Sterne. But they revealed more than the popular literary mode of the day: Karamzin was moving away from his liberal, Masonic past toward the conservative attitude of his later work.

In 1802 Karamzin founded the monthly *European Messenger,* one of the most important "thick journals" of the 19th century. He abandoned this in 1804 to devote himself to researching the history of the Russian state, an interest he pursued until his death. In 1811 he submitted to Alexander I his "Memoir on Ancient and Modern Russia," a firm historical defense of the time-honored virtues of the Russian autocracy. Meanwhile, Karamzin was working on his magnum opus, *Istoriya Gosudarstva Rossiiskago* (1819-1826; *History of the Russian Imperial State*), of which 11 of the 12 volumes were published before his death. His patriotic and conservative analysis corresponded to the chauvinism of Russian educated opinion in the traumatic aftermath of the French Revolution and the Napoleonic Wars.

Karamzin moved to St. Petersburg in 1816, where he established a close but guarded relationship with the Emperor. He gave the Emperor parts of his *History* to read, and he engaged the Emperor in many discussions on historical and political issues as a consequence of these readings. Karamzin always urged that the uniquely Russian state virtues not be abandoned in the artificial quest for European progress, although he did not wholly reject Western civilization. His own intellectual development had been under Western influence, so he found himself in the ambiguous position of seeking to discover and preserve the best of his own nation's historical character without fully denying the value of certain features of the Western tradition. He maintained a conservative, humane, and intelligent balance between Russia and the West.

In 1825 the unexpected death of Alexander and the Decembrist Revolt, carried out by radical, Western-oriented officers of the imperial army, undermined Karamzin's health. He died on May 22 (Old Style), 1826.

Further Reading

There is considerable information on Karamzin in his own *Memoir on Ancient and Modern Russia,* translated and with a long analysis by Richard Pipes (1959), and in his *Letters of a Russian Traveler, 1789-1790* (trans. 1957). Henry Nebel, Jr., translated and edited *Selected Prose of N.M. Karamzin* (1969) and wrote a study of his early literary efforts, *N.M. Karamzin: A Russian Sentimentalist* (1967). □

Donna Karan

Sometimes called the queen of American fashion, Donna Karan (born 1948) has earned a reputation as a world-class designer as well as a strong businesswoman in charge of a large retail corporation.

Donna Karan built her enormous fashion empire in less than a decade on one extraordinarily simple idea: If she needs a particular item of clothing—a bodysuit, a wrap skirt, a chiffon blouse, a longer jacket—then every other woman needs it too. This theory of visually inspired instincts made her one of the top fashion designers in the world. In 1992 Donna Karan New York, then totaling 14 divisions including fragrance, body care products, accessories, lingerie, and mens, womens, and childrenswear, grossed $275 million.

Karan was born Donna Faske in 1948 in New York and raised on Long Island. Her mother was a model and her father a haberdasher. Karan was fashion-obsessed from an early age, attending Parson's School of Design, which she left, without a degree, to take an assistant position at Anne Klein, one of the top design firms in the country.

She and Louis Dell'Olio became co-designers of Anne Klein after the designer's death in 1974. Jointly, they received many awards for their sporty, sophisticated womenswear. Japanese fashion financier Takihyo Tomio Taki had taken financial control of Anne Klein upon the founder's demise and his first gamble on Karan's genius was to appoint her to fill her boss's rather impressive pumps.

Earned Reputation as Versatile Innovator

Karan struck pay dirt in 1983 when she launched Anne Klein II, the first exciting "bridge" line priced between couture and affordable clothes for average women. The bridge line subsequently became a retailing phenomenon, creating a whole new shopping world for fashion-conscious yet budget-cautious women. Many other designers, from Calvin Klein to Geoffrey Beene, followed her stylish suit. In 1984 Takihyo, with his business partner Frank Mori, backed her first line on her own, called Donna Karan New York, pouring $10 million into the fledgling company. Her first collection was a retail hit of body-conscious but comfortable elegant jersey/wool clothing for the upscale working woman. Black predominated in her separates, designed to make life, work, and getting dressed in the mornings (and making appearances from office to evening affairs) much simpler.

But it was her launch of DKNY, a casual line of lower-priced clothes ($90 bodysuits, $300 blazers) in 1989 that made her ideas and her designer name vastly more accessible to working women wanting to don a designer name but unable to afford her couture prices. The philosophy was one of simplicity. She offered her version of wardrobe basics, which made dressing for any occasion easy.

In the early 1990s the DKNY line represented an estimated $285 million of projected total sales of $365 million. The line prospered by staying current with street fashion ideas incorporating the teenage grunge look (a mismatched sloppy style adopted by the youthful 90s counterculture) for mostly mainstream and older audiences.

In 1992 Karan came up with another idea: a basic line called Essentials—a capsule collection of blazers, pants, wrap skirts, and bodysuits that sold $15 million the first year, prompting her to add a line of Essentials for Men.

Her couture lines for men and women were decidedly high stakes, ranging up from $2,000 women's dresses and $2,500 men's suits. Essentials, only slightly lower-priced, was still a bit too costly for most fashion consumers. And yet, by the mid-1990s she sensed another opportunity for those seeking *greater* exclusivity—this time at top price points under a limited edition label with her signature. Called the Donna Karan Collection, it was distinguished by more detailing in luxurious, hand-painted or hand-dyed fabrics and retailed for up to $6,000.

Real Life, Real People Inspired Design

From the start, Karan was a designer's designer, using her own closet as a testing ground and inspiration for her fashions. For her youthful, funkier DKNY line, she looked to her daughter Gabrielle (born 1975). For suggestions for menswear designs, she used her husband and business partner, Stephan Weiss.

Her personal life also showed steady growth and determination. She married Long Island retailer Mark Karan in 1974 and had one daughter. While the couple divorced in 1978, they remained good friends. In 1983 she married Stephan Weiss, whom she had first met on a blind date ten years earlier. They lived in Manhattan and in a beach house on Long Island, where Weiss designed the home and grounds, leaving Karan to handle the interiors. Weiss, who was also a sculptor, designed the bottles for Karan's first signature fragrance, Donna Karan. The scent was a mix, in her words, of leather, cashmere, suede, and the "back of my husband's neck." But their minds haven't always met. Although she was the first American designer to suggest sarong skirts for men, her husband steadfastly refused to wear them.

Attempting to imitate all-American designer Ralph Lauren's lifestyle marketing ploy, Karan's "Woman-to-Woman" marketing campaign reflected her customer—a stylish, elegant, working woman. Striking a cord with independent career women, Karan explained, "I have hit upon a universality of design."

One of the Hottest Names In Fashion

Her connections to Hollywood and Washington, D.C., also helped to boost the designer's reputation. Singer/actress/director Barbra Streisand wore Karan constantly, as did television's Murphy Brown character actress Candace Bergen. Donning her menswear were singer Michael Bolton and actors Larry Hagman, Richard Gere, and Warren Beatty. First Lady Hillary Rodham Clinton slipped into her suits and dresses (after she wore the "cold shoulder" black dress at an inaugural bash, it immediately was "knocked off"—that is, copied at lower prices by everyone in the fashion world) and President Bill Clinton campaigned in her stylish navy wool crepe suits.

A far cry from her initial snug, simple jersey separates, a later line for women incorporated longer sheer chiffon dresses, Edwardian suits, empire waist dresses, and monastic long tunics over bell-bottom slacks with shoulder-slung chunky cross accessories.

Her reputation and identity as a world-class designer established, Karan expanded her vision into home furnishings and a women's body care line (moisturizers, bath soap, and shower gels). By the late 1990s, Karan had amassed a global business empire that included childrenswear, fragrances, skin-care products, hosiery, and eye wear, as well. The company had almost 300 foreign accounts, including 27 free-standing Donna Karan stores, with strong followings in Europe, the Far East, and Japan. In addition to attracting the loyalty of consumers, she won recognition from the global fashion press and top designers who voted her Best Woman Designer in the World and Best American Designer to Emerge in 20 Years.

Tested Business Acumen

Meanwhile, she shook up the fashion retailing world by attempting to gain further control of her company by going public with her company's stock. However, Karan's road to success was not always smooth. The first hurdle came in 1992 when the company expanded too rapidly, taking on more debt than warranted by its cash flow. Then came late deliveries and the mixed blessing of more demand than her supply could handle. "We had a vicious cycle of problems," recalled Karan. On top of these problems, the darling of Wall Street came under intense criticism as it became clear that the company was not strong enough to proceed with its plans for a public stock offering. The solution was to restructure the company's debt so that growth could continue.

A corner had been turned; new products were launched in the beauty and home lines, a licensing agreement was signed for jeans aimed at baby boomer jeans wearers, and revenues soared. By mid-1996, the company was ready to execute the initial public stock offering (IPO). Once again, Karan was hailed by the financial as well as the fashion world.

The ink was hardly dry before danger signals appeared. Never one to cut corners, Karan simply spent too much money, and expansion costs were growing faster than sales. Other obstacles also interfered. A plan to sell the cosmetics and fragrance division took longer than expected, and disagreements over production schedules and product lines dissolved the lucrative licensing arrangement for jeans. The company's stock plunged. Investors were furious, and demanded that more cost controls be implemented.

Found Wisdom in Letting Go

A new chapter began in the summer of 1997 when the company announced the appointment of John Idol as chief executive. Formerly a group president at Polo Ralph Lauren,

Idol brought badly needed expertise in licensing to the company. The key, however, laid in his reporting to the board rather than to Karan, who stepped down as chief executive but maintained her title as chairwoman of the company. The business of managing the bottom line was separated from the business of designing—and in turn was again hailed by Wall Street.

Further Reading

For further information on Donna Karan and the contemporary fashion industry see *Women of Fashion: Twentieth Century Designers* by Valerie Steele (1991); *Contemporary Designers,* edited by Ann Lee Morsan, (2nd ed. 1990); and *NY Fashion: The Evolution of American Style* by Caroline Rennolds Milbank (1985). Articles in periodicals include: *New York Times* (July 29, 1997, May 28, 1997, March 6, 1997, April 29, 1997); *Fortune* (January 13, 1997); *Town & Country* (December 1996); *Advertising Age* (August 5, 1996, October 7, 1996); and *Vogue* (December 1995 and January 1996). □

Maulana Karenga

Maulana Karenga (born 1941) introduced the holiday of Kwanzaa to African Americans. Kwanzaa, derived from African agricultural rites and communal activities, urges blacks to look back to their cultural roots as a source of celebration.

Known as the man who brought the cultural holiday of Kwanzaa to the United States in 1966, Maulana Karenga has played a key role in programs that have defined black identity and helped blacks connect themselves to their cultural roots. His identities since the mid-1960s have run the gamut from black power revolutionary and supporter of Malcolm X to mediator with whites in times of racial strife. Throughout, Karenga has stressed the importance of culture to blacks as a means of strengthening solidarity and overcoming oppression.

Karenga has played a great role in providing positive symbols to blacks through cultural reaffirmation. In speaking of his movement in *Emerge!,* he said, "As cultural nationalists, we believe that you must rescue and reconstruct African history and culture to revitalize African culture today in America." Karenga has acknowledged his debt to black thinkers of the past in shaping his view. Veronica Chambers wrote in *Essence* that Karenga's "intellectual voice is born of a mixed palette of teachings, from W. E. B. DuBois to Anna Julia Cooper, a legendary Black nineteenth-century feminist who attended the Sorbonne while in her sixties and received a Ph.D." The holder of two Ph.D.s of his own, Karenga pays particular homage to path-breaking blacks such as DuBois, Cooper, Fannie Lou Hamer, Malcolm X, Mary McLeod Bethune, Martin Luther King, Jr., and Frederick Douglass.

Leadership Skills Revealed in College

The son of a Baptist minister, Karenga was born on a poultry farm in Maryland. He moved to Los Angeles in the late 1950s to attend Los Angeles City College, and while there became the first black ever elected president of the student body. He earned his masters' degree in political science and African studies at the University of California at Los Angeles (UCLA) before embracing the black power movement.

After some initial interest in becoming a Black Muslim, Karenga became disenchanted with the religion and became a supporter of Malcolm X, although he did not agree with all of the black leader's teachings. Karenga thought that violence should be resorted to by blacks only as a self-defense measure, unlike radical black power advocates who supported more aggressive measures against the white establishment. In one of his first efforts to unify blacks in a positive rather than destructive manner, he helped establish the Black Congress among residents of Los Angeles' Watts district that helped restore the community after the 1965 race riots.

In the mid-1960s Everett started the group known as US (meant as a counterpoint to "them") that he "created as a social and culture change organization," according to *The Black 100*. It was at this time that he adopted the name Maulana Karenga—Maulana is Swahili for "master-teacher." All members of US were required to take on Afro-Swahili surnames, learn Swahili, shave their heads, and wear African-style attire. A central element of US was the embracing of the seven principles of the Nguzo Saba, a black value system that was to be a code of living for blacks. The principles consisted of Umjoya (unity), Kujichagulia (self-determination), Ujima (collective work and responsibility), Ujamaa (cooperative economics), Nia (purpose), Kuumba (creativity), and Imani (faith). The goal of this value system was to promote a national liberation of African Americans and US soon attracted a large following among blacks on the West Coast.

With US, Karenga was instrumental in building independent schools, black-studies departments, and black-student unions. As he gained status in the black power movement, he proceeded to organize a series of gatherings to provide blacks with a platform for social change. Working with other black leaders, he set up major black-power conferences in Washington DC, Philadelphia, and Newark, New Jersey, where he was instrumental in triggering development of an ideological framework for black politics in the years to come. Central to Karenga's efforts was the espousal of cultural nationalism to instill racial pride and confidence among American blacks.

Among the blacks who took leadership roles in the black cultural movement of the 1960s were LeRoi Jones (who became Amiri Baraka), Sonia Sanchez, Addison Gayle, Jr., Larry Neal, and Haki Madhubuti (formerly Don L. Lee). During this period Karenga worked alongside such people, founding the Brotherhood Crusade, as well as housing projects, community health centers, and other associations to aid blacks. "From the beginning, we were into institutional building for both the local and national community," he claimed in *Essence*. Karenga made it clear, however, that blacks had a right to act up if the system did not change. "Unless America awakens to the fact that she must contend with us as an enemy, or bargain with us as citizens, it will be to her serious disadvantage," he was quoted as saying in *Newsweek* in 1966.

Cultural Holiday Becomes Worldwide Phenomenon

One year after the creation of US, Karenga introduced a lasting source of black unity by introducing Kwanzaa to African Americans. Kwanzaa, which is Swahili for "first fruits," is a holiday based on African agricultural rites and communal activities that urges blacks to look back to their cultural roots as a source of celebration. On each of the seven days of Kwanzaa—from December 26 through January 1—a principle of the Nguzo Saba is acknowledged.

Although it coincides with the Christmas season, the holiday has no religious aspects and therefore allows people from all countries and backgrounds to join in without conflicts. A pan-Africanist, Karenga's support of Kwanzaa was an offshoot of his belief that blacks should consider themselves one people, regardless of their country. "Kwanzaa was created to reaffirm our culture and the bonds between us as a people," he told *Essence*. After initially being observed by a few hundred people, Kwanzaa celebrations have spread well beyond the borders of the United States in ensuing years.

Throughout the mid-1960s, Karenga's voice was clearly heard in speeches across the nation about the importance of racial pride. His reputation soared due to his role in helping the Los Angeles police limit black rioting after Martin Luther King, Jr.'s assassination in 1968. Karenga's mediating skills made him in demand for meetings with political leaders that included then-California Governor Ronald Reagan, ex-Los Angeles Mayor Sam Yorty, Senator Hubert Humphrey, and Ford Foundation head McGeorge Bundy. At the same time he was working with these leaders, Karenga's continued outspokenness also put him under surveillance by the FBI.

A number of factors isolated Karenga within the black-power movement. While some African Americans did not care for his overpowering manner, others disagreed with his philosophy for dealing with the problems of blacks; more extremist blacks spoke out against his dealing with whites. The cultural nationalists could not bridge the gap between blacks who wanted to overthrow the system and those who were willing to promote change through the normal political process.

Karenga's status was eroded considerably after the killing of Black Panther members John Huggins and Alprentice "Bunchy" Carter by US gunmen in 1969. It was also felt by many that the so-called cultural movement promoted by Karenga and Baraka compromised the rights of women. Karenga's male chauvinism came to the fore in 1971 when he was arrested and convicted of assaulting a female US member. After he was sent to prison to serve time for his offense, the US organization began to dissolve and was officially ended in 1974.

Ideological Shift During Imprisonment

In prison, Karenga actively complained that his sentence was more harsh than for others convicted of a similar offense, and noted that his repeated parole recommendations were ignored. During his incarceration he maintained a rigorous schedule of activity and received a steady flow of visitors. He would often endure 19-hour work days consisting of work in the prison library, running a humanist discussion group, and conducting research. His studies resulted in articles published in *Black Scholar* magazine that encompassed subjects ranging from feminism to pan-Africanism.

After three years, Karenga won his freedom due to the efforts of various black elected officials in California. After his release he admitted that US had made mistakes that weakened the movement and compromised its ability to change appropriately with the times. He also revealed an ideological reawakening by announcing his adherence to Marxist principles of class struggle. As Thomas L. Blair said in *Retreat to the Ghetto*, "In Karenga's new view, black nationalism is reactionary because in the pursuit of an elusive ideal of unity it makes class contradictions among blacks." Baraka also made the shift in philosophy, thus ending the militant cultural revolution of blacks started in the 1960s.

In the years that followed, Karenga would continue to rethink his position on black identity and once again embrace the principles of black culturalism. Prominent in his thoughts was the need for blacks to work together toward common goals and, especially for Africans to transcend borders of country and tribe. "In the final analysis shared social wealth and work are key to African economic development," he said, according to *The Black 100*.

Karenga's Marxist leanings continued to show in his negative opinion of black capitalism, which he felt subverted the black cause and resulted in blacks losing touch with their true identity. To further press the cause of black unity, Karenga and his wife Tiamoya increased their involvement with the Kwanzaa holiday over the years. By having no elements of elitism, exclusivity, or intellectualism, Kwanzaa is fully accessible to the masses and cannot be claimed as the special province of any one group, according to Karenga.

Voice of Reason During Los Angeles Riots

In addition to serving as professor and chairperson of the Department of Black Studies at California State University at Long Beach in the 1990s, Karenga became chairperson of the President's Task Force on Multicultural Education and Campus Diversity at the school. He also was appointed director of the African American Cultural Center in Los Angeles. After the 1992 riots in Los Angeles that followed the beating of Rodney King by police, Karenga once again became a voice of healing in the aftermath.

Karenga sponsored workshops and lectures to help close the racial wounds resulting from the event. Karenga remained reasonable and called for cool heads while the Rodney King trial was underway and blacks were threatening retribution if the jury gave the police a light sentence. "L.A. can be a model in a positive way or a negative way," he was quoted as saying in *Newsweek* while the trial was underway.

The Kwanzaa holiday remains Karenga's most important legacy to the black cause. His influence is demonstrated by the fact that by the 1990s Kwanzaa was celebrated by over 18 million blacks in the United States, Canada, the Caribbean, Europe, and Africa. He and his wife have presided over hundreds of Kwanzaas all over the world. "As cultural nationalists, we believe that you must rescue and reconstruct African history and culture to revitalize African culture today in America," he said in *Emerge*. "Kwanzaa became a way of doing just that. I wanted to stress the need for reorientation of values, to borrow the collective life-affirming ones from our past and use them to enrich our present."

Further Reading

Blair, Thomas L., *Retreat to the Ghetto, The End of a Dream,* Hill & Wang, 1977.
The Eyes on the Prize Civil Rights Reader, Penguin, 1991.
Salley, Columbus, *The Black 100,* Citadel Press, 1993.
Van Deburg, William L., *New Day in Babylon, The Black Power Movement and American Culture 1965-1975,* University of Chicago Press, 1992.
Black Enterprise, December 1991, p. 22; December 1993, p. 107.
Detroit Free Press Magazine, December 4, 1994, p. 6.

Ebony, September 1975, p. 170.

Essence, December 1989, p. 50; December 1992, pp. 96-98, 129.

Emerge, January 1992, pp. 11-12.

Newsweek, August 22, 1966, pp. 28-29; March 29, 1993, p. 30. □

Karim Khan Zand

Karim Khan Zand (died 1779), a ruler of Iran and founder of the short-lived Zand dynasty, was known for his humility, kindness, and gallantry.

Among the rulers of Iran, from 1500 to 1925, Karim Khan was the only one who was not of Turkish origin. He was a man of good character and a member of the Zand, which was part of the Aryan tribe of Lak in southern Iran.

When Nader Shah was assassinated in 1747, there were at least four rivals for his throne. Among these the least likely to succeed was Karim Khan. Not only was his tribe small, but he himself had been a common soldier in Nader Shah's army, rising to a position of leadership by his ability.

Struggle for Supremacy

Karim Khan joined with another Persian rival, Alimardan Khan of the Bakhtyari tribe, and they claimed to be "regents" in behalf of a minor Safavid prince. Later, when Alimardan was killed, Karim Khan was the sole ruler in southern Iran.

The third claimant was Azad, an Afghan general of Nader Shah who ruled in Azerbayjan. Azad went against Karim Khan and pushed him back all the way to Shiraz and beyond. Karim Khan, however, ambushed Azad and routed him in 1752. Azad took refuge in Baghdad and later in Tiflis but finally did not have any recourse but to put himself at the mercy of Karim Khan. He, behaving unlike the rulers of his time, treated Azad very kindly, and the two became close friends.

The last rival was Mohammad Hasan Khan Qajar, who ruled in northern Iran. Even though Karim Khan was no match for him in the field and was defeated in several battles, his popularity caused the allies of Qajar to desert to Karim Khan. In 1757 Mohammad Hasan was killed, and Karim Khan became the sole ruler of Iran.

For over 20 years Karim Khan gave the war-weary people of the country tranquility, security, and justice. The only exception was the short campaign against the Ottoman Empire, in which he captured Basra in order to save the trade of the Persian Gulf. From there he went and captured Baghdad in order to make it easy for the Persian Shiites to go on pilgrimage to Karbala.

Karim Khan never assumed the title of shah and was content with "vakil," or regent. He chose Shiraz for his capital and beautified that already beautiful city with mosques, bazaars, baths, and gardens which bear his name

to this day. At his death in 1779 the country was thrown again into chaos, and the struggle among his own relatives was the bloodiest.

Further Reading

There is not much material in English about Karim Khan. The best are Sir Percy Sykes, *History of Persia,* vol. 3 (3d ed., 1930), and Edward G. Browne, *A Literary History of Persia,* vol. 4 (1956).

Additional Sources

Perry, John R., *Karim Khan Zand: a history of Iran, 1747-1779,* Chicago: University of Chicago Press, 1979. □

Isabella Karle

By applying electron and X-ray diffraction to molecular structure problems, Isabella Karle (born 1921) was able to develop procedures for gathering information about the structure of molecules.

Isabella Karle is a renowned chemist and physicist who has worked at the Naval Research Laboratory in Washington, D.C., since 1946 and heads the X-Ray Diffraction Group of that facility. In her research, she applied electron and X-ray diffraction to molecular structure problems in chemistry and biology. Along with her husband Jerome Karle, she developed procedures for gathering information about the structure of molecules from diffraction data. For her work, she has received numerous awards such as the Annual Achievement Award of the Society of Women Engineers in 1968, the Federal Woman's Award in 1973, and the Lifetime Achievement Award from Women in Science and Engineering in 1986. Her work has been described in the book *Women and Success.*

Isabella Lugoski Karle was born on December 2, 1921, in Detroit, Michigan. Her parents were Zygmunt A. Lugoski, a housepainter, and Elizabeth Graczyk, who was a seamstress. Both her parents were immigrants from Poland, and Karle spoke no English until she went to school. While still in high school, she decided upon a career in chemistry, even though her mother wanted her to be a lawyer or a teacher. She received her B.S. and M.S. degrees in physical chemistry from the University of Michigan in 1941 and 1942. Determined to continue her studies, Karle ran into serious financial problems since teaching assistant positions at the University of Michigan were reserved exclusively for male doctoral students. She managed to stay in school on an American Association of University Women fellowship, however, and in 1943 also became a Rackham fellow. She received her Ph.D. in physical chemistry from the University of Michigan in 1944, at the age of twenty-two.

After receiving her doctorate, Karle worked at the University of Chicago on the Manhattan Project (the code name for the construction of the atomic bomb), synthesizing plutonium compounds. She then returned to the University of

Michigan as a chemistry instructor for two years. In 1942 she had married Jerome Karle, then a chemistry student. In 1946 she and her husband joined the Naval Research Laboratory, where she worked as a physicist from 1946 to 1959. In 1959 she became head of the X-ray analysis section, a position she maintained through the 1990s.

When Karle began her work at the Naval Research Laboratory, information about the structure of crystals was limited. Scientists had determined that crystals were solid units, in which atoms, ions, or molecules are arranged sometimes in repeating, sometimes in random patterns. These patterns or networks of fixed points in space have measurable distances between them. Although chemists had been able to investigate the structure of gas molecules by studying the diffraction of electron or X-ray beams by the gas molecules, it was believed that information about the occurrences of the patterns—or phases—was lost when crystalline substances scattered an X-ray beam. The Karles, working as a team, gathered phase information using a heavy-atom or salt derivative. The position of a heavy atom in the crystal could be located by scattered X-ray reflections, even though light atoms posed more serious problems. When a heavy atom could not be introduced into a crystal, its structure remained a mystery. In 1950 Jerome Karle, in collaboration with the chemist Herbert A. Hauptman, formulated a set of mathematical equations that would theoretically solve the problem of phases in light-atom crystals. It was Isabella Karle who solved the practical problems and designed and built the diffraction machine that photographed the diffracted images of crystalline structures.

While investigating structural formulas and the make-up of crystal structures using electron and X-ray diffraction, Karle made an important discovery. She found that only a few of the phase values—no more than three to five—are sufficient to evaluate the remaining values. She could then use symbols to represent these initial values and also numerical evaluations. This process for determining the location of atoms in a crystal was amenable to processing in high-speed computers. Eventually, it became possible to analyze complex biological molecules in a day or two that previously would have taken years to analyze. The rapid and direct method for solving crystal structure resounded through chemistry, biochemistry, biology, and medicine, and Karle herself has been active in resolving applications in a range of fields.

In addition to describing the structure of crystals and molecules, Karle also investigated the conformation of natural products and biologically active materials. After a crystallographer determines the chemical composition of rare and expensive chemicals, scientists can synthesize inexpensive substitutes that serve the same purpose. Karle headed a team that determined the structure of a chemical that repels worms, termites, and other pests and occurs naturally in a rare Panamanian wood. The team was then able to produce a synthetic chemical that mimics the natural chemical and is equally effective as a pest repellent. In another application, Karle studied frog venom. Using extremely minute quantities of purified potent toxins from tropical American frogs, the team headed by Karle established three-dimensional models, called stereoconfigurations, of many of the toxins and showed the chemical linkages of each of these poisons. The inexpensive substitutes of the toxins were of great importance in medicine. The venom has the effect of blocking nerve impulses and is useful to medical scientists studying nerve transmissions. Karle has also researched the effect of radiation on deoxyribonucleic acid (DNA), the carrier of genetic information. She demonstrated how the structural formulas of the configurations of amino acids and nucleic acids in DNA may be changed when exposed to radiation. Her research into structural analysis also established the arrangement of peptide bonds, or combinations of amino acids.

Karle has held several concurrent positions, such as member of the National Committee on Crystallography of the National Academy of Science and the National Research Council (1974–1977). She has long been a member of the American Crystallographic Society and served as its president in 1976. She was elected to the National Academy of Sciences in 1978. From 1982 to 1990 she worked with the Massachusetts Institute of Technology, and she has been a civilian consultant to the Atomic Energy Commission.

Karle has received numerous awards including the Superior Civilian Service Award of the Navy Department in 1965, the Hildebrand Award in 1970, and the Garvan Award of the American Chemical Society in 1976. She has received several honorary doctorates. Her most recent awards have been the Gregori Aminoff Prize from the Swedish Academy of Sciences in 1988, the Bijvoet Medal from the University of Utrecht, the Netherlands, in 1990, and a National Medal of Science in 1995, the United States' highest scientic honor. She has written over 250 scientific articles.

The Karles have three daughters, Louise Isabella, Jean Marianne, and Madeline Diane. All three have become scientists like their parents. Jerome Karle, who is chief scientist at the Laboratory for Structure and Matter of the U.S. Naval Laboratory, received the Nobel Prize in chemistry in 1985 for developing a mathematical method for determining the three-dimensional structure of molecules.

Further Reading

Kundsin, Ruth, *Women and Success,* Morrow, 1974.
McGraw-Hill Modern Scientists and Engineers, McGraw-Hill (New York), 1980, pp. 147–48.
Noble, Iris, *Contemporary Women Scientists of America,* Meissner, 1979.
Sankaran, Neeraja, *National Medal of Science Winners Contributed to Birth of Their Fields,* ''http://165.123.33.33/yr1995/oct/heros-951030.html,'' July 22, 1997. □

Andreas Bodenheim von Karlstadt

The German Protestant reformer Andreas Bodenheim von Karlstadt (ca. 1480-1541) was an early supporter of Luther. He later broke with Luther and became one of the more radical leaders of the Reformation.

K arlstadt was born at Karlstadt in Franconia. He attended the University of Erfurt, from which he received his bachelor's degree in 1502. He studied at Cologne and in 1504 went to the University of Wittenberg, where he rose to academic prominence. He won a doctor of laws degree at Siena in 1516. Introduced to the writings of St. Augustine by Martin Luther, Karlstadt soon shared the theological preoccupations that led to the start of the Reformation in 1517. In 1519 Karlstadt arranged the famous Leipzig Debates between himself and Johann Eck, but he made such a poor showing that his place had to be taken by Luther.

Karlstadt's career until 1519 was marked by considerable intelligence, a capacity for profound and original theological speculation, great energy, and fairness of mind. From 1519 until his death, however, other traits of character were also evident. His ambition and vanity became apparent, and his earlier tendency to follow intellectual and theological fashion drove him to theological and liturgical reforms which went far beyond those of Luther.

During Luther's seclusion in the Wartburg castle (1521-1522) Karlstadt made an abortive attempt to bring the Reformation to Denmark and then made himself the leader of the Reformation in Wittenberg. His doctrine of the common

priesthood of all believers took the form of ''the first Protestant communion,'' which he celebrated on Christmas Day 1521. In this rite Karlstadt omitted the consecration of the Host and allowed the laity to communicate in both species (bread and wine). These radical changes in Eucharistic doctrine and ritual led to his first break with Luther.

Karlstadt married in 1522 and associated briefly with Thomas Münzer and the Zwickau Prophets, who were ecclesiastical and social revolutionaries. In 1523 Karlstadt left Wittenberg to become the pastor of Orlamunde, but he was expelled from that post in 1524. He went to Strassburg and then to Basel, where his support of the Peasants' Rebellion endangered his life. Karlstadt had become reconciled with Luther, and he found shelter with him after the failure of the rebellion in 1525. But in 1527 he again broke with Luther on the question of the Eucharist.

With his wife and children Karlstadt then became a wanderer, proclaiming his theological doctrines and urging societal reforms somewhat similar to those proposed by the Anabaptists and Schwenckfelders. He finally found refuge in Zurich and in 1534 became a professor at the University of Basel. There Karlstadt continued his stormy career until his death of the plague.

Further Reading

There is no satisfactory biography of Karlstadt in English. There are useful discussions of his life in such histories of the Reformation as *The New Cambridge Modern History,* vol. 2: *The Reformation: 1520-1599* (1958), and George Huntston Williams, *The Radical Reformation* (1962). Karlstadt's life is so entwined with Luther's that studies of the latter also deal with Karlstadt, as Robert Herndon Fife, *The Revolt of Martin Luther* (1957), and Walter G. Tillmanns, *The World and Men around Luther* (1959).

Additional Sources

Pater, Calvin Augustine, *Karlstadt as the father of the Baptist movements: the emergence of lay Protestantism,* Lewiston, NY: E. Mellen Press, 1993. □

Babrak Karmal

A leading Afghan Marxist, Babrak Karmal (1929-1996) became Russian puppet ruler of the Democratic Republic of Afghanistan after the Russian invasion in December 1979 until his resignation ''because of ill health'' on May 4, 1986.

B abrak Karmal (roughly translated ''labor-loving little tiger'') was born into a wealthy Afghan family near Kabul, the capital of Afghanistan, January 6, 1929. His father, Maj. Gen. Mohammad Hussain, was a friend of the royal family, especially of Gen. Mohammad Daoud (prime minister 1953-1963; 1973-1978), cousin and brother-in-law of King Mohammad Zahir.

Karmal's ethnic background is rather hazy, as was common among those born in or near Kabul. He claimed to be Pushtun (the dominant ethnic group in Afghanistan). Most evidence, however, linked him to a Tajik or Qizilbash, Persian-speaking background. Ethnic origin was still important in the Afghan political system, even in the Marxist, Russian-dominated regime.

In 1948, Karmal graduated from the German language-oriented Nejat (also called Amani) High School, but was initially refused admission to Kabul University because of his outspoken leftist views. He was always a charismatic speaker and became involved in the student union and the *Wikh-i-Zalmayan* (Awakened Youth) Movement, which, along with other ethnically-oriented intellectual organizations, wanted to liberalize and permit broader participation in the political process.

Marxist Training

Admitted to the faculty of law and political science in 1951 after he promised to refrain from political involvement, Karmal nevertheless continued his leftist activities. When General Daoud seized power in 1953, he imprisoned most of the leftist hierarchy, and Karmal spent more than two years in prison. Mir Akbar Khyber, a cellmate of Karmal's, probably Afghanistan's best Marxist ideologue, gave Karmal the benefit of his learning. Prior to his incarceration, Karmal's exposure to Marxism had been haphazard.

Released from prison in 1956, Karmal worked in the Ministry of Education as a German and English translator, but was conscripted in 1957 for his two years of obligatory military service. After that, Karmal completed his education in the faculty of law and political sciences and returned to the Ministry of Education. Then, he moved to the Ministry of Planning in 1961.

Prime Minister Daoud resigned (under pressure) in 1963, and a constitutional experiment in monarchy began.Karmal resigned from the government in 1964 and from then on actively engaged in politics.

Start in Politics

Karmal became a frequent visitor to the Russian embassy, as did some other Marxist Afghan intellectuals. Most, including Karmal, were probably more nationalist and anti-royalist than pro-Russian. Also, Karmal was able to obtain medical treatment for his followers at the Russian embassy's dispensary. In addition, Karmal and Anahita Ratebzad (Karmal's mistress) held numerous soirées for young teachers and administrators who had come to the capital for training or reassignment. These parties included drinking and mixed dancing, anathema to conservative Muslims, but Karmal was busily developing a cadre loyal to his person.

Tacitly tolerated by the 1964 constitution, several political parties were launched, including the leftist-oriented People's Democratic Party of Afghanistan (PDPA), which was founded on January 1, 1965. Key among those elected to the central committee was Karmal. But from the very beginning a split began to develop. One group, *Khalq* (*The Masses*), emphasized the class struggle of classic Marxism. The other, to be called *Parcham* (*The Banner*) after the 1967

split, led by Karmal, wanted to create a united front of all anti-royalist groups.

The first elections under the 1964 constitution which were held the following year witnessed the election of three PDPA members to the lower house of parliament (*Wolesi Jirqah*): Nur Mohammad Nur, Anahita, and Karmal. The *Wolesi Jirqah* had 216 members, but the articulate PDPA members had impact far greater than their numbers would indicate.

Karmal's *Parcham* was largely responsible for confrontations with the authorities, which occurred during the first parliamentary sessions. Ultimately these led to the death of three Afghans and scores of wounded when troops fired into the demonstrators on October 25, 1965.

As the parliament shuffled along toward its inevitable failure, Karmal continued to maintain close contacts with the Russian embassy, recruit cadre, and meet with certain members of the royal family, especially ex-prime minister Daoud. Because of Karmal's easy access to royalty, many Afghans referred to *Parcham* as the "Royal Afghan Communist Party."

The 1969 elections saw only two PDPA leftists sent to the lower house: Karmal and Hafizullah Amin, an American-schooled educator. The period 1969-1973 witnessed a rapid deterioration of the parliamentary system as the *Wolesi Jirqah* emphasized investigations of corruption over positive legislative action.

Other forces were at play as well. Former Prime Minister Daoud, convinced that the constitutional experiment had failed, bided his time. Leftists and moderate socialists clustered about his person, and a coup was executed on July 17, 1973. *Parcham,* both military and civilian, participated, and Karmal openly boasted that he had brought Daoud back to power.

Daoud founded the Republic of Afghanistan and immediately began to defend his *Parcham* support. He dismissed some and sent others to the countryside, where they became disillusioned when they could make no impact on the local power elites. The prime minister introduced a liberalized constitution in February 1977, but many were disappointed in his regime.

In July, the two sections of the PDPA remarried after a ten year divorce, with the express purpose to oppose the Daoud regime. But it was a troubled union. Active Russian involvement in the reunion was still a question.

After 1978 Coup

A series of accidents led to an April 27-28, 1978, coup, and additional mishaps determined its outcome. The murder of Mir Akbar Khyber triggered a massive demonstration and led to the arrest of the Marxist leadership. Incidentally, Khyber was probably assassinated by the *Khalq* leadership. A 24-hour coup launched by Marxists in the military succeeded, and Daoud and most of his family died in the fighting.

The first cabinet of the new Democratic Republic of Afghanistan (DRA) acknowledged the following triumvirate: Nur Mohammad Taraki, prime minister, president of the

Revolutionary Council, general secretary of the PDPA; first deputy prime minister, Karmal; and Amin, deputy prime minister and foreign minister. A struggle for power began immediately. Karmal tried unsuccessfully to elicit support from the military, but the key officers remained loyal to Taraki and *Khalq*.

To protect itself, the Revolutionary Council exiled Karmal and most of the *Parcham* leadership to ambassadorships: Karmal was sent to Prague; Anahita to Belgrade; Nur to Washington.

But the *Khalq* leadership was not through with Karmal and *Parcham*. In late August 1978, the regime arrested a number of military officers and other professionals and charged them with plotting to overthrow the government. Those arrested confessed under torture and implicated Karmal and his followers. Karmal and the other *Parcham* ambassadors were ordered home, but under the circumstances they chose to remain in eastern Europe and Russia.

Meanwhile, the *Khalq* DRA announced a number of reform programs, which alienated virtually every segment of Afghan society. The reforms plus widespread brutal repression led to anti-DRA revolts in all of Afghanistan's 29 provinces. By fall 1979, it was obvious that the DRA would collapse under insurgent attacks unless the Russian military directly intervened. On Christmas Eve 1979 the invasion began. Russian troops killed Amin and Taraki.

Puppet Prime Minister

Karmal arrived in Kabul after Russian tanks had restored order. But the countryside, only partly involved before the Russian invasion, exploded into resistance. In spite of this, Karmal, now prime minister, president of the Politboro, and general secretary of the PDPA, thought he could put together a coalition government acceptable to all. He released the surviving political prisoners, which included a number of former cabinet members. Karmal asked them to help him form a new government. Most pleaded for time to recover from their experiences in prison, as all had been tortured. Those who could manage fled to Pakistan, India, Iran, and ultimately Western Europe or the United States.

Karmal's famed charisma had failed him, for few Afghans wanted to work with the puppet of a foreign power. Afghans quickly dubbed Karmal as "Shah Shuja the Second," a reference to an Afghan puppet of the British in the 19th century (1839-1842).

The DRA announced a number of reforms, which could not be implemented because of the war. So Karmal (and the world) watched the following patterns unfold. The first direct Russian military aggression since World War II on an independent, nonaligned nation led to the creation of one of the world's largest refugee problems. About a third of Afghanistan's population had fled the country by the end of 1985. In addition, increasingly effective guerrilla operations, both rural and urban, with little assistance from the outside world, underlined the fact that the Russians had been fighting in Afghanistan longer than they fought in World War II.

Additional evidence of Russian troubles in Afghanistan came with Karmal's resignation on May 4, 1986. He was replaced by Najibullah, the former head of the Afghan secret police, Khad.

Karmal's deposition and rise to power parallel the rise and fall of the Russian occupation of Afghanistan. After he was disposed, Karmal was exiled to Russia where he stayed until 1991 when he returned home. Karmal was in Moscow when he died from liver cancer in late 1996.

Further Reading

For the period and the man, see the following: Louis Dupree, *Afghanistan* (1980), and Red Flag over the Hindu Kush, *American Universities Field Staff Reports, Asia Series,* Nos. 44, 45, 46 (1979) and Nos. 23, 27, 28, 29, 37 (1980); Anthony Arnold, *Afghanistan's Two-Party Communism, Parcham and Khalq* (1983). A good contemporary account is Henry Bradsher, *Afghanistan and the Russian Union* (1983).

For additional information see Karmal's obituary in *Time* (December 16, 1996) and "An Ox Annoyed," *Economist* (July 27, 1991). □

Theodore von Kármán

The Hungarian-born American physicist Theodore von Kármán (1881-1963) made significant contributions to the fields of hydrodynamics, aerodynamics, and thermodynamics.

Theodore von Kármán was born on May 11, 1881, in Budapest. His father, a professor of education, founded the Minta Model Gymnasium, where Theodore was enrolled at the age of 9. There he learned the inductive reasoning approach which he practiced all his life. In 1898 he entered the Royal Joseph University of Polytechnics and Economics in Budapest, the only engineering school in Hungary, graduating with distinction in 1902. He served in the Austro-Hungarian Army for a year and then returned to the Royal Joseph as assistant professor.

Professional Accomplishments

Von Kármán's first major contribution to the study of engineering materials was the extension of the Euler theory of elastic-column buckling to an explanation of inelastic buckling (published 1906). That same year Von Kármán was granted a 2-year fellowship to study at the University of Göttingen under the famous aerodynamist Ludwig Prandtl. From Prandtl he learned the close relationship between design and theory and "the method of abstracting the basic physical elements of a complex process . . . and analyzing it with simplified methods of mathematics." Von Kármán was also greatly influenced by David Hilbert, Göttingen's greatest mathematician, who taught him that nature was inherently mathematical. Von Kármán completed his doctorate thesis in 1908, and it was published the following year.

In March 1908 Von Kármán left for the Sorbonne, where he attended lectures of Madame Curie. That fall he

accepted a position as a lecturer and assistant to Prandtl on a research project for Count Ferdinand von Zeppelin at the University of Göttingen. Here, in 1911 Von Kármán discovered that the oscillations of a cylinder in a flow tank were caused by the alternate shedding of vortices from the top and then the bottom of the cylinder. This phenomenon, called the Kármán vortex street, gives a scientific picture of the structure of the wake behind a moving body under certain conditions and enables the calculation of the drag of a sphere or cylinder. With this information engineers are able to minimize drag by streamlining. The Kármán vortex street also explains the oscillations of tall chimneys and radio towers as well as the collapse of the Tacoma Narrows Bridge in 1940.

In 1913 Von Kármán took the chair of aeronautics at the Aachen Technische Hochschule, where he set up a new program and constructed a wind tunnel which significantly advanced the knowledge of aerodynamics. When the war broke out in 1914, he was recalled by the army, and after a brief period he was transferred to the Luftarsenal, which marked the beginning of his association with military aviation. As director of the research laboratory, he pursued wind-tunnel experimentation, worked on machine gun-propeller synchronization, and pioneered an observational helicopter involving the use of counterrotating propellers. After the war Von Kármán spent a brief period as head of the Hungarian Department of Education. He returned to Aachen in 1919 to continue research and teaching. With the rise of Adolf Hitler, however, Von Kármán was convinced that he had to leave the increasingly oppressive envi-

ronment of Nazi Germany. He moved to the United States, where he served as director of the Guggenheim Aeronautical Laboratory (1930-1949) and the Jet Propulsion Laboratory (1942-1945).

Air Force Consultant

The U.S. Navy, and then the Army, began sending students to Von Kármán's classes at the California Institute of Technology in 1932. By 1939 he was a close adviser to Gen. Henry Arnold, commander of the Army Air Corps, and with Von Kármán's urgings the corps embarked upon an aeronautical research program. Having convinced the Air Force that it was possible and necessary to fly faster than the speed of sound, Von Kármán was instrumental in the decision to build the famous *Bell X-1* and later the *X-15*. Before the end of World War II Gen. Arnold requested Von Kármán to head the Science Advisory Board in Washington. As part of the effort to assess the technological progress created by the war, Von Kármán traveled to Germany to inspect laboratories and technical records and to talk with the country's scientists. Although he recognized the need to obtain the services of some German experts, he was opposed to the wholesale roundup of scientists as expressed in "Operation Paperclip," because he felt it would decimate European science and impede recovery. The outcome of these studies was the report "Where We Stand" (1945), which emphasized the technological character of World War II and the contribution of organized science.

Von Kármán felt that the enormous prestige of scientists could be used to bring about international peace; at the same time he maintained that the scientists as a group should act as adviser rather than advocate. It was his belief that "a scientist should be neither a [Edward] Teller nor an [Albert] Einstein insofar as public affairs are concerned." Near the end of his life he foresaw the creation of an international government and expressed great optimism in the role of science and technology in the future.

Further Reading

A useful autobiography, written with the help of Lee Edson and published after Von Kármán's death in 1963, is *The Wind and Beyond: Theodore von Kármán, Pioneer in Aviation and Pathfinder in Space* (1967), which also contains a list of his more than 100 books and papers.

Additional Sources

Gorn, Michael H., *The universal man: Theodore Von Kármán's life in aeronautics,* Washington: Smithsonian Institution Press, 1992. □

Sheikh Abeid Amani Karume

Sheikh Abeid Amani Karume (1905-1972), Tanzanian political leader, became the Zanzibari vice

president of the republic of Tanzania. He was one of Africa's least-known leaders.

Sheikh Abeid Karume was apparently the son of a slave woman from Ruanda-Urundi who moved to Zanzibar when the boy was young. He had little formal education, in 1920 becoming a seaman working cargo boats out of the island. He ultimately rose to quartermaster. A member of the British Seamen's Union, after 1938 he operated a syndicate of motorboats carrying passengers to and from harbor ships.

Karume first entered politics in 1954 when he was appointed town councilor. Later he became president of a social organization for black migrant workers called the Zanzibar African Association. In 1957 this group united with the Shirazi Association to form the pro-British AfroShirazi Party (ASP) with Karume as president. In July 1957, by appealing directly to the African community making up four-fifths of the population, the ASP won four of five seats in the colonial Legislative Council.

In the years before the 1964 revolution, Karume led the ASP in opposition to the ruling Arab coalition which was seemingly intent on maintaining the political economic dominance of the Arab community. ZanzibarPemba, an area the size of Rhode Island, became independent on Dec. 10, 1963. On Jan. 12, 1964, young ASP militants overthrew the Sultan and established African rule.

Karume was leader of the Revolutionary Council and subsequently became president of the new Zanzibar People's Republic. He was described as a big, slow, even phlegmatic, man who was honest, dependable, and strong-minded to the point of stubbornness. An eloquent Swahili orator, Karume spoke only halting English. He was a devout Moslem and the father of two sons. His role in the revolution was disputed; claims were made that he was a figurehead, even a prisoner of the real leadership which was said to center on Abdulrahma Babu, Kassim Hanga, and Hassan Moyo.

The revolutionary goal was to establish a wholly egalitarian society and, to this end, President Karume proclaimed the Zanzibar Manifesto on March 8. This nationalized and redistributed the land, 80 percent of which was held by the Arab 13 percent of the population.

In April 1964 Karume negotiated a union with mainland Tanganyika under which Zanzibar retained considerable authority in domestic affairs. He became first vice president of the United Republic, renamed Tanzania in October. Speculation was rampant whether Zanzibar was saved from becoming a Communist state or whether Tanganyika would go Communist along with the island.

After the union, despite extensive aid largely from East-bloc countries, Zanzibar's economy stagnated as each partner went its own way domestically. Karume both hailed the union as an example for other African states and raised objection to any further integration.

On April 7, 1972, Karume was assassinated by four gunmen in Dar es Salaam. Two members of the Revolutionary Council were wounded in the attack.

Further Reading

A good source for material on Karume's career is John Middleton and Jane Campbell, *Zanzibar: Its Society and Its Politics* (1965). Recommended for additional historical and political background are Michael F. Lofchie, *Zanzibar: Background to Revolution* (1965), and Allison Butler Herrick and others, *Area Handbook for Tanzania* (1968). □

Joseph Kasavubu

Joseph Kasavubu (ca. 1913-1969) was the first president of the Republic of the Congo and provided a continuous focus of power through the struggles of the former Belgian colony to independence.

Joseph Kasavubu was born in the village of Kuma-Dizi in the Mayombe district of Lower Congo. Having lost his mother at age 4, the boy was raised largely by his older brother, who sent him to a nearby Catholic mission, where he was baptized in 1925. After a few years of rudimentary schooling in the Kikongo language, Kasavubu attended a *petit séminaire* (1929-1936) and then a seminary in Kasai, from which he was dismissed in 1939 with the equivalent of an undergraduate degree in philosophy for reasons that were never made clear. He was nevertheless permitted to take a teacher's certificate and to work in mission schools but for such a meager pittance that the embittered Kasavubu eventually broke with the missions and got a bookkeeping job with the colonial administration in 1942.

Kasavubu's entry into public life in 1946 was sponsored by Jean Bolikango (later his rival for the presidency), who engineered his election as secretary of an alumni association, which position made him an ex officio member of UNISCO (Union des Intérêts Sociaux Congolais), a debating society tied to the Catholic missions. Kasavubu's maiden speech to this association, though cloaked in precautionary language, was sufficiently "radical" to be disavowed by his peers.

President of ABAKO

But Kasavubu's real debut in politics came in 1954, when he was elected president of the Bakongo tribal association (ABAKO) as a compromise candidate. Although political associations were not permitted at the time, Kasavubu transformed ABAKO in such a way as to make it a political party in all but name; when overt political activity emerged in 1956, Kasavubu was ready for action. His well-organized campaign in the first municipal elections (December 1957) resulted in a sweeping victory for ABAKO in the capital city of Léopoldville.

This victory had serious results for the Congo, however. ABAKO was interested only in mobilizing the Bakongo people and did not attempt to transform the party into a

nationwide organization. It created a resentment among non-Bakongo residents of the capital which prevented the emergence of a national coalition in which ABAKO might have played a senior role. In addition, the relatively high degree of political mobilization and radicalization achieved by the Bakongo, combined with their sense of national identity, led ABAKO to adopt a semidetached position on the Congolese political scene in the form of claims for separate independence or for pan-Congo "reunification" involving Cabinda and portions of Angola and French Congo. This attitude resulted in a policy of noncooperation, both among the Bakongo and on the part of Kasavubu himself, thus further contributing to ABAKO's reputation for intractability and to the speeding up of Belgium's plans for gradual decolonization.

President of the Republic

After a brief period in jail in early 1959 which made Kasavubu the Congo's first "prison graduate," he became a somewhat reluctant participant in the decolonization process. His unique position (as well as the nuisance value of ABAKO, which had less than 10 percent of the seats in the Congo's first Parliament) was recognized by Patrice Lumumba when he endorsed Kasavubu for the presidency, despite the fact that the ABAKO leader had sought to prevent Lumumba's accession to the premiership. The two men worked in uncomfortable partnership during the first few weeks of the Congo crisis, but on Sept. 5, 1960, through a literal interpretation of his presidential prerogatives, Kasavubu dismissed Lumumba, thus unleashing a chain of events which ultimately led to the prime minister's assassination.

Thereafter, Kasavubu withdrew to a position from which he tried to arbitrate between the various factions and, more importantly, to remain politically alive during the period that saw the gradual erosion and eventual reconstruction of the central government's authority. He lent the cover of his legitimacy to Joseph Mobutu's first coup, thus avoiding early retirement, and then supported the return to civilian government under Cyrille Adoula (1961-1964), only to maneuver the latter out of power in favor of Moïse Tshombe when the Congo rebellion threatened to engulf the entire country.

Although Kasavubu avoided being engulfed in the continent-wide reprobation directed against Tshombe, he also ran the risk of being increasingly treated as a superfluous quantity by those same powers that backed the prime minister. This was especially alarming in view of the fact that his own popularity among the Bakongo had come under serious questioning from a number of quarters. The threat to Kasavubu's position became more precise when Tshombe announced that he would seek the presidency—an office which Kasavubu himself had helped turn into a major power center through the 1964 adoption of a new constitution.

Deposed by Mobutu

With the two men thus bent on a collision course, Kasavubu announced his opposition to the employment of foreign mercenaries and summarily dismissed Tshombe from the premiership. As had been the case in 1960, however, he was unable to secure parliamentary endorsement for his handpicked successor, Evariste Kimba (a former associate of Tshombe), and the ensuing stalemate was eventually resolved in November 1965, when Mobutu dismissed all civilian politicians and established direct army rule.

His Retirement

Mobutu's own lack of a political base, however, soon led him to seek a reconciliation with Kasavubu as a means of securing some sort of legitimacy for his regime. Lacking any real alternative, the deposed president gave the new regime his measured endorsement and accepted an honorary seat in the Senate. He retired to a farm in Mayombe, where he died on March 24, 1969. His death and that of Tshombe (June 29, 1969) signaled the eclipse of the first generation of Congolese politicians.

Kasavubu's political career was helped primarily by his shrewdness and his retiring character. His main achievement, in the eyes of history, may well be to have retained his seat at a time when the Congo's need for some symbol of continuity was highest, although one might argue that this need itself contributed significantly to Kasavubu's relative longevity in office.

Further Reading

Studies of Kasavubu and the history of the Congo are in Alan P. Merriam, *Congo: Background of Conflict* (1961); Catherine Hoskyns, *The Congo since Independence, January 1960-December 1961* (1965); and Crawford Young, *Politics in the Congo: Decolonization and Independence* (1965). □

Nancy Kassebaum (Baker)

As a U.S. senator from Kansas, Nancy Landon Kassebaum Baker (born 1932) was a political maverick whose stands ranged from support of the Equal Rights Amendment and a woman's right to choose abortion to support for the failed nomination of Robert Bork to the Supreme Court.

Nancy Landon was born in Topeka, Kansas, on July 29, 1932, the daughter of Alfred M. Landon and his second wife, Theo (Cobb) Landon. She grew up in a political family. Her father, the Republican governor of Kansas, ran against President Franklin Delano Roosevelt in 1936, a race he lost by a landslide, carrying only two states, Maine and Vermont. Although she was only four years old when her father ran for president and remembered little of the contest, she later claimed she received a first-rate political education as she grew up by listening to her father and his friends through a heating vent from her bedroom.

Education and Early Career

She attended public schools in Topeka and graduated from the University of Kansas in Lawrence in 1954 with a B.A. in political science. After working for a year as a receptionist at Hallmark Cards, she married her college sweetheart, Philip Kassebaum, in 1956. The couple moved to Michigan, where she took an M.A. in diplomatic history while he finished law school at the University of Michigan. The next 20 years she spent on the family farm in Maize, Kansas, with her husband, who became a prominent Wichita lawyer. While raising four children, John Philip, Jr., Linda Josephine, Richard Landon, and William Alfred, Kassebaum worked as vice president of KFH and KBRA radio stations owned by Kassebaum Communications. She later confessed that there were times in high school and college when she considered a career in public life, but judged it "a daydream, a fantasy." She served on the Kansas Committee on the Humanities and Kansas Government Ethics Commission and was elected to the Maize school board, eventually becoming its president.

Kassebaum finally did enter public life in 1975 after separating from her husband. She moved to Washington, D.C., with her children, where she took a job as assistant to Kansas Senator James B. Pearson. During her ten months on his staff she acted as liaison between constituents and federal agencies. When Pearson decided not to seek reelection in 1978, Kassebaum cautiously considered entering the race. Her father publicly discouraged her, worried that Kansas was not yet ready for a woman senator. But her mother

and her husband, who remained a close confidant despite their separation and subsequent divorce in 1979, supported her decision to run for office.

Political Life

Kassebaum defeated eight Republican rivals in the Republican primary, including a more politically experienced woman, State Senator Jan Meyers. She managed to capture 31 percent of the vote. In the general election she faced Democrat William Roy, a lawyer and physician with a liberal record during his two terms as congressman from Topeka. Trading on her family name, she adopted as her slogan "A Fresh Face, a Trusted Kansas Name." The *New York Times* later commented that "if her middle name were Jones her campaign would have been a joke." Kassebaum responded, "It has been said I am riding on the coattails of my dad, but I can't think of any better coattails to ride on." Fortunately for his daughter, Landon's coattails proved stronger in 1978 than they had in 1936.

What Kassebaum lacked in political experience she made up for in political savvy. She proved a formidable candidate able to turn her lack of experience into a virtue. During the post-Watergate years, when the nation demonstrated its distrust of Washington insiders by electing Jimmy Carter president in 1976, Kassebaum presented herself as a common-sense homemaker. She won the support of the state's major newspapers, but not the Kansas Women's Political Caucus or the National Organization for Women. Despite her sympathy for the Equal Rights Amendment (ERA), she refused to support extension of the deadline for ratification. Kassebaum admitted to being a moderate feminist, but felt that humanist was a more accurate label.

A shrewd and tireless campaigner, she outmaneuvered and outspent her opponent. With a personal net worth of $2.5 million, she put $115,000 of her own money into the campaign budget of $841,287. Her finances became an issue late in the race when her opponent challenged her to make a full financial disclosure. She refused on the grounds that she still filed a joint tax return with her estranged husband and that disclosure would violate his right to privacy. She did reveal, however, that she earned $92,000 a year and paid only $5,075 in taxes. Although the issue hurt her popularity, she dismissed it as so much "barn waste" and held on to her lead, defeating her opponent by 85,752 votes.

From the moment Kassebaum won election on November 7, 1978, she moved into the national spotlight. She became the second (after Margaret Chase Smith of Maine) woman elected senator in her own right, not preceded by a husband or appointed to fulfill an unexpired term. Kassebaum asked for and received positions on key committees, although she had to wait two years for a berth on the Senate Foreign Relations Committee. She chaired the Senate half of the Military Reform Caucus and the Aviation Subcommittee of the Senate Commerce, Science, and Transportation Committee.

In the Senate she earned a reputation as a political independent. She did not share the social agenda of the Republican New Right and made no secret of her sympathy for the ERA and her support of a woman's right to choose abortion. After her election she was viewed generally favorably by women's movement leaders. "She's not hostile to the movement. She doesn't turn her back on the Equal Rights Amendment or on the cause of social justice," said Barbara Mikulski, a Democrat from Maryland, the only other woman serving with Kassebaum in the Senate.

On other issues she was closer to Republican conservatives. She supported the failed nomination of Robert Bork to the Supreme Court. She opposed the National and Community Service Act and the Act for Better Child Care on the grounds that they cost too much. Likewise, she supported Ronald Reagan's veto of a farm bill designed to bail farmers out of financial trouble when it became clear that such an expense would quickly climb to over a billion dollars. Yet her liberal stance on some foreign policy issues made her a Republican maverick. She supported the Panama Canal treaty, was skeptical of the Granada invasion, and called for a regional conference to solve the problems in Central America. But, in 1985, she refused to support sanctions against South Africa. At the same time, she attacked what she labeled the "tyranny of the Third World" in the United Nations by introducing an amendment in 1986 to limit U.S. support for the organization's budget to 20 percent unless the one-nation, one-vote rule be changed to reflect each country's financial contribution. At that time, the U.S. handled 25 percent of the budget, while the Soviet Union, as the second highest contributor, contributed 11.8 percent. At the low end of the financial supporters was a collective of 78 third world countries which together paid only 0.1 percent, according to Gertrude Samuels in the *New Leader*.

Kassebaum took over as head of the Senate Labor and Human Resources Committee following the Republican victories in the 1994 election. Generally known as a moderate, she said, "what I enjoy most is trying to figure out legislative answers." She is also quoted as having said, "I'm not a person who particularly seeks power, but I don't avoid it when I feel I can use it to accomplish a good result."

As her political stature grew she was mentioned frequently as a possible vice presidential candidate, first in 1984, before it became clear that Ronald Reagan would seek reelection, and again in 1988 as a possible running mate for George Bush. However, neither rumor came to fruition. In 1984 Kassebaum ran for reelection and defeated her Democratic opponent in a landslide, capturing 78 percent of the vote. Again in 1990 she won reelection easily, gaining more than 73 percent of the vote. In 1995 Kassebaum announced that she would not seek a fourth term in office. She married Howard Baker Jr., the former Tennessee senator and Republican majority leader, in December 1996.

Further Reading

Additional information on Nancy Kassebaum can be found in "Nancy Kassebaum and Barbara Mikulski," *Ms.* (September 1988); Gertrude Samuels, "The 20% Solution, Kassebaum vs Moynihan on the UN," in *New Leader* (May 5-19, 1986); Peggy Simpson, "Nancy Landon Kassebaum," in *Working Woman* (March 1984); Lynda Johnson Robb, "Nancy Kassebaum: Making Political History," in *Ladies Home Journal*

(April 1979); and Frank W. Martin, "Freed to Run by her Broken Marriage, Mrs. Kassebaum Goes to Washington," *People Magazine* (January 8, 1979). ☐

Sen Katayama

Sen Katayama (1860-1933) was a Japanese labor and Socialist leader who, influenced by the Christian social gospel and increasingly radical ideas, founded Japan's first modern settlement house, trade union movement, labor newspaper, and Socialist party.

Born on Jan. 8, 1860, as Sugataro Yabuki, the future Sen Katayama was the second son of an adopted (*yoshi*) father who 4 years later left the locally prominent Yabukis to become a monk. When he was 18, to circumvent military conscription, Sugataro was nominally adopted into the peasant household of Ikutaro Katayama, thereby obtaining his permanent name of Sen Katayama.

Katayama acquired a classical Confucian education in Okayama and then Tokyo, where he arrived at 21 at the height of the "people's rights" movement. His Confucian idealism got a populist twist; he never lost an unshakable faith in individual and social perfectibility.

With a warm, outgoing personality, Katayama made devoted friends, though a streak of irascibility also made him some enemies. One lifelong friend from this period was Seishichi Iwasaki of the Mitsubishi *zaibatsu* (a family-controlled commercial combine), who tolerated his friend's increasingly radical views and rescued him from debt, served as matchmaker in 1897, and later cared for his children. Iwasaki also helped him make his first trip to America (1884-1896), where after a year and more of odd jobs Katayama studied at Hopkins Academy, Maryville College, Grinnell College, Andover Theological Seminary, and Yale Divinity School.

Beginnings as Socialist

Back in Tokyo, Katayama soon began work at the Congregationalist Kingsley Hall, the first settlement house in Japan. This helped him come in contact with the incipient labor union movement, for which he founded *Rodo Sekai* (Labor World), the first labor paper in Japan. After helping organize the Society for the Study of Socialism in 1898, he joined those transforming it into the Socialist Society in 1900 and then became a founder of the abortive Social Democratic party of 1901, along with fellow Christians Isoo Abe, Kiyoshi Kawakami, Naoe Kinoshita, Kojiro Nishikawa, and atheist Denjiro (Shusui) Kotoku; though it had a mild, pacifistic platform, it was immediately dissolved by the authorities.

Katayama's second journey to the United States and Europe (1903-1907) spanned the Russo-Japanese War, which he dramatically opposed by shaking hands with the Russian Georgi Plekhanov at the Sixth Congress of the Second International at Amsterdam in 1904. In Japan again,

he encountered increasing governmental suppression of the Socialist movement, culminating in the precipitate execution of Kotoku in the "high treason trial" of 1910-1911. Katayama, nevertheless, fearlessly aided the Tokyo streetcar strike of 1911-1912 that won an outstanding victory for "organized" labor. But the costs were high. Katayama was imprisoned because of it; he felt forced to leave Japan in 1914.

In Exile

In America again, enduring hand-to-mouth poverty and suffering the divorce by his wife he had left in Japan with two children, having brought the older daughter to America, he played the role of interpreter of Japanese developments to the politically curious but ill-informed American Socialists. He ridiculed his more moderate rival labor leader, Bunji Suzuki, when he too visited the United States. In 1916 Katayama was invited to New York by the Dutch Socialist Rutgers, where he met Aleksandra Kollontai, Nikolai Bukharin, and Leon Trotsky and later helped found the American Communist party. In January 1920 he escaped the Palmer raids; in March 1921 he left for Mexico City for 8 months on an assignment for the Comintern, after which he was invited to Moscow to accept a high position in the Comintern.

The last 11 years of Katayama's life were spent serving the Comintern as one of the few Asians with a well-known revolutionary past. His knowledge of the Japanese Communist movement became increasingly vicarious. He traveled abroad again only briefly, to China in 1924. Toward the end of his life he became discouraged at the lack of success of the Communist movement in his own homeland. After his death on Nov. 5, 1933, his bier was borne by Stalin and other dignitaries, and he was honored by burial within the Kremlin walls.

Further Reading

Katayama's *The Labor Movement in Japan* (1918) is autobiographical to a degree, covering the years 1897 to 1912, but contains some errors. A superb biography is Hyman Kublin, *Asian Revolutionary: The Life of Sen Katayama* (1964), which is accurate, rounded, and fascinatingly written, and includes a bibliography. For background on the Socialist and Communist movements see Rodger Swearingen and Paul Langer, *Red Flag in Japan: International Communism in Action, 1919-1951* (1952); Robert A. Scalapino, *Democracy and the Party Movement in Prewar Japan: The Failure of the First Attempt* (1953); George Oakley Totten, *The Social Democratic Movement in Prewar Japan* (1966); and George M. Beckmann and Okubo Genji, *The Japanese Communist Party, 1922-1945* (1969). ☐

George S. Kaufman

American playwright George S. Kaufman (1889-1961) collaborated on a great number of successful plays that merged theatricality with satiric comedy.

George S. Kaufman was born in Pittsburgh, Pa., on Nov. 16, 1889. After attending public schools in Pittsburgh and Paterson, N.J., he studied law briefly. He worked as a clerk, stenographer, and ribbon salesman before he started contributing humorous verses to the newspaper column of Franklin P. Adams in 1908. With Adams's help, Kaufman joined the *Washington Times* in 1912. After working on the *New York Evening Mail* and the *New York Tribune,* he went to the *New York Times* in 1917 and remained as drama editor until 1930. In 1917 he married Beatrice Bakrow.

Tense and tireless, caustic and witty, Kaufman was somewhat eccentric in his personal mannerisms. His first successful play, *Dulcy* (1921), written with Marc Connelly, is a satire of a vapid woman who is wrecking her bright husband's plans. *To the Ladies* (1922) reverses this, as a bright woman saves her vapid husband's plans. For 20 years one Kaufman collaboration, and sometimes several, appeared annually on Broadway.

Among the best examples of Kaufman's satiric comedy were two collaborations with Edna Ferber: *The Royal Family* (1928) focuses on the American theater's first family, the Barrymores, and *Dinner at Eight* (1932) deals with social climbing. His musical satire, the Pulitzer Prize-winning *Of Thee I Sing* (1931), written with Morrie Ryskind, hilariously indicts the chicanery of politicians. He collaborated with Ryskind again on the musical *Let 'Em Eat Cake* (1933). In *First Lady* (1935) he again derided politicians.

Sometimes Kaufman succeeded with sheer theatricality, as in another Pulitzer Prize-winner, *You Can't Take It with You* (1936), written with Moss Hart. The classic *The Man Who Came to Dinner* (1939) was also written with Hart. Working with John P. Marquand on an adaptation of the latter's novel *The Late George Apley* (1944), Kaufman tossed barbs at the proper Bostonians.

After the death of his first wife in 1945, Kaufman married actress Leueen McGrath, whom he divorced in 1957; they wrote *The Small Hours* (1951). After World War II he worked increasingly as a play doctor. His knowledge of play structure was highly valued, and his plays rarely failed. He died on June 2, 1961, in New York City.

Further Reading

Kaufman and his work are discussed in John Mason Brown, *Two on the Aisle: Ten Years of the American Theatre in Performance* (1938) and *The Worlds of Robert E. Sherwood: Mirror to His Times* (1965); Edna Ferber, *A Peculiar Treasure* (1939; rev. ed. 1960); Edmond M. Gagey, *Revolution in American Drama* (1947); *Six Modern American Plays,* introduced by Allan G. Halline (1951); Moss Hart, *Act One* (1959); and Jean Gould, *Modern American Playwrights* (1966).

Additional Sources

Meredith, Scott, *George S. Kaufman and his friend,* Garden City, N.Y., Doubleday, 1974.
Goldstein, Malcolm, *George S. Kaufman: his life, his theater,* New York: Oxford University Press, 1979. □

Gerald Bernard Kaufman

A foreign policy spokesman of the British Labour Party, Gerald Bernard Kaufman (born 1930) became a member of Parliament in 1970.

Gerald Kaufman was born on June 21, 1930, and was the son of Louis and Jane Kaufman. As a Yorkshireman, he was educated in Leeds, an important textile and commercial center in the north of England, at city "council" schools in the primary grades and at Leeds Grammar School (high school). He went on to undergraduate education at Queen's College, Oxford.

His first real political job was assistant general secretary of the Fabian Society, which was the nucleus of British socialist intelligentsia. Kaufman only held this job for a year (1954-1955) and was pleased at obtaining the job as a journalist on the political staff of a popular newspaper, the *Daily Mirror,* for the next nine years (1955-1964). He moved to the *New Statesmen* in 1964-1965, in preparation for his five-year stint as the press adviser of Labour Prime Minister Harold Wilson (parliamentary press liaison officer, 1965-1970).

Kaufman's political career was given a boost by his successful election to a seat in the House of Commons in 1970. He failed in the elections of 1955 (Bromley) and 1959 (Gillingham), but he gained a victory in the election for

Manchester Ardwick on June 18, 1970. Kaufman was a member of Parliament at last. Ardwick, a working-class district, was merged into Manchester Gorton in June 1983; he successfully contested Gorton in 1983, and he retained the seat in the Commons into the 1990s.

Gorton, after redrawing, was one of the five new Manchester city seats, including the old working-class Ardwick division. Longsight, the southeastern part of Gorton, is a belt of inner-city desolation and votes strongly pro-Labour. Over 30 percent of its people are non-white. Rusholme and Fallowfield contain many owner-occupied houses (once part of Manchester's southern middle-class area), but the middle-class has fled out to the south towards Cheshire, the neighboring country. Although half its housing is owner-occupied, it is increasingly occupied by Asians. Gorton was a Labour stronghold in the early 1990s, so Kaufman had a safe seat for the foreseeable future.

In Gorton in 1983 the vote was Labour (Kaufman), 51.2 percent; Conservative, 28.5 percent; Liberal Alliance, 19 percent; Communist, 0.8 percent; and other, 0.5 percent. The Gorton 1987 parliamentary election, in which Kaufman was again successful, was much the same as 1983: Labour, 54.4 percent; Conservative, 23.3 percent; and Liberal Alliance, 21.7 percent. Kaufman had won for Labour 3.2 percent over the 1983 vote.

After 1987 Kaufman was what the British call "Shadow" foreign secretary (if, by any chance, the Labour government should be in power, he would be foreign secretary). With a safe seat behind him his star was rising. His

position in the Labour Party began ascending in 1974: parliamentary under-secretary of state for the Department of the Environment, March 1974-June 1975; under-secretary for the Department of Industry, June-December 1975; minister of state for the same department, December 1975-May 1979; privy councillor in 1978; opposition spokesman for the environment, 1979-1983; elected to the "Shadow" Cabinet, December 1980 (to the parliamentary committee of the Labour Party: the "PCP"); Shadow home secretary, 1983-1987; and finally, Shadow foreign secretary (in American parlance, secretary of state).

In 1987 Kaufman had a foreign policy trip to Central America in preparation for his new job. He had the disadvantage of being in Nicaragua while the Sandinistas were still in power and was full of pro-Sandinista arguments. The Nicaraguan people were "united by everyday wartime sacrifices"; they accepted hardships because "their government is doing its best" and sees to it that their shortages are "fairly shared"; and *most* Nicaraguans are "united in opposition to Reagan's attempt to destroy their Revolution." President Reagan should end his aid to the contra rebels. In the end, the Sandinista regime was voted out by the electors of Nicaragua (1990) and a new government was formed, partly by recognizing the contras. Gerald Kaufman was wrong about some aspects of the situation.

In a speech on South Africa to the House of Commons in 1988, Kaufman satirized Margaret Thatcher, the British Conservative prime minister, as being partly responsible for South Africa's social policy towards Blacks. He called her "the handmaiden of apartheid" and "the world's most effective ally of apartheid." It was an antagonistic political speech against Thatcher, heavy with "calculated excess and verbal gem-setting" (as a critic said). Thatcher was opposed to apartheid; she was anti-radical and anti-socialist, but she was no racist. Kaufman's speech was party-political, witty, and humorous, but left an impression that he was not taking the problems of South Africa seriously.

In 1990 he drew fire from Labour Party rank-and-file with a speech about the new democracies of Eastern Europe (the former East Germany, Poland, Czechoslovakia, Hungary, Bulgaria, and Romania), the ex-Communist regimes. Kaufman said a "Marshall Plan" should be devised by the rich nations to assist the new democracies; the role of the West was not to instigate change but to support the efforts for change. This speech did not go far enough for some of the rank-and-file. After all, he was the Shadow foreign secretary of the Labour Party; it was hardly a momentous speech.

At its party conference the British Labour Party in 1980 opted for *unilateral* nuclear disarmament. This standard of Labour foreign policy was reiterated in the British general election of 1983, which caused the breaking-away of some Labour supporters to join the Social Democratic Party in 1984. The disarmament policy was a product of the internal politics of the Labour Party and contributed to the loss of the 1987 general election, again. Kaufman, as the newest foreign policy spokesman, had a lot to worry about, despite his popularity within the PLP.

Kaufman was of the Jewish faith and traveled many times to Israel. He wrote a book about his trips, *Inside the Promised Land,* in 1986. He knew people in Israel and conversed with them on society and politics; his book basically was short, breezy, and personally informative, a short travelogue with political discussions. The "love of country" will continue to be the salvation of Israel as a nation, according to Kaufman. The book, however, was devoid of policy analysis.

In another book, *My Life in the Silver Screen* written in 1985, Kaufman reveals himself as a film buff with a nostalgic story of 50 years or so "going to the pictures" and what he saw there. In fact he saw the products of Hollywood, to a large extent, at the expense of European films. His book was smart, clever, and humorous, but not serious at all.

Kaufman was a promising British Labour Party politician, up against the ascendent Conservative Party in the 1990s, with John Major as the British prime minister. Major was in charge of the nation in the Gulf War of early 1991 and pursued the war to its successful conclusion. Kaufman had a long background of Labour foreign policy excesses and contradictions to account for as Labour's Shadow foreign secretary. Many critics believed that Kaufman's resignation in June 1992 clearly reflected the state of the Labour party (*Sunday Times* June 7, 1992). In the mid 1990s Kaufman served as the chairman of the House of Commons National Heritage Select Committee, which published reports on the United Kingdom film industry (*The Times,* March 25, 1995) and public ownership of the lottery (*The Guardian,* June 5, 1996). In politics, anything can happen, and usually does.

Further Reading

Additional information on Kaufman can be found in the *International Bibliography of the Social Sciences: Political Science* (London: 1953-to date) and in the *New Statesman* (December 13, 1985; September 11, 1987; March 4, 1988; and January 12, 1990); *The Economist* (November 2, 1985); and in the (London) *Times* (February 1 and 12, October 30, and November 25, 1989, and August 9, 1990).

In addition to the two books cited in the text, works by Gerald Kaufman include *How To Live Under Labour,* (with co-author; 1964); *The Left,* which he edited (1966); *To Build a Promised Land* (1973); *How To Be a Minister* (1980); and *Renewal: Labour's Britain in the 1980s,* which he edited (London: 1983). □

Ezekiel Kaufmann

The Jewish philosopher and scholar Ezekiel Kaufmann (1889-1963) founded a new school of biblical criticism.

Ezekiel Kaufmann was born in Dunayvtsy, Podolia. Following the advice of his teacher, the Hebrew poet Jacob Fichman, in 1906 he left for Odessa to study at the Great Yeshiva headed by the famed Rabbi Hayyim Tschernowitz. From there he traveled to St. Petersburg to take up Oriental studies. In 1913 he went to Switzerland and, concentrating in philosophy and Semitic philology, received his doctorate from the University of Berne. Following World War I, he moved to Germany. He worked on the German-Hebrew Jewish encyclopedia *Eshkol.* In Berlin he edited a periodical of Hebrew culture and education, *Atidenu,* assisted in the writing of Tschernowitz's *Abridgement of the Talmud,* and worked on the *Lexicon of Biblical and Talmudic Language.*

In 1929 Kaufmann emigrated to Palestine, where he was a teacher at the Reali School in Haifa until 1949. From that year, until his retirement in 1957, he was professor of Bible at the Hebrew University in Jerusalem. He began his literary career with a story published in the newspaper *Haolam.* His first outstanding critical article was devoted to a debate with Ahad Haam. He sought to argue against the latter's notion of the "national-survival instinct" as a substitute for religion in Judaism. Kaufmann's basic position was that the religious factor in Judaism was its mainspring, and nothing could replace it. This thesis was developed in *Golah ve nekar* (1929-1930), a historical and sociological study of the Jewish people from ancient through modern times. In this work he sought to disprove the accepted solutions for the problem of Jewish survival in the Diaspora and saw the land of Israel as manifesting only one of several territorial alternatives. He pondered the fate of the Jewish people in *Constraints of the Times* (1936), a collection of studies and articles, and in *Between Roads* (1944), a study in aspects of national philosophy.

In the early 1930s Kaufmann began to publish chapters of his monumental book *The History of Israelite Religion.* In this work he sought to negate the very foundations of modern biblical criticism, most notably the theories of Welhausen. While generally accepting the division into source documents, he rejected the evolutionary schema imposed upon those documents. In its stead he stressed the role of monotheism, its primacy, its revelational character, and its seminal role in the forging of the religion of Israel. In addition to this work, he published comprehensive introductions to, and commentaries upon, the biblical books of Joshua and Judges as well as a monograph, "The Biblical Account of the Conquest of Palestine."

Further Reading

There is very little writing in English on Kaufmann. A brief biography of him appears in the *Encyclopedia of Zionism and Israel,* edited by Raphael Patai and published by McGraw-Hill (1971). □

Kenneth David Kaunda

Kenneth David Kaunda (born 1924), first president of Zambia, was a leading figure in his country's independence movement. Until he stepped down in 1991, he maintained his critical position as the leader of a buffer country between white-ruled

states in southern Africa and hostile, independent black-ruled states to the north.

Kenneth David Kaunda was born on April 28, 1924, at Lubwa Mission near Chinsali in Northern Rhodesia. His father was a minister and teacher who had left Nyasaland (now Malawi) in 1904, and his mother was the first African woman to teach in colonial Zambia.

After completing his education in the early 1940s, Kaunda began teaching at Lubwa in 1943 and was headmaster there as well from 1944 to 1947. Then he moved to the copper mining area, where he founded a farmers' cooperative, was a mine welfare officer (1948), and became a boarding master at Mufulira Upper School from 1948 to 1949.

Political Career

The urbanized copper area was a natural setting for African nationalism. Resenting the racial discrimination that prevailed in central Africa, Kaunda helped to found the African National Congress (ANC), the first major anticolonial organization in Northern Rhodesia. He was its secretary general from 1953 to 1958 under ANC president Harry Nkumbula.

Early on, Kaunda became committed to the nonviolent principles of India's Mohandas Gandhi, a position strengthened by his visit to India in 1957. He broke with Nkumbula and became president of the Zambia African National

Union from 1958 through 1959. When civil disorder led to banning of this party, Kaunda was jailed for a period of nine months. On his release he became president of the new United National Independence party in 1960. On Oct. 30, 1962, he was elected to the Legislative Council. He formed a coalition government with Nkumbula's ANC and served as minister of local government and social welfare in 1962.

Zambia slowly moved through the complications of earning independence. Much of the success is attributed to the skillful diplomacy of Kenneth Kaunda, who succeeded in allaying the fears of the huge European and smaller Asian community that black leadership would ignore their interests. In October 1964, the new nation of Zambia was born, with Kaunda as its president.

The Aftermath of Independence

After independence, Kaunda made agreements with mining companies over copper royalties. He also had to deal with uprisings of the Lumpa religious sect under self-styled prophetess Alice Lenshina. His relations with neighboring white-ruled Rhodesia were unstable after the latter's 1965 illegal break with Britain, but he resisted those within and without his government who urged military action. Instead, Kaunda sought aid for a rail line to a Tanzanian port. This would offer an alternate route for landlocked Zambia's copper that prior to the rail line had to be exported through Rhodesia. These tensions heightened tribal differences and encouraged Kaunda's socialist leanings.

Kaunda, like other African leaders, faced the complex problems of independence and tribalism, although his diplomatic skills saved his country the trauma of civil war. However, political pressures within and without his borders led him to impose single- party rule in 1973. With civil war to the west in Angola in 1976 and continuing conflict in Rhodesia, Kaunda won, unopposed, a new five-year term. Pledging his government to enforce high standards of morality and concern for public welfare, he was able to put down several attempted coups over the next few years.

Kenneth Kaunda retired from office in 1991 when Frederick Chiluba came to power in the first multiparty election in Zambia following the legalization of opposition parties in 1990. He moved to London where he continued to be concerned with the policies and programs of his native country.

Further Reading

Kaunda's autobiography, *Zambia Shall Be Free* (1962); a biography by Merfyn Morley Temple, *Kaunda of Zambia* (1964); another biography by Richard Seymour Hall, *Kaunda: Founder of Zambia* (1964); Hall's *The High Price of Principles: Kaunda and the White South* (1970); also David C. Mulford, *Zambia: The Politics of Independence, 1957-1964* (1967). □

Kautilya

Kautilya (4th century B.C.), also known as Vishnugupta and Chanakya, is traditionally known as the author of the *Arthashastra*, the celebrated ancient Indian work on polity, and as the counselor of Chandragupta Maurya, the founder of the Maurya empire.

Most of the details of the life of Kautilya are uncertain and shrouded in myth and legend. Ancient Indian tradition describes him as a native of Taxila (near Peshawar in modern Pakistan) who had journeyed to Pataliputra (Patna), capital of the Nanda empire, in search of recognition of his learning. There he was insulted by Dhana Nanda, last of the Nanda rulers, and the irascible Brahmin swore vengeance on the house of the Nandas. Pursued by Nanda soldiers, Kautilya escaped into the forests, where he met the young Chandragupta Maurya. Kautilya took Chandragupta to Taxila. This was the time when Alexander's legions were invading northwestern India. Alexander retreated from the Punjab in 325 B.C., and soon thereafter Chandragupta worked his dynastic revolution, killing Dhana Nanda and becoming the ruler of India. Indian tradition asserts that Kautilya had masterminded this revolution and continued as Chandragupta's counselor.

The *Arthashastra*

Whatever the nature of accounts of Kautilya's life, it is certain that Kautilya was a historical figure and that he was responsible for the compilation of a work on polity, a work that has exerted a profound influence on the development of political ideas in traditional India. The *Arthashastra* was believed to have been lost and was known only through references to it and quotations from it in subsequent works on law and polity in Sanskrit. It was discovered and published in the 1920s and immediately provoked extensive discussion on the nature of its contents and their implications for understanding the traditional Indian polity.

The *Arthashastra* is not a work on political philosophy, which it treats only incidentally, but a manual of instruction on the administration of a state and ways to meet challenges to it. Kautilya is a thoroughgoing political realist and often gives the impression of being amoral. He views the state as a seven-limbed organism which grows in war and whose purpose is to destroy its enemies and extend the territory under its control by all means, including aggression against and subversion of its opponents.

The work treats of the many departments of governmental administration and pays special attention to war, preparation for it, and its triumphant execution. The bureaucracy, as envisioned by Kautilya, must be all-pervasive, efficient, and honest. The king is the central point of this vast and sprawling bureaucratic structure, and Kautilya's exhortation to him is to be on guard at all times. Kautilya's *Arthashastra* is often compared to Machiavelli's *Prince,* with which it shares many common philosophical and practical

views. In its spirit of realpolitik and machtpolitik it reveals an altogether surprising aspect of the Indian civilization.

Further Reading

The most scholarly edition and translation of the *Arthashastra* is by R. P. Kangle, *The Kautiliya Arthasastra* (3 vols., 1965). R. Shamasastry, *The Arthashastra* (1956), has long been a standard work of reference. M. V. Krishna Rao, *Studies in Kautilya* (1953; 2d rev. ed. 1958), presents the *Arthashastra* ideas in a popular style. U. N. Ghoshal, *A History of Indian Political Ideas* (1959), has extensive materials on the statecraft of Kautilya. □

Karl Johann Kautsky

The German-Austrian Socialist Karl Johann Kautsky (1854-1938) was the major theoretician of German Social Democracy before World War I and one of the principal figures in the history of the international Socialist movement.

Born in Prague, Karl Kautsky was the son of a Czech painter and his actress wife. His studies at the University of Vienna were mainly scientific, however, rather than artistic. Although he considered himself a Socialist by 1875, it was his encounter with Wilhelm Liebknecht and Eduard Bernstein about 1880 that brought him to Marxism, and in 1883 he became editor of *Die neue Zeit,* which soon became the leading Marxist theoretical journal in Germany and perhaps the world. In 1887 he published *The Economic Doctrines of Karl Marx,* which did much to popularize Marxist ideas.

Ideologically, Kautsky (along with August Bebel) represented the Socialist "center" which retained its belief in the inevitable—indeed imminent—collapse of capitalism, but which differed from the radical left in holding that socialism was possible only through political democracy. Unlike the Socialist right, however, Kautsky maintained that imperial Germany was too undemocratic for Socialists to participate in governmental coalitions and that therefore they must remain in the opposition. Kautsky was the author of much of the Erfurt program of 1891, strongly Marxist and revolutionary in tone, which was to remain the official program of the party throughout the imperial period, and he strongly resisted the revisionist tendencies associated with Bernstein that subsequently challenged many of the basic assumptions laid down at Erfurt.

Kautsky broke with the majority of the Social Democrats during World War I. Convinced of the war guilt of Germany and Austria, he joined the pacifist Independent Socialists (USPD), which cost him the editorship of *Die neue Zeit.* Though most of the Independent Socialists came from the radical wing of the prewar party, Kautsky did not share their enthusiasm for the Bolshevik revolution in Russia, and he became one of its most vocal Socialist opponents (especially in his *Dictatorship of the Proletariat,* 1918).

After the German revolution of 1918 Kautsky served briefly in the republican government in the Foreign Office and on the Socialization Commission. In 1919 he helped edit a collection of documents on the outbreak of the war, tending to show the guilt of the Kaiser. But in general Kautsky was without much influence in the post-war Social Democratic party or in the Weimar regime. He moved to Vienna, which he had to flee at the time of the Anschluss, just before his death in 1938.

Further Reading

Extensive material on Kautsky is in George Douglas Howard Cole, *A History of Socialist Thought* (4 vols., 1953-1958); Sidney Hook, *Marx and the Marxists: The Ambiguous Legacy* (1955); and J. P. Nettl, *Rosa Luxemburg* (2 vols., 1966). See also Merle Fainsod, *International Socialism and the World War* (1935), and George Lichtheim, *A Short History of Socialism* (1970).

Additional Sources

Geary, Dick, *Karl Kautsky,* New York: St. Martin's Press, 1987.
Kautsky, John H., *Karl Kautsky: Marxism, revolution & democracy,* New Brunswick, U.S.A.: Transaction Publishers, 1994.
Salvadori, Massimo L., *Karl Kautsky and the socialist revolution, 1880-1938,* London; New York: Verso, 1990.
Steenson, Gary P., *Karl Kautsky, 1854-1938: Marxism in the classical years,* Pittsburgh, Pa.: University of Pittsburgh Press, 1991. □

Yasunari Kawabata

Yasunari Kawabata (1899-1972) was a distinguished Japanese novelist who won the Nobel Prize in literature for exemplifying in his writings the Japanese mind.

Yasunari Kawabata was born in Osaka on June 11, 1899, into a cultured family, his father being a doctor of medicine. When Kawabata was 3, his father died; the next year his mother died, and Kawabata went to live with his grandparents. When he was 8, his grandmother died, and in 1914 his grandfather died. The child was thus constantly confronted with the death of members of his family, and it is thought that this experience left its mark on the writer, who often dwells on the problem of death, or loneliness of life. In *Diary of a Sixteen-year-old,* actually written on the eve of his grandfather's death but published in 1925, Kawabata gives vent to his emotions in a haunting memoir of early sorrow.

After the death of his grandfather, Kawabata became a ward of his mother's family. During grammar school he was inspired to be a painter. Indeed, he enjoyed a lifelong interest in art. Later, however, while attending high school in Tokyo and living with relatives in Asakusa, he decided to become a novelist. His literary career dates from about this time, when he began writing stories and essays for little magazines and local newspapers.

Kawabata read contemporary Japanese authors of the Shirakaba Ha, or White Birches school, and translations of Danish and Swedish writers. From the beginning of his career Kawabata was at odds with the currently popular naturalistic school, pursuing instead a more subtle, lyrically inspired tendency stemming from Japanese literary. During his student days he became acquainted with Kikuchi Kan, a writer of note and editor of the magazine *Bungei Shunju.* In 1923 Kawabata joined the magazine staff.

Graduating from the university in 1924, Kawabata together with other friends founded a literary magazine, *Bungei Jidai.* This journal was the starting point of a new school of writers, the Neoperceptionists, who reacted against both popular naturalism and the politically oriented Proletarian Writers' movement. Thereafter Kawabata wrote significant literary criticism and patronized young writers. In 1948 he became chairman of the Japanese PEN Club meetings, and in 1954 he was elected a member of the Japanese Academy of the Arts. Kawabata was awarded the Nobel Prize for literature in 1968. He committed suicide in Zushi on April 16, 1972.

Literary Career

Kawabata's fiction is distinguished by subtle psychological characterization and a lyrical style that is deceptively simple. His works might be called elegies of life. *The Dancing Girl of Izu* (1926) tells of a youth's sentimental love for a dancer in a troupe of entertainers who wander from one hot-spring resort to another. *The "Kurenaidan" of Asakusa* deals with the fascinating milieu of street gangs in

the Asakusa quarter of Tokyo. The author introduces himself as a character in the story, depicting a variety of low-life types who inhabit the back streets of Tokyo, their customs and mores.

Snow Country (1947), a stylistic tour de force, analyzes the love and loneliness of a country geisha in a mountain hot-springs resort who has an affair with an urbane dilettante from Tokyo. Living in two different types of isolation, the two find their love ultimately impossible. *A Thousand Cranes* (1949) depicts the tangled lives and hopelessly complicated emotions of a group of people, with the subtleties of the tea ceremony for a background. The shattering of a famous tea bowl, a kind of symbolic breaking of an evil spell, is perhaps the strangest in a long series of chapters on the strange life of objects. The principal characters are left, each with his own tragedy of loneliness. *Sleeping Beauty* (1961) reveals the faded memories of a man on the threshold of old age who indulges his erotic fantasies by visiting an establishment where young girls have been drugged to sleep and are unaware of his presence.

Further Reading

A biography of Kawabata is in the Kokusai Bunka Shinkokai, *Introduction to Contemporary Japanese Literature,* pt. 2 (1959). His career is also studied in Nakamura Mitsuo, *Contemporary Japanese Fiction, 1926-1968* (1969).

Additional Sources

Gessel, Van C., *Three modern novelists: Soseki, Tanizaki, Kawabata,* Tokyo; New York: Kodansha International, 1993. □

Rashidi Mfaume Kawawa

Rashidi Mfaume Kawawa (born 1929), Tanzanian political leader, devoted his career to policies designed to increase his fellow citizens' standard of living.

The son of an elephant hunter and the eldest of eight children, Rashidi Mfaume Kawawa was born in the Songea district of Tanganyika (now Tanzania) in eastern Africa. After primary schooling in Dar es Salaam, he finished his formal education at Tabora Government Secondary School (1951-1956), the alma mater of Julius Nyerere, leader in the fight for Tanganyika's independence. Kawawa refused the opportunity to continue his education at Uganda's Makerere College, thus enabling his father to use the family's limited resources to educate his siblings.

Early Career

Kawawa's first job was as a Public Works Department accounts clerk. This was a most difficult period for the young man. With the death of his father, he assumed the responsibility of supporting his younger brothers and sisters. In 1951 Kawawa realized a long-standing dream of becoming a social worker. He had actually inaugurated this career by organizing a literacy campaign for adults while a student in Dar es Salaam.

On his new job Kawawa joined a mobile film unit engaged in government literacy programs. When it was decided to use the unit for educational filming, he was chosen as the only Tanzanian leading actor. He also served as a scriptwriter and a producer. Perhaps the most important aspect of Kawawa's social worker career occurred when he was sent to central Tanzania (1953) to work among Kikuyu detainees held because of the Kenyan Mau Mau movement. He later described his successful work there as the "greatest challenge of my life."

Government Service

Kawawa joined the Tanganyika African Government Services Association, becoming its assistant general secretary in 1951 and its president in 1955. His main task was securing rights for government employees due them under Tanganyika's laws. Realizing the advantages of a nationwide organization, Kawawa helped found the Tanganyika Federation of Labor (TFL) and was elected its first general secretary in 1955.

The Tanganyikan independence movement was then underway, directed by Julius Nyerere of the Tanganyika African National Union (TANU). Kawawa's government employment prevented him from political participation, but his commitment to use the unions to further independence led to his resignation in February 1956 to devote his time

and talents to labor and political organization. Joining TANU, he became a central committee member (1957) and vice president (1960). In the meantime Kawawa had been appointed to the Legislative Council (1957), remaining a member until 1960. In September 1960, following his first appointment to Cabinet rank, he resigned from the TFL to concentrate on politics.

When Prime Minister Nyerere of the now independent Tanganyika resigned for a brief period in 1962, Kawawa replaced him until his return to office. After 1964 Kawawa held the office of second vice president of Tanzania (formed from the union of Tanganyika and the island republic of Zanzibar), serving as Nyerere's principal assistant for mainland affairs and as leader of the National Assembly.

Nyerere resigned as Tanzania's president in 1985, and Kawawa left government service as well. However, he was seen once more in the political spotlight when he attended the seventy-fifth birthday celebration of former president Nyerere in early 1997.

Further Reading

Judith Hare Listowell, *The Making of Tanganyika* (1965); *A Survey of East African History,* (1968) B. A. Ogot and J. A. Kiernan, eds.; Tanzanian delegation, UN. □

Elia Kazan

Elia Kazan (born 1909) is known as the preeminent director of works by Arthur Miller and Tennessee Williams. Kazan emerged as the leading exponent of psychological realism via his film and stage productions of the 1940s and 1950s. His works reflect both social struggle and personal pain.

Elia Kazan was born into a large family of Anatolian Greeks near Istanbul in 1909. Kazan's family came to the United States when he was four, and he grew up in the slums and suburbs of New York City. He was a reclusive child who read compulsively, often as an escape from working in the family business, the rug trade. Determined not to follow in his father's footsteps, the young Elia attended Williams College from 1926 to 1930, majoring in English literature. It was here that he developed his initial interest in theater, writing a prize-winning paper on the audience's emotional response to drama.

Kazan considered a career in the film industry and decided that more theatrical training would help him achieve that goal. He applied to the Yale School of Drama and was accepted, despite his lack of practical experience. From 1930 to 1932 Kazan immersed himself in all aspects of dramatic production at Yale. He found that he shared with several others an interest in social drama and the establishment of a left-wing alternative to Broadway theater. Before completing his degree, Kazan left graduate school to apprentice with the Group Theatre, an offshoot of the Theatre Guild.

The Group Theatre, fashioned after Stanislavski's famous Moscow Art Theatre, was founded by Cheryl Crawford, Lee Strasberg, and Harold Clurman. The company's productions were attempts to combine social consciousness and artistic excellence. Kazan worked for the group in a variety of capacities—as press agent, stage manager, and actor. In 1934, with Art Smith, he recruited new playwrights, an effort that resulted in Clifford Odets' *Waiting for Lefty.* In its initial performance Kazan played Agate, who delivers the play's final appeal for a strike of cab drivers.

His next association was with the Workers' Laboratory Theatre (re-named the Theatre of Action in 1935), where he realized his ambition to direct, beginning with Peter Martin's *The Young Go First* The production, implementing Group Theatre techniques of improvisation and rehearsal exercises, featured Alfred Saxe. The Theatre of Action's film division also employed Kazan as a director of left-wing movies. This unit evolved into Frontier Films, known for its documentary realism and called by *Variety* the "Group Theatre of motion pictures." In 1936 Kazan returned to the group, which was now headed by Clurman only. He stayed until 1941, acting in Odets' *Golden Boy* and other works. The departure of Strasberg and Crawford also allowed him to direct.

In the early 1940s Kazan began to concentrate solely on directing, and in the first few years of the decade he directed a number of plays, most notably Thorton Wilder's *The Skin of Our Teeth,* starring Tallulah Bankhead. This production earned Kazan the 1942 New York Drama Critics' Award for Best Director. By 1945 Kazan was receiving offers to direct from both Broadway and Hollywood. He continued to produce successes in both arenas, with the film *A Tree Grows in Brooklyn* and the play *All My Sons,* the latter by a then-unknown young playwright named Arthur Miller.

In 1947, with Cheryl Crawford and Robert Lewis, Kazan founded the Actors' Studio as a kind of revival of the Group Theatre, with a focus on actor training rather than producing plays. When Lee Strasberg was eventually recruited as the head of the studio, Kazan's position became that of an occasional instructor and patron.

Kazan returned to directing with the play with which he had the greatest personal relationship—Miller's *Death of a Salesman,* starring Lee J. Cobb. Believing that the protagonist, Willy Loman, was a man who was "socially mistaught," Kazan considered the play to be "a story of love—the end of tragic love" between father and son. He also noted that "this play has to be directed with COMPASSION." Jo Mielziner's famous setting for this production reflected the fragile physical and psychological realities of Willy Loman. The play was a tremendous success, ran more than 700 performances, and garnered the Pulitzer Prize among other major awards.

During the next few years, Kazan spent more of his time as a film director. Notable among this work are *A Streetcar Named Desire* (1951), *On the Waterfront* (1954), and *East of Eden* (1955). After the shooting of *Streetcar* Kazan was subpoenaed by the House UnAmerican Activities Committee to testify regarding any connection he had with members of the Communist Party working in the entertainment industry. Kazan, in a very painful position that would determine the future of his work, cooperated with the committee. He admitted that he had adopted communism for a time (which he had since renounced) and named several other party members with whom he had worked. He followed this up with newspaper ads, public addresses, and articles defending his testimony and anti-Communist position. Branded an "informer," Kazan found that a number of former associates would no longer work with him, including Harold Clurman and Arthur Miller.

Kazan threw himself back into his work, but his production of *Flight Into Egypt* closed on Broadway after only 46 performances. He then went to Germany to take over direction of *Man on a Tightrope,* but it also was a box-office failure. Kazan's next project was a Broadway production of Tennessee Williams' *Camino Real,* another financial disaster.

Kazan broke this string of disappointments with two Broadway successes, Robert Anderson's *Tea and Sympathy* and Williams' *Cat on a Hot Tin Roof,* and the Oscar-winning film *On the Waterfront,* as well as *East of Eden,* which gave James Dean his first starring role.

After this successful comeback, Kazan established his own film company and produced *Baby Doll* (1956), *A Face in the Crowd* (1957), and several others, but they fared poorly. Kazan returned to the theater in 1957 to direct William Inge's *Dark at the Top of the Stairs,* Archibald MacLeish's *J. B.,* and Williams' *Sweet Bird of Youth.*

In 1963 Kazan became co-director with Robert Whitehead of the Lincoln Center Repertory Theatre. The company's opening production was Arthur Miller's *After the Fall,* directed by Kazan. Miller and Kazan were re-united after a split of nearly a decade. The play was a success, but Kazan's subsequent production of *The Changeling,* just before the first anniversary of the Repertory Theatre, was a disastrous effort, and he resigned.

Kazan finally decided to produce his own screenplay, on which he had been working for several years. This was *America, America,* a fictionalized version of his own family's emigration to the United States. *The Arrangement,* his next film, was quasi-autobiographical and a financial disappointment.

Kazan then turned to writing novels (including *The Assassins*) and directed one film, *The Last Tycoon,* in 1976. His 1988 autobiography, *Elia Kazan: a Life,* touches on the entire fabric of people and productions in a fascinating life. In Kazan's mid-eighties, irony resonated as in a dark script when Arthur Miller's allegory of the Communist blacklisting era, *The Crucible,* was revived on the New York stage. At the same time, Kazan was denied a Life Achievement Award by the American film Institute because of his cooperation with the UnAmerican Activities Committee.

Further Reading

Thomas H. Pauly, *An American Odyssey: Elia Kazan and American Culture* (1983, paperback 1985); and in Michel Ciment, *Kazan on Kazan* (1974). Also see Kazan's 1988 autobiography, *Elia Kazan: A Life.* ☐

Nikos Kazantzakis

The Greek author, journalist, and statesman Nikos Kazantzakis (1883-1957) is considered the foremost figure in modern Greek literature. His work is marked by his search for God and immortality.

Nikos Kazantzakis was born on Feb. 18, 1883, in the town of Hērákleion, Crete, where he received his elementary and secondary education. His father was a primitive peasant, unsociable and uncommunicative, and his mother a sweet, submissive, and saintly woman. Nikos studied law in Athens (1902-1906) and graduated with honors. Before he left for Paris, where he studied philosophy (1907-1909), he had already made an appearance in Greek letters. His first work, an essay entitled "The Disease of the Century," was published by *Picture Gallery Magazine* and was followed by his first novel, *The Serpent and the Lily* (both 1906). Both works were under the pseudonym Carma Nirvani, one of the many he used the first years of his writing. His first play, *Daybreak,* was staged several months later at the Athenian Theater in Athens.

Early Career

While in Paris, Kazantzakis served as journalist for various Greek magazines. By 1910 he had completed a trilogy—*Broken Souls, The Empress Zoe,* and *God-Man;* a drama, *The Master Mason* (which won an award); and another play, *The Comedy.* The last two were published under the pseudonym Petros Psiloritis. In 1911, after a stormy relationship, he married Galatea Alexiou, a writer, and together they continued their writing in a small apartment in Athens.

During the Balkan Wars (1912-1913) Kazantzakis volunteered but served noncombatively with Special Services in the Premier's office. By 1916 he had written two more plays, *Hercules* and *Theofano* (he later developed the latter into *Nikiforos Phocas*), and mapped out three more. *The Master Mason* was staged as a musical drama at the Municipal Theater in Athens. By now his interest in Friedrich Nietzsche was at its peak, and he set off on a pilgrimage to Switzerland, visiting and studying the places associated with this philosopher. By 1920 Kazantzakis, now 37 years of age, was still undecided about his destiny. He felt he was an Odysseus who would never reach his Ithaca.

The years 1922-1924 were critical for Kazantzakis. He carried his inner struggles to Vienna and later Berlin. In Vienna he began to write the theatrical work *Buddha* (which after many revisions and additions was published in Athens in 1956) and completed the final draft of his romantic novel *A Year of Loneliness* (unpublished). In Berlin he drafted *Saviours of God,* a philosophic work into which he poured his longing for immortality and his belief that man's dedication to creative activity alone can save God.

In 1924 Kazantzakis completed *Buddha* and began *Odyssey: A Modern Sequel.* That summer he met Helen Samiou, a young Greek journalist, who later became his second wife. In November 1925 he went to the Soviet Union as a foreign correspondent for the Athenian newspaper *Free Speech.* Here he was greatly influenced by the new Russian movement. He then undertook new journeys—to Palestine and Cyprus (April-May 1926); Spain (August-September 1926); Italy (October 1926); where he had an audience with Mussolini; Egypt and Sinai (December 1926-January 1927). His journalistic interest in political events was a concession to the newspaper organizations which provided him with travel funds. In 1927 he settled for a short while on the island of Aegina to arrange selections from his travelogs into volumes that were later to appear as *Travels—Spain, Italy,* and so on.

In April 1928 Kazantzakis left again for the Soviet Union, where he wrote a screenplay for a Russian film entitled *The Red Kerchief.* (Its theme was the Greek Revolution of 1821.) Helen Samiou joined him, and together they toured the northern Soviet Union. From then on the couple were never separated except for short periods. Kazantzakis claimed that he owed his happiness to Helen and that without her he would have died many years sooner. She dedicated her life to him, acting as wife, secretary, nurse, companion, friend. In 1930 he worked on his *History of Russian Literature.* By 1932 he completed the manuscripts of *Buddha, Don Quixote, Muhammed, The Ten Days,* and

the first draft of his Greek translation of Dante's *Divine Comedy.*

Later Years

In 1936 Kazantzakis wrote two novels in French: *The Rock Garden* and *Mon Père.* (The latter was incorporated 14 years later in *Freedom or Death.*) By 1937 he had completed the seventh rewrite of his *Odyssey;* a new play, *Melissa;* and three cantas: *Alexander the Great Christ,* and *Grandfather-Father-Grandson.* He spent all of 1938 working on the final draft of the *Odyssey,* and in December of that year it was finally published in Athens. In 1941 he began his famous novel *Zorba the Greek.* In 1943 he completed *Zorba* and three plays, the *Prometheus Trilogy: Prometheus the Firebearer, Prometheus Bound,* and *Prometheus Freed.* Despite the hardships of the German occupation of Greece, his writing was not affected. He and Helen spent the occupation years on the island of Aegina, where he wrote feverishly. He completed a modern translation of Homer's *Iliad* and began his modern Greek translation of Homer's *Odyssey.* He brought all his manuscripts up to date and in 1944 he wrote the plays *Kapodistria* and *Constantine Paleologos.* When the German occupation ended, he returned to Athens and became active in various socialist groups. In August he was made president of the Socialist Workers Union and married Helen Samiou in the Greek Orthodox Church. A few months later he was appointed a minister in the Sofouli government of Greece and served until his resignation in 1946. Soon afterward, he and his wife took up residence in Paris. This was the beginning of their self-exile from Greece; Kazantzakis believed that his country had denied him too many times; he would continue his work on foreign shores.

In 1948 Kazantzakis wrote the play *Sodom and Gomorrha.* In July he began his famous novel *Christ Recrucified,* titled *The Greek Passion* in the English translation. By September the novel was completed, but, as was his custom, he did a full rewrite of the book by December. In 1949 he wrote *The Fratricides.* In April he wrote the play *Theseus,* which was published as *Kouros.* From May to July he wrote the play *Christopher Columbus,* and the next 2 months were spent rewriting *Constantine Paleologos.* In December he began *Freedom or Death* and completed the second rewrite by July 1950. He completed *The Last Temptation of Christ* by July 1951. In 1953, although in poor health, he completed *St. Francis of Assisi.* The Vatican issued an edict against *The Last Temptation of Christ* in April 1954. Kazantzakis replied with a telegram, quoting Tertullian: "In Your Courtroom, Lord, I Appeal." Among his last works was his spiritual semiautobiography, *Report to Greco* (1955).

Kazantzakis died on Oct. 26, 1957. He was buried in the town of his birth. A plain wooden cross marks his grave with the epitaph he had requested: "I have nothing . . . I fear nothing . . . I am free."

Further Reading

Two studies of Kazantzakis are Pandelis Prevelakis, *Nikos Kazantzakis and His Odyssey: A Study of the Poet and the*

Poem (trans. 1961), and Helen Kazantzakis, *Nikos Kazantzakis: A Biography Based on His Letters* (1968).

Additional Sources

Bien, Peter, *Nikos Kazantzakis,* New York, Columbia University Press, 1972. □

Denis Kearney

Denis Kearney (1847-1907), Irish-born American labor agitator, became the leader of unemployed workingmen of San Francisco during the 1870s.

Denis Kearney was born in County Cork on Feb. 1, 1847. He went to sea as a cabin boy at the age of 11 and rose to the rank of first mate by 1868, when he first arrived in San Francisco. For 4 years Kearney served as an officer on a coastal steamer but left his job after he was accused of deserting the ship in danger. He married in 1870 and in 1872 settled in San Francisco, where he purchased a hauling business. By 1877, when he emerged as a representative of the Draymen and Teamsters' Union, Kearney owned three wagons. He studied public speaking and frequented newspaper offices, where he exchanged views on current affairs and social philosophy.

Although he had no coherent ideology, Kearney seemed to attribute the distress of the working class to their shiftlessness; and on one occasion, at least, he stated that white workers should emulate the thrift and industry of the many Chinese on the West Coast. In 1877 he was elected secretary of the Workingmen's Trade and Labor Union of San Francisco.

However, in September 1877 Kearney called for the organization of an independent workingmen's party and initiated a series of meetings on a vacant lot adjoining City Hall. These "sandlot meetings," usually held on Sundays, were Kearney's focus of activity for 3 years. The crowds grew to over 2,000, and Kearney spoke eloquently on such themes as uniting all the poor and workingmen, land monopoly, and the "dangerous encroachments of capital." He warned especially that the presence of cheap Chinese labor robbed "Americans" of decent employment.

Kearney's platform manner was rude but effective, drawing on all the oratorical tricks of the day. His inflammatory speeches carefully stopped short of incitement to riot, but his followers frequently struck out at San Francisco's Chinese population. The Workingmen's party failed because of internal dissensions and the strong reaction against the party. Kearney was himself repudiated by the sandlotters when he supported the Greenback-Labor presidential candidate in 1880. Between 1880 and 1883 he spoke occasionally but could not command enthusiastic support. In 1883 he returned to private life, built up a profitable drayage business and employment agency, and invested successfully in stocks, real estate, and commodities. He died on April 24, 1907, a wealthy and even socially acceptable businessman.

Further Reading

There is no biography of Kearney or much information with which to work. Readers should consult these general works: James Bryce, *American Commonwealth* (3 vols., 1888; 2d rev. ed., 2 vols., 1896), which has the best account of Kearney; Lucile Eaves, *A History of California Labor Legislation* (1910); and Ira B. Cross, *A History of the Labor Movement in California* (1935). □

Stephen Watts Kearny

Stephen Watts Kearny (1794-1848), American soldier, played an important role in the conquest of New Mexico and California during the Mexican War.

Stephen W. Kearny was born on Aug. 30, 1794, in Newark, N.J. After attending common school in Newark and Columbia College, he joined the Army as a first lieutenant in 1812. During the War of 1812 he fought in Canada. He was promoted to captain in 1813 and remained in the Army after the war, serving mostly in the West.

In 1819 Kearny went to Camp Missouri (later Ft. Atkinson) near Omaha. In 1820 he journeyed through unknown land to Camp Cold Water (later Ft. Snelling) near St. Paul, Minn., and in 1825 he took part in an expedition to the mouth of the Yellowstone River. During the next 20 years he had a number of commands and supervised construction of several forts, including the famous fort on the Oregon Trail later named for him.

Shortly after the outbreak of war with Mexico in 1846, Kearny was named brigadier general and placed in command of the Army of the West. With almost 1,700 men he marched to Santa Fe and captured the city without opposition on August 18. After organizing a civil government in New Mexico, he left for California with a small force. En route to San Diego he repulsed a Mexican force at San Pasqual on December 6, suffering heavy casualties. Joining Commodore Robert F. Stockton at San Diego, Kearny led his depleted army to Los Angeles, captured the town in January 1847, and established an uneasy peace. Trouble developed between the American commanders after Lt. Col. John C. Frémont, whom Stockton had appointed civil governor, refused to recognize Kearny's authority to organize a new territorial government. Stockton left for Mexico; new orders from Washington confirmed Kearny's authority; and Frémont was sent back to Washington, where he was court-martialed and found guilty of mutiny, disobedience, and improper conduct.

After the trial Kearny went to Mexico and served for brief periods as civil governor of Veracruz and, later, of Mexico City. With his health weakened by yellow fever he

had contracted in Veracruz, he went to St. Louis, Mo. He died there on October 13, 1848.

Further Reading

The only full-length biography of Kearny is Dwight Clarke, *Stephen Watts Kearny: Soldier of the West* (1961). The standard history of the Mexican War is Justin Harvey Smith, *The War with Mexico* (2 vols., 1919). The story of the Army of the West is told by Ralph P. Bieber, ed., in his introduction to *Journal of a Soldier under Kearny and Doniphan, 1846-1847* (1935), which contains the diary of George Rutledge Gibson. Another firsthand account, Philip St. George Cooke, *The Conquest of New Mexico and California* (1878), has been reprinted many times. □

Paul John Keating

Federal treasurer of Australia (1983-1991) and Prime Minister (1991-1996), Paul John Keating (born 1944) was a dominant and powerful Australian Labour Party (ALP) politician, widely admired and equally widely vilified, who undeniably made his mark on the party.

aul John Keating was born on January 18, 1944, in the working-class western suburbs of Sydney, Australia. The eldest child of Irish, solidly Labor-oriented parents, Keating absorbed politics from childhood. His father, Matt Keating, was a leading local Labor Party member.

Keating was educated at De La Salle College in Bankstown, Sydney. But academic qualifications were not of interest to the impatient young Keating, and he left school in November 1958 to enter the workforce, which he did in January 1959, two days after his 15th birthday. He continued studies at night school while working as a clerk with the Sydney Country Council.

By his late teens Keating was an enthusiastic member of Young Labor, an earnest group of young people who regularly met to discuss the political issues of the day. It was a good training ground for many who were later to become Labor politicians. On the lighter side, Keating's interest had been caught by a rock band, the Ramrods, whom he heard play in the western Sydney pubs. Keating the aspiring entrepreneur wanted to make the Ramrods into something more professional and became their promoter. Under Keating's stewardship the group cut two records, both flops. Keating went on to develop his interest in politics.

During those years he had been learning, although not following a formal course of education. From the age of 18 Keating regularly visited Jack Lang, an old Labor political warhorse, then in his mid-eighties and still editing his newspaper, the *Century*. Lang, a one-time Labor premier and treasurer of New South Wales, was a controversial Labor figure even then, hated by some, a hero to others. To the young Keating he was a living Labor legend. From Lang, Keating learned much of Labor history and mythology and valuable lessons about government, politics, and the art of vitriolic rhetoric. Years later, Keating was at the vanguard of a push to have Lang re-admitted to the ALP, a few years before he died, at age 98, in 1975.

By the late 1960s, Keating's life had taken on a single focus: politics. With typical single-mindedness he dropped evening classes, the rock band, and social life to concentrate on building his base. It was a tough and tense fight, but in October 1969 Keating, age 24, had won nomination for the safe Labor seat of Blaxland.

Despite campaigning in a safe Labor seat, Keating threw all his energy into the 1969 federal election campaign. Taking a line from the Kennedy-style campaigning in the United States, he bought a bus and a loud hailer and cruised through the streets of Bankstown. The efforts paid off: at 25, Keating became New South Wales' youngest member of Parliament.

Once into Canberra and federal parliament, Keating was an ambitious young man in a hurry. But he had to wait until 1975 before winning a seat in a ministry—and then only briefly. At 31 he became the youngest minister in Labor's history when he was appointed minister for Northern Australia. Keating's achievement was short-lived. A few weeks later, on November 11, 1975, the Whitlam government was sacked from office. Labor, after being in office for the first time in almost a quarter of a century, was again relegated to the opposition benches.

For the bulk of the following opposition years Keating held the post of shadow spokesman on minerals and energy. But in January 1983, weeks before a federal election, Keating was reluctantly drafted into the role of shadow treasurer. Keating, although lacking the economics background, was chosen for his toughness and selling skills—and he needed all of those when Labor won government in March 1983.

Keating, with the reputation as a political killer with a sharp tongue, made his mark as federal treasurer. Labor in office embraced the free markets philosophy it had earlier opposed and, instead of reversing moves to liberalize the financial system, it advanced the process of financial deregulation that had begun under the Liberal coalition government. By the end of his first year as treasurer Keating had overseen a move to float the Australian dollar and remove virtually all exchange controls and was pushing to allow foreign banks to operate in Australia. The following year the influential magazine *Euromoney* voted Keating its finance minister of the year at the 1984 annual International Monetary Fund/World Bank meeting in Washington.

Tough years followed this accolade. In July 1985 Keating experienced his first serious setback when, at an ill-fated tax summit, his cherished plan for tax reform, based on a consumption tax, was rejected. But Keating won some significant tax measures, including a fringe benefits tax, a capital gains tax, and a move to end "double taxation" of company dividends. Problems intensified for Keating in 1986: Australia faced a burgeoning deficit on its current account and growing volume of foreign debt, factors which

sent the currency spiraling down. Keating delivered a colorful warning that the country was destined to become a "banana republic" if attitudes and policies were not adjusted.

Some improvement was made in the current account but foreign debt continued to rise, producing potentially crippling interest costs. Labor faced a tough election when it went to the polls in July 1987, but won a third term, albeit with the loss of some key seats. Keating had marketed his economic management well. He went on to consolidate the government's achievement in turning a budget deficit into a healthy surplus. The Labor government and Keating had made laudable progress in many areas under Prime Minister Robert Hawke. The progress included reforming the financial sector, the tax system, and superannuation and, through its wages accord with the unions, holding down wages. But by the end of the 1980s Australia, burdened with rising foreign debt, was confronting the threat of a real drop in living standards. Labor was praised for its achievements but criticized for relying too much on high interest rates to dampen demand for imports and for not succeeding in pushing through micro-economic reforms that would lift productivity, boost savings and investments, and improve international competitiveness.

But despite historically high interest rates that punished business and home buyers Labor was reelected for a record fourth term in March 1990, once again beating a weak Liberal opposition team. Keating, then treasurer for seven years, was also appointed deputy prime minister in April 1990. However, in 1991 he challenged Hawke for party leadership, lost, and was relegated to the "back bench" but won the post by year end. After serving as treasurer, Keating took on the position of Prime Minister in 1991. In September 1993, Keating formally notified Queen Elizabeth II of his proposal to create a federal republic in Australia to replace, by 2001, the long-standing constitutional monarchy. Keating remained Prime Minister until 1996 when he was defeated in the election by John Howard, thus ending the Labor Party's 13-year reign.

Further Reading

Who's Who in Australia carries a short biography of Keating; an unauthorized biography by E. Carew, *Keating, a biography* (1988); also P. Kelly's, *The Hawke Ascendancy* (1984); James Walsh wrote of Keating in "Destiny's Choice" *Time* (January 6, 1997). □

John Keats

The English poet John Keats (1795-1821) stressed that man's quest for happiness and fulfillment is thwarted by the sorrow and corruption inherent in human nature. His works are marked by rich imagery and melodic beauty.

John Keats was born on Oct. 31, 1795, the first child of a London lower-middle-class family. In 1803 he was sent to school at Enfield, where he gained a favorable reputation for high spirits and boyish pugnaciousness. His father died in an accident in 1804, and his mother in 1810, presumably of tuberculosis. Meanwhile, Keats's interest had shifted from fighting to reading.

When he left school in 1811, Keats was apprenticed to an apothecary-surgeon in Edmonton. Then it was that Edmund Spenser's *Faerie Queene* awakened him to the charm and power of poetry. The imaginative beauty of Spenser's world of fantasy fulfilled some romantic yearning in his adolescent mind, and he was even more impressed by the poet's mastery of language as evidenced in the aptness and the sensory intensity of his imagery. It was probably during his last months at Edmonton that Keats first tried his hand at writing: four stanzas entitled "Imitation of Spenser."

On Oct. 2, 1815, Keats was registered at Guy's Hospital, where he was to pursue his medical studies. He was a conscientious student, but poetry gained increasing hold on his imagination. Some growing sense of alienation may be perceived in his first published poem, the sonnet "O solitude! If I must with thee dwell," which Leigh Hunt printed in the *Examiner* on May 5, 1816.

Autumn 1816 brought decisive weeks in the maturation of Keats's art and personality. In late September he read George Chapman's translation of Homer, and this impressed upon him a new aspect of both Elizabethan and Greek poetry: no longer the mellow sensuousness, the ex-

quisite fantasy that he had found in Spenser, but a virility in theme and style that was to encourage him in his turn to "speak out loud and bold." In October he made the acquaintance of Hunt and of some of the young men who were to become his devoted friends and to whom he addressed so many admirable letters over the next 4 years. During November and December he wrote most of the poems for his first volume, which was published in March 1817.

Although it contains many felicitous, and at times arresting, phrases, the book testifies to the young poet's inexperience and immaturity. The derivative mannerisms of some of the sonnets, the easy sybaritic nature description in "I stood tiptoe," the romantic diffuseness and facile escapism of "Sleep and Poetry" do much to account for the criticism—though not the venomous malice—it received at the hands of *Blackwood's Magazine* in October. In retrospect, this first volume has a character of anticipation rather than achievement.

Publication of *Endymion*

The same cannot be said of *Endymion: A Poetic Romance,* to the writing of which Keats devoted most of his time from April to December 1817 and which appeared in May 1818. This mythical story of the Latmian shepherd's love for the moon goddess provided him with a narrative framework through which he hoped to discipline his exuberant imagination; within a firm structure that takes the hero through the bowels of the earth, under the sea, and through the sky, he could nevertheless give free rein to his fancy in a great variety of incidents. Keats turned the story of Endymion into an allegory of the romantic longing to overcome the boundaries of ordinary human experience. The similarity with Percy Bysshe Shelley's *Alastor,* which had been published in 1816, is obvious; but whereas the quest led Shelley's hero to despair and death, Endymion significantly realizes that ultimate identification with transcendence is not to be achieved through the unmediated vision he had sought, but through humble acceptance of human limitations and of the misery built into man's condition.

Keats's letters reveal that at this time several of his friends were ill or suffering from some sort of vexation. His brother was very unwell, and he himself, after a bad cold, prophetically feared in October 1817 that "I shall never be again secure in Robustness." Like other romantic writers, Keats had a central need somehow to adjust the evidence that, as he put it, "The world is full of troubles" with an exalted intuition of cosmic harmony; this preoccupation runs as a major trend through his letters.

Another basic problem with which Keats's letters deal is how to reconcile the rival claims of romantic subjectivity, which makes for sincerity, concreteness, intensity, and originality, and of esthetic objectivity, which alone raises poetry to universal meaningfulness. Such reconciliation, he thought, had been achieved by Shakespeare through a quality which Keats, in December 1817, had called "Negative Capability."

It may have been in a deliberate attempt to secure greater impersonality that in March-April 1818, after the allegory of *Endymion,* he turned to straightforward narrative in *Isabella,* which is based on a story by Boccaccio. Although the poem is distinctly inferior, its theme was connected with Keats's more philosophical preoccupations, as it centers on the beauty and greatness of tragic love.

On the whole, 1818 brought a lull in Keats's creative output. His letters, however, show that it was also a period of rapid inner growth. By May he had become articulately conscious of several pregnant verities: that experience, rather than unbridled fancy, is the key to true poetry; that sorrow and suffering are not to be eschewed but should be expected—in 1819 he was to say "greeted"—as a necessary step in the making of the soul; that no great poetry can be achieved if "high Sensations" are not completed by "extensive knowledge"; and that he himself, in his exploration of life's "dark passages," had not yet reached further than the "Chamber of Maiden-Thought."

Later Works

It was presumably in order to give poetic utterance to this enriched view of life and art that Keats started work on *Hyperion* in September 1818. This new poem linked up with *Endymion,* as an essential part of its purpose was to describe the growth of Apollo into a true poet through ever deeper acceptance and understanding of change and sorrow. But Keats was unable to get ahead with it for a number of reasons: a trip to Scotland had impaired his health; *Blackwood's* had published a vitriolic attack on *Endymion;* his brother, Tom, had died after several weeks' painful illness. Keats's friends were trying to entertain him, and he was reluctantly swept up in the absorbing trivialities of social life. Moreover, at this time he fell in love with Fanny Brawne.

In spring 1819 Keats sought creative relief from his failure to give satisfactory shape to his idea in new ventures which were apparently less ambitious, yet proved to be the crowning work of his *annus mirabilis.* Turning once more to verse narrative, he first produced the opulent *Eve of St. Agnes,* in deliberate revulsion against what he now saw as the "mawkish" sentimentality of *Isabella.* The rape of Madeline in this poem was soon to find its dialectical counterpart in the ghostlike idealism of *La Belle dame sans merci,* a ballad that tells of the mysterious seduction of a medieval knight by another of Keats's elusive, enigmatic, half-divine ladies. Each poem embodies an important trend in Keats's poetry: his sybaritic sense of exquisite sensuality verging at times on eroticism, and a longing mixed with fear and diffidence for some experience beyond human mortality.

These were followed in the spring and summer of 1819 by the first great odes: "Ode to Psyche," "Ode on a Grecian Urn," and "Ode to a Nightingale." These, together with the later "Ode on Indolence" and "Ode on Melancholy," are among the most acute imaginative explorations of the intricate relation between the contrasting experiences and aspirations whose interplay had always controlled Keats's inspiration: sorrow and bliss, art and reality, life and dream, truth and romance, death and immortality.

The triumphant balance and integration achieved in the odes was inevitably precarious. They coincided with the positive conception of the world as a "Vale of Soulmaking," which the poet had framed in April. But incipient financial trouble, together with his tortured love for Fanny, were beginning to press upon Keats. The three schemes that kept him busy during the latter half of 1819 illustrate his confusion and perplexity. In cooperation with one of his friends, he wrote his only drama, *Otho the Great,* in the futile hope of acquiring both money and public recognition. He also made his last attempt to define the function of the poet in *The Fall of Hyperion;* but this, like the former *Hyperion,* was never completed and remains a tantalizing fragment of cryptic, inconclusive beauty. Significantly, the last long poem that he managed to bring to completion was *Lamia,* a brilliantly ambiguous piece which leads to the disenchanted conclusion that both the artist and the lover live on deceptive illusions.

Keats's health had been declining for some time. In February 1820 a severe hemorrhage in the lungs revealed the seriousness of the disease. His third and last volume, *Lamia, Isabella, The Eve of St. Agnes and Other Poems,* was printed in July. In September, Keats left for Italy on an invitation from Shelley. He died in Rome on Feb. 23, 1821.

Further Reading

The best complete introduction to Keats, biographical and critical, is Douglas Bush, *John Keats* (1966). The standard biography is Walter Jackson Bate, *John Keats* (1963). For bibliography and general information on Keats see James Robertson MacGillivray, *Keats: A Bibliography and Reference Guide with an Essay on Keats' Reputation* (1949).

Clarence Dewitt Thorpe, *The Mind of John Keats* (1926; repr. 1964), combines critical insight into the poetry with illumination of Keats's personality. Extensive critical treatment of Keats's poetry is in Maurice Roy Ridley, *Keats' Craftsmanship* (1933); Claude Lee Finney, *The Evolution of Keats's Poetry* (1936); Walter Jackson Bate, *The Stylistic Development of Keats* (1945); Richard Harter Fogle, *The Imagery of Keats and Shelley* (1949); John Middleton Murry, *Keats* (1955); E. C. Pettet, *On the Poetry of Keats* (1957); Kenneth Muir, ed., *John Keats: A Reassessment* (1958); W. J. Bate, ed., *Keats* (1964); and Douglas Hill, *John Keats* (1969). For detailed analyses of individual poems see Earl R. Wasserman, *The Finer Tone* (1955); Harvey T. Lyon, *Keats' Well-read Urn* (1958); Jack Stillinger, ed., *Keats's Odes* (1968); and Albert S. Gérard, *English Romantic Poetry* (1968).

For general background the reader may consult Ian Jack, *English Literature, 1815-1832* (1963), which has very convenient bibliographies. □

Carey Estes Kefauver

United States Senator Carey Estes Kefauver (1903-1963) was an influential Tennessee Democrat who often broke ranks with his more conservative Southern colleagues to support economic and political

reform. He became the first candidate of his region to develop a national political following during his two campaigns for the presidency.

Estes Kefauver was born in Madisonville, Tennessee, on July 26, 1903, to Robert Cooke Kefauver and Phredonia (Estes) Kefauver. The Kefauvers were a politically distinguished family: Estes' paternal great-grandfather was a successful banker who was elected to the Tennessee State Senate in 1847, while his maternal great-grandfather ran for Congress unsuccessfully against David Crockett in 1828.

Kefauver graduated from the University of Tennessee in 1924 and three years later received a law degree *cum laude* from Yale University. He returned to Tennessee, established a practice in Chattanooga, and during the next 12 years became one of the city's most successful corporate attorneys. Despite extensive family and professional connections with wealthy, conservative Chattanoogans, Kefauver's political and philosophical sympathies gravitated toward reform and liberalism. He became the attorney for the *Chattanooga News,* the city's daily newspaper which championed publicly owned utilities, revision of Tennessee's constitution, reforms in local government, and improved labor conditions. Kefauver embraced most of these causes, and in 1936 he became president of the Volunteers, a coalition of young business and professional men and labor union leaders who wanted to reform county government. Kefauver's work with the Volunteers introduced him to the low wages

and poor working conditions in Chattanooga's textile mills, and his sympathy for workers won him union support throughout his political career.

Election to Congress

That career began in 1939 when Kefauver won a special election to fill the seat of Third District congressman Sam D. McReynolds, who died in office. During the campaign Kefauver supported President Franklin Roosevelt's New Deal program and advocated federal aid to education and support of the Tennessee Valley Authority (TVA), two positions he would maintain for the remainder of his legislative career. During nine years in the House of Representatives Kefauver successfully defended TVA from its critics, including powerful Tennessee senator Kenneth D. McKellar; advocated anti-monopoly legislation to protect small business from corporate takeover; and urged the elimination of the poll tax as a voting requirement.

In 1948 Kefauver, in his first campaign for the U.S. Senate, won an upset victory over Judge John A. Mitchell, the candidate of the Memphis-based political machine of Democratic boss Edward H. Crump. Kefauver assembled a coalition of labor, women's, African American, and professional groups as his chief supporters and adopted the coonskin cap as his trademark after Crump attacked him as a "pet coon."

Although Kefauver's surprising victory briefly attracted national attention, his early Senate years afforded prolonged nationwide exposure. In 1950 he coauthored the Kefauver-Cellar Act, which regulated corporate purchases of competitor's assets, and in 1950 and 1951 he chaired a special Senate committee appointed to investigate organized crime. The nationally televised "Kefauver Committee" hearings, held in a dozen major cities, generated little new information on the crime syndicate but gave the Tennessee senator important national publicity and influenced his decision to run for president in 1952. After entering the New Hampshire presidential primary and handily defeating President Harry S. Truman, who later withdrew from the race, Kefauver won 13 of the 15 remaining primaries, losing only in Florida and the District of Columbia. Although he seemed assured of the nomination, Kefauver's opponents—including President Truman, big city political bosses, and conservative Southern Democrats—combined to block his selection and eventually swung the convention to Illinois governor Adlai Stevenson. Stevenson and vice-presidential candidate John Sparkman of Alabama were in turn defeated by the Republican ticket of Gen. Dwight D. Eisenhower and California Congressman Richard Nixon.

Kefauver ran for the Democratic presidential nomination a second time in 1956, but the party again chose Adlai Stevenson. The Tennessee senator, however, did score a dramatic second ballot victory over Massachusetts senator John F. Kennedy for the vice-presidential nomination. Kefauver vigorously campaigned for the ticket, particularly in the Midwest and West, hoping to capitalize on farm belt resentment over President Eisenhower's agricultural policies, but the Democratic ticket was again defeated by President Eisenhower and Vice-President Nixon.

Successful Fight for Re-election

Many supporters urged Kefauver to make one last campaign for the presidency in 1960, but he decided instead to concentrate his efforts on his upcoming re-election campaign to the U.S. Senate. Kefauver's nearly decade long focus on national affairs and his liberal voting record had eroded his support among many Tennessee voters. His votes for both the 1957 and 1960 civil rights acts were cited by opponents as examples of his incompatibility with Tennessee and Southern politics; his 1958 Senate committee hearings on the pharmaceutical industry prompted out-of-state drug manufacturing companies to contribute substantial campaign funds to his opponent, Judge Andrew T. Taylor; and his bitter rivalry with former Tennessee governor Frank Clement and his successor, Buford Ellington, further hampered the senator's re-election efforts. Nevertheless, Kefauver waged an intense campaign which took him to each of the state's 95 counties. He pulled together the coalition that first propelled him to the Senate in 1948, and, after receiving timely endorsements from Democratic vice-presidential nominee Lyndon Johnson and other Southern senators, he was reelected to a third term by a 2 to 1 margin in what the *Nashville Banner* called "one of the most surprising votes in Tennessee's political history."

No longer engaged in national politics nor restricted by its demands and compromises, Estes Kefauver devoted his full attention to legislative matters. In 1962 he supported the 24th amendment to the Constitution, which abolished the poll tax, and coauthored the Kefauver-Harris Drug Control Act, which reduced the price and raised the safety requirements for prescription drugs. In 1963 he led the fight against American Telephone and Telegraph's efforts to dominate the telecommunications satellite program. As part of that campaign he introduced on August 8 an amendment to the National Aeronautics and Space Administration appropriation act to require A. T. & T. to reimburse NASA for research that would specifically benefit that corporation. During the debate over the appropriations bill amendment Kefauver suffered a heart attack, was hospitalized, and died the next day, August 10, 1963.

Further Reading

The best biographies of Kefauver are Charles L. Fontenay, *Estes Kefauver: A Biography* (1980); Harvey Swados, *Standing Up for The People: The Life and Work of Estes Kefauver* (1972); and Bruce Gorman, *Kefauver: A Political Biography* (1971). The Kefauver Senate Hearings on Organized Crime are discussed in William Howard Moore, *The Kefauver Committee and the Politics of Crime 1950-1952*. Kefauver wrote three books outlining his political views: *Crime in America* (1951), *In a Few Hands: Monopoly Power in America* (1965), and *A 20th Century Congress* (1947). See Robert Sobel, editor, *U.S. Congress, Senate, Biographical Directory of the American Congress, 1774-1971* (1971) for a discussion of Kefauver's legislative contributions. □

Modibo Keita

West African political leader Modibo Keita (1915-1977) led the fight for independence of the French Sudan and became the first president of the Republic of Mali.

Modibo Keita was born on June 4, 1915, in Bamako, the capital of French Sudan (now Mali), a landlocked nation in western Africa. After primary schooling, he was educated in neighboring Senegal and returned home in 1936 as a teacher.

Political Beginnings

Following World War II, France permitted its African territories to send representatives to the French Constituent Assembly in Paris. This marked the beginning of organized political activity in the Sudan. Keita joined the Rassemblement Démocratique Africain (RDA) and in 1947 was elected secretary general of the Union Soudanaise, the Sudan section of the RDA. In 1948 he was elected to the first territorial assembly of the French Sudan.

France opposed the RDA because of its close association with the French Communist party and its call for full equality. Considered a dangerous anticolonial, Keita was imprisoned briefly and released in 1947. In 1948, he was elected to the first territorial assembly of the French Sudan.

The Road to Independence

In 1952 and 1957, Keita was reelected to the territorial assembly and also served as mayor of Bamako. In 1956 he was elected deputy for the French Sudan to the French National Assembly and became that group's first African vice president. He twice held Cabinet posts in Paris: secretary of state for Overseas France and, later, secretary of state to the Presidency of the Council.

In November 1958, the Sudan became a self-governing republic within the French community and was renamed the Sudanese Republic. The following year, the republic joined with Senegal, Upper Volta, and Dahomey to form the Mali Federation. Keita was named president. Upper Volta and Dahomey soon withdrew, however, and the ill-fated union was plagued by disagreement and personality conflicts. The Mali Federation proclaimed its independence on June 20, 1960, but it broke apart in August when Senegal withdrew.

On September 23, 1960, Keita became president of the newly declared independent nation of Mali. He was also head of the Union Soudanaise, the country's only political party.

As president, Keita followed an austere socialist political path, moving his small country ideologically and economically closer to the Soviet Union and China. In 1963 he was awarded the Lenin Peace Prize for his attempts to rebuild the economy on socialist principles. Instead, Mali was beset by growing financial and economic problems, made worse by an especially poor harvest in 1968. This was the final straw that brought the government of Modibo Keita crashing down.

The president was ousted in a bloodless military coup on Nov. 19, 1968. He spent the remainder of his life, until his death on May 17, 1977, in military detention.

Further Reading

William J. Foltz, *From French West Africa to the Mali Federation* (1965); Frank Gregory Snyder, *One-party Government in Mali: Transition toward Control* (1965); Ruth Schachter Morgenthau, *Political Parties in French-speaking West Africa* (1964). □

Sir Arthur Keith

Sir Arthur Keith (1866-1955) was a British anatomist and physical anthropologist who specialized in the study of human evolution.

Arthur Keith was born on February 5, 1866, at Quarry Farm, Persley, near Aberdeen, Scotland, the sixth of ten children and the fourth son of John and Jessie (Macpherson) Keith. In his autobiography, Keith stated that as a youth he had been so impressed by Charles Darwin's then recently published book *Origin of Species* (1859) that he resolved to prepare for a medical education.

In 1884 he entered Marischal College of the University of Aberdeen, where he came under the influence of the botanist James Trail and (Sir) John Struthers, the anatomist.

On graduating with the highest honors in 1888, Keith accepted a post as medical officer to a mining company in Siam (Thailand). Although his original intention had been to use this as an opportunity to collect botanical specimens, he found himself becoming more interested instead in the local monkeys and apes. It was largely through his field observations and anatomical studies of the indigenous primates of Siam that his incipient interest in human evolution and physical anthropology in general began to take shape. It should be noted, however, that the botanical specimens he collected while in Siam were later used by H. N. Ridley in his comprehensive work on the *Flora of the Malay Peninsula* (1922-1925).

After three years in Siam, Keith returned home, and in 1894 he was awarded the degree of MD by the University of Aberdeen for a thesis entitled "The Myology of the Catarrhini: A Study in Evolution." He also passed the examination for the Fellowship of the Royal College of Surgeons. Armed with his MD and FRCS he won appointment as senior demonstrator in anatomy (1895) at the Medical School of the London Hospital. In 1908 he was elected to the conservatorship of the Royal College of Surgeons, and shortly thereafter he became president of the Royal Anthropological Institute of Great Britain (1912-1914); fellow of the Royal Society (1913); and Fullerian Professor of Physiology at the Royal Institution (1917-1923). It was during the last appointment that he received a knighthood (1921). In 1927 he was elected president of the British Association for the Advancement of Science, and three years later his professional career culminated with his election as rector of his alma mater, the University of Aberdeen (1930-1933).

Shortly after taking up his position at the London Hospital, Keith began work on *Man and Ape*, a book commissioned by the publisher John Murray. Between 1897 and 1900 Keith labored on what he considered to be his "magnum opus"—a compilation of the information on the comparative anatomy of living and fossil primates that he put together from his own research and from published anatomical descriptions. Although unpublished, the work is important as a historical document since it formed the basis for much of his later contributions to this area of research, as well as summarizing what was then known about apes and human comparative anatomy.

Although best remembered for his contributions to anthropology, Keith's earlier anatomical studies are noteworthy, particularly his researches into the causes of cardiac arrhythmia. He was responsible, in this regard, for describing (with Martin Flack), in 1906, the "sino-auricular node" of the heart and its role in the initiation and control of normal rhythmic contraction of the heart. He authored the well-known text *Human Embryology and Morphology*, which was published in 1902 and reached a sixth edition in 1948, and also edited and contributed to a number of textbooks dealing with surgical anatomy, such as (Sir Frederick) *Treve's Surgical Applied Anatomy* (1901, 1907, 1909). As these works indicate, it was not until after his appointment at the Royal College of Surgeons that he began to give his full attention to the questions of human evolution and racial diversification.

In his first major work in paleoanthropology, *Ancient Types of Men* (1911), Keith claimed a greater antiquity for *Homo sapiens* than had hitherto been generally accepted. In advocating this view, Keith joined forces with the French paleoanthropologist Marcellin Boule and others in rejecting the proposition that Neanderthals represented the antecedent form of modern humans—a position momentarily secured by the alleged discovery of the Piltdown hominid by the Sussex lawyer Charles Dawson in 1912. With the announcement of this ''discovery,'' Keith became embroiled in a heated controversy with Sir Arthur Smith Woodward and Sir Grafton Elliot Smith and others who claimed this ''fossil'' hominid manifested marked simian characteristics. Keith endeavored to demonstrate that the skull, if ''correctly'' reconstructed, was in fact morphologically similar to modern *Homo sapiens*. Although expressing some doubts about the generally accepted interpretation of the Piltdown hominid (now known to have been a forgery), Keith did not directly question either its authenticity or its antiquity. His conclusions can be found in his book *The Antiquity of Man* (1915), a widely read work reviewing all the fossil hominid remains known at that time. A second edition of this work was published in 1925, and six years later it was brought up to date with a supplementary volume, *New Discoveries Relating to the Antiquity of Man.*

During World War I Keith was occupied with problems of surgical anatomy related to war injuries and published a number of articles on this subject, as well as a book, *Menders of the Maimed* (1919), which is a historical critique of orthopedic surgery. It was during this period that he gave the Christmas juvenile lectures at the Royal Institution; these lectures were later published under the title *Engines of the Human Body* (1919), a second edition of which appeared in 1925.

After the war Keith's interests turned increasingly to general themes in medical history and to somewhat speculative considerations of the evolutionary processes involved in the emergence of modern *Homo sapiens*. Although he earned an international reputation as one of the foremost students of human evolution and was a self-proclaimed follower of Darwin, his work was in fact far removed from Darwin's mechanistic world view. Rejecting the role of chance in evolution, Keith adopted a distinctly vitalistic viewpoint remarkably similar to that of Ernst Haeckel, whom, incidentally, he uncritically admired. Keith developed the thesis that the spirit of nationalism is a potent factor in the evolutionary differentiation of human races. His opinions on race as represented in his book *A New Theory of Human Evolution* (1948) met with considerable debate and criticism at the time and widespread repudiation later.

Perhaps the most enduring of the many works Keith published during the last decades of his life is his comprehensive study of the hominid remains recovered from the caves of Mount Carmel (1929-1934), near Haifa, in what was then Palestine. The results of this study are summarized in a treatise he coauthored with Theodore D. McCown,

published under the title *The Stone Age of Mount Carmel: the Fossil Remains from the Levalloiso-Mousterian* (1939).

In 1933 recurrent ill-health forced Keith to resign from the conservatorship at the Royal College of Surgeons and to accept an appointment as master of the newly created Buckston Browne Research Institute at Downe, the country village south of London where Charles Darwin had once lived. It was here that Keith spent the remaining years of his life writing his memoirs and several books and essays on the physical and moral evolution of the human species. He died on January 7, 1955, in his 89th year.

Further Reading

In addition to his autobiography (London, 1950), further biographical information on Keith can be found in the memoirs of W. E. Le Gros Clark, ''Arthur Keith, 1866-1955,'' *Biographical Memoirs of Fellows of the Royal Society,* Volume 1 (1955), and in J. C. Brash and A. J. E. Cave, ''In piam memoriam: Sir Arthur Keith FRS,'' *Journal of Anatomy* 89 (1955). For a critical assessment of his views on evolution see C. L. Brace, ''Tales of the phylogenetic woods: the evolution and significance of evolutionary trees,'' *American Journal of Physical Anthropology* 56 (1981) and ''The roots of the race concept in American physical anthropology,'' in F. Spencer (editor), *A History of American Physical Anthropology, 1930-1980* (1982). □

Minor Cooper Keith

Minor Cooper Keith (1848-1929) was an American railroad and banana entrepreneur. He built a railroad from the Costa Rican Atlantic coast into the interior and developed bananas as one of the country's cash crops.

M inor Cooper Keith was one of the extraordinary men of both Costa Rican and railroading history. Born in Brooklyn, N.Y., on Jan. 19, 1848, soon after his twentieth birthday he was living in Costa Rica, where he spent the next 30 years building railroads and laying the foundations for what eventually became the United Fruit Company, one of America's great overseas private enterprises.

Building a Railroad

Though only 5 feet 5 inches tall and 140 pounds, Keith made up in energy and courage what he lacked in size. Before going to Costa Rica, he single-handedly started the cattle industry on Padre Island, on the Texas coastline. Simultaneously, his older brother Henry had won a contract to build a railway from Costa Rica's populated central highlands to the unpopulated and relatively unknown Atlantic coast. Minor joined him in Costa Rica to help with the project. Arriving in mid-1871, he was sent to the Atlantic coast hamlet of Port Limón to start building from that end, while Henry started work on the inland section.

On Aug. 10, 1871, Henry started in the highlands, and on November 15 Minor started from Port Limón. By Nov. 30, 1873, the first 27 miles of relatively easy highland construction was completed. For various reasons Henry was forced to halt construction at this point. Because he was unable to meet the terms of his contract, it was canceled by the Costa Rican government. Minor, by then established as a businessman and entrepreneur in Port Limón, negotiated a new contract with the Costa Rican government and in 1875 continued work on the lowland portion of the railroad. Nevertheless, there were several periods of relative inactivity in construction because of the extremely difficult terrain and the meager financial resources of Costa Rica, which then had but 146,000 inhabitants and no industry. Further problems included diseases from the swampy jungles (it is said 4,000 workers died building the railroad) and the difficulty of obtaining labor. To solve the labor problem, Keith imported many West Indians, especially Jamaicans, whose decendants to this day live in the Port Limón area, many still speaking West Indian-accented English. Another source of labor was Ferdinand de Lessep's failing Panama Canal project which released many workers.

In the early 1880s, to arrange financing for the last stretch between the completed high- and lowland sections of railroad, Keith negotiated a series of contracts, refinanced earlier loans, and on Aug. 20, 1886, began to build the final portion. This was completed 4 years later, and on Dec. 7, 1890, the first train covered the 97 miles of narrow-gage line to San José, Costa Rica's inland capital city, from Port Limón.

Founding of United Fruit Company

Simultaneously with the railroad construction, in 1884 Keith shrewdly obtained 800,000 acres of uncultivated land adjacent to the railroad right-of-way. On this land he planted the succulent Gros Michel strain of banana, which he had imported from Panama. Earlier, Keith had experimented with a small shipment to the United States and found them popular. Soon with his own crops, railroads to transport them, and his own port and vessels, with volume exports to the United States, Keith created a huge domestic American market. In order to stabilize this market, in 1899 he and several other banana importers organized several smaller companies into the pioneer banana giant, the United Fruit Company.

Though he is primarily associated with Costa Rica, Keith also developed extensive banana and railroad interests in Guatemala, El Salvador, Nicaragua, Panama, Colombia, Venezuela, Brazil, Jamaica, and the Dominican Republic. In fact, the very success of his banana activities often tided him over the financial shoals of his 20-year Costa Rican railroad-building enterprise.

In 1883 Keith married into one the most aristocratic Costa Rican families. As the 19th century drew to a close, he and his wife moved to Babylon, N.Y., where they lived on a baronial-sized estate. Though Keith maintained his extensive interests in Costa Rica, he sold his banana properties there to United Fruit. During the last 2 decades of his life he focused his interest on the Central American International

Railroad project. This would have meant a rail link from Mexico to Panama. Keith felt this would spur political integration, population movement, and economic growth. Though never completed, by the time of his death on June 14, 1929, the railroad had 887 miles of track laid in Guatemala and El Salvador, and the former country had an interoceanic rail link. The growth fostered by the later Pan-American Highway vindicated the accuracy of Keith's then visionary ideas.

Further Reading

The major monograph on Keith is Watt Stewart, *Keith and Costa Rica* (1964). Other works that deal in part with Keith's railroading projects are Frederick Upham Adams, *Conquest of the Tropics* (1914), and W. Rodney Long, *Railways of Central America and the West Indies* (1925). For the history of the United Fruit Company see Stacy May and Galo Plaza, *The United Fruit Company in Latin America* (1958). For general background on Costa Rica and Central America the following works are helpful: John and Mavis Biesanz, *Costa Rican Life* (1944); Stacy May and Associates, *Costa Rica: A Study in Economic Development* (1952); Hubert Herring, *A History of Latin America from the Beginnings to the Present* (1955; 3d rev. ed. 1968); and F. D. Parker, *The Central American Republics* (1964). □

Friedrich August Kekulé

The German chemist Friedrich August Kekulé (1829-1896) was the founder of structural organic chemistry.

August Kekulé, later Kekulé von Stradonitz, was born on Sept. 7, 1829, in the city of Darmstadt. After studies in the local gymnasium, young August, obedient to his father's wishes, enrolled in the school of architecture at the University of Giessen. At school Kekulé demonstrated a great talent for mathematics and drawing. It was in chemistry, however, a discipline then grappling with the complexities of the structure of organic molecules, that Kekulé's mathematical bent, excellent memory, and sense of space made him an ideal student of baffling structural problems.

Supported by his affluent family, Kekulé was able to study in Paris, where he gained the friendship of the eminent chemist Charles Gerhardt, from whose theory of types he later evolved his own theory of valency. He also moved in the scientific circles of Jean Baptiste Dumas and Charles Wurtz, whose school of organic chemistry was the only one in Europe that was able to rival the later German institutes. After his Paris studies Kekulé moved to London, where he worked as an assistant to John Stenhouse and later worked with William Williamson and Reinhold Hoffmann. From 1855 to 1858 Kekulé followed up his apprenticeship by serving as privatdozent at Heidelberg. Later in 1858 he was professor of chemistry at Ghent and ended his scientific career at the University of Bonn, where he served from 1867 until his death on July 13, 1896. During this long tenure

Kekulé contributed to the spectacular rise of organic chemistry and the chemical industry of Germany. His students came from all over Europe and went out to take leading professorships and to head industrial laboratories.

Kekulé was not a master experimentalist, but he became an inspired pedagogue. His mind was keyed to the problems of theory, particularly to the understanding of the architecture of the scores of new organic molecules that chemists were isolating from the plant and animal worlds and creating in their laboratories. It was Kekulé who brought order out of this chaos by grasping the fact that the secret of organic chemistry is contained in the tetravalency of the carbon atom and that this element has the unique capacity to link in long chains, with endless isomeric combinations possible.

Kekulé's supreme contribution to organic chemistry grew out of his solution to the problem of the structure of benzene (C_6H_6), the simplest of the aromatic series of carbon compounds. His solution to this puzzle, as told in his own words in 1865, was: "There I sat and wrote my *Lehrbuch*, but it did not proceed well, my mind was elsewhere. I turned the chair to the fireplace and fell half asleep. Again the atoms gamboled before my eyes. Smaller groups this time kept modestly to the background. My mind's eyes, trained by visions of a similar kind, now distinguished larger formations of various shapes. Long rows, in many ways more densely joined; everything in movement, winding and turning like snakes. And look, what was that? One snake grabbed its own tail, and mockingly the shape whirled before my eyes. As if struck by lightning I awoke. This time again I spent the rest of the night working out the consequences." From the dream of Kekulé had emerged the now familiar ring structure of benzene.

Further Reading

The definitive study of Kekulé is Richard Anschütz, *August Kekulé* (2 vols., 1929). He is also discussed in Eduard Farber, ed., *Great Chemists* (1961); Stephen Toulmin and June Goodfield, *The Architecture of Matter* (1962); and J. R. Partington, *A History of Chemistry,* vol. 4 (1964). □

Gottfried Keller

The Swiss short-story writer, novelist, and poet Gottfried Keller (1819-1890) was a master of the realistic novella and author of one of the outstanding German novels of his age.

Gottfried Keller was born in Zurich on July 19, 1819, and grew up in great poverty. He managed to go to Munich to study painting, but after 2 fruitless years his insufficient talent drove him home (1842), disillusioned and distraught.

Keller's life was marked by aimlessness and general inactivity, except for the publication of *Gedichten* (1846), a volume of poetry, until a government grant in 1848 permitted study at Heidelberg. There he met the atheistic philosopher Ludwig Feuerbach and the literary historian Hermann Hettner, who showed him where his real talents lay. Both greatly influenced his work.

During a 5-year stay in Berlin (1850-1855), Keller began writing in earnest. *Neuere Gedichte,* a second volume of poems, displayed notable lyric talent. *Der grüne Heinrich* (1854-1855; revised 1880), a *Bildungs-roman* (educational novel) like Goethe's *Wilhelm Meister,* is largely autobiographical, depicting the frustrations of a would-be artist. The work is regarded as one of the greatest German novels of the century.

In a series of stories called *Die Leute von Seldwyla* (1856), Keller's deep warmth and kindly humor manifest themselves as he points up the little failings of fictitious fellow Swiss with amiable indulgence and probing insight. The series contains *Romeo und Julia auf dem Dorfe,* a tragic story of two lovers thwarted by an unfriendly world, and is one of his finest narratives. Frederick Delius based an opera, *The Village Romeo and Juliet* (1907), on the story.

After returning to Zurich, Keller curtailed his writing, devoting his time to important duties as first secretary of the canton, an appointment he held until retirement (1876). His next work was *Sieben Legenden* (1872), a series of medieval legends told with disarming charm and simplicity. Its success established Keller's reputation. Five more stories in the *Seldwyla* series appeared in 1874, among them *Kleider machen Leute,* one of his best-known and best-loved tales.

The *Züricher Novellen* (1878), dealing with actual personalities from Zurich's past, again exhibits Keller's interest in the realistic portrayal of wholesome personality development. The cycle contains two of his finest stories: *Der Landvogt von Greifensee* and *Das Fähnlein der sieben Aufrechten. Das Sinngedicht* (1881) is a series of tales humorously describing a young man's search for a suitable mate. After publishing his collected poetry in 1882, Keller wrote his last work, *Martin Salander* (1886), a rather uninspired novel of Swiss political affairs.

Keller died in Zurich on July 15, 1890, acclaimed as a truly great figure of 19th-century German literature. Keller's writing displays uncommon geniality, zest for living, and rich humor. His gently moralizing style is direct, forceful, and vivid, revealing remarkable inventiveness and adroit characterization.

Further Reading

Most of Keller's works are available in English; see especially Kuno Francke, ed., *The German Classics,* vol. 14 (1914), for several of the novellas. *Der Grüne Heinrich* was translated as *Green Henry* by A. M. Holt (1960). Marie Hay, *The Story of a Swiss Poet* (1920), is a good general introduction, particularly valuable for its detailed account of the stories. A short but trenchant study appears as a chapter in Camillo von Klenze, *From Goethe to Hauptmann* (1926). Walter Silz, *Realism and Reality* (1954), contains an excellent evaluation of *Romeo und Julia auf dem Dorfe.* See also the biographical essay in Alex Natan, ed., *German Men of Letters* (1961). For general background see Edwin Keppel Bennett, *A History of the German Novelle* (2d ed. rev. by H. M. Waidson, 1961).

Additional Sources

Ruppel, Richard R., *Gottfried Keller: poet, pedagogue, and humanist,* New York: P. Lang, 1988. □

Helen Adams Keller

Though both blind and deaf, Helen Adams Keller (1880-1962), American lecturer and author, traveled the world over, crusading for improvement in the education and life of the physically handicapped.

Helen Keller was born in Tuscumbia, Ala., on June 27, 1880. Though she was born a normal child, at the age of 18 months an illness developed that left her blind and deaf. Yet, there were signs that she possessed high intelligence. When Helen was 6, her mother heard of the pioneer work being done at the Perkins Institution in Massachusetts for teaching deaf and blind people to communicate. In March 1887, Anne Sullivan, a product of the institution, came to serve as Keller's teacher. One month after her arrival, Sullivan had taught Keller the word "water." This sudden learning that things had names unlocked a whole, new universe for the child.

By the time she was 16, Keller had passed the admissions examinations for Radcliffe College; in 1904 she graduated *cum laude.* As a young woman, she became determined to learn about the world, and to improve the lives of others. With insight, energy, and deep devotion to humanity, she lectured throughout the world, lobbied in Congress, and wrote thousands of letters asking for contributions to finance efforts to improve the welfare of the blind. She visited hospitals and helped blind soldiers. She taught the blind to be courageous and to make their lives rich, productive, and beautiful for others and for themselves.

Keller associated with some of the greatest people of her times, including Alexander Graham Bell, Mark Twain, Andrew Carnegie, John D. Rockefeller, Sr., and presidents Grover Cleveland, Calvin Coolidge, and Woodrow Wilson. She authored such books as *Helen Keller's Journal, Optimism* (an essay), *Out of the Dark, Midstream: My Later Life, My Religion, The Song of the Stone Wall, The World I Live In,* and *The Story of My Life.*

Sullivan served as Keller's counselor and companion. When Keller died in 1962, her name was a worldwide symbol of what the human spirit could accomplish despite severe physical limitations.

Further Reading

One of the best books on Helen Keller's life is her autobiography, *The Story of My Life* (1903); John Albert Macy, husband of Anne Sullivan, prepared a supplement for this which includes information on Helen Keller's education as well as passages from her teacher's reports and letters. Important sources are Van Wyck Brooks, *Helen Keller: Sketch for a Portrait* (1956), containing new and detailed information, and Richard Harrity

and Ralph G. Martin, *The Three Lives of Helen Keller* (1962).
☐

Hall Jackson Kelley

Hall Jackson Kelley (1790-1874), American promoter, worked to encourage the settlement of the Oregon Territory.

Hall J. Kelley was born on Feb. 24, 1790, at Northwood, N.H. He attended school at Gilmanton, then began teaching school at the age of 16. In 1813 he graduated from Middlebury College, Vt., and 5 years later took charge of a public school in Boston, where he published several textbooks. He also wrote Sunday School lesson books, helping establish the Sunday School system in the process.

In 1823 the Boston school board terminated his contract, whereupon Kelley became a surveyor and engineer, for which he was qualified by a strong background in mathematics. Five years later he became an investor-employee of a manufacturing company, but the firm's failure in 1829 left him almost penniless.

Kelley had become increasingly interested in the Oregon country, and eventually he organized the American Society for Encouraging the Settlement of the Oregon Territory, incorporated under Massachusetts law in 1831. The congressional funding he requested failed to materialize, whereupon he determined to lead a party west himself. However, public ridicule of his project caused his prospective emigrants to abandon him; some of them did go to Oregon later under the leadership of Nathaniel J. Wyeth.

Kelley was determined to see Oregon at any expense. In 1833 he settled his wife and children with relatives and went to New Orleans, where he booked passage on a ship to Veracruz. He then went overland to a Pacific port and boarded another vessel that took him to California. There he met Ewing Young, a mountain man, with whom he journeyed to Oregon.

At Ft. Vancouver, Kelley, who had been ill during most of the trip to Oregon, was nursed back to health by Dr. John McLoughlin of the Hudson's Bay Company's post. He sent Kelley by company ship to Hawaii, where he boarded a vessel sailing for Boston, arriving in 1836.

Kelley began writing about Oregon just as the financial panic of 1837 was causing many people to think of moving west. His *Memoir,* a personal account of the geography of Oregon, was included in a report to Congress.

Kelley petitioned Congress for reimbursement for his expenses in visiting Oregon but was unsuccessful. He became a hermit at Three Rivers, Mass., doing occasional engineering work but mainly living on the charity of neighbors. He died on Jan. 20, 1874—blind and poverty-stricken. Although he had failed personally, his writings had helped change American attitudes toward Oregon, causing many to regard it as a good place to settle.

Further Reading

Fred W. Powell edited a collection of Kelley's works and letters, *Hall J. Kelley on Oregon* (1932), which includes biographical information. Powell also wrote a biography of Kelley, *Hall Jackson Kelley: Prophet of Oregon* (1917). See also John B. Horner, *A Short History of Oregon* (1924), and Arthur L. Throckmorton, *Oregon Argonauts* (1961). ☐

Oliver Hudson Kelley

The American agriculturalist Oliver Hudson Kelley (1826-1913) founded the Grange of the Patrons of Husbandry and was devoted to improving conditions for farmers.

Oliver Hudson Kelley was born and educated in Boston. He went west to Illinois for awhile, then to Minnesota in 1849, where he became a farmer and Indian trader. Kelley's wife died in 1851, and the following year he married a schoolteacher who also had come west from Boston.

Kelley quickly became a champion of Minnesota and of the farmer, whom he considered the indisputable source of wealth in America. Following a drought in 1862-1863, Kelley's Minnesota farm operations became unprofitable, and in 1864 he found employment as a clerk in the U.S. Department of Agriculture in Washington, D.C. He returned to Minnesota in 1865 to prepare a report for the Federal government on agricultural conditions. In January 1866 he was commissioned to make a survey of the agricultural situation in the South. He made a 3-month tour of the Carolinas, Georgia, Alabama, and Tennessee before returning to his Minnesota homestead.

For some time Kelley had toyed with the idea of establishing an organization of farmers for self-improvement, a secret fraternity patterned on the Masonic Order. However, this group would be closely allied to the Federal government, and women would participate equally with men. Together with a fellow government employee, he founded the Grange of the Patrons of Husbandry in 1867. Kelley zealously crusaded to organize local granges, and by 1874, 20,000 had been chartered, chiefly in the Middle West and South. Kelley emphasized the fraternal, social, psychological, and educational goals of the Grange, but it was later apparent that he had hoped to establish national solidarity among the farmers, thereby minimizing the sectional hatred that had been engendered by the Civil War.

Between 1870 and 1875 Kelley lived in Washington, D.C., as national secretary of the Grange. Turning his attention to real estate promotion in Florida, he moved to Carrabelle, a townsite he had founded. Three years later he resigned his position with the Grange to devote himself to land promotion. His life in Florida is little known; apparently he was not financially successful, for he returned to Washington and accepted a pension from the National Grange in 1905. The significant achievement of Kelley's life is detailed in his book, *Origin and Progress of the Order of the Patrons of Husbandry in the United States.*

Further Reading

The basic information on Kelley's life is in Solon J. Buck, *The Granger Movement* (1913). Additional evidence is in Thomas Clark Atkeson, *Semi-centennial History of the Patrons of Husbandry* (1916); Edward Weist, *Agricultural Organization in the United States* (1923); and Charles M. Gardner, *The Grange: Friend of the Farmer* (1949). □

Frank Billings Kellogg

Frank Billings Kellogg (1856-1937) negotiated the Kellogg-Briand Pact, intended to achieve international peace.

Frank B. Kellogg was born in Potsdam, N.Y., on Dec. 22, 1856. In 1867 the family moved to Minnesota, where Kellogg studied law and was admitted to the bar. He became a highly successful lawyer and was called to conduct a trust prosecution for the Federal government against the Standard Oil Company in 1911. His success led to election as president of the American Bar Association in 1912. In 1916 he was elected to the U.S. Senate but was defeated for reelection in 1922. He served as ambassador to Great Britain from 1923 to 1925.

In 1925 Kellogg was appointed secretary of state by President Calvin Coolidge. As secretary, he faced the problem of strained relations with Mexico over legislation against American oil interests, but the appointment of Dwight Morrow as ambassador relieved those tensions. Kellogg also found himself embroiled in Nicaragua, where civil war broke out against the government recognized by the United States. However, the mission of Henry L. Stimson to Nicaragua restored a measure of peace, which led, eventually, to the withdrawal of American troops. Kellogg was less successful in his attempt to bring about a reduction in naval armaments among the Great Powers.

Kellogg regarded his negotiation of the Kellogg-Briand Pact for the maintenance of world peace as his most important State Department work. Taking advantage of a French proposal to conclude a pact binding France and the United States to refrain from war with each other, Kellogg proposed a much more ambitious policy—a general international agreement for the preservation of peace. Signed in August 1928 and ratified by most of the nations of the world, this pact bound the signatory nations not "to resort to war as an instrument of national policy" and to settle all disputes by peaceful means. For this Kellogg received the Nobel Peace Prize in 1929 and was appointed a member of the Permanent Court of International Justice at The Hague, a post he held from 1930 to 1935.

In practice, the pact proved ineffectual in preventing war. It contained no provision for action against an aggressor nation and could not prevent the outbreak of World War II in 1939.

During Kellogg's tenure, the U.S. State Department took steps to allay Latin American worry over the Monroe Doctrine. In 1928 the Clark Memorandum sought to make it clear that the doctrine was not to be considered a justification for United States military intervention in the affairs of Latin America. Kellogg died on Dec. 22, 1937.

Further Reading

Old but still useful is David Bryn-Jones, *Frank B. Kellogg* (1937). Kellogg's conduct of foreign affairs is examined in Robert H. Ferrell, *Peace in Their Time: The Origins of the Kellogg-Briand Pact* (1952), and Lewis E. Ellis, *Frank B. Kellogg and American Foreign Relations, 1925-1929* (1961). □

Frances Kellor

Frances Kellor (1873–1952) was an activist who believed that the government could most effectively bring about social reform.

A social scientist who believed that government was the most effective vehicle for bringing about social reform, Frances Kellor played an important role in Theodore Roosevelt's 1912 presidential campaign. Her career in the 1910s illustrates the new political influence that educated women could exert through the application of their expertise on a range of social issues.

Early Achievements

Born in Columbus, Ohio on 20 October 1873, Francis Alice Kellor was raised by her mother, Mary Sprau Kellor, in a single-parent household. When Frances Alice Kellor was two, her mother took her two daughters to live in the small town of Coldwater, Michigan, where she supported her two children by working as a housekeeper and washerwoman. Kellor later listed her pastor at the First Presbyterian Church as one of the people who motivated her social reform. After earning a law degree from Cornell University in 1897, Kellor enrolled at the University of Chicago to study sociology part-time. There she studied aspects of unemployment and crime, arguing in her first book, *Experimental Sociology* (1901), that the origins of crime were to be located in disadvantaged childhoods, low levels of education, and unemployment and asserting the importance of reforming criminals in prisons. In 1900 she traveled in the southern states to study the living and working conditions of African Americans and subsequently published a series of articles recommending improvements in public schooling and the establishment of vocational-training schools, employment bureaus, and labor unions. In 1902 Kellor began studying women's employment bureaus in the urban North. The result of her research was *Out of Work: A Study of Employment Agencies* (1904), which concluded that the federal government ought to become involved in solving the systematic economic problems that led to unemployment. Her emphasis on government as the vehicle by which social reforms could best be achieved was the approach that many

social-science-minded reformers took during the Progressive Era.

Municipal Reform

In 1904 Kellor became general director of the Inter-Municipal Committee on Household Research, and the following year she moved to New York City to live with Mary Dreier, head of the organization's legislative committee, which prepared legislative bills on child labor, tenement-house law, and employment agencies. Kellor and Dreier lived together until Kellor's death in 1952. In 1906 Kellor was instrumental in organizing the National League for the Protection of Colored Women, which sought to educate African American women who had recently migrated to New York City and to assist those women in finding places to live and jobs. Kellor served as the first executive secretary of the organization. Appointed to the New York State Immigration Commission in 1908, Kellor joined the other commissioners in investigating urban immigrant living and working conditions, and—finding these conditions to be appallingly poor—they asserted the need for a state bureau to examine further their problems. Accordingly, in 1910 Kellor was appointed head of the New York State Bureau of Industries and Immigration. Under Kellor's direction the bureau championed worker safety and educational services.

Progressive Party

The Progressive Party of 1912 was an expression of the will to power of several groups in American society who agreed to work together in coalition to further each of their goals. Among the two most important elements in the Progressive Party that year were social scientists. For years social scientists such as Kellor had been urging social reform through the use of the state. Indeed, the Progressive Party platform adopted a plank on "social and industrial justice" that a group of social scientists had put forward at the annual National Convention of Charities and Corrections in June 1912. Kellor was head of the Progressive Party's National Service Committee, the party's administrative board. During the presidential campaign in 1912 Kellor led the party's research and publicity committee, prepared campaign statements, and roused support for Roosevelt and the party among other social reformers. She was also instrumental in shaping Roosevelt's campaign agenda. According to historian John Higham, Kellor "did more than anyone else to direct Roosevelt's growing reformist zeal toward the special plight of the urban immigrant."

New Interests

In the 1916 presidential campaign Kellor supported the candidacy of Republican Charles Evans Hughes. In the same year she also directed the National Americanization Committee, and following World War I she became an expert in international arbitration. She was a founding member of the American Arbitration Association in the mid-1920s, and published *Arbitration in the New Industrial Society* in 1934.

Further Reading

Ellen Fitzpatrick, *Endless Crusade: Women Social Scientists and Progressive Reform* (New York: Oxford University Press, 1990).
John Louis Recchiuti, "The Origins of American Progressivism: New York's Social Science Community" (Ph.D., Diss., Columbia University 1992). □

Ellsworth Kelly

Prolific American painter and sculptor Ellsworth Kelly (born 1923), a leader of the hard-edge school, is best known for his huge canvases of geometric forms in bright colors.

Ellsworth Kelly was born on May 31, 1923, in Newburgh, New York. He went to elementary and high schools in New Jersey, attended Pratt Institute in Brooklyn, New York, and served in the U.S. Army Engineer Corps during World War II (1943-1945). Ironically, in terms of his later use of color, he served in the camouflage unit in France.

Art Training and Early Work

Kelly got his initial training at the School of the Museum of Fine Arts in Boston (1946-1948), then went on to the École des Beaux-Arts in Paris. He had his first one-man show in Paris in 1951 and continued to live there until 1954, when he returned to New York City.

In New York, Kelly exhibited at the Betty Parsons Gallery in 1956, 1957, and 1959. By this time his work had begun to attract wider attention, and he was asked to participate in various group shows, the most important at the Brussels World's Fair (1958) and the Museum of Modern Art (New York, 1959). After 1960 Kelly gained increasing national and international recognition. He was invited to show at the São Paulo Biennial in 1961 and at the Seattle World's Fair in 1962.

Kelly's work can be seen in numerous museums. In addition, he executed several public commissions, the most notable being a painted metal relief for the Transportation Building in Philadelphia (1957), a plastic mosaic mural for the Eastman House in New York, and a mural for the New York State Pavilion at the New York World's Fair of 1964-1965. His awards include the Carnegie International of 1962 and 1964 and a fine-arts citation from Brandeis University in 1962.

Style

From his earliest work Kelly's style was consistently cool and hard-edged in orientation. Living in Paris, he was influenced by the geometric abstraction of such European artists as Piet Mondrian. This is especially apparent in his paintings of the early 1950s, many of which are based on strict geometric modules. Unlike Mondrian, however, Kelly frequently composed his paintings in separate panels that could be joined to form a large, single image. Many of these works are as much murals as easel paintings, and they

demonstrate how Kelly's art is amply suited to the demands of architectural settings.

Some of Kelly's finest individual paintings were executed during the 1960s. *Blue-White* (1962) consists of two large blue masses that barely converge within a white field; the clean simplicity of Kelly's drawing allows these forms to expand enormously, resulting in a work of truly monumental scale.

The Modern Era

Well into the 1990s, Kelly continued to gain in popularity and recognition. A quiet man who was seldom seen at functions of the art world, he once said, "I'm not interested in edges. I'm interested in mass and color."

In the 1980s, Kelly's works were exhibited at the Los Angeles City Museum of Art, the National Gallery in Washington, D.C., the Dallas Museum in Texas, and the Whitney Museum in New York City. In 1989, his works were part of an exhibition at the Guggenheim Museum in New York City, entitled Geometric Abstraction and Minimalization in America.

In 1991, Kelly was again part of an exhibition at the Whitney, and the following year he was shown again at the Guggenheim as part of the Art of This Century exhibit. In the fall of 1996, Kelly's works were presented in a major retrospective at the Guggenheim.

Further Reading

For more information see Edward Lucie-Smith, *Late Modern* (1969); *Who's Who in American Art; L.A. Times,* Feb. 21, 1997. □

Florence Kelly

Florence Kelley (1859-1932), American social worker and reformer, fought successfully for child labor laws and improved conditions for working women.

Florence Kelley was born on September 12, 1859, in Philadelphia, Pa., the daughter of U.S. congressman William Darrah Kelley. She entered Cornell University in 1876, but poor health kept her from graduating until 6 years later, as a Phi Beta Kappa. She then studied at the University of Zurich, where she was influenced by Marxist thought. In 1887 she published a translation of Friedrich Engels's *The Condition of the Working-class in England in 1844,* to which Engels added a preface in 1892.

In 1884 Kelley married a Polish-Russian physician, Lazare Wischnewetzky, and set up housekeeping in New York City. Their marriage was not happy, and she left him in 1889, moving to Chicago with their three children. Although they divorced and she reassumed the name of Kelley for herself and her children, she retained her title of "Mrs."

After 1889 Kelley turned in earnest to the study of social conditions, taking special interest in women and children working in the Chicago trades. In 1891 she joined Jane Addams and her associates at Hull House. Kelley's analyses of sweatshops and slum houses resulted in a new child labor law, and she was appointed chief factory inspector for Illinois. When she found her efforts to enforce the child labor law and the compulsory education law frustrated by uncooperative city attorneys, she decided to study law. She earned her law degree at Northwestern University in 1894. Her reports and legislative achievements were outstanding milestones in social investigation.

In 1899 Kelley returned to New York to become secretary of the National Consumers' League. She lived at the Henry Street Settlement House and worked with numerous reformers and reform organizations for minimum wage laws, woman's suffrage, and Federal aid for mothers and babies. Kelley considered herself a socialist, though she was not involved in the Socialist party. She wrote *Some Ethical Gains through Legislation* (1905) and helped establish what became known as the "Brandeis brief" (named for Justice Louis D. Brandeis), a process of integrating facts and experiences in legal action to demonstrate the need for changing laws according to human realities.

Kelley later wrote the *Modern Industry in Relation to the Family, Health, Education, Morality* (1914) and a compilation, *The Supreme Court and Minimum Wage Legislation* (1925). She died in Germantown, Pa., on February 17, 1932.

Further Reading

Josephine Goldmark, a friend and associate of Florence Kelley, wrote *Impatient Crusader: Florence Kelley's Life Story* (1953). Sketches of Kelley appear in Lillian D. Wald, *Windows on Henry Street* (1934); Jane Addams, *My Friend Julia Lathrop* (1935); and James Weber Linn, *Jane Addams: A Biography* (1935). ☐

Gene Kelly

Although Gene Kelly (1912-1996) established his reputation as an actor and dancer, his contribution to the Hollywood musical also embraces choreography and direction.

Gene Kelly's experiments with dance and with ways of filming it include combining dance and animation (*Anchors Aweigh* and *Invitation to the Dance*), and special effects (The "Alter Ego" number in *Cover Girl* and the split-screen dance of *It's Always Fair Weather*). His first attempts at film choreography relied on the established formulas of the film musical, but subsequently, particularly in the three films he co-directed with Stanley Donen, he developed a flexible system of choreography for the camera that took into account camera setups and movement, and editing.

Kelly was born in Pittsburgh, Pennsylvania, in 1912, and was the middle son of five children. His father was Canadian-born and loved sports, especially hockey. Every winter Kelly, Sr., would flood the family backyard and make an ice rink for hockey. As quoted in the *New Yorker,* Kelly remembered how the sport would later influence his dancing: "I played ice hockey as a boy and some of my steps come right out of the game—wide open and close to the ground." At 15 Kelly was playing with a semi-professional ice hockey team. Yet, he was also influenced by his mother's love of the theater. In fact, it was she who sent him to dancing lessons.

In 1929 Kelly left for Pennsylvania State college, but because of the Great Depression, his family lost their money, and Kelly had to move back home and attend the University of Pittsburgh in order to save the cost of room and board. Eventually, all five children would graduate from that school. While at Pitt, Kelly worked at a variety of odd jobs to pay his tuition: ditchdigger, soda jerk, gas pumper. Kelly's mother began to work as a receptionist at a local dance school, and she came up with the idea of the family running its own dance studio. They did and the studio was a big success.

After graduation from the University of Pittsburgh, Kelly attended law school. After only a month, he decided that law was not the career for him. He quit and continued to teach dance for another six years. In 1937 he left for New York, and was confident enough of his talent to believe that he would find work. He was right. He landed a job his first week in New York. Kelly's big break came in 1940 when he

was cast as the lead in the Rodgers and Hart musical *Pal Joey*. He played the part of an Irish nightclub singer who was a good-for-nothing loner.

The show was a hit and Kelly attracted the attention of producer-songwriter Arthur Freed, who convinced his boss, Hollywood studio executive Louis B. Mayer, to see the show. Mayer liked what he saw and told Kelly that he would like to have him under contract for the MGM studio. But it was Mayer's nephew, David O. Selznick, who signed Kelly to a contract in 1942. After six months, Kelly's contract was sold to MGM and he worked for MGM for the next 16 years.

His first Hollywood film was *For Me and My Gal* (1942), in which he starred opposite Judy Garland. Garland was only 20, but she had begun working in films at the age of 16. It was she who insisted that Kelly have the role, and she tutored him in how to act for the wide screen. "I knew nothing about playing to the camera," Kelly told *Architectural Digest*. "It was Judy who pulled me through." He learned quickly, however. After a couple of years doing stock musicals, Kelly made a breakthrough with *Cover Girl* (1944). Of his work in *Cover Girl*, Kelly told *Interview*: "[That's] when I began to see that you could make dances for cinema that weren't just photographed stage dancing. That was my big insight into Hollywood, and Hollywood's big insight into me."

Gene Kelly established his reputation as an actor and dancer, but his contribution to the Hollywood musical includes choreography and direction. His experiments with dance and with film technique include combining the two, as demonstrated in such films as *Anchors Aweigh* (1945) and *Invitation to the Dance* (1956). He also made use of special effects, as in the "Alter-Ego" number in *Cover Girl* (1944), where he danced with his reflection, or in the split-screen dance of *It's Always Fair Weather* (1957). His first attempts at film choreography relied on the established formulas of the film musical, but subsequently he developed a flexible system of choreography for the camera that took into account camera setups, movement, and editing.

Kelly consciously integrated dance into film in order to help the audience gain insight into the types of characters he played. For example, the song-and-dance man of *For Me and My Gal* is a common, unpretentious character, and his principal dances are tap routines—the kind of dance accessible to the general public of the era. The sailor of the "A Day in New York" sequence from *On the Town* is introspective and his dance is therefore more lyrical and balletic. The swashbuckler of the dream dances in *Anchors Aweigh* (1945) and *The Pirate* (1948) is an athletic performer, combining the forceful turns of ballet with acrobatic stunts.

Kelly often played a guy who feels that the best way to get what he wants is to impress people. He almost always realizes, however, that his brashness offends people, and that he will more easily succeed by being himself. The worldly wise sailor trying to impress Vera-Ellen in *On the Town* (1949) is really just a boy from Meadowville, Indiana. In *The Pirate* the actor Serafin pretends he is a treacherous pirate in order to win Judy Garland's heart, but it is the lowly actor that she really wants. In *An American in Paris* (1951) Kelly plays an aggressive painter, and in *It's Always Fair Weather* (1955) he portrays a cool and sophisticated New Yorker. Yet, underneath each of these characters' masks are the charming and clever "true" selves, which are expressed wittily through song and dance.

Though Kelly's characters are naturally high-spirited, they also have a somewhat sad aspect and tend to brood about their loneliness at key moments in the films. Kelly expresses the loneliness in dances that are almost meditations on the characters' feelings. After Gaby has lost Miss Turnstiles for the second time in *On the Town,* he dreams the ballet "A Day in New York." The isolation of his character is emphasized by the anonymity of the other dancers as well as the disappearance of Vera-Ellen. The ballet in *An American in Paris* serves a similar thematic purpose. The "Alter-Ego" dance in *Cover Girl* expresses Kelly's anxiety over losing his girlfriend, and the squeaky-board dance number in *Summer Stock* (1950) is a rumination on his new feeling for Judy Garland's character.

Kelly's performances left the impression that anyone—sailors, soldiers, ball players—could sing and dance. As he matured, his characters took on greater dimension, responding to the anxiety of city living, falling in love, and being lonely by distilling such experiences into dance.

And while most of his audiences were not really aware of Kelly's sophisticated techniques—thus the magic—virtually all found him uniquely appealing as a leading man. Nowhere was he more engaging than in 1952's *Singin' in the Rain*. One of the all-time great movie musicals, and perhaps the film most associated with Kelly, this comedy illustrates the late–1920s transition from silent pictures to "talkies." *Singin' in the Rain* showcased the considerable acting, singing, and dancing gifts of Debbie Reynolds and Donald O'Connor, but it is Kelly who dances away with the movie. His rendition of the title song has become an icon of American entertainment; Kelly makes a driving rain his partner, communicating the joy in movement at the heart of all his performances.

Gene Kelly will always be remembered for his incredible contribution—through dance performance, choreography, and photography—to the genre of the movie musical. While he had some success in nonmusical films—*Christmas Holiday, Marjorie Morningstar, Inherit the Wind*—his legacy lies in dance. Kelly died on February 2, 1996.

Further Reading

Griffith, Richard, *The Cinema of Gene Kelly,* New York, 1962.
Springer, John, *All Talking, All Singing, All Dancing,* New York, 1966.
Kobal, John, *Gotta Sing, Gotta Dance,* New York, 1970.
Burrows, Michael, *Gene Kelly,* Cornwall, England, 1971.
Thomas, Lawrence B., *The MGM Years,* New Rochelle, New York, 1972.
Knox, Donald, *The Magic Factory,* New York, 1973.
Hirschhorn, Clive, *Gene Kelly: A Biography,* London, 1974; rev. ed., 1984.
Thomas, Tony, *The Films of Gene Kelly, Song and Dance Man,* Secaucus, New Jersey, 1974; rev. ed., 1991.
Delameter, Jerome, *Dance in the Hollywood Musical,* Ann Arbor, Michigan, 1981.

Thomas, Tony, *That's Dancing,* New York, 1985.
Altman, Rick, *The American Film Musical,* Bloomington, Indiana, 1989.
Cinema, December 1966.
American Film (Washington, D.C.), February 1979.
Film Comment (New York), November/December 1984.
American Film (Washington, D.C.), March 1985.
Interview, May 1994.
Entertainment Weekly, 13 May 1994. □

Petra Kelly

Petra Kelly (1947-1992), West German pacifist and politician, had the reputation of being one of the most active and best known protagonists of the European peace and ecology movement.

Petra Karin Lehmann was born on November 29, 1947, in Günzburg, Bavaria. Her father left the family when she was five. In 1958 her mother married an American army officer, John E. Kelly. Petra Kelly was given the name of her step-father, but remained a West German citizen. She was educated in a Roman Catholic convent in Günzburg.

The family moved to the United States in 1959, where Kelly attended high school at Columbus/WestGeorgia. From 1966 to 1970 she studied political science at the American University's School of International Service in Washington, D.C.

Back on the continent she completed her studies at the University of Amsterdam in the Netherlands.She worked as a research assistant at the European Institute, finishing with a M.A. degree. Between 1971 and 1973 she gathered practical knowledge at the European Community Commission (ECC) in Brussels. In 1973 she finally became a full-time civil servant, employed by the European Community to deal with social and labor problems, public health, and various aspects of environmental protection.

The experiences of her teenage years in the United States had influenced her political socialization intensely. She witnessed the non-violent struggle of the African American civil rights movement and was deeply impressed. She was also concerned with the U.S. military engagement in Vietnam. In 1968 she campaigned for presidential candidate Robert Kennedy, who became her political idol, and after his murder for Hubert Humphrey.

Setting Her Goals

The brutal political violence expressed by the assassinations of the Kennedy brothers and Martin Luther King made a strong impression on Kelly. It directed her towards non-violence, Christian charity, solidarity, and foremost, world-wide peace. Witnessing the Soviet invasion of Czechoslovakia during a Prague visit in August 1968 caused her to adopt another principle: "Human rights may not be handled selectively."

The death of her sister Grace from eye cancer in February 1970 at the age of ten, demonstrated in Kelly's view a dangerous modern syndrome: she called it the "cancerisation of the world, which is caused mainly by world-wide nuclear pollution." The struggle against the civil and military use of nuclear power and for mutual disarmament became the focus of her political work during the 1970s.

She engaged in numerous activities of the European peace and anti-nuclear-power movement. Her involvement included protest against politics as a male domain and against patriarchal structures in everyday life. Her preoccupation with environmental issues arose from a genuine concern about the direct physical threat posed to human beings by the industrial deterioration of the environment and from a growing awareness of the limits of growth in modern postwar industrial societies.

In 1972 she supported Chancellor Willy Brandt and joined the Social Democratic Party (SPD). Becoming politically disappointed, she left the party in 1979. Her interest turned towards the work in the "umbrella" organization of the environmentalist movement, the Bund Bürgerinitiativen Umweltschutz (BBU), which was founded in 1972. Between 1976 and 1979 environmentalist initiatives scored successfully in communal and state elections. Kelly belonged to those prominent activists who tried to integrate ideas and supporters of the ecology movement in a common program and organization. In the meantime she had been elected to the executive committee of the BBU.

Forming the Green Party

In March 1979 she took part in founding the "Other Political Association," called the Greens. The new party maintained the traditional goals of the West German citizen initiatives movement of the 1970s: the pursuit of ecological, social, grass-roots democratic, and non-violent policies. The latter culminated in the protest against the 1979 NATO decision that scheduled the deployment of more U.S. first-strike missiles in the Federal Republic of Germany.

Her activities in the Green Party made Kelly known to a broader public. In 1979 she was nominated for the European Parliament in Strasbourg. In March 1980 she was elected member and speaker of the Green Party's executive committee. She campaigned in the federal elections of 1980 as well as in the Bavarian state elections of 1982 but lost. Finally the federal elections of 1983 brought an overwhelming success. The Green Party gained over two million votes. Kelly, as member and speaker of the Green faction, entered the parliament.

Within the broad and heterogeneous political spectrum of the Green Party, which ranged from trade unionists, socialists, and veterans of the student protest movement of the 1960s to Christian pacifists and conservatives, Kelly covered a key position in the fundamentalist wing. She defined the Greens as an "anti-party party" and the parliament primarily as a "market place" to espouse her views.

Her fears were that the Greens would become a catch-all party which "seeks only to gain power," which would not allow them to make utopian proposals and to ask fundamental questions any more. She wanted the Green Party to stay "fundamentalist and uncompromising in basic demands."

Kelly was labeled the "Jeanne d'Arc of the nuclear age," and a "secular nun." Her charismatic appeal was used to promote her beliefs in an idealistic, romantic, and utopian society without "egoism and profit, war and disease." This goal was achievable by changing oneself and by collective, creative, and colorful non-violent means of civil disobedience. She perceived herself in the political tradition of Martin Luther King, Gandhi, the Russian revolutionary writer and suffragette Alexandra Kollontai, and the German socialist Rosa Luxemburg.

Kelly's favorite works included the writings of Henry David Thoreau, Virginia Woolf, Anne M. Lindbergh, and William B. Yeats. On her own, she published a volume of her most important articles, speeches, appeals, and letters under the title *Fighting for Hope—the Non-violent Way to a Green Future*. The book included a foreword by the German writer and Nobel Peace Prize winner Heinrich Böll.

In 1992, Kelly had gone to New York to address the United Nations (UN) on Chinese human rights violations in Tibet and to attend International Women's Day ceremonies and festivities. In October of that year, Petra Kelly was found shot to death at her home in Bonn, Germany, in what was presumed to be a murder-suicide, committed by her companion, Gert Bastian.

Further Reading

Petra Kelly's biography *Petra Karin Kelly. Politikerin aus Betroffenheit* (Munich, 1983, and Hamburg, 1985) by Monika Sperr is in German; analytic surveys of the Green Party include Elim Papadakis' *The Green Movement in West Germany* (1984); and Charlene Spretnak's, *Green Politics. The Global Promise* (1984); see also "Germany: Petra Kelly's Death" by Andrew Giarelli in *World Press Review,* December 1994; and "Last Words From Petra Kelly" by Eric Williams in *The Progressive,* January 1, 1993, vol.57, no. 1. □

William Kelly

William Kelly (1811-1888), American iron manufacturer, invented a method of making inexpensive steel that anticipated the more famous and successful Bessemer process.

William Kelly was born in Pittsburgh, Pa., the son of a prosperous landowner. After William was educated in the common schools of the city, he entered the drygoods trade. By the age of 35 he was senior partner in the firm of McShane & Kelly. While on a business trip to Nashville, Tenn., he met and fell in love with Mildred Gracy. She was from the town of Eddyville, Ky., which he often visited, eventually purchasing some nearby iron lands and a furnace. After their marriage he set himself up as an iron manufacturer.

At this time iron was sold in three forms, each distinguished by the amount of carbon present in the iron. Cast iron was highest in carbon content. Some cast iron was converted in forges to wrought iron, which contained no carbon. Intermediate was steel, which was the strongest form. Steel was made by slowly heating iron to high temperatures; this was an expensive process and therefore little used.

Beginning in 1847, Kelly made a series of experiments in an attempt to save on fuel costs in his furnace. He discovered that a blast of air would increase the temperature of the molten cast iron, since the carbon impurity acted as a fuel. Kelly hoped to save fuel by this process, and between 1851 and 1856 he built a series of experimental furnaces in the woods behind his plant. The work was done in secret because he was afraid that customers would not trust the metal made by the new process. In 1856 he learned that Henry Bessemer, working in England, had patented a similar process and that a patent was being applied for in the United States. Even though Bessemer was trying to make steel (rather than to save fuel) and had proved his method a success (which Kelly had not), Kelly objected to Bessemer's patent application and revealed his own experiments. In 1857 he was granted a patent for his process.

Though Kelly conducted one further experiment, his process was never successfully applied. In 1861 he merged with the firm that represented the Bessemer interests. The Kelly interests received three-tenths of the stock of the new

firm, and the Bessemer people took seven-tenths. Kelly was not directly involved in these later commercial activities but lived in quiet retirement in Louisville, Ky., until his death in 1888.

Further Reading

The standard biography of Kelly, John Newton Boucher, *William Kelly: A True History of the So-Called Bessemer Process* (1924), is not entirely reliable. It should be supplemented with Philip W. Bishop, "The Beginnings of Cheap Steel," in United States National *Museum, Bulletin 218* (1959). □

Unlike most of the servants of the company, Kelsey showed no hesitation in striking inland from the shores of the bay. This venturesome spirit was noted by the committee in London, which directed the resident governor "that the boy, Henry Kelsey bee sent to Churchill River because Wee are informed hee is a very active lad Delighting much in Indian Company being never better pleased than when he is travelling among them." From 1690 to 1692 he ranged far inland and was the first European ever to visit the Canadian prairies. His journal described the immense grasslands of the interior, the awesome spectacle of the vast buffalo herds, and an exciting vignette of his encounter with a grizzly bear. Kelsey also developed a rare talent for understanding Indian dialects.

In 1694 Kelsey was captured by D'Iberville, the commander of a French expeditionary force. France and England were then engaged, on opposite sides, in the War of the Spanish Succession. Kelsey's confinement was not arduous, but he was relieved in the summer of 1696, when the Royal Navy appeared in the bay and Ft. York was retaken. For the next 20 years he was a mariner in the employ of the company.

Kelsey was named deputy governor in the bay in 1714 and was present to receive the surrender of Ft. York from the French (who had again captured it). In 1718 he succeeded to the resident governorship, a post which he held for 4 years. He went back to England in 1722 and died there 2 years later while awaiting the captaincy of a ship in order to return to Hudson Bay.

Further Reading

The major sources for information on Kelsey are *The Kelsey Papers* (1929), edited with an introduction by Arthur G. Doughty and Chester Martin, and a biography by A. M. Johnson in *Hudson's Bay Record Society,* vol. 25 (1965). Also of some use is J. W. Whillans, *First in the West: The Story of Henry Kelsey* (1955). Briefer but good accounts are in Arthur S. Morton, *A History of the Canadian West to 1870-71* (1939), and Glyndwr Williams, *The British Search for the Northwest Passage in the Eighteenth Century* (1962). □

Henry Kelsey

Henry Kelsey (ca. 1667-1724) was an English-born Canadian explorer and overseas governor of the Hudson's Bay Company. He was the first European to visit the interior of western Canada and to winter on the prairies.

Henry Kelsey was apprenticed in 1684 to the Hudson's Bay Company for a term of 4 years. He would eventually serve the company for almost 40 years, spending all but 3 in the environs of the bay. He was sent out immediately, "his time to commence at his arrival in the Bay and to terminate from his coming from thence who is to have £8 and two suites of apparell."

Baron Kelvin of Largs

The Scottish physicist William Thomson, Baron Kelvin of Largs (1824-1907), was the originator of the absolute scale of temperature and was one of the founders of thermodynamics.

William Thomson was born on June 26, 1824, at Belfast, Ireland. His father taught mathematics and joined the University of Glasgow faculty in 1831. He devoted much of his time to the education of his sons and arranged for them to audit university classes. Thus when William was 10, he matriculated in the university and did well. After a tour of the Continent, Thomson entered Peterhouse, Cambridge, in 1841.

In 1846 Thomson was appointed professor of natural philosophy at the University of Glasgow. He held this position for 53 years. In addition to teaching and inaugurating the first physics laboratory for students in the British Isles, he continued his mathematical and physical studies.

In 1847 Thomson learned of James Joule's work on the relationships between heat and work. In 1848 he originated his absolute temperature scale, and in 1851, independently of the findings of R. J. E. Clausius in the preceding year, he proposed the second law of thermodynamics.

From 1850 until 1860 Thomson's researches focused on thermoelectric effects, resulting in his discovery of the "Thomson heat effect." His other work on the principles of cyclic heating and refrigeration and his collaborative work with Joule on the cooling of gases by expansion are part of the contributions which justify listing him as one of the founders of thermodynamics.

By the end of 1855 Thomson, then 31, had published 96 papers and had reached his peak in pure physics. He devoted the remainder of his life chiefly to the application of physics, especially in the field of electricity. Between 1855 and 1865 he wrote a series of papers on telegraphic signaling by wire which were important to the laying of the first Atlantic cable. He developed and patented much equipment, such as the mirror galvanometer (1858), the quadrant electrometer, the siphon recorder for telegraphy (1867), and stranded conductors. As a leading member of the British Association Committee on Electrical Standards, he was instrumental in the adoption of the system of electrical units which later was adopted internationally.

Thomson became wealthy through his many discoveries and inventions and famous as well. In 1866 he was knighted and in 1892 was elevated to the peerage as Baron Kelvin of Largs. Almost every honor that can come to a scientist was awarded to him, including burial in Westminster Abbey. He died on Dec. 17, 1907, at his country home "Netherhall," near Largs.

Further Reading

Agnes G. King, *Kelvin the Man* (1925), provides an interesting view of Kelvin. See also Silvanus P. Thompson, *The Life of William Thomson* (1910). A more recent study is in David K.C. MacDonald, *Faraday, Maxwell, and Kelvin* (1964). A detailed biographical account of Kelvin is in James Gerald Crowther, *Men of Science* (1936). A short study is in Bryan Morgan, *Men and Discoveries in Electricity* (1952). □

Yashar Kemal

Yashar Kemal (born 1922) was the most successful and most widely known of modern Turkish novelists. His works, which also include short stories and essays, are local in color and infused with the spirit of Turkish folk traditions. They show the influence of world classics from Homer to Stendal, Steinbeck, and Faulkner.

Yashar Kemal was born Kemal Sadik Göçeli in southwestern Turkey in the small village of Hemite near Osmaniye in the province of Adana. His father came from a line of feudal landlords and his mother from a family of famous brigands in eastern Anatolia. At the age of five Yashar Kemal saw his father shot to death while praying in the mosque and, in the same incident, lost one of his eyes. He did not attend school until he was nine (walking two hours a day in order to do so) and had no formal education beyond eighth grade.

From early childhood, however, he imbibed the oral literature of the Turkish people by listening to storytellers and minstrels and the songs of the villagers as they worked or experienced the joys and tragedies of life. He himself became an accomplished folk singer and extempore minstrel at a young age and in his late teens began serious collection and study of the oral literature. He started to earn a living as a jack-of-all-trades—including construction worker, cobbler's assistant, watchman, and cotton picker. He first went to Istanbul in the early 1940s and worked as a clerk in the gas company. At that time he became acquainted with a group of intellectuals who introduced him to the works of classical and European writers and to art and modern painting.

Beginnings as Writer and Reporter

After a period back in the southwest as a public writer of petitions in the little town of Kadirli, and having been acquitted of a charge of disseminating Communist propaganda, he returned to Istanbul and became a roving reporter for the daily *Cumhuriyet.* He was later given a weekly column and appointed chief of the paper's Anatolian Bureau. He resigned from *Cumhuriyet* in 1963, after which he devoted himself to literature—from 1967 to 1971 he also published a leftist political weekly of which he was a co-founder—and continued to contribute to a variety of journals and newspapers. He was among those who founded the Writers Union of Turkey and served as its first chairman during the years 1974 through 1976.

Yashar Kemal's early attempts as a writer were in the realm of poetry, the first of his poems to be published appearing in 1939 in the journal of the Adana *Halkevi* ("People's House," one of the cultural centers established by the Republican People's Party in the early days of the Turkish Republic). The *Halkevi* also published his earliest folklore studies (a collection of ballads in 1942 and a study of elegies in 1943). All of these works, as well as poems accepted by journals in the early 1940s, were signed with his real name, Kamal Sadik Göğçeli. He changed his name to Yashar Kemal when he moved to Istanbul in 1951.

Yashar Kemal began to write fiction in the late 1940s and became known in Istanbul as a short story writer as well as an outstanding journalist with a special gift for travelogues. Various collections of his journalistic writings and of his short stories have been published in Turkey, and English translations of some of his best short stories are available in *Anatolian Tales,* published in New York in 1969.

Career as Novelist

It was not until he was 33 years old that he published his first novel, *Ince Memed* (1955; *Mehmet My Hawk,* 1961). Set in the Taurus-Chukurova area that he knew so well, it tells of a young village boy who, driven to banditry through the tyranny of the local landowner, becomes a Robin Hood-like figure, an outlaw fighting against injustice, and a legend and inspiration to the villagers of the area. Two sequels, *Ince Memed 2* (1969; *They Burn the Thistles,* 1973) and *Ince Memed 3* (1984), continue the saga of this folk hero.

Ortadirek (1960; *The Wind from the Plain,* 1962), *Yer demir gök bakir* (1963; *Iron Earth, Copper Sky,* 1974) and *Ölmez otu* (1968; *The Undying Grass,* 1978) form a trilogy that again deals with the ordeals of the poverty-stricken villagers in the Taurus Mountains. Confronted by the forces of nature and the rapacity of landlords, these people survive only by an annual migration to the coastal plain to earn money picking cotton. Set in the same milieu, the novel *Akçasazin ağalari* centers on the problems of the landlords themselves, especially the old blood feud, and shows the effects of the breakdown of the feudal and tribal orders. It appeared in two volumes: *Demirciler çarşisi cinayeti* (1974; *The Lords of Akchasaz: Murder in the Ironsmiths Market,* 1979) and *Yusufcuk Yusuf* ("Turtledove Yusuf," 1975).

Later Yashar Kemal wrote also of underprivileged groups in other parts of Turkey. *Al gözüm seyreyle Salih* (1976; *Seagull,* 1981) is set in a Black Sea fishing town; *Deniz küstü* (1978; *The Sea-crossed Fisherman,* 1985) and *Kuşlar da gitti* (1978; *Alors les oiseaux sont partis,* 1981) take the reader to Istanbul and its environments.

Much of Yashar Kemal's writing was inspired by the folklore of Anatolia, drawing on well-known tales or the lives of individuals famous in the folk tradition. Such works include *Üç Anadolu Efsanesi* (1967; *Three Anatolian Tales,* 1975), *Ağridağ Efsanesi* (1970; *The Legend of Ararat,* 1975), *Binboğalar Efsanesi* (1971; *The Legend of the 1000 Bulls,* 1976), and *Çakicali Efe* (*The Swashbuckler from Chakija,* 1972). His language also derives much from the ordinary Turkish people, its texture at once epic and lyrical.

Yashar Kemal's general style had a great influence on modern Turkish writing. From the beginning he was noted as a first-rate storyteller and as a social realist. Yet he blended stark realism with scenes of epic grandeur and tempered it by the unreality of myth. He alternated description of the environment (sometimes painted with panoramic strokes, sometimes etched with minute attention to detail) with stream of consciousness writing. He won many awards in Turkey and abroad. The universal appeal of his work is attested by the many translations available in more than 20 languages.

Kemal was accused by the Turkish government of promoting separatism through an article he had written for the German publication, *Der Spiegel,* and was arrested in 1995. Kemal was given a suspended 20-month sentence in 1996 for speaking out against the government's actions regarding the Kurds.

Further Reading

Edebiyat 5 (Nos. 1 and 2, 1980), available through the Middle East Center at the University of Pennsylvania in Philadelphia, is a special issue devoted to Yashar Kemal. Also see ''Yashar Kemal's epic struggle'' by Nicole Pope in *World Press Review,* July 1996, vol. 43, no. 7, p. 40; and a Web site maintained by the Armenian National Committee of Canada, http://armen-info.com/lacuse/publes/95loel.htm. □

Frances Anne Kemble

Born into a famous English theatrical family, Frances Anne Kemble (1809-1893), known as Fanny Kemble, went to America in 1832, where she was celebrated both for her dramatic talent and her cultural observations.

Frances Anne Kemble was born on November 27, 1809. The daughter of actor Charles Kemble and his actress wife Maria Theresa De Camp, she could claim full membership in the aristocracy of the British theater. By the time she traveled with her father to their New York opening in 1832, she was an established dramatic star. For two seasons Kemble and the company toured the United States, playing to wildly enthusiastic audiences. But in spite of her success, Kemble hated what she thought of as the artificiality of acting. She was happy to retire in 1834 to become the wife of Pierce Butler, heir to a rich Georgia plantation.

Kemble published a record of her 2-year theatrical tour, *Journal of a Residence in America* (1835). It was an incisive and genuinely good-humored account, but such publications by foreigners were the rage then and thin-skinned critics made her the target of journalistic wrath. Kemble's marriage, in the meantime, was becoming troubled. Her romantic notions about life on a plantation were rudely shocked by the facts. Unable to live with slavery, she withdrew, first visiting England in 1841 and breaking formally with her husband in 1846. For a year she returned to the British stage and in 1847 moved to Italy, where she wrote *A Year of Consolation* (1848). In 1848 Butler sued for divorce in a widely celebrated case. After a year the divorce was granted, with custody of their two daughters going to Butler.

Kemble returned to the United States, making a career of giving public readings from Shakespeare. This innovation brought her enthusiastic applause and a more than decent income. In 1863, in a very successful attempt to influence British public opinion against the Confederate states, she published an account of her plantation experience, *Journal of a Residence on a Georgia Plantation.* She published several later volumes of autobiography and also literary criticism, as well as a novel, *Far Away and Long Ago* (1889).

Further Reading

There is only one full-length, thoroughly documented study of Fanny Kemble: Margaret N. Armstrong, *Fanny Kemble: A Passionate Victorian* (1938). As a cultural commentator, she is examined in Una Pope-Hennessy, *Three English Women in America* (1929), which also discusses Frances Trollope and Harriet Martineau. A study of her as a theatrical figure is included in Edward Robins, *Twelve Great Actresses* (1900).

Additional Sources

Furnas, J. C. (Joseph Chamberlain), *Fanny Kemble: leading lady of the nineteenth-century stage: a biography,* New York: Dial Press, 1982.

Kemble, Fanny, *The terrific Kemble: a Victorian self-portrait from the writings of Fanny Kemble,* London: H. Hamilton, 1978.

Marshall, Dorothy, *Fanny Kemble,* New York: St. Martin's Press, 1978, 1977. □

Jack French Kemp Jr.

A conservative on economic issues and a liberal on social questions, Jack French Kemp, Jr. (born 1935), was an articulate spokesperson for the Republican Party for many years. He was the vice presidential candidate on the Republican Party's ticket in Sen. Bob Dole's failed run for the presidency in 1996.

Jack French Kemp, Jr., was born in Los Angeles, California, on July 13, 1935. He attended public elementary and high schools in Los Angeles. In 1957 he received his Bachelor of Arts degree from Occidental College in Los Angeles, where he was the starting quarterback and team captain of the football team. Kemp did post-graduate work at Long Beach State University and California Western University in political science and education.

Between 1958 and 1962 Kemp was a member of the United States Army Reserves, serving in active duty during 1958. He was drafted by the San Diego Chargers football team, with whom he played for five years. During his stay with San Diego he was selected as the captain of the team in 1961 and 1962. He was then traded to the Buffalo Bills and led them to the American Football League championship for two consecutive years, 1964 and 1965. In 1965 he was voted the league's most valuable player. During his athletic career Kemp co-founded the American Football League Players Association (1956) and between 1956 and 1970 he was elected its president five times.

During the later years of his football career Kemp began to develop his political background by associating with a newly elected governor of California, Ronald Reagan. In 1967 Kemp was appointed to the position of special assistant to the governor, gaining political experience and some notoriety during Reagan's governorship. He furthered his experiences by winning a position as the special assistant to the chairman of the Republican National Committee in 1969. He continued his football career until 1970, when he retired to pursue a career in politics.

Kemp's leadership skills led him to be oriented toward a variety of community activities in the Buffalo, New York, area. His dedication gained the respect of the community and led him to be the recipient of a series of awards. He was given the Distinguished Service Award by the New York State Jaycees. He also was given an Outstanding Citizen Award by the *Buffalo Evening News* in 1965 and 1974.

With the support of a popular football career and the experiences gained from his activities with the players' association, Kemp launched a political career that led him to a seat in Congress. On January 3, 1971, he was sworn into the House of Representatives for a district comprised of several Buffalo suburbs and western New York state as a member of the Republican Party. A member of the 92nd Congress of the United States, Kemp remained for nine terms, until 1989. During his years as a congressman Kemp served for seven years in the Republican Party leadership as chairman of the House Republican Conference.

During the Nixon and Ford administrations Kemp maintained middle-of-the-road positions due in part to his inexperience and the domination by the Democratic majority in the House. After gaining experience in the House through diligence in informing himself on issues, he became known as a strong Republican voice on economic issues.

When the political leadership in the White House switched from Jimmy Carter to Ronald Reagan, Kemp found his political views commanding significant interest, primarily through President Reagan's economic strategy. Kemp became a major voice for "supply-side economics," which President Reagan accepted as a driving force in his domestic policies. Kemp co-authored a 30 percent tax reduction plan that would cut personal taxes over the first three years of Reagan's term, known as the Kemp-Roth plan. The proposal was adopted in modified form by Congress in 1981 (he had worked to secure the support of nearly all Republicans by 1978). As a strong advocate of a supply-side economic strategy, Kemp aimed to reduce the corporate and individual tax rates to encourage business growth and create jobs. He also voiced strong views on abortion and on the need to continue a strong military build-up.

Kemp's viewpoints tended to the left on some issues, which lowered acceptance of him by the more conservative Republicans. Kemp fought cuts on Social Security and expressed a lot of concern for child nutrition funding. He also supported economic provisioning for revitalization of inner cities. While these viewpoints balanced his political platform, they confused some Republican voters. Some felt he was unqualified to hold higher political office because of these inconsistencies.

Kemp continued with his strong economic plans, expressing much concern for a reduction in inflation. He rounded up enough congressional support to pass an amendment to Congress' 1986 budget plan. The resolution called for an international conference with the goal of reforming the world monetary system. The ideals of Kemp's efforts were appreciated but he failed to stick to a solid plan of action, confusing his supporters.

Kemp hinted at running for governor of New York in 1980 and for the Senate later that term. He held back from officially declaring any run for higher office until he unsuccessfully attempted to gain the candidacy for the Republican nomination for president in 1988.

Under the Bush administration Kemp was appointed secretary of housing and urban development (HUD) on February 13, 1989. Kemp was faced with the task of rehabilitating a department that during the Reagan administration was left to waste. He shut down questionable HUD programs and tightened control of others. A lack of financial support prevented him from producing any noticeable growth in HUD programs, and he received some negative press for the lack of growth in these programs.

Although out of office, Kemp remained oriented toward furthering his political goal: the presidency. In January 1993, he co-founded Empower America, a public policy and advocacy organization designed to expand on democratic capitalism and advancing social policies. Kemp also served as a distinguished fellow at the Heritage Foundation and as a visiting fellow at the Hoover Institute, two conservative think tanks.

Still, Kemp considered not even attending the 1996 Republican Convention, telling reporters that his political life was over and that he was a "has been." A few days later, he was named Bob Dole's vice presidential running mate despite past differences.

After Clinton's landslide win, Kemp rejoined the board of directors of Carson Inc., an African-American company with a growing international base. He lost no time in aiming for another shot at the presidency in 2000. In early 1997, he told reporters that the last election had only "whetted my appetite" for the job. He plotted a strategy of inclusion of African Americans and the poor, saying he wanted the party to return to its roots in the days of Abraham Lincoln. "I believe with all my heart that there is a struggle going on for the heart and soul of the Republican Party. That party must be inclusive, not exclusive, it must be progressive and conservative, not reactionary and conservative."

Jack Kemp married Joanne Main during his collegiate years in California. They had four children: Jeffery, Jennifer, Judith, and James.

Further Reading

The American Idea, Ending Limits to Growth, published in 1984, and *An American Renaissance: A strategy for the 1980's,* published in 1979, both by Jack Kemp; articles by Kemp include "Better than Affirmative Action" in the *Washington Post* July 8, 1997. □

Thomas à Kempis

The spiritual writer Thomas à Kempis (ca. 1380-1471) was a Roman Catholic monk in Holland whose "The Imitation of Christ" became a classic in religious literature.

homas à Kempis, whose family name was Hammercken, was born in the Rhineland town of Kempen near Düsseldorf in Germany. The school he attended at nearby Deventer in Holland had been started by Gerard Groote, founder of the Brothers of the Common Life. These were men devoted to prayer, simplicity, and union with God. Thomas of Kempen, as he was known at school, was so impressed by his teachers that he decided to live his own life according to their ideals. When he was 19, he entered the monastery of Mount St. Agnes, which the Brothers had recently started near Zwolle in Holland and which was then being administered by his older brother John. He spent the rest of his long life behind the walls of that monastery.

The pattern of Thomas's life remained the same over the years. He devoted his time to prayer, study, copying manuscripts, teaching novices, offering Mass, and hearing the confessions of people who came to the monastery church. From time to time Thomas was given a position of authority in the community of monks, but he consistently preferred the quiet of his cell to the challenge of administration. He was pleasant but retiring. The other monks eventually recognized Thomas's talent for deep thought and stopped troubling him with practical affairs.

Thomas wrote a number of sermons, letters, hymns, and lives of the saints. He reflected the mystical spirituality of his times, the sense of being absorbed in God. The most famous of his works by far is *The Imitation of Christ*, a charming instruction on how to love God. This small book, free from intellectual pretensions, has had great appeal to anyone interested in probing beneath the surface of life. "A poor peasant who serves God," Thomas wrote in it, "is better than a proud philosopher who ... ponders the courses of the stars." The book advised the ordering of one's priorities along religious lines. "Vain and brief is all human comfort. Blessed and true is that comfort which is derived inwardly from the Truth." Thomas advised where to look for happiness. "The glory of the good is in their own consciences, and not in the mouths of men." *The Imitation of Christ* has come to be, after the Bible, the most widely translated book in Christian literature. Thomas died in the same monastic obscurity in which he had lived, on Aug. 8, 1471.

Further Reading

The most convenient modern edition of *The Imitation of Christ* is the translation by Justin McCann (1952). There are no modern works on the life of Thomas à Kempis, but several older books are still valuable: Francis R. Cruise, *Thomas à Kempis* (1887), and J. E. G. De Montmorency, *Thomas à Kempis: His Age and Book* (1906). □

Amos Kendall

Amos Kendall (1789-1869), American journalist and politician, was postmaster general under President Jackson and a leading member of his "Kitchen Cabinet."

Amos Kendall was born in Dunstable, Mass., on Aug. 16, 1789. As a child, he worked long hours on his father's farm, attending the free public schools when he could. He graduated at the head of his class from Dartmouth College in 1811. He studied law for 2 years but, undecided about his future, traveled to Kentucky and spent a year as tutor in the family of Henry Clay. In 1816 he became editor of the *Argus of Western America* in Frankfort, Ky., demonstrating exceptional journalistic ability. He married Mary B. Woolfolk in 1818; she died in 1823, and in 1826 he married Jane Kyle.

In 1828 Kendall switched allegiance from Clay to work effectively for the election of Andrew Jackson. Following Jackson's victory Kendall went to Washington, D.C., to become fourth auditor of the Treasury. More importantly, he became the President's intimate adviser. He proved an able administrator and in 1834 became postmaster general, holding office until 1840.

Kendall suffered financial reverses in the early 1840s. He had founded an unsuccessful paper, *Kendall's Expositor,* and became tangled in litigation over earlier disputes with mail contractors. He was found guilty of refusal to pay debts, but he was exonerated in his appeal to the Supreme Court. In 1845 Kendall's fortunes improved. He was engaged as business manager by Samuel F. B. Morse to exploit Morse's newly invented telegraph, and during the next 15 years both men made fortunes.

Kendall retired in 1860 to live out his life as a philanthropist, contributing mainly to churches and establishing an institution for the deaf and dumb. He remained a Democrat during the Civil War but supported the Union. He died on Nov. 12, 1869.

Kendall's importance to American history rests on his labors as Jackson's assistant and his influence upon both the form and substance of Jacksonian Democracy. He wrote most of the President's annual addresses and drafted Jackson's veto of the bill to recharter the Second Bank of the United States. He also produced much of the newspaper material that appeared throughout the country to build support for Jackson's programs. Kendall left his mark upon American society in a crucial period of its development.

Further Reading

Kendall's son-in-law, William Stickney, edited the *Autobiography of Amos Kendall* (1872), which has much material on his life. Descriptions of Kendall and his work are in the writings of his contemporaries, such as that of journalist Ben Perley Poore, *Perley's Reminiscences of Sixty Years in the National Metropolis* (2 vols., 1886). Information on him is available in the voluminous literature on the Jacksonians. Arthur M. Schlesinger, Jr., analyzes Kendall's career and influence in *The Age of Jackson* (1949). □

Edward Calvin Kendall

Edward Calvin Kendall (1886-1972), American biochemist and Nobel Prize winner, isolated the hormone thyroxin and played a leading role in the isolation and synthesis of the hormone cortisone.

On March 8, 1886, E. C. Kendall was born in South Norwalk, Conn. He received a bachelor of science degree in 1908, a master of science degree in 1909, and a doctorate in chemistry in 1910 from Columbia University. The following year Kendall was a research chemist with Parke, Davis and Company in Detroit, and from 1911 to 1914 he worked at New York City's St. Luke's Hospital. During these years he was engaged in research on the thyroid gland. In 1914 he succeeded in isolating the thyroid hormone thyroxin. His discovery was reported in the *Journal of the American Medical Association* for 1915. Also in that year, he married Rebecca Kennedy.

In 1914 Kendall had accepted a position as head of the section of biochemistry at the Mayo Clinic Graduate School in Rochester, Minn., and in 1921 he was named professor of physiological chemistry. At the Mayo Clinic he and his coworkers made important scientific contributions, including studies on oxidation in the animal organism, but Kendall's most significant achievement was the isolation and synthesis of cortisone, a hormone produced by the adrenal cortex.

The adrenal glands had been observed first in the 16th century, and by the 19th century it was suspected that the adrenals were related to certain diseases. In the 1930s several researchers began to study them in an effort to determine what the active substance of the glands was. This proved a very complex problem since the adrenal cortex alone produces a series of closely related hormones. Kendall's research team isolated several of these hormones, including one that was renamed cortisone in 1939.

Kendall's early reports on the isolation of cortisone and other hormones of the adrenal cortex appeared in the *Proceedings of the Mayo Clinic* (1934) and the *Journal of Biological Chemistry* (1936). He then guided work toward the synthesis of cortisone, which was accomplished between 1946 and 1948.

Kendall had a major role in the introduction of cortisone for treatment of rheumatoid arthritis and rheumatic fever, although Dr. Philip S. Hench of the Mayo Clinic directed the early testing. In 1950 Kendall and Hench shared the Nobel Prize in physiology or medicine with Tadeus Reichstein for their work on cortisone. Kendall retired from the Mayo Clinic in April 1951 and became visiting professor in the department of biochemistry at Princeton University. He died on May 4, 1972, in Princeton.

Further Reading

A short sketch of Kendall is in Theodore L. Sourkes, *Nobel Prize Winners in Medicine and Physiology* (new and rev. ed. 1967). A slightly more detailed biography is in Nobel Foundation, *Nobel Lectures in Physiology or Medicine, 1942-1962,* vol. 3 (1964), which includes information on the events and discoveries leading to Kendall's work as well as a discussion of the work itself. □

John C. Kendrew

John C. Kendrew (born 1917) was awarded the Nobel Prize in chemistry (with Max Perutz) in 1962 for his work in determining protein structures.

John Cowdery Kendrew was born in Oxford, England, on March 24, 1917, the son of Wilfred George and Evelyn May Graham (Sandberg) Kendrew. His father was a climatologist at the university; thus young Kendrew was raised in a highly enriched, scientific atmosphere. He trained as a physical chemist upon entering Cambridge, taking his B.A. from Trinity College in the spring of 1939. After graduation he considered switching to biology for further study, but without clear direction, and with the outbreak of World War II he joined the Air Ministry and worked on the application of airborne radar to the war effort and as a civilian scientist for the Royal Air Force. Kendrew worked for the RAF until 1945, first in England, then in the Middle East, and finally in Southeast Asia.

Early Interest in Structural Chemistry

It was in the Far East that he first became acquainted with J. D. Bernal, the great structural chemist and later scientific adviser to Lord Mountbatten. Ironically, Bernal had been working at Cambridge throughout the 1930s utilizing x-ray diffraction to determine the structure of crystals. This is accomplished by directing a beam of x-rays upon a crystal and capturing the diffraction pattern established upon a photographic plate. Bernal was at that time excited about the possibility of determining the structure of proteins through the use of x-rays, and he convinced Kendrew that the field was ready for cultivation. Kendrew's mind was thus at work upon structures when, on a military trip to California, he met Linus Pauling and learned of his interest in protein and amino acid structures. The combined influence of Bernal and Pauling persuaded him to switch from chemistry to biology, and with the war's end he returned to Cambridge to pursue his doctorate.

Work with Myoglobin

Max Perutz, a former student of Bernal's, was already working on the structure of hemoglobin at Cambridge's Cavendish Laboratory when Kendrew joined him in 1946. From Perutz he learned the elements of crystallography, and he began his doctoral research on the protein myoglobin. Kendrew chose this protein because of its close relation to hemoglobin, but also because it was one-quarter the size (2,500 atoms to hemoglobin's 10,000). While actively engaged in this research, and though he had not yet finished

his doctoral requirements, Kendrew rose rapidly in the post-war academic hierarchy. In 1947 he was named department chairman of the Medical Research Council Laboratory for Molecular Biology, also in the Cavendish Laboratory under Sir Lawrence Bragg but later in its own building, a post he held at Cambridge until 1975—a period concurrent with his being a fellow of Peterhouse. In 1949 he finished his Ph.D., but he continued to work on the structure of myoglobin as the determination of its crystalline arrangement was still unsolved.

In 1953 Perutz discovered a new technique that was to unravel the mystery of the protein. He showed that attaching a single atom, such as gold or mercury, to a hemoglobin molecule slightly altered the diffraction pattern. By a comparison of before and after photographs it was possible to determine the heavy atoms' positions in the hemoglobin crystal. This method, known as isomorphic replacement, could potentially solve the entire puzzle of hemoglobin structure. Kendrew applied it to the simpler molecule myoglobin, succeeding by 1957—after thousands of photographs and repeated measurements—in unraveling the first protein structure. This first picture was rather blurred, but by 1959, after many more photographs and measurements, Kendrew and his associates achieved a very high resolution, such that most of the individual atoms were now "visible." Eventually, nearly every atom's location in the molecule was determined, but at the time the polypeptide chain was shown to coil about in a spiral manner already described theoretically by Pauling in 1951 and called the alpha-helix.

For their work Perutz and Kendrew were awarded the 1962 Nobel Prize in chemistry. Kendrew received other recognition for his work in what is now commonly known as molecular biology—a 1960 fellow of the Royal Society; decorated knight bachelor and commander, Order of the British Empire; and foreign associate, National Academy of Sciences (United States). After 1959 he was editor-in-chief of the *Journal for Molecular Biology,* and in 1970 he left Cambridge for the post of director-general of the European Molecular Biology Laboratory in Heidelberg, Germany, which he held until 1982.

Further Reading

Horace Judson's *The Eighth Day of Creation* (1979) tells the story of molecular biology; the *Thread of Life* (1966), by Kendrew, non-technical overview with x-ray crystallographic photographs. See also: "How Molecular Biology Got Started" in *Scientific American,* vol. 216, 1967, pp. 141-143; and "Myoglobin and the Structure of Proteins (Nobel Address)" in *Science,* Vol. 139, 1963, pp. 1259 - 1266; *Biochemistry* by Lubert Stryer (1988). □

George F. Kennan

Combining the talents of the diplomat with the wisdom of the scholar, George F. Kennan (born 1904) left a powerful impression on his age. Author of the famed "Doctrine of Containment," he helped to de-

fine the issues and values dividing America and Russia at the onset of the Cold War.

Until he won White House and State Department recognition as a creative and farsighted thinker by his "Long Telegram" of 1946, George Frost Kennan was one of many first-rate Foreign Service officers representing American interests abroad. After the telegram brought him to the attention of his superiors and his *Foreign Affairs* article in 1947 earned him a national following, George F. Kennan was assured his place in history.

Born in Milwaukee, Wisconsin, on February 16, 1904, he came from" . . . a straight line of pioneer farmers . . ." of 18th-century English-Scottish-Ulster stock. After graduation from a secondary school military academy, he entered Princeton, graduating in 1925. College was more an ordeal than a career for him, as he recounted in his Pulitzer prize winning *Memoirs* 1925-1950. He described himself with simple severity as" . . . an oddball, not eccentric, not ridiculed or disliked, just imperfectly visible to the naked eye." History impressed him most, although he also loved literature.

Becoming an Expert on Russia

He entered the newly-created Foreign Service School in 1926 after passing a stiff competitive examination. Brief assignments in Geneva and Hamburg sharpened his language skills and exposed him to minor diplomatic tasks, but left him convinced of the need for more education. He was on the point of resigning when an in-service program opened up offering three years of study in Europe. As his field, he selected Russian and Russia.

Kennan's choice of Russia reflected a family link dating to the previous century. An elder cousin of the same name had carved a career out of studying Russian tsardom, producing a landmark work entitled *Siberia and the Exile System.* In his *Memoirs,* the younger Kennan expressed the feeling " . . . that I was in some strange way destined to carry forward as best I could the work of my distinguished and respected namesake."

The next few years were spent on the periphery of Bolshevism, in then independent Estonia and Latvia, in travels to Finland; but always on the outside, looking in. He progressed well as a student, translating Russian into German and vice versa, deepening his knowledge of Russian history, and preparing for what almost seems a preordained future.

In 1931 he married a Norwegian woman named Annelise Soerensen. Four children were born to them.

Posted to Moscow

Two years later, diplomatic relations were restored between the United States and the Soviet Union. Kennan's linguistic ability and his familiarity with economic conditions in Russia made him a logical choice to accompany William C. Bullitt, President Franklin D. Roosevelt's nominee as ambassador, on the initial trip to Moscow. He had

found his niche; those early years were " . . . a wonderful and exciting time." Even the " . . . Moscow winter was healthy and exhilarating" to a Milwaukean entering his thirties.

He gained invaluable experience during the 1930s in Vienna, Moscow, Prague, and Berlin. Stationed in the latter city when the Nazis declared war on the United States in 1941, he spent six months in an internment camp until repatriated in 1942 and reassigned to Lisbon.

He returned to Moscow in the spring of 1944 and remained there for two crucial years. His career to this point had been an enviable one which would reflect credit on any diplomat, but he had not yet made that breakthrough which would take him from competence to greatness. His opportunity came at the age of 42. By 1946 he was convinced that few Americans in leadership positions understood Russia, Stalin, or Communism and, further, that his efforts to remedy this were largely ignored. But a query from the Treasury Department seeking information on economic and financial matters gave him the forum he needed. The result was an 8,000 word cable (the "Long Telegram") describing the world from the Soviet perspective.

He defined Soviet premises as based on beliefs that capitalism would generate debilitating international competition and divisive internal conflict. Capitalist countries harboring socialist and social democratic movements were especially suspect, since their tenets were masks hiding bourgeois values. From these premises, Kennan predicted certain Soviet actions would flow. Russia and its allies must grow stronger to take advantage of capitalism's weaknesses, for example, and left wing leaders and groups must be firmly dealt with.

War between the United States and Russia was not inevitable, Kennan argued, and coexistence between their differing social and economic systems was entirely possible. The best way to compete with Communism was by educating the public to a true understanding of Russia and its people. In a powerful conclusion, he observed that " . . . every courageous and incisive measure to solve internal problems of our own society . . . is a diplomatic victory over Moscow worth a thousand diplomatic notes and communiques." This is so because " . . . Communism is like a malignant parasite which feeds only on diseased tissue."

Winning Respect for His Views

Notwithstanding the stilted telegraphic style, Kennan's power to articulate the main outlines of American-Soviet relations made him an overnight sensation in Washington's highest circles. From President Truman down through the top few thousand members of America's governing officials Kennan became required reading. "My voice now carried," he observed tersely in later years.

Returning to Washington shortly after sending the cable, he was sent around the country by the State Department to address diverse groups in the Mid-and Far-West. He was also named to a key position in the newly created National War College.

His growing influence within and outside the government gave him the opportunity for critical input into the Truman Doctrine and Marshall Plan developments. In 1947 Secretary of State George C. Marshall selected him to head the Policy Planning Staff, a key agency for formulating national policy. Cutting back on his other activities, he threw himself wholeheartedly into the task of organizing and staffing an effective advisory body.

The next step in Kennan's path to fame was taken with the publication in July 1947 of "The Sources of Soviet Conduct" in the magazine *Foreign Affairs,* the prestigious journal of the Council of Foreign Relations. Publication of this article gave a name to President Truman's developing policy toward Communism—"The Doctrine of Containment."

"The Doctrine of Containment"

A more succinct or complete exposition of the Russian roots of Soviet behavior would be difficult to find. Everything is in this article: the fanatical characters of Lenin and Stalin, their sense of total infallibility, their intransigeant contempt for capitalism, and the chilling conviction that they were incapable of defeat in the long run. Only a very stable society, sure of its own " . . . spiritual vitality . . . , and possessed of . . . a policy of firm containment," could cope with such a monolithic threat. Whether Americans were up to this " . . . duel of infinite duration" only time could tell, but it was clear to Kennan that containing Communism was not essentially a military matter. The patience and strength and other virtues he referred to were part of the national character, not the nation's arsenal.

But to his dismay, his readers in the Truman administration transformed the "Doctrine of Containment" into a military strategy hinging on international alliances. Central to this was an arms build-up based on stockpiling atomic weapons and the decision to develop the hydrogen bomb, a decision Kennan would at least have deferred until the issue of whether we would ever use this weapon on a first strike basis had been resolved.

This issue and the concurrent loss of influence of the Policy Planning Staff under newly appointed Secretary of State Dean G. Acheson built sufficient frustration in Kennan to cause him to secure a temporary leave of absence. He joined the Institute for Advanced Study at Princeton.

During the next four decades Kennan became one of America's greatest scholars, capturing two Pulitzer prizes, a Bancroft, a Parkman, and many other honors. Only twice did he venture out of academe. He served for six months as ambassador to the Soviet Union at Secretary Acheson's request in 1952 but was ousted by the Russians for what they took to be criticism of their regime. In 1961 President John F. Kennedy appointed him ambassador to Yugoslavia, a post he held for two years.

A Legacy of First-Class Histories

His writings are models of literary elegance and relentlessly exact scholarship. *American Diplomacy,* his first effort, appeared in 1950, sketching the development of a national foreign policy from 1898 to the early days of the Cold War. Volume after volume followed, sometimes on contemporary issues, such as *Realities of American Foreign Policy* (1954), *Russia, the Atom and the West* (1958), or *The Nuclear Delusion* (1976). These were usually built out of lectures he had given and were invariably and uniformly instructive.

But his writings on Russian history took the prizes for their pith and insight. *Russia Leaves the War* (1956), *The Decision To Intervene* (1958), and *Russia and the West Under Lenin and Stalin* (1961) established him as the nation's foremost kremlinologist. To these must be added *The Marquis de Custine and His Russia in 1839* (1971) and *The Decline of Bismarck's European Order* (1979), the latter a study of Franco-Russian relations before World War I.

His *Memoirs 1925-1950* are in a class by themselves, revealing a gentle man whose fiercely held convictions never overruled his basic civility and integrity. They also show that Kennan was often decades ahead of others in his thinking. He understood Communist paranoia before most Americans were aware of the Russian menace. And he became convinced that nuclear war was unthinkable almost before it was possible.

He owned a 235-acre farm in Pennsylvania on which the family worked on weekends in what was an apparent effort to continue the "Pioneer farmer" line for one more generation. Into his nineties he continued to write forcefully and innovatively. A *Foreign Affairs* article published in 1986 under the title "Morality and Foreign Policy" drew together his interest in Russia, his horror of nuclear war, and his attachment to the soil. The twin "apocalyptic dangers" of our time, he wrote, are war among nuclear-armed industrial nations and man's disturbing habit of fouling his environment. He published two books in the 1990s. The first, *Around the Cragged Hill: A Personal and Political Philosophy* (1993), discusses both U.S. foreign and domestic policies and Kennan shares thoughts on each. He also comments on various aspects of society, including computers and automobiles and their relative merits and evils. The second, *At A Century's Ending: Reflections, 1982-1995* (1996), is a collection of his essays and speeches from those years.

Further Reading

Memoirs 1925-1950 by Kennan; "The Great Foreign Policy Fight," by Gregg Herken, *American Heritage* (April, May 1986) offers great insight into Kennan's ideas and details his career well; also Barton Gellman's *Contending with Kennan* (1984); Walter Isaacson and Evan Thomas included Kennan as one of *The Wise Men: Six Friends and the World They Made* (1986) in this study of the years immediately after World War II.

Kennan's own works include *Around the Cragged Hill; A Personal And Political Philosophy* (1993); and *At A Century's Ending: Reflections, 1982-1995* (1996). □

Anthony M. Kennedy

U.S. Supreme Court Justice Anthony M. Kennedy (born 1936) was appointed by Ronald Reagan in 1988. His votes generally tipped the balance in favor of conservative decisions.

Anthony M. Kennedy, who was named to the United States Supreme Court after President Ronald Reagan's first two nominations for Justice Lewis Powell's seat were unsuccessful, was born on July 23, 1936, in Sacramento, California. He reportedly experienced a remarkably trouble-free boyhood that included regular service as an altar boy at his Roman Catholic parish church. In fact, Kennedy used to joke with his young friends that his father in a fit of affectionate despair had offered to pay him $100 if just once he would do something requiring his parents to come pick him up at the local police station! The youngster never collected on the dare.

An honor roll student at McClatchy High School in Sacramento, Kennedy always assumed that he would attend Stanford University like his mother and become a lawyer like his father. Indeed, Kennedy was to follow in his parents' footsteps. As an undergraduate, the future justice continued his outstanding academic career. He was particularly captivated by constitutional law, and his professor for that class described him as "brilliant." Kennedy completed his graduation requirements in three years, but his father ap-

parently thought his son was too young to enroll immediately in law school, so young Kennedy spent a year at the London School of Economics. Upon his return in 1958, he received his B.A. degree from Stanford, where he was elected to Phi Beta Kappa. He then attended Harvard Law School, from which he obtained his LL.B. degree, *cum laude,* in 1961.

Becomes Expert on Constitutional Law

Kennedy began his practice of law in the prestigious San Francisco firm of Thelen, Marrin, John & Bridges, but within two years he was back in Sacramento to assume the law practice of his father, who had died suddenly of a heart attack in 1963. Described as an "intellectual," Kennedy seemingly disliked the flesh-pressing required of lobbying work in the state capital. Eventually, he found an outlet for his more academic interest in the law when the dean of the McGeorge School of Law of the University of the Pacific offered him a part-time teaching position. Just as in his student days, he thrived in the classroom and would often amaze his own students by lecturing for three hours on constitutional law without referring to a note.

Like his father before him, Kennedy was a Republican, if not a particularly active one. Nevertheless, in the early 1970s he was asked to serve on a commission to draft a tax-limitation initiative known as Proposition 1 for Ronald Reagan, then the governor of California. Although the ballot proposition failed in 1973, Kennedy had impressed the Reagan camp with his constitutional expertise. When an opening became available on the U.S. Court of Appeals for the Ninth Circuit in 1975, President Gerald Ford was persuaded to appoint Kennedy to the circuit bench, making the 38-year-old Californian one of the youngest appellate justices in the nation's history.

"Unknown" Philosophy Leads to High Court

Significantly for the ideological fallout over the abortive nomination of Judge Robert Bork in 1987, Kennedy was described as a moderate conservative cast in the Gerald Ford, rather than in the Barry Goldwater, mold. Liberals were quick to label Kennedy "open-minded" in contrast to the "reactionary" Bork. Yet the more accurate picture of Kennedy's ideology in contrast to Bork's was not that it was less conservative but that it was virtually unidentifiable. The 430 opinions that Kennedy had drafted in his tenure on the Ninth Circuit did not reveal a clear jurisprudential posture on such controversial issues as civil rights, women's rights, and the issue which was Bork's downfall, the right to privacy. Unlike Bork's academic penchant for writing and speaking, Kennedy had left no paper trail of law review articles and speeches.

Thus, Kennedy's personal integrity, his judicial experience, and his less dogmatic ideology made him the perfect candidate to fill Justice Powell's "swing" seat on the Supreme Court after the turmoil surrounding the Senate's defeat of Bork in October 1987 and the withdrawal of Judge Douglas Ginsburg's nomination several weeks later when it was disclosed that he had used marijuana both as a student and as a law professor. After a seven-month ordeal to fill the Court's ninth seat, the Senate voted unanimously (97:0) on February 3, 1988, to confirm the Kennedy nomination. At the age of 51, Kennedy became the Court's youngest member.

Kennedy's early years on the high court by no means offered a definitive portrait of his Supreme Court jurisprudence, but his initial votes and opinions began to reveal identifiable trends. As occupied by Justice Kennedy, the Court's swing seat, which Justice Powell had captured for the moderate center, no longer functioned as a vote that balanced the liberal and conservative blocs by siding with one or the other from case to case. Instead, Kennedy's vote became a tie-breaker that consistently tipped the balance in favor of the conservatives.

Conservative Voting Record

In the abortion realm, for example, Kennedy voted with the 5:4 majority to allow states the right to impose substantial new restrictions on abortion (*Webster* v. *Reproductive Health Services* [1989]). Kennedy also arrived at a conservative result on the matter of the right to privacy vis-à-vis the drug-testing issue. In *Skinner* v. *Railway Labor Executives* (1989) and *National Treasury Employees* v. *Von Raab* (1989), he wrote both majority opinions for the Court's constitutional sanction of the federal government's efforts to create a drug-free workplace.

It is in the area of affirmative action, however, that Justice Kennedy's vote began to distinguish him most fundamentally from Justice Powell. In early 1989 Kennedy voted with the 6:3 majority in invalidating a *local* set-aside law in Richmond, Virginia, that channeled 30 percent of public works funds to minority-owned construction companies (*City of Richmond* v. *J.A. Croson Co.*). He also cast his vote with the narrow 5:4 majority that ruled that court-approved affirmative action settlements may subsequently be challenged by disappointed white workers (*Martin* v. *Wilks* [1989]). The Court reached an equally conservative result, with Kennedy casting a fifth vote for the majority, in *Wards Cove Packing* v. *Atonio* (1989), which ruled that employee discrimination claims based on a statistical showing of underutilization of women or minorities must prove that the policies they are challenging cannot be justified as necessary to the employer's business.

Kennedy's most notable contribution to the Court's more conservative tack in employment discrimination cases was his majority opinion in *Patterson* v. *McLean Credit Union* (1989), which upheld the use of the 1866 Civil Rights Act for claims of discrimination at the initial hiring stage, but barred use of the statute for claims of on-the-job bias.

In church-state matters Kennedy revealed an accommodationist stance, particularly in simultaneous rulings on Christmas-season displays sponsored by city and county governments in Pittsburgh. He dissented from a decision declaring that a Nativity scene, unaccompanied by any more secular symbols of the season, amounted to an unconstitutional endorsement of the Christian faith. He found himself in the majority, however, when the Court permitted a Hanukkah menorah to be displayed next to a Christmas

tree (*Allegheny County* v. *Greater Pittsburgh A.C.L.U.* [*1989*]).

Another First Amendment case, this time in the free speech realm, found Kennedy uncharacteristically joining in a liberal decision which declared that burning the American flag as a political protest is a form of protected symbolic speech (*Texas* v. *Johnson* [1989]). Despite his vote in the controversial flag-burning case, Kennedy seemed to be clinging to a cautious conservatism bolstered by a professed adherence to judicial restraint.

According to the *New Yorker* (November 11, 1996), "Kennedy has disappointed conservatives by upholding liberal precedents on the crucial social issues of abortion, flag-burning, gay rights and school prayer.." A writer for (*n*= "1"]*Washingtonian* December 1996) magazine noted that Kennedy and fellow justice Sandra Day O'Connor have become an "important tandem" because of their unpredictability. A critic retorted that Kennedy and O'Connor "should really be thrown to the alligators." (*National Review* June 17, 1996). But others state he is doing what he was appointed to do, as "he refuses to impose his personal views on the nation." (*New Yorker* November 11, 1996).

Kennedy married Mary Davis on June 29, 1963, and was the father of two sons and a daughter.

Further Reading

A short biographical sketch may be found in the Congressional Quarterly *Guide to the U.S. Supreme Court,* 2d edition (1990). An informative analysis of Kennedy also appeared in the *New York Times* (November 12, 1987). The Senate Judiciary Committee's report of the hearings on Kennedy's Supreme Court nomination provided a wealth of material (100th Cong., 1st sess.).

See also *New Republic* (June 10, 1996); *National Review* (June 17, 1996); *New Yorker* (November 11, 1996); *Washingtonian* (December 1996); and *U.S. News & World Report* (July 7, 1997). □

Edward M. Kennedy

Edward M. Kennedy (born 1932), youngest brother of President John F. Kennedy and Robert F. Kennedy, entered the U.S. Senate at age 30 and steadily gained influence as he continued to win re-election. Largely because of the glamorous "Kennedy legacy," he was considered a potential Democratic presidential nominee starting in 1968.

Edward M. Kennedy was born February 22, 1932, fourth son and last of nine children of Joseph P. and Rose Fitzgerald Kennedy. Because of his wealthy family's frequent shuttling among Boston, New York, and Palm Beach (and—while his father was ambassador to London—England), Kennedy attended several different private schools before enrolling in Milton Academy in 1946. Upon graduation from Milton in 1950 he enrolled at Harvard—

like his older brothers before him. At the end of his freshman year, however, he was expelled for having another student take a Spanish final examination in his stead. Kennedy then enlisted for a two-year stint in the army. Perhaps the advantage of his father's influence won him assignment to SHAPE (Supreme Headquarters Allied Powers, Europe) headquarters in Paris.

Preparation for Public Service

After his discharge Kennedy returned to Harvard, graduating in 1956. He then enrolled in the University of Virginia Law School, where his talent for debate, always apparent, was sharpened. He received his law degree in 1959 and was admitted to the Massachusetts bar in the same year. In November 1958 Kennedy married Virginia Joan Bennett. Together they had three children: Kara Anne; Edward M., Junior; and Patrick Joseph.

While still a law student Edward Kennedy managed the successful Senate re-election campaign in Massachusetts of his brother John (JFK). Then, in 1960 he served as Western states coordinator for JFK's campaign for the Democratic presidential nomination. After his brother's victory in the 1960 election, Edward took a position (on a "dollar-a-year" basis) as assistant to the Suffolk County (Massachusetts) district attorney. As preparation for running in 1962 for the remainder of JFK's unexpired Senate term, Edward traveled widely and filled numerous speaking engagements.

Becoming a National Figure

At the minimum age (30), Kennedy easily won election to the Senate in 1962 over Republican George Lodge after winning a bruising primary against the nephew of U.S. House Speaker John W. McCormack. Kennedy's slogan was: "I can do more for Massachusetts." As a junior legislator, Kennedy deferred to his Senate seniors, surprising some observers who expected greater aggressiveness. A year after JFK's 1963 assassination, Edward won election to his first full Senate term with 74.4 percent of the vote. He won despite (or perhaps partially because of) suffering a critical back injury in a plane crash in June which incapacitated him throughout the campaign.

Also elected to the Senate in 1964 (in New York) was Edward Kennedy's only surviving brother, Robert. Though he was Robert's senior in the Senate, Edward remained—partially by choice—in the former's shadow during the mid-1960s. But in 1965 he scored his first major legislative victory, leading the fight for passage of the Immigration and Nationality Act, which ended the national origins quota system.

Kennedy began to speak out against the Vietnam War by 1967, focusing mainly on the need for draft reform and the U.S. failure to provide for the Vietnamese war victims. After visiting South Vietnam in early 1968 he became more critical, yet managed to stay on good terms with the administration of President Lyndon Johnson.

Kennedy's life was strongly affected by his brother Robert's assassination in June 1968. After a period of withdrawal, he became more strident in denouncing the Vietnam War and in pressing for selected social reforms. Though he resisted efforts to draft him for the 1968 Democratic nomination (which went to Hubert Humphrey), his actions clearly established him as heir to the "Kennedy legacy."

Perennial Presidential Possibility

The year 1969 began well for Kennedy, with his election as Senate majority whip in January. Six months later, however, his career suffered a devastating—some thought fatal—blow when, following a party he drove his car off a narrow bridge on Chappaquiddick Island, resulting in the drowning of his companion, Mary Jo Kopechne. Kennedy's failure to report the accident for nearly nine hours was harshly condemned by press and public alike. In a televised speech a week later he asked the voters to advise him as to whether he should remain in office. The response was positive, as was the local court's verdict: Kennedy's sentence—for leaving the scene of an accident—was suspended.

Chappaquiddick provided grist for several pot-boiling books and posed a lasting threat to Kennedy's presidential hopes, but it did not hamper him in the Senate. He energetically opposed Nixon's ABM (anti-ballistic missile) deployment proposal, backed various measures to end the Vietnam War, and led the fight for the 18-year-old vote. After winning easy re-election in 1970, however, Kennedy lost his majority whip post to Senator Robert Byrd by a close vote in 1971. Freed from the constraints of his formal leadership post, he resumed more energetically than ever his outspoken opposition to the Nixon administration. Suspected of harboring hopes for the 1972 Democratic presidential nomination, he again renounced any such ambitions. He did not attend the convention and refused nominee George McGovern's offer of the vice-presidential nomination.

In the 1970s Kennedy became closely identified with the issues of handgun control and compulsory national health insurance (his 1972 book, *In Critical Condition,* was a sweeping indictment of the U.S. health care industry). He also took strong positions favoring bussing for racial balance, amnesty for Vietnam-era draft evaders, and the right of women to receive federal assistance for abortions. He was well aware that his views were controversial, once remarking that he would "love to campaign against" his record.

Kennedy dispelled the inevitable rumors of his availability for the presidency in 1976, announcing in late 1974 that he would not run—despite his commanding position in the early polls. Running instead for re-election to the Senate in 1976, he won with an impressive 70 percent of the vote. Now one of the Senate's most powerful figures, Kennedy became chairman of the Judiciary Committee and pushed for airline deregulation, no-fault insurance, and consumer-oriented modifications in the anti-trust laws. He loyally backed Democratic President Jimmy Carter's foreign policy initiatives, including normalization of U.S.-China relations and the Panama Canal treaties.

Though Kennedy disavowed interest in the 1980 presidential nomination during the early part of Carter's term, he again emerged as the favorite in public opinion polls. Finally yielding to temptation, he announced in November 1979 that he would challenge Carter for the nomination. His candidacy began miserably, however, when he performed poorly in a televised interview (which revived the "Chappaquiddick issue"); also the Iranian hostage crisis and Russian invasion of Afghanistan increased public support for incumbent Carter, at least temporarily. Kennedy lost important early caucus contests and primaries to Carter, fatally damaging his "winner's" mystique. Well before the convention, Carter's nomination was assured. Kennedy, however, dominated the convention itself with one of his most stirring speeches.

A Leader on National Issues

When the Republicans gained control of the Senate in 1981, Kennedy lost his Judiciary Committee chairmanship and once again focussed his energies primarily on social programs and labor issues. Rising to seventh in Democratic seniority in the Senate after his fourth re-election in 1982 (with 60 percent of the vote), Kennedy emerged as an influential and constant critic of Ronald Reagan's domestic and foreign policies, opposing "supply-side" economic measures, U.S. aid to rightist forces in Central America, and proposals to bar federal courts from requiring bussing in local school districts.

In late 1982 Kennedy removed himself from contention for his party's presidential nomination. By mid-decade, he was still only in his fifties. Despite the break-up of his marriage of nearly 25 years and the lingering stigma of Chappaquiddick, he retained his high standing in public opinion polls. Heir to a glamorous political tradition, committed to an expanded federal role in pursuit of social and economic justice, yet clearly capable of pragmatic trimming when necessary.

Kennedy has proven himself a staunch proponent of national health insurance and tax reform. He co-sponsored the Kassebaum-Kennedy bill making health insurance available to people who change jobs and/or have pre-existing health conditions. Kennedy and Senator Orrin Hatch proposed to raise the cigarette tax to expand the availability of health insurance for children. The bill, introduced April 8, 1997, was defeated by a close margin on May 21, 1997.

Kennedy's son, Patrick Kennedy, is an assistant secretary of state in the Clinton administration.

Further Reading

James McGregor Burns, *Edward Kennedy and the Camelot Legacy* (1976), is the most thorough biographical treatment of the youngest Kennedy; David Burner and Thomas R. West, in *The Torch Is Passed: The Kennedy Brothers and American Liberalism* (1984), give substantial attention to Edward in the context of the political tradition established by his elder brothers; other useful sources include: Theo Lippman, *Senator Ted Kennedy* (1970); William Honan, *Ted Kennedy: Profile of a Survivor* (1972); Burton Hersh, *The Education of Edward Kennedy: A Family Biography* (1972); and Murray Levin and T. A. Repak, *Edward Kennedy: The Myth of Leadership* (1980); "What Democrats should fight for" by Edward M. Kennedy in *Vital Speeches of the Day,* vol. 61, no. 8, February 1, 1995; and "Happy Birthday Teddy" by Martin F. Nolan in *Washingtonian,* vol. 32, no. 5, February 1997, pp. 54-57; Critical assessments focussing on the Chappaquiddick incident include Jack Olsen, *The Bridge at Chappaquiddick* (1970) and Robert Sherrill, *The Last Kennedy* (1976); Kennedy himself has written *Decisions for a Decade: Policies and Programs for the 1970s* (1968) and *In Critical Condition: The Crisis in America's Health Care* (1972). ▫

John Fitzgerald Kennedy

John Fitzgerald Kennedy (1917-1963) served in both houses of Congress before becoming the thirty-fifth president of the United States. His assassination shocked the world.

John F. Kennedy once summed up his time as "very dangerous, untidy." He was the child of two world wars, of the Great Depression, and of the nuclear age. "Life is unfair," he remarked. And so it was to Kennedy, heaping him with glory, burdening him with tragedy. Yet, he never lost his grace, his sense of balance, or his indomitable gaiety.

Kennedy was born in Brookline, Mass., on May 29, 1917. He was the second son of business executive and financier Joseph P. Kennedy and Rose Fitzgerald Kennedy. His great-grandfather had emigrated in 1850 from Ireland to

Boston, where he worked as a cooper. His paternal grandfather had served in the Massachusetts Legislature and in elective offices in Boston. Kennedy's maternal grandfather, John Francis Fitzgerald, had been a state legislator, mayor of Boston, and U.S. congressman. Kennedy's father served as ambassador to Great Britain (1937-1940), having been chairman of the Securities and Exchange Commission and of the U.S. Maritime Commission. Thus Kennedy was born into a wealthy family oriented toward politics and public service.

Education and Youth

Kennedy attended the Canterbury parochial school (1930-1931), completing his preparatory education at the Choate School (1931-1935). He enrolled at Princeton University in 1935, but illness soon forced him to withdraw. Upon recovery he went to Harvard University. During his junior year he traveled in Europe, observing the political tensions that were leading to World War II. He was gathering materials for his senior thesis, which, reflecting some of the isolationist views of his father, later became the best-selling book *Why England Slept* (1940).

After graduating from Harvard *cum laude* with a bachelor of science degree in 1940, Kennedy enrolled at Stanford University for graduate studies. In April 1941 he tried to enlist in the U.S. Army but was rejected for physical reasons (a back injury received while playing football). Months later, his back strengthened through a regimen of exercises, the Navy accepted him. He became an intelligence officer with the rank of lieutenant junior grade in Washington, D.C.

After the Japanese attack on Pearl Harbor he requested active duty at sea; this assignment was not granted until late in 1942.

War Hero

Following his training with the Motor Torpedo Boat Squadron, Kennedy was shipped to the South Pacific into the war against Japan. In March 1943 he received command of a PT boat. That August, when his boat was sliced in two by a Japanese destroyer, two of his crew were killed, while Kennedy and four others clung to the half of the PT boat that remained afloat. Six other men survived in the nearby water, two wounded. In a 3-hour struggle Kennedy got the wounded crewmen to the floating hulk. When it capsized, he ordered his men to swim to a small island about 3 miles away, while he towed one man to shore in a heroic 5-hour struggle. Several days later, having displayed exceptional qualities of courage, leadership, and endurance, Kennedy succeeded in having his men rescued.

Kennedy did not see further action, for he suffered an attack of malaria and aggravation of his back injury. In December he returned to the United States. After a hospital stay he became a PT instructor in Florida, until he was hospitalized again. He was retired from the service in the rank of full lieutenant in March 1945, having undergone a disk operation. Returning to civilian life, Kennedy did newspaper work for several months, covering the United Nations Conference on International Organization in San Francisco, the Potsdam Conference, and the British elections of 1945.

House of Representatives

However, Kennedy desired a political career. In 1946 he became a candidate for the U.S. House of Representatives from the Massachusetts eleventh congressional district. Realizing that, despite his family's background in Democratic politics, he was unknown to the district's electorate, Kennedy built a large personal organization for his campaign. On whirlwind tours he met as many voters as possible, addressing them in a direct, informal style on timely topics. In this campaign, as in all the others, his brothers, sisters, and mother supported him. His brothers, Robert and Ted, acted as his managers, while his sisters and mother held social events.

Kennedy was a driven man. "The Kennedys were all puppets in the hands of the old man," Washington newspaperman Arthur Krock once observed. "I got Jack into politics," his father said, although he admitted that neither he nor his wife could picture their son as a politician. "I told him Joe [the oldest brother, who died a hero in World War II] was dead . . . and I told him he had to." Kennedy fell heir to the political know-how of his grandfather, the legendary "Honey Fitz," who had charmed and utilized the tough Boston Irish electorate. Meanwhile, Kennedy climbed more stairs and shook more hands and worked harder than the 10 other contenders for the candidacy combined.

Kennedy won the primary, the fall election, and reelection to the House in 1948 and in 1950. He kept his campaign pledges to work for broader social welfare programs, particularly in the area of low-cost public housing. Kennedy was a staunch friend of labor. In 1949 he became a member of the Joint Committee on Labor-Management Relations. He battled unsuccessfully against the Taft-Hartley Bill and later supported bills that sought to modify its restrictive provisions. Although Kennedy supported President Harry Truman's social welfare programs, progressive taxation, and regulation of business, he did not follow administration policies in foreign relations. He opposed the fighting in Korea "or any other place in Asia where we cannot hold our defenses."

In 1951 Kennedy spent 6 weeks traveling in Great Britain, France, Italy, Spain, Yugoslavia, and West Germany. On his return he advised the Senate Committee on Foreign Relations that he believed defending Western Europe was strategically important to the United States but that he felt Western Europeans should do more on their own behalf and not rely so strongly on the United States. That autumn he traveled around the world. His visits to the Middle East, India, Pakistan, Indochina, Malaya, and Korea caused him to reverse a previous position and support Point Four aid for the Middle East. He also urged that France get out of Algeria.

The Senate

In April 1952 Kennedy announced his candidacy for the U.S. Senate, running against the strongly entrenched Henry Cabot Lodge, Jr., a Republican liberal. Kennedy won by over 70,000 votes. Lodge reeled under the impact: "those damned tea-parties," he said. He had not run against a man, but a family—the Kennedy women having acted as hostesses to at least 70,000 Massachusetts housewives. In 1958 Kennedy was reelected.

On Sept. 12, 1953, Kennedy married Jacqueline Lee Bouvier, daughter of a New York City financier, at Newport, R. I. Arthur M. Schlesinger, Jr., noted of Mrs. Kennedy that "under a veil of lovely inconsequence" she possessed "an all-seeing eye and ruthless judgment." Four children were born, of whom two survived infancy: Caroline Bouvier and John Fitzgerald.

Taking his seat in the Senate in January 1953, Kennedy served on the Labor and Public Welfare Committee, the Government Operations Committee, the Select Committee on Labor-Management Relations, the Foreign Relations Committee, and the Joint Economic Committee. He secured passage of several bills to aid the Massachusetts fishing and textile industries and fought to ameliorate New England's economic problems. In 1954 he voted to extend the president's powers under the reciprocal trade program.

A recurrence of his old back injuries forced Kennedy to use crutches during 1954. An operation in October was followed by another in February 1955. He spent his months of illness and recuperation writing biographical profiles of Americans who had exercised moral courage at crisis points in their lives. *Profiles in Courage* (1956), a best seller, won the Pulitzer Prize for biography in 1957.

Kennedy's back operations were not completely successful, and he was never again entirely free from pain. He resumed his senatorial duties in May 1955. During the next years he opposed reform in the electoral college, favored

American aid to help India stabilize its economy, and became a strong advocate of civil rights legislation. Social welfare legislation was of primary concern. The Kennedy-Douglas-Ives Bill (1957) required full disclosure and accounting of all employee pension and welfare funds. The Kennedy-Byrd-Payne Bill was a budgeting and accounting bill that placed the financial structure of the government on an annual accrued expenditure basis. Kennedy also sponsored bills for providing Federal financial aid to education and for relaxing United States immigration laws.

Campaign for the Presidency

Kennedy's record in Congress, together with his thoughtful books and articles, had attracted national attention. At the Democratic National Convention in Chicago in 1956, when presidential nominee Adlai E. Stevenson left the choice of his running mate open, Kennedy was narrowly defeated by Estes Kefauver. From then on, however, Kennedy was running for the presidency. He began building a personal national organization. Formally announcing his candidacy in January 1960, Kennedy made whirlwind tours and won the Democratic primaries in New Hampshire, Wisconsin, Indiana, Ohio, Oregon, Maryland, and Nebraska, plus an upset victory over Hubert Humphrey in West Virginia. On July 13, 1960, Kennedy was nominated on the first ballot, with Lyndon B. Johnson as his running mate.

"Jack In Walk" shouted the *Boston Globe* after Kennedy gained the nomination. But it would be no walk to the White House against the Republican candidate, Richard Nixon. Kennedy's candidacy was controversial because he was a Roman Catholic; religious prejudice probably cost him a million votes in Illinois alone. But his "Houston speech" on Sept. 11, 1960, met the religious issue head on. He believed in the absolute separation of church and state, he said, in which no priest could tell a president what to do and in which no Protestant clergyman could tell his parishioners how to vote.

A series of televised debates with Nixon was crucial. Kennedy "clobbered" the Republican leader with his "style." Skeptical and laconic, careless and purposeful, Kennedy displayed wit, love of language, and a sense of the past. On November 9 Kennedy became the youngest man in American history to win the presidency and the only Roman Catholic to do so. The election was one of the closest in the nation's history; his popular margin was only 119,450 votes. On December 19 the electoral college cast 303 votes for Kennedy and 219 for Nixon.

The Presidency

The inauguration on Jan. 20, 1960, of the first president born in the 20th century had a quality of pageant, as the old poet Robert Frost, the old priest Cardinal Richard Cushing, and the old president Dwight Eisenhower watched the torch being passed to a new generation. Then the challenge of Kennedy's inaugural address rang out: "Ask not what your country can do for you, but rather what you can do for your country." The new "First Family" quickly captured the public imagination: Jacqueline, with her cameo beauty and her passion for excellence; 3-year-old Caroline; and new-born John.

Although happy that he could do something about "the problems that bedeviled us," Kennedy was aware that his razor-thin victory had narrowed his options. Congress was unyielding—it had seen presidents come and go, and it distrusted Kennedy's youth and wit and gaiety. Kennedy was never able to "escape the congressional arithmetic." Unlike his successor, Lyndon B. Johnson, Kennedy had no past political favors to draw upon. Therefore, most of his program—tax reform, civil rights, a Medicare system, and the establishment of a department of urban affairs—bogged down in Congress. Ironically, his education bill was defeated largely through the efforts of the Roman Catholic hierarchy.

The Cuban invasion burst over the Kennedy administration like a bombshell in April 1961. On April 17 it became known that 1,400 exiled Cubans had invaded Cuba's Las Villas Province and had penetrated 10 miles inland. On April 18 Soviet premier Nikita Khrushchev sent a note to Kennedy stating that his government was prepared to come to the aid of the Cuban government to help it resist armed attack. By April 20 the invasion was clearly a failure. Who was responsible for American involvement in this shabby operation? Kennedy shouldered the responsibility for the fiasco, but his biographers have since noted that "Operation Pluto," committing the Central Intelligence Agency (CIA) to train Cuban guerrillas, was a project of Dwight D. Eisenhower's administration. Kennedy, initially overawed by the CIA and the joint chiefs of staff, in the end refused to commit the necessary American troops. He was aware that if the Cuban people did not rise up and back the invaders, the United States could not impose a regime on them. Furthermore, he was apprehensive that if America moved in Cuba the Soviet Union might move in Berlin. The Bay of Pigs fiasco proved Kennedy's ability to face disaster. When it was over, he was "effectively in control."

Kennedy rapidly learned the great limitations on a president's ability to solve problems. He wanted the United States to reexamine its attitude toward the Soviet Union, and he wanted to act upon both nations' mutual "abhorrence of war." His separate meetings with Gen. Charles De Gaulle, the president of France, and Khrushchev in the spring of 1961 were social triumphs but political defeats. Kennedy failed to dissuade De Gaulle from pulling France out of the North Atlantic Treaty Alliance, and he could reach no agreement with the Soviet chief on the status of Berlin. He did voice to Khrushchev, however, America's determination to stay in Berlin. Each threatened to meet force with force. In August the Berlin crisis exploded. The East Germans tightened border curbs and erected a wall of concrete blocks along most of the 25-mile border between East Berlin and West Berlin. Kennedy unequivocally stated that the United States would not abandon West Berlin.

Kennedy's civil rights bills bogged down in Congress. Civil rights was the President's foremost domestic concern. When the showdown came, "the Kennedys," as the President and his brother Robert, the attorney general, shamed southern governors. They sent 600 Federal marshals to Ala-

bama in 1961 to protect the "Freedom Riders." In 1962 they forced Mississippi's governor, Ross Barnett, to send his troopers back to the state university, while dispatching hundreds of Federal marshals into an all-night battle to protect the right of one African American student to attend the university.

Kennedy appealed by television to the conscience of the nation. "We are confronted with a moral issue. It is as old as the Scriptures and it is as clear as the American Constitution." He called upon the American people to exhibit a sense of fairness. The political costs were high because Kennedy already had the African American vote.

Nuclear Confrontation

On Oct. 22, 1962, Kennedy addressed the nation on a grave matter. The Soviet Union, he said, had deployed nuclear missiles in Cuba, and the United States had declared a quarantine on all shipments of offensive military equipment into Cuba. The United States would not allow Cuba to become a Soviet missile base, and it would regard any missile launched from Cuba "as an attack by the Soviet Union on the United States, requiring a full retaliatory response."

This direct confrontation was brinkmanship. For a week the details had been "the best kept secret in government history." Through 7 days of gripping tension and soul-searching, the administration had maintained a facade of normal social and political activities. Meanwhile, American military units throughout the world were alerted.

As messages went back and forth between Kennedy, Khrushchev, and Pope John, who volunteered his aid as peacemaker, Soviet ships were moving toward Kennedy's invisible line in the Atlantic. Would they stop? They slowed, then stopped, and on October 28 the news came that the Soviet Union would remove its missiles from Cuba. For a time Kennedy seemed at least 10 feet tall, but his own wry comment on the crisis was, "Nobody wants to go through what we went through in Cuba very often."

Out of this confrontation came the greatest single triumph of the Kennedy administration: the nuclear testban treaty with the Soviet Union. Kennedy called this treaty "the first step down the path of peace." Before negotiations for the treaty were completed, Khrushchev had defiantly reopened the nuclear race. Kennedy, however, held firm, and the treaty was signed on July 25, 1963. "Yesterday a shaft of light cut into the darkness," Kennedy said. A "hot line" for emergency messages was also established between Washington, D.C., and Moscow.

Vietnam Commitments

According to Kennedy's biographer Arthur M. Schlesinger, Jr., Vietnam "was his great failure." Certainly it consumed more of his time than any other problem. Kennedy had inherited the commitment, but he stepped up the conflict, despite his assertion that "full-scale war in Vietnam . . . was unthinkable." Kennedy had opposed the French military operations in Algeria and was aware of Gen. Douglas MacArthur's and Eisenhower's warnings against a land war in Asia. Yet he tripled American forces in Vietnam at a time when South Vietnamese troops greatly outnumbered the enemy. Why? Senator William Fulbright has suggested that Kennedy put troops in Vietnam to prove to Khrushchev that "he couldn't be intimidated."

Kennedy was well aware of the dangers of the presidency. One of his favorite poems was "I Have a Rendezvous with Death," and he had always been haunted by the poignancy of those who die young. "Who can tell who will be president a year from now?" he would ask. On the fatal day of his arrival in Dallas, Tex., he remarked that if anyone wanted to kill a president he needed only a high building and a rifle with a telescopic lens.

That day—Nov. 22, 1963—Kennedy was assassinated by a lone sharpshooter, Lee Harvey Oswald, who fired on Kennedy's motorcade with a rifle equipped with a telescopic lens. Within hours, that "live, electric" figure was dead. Gone was all that brilliance and wit and purpose. In Indonesia, flags were lowered to half-mast; in New Delhi, India, crowds wept in the streets; in Washington, D.C., "grief was an agony."

His Legacy

Kennedy was the first president to face a nuclear confrontation; the first to literally reach for the moon, through the nation's space programs; the first in half a century to call a White House conference on conservation; the first to give the arts a prominent place in American national councils; the first since Theodore Roosevelt with whom youth could identify. He made the nation see itself with new eyes.

Yet his most cherished dreams foundered without the influence of his inspiration and guiding hand. The Alliance for Progress, his program to revitalize life throughout the poor nations of South America, disintegrated—Latin American leaders were simply not committed to democratic change. The youthful idealism of the Peace Corps eroded under the impact of disillusionment and reality. The romantic "Green Berets" degenerated into a cloak-and-dagger outfit.

What Kennedy accomplished was not as important as what he symbolized. He enjoyed unique appeal for the emerging Third World. As the African magazine *Transition* expressed it, murdered with Kennedy was "the first real chance for an intelligent and new leadership in the world. His death leaves us unprepared and in darkness."

Further Reading

Perhaps the most objective, scholarly biographical account of Kennedy is Theodore Sorenson, *Kennedy* (1965), combining the insights of the "insider" with the detachment of the historian. Intimate but more romanticized is Arthur M. Schlesinger, Jr., *A Thousand Days* (1965), winner of a Pulitzer Prize. Useful books by intimates of Kennedy include Evelyn Lincoln, *My Twelve Years with John F. Kennedy* (1965), and Pierre Salinger, *With Kennedy* (1966). The most critical, but well-annotated, study is Victor Lasky, *J. F. K.: The Man and the Myth* (1963). Valuable insights are in the anthology by Donald S. Harrington, *As We Remember Him* (1965), and in Tom Wicker, *JFK and LBJ: The Influence of Personality upon Politics* (1968). Kennedy's election to the presidency is detailed in Arthur M. Schlesinger, Jr., *History of American Presidential*

Elections (4 vols., 1971). Robert Kennedy, *Thirteen Days* (1969), illumines the tensions of the Cuban missile crisis. William Manchester, *The Death of a President* (1967), is the definitive work on the assassination. See also Hugh Sidey, *John F. Kennedy, President* (1963), and Alex Goldman, *John Fitzgerald Kennedy: The World Remembers* (1968). □

John Pendleton Kennedy

John Pendleton Kennedy (1795-1870), a prominent American novelist in his time, served briefly as President Millard Fillmore's secretary of the Navy.

John Pendleton Kennedy was the scion of a cultivated Baltimore, Md., family. He graduated from Baltimore College in 1812 and served for 2 years in the Maryland militia. In 1816 he began practicing law. He disliked the law, however, and by 1829 (thanks to a legacy from a wealthy uncle) was able to withdraw from the courtroom and begin his long literary and public career.

Kennedy contributed sketches and satires to various publications. In 1832 he published his first book, *Swallow Barn,* a series of sketches depicting plantation life in Virginia, written under the pseudonym Mark Littleton. Under the same name he published his most successful novel, *Horse-Shoe Robinson (1835).* In 1838 he not only produced another novel, *Rob of the Bowl,* but was also elected to the U.S. House of Representatives as a Whig. He lost and regained the seat several times. During this period he began to turn from fiction to more overtly political writing.

In 1840 Kennedy's satire on Jacksonian democracy was published. In 1843 his *Defense of the Whigs* attacked John Tyler's defection from party policy on assuming the presidency after the death of William Henry Harrison. Kennedy produced his last important literary effort, a two-volume biography of the great lawyer William Wirt, in 1849.

Kennedy penetrated most deeply into national politics in 1852, when he was appointed secretary of the Navy by President Millard Fillmore. During his 8-month tenure he helped organize Adm. Matthew Perry's expedition to Japan and dispatch the search party trying to find the missing explorer Sir John Franklin and his expedition.

At the outset of the Civil War, Kennedy, who had fought secession on the one hand and republicanism on the other, finally cast his lot with the Union. The genial community of Baltimore gentlemen disintegrated over this question, and Kennedy's last years were lived out in a stern atmosphere. In 1865 he published *Mr. Ambrose's Letters on the Rebellion,* in which he pleaded for compassion toward the fallen South. *Occasional Addresses, Political and Official Papers,* and *At Home and Abroad* (all 1872) were published posthumously.

Further Reading

The "official" biography is Henry T. Tuckerman, *The Life of John Pendleton Kennedy* (1871). A very strong, recent study is Charles H. Bohner, *John Pendleton Kennedy: Gentleman*

1867. During the decade of their partnership the firm dealt with several southern and western developmental railroads.

In 1868 Kennedy opened his own railroad commission merchant and private banking firm, J.S. Kennedy & Co. It combined credit with trade and specialized in the discounting and creation of commercial paper; growth allowed specialization in the banking function. J.S. Kennedy & Co. bought and sold railway bonds and stocks and negotiated loans, drew bills in London, and was a fiscal agent and banker for railroads. Engaging in the process of financing Anglo-American trade and financial intermediation, Kennedy mobilized and funneled the capital of a multitude of American and European investors to promote American economic development. He emerged as an independent entrepreneur just as changes in the railroads, the manufacturers of specific railroad products, and the capital market combined to make the railroad commission merchant obsolescent.

Consequently, he and his competitors gradually shifted from an emphasis on acting as a commission merchant to financing as a private banker. Kennedy had business relations in his own name with southern and western developmental railroads, especially the St. Paul, Minneapolis & Manitoba. Also, he represented both British and American iron manufacturers.

In 1878 Kennedy completed the sale of the two bankrupt St. Paul & Pacific railroads to George Stephen Associates. A year later the property was reorganized as the St. Paul, Minneapolis & Manitoba. This railroad transaction transformed Kennedy from merely rich to one of the most wealthy Americans of his time.

Like other private international banking houses, J.S. Kennedy & Company mobilized and transferred the savings of numerous European investors to the United States. Kennedy participated in 1873 in the launching of the Scottish American Investment Company. Kennedy acted as its New York agent from 1873 to 1883 and for 15 years thereafter remained a member of the advisory board.

During his 15 years as a railroad commission merchant and private international banker, J.S. Kennedy & Co. took large risks, and Kennedy amassed an ever larger personal fortune. J.S. Kennedy & Co. reorganized and supplied railroads. It acted as agent for bankers and railroads, issuing commercial credits and letters of credit and collecting dividends, coupons, and foreign and inland drafts. Kennedy liquidated his firm in 1883, owing to nervous and physical exhaustion.

Kennedy's 1883 "retirement" broadened his role as a financier with diverse interests in leading New York financial intermediaries. Kennedy held the post of president *pro tem* of the Bank of the Manhattan Company, 1883-1884, when he became vice president until he resigned for reasons of health in 1888.

Kennedy also served as a trustee of the Central Trust Company from 1882 until he died. Kennedy held similar positions with the National Bank of Commerce (1887-1909), the New York Life Insurance Company (1903-1906), the Title Guarantee and Trust Company (1895-1909), and

from Baltimore (1961). Joseph V. Ridgely, *John Pendleton Kennedy* (1966), provides a helpful handbook approach. For background see Vernon L. Parrington, *Main Currents in American Thought,* vol. 2 (1927), and Alexander Cowie, *The Rise of the American Novel* (1948). □

John Stewart Kennedy

Although most of his contributions to railroad building, finance, and charity took place in the late 1800s, the works of John Stewart Kennedy (1830-1909) carried well into the 20th century.

John Stewart Kennedy supplied and financed American railroads during the great age of railroad building, becoming James J. Hill's financial intermediary when Hill obtained control of the St. Paul, Minneapolis & Manitoba Railway in 1878. From the early 1880s until his death in 1909 Kennedy was a director of the Bank of the Manhattan Company and other financial institutions.

Born in 1830 near Glasgow, Scotland, Kennedy first visited the United States in 1850 as a representative for an iron firm that sold railroad-related products. On that trip he met his future partner, Morris Ketchum Jesup, a railroad commission merchant and private banker. Kennedy became a significant player in American economic and business history as a partner in M.K. Jesup & Co. from 1857 to the United States Trust Company of New York (1896-1909). As a result of his varied banking activities, Kennedy became a central figure in the history of American banking and in the New York business community.

The scale of Kennedy's bequests dwarfs that of many of his contemporaries with comparable financial resources, perhaps because he had no children. Although the magnitude of his gifts certainly warranted it, by his own choice nothing was ever named after Kennedy to perpetuate his name. Equally important, unlike many contemporary philanthropists, he did much more than merely dole out his millions with an open hand. Instead, Kennedy took an active part in the management of those institutions (the New York Public Library, the Metropolitan Museum of Art, and the Presbyterian Hospital) to which he entrusted his funds, becoming a member of their boards of trustees and an officer. His contributions to New York City and national cultural, social, and civic institutions were consequential. He enriched libraries and universities, hospitals and charities with his money, his presence, and his administrative skill.

Kennedy died in 1909 as one of America's richest men. He accumulated a fortune of $60 million and gave away roughly half this sum in his will to institutions in which he had been involved.

Further Reading

For additional information on Kennedy and his times see Albro Martin, *James J. Hill and the Opening of the Northwest* (1976) and Ralph W. Hidy, Muriel E. Hidy, and Roy V. Scott with Don L. Hofsommer, *The Great Northern Railway: A History* (1988).

Additional Sources

Engelbourg, Saul, *The man who found the money: John Stewart Kennedy and the financing of the the western railroads,* East Lansing: Michigan State University Press, 1996. □

Robert Francis Kennedy

Robert Francis Kennedy (1925-1968), a U.S. senator and the attorney general in the administration of his brother John F. Kennedy, was assassinated during his 1968 race for the Democratic presidential nomination.

Robert Kennedy was born on November 20, 1925, in Brookline, Mass. He graduated from Milton Academy before entering Harvard. His college career was interrupted during World War II; just after his oldest brother, Joseph, was killed in combat, Robert joined the Navy and was commissioned a lieutenant. In 1946 he returned to Harvard and took his bachelor of arts degree in 1948. He earned his law degree from the University of

Virginia Law School and was admitted to the Massachusetts bar in 1951. A year earlier he had married Ethel Shakel, by whom he had 11 children, one born posthumously.

In 1951 Kennedy joined the Criminal Division of the U.S. Department of Justice. He resigned the following year to run John F. Kennedy's successful campaign for U.S. senator. In 1953 Robert was appointed one of 15 assistant counsels to the Senate subcommittee on investigations under Senator Joe McCarthy. But later that year, when Democratic members of this subcommittee walked out in protest against McCarthy's harassing methods of investigation, Kennedy resigned.

Kennedy rejoined the Senate's permanent subcommittee on investigations as chief counsel for the Democratic minority in 1954. The following year, when the Democrats reorganized this committee under Senator George McClellan, Kennedy became chief counsel and staff director. That year the U.S. Junior Chamber of Commerce elected him one of "ten outstanding young men." In 1955, at his own expense, Kennedy joined Supreme Court Justice William O. Douglas on a tour of several Soviet republics.

Kennedy became chief counsel to the Senate Select Committee on Improper Activities in the Labor or Management Field organized under McClellan in 1957, and he directed a staff of 65. His major accomplishment was the investigation of corruption in the International Brotherhood of Teamsters. The hearings became nationally prominent, particularly Kennedy's prosecution of the union's president, James Hoffa, which to some union leaders seemed more

like persecution. Kennedy was responsible for several additional investigations of labor and management abuses.

In 1960 Kennedy managed his brother's successful presidential campaign, and when John as incoming president appointed Robert U.S. attorney general, nationwide cries of nepotism arose. Robert's role in his brother's Cabinet was unique. He was virtually the President's other self. Shoulder to shoulder, the brothers stood together—through the Cuban missile crisis, the civil rights cases, and the growing war in Vietnam.

Soon after President Kennedy's assassination in 1963, Robert resigned from Lyndon Johnson's administration to run successfully for New York State senator in 1964. Naive liberals wondered why he chose to run in New York—thus knocking out a good liberal senator, Kenneth Keating—when he might have opposed Harry Byrd in his resident state of Virginia; but Kennedy was thinking of the presidency by now, and Virginia was no power base. As senator, Kennedy achieved a splendid record.

Kennedy leaped into the presidential sweepstakes in 1968, abruptly following Eugene McCarthy's solitary effort to dramatize the issue of the war in Vietnam. Kennedy's entrance into the Democratic primaries bitterly divided liberal Democrats. By this time Kennedy, who had come to sympathize with the African Americans' drive for ''black power,'' was the joy of radical activists. He could reach and unite young people, revolutionaries, alienated African Americans, and blue-collar Roman Catholics. Meanwhile, the white South hated him; big business distrusted him; and middle-class, reform Democrats were generally suspicious of him.

On the night of June 4, 1968, following a hard-fought, narrow victory in the California primaries, Kennedy was killed by an assassin's bullet. Robert had been no carbon copy of John. In some ways he was more intense, more committed than John had been, yet he shared John's ironic sense of himself and his conviction that one man could make a difference.

Further Reading

There is no definitive study of Kennedy. Good general treatments are William V. Shannon, *The Heir Apparent* (1967), and Jack Newfield, *Robert Kennedy* (1969). See also Nick Thimmesch, *Robert Kennedy at 40* (1965), and William J. Vanden Heuvel and Milton Gwirtzman, *On His Own* (1970). Victor Lasky, *Robert F. Kennedy: The Myth and the Man* (1968), is a hostile account. Valuable insights on him are in books about his brother: Theodore Sorenson's *Kennedy* (1965) and *The Kennedy Legacy* (1969); Arthur M. Schlesinger, Jr., *A Thousand Days* (1965); and Donald S. Harrington, *As We Remember Him* (1965). Dealing with political campaigns are Gerald Gardner, *Robert Kennedy in New York* (1965); David Halberstam, *The Unfinished Odyssey of Robert Kennedy* (1969), an account of his campaign for the presidential nomination; and Jules Witcover, *85 Days: The Last Campaign of Robert Kennedy* (1969). □

Elizabeth Kenny

Elizabeth Kenny (1886-1952) was an Australian nursing sister who pioneered a method of treatment for infantile paralysis. Her determination and persistence helped to focus efforts on finding a cure or a preventive vaccine for polio.

Elizabeth Kenny was born at Warialda in New South Wales, the daughter of an Irish immigrant veterinary surgeon. She trained as a nurse in a private hospital in Sydney, graduating in 1911. After a period of bush nursing in the Queensland Outback, she served during World War I as a nurse to the Australian military forces, caring for the wounded on hospital ships. Her inventive talent emerged during this time, and she patented an improved stretcher for use in the field.

After the war Sister Kenny's attention was attracted to the treatment of poliomyelitis and cerebral palsy. A polio epidemic in Queensland in 1933 led her to concentrate her efforts in that field, and she opened a clinic in Townsville which was granted public recognition and government support the next year. From 1934 to 1937 she helped establish new clinics in Queensland, New South Wales, Victoria, and, after a journey to Britain in 1937, in Surrey.

Sister Kenny's method was in opposition to the current orthodoxy, which generally called for the complete immobilization of polio patients, many of whom were placed in heavy splints. She maintained that the key to the disease lay in the muscular framework of the body rather than in the nervous or spinal systems; and her forcefulness and popularity inevitably made her into something of a cause célèbre. A royal commission was appointed in 1935 to examine her ideas, and when it reported in 1938, the verdict of the commissioners was unfavorable. About the same time in London a committee of medical experts contradicted her theories, although public opinion remained sympathetic.

Sister Kenny arrived in the United States in 1940 and was received enthusiastically. Her lectures in Minneapolis were given much publicity, and in 1941 a medical committee of the National Foundation for Infantile Paralysis declared itself in agreement with her basic practice and approach. She became a guest instructor at the University of Minnesota Medical School in 1942, and the Elizabeth Kenny Institute at Minneapolis was founded. Clinics using her treatment sprang up throughout the United States, and she was showered with degrees and approval.

In 1950 a special act of Congress was passed which enabled Sister Kenny to enter and leave the United States as she wished—a historic honor shared only with the Marquis de Lafayette. Although she claimed that over 85 percent of her more than 7,000 patients at Minneapolis recovered as against 13 percent treated in the more conservative manner, medical opinion remained divided. She had great powers of persuasion and a lively appreciation of the value of publicity. There seems, however, to be little doubt that her courage, tenacity, and independence helped greatly to focus public attention on the problems of polio victims and led to an improvement of facilities available to assist in their therapy and rehabilitation.

Sister Kenny died in Toowoomba, Queensland, on Nov. 30, 1952. Among her books should be noted *Infantile Paralysis and Cerebral Diplegia: Methods Used for the Restoration of Function* (1937) and *The Treatment of Infantile Paralysis in the Acute Stage* (1941).

Further Reading

Sister Kenny's own account of her work and goals are in her *And They Shall Walk* (1943), written with Martha Ostenso, and *The Kenny Concept of Infantile Paralysis and Its Treatment* (1943), written in collaboration with J. F. Pohl. A biography is Maurice Colbeck, *Sister Kenny of the Outback* (1965).

Additional Sources

Cohn, Victor, *Sister Kenny: the woman who challenged the doctors,* Minneapolis: University of Minnesota Press, 1975.
Kenny, Elizabeth, *And they shall walk,* New York: Arno Press, 1980, 1943. □

James Kent

James Kent (1763-1847), influential American jurist, is best known for his *Commentaries on American Law*. He was a leading conservative of his time.

James Kent was born on July 3, 1763, at Fredericksburgh, N.Y. His father was a lawyer and farmer. James entered Yale College in 1777 at the age of 14 and graduated 4 years later with honors. After studying law with a prominent Poughkeepsie, N.Y., attorney, he was admitted to the bar in 1785. In April he married Elizabeth Bailey; it was a most happy marriage and they had four children.

Kent thought that the legal profession would "always enable Gentlemen of active Geniuses to attain a decisive Superiority in Government," and his career showed this concept to be valid. From 1785 to 1793 Kent practiced in Poughkeepsie. He served two consecutive terms in the New York Assembly, starting in 1791. He moved to New York City in 1793, and the following year he was appointed Columbia College's first law professor. After an auspicious start, attendance dropped noticeably, and he resigned in the spring of 1797. Kent was elected to another term in the Assembly in 1796. John Jay, governor of New York, appointed him master in chancery in 1796 and recorder of the city in 1797.

In 1798 Kent was made a justice on the New York Supreme Court, the main function of which was appellate. Kent helped adjust the law to contemporary conditions. His rigorous and systematic work habits set a good example for his fellow judges, and he was responsible for adoption of the practice of writing opinions, which in a short time led to published reports in New York. He was promoted to chief justice in 1804 and remained on the court until 1814, when he was appointed chancellor, a position he held until reaching the mandatory retirement age of 60. As chancellor, Kent

was largely responsible for the creation of equity jurisdiction in the United States.

By a quirk in the constitution of 1777, Kent and his fellow judges reviewed all bills passed by the legislature. Thus he was part of the governing process for 25 years. Kent and other conservative judges incurred the wrath of the majority of the electorate, culminating in the calling of a constitutional convention in 1821. As a delegate, Kent was one of a small but articulate group that fought unsuccessfully against such changes as a sharp reduction in property requirements for voting. The convention reaffirmed the provision that the judiciary retire at 60 and thus guaranteed Kent's retirement.

After Kent retired, he left Albany, where he had resided since 1798, and returned to New York City. In 1824 he began another series of law lectures at Columbia, based on the immense research that had gone into his judicial opinions. This research also provided the basis for *Commentaries on American Law*. For the rest of his life he was constantly revising the book and had just completed the sixth edition when he died on Dec. 12, 1847.

Further Reading

William Kent, *Memoirs and Letters of James Kent* (1898), provides some interesting letters and excerpts from autobiographical sketches. John Theodore Horton, *James Kent: A Study in Conservatism, 1763-1847* (1939), successfully relates Kent's work and thought to his environment. □

Rockwell Kent

The American painter and illustrator Rockwell Kent (1882-1971) fitted into the realist tradition that was a revolutionary force early in the 20th century and then gradually developed a stylized approach to subjects taken from the working class.

Born in Tarrytown Heights, N.Y., on June 21, 1882, Rockwell Kent studied architecture at Columbia University. However, he became a painter, studying with William Merritt Chase, Robert Henri, and others. A socialist from an early age, he apparently saw his work as growing out of a general socialist respect for workers. He was deeply involved in the agitation against the National Academy of Design led by Henri and John Sloan and was an exhibitor in the famous Armory Show of 1913. This was the limit of his commitment to revolutionary art, however, for the workers he idealized in his paintings and drawings were usually outdoorsmen and other solitary types—trappers, fishermen, and other such individualists—rather than the urban, assembly-line workers most often thought of as the subject of socialist concern.

Kent was a remarkable man. Perhaps because of his political beliefs, but probably out of some deeper feeling for reality, he worked at various times in his life as a lobsterman and carpenter along the coast of Maine and as a ship's carpenter. He lived in Alaska, Newfoundland, and Greenland, drawing many of his best-known pictures of the people and their activities there. In a small boat he explored the waters off the southern tip of South America.

Kent wrote and illustrated *Wilderness* (1920) and *Voyaging Southward* (1924), which many critics consider the best American books ever produced in terms of harmonious balance between text and pictures. Along with Fritz Eichenberg, Kent is as responsible as any artist for the high level of American book illustration during the first half of the 20th century. His illustrations, like his paintings, often create a mood of loneliness and a sense of man's small resources against the might of nature. Among the authors he illustrated are Shakespeare, Chaucer, and Herman Melville. He died on March 13, 1971, at the age of 88.

Further Reading

The best source of information on Kent and his art is his own works. In addition to the two mentioned in the text see *Rockwellkentiana*, written in collaboration with Carl Zigrosser (1933); *This Is My Own* (1940); and *It's Me O Lord* (1955), an autobiography. Richard Williamson Ellis, *Book Illustration* (1952), includes a discussion of Kent.

Additional Sources

Kent, Rockwell, *It's me, O Lord: the autobiography of Rockwell Kent*, New York: Da Capo Press, 1977, 1955.
Traxel, David, *An American saga: the life and times of Rockwell Kent*, New York: Harper & Row, 1980. □

Jomo Kenyatta

Jomo Kenyatta (1891-1978) was a Kenyan statesman and the dominant figure in the development of African nationalism in East Africa. His long career in public life made him the undisputed leader of the African people of Kenya in their struggle for independence.

In the modern political history of Africa very few of the representatives of African peoples have had the opportunity for a sustained position of leadership. The lack of a Western education and the limiting horizons of tribal politics hindered the rise of an African political elite, especially in the British East African possessions, in the years before World War II. Kenyatta is one of the outstanding exceptions of this process; his public career of over 40 years established him as one of the most significant African leaders of the twentieth century.

Jomo Kenyatta, who was known as a child as Johnstone Kamau Ngengi, was born, according to most biographies, on October 20, 1891 at Ichaweri. There have always been questions about his birth date created by the unusual way the Kikuyu kept records and Kenyatta's own convenient ability to deny his correct age. His parents were Muigai, a Kikuyu farmer, and Wambui.

Little is known of the early years of his life. He was baptized in August 1914 and received the first 5 years of his education at the Church of Scotland Mission in Kikuyu near Nairobi. From 1921 to 1926 he was employed by the water department of the Nairobi Town Council. He also served as an interpreter to the Kenya Supreme Court. It is said that his use of the name Kenyatta dates from this period, deriving from the Kikuyu-language designation for the beaded workers' belt he wore while at work called a *mucibi wa kinyata* .

Early Political Career

In the Kenya of the 1920s the emerging nationalism of the African inhabitants was dominated by the dynamic Kikuyu peoples, the country's largest tribal grouping. They had proved receptive to some aspects of European culture, especially in education, and they began to attempt using the techniques of British democracy to secure their desired goals.

A particularly vital problem to the Kikuyu was the question of land ownership within the colony; they held that the British had unjustly seized much Kikuyu land. Various political organizations, such as the Young Kikuyu Association and the East African Association, were formed to advance their case. Kenyatta, as one of the few educated Kikuyu, joined the Young Kikuyu Association in 1922. British opposition, however, prevented these organizations from achieving any success. The Kikuyu Central Association was created from the Young Kikuyu Association and the East Africa Association and, like all the former groupings, needed men trained in English.

In 1927 Kenyatta, one of the elite as an educated Kikuyu, was asked to become its general secretary, a position which he accepted in early 1928. His office entailed work to encourage the growth of a modern political consciousness among the Kikuyu and thus to develop a broad basis of support for the organization. This required extensive traveling throughout the extensive Kikuyu territory. During 1929 the organization decided to issue its own publication, the Kikuyu-language monthly *Mwigwithania* (The Reconciler), and Kenyatta was selected as its editor. It was probably the first newspaper produced by Africans in Kenya.

Residence in Britain

Kenyatta's chance for a broader role arrived in 1928, when he testified before the Hilton-Young Commission, which had been sent to East Africa to investigate the project for a federation of British East African Territories. In February 1929 the Kikuyu Central Association decided to send Kenyatta to London to testify against the proposed union of Kenya, Tanganyika, and Uganda. He was refused an opportunity before the commission, but the experience of visiting Europe was valuable. He became involved with some radical anti-colonial organizations and traveled to the communist-sponsored International Trade Union of Negro Workers in Hamburg. He also traveled to Berlin and spent several weeks in the Soviet Union in August 1929.

He returned to Kenya in the fall of 1930 and gained permission for the Kikuyu to control their own independent schools despite opposition from the Christian missionary schools. In May 1931 he and Parmenas Githendu Mockerie were dispatched to London by the Kikuyu Central Association to testify before a select parliamentary committee studying the East Africa federation plans by the Colonial Office. He remained in Europe for 15 years, married an English woman, and had a son, Peter. He studied English at the Quaker College of Woodbrooke and at Selly Oak in Birmingham. Among the positions Kenyatta held was that of assistant in phonetics at London University's School of Oriental and African Studies from 1933 to 1936.

In 1936 Kenyatta enrolled at the London School of Economics as a postgraduate student. In the course of his studies he presented a series of papers to the seminar directed by the eminent anthropologist Bronislaw Malinowski. They were published in 1938 as *Facing Mount Kenya*. This work, which has been labeled as "a text in cultural nationalism" since it was one of the earliest publications by an African discussing his own culture without apology, made considerable impact.

Kenyatta asserted the right of Africans to speak for themselves, and not only to be discussed by foreign anthropologists or missionaries and, more important, he declared that Africans should be proud of their own cultural heritage. He especially developed his case around the then important issue of female circumcision, currently under attack by Christian missionaries, demonstrating the relevance of the ceremony to the total Kikuyu culture and indicating how Europeans had ignored this ritual aspect of the study of any African cultural facet. *Facing Mount Kenya* remains a classic among studies relating to the Kikuyu way of life.

When World War II began, Kenyatta worked on a farm in Surrey and lectured to the British army and the Worker's Educational Association on Africa. He became intensely active in general African movements; along with other pioneers of African nationalism, including Kwame Nkrumah and George Padmore, he founded the Pan African Federation and organized the fifth Pan African Congress at Manchester in March 1945 with the theme "Africa for the Africans." One great advantage of these long years away from Kenya was to isolate Kenyatta from the many divisions and rivalries of his homeland's nationalist movements, brought about by the frustrations imposed on Africans trying to organize in the British-dominated territory.

Politics in Kenya

Thus when Kenyatta returned to Kenya in September 1946, he was generally recognized by politically conscious Africans as the most effective leader for their new moves toward greater freedom. Many Europeans reacted also by regarding him as a potentially effective threat to their position of privilege. Kenyatta immediately began organizing a political movement which would be represented all over Kenya. In June 1947 he became president of the most effective African political movement to that time, the Kenya African Union. His efforts to encourage non-kikuyu to join the movement were successful and membership in the Kenyan African Union increased by over 100,000.

In 1947 Kenyatta also accepted the position of principal of the independent Teachers' Training College at Githanguri, thus bringing another facet of Kenyan protest under his influence. But despite his considerable success, the European settler dominated government of Kenya managed to keep control of the country's evolution. Many Africans therefore became increasingly frustrated by their lack of progress, and extremist groups began to prepare for a direct challenge to European domination.

Trial and Imprisonment

Kenyatta was unable to control the extremists, and by 1952 the violence had risen to such a level, particularly in the so-called Mau Movement, that the British reacted by declaring a state of emergency. Kenyatta was arrested on October 20, the government considering that if the leader of the Kenya African Union were removed from political life the Mau Mau crisis, which had claimed nearly 200 European and 12,000 Mau Mau lives, would cease. They planned no reforms to meet African aspirations.

A world-famous trial for Kenyatta was held at the remote location of Kapenguria in November. In conditions of intense military security, the government aimed to prove that Mau Mau was a part of the Kenya African Union and Kenyatta its leader. The judgment of the court in April 1953 gave Kenyatta and five other defendants the maximum sentence of 7 years at hard labor, but the trial was conducted in such a manner that many doubted the justice of the sentence.

Achieving Independence

During the state of emergency all Kenya-wide African political organizations had been restricted. But as the British began to regain control of affairs after 1955, African parties were allowed to reemerge at the local level, a decision which harmed future African developments by encouraging separatism among African leaders. Nevertheless, the Mau Mau crisis had forced the British government to realize the futility of continuing the evolution of Kenya through the existing colonial government.

The Colonial Office took a firm direction in moving the country toward independence through a series of new constitutions (in 1954, 1957, and 1960) designed to increase African participation in governing their homeland. But although African leaders seized the advantages offered to them, continually striving to wrest control from the European settlers, they made Kenyatta's participation in any government leading to independence one of their essential demands.

Kenyatta was freed from the desert prison of Lokitaung in northwestern Kenya in 1959 but was restricted to house arrest for two years in the Northern Frontier District town of Lodwar. In March 1960 the Kenya African National Union was formed and elected Kenyatta as its president in absentia. On August 14,1961, after nine years of detention, Kenyatta assumed the presidency of the Kenya African National Union party.

On January 12, 1962, Kenyatta was elected to the Kenyan Legislative Assembly to represent the constituency of Fort Hall. On April 10, he agreed to serve in a coalition government as minister of state for constitutional affairs and economic planning. In the May 28, 1963 elections Kenyatta led his African National Union party to victory. Kenyatta was invited to form a government and became self-governing Kenya's first prime minister on June 1. He took steps to reassure the European farmers about their future and also appealed to the freedom fighters and members of the Mau Mau to lay down their arms and join the new nation.

On December 12, 1963 Kenya became the 34th African state to gain independence. The duke of Edinburgh was in attendance as the colonial flag was lowered at midnight and the new Kenyan flag raised.

Ruling Kenya

The first years of Kenyan independence were dominated by restructuring and rebuilding the nation. In November of 1964 Kenyatta convinced the rival Kenya African Democratic Union and its leader, Ronald Ngala, to dissolve and join Kenyatta's Kenyan African National Union party to form a single chambered National Assembly. Ngala had been Kenyatta's greatest political rival because his party stood for regional autonomy while Kenyatta's party stood for a strong central government.

The European settler problem disappeared, since most of those antagonistic to African rule left the country, but the problem of integrating the various African and Indian citizens of the new republic continued.

The greatest political challenge to Kenyatta was a dispute with Dginga Odinga, the leader of the powerful Luo tribe. Odinga had served as home affairs minister and later as vice president. Odinga was accused by other cabinet ministers of accepting financial aid from Communist China and using the money to buy influence with members of parliament. In March 1964, Kenyatta, who had given Odinga the benefit of the doubt for past loyalty, finally abolished Odinga's position as deputy president of the ruling Kenya African National Union party. In 1966 Odinga resigned as Kenya's national vice president and formed the Kenya Peoples' Union as a leftist opposition party.

On July 5, 1969, Tom Mboya, a popular Luo politician, was assassinated by a Kikuyu. The assassin was tried and executed, but Luo anger still ran high. In October 1969, Kenyatta's appearance in Luo territory set off riots and threatened to divide the new nation. After initially ignoring the problem, Kenyatta imposed a curfew, detained Odinga and his leaders, and banned the Kenya Peoples' Union party. Kenyatta moved the election date to early December 1969 and declared anyone could run for a seat if they were a member of the Kenya African National party. Several members of Kenyatta's party were defeated, but his government survived the election. Despite Luo anger and rumors of military plots, Kenya regained a surface calm which continued through Kenyatta's presidency.

Kenyatta made Kenya a showcase nation among the former African colonial states. Leading his nation on a relatively conservative course, he provided for peace and prosperity in his nation while improving health, agriculture, tourism, business, and manufacturing. Although Kenyatta utilized both communist and capitalist financial and technical aid, which helped Kenya take the lead in economic

development in East Africa, he came down heavily and communist efforts to infiltrate the country.

Kenyatta followed a nonaligned, but pro-western, foreign policy and pursued an orthodox African policy towards the apartheid tactics of Rhodesia and South Africa. In 1971 he became the unmitigated leader in East Africa and achieved his greatest foreign policy success when he helped to settle a border dispute between Uganda and Tanzania.

Kenyatta died peacefully in Mombassa on August 22, 1978. His successor, Daniel arap Moi, was Kenya's vice president. The transition of power was seamless and Moi suggested a continuation in Kenyatta's policies by calling his own program *Nyayo* or "footsteps."

Further Reading

Kenyatta's own writings include: *Facing Mount Kenya* (1938); *My People of Kikuyu and the Life of Chief Wangombe* (1944); *Kenya: The Land of Conflict* (1944); and *Harambee!* (1964); an account of the early life and times of Kenyatta and of Mau Mau groups is by Carl G. Rosberg, Jr., and John Nottingham, *The Myth of "Mau Mau": Nationalism in Kenya* (1966); for general historical background are *Kenya, a Political History: The Colonial Period* (1963), by George Bennett; and *History of East Africa*, vol. 2 (1965) by Vincent T. Harlow and E. M. Chilver; the life and career of Kenyatta is traced in the Anthony Howarth and David Koff film *Kenyatta* (1979); Kenyatta is also listed with a brief biography in the A&E Television Networks online biography at www.biography.com (1997); and mentioned in relationship to Kenya's present government in the JamboKenya homepage at sbwm.erols.com. □

Johannes Kepler

The German astronomer Johannes Kepler (1571-1630) was one of the chief founders of modern astronomy because of his discovery of three basic laws underlying the motion of planets.

Johannes Kepler was born on Dec. 27, 1571, in the Swabian town of Weil. His father, Heinrich Kepler, was a mercenary; although a Protestant, he enlisted in the troops of the Duke of Alba fighting the Reformed insurgents in the Low Countries. Kepler's grandmother brought him up; for years he was a sickly child. At 13 he was accepted at a theological seminary at Adelberg.

Kepler wanted to become a theologian, and following his graduation from the University of Tübingen, as bachelor of arts in 1591, he enrolled in its theological faculty. But he was also interested in French literature and astronomy. His poor health and proclivity to morbidness singled him out no less than did his precocious advocacy of the doctrine of Copernicus.

It seems that the University of Tübingen gladly presented Kepler for the post of the "mathematician of the province" when request for a candidate came from Graz. He arrived there in April 1594 and set himself to work on one of his duties, the composition of the almanac, in which the main events of the coming year were to be duly predicted. His first almanac was a signal success. The occurrence of two not too unlikely events, an invasion by the Turks and a severe winter, which he had predicted, established his reputation.

Far more important for astronomy was the idea that seized Kepler on July 9, 1595. It appeared to him that the respective radii of the orbits of the planets corresponded to the lengths determined by a specific sequence in which the five regular solids were placed within one another, with a sphere separating each solid from the other. The sphere (orbit) of Saturn enveloped a cube which in turn enveloped another sphere, the orbit of Jupiter. This circumscribed a tetrahedron, a sphere (the orbit of Mars), a dodecahedron, a sphere (the orbit of earth), an icosahedron, a sphere (the orbit of Venus), an octahedron, and the smallest sphere (the orbit of Mercury). The idea was the main theme of his *Mysterium cosmographicum* (1596).

The next year Kepler married Barbara Muehleck, already twice widowed, "under an ominous sky," according to Kepler's own horoscope. Of their five children only one boy and one girl reached adulthood. It was with reluctance that Kepler, a convinced Copernican, first sought the job of assistant to Tycho Brahe, the astrologer-mathematician of Rudolph II in Prague. He took his new position in 1600. On the death of Tycho the following year, Kepler was appointed his successor.

His Three Laws

Kepler's immediate duty was to prepare for publication Tycho's collection of astronomical studies, *Astronomiae instauratae progymnasmata* (1601-1602). Kepler fell heir to Tycho's immensely valuable records. Their outstanding feature lay in the precision by which Tycho surpassed all astronomers before him in observing the position of stars and planets. Kepler tried to utilize Tycho's data in support of his own layout of the circular planetary orbits. The facts, that is, Tycho's observations, forced him to make one of the most revolutionary assumptions in the history of astronomy. A difference of 8 minutes of arc between his theory and Tycho's data could be explained only if the orbit of Mars was not circular but elliptical. In a generalized form this meant that the orbits of all planets were elliptical (Kepler's first law). On this basis a proper meaning could be given to another statement of his which he had already made in the same context. It is known as Kepler's second law, according to which the line joining the planet to the sun sweeps over equal areas in equal times in its elliptical orbit.

Kepler published these laws in his lengthy discussion of the orbit of the planet Mars, the *Astronomia nova* (1609). The two laws were clearly spelled out also in the book's detailed table of contents. Thus they must have struck the eyes of any careful reader sensitive to an astronomical novelty of such major proportion. Still, Galileo failed to take cognizance of them in his printed works, although he could have used them to great advantage to buttress his advocacy of the Copernican system.

The relations between Galileo and Kepler were rather strange. Although Galileo remained distinctly unappreciative of Kepler's achievements, the latter wrote a booklet to celebrate Galileo's *Starry Messenger* immediately upon its publication in 1610. On the other hand, Kepler argued rather vainly in his *Conversation with the Starry Messenger* (1610) that in his *Astronomiae pars optica* (1604), or *Optics,* which he presented as a commentary to Witelo's 13th-century work, one could find all the principles needed to construct a telescope.

In 1611 came Rudolph's abdication, and Kepler immediately looked for a new job. He obtained in Linz the post of provincial mathematician. By the time he moved to Linz in 1612 with his two children, his wife and his favorite son, Friedrich, were dead. Kepler's 14 years in Linz were marked, as far as his personal life was concerned, with his marriage in 1613 to Suzanna Reuttinger and by his repeated efforts to save his aged mother from being tried as a witch.

As for Kepler the scientist, he published two important works while he was in Linz. One was the *Harmonice mundi* (1618), in which his third law was announced. According to it the squares of the sidereal periods of any two planets are to each other as the cubes of their mean distances from the sun. The law was, however, derived not from celestial mechanics (Newton's *Principia* was still 6 decades away) but from Kepler's conviction that nature had to be patterned along quantitative relationships since God created it according to "weight, measure and number." Shortly after his first book appeared, he wrote in a letter: "Since God established everything in the universe along quantitative norms, he endowed man with a mind to comprehend them. For just as the eye is fitted for the perception of colors, the ear for sounds, so is man's mind created not for anything but for the grasping of quantities." In the *Harmonice mundi* he wrote merely a variation on the same theme as he spoke of geometry which "supplied God with a model for the creation of the world. Geometry was implanted into human nature along with God's image and not through man's visual perception and experience." The second work was the *Epitome astronomiae Copernicanae,* published in parts between 1618 and 1621. It was the first astronomical treatise in which the doctrine of circles really or hypothetically carrying the various planets was completely abandoned in favor of a physical explanation of planetary motions. It consisted in "magnetic arms" emanating from the sun.

Kepler was already in Ulm, the first stopover of the wanderings of the last 3 years of his life, when his *Tabulae Rudolphinae* (1628) was published. It not only added the carefully determined position of 223 stars to the 777 contained in Tycho's *Astronomiae instauratae progymnasmata* but also provided planetary tables which became the standard for the next century. Kepler died on Nov. 15, 1630. He was a unique embodiment of the transition from the old to the new spirit of science.

Further Reading

The standard modern biography of Kepler was written by Max Caspar and was translated and edited by C. Doris Hellmann as *Kepler* (1959). The section on Kepler in Arthur Koestler's *The Sleepwalkers* (1959) is also available as a separate volume, *The Watershed: A Biography of Johannes Kepler* (1960). For a rigorous discussion of Kepler's astronomical theories see Alexander Koyré, *The Astronomical Revolution: Copernicus, Kepler, Borelli* (1961; trans. 1969). ☐

Aleksandr Fedorovich Kerensky

The Russian revolutionary and politician Aleksandr Fedorovich Kerensky (1881-1970) was the central figure around whom the fate of representative government and socialism revolved in Russia during the Revolution of 1917.

Aleksandr Kerensky was born on April 22, 1881, in Simbirsk (now Ulyanovsk), the son of a teacher who also served as a middle-ranked provincial official. He entered St. Petersburg University (1899), where he studied jurisprudence, philology, and history. By 1904 he had completed his formal training and joined the St. Petersburg bar. He gained a reputation for public controversy and civil liberty; among other things, he worked with a legal-aid society and served as a defense lawyer in several celebrated political cases.

Kerensky's formal political career began when he stood successfully for election to the Fourth Duma (legislative assembly) in 1912. As a candidate of the Labor (Trudovik) party, he continued to champion civil rights. By 1914 he had been imprisoned twice for acts considered unfriendly or seditious by the government.

With the outbreak of World War I (1914), Kerensky was one of the few Duma members to speak against it, denouncing, in a public speech, the "devouring, fratricidal war." As Russian defeat followed defeat, support for the government dwindled and then disappeared, setting the stage for the Revolution of 1917 that swept Kerensky to power for a brief time.

During the revolutionary months of 1917, power in the major cities of Russia and at many points of military concentration was effectively divided between the provisional government, which derived its authority from the Duma, and the soviets—or representative councils—of workers' and soldiers' deputies. Among the members of the provisional government, Kerensky had a unique position because, for a time, he bridged the gap between these competing agencies of the revolution. Although a well-known member of the Duma, he was an articulate spokesman for the left and a member of the executive committee of the Petrograd soviet.

Kerensky was minister of justice in the first provisional government, organized by a liberal, Prince Lvov. This government's policy of honoring the war aims and obligations of the czarist government proved sufficiently unpopular that the minister of foreign affairs (Pavel Miliukov) and the minister of war and navy (Aleksandr Guchkov) were forced to resign; Kerensky succeeded to the latter position. He fared

little better in this position than had Guchkov, however. In spite of initial successes, a major offensive, which Kerensky inspired, resulted in fresh military disasters (June 1917). Thus, amidst military failure and broadly based, disruptive demonstrations, Lvov resigned as prime minister in July and Kerensky succeeded him.

Kerensky's own view was that in the succeeding weeks the Russian political situation was tending toward stability. Radical leftist agitators (including Lenin and Trotsky) had been imprisoned or forced to flee the country, and Kerensky himself enjoyed a certain amount of popularity. Moreover, the time was thought to be drawing closer when it would be possible to convene a constituent assembly that would formally establish a democratic regime. The stroke that destroyed these hopes came unexpectedly from the right in the form of the Kornilov uprising (September 9-14), which was an attempt to establish a conservatively backed military government. Kerensky managed to halt the attempted coup only by calling upon the radical left for support. Similarly, he was unable from this time forward to count on the military leadership for support against this same radical left. Soon after, Lenin and Trotsky, at large again, planned their own coup, the Bolshevik Revolution of November. When the blow fell, Kerensky was out of Petrograd searching for troops loyal enough to defend the government against the Bolsheviks. Failing in this, he returned to Petrograd and then Moscow, futilely attempting to organize opposition against the revolution.

In the spring of 1918 Kerensky finally fled Russia, and, for a short time thereafter, he strove to rally international opposition against the Bolshevik government. Failing this, he began to write and lecture in Europe on the affairs of his native land. In 1940 he moved to the United States, writing, lecturing, and teaching at Stanford University. He died on June 11, 1970, in New York City.

Further Reading

The most important sources on Kerensky's political work remain his own writings: *Prelude to Bolshevism: The Kornilov Rising* (1919); *The Catastrophe: Kerensky's Own Story of the Russian Revolution* (1927); *Russia and History's Turning Point* (1965). Kerensky also made a significant contribution to the background material on this period by his work, edited with Robert Paul Browder, *The Russian Provisional Government, 1917* (3 vols., 1961).

Additional Sources

Abraham, Richard, *Alexander Kerensky: the first love of the revolution,* New York: Columbia University Press, 1987. □

Jerome David Kern

Jerome David Kern (1885-1945), American composer, wrote the scores for several of the musical theater's greatest successes.

Jerome Kern was born in New York City on Jan. 27, 1885. His first music teacher was his pianist-mother. He later studied at the New York College of Music as well as in Europe.

After working in the London theater, Kern returned to America, where the only work he could find was as a song plugger and pianist with a music publishing company. From 1905 to 1908 he was associated with a music company, rising to the vice presidency. He married Eva Leale in 1910, and they had a daughter. His first published score was an operetta, *The Red Petticoat* (1912).

Between 1914 and 1929 Kern was represented on Broadway by at least one show a season. His prolific output included *Rock a Bye Baby* (1918), *Sally* (1920), and *Sunny* (1925). In 1926 he wrote the score for a Broadway adaptation of an Edna Ferber novel, and Oscar Hammerstein II wrote the lyrics. The result was the musical classic *Show Boat*. It opened in 1927 and ran for 572 performances. It was later twice made into a Hollywood film. One of its songs, "Ol' Man River," is perhaps Kern's most famous. In 1941 *Show Boat* was transposed into symphonic form and performed by the New York Philharmonic Orchestra.

Other Kern successes include *Music in the Air* (1932) and *Roberta* (1933) and, for the movies, *Swing Time* (1936), *You Were Never Lovelier* (1942), and *Centennial Summer* (1946). Among his most popular songs are "My Bill," "Smoke Gets in Your Eyes," "Who?," "They Didn't Believe Me," "Look for the Silver Lining," and "The Last Time I Saw Paris" (his only hit song not written for a specific show).

In the realm of serious music, Kern composed *Portrait for Orchestra (Mark Twain)*, which had its world premiere in 1942 by the Cincinnati Symphony Orchestra, and *Montage for Orchestral Suite* for full orchestra and two pianos.

Kern was interested in a number of scholarly pursuits. His collection of rare books brought nearly $2 million at auction in 1929. He was also a collector of art, a numismatist, and philatelist.

In his 40-year career Kern wrote 104 stage and screen vehicles. At the time of his death on Nov. 11, 1945, he was in New York to cosponsor a new production of *Show Boat*. A film biography, *Till the Clouds Roll By* (1946), was one of many tributes paid to him.

Further Reading

An entertaining account of Kern's life is David Ewen, *The Story of Jerome Kern* (1953), which makes it clear that Kern was the first to break from the style of European operettas. See also Ewen's *The World of Jerome Kern* (1960). Background studies include Cecil M. Smith, *Musical Comedy in America* (1950), and David Ewen, *The Story of America's Musical Theater* (1961; rev. ed. 1968) and *Great Men of American Popular Song* (1970).

Additional Sources

Bordman, Gerald Martin, *Jerome Kern: his life and music,* New York: Oxford University Press, 1980.
Lamb, Andrew, *Jerome Kern in Edwardian London,* Brooklyn, N.Y.: Institute for Studies in American Music, Conservatory of

Music, Brooklyn College of the City University of New York, 1985.

Freedland, Michael, *Jerome Kern,* New York: Stein and Day, 1981, 1978. ☐

Jean-Louis Lebris de Kerouac

Jean-Louis Lebris de (Jack) Kerouac (1922-1969), American writer, experimented with spontaneous autobiographical fiction chronicling his travels into the American West. He is known as the father of the Beat Generation.

Rambling. Wandering. Overflowing. Like his fiction, Jack Kerouac covered a great deal of territory in a short period of time. Known as the father of the Beat Generation, Kerouac's freewheeling life on the road and his chronicles of that life paved the way for the youth counter-culture of the 1960s.

Born March 12, 1922, in Lowell, Massachusetts, Jean-Louis Lebris de Kerouac was the son of a French-Canadian printer. Kerouac, who wanted to be a writer from his earliest childhood, did not speak a word of English until he was five years old. He had an older brother, Gerard, who died at age nine, and an older sister Caroline. At age 11 Kerouac began writing adolescent novels and fictionalized newspaper accounts of horse racing, football, and baseball.

A gifted athlete, Kerouac was recruited by Columbia University for the football team. At age 17 he went off to Horace Mann High School in New York to boost his grades and his weight in preparation for Columbia. In 1940 Kerouac arrived at Columbia. In his second game as a freshman Kerouac returned a kick 90 yards, but on his next return he broke his leg. The injury freed him to pursue his true passion—literature.

During this period, Kerouac once bragged, he set a Columbia record for cutting classes. The young writer studied the rolling style of Thomas Wolfe and plunged deep into the New York street scene. In 1941, his leg healed, Kerouac had a falling out with Columbia's football coach. When he left school Jack Kerouac took his first road trip, to Washington, D.C.

Kerouac pumped gas for a while in Connecticut, where his family had moved; worked briefly as a sports reporter for the *Lowell Sun* when his family returned there; and found himself a scullion on the S. S. *DORCHESTER* bound for Greenland. Two days after that trip Kerouac was back at Columbia for a second, short stay. In 1943 he joined the Navy, but was honorably discharged as a discipline problem after six months. Kerouac spent the war years working as a merchant seaman and hanging around Columbia with free-thinking Bohemians, including William Burroughs, Lucian Carr, Edie Parker, and Allen Ginsburg. He wrote two novels during the war, *The Sea Is My Brother* and *And The Hippos Were Boiled In Their Tanks,* with Burroughs.

Kerouac married Parker in 1944, but the marriage broke up after two months. His father died in 1946, and in 1947 Kerouac found his guiding light—Neal Cassady.

Cassady's reputation among the New York crowd was of mythical proportions. Mad genius, admired by women, car thief, Cassady visited New York and had Kerouac give him writing lessons. When Cassady returned to Denver, Kerouac followed. After a few weeks in Denver with Cassady, Kerouac wandered into California. During the next four years he travelled throughout the West. When not on the road, he worked on his novel *The Town and The City* in New York. The novel was published in 1950.

Now married to Joan Haverty, a woman he knew only a few days before proposing, Kerouac began to experiment with a more spontaneous writing style. He wanted to write the way he lived: once and with no editing. In April 1951 Kerouac threaded a huge roll of teletype paper into his typewriter and wrote the single 175,000-word paragraph that was to be *On The Road* . The more than 100-foot scroll was written in three weeks but took more than seven years to be published.

On The Road chronicles the travels of Dean Moriarity—a Cassady figure—and Sal Paradise—Kerouac as narrator. They travel from New York to Denver, San Francisco, and Mexico City. In it, Sal, the Eastern college square, absorbs the meaning of the West and Kerouac carves out his legacy as a writer and immortalizes the philosophy of the Beat Generation.

On The Road, which despite Kerouac's attempts at spontaneity took shape over a period of three and a half years, was written in at least five different versions. There are three in print. *On The Road* was the fourth version; *Pic,* written in 1950 and published after Kerouac's death, was the third; and *Visions of Cody,* written in 1951-1952, was the final version. The author's changing image of what it means to be on the road can also be applied to his view of what it means to be a writer. In its first version, the road is a specific place. In the second, it is a symbol, and in the final three versions the road is a mix of the imaginative and the real.

The episodic, apparently rambling, prose of *On The Road* instills its characters with a disdain for established values and a romantic code born out of the West. Sal and Neal are "performing our one noble function of the time, *move.*" And with movement comes wisdom and meaning in a repressive society.

In the time between writing *On The Road* and its publication Kerouac took numerous exhausting road trips, ended his second marriage, fell into great depression and drug and alcohol addiction, and did his most ambitious experimentation with the narrative form. Always after spontaneity, Kerouac wrote in great bursts of athletic energy—writing complete works through all-night, week-long binges. In 1952 he wrote *Visions of Cody, Dr. Sax,* and "October in Railroad Earth." In 1953 he completed *Maggie Cassidy* (a romantic tale of his teenage days), *The Subterraneans,* and a statement of his writing principles, "The Essentials of Spontaneous Prose." In 1955 Kerouac wrote *Mexico City Blues* and *Tristessa,* and in 1956 he wrote *Visions of Gerard, The Scripture of the Golden Eternity,* and *Old Angel Midnight* as well as book one of *Desolation Angels.*

When *On The Road* was published, Kerouac became an instant celebrity and spokesman for the Beat Generation. He handled the notoriety poorly. As a spokesman he was contrary and unintelligible. He often appeared drunk, and interviews frequently dissolved into didactic arguments. In 1958 he wrote *The Dharma Bums* as a commercial followup to *On The Road,* but then fell silent for four years before writing again. By 1960 Kerouac was a sick and dying alcoholic; he suffered a nervous breakdown.

Again remarried, Kerouac died of a massive abdominal hemorrhage on October 21, 1969, with a pad in his lap and pen in his hand. He was buried in the family plot near Lowell, Massachusetts.

Further Reading

Tom Clark's *Jack Kerouac* (1984) is an extremely thorough biography of the author's life, but is short on criticism of Kerouac's work. A helpful package is *On The Road, Text and Criticism,* edited by Scott Donaldson (1979). In addition to the novel, the package includes a number of insightful articles, including pieces by Kerouac, John Clellon Holmes, Timothy Hunt, and the transcript of an interview with the author by Ted Berrigan. *Lonesome Traveler* by Jack Kerouac (1960) is a collection of autobiographical pieces, useful for their style as

much as for their content. *Jack Kerouac* by Harry Russell Huebel (1979) is a quick biography, and *Jack's Book, An Oral Biography of Jack Kerouac* by Barry Gifford and Lawrence Lee (1978) is also interesting. □

Clark Kerr

Clark Kerr (born 1911) was an economist and labor/ management expert who served as president of the multi-campus University of California from 1952 to 1967, a period of rapid growth and expansion. He was concerned about the role of the university in society and created a master plan for coordinating the programs of all of the state's colleges and universities.

Clark Kerr was born May 17, 1911, in Stony Creek, Pennsylvania, to Samuel William Kerr and Carolina Clark Kerr. He received a B.A. from Swarthmore College in 1932 and an M.A. from Stanford the following year. He attended the London School of Economics during 1935-1936 and in 1939 was awarded a Ph.D. in economics from the University of California, Berkeley. He was subsequently awarded numerous honorary degrees from the most prominent American colleges and universities. Kerr married Catherine Spaulding Kerr, and they had three children, two boys and a girl.

Kerr began his teaching career in 1936 with successive one year stints at Antioch College, Stanford University, and the University of California before accepting a professorship at the University of Washington in 1940. An expert on labor, he was named to the U.S. War Labor Board in 1942 to arbitrate wage disputes between unions and companies. His expertise as a labor/management consultant became widely known, and he soon became the highest paid negotiator on the West Coast. Following five years at the University of Washington, Kerr returned to Berkeley to establish the Institute of Industrial Relations and serve as its director while teaching a regular load of classes. In 1952 he was appointed chancellor of the Berkeley campus, and in 1958 he succeeded Robert Gordon Sproul as president of the multi-campus University of California.

The rapid growth of universities in response to the postwar baby boom had begun when Kerr took office. Rapid growth and expansion of the university system was on the horizon, and during his tenure the university doubled its enrollment to more than 50,000 students. The previous president had kept a tight reign on campus political activities to the extent that even Adlai Stevenson was not allowed to speak on the Berkeley campus. In 1949 Kerr had fought the application of faculty loyalty oaths, and that action identified him as a liberal in the eyes of many. Upon becoming system president he lifted the speaker ban on Communist speakers—winning him the American Association of University Presidents Meiklejohn Award—and liberalized a few other rules.

His policies were put to the test by the growth of activist groups on campus during the civil rights thrust of 1963-1964. Students aggressively pushed for remedies to racial discrimination in the university community and confronted local businesses, often leading to demonstrations and arrests. This antagonism led to Kerr's banning of on-campus recruiting and solicitation of funds for off-campus groups. Students denounced the president's action, and the Free Speech Movement was formed. In the fall of 1964 police attempted to arrest a non-student manning a table for the Congress of Racial Equality and were denied access to this individual by a massive 30-hour sit-in. Further incitement was provided by the Free Speech Movement (F.S.M.). Kerr met with Marco Savio, leader of the protesters, and was assumed to have resolved the disagreement, but Governor Brown intervened the next day and ordered the arrest of the students. There was immediate campus outrage, and the Berkeley faculty voted overwhelmingly to meet the F.S.M. demands.

The next three years of Kerr's administration were marked by constant attempts at mediation between the university and various interests, including the California state government. Ronald Reagan became governor in 1967, and conflict developed immediately between his administration and Kerr over proposed cuts in operating funds and the proposal to end free education by imposing tuition and other fees. An impasse developed, and on June 20, 1967, the California State Board of Regents voted to dismiss him as president, pointing to what they saw as his mishandling of the 1964 unrest at Berkeley.

Clark Kerr's accomplishments as president lay primarily in the evolution of the University of California into a "multiversity," a term he coined. He argued that a university must of necessity cater to the elite, but in an egalitarian society its role is that of a "prime instrument of national purpose." It must serve many constituencies, including government, industry, and the general public as well as its students and faculty. He devised a master plan to coordinate programs of all the state's colleges and universities. The result was a hierarchy of higher education, with the top 12 percent of high school graduates attending the universities, the rest of the upper third attending the colleges, and the remainder attending the junior colleges. This model was considered by many to be a proper national goal.

Kerr continued to hold his faculty position at Berkeley's School of Business Administration following his dismissal as president. His administrative innovations led to his appointment as head of a Carnegie Commission study of the structure and finance of higher education. In 1968 the commission called for a federal civilian "bill of educational rights" to guarantee a college education to any qualified student regardless of his/her ability to pay. Kerr's committee evolved into the Carnegie Council on Policy Studies in Higher Education, whose final report *Three Thousand Futures: The Next Twenty Years in Higher Education* has become the benchmark for reform in higher education. Clark Kerr's membership on numerous governmental and industrial commissions throughout his career bore witness to his position of respect and influence. He was also an extremely active worker in the Committee for a Political Settlement in Vietnam. He and his wife lived in El Cerrito, California, in a home overlooking the San Francisco Bay, a tranquil site where he wrote and pursued his favorite leisure activity of gardening.

Kerr held memberships in many professional and honorary organizations, including the American Academy of Arts and Sciences, Royal Economic Society, American Economic Association, National Academy of Arbitrators, and the Rockefeller Foundation.

Kerr continued to publish through the 1980s. *Economics of Labor in Industrial Society,* edited by Clark Kerr and Paul D. Staudohar and *Industrial Relations in a New Age: Economic, Social, and Managerial Perspectives,* edited by Kerr and Staudohar appeared at the end of the decade. Kerr also co-authored *The Guardians: Boards of Trustees of American Colleges and Universities* with Martin L. Gade in 1989. The book discusses problems with the governing boards of various universities and suggests a number of reforms.

Further Reading

Industrialism and Industrial Man (1964); *Labor and Management in Industrial Society* (1972); *Marshall, Marx, and Modern Times* (1969); *The Future of Industrial Societies* (1983); *The Uses of the University* (1972); and *Unions, Management, and the Public* (1967) all by Clark Kerr; for reviews of his work, see: *Monthly Labor Review,* March 1988, vol. 111, no. 3, p. 51-52 in which Morris Weisz reviews *Economics of Labor in Industrial Society* and *Industrial Relations in a New Age: Economic, Social, and Managerial Perspectives,* both edited by Kerr and Paul D. Staudohar; and a review of *The Guardians: Boards of Trustees of Americas Colleges and Universities,* by Carolyn J. Mooney in *The Chronicle of Higher Education,* May 17, 1989. ☐

J. Robert Kerrey

Elected senator from Nebraska in 1988, J. Robert (Bob) Kerrey (born 1943) made an unsuccessful bid for the Democratic nomination for president in 1992. He made a name for himself as being a maverick and a deficit hawk.

Robert Kerrey was born in 1943 in Lincoln, Nebraska, where he was raised and educated. Upon completion of college at the University of Nebraska (B.S. in pharmacy in 1966), Kerrey entered the military service as a Navy SEAL (the Navy equivalent of the Green Berets). During his service in Vietnam in 1969 he was wounded in battle, which required the amputation of his right leg just below the knee. In 1970 he was awarded the Congressional Medal of Honor for "conspicuous gallantry." He is the only current member of the Senate holding the Medal of Honor. In the history of the United States Senate only four other members have been Medal of Honor recipients—all for service during the Civil War. While convalescing and rehabilitating in a military hospital in Philadelphia, however, he developed a strong conviction against the war in which he served and later opposed several armed conflicts involving U.S. military personnel. Notwithstanding a prosthesis, Kerrey was an avid runner, finishing a marathon and logging six miles a day.

Launches Restaurant Chain

Upon completion of his military service, he returned to Lincoln with the intention of opening a pharmacy (his undergraduate major). He decided against pursuing this profession because he thought there already were too many pharmacies operating in the area. Instead, he developed a string of restaurants with his brother-in-law (Grandmother's Restaurants—so named because they wanted to provide food just like grandmother's). The success of this venture along with the development of fitness centers in Nebraska made him a millionaire.

In 1983 he entered into politics for the first time and defeated an incumbent governor to take office as the head of the state of Nebraska. Inheriting a large budget deficit and a farm crisis that struck the Midwest during the early 1980s, his popularity and approach to governing facilitated a quick turnaround of the state's fortunes. By cutting some programs, increasing taxes, and expanding the tax base, he was able to reverse the state's deficit and replace it with a $49 million surplus by the end of his first term. He decided to forego what many considered certain reelection (he enjoyed an approval rating above 70 percent) and dropped from the political scene when his term ended in 1986.

His self-imposed suspension from the political arena was short-lived, however. In 1988, perhaps realizing that a rare opportunity presented itself for a chance at the Senate, he decided to challenge Republican David Karnes, an attorney from Omaha who was appointed to finish the term of Senator Edward Zorinsky, a Democrat, who died suddenly in 1987. He handily won election and took office in 1989. While still learning the ropes of the Senate, he decided to enter the Democratic presidential sweepstakes as a candidate, attempting to wrestle the White House from 12 years of Republican occupancy.

Failed Presidential Bid

His presidential bid in 1992 was limited, as he was unable to mount a successful challenge to the eventual Democratic nominee and president, Bill Clinton. He did strike hard at the sitting president (George Bush) as one of only three members of the Senate voting against support for the Gulf War in Iraq. Even with a capacity for inspiring speeches and a press corps that gave him considerable attention, he was unable to convince voters that he should be the Democratic party's presidential candidate in November. He only managed a disappointing third-place finish in the New Hampshire primary and won in South Dakota (40 percent to 25 percent over Senator Tom Harkin of Iowa). Nonetheless, he was unable to gather any further significant support as he finished fourth or fifth in five other primary states a week after the South Dakota victory and abruptly dropped from the race.

Kerrey continued his efforts in the Senate, establishing his credentials as someone who worked hard at understanding issues. His general views on policies appeared to favor cutting spending wherever possible in order to reduce the deficit (he argued against uncontrollable entitlement programs that lock in expenditures and contribute to a large budget deficit). Of this problem, he told *The Washington Times* in 1996, "We (will) have converted the federal government into an ATM (automatic teller machine)."

He held positions on the Senate Appropriations and Agriculture Committees. While he was not categorized as a traditional "tax and spend" senator, he was willing to consider tax increases where appropriate to cover necessary governmental spending. He argued for a health care trust fund to finance the federal government's health programs and worked for programs that benefited Nebraska's farming economy, including export assistance, crop insurance, and wetlands laws.

Kerrey was considered in some circles to be a maverick. He articulated positions that made him a voice for a new vision of the Democratic party. He had characteristics that some attribute to the new Democratic party: He was traditionally liberal on lifestyle issues, civil rights issues (he argued against flag burning legislation), and child and nutrition issues. Yet he also took more conservative positions on economic policies—the need to eliminate the budget deficit by cutting entitlements and a generally reduced role for the federal government. He co-sponsored legislation with Senator Joseph Lieberman (Connecticut) to set up a bipartisan commission (similar to the base-closing commission) to streamline the federal government.

Entitlement Reform Ignored

His relationship with President Clinton's administration was at times a rocky one. He cast the key vote in the Senate in 1993 that led to the passage of the president's tax increase and budget deficit reduction plan. As a condition, he wrangled a promise from Clinton to support a commission on entitlement reform. Its recommendations, however, were largely ignored. He was re-elected to the Senate in 1994. He chose not to challenge Clinton for the 1995 Democratic nomination instead heading up the job of chairman of the Democratic Senatorial Campaign Committee. Kerrey continued his outspoken ways when he told *Esquire Magazine* in January 1996 that "Clinton is an unusually good liar. Unusually good. Do you realize that?"

Kerrey remained close to his children, a son, Ben, and a daughter, Lindsey, who resided in Omaha with their mother, from whom he was divorced. An avid reader, he suggested that members of Congress should read only fiction, and he enjoyed a reputation as a member of the Senate who was always prepared.

Further Reading

Kerrey's speeches on the Senate floor are interesting reading—see the *Congressional Record;* also see Michael Barone and Grant Ujifusa, *The Almanac of American Politics* (1994); and "Grave Doubts," *Esquire Magazine* (January 1996). □

Albert Field Marshal Kesselring

Field Marshal Albert Kesselring (1885-1960), one of the most prominent German air and field commanders in World War II, surrendered the southern part of the German troops to the Americans in 1945.

Albert Kesselring was born in Markstedt near Bayreuth, Bavaria, on Nov. 20, 1885. Upon completion of a traditional classical education, he joined the Bavarian foot artillery in 1904 and was commissioned officer in 1906. During World War I and most of the postwar years he served as an army staff officer at the disguised general staff or "Troops Office" and later at the War Ministry. After the Nazi take-over in 1933, he was formally discharged from the army and put in charge of the administration office of the incipient and still undercover air force under the command of his old comradein-arms Hermann Göring.

In June 1936 Kesselring became Göring's chief of staff; one year later he commanded Air Region III (southeastern Germany) and finally, from the spring of 1938 on, commanded Air Fleet I in Berlin. After the outbreak of World War II he first directed the air attacks of Air Fleet I over Poland, then in the summer and fall of 1940 led the operations of Air Fleet II over France, in the air support over Dunkirk, and finally in the Battle of Britain. On June 30, 1940, he was promoted to the rank of field marshal. During Operation Barbarossa of June 1941 he again commanded Air Fleet II on the central Russian front.

In September 1941 Kesselring was transferred to Rome as commander in chief south, with the task of coordinating the Italo-German war effort in the Mediterranean area. From there he shared in the direction of the campaign of Rommel in North Africa and oversaw the defensive battles in Tunis, Sicily, and then on the Italian peninsula. With the defection of Italy in September 1943, he was supreme commander in Italy and the Mediterranean and from 1943 to 1945 directed the steady retreat of the German armies under the onslaught of the Allied troops and Italian partisans. From March 10, 1945, he headed Hitler's last stand on the Rhine. On May 7 he surrendered the southern half of the German forces to the Americans.

Kesselring was tried by a British military court in Venice in May 1947 and was sentenced to death for the shooting of 320 Italian hostages (Ardeatine Caves massacre) in March 1944. In October 1947 the sentence was commuted to life imprisonment; in October 1952 he was released for reasons of ill health. He died in Bad Nauheim, Bavaria, on July 16, 1960.

Further Reading

Kesselring's highly defensive memoirs were published under two different titles in English: *The Memoirs of Field Marshal Kesselring* (1953) and *Kesselring: A Soldier's Record* (1954). The documents of Kesselring's trial in Venice were ably edited in a dual-language edition by Lt. Col. A. P. Scotland, *Der Fall Kesselring: The Kesselring Case* (1952). Interesting sidelights on Kesselring's career and personality are in Siegfried Westphal, *The German Army in the West* (1950; trans. 1951), by a former military aide to Kesselring who tries to shift the onus for the war from the German army to Hitler. Kesselring's military actions during World War II are analyzed in W. G. F. Jackson, *The Battle for Italy* (1967); Fred Majdalany, *The Fall of Fortress Europe* (1968); and Peter Townsend, *Duel of Eagles* (1970).

Additional Sources

Kesselring, Albert, *The memoirs of Field-Marshal Kesselring,* Novato, CA: Presidio, 1989, 1953.
Macksey, Kenneth, *Kesselring: the making of the Luftwaffe,* London: Batsford, 1978. □

David A. Kessler

Appointed commissioner of the Food and Drug Administration in December 1990 by President George Bush, David A. Kessler (born 1951) was reappointed by President Bill Clinton in 1993. He stepped down in 1997 to become dean of the Yale University School of Medicine. He will be remembered as a consumer's advocate and a vigilant watchdog over the industries which produce food and drugs.

David Kessler was born on May 31, 1951, in New York City. He graduated from Amherst College *magna cum laude* in 1973 with a Bachelor of Arts degree. He was elected to Phi Beta Kappa, the liberal arts honorary fraternity, and to Sigma Xi, the Scientific Research Society of North America. At Amherst he received the Harvey Blodgett Award in Biology and the John Woodruff Simpson fellowship for the study of medicine.

From 1973 to 1979 he went to Harvard Medical School, receiving his doctorate in 1979. In 1977-1978 he was a special student at the Harvard Law School. In 1978 he earned his J.D. (Doctor of Law) degree from the law school of the University of Chicago, which he attended from 1975 to 1977. He was an associate editor of the law review there.

New York University's Graduate School of Business Administration, which he attended from 1984 to 1986, awarded him an advanced professional certificate in management. He also studied advanced management in health care at the Yale School of Organization and Management.

Specialized in Pediatrics

Kessler's medical specialty was pediatrics. He served as an intern and resident in the Department of Pediatrics of the Johns Hopkins University Hospital in Baltimore. He was also a professor at the Albert Einstein College of Medicine, the Bronx, New York, teaching in the Department of Pediatrics, Epidemiology and Social Medicine. While medical director of the Albert Einstein Hospital he continued prac-

ticing his specialty, attending children regularly in the emergency rooms of the city's public hospitals. He was certified by the American Board of Pediatrics and the National Board of Medical Examiners.

In his administrative post at Albert Einstein Hospital he introduced a new emergency evaluation system; reorganized the medical service; opened new facilities for cancer, adult kidney dialysis, and blood donation; and expanded dialysis facilities for children. He introduced a training program for physician assistants that became a model for other teaching hospitals in the state and a quality assurance system for Einstein Hospital.

Kessler's research included experience at the Children's Hospital Medical Center, Boston, Massachusetts; the Marine Biological Laboratory, Woods Hole, Massachusetts; and the Sloan-Kettering Institute for Cancer Research, New York City.

From 1981 to 1984 Kessler was a special consultant to Senator Orrin G. Hatch (Republican, Utah), then chairman of the United States Senate Labor and Human Relations Committee, on food and drug related questions. He began teaching food and drug law in the Julius Silver Program in Law, Science and Technology at Columbia University's School of Law in New York City in 1986.

His articles on food labeling and the safety of new pharmaceuticals and medical devices appeared in the *New England Journal of Medicine,* the *Journal of the American Medical Association,* the *Harvard Journal of Legislation,* the *University of Chicago Law Review,* and other professional publications. He edited, with Carl Eisdorfer and Abby Spector, *Caring for the Elderly: Reshaping Health Policy.* He was chair of a committee advising the secretary of the Department of Health and Human Services on the missions of the department and the Food and Drug Administration (FDA) before assuming the position of commissioner, and he continued as a nonvoting member after his appointment.

The Food and Drug Administration monitors cosmetics, foods, food supplements (such as vitamins), prescription and non-prescription animal and human drugs, and a wide range of other medical, prosthetic, and surgical products used by Americans. In the 1960s the agency had achieved international fame for keeping thalidomide off the market in the United States; in other countries the drug caused a range of birth abnormalities. Experts estimate that about a quarter of all goods bought by American consumers must meet FDA scrutiny.

Named to Head FDA

He was named to head the agency by President George Bush's administration in 1990. Before Kessler's assumption of the FDA commissionership, certification of the efficacy and safety of drugs and vitamin pills had been long and cumbersome. The agency had got entangled in allegations of fraud concerning generic drugs. It had been charged with ignoring dishonest labeling of food products such as orange juice and with the improper approval of potentially dangerous implants in breast surgery.

Kessler moved quickly to restore public and industry confidence in the FDA's missions and operation. He reorganized the bureaucracy, borrowing personnel and practices from private industry. Congress approved Kessler's request to charge pharmaceutical houses $100,000 to evaluate each new drug and to provide funds to hire additional reviewers. The agency raised standards for the approval of new drugs and medical and surgical appliances. It rewrote and quickly reissued the vast array of rules governing the labeling of foods. Kessler launched a continuing public information campaign to educate the public about the FDA's work.

Kessler also caused controversy as he tackled issues such as tobacco regulation, food labeling, breast implants, and fake fat olestra. Labels detailing the fat, fiber, and caloric contents of foods debuted in May 1994. He banned silicone gel breast implants because of safety concerns. His most difficult challenge was taking on the tobacco industry when he insisted that it be regulated as an addictive drug and called for restrictions in cigarette ads aimed at minors. His crowning achievement came as he left office. That was when the first-ever FDA regulations of tobacco went into effect on Feb. 28, 1997, forbidding merchants from selling tobacco to minors.

On leaving the agency, Kessler wrote in *Newsweek*, "Both the agency and I have been vilified. I feel very strongly, however, that if you believe in what you're doing, all the name-calling in the world won't stop you." He became dean of the Yale University School of Medicine on July 1, 1997.

Kessler was married to Paulette Steinberg Kessler, an attorney. They had two children, Elise and Benjamin.

Further Reading

Additional material may be found in Kessler's own works, especially in such articles as "Addressing the Problem of Misleading Advertising" in *Annals of Internal Medicine* (June 1, 1992) and "Regulating the Prescribing of Human Drugs for Nonapproved Uses Under the Food, Drug, and Cosmetic Act," *Harvard Journal of Legislation* (1978); in published speeches such as "Remarks by the Commissioner of Food and Drugs," in *Food and Drug Cosmetic Law Journal* (November 1991); and "Remarks Upon Taking the Oath of Office," in *Journal of the Association of Food and Drug Officials* (April 1991); and in his book, *Caring for the Elderly: Reshaping Health Policy* (1989); *Business Week* (October 25, 1993) reviews Kessler's work in "Getting the Lead Out at the FDA" by John Carey; *Time* magazine discusses "The Commish Under Fire," (January 8, 1996) and in "A Commish Many Will Miss" (Dec. 9, 1996); Kessler addresses his leaving the FDA in *Newsweek* "We've Fought the Good Fight" Dec. 9, 1996. ☐

Charles F. Kettering

An engineer, industrial pioneer, and apostle of progress, Charles F. Kettering (1876-1958), first as an independent inventor and later as General Motors Corporation's research chief, conducted research

which established him as one of the most creative Americans of his generation.

Charles Francis Kettering, born on August 29, 1876, on a farm near Loudonville, Ohio, taught three years in country and small-town schools to finance his higher education. Entering Ohio State University at age 22, he dropped out in his sophomore year because of poor eyesight. He worked two years as a telephone lineman, then returned to Ohio State, graduating at age 28 in 1904.

The NCR and Delco Era

Upon receiving his degree, Kettering became an experimental engineer with National Cash Register Company (NCR) in Dayton. During his five years with NCR he created a low-cost printing cash register; electrified the cash register, doing away with the hand crank; developed a system that tied charge phones to cash registers; and originated an accounting machine for banks. Meantime, in 1905 he was married to Olive Williams of Ashland, Ohio. The couple had one son, Eugene Williams, in adulthood president of the Charles F. Kettering Foundation.

Having developed a better ignition system for autos while working "on the side" for NCR, Kettering, with the financial backing of NCR's general manager Col. Edward A. Deeds and other capitalists, organized Dayton Engineering Laboratories Company (Delco) in 1909. That year an order from Cadillac for 8,000 ignition systems led to creation of an

electric starter, first offered on Cadillac cars in 1912 and on many more makes the following year. In addition to working on the self-starter, Kettering and Delco also improved auto lighting systems and developed a dependable means of generating electricity on farms. Meantime, Delco became a sizable manufacturing firm, as well as a research facility.

The GM Years

In 1915 Colonel Deeds, a top-notch administrator, joined Delco, complementing Kettering, who preferred to devote himself to research. In 1916 Delco, in exchange for nine million dollars, became a subsidiary of United Motors Corporation, an automotive parts and accessories combine. United Motors, in turn, was acquired by General Motors in 1918. Kettering was invited to organize and direct General Motors Research Corporation, headquartered in Dayton at the inventor's insistence. The labs were incorporated as General Motors Research Corporation in 1920, at which time Kettering—simultaneously named a GM vice-president and board member—agreed to move the bulk of research activity to Detroit. In 1925, when the labs were transferred to a new 11-story building, Kettering and his wife moved to Detroit, occupying a suite atop the Motor City's tallest hotel until Kettering's retirement.

As head of GM's research function for 27 years, Kettering guided research on and the improvement of many products, acquiring 140 patents in his name. His most notable achievements included the development of "Ethyl" leaded gasoline to eliminate engine knock; the high-compression automobile engine; the non-toxic, non-inflammable refrigerant "Freon"; and faster-drying and longer-lasting finishes for automobiles. He also created the lightweight diesel engine, which, in one of its applications, revolutionized the motive power of railroads.

Philosopher and Humanitarian

In addition to earning acclaim as a scientist and engineer, Kettering was highly regarded as a public speaker and social philosopher. "I am for the double-profit system," he said, "a reasonable profit for the manufacturer and a much greater profit for the customer." "I object to people running down the future," he also remarked; "I am going to live all the rest of my life there, and I would like it to be a nice place, polished, bright, glistening, and glorious." Kettering always regarded himself as a professional amateur. "We are amateurs," he observed, "because we are doing things for the first time." "Do something different," he continually admonished, "My God, do something different."

Kettering retired from General Motors in 1947, while continuing to serve as a director and research consultant until his death in Dayton on November 25, 1958. He received more than three dozen honorary doctor's degrees and additional dozens of awards, citations, and medals. His name is memorialized in the Charles F. Kettering Foundation, which he organized for medical research in 1927, and the Sloan-Kettering Institute for Cancer Research, founded by GM chairman Alfred P. Sloan, Jr. in 1945.

Further Reading

The most informative book on Kettering is *Professional Amateur: The Biography of Charles Franklin Kettering* (1957), a sympathetic portrait by T. A. Boyd, a longtime associate. Boyd also edited the useful *Prophet of Progress: Selections from the Speeches of Charles F. Kettering* (1961), which draws from the lengthy list of published speeches, articles, and interviews cited in an appendix. Kettering himself, with Allan Orth, wrote *American Battle for Abundance: A Story of Mass Production* (1947). The inventor also is discussed in Arthur Pound's *The Turning Wheel: The Story of General Motors Through Twenty-five Years 1908-33* (1934). □

Francis Scott Key

Francis Scott Key (1779-1843) was a successful attorney and amateur poet whose one notable verse, "The Star-Spangled Banner," became the national anthem of the United States.

Poet and attorney Francis Scott Key was a witness to the relentless bombing of Baltimore's Fort McHenry by the British during the War of 1812. Inspired by the sight of the battered American flag that flew over the fort throughout the conflict, he penned the lines of the future national anthem of the United States on the back of an envelope. His poem, "The Star-Spangled Banner," soon appeared in newspapers across the country and was set to the tune of a popular English drinking song. Congress officially named it the national anthem in 1931.

Key was born on his family's 2,800-acre estate, Terra Rubra, near Frederick County, Maryland, on August 1, 1779. He was the son of John Ross Key, a soldier who had distinguished himself in battle during the Revolutionary War. The Keys were known for their hospitality, and in July 1791 President George Washington visited their home on his way to Philadelphia. As a boy, Key became an excellent horseman. He attended prep school at St. John's College in Annapolis, graduating in 1796. Key then remained at St. John's to earn a degree in law.

A Religious Pacifist

Key established a law practice in Frederick in 1801. The following year he married Mary Tayloe Lloyd, who also came from a prominent Maryland family. The couple eventually had eleven children, six boys and five girls. In 1803 Key and his family moved to Georgetown, in the District of Columbia. Key became a partner in the law practice of his uncle, Philip Barton Key, taking over the practice two years later.

A deeply religious man, Key was an active member of St. John's Episcopal Church and sang with the Georgetown Glee Club. He even composed a popular hymn, "Lord, with Glowing Heart I'd Praise Thee." His faith led him to maintain a pacifist stance when relations between England and the United States grew increasingly tense in the early 1810s. The British, then engaged in a war with France, frequently

"impressed" American ships and crews into British service against their will. There were also disputes between British and American troops along the Canadian border and on the western frontier. Responding to the increasing British threat, the United States declared its "second war for independence" in 1812.

Became a Patriot and Enlisted

When England defeated France in 1814 and turned its full attention to fighting the United States, Key reversed his position against the war and became an avowed patriot. In 1814 he enlisted in the District of Columbia militia and became an aide to General Walter Smith. The American forces clustered around Baltimore, anticipating that it would be the main target of British attacks. Instead, the British landed near Washington, D.C., and in August 1814 they managed to capture the city and burn down the Capitol building and the White House. During the attack, Key's friend William Beanes, a Maryland physician and important patriot strategist, was captured and imprisoned aboard a British warship. The American military leaders decided to send Key to meet with the British and try to secure Beanes's release.

Key embarked on the mission on September 3, 1814. On his way, he stopped to retrieve letters written by British prisoners of war describing their good treatment by the Americans. On September 7, he sailed out to meet the British fleet at the mouth of the Potomac River. At first the captors refused to release Beanes, but they eventually agreed after reading the testimonials Key had secured. The

two men's departure was delayed, however, to prevent them from revealing British plans to launch a full-scale attack on Baltimore. Their boat was put in tow behind the British fleet as it approached Fort McHenry.

Poem Conveyed Patriotic Feelings

As sixteen British warships formed a semicircle around the fort, Key noticed a thirty-by-forty-two-foot American flag flying over it. The ships commenced bombing on September 13 and continued for the next twenty-four hours. Key watched from aboard his ship as some 1,800 shells exploded in and around the fort, lighting up the night sky. American forces on land and on sea counterattacked. When the shelling finally stopped it was still dark, and Key waited impatiently to learn how the fort had fared. At dawn he saw the American flag still flying defiantly over Fort McHenry, proving that the American forces had prevailed.

In the early morning hours of September 14, 1814, Key wrote a poem conveying his patriotic feelings about the battle. He and Beanes were allowed to return to Baltimore later that morning, where Key's poem was soon published as a broadside entitled "The Defense of Fort McHenry." The verse quickly gained popularity as it was reprinted in newspapers across the country and set to the tune of a popular song, "To Anacreon in Heaven." Key's song, renamed "The Star-Spangled Banner" in 1815, was adopted by the Union army during the Civil War and was declared the anthem of the American military during World War I. After several failed attempts, it was finally recognized by Congress as the national anthem of the United States in 1931.

A Respected Attorney

After the War of 1812, Key enjoyed a flourishing law practice. He was appointed district attorney for the District of Columbia in 1833 and held the post through 1841. In this position, Key negotiated several important agreements between the government and Native Americans. He also became active in the anti-slavery movement. Key became ill during a trip to Baltimore and died of pneumonia at the home of his daughter on January 11, 1843.

The "Star-Spangled Banner" has been criticized in some quarters, mostly due to its musical difficulty, and some minor attempts have been made to replace it as the national anthem. "No matter how many critics our anthem might have," composer John Philip Sousa asserted in *Francis Scott Key and the Star Spangled Banner,* "none of them can dispute the fact that it was a very satisfactory anthem during the World Wars and played an enormous part in arousing enthusiasm and patriotism. It would be as easy to make a stream run uphill as to secure a new national anthem. . . . The only possible chance that we might have a new national anthem would be when the eyes of all Americans are directed toward some particular cause and another genius captures the spirit of the moment in a thrilling song of patriotism. Until that time I do not believe the veneration for Francis Scott Key's anthem will ever be displaced." The flag that inspired Key, as well as his original manuscript, are on display at the Smithsonian Institution.

Further Reading

Silkett, John T., *Francis Scott Key and the History of the Star Spangled Banner,* Vintage American Publishing, 1978.
Weybright, Victor, *Spangled Banner: The Story of Francis Scott Key,* Farrar and Rinehart, 1935. □

Vladimir Orlando Key Jr.

The American political scientist Vladimir Orlando Key, Jr. (1908-1963), played an extremely influential role in the development of the now predominant behavioral, or empirical, approach to the study of politics.

After spending his early life in Texas and receiving much of his education there, V. O. Key attended McMurray College in Abilene for 2 years and then the University of Texas, where he received a bachelor of arts degree in 1929 and a master of arts degree in 1930. He went to the University of Chicago for his doctoral work. There he came under the influence of Charles E. Merriam, the leading figure in the "Chicago school" of political science. The intention of the Chicago school was to explore and develop new methods of studying political and administrative behavior. It pioneered in the use of statistics, the use of filed methods, the study of the role of psychology in politics, and especially the realistic approach that focused on power and power relations. In this atmosphere Key wrote his doctoral dissertation, *The Techniques of Political Graft in the United States.* His approach was not to moralize about graft but to analyze it from the standpoint of the function it played in the political system.

After teaching for a short time at the University of California at Los Angeles, Key went to Washington in 1936, where he was first associated with the Social Science Research Council, and he later served as a staff member of the National Resources Planning Board. In 1938 he was appointed to the faculty of Johns Hopkins University. At the outset of World War II, however, he returned to Washington, where he served several years with the U.S. Bureau of the Budget.

Key's pioneering approach to the study of politics was evident in 1942 in the first of many editions of his extremely influential text *Politics, Parties, and Pressure Groups.* Unlike earlier studies which were merely party histories, Key focused on the interest groups that contend for power and on their functions in the party system and the whole political process. Following World War II, he published his landmark work *Southern Politics in State and Nation* (1949). The work received the Woodrow Wilson Foundation Award for 1949 and inspired a number of other regional studies. Innovative in its approach, it analyzed local election returns and extensive in-depth interviews.

Following the publication of *Southern Politics,* Key was appointed Alfred Cowles professor of government and chairman of the department at Yale University. Preferring research to such administrative duties, he moved to Harvard in 1951 as Jonathan Trumbull professor of history and government. In 1954 he published *A Primer of Statistics for Political Scientists,* a general introduction to statistics with advice on research strategy. The work accomplished its purpose, giving considerable impetus to the study of statistics and the use of quantitative methods in political science.

In 1956 Key published *American State Politics,* a pioneering study of the functioning of two-party and one-party states in which he utilized aggregate election returns. While troubled by ill health during much of this period, Key nevertheless managed to accomplish a prodigious amount of work and in 1958 was elected to the presidency of the American Political Science Association. In 1959 he coauthored with Frank Munger "Social Determinism and Electoral Decision," a paper critical of the early sociological approach to the study of voting which maintained that social characteristics determined political preference.

In 1961 Key published *Public Opinion and American Democracy,* a massive study on American political culture, in which he attempted to explore the patterns and distribution of opinions, the ways in which they are formed, and the links between mass opinions and the operations of the structural machinery of government.

Although his health had become much worse, Key continued working to the very end. His last work was *The Responsible Electorate,* published posthumously with the assistance of his former student Milton Cummings, Jr., in 1966. This work challenged the conclusions of many leading works on the study of voting behavior by arguing that there was a greater degree of rationality involved in voting than had been commonly inferred.

Further Reading

No biographical work on Key exists. Useful background works for the problems with which he was concerned are David Easton, *The Political System: An Inquiry into the State of Political Science* (1953), and William T. Bluhm, *Theories of the Political System* (1965). □

John Maynard Keynes

John Maynard Keynes 1st Baron of Tilton (1883-1946), was an English economist who revolutionized economic theory and policy by linking employment and income to public and private expenditure. He is also known for his role in the creation of new international monetary institutions in World War II.

John Maynard Keynes was born on June 5, 1883, the son of John Neville Keynes, registrar of the University of Cambridge and eminent logician and economist. John Maynard's mother, a charming and talented woman, was onetime mayor of Cambridge. He was educated at Eton and King's College, Cambridge, and began a career in the civil service, where he was assigned to the India Office from 1906 to 1909. There he acquired an intimate knowledge of the government service and an interest in Indian currency and finance that was to bear fruit a few years later.

His Writings

In 1909 Keynes was elected fellow of King's College and returned to Cambridge. In 1911 he was chosen, in spite of his youth and inexperience, as editor of the *Economic Journal,* the publication of the Royal Economic Society and one of the leading professional journals. From that time until 1945 his duties were carried out with outstanding promptness and efficiency. In 1913 his first book, *Indian Currency and Finance,* was published shortly after he was appointed to the Royal Commission on Indian Currency and Finance. His book has been referred to as the best in the English language on the gold exchange standard.

With the outbreak of World War I Keynes entered the Treasury, first as an unofficial and unpaid assistant. Before the end of the war he held a position equivalent to an assistant secretary and was largely responsible for handling Interallied finances.

At the conclusion of the war Keynes went to the Paris Conference as principal representative of the Treasury and deputy for the chancellor of the Exchequer on the Supreme Economic Council. It soon became apparent to him that the economic terms of the treaty and particularly the reparations settlement were impossible of fulfillment. He resigned in June 1919 and set forth his case in *The Economic Consequences of the Peace* (1919). Although the book aroused

John Maynard Keynes (right)

tremendous controversy, subsequent events have demonstrated the substantial correctness of his position.

Having left the public service, Keynes returned to Cambridge as second bursar of King's College. In 1921 he assumed the first of a number of important company directorships. Also that year, he published *A Treatise on Probability* and, a year later, *A Revision of the Treaty,* a sequel to *The Economic Consequences* . In 1923 his *Tract on Monetary Reform* appeared. From 1924 until his death he was first bursar of King's College and through his expert management made King's what a contemporary has described as "indecently rich."

In 1925 Keynes married Lydia Lopokova, a Russian ballerina, who was as outstanding a person in her own way as he was in his. Although he had for many years been a collector of rare books and fine art, he now became an active patron of the theater, helping in later years (1932) as treasurer of the Camargo Society to bring about a union of the resources of the Camargo, the Vic-Wells, the Rambert Ballet, and others. In 1936 he founded and generously financed the Cambridge Arts Theatre.

Keynes's *Treatise on Money,* a two-volume work that generations of students have found full of brilliant insights but incomprehensible as a whole, was published in 1930. In it Keynes attempted with little success to break free of the shortcomings and limitations of the Cambridge version of the quantity theory of money. In retrospect, one can see the germ of many of the ideas that distinguish his later work—but as isolated flashes of insight lacking the proper framework and, as a result, not leading to any very useful or interesting conclusions.

Finally, in 1936, came Keynes's *General Theory of Employment, Interest and Money,* a book that not only revolutionized economic theory but also had a direct impact on the lives of a large proportion of the world's population. Here Keynes took issue with the classical theory which found in a competitive capitalist economy a set of mechanisms that automatically move the economy toward a state of full employment. (The term "classical" is used here to mean the mainstream of orthodox economic theory beginning with Adam Smith and running through the work of Ricardo, Mill, Marshall, and others.) These mechanisms functioned in the labor market and in the market for goods and services.

Classical Position

In the labor market, competition among workers assures full employment on the condition that the real rate of wages responds to the forces of supply and demand. In the market for goods and services, however, the question arises if there is any assurance that all of the output produced at full employment will find buyers. The classical economists found the answer to this question to be in the affirmative. To understand the rationale of their position, it is necessary to keep firmly in mind the truism that, in the aggregate, the value of output and income are identical. It follows from that truism that if all output is to be purchased, expenditures must be exactly equal to income.

Given this truism, how did the classical economists see this mechanism working? There are two types of expenditures made, those on goods and services for consumption purposes and those for goods and services purchased with an eye for resale or to be used to produce more goods and services. The first type of expenditure is called consumption, and the second, investment. If that part of income that is *not* spent on consumers goods is called "saving," then income and expenditures will be equal if saving is equal to investment. Hence, expenditures are equal to the value of output.

The classical economists believed that saving and investment were both functions of the rate of interest, with savers saving more and investors investing less as the rate of interest rises, and the reverse happening when the rate of interest falls. The interest rate would always adjust in such a way as to assure that all of current output would be purchased.

Keynes's Theory

Keynes disagreed with both the labor market analysis and the goods market analysis of the classicists. He argued that changes in money wage rates do not result in corresponding changes in real wages because of their impact on the incomes and, therefore, on the expenditures of wage earners. Lower money wages, he argued, would force lower demand for goods and services and therefore lower their prices. Real wages would be unchanged.

With respect to the product market, Keynes held that saving is a function of the level of income rather than of the rate of interest. There is no reason to believe that the amount that investors will be willing to invest (determined, according to Keynes, by the rate of interest and by the expectations about the future held by potential investors) will turn out to be equal to the amounts that savers wish to save out of a full employment level of income. Where savers wish to save more than investors wish to invest, part of current output will go unsold. This will lead producers to cut back on current output and therefore on employment and income. As income falls, saving will fall. Income will keep on falling until savers are willing to save no more than investors wish to invest.

Liquidity Trap

Since the system, as Keynes saw it, does not tend to seek full employment when left to itself, it is necessary for policy makers to do so. Basically, two possibilities exist: monetary authorities may induce investors to invest the desired amounts through their control over the rate of interest, or fiscal authorities may close the gap between investment and full employment levels of saving with government expenditures.

Keynes was somewhat pessimistic about the ability of monetary authorities to bring about the necessary changes in private investment expenditures. Under some circumstances the central bank can drive interest rates down by increasing the money supply. The public, finding itself with more money than it wishes to hold, will attempt to convert it into interest-earning assets. This will drive the prices of securities up and, consequently, interest rates down.

Once the interest rate is driven down to a level at which the public believes that it must rise again, holding securities entails the risk of taking a capital loss. Under these circumstances the public will not convert additional money balances into securities, and the interest rate will not be driven down any further. This floor on interest rates is known as the liquidity trap and represents a severe limitation on the central bank's ability to stimulate private investment.

Keynes also saw another and perhaps more serious limitation to monetary policy. Private investors, he maintained, make their decisions not only on the basis of the interest rate but also on the basis of their expectations about costs and demand for their product in the future. All of these expectations are lumped together for convenience's sake into what he called the marginal efficiency of capital. The important thing about the marginal efficiency of capital is that it is based, not upon known facts, but upon expectations about the future which must, of necessity, be very uncertain. The uncertainty means that the marginal efficiency is likely to be very unstable. Keynes regarded it as entirely possible that the marginal efficiency of capital could be so low that even a rate of interest of zero would not be sufficient to stimulate a full employment level of investment.

Thus, although in later years he was less pessimistic about the usefulness of monetary policy, Keynes was inclined to believe that fiscal policy would have to bear the main part of the burden of assuring full employment. Further, he was inclined to believe that in mature economies, such as those of the United States and western Europe, high levels of income had led the public to save large proportions of their income, while the factors that had historically provided expanding investment opportunities were disappearing. This idea is known as the stagnation hypothesis and enjoyed a wide acceptance during the 1930s and 1940s.

Return to Public Service

With the beginning of World War II, Keynes again entered the public service. In July 1940 he was asked to serve as adviser to the chancellor of the Exchequer, and he was soon after elected to the Court of the Bank of England and was raised to the peerage as Lord Tilton in 1942. Through his work, national income and expenditure accounts were developed and utilized in the preparation of wartime budgets. In addition to internal finance, he had special responsibility for intergovernmental finance, lend-lease, and mutual aid. This work required that he become a sort of special envoy to Washington and Ottawa in particular.

In the closing days of the war, Keynes played a major role in negotiating the United States loan to Great Britain and in the establishment of the International Monetary Fund and the Bank for Reconstruction and Development. Keynes died of a heart attack on Easter Sunday, April 21, 1946, shortly after having returned from the inaugural meetings of the International Monetary Fund and the World Bank in Savannah, Ga.

Further Reading

The most definitive study of Keynes's life and work is *The Life of John Maynard Keynes* (1951), written by R. F. Harrod, who was a friend and an eminent economist in his own right. A shorter but highly readable biography is Seymour E. Harris, *John Maynard Keynes, Economist and Policy Maker* (1955). Robert Lekachman, *The Age of Keynes* (1966), contains some material not found in the earlier volumes, including an up-to-date appraisal of Keynes's influence. See also Lawrence R. Klein, *The Keynesian Revolution* (2d ed. 1966). □

Aram Ilich Khachaturian

Soviet composer Aram Ilich Khachaturian (1903-1978) is best known for two works: *Piano Concerto* (1936) and the ballet *Gayane* (1942), which includes the popular and rhythmic *Sabre Dance*. His compositions incorporate the folk tunes of his native Armenia and other parts of Russia.

Aram Khachaturian was born on June 6, 1903, in the Armenian community of Tiflis, Georgia, Russian Empire (later part of the U.S.S.R. and now Tbilisi in the Republic of Georgia). Music was not on his mind at the Tiflis Commercial School where he debated between a career in medicine or engineering. In 1920, however, Georgia became part of the new Soviet Union. The following year,

Khachaturian, then 17, went to Moscow with his oldest brother, Suren, who was director of the Moscow Art Theater. Like his brother, Khachaturian Russianized name to Khachaturov, which he used for a period of 18 years. Influenced by his brother's work in Moscow, Khachaturian fell under the magic spell of the music world. Although he began to study biology at Moscow University, he took cello lessons as well at the Gnessin Music School.

Early Music Career

Khachaturian had hardly mastered the basics of musical composition when he completed his first work, *The Dance* for violin and piano (1926). By the following year, with the publication of *Poem in C Sharp Minor,* his extensive use of folk music from his native land was already evident. Said Gerald Abraham in *Monthly Musical Record,* "The Khachaturian of this period was in the position of an eager, intelligent child who has just been given the run of a toyshop ... Like many other young musicians with fuller cultural backgrounds, Khachaturian discovered music through contemporary music, and only later developed a love of the classics."

Over the next several years, Khachaturian studied and also taught at the Moscow Conservatory. Influenced by contemporary Western music, particularly the works of Maurice Ravel, his compositions began to show the maturity, mastery, and rich stirring color that so dominated his music.

The Compositions

The first of Khachaturian's two best-known works, *Piano Concerto* (1936) was first performed in the United States at the Juilliard Graduate School of Music in New York City on March 15, 1942, followed by the first public performance, by the Boston Symphony Orchestra, that July. Said the music critic of the *World-Telegram,* "There is no piano concerto in the entire literature to equal this one in sheer energy, speed, and sheer drive .... It happens also to be pretty good music. . . ."

Other works followed, most notably: *Happiness,* a ballet (1939); *Violin Concerto in D Minor* (1940), for which he won the Stalin Prize, Second Degree; *Second Symphony* (1943), written for the 25th anniversary of the Russian revolution; *Masquerade* (1944), a symphonic suite in the tradition of lavish classical Russian music; and *Spartak,* a ballet (1953). In addition, he composed violin and cello concerto and numerous minor works.

The second of Khachaturian's best-known works is *Sabre Dance* from his ballet *Gayane* (1942). This rhythmically stirring piece has received popular recognition since it was first performed. It is generally played in four-quarter rather than the three-quarter time in which it was written. First performed by the Leningrad Kirov Theatre of the Opera and Ballet, it is set on a collective Soviet farm just before World War II. He received his second Stalin Prize for this piece.

Criticism and Restoration

Khachaturian wrote numerous musical works, including marches, dances, chamber music, and film scores. During World War II, he was president of the Moscow Union of Composers and belonged to the Battle Song Staff, which wrote songs for the Russian army.

After the war, however, in 1948, Khachaturian, along with leading composers Sergei Prokofiev and Dmitri Shostakovich, was accused by the Central Committee of the Russian Communist party of having "antidemocratic tendencies" in his music. He was censured by the critics even after he admitted to such charges in public. However, he was restored to favor later that yer when he was praised for his film biography of Lenin. In 1954, he was named People's Artist of the Soviet Union. Five years later, he was awarded the Lenin Prize in recognition of his work. Although the official criticism was later charged to excesses of the Stalin period, it moved Khachaturian closer to Soviet political thinking in the arts. He frequently appered in world forums in the role of champion of an apologist for the Soviet idea of creative orthodoxy. His later works were often criticized as repetitive and eclectic.

Khachaturian's wife, Nina, was also prominent in Soviet cultural life and wrote songs under the name of Nina Makarova. Khachaturian lived in Moscow until his death on May 1, 1978.

Further Reading

Gustav Schneerson, *Aram Khachaturian,* translated into English by Xenia Denko in 1959, was published by the Moscow Foreign Language Publishing House and reflects Soviet views; Gerald Abraham's, *Eight Soviet Composers* (1943), includes a chapter on Khachaturian. □

Sayyid Abdullah Khalil

Sayyid Abdullah Khalil (1892-1970) was a Sudanese military officer and political leader and the second prime minister of the Republic of the Sudan.

Abdullah Khalil was born into a Mahdist farming family in the western Sudan. He was educated in the military school in Khartoum and subsequently served as an engineer in the Egyptian army and after 1925 in the Sudan Defense Force. During his military career he served in the Dardanelles campaign during World War I and against the Italians in Ethiopia in World War II. He retired in 1944 with the rank of brigadier general.

Khalil first became involved in politics in the early 1920s, when he was an active member of the Sudanese Union, a group of young, educated Sudanese who sought closer ties between Egypt and the Sudan. His political activities on behalf of Egypt ended in 1924, when the Egyptian government failed to support a pro-Egyptian mutiny among Sudanese soldiers stationed in Khartoum. After his retirement from the army he became active in politics again, this time as a leader in the moderate anti-Egyptian Umma (Nation) party, which was formed to oppose the pro-Egyptian Ashiqqa party led by Ismail al-Azhari.

Politics in the Sudan during the period before independence was dominated by the future relationship between the Sudan and Egypt. The simple division between those who desired "unity of the Nile Valley" and those, like Khalil, who sought a Sudan independent of both British and Egyptian rule was complicated by deep religious rivalries in the Sudan. On the one hand, Khalil's Umma party was strongly supported by the Mahdists, who had driven the Egyptians from the Sudan in the late 19th century. On the other, al-Azhari's Ashiqqa party and later his National Unionist party (NUP) was supported by the Khatmiyya sect, which had a long history of friendship with Egypt. These sectarian divisions split and confused the nationalist movement almost from its inception.

Desire for Independence

Between 1948 and 1956 power shifted from one side to the other. In 1948 the Umma party received a majority of the seats in the new Legislative Assembly, in which Abdullah Khalil quickly emerged as the principal leader. His willingness to cooperate with the British weakened the position of the Umma leaders, however, and in 1953 al-Azhari's NUP won a stunning victory in the nationwide elections for the first independent Sudanese Parliament. Khalil and the Umma party bitterly resigned themselves to opposing al-Azhari's government, adamantly objecting to any future but an independent Sudan.

Recognizing that his pro-Egyptian policy did not have the support of the majority of the Sudanese people, al-Azhari declared the Sudan an independent republic on Jan. 1, 1956. This victory for the Umma party's program signaled the end of al-Azhari's dominance. In February he invited Khalil to join a "ministry of all talents," but this temporary expedient could not prevent his downfall. In June, when some of his former supporters founded the People's Democratic party (PDP), which established a coalition with the Umma party, al-Azhari was forced to resign, and Khalil became his country's second prime minister on July 5.

Internal Divisions

Khalil's government, however, was from the beginning a coalition of convenience. The Umma party and the PDP could find common cause in their opposition to al-Azhari; they could not, however, agree on a common program to deal with the major problems facing the newly independent Sudan. The principal task facing Khalil's government was to prepare a constitution acceptable to all segments of the population.

The Umma party wanted a strong presidential system, like that of the United States, which they felt would be dominated by the leader of the Mahdist sect, Abd al-Rahman al-Mahdi. Neither the PDP, which was dominated by Khatmiyya supporters, rivals to the Mahdists, nor al-Azhari's NUP would accept this solution, arguing for a parliamentary constitution similar to Great Britain's. The southern Sudanese distrusted both claims, wanting a federation which would grant the south substantial internal autonomy. Faced with these opposing views, Khalil's coalition became increasingly unable to lead or even govern the country.

During 1957 and early 1958 the political situation in the Sudan continued to deteriorate. In the south the government launched a program to Arabicize and Islamize the southern peoples. In the north relations with Egypt became increasingly strained over a series of border incidents along the Sudanese-Egyptian frontier, continued disagreement over the future division of the vital Nile water, and the strident antigovernment propaganda launched by the Egyptians. In addition, an economic recession hit the Sudan when the world price of cotton, the Sudan's major export, fell below the price the government needed to maintain a favorable balance of payments and to support their development projects.

When Khalil attempted to rectify the situation by artificially holding prices above the world market, Sudanese cotton remained unsold. When he negotiated an aid agreement with the United States, he encountered such strong opposition that his government nearly fell. Soon party politics and intrigue replaced parliamentary principles. Corruption was widespread, while the political maneuvering increasingly involved Egypt, raising fears among Khalil, the Umma, and the army that the Sudan might easily become a political dependency of Egypt.

Bloodless Coup

By November 1958 the situation had reached a crisis. Khalil was desperately trying to serve his government by including his old opponent, al-Azhari, in the coalition. Al-Azhari, meanwhile, was rumored to have been negotiating with President Nasser of Egypt. Unable to govern, on the one hand, while fearing an increase of Egyptian influence, on the other, Khalil did not oppose the intervention of the army. On the night of Nov. 16, 1958, the army under Gen. Ibrahim Abboud occupied Khartoum and seized power. The military coup d'etat was unopposed and bloodless, and the civilian government collapsed with little protest. The military take-over ended Abdullah Khalil's career as a powerful political leader in the Sudan and relegated him to quiet obscurity. He died on Aug. 23, 1970, in Khartoum.

Further Reading

For background material on Khalil and the Sudan see J. S. R. Duncan, *The Sudan: A Record of Achievement* (1952); Henry C. Jackson, *Behind the Modern Sudan* (1956); and Mandour El Mahdi, *A Short History of the Sudan* (1965). □

Sir Seretse M. Khama

Seretse M. Khama (1921-1980), first president of Botswana after it gained independence from Great Britain in 1966, was a major figure in his country's political history. He was also the grandson of Khama III the Good, who allied his kingdom of Bechuanaland with British colonizers in the late 19th century. As such, Khama carried the title of Sir Seretse, chieftain of the Ngwato (or Bamangwato) tribe.

Seretse M. Khama was born in the British Protectorate of Bechuanaland (now Botswana) in southern Africa, on July 1, 1921. He was heir to the chieftainship of the Ngwato (or Bamangwato) people, the largest of the Bechuanaland tribes. His uncle, Tshekedi Khama, acted as regent and groomed the boy to take over the chieftainship. He was schooled at home until the age of ten when he was sent to South Africa, where he attended Tiger Kloff, Adams College, and Lovedale, graduating in 1940. He received a bachelor of arts degree from Fort Hare University College and went on to study law at the University of the Witwatersrand. During his first year there, his uncle decided it was time for the young man to become chief, but Khama asked for permission to continue his studies in England, where he attended Oxford University.

A Troubling Marriage

After three years at Oxford and as a law student in London, Khama informed his uncle that he was going to marry an English woman, Ruth Williams. She was a typist with a local insurance company. Everyone but the young couple was deeply distressed—Uncle Tshekedi, Williams's parents, and even the government of South Africa, which warned the British Colonial Office that trouble would come from this interracial marriage.

The uncle's basic objection was that Khama, as chief-designate, had violated tribal law and custom by taking a wife without the prior assent of the tribe. Moreover, Tshekedi Khama was aware of the possible consequences of a mixed marriage in this exposed territory, overshadowed by its white-supremacist neighbors, South Africa and Southern Rhodesia. The marriage was discussed at three large *kgotlas* (tribal meetings) held between November 1948 and June 1949.

At the first *kgotla,* nearly all the speakers opposed the marriage, and it was resolved not to accept Ruth Williams as the wife of a future chief. Furthermore, she was not to be allowed to enter Ngwato country. More people were won over to Seretse's side at the second *kgotla* in December 1948, but most tribesmen still expressed hostility. By now, however, rumors (which were false) were circulating that the uncle himself had designs on the chieftainship. At the final *kgotla* in June 1949, tribal feeling had turned decisively against Tshekedi Khama. In a short speech, Seretse Khama asked the tribe if they were in favor of him and his wife, and most shouted their approval.

International Complications

Khama and Ruth Williams were married in a civil ceremony, because all London churches closed their doors to the couple, on Sept. 29, 1948. Approval of the marriage by the *kgotla* did not, however, end the trouble. The British government instituted a commission of inquiry to examine the dispute and ascertain whether Khama was "a fit and proper person to discharge the functions of chief." The British may have been responding to South African pressures. Dr. D. F. Malan, the South African prime minister, had expressed bitter opposition to the marriage and had declared that Seretse Khama was prohibited from entering South Africa. (This was a serious restriction as the capital of Bechuanaland was then the South African town of Mafeking.) It was thought that South Africa would intensify its demand to incorporate the territory, as it had long wished to do, and that it might apply economic pressures that could cripple Bechuanaland, which was utterly dependent upon South Africa.

The findings of the commission were never published, but in 1950 the British government decided to withhold recognition from Khama as chief for at least five years. During this time he was prohibited from entering Bechuanaland without special permission. Subsequently, in 1952 the British offered Khama an official post in Jamaica if he would give up his claim to the chieftainship. He refused. Pressure from the Ngwato failed to induce the British government to alter its stand.

Return Home

Finally, in 1956, Khama, who had been living in London for some years, and his uncle both renounced their children's claims to the chieftainship. That year, Khama, his wife, and four children, Jacqueline, Ian Seretse, and twins Tshekedi Stanford and Anthony Paul, returned to Bechuanaland as private citizens.

Not barred from participating in local politics, Khama soon became an important member of the Ngwato Tribal Council, the African Advisory Council, and the Joint Advisory Council. He supported a motion for the introduction of a legislative council and spoke out strongly against racial discrimination. In 1961 Khama became a member of the new Legislative Council and was subsequently appointed to the Executive Council. In 1962 he was instrumental in founding the Bechuanaland Democratic party.

Constitutional development proceeded rapidly in the early 1960s. By March 1965, after Khama's party had won 28 out of the 31 contested constituencies, Bechuanaland was granted self-government and Khama became prime minister. Full sovereign independence was granted on September 30, 1966, when Bechuanaland became the Republic of Botswana (an old tribal name for the country). Seretse Khama became its first president and was knighted by Queen Elizabeth II.

As the new leader, Sir Seretse Khama showed great determination to develop his poverty-stricken and drought-ravaged country. He achieved free universal education and tried to strengthen the nation's economy. His major challenge was South Africa. Despite an overwhelming economic dependence on its southern neighbor, Khama had always made clear his abhorrence of apartheid, South Africa's policy of racial apartness. He had even deported a South African citizen for making racist statements. Despite a fundamental difference of philosophy, however, Khama managed to maintain reasonably cordial relations with his powerful neighbor and at the same time preserve an undisputed independence.

In time, even Khama's in-laws softened on the marriage and often visited the state house in Gaborone. Khama was reelected to successive terms and remained president of Botswana until his death on July 13, 1980.

Further Reading

There is no full-length biography of Seretse. Information on him is contained in John Redfern, *Ruth and Seretse: "A Very Disreputable Transaction"* (1955); Mary Benson, *Tshekedi Khama* (1960); and S. M. Gabatshwane, *Seretse Khama and Botswana* (1966). Recommended for general historical background are William Malcolm Hailey, *The Republic of South Africa and the High Commission Territories* (1963), and Richard P. Stevens, *Lesotho, Botswana, and Swaziland* (1967). □

Ayatollah Sayyid Ali Khamenei

Ayatollah Sayyid Ali Khamenei (born 1939) followed Ayatollah Rohollah Khomeini as supreme spiritual and political leader of the Islamic Republic of Iran. A favored Khomeini disciple, key revolutionary strategist, and innovative president, Khamenei was elected supreme leader by a Council of Islamic Experts on June 5, 1989.

Born in 1939, Sayyid Ali Khamenei was raised in a family of Islamic scholars in Meshed, a key city in northeast Iran. At 18 he began advanced religious training at Najaf, Iraq. Some sources claim that Khamenei also undertook limited paramilitary training in Palestinian camps in Lebanon and Libya. He moved to Qom, Iran, in 1958, where he became a close student of Ayatollah Khomeini. In 1963 Khamenei was involved in the massive student protests against the shah's Western-oriented reforms. The protests were brutally crushed, and Khomeini was exiled. Khamenei continued his studies in Meshed, eventually achieving recognition as *hojatolislam* ("authority on Islam"), a rank only one step beneath ultimate esteem as an ayatollah.

Khamenei's Farsi, Arabic, and Turkish language skills helped him as a literary critic and translator of works on Islamic science, history, and Western civilization. Khamenei's own books include a study of "the role of Muslims in the liberation of India."

Revolutionary Strategist

Khamenei's teachings drew the wrath of the shah's agents. Frequent arrests and three years of imprisonment were followed by a year of internal exile in the Baluchi desert region. Undaunted, Khamenei returned to Meshed in time to help orchestrate the nationwide street battles that resulted in the shah's overthrow and the triumphant return of Khomeini in 1979.

Khamenei rose rapidly as the clerics gradually consolidated their control over the revolution. An original Revolutionary Council member, Khamenei cofounded the Islamic Republican Party, was designated the prestigious Friday prayer leader for the capital city of Tehran, and was elected to the *Majlis* (consultative assembly). Khamenei's early tasks also included the ideological indoctrination of the shah's military and the formation of the autonomous and ideologically driven Revolutionary Guards. Khamenei staunchly defended the militant students who held 52 American diplomats for 444 days (1979-1981). After Iraq invaded Iran, Khamenei was Khomeini's first personal representative on the powerful Supreme Defense Council, from where he helped discredit then president Bani-Sadr for being inclined to accept Iraqi cease-fire offers. Khamenei viewed hard-line stands as beneficially producing a "born again" self-confidence in the Iranian people.

Khamenei was elected president on October 2, 1981, almost by default, since scores of top revolutionary clerics had been killed by bombs planted by the *Mujahedeen-e-Khalq* (Islamic-Marxist guerrillas). Khamenei himself barely survived a tape-recorder bomb; his right arm and voice remained damaged.

Presidential Years

As president, Khamenei's authority was significantly checked by Iran's complicated constitutional structure. Khomeini's original choice for prime minister, Ali-Akbar Velayati, was rejected by the Majlis in favor of the independent-minded Hussein Moussavi. Like the French system, Iran's divided executive increasingly suffered from bureaucratic confusion and tensions. Velayati, for example, became foreign minister, but many of his deputies were more beholden to Moussavi.

Khamenei's policy positions did not necessarily follow his earlier hard-line reputation. In social matters Khamenei tended to advocate stern social and cultural purity. Yet, he was quick to encourage skilled Iranians to return from abroad, regardless of their fidelity to revolutionary norms. In economics Khamenei's defense of the *Bazaaris* (merchants) against un-Islamic socialism clashed sharply with Moussavi's enactment of radical land and business reforms. When such disputes became severe, the theoretically supreme Ayatollah Khomeini tended merely to endorse such "constructive debate" and to praise the loyal service of both Moussavi and Khamenei. Though Moussavi's measures were often vetoed by Iran's conservative Council of Guardians, some observers viewed Khamenei's presidency as becoming ceremonial.

Khamenei's most significant presidential contribution was in foreign policy. As Iran struggled to break its pariah status, Khamenei launched in 1984 what became known as an "open door" policy. With Khomeini's blessing, Khamenei transformed the "neither east nor west" revolutionary slogan away from isolationism to mean neither eastern nor western domination. "Rational, sound, and healthy relations with all countries" will help Iran meet its "needs," he said, while aiding in the non-violent spread of Iran's revolutionary message. Khamenei insisted that reciprocity and mutual respect were Iran's criteria for good relations, not ideological conformity. Thus, even unconverted "Satans" like the United States could become friends.

Khamenei's "open minded policy" was frequently denounced by radical hardliners, particularly after the revelations of covert dealings with the United States. Still, the pragmatic analyses of Khamenei and Majlis speaker Rafsanjani arguably were behind Iran's "surprise" acceptance of a cease-fire with Iraq in August of 1988. The Salman Rushdie uproar was a subsequent setback for the pragmatists. When Khamenei suggested that the condemned author could redeem himself, Khomeini publicly reversed Khamenei, saying that Rushdie could not repent from intentional blasphemy.

Supreme Leader

Despite past controversial stands, the 49-year-old Khamenei was swiftly selected as the new supreme leader after Ayatollah Khomeini's death by an 80-member Council of Islamic Experts. The context for Khamenei's selection had been set by Khomeini's demotion of his previously designated successor, Ayatollah Hossein Montazeri, for his hardline international views and brazen criticisms of postwar executions of Mujahedeen leaders. Though elevated to ayatollah status, Khamenei's credentials were challenged by more senior Islamic clergy, including Montazeri. Yet, Khamenei's loyalty to Khomeini and his "skills gained during eight years as president" were deemed to take "priority" over religious training.

As spiritual leader, Khamenei followed Khomeini's tendency to seek conciliation among factions. To placate the marginalized radicals, Khamenei occasionally cautioned the powerful new president, Ali Rafsanjani, not to lose sight of revolutionary principles. Yet Khamenei's sanctioning of careful international financing of reconstruction exemplified his continued emphasis on pragmatic needs.

No longer as immersed in policy making, Khamenei's sermons took on the air of a detached theoretical historian. Such reasoned discourses on the unique and lasting aspects of Iran's Islamic revolution can still be displaced by fiery rhetoric. Amidst the 1990-1991 Persian Gulf crisis, Khamenei proclaimed a "Holy War" against notions of permanent U.S. bases in Saudi Arabia, even as he supported "international" efforts to remove Iraq from Kuwait.

Kamenei continued his defiance of the U.S. during the 1990s. In a ceremony marking the sixth anniversary of the death of Khomeini, he accused Washington of interfering in the affairs of Iran, saying; "It is very clear that the government of Iran is against U.S. interests." Anything with an American flavor came under his attack. With Khamenei's religious ruling, both Coke and Pepsi were banned in Iran. He launched a drive to make the universities more Islamic, and to increase censorship of newspapers, books, and films. While many in the public sector had little enthusiasm for continuing the revolutionary fervor, Khamenei with an extremist viewpoint attempted to keep Iran from moderating its stance. During the 1997 elections, Khamenei's choice for president, Ali Akbar Nateq-Noori, was defeated by Moham-med Khatami in a referendum by the general public for more freedom and liberty.

Further Reading

Within the growing literature on Iran's revolution and its regional and world impact, several well written and widely circulated English studies stand out: Shaul Bakhash, *The Reign of the Ayatollahs: Iran and the Islamic Revolution* (1984); R.K. Ramazani, *Revolutionary Iran: Challenge and Response in the Middle East* (1988); Robin Wright, *In the Name of God: The Khomeini Decade* (1989); and R.K. Ramazani, editor, *Iran's Revolution: The Search for Consensus* (1990). English translations of key Iranian speeches can be found in the Foreign Broadcast Information Service, available at most U.S. Government depository libraries. Khamenei's fundamentalism and politics is discussed by David Hirst in the *The Guardian* (February 3, 1997). □

Ayatollah Ruhollah Musavi Khomeini

Ayatollah Ruhollah Musavi Khomeini (1902-1989) was the founder and supreme leader of the Islamic Republic of Iran. The only leader in the Muslim world who combined political and religious authority as a head of state, he took office in 1979.

Ayatollah Khomeini was born on September 24, 1902, according to most sources. The title Ayatollah (the Sign of God) reflected his scholarly religious standing in the Shia Islamic tradition. His first name, Ruhollah (the Spirit of God), is a common name in spite of its religious meaning, and his last name is taken from his birthplace, the town of Khomein, which is about 200 miles south of Tehran, Iran's capital city. His father, Mustapha Musavi, was the chief cleric of the town where he was murdered only five months after the birth of Ruhollah. The child was raised by his mother (Hajar) and aunt (Sahebeh), both of whom died when Ruhollah was about 15 years old.

A Religious Scholar

Ayatollah Khomeini's life after childhood went through three distinct phases. The first phase, from 1908 to 1962, was marked mainly by training, teaching, and writing in the field of Islamic studies. At the age of six he began to study the Koran, Islam's holy book, and also elementary Persian. Subsequently he was taught Islamic jurisprudence by his older brother, Morteza Pasandideh, who was also an ayatollah in the holy city of Qom in Iran. He completed his studies in Islamic law, ethics, and spiritual philosophy under the supervision of Ayatollah Abdul Karim Haeri-ye Yazdi, first in Arak, a town near Khomein, and later in Qom, where he also got married and had two sons and three daughters. His older son, Hajj Mustafa, died (allegedly killed by the Shah's security agents), but the younger one,

Ahmad, was relatively active in revolutionary politics in Tehran.

Although during this scholarly phase of his life Khomeini was not politically active, the nature of his studies, teachings, and writings revealed that he firmly believed from the beginning in political activism by clerics. Three factors support this suggestion. First, his interest in Islamic studies surpassed the bounds of traditional subjects of Islamic law (*Sharia*), jurisprudence (*Figh*), and principles (*Usul*) and the like. He was keenly interested in philosophy and ethics. Second, his teaching focused often on the overriding relevance of religion to practical social and political issues of the day. Third, he was the first Iranian cleric to try to refute the outspoken advocacy of secularism in the 1940s. His now well-known book, *Kashf-e Assrar* (*Discovery of Secrets*) was a point by point refutation of *Assrar-e Hezar Saleh* (*Secrets of a Thousand Years*), a tract written by a disciple of Iran's leading anti-clerical historian, Ahmad Kassravi.

Preparation for Political Leadership

The second phase of Khomeini's life, from 1962 to 1979, was marked by political activism. During this phase he carried his lifelong fundamentalist interpretation of Shia Islam to its logical and practical conclusions. Logically, in the 1970s, as contrasted with the 1940s, he no longer accepted the idea of a limited monarchy under the Iranian Constitution of 1906-1907, an idea that was clearly evidenced by his book *Kashf-e Assrar*. In his *Islamic Government* (*Hokumat-e Islami*) —which is a collection of his lectures in Najaf (Iraq) published in 1970—he rejected both the Iranian Constitution as an alien import from Belgium and monarchy in general. He believed that the government was an un-Islamic and illegitimate institution usurping the legitimate authority of the supreme religious leader (*Faqih*), who should rule as both the spiritual and temporal guardian of the Muslim community (*Umma*). Practically, he launched his crusade against the shah's regime in 1962, which led to the eruption of a religiopolitical rebellion on June 5, 1963. This date (15th of Khurdad in the Iranian solar calendar) is regarded by the revolutionary regime as the turning point in the history of the Islamic movement in Iran. The shah's bloody suppression of the uprising was followed by the exile of Khomeini in 1964, first to Iraq until expelled in 1978 and then to France.

Radicalization of Khomeini's religiopolitical ideas and his entry into active political opposition in the second phase of his life reflected a combination of circumstances. First, the deaths of the leading, although quiescent, Iranian religious leader, Ayatollah Sayyed Muhammad Burujerdi (1961), and of the activist cleric Ayatollah Abul Qassem Kashani (1962) left the arena of leadership open to Khomeini, who had attained a prominent religious standing by the age of 60. Second, although ever since the rise of Reza Shah Pahlavi to power in the 1920s the clerical class had been on the defensive because of his secular and anticlerical policies and those of his son, Muhammad (Mohammad) Reza Shah, these policies reached their peak in the early 1960s. The shah's so-called White Revolution (1963) in particular was considered by the religious leaders as detrimental to not only the Shia cultural tradition, but also to their landed and educational interests. And third, the shah's granting of diplomatic privileges and immunities to the American military personnel and their dependents (1964) was viewed as degrading to the Iranian sense of national independence.

Founding the Islamic Republic of Iran

The third phase of Khomeini's life began with his return to Iran from exile on February 1, 1979—Muhammad Reza Shah had been forced to abdicate two weeks earlier. On February 11 revolutionary forces allied to Khomeini seized power in Iran. The hallmark of this phase was the emergence of Khomeini as the founder and the supreme leader of the Islamic Republic of Iran. Throughout this phase, Khomeini was preoccupied with the fundamental goal of engineering an ideal Islamic society in Iran. From the perspective of Khomeini and his leading disciples, the Iranian Revolution went through three major periods. The first one began with Khomeini's appointment of Mehdi Bazargan as the head of the "provisional government" on February 5, 1979, and ended with his fall on November 6, two days after the seizure of the U.S. embassy in Tehran. This, according to Khomeini, marked the beginning of the second revolution, which was in his view better than the first one that had resulted in the departure of the shah (January 16, 1979). The hallmark of this so-called second revolution was the elimination of mainly nationalist forces from politics. As early as August 20, 1979, 22 opposition newspapers were ordered closed. In terms of foreign policy, the landmarks of the second revolution were the destruction of U.S.-Iran relations and the Iranian defense against the Iraqi invasion of the Shatt-al-Arab (September 22, 1980). The admission of the shah to the United States on October 22, 1979; Khomeini's instruction to Iranian students on November 1 to "expand with all their might their attacks against the United States" in order to force the extradition of the shah; and the seizure of the American embassy on November 4 led to 444 days of agonizing dispute between the United States and Iran until the release of the hostages on January 21, 1981.

The so-called third revolution began with Khomeini's dismissal of President Abul Hassan Bani-Sadr on June 22, 1981. In retrospect, the fate of Bani-Sadr, as that of Bazargan, reflected Khomeini's singleminded determination to eliminate from power any individual or group that could stand in the way of his engineering the ideal Islamic Republic of Iran which he had formally proclaimed on April 1, 1979, and which he called "the first day of the Government of God." This government, however, had yet to be molded thoroughly according to his fundamentalist interpretation of Islam. In terms of foreign policy, the main characteristics of the third revolution were the continuation of the Iraq-Iran war, increasing rapprochement with the Soviet Union, and expanded efforts to export the "Islamic revolution."

In the opinion of this author, the revolution began going through yet a fourth phase in late 1982. Domestically, the clerical class had consolidated its control, prevented land distribution, and promoted the role of the private sector in the economy. Internationally, Iran sought a means of ending its pariah status and tried to distance itself from terrorist groups. It expanded commercial relations with Western Europe, China, Japan, and Turkey; reduced interaction with the Soviet Union; and claimed that the door was open for reestablishing relations with the United States. Late in 1985 a special 60-member assembly of religious figures designated as Khomeini's eventual successor for the office of "Supreme Jurisprudent", a close ally—Ayatollah Hussein Ali Montazeri (born 1922).

In November of 1986 President Reagan acknowledged that the United States had secretly supplied some arms to Iran. The disclosure and subsequent handling of the purchase money led to a lengthy congressional investigation and the appointment of an independent counsel to see if federal statutes had been violated.

In 1988, Khomeini and Iran accepted the United Nation's call for a cease-fire with Iraq. On February 14, 1989, Khomeini sentenced writer Salman Rushdie to death, without a trial, in a legal ruling called a *fatwa*. Khomeini deemed Rushdie's novel *The Satanic Verses* to be blasphemous because of its unflattering portrait of Islam. Before his death from cancer in Iran on June 3, 1989, Khomeini designated President Ali Khamenei to succeed him. Khomeini is still a revered figure to Iranians. Each year on the anniversary of his death, hundreds of thousands of people attend a ceremony at his shrine at the Behesht-e-Zahra cemetery.

Further Reading

The main sources of biographical information on Khomeini are in Persian. Two of these are Hamid Rouhani, *Nehzat-e Imam Khomeini* (1977) and volumes 3, 7, and 8 of 11 volumes by Ali Davani, *Nehzat-e Rouhaniyun-e Iran* (1981). For relevant detailed accounts of the revolutionary periods in English, see Shaul Bakhash, *The Reign of the Ayatollahs: Iran and the Islamic Revolution* (1984) and Dilip Hiro, *Iran Under the Ayatollahs* (1985). On the foreign policy of Iran since the revolution see this author's, "Khumayni's Islam in Iran's Foreign Policy" in Adeed Dawisha (editor), *Islam in Foreign Policy* (1983); "Iran's Islamic Revolution and the Persian Gulf," *Current History* (January 1985); and "Iran: Burying the Hatchet," *Foreign Policy* (Fall 1985). For a concise treatment of Khomeini's life and especially of his political ideas, see Farhang Rajaee, *Islamic Values and World View: Khomeyni on Man, the State and International Politics* (1983) and Amir Taheri, *The Spirit of Allah* (1985). A grim picture of the 14-month ordeal of the American captives is told in Moorhead Kennedy, *The Ayatollah in the Cathedral: Reflections of a Hostage* (1986). See also: "Assaying the Khoeneini Legacy" by G. H. Jansen in *World Press Review*, August 1, 1989, vol. 36, no. 8; and *Religion and Politics in Iran* ed.by Nikki R. Keddie, Yale University Press (1983). For more on the Rushdie sentence, see: "The Rushdie Affair" by Lewis Vernard in *American Scholar*, Spring 1991, vol. 60, no. 2, pp. 185-196; and "The Satanic Fatwa," by Djalal Gandjeih in *Utne Reader*, September 1994, pp. 131-133. □

Har Gobind Khorana

Har Gobind Khorana (born 1922) was an Indian organic chemist and cowinner of the 1968 Nobel Prize for physiology or medicine. His research in chemical genetics vastly extended our understanding of how the chemicals of a cell nucleus transmit information to succeeding generations of cells.

Har Gobind Khorana was born in Raipur on January 9, 1922. After obtaining a doctorate in chemistry from the University of Liverpool, he worked with V. Prelog at the Federal Institute of Technology in Zurich and with Sir Alexander Todd at Cambridge University. From 1952 to 1960 he was head of the Organic Chemistry Group of the British Commonwealth Research Council in Vancouver, and for part of this period he was visiting research professor at the Rockefeller University in New York City. He moved to the University of Wisconsin in 1960 and in 1964 was named to the Conrad A. Elvehjem chair in life sciences at the Institute of Enzyme Research.

Khorana's research embraced many fields: peptides and proteins; chemistry of phosphate esters, nucleic acids, and viruses; and chemical genetics. It was his work in chemical genetics that secured for him three coveted prizes: the Merck Award of the Chemical Institute of Canada in 1958, the Louisa Gross Horwitz Prize of Columbia University in 1968, and the Nobel Prize in the same year.

In 1970 Khorna left the University of Wisconsin for the Massachusetts Institute of Technology, becoming the Alfred P. Sloan Professor. He was associated with Cornell University from 1974 to 1980 as well. Also in 1970, Khorana made a major breakthrough when he announced the synthesis of the first artificial gene. Six years later, Khorana and his team created a second artificial gene, this one capable of functioning in a living cell. This valuable work laid the foundation for a future in which scientists could use artificial genes to synthesize important proteins or to cure hereditary diseases in humans. In recent years, Khorana has synthesized the gene for bovine rhodopsin, the retinal pigment that converts light energy into electrical energy.

Khorana, who became an American citizen in 1966, has developed a reputation as a tireless worker who once went 12 years without a vacation. He enjoys hiking, listening to music, and often takes his scientific inspiration from long daily walks. With his wife, Esther Elizabeth Sibler, he raised two daughters, Julia Elizabeth and Emily Anne, and one son, Dave Roy.

Further Reading

An autobiographical sketch by Khorana, his Nobel lecture, and the presentation speech of the Nobel Committee (all in English) appear in the annual *Les Prix Nobel en 1968* (1969). A good source for understanding genetical research and Khorana's work is Robert H. Haynes and Philip C. Hanawalt, eds., *The Molecular Basis of Life: An Introduction to Molecular Biology* (1968). His work is also discussed in Carl R. Woese, *The Genetic Code: The Molecular Basis for Genetic Expression* (1967). □

Khorana's work supplements the research of Marshall Nirenberg and Robert Holley. In 1961, while experimenting with the intestinal bacterium *Escherichia coli,* Nirenberg had deciphered the coded messages that DNA (deoxyribonucleic acid) sends to RNA (ribonucleic acid), which in turn prescribes the synthesis of new proteins. Further experiments revealed codes for most of the known amino acids normally present in proteins. But, although the nucleotide composition became known, gaps in the knowledge about the order of the nucleotide remained.

With his coworkers Khorana resolved this gap by synthesizing all of the 64 possible trinucleotides. He used synthetic polydeoxyribonucleotides of known sequence to direct the synthesis of long, complementary, polyribonucleotides in reactions catalyzed by the enzyme RNA polymerase. By preparing RNA-like polymers with alternating sequence, he demonstrated that such a polymer directs the synthesis of a polypeptide with alternating amino acids—leucine and serine.

After testing a large number of such polymers, Khorana afforded a clear proof of codon assignments and confirmed that the genetic language is linear and consecutive and that three nucleotides specify an amino acid. In addition, he proved the direction in which the information of the messenger RNA is read and that the code words cannot overlap. The manner in which polyribonucleotides are manufactured afforded the clearest proof that the sequence of nucleotides in DNA specifies the sequence of amino acids in proteins through the intermediary of an RNA.

Khosrow I

Khosrow I (531-576) was a Persian king and the most illustrious member of the Sassanid dynasty. He is distinguished for both his military achievements and his far-reaching administrative and social reforms.

U nder his father, Kavat, Khosrow played a leading role in subduing the followers of Mazdak, a religious leader who preached a communistic creed aiming at the elimination of the causes of hostility among men. The movement gained popularity and for a time enjoyed the support even of the reform-minded Kavat. In the end, however, Kavat gave in to Khosrow's insistence on crushing the movement, a plan which was executed with utter ruthlessness.

Interior Administration

Khosrow, who had been appointed crown prince by kavat, first encountered the opposition of his two older brothers. He ended this opposition effectively by putting his brothers and some of their children to death. He then turned his attention to the Mazdakites, who still posed a threat to his rule, and massacred a large number of them, among whom Mazdak also perished. Khosrow's severity, however, was matched by a firm resolve for reforms and deep concern for the administration of justice. He was strictly a man of law and order who believed in the intimate relationship of church and state and in upholding a clear distinction between the different classes of society.

In order to stamp out the causes of widespread dissatisfaction, Khosrow reorganized the Sassanid state and instituted far-ranging reforms. He divided the country into four main provinces, for each of which he appointed a governor (*patkospan*), a military commander, and a chief inspector. He also thoroughly overhauled the tax system with a view to both stabilizing the state's revenues and correcting tax inequities. He instituted periodic surveys of the land and produce to prevent the recurrence of former abuses. Arab and Persian historians call him Anushervan (''of immortal soul'') the Just, a reflection of his reputation of being firm but even-handed.

Foreign Policy

Khosrow's foreign policy was marked by his determination to withstand any encroachment upon the Persian borders and by his ambition to extend the Persian frontiers. In these matters he was remarkably successful. In 533, when Khosrow was still beset by the Mazdakite problem, he signed a peace treaty with Rome, stipulating that Rome pay 1,100 pounds of gold toward the upkeep of Darband and other fortresses in the Caucasus against nomadic inroads, that Rome keep the fortress of Dara but not its headquarters in Mesopotamia, and that fortresses captured by each side in Lazica during previous wars be restored.

Justinian, Khosrow's able counterpart, welcomed the peace treaty in order to pursue his conquests in Italy and North Africa, but his successes alarmed Khosrow, who felt equally concerned about Armenia, a Persian protectorate courting Rome. War broke out between the two countries, and Khosrow's armies scored a number of victories. More than once, terms of peace were agreed upon, only to be broken again, sometimes by Rome, sometimes by Persia—a course typical of Persic-Roman relations in medieval times. The conflict with Rome survived Khosrow, whose military operations against Rome were generally more successful than not and who personally conducted his armies even in his old age.

A peace treaty with Rome in 562 allowed Khosrow to turn his attention to the East, where, in alliance with the Khaghan of the Turks, he invaded the territory of the Ephthalites. These were most probably a group of White Huns who had pushed westward and settled on the Persian frontier.

Military Conquests

Khosrow's victory extended the frontiers of Persia to the Oxus River and brought Kabolestan, Zabolestan, and Arachosia, among other provinces, under Persian rule. This expansion also made the Sassanid state a direct neighbor of the Turks.

Other military successes by Khosrow included his defeat of the Khazars, an Altaic people who had their capital near the Volga estuary; his campaign in 569 on the north-

eastern frontier against the Turks who had invaded Persian territory; and his campaign in Arabia in 576 against the Abyssinian conquerors of Yemen. The last campaign extended Persian rule into southern Arabia.

In Persian literature, Khosrow I is credited with justice, wisdom, and military prowess. His reforms imparted new life to the Sassanid dynasty, and his suppression of the Mazdakite movement made the Zoroastrian Church once again supreme. Bozorgmehr, the sage who is reported to have been his vizier and chief adviser, however, is not confirmed as a historical figure.

Further Reading

The Letter of Tansar, translated by Mary Boyce (1968), is a primary source concerning Khosrow's internal reforms. For an account of his reign see George Rawlinson, *The Seventh Great Oriental Monarchy* (1882), and Percy Sykes, *A History of Persia,* vol.1 (3d ed. 1930). ☐

Nikita Sergeevich Khrushchev

The Soviet political leader Nikita Sergeevich Khrushchev (1894-1971) was a major force in world politics in the post-Stalin period.

Nikita Khrushchev was born in Kalinovka in southern Russia on April 17, 1894. At 15 he became an apprentice mechanic in Yuzovka, where his father was working as a miner. When his apprenticeship ended, he was employed as a machine repairman in coal mines and coke plants of the region.

In 1918 Khrushchev joined the Communist party, and he enrolled in the Red Army to fight in the civil war then in progress. After nearly 3 years of service, he returned to Yuzovka and was appointed assistant manager of a mine. Soon thereafter, he entered the Donets Industrial Institute, from which he graduated in 1925. He then took up his career as a full-time party official, beginning as secretary of a district party committee near Yuzovka.

Four years later Khrushchev attended the Industrial Academy in Moscow for training in industrial administration, leaving in 1931 to become secretary of a district party committee in Moscow. Within 4 years he became head of the party organization of Moscow and its environs, thus joining the highest ranks of party officialdom. In Moscow he used his industrial training as he helped to supervise the construction of the city's subway system.

When Stalin began purging the Communist party's leadership of those he mistrusted, Khrushchev was fortunate to be one of the trusted. In 1938, when most of the chief party leaders in the Ukraine were purged, he was made first secretary of the Ukrainian Communist party and at the same time was named to the Politburo, the ruling body of the Soviet Communist party. As first secretary, he was in fact,

which the government had been following since 1953, for the purpose of ending the worst practices of the Stalin dictatorship. Although the Soviet Union under Khrushchev continued to be a one-party totalitarian state, its citizens enjoyed conditions more favorable than had been possible under Stalin. The standard of living rose, intellectual and artistic life became somewhat freer, and the authority of the political police was reduced. In addition, relations with the outside world were generally improved, and Soviet prestige rose.

Khrushchev's fortunes eventually began to take a downward turn, however. Some of his ambitious economic projects failed; his handling of foreign affairs resulted in a number of setbacks; and de-Stalinization produced discord in the Communist ranks of other countries. These developments caused concern among party leaders in the U.S.S.R., many of them already fearful that Khrushchev might be planning to extend his power. In October 1964, while Khrushchev was away from Moscow, they united in an effort whereby they managed to deprive him of his office and require his retirement. He died on Sept. 11, 1971, in Moscow.

Further Reading

Khrushchev's purported memoirs are *Khrushchev Remembers,* with an introduction, commentary, and notes by Edward Crankshaw (1970). Crankshaw's *Khrushchev: A Career* (1967) is a well-written account covering many phases of his career. Myron Rush, *The Rise of Khrushchev* (1965), concentrates on Khrushchev's ascent to power. An incisive biography is Mark Frankland, *Khrushchev* (1967). *Khrushchev and the Arts: The Politics of Soviet Culture, 1962-1964,* selected and edited by Priscilla Johnson and Leopold Labedz (1965), deals with the de-Stalinization of Soviet literature, in which Khrushchev played a crucial role. Although all data are not yet available, William Hyland and Richard Shryock, *The Fall of Khrushchev* (1968), attempts to account for the change in Soviet leadership in 1964. Michel Tatu, *Power in the Kremlin: From Khrushchev to Kosygin* (1967; trans. 1969), and Adam B. Ulam, *Expansion and Coexistence: The History of Soviet Foreign Policy, 1917-67* (1968), are recommended for general background. □

though not in name, the chief executive of the Ukraine. Except for a short interval in 1947, he retained his authority in that area until 1949.

During World War II, while still first secretary of the Ukrainian Communist party, Khrushchev served in the Red Army both in the Ukraine and in other southern parts of the former U.S.S.R., finally advancing to the rank of lieutenant general.

In 1949 Khrushchev was summoned to Moscow to serve in the party's Secretariat, directed by Stalin. Then, after Stalin's death in 1953, Khrushchev was among the eight men in whose hands power became concentrated. In the allocation of the various spheres of power, the party was recognized as his sphere; within a few months he became first secretary of the Central Committee of the Soviet Communist party—that is, its chief official.

By installing his supporters in important party positions and making some shrewd political alliances, Khrushchev gained ascendancy over the seven who shared power with him; by 1955 he was clearly the foremost political figure in the Soviet Union. Even that prestigious status was enhanced 3 years later, when he became chairman of the Council of Ministers, succeeding Nikolai Bulganin. With that, he became the most powerful man in the country: as chairman of the Council of Ministers, he was head of the government; and, as first secretary of the Soviet Communist party's Central Committee, he was head of the party.

Instead of emulating Stalin by becoming a dictator, Khrushchev encouraged the policy of de-Stalinization,

Khufu

Khufu (reigned 2590-2568 B.C.), or Cheops, was an Egyptian king who built the Great Pyramid at Giza and ruled as the second king of the Fourth Dynasty.

The son and immediate successor of Queen Hetepheres and King Snefru, the founder of the Fourth Dynasty (ca. 2613-2494 B.C.), Khufu is perhaps better known by his Greek name, Cheops. His Great Pyramid at Giza marks the climax in pyramid building in respect to both size and quality of construction. No monument in Egypt has been surveyed and measured so often and so carefully. Its base covers an area of 13.1 acres, and a survey undertaken in 1925 showed that the difference between the longest and shortest sides was only 7.9 inches. When complete, it rose to a height of 481.4 feet, the top 31 feet of which are now missing.

It has been estimated that the core of local stone and the outer facing of the completed pyramid were composed of about 2,300,000 separate blocks, each averaging about 2 1/2 tons. The outer facing was originally of Tura limestone, but with the exception of a few pieces at the base, all this has been stripped off the sides. The capstone, which was possibly of granite, has also been removed.

The original entrance was in the north face at a height of about 55 feet measured vertically above ground level. According to a Moslem tradition, a large opening a little below it was made during the 9th century A.D. at the command of the caliph al-Mamun, who mistakenly believed that the pyramid contained hidden treasure.

The internal arrangements show two changes of plan, the latter of which involved the construction of the famous Grand Gallery, which slopes upward to the burial place, now known as the King's Chamber. Adjoining the east face of the pyramid was the Mortuary Temple.

Little is known of the events of this King's reign, but some indication of the extent of Egypt's power and influence at this time is afforded by the occurrence of his name on monuments ranging from Nubia to Sinai and even farther afield. A stele bearing his name was found in the diorite quarries northwest of Toshka in the Nubian Desert, and a relief at Wadi Maghara in Sinai depicts him smiting the local Bedouin.

Further Reading

What is known of the events of Khufu's reign is discussed by William Stevenson Smith in *The Cambridge Ancient History,* vol. 1 (2d ed. 1962). For information on the Great Pyramid at Giza see Iowerth Eiddon Stephen Edwards, *The Pyramids of Egypt* (rev. ed. 1961), and on the tomb of Khufu's mother, Hetepheres, see "The Tomb of Hetep-heres" in volume 2 of George Andrew Reisner and William Stevenson Smith, *A History of the Giza Necropolis* (2 vols., 1942-1955). A background work is Sir A. H. Gardiner, *Egypt of the Pharaohs* (1961). □

Muhammad ibn Musa al-Khwarizmi

Muhammad ibn Musa al-Khwarizmi (died ca. 850) was a Moslem mathematician, astronomer, and geographer and one of the most seminal scientific minds of early Islamic culture.

Al-Khwarizmi flourished at the court of the Abbasid caliph al-Mamun (reigned 813-833), whose interest in science and philosophy gave great impetus to scholarly investigation and to a copious translation movement from Greek via Syriac into Arabic. Very little is known of al-Khwarizmi's life, although his name indicates at least a

family origin in the Persian culture of the Oxus River (Amu Darya) delta. He may have been attached to al-Mamun's scientific academy in Baghdad, the House of Wisdom (Arabic, *Bayt al-Hikma*), and it is probable that he participated in the calculation of the length of a degree of latitude, which took place during al-Mamun's reign.

To al-Khwarizmi we owe the world "algebra," from the title of his greatest mathematical work, *Hisab al-Jabr wa-al-Muqabala* (Calculation for Integration and Equation). The book, which was twice translated into Latin, by both Gerard of Cremona and Robert of Chester in the 12th century, works out several hundred simple quadratic equations by analysis as well as by geometrical example. It also has substantial sections on methods of dividing up inheritances and surveying plots of land. Al-Khwarizmi was one of the early popularizers in the Islamic world of the numeral system, which, along with the zero concept, is called Arabic in the West but which was borrowed at about this time from India. A technical term for the Arabic numerals, no longer much in use, is derived from the very name al-Khwarizmi: algorism.

Al-Khwarizmi also wrote a treatise on arithmetic which has survived only in a medieval Latin translation; Arabic bibliographies of the period mention two books by him on the astrolabe and one on sundials, although none of these seems to have come down to us. Al-Khwarizmi also compiled the first astronomical tables known in the Moslem world. They were translated into Latin, together with their lengthy introduction, by Adelard of Bath in 1126.

Of great importance also was al-Khwarizmi's contribution to medieval geography. His improvement upon Ptolemy's work is entitled *Surat al-Ard* (The Shape of the Earth). The text exists in a manuscript; the maps have unfortunately not been preserved, although modern scholars have been able to reconstruct them from al-Khwarizmi's descriptions.

Further Reading

The *Hisab al-Jabr* was translated into English with a useful biographical introduction and notes by Louis Charles Karpinski, *Robert of Chester's Latin Translation of the Algebra of al-Khowarizmi* (1915). Seyyed Hossein Nasr, *Science and Civilization in Islam* (1968), has extensive material on al-Khwarizmi. For the intellectual setting of his era see "The Time of al-Khwarizmi" in volume 1 of George Sarton, *Introduction to the History of Science* (3 vols. in 5, 1927-1948). □

Alfred Vincent Kidder

The American archaeologist Alfred Vincent Kidder (1885-1963) directed expeditions which excavated important prehistoric ruins in the American Southwest and Middle America.

Alfred Kidder was born on Oct. 29, 1885, in Marquette, Mich., the son of a mining engineer. He entered Harvard College with the intention of qualifying for the medical school but was appalled by the premedical courses, and so he applied for a summer job in archeology. He spent two successive summers in the mesa and canyon country of southwestern Colorado and southeastern Utah. He obtained his bachelor's degree at Harvard in 1908 and a doctorate in anthropology in 1914.

Kidder then embarked on a series of Peabody Museum expeditions to the Southwest, mostly in northeastern Arizona, where, with Samuel J. Guernsey, he established the validity of chronological cultural periods. Kidder brought to the attention of scholars in the United States and abroad that valuable deductions about the development of human cultures could be obtained through archeological excavation in the United States as well as in the Old World.

In 1915 the R. S. Peabody Foundation of Phillips Academy, Andover, Mass., selected Kidder to conduct excavations at Pecos Pueblo in the Rio Grande drainage of New Mexico, for centuries a crossroads for the exchange of trade and ideas between Pueblo and Plains Indians. Now a national monument, Pecos Pueblo was a landmark in American archeology and a training ground for many of the men who were to mold its development. There Kidder inaugurated the annual Pecos Conference, which continues today, bringing together for fruitful cooperation archeologists and ethnologists working in the Mountain and Plains states.

After field work at Pecos ended in 1929, Kidder became increasingly involved in Middle American archeology. Since 1926 he had been adviser to the Carnegie Institution of Washington in its surveys and excavations of Yucatán. In 1929 he was appointed head of the institution's Division of Historical Research. Here he applied his experiences in the Southwest to the study of one of the highest and most elaborate civilizations of ancient times. He instigated what he called a "panscientific" approach, utilizing a wide range of modern scientific disciplines, including physical anthropology, ethnology, geography, geology, plant and animal biology, agronomy, medicine, and the documentary history of the aborigines.

Kidder was a member of the faculty (governing board) of the Peabody Museum at Harvard University from 1939 until 1950, president of the Society of American Archeology in 1937 and of the American Anthropological Association in 1942, and a member of the National Academy of Sciences. To Kidder, more than to any other person, is owed the transformation, during the first half of the 20th century, of American archeology from an antiquarian avocation to a scientific discipline.

Further Reading

Background on Kidder's life and work appears in the National Academy of Sciences of the United States of America, *Biographical Memoirs,* vol. 39 (1967). Brief mention is made of him in Gordon R. Willey and Philip Philipps, *Method and Theory in American Archeology* (1958).

Additional Sources

Givens, Douglas R., *Alfred Vincent Kidder and the development of Americanist archaeology,* Albuquerque: University of New Mexico Press, 1992. □

Sidney Kidman

From a humble background as a stockman, Sidney Kidman (1857-1935) went on to own, control, or have a financial interest in more pastoral land than anyone else in modern history. He was known in Australia and throughout the world as "The Cattle King."

When Australia had few railways and fewer telegraphs and when there was no such thing as wireless, motor transport, or airplanes, Sidney Kidman started to build and steadily added to two big chains of stations that stretched almost the length and breadth of Australia. With the aid of his phenomenal memory and his intensive knowledge of the geography of the bush, plus a small army of dedicated men, Kidman controlled the movement of great herds of cattle hundreds of miles apart and sent stock from his semi-arid lands in an evenly flowing stream to markets. Kidman used more than 150 stations covering more than 160,000 square miles of country (an area larger than the state of California).

Kidman was born on May 9, 1857, in Adelaide, South Australia, the fifth son of George and Elizabeth Mary Kidman. His father died when he was 14 months old. In 1870, when Sidney was 13, he ran away from home to join his older brothers George, Frederick, Thomas, and Sackville, who were working as stockmen and drovers in the Barrier region of New South Wales (now Broken Hill). He was given a job with Harry Raines, a nomadic herdsman who squatted with cattle where he found good feed. Raines was forced to move on when Abe Wallace arrived to take up the land legally, and Kidman found a job at Mount Gipps station in the area as a stockhand at 10 shillings a week. When he asked for a raise in pay in 1873 he was fired. He later claimed it was the best thing that ever happened to him in his life because it forced him to become an independent operator. Kidman never worked for another boss again.

Taking on Many Businesses

In 1875 he set up as a butcher in the canvas town of Cobar, New South Wales, where copper had been found and made money selling meat to miners from his boughshed butcher's shop. Seeing the money that could be made from transport, he acquired drays to cart provisions (flour, tea, sugar, jam, and soap) to the miners. The drays were also used to cart copper ore to the river ports of Wilcannia and Bourke. When gold was found in the Mount Browne area of New South Wales in 1881, Kidman was again in early providing rations and transport for the miners. He set up the first ration store in Tibooburra.

In 1878 he inherited 400 pounds from his grandfather. He used it to increase his dealing and trading, especially with horses. For a while he had a partnership with Bill Emmett (also known as Hammett) in Wilcannia and made frequent trips to Adelaide buying and selling horses and droving cattle.

He seized every opportunity and tried to make it a profitable one. In 1884 he secured a one-fourteenth share in the Broken Hill Mining Company for 60 pounds, selling it soon after at a profit of 40 pounds. Had he held onto it, his profit would have extended to many millions of pounds.

In 1885 he married a schoolteacher, Isabel Brown Wright, at Kapunda, South Australia. They had six children—Gertie, Elma, Edna (Edith and Norman, who died in infancy), and Walter.

Kidman joined his brother Sackville in a butchering business partnership at Broken Hill to accommodate the miners; the business extended into coaching in the late 1880s when the Kidman brothers' coaching business became second only to that of Cobb and Co. The coaches ran throughout New South Wales, Queensland, and South Australia, and also in Western Australia in the 1890s when another gold rush broke out.

Buying Land in the Bush

The 1890s was a time of major business recession, and many pastoral land holders were forced to give up their land. The Kidman brothers were in a sound financial position to buy up suitable large tracts of land on which they had had their eyes for some time. Their lust for land was not without purpose.

They sought no land near the coast or in the more reliable rainfall areas but the semi-arid lands of remote country. Sidney Kidman had realized that land where little or no rain fell could still be worked profitably where it incorporated rivers that rolled down from the north. After monsoon rains, the rivers burst their banks in south-western Queensland, providing untold miles of flood plain country which quickly responded with good fattening pasture for stock. He sought to buy such country and link it together in a vast chain of stations from the Gulf of Carpentaria south through western Queensland to Broken Hill and then into South Australia towards Adelaide. The chain would be watered by Cooper Creek and the Georgina and Diamantina rivers, which even when not in flood contained many good, permanent water holes. He also concentrated on a second chain of stations that ran from the Fitzroy River and Victoria River Downs in the Northern Territory to the Macdonnell Ranges, to the Oodnadatta area of South Australia, and down to the Flinders Ranges. The major chain was the north-south chain and the auxiliary chain, the central-South Australian chain. The aim of the strategy was to make the chains drought-proof or drought-resistant and to keep stock on the move where good feed prevailed and to stage them continually towards a market.

In 1895 the Kidmans bought their first station, Cowarie, in South Australia, and the following year, Owen Springs in the Northern Territory. Owen Springs was bought mainly for the 4,000 horses on the 600 square mile run that could be used for the coaching business. By 1899 the brothers had a further 14 stations amounting to some 11,000 square miles when Sackville died, and Sidney continued to buy up more solidly than ever. Victoria River Downs, some 12,500 square miles, was added, and when the turn of the century drought struck with great severity Kidman sustained stock losses of between 500,000 pounds and 700,000 pounds because his chains were still in fledgling formation.

In 1900 Kidman started his horse sales at Kapunda, South Australia, where as many as 2,000 horses from his stations were sold annually until 1935. The annual sales often went on for a fortnight and were said to be the biggest held in the world. By 1908, when Kidman made his first visit to England, he had 50,000 square miles of country and was acknowledged as the largest land holder in the British Empire; the United States could produce no one to trump him and called him the biggest pastoral landholder in the world.

In World War I his name became a by-word for generosity as he gave fighter planes, ambulances, shipments of beef and wool, and horses to be used in the Middle East to the war effort. He gave at a time when he was financially stressed by another drought and his stock losses amounted to more than 1 million pounds from his now much-strengthened chains, which stood at more than 100,000 square miles. He was knighted in 1921 for his war-time efforts.

The Man and His Legacy

He continued to buy up land in the 1920s, holding about 130,000 square miles of country in four states and the Northern Territory at the time of his retirement in 1927 when other members of his family assumed control of the day-to-day running of the business. He was again hit badly by the 1926-1930 drought, when his losses tallied 1.5 million pounds.

In 1932 when he turned 75 he was given a "public" birthday party by his station managers and stockmen in the form of a rodeo put on in Adelaide. Some 50,000 people broke down walls and fences to gain entry, and the party made headlines around Australia and overseas. When he died on September 1, 1935, at the age of 78, his death drew wide coverage throughout the world; he was the best known Australian internationally at the time.

He surprised people by leaving so little money—only 300,000 pounds, mainly to his family, but with generous bequests to charities. In order to avoid both state and federal income tax and state and federal death duties, his empire had been restructured in the 1920s to escape the clutches of the tax man.

He was a controversial figure in his day. Many people resented the fact that he had climbed to success on the financial misfortunes of others and condemned him for holding so much land. He was also accused of either "abusing" his land or of not improving it with fences and additional water, and he faced several commissions of inquiry to give evidence into matters relating to beef and land monopolies and pastoral mismanagement. He always emerged unscathed, in part because of his constant claim that he would sell off or hand back any of his land to anyone or any government who would either take it on or do a better job.

Much of the condemnation that came his way resulted from pure jealousy. The men who worked for him—and there were hundreds of them—regarded him with a mysterious and even savage loyalty. His managers, stockmen, and drovers were men of superior calibre—they were the experts of the day, and one of the reasons for his great pastoral success was his ability to select and retain men who were top notch in their field.

One of his earliest friends as a 14-year-old boy was an aboriginal, Billy, during the time he spent with the nomad herdsman Harry Raines. They worked together, and Billy was instrumental in teaching Kidman the bush knowledge that gave him an edge on many others of his time. Kidman admired the aboriginals who lived and worked on his stations and always saw that they were well-treated.

He did not live on any of his outback holdings, but at first at Kapunda and then at Unley Park, Adelaide. However, he made frequent inspections of his places—first on horseback, then by buggy with his wife at his side, and later by motor car—to see how his chain strategy was working. He considered visits a ''must'' during drought times. His men—and the aboriginals—were always pleased to see him. The aboriginals called him ''Big fella Kidman, King of all Adelaide.'' They often insisted they would make rain for him if he gave them ''wheelbarrows'' (buggies), trousers, shirts, blankets, tobacco, jam, and other goods for their special efforts. Kidman was always happy to oblige.

A bitter family split and the refusal by Kidman to allow the New South Wales Western Lands' Commission to take back portions of his holdings in western New South Wales for soldier settlement led to the disintegration of his vast empire soon after his death. The Western Lands' Commission did resume many holdings as the leases expired and cut them into smaller places. It did not prove to be a wise move, since many smaller places overstocked to make money and were reduced to dustbowls.

Kidman's interests after his death were managed by his son, Walter, until his death in 1970 and then by Kidman's grandson, John Ayers, Sr., until his death in 1981. They were later managed by his great-grandson, John Ayers, Jr., and even today they are not inconsiderable—amounting to more than 45,000 square miles, about one-third of what Kidman once owned.

Further Reading

The first account of Sidney Kidman's life was the book ''The Cattle King'' written by Ion Idriess and published by Angus & Robertson in 1936, the year after Kidman died. It is a somewhat romantic and fictitious look at his life. A more detailed and historically accurate account is given in a biography by Jill Bowen published in 1986-1987 by Angus and Robertson. (The title of the book and the time of publication had yet to be decided when this entry was prepared.)

The Kidman business records were, for the most part, destroyed in two office fires in 1904 and in 1924. The Bank of New South Wales archives has details of Kidman's banking records. Other details of Kidman's business activity can be found at the Australian National University Business and Labour

Archives in the Goldsbrough Mort, Dalgety, and A.M.L. and F records. There is more information on Kidman in both the Northern Territory Archives, Darwin, and the Queensland State Archives, Dutton Park, Brisbane, than there is in the state libraries of New South Wales and South Australia. Most Australian newspapers on June 3, 1921, carried details about Kidman's life at the time he was knighted, and most Australian newspapers and many overseas newspapers, including the London and New York *Times,* carried fuller reports of his life and achievements from September 1, 1935, when he died, to September 3, 1935, when his funeral took place. □

Anselm Kiefer

The controversial work of the German artist Anselm Kiefer (born 1945) was a complex examination of many themes, from alchemy to his country's Nazi past, often explored through such unconventional materials as lead and straw.

Anselm Kiefer was born in Donaueschingen, southern Germany, on March 8, 1945, during the final days of the collapse of the Third Reich. Growing up in a divided postwar Germany, he would eventually confront through his art the German burden of the Nazi legacy. As a young man in the mid 1960s he first studied French and law before pursuing the study of art at academies in Freiburg and Karlsruhe in the late 1960s.

An early conceptual art exercise entitled *Occupations* (1969) remains one of his most controversial works. It consisted of a series of photographs of Kiefer dressed up in military garb while performing a Sieg Heil salute in such countries as France and Italy. He acted out this pompous military act of occupation from the Roman Colosseum to the seashore. Was this a disturbing nostalgia for past Nazi glory or was it a satire of dreams of empire? ''I do not identify with Nero or Hitler,'' Kiefer once stated, ''but I have to reenact what they did just a little bit in order to understand the madness. That is why I make these attempts to become a fascist.''

In the early 1970s Kiefer studied occasionally with the artist Joseph Beuys in Düsseldorf. Kiefer's art would not follow the public performances and personal myth-making of Beuys' art. Nonetheless, Beuys was one of Kiefer's strongest influences, as can be seen in his desire to create art that was in a dialogue with history and the role of the artist in transforming materials.

In 1971 Kiefer married and moved to the small village of Hornbach in the Oden Forest of West Germany. He began to lead a reclusive life in an old schoolhouse that became his home and studio. Except for personal photographs that he used in his art, he did not want to be photographed and granted few interviews (he preferred to be paraphrased rather than quoted). In 1976 he wrote a cryptic autobiography that consists of a brief list of names, words, and phrases of personal significance.

Kiefer's art of the 1970s began to grapple with complex investigations of myth, religion, and history. At first the settings for his paintings were the dense forests of his region and the heavy timber structure of his attic studio in the schoolhouse, as seen in *Father, Son, Holy Ghost* (1973) where three burning chairs represent the Christian Trinity. His art began to present the mythic and historical figures of German culture, especially those who had been celebrated during the Third Reich. He explored such Wagnerian themes as *Brunhilde-Grane* (1978) and created pantheons of German cultural heroes, as in the assembled woodcut portraits of *Ways of Worldly Wisdom—Arminius's Battle* (1978-1980). Kiefer's paintings often have their titles written boldly across them (and sometimes specific names as well), allowing the works to be read both as images and conceptually as linguistic fragments. He did not create an easy art; many of his works require a rather extensive understanding of literature and history.

A recurrent theme that began to emerge in 1974 was the land, often specific German landscapes that are broad, cultivated plains. However, these were not pantheistic tributes to a bountiful nature, but were dark, tortured fields suggestive of scorched earth after some apocalyptic battle. The romantic love of German land evoked by the 19th-century painter Casper David Friedrich now reached an angst-ridden dead end in the tar-like blacks and ash-like grays of Kiefer's paintings.

Kiefer also examined that taboo subject in postwar Germany, the Third Reich. By the early 1980s many of his paintings were based upon images of the sterile and overscaled Neo-Classical architecture of Hitler's megalomaniacal dreams.

One of Kiefer's most powerful series of paintings was based upon Paul Celan's 1945 poem "Death Fuge," which was written in a Nazi concentration camp. The poem contrasted the Aryan blonde hair of Margarete and the dark "ashen hair" of the Jewess Shulamite. In *Your Golden Hair, Margarete* (1981) a limp arc of bundled yellow straw is attached to a painting of one of Kiefer's devastated fields, as the Nazi blonde ideal was made grotesque. For *Shulamite* (1983) he painted a cavernous room based upon a Nazi memorial hall. The room appeared to be blackened with soot as a candelabrum burns in the back. This hellish, over-like environment was evocative of the Holocaust that consumed Shulamite. Fire, both as a destructive and redemptive force, was a common theme in Kiefer's art.

Kiefer was deeply interested in alchemy—the medieval folly of attempting to change such base materials as lead into precious gold. For Kiefer, the artist was an alchemist, converting raw materials such as paint and canvas into objects of great profundity. The aspirations and limits of art were symbolized by the motif of the winged palette that seems to be woefully earth bound, such as in the 1985 sculpture *Palette with Wings* where the wings were made of such metals as lead. In 1989 he exhibited sculptures of grounded lead bombers evocative of this same Icarus-like theme.

By the mid-1980s Kiefer was moving away from specifically German subject matter to more universal themes, often dealing with a "New World" where Kiefer freely manipulated the culture of the past into painted environments of the artist's making. After a trip to Israel in 1984, he began to draw extensively from such ancient sources as the Old Testament. In his painting of the Holy City *Jerusalem* (1986), an alchemist field containing lead and gold leaf was presented with the "ironical" addition of attached iron skis. For such complicated paintings as *Osiris and Isis* (1985-1987) he juxtaposed ancient Roman ruins and Egyptian mythology with the transforming power of nuclear energy.

Throughout his career Kiefer was a maker of books, one-of-a-kind works like medieval manuscripts. His most monumental expression of this interest is *The High Priestess/Zweistromland* [Land of Two Rivers] (1985-1989). This sculpture consists of two bookcases (labeled after the rivers Tigris and Euphrates) containing about two hundred lead books, all on a superhuman scale. Some of the books were blank; others contained such things as obscure photographs of clouds or dried peas. It was a many layered work dealing with the artifacts of knowledge.

Kiefer's art began in the milieu of the late 1960s; the conceptual side of his work has often been present, as has the use of unconventional materials associated with process art (in Kiefer's case, lead, straw, sand, etc.). His mature works were expressively painted, often on an enormous scale, which led to comparisons by critics with Jackson Pollock, the great American Abstract Expressionist. Kiefer's rise to public prominence in the early 1980s coincided with the emergence of Neo-Expressionism, the Post-Modern return to painting and historical subject matter, as well as the growing international interest in contemporary German art. A major retrospective of Kiefer's art toured the United States in 1987-1989.

Kiefer's art was often more appreciated outside of Germany. When his work was featured by West Germany at the 1980 Venice Biennale it caused a great deal of controversy at home for his resurrection of the ghosts of German nationalism, particularly Hitler's Third Reich. However, a neo-Nazi interpretation of Kiefer's art was dismissed by many as a superficial reading of his work. He even received an individual exhibition at the Israel Museum, Jerusalem, in 1984.

Anselm Kiefer was considered by some to be the most significant artist of his day. While his art emerged during a time when Germans began to discuss their country's difficult past, it evolved into a more universal examination of the complexities of art, culture, and human existence. He published *A Book by Anselm Kiefer* in 1988.

Further Reading

The most thorough discussion of Kiefer to be found in English was the exhibition catalogue *Anselm Kiefer* by Mark Rosenthal (1987). Specific works are featured in *A Book by Anselm Kiefer,* introduction by Theodore E. Stebbins, Jr., and Susan Cragg Ricci (1988) and in Armin Zweite, *Anselm Kiefer: The High Priestess* (1989). An informative discussion can be found in Paul Taylor, "Painter of the Apocalypse" in *The New York Times Magazine* (October 16, 1988). A good example of a critical critique was Andreas Huyssen, "Anselm Kiefer: The Terror of History, the Temptation of Myth" in *October* (spring, 1989). Kiefer's art was placed into the broader context of contemporary German art in Jack Cowart, editor, *Expressions: New Art from Germany* (1983); Christos M. Joachimides, Norman Rosenthal, and Wieland Schmied, editors, *German Art in the 20th Century: Painting and Sculpture 1905-1985* (1985); and Thomas Krens, Michael Govan, and Joseph Thompson, editors, *Refigured Painting: The German Image 1960-88* (1989). For a summary of Kiefer's art see Howard Smagula, *Currents: Contemporary Directions in the Visual Arts* (second edition, 1989).

For additional information, see *School Arts* (March 1993); *Art in America* (September 1993); and The *Independent* (May 5, 1995). □

Edward Kienholz

Edward Kienholz (1927-1994) first gained recognition as a member of the Pop Art generation. His "constructions" and "tableaux" were comprised of commonplace objects and cast figures which are combined to form familiar environments. These environments illuminated his vision of the decadence and hypocrisy of American values, culture, and society.

E dward Kienholz was born in Fairfield, Washington, in 1927. Kienholz' rural upbringing provided him with the skills of mechanics and carpentry that would later prove so useful in the creation of his detailed "constructions" and "tableaux." Between 1945 and 1953 Kienholz led a rather itinerant life. He held various jobs, travelled, and attended several colleges, including Washington State College, Eastern Washington College of Education, and Whitworth College. In 1953 he settled in Los Angeles.

Works Combine Visual and Verbal Puns

Once in Los Angeles, Kienholz ran a succession of art galleries while embarking on his artistic career. His earliest works consisted of painted wood panels. Even in these early works we sense the bitterness and irony so characteristic of his later mature work. An early painting entitled *George Warshington in Drag* (1957) presents us with an image of our heroic first president in drag. The title, often an important ingredient in Kienholz' work, had been inscribed on the painting's surface. Walter Hops has suggested that the artist "mixed, in a sort of pun, two national compulsions: cleanliness and aggressiveness" by a simultaneous reading of the words "wash" and "war." The combination of both visual and verbal puns is a characteristic of Kienholz' art. This technique allowed him to comment effectively on American society and its values.

Works Recall Social Issues

By the late 1950s Kienholz broke free from the two-dimensional surface altogether and began to create three-dimensional "constructions" through the assembly and combination of everyday objects. One of Kienholz' earliest constructions, entitled *John Doe* (1959), is at once a jolting and bitterly humorous comment on the anonymity of the individual in America's commercial society. By thrusting a paint-splattered mannequin's head and torso into a baby carriage, Kienholz created a shocking, even repulsive, commentary on the way in which contemporary values and social conditions affect the individual.

Another construction—*The Illegal Operation* (1962)—also revolves around an issue of great social concern—illegal abortion. It is a ferocious image riddled with visual puns. An ordinary shopping cart has been converted into a surgical table. Upon this makeshift table rests a soiled and bloody mattress, the end of which has been ripped open suggestively. On the floor rests a hospital bedpan and bucket full of blood-stained refuse and rags. In the foreground sits a small stool beside a saucepan filled with crude surgical instruments. An old household floor lamp provides the only source of light for this back room operation. The detail and staging seen in *The Illegal Operation* anticipates Kienholz' more elaborate "tableaux" later in the decade.

Life-Sized "Tableaux"

During the mid-1960s Kienholz' constructions were expanded into life-sized environments referred to as "tableaux." These elaborate tableaux are typically composed of a life-size cast or assembled figures set within a familiar environment. In this respect, Kienholz' art shared an affinity with that of George Segal, but Kienholz combined the elements of fantasy, wit, irony, and sarcasm with reality. The result was always a rather moralistic criticism of American life.

Kienholz' tableau *The State Hospital* (1964-1966) is a gruesome image of institutionalism. Within the austere confines of a constructed cell, a nude mental patient with a fishbowl containing live fish for a head is otherwise modelled with revolting realism. The figure lies strapped to his bed. In the adjoining bunk above lies an identical figure surrounded with a cartoon bubble which points to the figure below. The implications are clear. The figure is both physically and mentally confined. His thoughts are restricted, like the fish in his bowl head, to himself and his self image. The spectator peering into this barren cell becomes a part of the patient's dismal world. His space becomes the viewer's, and the viewer suddenly loses his/her self-complacent attitude before such a grisly image. Through the realistically rendered environment and shocking imagery, Kienholz forced viewers to recognize what he saw as universal aspects of the human condition—loneliness and despair, both caused by society.

In another tableau, *The Wait* (1964-1965), Kienholz turned to the themes of old age and death. An old woman fashioned from animal bones sits in an antique chair. A glass jar containing a faded photograph serves as her head. Homey, domestic comforts surround her: an old lamp, a braided rug, a lapped cat, and a sewing basket on the floor. On the table to the right sits a collection of old family photographs representing her past. This lonely woman whose life has already passed must now await the inevitability of death. The overriding theme of death is ironically juxtaposed with the inclusion of a live bird which chatters away as the beholder remains frozen before this pathetic widow.

Kienholz' work during the 1970s and 1980s became more sophisticated and elaborate. In a later example entitled *Sollie 17* (1979-1980) Kienholz placed three cast images of the same man within a realistically constructed dilapidated urban dwelling. Clad only in a pair of baggy undershorts, the old man is seen lying on a soiled bed reading a pulp Western. On the right edge of the bed the same man sits. His head—a framed photograph attached to the cast body—is downcast as the lonely man plays a game of cards. Finally the man is seen to the rear gazing out a window which opens onto an urban cityscape. The barrenness of the man's life is echoed in the bare bulb that illuminates this sordid interior from above. This is a powerful image of alienation and the despair of a vacuous life; a life wherein time is not measured by a clock but by the water that drips from a faulty tap.

Kienholz reproduced familiar environments by taking discarded objects from everyday life and assembling them in such a way that they took on a renewed significance. With an uncanny eye for detail and arrangement Kienholz orchestrated frozen dramas. By demanding that the viewers take an active part in his play he confronts them with images of themselves and the world around them. Everything suddenly becomes imbued with an allegorical significance and a once familiar world becomes hostile.

Kienholz acknowledged that his wife often assisted him in his work. After 1973 Kienholz spent six months of each year in Berlin and the other six months in Hope, Idaho.

Kienholz died of a heart attack on June 10, 1994 in Hope, Idaho. His burial was reminiscent of his "tableaux." He was buried in the passenger seat of a 1940 Packard coupe with the ashes of his dog in the back seat and, in the glovebox, a bottle of vintage wine. In 1996, a retrospective of his work was shown at the Whitney Museum of American Art in New York.

Further Reading

There are many articles and numerous museum catalogues that are concerned with Kienholz. Some useful sources containing excellent background material are Lucy Lippard, *Pop Art* (1966); H. H. Arnason, *History of Modern Art* (1968); John Russell and Suzi Gablik, *Pop Art Redefined* (1969); and John Wilmerding, *American Art* (1976). See also: "All-American barbaric yawp" by Robert Hughes in *Time,* May 6, 1996, vol. 147, no. 19; and "Ed and Nancy: The Kienholzes' Art of Collaboration," by Kay Larson in *The Village Voice,* March 12, 1996. ☐

Søren Aabye Kierkegaard

The Danish philosopher and religious thinker Søren Aabye Kierkegaard (1813-1855) was the progenitor of 20th-century existential philosophy.

Søren Kierkegaard was born in Copenhagen on May 5, 1813. His father, Michael Pedersen Kierkegaard, was a self-made man who had amassed a considerable fortune as a wool merchant. At the age of 40 he retired and devoted himself exclusively to the intellectual life. His house became a meeting place for university professors, prominent clergymen, and writers of the day. Søren, the youngest of seven children, had a slight physical handicap. He was sickly, and frail, yet highly gifted, and his father's favorite. He was brought up in a house where discussion and debate were as familiar as the furniture.

At the time of Søren's birth Michael Kierkegaard was 57, a highly respected and rather formidable patriarch who attempted to instill an austere and demanding Christianity into his children. The young Søren idolized his father, who in bad weather used to take him for imaginary walks up and down his study, discoursing all the while on make-believe sights. This no doubt helped develop the inexhaustible power of imagination which is a hallmark of Kierkegaard's writing. He agreed with his father's wish that he study theology and entered the University of Copenhagen in 1831.

On his twenty-second birthday Kierkegaard records in his *Journals* a shattering experience, "the great earthquake"—a sudden and terrifying disillusionment about his father. Kierkegaard had long wondered about the causes for the gloom and depression that always hovered around his father. He had thought it was bereavement, for the old man had lost his wife and five children within a few years. But his

father told him that his gloom was actually guilt feelings about two grave misdeeds. As a young boy, he had cursed God for his ill fortune. Still worse, shortly after the death of his first wife in pregnancy, he had conceived a child by a female servant. Overwhelmed with guilt, he married the girl, and she became the mother of his seven children.

The highly sensitive and idealistic Søren was shaken. He stopped coming home for meals, neglected his studies, and finally left home altogether, determined to lead the life of an esthete, as a deliberate reproach to the stern training his father had given him. He began to live in high style, carousing and drinking, and even had, while drunk, an encounter with a prostitute—which built up in him a guilt equal to his father's. After 6 months of estrangement, he returned home in response to his father's agonized entreaties. They were reconciled, and a year later the father died. But Søren was haunted throughout his life by the idea of a curse on the family and by a profound inner melancholy.

At the age of 27 Kierkegaard became engaged to Regine Olsen, who was 10 years younger than he and the daughter of a prominent government official. A beautiful girl of modest intellectual gifts but endowed with a warm and open nature, she was dazzled by the sparkling conversation of her suitor, who usually managed to cover up his melancholy with wit and affability. Two days after his proposal had been accepted, he "saw that he had blundered." He could not ask her to take on his burden of guilt and melancholy. He began to look for some way out which would do the least damage to Olsen. He now deliberately played the

aloof and cynical dandy in an effort to break her affection for him and so free her. But the bewildered girl only grew more fascinated. Partly suspecting what lay behind his reversal, she sought to heal him of his fear and scruples. But he was unable to accept this, and finally, after 13 months of pain and heartbreak, he forced her to break off the engagement.

Kierkegaard sailed for Berlin, still agonizing over his decision. Olsen, basically a healthy-minded and uncomplicated person, recovered quickly and within 2 years had accepted an earlier suitor and married. Characteristically, Kierkegaard was now furious at her "unfaithfulness." Yet even after her marriage, he still hoped for some form of relationship with her—a platonic friendship—so that he could publicly honor her with his books. What he had wanted all along was a muse, not a wife. Many of his writings, especially of the early period, contain quite open allusions and appeals to Olsen, justifications of his strange behavior, and pledges of his continuing faithfulness. Apparently she never acknowledged these strange appeals.

His Writings

Kierkegaard had gone to Berlin to study philosophy and for a short while followed F. W. J. von Schelling's lectures with increasing disenchantment. But then he discovered his true vocation: to be a writer. The creative energy which had been building up in him throughout the long struggle with his father and Olsen now burst forth in a torrent of writings. The first of these, *Either/Or* (1843), confronts the reader with an existential choice between two incompatible attitudes toward life: the esthetic and the ethical. The book does not present arguments but rather character portraits, situations, vignettes—written with remarkable verve and psychological insight. The author does not judge between the attitudes. His point to the reader is: each one must choose for himself and no one will find a convincing proof for his choice.

Kierkegaard's own choice is made clear in the two following works, published in the same year. He rejects both alternatives in favor of a third. *Fear and Trembling and Repetition,* through the figure of Abraham and his sacrifice of Isaac, reflect on his own experiences with his father and Olsen while outlining a third fundamental attitude: the religious—an attitude of unconditional obedience to God. In the first of these books Kierkegaard describes what is entailed by faith: the acceptance of paradox, sacrifice, and suffering. In the second he discusses the psychology of the believer. Still in the same year he brought out three volumes of *Edifying Discourses.* In these he spoke in his own name directly to the reader. The other works were published under various pseudonyms. In all, he used 19 distinct pseudonyms in his work according to an elaborate private plan. This was not to hide his identity—everyone knew who the author was—but to indicate that these were possible lifestyles, not necessarily his own.

The following year brought another creative burst of six more works, of which the common theme is a resistance to certain features of G. W. F. Hegel's philosophy, in particular, to Hegel's tendency to mediate all oppositions and to hold out the prospect of complete understanding. Hence,

Kierkegaard deliberately plays up the surd, suprarational character of Christianity and its demand for a radical choice (not a mediation) between good and evil. The two most important books of 1844 are the *Philosophical Fragments,* which shows that freedom is the necessary condition for Christianity and that freedom is the necessary condition for Christianity and that freedom cannot be understood or proved, and *The Concept of Dread,* which shows that it is in the experience of dread or anxiety that man apprehends his freedom to choose and hence his responsibility.

The year 1845 saw two more large-scale works: *Stages on Life's Way,* in which he once more went over the ground covered by *Either/Or,* this time making plain that religion forms a special sphere of existence; and *Concluding Unscientific Postscript,* a detailed attempt to show, against Hegel, that it is impossible to understand human existence intellectually. The truth about one's own life is not to be attained in conceptual thought; it is a truth that is chosen, and lived in fidelity to that choice. With this tremendous labor completed in less than 4 years, Kierkegaard believed he had finished his task. He was ready to put down his pen and now began to wonder if, as his father had wished, he should not accept ordination and a parsonage in the country.

Conflicts with Society

All these works had been published at Kierkegaard's own expense, out of his inheritance. Apart from a brief flurry, mostly favorable, over *Either/Or,* there had been virtually no public response to his work. Now there appeared a generally favorable review but in a new journal, the *Corsair,* which, though eagerly read, was widely regarded as scurrilous and lacking in taste. Sharing this opinion, Kierkegaard wrote a sarcastic letter saying that in such a journal he would rather be abused than praised. The response of the editor was to launch a sustained and merciless series of cartoons depicting the writer. His hunchback and eccentric dress made him an easy mark for the cartoonist. For a whole year he was satirized and lampooned. He found strangers gaping and giggling at him wherever he went in Copenhagen, then still a small, enclosed town. Deeply hurt, he moved to counterattack. He began to write furious denunciations of the power of the press, of mindless public opinion, even of the concept of democracy. Some of these opinions he confided only to his *Journals;* others were published as *The Present Age* (1846). Ordination was now out of the question.

Conflict with the Church

The Danish State Lutheran Church, in which Kierkegaard had thought of taking orders, was presided over by Bishop J. P. Mynster, an old friend of his father. As Kierkegaard's work became more and more critical of the notion of an established and comfortable Christianity, the bishop grew alarmed. Kierkegaard's *Training in Christianity* (1849) set very high standards for anyone claiming to be a Christian and was widely taken as a slap at the bishop. Many in and out of the clergy were incensed.

In early 1854 Mynster died, and Kierkegaard, who had been holding back certain charges out of personal respect for the man, now felt free to speak out. At his death Mynster had been called "a witness to the truth." This phrase, originally used of the Christian martyrs, was the last straw for Kierkegaard. He exploded with a frontal assault on the establishment. Using his erstwhile enemy, the press, Kierkegaard issued a series of broadsides, 21 in all, in which he condemned the compromises of the Church, the comfortable and worldly lives of the clergy, and the watered-down doctrine. The main burden of all these attacks was not that men failed to live up to the severe demands of Christianity—he admitted this was impossible—but rather the pretense of doing so. Hypocrisy was his target.

Exhausted by these labors and the overwork of a dozen years, Kierkegaard collapsed on the street with a paralyzing stroke. He lingered for a month, refusing to take communion unless from the hands of a layman, and died on Nov. 11, 1855. Nearly 70 years passed before his work began to be known outside Denmark, but he has become one of the strongest influences on 20th-century thought.

Further Reading

Kierkegaard reveals himself in nearly all his writings, but most directly in his *Journals.* An English selection of these numerous volumes was published in 1938; the first volume of a new, complete translation appeared in 1967. The secondary literature on Kierkegaard is voluminous. Peter Preisler Rohde, *Søren Kierkegaard: An Introduction to His Life and Philosophy,* translated by Alan Moray Williams (1963), is a good place for the student to begin. Another introduction to Kierkegaard, with an emphasis on his religious thought, is Hermann Diem, *Kierkegaard: An Introduction,* translated by D. Green (1966). George Bartholomow and George E. Arbaugh, *Kierkegaard's Authorship: A Guide to the Writings of Kierkegaard* (1968), is a very helpful guide to all of Kierkegaard's writings.

Additional Sources

Lebowitz, Naomi, *Kierkegaard, a life of allegory,* Baton Rouge: Louisiana State University Press, 1985.

Encounters with Kierkegaard: a life as seen by his contemporaries, Princeton, N.J.; Princeton University Press, 1996.

Collins, James Daniel, *The mind of Kierkegaard,* Princeton, N.J.: Princeton University Press, 1983. □